SQL Tips and Techniques

SQL Tips and Techniques

Konrad King

Contributing Editor
Kris Jamsa, Ph.D., M.B.A.

Premier
Press

Publisher: Stacy L. Hiquet

Marketing Manager: Heather Buzzingham

Managing Editor: Sandy Doell

Editorial Assistant: Margaret Bauer

Technical Reviewers: David Fields, Michael Stavros

Book Production Services: Argosy

Cover Design: Phil Velikan

Important: Premier Press cannot provide software support. Please contact the appropriate software manufacturer's technical support line or Web site for assistance.

Premier Press and the author have attempted throughout this book to distinguish proprietary trademarks from descriptive terms by following the capitalization style used by the manufacturer.

Information contained in this book has been obtained by Premier Press from sources believed to be reliable. However, because of the possibility of human or mechanical error by our sources, Premier Press, or others, the Publisher does not guarantee the accuracy, adequacy, or completeness of any information and is not responsible for any errors or omissions or the results obtained from use of such information. Readers should be particularly aware of the fact that the Internet is an ever-changing entity. Some facts may have changed since this book went to press.

ISBN: 1-931841-45-4

Library of Congress Catalog Card Number: 00104878

Printed in the United States of America

02 03 04 05 06 RI 10 9 8 7 6 5 4 3 2 1

Acknowledgments

It is especially difficult to thank everyone involved in the process of converting an author's expertise and experiences into a finished manuscript available at the reader's fingertips. Please take a few moments to review the list of dedicated professionals on the Premier Press and Argosy teams that made this book a reality. Without them, the information within these pages would not be before you today. The excellent quality of the book's content is a direct result of their efforts.

First, let me express additional thanks to Stacy Hiquet, who saw both the book's potential and provided the firm hand and patience to keep the project moving along. Throughout the process, Stacy always had a kind word and a cheerful attitude that made writing the book a pleasure. Thank you, Stacy, for giving me a chance to produce some of my best work.

Thanks also to Daniel Rausch and Adriana Lavergne at Argosy for making available the editorial staff that had both in-depth technical knowledge and a firm grasp of how to present difficult concepts in a clear and concise manner. The quality and consistency of the book's text and illustrations would not have been possible without the superb efforts of its project managers.

A special thanks also to Lorraine Cooper, Krista Hansing, Elizabeth Agostinelli, David Fields, and the rest of the editorial team that spent their valuable time editing, organizing, and making the technical content both interesting and easy to read. Working behind the scenes, the editorial staff is often underappreciated. Thank you all so much for your insights, candor, and selfless contributions of content that brought the book's quality to the excellent level readers expect from Premier Press books. I look forward to the challenge of submitting work that meets your high standards again on future projects.

Thanks also to my friend Kris Jamsa whose technical expertise on a seemingly limitless range of subjects never ceases to amaze me. Kris, thank you for giving me the opportunity to work with you on projects and for raising the bar of writing excellence ever higher with each book. Every author needs a great coach to produce his best work and every person needs true friends to make it through the trials and tribulations of life. You're both a great coach and excellent friend who has changed my life (and writing) for the better over the years.

Last, and definitely not least, a very special thanks goes to my wife and love of my life, Karen King. Her encouragement gets me over the "blank page" stage at the start of each chapter, helps me work through the "Why isn't this code working?" rough spots in the middle, and she makes sure that I finish every project with an "atta-boy" and "just do it!" attitude that keep me working. Karen, I love you and I couldn't (and wouldn't want to) do it without you!

About the Author

Konrad King has been writing programs and working with computers since taking night school classes at Lancaster Community College (studying COBOL) while a junior in high school. After graduating as class valedictorian from Mojave High School, Konrad attended the U.S. Air Force Academy and earned a bachelor of science degree in computer science. In addition to other academic awards, Konrad graduated third in his class overall from the Air Force Academy and was presented the Eagle and Fledglings award as the top computer science major.

In 1984, Konrad entered the Air Force as a commissioned officer and served for four years as the systems manager for the Data General MV series of minicomputers. In this capacity, Konrad worked with the vendor on hardware and software maintenance agreements; oversaw the purchase of several millions of dollars in equipment; implemented a comprehensive backup strategy; managed and maintained all computer systems and application programs; and also wrote real-time data collection programs in FORTRAN.

After leaving the Air Force in 1988, Konrad started his own consulting business in Las Vegas. His primary focus has been on developing enterprise database systems that allow his clients to run all aspects of their business by using a set of custom, user-friendly applications. To this end, Konrad has written interface programs in both Dbase and Dataflex relational database systems, and more recently Visual C++ and Visual Basic applications for Microsoft, Oracle, and Sybase SQL DBMS products. In addition to honing his programming skills by writing countless lines of code that capture data and produce critical management and production reports, Konrad has amassed a large pool of knowledge in the areas of Windows (NT/2000/XP) networking, Novell networks, and SQL DBMS installation, backup, and performance. Konrad has worked with mainframes, minicomputers, PCs both on a software and hardware level—having built both PCs and PC-based networks from the ground up.

Konrad's latest efforts include designing and implementing several Web sites that allow his clients to improve customer relationships and expand their businesses through e-commerce. Using a combination of ASP Scripts, Java applets, and ActiveX Objects, Konrad's Web sites allow customers to contact service personnel by establishing two-way communication across the Internet, view their SQL server based account information online, and use credit cards to make purchases on secure Web servers.

In his spare time, Konrad has further augmented his 21-year career in the computer industry by authoring, co-authoring, and technical editing several computer books by award-winning authors. His authoring credits include books on PowerPoint, FrontPage, Microsoft SQL Server, and Oracle SQL database installation, performance tuning, and programming, Web server security and installation, and Web site design and implementation using Active Server Pages, Perl, JavaScript, and Visual Basic.

You can reach Konrad at kki@NVBizNet.com.

Contents at a Glance

Contents

Understanding SQL Basics and Creating Database Files

Using SQL Data Definition Language (DDL) to Create Data Tables and Other Database Objects

Using SQL Data Manipulation Language (DML) to Insert and Manipulate Data Within SQL Tables

Working with Queries, Expressions, and Aggregate Functions

Understanding SQL Transactions and Transaction Logs

Using Data Control Language (DCL) to Set Up Database Security

Creating Indexes for Fast Data Retrieval

Using Keys and Constraints to Maintain Database Integrity

Performing Multiple-table Queries and Creating SQL Data Views

Working with Functions, Parameters, and Data Types

Working with Comparison Predicates and Grouped Queries

Working with SQL JOIN Statements and Other Muliple-table Queries

Understanding SQL Subqueries

Understanding Transaction Isolation Levels and Concurrent Processing

Writing External Applications to Query and Manipulate Database Data

Retrieving and Manipulating Data Through Cursors

Understanding Triggers

Working with Data Blobs and Text

Working with MS-SQL Server Information Schema View

Monitoring and Enhancing MS-SQL Server Performance

Working with Stored Procedures

Repairing and Maintaining MS-SQL Server Database Files

Writing Advanced Queries and Subqueries

Exploiting MS-SQL Server Built-in Stored Procedures

Working with SQL Database Data Across the Internet

1 Understanding the Definition of a Database

Many people use the term *database* to mean any collection of data items. Working as a consultant, I've been called onsite to repair a database, only to find that the client was referring to a customer list in a Corel WordPerfect document that appeared "corrupted" because someone had changed the document's margins. Microsoft and Lotus have also blurred the lines between application data and a database by referring to "database" queries in help screens about searching the information stored in the cells that make up their competing spreadsheet products.

As the name implies, a *data*base contains data. The data is organized into records that describe a physical or conceptual object. Related database records are grouped together into tables. A customer record, for example, could consist of data items, or attributes, such as name, customer number, address, phone number, credit rating, birthday, anniversary, and so on. In short, a customer record is any group of attributes or characteristics that uniquely identify a person (or other business), making it possible to market the customer for new business or to deliver goods or services. A customer table, then, is a collection of customer records. Similarly, if a business wants to track its inventory (or collection of goods for sale), it would create an inventory table consisting of inventory records. Each inventory record would contain multiple attributes that uniquely describe each item in the inventory. These attributes might include item number, description, cost, date manufactured or purchased, and so on.

While a flat file (which we'll discuss in Tip 2, "Understanding Flat Files,") contains only data, a database contains both data and metadata. Metadata is a description of:

- The fields in each record (or columns in a table)
- The location, name, and number of records in each table
- The indexes used to find records in tables
- The value constraints that define the range of values that can be assigned to individual record attributes (or fields)
- The key constraints that define what records can be added to a table and that limit the way in which records can be removed; also the relationship between records in different database tables

While the data in a database is organized into related records within multiple tables, the metadata for a database is placed in a single table called the data dictionary.

In short, a database is defined as a self-describing collection of records organized into tables. The database is self-describing because it contains metadata in a data dictionary table that describes the fields (or attributes) in each record (or table row) and the structure that groups related records into tables.

2 Understanding Flat Files

Flat files are collections of data records. When looking at the contents of a flat file, you will not find any information (metadata) that describes the data in the file. Instead, you will see row after row of data such as the following:

```
010000BREAKFAST JUICES                 F00.000000
010200TREE TOP APPLE JUICE         12OZF01.100422
010400WELCHES GRAPE JUICE          12OZF00.850198
010600MINUTE MAID LEMONADE         12OZF00.850083
010800MINUTE MAID PINK LEMONADE    12OZF00.890099
011000MINUTE MAID ORANGE JUICE     12OZF01.260704
011400MINUTE MAID FRUIT PUNCH      12OZF00.820142
011600CAMPBELLS CAN TOMATO JUICE   46OZG01.200030
020000FAMOUS BRAND CEREALS             G01.200000
020200GENERAL MILLS CHEERIOS       15OZG03.010050
```

Looking at the flat file listing, you can see that the file contains only data. Spaces are used to separate one field from another and each non-blank line is a record. Each application program reading the data file must "know" the number of characters in each "field" and what the data means. As such, programs must have lines of code that read the first 6 characters on a line as an item number and the next 32 characters as a description, followed by a 1-character department indicator, followed by a 5-character sales price, and ending with a 4-digit average count delivered each week. COBOL programs using flat files had a "File Description" that described the layout of each line (or record) to be read. Modern programming languages such as Pascal, C, and Visual Basic let you read each line of the flat file as a text string that you can then divide into parts and assign to variables whose meanings you define elsewhere in the application. The important thing to understand is that every program using a flat file must have its own description of the file's data. Conversely, the description of the records in a database table is stored in the data dictionary within the database itself. When you change the layout of the records in a flat file (by inserting a five-character item cost field after the sales price, for example), you must change all of the programs that read data from the flat file. If you change the fields in a database record, you need change only the data dictionary. Programs reading database records need not be changed and recompiled.

Another difference between flat files and a database is the way in which files are managed. While a database file (which consists of one or more tables) is managed by the database management system (DBMS), flat files are under the control of the computer operating system's file management system. A file management system, unlike a DBMS, does not keep track of the type of data a file contains. As such, the file system handles word-processing documents, spreadsheets, and graphic images the same way—it keeps track of each file's location and size. Every program that works with a flat file must have lines of code that define the type of data inside the file and how to manipulate it. When developing applications that work with database tables, the programmer needs to specify only what is to be done with the data. While the programmer working with a flat file must know how and where the data is stored, the database programmer is freed from having to know these details. Instead, of having to program how the file manager is to read, add, or remove records, the database programmer needs to specify only which actions the DBMS is to take. The DBMS takes care of the physical manipulation of the data.

Unfortunately, each operating system (DOS, Windows, Unix, and OS2, to name a few) has a different set of commands that you must use to access files. As a result, programs written to use flat file data are not transportable from one operating system to another since the data-manipulation code is often specific to a particular hardware platform. Conversely, programs written to manipulate database data are transportable because the applications make use of high-level read, write, and delete commands sent to the DBMS, which performs the specific steps necessary to carry them out. A delete command sent to the DBMS by an application running on a Unix system is the same delete command a DBMS running on Windows NT expects to see. The physical steps taken to carry out the command differ, but these steps are handled by the DBMS and hidden from the application program.

Thus, the major differences between a flat file and a database are that the flat file is managed by the operating system's file management system and contains no description of its contents. As a result, application programs working with a flat file must include a definition of the flat file record layout, code that specifies the activity (read, write, delete) to be performed, and low-level operating system-specific commands to carry out the program's intent. A database, on the other hand, is managed by the DBMS that handles the low-level commands that manipulate the database file data. In short, programs that work with flat files define the data and the commands that specify what to do and how to do it. Programs that work with a database specify only what is to be done and leave the details of how it is to be done to the DBMS.

3 Understanding the Hierarchical Database Model

A hierarchical database model consists of data arranged into a structure that looks a lot like a family tree or company organizational chart. If you need to manage data that lends itself to being represented as parent/child relationships, you can make use of the hierarchical database model. Suppose, for example, that you have a home food delivery service and need to know how much of each grocery item you have to purchase in order to fill your customer orders for a particular delivery date. You might design your database using the hierarchical model similar to that shown in Figure 3.1.

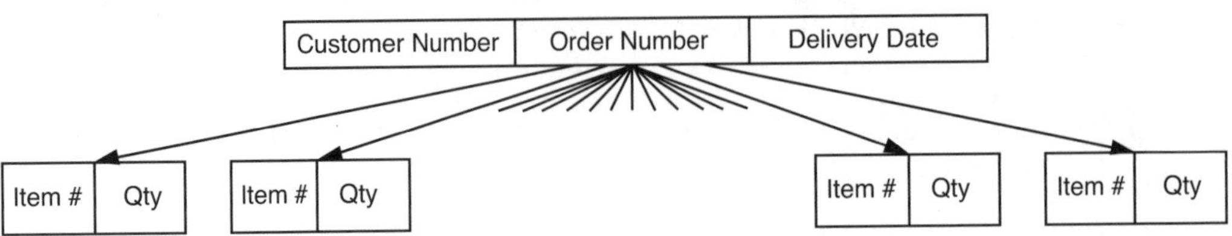

Figure 3.1 Hierarchical database model with ORDER/ITEM parent/child relationships

In a hierarchical database, each parent record can have multiple child records; however, each child must have one and only one parent. The hierarchical database for the home food delivery service orders consists of two tables: ORDER (with fields: CUSTOMER NUMBER, ORDER NUMBER, DELIVERY DATE) and ITEM (with fields: ITEM NUMBER, QUANTITY). Each ORDER (parent) record has multiple ITEM (child) records. Conversely, each ITEM (child) record has one parent—the ORDER record for the date on which the item is to be delivered. As such, the database conforms to the hierarchical database model.

To work with data in the database, a program must navigate its hierarchical structure by:

- Finding a particular parent or child record (that is, find an ORDER record by date, or find an ITEM by ITEM NUMBER)
- Moving "down," from parent to child (from ORDER to ITEM)
- Moving "up," from child to parent (from ITEM to ORDER)
- Moving "sideways," from child to child (from ITEM to ITEM) or parent to parent (from ORDER to ORDER)

Thus, to generate a purchase order for the items needed to fill all customer orders for a particular date, the program would:

1. Find an ORDER record for a particular date.
2. Move down to the first ITEM (child) record and add the amount in the quantity field to the count of that item number to be delivered. For example, if the first item were item number 10 with a quantity of 5, the program would add 5 to the count of item 10s to be delivered on the delivery date.
3. Move sideways to the next ITEM (child) record and add the amount in its quantity field to the count of that item number to be delivered. For example, if the next ITEM (child) record for this order were 15 with a quantity of 4, the program would add 4 to the count of item 15s to be delivered on the delivery date.
4. Repeat Step 3 until there are no more child records.
5. Move up to the ORDER (parent) record.
6. Move sideways to the next ORDER (parent) record. If the ORDER record has a delivery equal to the one for which the program is generating the purchase order, continue at

Step 2. If there are no more ORDER records, or if the delivery date in the ORDER record is not equal to the date for which the program is generating a purchase order, continue at Step 7.

7. Output the purchase order by printing the item number and quantity to be delivered for each of the items with a nonzero delivery count.

The main advantages of the hierarchical database are:

- **Performance.** Navigating among the records in a hierarchical database is very fast because the parent/child relationships are implemented with pointers from one data record to another. The same is true for the sideways relationships from child to child and parent to parent. Thus, after finding the first record, the program does not have to search an index (or do a table scan) to find the next record. Instead, the application needs only to follow one of the multiple child record pointers, the single sibling record pointer, or the single parent record pointer to get to the "next" record.
- **Ease of understanding.** The organization of the database parallels a corporate organization chart or family tree. As such, it has a familiar "feel" to even nonprogrammers. Moreover, it easily depicts relationships where A is a part of B (as was the case with the order database we discussed, where each item was a part of an order).

The main disadvantage of the hierarchical database is its rigid structure. If you want to add a field to a table, the database management system must create a new table for the larger records. Unlike an SQL database, the hierarchical model has no ALTER TABLE command. Moreover, if you want to add a new relationship, you will have to build a new and possibly redundant database structure. Suppose, for example, that you want to track the orders for both a customer and all of the customers for a salesperson; you would have to create a hierarchical structure similar to that shown in Figure 3.2.

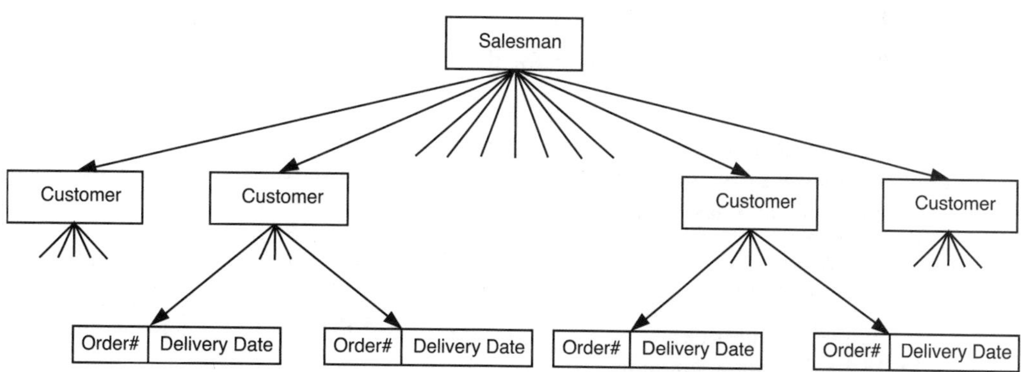

Figure 3.2 Hierarchical database model with SALESMAN, CUSTOMER, and ORDER relationships

If you just rebuild the ORDER records to include the salesman and leave the database structure as shown in Figure 3.1, your application would have to visit each and every ORDER record to find all of the customers for a particular salesman or all of the orders for a particular customer. Remember, each record in the hierarchical model has only one sibling pointer for use in moving laterally through the database. In our example database, ORDER records are linked by delivery date to make it easy to find all orders for a particular delivery date. Without knowing the date range in which a particular customer placed his or her order(s), you have to visit every ORDER record to see if it belongs to a specific customer. If you decide to restructure the original database instead of creating the redundant ORDER table, you increase the time it takes to find all of the orders for a particular delivery date. In the restructured database, moving laterally at the ORDER record level of the tree gives you only the ORDER records for a particular customer, since ORDER records are now children of a CUSTOMER record parent.

4 Understanding the Network Database Model

The network database model extends the hierarchical model by allowing a record to participate in multiple parent/child relationships. In order to be helpful, a database model must be able to represent data relationships in a database to mirror those we see in the real world. One of the shortcomings of the hierarchical database model was that a child record could have one and only one parent. As a result, if you needed to model a more complex relationship, you had to create redundant tables. For example, suppose you were implementing an order-processing system. You would need at least three parent/child relationships for the same ORDER record, as shown in Figure 4.1.

You need to be able to print out an invoice for the orders placed by your customers, so you need to know which orders belong to which customer. The salesmen need to be paid commissions, so you need to know which orders each of them generated. Finally, the production department needs to know which parts are allocated to which orders so that it can assemble the orders and maintain an inventory of products to fill future orders.

If you were to use the hierarchical model, you would have to produce three ORDER tables, one for each of the three parents of each ORDER record. Redundant tables take up additional disk space and increase the processing time required to complete a transaction. Consider what happens if you need to enter an order into a hierarchical database that has redundant ORDER tables. In the current example with three parent/child relationships to ORDER records, the program must insert each new ORDER record into three tables. Conversely, if you had a database that allowed a record to have more than one parent, you would have to do only a single insert.

In addition to allowing child records to have multiple parents, the network database model introduced the concepts of "sets" to the database processing. Using the network database model, you could structure the order-processing database relationships shown in Figure 4.1 as shown in Figure 4.2.

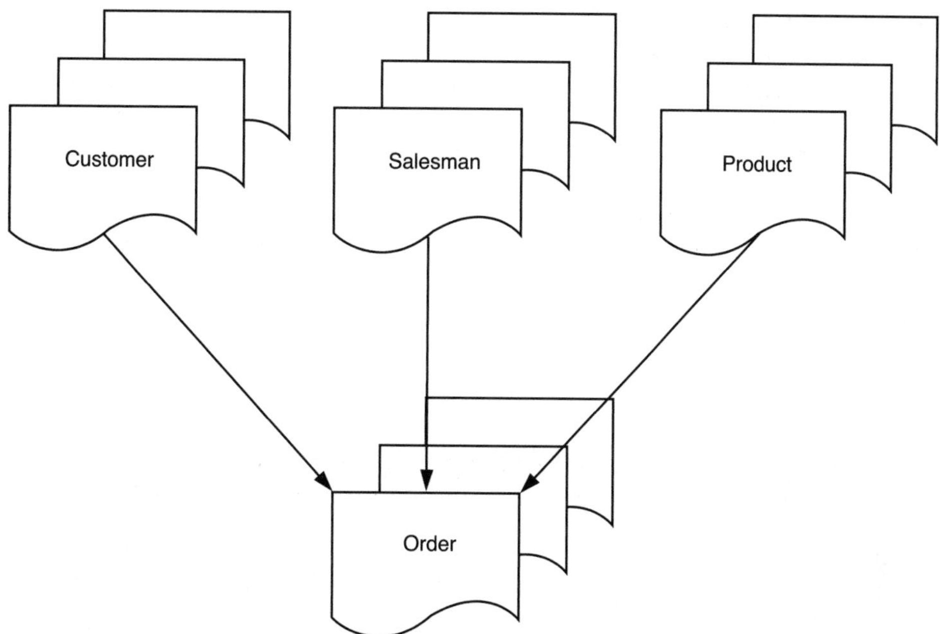

Figure 4.1 Database requiring multiple parent/child relationships

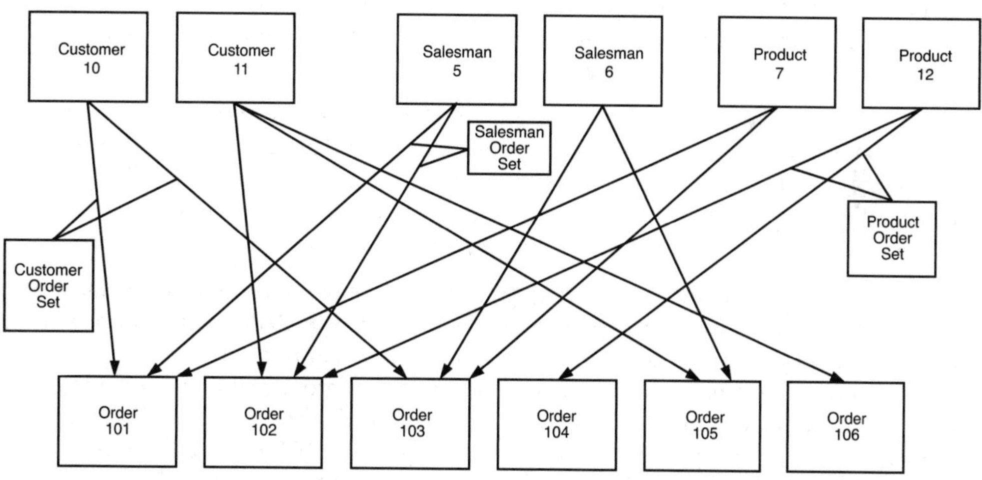

Figure 4.2 A database for an order-processing system based on the network database model

Look at Figure 4.2, and you will see that ORDER 101 and ORDER 103 belong to (or are the children of) CUSTOMER 10. Meanwhile, ORDER 102, ORDER 105, and ORDER 106 belong to CUSTOMER 11. As mentioned previously, the network database model applies set concepts to database processing. Refer again to Figure 4.2, and note that the orders that belong to CUSTOMER 10 (ORDER 101 and ORDER 103) are defined as the Customer

Order Set for CUSTOMER 10. Similarly, ORDERS 102, 105, and 106 are the Customer Order Set for CUSTOMER 11. Moving next to the SALESMEN records, you can see that SALESMAN 5 was responsible for ORDER 101 and ORDER 102. Meanwhile SALESMAN 6 was responsible for ORDER 103 and ORDER 105. Thus, the Salesman Order Set for SALESMAN 5 consists of ORDERS 101 and 102, and the Salesman Order Set for SALESMAN 6 includes ORDERS 103 and 105. Finally, moving on to the PRODUCTS table, you can see that that PRODUCT 7 is on ORDER 101 and ORDER 103. PRODUCT 12, meanwhile, is on ORDER 102 and ORDER 104. As such, the Product Order Set for PRODUCT 7 consists of ORDERS 102 and 104; while the Product Order Set for PRODUCT 12 includes ORDERS 102 and 104.

Note: *The company will, of course, have more customers, salesmen, products, and orders than those shown in Figure 4.2. The additional customers, salesmen, and products would be represented as additional parent records in their respective tables. Meanwhile, each of the additional ORDER (child) records in the ORDER table would be an element in each of the three record sets (Customer Order Set, Salesman Order Set, and Product Order Set).*

To retrieve the data in the database, a program must navigate the hierarchical structure by:

- Finding a parent or child record (finding a SALESMAN by number, for example)
- Moving "down," from parent to the first child in a particular set (from SALESMAN to ORDER, for example)
- Moving "sideways," from child to child in the same set (from ORDER to ORDER, for example), or from parent to parent (from CUSTOMER to CUSTOMER, SALESMAN to SALESMAN, or PRODUCT to PRODUCT)
- Moving "up," from child to parent in the same set, or from child to parent in another set (from ORDER to SALESMAN or from ORDER to PRODUCT or from ORDER to CUSTOMER)

Thus, getting information out of a network database is similar to getting data out of the hierarchical database—the program moves rapidly from record to record using a pointer to the "next" record. In the network database, however, the programmer must specify not only the direction of the navigation (down, sideways, or up), but also the set (or relationship) when traveling up (from child record to parent) and sideways (from child to child in the same set).

Because the network database model allows a child record to have multiple parent records, an application program can use a single table to report on multiple relationships. Using the order-processing database example, a report program can use the ORDER table to report which orders include a particular product, which customers bought the product, and which salesmen sold it by performing the following steps:

1. Find a PRODUCT record by description or product number.
2. Move down to the first ORDER record (which contains the product) in the Product Order Set.

3. Find the CUSTOMER that ordered the product (placed the order) by moving up to the parent of the Customer Order Set.
4. Return to the child ORDER record by moving back down the link ascended in Step 3.
5. Find the SALESMAN that sold the product (got the customer to place the order) by moving up to the parent of the Salesman Order Set.
6. Return to the child ORDER record by moving back down the link ascended in Step 5.
7. Move sideways to the next ORDER (child) record in the Product Order Set. If there is another child record, continue at Step 2.

The main advantages of the hierarchical database are:

- **Performance.** Although the network database model is more complex than the hierarchical database model (with several additional pointers in each record), its overall performance is comparable to that of its predecessor. While the DBMS has to spend more time maintaining record pointers in the network model, it spends less time inserting and removing records due to the elimination of redundant tables.
- **Ability to represent complex relationships.** By allowing more than one parent/child link in each record, the network database model lets you extract data based on multiple relationships using a single table. While we explored using the network database to get a list of all customers that purchased a product and all salesmen that sold the product, you could also get a list of the orders placed by one or all of the customers and a list of sales made by one salesman or the entire sales force using the same network database structure and the same set of tables.

Unfortunately, the network database model, like its hierarchical rival, has the disadvantage of being inflexible. If you want to add a field to a table, the DBMS must create a new table for the larger records. Like the hierarchical model (and, again, unlike an SQL relational database), the network model has no ALTER TABLE command. Moreover, rebuilding a table to accommodate a change in a record's attributes or adding a new table to represent another relationship requires that a majority of the network database's record links be recalculated and updated—this translates into the database being inaccessible for extended periods of time to make even a minor change to a single table's fields.

5 Understanding the Relational Database Model

While the relational database model did not appear in commercial products until the 1980s, Dr. Edgar F. Codd of IBM defined the relational database in 1970. The relational model simplifies database structures by eliminating the explicit parent/child relationship pointers. In a relational database, all data is organized into tables. The hierarchical and network database records are represented by table rows, record fields (or attributes) are represented as table columns, and pointers to parent and child records are eliminated.

A relational database can still represent parent/child relationships, it just does it based on data values in its tables. For example, you can represent the complex Network database model data shown in Figure 4.2 of Tip 4 with the tables shown in Figure 5.1.

Customer Table

CUST_NO	LAST_NAME	FIRST_NAME
10	FIELDS	SALLY
11	CLEAVER	WARD

Salesman Table

SALESMAN_NO	LAST_NAME	FIRST_NAME
5	KING	KAREN
6	HARDY	ROBERT

Product Table

PRODUCT_NO	DESCRIPTION	SALES_PRICE	INV_COUNT
7	100 WATT SPEAKER	75.00	25
8	DVD PLAYER	90.00	15
9	AMPLIFIER	450.00	305
10	RECEIVER	750.00	25
11	REMOTE CONTROL	25.00	15
12	50 DVD PACK	500.00	25

Order Table

ORDER NO	DEL DATE	PRODUCT_NO	SALESMAN_NO	CUST_NO
101	01/15/2000	7	5	10
102	01/22/2000	12	5	11
103	03/15/2000	7	6	10
104	04/05/2000	12	7	12
105	07/05/2000	9	6	11
106	08/09/2000	7	8	11

Figure 5.1 ORDER_TABLE with relationships to three other tables

In place of pointers, the relational database model uses common columns to establish the relationship between tables. For example, looking at Figure 5.1, you will see that the CUSTOMER, SALESMAN, and PRODUCT tables are not related because they have no columns in common. However, the ORDER table is related to the CUSTOMER table by the CUS-

TOMER_NO column. As such, an ORDER table row is related to a CUSTOMER table row where the CUSTOMER_NO column has the same value in both tables. Figure 5.1 shows CUSTOMER 10 owns ORDER 101 and ORDER 103 since the CUST_NO column for these two ORDER rows is equal to the CUSTOMER_NO column in the CUSTOMER table. The SALESMAN and PRODUCT tables are related to the ORDER table in the same manner. The SALESMAN table is related to the ORDER table by the common SALESMAN_NO column, and the PRODUCT table is related to the ORDER table by the PRODUCT_NO column.

As you may have noticed from the discussion of the hierarchical model in Tip 3, "Understanding the Hierarchical Database Model," and the network model in Tip 4, applications written to extract data from either of these models had the database structures "hard-coded" into them. To navigate the records in the network model, for example, the programmer had to know what pointers were available and what type of data existed at each level of the database tree structure. Knowing the names of the pointers let the programmer move up, down, or across the database tree; knowing what data was available at each level of the tree told the programmer the direction in which to move. Because record relationships based on pointers are hard-coded into the application, adding a new level to the tree structure requires that you change the application program's logic. Even just adding a new attribute to a network database record changes the location of the pointer within the record changes. As a result, any changes to a database record require that the application programs accessing the database be recompiled or rewritten.

When working with a relational database, you can add tables and add columns to tables to create new relationships to the new tables without recompiling existing applications. The only time you need to recompile an application is if you delete or change a column used by that program. Thus, if you want to relate an entry in the SALESMAN table to a customer (in the CUSTOMER table), you need only add a SALESMAN_NO column to the CUSTOMER table.

6 Understanding Codd's 12-Rule Relational Database Definition

Dr. Edgar F. Codd published the first theoretical model of a relational database in an article entitled "A Relational Model of Data for Large Shared Data Banks" in the *Communications of the ACM* in 1970. The relational model was theoretical at the time because all commercially available database management systems were based on either the hierarchical or the network database models. Although Dr. Codd worked for IBM, it was Oracle that brought the first database based on the relational model to market in 1980—10 years later! While Dr. Codd's 12 rules are the semi-official definition of a relational database, and while many commercial databases call themselves relational today, no relational database follows all 12 rules.

Codd's 12 rules to define a relational database are:

1. **The Information Rule.** All information in a relational database must be represented in one and only one way, by values in columns within rows of tables. SQL satisfies this rule.
2. **The Guaranteed Access Rule.** Each and every datum (or individual column value in a row) must be logically addressable by specifying the name of the table, primary key value, and column name. When addressing a data item, the name of the table identifies which database table contains the item, the column identifies a specific item in a row of the named table, and the primary key identifies a single row within a table. SQL follows this rule for tables with primary keys. However, SQL does not require that a table have a key.
3. **Systematic Treatment of Null Values.** The relational database management system must be able to represent missing and inapplicable information in a systematic way that is independent of data type, different than that used to show empty character strings or a strings of blank characters, and distinct from zero or any other number. SQL uses NULL to represent both missing and inapplicable information—as you will learn later, NULL is *not* zero, nor is it an empty string.
4. **Dynamic Online Catalog Based on the Relational Model.** The database catalog (or description) is represented in the same manner as ordinary data (using tables), so authorized users can use the same relational language to work with the online catalog and regular data. SQL does this through system tables whose columns describe the structure of the database.
5. **Comprehensive Data Sublanguage Rule.** The system may support more than one language, but at least one language must have a well-defined syntax that is based on character strings and that can be used both interactively and within application programs. The language must support:
   - Data definitions
   - View definitions
   - Data manipulation (both update and retrieval)
   - Security
   - Integrity constraints
   - Transaction management operations (Begin, Commit, Rollback)

   SQL Data Manipulation Language (DML) (which can be used both interactively and in application programs) has statements that perform all of the required operations.
6. **View Updating Rule.** All views that are theoretically updateable must be updateable by the system. (Views are virtual tables that give users different "pictures" or representations of the database structure.) SQL does not fully satisfy this rule in that it limits updateable views to those based on queries on a single table without GROUP BY or HAVING clauses; it also has no aggregate functions, no calculated columns, and no SELECT DISTINCT

clause. Moreover, the view must contain a key of the table, and any columns excluded from the view must be NULL-able in the base table.

7. **High-Level Insert, Update, and Delete.** The system must support multiple-row and table (set-at-a-time) Insert, Update, and Delete operations. SQL does this by treating rows as sets in Insert, Update, and Delete operations. Rule 7 is designed to exclude systems that support only row-at-a-time navigation and modification of the database, such as that required by the hierarchical and network database models. SQL fully satisfies this rule.
8. **Physical Data Independence.** Application programs and interactive database access methods don't have to change due to a change in the physical storage device or method used to retrieve data from that device. SQL does this well.
9. **Logical Data Independence.** Application programs and interactive database access methods don't have to change if tables are changed in a way that preserves the original table values. SQL satisfies this requirement—the results of queries and action taken by statements do not depend on the arrangement of columns in a row, the position of rows in a table, or the structure used to represent the table inside the computer system.
10. **Integrity Independence.** All integrity constraints specific to a particular relational database must be definable in the relational sub-language, be specified outside of the application programs, and stored in the database catalogue. SQL-92 has integrity independence.
11. **Distribution Independence.** Applications and end users should not be aware of whether the database data exists in a single location or whether it is replicated on and distributed among many computers on a network. Thus, the database language must be able to use the same commands to query and manipulate distributed data located on both local and remote computer systems. Distributed SQL database products are relatively new, so the jury is still out as to how well they will satisfy this criterion.
12. **The Nonsubversion Rule.** If the system provides a low-level (record-at-a-time) interface, the low-level statements cannot be used to bypass integrity rules and constraints expressed in the high-level (set-at-a-time) language. SQL-92 complies with this rule. Although one can write statements that affect individual table rows, the system will still enforce security and referential integrity rules.

Just as no SQL DBMS complies with all of the specifications in the SQL-92 standard, none of the commercially available relational databases follow all of Codd's 12 rules. Rather than comparing scorecards on the number of Codd's rules a relational database satisfies, companies normally select a particular database product based on performance, features, availability of development tools, and quality of vendor support. However, Codd's rules are important from a historical prospective, and they do help you decide whether a DBMS is based on the relational model.

7 Understanding Terms Used to Define an SQL Database

Tables

Every SQL database is based on the relational database model. As such, the individual data items in an SQL database are organized into *tables*. An SQL table (sometimes called a relation), consists of a two-dimensional array of rows and columns. As you learned in Codd's first two rules in Tip 6, "Understanding Codd's 12-Rule Relational Database Definition," each cell in a table contains a single valued entry, and no two rows are identical. If you've used a spreadsheet such as Microsoft Excel or Lotus 1-2-3, you're already familiar with tables, since spreadsheets typically organize their data into rows and columns. Suppose, for example, that you were put in charge of organizing your high school class reunion. You might create (and maintain) a table of information on your classmates similar to that shown in Figure 7.1.

Notice that when you look vertically down the table, all of the values in any one column have the same meaning in each and every row of the table. As such, if you see a student ID in the first column of the tenth row of the table, you know that every row in the table has a student ID in its first column. Similarly, if you find a street address in the third column of the second row of a table, you know that the remaining rows of the table have a street address in the third column. In addition to a column having a consistent data type throughout the rows of the table, each column's data is also independent of other columns in the row. For example, the NAME column will contain student names whether it is the second column (as shown in Figure 7.1), the fifth column, or the tenth column in the table.

The "sameness" of the values in a column and the independence of the columns, allow SQL tables to satisfy Codd's relational database Rule 9 (Logical Data Independence). Neither the order of the rows in the table nor the order of its columns matters to the database management system (DBMS). When you tell the DBMS to execute an SQL statement such as

```
SELECT NAME, PHONE_NUMBER
  FROM STUDENT
```

the DBMS will look in the system table (or catalog) to determine which column contains the NAME data and which column has the PHONE_NUMBER information. Then the DBMS will go through the rows of the table and retrieve the NAME and PHONE_NUMBER value from each row. If you later rearrange the table's rows or its columns, the original SQL statement will still retrieve the same NAME and PHONE_NUMBER data values—only the order of the displayed data might change if you changed the order of the rows in the table.

Columns

Row

Student_ID	Name	Street_Address	City	State	ZIP	Phone_Number
812542	Joseph Archer	15 Main Ave	Pembroke	DE	02053	111-223-5241
752486	Jay Harker	109 Park St	Pleasantville	MA	05088	521-714-5542
635148	Laura Ross	5 Brooks Rd	Smalltown	WY	07564	215-305-3051
335375	Kelly Sharp	23 Smith Dr	Edison	KS	05678	732-589-5741
100548	Carl Layton	71 Argosy Rd	Washington	NC	03045	552-251-4152
101588	Victoria Carter	1223 Simmons Ave	White Falls	NJ	07823	980-987-5412
996688	Shirley Ivins	85 Fox Run	Mt. Killing	OH	09654	351-333-8520
005008	Miranda Wan	12 Waterfront Blvd	Laurel	TX	03155	663-658-6574
607845	David Bergen	6 Front Street, Apt 2	Red Hill	AL	03405	888-564-9860
144637	Samual Witt	3 Whatchamacallit Dr	Hartford	PA	03005	504-854-9999
635892	Marc Levine	111 Side View Rd	Waltham	CT	07845	500-698-3235
195784	Craig Stricklin	601 New York Ln	Bricktown	NJ	05566	780-115-5000
004920	Tom Curry	224 Arnold Ave	Amarillo	NM	04305	985-665-6655
360755	Jessica Speigel	17 Greenwood Loop	Long Beach	UT	01520	301-504-5623
092868	Gabriel Walker	3 West Main Street	Landbrige	VA	05060	802-998-4452

Figure 7.1 Relational database table of student information

If you look horizontally across the table, you will notice that all of the columns in a single row are the attributes of a single entity. In fact, we often refer to individual table rows as records (or tuples), and the column values in the row as fields (or attributes). Thus, you might say that Figure 7.1 consists of 15 customer records and that each record has the fields STUDENT_ID, NAME, STREET_ADDRESS, CITY, STATE, ZIP_CODE, and PHONE_NUMBER.

Views

A database *view* is not an opinion, nor is it what you see when you look out of a window in your home. Rather, a database view is the set of columns and rows of data from one or more tables presented to a user as if it were all of the rows and columns in a single table. Views are sometimes called "virtual" tables because they look like tables; you can execute most SQL statements on views as if they were tables. For example, you can query a view and update its data using the same SQL statements you would use to query and update the tables from which the view was generated. Views, however, are "virtual" tables because they have no independent existence. Views are a way of looking at the data, but they are not the data itself.

Suppose, for example, that your school had a policy of calling the homes of students too sick to attend classes (why else would you miss school, right?). The attendance clerk would need only a few columns (or attributes) from the STUDENT table and only those rows (or records) in which the student is absent. Figure 7.2 shows the attendance clerk's view of the data.

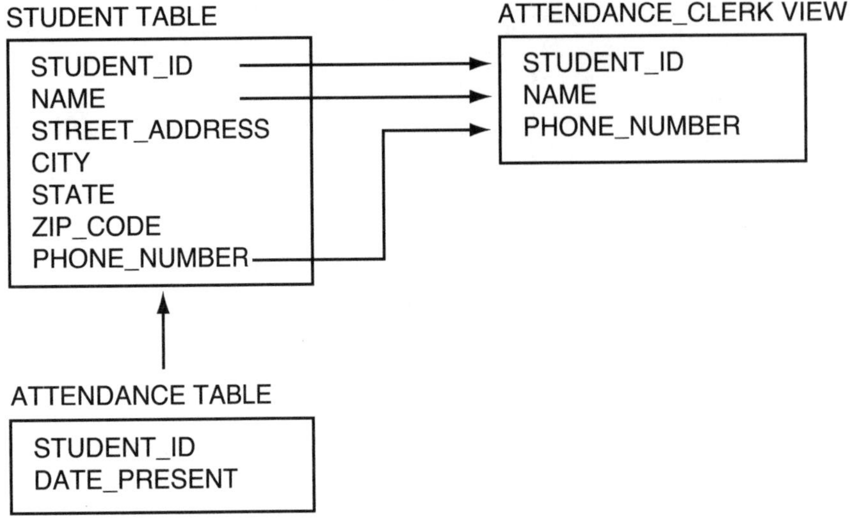

Figure 7.2 Attendance clerk database view derived from a single table

Although the student database has seven fields, the attendance clerk sees only three on his screen: STUDENT_ID, NAME, and PHONE_NUMBER. Since the attendance clerk is to call the homes of only the students absent from school, you would write a query that selected the rows of the STUDENT table that did not have a matching row in the ATTENDANCE table. Then you would have your query display only the three fields shown in the ATTENDANCE_CLERK view in Figure 7.2. Thus, the attendance clerk would see only the STUDENT_ID, NAME, and PHONE_NUMBER fields of absent students.

Now, suppose you needed to print the class schedule for the students. Well, each student needs only his or her own class information, as show in Figure 7.3.

The STUDENT_SCHEDULE view includes the majority of columns from the CLASS_DETAIL table and only two columns from the STUDENT_TABLE. Thus, one student's view of the database is very different than that shown to the attendance clerk. While the attendance clerk sees the database as a list of names and phone numbers of students absent on a particular day, the student sees the database as a list of classes he is scheduled to attend. As such, you can hide table columns from view, combine columns from multiple tables, and display only some of the rows in one or more tables.

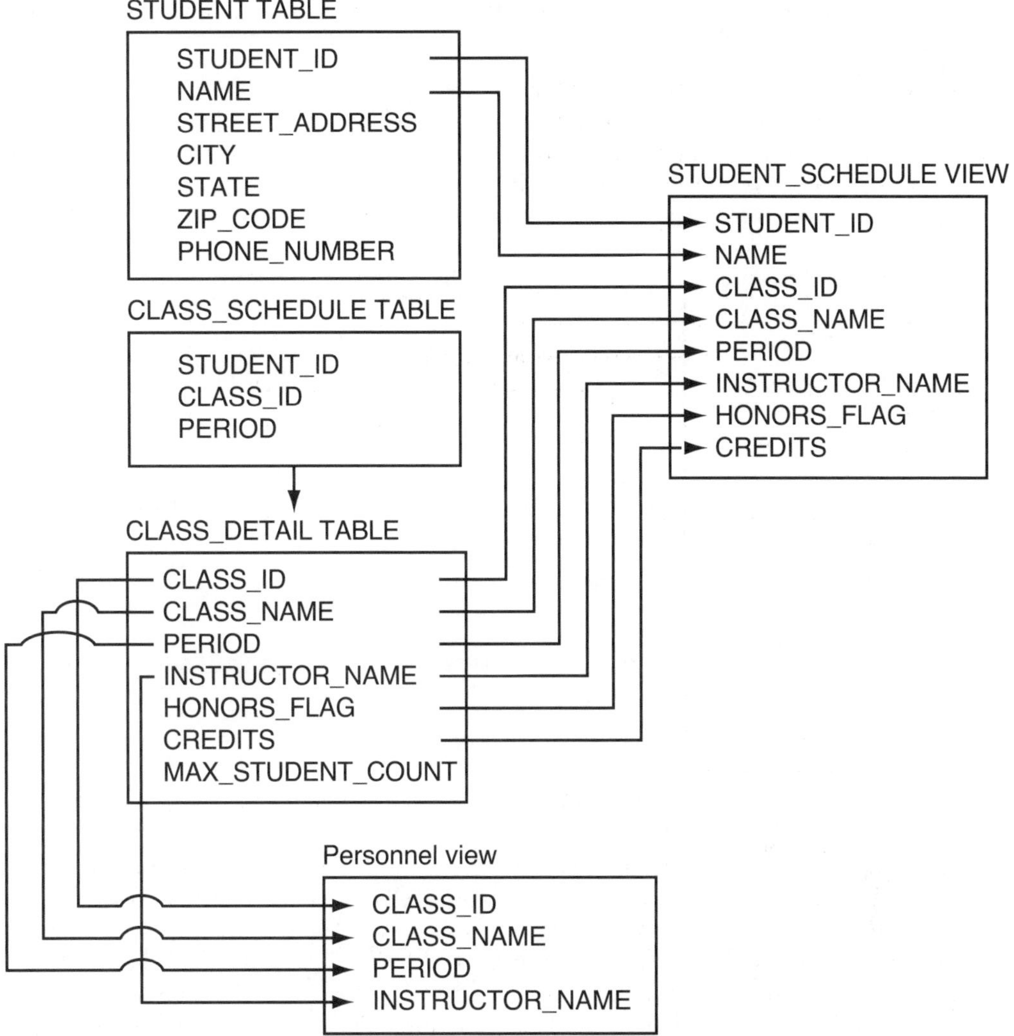

Figure 7.3 Student schedule and personnel views derived from multiple tables

As far as the user is concerned, the view itself is a table. As mentioned previously in the current example, the student thinks there is a table with his name and class schedule, and the attendance clerk thinks there is a table of absent students. In addition to displaying data as if it were a table, a view also allows a user with update access to change values in the base tables. (Base tables are those tables from which the view [or virtual table] is derived.) Notice the PERSONNEL view shown in Figure 7.3. Suppose that you had a personnel clerk responsible for entering the names of the instructors for each of the classes. The clerk's screen (view) would show the information on a particular class and allow the clerk to update the name of the instructor for that class. When the clerk changes the name in the INSTRUCTOR_NAME column of the PERSONNEL view, the DBMS actually updates the value in the INSTRUCTOR_NAME column of the CLASS_DETAIL table in the row from which the PERSONNEL view was derived.

Schemas

The database *schema* is a set of tables (often called the system catalog) that contain a full description of the entire database. Although Figure 7.1 shows the names of the columns as part of the table, and Figure 7.2 and Figure 7.3 show the names of the columns in place of data, actual database data tables contain only data values. Thus, the actual database table shown in Figure 7.1 would have only the information shown below the column headings. Similarly, the table rows (or records) represented by the rectangles in Figure 7.2 and Figure 7.3 would have the actual student, attendance, and class information. The database schema has tables that contain:

- The name of each data table
- The names of each data table's columns, the type of data the column can hold, and the range of values that a column can take on
- A list of database views, how the views are derived, and which users are allowed to use which views
- A list of constraints, or rules, that limit the range of values one can enter into a column, rows one can delete from a table, and rows one can add
- Security information on who can view (query) an existing table, remove a table, or create a new one
- Security information on who can update each table's contents and which columns he or she can change
- Security information on who can add rows to or delete rows from each table

You will learn more about the database schema in Tip 12, "Understanding Schemas." For now, the important thing to know is that the database schema contains a complete description of the database.

Domains

Each column of a table (or attribute of a relation) contains some finite number of values. The *domain* of the table column (or attribute) is the set of all possible values one could find in that column. Suppose, for example, that you had a table of coins in a U.S. coin collection. The DENOMINATION column could have only the values 0.01, 0.05, 0.10, 0.25, 0.50, and 1.00. Thus, the "domain" of the DENOMINATION table is [0.01, 0.05, 0.10, 0.25, 0.50, 1.00], and all of the rows in the table must have one of these values in the DENOMINATION column.

Constraints

Constraints are the rules that limit what can be done to the rows and columns in a table and the values that can be entered into a table's attributes (columns). While the domain is the range of all values that a column can assume, a column constraint (such as the CHECK constraint, which you will learn about in Tip 193, "Using the CHECK Constraint to Validate a Column's Value") is what prevents a user from entering a value outside the column's domain.

In addition to limiting the values entered into a field, constraints specify rules that govern what rows can be added to or removed from a table. For example, you can prevent a user from adding duplicate rows to a table by applying the PRIMARY KEY constraint (which you will learn about in Tip 173, "Understanding Foreign Keys") to one of a table's columns. If you apply the PRIMARY KEY constraint to the STUDENT_ID column of the STUDENT table in Figure 7.1, the DBMS will make sure that every value in the STUDENT_ID column remains unique. If you already have a STUDENT_ID 101 in the STUDENT table, no user (or application program) can add another row with 101 in the STUDENT_ID column to the table. Similarly, you can apply the FOREIGN KEY constraint (which you will learn about in Tip 174, "Understanding Referential Data Integrity Checks and Foreign Keys") to a column to prevent related rows in another table from being deleted. Suppose, for example, that you had a CUSTOMER and ORDER table similar to that shown in Figure 7.4.

CUSTOMER table

CUSTOMER_ID	NAME	ADDRESS
10	Konrad King	765 Wally Way

ORDER table

Order_No	CUSTOMER_ID	Item	Quantity	Order Date
1	10	789	12	4/12/2000
2				
3				
4				
5				

Figure 7.4 ORDER and CUSTOMER table related by CUSTOMER_ID

The rows (or records) in the ORDER table are related to the CUSTOMER table by the value in the CUSTOMER_ID column. Thus, a row (or order) in the ORDER table with a CUSTOMER_ID of 10 was placed by Customer 10 (the row in the CUSTOMER table with a 10 in the CUSTOMER_ID column). If someone removed Customer 10 from the CUSTOMER table, you would no longer have any information (other than customer number) on the person that placed Order 1. You can prevent the loss of information by placing the FOREIGN KEY constraint on the CUSTOMER_ID column of the ORDER table. Once in place, the constraint will prevent anyone from deleting Customer 10 from the CUSTOMER table, as long as at least one row (order) in the ORDER table has a 10 in the CUSTOMER_ID field.

In short, constraints are the rules that maintain the domain, entity, and referential integrity of your database. You will learn all about the database integrity and the importance of maintaining it in Tips 175–190.

8 Understanding the Components of a Table

An SQL table consists of scalar (single-value) data arranged in columns and rows. Relational database tables have the following components:

- A unique table name
- Unique names for each of the columns in the table
- At least one column
- Data types, domains, and constraints that specify the type of data and its range of values for each column in the table
- A structure in which data in one column of the table has the same meaning in every row of the table
- Zero or more rows that represent physical or logical entities

When naming a table, bear in mind that no two tables you create can have the same name. However, table names in the SQL database need be unique only among all of the tables created (or owned) by an individual user. As such, if two users—Joe and Mark, for example—were to create tables in an SQL database, both of them could create a table named Stocks. However, neither of them could create two tables named Stock in the same schema. In Tip 9, "Understanding Table Names," you'll learn more about table names and how the DBMS uses the owner name and schema name to make the names unique across all of the tables in the database. For now, the important thing to know is that you must give your table a name, and you don't have to worry about what other people have named their tables. When selecting a table name, analyze the columns you plan to include in the table, and use a name that summarizes the table's contents. Figure 8.1, for example, contains columns of data that deal with phone call data: PHONE_REP_ID (who made the call), PHONE_NUMBER (the phone number called), DATE_TO_CALL and TIME_TO_CALL (the date and time the call was to be made), DATE_CALLED and TIME_CALLED (the date and time the call was made),

HANGUP_TIME (the time the call ended), and DISPOSITION (what happened as a result of the call). The column titles indicate that the table will contain phone call data. Therefore, CALL_HISTORY is an appropriate table name since the name describes the type of data that can be retrieved from the table.

CALL_HISTORY table

PHONE_REP_ID	PHONE_NUMBER	DATE_TO_CALL	TIME_TO_CALL	DATE_CALLED	TIME_CALLED	HANGUP_TIME	DISPOSITION

Figure 8.1 Relational database table of phone call history data

Each horizontal row in a relational database table represents a physical or logical entity. In the CALL_HISTORY table, for example, each row represents a phone call. The columns in a row represent data items. Although neither the relational database rules nor the SQL-92 specification dictates that columns in a table must be somehow related, you will seldom (if ever) see a database table where the columns are just a random mix of data. Typically (if not by convention), data in the columns of a row details the attributes of the entity represented by that row. Notice that the columns in the CALL_HISTORY table shown in Figure 8 all describe some attribute of a phone call.

All relational database tables have at least one column. (A table may have no rows but must have at least one column.) The SQL standard does not specify the maximum number of columns, but most commercial databases normally limit the number of columns in a table to 255. Similarly, the SQL standard places no limit on the number of rows a table may contain. As a result, most SQL products will allow a table to grow until it exhausts the available disk space—or, if they impose a limit, they will set it to a number in the billions.

The order of the columns in a table has no effect on the results of SQL queries on the database. When creating a table, you do, however, have to specify the order of the columns, give each column a unique name, specify the type of data that the column will contain, and specify any constraints (or limits) on the column's values. To create the table shown in Figure 8.1, you could use this SQL statement:

```
CREATE TABLE CALL_HISTORY
  (PHONE_REP_ID CHAR(3) NOT NULL,
   PHONE_NUMBER INTEGER NOT NULL,
   DATE_TO_CALL DATE,
   TIME_TO_CALL INTEGER,
   DATE_CALLED  DATE    NOT NULL,
   TIME_CALLED  INTEGER NOT NULL,
   HANGUP_TIME  INTEGER NOT NULL,
   DISPOSITION  CHAR(4) NOT NULL)
```

When you look vertically down the columns in a relational database table, you will notice that the column data is self-consistent, meaning that data in the column has the same meaning in every row of the column. Thus, while the order of the columns is immaterial to the query, the table must have some set arrangement of columns that does not change from row to row. After you create the table, you can use the ALTER TABLE command to rearrange its columns; doing so will have no effect on subsequent SQL queries on the data in the table.

Each column in the table has a unique name, which you assign to the column when you execute the CREATE TABLE statement. In the current example, the column heading names are shown at the top of each column in Figure 8.1. Notice that the DBMS assigns column names from left to right in the table and in the order in which the names appear in the CREATE TABLE statement. All of the columns in a table must have a different (unique) name. However, the same column name may appear in more than one table. Thus, I can have only one PHONE_NUMBER column in the CALL_HISTORY table, but I can have a PHONE_NUMBER column in another table, such as CALLS_TO_MAKE, for example.

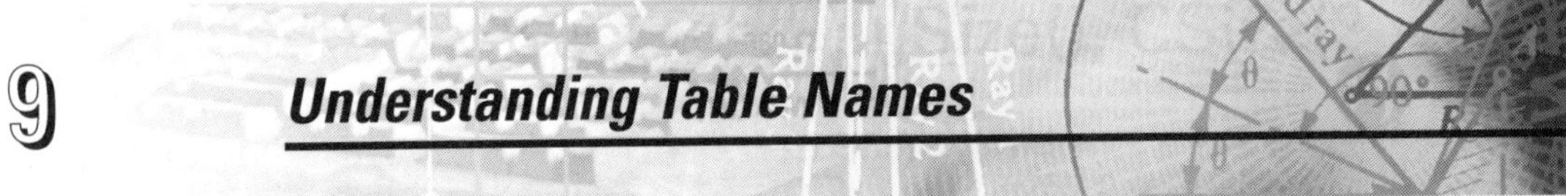

9 Understanding Table Names

When selecting the name for a table, make it something short but descriptive of the data the table will contain. You will want to keep the name short since you will be typing it in SQL statements that work with the table's data. Keeping the name descriptive will make it easy to remember which table has what data, especially in a database system with many (perhaps hundreds) of tables. If you are working on a personal or departmental database, you normally have carte blanche to name your tables whatever you wish—within the limits imposed by your DBMS, of course. SQL does not specify that table names begin with a certain letter or set of letters. The only demand is that table names be unique by owner. (We'll discuss table ownership further in a moment.) If you are working in a large, corporatewide, shared database, your company will probably have some restrictions on table names to organize the tables by department (perhaps) and to avoid name conflicts. In a large organization, for example, tables for sales may all begin with "SALES_," those for human resources might begin with "HR_," and those for customer service might start with "SERVICE_." Again, SQL makes no restrictions on the table names other than they be unique by owner—a large company with several departments may want to define its own set of restrictions to make it easier to figure out where the data in a table came from and who is responsible for maintaining it.

In order to create a table, you must be logged in to the SQL DBMS, and your username must have authorization to use the CREATE TABLE statement. Once you are logged in to the DBMS, the system knows your username and automatically makes you the owner of any table you create. Therefore, if you are working in a multi-user environment, the DBMS may indeed have more than one table named CUSTOMER—but it has only one CUSTOMER table owned by any one user. Suppose, for example, that DBMS users Karen and Konrad each create a CUSTOMER table. The DBMS will automatically adds the owner's name (by default, the table owner is the user ID of the person creating the table) to the name of the table to form a *qualified table name* that is then stored in the system catalog. Thus, Karen's CUSTOMER table would be stored in the system catalog as KAREN.CUSTOMER, and Konrad's table would be stored as KONRAD.CUSTOMER. As such, all of the table names in the system catalog are still unique even though both Konrad and Karen executed the same SQL statement: CREATE TABLE CUSTOMER.

When you log in to the DBMS and enter an SQL statement that references a table name, the DBMS will assume that you are referring to a table that you created. As such, if Konrad logs in and enters the SQL statement SELECT * FROM CUSTOMER, the DBMS will return the values in all columns of all rows in the KONRAD.CUSTOMER table. Likewise, if Karen logs in and executes the same statement, the DBMS will display the data in KAREN.CUSTOMER. If another user (Mark, for example) logs in and enters the SQL statement SELECT * FROM CUSTOMER without having first created a CUSTOMER table, the system will return an error, since the DBMS does not have a table named MARK.CUSTOMER.

In order to work with a table created by another user, you must have the proper authorization (access rights), and you must enter the qualified table name. A qualified table name specifies the name of the table's owner, followed by a period (.) and then the name of the table (as in <owner>.<table name>). In the previous example, if Mark had the proper authorization, he could type the SQL statement SELECT * FROM KONRAD.CUSTOMER to display the data in Konrad's CUSTOMER table, or SELECT * FROM KAREN.CUSTOMER to display the contents of Karen's CUSTOMER table. You can use a qualified table name in an SQL statement wherever a table name can appear.

The SQL-92 standard further extends the DBMS's ability to work with duplicate tables by allowing a user to create tables within a schema. (You will learn more about schemas in Tip 12, "Understanding Schemas," and about creating tables within schemas in Tip 506, "Using the CREATE SCHEMA Statement to Create Tables and Grant Access to Those Tables.") The fully qualified name of a table created within a schema becomes the schema name, followed by a period (.) and then the name of the table (for example, <schema>.<table name>). Thus an individual user could create multiple tables with the same name by putting each of the tables in a different schema. For now, the important thing to know is that every table must have a unique qualified table name. As such, a user cannot use the same name for two tables unless he creates the tables in different schemas (which you will learn how to do in Tip 506).

10 Understanding Column Names

The SQL DBMS stores the names of the columns along with the table names in its system catalog. Column names must be unique within a table but can appear in multiple tables. For example, you can have a STUDENT_ID column in both a STUDENT table and a CLASS_SCHEDULE table. However, you cannot have more than one STUDENT_ID column in either table. When selecting a column name, use a short, unique (to the table being created) name that summarizes the kind of data the column will contain. If you plan to store an address in a column, name the column ADDRESS or STREET_ADDRESS, use CITY as the name for a column that holds the city names, and so on. The SQL specification does not limit your choice as to the name you use for a column (other than that a column name can appear only once in any one table). However, using descriptive column names makes it easier to know which columns to use when you write SQL statements to extract data from the table.

When you specify a column name in an SQL statement, the DBMS can determine the table to which you are referring if the column name is unique to a single table in the statement. Suppose, for example, that you had two tables with column names defined as shown in Figure 10.1.

The DBMS would have no trouble determining which columns to display in the following SQL statement:

```
SELECT
  STUDENT_ID, STUDENT_NAME, SUBJECT, TEACHER_NAME
FROM
  STUDENT, TEACHER
WHERE
  CLASS1_TEACHER = TEACHER_ID
```

Since STUDENT_ID and STUDENT_NAME appear only in the STUDENT table, the DBMS would display the values in the STUDENT_ID and STUDENT_NAME columns of the STUDENT table. Similarly, SUBJECT and TEACHER_NAME are found only in the TEACHER table, so the DBMS would display SUBJECT and TEACHER_NAME information from the TEACHER table as it executes the SELECT statement. Thus, if you use columns from more than one table in an SQL statement, the DBMS can figure out which column name refers to which table if none of the column names in the SQL statement appears in more than one table listed in the FROM clause.

STUDENT table

STUDENT_ID
STUDENT_NAME
STREET_ADDRESS
CITY
STATE
ZIP_CODE
PHONE_NUMBER
CLASS1_TEACHER
CLASS2_TEACHER
CLASS3_TEACHER
CLASS4_TEACHER

TEACHER table

TEACHER_ID
TEACHER_NAME
SUBJECT
PHONE_NUMBER

Figure 10.1 Example STUDENT table and TEACHER table with duplicate column names

If you want to display data from one or more columns that have the same name in more than one table used in an SQL statement, you will need to use the *qualified column name* for each of the duplicate columns. The qualified column name is the name of the table, followed by a period (.) and then the name of the column. As such, if you wanted to list the student's phone number (found in the PHONE_NUMBER column in the STUDENT table), you could use the following SQL statement:

```
SELECT
  STUDENT_ID, STUDENT_NAME, STUDENT.PHONE_NUMBER, SUBJECT,
  TEACHER_NAME
FROM
  STUDENT, TEACHER
WHERE
  CLASS1_TEACHER = TEACHER_ID
```

If you specified only PHONE_NUMBER after STUDENT_NAME, the DBMS would not know if it were supposed to display the student's phone number or the teacher's phone number, since both tables have the column named PHONE_NUMBER. By using the qualified column name (STUDENT.PHONE_NUMBER, in this example), you specify not only the column whose data you want, but also the table whose data the DBMS is to use. In general, you can use qualified column names in an SQL statement wherever unqualified column names can appear.

As you learned in Tip 9, "Understanding Table Names," you need to use qualified table names whenever you want to work with a table that you do not own. Thus, you must use the qualified table name (the name of the table, followed by a period [.] and then the table name) in your SQL statement wherever the name of the table that you do not own appears. Thus, in the current example, if you own the TEACHER table but you did not create the STUDENT table (and Konrad, who created the table, gave you access to the table but did not assign its ownership to you), you would modify the SQL statement as follows:

```
SELECT
  STUDENT_ID, STUDENT_NAME, KONRAD.STUDENT.PHONE_NUMBER,
  SUBJECT, TEACHER_NAME
FROM
  KONRAD.STUDENT, TEACHER
WHERE
  CLASS1_TEACHER = TEACHER_ID
```

By using the qualified table name KONRAD.STUDENT in place of STUDENT in the SELECT statement, you tell the DBMS to extract data from the STUDENT table owned by Konrad instead of trying to get data from a nonexistent STUDENT table created (or owned) by you.

11 Understanding Views

As you learned in Tip 7, "Understanding Terms Used to Define an SQL Database," views are virtual tables. A view looks like a table because it appears to have all of the essential components of a table—it has a name, it has rows of data arranged in named columns, and its definition is stored in the database catalog right along with all of the other "real" tables. Moreover, you can use the name of a view in many SQL statements wherever a table name can appear. What makes a view a *virtual* vs. *real* table is that the data seen in a view exists in the tables used to create the view, not in the view itself.

The easiest way to understand views is to see how they are created, what happens when you use the name of a view in an SQL query, and what happens to the view upon completion of the SQL statement.

To create a view, use the SQL CREATE VIEW statement. Suppose, for example, that you have relational database tables with salesman and payroll data similar to that shown in Figure 11.1.

SALES_REPS table

EMP_NUM	NAME	APPT_COUNT	SALES_COUNT	SSAN	ADDR
1	Tamika James	10	6		
2	Sally Wells	23	9		
3	Robert Hardy	17	12		
4	Jane Smith	12	8		
5	Rodger Dodger	22	17		
6	Clide Williams	19	16		

PAYROLL table

EMP_NUM	YTD_SALARY	YTD_COMMISSION
1	$69,595.00	$2,595.00
2	$89,498.00	$16,323.00
3	$45,000.00	$27,123.00
4	$75,000.00	$17,000.00
5	$63,000.00	$5,000.00
6	$72,898.00	$2,993.00

Figure 11.1 Example relational database tables to use as base tables for a view

When you execute this SQL statement

```
CREATE VIEW APPT_SALES_PAY
  (NAME,APPTS,SALES,SALES_PCT,YTD_SALARY,YTD_COMMISSION) AS
SELECT
  NAME, APPT_COUNT, SALES_COUNT, ((APPT_COUNT / SALES_COUNT)
  * 100), YTD_SALARY, YTD_COMMISSION
FROM
  SALES_REPS, PAYROLL
WHERE
  SALES_REPS.EMP_NUM = PAYROLL.EMP_NUM
```

the DBMS stores the definition of the view in the database under the name APPT_SALES_PAY. Unlike the CREATE TABLE statement that creates an actual empty database table in addition to storing the definition of the table in the system catalog, the CREATE VIEW statement only stores the definition of the view.

The DBMS does not create an actual table when you create a view because, unlike a real table, the view does not exist in the database as a set of values in a table. Instead, the rows and columns of data you see through a view are the results produced by the query that defines the view.

After you create a view, you can use it in a SELECT statement as if it were a real table. For example, after you create the APPT_SALES_PAY view (using the CREATE statement that follows Figure 11.1), you can display the results of the query that defines the view by using this SQL statement:

```
SELECT * FROM APPT_SALES_PAY
```

When the DBMS sees the reference to a view in an SQL statement, it finds the definition of the view in its system tables. The DBMS then transforms the view references into an equivalent request against the base tables and executes the equivalent SQL statements. For the current example, the DBMS will execute a multi-table select statement (which you will learn about in Tip 205, "Using a SELECT Statement with a FROM Clause for Multi-table Selections") to form the virtual table shown in Figure 11.2, and then display the values in all of the columns in each row of the virtual table.

For simple views, the DBMS will construct each row of the view's virtual table "on the fly." Thus, in the current example, the DBMS will extract data from the columns specified in the view definition from one row in the SALES_REPS and PAYROLL tables to create a row in the virtual APPT_SALES_PAY table. Next, the DBMS will execute the SELECT statement to display the fields in the newly created row (of the virtual table). The DBMS will then repeat the procedure (create a virtual row from the two tables and then display the columns of the virtual row), until no more rows in the base tables satisfy the query in the view.

To execute more complex views (such as those used in SQL statements that update data in the base tables), the DBMS must actually *materialize* the view, meaning that the DBMS will perform the query that defines the view and store the results in a temporary table. The DBMS will then use the temporary table to execute the SQL statement (such as SELECT * FROM APPT_SALES_PAY) that references the view. When the DBMS no longer needs the temporary table (at the completion of the SQL statement), the DBMS discards it. Remember, views do not hold data; they merely display the data stored in their base tables (SALES_REPS and PAYROLL, in the current example).

Whether the DBMS handles a particular view by creating rows on the fly or by pulling the view data into a temporary table, the end result is the same—the user can reference views in SQL statements as if they were real tables in the database.

There are several advantages in using views:

- **Provide security.** When you don't want a user to see all of the data in a table, you can use a view to let the user see only specific columns. Thus, someone working in the personnel department can see the employee name and address information through a view, while the salary or hourly pay can remain hidden by being excluded from the view.

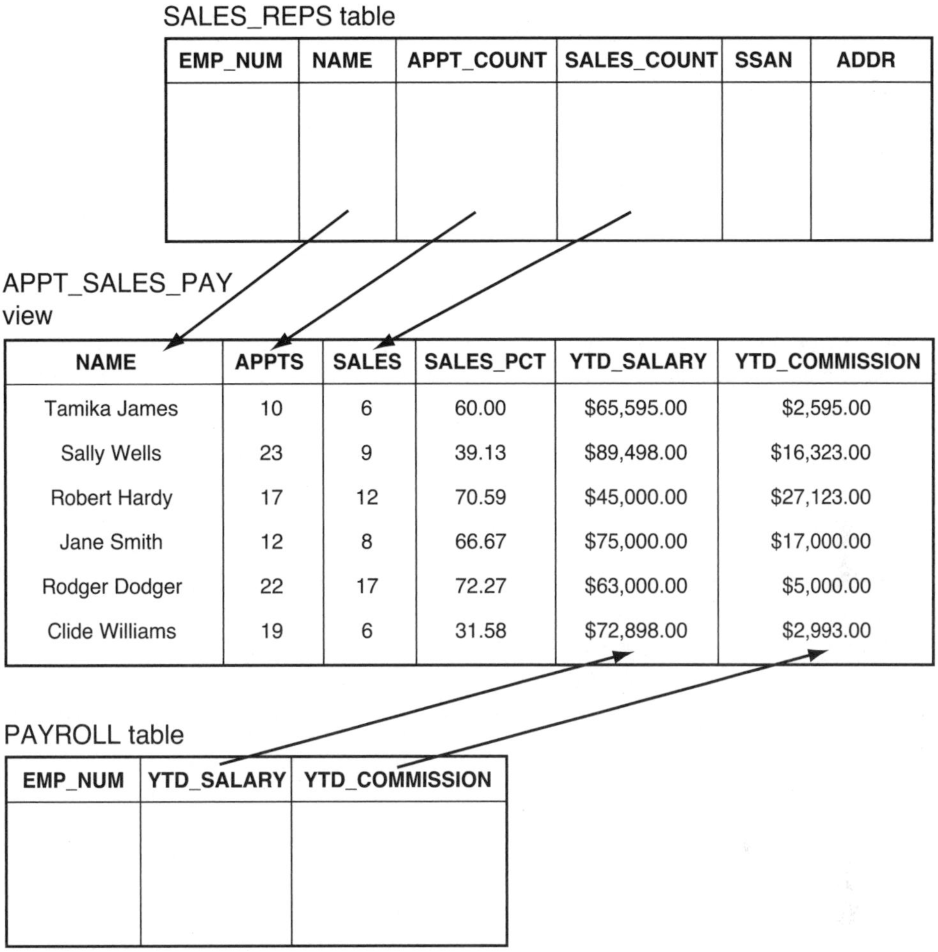

SALES_REPS table

EMP_NUM	NAME	APPT_COUNT	SALES_COUNT	SSAN	ADDR

APPT_SALES_PAY view

NAME	APPTS	SALES	SALES_PCT	YTD_SALARY	YTD_COMMISSION
Tamika James	10	6	60.00	$65,595.00	$2,595.00
Sally Wells	23	9	39.13	$89,498.00	$16,323.00
Robert Hardy	17	12	70.59	$45,000.00	$27,123.00
Jane Smith	12	8	66.67	$75,000.00	$17,000.00
Rodger Dodger	22	17	72.27	$63,000.00	$5,000.00
Clide Williams	19	6	31.58	$72,898.00	$2,993.00

PAYROLL table

EMP_NUM	YTD_SALARY	YTD_COMMISSION

Figure 11.2 APPT_SALES_PAY view generated from base tables SALES_REPS and PAYROLL

- **Simplify data structures.** You can present the database as a "personalized" set of tables. Suppose, for example, that you have separate employee and payroll tables. You can use a view to display employee names and pay figures in a single virtual table for the company's managers.

- **Abstract data structures.** As time goes on, some users will save SQL queries that they use often, and others may even write Visual Basic or C++ programs that extract data from the database to produce reports. If someone (such as the table owner or database administrator) changes the physical structure of a table by splitting it into two tables, for example, saved user queries may no longer function and application programs may try to access columns that no longer exist. However, if users write their queries or application programs to access data in the "virtual" view tables, you can insulate them from changes to the underlying database structures. When you split a table, for example, you need change the view's query so that it recombines the split tables into the set of columns found in the original view.

- **Simplify queries.** By using a view to combine the data from several tables into a single virtual table, you make it possible for a user to write SQL queries based on a single table, thus avoiding the complexity of using multi-table SELECT and JOIN statements.

While views provide several advantages, there are two main disadvantages to using them:

- **Performance.** Since a view is a virtual table, the DBMS must either materialize the data in a view as a temporary table or extract the data in the view's rows on the fly (one row at a time) whenever you use a view in an SQL statement. Thus, each time you use an SQL statement that contains a view reference, you are telling the DBMS to perform the query that defines the view in addition to performing the query or update in SQL statement you just entered.
- **Update restrictions.** Unfortunately, SQL violates Rule 6 of Codd's rules (you learned about this in Tip 6, "Understanding Codd's 12-Rule Relational Database Definition"), in that not all views are updateable. Currently, SQL limits updateable views to those based on queries on a single table without GROUP BY or HAVING clauses. In addition, to be updateable a view cannot have aggregate functions, calculated columns, or a SELECT DISTINCT clause. And, finally, the view must contain a table key column, and any columns excluded from the view must be NULL-able in the base table.

Due to SQL limitations on what views you can use for updating base tables, you cannot always create views to use in place of base tables. Moreover, in those cases where you can use a view, always weigh the advantages of using the view against the performance hit you take in having the DBMS create virtual tables every time it executes an SQL statement that references a view.

12 *Understanding Schemas*

A table consists of rows and columns of data that deal with a specific type of entity such as marketing calls, sales statistics, customers, orders, payroll, and so on. A schema is the collection of related tables. Thus, a schema is to tables what tables are to individual data items. While a table brings together related data items so that they describe an entity when considered a row at a time in a table, the schema is the set of related tables and organizational structure that describe your department or company.

Suppose that you worked in a sales organization with five departments as shown in Figure 12.1.

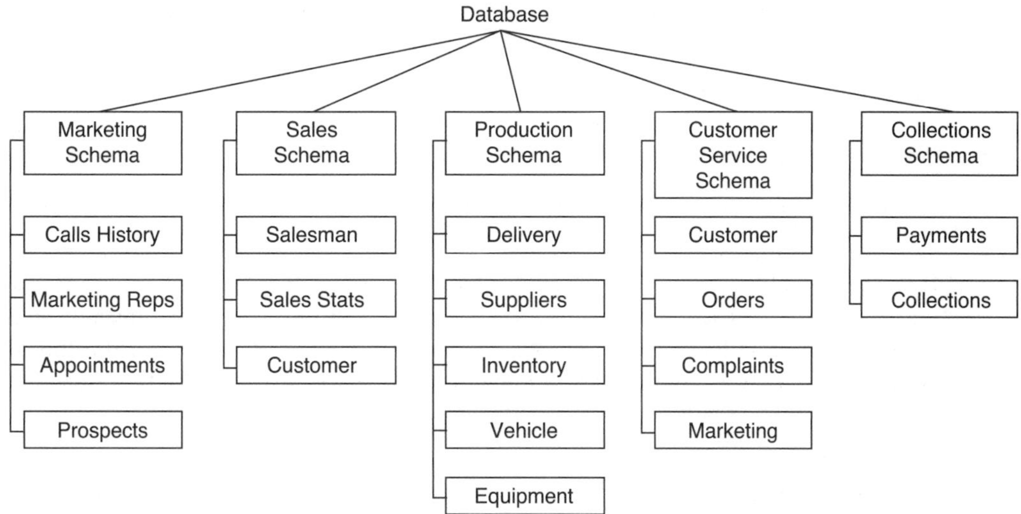

Figure 12.1 Database with tables grouped into five schemas, one for each department in the company

The tables in the marketing department, for example, might include tables showing the history of marketing calls made, marketing representative appointment setting statistics, an appointment list, and demographic data on prospects. The collections department, meanwhile, would have tables that deal with customer information, payments made on accounts, and collections activity such as scheduling dunning letters and field calls for payment pickups. All of the tables shown in Figure 12.1 would exist in a single database. However, each department has its own set of activities, as reflected in the set tables of data it maintains. Each department's tables could be organized into a separate schema within the company's database.

The schema is more of a "container" for objects than just a "grouping" of related tables because a schema includes:

- **Tables.** Related data items arranged in columns of rows that describe a physical or logical entity. The schema includes the tables as well as all of the components of a table (described in Tip 8, "Understanding the Components of a Table"), which include the column domains, check constraints, primary and foreign keys, and so on).
- **Views.** Virtual tables defined by an SQL query that display data from one or more base tables (as described in Tip 11, "Understanding Views"). The schema includes the definition of all views that use base tables of "real" data included in the schema. (As you learned in Tip 11, the virtual tables exist only for the duration of the SQL statement that references the view.)
- **Assertions.** Database integrity constraints that place restrictions on data relationships between tables in a schema. You will learn more about assertions in Tip 33, "Understanding Assertions."

- **Privileges.** Access rights that individual users and groups of users have to create or modify table structures, and to query and/or update database table data (or data in only specific columns in tables through views). You will learn all about the SQL security privileges in Tips 135–158.
- **Character sets.** Database structures used to allow SQL to display non-Roman characters such as Cyrillic (Russian), Kanji (Asian), and so on.
- **Collations.** Define the sorting sequences for a character set.
- **Translations.** Control how text character sequences are to be translated from one character set to another. Translations let you store data in Kanji, for example, and display it in Cyrillic, Kanji, and Roman—depending on the user's view of the data. In addition to showing which character(s) in one character set maps to which character(s) in another, translations define how text strings in one character set compare to text strings in another when used in comparison operations.

In short, the schema is a container that holds a set of tables, the metadata that describes the data (columns) in those tables, the domains and constraints that limit what data can be put into a table's columns, the keys (primary and foreign) that limit the rows that can be added to and removed from a table, and the security that defines who is allowed to do what to objects in the schema.

When you use the CREATE TABLE statement (which you will learn about in Tip 46, "Using the CREATE TABLE Statement to Create Tables"), the DBMS automatically creates your table in the default schema for your interactive session, the schema named <user ID>. Thus, if users Konrad and Karen each log in to the database and execute the SQL statement

```
CREATE TABLE CALL_HISTORY
  (PHONE_REP_ID CHAR(3) NOT NULL,
   PHONE_NUMBER INTEGER NOT NULL,
   DATE_TO_CALL DATE,
   TIME_TO_CALL INTEGER,
   DATE_CALLED  DATE    NOT NULL,
   TIME_CALLED  INTEGER NOT NULL,
   HANGUP_TIME  INTEGER NOT NULL,
   DISPOSITION  CHAR(4) NOT NULL)
```

the DBMS will add a table to each of two schemas, as shown in Figure 12.2.

In short, anytime you use the CREATE statement to create a database object such as a table, view, domain, assertion, and so on, the DBMS will create that object in the default "container" schema.

If you want to create an object in a specific schema "container," the container must exist and you must use the qualified name for the object you are creating. Qualified object names are an extension of the qualified table names you learned about in Tip 9, "Understanding Table Names." Instead of using <owner>.<object name>, use <schema name>.<object name> to place an object in a specific schema.

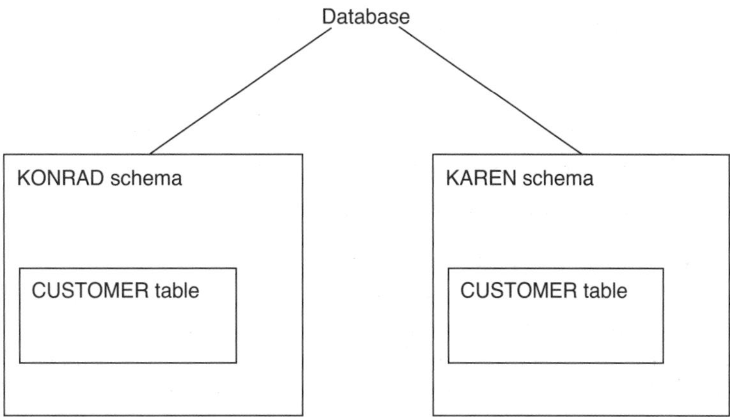

Figure 12.2 Database with two schemas, KONRAD and KAREN

For example, to create the MARKETING schema shown in Figure 12.1, you could use the SQL statement

```
CREATE SCHEMA MARKETING AUTHORIZATION KONRAD
  CREATE TABLE CALLS_HISTORY
    (PHONE_REP_ID CHAR (3) NOT NULL,
     PHONE_NUMBER INTEGER, NOT NULL,
     DATE_CALLED  DATE)
  CREATE TABLE  MARKETING REPS
    (REP_ID   CHAR(3),
     REP_NAME CHAR(25))
  CREATE TABLE APPOINTMENTS
    (APPOINTMENT_DATE  DATE,
     APPOINTMENT_TIME INTEGER,
     PHONE_NUMBER       INTEGER)
  CREATE TABLE PROSPECTS
    PHONE_NUMBER INTEGER,
    NAME         CHAR(25),
    ADDRESS      CHAR(35))
```

to create the MARKETING schema and the structure for its four tables. The AUTHORIZATION predicate in the CREATE SCHEMA statement authorizes Konrad to modify the schema and its objects. As such, Konrad could then use an ALTER TABLE MARKETING.<table name> statement to change the columns, domains, and constraints of columns in the tables included in the MARKETING schema. Moreover, Konrad can create additional tables in the MARKETING schema by specifying the schema name in a CREATE TABLE statement, such as:

```
CREATE TABLE MARKETING.CONTESTS
  (DESCRIPTION CHAR(25),
   RULES       VARCHAR(100),
   WIN_LEVEL1  MONEY,
```

```
WIN_LEVEL2  MONEY,
WIN_LEVEL3  MONEY)
```

All DBMS products have schema, or "containers," that hold a collection of tables and related objects. However, the name you can give to a schema varies from product to product. Oracle, Informix, and Sybase, for example, require that the schema name and username be the same. Each also limits the types of objects you can define in the CREATE SCHEMA statement. Thus, you must check the syntax of the CREATE SCHEMA statement in your DBMS manual (or Help system) to see what objects can be grouped together in schema "containers" and what names you can give to schema itself.

13 Understanding the SQL System Catalog

The system catalog is a collection of tables that the DBMS itself owns, creates, and maintains in order to manage the user-defined objects (tables, domains, constraints, schemas, other catalogs, security, and so on) in the database. As a collection, the tables in the system catalog are often referred to as the *system* tables because they contain data that describes the structure of the database and all of its objects and are used by the database management system in some way during the execution of every SQL statement.

When processing SQL statements, the DBMS constantly refers to the tables in the system catalog to:

- Make sure that all tables or views referenced in a statement actually exist in the database
- Make sure the columns referenced in the SQL statement exist in the tables listed in the target tables list portion of the statement (for example, the FROM section of a SELECT statement)
- Resolve unqualified column names to one of the tables or views referenced in the statement
- Determine the data type of each column
- Check the system security tables to make sure that the user has the privilege necessary to carry out the action described in the SQL statement on the target table (or column)
- Find and apply any primary key, foreign key, domain, and constraint definitions during INSERT, UPDATE, or DELETE operations

By storing the database description as a set of system tables, SQL meets the requirement for a "Dynamic Online Catalog Based on the Relational Model," listed as Rule 4 of Codd's 12 rules that define a relational database (which you learned about in Tip 6, "Understanding Codd's 12-Rule Relational Database Definition").

Not only does an SQL database use the system tables in the system catalog to validate and then execute SQL statements issued by the user or application programs, but the DBMS also makes the data in the system catalog available either directly or through views.

Note: *The database administrator may limit access to the tables in the system catalog due to security concerns. After all, if you knew the primary key constraints, column name, and data domains for a particular table, you could determine the contents of the column(s) in the primary key—even if you did not have SELECT access to the table itself. Moreover, the structure of the database may itself be a trade secret if table and/or column names give information as the types of data a company in a particular market would find important enough to collect.*

Since the DBMS maintains the data in the system tables so that it accurately describes the structure and contents of the database, user access to the system catalog is strictly read-only. Allowing a user to change the values in system tables would destroy the integrity of the system catalog. After all, if the DBMS is doing its job of maintaining the tables to accurately describe the database, any changes made to the catalog by the user would, by definition, change a correct value into an incorrect one.

The main advantage of user-accessible system tables is that they allow applications programmers to write general-purpose database tools that allow users to access SQL databases without having to know SQL. For example, by querying the system tables, an application program can determine the list of tables and views to which a user has access. The program could then allow the user to select the table(s) of interest and list the columns available for display in the selected table(s). Next the application program could allow the user to enter any "filtering" or search criteria. After the user has selected the table and columns and entered selection criteria, the application program could generate the SQL statements necessary to extract the data and format and display the query results to the user.

Without the system tables, the table and column names and the access rights would have to be hard-coded into the application programs, making general-purpose third-party applications impossible to write. Due to the demand for such third-party software solutions (owing perhaps to the scarcity of good SQL programmers), most major SQL database products are moving to support a common a set of system catalog views know collectively as the INFORMATION_SCHEMA.

You will learn more about the INFORMATION_SCHEMA and system tables in Tips 472–493, which discuss the INFORMATION_SCHEMA and the system tables on which it is based, and Tip 494 "Understanding the MS-SQL Server System Database Tables," which reviews the MS-SQL Server system tables. For now, the important thing to know is that the INFORMATION_SCHEMA views will allow the same application program to access system table information in different database products even though the structure of the catalog and the tables it contains varies considerable from one brand of DBMS to another.

14 Understanding Domains

A domain is the set of all values that are legal for a particular column in a table. Suppose, for example, that your EMPLOYEE table had a DEPENDANT field that your company policy states must be an INTEGER between 0 and 14. The domain of DEPENDANT would then be 0,1,2,3,4,5,6,7,8,9,10,12,13,14. Or, suppose you were maintaining a table for a tablecloth inventory that has a COLOR column, and all of your tablecloths were white, beige, or blue. The domain of the COLOR column would then be WHITE, BEIGE, BLUE.

Once you define a domain using the CREATE DOMAIN statement (which we will discuss in Tip 170, "Using the CREATE DOMAIN Statement to Create Domains"), you can use the domain as a data type when defining a column. Suppose, for example, that you had a CUSTOMER table with a STATE field. You could define the domain of the STATE field by creating a STATE_CODE domain using this SQL statement:

```
CREATE DOMAIN STATE_CODE AS CHAR(2)
  CONSTRAINT VALID_STATE_ABBREVIATION
  CHECK (VALUE IN ('AL', 'AK', 'AZ', 'CO', 'CT', ...  ))
```

Note: *You would list the remaining 45 state codes in place of the "..." in the VALUE IN section of the CREATE DOMAIN statement.*

To have the DBMS validate data as it is entered into the STATE field of the CUSTOMER table, use the STATE_CODE domain as the data type for the state field when creating the table, as shown in this SQL statement:

```
CREATE TABLE CUSTOMER
  (NAME      VARCHAR(25),
   ADDRESS   VARCHAR(35),
   CITY      VARCHAR(20),
   STATE     STATE_CODE,
   ZIP_CODE  INTEGER)
```

The beauty of defining a domain is that you can change it on the fly without having to alter the structure of the table or recompile any existing stored procedures or application programs.

Suppose, for example, that Puerto Rico were to become a state; you could use the ALTER DOMAIN statement to add PR to the list of valid state abbreviations. The DBMS would then automatically allow the user to enter PR for the STATE field, since the updated STATE_CODE domain (stored in the system tables) would include PR as a valid state code the next time the DBMS referred to it in checking the value in the STATE field of a row to be added to the CUSTOMER table.

15 Understanding Constraints

Constraints are database objects that restrict the data that a user or application program can enter into the columns of a table. There are seven types of constraints: assertions, domains, check constraints, foreign key constraints, primary key constraints, required data, and uniqueness constraints. Each type of constraint plays a different roll in maintaining database integrity:

- **Assertions.** Allow you to maintain the integrity of a relationship among data values that cross multiple tables within a database. Suppose, for example, that you have a marketing room with four teams of sales representatives, and each of the sales representatives has a quota for the number of sales he or she is to make on a daily basis. If your marketing manager has a daily quota, you would use an assertion to ensure that the ROOM_QUOTA column in the marketing manager record (row) of the MANAGER table did not exceed the sum of the values in the REP_QUOTA column in the PHONE_REP table. You will learn more about assertions in Tip 33, "Understanding Assertions," and Tip 199, "Using the CREATE ASSERTION Statement to Create Multi-table Constraints."
- **Domains.** Ensure that users and applications enter only valid values into table columns. Every column in a table has a certain set of values that are legal for that column. For example, if the MONTHLY_SALARY column in a PAYROLL table must always have values between $0.00 and $100,000.00, you can apply a domain constraint to tell the DBMS to prevent values outside of that range from being entered into the database. (Of course, high-stress jobs, such as SQL DBA, will require that the upper limit of the MONTHLY_SALARY domain be higher.)
- **Check constraints.** In addition to being used to define domains and assertions, this constraint can be applied directly to table columns in CREATE TABLE or ALTER TABLE statements. Whether a check constraint is given a name (using the CREATE DOMAIN or CREATE ASSERTION statement) or is added directly to a table definition, it performs the same function.

As you learned in Tip 14, "Understanding Domains," you create a domain by giving a name to a check constraint with a constant set of data values. Instead of using the CREATE DOMAIN statement, you can include CHECK constraint (which you will learn about in Tip 193, "Using the CHECK Constraint to Validate a Column's Value") directly to a column in the CREATE TABLE or ALTER TABLE statement.

As you will learn in Tip 33, an assertion is really another name for a CHECK constraint to which you've assigned a name using the CREATE ASSERTION statement. You can use assertions or multi-table CHECK constraints to apply business rules to the values of columns in a table. Suppose, for example, that your company did not allow back orders. As such, you could use a query in the CHECK constraint on the QUANTITY column of the ORDER table that would allow only values that were less than the total of the product currently on hand, as shown in the INVENTORY table. You will learn more about using search conditions in the CHECK constraint in Tip 444, "Understanding When to Use a CHECK Constraint Instead of a Trigger."

- **Foreign key constraints.** Are used to maintain referential integrity within the database by making sure that the parent record is not removed if there are still child records. Conversely, the FOREIGN KEY constraint also makes sure that you do not add a child record (row) to a table if there is no corresponding parent. Suppose, for example, that you had two tables, STUDENT and GRADES. You would apply the FOREIGN KEY constraint (which you will learn about in Tip 174, "Understanding Referential Data Integrity Checks and Foreign Keys") to one of the columns (such as STUDENT_NUMBER) in the child (GRADES) table to tell the DBMS that the value inserted in that column must also be present in the PRIMARY KEY column in one of the rows in the parent (STUDENT) table. Thus, if STUDENT_ID were the PRIMARY KEY in the (parent) STUDENT table, the DBMS would allow the insertion of a row into the GRADES table only if the student record (row) had a STUDENT_NUMBER equal to one of the STUDENT_IDs in the STUDENT table. Conversely, the DBMS would prevent the deletion of any student record (row) from the STUDENT table if one or more grades records (rows) had a STUDENT_NUMBER equal to the STUDENT_ID in the row to be deleted.
- **Primary key constraints.** Maintain entity integrity by specifying that at least one column in a table must have a unique value in each and every row of the table. Having a column with a different value in every row of the table prevents two rows of the table from being identical, thereby satisfying Codd's Rule #2 ("The Guaranteed Access Rule," discussed in Tip 6, "Understanding Codd's 12-Rule Relational Database Definition"). If you have a STUDENT table, for example, you would want one and only one row in the table to list the attributes (columns) for any one student. As such, you would apply the PRIMARY KEY constraint (which you will learn about in Tip 173, "Understanding Foreign Keys") to the STUDENT_ID column of the STUDENT table in order to ensure that no two students were given the same student ID number.
- **Required data.** Some columns in a table must contain data in order for the row to successfully describe a physical or logical entity. For example, suppose you had a GRADES table that contained a STUDENT_ID column. Each and every row in the table must have a value in the STUDENT_ID column in order for that grade record (row) to make sense—after all, a grade in a class is meaningless unless it is associated with the specific student (identified by the STUDENT_ID) that earned it. You will learn about the NOT NULL (required data) constraint in Tip 191, "Using the NOT NULL Column Constraint to Prevent NULL Values in a Column."
- **Uniqueness constraints.** While each table can have only one PRIMARY KEY, there are times when you may want to specify that more than one column in a table should have a unique value in each row. You can apply the UNIQUE constraint (which you will learn about in Tip 192, "Using the UNIQUE Column Constraint to Prevent Duplicate Values in a Column") to a table column to ensure that only one row in the table will have a certain value in that column. Suppose, for example, that you have a TEACHERS table and want to have only one teacher available for each subject offered at the school. If the table's PRIMARY KEY constraint were already applied to the TEACHER_ID column, you could

apply the UNIQUE constraint to the SUBJECT column to tell the DBMS not to allow the insertion of a row where the value in the SUBJECT column matched the value in the SUBJECT column of a row already in the table.

The DBMS stores a description of each constraint in its system tables when the constraint is normally specified as part of a table definition (CHECK, FOREIGN KEY, PRIMARY KEY, NOT NULL [required data], UNIQUE), or by using the CREATE statement (ASSERTION, DOMAIN). All constraints are database objects that either limit the values that you can put into a table's columns or limit the rows (combination of column values) that you can add to a table.

16 Understanding the History of SQL

Both SQL and relational database theory originated in IBM's research laboratories. In June 1970, Dr. Edgar F. Codd, an IBM engineer, wrote a paper outlining the mathematical theory of how data could be stored in tables and manipulated using a data sublanguage. The article, entitled "A Relational Model of Data for Large Shared Data Banks," was published in the *Communications of the Association for Computing Machinery* (ACM) and led to the creation of relational database management systems (DBMS) and Structured Query Language (SQL).

After Dr. Codd published his article, IBM researchers began work on System /R, a prototype relational DBMS. During the development of System /R, the engineers also worked on a database query language—after all, once data was stored in a DBMS, it would be of no use unless you could combine and extract it in the form of useful information. One of the query languages, SEQUEL (short for Structured English Query Language), became the de facto standard data query language for relational DBMS products. The SQL we use today is the direct descendant of IBM's original SEQUEL data sublanguage.

Although IBM started the research in 1970 and developed the first prototype relational DBMS (System /R) in 1978, it was Oracle (then known as Relational Software, Inc.) that introduced the first commercial relational DBMS product in 1980. The Oracle DBMS (which ran on Digital Equipment Corp [DEC] VAX minicomputers) beat IBM's first commercial DBMS product (SQL/DS) to market by two years. While Oracle continued to refine its product and released version 3, which ran on mainframes, minicomputers, and PCs, in 1982, IBM was working on Database 2 (DB2) which it announced in 1983 and began shipping in 1985.

DB2 operated on IBM's MVS operating system on IBM mainframes that dominated the large data center market at the time. IBM called DB2 its flagship relational DBMS, and with IBM's weight behind it, DB2's SQL became the de facto standard database language.

Although initially slower than other database models (such as the hierarchical model that you learned about in Tip 3, "Understanding the Hierarchical Database Model," and the network model that you learned about in Tip 4, "Understanding the Network Database Model"), the relational model had one major advantage—you didn't need a programmer to get information from the database. The relational query languages let users pose ad hoc, English-like queries to the database and get immediate answers—without having to write a program first.

As the performance of relational DBMS products improved through software enhancements and increases in hardware processing power, they became accepted as the database technology of the future. Unfortunately, compatibility across vendor platforms was poor. Each company's DBMS included its own version of SQL. While every flavor of SQL contained the basic functionality of IBM's DB2 SQL, each extended it in ways that took advantage of the particular strengths of the vendor's relational DBMS and hardware platform.

In 1986 the American National Standards Institute (ANSI) and the International Organization for Standardization (ISO) published the first formal ANSI/ISO standard for SQL. SQL-86 (or SQL1) gave SQL "official" status as *the* relational DBMS data language. ANSI updated the standard in 1992 to include "popular" enhancements/extensions found across DBMS products and added a "wish list" objects and methods that a DBMS *should* have.

SQL-92 (or SQL2), published in ANSI Document X3.135-1992, is the most current and comprehensive definition of SQL. At present, no commercial DBMS fully supports all of the features defined by SQL-92, but all vendors are working toward becoming increasingly compliant with the standard. As a result, we are getting closer to the goal of having a data language (SQL) that is truly transportable across DBMS products and hardware platforms.

17 Understanding the Difference Between SQL and a Programming Language

To solve problems in a procedural programming language (such as Basic, C, COBOL, FORTRAN, and so on), you write lines of code that perform one operation after another until the program completes its tasks. The program may execute its lines of code in a linear sequence or loop to repeat some steps or branch to skip others. In any case, when writing a program in a procedural language, the programmer specifies what is to be done and how to do it.

SQL, on the other hand, is a nonprocedural language in that you tell SQL *what* you want to do without specifying exactly *how* to accomplish the task. The DBMS, not the programmer, decides the best way to perform the job. Suppose, for example, that you have a CUSTOMER table and you want a list of customers that owe you more than $1,000.00. You could tell the DBMS to generate the report with this SQL statement:

```
SELECT
  NAME, ADDRESS, CITY, STATE, ZIP, PHONE_NUMBER,
  BALANCE_DUE
FROM
  CUSTOMER
WHERE
  BALANCE_DUE > 1000.00
```

If writing a procedural program, you would have to write the control loop that reads each row (record) in the table, decides whether to print the values in the columns (fields), and moves on to the next row until it reaches the end of the table. In SQL, you specify only the data you want to see. The DBMS then examines the database and decides how best to fulfill your request.

Although it is an acronym for "Structured Query Language," SQL is more than just a data retrieval tool. SQL is a:

- **Data definition language (DDL),** for creating (and dropping) database objects such as tables, constraints, domains, and keys.
- **Data manipulation language (DML),** for changing values stored in columns, inserting new rows, and deleting those you no longer want.
- **Data control language (DCL),** for protecting the integrity of your database by defining a sequence of one or more SQL statements as a transaction in which the DBMS must complete all statements successfully or have none of them affect the database. DCL also lets you set up the security structure for the database.
- **Query language,** for retrieving data.

In addition to the DDL, DML, DCL, and query functions, SQL maintains data integrity and coordinates concurrent access to the database objects. In short, SQL provides all of the tools you need for controlling and interacting with the DBMS.

Despite all that it does, SQL is not a complete computer language (like Basic, C, or FORTRAN) because it contains no block (BEGIN, END) statements, conditional (IF) statements, branch (GOTO) statements, or loop (DO, WHILE, FOR) statements. Because it lacks input statements, output statements, and common procedural language control methods, SQL is considered a data *sublanguage.* What SQL lacks in procedural language components, it makes up for in the database realm with statements specialized for database management and data retrieval tasks.

You can get information from an SQL database by submitting ad hoc queries during an interactive session or by embedding SQL statements in a procedural application program. Issuing queries during an interactive session is most appropriate when you want a quick answer to a specific question that you may ask only once. If, on the other hand, you need the same information repeatedly and want to control the format of the output, embedding SQL statements in an application program or having the program send SQL commands to the DBMS via a call-level interface makes the most sense.

*Note: Most major database vendors are adding procedural programming language-like features to their SQL products by allowing you to create stored procedures. Stored procedures are sequences of SQL statements that you tell the DBMS to execute by entering the stored procedure's name at the console during an interactive session, or by sending the name as a command to the DBMS within an application program. The stored procedure itself contains SQL statements and code written in the vendor's extensions to SQL that provide procedural language facilities such as BEGIN-END blocks, IF statements, functions, procedures, WHILE loops, FOR loops, and so on. Oracle, for example, extends SQL with PL/SQL and SQL*Plus, while Microsoft lets you use its Transact-SQL extensions in stored procedures.*

18 Understanding Data Definition Language (DDL)

Data definition language (DDL) is the set of SQL statements (ALTER, CREATE, DROP, GRANT) that let you create, alter, or destroy (drop) the objects that make up a relational database. To put it another way, you use DDL to define the structure and security of a database. SQL-89 (the first ANSI/ISO standard written for SQL) defines data manipulation language (DML) and DDL as two distinct and relatively unrelated languages. Moreover, DML statements, which allow you to update the data in the database, must be available for use while users are accessing the database, for obvious reasons. SQL-89 does not require that the DBMS accept DDL statements during its normal operation. Thus, the standard allows a static database structure similar to that of the hierarchical model (see Tip 3, "Understanding the Hierarchical Database Model") and the network model (see Tip 4, "Understanding the Network Database Model").

The most basic (and powerful) DDL statement is the CREATE statement. Using CREATE, you build the database schema (which you learned about in Tip 12, "Understanding Schemas"). For example, to build a database with two schemas as shown in Figure 18.1, you could use the following SQL statements:

```
CREATE SCHEMA AUTHORIZATION KONRAD
  CREATE TABLE EMPLOYEES
    (ID           CHAR(3),
     NAME         VARCHAR(35),
     ADDRESS      VARCHAR(45),
     PHONE_NUMBER CHAR(11),
     DEPARTMENT   CHAR(10),
     SALARY       MONEY,
     HOURLY_RATE  MONEY)
  CREATE CUSTOMERS
    (NAME         VARCHAR(35),
     ADDRESS      VARCHAR(45),
     PHONE_NUMBER CHAR(11),
```

```
     FOOD_PLAN     CHAR(2))
  CREATE TABLE        APPT_SCHEDULE
    (APPT_DATE        DATE,
     APPT_TIME        INTEGER,
     APPT_DISPOSITION CHAR(4),
     APPT_SALESMAN_ID CHAR(3))
GRANT SELECT, UPDATE
  ON EMPLOYEES
  TO HR_DEPARTMENT
GRANT ALL PRIVILEGES
  ON CUSTOMERS
  TO MARKETING_REPS, OFFICE_CLERKS
GRANT SELECT
  ON APPT_SCHEDULE
  TO PUBLIC
GRANT SELECT, INSERT
  ON APPT_SCHEDULE
  TO MARKETING REPS
CREATE SCHEMA AUTHORIZATION KAREN
  CREATE TABLE EMPLOYEES
    (ID            CHAR(3),
     NAME          VARCHAR(35),
     ADDRESS       VARCHAR(45),
     PHONE_NUMBER  CHAR(11),
     EMPLOYEE_TYPE CHAR(2),
     SALARY        MONEY,
     HOURLY_RATE,  MONEY)
  GRANT SELECT, UPDATE
    ON EMPLOYEES
    TO HR_DEPARTMENT
  CREATE PATIENTS
    (ID            INTEGER
     SPONSOR_SSAN  CHAR(11),
     NAME          VARCHAR(35),
     ADDRESS       VARCHAR(45),
     PHONE_NUMBER  CHAR(11),
     AILMENT_CODES VARCHAR(120))
  GRANT SELECT, UPDATE
    ON PATIENTS
    TO DOCTORS, NURSES, CLERKS
  CREATE TABLE APPT_SCHEDULE
    (APPT_DATE          DATE,
     APPT_TIME          INTEGER,
     REASON_CODES       VARCHAR(120),
     DOCTOR_ID          CHAR(3),
     NURSE_ID           CHAR(3),
     REFERRAL_DOCTOR_ID CHAR(15))
  GRANT SELECT, UPDATE
    ON APPT_SCHEDULE
    TO PUBLIC
```

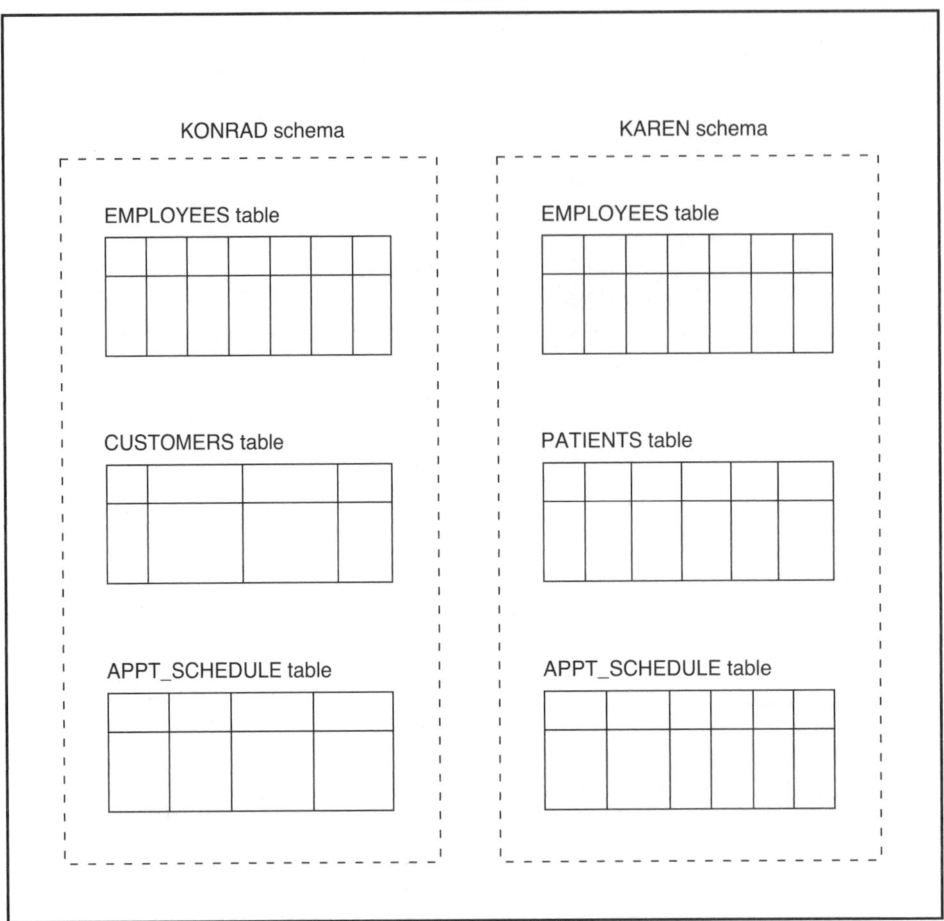

Figure 18.1 Example database with two schemas named KONRAD and KAREN, each containing three tables

---

Note: *The CREATE SCHEMA statement uses AUTHORIZATION in place of USER in naming the schema (such as CREATE SCHEMA AUTHORIZATION KONRAD, in the example). Not only does the SQL-89 specification refer to users as "authorization IDs," but the term* authorization ID *is more applicable on those occasions when you are creating a schema for a department vs. an individual. Moreover, even when creating schemas for individual authorization ID "works," the user ID (or username) is the ID that is authorized to the rights of ownership over the objects in the schema.*

If you were working in an environment using a static DDL, you would submit the CREATE SCHEMA statements to the database builder program, which would create the tables and set up the security scheme. The database structure would then be "frozen." Users could log in (and application programs could attach) to the database and send DML commands to work with the data in the database, but no tables could be removed or added.

In support of the static nature of the database structure, the SQL-89 specification did not include DROP TABLE and ALTER TABLE statements in the DDL definition. If you needed to change the structure of the database (by adding or removing a table, for example), you would have to get everyone to log out of the database and stop all DBMS access and processing. Then you would unload the data, submit a revised schema to the builder application, and then reload the data.

Although the SQL-89 standard permits a static database structure, no SQL database ever used this approach. Even the earliest releases of the IBM SQL products included the DROP TABLE and ALTER TABLE statements. Full compliance with SQL-92 eliminates the static database structure in that the current (as of this writing) SQL standard includes both DROP and ALTER statements—which require that users be able to remove or modify the structure of tables on the fly (that is, during the normal operation of the DBMS).

Although only the CREATE SCHEMA statement was shown in detail in this tip, other tips in this book will show how to use each of the DDL statements to:

- **CREATE/DROP/ALTER ASSERTION.** Limits the values that can be assigned to a column based on single or multiple table column relationships. DDL assertion statements are discussed in Tip 199, "Using the CREATE ASSERTION Statement to Create Multi-table Constraints."
- **CREATE/DROP/ALTER DOMAIN.** A named set of valid values for a column. DDL domain statements are discussed in Tip 170, "Using the CREATE DOMAIN Statement to Create Domains."
- **CREATE/DROP INDEX.** Structures that speed up database access by making it easier for SQL query statements to find the set of rows with columns that meet the search criteria. DDL index statements are discussed in Tip 161, "Using the CREATE INDEX Statement to Create an Index," and Tip 163, "Using the MS-SQL Server Enterprise Manager to Create an Index."
- **CREATE/DROP SCHEMA.** a set of related tables, views, domains, constraints, and security structure. Discussed in Tip 506, "Using the CREATE SCHEMA Statement to Create Tables and Grant Access to Those Tables."
- **CREATE/DROP/ALTER TABLE.** Rows of related columns (of data). DDL table statements are discussed in Tip 46, "Using the CREATE TABLE Statement to Create Tables"; Tip 56, "Understanding the ALTER TABLE Statement"; Tip 57, "Using the ALTER TABLE Statement to Add a Column to a Table"; Tip 60, "Using the ALTER TABLE Statement to Change Primary and Foreign Keys"; and Tip 63, "Using the DROP TABLE Statement to Remove a Table from the Database."
- **CREATE/DROP/ALTER VIEW.** Virtual tables that display columns of data from rows in one or more base tables. DDL view statements are discussed in Tip 64, "Using the DROP VIEW Statement to Remove a View"; Tip 206, "Using a View to Display Columns in One

or More Tables or Views"; and Tip 460, "Using the ALTER VIEW Statement to Modify a View."

- **GRANT.** Gives specific SQL statement access on individual database objects to a user or group of users. The GRANT statement is discussed in Tip 145, "Using the GRANT Statement WITH GRANT OPTION to Allow Users to Give Database Object Access to Other Users."

The important thing to know now is that DDL consists of the statements that let you create, alter, and destroy objects (tables, views, indexes, domains, constraints) in your database. DDL also has the GRANT statement that you can use to set up database security by granting users or groups DDL and DML statement access on a statement-by-statement and object-by-object basis.

Note: *The GRANT statement is part of the DDL and the data control language (DCL). When used in a CREATE SCHEMA statement, GRANT acts as a DDL statement. When used to give users (or groups) additional privileges outside a schema definition, GRANT is a DCL statement. As such, you will find GRANT and its opposite (REVOKE) in Tip 20, "Understanding Data Control Language (DCL)," which describes the SQL DCL statements.*

---

19 Understanding Data Manipulation Language (DML)

Data manipulation language (DML) lets you do five things to an SQL database: add data to tables, retrieve and display data in table columns, change data in tables, and delete data from tables. As such, basic DML consists of five statements:

- **INSERT INTO.** Lets you add one or more rows (or columns) into a table.
- **SELECT.** Lets you query one or more tables and will display columns in rows that meet your search criteria.
- **UPDATE.** Lets you change the value in one or more columns in table rows that meet your search criteria.
- **DELETE FROM.** Lets you remove one or more table rows that meet your search criteria.
- **TRUNCATE.** Lets you remove all rows from a table.

In theory, data manipulation is very simple. You already understand what it means to add data. Tip 67, "Using the INSERT Statement to Add Rows to a Table," will show you how to INSERT (add) data directly into to a table; Tip 68, "Using the INSERT Statement to Insert Rows Through a View," will show you how to INSERT data into a table through a view; and Tip 71, "Using the SELECT Statement to INSERT Rows from One Table into Another," will show you how to copy rows from one table into another.

The hardest part of data manipulation is selecting the rows you want to display, change, or delete. Since a relational database can have more than one schema, there is no guarantee that all data items (column values) in a database are related to each other in some way. What you do know is that sets of data items (columns in tables and tables in a schema) are related. You will use the SELECT statement to describe the data you want to see, and then the DBMS will find and display it for you. Tip 86, "Understanding the Structure of a SELECT Statement," shows you the structure of the SELECT statement, and Tip 87, "Understanding the Steps Involved in Processing an SQL SELECT Statement," shows you what you can expect after executing an SQL query.

Because databases model a constantly changing world, the data in a database will require frequent updates. The update process involves finding the row(s) with the data item(s) (column[s]) you want to change and then updating the values in those columns. Tips 73–77 show you how to use the UPDATE statement in conjunction with the SELECT statement to update column values in rows that meet your search criteria.

Once data gets old and loses its usefulness, you will want to remove it from the table in which it resides. Outdated or unneeded data in table rows slows performance, consumes memory and disk space, and can confuse users if returned as part of a query. Thus, you will want to use the DELETE statement to remove unneeded rows from a table. Tip 79, "Using the DELETE Statement to Remove a Row from a Table," shows you how to use the DELETE statement to remove a single row from a table; Tip 80, "Using the DELETE Statement with a Conditional Clause to Remove Multiple Rows from a Table," and Tip 81, "Using the DELETE Statement with a Subquery to Remove Multiple Rows from a Table," show you how use the DELETE statement to remove multiple rows from a table; and Tip 82, "Using the TRUNCATE Statement to Remove All Rows from an MS-SQL Server Table," shows you how to use the TRUNCATE statement to remove all rows from a table.

Although basic DML consists of only five statements, it is a powerful tool for entering, displaying, changing, and removing data from your database. DML lets you specify exactly what you want to do to the data in your database.

20 Understanding Data Control Language (DCL)

While DML lets you make changes to the data in your database, data control language (DCL) protects your data from harm. If you correctly use the tools that DCL provides, you can keep unauthorized users from viewing or changing your data, and prevent many of the problems that can corrupt your database. There are four DCL commands:

- **COMMIT.** Tells the DBMS to make permanent changes made to temporary copies of the data by updating the permanent database tables to match the updated, temporary copies. The COMMIT statement is discussed in Tip 129, "Understanding When to Use the COMMIT Statement."
- **ROLLBACK.** Tells the DBMS to undo any changes made to the DBMS after the most recent commit. The ROLLBACK statement is discussed in Tip 130, "Using the ROLLBACK Statement to UNDO Changes Made to Database Objects."
- **GRANT.** Gives specific SQL statement access on individual database objects to a user or group of users. The GRANT statement is discussed in Tip 145, "Using the GRANT Statement WITH GRANT OPTION to Allow Users to Give Database Object Access to Other Users."
- **REVOKE.** Removes specific SQL statement access previously granted on individual database objects from a user or group of users. The REVOKE statement is discussed in Tip 147, "Using the REVOKE Statement with the CASCADE Option to Remove Privileges."

A database is most vulnerable to damage while someone is changing it. If the software or hardware fails in the middle of making a change, the data will be left in an indeterminate state—part of what you wanted done will be completed, and part will not. Suppose for example that you told SQL to move money from one bank account to another. If the computer locks up while it is doing the transfer, you won't know if the DBMS debited the one account or if it got around to crediting the second account.

By encapsulating the debit and credit UPDATE statements within a transaction, you can make sure that the DBMS executes both statements successfully before executing the COMMIT command to write the updated balances permanently to the database.

If the DBMS does not successfully complete all of the statements in a transaction, you issue a ROLLBACK command. The DBMS will back out any changes made to the database since the last COMMIT command was executed. In the case of our failed money transfer example, the DBMS would back out any and all updates so that the balances in the accounts would be as they were before the DBMS attempted to move money from one account to another—it would be as if the transaction never happened.

Aside from data corruption caused by hardware or software failures, you also have to protect your data from the users themselves. Some people should have no access to the database. Others should be able to see some but not all of the data, while not being able to update any of it. Still others should have access to see and update a portion of the data. Thus, you must be able to approach database security on a user-by-user and group-by-group basis. DCL gives you the GRANT and REVOKE commands to use in assigning access privileges to individual users and groups of users. The DCL commands used to control security are:

- **GRANT SELECT.** Lets the user or group see the data in a table or view. Tip 149 discusses the GRANT and REVOKE SELECT statements.

- **REVOKE SELECT.** Prevents the user or group from seeing data in a table or view. Tip 149 discusses the GRANT and REVOKE SELECT statements.
- **GRANT INSERT.** Lets the user or group to add row(s) to a table or view. Tip 151 discusses the GRANT INSERT statement
- **REVOKE INSERT.** Prevents users or groups from adding row(s) to a table or view. Tip 151 discusses the REVOKE INSERT statement.
- **GRANT UPDATE.** Lets the user or group of users change the values in the columns of a table or view. Tip 152 discusses the GRANT UPDATE statement.
- **REVOKE UPDATE.** Prevents the user or group of users from changing the values in the columns of a table or view. Tip 152 discusses the REVOKE UPDATE statement.
- **GRANT DELETE.** Allows a user or group of users to delete row(s) in table or view
- **REVOKE DELETE.** Prevents a user or group of users from deleting row(s) in a table or view.
- **GRANT REFERENCES.** Lets a user or group of users to define a FOREIGN KEY reference to the table. Tip 153 discusses the GRANT REFERENCES statement.
- **REVOKE REFERENCES REVOKE REFERENCES.** Prevents the user or group of users from defining a FOREIGN KEY reference to the table. Tip 153 discusses the REVOKE REFERENCES statement.

Thus, DCL contains commands you can use to control who can access your database and what those users can do once they log in. Moreover, the DCL gives you control over when the DBMS makes permanent (COMMITs) changes to your database and lets you undo (ROLLBACK) changes not yet committed.

21 Understanding SQL Numeric Integer Data Types

Columns of type INTEGER can hold whole numbers—numbers without a fractional part (nonzero digits to the right of the decimal point). The maximum number of digits, or precision, of an INTEGER column is implementation-dependant. As such, you cannot control the maximum positive and negative value you can assign to an INTEGER column (check your SQL manual for the precision of integers on your system).

***Note:** An implementation is a DBMS product running on a specific hardware platform.*

There are two standard SQL INTEGER types: INTEGER (also INT) and SMALLINT. The precision of INTEGER is twice that of SMALLINT. MS-SQL Server running on a Windows NT platform, for example, can store an INTEGER value in the range –2,147,483,648 to

+2,147,486,647 (–[2**31] to 2**31). Each MS-SQL INTEGER consists of 4 bytes (32 bits)—31 bits for the magnitude (precision) and 1 bit for the sign. (Note that the term "precision" as used here is the number of digits in the number and not its accuracy.)

An MS-SQL Server SMALLINT, on the other hand, can hold numbers in the range –32,768 to 37,267 (–[2**15] to 2**15). Each MS-SQL Server SMALLINT consists of 2 bytes (16 bits)—15 for the magnitude (precision) and 1 bit for the sign.

The amount of storage space required to save an integer value to disk depends on its precision, not the actual number being stored. Thus, if you declare a column to be of type INTEGER, the system will take 8 bytes to store 1, 10,000, 1,000,000, or 2,000,000,000 in that column. Similarly, if you declare a column to be of type SMALLINT, the DBMS will take 4 bytes (instead of 8) to store a value, whether it is 2, 2,000, or 32,000.

Even in this day of large, inexpensive disks, it is best to conserve disk space by using the appropriate integer type (INTEGER or SMALLINT) based on the precision that you will need to store the values in a column. Thus, if you know that the value in a column will be no more than 32,767 and no less than –32,768, define the column as a SMALLINT, not an INTEGER. Both will hold whole numbers, but the SMALLINT data type will store those numbers using 4 bytes fewer than that used to store the same value in a column of type INTEGER.

Some SQL servers will even allow you to store a whole number value using as little as 1 byte. MS-SQL Server, for example, has the TINYINT data type. Columns of type TINYINT can hold positive whole numbers in the range 0 to 255. Thus, if you know that you will be using a column to store numbers no smaller than 0 and no larger than 255, define the column as TINYINT instead of INTEGER, and save 6 bytes per value stored.

The DBMS will automatically prevent the insertion of any rows where the value in a column is outside the acceptable range of values for that column's data type. Thus, if you create a table using:

```
CREATE TABLE integer_table
  (integer_max  INT,
   smallint_max SMALLINT,
   tinyint_max  TINYINT)
```

and then try to INSERT a row using:

```
INSERT INTO INTEGER_TABLE
  VALUES (1,2,256)
```

the DBMS will reject the row and return an error message similar to:

```
Server: Msg 220, Level 16, State 2, Line 1
Arithmetic overflow error for type tinyint, value = 256.
The statement has been terminated.
```

You will learn all about the INSERT statement in Tip 67, "Using the INSERT Statement to Add Rows to a Table." For now the important thing to know is that the VALUES clause in the INSERT statement tells the DBMS to insert the listed values by position. In the current example, the DBMS tries to assign the value 1 to the INTEGER_MAX column, the value 2 to the SMALLINT_MAX column, and the value 256 to the TINYINT_MAX column. The DBMS is able to carry out the first two assignments, but the third (assigning 256 to TINYINT_MAX, of data type TINYINT) causes an error since the maximum value of a column of type TINYINT is 255.

To summarize, SQL numeric INTEGER types are as shown in the following table:

Type	*Precision*	*Storage Space*
INTEGER (or INT)	–2,147,483,648 to +2,147,486,647	4 bytes (32 bits)
SMALLINT	–32,768 to 32,767	2 bytes (16 bits)
TINYINT	0 to 255	1 byte (8 bits)

Table 21.1 Numeric Integer Data Types and Storage Requirements

The precision and storage space are those for an MS-SQL Server running on a Windows NT server. Moreover, TINYINT is an MS-SQL Server-specific data type. You will need to check your system manuals to determine the precision, storage requirements, and other whole number types for your DBMS.

Note: *If you want to make your tables transportable, stick with the standard SQL INTEGER types: INTEGER (or INT) and SMALLINT. Otherwise, you may have to change your table definitions to create the same tables under different DBMS products if one supports a data type (such as TINYINT) and the other does not.*

22 Understanding SQL Numeric Floating-Point Data Types

You can use floating-point columns to store both whole numbers and numbers with a fractional part—numbers with nonzero digits to the right of the decimal point. Unlike the INTEGER data types (INTEGER, SMALLINT, TINYINT), which have precision set by the implementation, you control the precision of the columns you define as NUMERIC or DECIMAL. (The precision of the other floating-point data types—REAL, DOUBLE PRECISION, and FLOAT—is machine-dependent.)

The SQL floating-point data types are:

- NUMERIC (precision, scale)
- DECIMAL (precision, scale) or DEC (precision, scale)

- REAL
- DOUBLE PRECISION
- FLOAT (precision)

NUMERIC Data Type

When identifying a column as type NUMERIC, you should specify both the precision and the scale the DBMS is to use in storing values in the column. A number's precision is the total number of digits in a number. The scale is the maximum number of digits in the fractional part of the number. Thus, to allow for numeric data in the range –9999.999 to 9999.9999 you could use the following SQL statement:

```
CREATE TABLE numeric_table
  (numeric_column NUMERIC(8,4))
```

Both the precision and the scale of a NUMERIC column must be positive, and the scale (digits to the right of the decimal) cannot be larger than the precision (the maximum number of digits in the number). In the current example, the column NUMERIC_COLUMN has a precision of 8 and a scale of 4, meaning it can hold a number with, at most, eight digits, with four of them to the left and four of them to the right of the decimal point. Thus, if you attempt to insert the value 12345.6 into the column, the DBMS will return an arithmetic overflow error because your value has more than four digits to the left of the decimal. Similarly, if you insert the value 123.12345 into the column, the DBMS will round the value to 123.1235 because the scale is, at most, four digits (to the right of the decimal point).

Note: *If you don't specify the precision and scale when you identify a column of type NUMERIC, you will get the DBMS default for precision and scale. For example, if you are using MS-SQL Server and enter the following SQL statement*

```
CREATE TABLE numeric_table
  (numeric_column NUMERIC)
```

MS-SQL Server will give you a precision of 18 and a scale of 0. Thus, you can enter whole numbers 18 digits—the DBMS ignores any digits you enter to the right of the decimal point since the default scale is 0. Other DBMS products may give you a scale that is half of the precision. Thus, if the default precision is 18, the scale would be 9. When using the NUMERIC type, don't leave the precision and scale up to the DBMS—specify both. Otherwise, you may find that applications using your tables on one DBMS work fine but fail when running on another DBMS because the default precision and scale are different between the two products.

DECIMAL and DEC Data Types

The DECIMAL data type is similar to NUMERIC in that you specify both the precision and the scale of the numbers the DBMS is to store in columns of type DECIMAL. When a column is of type decimal, however, it may hold values with a greater precision and scale than you specify if the DBMS and the computer on which it is running allow for a greater precision. Thus, if you use the SQL statement

```
CREATE TABLE decimal_table
  (decimal_column DECIMAL (6,2))
```

you can always put values up to 9999.99 into the column DECIMAL_COLUMN. However, if the implementation uses a greater precision, the DBMS will not reject values with values greater than 9999.99.

Note: An implementation is a DBMS product running on a specific hardware platform.

REAL Data Type

Unlike the NUMERIC, DECIMAL, and DEC data types, which define columns with precise values, REAL, DOUBLE PRECISION, and FLOAT are *approximate* data types. When you define a column of TYPE NUMERIC(5,2), the computer will store the *exact* value of the number. You can specify the precision and scale for the precise floating point types (NUMERIC, DECIMAL, DEC), but there is a limit to the largest value you can store "exactly." Using MS-SQL Server running on an NT platform, for example, you can store a NUMERIC value with up to 38 digits. Therefore, if you need to store very large or very small numbers, you will need to use the REAL, DOUBLE, or FLOAT approximate data types.

The precision of the REAL data type depends on the platform on which you're running. A 64-bit machine (such as one based on the Alpha processor) will give you more precision than a 32-bit machine (such as one based on the Intel processor). When you define a column to be of type REAL using MS-SQL Server running under Windows NT on an INTEL platform, for example, the column can hold values with up seven digits of precision in the range 3.4E–38 to 3.4E+38.

In case, you're a bit "rusty" on the *scientific notation* you learned in high school, let's digress for a quick review. As you know (or knew), you can represent any number as a *mantissa* and an *exponent*. For example, if you have the number 32,768, you can express it as 3.2768E+4, which is the *mantissa* (3.2768, in this example) multiplied by 10 raised to the power or *exponent* (4, in this example). Thus, writing 3.2768E+4 is the same as writing 3.2768 * 10**4, which equals 32,768. Similarly, you could write 0.000156 as 1.56E-4.

A column of type REAL in an MS-SQL Server database running on an Intel platform can hold up to eight digits in the mantissa and have a value in the range 3.4E–38 to 3.4E+38.

Note: Check your system manual to find out the exact precision and value range of REAL numbers for your implementation.

DOUBLE PRECISION Data Type

When you define a column as being a DOUBLE PRECISION type, you are telling the DBMS that you want to store values with *double* the precision of a REAL data type. Like the REAL data type, the actual precision of a DOUBLE PRECISION column depends on the implementation (the combination of DBMS and platform on which it is running). The SQL-92 specification does not specify exactly what DOUBLE PRECISION means. It requires only that the precision of a DOUBLE PRECISION number be greater than the precision of a REAL (or single precision) number.

In some systems, the DOUBLE PRECISION data type will let you store numbers with twice the number of digits of precision defined for the REAL data type and twice the exponent. Other systems will let you store less than double the number of REAL digits in the mantissa, but let you store much larger (or smaller) numbers by letting you more than double the exponent allowed for the REAL data type.

The DOUBLE PRECISION data type for MS-SQL Server running under Windows NT on an INTEL platform gives you 16 digits of precision (17 digits total) for the mantissa and much more than twice the exponent of a REAL number. While an MS-SQL Server column of type REAL can hold values with up to 8 digits (7 digits of precision) and be in the range 3.4E–38 to 3.4E+38, a DOUBLE PRECISION column on the same system can hold 17-digit mantissas (16 digits of precision) and be in the range of 1.7E–308 to 1.7E+308.

Check your system manual to find out the exact precision and value range of DOUBLE PRECISION numbers for your implementation. Don't assume that DOUBLE PRECISION means twice the precision and twice the exponent.

FLOAT Data Type

Whether the FLOAT data type has the precision and range of a REAL number or a DOUBLE PRECISION number depends on the precision you specify when defining a column to be of type FLOAT.

When you define a column of type FLOAT, you specify the precision you want. If the hardware on which you are running the DBMS will support the precision using single-precision (REAL) registers, then you will get the default precision for REAL numbers. If, on the other hand, the hardware supports only the precision you specified for the FLOAT data type using DOUBLE PRECISION registers, the DBMS will store values of type FLOAT using the default precision for the DOUBLE PRECISION data type.

In reality, you will have to check your system manual or experiment with storing numbers in columns of type FLOAT to see the actual precision you will get based on the precision you specify for the FLOAT data type. For example, when running MS-SQL Server under Windows NT on an INTEL computer, the SQL statement

```
CREATE TABLE float_table
  (float_column FLOAT (15))
```

will result in only seven digits of precision (eight digits total). Thus, MS-SQL Server will insert 123456789012 as 1.2345679E+11 in the FLOAT_COLUMN, even though you specified a precision as 15. In fact, any precision less than 25 will result in only a single-precision (REAL) 7 digits of precision. If you specify a FLOAT precision of 26–53 (or omit the precision), the DBMS will store values using the DOUBLE PRECISION 16 digits of precision (17 digits total).

23 Understanding SQL Character Data Types

Table columns defined as being of one of the character data types can hold letters, numbers, and special characters (such as !,@,#,$,%,^, and so on). There are four character data types, each with one or two synonyms. The SQL character data types are:

Character Type	*Description*
CHAR(length) CHARACTER(length)	Fixed-length character string
VARCHAR(length) CHAR VARYING(length) CHARACTER VARYING(length)	Variable-length character string
NCHAR(length) NATIONAL CHAR(length) NATIONAL CHARACTER(length)	Fixed-length Unicode character string
NCHAR VARYING(length) NATIONAL CHAR VARYING(length) NATIONAL CHARACTER VARYING(length)	Variable-length Unicode character string

Table 23.1 SQL Character Data Types

When declaring a column as one of the character types, you specify both the character data type and its length. (The length of a character string is the maximum number of letters, symbols, and numbers the string can hold.) Thus, given the SQL table declaration

```
CREATE TABLE character_table
  (char_column          CHAR(10),
   char_column2         CHAR(100),
   varchar_column       VARCHAR(100),
   nchar_column         NCHAR(20)
   nchar_varying_column NCHAR VARYING (200))
```

you can store 10 characters in the column CHAR_COLUMN, 100 characters in CHAR_COLUMN2, 100 characters in the VARCHAR_COLUMN column, 20 characters in the column NCHAR_COLUMN, and 200 characters in the NCHAR_VARYING_COLUMN column.

To insert values that include letters or symbols into a CHARACTER data type column, enclose the string you want to insert in either single or double quotes. In our current example, executing the SQL INSERT statement

```
INSERT IN character_table
  VALUES ("Konrad", 9, 5+4, '5+4')
```

you would store Konrad in CHAR_COLUMN, 9 in VARCHAR_COLUMN, 9 in NCHAR_COLUMN, and 5+4 in NCHAR_VARYING_COLUMN. As you can see, if a character string includes only numbers, you need not enclose it in quotes. However, if the character string is a numeric expression, you must enclose it in quotes if you want the DBMS to store the numeric expression instead of the results of the numeric expression.

Fixed-Length CHARACTER Data Types

When you store data in a CHAR or CHARACTER column, each character, symbol, or number uses 1 byte of storage space. CHAR and CHARACTER are fixed-length data types, and the DBMS will pad (add blanks to) your string to make it the length specified in the column type definition. In the current example, the CHAR_COLUMN can store 10 characters. As such, the DBMS will store 10 characters in the CHAR_COLUMN column—the character string Konrad followed by four blanks. Similarly, the 9 in CHAR_COLUMN2 is stored as the character 9 followed by 99 blank spaces, since column CHAR_COLUMN2 was declared as a fixed-length character field of 100 characters.

You can store up to 8,000 characters in a column of type CHAR or CHARACTER.

Variable-Length CHARACTER Data Types

VARCHAR, CHAR VARYING, and CHARACTER VARYING are variable-length character strings, meaning that the length in the declaration is the maximum number of characters the column can hold, but the character string in the column may actually have less characters. Thus, in the current example, the NCHAR_COLUMN holds the character 9, using only one byte of storage. Similarly, the column NCHAR_VARYING_COLUMN holds the character string 5+4, using 3 bytes of data. Conversely, the DBMS uses 100 bytes to store the character 9 in CHAR_COLUMN2 and 10 bytes to store the character string Konrad because CHAR_COLUMN and CHAR_COLUMN2 are fixed-length character fields that must have the number of characters given as the column length in the table declaration.

You can store up to 8,000 characters in a column of type VARCHAR, CHAR VARYING, or CHARACTER VARYING.

Fixed- and Variable-Length Unicode CHARACTER Data Types

Computers store characters (whether symbols, letters, or numbers) as a numeric value. As such, every character, symbol, and number in the English language is represented on the computer as a unique sequence of 1s and 0s. Because different languages have characters that differ from any characters in another language, each has its own in encoding scheme. Thus, an A in German will have a different encoding (be represented as a different sequence of 1s and 0s) than an A in Russian. In fact, the European Union requires several different encodings to cover all of its languages.

Unicode was designed to provide a unique number for every character, no matter what platform, program, or language. Thus, the Unicode encoding for the letter A will have the same numeric value whether the A is found in a table on a system in Russia, Greece, or Japan.

The advantage of using Unicode is that you don't have to program in all of the possible numeric values for each symbol, letter, and number for all of the languages whose text you want to store in your database. The disadvantage of using Unicode is that due to the large number of Unicode characters (remember, Unicode is a combination of common and unique characters from any different character sets), it takes 2 bytes instead of 1 to represent each Unicode character. As a result, a Unicode string of type NCHAR(20) takes 40 bytes of storage, while a string of type CHAR(20) takes only 20 bytes.

When you define a column of type NCHAR, NATIONAL CHAR, or NATIONAL CHARACTER, you are telling the DBMS to store a fixed-length character string in the column using the Unicode encoding for each character in the string. Thus, a column of type NCHAR(length) (NATIONAL CHAR(length) and NATIONAL CHARACTER(length)) is a fixed-length character string like a column of type CHARACTER(length). Both contain the number of characters specified by (length). Thus, in our example, the NCHAR_COLUMN defined as data type NCHAR(20) can hold a character string of 20 characters. If you insert a character string of less than 20 characters into an NCHAR(20) column, the DBMS will add spaces to the end of the string to bring it to 20 characters.

You can store up to 4,000 characters in a column of type NCHAR, NATIONAL CHAR, or NATIONAL CHARACTER.

NCHAR VARYING is the Unicode equivalent of the VARCHAR data type. Like VARCHAR, columns of data type NCHAR VARYING(length) (NATIONAL CHAR VARYING (length) and NATIONAL CHARACTER VARYING(length)) hold variable-length character strings up to the number of characters specified by *length*. Thus, in our example, the NCHAR_VARYING_COLUMN defined as data type NCHAR VARYING(200) can hold a character string of up to 200 characters. If you insert a string of less than 200 characters into an NCHAR VARYING(200) column, the DBMS will not add blanks to the end of the character string. As such, the length of a character string stored in an NCHAR VARYING column can be less than the maximum length (number of characters) specified for the column in the table declaration.

You can store up to 4,000 characters in a column of type NCHAR VARYING, NATIONAL CHAR VARYING, or NATIONAL CHARACTER VARYING.

Note: *If you insert a character string longer than the length specified by the character type, the DBMS will truncate (or cut off) the extra characters and store the shortened string in the column without reporting an error. Therefore, if you have a column defined as being of type CHAR(10) and you attempt to insert the string abcdefghijklmnop, the*

DBMS will store abcdefghij in the column, shortening the maximum number of characters you specified for the character string. When storing a character string, the DBMS will truncate (shorten) a string longer than the maximum specified length, whether the character type is fixed-length or variable-length.

24 Understanding the Advantages of Using the VARCHAR Data Type

If you have a text column where the number of characters you want to store varies from to row, use a variable-length character string to save disk space. Suppose, for example, that you define an order table as follows:

```
CREATE TABLE order_table
  (customer_number        INTEGER,
   delivery_date          DATE,
   item_number            SMALLINT,
   quantity               SMALLINT,
   special_instructions CHAR(1000))
```

By using a fixed CHARACTER type, the DBMS will make the SPECIAL_INSTRUCTIONS column in every row 1,000 characters in length, even if you enter SPECIAL_INSTRUCTION strings for only a few items. As you learned in Tip 23, "Understanding SQL Character Data Types," the DBMS adds blanks to the end of a fixed-length character string if you insert a string with less than the number of characters you define as the string's length—in this case, 1,000 characters. Therefore, if you have one item that requires special instructions in a 10,000-row table, you will waste 9.9MB of disk spaces because the system will store 1,000 blank characters in each of the 9,999 rows that don't have any special instructions.

If on the other hand, you were to create the same ORDER_TABLE using the SQL statement

```
CREATE TABLE order_table
  (customer_number        INTEGER,
   delivery_date          DATE,
   item_number            SMALLINT,
   quantity               SMALLINT,
   special_instructions VARCHAR(1000))
```

the DBMS would not add blanks to the character string you insert in the SPECIAL_INSTRUCTIONS column. Thus, for the current example, where only 1 row has SPECIAL_INSTRUCTIONS, your 10,0000-row table will be 9,999,000 bytes (9MB) smaller than the table with identical data whose SPECIAL_INSTRUCTIONS column is declared as a fixed-length character type of 1,000 bytes.

The variable-length data types are:

- VARCHAR
- CHAR VARYING
- CHARACTER VARYING
- NCHAR VARYING
- NATIONAL CHAR VARYING
- NATIONAL CHARACTER VARYING

Review Tip 23 for additional information on how to declare a column using each of these data types.

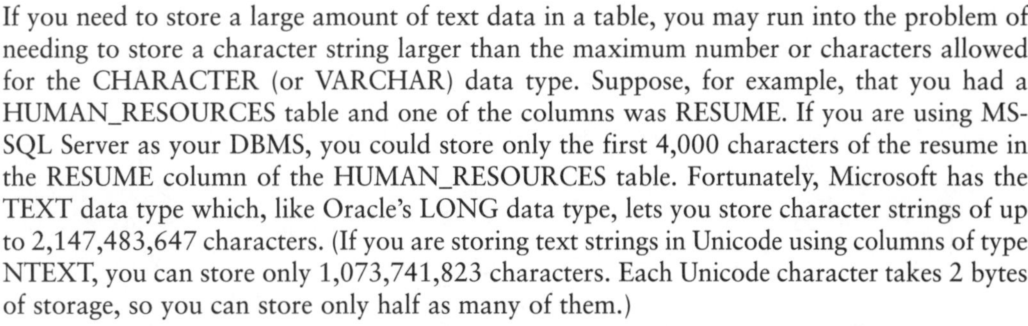

25 Understanding the LONG (Oracle) or TEXT (MS-SQL Server) Data Type

If you need to store a large amount of text data in a table, you may run into the problem of needing to store a character string larger than the maximum number or characters allowed for the CHARACTER (or VARCHAR) data type. Suppose, for example, that you had a HUMAN_RESOURCES table and one of the columns was RESUME. If you are using MS-SQL Server as your DBMS, you could store only the first 4,000 characters of the resume in the RESUME column of the HUMAN_RESOURCES table. Fortunately, Microsoft has the TEXT data type which, like Oracle's LONG data type, lets you store character strings of up to 2,147,483,647 characters. (If you are storing text strings in Unicode using columns of type NTEXT, you can store only 1,073,741,823 characters. Each Unicode character takes 2 bytes of storage, so you can store only half as many of them.)

It would be wasteful to preallocate 2GB of disk space for each column you declare as type TEXT. As such, MS-SQL Server preallocates only a small portion (8K) of the maximum TEXT space and allocates the remainder in 8K (8,192 byte) increments as you need it. As such, when it is ready to save character 8,193 of a TEXT string to disk, the DBMS allocates another block (page) of 8,192 bytes and creates a link from the page holding the previous 8,192 bytes to the page holding the next 8,192 bytes.

Once the DBMS stores the data in the TEXT column to disk, the entire TEXT block is logically contiguous. This is to say that the DBMS "sees" the TEXT block as one huge character string, even if the individual 8K blocks (pages) that make up the TEXT block are not physically contiguous. As such, you can display the entire contents of a TEXT column using a single SELECT statement such as:

```
SELECT resume FROM human_resources
```

if, for example, HUMAN_RESOURCES were a table defined as:

```
CREATE TABLE human_resources
  (id               INTEGER,
   name             VARCHAR(25),
   department_code TINYINT,
   data_of_hire     DATE,
   resume           TEXT)
```

Note: *The actual number of characters of TEXT data displayed by the SELECT statement is limited by the value of the Global Variable @@Textsize. If you don't change the value of @@Textsize, MS-SQL Server limits the number of TEXT characters displayed to 64K (64,512) by default.*

26 Understanding the MS-SQL Server IMAGE Data Type

The MS-SQL Server IMAGE data type is similar to the TEXT data type in that it you can store 2,147,483,647 bytes of data in a column declared as data type IMAGE. You would use an image type, for example, if you wanted to create a table of graphics images such as:

```
CREATE TABLE graphic_images
  (id          INTEGER,
   description VARCHAR(250),
   picture     IMAGE)
```

Typically, you won't use an INSERT statement to enter binary data into an IMAGE column. Instead, you will use an application program that passes the binary (picture) data to the DBMS for storage in the table.

Similarly, an IMAGE column is not meant for direct output using a SELECT statement, although such a SELECT statement is not prohibited. Instead, you would have the DBMS pass the image data to a graphics program (like WinJPeg) or to a Web browser for display.

If you do display an IMAGE column using the SELECT statement, you will find that the SELECT statement does not translate the values in the IMAGE column to ASCII. For example, suppose that you use the INSERT statement

```
INSERT INTO graphic_images
  VALUES (123,'Picture123','Picture123')
```

to place data into a row in the GRAPHICS_IMAGES table created as the example at the beginning of this tip. If you use the SELECT statement

```
SELECT * FROM graphic_images
```

MS-SQL Server would display:

```
id          description    picture
--------------------------------------------------------
123         Picture123     0x5069637475726531323 3
```

By not translating the hexadecimal representation of data in the IMAGE column to ASCII when SELECTED, the DBMS makes it easy to pass the actual "raw" picture file to a graphics program in answer to a query sent to the DBMS by an application program.

27 Understanding Standard SQL Datetime Data Types and the DATETIME Data Type

Although you can store dates and times in columns of type CHAR or VARCHAR, you will find it more convenient to use datetime columns instead. If you put dates and times into datetime columns, the DBMS will format the dates and times in a standard way when you display the contents of the columns as part of SELECT statements. More importantly, by using datetime columns, you will be able to use specialized date and time functions (such as INTERVAL and EXTRACT) to manipulate date and time data.

The SQL-92 standard specifies five datetime data types:

- **DATE.** Uses 10 characters to store the four-digit year, two-digit month, and two-digit day values of the date in the format 2000-04-25. Because the DATE data type uses a four-digit year, you can use it to represent any date from the year 0001 through the year 9999. Thus, SQL will have a year 10K problem, but I, for one, will let future generations worry about it.
- **TIME.** Uses eight characters, including the colons, to represent the two-digit hours, two-digits minutes, and two-digit seconds in the format 19:22:34. Because the SQL formats time using the 24-hour clock, 19:22:34 represent 22 minutes and 34 seconds past 7 P.M., whereas 07:22:34 represents 22 minutes and 34 seconds past 7 A.M. If you define a column as type TIME, the default is for the DBMS to display only whole seconds. However, you can tell the DBMS to store (and display) fractions of seconds by adding the precision you want to the TIME data type when using it to define a column of type TIME. For example, if you create a table with the SQL statement

```
CREATE TABLE time_table
    (time_with_seconds TIME(3))
```

  the DBMS will store time data including up to three digits representing thousandths of seconds.

- **TIMESTAMP.** Includes both date and time using 26 characters—10 characters to hold the date, followed by a space for separation, and then 15 characters to represent the time, including a default of fractions of seconds to six decimal places. Thus, if you create a table using

```
CREATE TABLE time_table
    (timestamp_column              TIMESTAMP,
     timestamp_column_no_decimal TIMESTAMP (0))
```

  the DBMS will store the date and time in TIMESTAMP_COLUMN formatted as 2000-04-25 19:22:34.123456, and the date and time in TIMESTAMP_COLUMN_NO_DECIMAL formatted as 2000-04-25 19:25:34. (The number in parenthesis (()) after TIMESTAMP specifies the precision of the fractions of seconds portion of the time—0, in the example.)

- **TIME WITH TIME ZONE.** Uses 14 characters to represent the time and the offset from Universal Coordinated Time (UTC)—eight characters to hold the time followed by the offset of the local time from (UTC)—formerly known as Greenwich Mean Time or GMT. Therefore, if you create a table using

```
CREATE TABLE time_table
    (time_with_gmt          TIME WITH TIME ZONE,
     time_with_seconds_gmt TIME (4) WITH TIME ZONE)
```

  the DBMS will store the time in TIME_WITH_GMT formatted as 19:22:24-05:00, and in TIME_WITH_SECONDS_GMT formatted as 19:22:24.1234-05:00. (The (4) in the data type for the TIME_WITH_SECONDS_GMT column in the example represents the optional precision you can specify to represent the fractions of seconds in the time.)

- **TIMESTAMP WITH TIME ZONE.** Uses 32 characters to represent the date, the time, and the offset from Universal Coordinated Time (UTC)—10 characters to hold the date, followed by a space for separation, and then 21 characters to represent the time, including a default of fractions of seconds given to six decimal places and the office from UTC (GMT). Thus, if you create a table using

```
CREATE TABLE time_table
    (timestamp_column TIMESTAMP WITH TIME ZONE,
     timestamp_no_dec TIMESTAMP(0)WITH TIME ZONE)
```

  the DBMS stores the date and time in TIMESTAMP_COLUMN formatted as 2000-04-25 19:22:34.123456+04:00 and in TIMESTAMP_NO_DEC using the format 2000-04-25 19:25:34+01:00 (The number in parenthesis (()) after TIMESTAMP specifies the precision of the fractions of seconds portion of the time—0, in the example.)

Unfortunately, not all DBMS products support all five of the standard SQL datetime data types. In fact, some DBMS products even use TIMESTAMP for purposes other than defining columns that hold date and time data. As such, check your system manual to see which of the SQL datetime data types your DBMS supports.

Don't be surprised to find that your system uses a nonstandard data type such as DATETIME (used by SQLBase, Sybase, and MS-SQL Server) to format columns that will hold dates and times.

If your system uses the DATETIME data type, you can define a column to hold date and time using an SQL statement similar to:

```
CREATE TABLE date_table
  (date_time DATETIME)
```

To insert a date and time into a DATETIME column, enclose the date and time in single quotes using an INSERT statement similar to:

```
INSERT INTO date_table
  VALUES ('04/25/2000 21:05:06:123')
```

If you are using MS-SQL Server and execute the SQL statement

```
SELECT * FROM date_table
```

the DBMS will display the value in the DATE_TIME column as: 2000-04-25 21:05:06.123.

MS-SQL Server lets you specify the date in the INSERT statement using any one of a variety of formats, including but not limited to:

- Apr 25 2000
- APR 25 2000
- April 25, 2000
- 25 April 2000
- 2000 April 25
- 4/25/00
- 4-25-2000
- 4.25.2000

MS-SQL Server also gives you a number of ways to express the time you want to insert into a DATETIME column. Valid ways to express time include:

- 9:05:06:123pm
- 9:5:6:123pm
- 9:05pm
- 21:00
- 9pm
- 9PM
- 9:05

(Note that the last entry in this example ["9:05"] will insert 9:05am and not 9:05pm.) If you insert a date without a time, MS-SQL Server will append 00:00:00:000 to your date. Thus, the SQL statement

```
INSERT INTO date_table VALUES ("2000 Apr 25")
```

will set the value of DATE_TIME to 2000-04-10 00:00:00.000. (MS-SQL Server will replace the portion of the time you leave off with zeroes.)

If you insert only a time into a DATETIME column, MS-SQL Server will replace the omitted date with 01/01/1900.

28 Understanding the SQL BIT Data Type

When you are working with data that can take on only one of two values, use the BIT data type. For example, you can use BIT fields to store the answers to yes/no or true/false survey questions such as: these "Are you a homeowner?" "Are you married?" "Did you complete high school?" "Do you love SQL?"

You can store answers to yes/no and true/false questions in CHARACTER columns using the letters Y, N, T, and F. However, if you use a column of type CHARACTER, each data value will take 1 byte (8 bits) of storage space. If you use a BIT column instead, you can store the same amount of data using 1/8 the space.

Suppose, for example, that you create a CUSTOMER table using the SQL statement:

```
CREATE TABLE customer
  (id                  INTEGER,
   name                VARCHAR(25),
   high_school_graduate BIT,
   some_college        BIT,
   graduate_school     BIT,
   post_graduate_work  BIT,
   male                BIT,
   married             BIT,
   homeowner           BIT,
   US_citizen          BIT)
```

If you follow normal conventions, a 1 in a BIT column would represent TRUE, and a 0 would represent FALSE. Thus, if the value of the MARRIED column were 1, that would mean that the CUSTOMER is married. Similarly, if the value in the US_CITIZEN column were 0, that would mean that the CUSTOMER is not a U.S. citizen.

Using the BIT data type instead of a CHARACTER data type for the eight two-state (BIT) columns in the current example not only saves 56 bytes of storage space per row, but it also simplifies queries based on the two-state column values.

Suppose, for example, that you wanted a list of all male customers. If the MALE column were of type CHARACTER, you would have to know whether the column would contain a T, t, Y, y, or some other value to indicate that the CUSTOMER is a male. When the column is a BIT column, you know that the value in the male column can only be a 1 or a 0—and will most likely be a 1 if the CUSTOMER is a male, since a 1 would, by convention, indicate TRUE.

You can use a BIT column to select rows that meet a specific condition by checking the value of the column in the WHERE clause of your SQL statement. For example, you could make a list of all customers that are high school graduates using the SQL SELECT statement:

```
SELECT id, name
FROM   customer
WHERE  high_school_graduate = 1
```

Selecting rows that meet any one of several criteria is also easy. Suppose, for example, that you want a list of all customers that are either married or homeowners. You could use the SQL SELECT statement:

```
SELECT id, name
FROM   customer
WHERE  married = 1 OR homeowner = 1
```

If, on the other hand you want to select only married homeowners, you would use an AND in place of the OR in the WHERE clause.

29 Understanding Constants

SQL does not have a CONSTANT data type, like that found in programming languages such as Pascal, Visual Basic, and C++. However, you do not have to put data values into columns in order to use those values in SQL statements. Valid SQL statements can and often do include literal string, numeric, and date and time constants, and symbolic constants (also referred to as system maintained constants).

Numeric Constants (Exact and Approximate Numeric Literals)

Numeric constants include integers, decimals, and floating-point numbers. When using integer and decimal constants (also called exact numeric literals) in SQL statements, enter them as decimal numbers. Write negative numbers using a leading (vs. trailing) minus sign (dash), and you can precede positive numbers with an optional plus sign. Whether writing positive or negative constants, omit all commas between digits.

Examples of well-formed SQL exact numeric literals are: 58, –47, 327.29, +47.89, –785.256.

In addition to integers and decimals, SQL lets you enter floating-point constants (also called approximate numeric literals). Use E (or scientific) notation when using floating-point numbers in an SQL statement. Floating-point numbers look like a decimal number (called the mantissa), flowed by an E and then a positive or negative integer (the exponent) that represents the power of 10 by which to multiply the number to the left of the E (the mantissa).

Examples of well-formed SQL approximate numeric literals are: 2.589E5, –3.523E2, 7.89E1, +6.458E2, 7.589E–2, +7.589E–6, which represent the numbers 258900, –352.3, 78.9, +645.8, 0.07589E–2, and +0.000007589, respectively.

String Constants (Literals)

The SQL-92 standard specifies that you enclose SQL character constants in single quotes.

Well-formed string constants include: 'Konrad King,' 'Sally Fields,' 'Nobody doesn"t like Sarah Lee.'

Notice that you can include a single quote within a string constant, (the word *doesn't,* in the current example) by following the single quote that you want to include with another single quote. Thus, to include the contraction *doesn't* in the string constant, you write "doesn"t."

Some DBMS products (such as MS-SQL Server) allow you to enclose string constants within double quotes. Valid string constants for such DBMS products include: "Konrad King," "Sally Fields," "Nobody doesn't like Sara Lee." Notice that if you enclose a string constant in double quotes, you do not have to use two single quotes to form the contraction *doesn't.*

Date and Time Constants

Using date and time constants in an SQL statement is a bit more involved than including numeric and string literals. Every DBMS supports the use of characters and number strings. However, as you learned in Tip 27, "Understanding Standard SQL Datetime Data Types and the DATETIME Data Type," not all DBMS products support all five of the SQL standard datetime data types—in fact, MS-SQL Server does not support any of them, opting instead to support its own DATETIME data type. As such, before you can use a date or time constant in an SQL statement, you must first know the proper format for entering dates and times on your DBMS. So, check your system manual.

Once you know the correct date and time format for your DBMS product, you can use date and time constants by enclosing valid date and time values within single quotes.

For MS-SQL Server, valid date and time constants include: '27 Apr 2000,' '4-27-2000,' '4.27.2000,' '2000 Apr 27,' '2000.4.27,' '5:15:00 pm,' '17:23:45,' '4-27-2000 5:15:23.'

Symbolic Constants (System-Maintained Constants)

The SQL-89 standard specified only a single symbolic constant: USER. SQL-92 includes USER, SESSION_USER, SYSTEM_USER, CURRENT_DATE, CURRENT_TIME, and CURRENT_TIMESTAMP. Unfortunately, many DBMS products support only some or none of the symbolic constants to varying degrees. MS-SQL Server, for example, supports USER, CURRENT_USER, SESSION_USER, SYSTEM_USER, CURRENT_TIMESTAMP, and APP_NAME—but only when used as part of a DEFAULT constraint in a CREATE or ALTER TABLE statement. Thus, the SQL statement

```
SELECT customer_name, balance_due, date_due
FROM   customer_ar
WHERE  date_due < CURRENT_DATE
```

may be perfectly acceptable in your DBMS product but unacceptable to MS-SQL Server.

Note: *MS-SQL Server gives you access to system-maintained constants through built-in functions instead of through symbolic constants. As such, MS-SQL Server would return the customers with past due balances as requested by the example query if you wrote the SQL statement as:*

```
SELECT customer_name, balance_due, date_due
FROM   customer_ar
WHERE  date_due < GETDATE()
```

Before using symbolic constants, check your system manual to determine which of the symbolic (or system-maintained) constants your DBMS supports. Also check your manual to see if your DBMS has built-in functions that return the values of system-maintained constants not included in the list of symbolic constants.

30 Understanding the Value of NULL

When a DBMS finds a NULL value in a column, it interprets it as undefined or unavailable. The SQL-92 standard specifies that a DBMS cannot assign or assume an explicit or implicit value to a NULL column.

A NULL is not the same as a space (in a character column), a zero (in a numeric column), or a NULL ASCII character (which is all zeroes) (in a character column). In fact, if you execute the SQL statement

```
SELECT * FROM customer WHERE education = NULL
```

the DBMS will not display any rows, even if the education column in some of the rows in the CUSTOMER table has a NULL value. According to the SQL standard, the DBMS cannot make any assumption about a NULL value in a column—it cannot even assume that a NULL value equals NULL!

There are several reasons that a column may be NULL, including:

- **Its value is not yet known.** If your STUDENT table includes a RANK_IN_CLASS column, you would set its value to NULL on the first day of school.
- **Its value does not yet exist.** If your MARKETING_REP table includes an APPOINTMENT_QUOTA, the column's value would be NULL until set by the marketing room manager after the marketing rep completes his or her training.
- **The column is not applicable to the table row.** If your EMPLOYEE table includes a MANAGER-ID column, you would set the column to NULL for the company owner's row.

Be selective about the columns in which you allow the DBMS to store NULL values. A PRIMARY KEY column (which you will learn about in Tip 172, "Using the PRIMARY KEY Column Constraint to Uniquely Identify Rows in a Table"), cannot have a NULL in any of its rows. After all, a PRIMARY KEY column must be unique in each and every row. Since the DBMS cannot make any assumptions about the value of a NULL, it cannot say with certainty that the NULL value in one row would be the same as the value in another row once the column's value is no longer unknown (or becomes defined).

Also, if you plan to use a column in functions such as MIN, MAX, SUM, AVG, and so on, be sure to apply the NOT NULL constraint (which you will learn about in Tip 191, "Using the NOT NULL Column Constraint to Prevent NULL Values in a Column") to the column. If you use one of the aggregate functions on a column that has a NULL in a row, the result of the function will be indeterminate (that is, NULL). After all, the DBMS cannot compute the SUM of the values in a column if there are one or more rows in the table whose column value is unknown.

In summary, think of NULL as an indicator rather than a value. When the DBMS finds a NULL in a column of a row in a table, the DBMS "knows" that data is missing or not applicable.

31 Understanding the MS-SQL Server ISNULL() Function

You can use the MS-SQL Server ISNULL() built-in function to return a value other than NULL for columns that are NULL. Suppose, for example, that your EMPLOYEE table has data in columns as shown in Figure 31.1.

EMPLOYEE table

ID	NAME	DATE_HIRED	QUOTA
1	Sally Smith	04/27/00	NULL
2	Wally Wells	04/13/99	5
3	Greg Jones	05/12/97	7
4	Bruce Williams	04/15/00	NULL
5	Paul Harvey	06/05/99	9

Figure 31.1 EMPLOYEE table with sample data and NULL values

If you execute the SQL SELECT statement

```
SELECT id, name, date_hired, quota FROM employee
```

MS-SQL Server will display output similar to the following:

```
id  name            date_hired          quota
---------------------------------------------
1   Sally Smith     04/27/00 00:00:00   NULL
2   Wally Wells     04/13/99 00:00:00   5
3   Greg Jones      05/12/97 00:00:00   7
4   Bruce Williams  04/15/00 00:00:00   NULL
5   Paul Harvey     06/05/99 00:00:00   9
```

If you don't want to explain what a NULL is to your users, you can use the built-in ISNULL() to replace "(null)" in the output with another text string or number.

The syntax of the ISNULL() function is:

```
ISNULL(expression,value)
```

Substitute the name of the column that contains NULLs for *expression* and the character string or number you want displayed in place of "(null)" for *value*. Therefore, if you want MS-SQL Server to replace "(null)" in the QUOTA column with "In Training," use the SQL statement

```
SELECT
  id, name, date_hired, 'quota'=ISNULL(quota,'In Training')
FROM
  employee
```

to have MS-SQL Server output the following for our example data:

```
id  name            date_hired          quota
--------------------------------------------------
1   Sally Smith     04/27/00 00:00:00   In Training
2   Wally Wells     04/13/99 00:00:00   5
3   Greg Jones      05/12/97 00:00:00   7
4   Bruce Williams  04/15/00 00:00:00   In Training
5   Paul Harvey     06/05/99 00:00:00   9
```

You can also use the MS-SQL Server ISNULL() function to select either rows where a column is NULL or rows where a column is not NULL. For example, if you want to see the rows in the EMPLOYEE table where the quota is null, you could use an SQL SELECT statement similar to:

```
SELECT id, name, date_hired, ISNULL(quota,'In Training')
FROM   employee
WHERE  ISNULL(quota,-999) = -999
```

If, on the other hand, you want to see only those reps who have a defined quota, replace the = in the WHERE clause with <>, similar to the following:

```
SELECT id, name, date_hired, quota
FROM   employee
WHERE  ISNULL(quota,-999) <> -999
```

32 Understanding the MS-SQL Server IDENTITY Property

You can apply the IDENTITY property to one (and only one) of the columns in a table to have MS-SQL Server supply an incrementing, non-NULL value for the column whenever a row is added that does not specify the column's value. Suppose, for example, that you wanted to create an EMPLOYEE table that included an EMPLOYEE_ID column, but you did not want to supply the EMPLOYEE_ID each time you added a new employee to the table. You can have MS-SQL Server supply the "next" EMPLOYEE_ID each time a row is added by creating the EMPLOYEE table using an SQL statement similar to the following:

```
CREATE TABLE employee
  (id    INTEGER IDENTITY(10,10),
   name  VARCHAR(35),
   quota SMALLINT)
```

The format of the IDENTITY property is:

```
IDENTITY (initial_value, increment)
```

If you omit the *initial_value* and increment, MS-SQL Server will set both the initial_value and the increment to 1.

The CREATE TABLE statement in the current example tells MS-SQL Server to assign a 10 to the ID column of the first row added to the EMPLOYEE table. Then, when you add subsequent rows to the table, MS-SQL Server will add 10 to the ID value in the last row of the table and assign that value to the ID column of the new row to be added. Thus, executing the SQL statements

```
INSERT INTO employee (name, quota)
  VALUES ('Sally Smith', NULL)
INSERT INTO employee (name, quota)
  VALUES ('Wally Wells', 5)
INSERT INTO employee (name, quota)
  VALUES ('Greg Jones', 7)
SELECT * FROM employee
```

MS-SQL Server will insert the three employee rows into the display and display them similar to the following:

```
id  name            quota
---------------------------
10  Sally Smith     NULL
20  Wally Wells     5
30  Greg Jones      7
```

You can apply the IDENTITY property only to columns of type INTEGER, INT, SMALLINT, TINYINT, DECIMAL, or NUMERIC—and only if the column does not permit NULL values.

Note: *Specifying the IDENTITY property for a column does not guarantee that each row will have a unique value in that column. Suppose, for example, that you executed the SQL statements on the table in the current example:*

```
SET IDENTITY_INSERT employee ON
INSERT INTO employee (id, name, quota)
  VALUES(20, 'Bruce Williams', NULL)
SET IDENTITY_INSERT employee OFF
INSERT INTO employee (name, quota)
  VALUES('Paul Harvey', 9)
SELECT * FROM employee
```

MS-SQL Server will display table rows similar to the following:

```
id  name            quota
---------------------------
10  Sally Smith     (null)
20  Wally Wells     5
30  Greg Jones      7
20  Bruce Williams  (null)
40  Paul Harvey     9
```

Because the first INSERT statement specifies the value for the ID column, the DBMS puts a 20 in the ID column of the Bruce Williams row. The second INSERT statement does not include a value for the ID column. As a result, the DBMS adds 10 (the increment) to the highest ID (30) and uses the result (40) as the ID for the new Paul Harvey row.

If you want to guarantee that the IDENTITY column contains a unique value in each row of the table, you must create a unique index based on the IDENTITY column, which you will learn how to do in Tip 161, "Using the CREATE INDEX Statement to Create an Index."

33 Understanding Assertions

As you learned in Tip 15, "Understanding Constraints," a constraint is a database object that restricts the data a user or application program can enter into the columns of a table. An assertion is a database object that uses a check constraint to limit data values you can enter into the database as a whole.

Both assertions and constraints are specified as check conditions that the DBMS can evaluate to either TRUE or FALSE. However, while a constraint uses a check condition that acts on a single table to limit the values assigned to columns in that table; the check condition in an assertion involves multiple tables and the data relationships among them. Because an assertion applies to the database as a whole, you use the CREATE ASSERTION statement to create an assertion as part of the database definition. (Conversely, since a constraint applies to only a single table, you apply [define] the constraint when you create the table.)

For example, if you want to prevent investors from withdrawing more than a certain amount of money from your hedge fund, you could create an assertion using the following SQL statement:

```
CREATE ASSERTION maximum_withdrawal
  CHECK (investor.withdrawal_limit >
         SELECT SUM(withdrawals.amount)
         FROM   withdrawals
         WHERE  withdrawals.investor_id = investor.ID)
```

Thus, the syntax used to create an assertion is:

```
CREATE ASSERTION <assertion name> <check condition>
```

Once you add the MAXIMUM_WITHDRAWAL ASSERTION to the database definition, the DBMS will check to make sure that the assertion remains TRUE each time you execute an SQL statement that modifies either the INVESTOR or WITHDRAWALS tables. As such, each time the user or application program attempts to execute an INSERT, UPDATE, or DELETE statement on one of the tables in the assertion's CHECK clause, the DBMS checks the check condition against the database, including the proposed modification. If the check condition remains TRUE, the DBMS carries out the modification. If the modification makes the check condition FALSE, the DBMS does not perform the modification and returns an error code indicating that the statement was unsuccessful due to an assertion violation.

34 Understanding the SQL DBMS Client/Server Model

Client/Server computing (often called n-tier computing when you use the Internet to connect the client to the server), involves distributed data processing, or multiple computers working together to perform a set of operations. In the client/server model, the client (workstations) and server (DBMS) work together to perform operations that create objects and manipulate the data in a database. Although they work together in the overall scheme of things, the tasks the server performs are different than the work accomplished by the clients.

The relational DBMS model and SQL are particularly suited for use in a client/server environment. The DBMS and data reside on a central server (computer), and multiple clients (network workstations) communicate requests for data to the server across connections on the local area network (LAN). The application program running on the client machine accepts user input and formulates the SQL statements, which it then sends to the DBMS on the server. The DBMS then interprets and executes the SQL commands, and sends the results back to the client (workstation). Finally, the application program running at the workstation formats and displays the results for the user.

Using the SQL client/server relationship is a much more efficient use of bandwidth as compared to a simple database file-sharing system where the workstation would copy large amounts of data from the fileserver, manipulate the data locally, and then send large amounts of data back to the fileserver to be stored on the network disk drives. Put another way, the older, more inefficient shared file access method involves sending you the entire filing cabinet and all of its folders. Your application program then has to sift through everything available to find the file folder it needs.

In the client/server model, the server rummages the filing cabinet for you and sends only the desired file folder to the application program. The user uses an application program running on a network workstation (the client) to send requests (using SQL statements) for data to the DBMS (the server). The DBMS and data reside on the same system, so the DBMS can execute the SQL statements and send only the data the user needs across the LAN to the workstation.

A DBMS (the server) has nothing to do until it receives a request (one or more SQL statements) from the client (network workstation). The server is responsible for storing, manipulating, and retrieving data for multiple clients. As such, the server hardware typically has multiple, high-end processors to handle simultaneous data requests and large amounts of fast storage, and it is optimized for fast data access and retrieval.

When processing SQL statements, the DBMS (server) interprets the commands and translates them into database operations. After executing the operations, the server then formats and sends the results to the client. Thus, the server's job is relatively straightforward: read, interpret, and execute SQL statements. Moreover, the server has no responsibility for presenting the information to the user—that job is left to the client.

The client portion of the SQL client/server system consists of hardware (often similar in processing power to the server) and software, the user's interface to the DBMS. When working with SQL, the user often does not even realize that there is a separate DBMS server involved. As far as the user is concerned, the application program (such as an order entry system) running on his or her computer is acting on data stored on a shared network drive. In reality, the client (application program) accepts user input, translates what the user enters into SQL commands, and sends the commands along with any data entered to the DBMS server. The application then waits for the server to send back the results, which the program then displays to the user.

In the client/server environment, the client is responsible for:

- Accepting needed information from the user (or another application program)
- Formulating the data retrieval, removal, or update request for the server
- Displaying all information (data and server messages) to the user
- Manipulating individual data items (the server takes care of the physical storage, removal, and retrieval of data, but data values are determined on the client side of the client/server model)
- Formatting the information and producing any reports (both printed and online)

Note: *You can reduce network traffic and server workload by duplicating some data validity checks in the client application. For example, having the application program force the user to enter a valid quantity before sending the columns in an order row to the DBMS will avoid sending the data to the server, having the DBMS parse the SQL statement only to send it back to the client as invalid.*

Be sure to use validity checks on the client side of the client/server model in addition to (and not in place of) the server's SQL-defined data integrity mechanisms. By consolidating validation on the server (and duplicating it on the client where it makes senses), you ensure that EVERY application's data is validated using the same set of rules. If you trust the application to perform its own validation, you will invariably run into problems where validation code, omitted during the testing phase, is inadvertently left out of the production system as well. Moreover, if you need to change or add new business rules, changing server validity checks in one place (on the server) is relatively simple as compared to contacting each software vendor (or in-house programming staff) to update individual application programs.

35 Understanding the Structure of SQL Statements

When using SQL to send commands to the DBMS, you first tell the DBMS what you want to do and then describe the data (or structure) on which you want the DBMS to take the action. SQL is similar to the German language in that you put the action word (the verb) at the beginning of the sentence (the SQL statement) and then follow the verb with one or more clauses that describe the subject (the database object, or set of rows) on which you want the DBMS to act. Figure 35.1 shows the basic form of SQL statements.

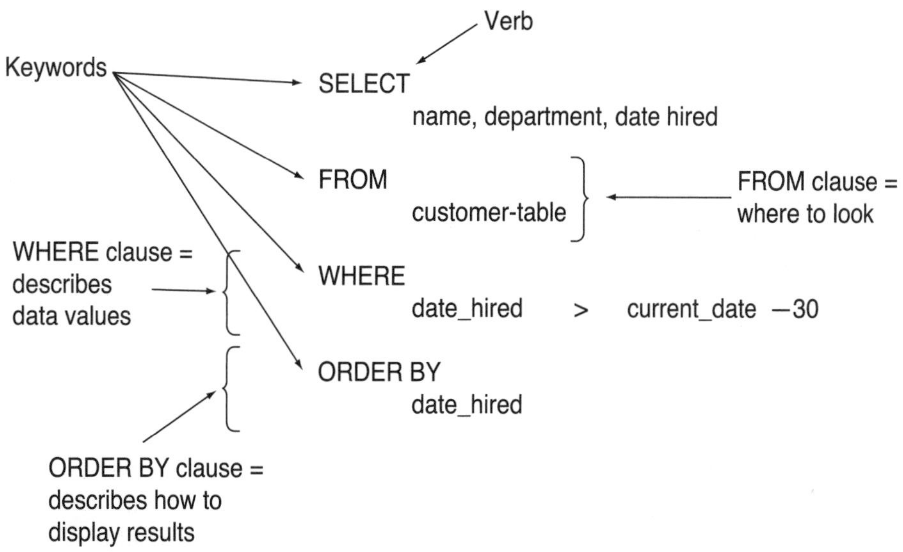

Figure 35.1 Basic structure of an SQL statement

As shown in Figure 35.1, each SQL statement begins with a keyword that describes what the statement does. Keywords you'll find at the beginning of SQL statements include: SELECT, INSERT, UPDATE, DELETE, CREATE, or DROP. After you tell the DBMS what you want done, you tell it the columns of interest and the table(s) in which to look. You normally identify the columns and tables you want to use by listing the columns after the verb (at the start of the SQL statement) and by listing the table(s) after the keyword FROM.

After you tell the DBMS what to do and identify the columns and tables to which to do it, you finish the SQL statement with one or more clauses that either further describe the action the DBMS is to take, or give a description of the data values that identify tables rows on which you want you want to DBMS to act. Typical descriptive clauses begin with the keywords: HAVING, IN, INTO, LIKE, ORDER BY, WHENEVER, WHERE, or WITH.

ANSI/ISO SQL-92 has approximately 300 reserved words of which you will probably use about 30 to do the majority of your work with the database. Table 35.1 lists some of the most commonly used keywords. Although some of the keywords are applicable only to MS-SQL Server, you will find keywords that perform similar functions if you are using another vendor's DBMS.

Keyword	***Description***
Data Definition Language (DML)	
CREATE DATABASE	(MS-SQL Server). Creates a database and transaction log. A database has one or more schemas, which contain database objects such as tables, views, domains, constraints, procedures, triggers, and so on.
DROP DATABASE	(MS-SQL Server). Erases a database and transaction log.
CREATE SCHEMA	Adds a named container of database objects to the database. A database may have more than one schema. All database objects (tables, views, domains, constrains, procedures, triggers, and so on) reside in one of the schemas within the database.
DROP SCHEMA	Removes a schema from a database.
CREATE DOMAIN	Creates a named list of allowable values for columns in database tables. You can use domains as data types for columns in multiple tables.
DROP DOMAIN	Removes a domain definition from the database.
CREATE TABLE	Creates a structure (table) of columns and rows to hold data.
ALTER TABLE	Adds columns to a table, removes columns from a table, changes column data types, or adds column constraints to a table.
DROP TABLE	Removes a table from the database.
CREATE VIEW	Creates a database object that displays rows of one or more columns from one or more tables. Some views allow you to update the base tables.
DROP VIEW	Drops a database view.
CREATE INDEX	Creates a structure with values from a table column, which speeds up the DBMS's ability to find specific rows within the table.
DROP INDEX	Removes an INDEX from the database.

Keyword	*Description*
Data Manipulation Language (DML)	
INSERT	Adds one or more rows to a table.
SELECT	Retrieves database data.
UPDATE	Updates data values in a table.
DELETE	Removes one or more rows from a table.
TRUNCATE	(MS-SQL Server). Removes all rows from a table.
Data Control Language (DCL)	
ROLLBACK	Undoes changes made to database objects, up to the last COMMIT or SAVEPOINT.
COMMIT	Makes proposed changes to the database permanent. (COMMITTED changes cannot be undone with a ROLLBACK.)
SAVEPOINT	Marks points in a transaction (set of actions) that can be used to ROLLBACK (or undo) a part of a transaction without having to undo the entire transaction.
GRANT	Gives access to database objects or SQL statements.
REVOKE	Removes access privileges to database objects or executes specific SQL statements.
Programmatic SQL	
DECLARE	Reserves server resources for use by a cursor.
OPEN	Creates a cursor and fills it with data values selected from columns in one or more rows in one or more database tables.
FETCH	Passes data values from a cursor to host variables.
CLOSE	Releases the resources used to hold the data copied from the database into a cursor.
DEALLOCATE	Releases server resources reserved for use by a cursor.
CREATE PROCEDURE	(MS-SQL Server). Creates a named list of SQL statements that a user (with the correct access rights) can execute by using the name as he or she would any other SQL keyboard.
ALTER PROCEDURE	(MS-SQL Server). Changes the sequence of SQL statements that the DBMS will perform when the user calls a procedure.
DROP PROCEDURE	(MS-SQL Server). Removes a procedure from the database.

Keyword	*Description*
CREATE TRIGGER	(MS-SQL Server, DB2, PL/SQL). Creates a named sequence of SQL statements that the DBMS will execute automatically when a column has a specific data value or when a user attempts a specific database command (the triggering event).
ALTER TRIGGER	(MS-SQL Server, DB2, PL/SQL). Changes the SQL statements executed when the DBMS detects the triggering event, or changes the nature of the event.
DROP TRIGGER	(MS-SQL Server, DB2, PL/SQL). Removes a trigger from the database.
DESCRIBE INPUT	Reserves an input area an application program will use to pass values to the DBMS during a dynamic SQL statement.
GET DESCRIPTOR	Tells the DBMS to use the DESCRIPTOR area to retrieve data values placed there by an application program during a dynamic SQL statement.
DESCRIBE OUTPUT	Reserves an output area the DBMS will use to pass data from the database to an application program during a dynamic SQL statement.
SET DESCRIPTOR	Tells the DBMS to place data into the DESCRIPTOR area for retrieval by an application program during a dynamic SQL statement.
PREPARE	Tells the DBMS to create an execution plan or compile the SQL statement(s) in a dynamic SQL statement.
EXECUTE	Tells the DBMS to execute a dynamic SQL statement.

Table 35.1 Commonly Used SQL and MS-SQL Server Keywords

You will find several tips on each of the common SQL statements (and others that are important, though not commonly used), throughout this book. The important thing to know now is that all SQL statements begin with a keyword (verb), have a list of objects on which to act, and may have one or more clauses that further describe the action or identify the rows on which to act at the end of the statement. If the SQL statement does not contain clauses that limit the action to rows with specific column data values, the DBMS will take action on all of the rows in a table (or multiples tables through a VIEW).

36 Understanding How the DBMS Executes SQL Statements

When processing an SQL statement, the DBMS goes through five steps:

- **Parse.** The DBMS goes through the SQL statement word by word and clause by clause to make sure that all of the keywords are valid and all of the clauses are well-formed. The DBMS will catch any syntax errors (badly formed SQL expressions) or typographical errors (misspelled keywords) during the parsing stage.
- **Validate.** The DBMS will check to make sure that all tables and columns named in the statement exist in the system catalog, as well as make sure there are no ambiguous column name references. During the validation step, the DBMS will catch any semantic errors (invalid references or valid references to nonexistent objects) and access violations (attempts to access database objects or attempts to execute SQL statements to which the user does not have sufficient privilege).
- **Optimize.** The DBMS runs an optimizer to decide on the best way to carry out the SQL statement. For a SELECT statement, for example, the optimizer checks to see if it can use an INDEX to speed up the query. If the query involves multiple tables, the optimizer decides if it should join the tables first and then apply the search condition, or vice versa. When the query appears to involve a scan of all rows in the table, the optimizers determines if there is a way to limit the data set to a subset of the rows in order to avoid a full table scan. Once the optimizer runs through all of the possibilities and gives them a rating based on speed (efficiency) and safety, the DBMS chooses one of them.
- **Generate execution plan.** The DBMS generates a binary representation of the steps involved in carrying out the SQL statement based on the optimization method suggested by the optimizer. The execution plan is what is stored when you create an MS-SQL Server procedure and what is generated when you prepare a dynamic SQL query. Generating the execution plan is the DBMS equivalent of compiling an application program to produce the .EXE file (the executable code).
- **Execute.** The DBMS carries out the action specified by the SQL statement by executing the binary execution plan.

Different steps in the process put different loads on the DBMS and server CPU. The parsing requires no database access and very little CPU time. Validation requires some database access but does not put too much of a load on the DBMS. The optimization step, however, requires a lot of database access and CPU time. In order to optimize a complex, multi-table query, for example, the optimizer may explore more than 20 ways to execute the statement.

The reason you don't just skip the optimization step is because the "cost" of doing the optimization is typically much less than the cost of performing the SQL statement in less than the most efficient manner. To put it another way, the reduction in time it takes to complete a well-optimized query more than makes up for the time spent in optimizing the query. Moreover, the more complex the query, the greater the benefits of optimization.

One of the major benefits of using procedures is being able to avoid performing the same parsing, validation, and (especially) optimization steps over and over again. When you enter an SQL query using an interactive tool (such as the MS-SQL Server Query Analyzer), the DBMS has no choice but to go through the entire five-step execution processor, even if you type in the same query multiple times.

If you put your SQL statement (or statements) into a stored procedure, however, the DBMS can parse, validate, optimize, and develop the execution plan in advance. Then, when you call the procedure, the DBMS needs only to execute the already compiled execution plan. Precompiled procedures let the DBMS avoid the "expensive" optimization phase the second and subsequent times you execute the SQL statements in the procedure. Thus, procedures let you move the first four steps of the execution process to the development environment, which reduces the load on the online production DBMS (and server).

37 Understanding SQL Keywords

SQL keywords are words that have a special significance in SQL and should not be used as user-defined names for database objects such as tables, columns, domains, constraints, procedures, variables, and so on. There are two types of keywords, reserved and nonreserved. The difference between reserved and nonreserved keywords is that some database products let you (although you should not) use nonreserved keywords to name database objects and variables. To make your SQL statements portable and less confusing, avoid using reserved words as identifiers.

When writing SQL statements, use all capital letters for keywords and lowercase letters for nonkeywords (or vice versa). Keywords are case-insensitive, meaning that the DBMS will recognize a keyword whether you type it using all capital letters, lowercase letters, or a combination of both. Making the case (capital vs. lower case) of reserved words different than nonreserved words in SQL statements makes the SQL statements easier for you (and those responsible for maintaining your database creation) to read.

Since each DBMS product supports most SQL-92 reserved words and adds a few of its own, the system manual and online help system are your best source for a list of reserved words. For example, to review MS-SQL Server's list of reserved words, perform the following steps:

1. Click on the Start button. Windows will display the Start menu.
2. Select Programs, Microsoft SQL Server 7.0 option, and click on Books Online. Windows will start the MS-SQL Server Help system.

3. Click on the Index tab and enter **KEYWORDS** in the Type in the Keyword to Find field. The MS-SQL Server Help system will display an alphabetical list of terms starting with Keywords.
4. To see a list of reserved keywords, click on Reserved and then click on the DISPLAY button. The Help system will display a dialog box asking you to select the type of reserved words on which you want its assistance.
5. Click on Reserved Keywords (T-SQL) and then click on the DISPLAY button. The MS-SQL Server Help system will display a list of T-SQL (Transact-SQL) reserved words, followed by a list of ODBC reserved words. The ODBC reserved words include the SQL-92 reserved words that MS-SQL Server supports. (Transact-SQL is MS-SQL Server's own procedural SQL language; Oracle uses PL/SQL and SQL Plus*.)

To exit the Help system, click on the close button (the X) in the upper-right corner of the Help application window.

38 Using the MS-SQL Server Query Analyzer to Execute SQL Statements

You can use the MS-SQL Server Query Analyzer (QA) to execute any SQL statement supported by MS-SQL Server. (As mentioned in previous tips, no commercially available database supports everything in the SQL-92 standard.) QA has a graphical user interface (GUI) you can use to pose ad hoc (interactive) queries and to send SQL commands to an MS-SQL Server. (MS-SQL Server also provides a command-line interface to the database through ISQL, which you will learn about in Tip 39, "Using the MS-SQL Server ISQL to Execute SQL Statements from the Command Line or Statements Stored in an ASCII File.")

Note: *You will need to install MS-SQL Server prior to using the Query Analyzer. Tip 527 gives you step-by-step instructions for installing MS-SQL Server, if you have not yet installed it on your computer system.*

To start to start MS-SQL Server QA, perform the following steps:

1. Click on the Start button. Windows will display the Start menu.
2. Select Programs, Microsoft SQL Server 7.0 option; click on Query Analyzer. Windows will start QA and display a Connect to SQL Server dialog box similar to that shown in Figure 38.1.

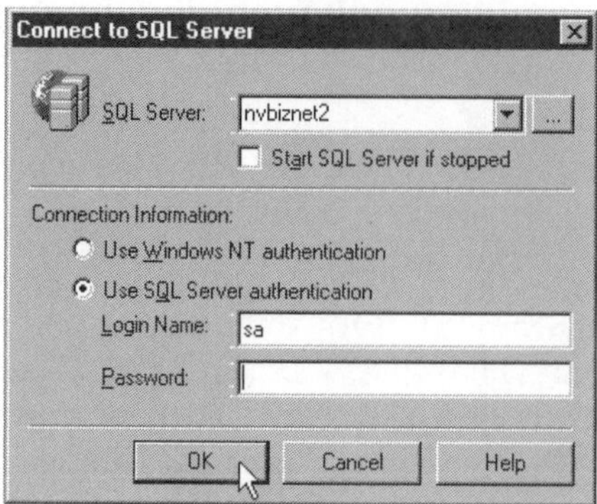

Figure 38.1 MS-SQL Server Query Analyzer, Connect to SQL Server dialog box

3. Enter the name of the SQL Server to which you wish to connect in the SQL Server field. (The name of the SQL Server is typically the same as the name of the Windows NT Server on which you installed the MS-SQL Server.)
4. Enter your login name in the Login Name field. When you install MS-SQL Server, the program automatically creates the sa (system administrator) account without a password. If you are working with your own installed copy of the MS-SQL Server, use the sa account; if not, enter the Login Name and Password your system administrator (or database administrator) assigned to you.
5. Click on the OK button. QA will log in to the MS-SQL Server you specified in Step 4 and display the Query pane in the QA application window, similar to that shown in Figure 38.2.

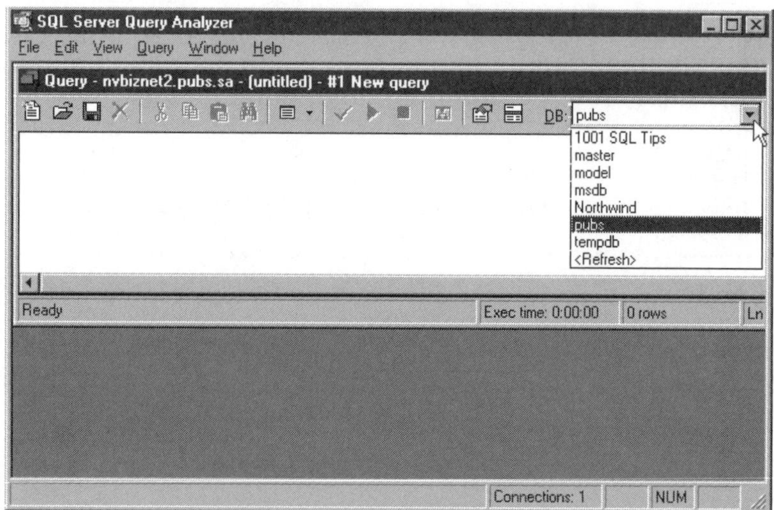

Figure 38.2 The MS-SQL Server Query Analyzer Query pane in the Query Analyzer window

When you install MS-SQL Server under Windows NT, the installation program creates several databases, as shown in the DB drop-down list in the right corner of the Query pane in Figure 38.2. Before using QA to send SQL statements to the MS-SQL Server, you must select a database.

To work with the pubs (sample) database, perform the following steps:

1. Click on the drop-down button to the right of the DB field (in the upper-right corner of the QA Query pane) to list the databases on the SQL Server to which you are connected.
2. Click on a database to select it. For the current example, click on pubs.
3. Place your cursor in the Query pane by clicking anywhere within it. QA will place the cursor in the upper-left corner of the Query pane.
4. Enter your SQL statement in the Query pane. For the current example, enter **SELECT * FROM authors.**
5. To execute the query (entered in Step 4), either press F5 or Ctrl+E, or select the Query menu Execute option. For the current example, press F5. QA will display your query results in a Results pane below the Query pane, similar to that shown in Figure 38.3.

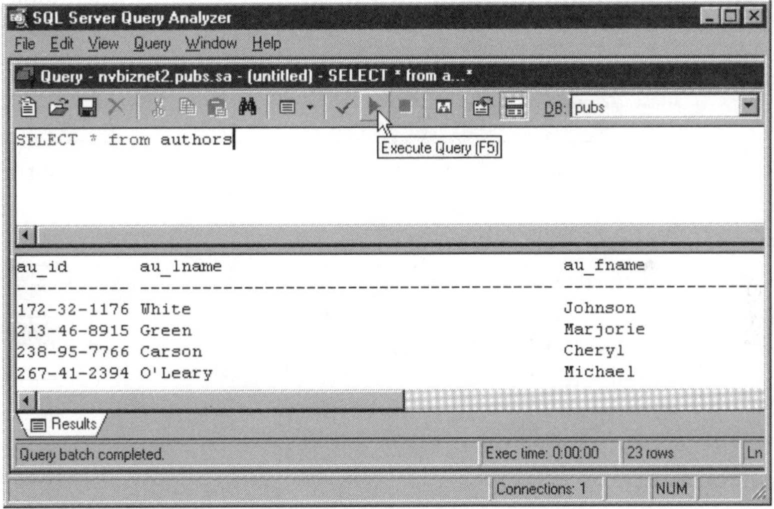

Figure 38.3 The Query Analyzer, with a query in the Query pane and query results in a Results pane

Whenever you tell QA to execute the SQL in the Query pane, QA will send all of the statements in the Query pane to the SQL Server for processing, unless you select a specific statement (or set of statements) you want to execute. So, be careful you don't press Ctrl+E (or press F5, or select the Query menu Execute option), thinking that QA will send only the last statement you typed to the SQL server.

If you have multiple statements in the Query pane, either remove the ones you don't want to execute, or highlight the statement(s) that want QA to send to the SQL Server for processing. For example, if you, you had the following statements in the Query pane

```
SELECT * FROM authors
SELECT * FROM authors WHERE au_lname = 'Green'
```

and you only wanted to execute the second statement, highlight the second query to select it and then select the Query menu Execute option (or click on the green Execute Query button on the standard toolbar). QA will send only the second select statement to the SQL Server and display the results in the Results pane, similar to that shown in Figure 38.4.

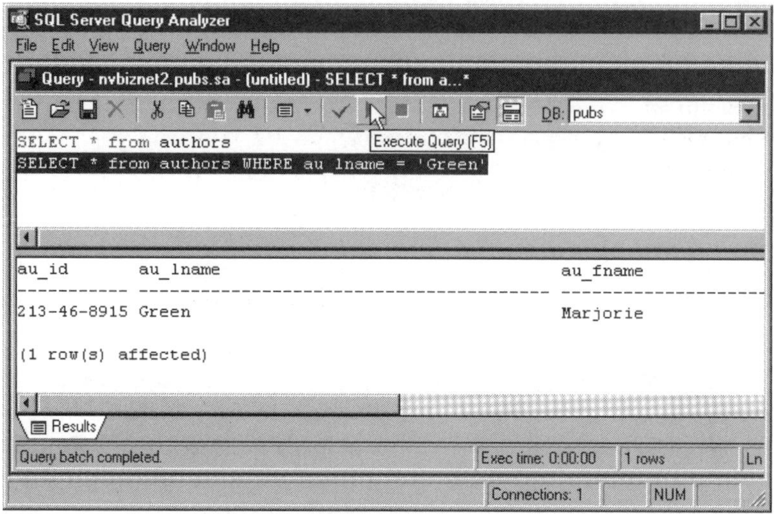

Figure 38.4 The Query Analyzer after executing the highlight statement when the Query pane contains multiple statements

Having QA retain SQL statements in the Query pane after it executes them can save you a lot of typing, especially if you enter a complex query and don't get the results you expect. If you need to change the logic of your query's selection clause, you need only click your cursor in the SQL statement and make your change, without having to retype the entire statement.

39 Using the MS-SQL Server ISQL to Execute SQL Statements from the Command Line or Statements Stored in an ASCII File

In Tip 38, "Using the MS-SQL Server Query Analyzer to Execute SQL Statements," you learned how to use the MS-SQL Query Analyzer GUI query tool. MS-SQL Server also includes two command-line query tools: ISQL.EXE and OSQL.EXE. You'll find both of these tools in MS-SQL Server's BINN subdirectory. (If you installed MS-SQL Server to the default C:\MSSQL7 folder, you will find ISQL and OSQL in the C:\MSSQL7\BINN subfolder.)

Aside from the name, the only difference between ISQL and OSQL is that ISQL uses DB-LIB to connect to the database, whereas OSQL uses ODBC. Although we'll use ISQL to access that database in this tip, the important thing to know is that you can execute the same statements using OSQL. Thus, if you have only OSQL on your system, just use it in place of ISQL in the following example.

The command-line query tools are useful if you find yourself running a series of SQL statements. You can use ISQL (or OSQL) to execute the statements one after another by typing them into an ASCII that you pass to ISQL or OSQL for processing. The command-line tools also give you a quick, low overhead way to test your SQL queries.

Note: *You will need to install MS-SQL Server prior to using either of the two command-line query tools (ISQL or OSQL). Tip 527 gives you step-by-step instructions for installing MS-SQL Server, if you have not yet installed it on your computer system.*

If you are using the computer on which you installed MS-SQL Server, you need type only **I SQL** or **OSQL** at the MS-DOS prompt to start the query tool because the installation program added the C:\MSSQL7\BINN folder in your path. If you are attaching to the MS-SQL Server across a network, have your system administrator give you access to the MSSQL7\BINN\OSQL.EXE on the server. (In order to use ISQL.EXE, you must install NTWDBLIB.DLL on your computer—OSQL.EXE does not require an additional DLL file.)

Before you can start using ISQL, you must get to an MS-DOS prompt. If you have an MS-DOS icon on your desktop, double-click on it. Otherwise, click your mouse on the Start button, select Programs, and then click your mouse on Command Prompt. Windows will start an MS-DOS session.

The format of the command to start ISQL is:

```
ISQL -S<server name> -U<username> -P<password>
```

(If you want to see the list of all ISQL command line parameters, type **ISQL-?** and then press the Enter key.)

To use ISQL to attach to your MS-SQL Server, replace <server name> with the name of your MS-SQL Server, and replace <username> and <password> with your login name and password. For example, to attach to the MS-SQL Server NVBizNet2 using the login name sa, which has no password, type

```
ISQL -SNVBizNet2 -Usa -P
```

and then press the Enter key. ISQL will display its equivalent of the MS-DOS prompt, similar to that shown in Figure 39.1.

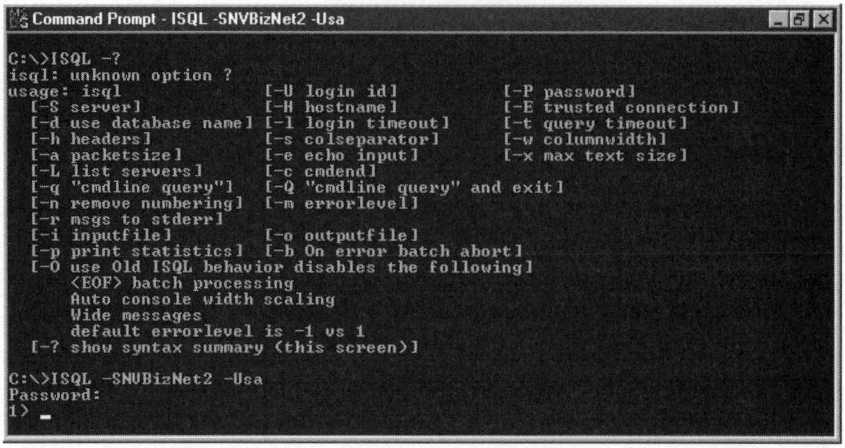

```
Command Prompt - ISQL -SNVBizNet2 -Usa

C:\>ISQL -?
isql: unknown option ?
usage: isql                  [-U login id]          [-P password]
  [-S server]                [-H hostname]          [-E trusted connection]
  [-d use database name]     [-l login timeout]     [-t query timeout]
  [-h headers]               [-s colseparator]      [-w columnwidth]
  [-a packetsize]            [-e echo input]        [-x max text size]
  [-L list servers]          [-c cmdend]
  [-q "cmdline query"]       [-Q "cmdline query" and exit]
  [-n remove numbering]      [-m errorlevel]
  [-r msgs to stderr]
  [-i inputfile]             [-o outputfile]
  [-p print statistics]      [-b On error batch abort]
  [-O use Old ISQL behavior disables the following]
      <EOF> batch processing
      Auto console width scaling
      Wide messages
      default errorlevel is -1 vs 1
  [-? show syntax summary (this screen)]

C:\>ISQL -SNVBizNet2 -Usa
Password:
1> _
```

Figure 39.1 The ISQL response to the -? parameter, followed by the ISQL Ready prompt (1>) after ISQL successfully attached to the NVBizNet2 SQL Server

Once you see the ISQL Ready prompt, perform the following steps to send SQL statements to the SQL server:

1. Type an SQL statement at the Ready (1>) prompt. For the current example, type **USE pubs** (to tell the SQL Server you want to use the PUBS database), and then press the Enter key. ISQL will respond with the Ready prompt 2>, indicating that it is ready for you to enter the second line of commands.
2. Type an SQL statement. For the current example, type **SELECT * FROM authors WHERE zip = 94609** and then press the Enter key. ISQL will respond with the Ready prompt 3>, waiting for the third statement or command.
3. If you have additional statements you want ISQL to send to the server as a group, repeat Step 2 until you finish entering.
4. Type **GO** and the press the Enter key to tell ISQL to send your SQL statements to the SQL server.

After you complete Step 4, ISQL will send the SQL statements you entered prior to the GO command to the DBMS, display the results, and then indicate that it is ready for your next command by displaying another Ready prompt (1>).

The important thing to understand is that ISQL sends your SQL statements to the SQL Server only after you type **GO** at a ready prompt and press the Enter key.

To exit ISQL, type **EXIT** at a ready prompt and then press the Enter key. ISQL will terminate and your computer will return to the MS-DOS prompt.

To exit your MS-DOS session and return to the Windows desktop, type **EXIT** at the MS-DOS prompt and press the Enter key.

Note: *By typing USE* ***pubs*** *in Step 2, you told the DBMS that you wanted to use the PUBS database. Instead of having ISQL send the USE statement to the DBMS, you can select the database you want to use by adding –d<use database name> when you start ISQL. In the current example, you would have entered:*

```
ISQL -SNVBizNet2 -Usa -P -dpubs
```

To start ISQL, log in to the sa account on the NVBizNet2 SQL Server and select PUBS as the database to use in subsequent SQL statements.

As mentioned at the beginning of this tip, you can type SQL statements into an ASCII file and then have ISQL (or OSQL) execute them. To do so, add the –i<input file> parameter when typing the ISQL startup command. Suppose, for example, that you had the following statements in a file named INFILE39.SQL:

```
USE pubs
SELECT au_ID, au_lname, zip FROM authors WHERE zip = 94301
GO
```

You could tell ISQL to send the two statements in INFILE39.SQL to the DBMS and display the results to the screen by starting ISQL with the command line:

```
ISQL -SNVBizNet2 -Usa -P -dpubs -iInFile39.sql -n
```

The –n tells ISQL not to display statement numbers. Without the –n, ISQL will display a statement number and the greater than (>) symbol for each of the three SQL statements. As a result, the headings won't line up with the column data. The –n tells ISQL not to display the statement line numbers. After you enter the command line, press the Enter key. ISQL will send each of the statements in the input file InFile39.sql to the DBMS and display output similar to:

```
au_ID        au_lname     zip
-----------  -----------  -----
427-17-2319  Dull         94301
846-92-7186  Hunter       94301
```

As a final permutation, to store the query results in a file instead of displaying them to the screen, add the –o<output file> parameter to the ISQL startup command. Suppose, for example, that you want to store the query results from executing the statements in the input INFILE39.SQL into the output file OUTFLE39. You would type

```
ISQL -SNVBizNet2 -Usa -P -iInFile39.sql -n -oOutFle39
```

at the MS-DOS prompt and then press the Enter key to start ISQL.

40 Using the ED Command Within ISQL to Edit SQL Statements

Before sending SQL statements to the DBMS when you enter the GO command, ISQL acts as a line editor. As you learned in Tip 39, "Using the MS-SQL Server ISQL to Execute SQL Statements from the Command Line or Statements Stored in an ASCII File," the format of the command to start ISQL at the MS-DOS command line is:

```
ISQL -S<server name> -U<username> -P<password>
```

Note: *Substitute the name of your SQL Server for NVBizNet2, and use your own username and password for login if the sa account is not available to you.*

Thus, to log in to the NVBizNet2 MS-SQL Server as username sa, perform the following steps:

1. Click your mouse on the Start button, select Programs, and click your mouse on Command Prompt. Windows will start an MS-DOS session.
2. To start ISQL, type **ISQL –SNVBizNet2 –Usa –P** and press the Enter key. ISQL will display its Ready prompt (1>).
3. Next, enter the SQL SELECT statement:

```
SELECT * FROM authors
```

4. Press the Enter key. After ISQL puts your statement in its statement buffer, your screen will appear similar to the following:

```
ISQL -SNVBizNet2 -Usa -P
1> SELECT * FROM authors
2>
```

Since you did not identify the database you want to use, ISQL will display the following if you enter **GO** and press the Enter key at the Ready prompt (2>).

```
Msg 208, Level 16, State 1, Server NVBIZNET2, Line 1
Invalid object name 'authors'.
```

Because ISQL is a line editor interface, you cannot move your cursor in front of SELECT and insert a statement. Thus, if you had only ISQL, your only choice would be to enter **EXIT** or **QUIT** at the Ready prompt (2>) and start over, this time either adding the **–d <use database name>** parameter to the ISQL command line or typing **USE <database name>** in response the first Ready prompt (1>).

Fortunately, ISQL lets you use the MS-DOS full-screen editor.

To start the full screen editor, type **ED** at a ready prompt (2>) and press the Enter key. ISQL will start the MS-DOS editor and transfer the contents of its statement buffer, similar to that shown in Figure 40.1.

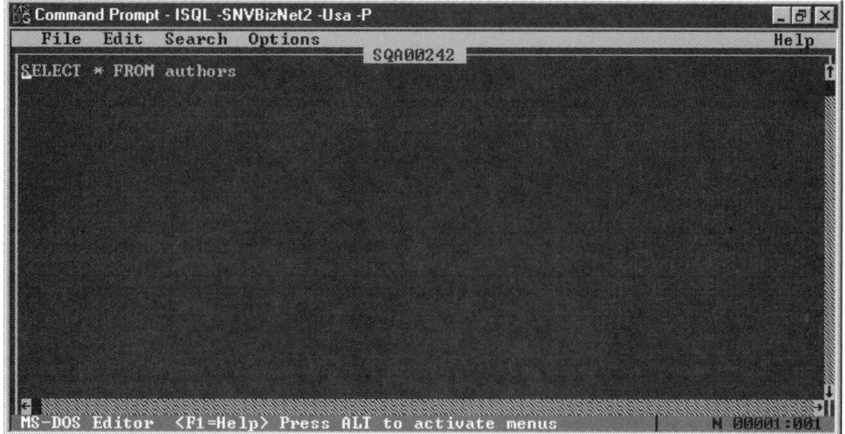

Figure 40.1 The MS-DOS full-screen editor as started by ISQL

To insert the USE statement in front of the SELECT statement, move your cursor in front of the word SELECT. Type **USE pubs** and press the Enter key. Once you've done that, you will have two statements in the text editor:

```
USE pubs
SELECT * FROM authors
```

To transfer the contents of the full-screen editor to the ISQL statement buffer, select the File, Exit option. When the editor prompts you to save your changes, press Y. The MS-DOS editor will send its contents to ISQL which will display them as individual lines similar to:

```
1> USE pubs
2> SELECT * FROM authors
3>
```

Now, type **GO** and press the Enter key to send the USE and SELECT statements to the DBMS. After ISQL displays the query results, type **EXIT** and press the Enter key to exit ISQL and return to the MS-DOS prompt.

The important things to know are:

- You can work in single-line edit mode by typing your SQL statements in response to each ISQL Ready prompt.
- ISQL stores each statement you enter in its statement buffer.
- You can use a full-screen editor by entering **ED** in response to an ISQL Ready prompt.

- When you start the full-screen editor (with the ED command), ISQL copies the contents of its statement buffer to the editor screen.
- When you leave the full-screen editor (by selecting the File menu Exit option), ISQL reads the contents of the editor screen into its statement buffer as one statement per editor line.

41 Using the CREATE DATABASE Statement to Create an MS-SQL Server Database and Transaction Log

Unlike many other DBMS products, MS-SQL Server lets you create multiple databases for each MS-SQL Server. Most commercial DBMS products do not even have a CREATE DATABASE command. Instead, the installation program creates the one database file the SQL Server will use. The database administrator (dba) and privileged users then create all of the database objects in the one database. As a result, the typical database contains a mix of both related and unrelated tables.

MS-SQL Server gives you the best of both worlds. If you want, you can create a single database for all of your tables, or you can separate totally unrelated tables into separate databases. Suppose, for example, that you and your spouse each run your own home business. Using the typical DBMS, you would create one database to hold both your (mail order) CUSTOMER list and your spouse's (accounting) CLIENT list, even though the two tables are completely unrelated.

Having a single database means that both businesses would lose database access during backup and (if necessary) recovery operations. If the two were separate, you could still use a single server (to save a bit of hard-earned cash on software and hardware), but you would not be affected by database problems or maintenance activities that have nothing to do with your own tables.

Finally, MS-SQL Server's multiple database strategy makes it possible to create a development database that uses the same database objects and security setup as its production counterpart. Having an identical database structure and security setup makes it easier to test how proposed changes will affect online application programs, database stored procedures, views, and triggers. Moreover, once you've fully tested new or modified code on the development system, you will be able to install procedures, triggers, and views on the production system without further modification. Finally, you can import data from tables in the production database into identical tables in the development database, making it easy to use the development system to "freeze" database data and reproduce errors that seem to occur at random intervals.

The syntax of the CREATE DATABASE statement is:

```
CREATE DATABASE <database name>
[ON {[PRIMARY] <filespec>} [,...<last filespec>]]
[LOG ON { <filespec>} [,...<last filespec>]]
[FOR RESTORE]
<filespec> is defined as:
   (NAME = <logical file name>,
    FILENAME = '<physical file name>'
    [, SIZE = <initial file size>]
    [, MAXSIZE = {<maximum file size> | UNLIMITED}]
    [, FILEGROWTH = <file extension inc>])
```

Review Table 41.1 for a brief explanation of CREATE DATABASE keywords and options.

Keyword / Option	***Description***
database name	The name of the database.
ON <filespec>	The name(s) of the disk file(s) that will hold the data portion of the database. MS-SQL Server lets you split a single database into multiple files.
PRIMARY	If you split the database into multiple files, PRIMARY identifies the file that contains the start of the data and the system tables. If you don't specify a PRIMARY file, MS-SQL Server will use the first file in the list as the PRIMARY file.
LOG ON <filespec>	The name(s) of the disk file(s) that will hold the transaction log.
FOR RESTORE	Do not allow access to the database until it is filled with data by a RESTORE operation.
<logical file name>	The name the MS-SQL Server will use to reference the database or transaction log.
<physical file name>	The full pathname to the database or transaction log file.
<initial file size>	The initial size, in megabytes, of the database or transaction log. If you don't specify an initial size for the transaction log, the system will size it to 25 percent of the total size of the database files.
<maximum file size>	The maximum size to which the database or transaction log can grow. If you specify UNLIMITED, the files can grow until they exhaust the physical disk space.
<file extension inc>	The number of bytes to add to the size of the transaction log or database file when the current free space in the file is used up.

Table 41.1 Definition of CREATE DATABASE Statement Keywords and Options

To create a database using the MS-SQL Server Query Analyzer, perform the following steps:

1. Click your mouse on the Start button. Windows will display the Start menu.
2. Move your mouse pointer to Programs on the Start menu, select the Microsoft SQL Server 7.0 option, and click your mouse on Query Analyzer. Query Analyzer will display the Connect to SQL Server dialog box similar to that shown in Figure 41.1.

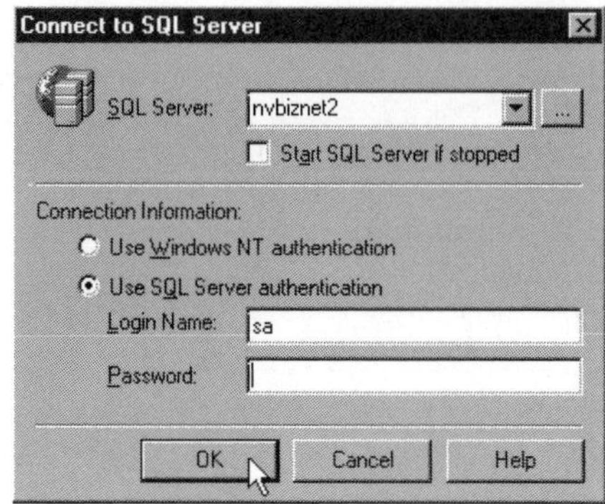

Figure 41.1 The Query Analyzer Connect to SQL Server dialog box

3. Enter the name of your SQL Server in the SQL Server field.
4. Enter your username in the Login Name field, and enter your password in the Password field.
5. Click on the OK button. Query Analyzer will connect to the SQL Server you entered in Step 3 and display the Query pane in the SQL Server Query Analyzer application window.
6. Enter the CREATE DATABASE statement. For the current example, enter:

```
CREATE DATABASE SQLTips
ON      (NAME        = SQLTips_data,
         FILENAME    = 'c:\mssql7\data\SQLTips_data.mdf',
         SIZE        = 10,
         FILEGROWTH = 1MB)
LOG ON (NAME = 'SQLTips_log',
         FILENAME = 'c:\mssql7\data\SQLTips_log.ldf',
         SIZE = 3,
         FILEGROWTH = 1MB)
```

7. Click on the green arrow Execute Query button on the standard toolbar (or select the Query menu Execute option). Query Analyzer will create the database on the SQL Server to which you connected in Step 5.

After you complete Step 7, the Query Analyzer will display the results of the CREATE DATABASE execution in the Results pane in the SQL Server Query Analyzer application window. If Query Analyzer is successful in executing your CREATE DATABASE statement, the program will display the following in the Results pane:

```
The CREATE DATABASE process is allocating 10.00 MB on disk 'SQLTips_data'.
The CREATE DATABASE process is allocating 3.00 MB on disk "SQLTips_log'.
```

42 Using the MS-SQL Server Enterprise Manager to Create a Database and Transaction Log

In Tip 41, "Using the CREATE DATABASE Statement to Create an MS-SQL Server Database and Transaction Log," you learned that MS-SQL Server lets you create multiple databases on a single server, and you also learned how to use the CREATE DATABASE statement. Like most database management tools, MS-SQL Server gives you not only a command line (SQL or Transact-SQL) statement, but also a graphical user interface (GUI) tool to perform the same function. To create a database using the MS-SQL Server Enterprise Manager, perform the following steps:

1. Click your mouse on the Start button. Windows will display the Start menu.
2. Move your mouse pointer to Programs on the Start menu, select the Microsoft SQL Server 7.0 option, and click your mouse on Enterprise Manager. Windows will start the Enterprise Manager in the SQL Server Enterprise Manager application window.
3. Click your mouse on the plus (+) to the left of SQL Server Group to display the list of MS-SQL Servers available on your network.
4. Click your mouse on the plus (+) to the left of the SQL Server on which you wish to create a database. Enterprise Manager, in turn, will display a Database Properties dialog box similar to that shown in Figure 42.2
5. Click your mouse on the Databases folder to display the list of databases currently on the server, similar to that shown in Figure 42.1.
6. Select the Action menu New Database option. Enterprise Manager displays a Database Properties dialog box similar to that shown in Figure 42.2.

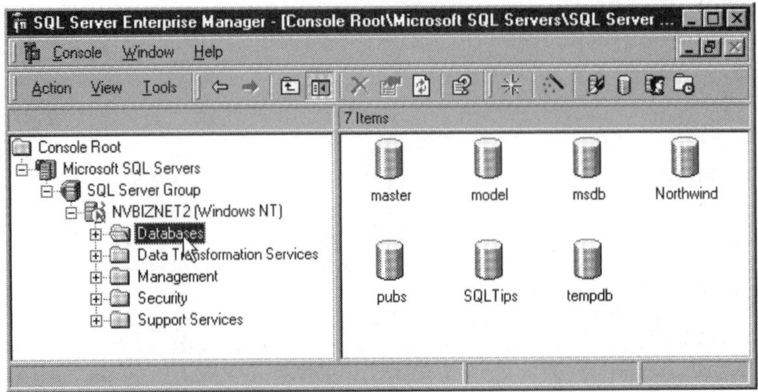

Figure 42.1 The SQL Server Enterprise Manager application window

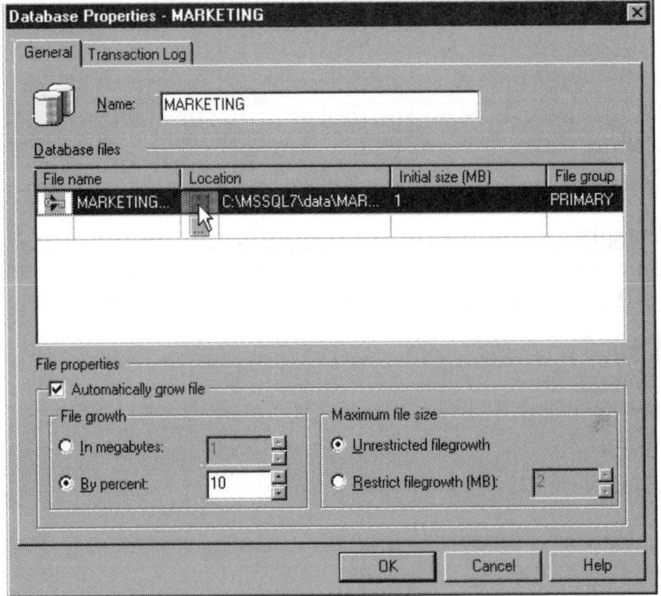

Figure 42.2 The Enterprise Manager Database Properties dialog box

7. Enter the name of the database in the Name field. For the current project, enter **MARKETING**. The Enterprise Manager will automatically fill in the pathname and initial database size in the Database Files section of the Database Properties dialog box.

Note: *If you want to put the database in a folder other than the default folder or change the physical file name, click your mouse on the Search button in the Location field in the Database Files area of the Database Properties dialog box. Enterprise Manager will* *display the Locate Database File dialog box so you can select a folder or change the database's physical file name.*

8. Click on the Initial size (MB) field and enter the initial size of the database file. For the current project, enter **10**.
9. Set the database File Growth and Maximum File Size options. For the current project, accept the defaults, which allow the database file to grow by 10 percent each time it fills up and place no restriction on its maximum size.
10. Click on the Transaction Log tab.
11. If you want to change the pathname (the file name and physical location) of the transaction log file, click on the Search button in the Location field to work with the Locate Transaction Log File dialog box. For the current project, accept the default pathname for the transaction log.
12. Click on the Initial size (MB) field, and enter the initial size of the transaction log. For the current project, enter **3**.
13. Set the database File Growth and Maximum File Size options. For the current project, accept the defaults, which allow the transaction log to grow by 10 percent each time it fills up and place no restriction on its maximum size.
14. Click on the OK button.

After you complete Step 14, the Enterprise Manager will create the database (MARKETING, in the current example) according to the options you selected and return to the SQL Server Enterprise Manager application window.

The important thing to know now is that MS-SQL Server gives you two ways to create a database. You can use the CREATE DATABASE statement or use the Enterprise Manager's Action menu New Database option. Whether you use CREATE DATABASE or the Enterprise Manager, you can set database and transaction log options that specify:

- The physical locations (pathnames) of the database and transaction log file(s)
- The initial size of the database and transaction log
- The increment by which the database and transaction log will grow
- The maximum size to which the database and transaction log file(s) can grow

If you are using CREATE DATABASE, you specify the database and transaction log properties in separate clauses within the statement. When you use the Enterprise Manager to create a database, you can still specify different properties for the database and transaction log file(s) by using the Database Properties dialog box General tab to specify database options and using the Transaction Log tab to select transaction log options.

43 Using DROP DATABASE to Erase an MS-SQL Server Database and Transaction Log

Dropping (deleting) databases you no longer need frees up disk space. The primary rule to follow: *Be careful!* You cannot easily undo an executed DROP DATABASE statement. As such, always back up the database before dropping (erasing) it. Having a full backup will save you a lot of headaches if the user decides he or she needs "one more thing" from the database—right after you erase it, of course.

Only the system administrator (sa) or a user with dbcreator or sysadmin privilege can drop a database. You cannot drop the MASTER, MODEL, or TempDB database.

The syntax of the DROP DATABASE statement is:

```
DROP DATABASE <database name>
              [,<database name>, <last database name>]
```

Thus, to remove the MARKETING database you created in Tip 42, "Using the MS-SQL Server Enterprise Manager to Create a Database and Transaction Log," perform the following steps:

1. Start the MS-SQL Server Query Analyzer (as you learned to do in Tip 38, "Using the MS-SQL Server Query Analyzer to Execute SQL Statements"), or start the Enterprise Manager (as you learned to do in Tip 42) and select the Tools menu, SQL Server Query Analyzer option.
2. Enter the DROP DATABASE statement in the Query Analyzer's Query pane. For the current project, type

```
DROP DATABASE marketing.
```

3. Press Ctrl+E (or select the Query menu, Execute option).

After you complete Step 3, the Query Analyzer will attempt to delete the database and log file. If Query Analyzer successfully deletes the MARKETING database and transaction log, it will display the following in the Results pane of the Query Analyzer application window:

```
Deleting database file 'C:\MSSQL7\data\MARKETING_Data.MDF'.
Deleting database file 'C:\MSSQL7\data\MARKETING_Log.LDF'.
```

44 Understanding How to Size MS-SQL Server Databases and Transaction Logs

MS-SQL Server puts all database objects (tables, views, procedures, triggers, indexes, and so on) into a single large file. Whenever you make a change to the database (add an object, alter an object, delete a row, update a column value, insert a row, and so on), the DBMS makes an entry in a second file, the transaction log. Thus, every database has two files: the database file, which contains all of the database objects; and the transaction log, which contains an entry for each change made to the database (since the last time the log was cleared).

Note: *The database file and transaction log can each be made up of more than one physical file. However, the DBMS treats the set of physical files used to hold the database data as a single, logical "database file" and the set of physical files used to hold the transaction log as a single, logical "transaction log" file. You can set the initial size of each individual file, but the FILEGROWTH option applies to the logical database file and transaction log, not to each physical file used to store them on disk.*

As you learned in Tip 41, "Using the CREATE DATABASE Statement to Create an MS-SQL Server Database and Transaction Log," and Tip 42, "Using the MS-SQL Server Enterprise Manager to Create a Database and Transaction Log," you use the SIZE option to specify the initial size of the database and transaction log when you create them. For example, in Tip 41, you executed the SQL statement

```
CREATE DATABASE SQLTips
ON      (NAME        = SQLTips_data,
         FILENAME    = 'c:\mssql7\data\SQLTips_data.mdf',
         SIZE        = 10,
         FILEGROWTH = 1MB)
LOG ON (NAME = 'SQLTips_log',
         FILENAME = 'c:\mssql7\data\SQLTips_log.ldf',
         SIZE = 3,
         FILEGROWTH = 1MB)
```

which created the SQLTips database file (SQLTIPS_DATA.MDF) with an initial size of 10MB and the transaction log for the database (SQLTIPS_LOG.LDF) with an initial size of 3MB. As you add rows to tables in the database, you use up the free space in the database file. If you add data to a table where each row consists of 10 columns of type CHAR(100), you use up 1,000 bytes (10 columns × 100 bytes / column) of the 10MB available each time you add a row to the table.

Once you've used all of the free space in a database file (10MB, in the current example) you can no longer add data to the database, even if there is a large amount of physical disk storage space available. To avoid running out of room in the database file before exhausting the physical disk space, use the FILEGROWTH option when you create a database. The FILEGROWTH option tells MS-SQL Server to extend the size of the database file each time it gets full.

In the current example, you set FILEGROWTH to 1MB, which means that each time you use up the space allocated to the database file, the DBMS will increase the size of the file by 1MB. Moreover, since you did not specify a maximum database file size, the DBMS will extend the database file 1MB at a time (as necessary) until it exhausts the physically disk storage space.

Each time you make a change to the database, the DBMS stores the original data values and makes a notation detailing what was done in the transaction log. As such, the DBMS may use up the 3MB allocated to the transaction log in the current example rather quickly if you are making a lot of changes to the database. Fortunately, you can have MS-SQL Server extend the size of the transaction log, just as it does the size of the database file.

In the current example, the DBMS will add 1MB of free space to the transaction log each time the transaction log file fills up.

Note: *Although the current example uses the same FILEGROWTH value for the database file and the transaction log, the two are independent. For example, you can set the FILEGROWTH at 5MB for the database file and 3MB for the transaction log—one does not depend on the other.*

Be sure to specify a large enough initial database file size and growth factor so that your DBMS isn't spending the majority of its time extending the size of the database file as you add table rows. To determine the initial database file size, perform the following analysis on each table in the database:

1. List the column name, data type, and number of bytes of disk space the DBMS will need to store a value in the column. (Your system manual will have a breakdown of the storage required for the data types your DBMS supports.)
2. Determine the number of rows you expect the table to hold within the first six months (or year) of operation.
3. Multiply the number of bytes per row times the number of rows in the table to determine the storage requirements of the table.

Once you know the storage required for each table in your database, set the initial size of the database file to 25–50 percent more than the sum of the space required by all of its tables. The extra space (50 percent, if possible), allows for a margin of error for your guess as to the number or rows you expect each table to hold, leaves space for indexes the DBMS can add to speed up data access, and gives the DBMS room for system cursors and for temporary tables it creates when processing complex queries with large result sets.

Set the FILEGROWTH option to 10 percent of the initial database file size, rounded up to the nearest whole number. Thus, if your initial database file size is 25MB, set your FILEGROWTH to 3MB. Monitor the size of your database file, especially during the first several months of operation. If you find the database file growing at more than 10 percent in a month, increase the FILEGROWTH option so that the DBMS has to extend the database file size only once a month.

As a general rule of thumb, set the initial size of your transaction log file to 25 percent of the initial size of your database file, and set its FILEGROWTH to 10 percent of its initial size. Thus, if your initial database file size is 250MB, set the transaction log file to start at 25MB and grow by 3MB. Monitor the growth in size of your transaction log, and adjust its growth factor so that the DBMS has to extend it at most only once per month.

You learned how to set the initial file size and the growth increment (FILEGROWTH) for your database and transaction log files using the CREATE DATABASE statement in Tip 41 and using the MS-SQL Server Enterprise Explorer in Tip 42. After you've created the database file and transaction log, you can use the Enterprise Manager to change the size of either the file or its growth factor by performing the following steps:

1. To start the Enterprise Manager, click on the Start button, move your mouse pointer to Programs on the Start menu, select Microsoft SQL Server 7.0, and click your mouse on Enterprise Manager.
2. To display the list of SQL Servers, click on the plus (+) to the left of SQL Server Group.
3. To display the list of resources on the SQL Server with the database file or transaction log you want to modify, click on the plus (+) to the left of the SQL Server's name. For example, if you want to work with the SQL Server NVBizNet2, click on the plus (+) to the left of NVBizNet2. Enterprise Manager will display a list of folders that represent the resources managed by the SQL Server NVBizNet2 (in the current example).
4. Click on the Databases folder. The Enterprise Manager will display the databases on the SQL Server in its right pane.
5. Double-click your mouse on the database icon whose database file or transaction log you want to modify. For the current example, double-click your mouse on SQLTips (if you created the database in Tip 41). Enterprise Manager will display the General tab of the SQLTips Properties dialog box similar to that shown in Figure 44.1. (The name of the dialog box is <database name> Properties.) As such, your dialog box will be SQLTips Properties only if you double-clicked your mouse on the SQLTips database.
6. Click on the Space Allocated field in the Database files area of the dialog box. For the current example, change the 10 to 15.
7. To have the database file grow by a percentage of its current size instead of by a constant number of megabytes, click your mouse on the By Percent radio button in the File Properties area of the dialog box. For the current example, leave the percentage the default, 10 percent.

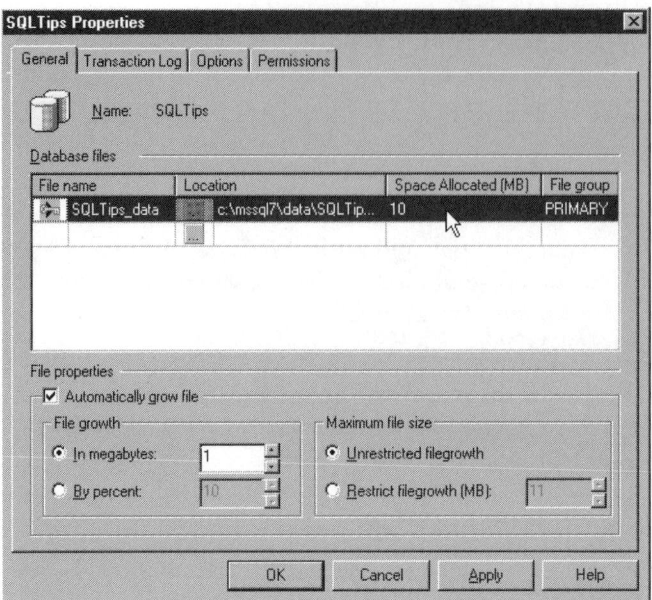

Figure 44.1 The Enterprise Manager database properties dialog box

8. If you want to restrict the database file growth to a certain number of megabytes, click on the Restrict Filegrowth (MB) radio button and enter the maximum file size in megabytes. For the current example, allow for unrestricted file growth by clicking on the Unrestricted Filegrowth radio button.
9. Click on the Transaction Log tab to work with the transaction log properties. For the current example, leave the transaction log properties unchanged. However, if you did want to change the transaction log options, you would follow Steps 6 to 8, substituting "transaction log" for "database file" in each step.
10. Click on the OK button. The Enterprise Manager will apply your changes to the SQLTips database and return to the Enterprise Manager application window.

The optimal initial size and growth increment for a database and transaction log depend on the amount of data, amount of physical storage space available, and volume of transactions you expect the DBMS to handle. If you're converting from one DBMS product to another, base your size and increment settings on historical requirements. Otherwise, use the figures in this tip as a reasonable starting point. The important thing to understand is that while you don't want to allocate space you'll never need, you also want the DBMS to spend as little time as possible increasing the size of the database file and transaction log.

45 Understanding the MS-SQL Server TempDB Database

Each time you start MS-SQL Server, the DBMS creates a special database named TempDB. The server uses the TempDB database for such things as temporary tables, cursor data, and temporary, user-created global variables. In short, the TempDB database is the system's scratchpad. However, you can use it as well.

The advantage of using TempDB is that activities you perform to TempDB objects (tables, views, indexes, and so on) are not logged. As such, the DBMS can manipulate data in TempDB faster than it does in other databases.

Prior to changing database objects and data values (other than TempDB objects and data), the DBMS must store the preupdate (original) object structures and values in the transaction log. Thus, for non-TempDB data, every data manipulation involves two save operations—save the original and then save the updated value. Saving the original data values can impose significant overhead if you are making a large number of changes. When using TempDB objects, however, the DBMS has to perform storage operations only once—to save the updated values to disk.

The downside of using TempDB objects is that you cannot roll back (or undo) manipulations made on TempDB objects. Moreover, each time you shut down the DBMS and restart it, TempDB (and all of its objects) is erased. As such, any information stored in TempDB is lost each time the DBMS restarts (and re-creates TempDB). Therefore, do not rely on the existence of any information in TempDB from one session to the next.

Use TempDB as a scratchpad (as MS-SQL Server does) to hold temporary data values and tables. TempDB is especially useful for aggregating data values from multiple tables in order to generate a summary report. Rather than trying to write an SQL statement that both selects and summarizes data, you can simplify your task by writing a query that aggregates the data you want in a temporary TempDB table, and then execute a simple second query to produce your final report.

46 Using the CREATE TABLE Statement to Create Tables

Tables are the primary structures used to hold data in a relational database. In a typical multi-user environment, the database administrator (dba) creates the tables that serve as the data stores for the organization's data. Users normally create their own temporary tables used to store data extracted from the main organizational tables.

For example, the dba would create the CUSTOMER and ORDERS tables to hold a permanent record of all of the company's customers and their orders. If you then need to produce several reports for a particular quarter, you would create a temporary table to hold a portion of the company's data. By extracting a portion of the overall table into a temporary table, you have to do the data selection only once, and you can use the results of the selection for multiple reports such as quarter-to-quarter comparisons, a list of the top customers based on amount purchased, or a summary of items sold during the period.

Whether you are creating permanent or temporary tables, you use the same SQL CREATE TABLE statement. The syntax of the CREATE TABLE statement is:

```
CREATE TABLE <table name>
 (<column definition> [,...<last column definition]
   [<primary key definition>]
   [<foreign key definition>])
<column definition> is defined as:
   <column name> <data-type> [DEFAULT <value>]
   [NOT NULL][UNIQUE][<check constraint definition>]
<check constraint definition> is defined as:
   CHECK (<search condition>)
<primary key definition> is defined as:
   PRIMARY KEY (<column name> [, <column name>])
<foreign key definition> is defined as:
   FOREIGN KEY (<column name>) REFERENCES <table name>
```

Review Table 46.1 for a brief explanation of CREATE TABLE keywords and options.

Keyword / Option	***Description***
table name	The name of the table—must be unique by owner within a database. (See Tip 9, "Understanding Table Names.")
column name	The name of a column—must be unique within the table.
data-type	One of the SQL data types (see Tips 21–26) or a named domain (see Tip 14, "Understanding Domains").
DEFAULT <value>	Value assigned to a column if you create a row and do not give the column an explicit initial value. (See Tip 51, "Using the DEFAULT Clause in a CREATE TABLE Statement to Set Default Column Values.")
NOT NULL	Constraint to prevent the assignment of a NULL value to a column. (See Tip 191, "Using the NOT NULL Column Constraint to Prevent Null Values in a Column.")

Keyword / Option	***Description***
UNIQUE	Constraint that prevents adding two table rows with the same value in the *unique* column. (See Tip 192, "Using the UNIQUE Column Constraint to Prevent Duplicate Values in a Column.")
CHECK <search condition>	The search condition can be any SQL statement that evaluates to either TRUE or FALSE. The check constraint prevents adding rows to a table where the search condition evaluates to FALSE. (See Tip 193, "Using the CHECK Constraint to Validate a Column's Value.")
PRIMARY KEY	Constraint that prevents adding two table rows with the same value in the column or set of columns. A table can have only one PRIMARY KEY. The PRIMARY KEY is column (or set of columns) that can be referenced as a FOREIGN KEY in another table. (See Tip 172, "Using the PRIMARY KEY Column Constraint to Uniquely Identify Rows in a Table.")
FOREIGN KEY	Column whose value can be found as the PRIMARY KEY in table specified by REFERENCES <table name>. (See Tip 174, "Understanding Referential Data Integrity Checks and Foreign Keys.")

Table 46.1 Definition of CREATE TABLE Statement Keywords and Options

For example, if you execute the CREATE TABLE statements

```
CREATE TABLE item_master
  (item_number INTEGER,
   description VARCHAR(35) NOT NULL
   PRIMARY KEY (item_number))
CREATE TABLE orders
  (order_number    INTEGER UNIQUE NOT NULL,
   item_number     INTEGER NOT NULL,
   quantity        SMALLINT DEFAULT 1,
   item_cost       DECIMAL (5,2),
   customer_number INTEGER
   PRIMARY KEY (order_number, item_number)
   FOREIGN KEY (item_number) REFERENCES item_master)
```

the DBMS will create two tables, ITEM_MASTER and ORDERS. The ITEM_MASTER table has two columns, DESCRIPTION and ITEM_NUMBER. The ITEM_NUMBER is the PRIMARY KEY for the ITEM_MASTER table, meaning that each item (row) in the table will have a unique ITEM_NUMBER. Put another way, no two item descriptions will have the same item number.

The second table, ORDERS, has five columns. The PRIMARY KEY of the ORDERS table is a composite key, meaning that it is made up of two or more columns. In the current example, the PRIMARY KEY for ORDERS consists of the ORDER_NUMBER and ITEM_NUMBER columns, meaning that the same ORDER_NUMBER (like 123, for example) may appear in several rows of the table, but each row for the same ORDER_NUMBER will have a unique ORDER_NUMBER-ITEM_NUMBER pair.

The FOREIGN KEY constraint in the ORDERS table tells the DBMS that the value in the ITEM_NUMBER column in the ORDERS table REFERENCES the PRIMARY KEY in the ITEM_MASTER table. Thus, the DBMS can take the value in the ITEM_NUMBER column and uniquely identify a single row in the ITEM_MASTER table. Moreover, the DBMS will not allow you to add a row to the ORDERS table if the ITEM_NUMBER value in the row to be inserted does not exist in the ITEM_MASTER table. Conversely, you will not be able to delete a row in the ITEM_MASTER file if its ITEM_NUMBER value exists as an ITEM_NUMBER in the ORDERS table. (You will learn more about the FOREIGN KEY constraint in Tip 174.)

From its syntax and the examples in this tip, you can see that the CREATE TABLE statement lets you define database tables. When creating a table, you give the names of the columns and the data type of each column, and specify any constraints as to the data values the columns can hold. Moreover, you can identify one of the columns or a set of columns as the PRIMARY KEY for the table, meaning that each row in the table has a unique value in the column (or set of columns) that make up the PRIMARY KEY. Finally, you can use the FOREIGN KEY constraint to identify parent/child relationships between tables. In the current example, ORDERS is the child of the ITEM_MASTER parent.

47 Using the MS-SQL Server Enterprise Manager to Create Tables

In addition to typing CREATE TABLE statements into the MS-SQL Server Query Analyzer's Query pane or at the ISQL (or OSQL) Ready prompts, MS-SQL Server gives you a GUI tool you can use. To create a table using the Enterprise Manager, perform the following steps:

1. To start the Enterprise Manager, click on the Start button, move your mouse pointer to Programs on the Start menu, select Microsoft SQL Server 7.0, and click your mouse on Enterprise Manager.
2. To display the list of SQL servers, click on the plus (+) to the left of SQL Server Group.
3. To display the list of resources on the SQL Server on which you wish to create a table, click on the plus (+) to the left of the SQL Server's name. For example, if you want to work

with the SQL Server, NVBizNet2, click on the plus (+) to the left of NVBIZNET2. Enterprise Manager will display a list of folders that represent the resources managed by the SQL Server NVBizNet2 (in the current example).

4. Click on the Database folders. The Enterprise Manager will display the databases on the SQL Server in its right pane.
5. Right-click your mouse on the database in which you wish to create the table. For the current example, right-click your mouse on the SQLTips database. (If you did not create the SQLTips database, right-click your mouse on the TempDB database.) The Enterprise Manager will display a pop-up menu.
6. Move your mouse pointer to New on the pop-up menu, and then select Table. Enterprise Manager will display the Choose Name dialog box.
7. Enter the table name in the Enter a Name for the Table field of the Choose Name dialog box. For the current example, enter **Item_Master** and then click on the OK button. Enterprise Manager will display the SQL Server Enterprise Manager–New Table window shown in Figure 47.1.
8. Prepare to enter the first column name by clicking your mouse on the first cell in the Column Name column.
9. Enter the name of the column. For the current example, enter **item_number**. Next, press the Enter key to move to the input cursors to the Datatype field.
10. Select the field's data type. Either click on the drop-down arrow to the right of the Datatype field and select the data type, or enter the data type into the Data Type field. For the current example, enter **INT**. Next, press the Enter key to move to the insert cursor to the Length field.

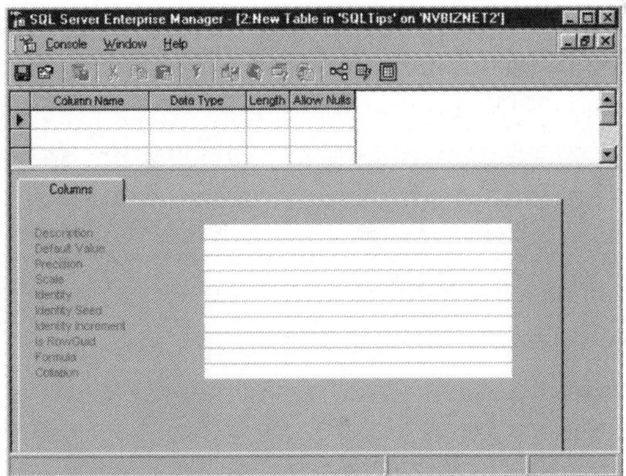

Figure 47.1 The MS-SQL Server Enterprise Manager New Table window

11. If you are working with a character, image, or text type, enter the length of the character. In the current example, you are working with an integer, so the Length field is not applicable. Press the Enter key to move the input cursor to the Precision field.
12. If you are working with a decimal or floating-point (nonwhole) number, enter the total number of digits in the number into the Precision field. In the current example, you are working with an integer, so the precision is set to the default precision for your implementation (which you cannot change). Press the Enter key to move the input cursor to the Scale field.
13. If you are working with a decimal or floating-point (nonwhole) number, enter the number of digits you want to carry to the right of the decimal point into the Scale field. In the current example, you are working with an integer, so the Scale field is not applicable. Press the Enter key to move to the Allow Nulls check box.
14. To allow the field to hold a NULL value, click on the Allow Nulls check box until the check mark appears. For the current example, clear the Allow Nulls check box—every item in the ITEM_MASTER table must have an ITEM_NUMBER.
15. If you want to set the column to a constant default value if you don't supply an explicit value for the column when inserting a row into the table, enter the value into the Default Value field. For the current example, leave the Default Value field blank.
16. To have the DBMS supply an incrementing value for the column if you don't supply an explicit value for the column when inserting a row into the table, click on the Identity check box until the check mark appears. For the current example, click a check mark into the Identity check box—you want the system to supply the item numbers for new items you add to the ITEM_MASTER table. Then press the Enter key to move the input cursor to the Identity Seed field.
17. Enter the first value the DBMS should supply for the column—applicable only if you've identified the column as having the IDENTITY property. For the current example, enter **1000**. Then press the Enter key to move the input cursor to the Identity Increment field.
18. Enter the value by which the DBMS is to increment the previous number it supplied for the column when inserting a new table row—applicable only if you've identified the column as having the IDENTITY property. For the current example, enter **100**.
19. Click on the next empty cell in the Column Name field to enter another column name.
20. Repeat Steps 9–19 until you've defined all of the columns in your table. For the current example, add a second column named Description, with data type VARCHAR of length 35, which does not allow NULL values. Enterprise Manager will display your table definition similar to that shown in Figure 47.2.
21. To identity a column as the PRIMARY KEY, right-click your mouse on any field in the column, and select Set Primary Key from the pop-up menu. For the current example, right-

click your mouse on ITEM_NUMBER in the Column Name field, and then select Set Primary Key from the pop-up menu.

Note: *If you want to use a multiple-column (composite) PRIMARY KEY, right-click your mouse on any cell in the table and select Properties from the pop-up menu. The Enterprise Manager will display the Properties dialog box. Click on the Indexes/Keys tab and select the columns you want to include in the PRIMARY KEY in the Column Name list field in the Type area of the Indexes/Keys tab. When you are finished selecting columns for the PRIMARY KEY, click on the Close button. (You will learn more about using Enterprise Manager to create indexes in Tip 162, "Understanding MS-SQL Server CREATE INDEX Statement Options.")*

---

22. To save your table definition, click on the Save button (first button on the left with the floppy disk icon) on the New Table standard toolbar.
23. To close the MS-SQL Server Enterprise Manager New Table window, click on the close button (the X) in the upper-right corner of the application window.

You can use the CREATE TABLE statement (which you learned about in Tip 46, "Using the CREATE TABLE Statement to Create Tables") or the Enterprise Manager GUI New Table tool to create MS-SQL Server tables. Both SQL and GUI allow you to define columns, set constraints, and identify table keys. If you have MS-SQL Server Enterprise Manager installed on your computer, the method you select to create your tables is a matter of personal preference (command line vs. GUI).

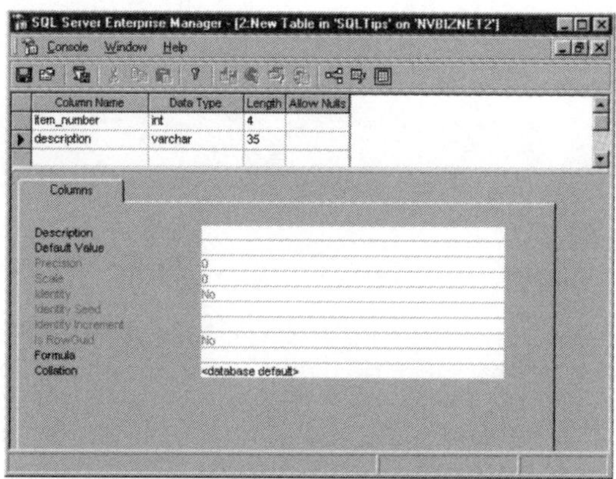

Figure 47.2 The MS-SQL Server Enterprise Manager New Table window after defining two columns for the ITEM_MASTER table

48 Creating MS-SQL Server Temporary Tables

MS-SQL Server lets you create two types of temporary tables: global and local. Local temporary tables are available only to the session in which they are created, and the DBMS automatically erases local temporary tables when the session ends. Global temporary tables are available to multiple database sessions. The DBMS drops a global temporary table after the last user using the table terminates his or her session.

Each login to the database starts a new session. As such, when you use Query Analyzer to attach to a database, you start a session. When you log off or terminate Query Analyzer, the DBMS ends your session. If you're logged in to the database, each time you execute a stored procedure or run an application program that logs in to the same or another database, the DBMS starts a new session. If you log in to the same database a second time, the DBMS keeps your original session open, but information in temporary tables created in the first session is not available to the second session.

Temporary tables are useful when you need to do several operations on the same set of data, such as creating summary reports on a subset of the data from multiple tables. By selecting and combining the raw data you need into a single table, you avoid having the DBMS extract and combine the data multiple times. In addition to eliminating multiple select operations, using a single temporary table increases execution speed because the MS-SQL Server can retrieve data faster from a single table than it can through references to multiple base tables.

To create a *local* temporary table, start the table name with a single pound (#) sign. As such, executing the statement

```
CREATE TABLE #customer_orders
  (customer_number INTEGER,
   customer_name   VARCHAR (35),
   order_date      DATETIME,
   amount          MONEY)
```

will create a local temporary table. The #CUSTOMER_ORDERS table is accessible only to the person who created it. Moreover, the DBMS will automatically DROP the table when the user logs out.

If you want to create a *global* temporary table, start the table name with two pound (#) signs. Thus, if you want to create a temporary table that is accessible to multiple users (and sessions), use a double pound (#) sign with a CREATE TABLE statement similar to:

```
CREATE TABLE ##customer_orders
  (customer_number INTEGER,
   customer_name   VARCHAR (35),
   order_date      DATE_TIME,
   amount          MONEY)
```

The DBMS will not DROP the global temporary table until the last user that referenced the table during his or her session logs out.

49 Using the Transact-SQL CREATE DEFAULT Statement to Set a Column Default

MS-SQL Server lets you create named, default values you can *bind* to columns and user-defined data types. Once you bind a default to a table column, the DBMS will supply the default value for the column (instead of NULL) if you insert a row that includes the column without specifying its value. The advantages of creating a default outside the CREATE TABLE statement are that you can use a descriptive name for the default, apply the same default to multiple columns in the same or different tables, and change or drop the default at any time.

The syntax of the Transact-SQL CREATE DEFAULT statement is:

```
CREATE DEFAULT [<owner name>.]<name of default>
AS <constant expression>
```

Note: *Transact-SQL consists of Microsoft's additions to standard SQL. No commercial DBMS product fully supports everything in the SQL-92 standard. Conversely, every vendor adds its own SQL extensions (such as CREATE DEFAULT) and provides procedural language constructs. Microsoft calls its SQL and extensions and procedural language additions Transact-SQL. Oracle uses PL/SQL and SQL*Plus. While most standard SQL-92 code is transportable across DBMS products, specific product extensions (such as Transact-SQL statements) are not. If you need to use a Transact-SQL statement in an Oracle DBMS, check your system manual. You will probably find a PL/SQL statement that performs the same function but has a different name syntax.*

Defaults you create must comply with the following rules:

- You do not have to supply the <owner name> for the default. However, if you do not, the DBMS will supply your login name as the default for <owner name>.
- The name you use for the default (<name of default>) must be unique by owner.
- The <constant expression> must contain only constant values such as numbers, character strings, built-in functions, or mathematical expressions. The <constant expression> cannot include any columns or other database objects.
- After creating a default, you must use the stored procedure sp_bindefault to bind the default value to a column before the DBMS will supply the value for the column when inserting a row.
- The default must be compatible with the column to which you bind it. If you bind a character string to a numeric column, for example, the DBMS will generate an error message and not insert the row each time it has to supply the default value for the column.

- If you supply a character string default for a character column and the default is longer than the column length, the DBMS will truncate the default value to fit into the column.
- If a column has both a default and a constraint, the default value cannot violate the constraint. If a column's default value violates a column constraint, the DBMS will generate an error message and not insert the row each time it has to supply the default value for the column.

Suppose, for example, you had a table defined by

```
CREATE TABLE employee
  (employee_ID              INTEGER,
   first_name               VARCHAR(20),
   last_name                VARCHAR(30),
   social_security_number CHAR(11),
   street_address           VARCHAR(35),
   health_card_number       CHAR(15),
   sheriff_card_number      CHAR(15)
   PRIMARY KEY (employee_ID))
```

and you want to supply "applied for" and "unknown" in place of NULL values if you don't know the Social Security number, health card number, or sheriff card number when adding a new employee to the EMPLOYEE table. You can create the defaults you need by executing the Transact-SQL statements:

```
CREATE DEFAULT ud_value_unknown AS "Unknown"
CREATE DEFAULT ud_applied_for AS "Applied for"
```

Note: *You can only enter one CREATE DEFAULT statement at a time into the Query Analyzer's Query Pane, or into the ISOQL (or OSOQL) command buffer.*

Before the DBMS will use a default, you must execute the sp_bindefault stored procedure to *bind* the default value to a user-defined data type or a table column. You will learn how to bind default values to a table column in Tip 50 and how to bind a default to a user-defined data type in Tip 594.

You can use the stored procedure sp_help to display a list of user and system-defined defaults. Since sp_help will display all defaults, not just the ones you create, you may want to group all of your defaults together in the list. To do so, use the same first one or two characters for the names of the defaults (such as UD_, short for USER DEFAULTS). Then, when you use sp_help to list the database defaults, the stored procedure will group all of the defaults you create together in its semi-alphabetized list of all defaults.

50 Using the MS-SQL Server Stored Procedure sp_bindefault to Bind a User-Created Default to a Table Column

As mentioned in Tip 49, "Using the Transact-SQL CREATE DEFAULT Statement to Set a Column Default," you must *bind* defaults to table columns so the DBMS knows which columns it is supposed to set to which default values. The syntax to use when executing the stored procedure sp_bindefault to bind a default value to a table column is

```
EXEC sp_bindefault
  @DEFNAME=<name of default>,
  @OBJNAME=<table name>.<column name>
```

where <name of default> is the name you gave the default in the CREATE DEFAULT statement, and <table name>.<column name> is the name column in the table for which you want the DBMS to supply the default value.

For example, if you executed the Transact-SQL CREATE DEFAULT statements

```
CREATE DEFAULT ud_value_unknown AS "Unknown"
CREATE DEFAULT ud_applied_for AS "Applied for"
```

the DBMS would store the default values UD_VALUE_UNKNOWN and UD_APPLIED_FOR in the database system tables. Once it's created, you can use the stored procedure sp_bindefault to bind the defaults to columns in tables (such as the EMPLOYEE table defined by example in Tip 49).

To bind the default ud_value_unknown ("Unknown") to the SOCIAL_SECURITY_NUMBER column in the EMPLOYEE table, execute the Transact-SQL statement:

```
EXEC sp_bindefault
  @defname=ud_value_unknown,
  @objname='employee.[social_security_number]'
```

To bind the default ud_applied_for ("Applied For") to the SHERIFF_CARD_NUMBER column in the EMPLOYEE table, execute the Transact-SQL statement:

```
EXEC sp_bindefault
  @defname=ud_applied_for,
  @objname='employee.[sheriff_card_number]'
```

To bind the default ud_applied_for ("Applied For") to the HEALTH_CARD_NUMBER column in the EMPLOYEE table, execute the Transact-SQL statement:

```
EXEC sp_bindefault
  @defname=ud_applied_for,
  @objname='employee.[health_card_number]'
```

After you bind defaults to the EMPLOYEE table columns, the DBMS will supply the default value for the default-bound columns when you execute an INSERT statement on the EMPLOYEE table, such as:

```
INSERT INTO employee (employee_ID, first_name, last_name)
  VALUES (1, 'Konrad', 'King')
```

In the current example, the DBMS will supply "Unknown" for SOCIAL_SECURITY_NUMBER, "Applied For" for SHERIFF_CARD_NUMBER and HEALTH_CARD_NUMBER, and NULL for STREET_ADDRESS.

51 Using the DEFAULT Clause in a CREATE TABLE Statement to Set Default Column Values

A default column value is the character string or number that you want the DBMS to enter into a column when you don't provide a value for the column. You learned how to create default column values in Tip 49, "Using the Transact-SQL CREATE DEFAULT Statement to Set a Column Default," and how to bind them to multiple columns in one or more tables in Tip 50, "Using the MS-SQL Server Stored Procedure sp_bindefault to Bind a User-Created Default to a Table Column." Unfortunately, the Transact-SQL CREATE DEFAULT statement and the sp_bindefault stored procedure are available to you only if you are working with MS-SQL Server.

The standard SQL-92 CREATE TABLE statement (available on all SQL relational DBMS products) gives you the ability to define default values for columns when you create a table. Not only is setting default column values standard across DBMS products, but it is also simpler than the Transact-SQL default value creation and binding process.

To define a column default value, simply add the keyword DEFAULT followed by the default value to the column definition in a CREATE TABLE statement. For example, the SQL CREATE TABLE statement

```
CREATE TABLE employee
(employee_ID              INTEGER,
 first_name               VARCHAR(20)  NOT NULL,
 last_name                VARCHAR(30)  NOT NULL,
 social_security_number   CHAR(11)     DEFAULT 'Unknown',
 street_address           VARCHAR(35)  DEFAULT 'Unknown',
 health_card_number       CHAR(15)     DEFAULT 'Applied For',
 sheriff_card_number      CHAR(15)     DEFAULT 'Applied For',
 hourly_rate              NUMERIC(5,2) DEFAULT 10.00,
 bonus_level              INTEGER      DEFAULT 1,
```

```
    job_rating_90days        SMALLINT,
    job_rating_180days       SMALLINT,
    job_rating_1year         SMALLINT
    PRIMARY KEY (employee_ID))
```

defines default values for SOCIAL_SECURITY_NUMBER, STREET_ADDRESS, HEALTH_CARD_NUMBER, SHERIFF_CARD_NUMBER, HOURLY_RATE, and BONUS_LEVEL. As such, when you execute the SQL INSERT statement

```
INSERT INTO employee
   (employee_ID, first_name, last_name,
    social_security_number, street_address)
VALUES (1, 'Konrad', 'King', NULL, '77 Sunset Strip')
```

the DBMS will set the HEALTH_CARD_NUMBER and SHERIFF_CARD_NUMBER columns to "Applied For," the HOURLY_RATE column to 10.00, and the BONUS_LEVEL column to 1. Although the SOCIAL_SECURITY_NUMBER and STREET_ADDRESS columns have defaults, the default values were not used for the columns since the INSERT statement set the SOCIAL_SECURITY_NUMBER column to NULL and the STREET_ADDRESS column to "77 Sunset Strip." Finally, since the CREATE TABLE in the current example, did not define default values for the three job rating columns (JOB_RATING_90DAYS, JOB_RATING_180DAYS, and JOB_RATING_1YEAR), the DBMS will set these columns to NULL.

Note: *Before you set column default values in the CREATE TABLE statement, check to see if your DBMS will allow you to change or stop using the defaults after you've created the table. MS-SQL Server will not let you use the ALTER TABLE statement to add, change, or drop (remove) any column defaults you define in a CREATE TABLE statement. (You can use the ALTER TABLE statement to add a new column and assign a default value to the column. However, once the column is part of a table, you cannot change its default value). If you are using MS-SQL Server, you can get around this shortcoming by using the Transact-SQL CREATE DEFAULT statement to create a named column default object outside the table definition. MS-SQL Server lets you bind a name column default to a column using the sp_bindefault stored procedure. You can change the value of a named column default at any time by unbinding the default from all columns, dropping it, re-creating the column default with a new value, and then re-binding it to the columns in one or more tables.*

---

52 Using the MS-SQL Server Enterprise Manager to Create a Default for a User-Defined Data Type or Table Column

As usual, MS-SQL Server has both a command-line Transact-SQL statement way to create a default (which you learned about in Tip 49, "Using the Transact-SQL CREATE DEFAULT Statement to Set a Column Default") and a GUI method using the MS-SQL Server Enterprise Manager. The advantages of creating a default outside the CREATE TABLE statement are that you can give the default a meaningful name, use it for user-defined data types or multiple columns in one or more tables, change the default value at any time, or stop using it altogether.

To create a default using the MS-SQL Server Enterprise Manager, perform the following steps:

1. To start the Enterprise Manager, click your mouse on the Start button, move your mouse pointer to Programs on the Start menu, select Microsoft SQL Server 7.0, and click your mouse on Enterprise Manager.
2. To display the list of SQL servers, click your mouse on the plus (+) to the left of SQL Server Group.
3. To display the list of resources on the SQL Server with the database in which you wish to create the default, click your mouse on the plus (+) to the left of the SQL Server's name. For example, if you want to work with the SQL Server NVBizNet2, click your mouse on the plus (+) to the left of NVBizNet2. Enterprise Manager will display a list of folders that represent the resources managed by the SQL Server, NVBizNet2 (in the current example).
4. Click your mouse on the Databases folder. The Enterprise Manager will display the databases on the SQL Server in its right pane.
5. Click your mouse on the icon for the database in which you wish to create the default. For the current example, click your mouse on SQLTips (if you created the database in Tip 41). (If you don't have an SQLTips database, click your mouse on Northwind, the example database.)
6. Select the Action menu New option, and click your mouse on Default. The Enterprise Manager will display a Default Properties dialog box similar to that shown in Figure 52.1.
7. Enter the name of the default into the Name field. For the current example, enter **ud_minimum_wage** and then press the Tab key.

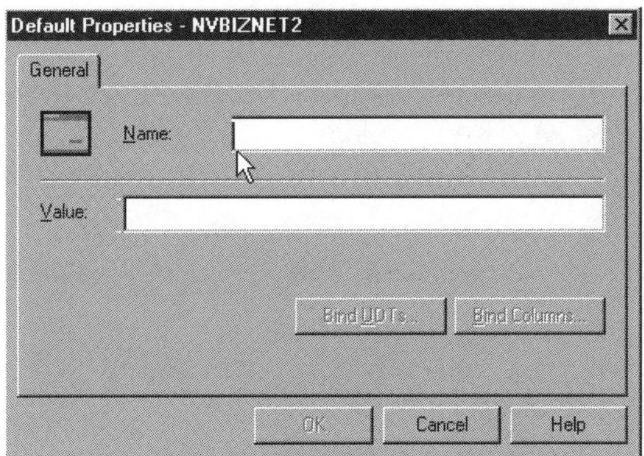

Figure 52.1 The Enterprise Manager Default Properties dialog box

8. Enter the default value into the Value field. You can enter either a number, a character string, a built-in function, or a mathematical expression. The value cannot include any columns or other database objects. For the current example, enter **7.35** into the Value field.
9. Click your mouse on the OK button. The Enterprise Manager will add the UD_MINIMUM_WAGE default definition to the system tables and close the Default Properties dialog box.

As you learned in Tip 51, "Using the DEFAULT Clause in a CREATE TABLE Statement to Set Default Column Values," you must bind the default value to a column or user-defined data type in order for the DBMS to actually use the default you created. In Tip 51, you used the stored procedure sp_bindefault to bind a default to a table column. In Tip 54, "Using the MS-SQL Server Enterprise Manager to Bind a Default to a Data Type or Table Column," you will learn how to use the Enterprise Manager to bind a default to a user-defined data type and a table column.

53 Using the MS-SQL Server Enterprise Manager to Create a User-Defined Data Type

You learned about SQL data types in Tips 21–26, and you used them when you learned to create a table in Tip 46, "Using the CREATE TABLE Statement to Create Tables." As you now know, each table column must have a data type that defines the type of data you can put into the column. For example, if a column is of type INTEGER, you can store only whole numbers—characters and numbers with a decimal point are not allowed. Similarly, when you define a column as being of type CHAR(10), you know that it can hold up to 10 characters, symbols, or numeric digits.

A user-defined data type lets you use one of the standard SQL data types or domain you've created to define a descriptive name for the type of data a user will find in a column you define as being of that (user-defined) data type. Suppose, for example, that you were working with the REGULAR_PAY_RATE column in an EMPLOYEE table; you could define the column's data type as NUMERIC(5,2), or you could use a more descriptive user-defined data type such as HOURLY_PAY_RATE.

To use Enterprise Manager to create a user-defined data type, perform the following steps:

1. To start the Enterprise Manager, click your mouse on the Start button, move your mouse pointer to Programs on the Start menu, select Microsoft SQL Server 7.0, and click your mouse on Enterprise Manager.
2. To display the list of SQL servers, click your mouse on the plus (+) to the left of SQL Server Group.
3. To display the list of resources on the SQL Server with the database in which you wish to create the data type, click your mouse on the plus (+) to the left of the SQL Server's name. For example, if you want to work with the SQL Server NVBizNet2, click your mouse on the plus (+) to the left of NVBIZNET2. Enterprise Manager will display a list of folders that represent the resources managed by the SQL Server NVBizNet2 (in the current example).
4. Click your mouse on the plus (+) to the left of the Databases folder. The Enterprise Manager will expand the server list to show the list of databases on the SQL Server you selected in Step 3.
5. Click your mouse on the plus (+) to the left of the database in which you wish to create the data type. For the current example, click your mouse on the plus (+) to the left of SQLTips (if you created the database in Tip 41, "Using the CREATE DATABASE Statement to Create an MS-SQL Server Database and Transaction Log"). (If you don't have an SQLTips database, click your mouse on the plus (+) to the left of Northwind, the example database.) Enterprise Manager will display a list of database object types.
6. Click your mouse on User-Defined Data Types. Enterprise Manager will display the existing user-defined data types in the right pane of the application window.
7. Select the Action menu New User-Defined Data Type option. The Enterprise Manager will display a User-Defined Data Type Properties dialog box similar to that shown in Figure 53.1.
8. Enter the name of the data type into the Name field. For the current example, enter **hourly_pay_rate**.
9. Click your mouse on the drop-down list button to the right of the Data Type field to list the available SQL data types and select one for your user-defined data type. (Your are not actually creating a *new* data type. Rather, you are simply applying a descriptive name to an existing SQL data type.) For the current example, select money.

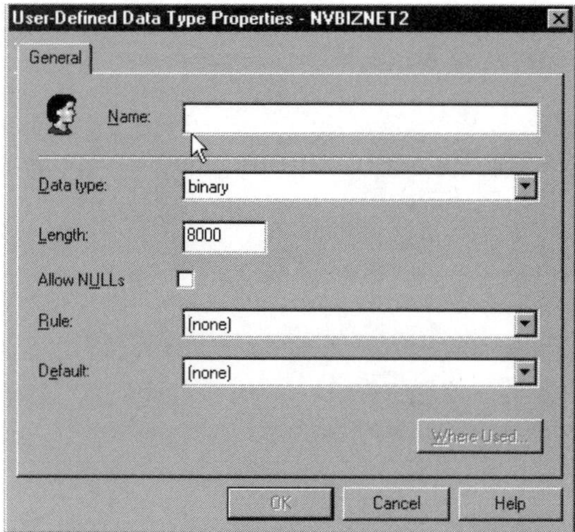

Figure 53.1 The Enterprise Manager User-Defined Data Type Properties dialog box

10. If you want to allow NULL values for columns of your user-defined data type, click your mouse on the All NULLS check box until the check mark appears. For the current example, click your mouse on the check box until the check mark appears—you want to allow a NULL value for the hourly pay rate if the employee is salaried or gets paid only on commission.

11. If you want to use a database rule to apply a constraint to limit the values a user can enter into columns defined as being of the data type you are defining, use the drop-down list button to the right of the Rule field to display the list of database rules and select the one you want. (You will learn how to create Rules in Tip 195, "Using the Transact-SQL CREATE RULE Statement to Create an MS-SQL Server Rule.") For the current example, select (none).

12. If you want the DBMS to supply a default value when a user does not provide a value when inserting rows that include columns defined as being of the data type you are defining, use the drop-down list button to the right of the Default Name field to display the list of defined defaults, and select the one you want. For the current example, select (none).

13. Click your mouse on the OK button.

After you complete Step 13, the Enterprise Manager will store your data type definition in the DBMS system tables. You can then use the data type you defined in the database anywhere you can use a standard SQL data type. In the current example, the SQL statement

```
CREATE TABLE employee
  (id                INTEGER,
   name              VARCHAR(35),
   regular_pay_rate hourly_pay_rate)
```

would be valid once you performed the steps to create the HOURLY_PAY_RATE data type.

Note: *User-defined data type names in a database must be unique by owner and must be defined in the database in which you want to use them. For example, if you define HOURLY_PAY_RATE in the SQLTips database, you must also define it in the Northwind database if you want to use HOURLY_PAY_RATE as a data type for columns in both SQLTips database tables and Northwind database tables.*

54 Using the MS-SQL Server Enterprise Manager to Bind a Default to a Data Type or Table Column

Before MS-SQL Server will use a default value you've created, you must bind the default to a table column or a user-defined data type. In Tip 50, "Using the MS-SQL Server Stored Procedure sp_bindefault to Bind a User-Created Default to a Table Column," you learned how to use the stored procedure sp_bindefault to bind a default to a table column. In this tip, you will learn how to use the Enterprise Manager.

To use Enterprise Manager to bind a default to a table column, perform the following steps:

1. To start the Enterprise Manager, click your mouse on the Start button, move your mouse pointer to Programs on the Start menu, select Microsoft SQL Server 7.0, and click your mouse on Enterprise Manager.
2. To display the list of SQL Servers, click your mouse on the plus (+) to the left of SQL Server Group.
3. To display the list of resources on the SQL Server with the database in which you wish to bind the default to a column, click your mouse on the plus (+) to the left of the SQL Server's name. For example, if you want to work with the SQL Server NVBizNet2, click your mouse on the plus (+) to the left of NVBizNet2. Enterprise Manager will display a list of folders that represent the resources managed by the SQL Server NVBizNet2 (in the current example).
4. Click your mouse on the plus (+) to the left of the Databases folder. The Enterprise Manager will expand the database branch of the SQL Server list to show the list of databases on the SQL Server you selected in Step 3.
5. Click your mouse on the plus (+) to the left of the database in which you wish to bind the default. For the current example, click your mouse on the plus (+) to the left of SQLTips (if you created the database in Tip 41, "Using the CREATE DATABASE Statement to Create an MS-SQL Server Database and Transaction Log"). (If you don't have an SQLTips database, click your mouse on the plus (+) to the left of Northwind, the example database.) Enterprise Manager will display a list of database object types.

6. Click your mouse on the Defaults icon in the list of database object types. Enterprise Manager will use its right pane to display the list of user-defined defaults in the database you selected in Step 5, similar to that shown in Figure 54.1.

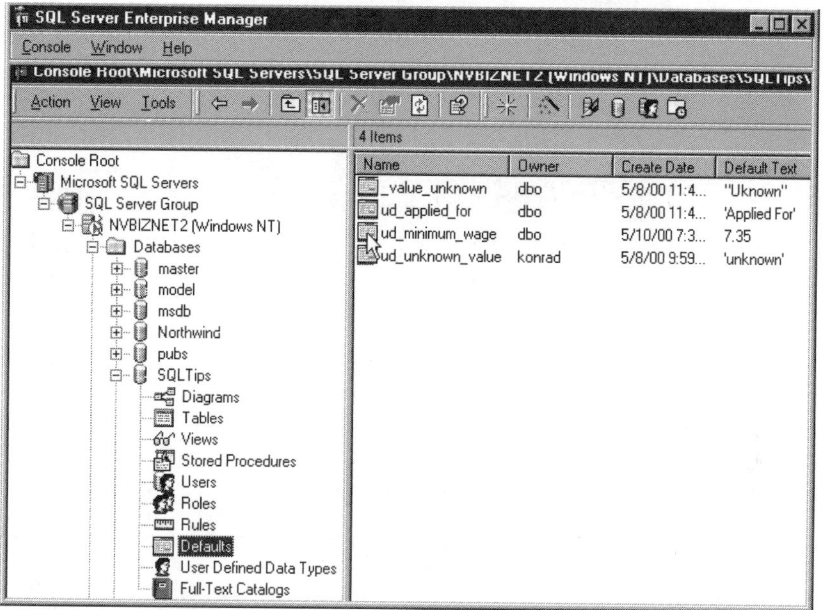

Figure 54.1 The Enterprise Manager application window displaying the user-defined defaults for a database

7. Double-click your mouse on the name of the default you want to bind to a table column. For the current example, double-click your mouse on ud_minimum_wage (if you created the UD_MINIMUM_WAGE default in Tip 52, "Using the MS-SQL Server Enterprise Manager to Create a Default for a User-Defined Data Type or Table Column"). Enterprise Manager will display a Default Properties dialog box similar to that shown in Figure 54.2.

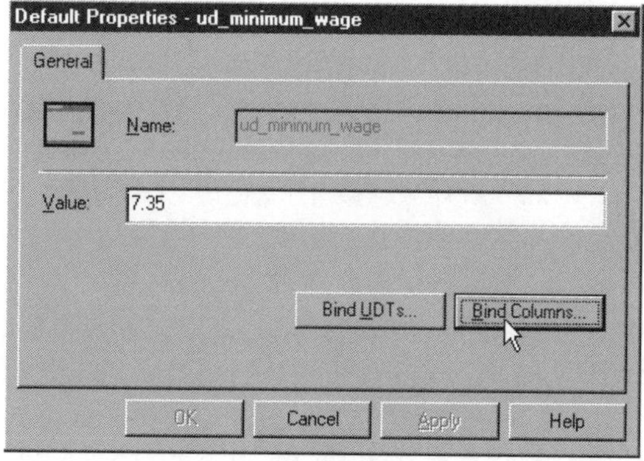

Figure 54.2 The Default Properties dialog box after selecting the UD_MINIMUM_WAGE default

8. Click your mouse on the Bind Columns button. Enterprise Manager will display a Bind Default to Columns dialog box similar to that shown in Figure 54.3.

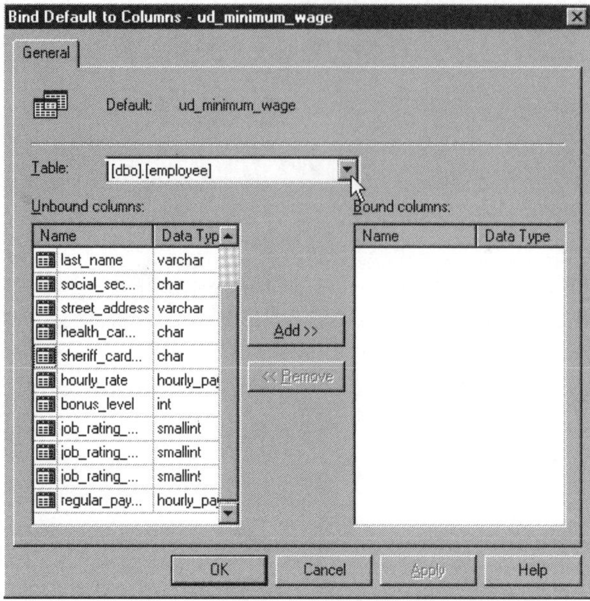

Figure 54.3 The Bind Default to Columns dialog box

9. Click your mouse on the drop-down list button to the right of the Table field to display the list of tables in the database. Click your mouse on the table with the column to which you want to bind a default. For the current example, click your mouse on the EMPLOYEE table. Enterprise Manager will display a list of the table's columns in the Unbound columns list.

10. Find the column to which you wish to bind the default in the Unbound defaults list along the lower-left side of the Bind Default to Columns dialog box, and click your mouse on it. For the current example, click your mouse on REGULAR_PAY_RATE.

11. Click your mouse on the ADD button. Enterprise Manager will *add* the REGULAR_PAY_RATE column to the Bound columns list. (Since the left list shows only unbound columns, you will see that Enterprise Manager removed REGULAR_PAY_RATE from the Unbound columns list when it placed the column name in the Bound columns list.)

12. Click your mouse on the OK button. Enterprise Manager will return to the Default Properties dialog box.

After you complete Step 12, Enterprise Manager will note your default bindings in the database system tables. The DBMS will then set the column to the default value whenever a user adds a row to the table without giving the value of the column to which you've bound a default.

If you later decide that you no longer want the DBMS to supply a default for a particular column execute the stored procedure sp_unbindefault, or perform Steps 1–9 of the procedure to bind a default to a column. Then, instead of selecting an *unbound* column in Step 10, select the column you want to unbind from the Bound columns list in the lower-right side of the Bind Default to Columns dialog box. Next, in Step 11, click your mouse on the Remove button. Finally, finish unbinding the default by clicking on the OK button in Step 12.

In addition to binding defaults to table columns, you can also bind a default to a user-defined data type. Once you do so, the DBMS will supply the default value instead of NULL whenever a user does not supply a value for a table column defined as being of the data type to which you've bound the default.

For example, to bind the UD_MINIMUM_WAGE default to the HOURLY_PAY_RATE data type you defined in Tip 53, "Using the MS-SQL Server Enterprise Manager to Create a User-Defined Data Type," perform the following steps:

Note: *If you exited the Default Properties dialog box or did not perform the bind default procedure at the beginning of this tip, perform Steps 1–7 of the bind defaults procedure, as necessary, to display the Default Properties dialog box.*

---

1. Click your mouse on the Bind UDTs button on the Default Properties dialog box. Enterprise Manager will display defaults you've defined in a Bind Default to User-Defined Data Types dialog box similar to that shown in Figure 54.4.

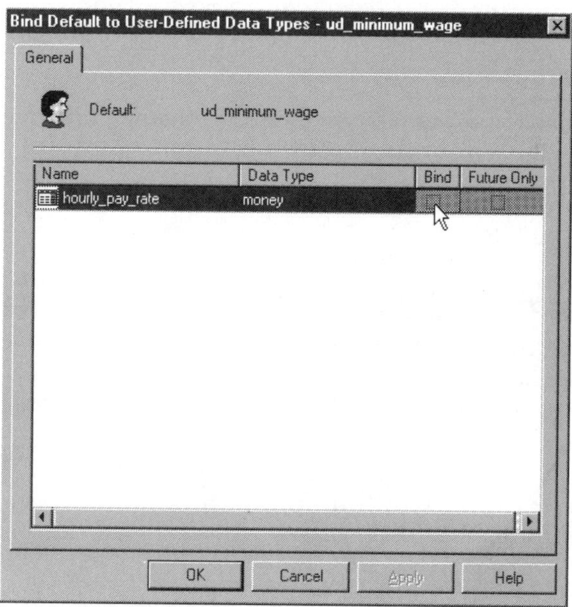

Figure 54.4 The Bind Default to User-Defined Data Types dialog box

2. Find the data type to which you wish to bind the default, and click your mouse on the check box in the Bind column until the check mark appears. For the current example, click your mouse on the check box to the right of the HOURLY_PAY_RATE data type (if you created it in Tip 53).

3. If you want a default value bound only to future columns defined as being of the data type to which you are binding the default, click your mouse on the Future Only check box until the check mark appears. For the current example, leave the Future Only check box clear—the DBMS will then use the default both for columns already declared as being of the HOURLY_PAY_RATE data type as well as those for you will define as being of the data type in the future.

4. Click your mouse on the OK button. Enterprise Manager will note your default bindings in the DBMS system tables and return to the Default Properties dialog box.

If you later decide you that you no longer want the DBMS to supply a default for a particular columns defined as a specific user-defined data type to which you've bound a default, you can execute the stored procedure sp_unbindefault (which you will learn about in Tip 650), or return to the User-Defined Data Types dialog box and clear the Bind check box for the user-defined data type.

When you unbind a default from a data type, you must decide whether or not you want the default to remain bound to existing columns of the data type. If you click a check mark into the Future Only check box, the DBMS will continue supplying the default value for existing columns of the user-defined data type. If you clear the Future Only check box, the DBMS will supply NULL (stop supplying the default value) for both existing columns of the data type and any that you create in the future.

To return to the Enterprise Manager application window, click your mouse on the OK button on the Default Properties dialog box.

55 Using the Transact-SQL DROP DEFAULT Statement to Remove a Default from a Database

When you no longer need a default you've created, you can use the Transact-SQL DROP DEFAULT statement to permanently remove the default from the database in which you created it. The syntax of the DROP DEFAULT statement is

```
DROP DEFAULT <default name>
  [, <default name>, ... ,<last default name>]
```

where the <default name> is the name you gave the default when you defined it. As you can see from the syntax of the statement, you can drop multiple defaults with a single DROP DEFAULT.

In Tip 49, "Using the Transact-SQL CREATE DEFAULT Statement to Set a Column Default," you used the Transact-SQL statements

```
CREATE DEFAULT ud_value_unknown AS "Unknown"
CREATE DEFAULT ud_applied_for AS "Applied for"
```

to create two defaults: UD_VALUE_UNKNOWN and UD_APPLIED_FOR. If you no longer need these defaults, execute the Transact-SQL statement

```
DROP DEFAULT ud_value_unknown, ud_applied_for
```

to remove them from the database.

One important thing to know is that you cannot drop a default that is currently bound to either columns or user-defined data types. You must first use either the Enterprise Manager or the stored procedure sp_unbindefault to unbind the default from all columns and user-defined data types. Once you've completely unbound the default, you can remove it from the database.

If you create and use defaults, it is essential that you keep an accurate list of them and (perhaps more importantly) the columns and user-defined data types to which they are bound. Unfortunately, the error message the DBMS returns if you try to drop a column with a bound default states only the error and does not identify the bindings that caused it. For example, if you execute the statement

```
DROP DEFAULT ud_applied_for
```

and UD_APPLIED_FOR is bound to a column or data type, the statement will fail and the DBMS will display the error message:

```
The default 'ud_applied_for' cannot be dropped because it
is bound to one or more column.
```

To successfully execute the DROP DEFAULT statement, you will need to run the stored procedure sp_unbindefault. However, sp_unbindefault requires that you supply both the table and the column name in order to unbind a default. Moreover, MS-SQL Server does not have a stored procedure that will list the columns to which a default is bound, so you will need to refer to your documentation.

If you don't have a list of bindings for the default you want to remove, or if you prefer to use a GUI tool, you can use the MS-SQL Server Enterprise Manager to unbind and drop a default. First, perform the first eight steps of the bind default procedure in Tip 54, "Using the MS-SQL Server Enterprise Manager to Bind a Default to a Data Type or Table Column." After you complete Step 8, the DBMS will display the Bind Default to Columns dialog box (refer to Figure 54.3, in Tip 54).

Once you have the Bind Default to Columns dialog box on your screen, perform the following steps to unbind the default:

1. To find a table with one or more bindings to the default you want to remove, click your mouse on the drop-down list box to the right of the Table field. Enterprise Manager will display the list of database tables in the drop-down list box.

2. If you know the name of the table you want, select it from the drop-down list. (If you don't know the table you want, you will have to select each of the tables in the database, one at a time.) The Enterprise Manager will display the table columns bound to your default in the Bound Columns list.
3. To unbind the default from a column, click your mouse on the column name in the Bound Columns list, and then click your mouse on the Remove button.
4. Repeat Step 3 until you've removed all of the column names from the Bound Columns list.
5. If your documentation lists other tables to which the default is bound (or if you don't have documentation and you have not made it through the list of database tables), click your mouse on the Apply button and then continue at Step 3 to select the next table with which you want to work.
6. When you are finished unbinding the default from table columns, click your mouse on the OK button. Enterprise Manager will return to the Default Properties dialog box (similar to that shown in Figure 54.2, in Tip 54).
7. Click your mouse on the OK button. Enterprise Manager will return to its application window with defaults displayed in the right pane, similar to that shown in Figure 54.1, in Tip 54.

Now that you've unbound the default, you can perform the following steps to delete (drop) the default:

1. To select the default you want to delete (drop), click your mouse on the name of the default in the list of defaults in the right pane of the Enterprise Manager's application window.
2. To delete the default, click your mouse on the Delete button (the red X) on the Standard Toolbar (or select the Action menu Delete option). Enterprise Manager will display the name, owner, and type of the default you selected in the Drop Objects dialog box.
3. Click your mouse on the Drop All button.

To exit Enterprise Manager, click on the application window's close button (the X in the upper-right corner), or select the Console menu Exit option.

56 Understanding the ALTER TABLE Statement

No amount of prior planning completely eliminates the need for changing the structure of tables over the course of time. This is not to say that you should spend little time designing tables because they are going to change anyway. Quite the opposite—the more time you spend on design and deciding exactly what data goes in what tables, the less time you will spend later changing your tables and trying to input several months' worth of information that you initially omitted from the database.

That being said, changes to database tables, like changes in life, are inevitable. Perhaps you created your customer table before *everyone* had an e-mail address (yes, that was not too many years ago). So, now you need to add not only an e-mail address but also a Web (home page) address to the customer record. Or, maybe your company no longer accepts back orders. As such, your inventory table now needs a "minimum_stock_level" column so the DBMS can alert you to order parts from your supplier before you run out and can't take a customer's order. Finally, suppose that your company expands its product line and now makes purchases from multiple vendors. You may need to add a foreign key linking a new "vendor" column in the item master table to a newly created vendors table. None of these changes are necessitated by poor design. The database tables must change because the entities they represent (the business, business rules, and relationships) do not remain constant.

Fortunately, the SQL ALTER TABLE statement allows you to:

- Add a column to a table
- Drop a column from a table
- Change or drop a column's default value
- Add or drop individual column constraints
- Change the data type of a column
- Add or drop a table's primary key
- Add or drop foreign keys
- Add or drop table check constraints

The syntax of the ALTER TABLE statement is:

```
ALTER TABLE <table name>
  {ADD <column definition>}
  {[WITH CHECK | WITH NO CHECK] ADD <table constraint>}
  {ALTER COLUMN <column name> <new data type>
     [(precision,scale)][NULL | NOT NULL]}
  {DROP COLUMN <column name>
     [,<column name>...,<last column name]}
  {DROP [CONSTRAINT] <constraint name>}
  {CHECK | NO CHECK CONSTRAINT [ALL |
     <constraint name>
     [,<constraint name>...,<last constraint name>]}
```

```
  {ENABLE | DISABLE TRIGGER [ALL |
     <trigger name>
     [,<trigger name>...,<last trigger name>]}

<column definition> is defined as:
   <column name> <data type>
   [IDENTITY [(seed,increment)]|[NOT NULL]
   [DEFAULT <value>]][UNIQUE]
   [<check constraint definition>]

<check constraint definition> is defined as:
   CHECK (<search condition>)

<table constraint> is defined as:
   [CONSTRAINT <constraint name>]
        <primary key definition>
      | <foreign key definition>
      | DEFAULT <constant expression>
          FOR <column name>
      | CHECK (<search condition>)

<primary key definition> is defined as:
   PRIMARY KEY (<column name> [, <column name>])

<foreign key definition> is defined as:
   FOREIGN KEY (<column name>) REFERENCES <table name>
```

Note: *Do not include the ellipses ({}) in your ALTER TABLE statement. The ellipses delineate the different forms of the ALTER TABLE statement, and you must select one (and only one) of the forms per statement. Thus,*

```
ALTER TABLE <table name> ADD <column definition>
```

is one valid choice, as is this

```
ALTER COLUMN <column name> <new data type>
  [(precision,scale)][NULL | NOT NULL]
```

and so on.

Also, do not put the pipe (|) symbol in your ALTER TABLE statement. The pipe symbol indicates "or," meaning you must select one clause or another. As such, when specifying a table constraint, either define a primary key, a foreign key, a default, or a check constrain, but not all four.

SQL ALTER TABLE statement clauses tend to be very DBMS-specific. All products allow you to add columns. However, not all products let you drop columns. (Using the ALTER STATEMENT to drop a column is not part of the SQL-92 specification.) Some products allow you to add and drop individual column constraints on existing columns; others, including MS-SQL Server, do not.

In short, each DBMS vendor adds what it considers to be important features to the ALTER TABLE statement and removes those clauses more easily implemented with other vendor-specific constructs. MS-SQL Server, for example, does not let you use the ALTER TABLE statement to change defaults on or add defaults to existing columns, even though other DBMS vendors do. Instead, MS-SQL Server, through Transact-SQL and stored procedures, provides CREATE DEFAULT, sp_bindefault, sp_unbindefault, and DROP DEFAULT to manage column default apart from the ALTER TABLE statement.

We will discuss many of the ALTER TABLE clauses later in this book. The important thing to know is that every DBMS has an ALTER TABLE statement you can use to change a table's structure. Check your DBMS documentation for the specific clauses available to the ALTER TABLE statement in your DBMS product.

57 Using the ALTER TABLE Statement to Add a Column to a Table

Adding a column to a table is perhaps the most common use of the ALTER TABLE statement. The syntax of the ALTER TABLE statement to add a column is:

```
ALTER TABLE <table name>
  ADD <column name> <data type> [DEFAULT <value>]
   [NOT NULL][IDENTITY][UNIQUE][CHECK (<search condition>)]
```

For example, to add a BADGE_NUMBER column to an EMPLOYEE table defined by

```
CREATE TABLE employee
  (employee_id             INTEGER,
   first_name              VARCHAR(20),
   last_name               VARCHAR(30),
   social_security_number CHAR(11),
   street_address          VARCHAR(35)
   PRIMARY KEY (employee_id))
```

you could use the ALTER TABLE statement:

```
ALTER TABLE employee ADD badge_number INTEGER IDENTITY
```

The DBMS will add a new column, BADGE NUMBER, to the EMPLOYEE table. In addition (MS-SQL Server only), IDENTITY characteristic in the current example will have MS-SQL Server set the value of the BADGE_NUMBER column in each row, starting with 1 and incrementing the value by 1 for each subsequent row.

When you use the ALTER TABLE statement to add a new column to a table, the DBMS adds the column to the end of the table's column definitions, and it will appear as the rightmost column in subsequent queries. Unless you specify a default value (or use the IDENTITY constraint on MS-SQL Server), the DBMS assumes NULL for the value of the new column in existing rows.

Since the DBMS assumes NULL for the new column in existing rows, you cannot simply add the NOT NULL constraint when you use the ALTER TABLE statement to add a column. If you add the NOT NULL constraint, you must also provide a default. After all, the DBMS assumes NULL for the new column in existing rows if you don't provide a default value, and thus would immediately violate the NOT NULL constraint.

When you add column to a table, the DBMS does not actually expand existing rows. Instead, it expands only the description of the table to include the new column(s) in the system tables. Each time you ask the DBMS to read an existing row, it adds one (or more) NULL values for the new column(s) before presenting query results. The DBMS will add the new column(s) to new rows and to any existing rows as the DBMS stores updates to them.

58 Using the MS-SQL Server ALTER TABLE, DROP COLUMN Clause to Remove a Table Column

The SQL-92 standard does not specify a DROP COLUMN clause as part of the ALTER TABLE statement. As a result, some DBMS products require that you unload data from the table, use the DROP TABLE statement to erase the table, execute the CREATE TABLE statement to re-create the table without the column you want to drop, and then reload the data you unloaded before dropping the table. (Given the steps involved, you might be tempted to just ignore the column you want to drop.)

Fortunately, MS-SQL Server provides a DROP COLUMN clause as part of its ALTER TABLE statement. The syntax for dropping a column is:

```
ALTER TABLE <table name>
  DROP COLUMN <column name>
  [,<column name>...,<last column name]
```

Thus, to drop columns from an EMPLOYEE table defined by

```
CREATE TABLE employee
  (employee_id               INTEGER,
   first_name                VARCHAR(20),
   last_name                 VARCHAR(30),
   social_security_number CHAR(11),
   street_address            VARCHAR(35),
   health_card_number        CHAR(15),
   sheriff_card_number       CHAR(15),
```

```
    badge_number            IDENTITY(100,100)
    PRIMARY KEY (employee_id))
```

you could use the ALTER TABLE statement

```
ALTER TABLE employee
  DROP COLUMN health_card_number, sheriff_card_number
```

to drop the HEALTH_CARD_NUMBER and SHERIFF_CARD_NUMBER columns.

MS-SQL Server will prevent you from dropping a column to which a constraint or default value is assigned. Moreover, you cannot drop a column identified as a FOREIGN KEY in another table. For example, if you attempt to drop the EMPLOYEE_ID from the EMPLOYEE table, MS-SQL Server will respond with the error message

```
Server: Msg 4922, Level 16, State 3, Line 1
ALTER TABLE DROP COLUMN employee_id failed because PRIMARY
  KEY CONSTRAINT PK__employee__6E01572D access this column.
```

and the ALTER TABLE statement will fail.

In order to drop a column with a default value or constraint, you must first drop the constraint using an ALTER TABLE statement in the form:

```
ALTER TABLE <table name> DROP CONSTRAINT <constraint name>
```

In the current example, the CREATE TABLE statement did not specify a name for the PRIMARY KEY constraint on the EMPLOYEE_ID column of the EMPLOYEE table. As a result, the DBMS created the unique constraint name PK__employee__6E01572D for the PRIMARY KEY constraint. Thus, in order to remove the PRIMARY KEY constraint from the EMPLOYEE table in the example, use the Transact-SQL statement:

```
ALTER TABLE employee DROP CONSTRAINT PK__employee__6E01572D
```

Note: *The name the DBMS assigns to an unnamed constraint will differ each time you create a constraint, even if you drop and respecify the same constraint. Also, when dropping a constraint with a DBMS-generated name, be sure to note and use double (vs. single) underscores (__) in the constraint name.*

If you want to drop a column that is a FOREIGN KEY in another table, you must first use the ALTER TABLE statement to drop the FOREIGN KEY reference in the other table, and then you drop the column in the current table. (You will learn more about using the ALTER TABLE statement to work with FOREIGN KEY constraints in Tip 60.)

59 Using the ALTER TABLE Statement to Change the Width or Data Type of a Column

Unlike many DBMS products, MS-SQL Server allows you to change not only the width of a column but also its data type. There are, however, a few restrictions on data type changes. You cannot change the data type of a column if the column:

- Is of type TEXT, IMAGE, NTEXT, or TIMESTAMP
- Is part of an index, unless the original data type is VARCHAR or VARBINARY and you are not changing the original data type or making the column width shorter
- Is part of a PRIMARY KEY or FOREIGN KEY
- Is used in a CHECK constraint
- Is used in a UNIQUE constraint
- Has a default associate with it
- Is replicated
- Is computed or used in a computed column

When changing a column's data type, all of the existing data in the column must be compatible with the new data type. As such, you can always convert from INTEGER to character since a CHARACTER column can hold numeric digits, letters, and special symbols. However, when converting a CHARACTER column to INTEGER, you must ensure that every row of the table has numeric digits or NULL in the CHARACTER field you are converting.

Once you've identified the column as one whose type you can change, use the ALTER TABLE statement in the form

```
ALTER TABLE <table name>
  ALTER COLUMN <column name> <new data type>
```

to change the width or data type of a column. For example, if you have an EMPLOYEE table defined by

```
CREATE TABLE employee
  (employee_id            INTEGER,
   first_name             VARCHAR(20),
   last_name              VARCHAR(30),
   social_security_number CHAR(11),
   street_address         CHAR(30),
   health_card_number     CHAR(15),
   sheriff_card_number    CHAR(15),
   PRIMARY KEY (employee_id))
```

you can use the ALTER TABLE statement

```
ALTER TABLE employee
  ALTER COLUMN street_address CHAR(35)
```

to change the width of the STREET_ADDRESS column from CHAR(30) to CHAR(35).

You can also use the ALTER TABLE statement to change a column's data type. For example, to change the HEALTH_CARD_NUMBER from CHAR(15) to INTEGER, use the ALTER TABLE statement:

```
ALTER TABLE employee
  ALTER COLUMN health_card_number INTEGER
```

When converting a column from one data type to another, remember that all of the existing data in the column must be compatible with the new data type. Thus, the conversion of HEALTH_CARD_NUMBER from character to integer will work only if all of the current health card numbers are NULL or if they are all composed of only digits. As such, if any health card number includes a non-numeric character, the ALTER TABLE statement converting the column's data type from CHARACTER to INTEGER will fail.

60 Using the ALTER TABLE Statement to Change Primary and Foreign Keys

In addition to changing the width and data type of a column, you can use the ALTER TABLE statement to add table constraints such as a PRIMARY KEY and FOREIGN KEY. Tip 61, "Using the CREATE TABLE Statement to Assign the Primary Key," and Tip 62, "Using the CREATE TABLE Statement to Assign Foreign Key Constraints," will show you how to define keys as part of the CREATE TABLE statement when creating a new database table. For existing tables, use the ALTER TABLE statement to add named and unnamed PRIMARY KEY and FOREIGN KEY constraints.

Both PRIMARY KEY and FOREIGN KEY constraints are database "keys," which means that each is a column or a combination of columns that uniquely identifies a row in a table. While a PRIMARY key uniquely identifies a row in the table in which it is defined, a FOREIGN KEY uniquely identifies a row in another table. (A FOREIGN KEY in one table always references the PRIMARY key in another table.)

A table can have only one PRIMARY KEY, but it can have several FOREIGN KEYS. While the value of the column or combination of columns that makes up a PRIMARY key must be unique for each row in the table, the value of the column or combination of columns that makes up a FOREIGN KEY need not be (and most likely are not) unique within the table in which the FOREIGN KEY is defined.

You will learn more about the PRIMARY KEY constraint in Tip 172, "Using the PRIMARY KEY Column Constraint to Uniquely Identify Rows in a Table," and the FOREIGN KEY constraints in Tip 173, "Understanding Foreign Keys."

The syntax for using the ALTER TABLE statement to add a PRIMARY KEY constraint to a table is:

```
ALTER TABLE <table name> ADD CONSTRAINT
  <constraint name> PRIMARY KEY (<column name>
  [,<column name>...,<last column name>])
```

Therefore if you have a table created by

```
CREATE TABLE employee
  (employee_id  INTEGER NOT NULL,
   badge_number SMALLINT NOT NULL,
   first_name   VARCHAR(20),
   last_name    VARCHAR(30))
```

you can add a single column PRIMARY KEY based on the EMPLOYEE_ID using the statement:

```
ALTER TABLE employee
  ADD CONSTRAINT pk_employee PRIMARY KEY (employee_id)
```

If the values in a single column are not unique in each row of the table, but the values in a combination of columns are, you must use a composite, or multi-column PRIMARY KEY. Suppose, for example, that you had an EMPLOYEE table where two employees could have the same employee number, but no two employees with the same employee number would have the same badge number. To add the PRIMARY KEY to the table, use the ALTER TABLE statement

```
ALTER TABLE employee
  ADD CONSTRAINT pk_employee
  PRIMARY KEY (employee_id,badge_number)
```

to combine EMPLOYEE_ID and BADGE_NUMBER into a single, unique key value for each row of the table.

Note: *Since a table can have only one PRIMARY KEY, you just first use the ALTER TABLE statement*

```
ALTER TABLE <table name> DROP CONSTRAINT <constraint name>
```

if you want to change a table's PRIMARY KEY. In other words, you must remove a table's existing PRIMARY KEY before you can use the ALTER TABLE statement to add a new PRIMARY KEY constraint to the table.

Adding FOREIGN KEY constraints to a table is similar to defining the PRIMARY KEY. However, when working with a FOREIGN KEY, you must identity not only the columns in the current table that make up the FOREIGN KEY but also the PRIMARY KEY columns in the table referenced by the FOREIGN KEY.

A FOREIGN KEY constraint is normally used to represent a parent/child relationship between two tables. When you place a FOREIGN KEY constraint on a column or combination of columns, you are saying that the value in the column (or combination of columns) in the child record (row in the child table) can be found in the column (or combination of columns) that makes up the PRIMARY KEY in the parent record (row in the parent table).

The syntax for using the ALTER TABLE statement to add a FOREIGN KEY constraint to a table is:

```
ALTER TABLE <table name>
  [WITH NOCHECK]
  ADD [CONSTRAINT <constraint name] FOREIGN KEY
    (<column name>[,<column name>...,<last column name>]
  REFERENCES <foreign table name>
    (<foreign column name>
    [,<foreign column name>...,<last foreign column name>])
```

As such, to create a parent/child relationship between a (parent) CUSTOMER table created by

```
CREATE TABLE customer
  (customer_number INTEGER PRIMARY KEY,
   first_name      VARCHAR(20),
   last_name       VARCHAR(30),
   address         VARCHAR(35))
```

and a (child) ORDER table created by

```
CREATE TABLE order
  (placed_by_customer_num INTEGER,
   order_date             DATETIME,
   item_number            INTEGER,
   quantity               SMALLINT)
```

you might use the ALTER TABLE statement

```
ALTER TABLE order ADD
  CONSTRAINT fk_order_column
  FOREIGN KEY (placed_by_customer_num)
  REFERENCES customer (customer_number)
```

which links each row in the ORDER table to one (and only one) of the rows in the CUSTOMER table. In other words, each and every value in the PLACED_BY_CUSTOMER_NUM column in the ORDER table can be found in the CUSTOMER_NUMBER column of the customer table. Thus, every order (child) must have an associated customer (parent) that placed the order.

Note: *When you use the ALTER TABLE statement to add a FOREIGN KEY to a table, the DBMS will check existing data to make sure it does not violate the constraint. In the current example, the DBMS will ensure that every value in the PLACED_BY_CUSTOMER_NUM of the ORDER table exists in the CUSTOMER_NUMBER table of* *the CUSTOMER table. If the check fails, the DBMS will not create the FOREIGN KEY, thereby maintaining referential data integrity.*

If you are sure that existing data will not violate the FOREIGN KEY constraint, you can speed up the execution of the ALTER TABLE statement by adding the WITH NOCHECK clause. If you do so, the DBMS will not apply the FOREIGN KEY constraint to existing rows of the table. Only rows subsequently updated or inserted will be checked to make sure that the FOREIGN KEY value exists in the PRIMARY KEY of the referenced (parent) table.

61 Using the CREATE TABLE Statement to Assign the Primary Key

A *key* is a column or combination of columns that uniquely identifies a row in a table. As such, a key gives you way to distinguish one particular row in a table from all of the others. Because a key must be unique, you should not include NULL values in any of the columns that make up a key. Remember, the DBMS cannot make any assumptions about the actual value of NULL in a column. Thus, a row with NULL in a key column will be indistinguishable from any other row in the table because the NULL value could, in fact, be equal to the value in any other row.

Each table can have one (and only one) PRIMARY KEY. Because the PRIMARY KEY must uniquely identify each row in a table, the DBMS automatically applies the NOT NULL constraint to each of the columns that make up the PRIMARY KEY. When creating a new table, you can create a single-column PRIMARY KEY by including the key words "PRIMARY KEY" in the column definition.

The syntax of a PRIMARY KEY definition in a CREATE TABLE statement comes in one of two forms

```
[CONSTRAINT <constraint name>] PRIMARY KEY
```

if the PRIMARY KEY is an unnamed constraint defined as part of the PRIMARY KEY column's definition, or

```
CONSTRAINT <constraint name>
  PRIMARY KEY (<column name>
    [,<column_name...[,<last column name>]])
```

for a multiple-column (or composite) PRIMARY KEY or a single-column named PRIMARY KEY.

For example, the CREATE TABLE statement

```
CREATE TABLE employee
  (employee_id INTEGER PRIMARY KEY,
```

```
  first_name   VARCHAR(20),
  last_name    VARCHAR(30))
```

identifies the EMPLOYEE_ID column as the PRIMARY KEY in the EMPLOYEE record. As such, every row in the EMPLOYEE table must have a unique, non-NULL value in the EMPLOYEE_ID column.

The system stores the PRIMARY KEY as a constraint in the system tables. As such, if you don't give the PRIMARY KEY a name, the DBMS will generate one for you. The name the system assigns becomes important to you if you ever want to drop a table's PRIMARY KEY so that you can change it. (Since a table can have only one PRIMARY KEY, you will need to drop the existing PRIMARY KEY and create a new one when if you want to change its column[s].)

Note: *If you are using MS-SQL Server, you can call the stored procedure sp_help to display the name that the DBMS assigned to the PRIMARY KEY by executing the command*

```
EXEC sp_help <table name>
```

(where <table name> is the name of the table with the PRIMARY KEY whose name you want to know).

MS-SQL Server will respond with a description of the table identified by <table name>. Look in the index_name column of the section of the report titled PRIMARY to see the name the DBMS assigned to the PRIMARY KEY.

If you don't want the DBMS to generate its own name for the PRIMARY KEY, you can name it yourself by specifying the name when you identify the column that makes up the PRIMARY KEY. For example, to give the name pk_employee_table to the PRIMARY KEY in the current example, use the CREATE TABLE statement:

```
CREATE TABLE employee
  (employee_id INTEGER,
     CONSTRAINT pk_employee_table PRIMARY KEY,
   first_name   VARCHAR(20),
   last_name    VARCHAR(30))
```

Sometimes no single column in a table has a unique value in every row. Suppose, for example, that each division in your company issues its own employee numbers. Division #1 has employees #123, #124, and #126; division #2 has employees #121, #122, and #123. If you identify EMPLOYEE_ID as the PRIMARY KEY, you will be able to insert all division #1 employees into the EMPLOYEE table. However, when you try to insert division #2 employee #123, the DBMS will not allow you to do so. Because the EMPLOYEE table already has a row with an EMPLOYEE_ID of 123, the DBMS rejects your attempt to add a second row with 123 in the EMPLOYEE_ID column because EMPLOYEE_ID, the PRIMARY KEY, must be unique in each row of the table.

You can still create a PRIMARY KEY for the table where no single column is unique by identifying a set of multiple columns that, when taken together, is different in every row of the table. In the current example, you know that employee numbers are unique by division. Thus, you can use a two-column PRIMARY KEY consisting of EMPLOYEE_ID and DIVISION, such as

```
CREATE TABLE employee
  (employee_id INTEGER,
   division    SMALLINT,
   first_name  VARCHAR(20),
   last_name   VARCHAR(30)

   CONSTRAINT pk_employee_table
     PRIMARY KEY (employee_id, division))
```

to create a PRIMARY KEY for the EMPLOYEE table.

Note: *The placement of the PRIMARY KEY definition within the CREATE TABLE statement is not important. As such, the CREATE TABLE statement*

```
CREATE TABLE employee
  (employee_id               INTEGER
   CONSTRAINT pk_employee_table
     PRIMARY KEY (employee_id, division),
   division                  SMALLINT,
   first_name                VARCHAR(20),
   last_name                 VARCHAR(30))
```

is equivalent to the one in the example just prior to this note.

---

62 Using the CREATE TABLE Statement to Assign Foreign Key Constraints

As was previously discussed, a database *key* uniquely identifies a row in a table. In Tip 61, "Using the CREATE TABLE Statement to Assign the Primary Key," you learned that each row in a PRIMARY KEY uniquely identifies single row within the table in which the PRIMARY KEY is declared. A FOREIGN KEY, on the other hand, references the PRIMARY KEY in a table other than the one in which the FOREIGN KEY is declared. As such, each row within a FOREIGN KEY in one table uniquely identifies a single row in another table. While each PRIMARY KEY value must be unique within a table, the values within a FOREIGN KEY need not be (and most likely is not) unique.

A FOREIGN KEY is normally represents a parent/child relationship between two tables. When you place a FOREIGN KEY constraint on a column or combination of columns, you are saying that the value in a column (or combination of columns) within the row in the child table can be found in the column (or combination of columns) that makes up the PRIMARY KEY value of a specific row within the parent table.

The syntax of the FOREIGN KEY constraint declaration is:

```
[CONSTRAINT <constraint name>]
  FOREIGN KEY (<column name>
    [,<column name>...[,<last column name>]])
  REFERENCES <foreign table name>
    (<foreign table column name>
       [,<foreign table column name>...
       [,<last foreign table column name>]])
```

Suppose, for example, that you want to track customer orders using the CUSTOMER (parent) table and ORDER (child) table created by:

```
CREATE TABLE customer
  (customer_number          INTEGER,
   first_name               VARCHAR(20),
   last_name                VARCHAR(30),
   address                  VARCHAR(35),
   CONSTRAINT pk_customer_table
     PRIMARY KEY (customer_number))

CREATE TABLE order
  (placed_by_customer_num INTEGER
     FOREIGN KEY (placed_by_customer_num) REFERENCES
       customer(customer_number),
   order_date               DATETIME,
   item_number              INTEGER,
   quantity                 SMALLINT,

   CONSTRAINT pk_order_table
     PRIMARY KEY
     (placed_by_customer_num, order_date, item_number))
```

The FOREIGN KEY defined in the ORDER table tells you that you can find the value in the PLACED_BY_CUSTOMER_NUM column (of the child table ORDER) in the PRIMARY KEY column CUSTOMER_NUMBER of a row in the CUSTOMER (parent) table.

Because the column PLACED_BY_CUST_NUM is a *foreign* and not a *primary* key in the ORDER table, you can have more than one ORDER row with the same value in the PLACED_BY_CUST_NUM column, indicating that an individual customer ordered more than one item or placed more than one order.

The FOREIGN KEY constraint on the PLACED_BY_CUSTOMER_NUM column also tells you that the value in the PLACED_BY_CUST_NUM column will appear once and only once in the CUSTOMER_NUMBER field of the CUSTOMER table (because a FOREIGN KEY in a table always refers to the PRIMARY KEY in another table). As such, you will be able to uniquely identify the customer that placed the order because the FOREIGN KEY value

(PLACED_BY_CUSTOMER_NUM) in the current table uniquely identifies a row (a customer) in the *foreign* (CUSTOMER) table.

When you do not provide a name for a FOREIGN KEY constraint, the system will generate one for you so that it can store the constraint in its system tables. In the current example, the FOREIGN KEY in the ORDER table was not explicitly named. As such, the system will generate a name.

If you are using MS-SQL Server, you can determine the name of the FOREIGN KEY by executing the stored procedure sp_help and supplying the name of the parent table (CUSTOMER, in the current example) for <table name> in the statement:

```
EXEC sp_help <table name>
```

MS-SQL Server will respond with a description of the table and will list the FOREIGN KEY names in the "Table Is Referenced By" section of the report.

If you want to select a name for the FOREIGN KEY (instead of having the DBMS generate one), change the CREATE TABLE statement in the current example to:

```
CREATE TABLE order
  (placed_by_customer_num INTEGER
     CONSTRAINT fk_customer_table FOREIGN KEY
        (placed_by_customer_num) REFERENCES
         customer(customer_number),
   order_date                DATETIME,
   item_number               INTEGER,
   quantity                  SMALLINT,
   CONSTRAINT pk_order_table
     PRIMARY KEY
     (placed_by_customer_num, order_date, item_number))
```

As you learned in Tip 61, a PRIMARY KEY may consist of more than one column. When a FOREIGN KEY in one table references a composite (or multi-column) PRIMARY KEY in another table, the FOREIGN key, too, will consist of multiple columns. Suppose, for example, that the ITEM_MASTER table for the orders in the current example was defined by:

```
CREATE TABLE item_master
  (item_number       INTEGER,
   vendor_id         INTEGER,
   quantity_on_hand SMALLINT

   CONSTRAINT pk_item_master_table
     PRIMARY KEY (item_number, vendor_id))
```

You could reference the composite PRIMARY KEY in the ITEM_MASTER table with the FOREIGN KEY constraint FK_ITEM_MASTER_TABLE using the CREATE TABLE statement:

```
CREATE TABLE order
  (placed_by_customer_num INTEGER
   order_date              DATETIME,
```

```
  item_number              INTEGER,
  vendor_id_number         INTEGER,
  quantity                 SMALLINT,

  CONSTRAINT fk_item_master_table FOREIGN KEY
    (item_number, vendor_id_number) REFERENCES
     item_master (item_number,vendor_id),

  CONSTRAINT fk_customer_table FOREIGN KEY
    (placed_by_customer_num) REFERENCES
     customer(customer_number),

  CONSTRAINT pk_order_table
    PRIMARY KEY
    (placed_by_customer_num, order_date, item_number))
```

The important thing to know about the FOREIGN KEY constraint is that it specifies that the value in the column or combination of columns in one table must be found as the value in the PRIMARY KEY of the table, which it references. As such, if you have a single-column PRIMARY KEY, you will use a single-column FOREIGN KEY. Conversely, if you need to reference a multi-column or composite PRIMARY KEY, you will use a multi-column FOREIGN KEY.

63 Using the DROP TABLE Statement to Remove a Table from the Database

When you no longer need a table, use the DROP TABLE statement to remove it from the database. Before dropping a table, however, make sure that you no longer need it! When the DBMS executes the DROP TABLE statement, it erases the table data and index(es) from the database and removes the definition of the table and its constraints from the system tables. Thus, the only way to recover a dropped table is to re-create the table and restore data by reading it from the most recent backup. As such, make sure you really no longer need the table or its data before you execute the DROP TABLE statement.

The syntax of the DROP TABLE statement is:

```
DROP TABLE
  [[<schema name>.]<table owner name>.]]<table name>
```

Thus, to drop the CUSTOMER table in Tip 62, "Using the CREATE TABLE Statement to Assign Foreign Key Constraints," you would execute the SQL statement:

```
DROP TABLE customer
```

When it receives the DROP TABLE command, the DBMS checks to see if the table you want to drop is referenced by a FOREIGN KEY in another table. If it is (as is the case with CUSTOMER in the current example), the DROP TABLE statement will fail, and the DBMS will display an error message similar to:

```
Server: Msg 3726, Level 16, State 1, Line1
Could not drop object 'customer' because it is referenced
by a FOREIGN KEY constraint
```

Before you can remove a table reference by a FOREIGN KEY, you must first use the ALTER TABLE statement to remove the FOREIGN KEY constraint from the other table. In the current example, you must execute the ALTER TABLE statement

```
ALTER TABLE order DROP CONSTRAINT fk_customer_table
```

before the DBMS will let you drop the CUSTOMER table.

Note: *While the DBMS checks its system tables for FOREIGN KEY references to the table you want to remove, it does not check VIEWs (which you learned about in Tip 11, "Understanding Views") and stored procedures to see if they reference the table or its columns. Stored procedures that reference a dropped table will fail to run, and the DBMS will return an error message in place of VIEW's data that includes columns from a dropped table. As such, check your database documentation carefully to make sure that you are the only one that uses the table you are about to drop*—before *you drop the table.*

---

64 Using the DROP VIEW Statement to Remove a View

To remove a database view that you no longer need, execute the DROP VIEW statement. Unlike the DROP TABLE statement, the DROP VIEW command does not erase any database tables or data. When you DROP a view, the DBMS simply removes its definition (the name and the SELECT statement that defines the view) from the system tables. If you later decide you need the view again, simply use the CREATE VIEW statement or a tool like the MS-SQL Server Create View Wizard to re-create the view. As long as the underlying table is still in the database, re-creating the view will bring back the virtual table and its data.

The syntax of the DROP VIEW statement is:

```
DROP VIEW <view name> [,<view name>...[,<last view name>]]
```

As such, to remove a VIEW named VW_SALES_PRODUCTION from the database, you would execute the SQL statement:

```
DROP VIEW vw_sales_production
```

You can remove several views at once by separating the names of the views with commas in a single DROP VIEW statement. For example, to remove views VW_SALES_PRODUCTION_EAST and VW_SALES_PRODUCTION_WEST, you would use the SQL statement:

```
DROP VIEW
  vw_sales_production_east, vw_sales_production_west
```

Although no data is erased when you drop a view, you do need to make sure that no stored procedures or other views reference the view you are about to drop. If you run a stored procedure or use view that references a dropped view, the DBMS will respond with an error message in the form:

```
Server: Msg 208, Level 16, State 1, Procedure
  <name of referencing view>, Line 2
Invalid object name '<name of dropped view>'.

Server: Msg 4413, Level 16, State 1, Line 1
Could not use view '<name of referencing view>' because of
  previous binding errors.
```

(The DBMS, of course, substitutes the actual name of the dropped view for "<name of dropped view>" and the actual name of the view that references the dropped view for "<name of referencing view>.")

65 Using the MS-SQL Server Enterprise Manager Create View Wizard to Create a View

Views are virtual tables. Although they look and act like regular relational database tables, views contain no data. Rather, a view is a set of instructions for the DBMS that tells it what data stored in physical (real) tables to display and how to display it. MS-SQL Server gives you two ways to define a view. You can use the CREATE VIEW statement (which you will learn about in Tip 206, "Using a View to Display Columns in One or More Tables or Views"), or you can use the MS-SQL Server's Create View Wizard. Whichever method you use to create the view, the DBMS will store its name in the system tables along with the SELECT statement that lists the view's columns and search criteria (its WHERE clause).

At the lowest level, all views are based on one or more physical database tables. (You can create views based on other views. However, at some point, one of the views in the chain has to be based on an actual database table.) Therefore, to see how you can use the Create View Wizard to create a view, you must start by deciding on the data you want to display. Suppose, for example, that you want to create a view based on the data in the PRODUCTION table shown in Figure 65.1.

PRODUCTION table

Rep_ID	Call	Appointments	Sales	Deliveries
1	100	4	3	2
2	255	7	4	4
3	750	12	6	5
4	400	15	9	7
5	625	10	8	6
6	384	11	6	4
7	295	17	4	1

Figure 65.1 PRODUCTION table with sample data to use in creating a view

To use the Create View Wizard to create a view that displays data from a single table, perform the following steps:

1. Start the Enterprise Manager by clicking your mouse on the Start button. When Windows displays the Start menu, move your mouse pointer to Programs, select Microsoft SQL Server 7.0, and then click your mouse on Enterprise Manager.
2. To display the list of SQL servers, click your mouse on the plus (+) to the left of SQL Server Group.
3. Click your mouse on the icon for the SQL Server with the database in which you wish to create the view. For example, if you want to create a view in a database on a server named NVBIZNET2, click your mouse on the icon for NVBIZNET2.
4. Select the Tools menu Wizards option (or click your mouse on the Wizards button, the magic wand on the Standard Toolbar). Enterprise Manager will display the Select Wizard dialog box so that you can select the wizard you want to use.
5. Click your mouse on the plus (+) to the left of Database to display the list of database object wizards.
6. Click your mouse on Create View Wizard to select it, and then click your mouse on the OK button. Enterprise Manager will start the Create View Wizard, which displays its "Welcome to the Create View Wizard" screen.
7. Click your mouse on the Next button. The Create View Wizard will display the Select Database dialog box.
8. Click your mouse on the drop-down list button to the right of the Database Name field to display the list of databases on the SQL Server you selected in Step 3.
9. Click your mouse on the database in which you wish to create the view. For the current example, click your mouse on SQLTips to select the SQLTips database.

10. Click your mouse on the Next button. The Create View Wizard will display a Select Tables dialog box, similar to that shown in Figure 65.2.

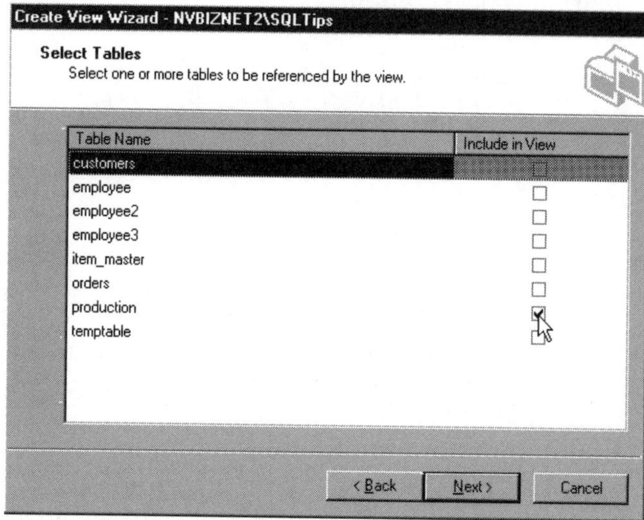

Figure 65.2 The MS-SQL Server Create View Wizard's Select Tables dialog box

11. Click your mouse on the check boxes of the tables whose data you want to include your view. For the current example, click your mouse on the check box for the PRODUCTION table until the check mark appears.

12. Click your mouse on the Next button. The Create View Wizard will display a Select Columns dialog box, similar to that shown in Figure 65.3.

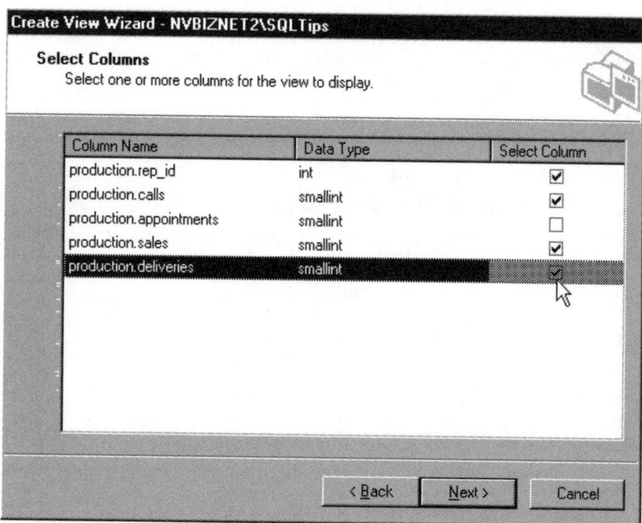

Figure 65.3 The MS-SQL Server Create View Wizard's Select Columns dialog box

13. Click your mouse on the check boxes of the columns you want to display. For the current example, select: PRODUCTION.REP_ID, PRODUCTION.CALLS, PRODUCTION.SALES, and PRODUCTION.DELIVERIES.

Note: *The list of columns in the selection area of the Select Columns dialog box includes all of the columns for all of the tables selected in Step 11. The Create View Wizard shows you which columns belong in which tables by using the qualified column name for each column—that is, it displays the column name as <table name>.<column name> (where <table name> is the name of the table that contains <column name>).*

---

14. Click your mouse on the Next button. The Create View Wizard will display the Define Restriction dialog box. If you do not want to display all of the rows in the tables you selected (in Step 11), enter the WHERE clause that you want the DBMS to use as the criteria for selecting the rows to display. For the current example, enter **WHERE PRODUCTION.SALES > 4** to have the DBMS display only rows where the value in the SALES column of the PRODUCTION table is greater than 4.
15. Click your mouse on the Next button. The Create View Wizard will display the Name the View dialog box.
16. Enter a name for the view in the View Name field. For the current example, enter **vw_sales_production** into the View Name field.

Note: *It is best to keep view names consistent so that you can distinguish them from actual tables when looking at a list of database objects. For example, if you start all of your view names (and only your view names) with "vw_", you will know that any database object starting with "vw_" is a view.*

---

17. Click your mouse on the Next button. The Create View Wizard will display the SQL statements the DBMS will use to create the view, in a Completing the Create View Wizard dialog box similar to that shown in Figure 65.4.
18. Make any necessary corrections to the WHERE clause and any other changes necessary to further refine the view. (You can add or remove columns, change the view name, change the selection criteria in the WHERE clause, and so on.)
19. Click your mouse on the Finish button.

After you complete Step 19, the Create View Wizard will check the syntax of the statements in the Completing the Create View Wizard dialog box and will prompt you to correct any errors. (If there are any errors, the problem will most likely be with the WHERE clause you entered in Step 14.)

Repeat Steps 18 and 19 until the Create View Wizard displays the "Wizard Complete!" message box, with the message "The view was created successfully." Once you see the message box, click your mouse on its OK button to return to the MS-SQL Server Enterprise Manager application window.

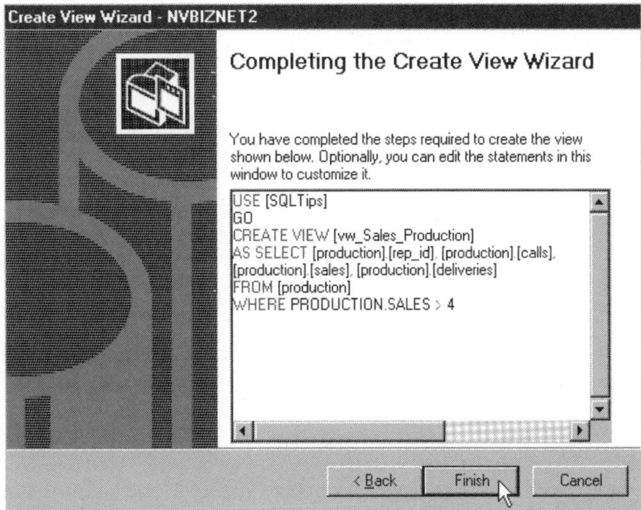

Figure 65.4 The MS-SQL Server Create View Wizard's Completing the Create View Wizard dialog box

Once the DBMS stores your view in its system tables, use the SELECT statement to display the view data. For example, to display all of the columns and rows in the view you created in the current example, execute the SELECT statement:

```
SELECT * FROM vw_sales_production
```

Given that the PRODUCTION table has the data shown in Figure 65.1, MS-SQL Server will display the virtual contents of your view table, VW_SALES_PRODUCTION as

```
rep_id      calls  sales  deliveries
----------- ------ ------ ----------
3           750    6      5
4           400    9      7
5           625    8      6
6           384    6      4
(4 row(s) affected)
```

66 Understanding the CASCADE and RESTRICT Clauses in a DROP VIEW Statement

As mentioned in Tip 64, the DBMS will not erase any database data when you drop a view. However, you still have to be careful that the view you are dropping is not referenced by another view. Some DBMS products let you add the CASCADE or RESTRICT clause to a DROP VIEW statement to control the behavior of the DBMS when you tell the system to DROP a view that is referenced by another view.

If you execute the DROP VIEW statement with the CASCADE clause, the DBMS will not only remove the view you name in the DROP VIEW statement, but also any other view that references the view in the DROP VIEW statement. For example, if you have two views as defined by

```
CREATE VIEW vw_sales_production AS
 SELECT rep_id, calls, sales, deliveries FROM production
```

and

```
CREATE VIEW vw_delivered_sales_commissions
  (rep_id, deliveries, commission) AS
SELECT rep_id, deliveries, deliveries * 150.00
FROM vw_sales_production
```

when you execute

```
DROP VIEW vw_sales_production
```

the DBMS will remove only the VW_SALES_PRODUCTION view from the system tables. If you execute the SELECT statement

```
SELECT * FROM vw_delivered_sales_commissions
```

after you DROP the VW_SALES_PRODUCTION view, the DBMS will respond with an error message in the form:

```
Server: Msg 208, Level 16, State 1,
  Procedure vw_delivered_sales_commissions, Line 1
Invalid object name 'vw_sales_production'.

Server: Msg 4413, Level 16, State 1, Line 1
Could not use view 'vw_delivered_sales_commissions'
  previous binding errors.
```

If, on the other hand, you DROP the VW_SALES_PRODUCTION view with the DROP VIEW statement

```
DROP VIEW vw_sales_production CASCADE
```

the DBMS will remove both VW_SALES_PRODUCTION and VW_DELIVERED_SALES_COMMISSIONS (which references it) from the system tables.

Conversely, some DBMS products allow you to add the RESTRICT clause to the DROP VIEW statement. The RESTRICT clause will prevent you from dropping a view that is referenced by another view Thus, in the current example, executing the "restricted" DROP VIEW statement

```
DROP VIEW vw_sales_production RESTRICT
```

will fail because the view VW_SALES_PRODUCTION view is referenced by the VW_DELIVERED_SALES_COMMISSIONS view.

Note: *Not all DBMS products provide the CASCADE and RESTRICT clauses for the DROP VIEW statement—MS-SQL Server, for example, does not. As such, check your system documentation to see if you can add the CASCADE or RESTRICT clause to the DROP VIEW statement in your DBMS product.*

67 Using the INSERT Statement to Add Rows to a Table

Use the INSERT statement to add data to a database table one row at a time. The syntax of the INSERT statement is:

```
INSERT INTO <table name>
  [(<column name>...[,<last column name>])]
 VALUES (<column value>...[,<last column value>])
```

This tells the DBMS to insert the values (listed in the VALUES clause) into the columns (listed after the <table name> in the INTO clause) in the table given by <table name>.

Although the word INSERT seems to imply that you are placing the new row of data in front of or between existing rows in the table, the INSERT statement merely builds a single row of data that matches the column structure of the table. Once it receives the INSERT statement, the DBMS decides on the physical location in the table for the new row. As a result, a new row of data may end up at the beginning, the end, or somewhere else among the existing rows in a table.

Note: *As you learned from Tip 6, "Understanding Codd's 12-Rule Relational Database Definition," a relational database must exhibit logical data independence (Rule 9). As such, the actual order of the columns in a row (as long as it is consistent throughout the table) and the order of the rows in the table have no effect on information retrieved when you query the database. Therefore, where the DBMS places a new row of data in a table is unimportant.*

Suppose, for example, that you have an ORDERS table created with the statement:

```
CREATE orders
  (order_number          INTEGER NOT NULL,
   customer_number       INTEGER NOT NULL,
   item_number           INTEGER NOT NULL,
   quantity              SMALLINT DEFAULT 1,
```

```
   order_date              DATETIME,
   special_instructions VARCHAR(30))
```

You would use the INSERT statement

```
INSERT INTO orders
  (order_number, customer_number, item_number, quantity,
   order_date, special_instructions)
 VALUES (1, 10, 1001, 5, '05/18/00', 'keep frozen')
```

to add an order with order number 1, placed on 05/18/00, by customer 10, for 5 of item 1001, which must be kept frozen to the ORDERS table.

The names of the columns listed after the keyword INSERT must be in the definition of the table into which the DBMS is to insert a row. The names need not be in the same order as the columns in the table, nor do you have to list all of the table's columns (as you will learn in Tip 70, "Using the INSERT Statement to Add Data to Specific Columns in a Row"). As such, the INSERT statement

```
INSERT INTO orders
  (customer_number, order_number, order_date, item_number,
   quantity, special_instructions)
 VALUES (10, 1, '05/18/00', 1001, 5, 'keep frozen')
```

is equivalent to that given in the preceding paragraph, even though the column names and values are listed in a different order.

Starting from left to right, the DBMS will take the first value in the VALUES clause and place it into the table column given by the first name in the list of column names; it will take the second value from the list of values and place it in the table column given by the second name in the list of column names, and so on. The list of columns and the list of values must both contain the same number of items. Moreover, the data type of each value in the values list must be compatible with the data type of the corresponding table column into which the DBMS is to place it.

Note: *Most DBMS products will allow you to omit the list of columns from the INSERT statement. If you don't provide the column list, the DBMS assumes a column list that includes all of the columns in the table in the order in which they appear in the table definition. As such, in the current example*

```
INSERT INTO orders
VALUES (1, 10, 1001, 5, '05/18/00', 'keep frozen')
```

is equivalent to:

```
INSERT INTO orders
  (order_number, customer_number, item_number, quantity,
   order_date, special_instructions)
 VALUES (1, 10, 1001, 5, '05/18/00', 'keep frozen')
```

To get a list of a table's columns and the order in which they appear in each row of the table, without listing any of the table's data, execute the SELECT statement:

```
SELECT * <table name> WHERE NULL = NULL
```

(Substitute the name of the table whose columns you want to display for <table name>, of course.)

(In Tip 317, "Understanding Why the Expression NULL = NULL Evaluates to False," you will learn why the WHERE clause NULL = NULL is FALSE and will therefore cause the SELECT statement to display only the column names and none of the table's data.)

68 Using the INSERT Statement to Insert Rows Through a View

In addition to using a view to display table data, you can use a view in an INSERT statement to add data to the view's underlying table. The syntax for inserting data into a table through a view is the same as that used to INSERT data directly into a table—except that you use the name of the view instead of the name of the table as the target of the INSERT statement's INSERT clause. Thus, the syntax of the INSERT statement to add rows to a table through a view is:

```
INSERT INTO <view_name>
  [(<view column name>...[,<view column name>])]
VALUES (<view column value>...[,<last value column value>])
```

For example, given a table created with the SQL statement

```
CREATE orders
  (order_id    INTEGER IDENTITY,
   cust_id     INTEGER NOT NULL,
   item        INTEGER NOT NULL,
   qty         SMALLINT DEFAULT 1,
   order_date  CHAR(10),
   ship_date   CHAR(10),
   handling    VARCHAR(30) DEFAULT 'none')
```

and a view defined by

```
CREATE VIEW vw_shipped_orders AS
  SELECT order_id, cust_id, item, qty, order_date,
         ship_date
FROM orders
WHERE ship_date IS NOT NULL
```

you can use the INSERT statement

```
INSERT INTO vw_shipped_orders
  (cust_id, item, qty, order_date, ship_date)
 VALUES (1002, 55, 10, '2000-05-17', '2000-18-00')
```

to add a row the underlying table, ORDERS.

Executing the SELECT statement

```
SELECT * FROM vw_shipped_orders
```

on the view yields the result:

```
order_id cust_id item qty order_date ship_date
-------- ------- ---- --- ---------- ---------
1        1002    55   10  2000-05-17 200-15-18
 (1 row(s) affected)
```

Executing the SELECT statement

```
SELECT * FROM orders
```

on the underlying ORDERS table, yields the result:

```
order_id cust_id item qty order_date ship_date handling
-------- ------- ---- --- ---------- --------- --------
1        1002    55   10  2000-05-17 200-15-18 none
(1 row(s) affected)
```

Notice that when you INSERT data through a view, you need not include values for all of the columns in the view. In the current example, the ORDER_ID column included in the view definition was omitted from the INSERT statement.

As is the case with an INSERT directly into the underlying table, the DBMS will use the table columns default value for any column for which the INSERT statement does not specify a value. In the current example, the DBMS will supply the "next" unique INTEGER value for the ORDER_ID column because the table definition specifies the IDENTITY characteristic for the ORDER_ID column, and the INSERT statement does not include a value for the column. (You learned about the MS-SQL Server IDENTITY property in Tip 32, "Understanding the MS-SQL Server IDENTITY Property.") Similarly, the DBMS will use the defined default value of "none" for the HANDLING column, since the values list in the INSERT statement does not include a HANDLING value.

Note: *If a column does not have a default value and the INSERT statement does not include an explicit value for it, the DBMS will set the column to NULL when it executes the INSERT statement.*

Note: *When inserting a row into an underlying table through a view, you can supply values for the columns only in the view definition. In the current example, the HANDLING column is not a part of the view definition. As such, you cannot supply a value for the HANDLING column when adding rows to the ORDERS table through the VW_SHIPPED_ORDERS view.*

An interesting anomaly can occur when you INSERT data into a table through a view—a row from a successfully executed INSERT statement may seem to "disappear" when you use the view to display table data. For example, execute the INSERT statement

```
INSERT INTO vw_shipped_orders
  (cust_id, item, qty, order_date)
VALUES (2004, 110, 20, '2000-05-01')
```

to add a row to the ORDERS table through the VW_SHIPPED_ORDERS view. Next, execute the SELECT statement:

```
SELECT * FROM vw_shipped_orders
```

The DBMS will return the results:

```
order_id cust_id item qty order_date ship_date
-------- ------- ---- --- ---------- ---------
1        1002    55   10  2000-05-17 200-15-18
(1 row(s) affected)
```

What happened to the second order?

If you execute the SELECT statement

```
SELECT * FROM orders
```

on the underlying ORDERS table, the DBMS will return:

```
order_id cust_id item qty order_date ship_date handling
-------- ------- ---- --- ---------- --------- --------
1        1002    55   10  2000-05-17 200-15-18 none
2        2004    110  20  2000-05-01 NULL      none
(2 row(s) affected)
```

So, the second order is indeed in the table!

The reason the SELECT on the view did not display the second order while the SELECT on the underlying ORDERS table did is that the value in the SHIP_DATE column is NULL in the second order. Since the WHERE clause in the view definition specifies that the view is to display only rows where the SHIP_DATE is not NULL, the view will not display the second order. (The DBMS set the SHIP_DATE column to NULL because the INSERT statement did not include a value for the column, and the table definition did not define a default value.)

69 Using the MS-SQL Server Enterprise Manager to Define or Change a Primary Key Constraint

As you learned in Tip 61, "Using the CREATE TABLE Statement to Assign the Primary Key," a PRIMARY KEY uniquely identifies each row in the table in which it is defined. MS-SQL Server gives you three ways to add key constraints to your tables: as part of a CREATE TABLE statement (as you learned in Tip 61 and Tip 62, "Using the CREATE TABLE Statement to Assign Foreign Key Constraints"), as part of an ALTER TABLE statement (as you learned in Tip 60, "Using the ALTER TABLE Statement to Change Primary and Foreign Keys"), and by using the MS-SQL Server Enterprise Manager.

To use MS-SQL Server Enterprise Manager to add or change a table's PRIMARY KEY constraint, perform the following steps:

1. Start the Enterprise Manager by clicking your mouse on the Start button. When Windows displays the Start menu, move your mouse pointer to Programs, select Microsoft SQL Server 7.0, and then click your mouse on Enterprise Manager.
2. To display the list of SQL Servers, click your mouse on the plus (+) to the left of SQL Server Group.
3. Click your mouse on the plus (+) to the left of the icon for the SQL Server with the database containing the tables to which you wish to add key constraints. For example, if you want to work with tables in a database on a server named NVBizNet2, click your mouse on the plus (+) to the left of the icon for NVBizNet2. The Enterprise Manager will display folders containing databases and services available on the MS-SQL Server you selected.
4. Click your mouse on the plus (+) to the left of the Databases folder. The Enterprise Manager will display a list of databases on the SQL Server you selected in Step 3.
5. Click your mouse on the plus (+) to the left of the database with the table to which you wish to add key constraints. For the current example, click your mouse on the plus (+) to the left of the SQLTips database icon. Enterprise Manager will display a list of icons representing database objects.
6. Click your mouse on the Tables icon. Enterprise Manager will display the list of tables in the database (whose object list you expanded in Step 5) in the application window's right pane.

7. Click your mouse on the name of the table to which you wish to add a key constraint. For the current example, click your mouse on EX_ORDERS.

8. Select the Action menu Design Table option. The Enterprise Manager will display a Design Table window similar to that shown in Figure 69.1.

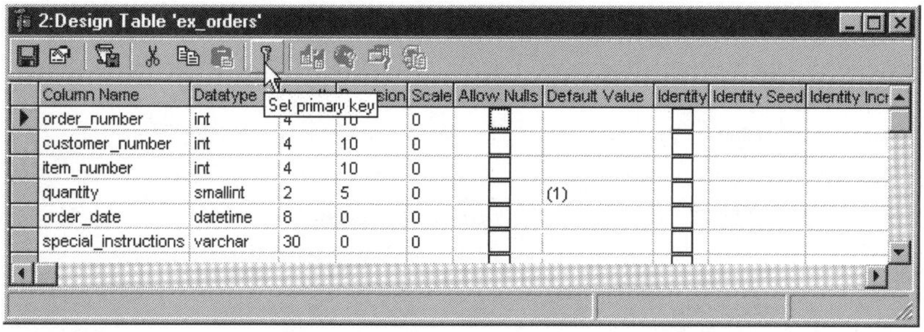

Figure 69.1 The MS-SQL Server Enterprise Manager's Design Table window

9. To select a single column for the table's PRIMARY KEY, click your mouse on the selection button to the left of the name of the column that will make up the key. If you want to create a composite or multi-column PRIMARY KEY, hold down the Ctrl key as you click your mouse on the selection buttons to the left of the names of the columns to include in the key, and then release the Ctrl key. For the current example, click your mouse on the selection button to the left of ORDER_NUMBER.

Note: *Be sure to clear the Allow Nulls check box for every column in your PRIMARY KEY. NULL values are not allowed in the columns that make up the PRIMARY KEY.*

---

10. To tell the Enterprise Manager to create the PRIMARY KEY, either click your mouse on the Set Primary Key button on the Design Table Standard toolbar, or right-click your mouse on one of the columns in the PRIMARY KEY and then select the Set Primary Key option on the pop-up menu.

11. To save your changes, click your mouse on the Save button (the floppy disk icon), the first button from the left on the Design Table Standard toolbar.

12. Click your mouse on the Close button (the X) in the upper-right corner of the Design Table window.

When you complete Step 12, Windows will close the Design Table window and return to the Enterprise Manager application window.

70 Using the INSERT Statement to Add Data to Specific Columns in a Row

The most common form of the INSERT statement is as a row value expression. Although you can use the INSERT statement to add a single value to a table, you will normally use it to add a row of data a time. For example, the INSERT statement

```
INSERT INTO employee VALUES (1,'Konrad','King',
  '555-55-5555','7810 Greenwood Ave',NULL,NULL)
```

will add a row to a table created with the statement

```
CREATE TABLE employee
  (employee_id            INTEGER,
   first_name             VARCHAR(20),
   last_name              VARCHAR(30) NOT NULL,
   social_security_number CHAR(11),
   street_address         CHAR(30),
   health_card_number     CHAR(15),
   sheriff_card_number    CHAR(15),
   PRIMARY KEY (employee_id))
```

by transferring the data values in the VALUES clause into the columns of the table row based on position. "Based on position" means the DBMS will put the first value, 1 into the first column, employee_id; the second value, Konrad into the second column, first_name; the third value, King into the third column, last_name, and so on.

The syntax of the INSERT statement is:

```
INSERT INTO <table name>
  [(<column name>[...,<last column name>])]
VALUES (<column value>[...,<last column value>])
```

If you omit the optional column list following the <table name>, the DBMS sets the column list to include all of the columns in the table in the order in which they appear in the table definition. In the current example, the DBMS treats the statement

```
INSERT INTO employee VALUES (1,'Konrad','King',
  '555-55-5555','7810 Greenwood Ave',NULL,NULL)
```

as if it were written as:

```
INSERT INTO employee
  (employee_id, first_name, last_name,
   social_security_number, street_address,
   health_card_number, sheriff_card_number)
VALUES (1, 'Konrad', 'King', '555-55-5555',
        '7810 Greenwood Ave',NULL,NULL)
```

While the data values in the VALUES clause must match the number of columns specified in the column list (which follows the table name), you need not list all of the table row's columns in the column list. For example, if you want to provide only EMPLOYEE_ID, FIRST_NAME, and LAST_NAME, you could use the INSERT statement:

```
INSERT INTO employee
  (employee_id, first_name, last_name)
VALUES (2, 'Sally', 'Fields')
```

The DBMS will then set the EMPLOYEE_ID column to 2, FIRST_NAME to Sally, LAST_NAME to Fields, and the remaining columns in the row to their default values (which is NULL unless set to another value by a DEFAULT clause in the CREATE statement or previously bound to a default value using the sp_bindefault stored procedure).

Thus, from the current example, you can see that while every column name in the INSERT statement's column name list must match a column name in the table into which you are inserting data, the INSERT statement's column list need not contain the names of all of the table's columns. Moreover, the column names in the column list need not be listed in the order in which they appear in a table row. For example, the INSERT statement

```
INSERT INTO employee
  (first_name, employee_id, last_name)
VALUES ('Sally', 2, 'Fields')
```

is equivalent to:

```
INSERT INTO employee
  (employee_id, first_name, last_name)
VALUES (2, 'Sally', 'Fields')
```

The advantage in listing column names in an INSERT statement is that the statement with a column list will still execute properly after a user adds a column to the table. For example, if the user executes the statement

```
ALTER TABLE employee ADD COLUMN hourly_pay_rate NUMERIC
```

the INSERT statement

```
INSERT INTO employee VALUES (1,'Konrad','King',
  '555-55-5555','7810 Greenwood Ave',NULL,NULL)
```

will fail to execute because the VALUES clause does not have a value for the HOURLY_PAY_RATE column. (Remember, if you do not supply a column list, the DBMS sets the column list to include all of the column names from the table definition. Thus, the INSERT statement in the current example fails to execute, because the column name list includes one more column name than the number of values in the VALUES clause.)

Conversely, after using the same ALTER TABLE statement (cited in the previous paragraph) to add a new column to the table, the statement

```
INSERT INTO employee
  (first_name, employee_id, last_name)
VALUES ('Sally', 2, 'Fields')
```

will still execute properly. It tells the DBMS to put values into the FIRST_NAME, EMPLOYEE_ID, and LAST_NAME columns, and to set the remaining columns (including the new HOURLY_PAY_RATE column) to the column's default value (NULL, unless otherwise defined).

Note: *When listing columns in an INSERT statement, you must include values for any columns with a NOT NULL constraint unless the column has a non-NULL default value. In the current example, an INSERT statement must include values for both the EMPLOYEE_ID and LAST_NAME columns, since both columns are governed by a NOT NULL constraint and neither of them has a non-NULL default value. (The PRIMARY KEY constraint on the EMPLOYEE_ID column adds the NOT NULL constraint to the column by default.) As such, the INSERT statement*

```
INSERT INTO employee
  (first_name, last_name) VALUES ('Sally', 'Fields')
```

will fail when the DBMS attempts to set the EMPLOYEE_ID column to NULL.

Note: *If you want the DBMS to supply a unique non-NULL value for a single-column PRIMARY KEY, add the IDENTITY property to column. (You learned about the IDENTITY property in Tip 32, "Understanding the MS-SQL Server IDENTITY Property.") If the EMPLOYEE_ID column in the EMPLOYEE table in the current example had the IDENTITY property, the DBMS would successfully execute the INSERT statement in the previous note by supplying a unique, non-NULL EMPLOYEE_ID.*

---

71 Using the SELECT Statement to INSERT Rows from One Table into Another

Although used primarily to add one row of data to a table, you can use a single INSERT statement to add multiple rows to table at once. In fact, you can use an INSERT statement to copy all or part of one table into another.

As you learned in Tip 70, "Using the INSERT Statement to Add Data to Specific Columns in a Row," the syntax of the basic INSERT statement is:

```
INSERT INTO <table name>
  [(<column name> [...,<last column name>])]
VALUES (<column value>[...,<last column value>])
```

Well, the VALUES clause of the INSERT statement should actually be written as:

```
INSERT INTO <table name>
  [(<column name> [...,<last column name>])]
VALUES (<row value constructor>
        [...,<last row value constructor>])
```

Here, each <row value constructor> is a list of column values that matches the number (and type) of columns in the statement's column name list (which follows the table name).

Thus, while you used the INSERT statement to add a single row to the table in Tip 70, you can add additional row values to the same statement when you want to add multiple rows to the table at once. For example, the statement

```
INSERT INTO employee VALUES (1,'Konrad','King',
  '555-55-5555','7810 Greenwood Ave',NULL,NULL)
```

with one *row value constructor* (introduced by the keyword VALUES) will add one row to the employee table, while the statement

```
INSERT INTO employee
   (employee_id, first_name, last_name,
   social_security_number, street_address,
   health_card_number, sheriff_card_number)
VALUES (1, 'Konrad', 'King', '555-55-5555',
        '7810 Greenwood Ave',NULL,NULL),
       (2, 'Sally', 'Fields', '556-55-5555',
        '77 Sunset Strip',NULL,NULL),
       (3, 'Wally', 'Wallberg', '557-55-5555',
        '765 E. Eldorado Lane',NULL,NULL)
```

with three row value constructors (following the keyword VALUES) will add three rows to the same table.

Note: *As you learned previously, the column list (following the table name) in the two example INSERT statements in the previous paragraph are equivalent. When you do not specify column names (as is the case in the first INSERT statement), the DBMS supplies the INSERT statement with a column name list that consists of all columns in the table (as is explicitly enumerated in the second INSERT statement).*

Thus far, the example INSERT statements in this tip list values for all columns in a table row. However, as is the case with a single-row INSERT statement, multi-row INSERT statements can supply values for all or part of a row's columns. For example, the statement

```
INSERT INTO employee (employee_id, first_name, last_name)
VALUES (4, 'Joe', 'Kernan'), (5, 'David', 'Faber'),
       (3, 'Brad', 'Woodyard')
```

will add three rows to the EMPLOYEE table. (The DBMS will assign the column default value [NULL, in the current example] to each of the columns not list in the column name list.)

Because SQL lets you use a single INSERT statement to add multiple rows to a table at once, you can replace the VALUES clause with a SELECT statement—as long as the rows constructed by the SELECT statement have the same number and type of columns as those found in the column name list (which follows the table name in the INSERT statement).

Thus, to INSERT rows from one table into another, use the INSERT statement syntax:

```
INSERT INTO <table name>
  [(<column name> [...,<last column name>])]
SELECT <column name> [...,<last column name>]
FROM <table name>
[WHERE <search condition>]
```

As such, to insert all employees in the EMPLOYEE table into a second employees table, EMPLOYEE2, you could use the INSERT statement:

```
INSERT INTO employee2 SELECT * from employee
```

Note: *In order for the* ***SELECT **** *clause in the example INSERT statement to work, both EMPLOYEE and EMPLOYEE2 must have the same number of columns in the same order. In the following paragraphs, you will learn how you can get around this restriction by listing column names explicitly vs. using the column name list implicit in the* ***SELECT **** *clause. The important thing to know now is that you can copy data from one table into another either by listing the specific columns whose data you want copied or by omitting the column list, in which case the DBMS assumes that you want to copy all of the column values from one table into another.*

If you have several queries to run against data from multiple tables, you will find that your queries are simpler and execute more quickly if you first consolidate the data from multiple tables into one temporary table and then execute your SQL statements as single table queries against the new aggregate table. Accumulating data into a single data avoids having the DBMS search multiple tables multiple times, repeatedly reading and eliminating the same data that does not meet your search criteria.

For example, given CUSTOMERS, EMPLOYEES, and ORDERS tables defined as follows

```
CREATE TABLE customers
  (customer_id  INTEGER,        first_name   VARCHAR(30),
   last_name    VARCHAR(30),    address      VARCHAR(35),
   city         VARCHAR (20),   state        CHAR(2),
   zip_code     INTEGER,        phone_number CHAR(12),
   salesperson  INTEGER         net_due_days SMALLINT,
   credit_limit NUMERIC)
CREATE TABLE employees
  (employee_id       INTEGER,      first_name     VARCHAR(30),
   last_name         VARCHAR(30),  address        VARCHAR(35),
   ssan              CHAR(11),     salary         NUMERIC,
   low_quota         SMALLINT,     medium_quota SMALLINT,
   high_quota        SMALLINT,     sales_commission NUMERIC)
CREATE TABLE orders
```

```
  (order_id    INTEGER,  order_date  DATETIME,
   item_number INTEGER,  quantity    SMALLINT,
   customer_id INTEGER,  salesman_id INTEGER)
CREATE TABLE products
  (product_id       SMALLINT, description VARCHAR(40),
   quantity_on_hand SMALLINT, item_cost   NUMERIC)
```

you can combine data into a single table defined by

```
CREATE TABLE temp_report_table
  (customer_ID         INTEGER,
   cust_first_name     VARCHAR(30),
   cust_last_name      VARCHAR(30),
   salesman_ID         INTEGER,
   salesman_first_name VARCHAR(30),
   salesman_last_name  VARCHAR(30),
   order_date          DATETIME,
   order_item_number   SMALLINT,
   order_item_quantity SMALLINT,
   order_total         NUMERIC,
   order_item_desc     VARCHAR(40))
```

by using the INSERT statement:

```
INSERT INTO temp_report_table
  (customer_id, cust_first_name, cust_last_name,
   salesman_id, salesman_first_name, salesman_last_name,
   order_date, order_item_number, order_item_quantity,
   order_total, order_item_desc)
SELECT
   customers.customer_id, customer.first_name,
   customers.last_name, employee_id, employees.first_name,
   employees.last_name, order_date, item_number, quantity,
   (quantity * item_cost), description
FROM orders, customers, products, employees
WHERE orders.customer_id = customers.customer_id
AND   product_id         = item_number
AND   employee_id        = salesman_id
```

Once you've combined the data from the four tables into one, you can use a single-table SELECT statement to display data from one or more of the tables. For example, the SELECT statement

```
SELECT
  cust_first_name, cust_last_name, salesman_first_name,
  salesman_last_name, order_item_quantity, order_total,
  order_item_desc
FROM temp_report_table WHERE order_item_number = 5
```

will display the names of the salesmen that sold item 5; the names of the customers that purchased it; and the date, quantity, total, and item description for orders for item 5.

You can also use the simple single-table query

```
SELECT salesman_id, salesman_first_name,
        salesman_last_name, order_total
FROM temp_report_table
WHERE order_total =
       (SELECT MAX(order_total) FROM temp_report_table)
```

to display the amount of the largest order and the name of the salesman who sold it.

In both single-table query examples, you would have had to perform a SELECT and a multiple-table JOIN (as you will learn to do in Tip 283, "Understanding Joins and Multi-table Queries") to display the same information, had you not first combined all of the data you needed into a single table.

72 Setting the MS-SQL Server SELECT INTO/BULKCOPY Database Option to TRUE to Speed Up Table-to-Table Data Transfers

One of the strengths of the SQL relational DBMS model is its ability to perform transaction processing. By grouping sets of SQL statements together as a single transaction, the DBMS can maintain data—even when an action requires the successful execution of multiple SQL statements. If a portion of a transaction fails, the DBMS uses the database transaction log to "back out" the partially executed transaction and restores pretransaction data values to the affected tables. Once uncommitted statements are rolled back, the tables appear as if none of the SQL statements in the transaction was executed.

The ability to rollback partially executed and even successfully complete but erroneous transactions normally more than justifies the overhead involved in maintaining the transaction log—just ask any database administrator who was able to "undelete" rows of critical (and perhaps irreplaceable) data mistakenly removed by a user executing a DELETE statement with a faulty search condition.

Although it is a critical safeguard for normal processing, maintaining the transaction log imposes unnecessary overhead when you are consolidating large amounts of data from multiple tables into a single, redundant temporary table (as you did in Tip 71). After all, if the SELECT statement fails partway through execution, you still have the original data values in the original tables. As such, you can TRUNCATE (remove the data from) the temporary table and restart the data consolidation.

If many users are copying large numbers of rows into redundant (and many times, temporary) tables, you can improve the overall performance of the DBMS (and speed up the data transfers) by setting the database SELECT INTO/BULKCOPY option to TRUE. Setting the SELECT INTO/BULKCOPY option to TRUE tells the DBMS to treat table-to-table data transfers as bulk inserts. The DBMS stores less information in its transaction log during a bulk insert, which reduces the overhead necessary to maintain the transaction log and consequently lets the DBMS use additional resources to complete the table-to-table transfer in a shorter period of time.

Note: *Setting the SELECT INTO/BULKCOPY option to TRUE has database-wide ramifications. While SELECT INTO/BULKCOPY is set TRUE, the DBMS will store less than full transaction log information about all INSERT statements that have a SELECT INTO clause. The abbreviated transaction log data will prevent you from performing an undo or rollback for these INSERT statements. However, the lack of an "undo" option is not a problem since you still have the data in the original tables, just in case.*

To reduce the amount of information written to the transaction log during table-to-table data transfers, execute the sp_dboption stored procedure using the syntax:

```
sp_dboption <database name>, 'SELECT INTO/BULKCOPY', TRUE
```

As such, to speed up the transfer of data between tables in the SQLTips database, you would execute the statement:

```
EXEC SP_DBOPTION SQLTips, 'SELECT INTO/BULKCOPY', TRUE
```

If you later want to maintain a full transaction log for all updates (including table-to-table data transfers), execute the statement:

```
EXEC <database name>, 'SELECT INTO/BULKCOPY', FALSE
```

Here, <database name> is the name of the database in which you wish to turn off the bulk copy treatment of INSERT statements that include a SELECT INTO clause.

Note: *If you are loading table data from another computer system, from another DBMS, or from large sequential files, use the MS-SQL Server BULK INSERT statement or BCP utility—they allow you to set transaction log and other options on an individual table basis (vs. database-wide, as the SELECT INTO/BULKCOPY database option does). The BCP utility, for example, lets you define the format of the source data and will load data into tables much more quickly than repeated single-row INSERT statements. (See the MS-SQL Server "Books Online" documentation for more help on the BCP utility.)*

---

73 Using the UPDATE Statement to Change Column Values

To change one or more data values in a database, execute an UPDATE statement. You can use a single UPDATE to change the value of one or more columns of a single row or to change multiple column values in selected rows in a single table. Of course, in order to modify the data in the table named in the UPDATE statement, you must have UPDATE access to the table. (You will learn about SQL Object Privileges in Tip 142.)

The syntax of the UPDATE statement is:

```
UPDATE <table name | view name>
SET <column name> = <expression>
      [..., <last column name> = <last expression>]
[WHERE <search condition>]
```

As such, when salesperson #3, Joe Smith, gets promoted to area supervisor, you can reassign all of Joe Smith's customers to their new salesperson #9, Sally Fields, using the UPDATE statement:

```
UPDATE customers SET salesperson = 9 WHERE salesperson = 3
```

Or, you can set the credit limit to $10,000 and the payment terms to net 120 for customer Konrad King using the UPDATE statement:

```
UPDATE customers
SET    credit_limit = 10000,  net_due_days = 120
WHERE  first_name = 'Konrad' AND last_name = 'King'
```

The WHERE clause in the UPDATE statement identifies the row or rows in the table (given by <table name>) whose column values are to be modified. The SET provides the list of column values to be assigned to the rows that satisfy the search criteria in the WHERE clause. In short, the UPDATE statement goes through a table (of customers, in the current examples) one row at a time and updates column values in rows for which the search conditions yields TRUE. Conversely, the UPDATE statement leaves column data unchanged in rows where the search condition (in the WHERE clause) evaluates to FALSE or NULL.

As you can see from the syntax of the UPDATE statement, the SET clause contains a list of column assignment expressions. A table column name can appear as the target of an assignment only once in the assignment list. Moreover, the expression must yield a value compatible with the data type of the column to which it is to be assigned. (You cannot, for example, assign a character string to a column with a NUMERIC data type.) Moreover, the expression must be computable based on the values in the columns of the row currently being updated, and it may not contain any subqueries or column functions (such as SUM, AVG, COUNT).

Note: *Column values not referenced in the expressions or in the WHERE clause of an UPDATE statement, maintain the value they had prior to any updates throughout the entire statement. Thus, the UPDATE statement*

```
UPDATE employees
SET low_quota = (low_quota * 2), medium_quota =
  (low_quota * 4), high_quota = (medium_quota * 8)
WHERE low_quota = 1 AND medium_quota = 2
```

*will set the LOW_QUOTA to 2, the MEDIUM_QUOTA to 4 (4 * 1, not 4 *2), and the HIGH_QUOTA to 16 (8 * 2, not 8 * 4).*

Make sure you *do not* omit the WHERE clause unless you want to UPDATE all of the rows in a table. For example,

```
UPDATE employees SET low_quota =  low_quota * 1.5
```

will increase the LOW_QUOTA value by 150 percent for all employees (rows) in the EMPLOYEES table.

Note: *Before executing a new UPDATE statement (especially one with complex selection criteria), execute a* **SELECT COUNT(*)** *statement using the UPDATE statement's WHERE clause. For example, the statement*

```
SELECT COUNT(*) FROM customers WHERE salesperson = 3
```

will tell you the number of rows the DBMS will modify when you execute the UPDATE statement:

```
UPDATE customers SET salesperson = 9 WHERE salesperson = 3
```

By seeing the number of rows the UPDATE statement will change, you're likely to catch mistakes in the selection criteria—if you have some idea as to the number of rows that you expect to modify.

74 Using the UPDATE Statement with a Conditional Clause to Change Values in Multiple Rows at Once

You can use the UPDATE statement to modify column values in one, some, or all of the rows in a table. The syntax of the UPDATE statement is:

```
UPDATE <target table name | view name>
SET <column name> = <expression>...
      [, <last column name> = <last expression>]
[WHERE <search condition>]
```

If you want to update columns in all of the rows in a table, use an UPDATE statement without a WHERE clause, such as

```
UPDATE employee SET YTD_fed_tax_withheld = 0.00,
  YTD_FICA_Employer = 0.00, YTD_FICA_Employee = 0.00,
  YTD_gross_pay = 0.00
```

which sets the value of the YTD_FED_TAX_WITHHELD, YTD_FICA_EMPLOYER, YTD_FICA_EMPLOYEE, and YTD_GROSS_PAY columns to 0.0 in all of the rows in the EMPLOYEE table.

To modify the columns in only some of the rows in a table, add a WHERE clause to the UPDATE statement. When the DBMS executes an UPDATE statement that has a WHERE clause, it selects the rows that meet the search criteria and then goes through those rows one at a time, updating the column values as specified by the UPDATE statement's SET clause.

For example, the UPDATE statement

```
UPDATE employees SET low_quota = 1, medium_quota = 2,
  high_quota = 4
WHERE low_quota IS NULL
```

will set the three columns LOW_QUOTA, MEDIUM_QUOTA, and HIGH_QUOTA to 1, 2, and 4, respectively, in those rows where the LOW_QUOTA is NULL prior to the execution of the UPDATE statement.

The column names in the UPDATE statement's SET clause must be columns in the target table (the table named after the keyword UPDATE). Moreover, expressions in the UPDATE statement's SET clause cannot include any subqueries or column functions and must evaluate to a data type compatible with the data type of the columns to which they are to be assigned.

Do not worry about the order of the expressions in the SET clause. Since the value of each column used in an expression (and in the WHERE clause) is set to the column's value before any updates are applied, changes to a column's value made by one expression have no effect on any other expressions in the same UPDATE statement.

For example, suppose you were to execute the UPDATE statement

```
UPDATE employees
SET department = ' Main Room', sales = 0,
    low_quota = sales, medium_quota = low_quota + 5,
    high_quota = medium_quota + 5
WHERE sales > low_quota AND department ='Training'
```

on a table row where the SALES column has a value of 10 and LOW_QUOTA, MEDIUM_QUOTA, and HIGH_QUOTA columns have values of 1, 2, and 4, respectively.

The UPDATE statement will set DEPARTMENT to Main Room, SALES to 0, LOW_QUOTA to 10, MEDIUM_QUOTA to 6, and HIGH_QUOTA to 7. Even though it changed the value of LOW_QUOTA from 1 to 10, before it set the value of MEDIUM_QUOTA to LOW_QUOTA + 5, the UPDATE statement uses the preupdate value of all columns (including LOW_QUOTA) throughout the expressions in the SET clause. As such, the UPDATE statement sets the value of MEDIUM_QUOTA to 1 + 5, or 6, and HIGH_QUOTA to 2 + 5, or 7—even though both LOW_QUOTA and MEDIUM quota have new higher values by the time the DBMS evaluates the expressions.

(If you wanted to set the values of the quotas based on the value of the SALES column in the current example, you would use SALES in each expression. The UPDATE statement

```
UPDATE employees
SET department = ' Main Room', sales = 0,
    low_quota = sales, medium_quota = sales + 5,
    high_quota = sales + 10
WHERE sales > low_quota AND department ='Training'
```

would yield the desired quota values of 10, 15, and 20.

75 Using a Subquery in an UPDATE Statement to Change Values in Multiple Rows at Once

Tip 73, "Using the UPDATE Statement to Change Column Values," and Tip 74, "Using the UPDATE Statement with a Conditional Clause to Change Values in Multiple Rows at Once," show example UPDATE statements using WHERE clauses that determine a row's eligibility by using one of the comparison operators (=, >, <, <>, IS). The UPDATE statement will also let you use the results of a SELECT statement to specify which rows you want to UPDATE in the target table.

For example, suppose you want to reassign employees with a less than average number of sales to the training department. You could use the UPDATE statement:

```
UPDATE employees SET department = 'Training'
WHERE department <> 'Training'
AND   sales < (SELECT AVG(sales)
               FROM employees
               WHERE department <> 'Training')
```

As another example, suppose you want to change the job title of all supervisors in charge of more than five employees to manager. You could use the UPDATE statement:

```
UPDATE employees SET job_title = 'Manager'
WHERE job_title = 'Supervisor'
AND   5 < (SELECT COUNT (*)
 FROM employees WHERE reports_to = employee_id)
```

(In the current example, you could not omit the job_title = 'Supervisor' search condition because a vice president responsible for more than five employees would have his job title changed to manager.)

You can nest subqueries in the WHERE clause to any level, meaning that the SELECT statement in the UPDATE statement's WHERE clause can have a SELECT statement in its WHERE clause, which can have a SELECT statement in its WHERE clause, and so on.

SQL-89 prevented the SELECT statement in the WHERE clause of an UPDATE statement from referencing the table being updated at any level. SQL-92 eliminates this restriction by evaluating the references to columns in the target table as if none of the rows of the target table were updated. As such, the SELECT statement in the first example will use the same average of SALES for every row of the EMPLOYEES table, even though the average of SALES made by employees not in training changes as low-producing employees are moved to the training department as the DBMS works it way through the table.

76 Using the UPDATE Statement to Change Column Values in Rows Selected Based on a Computed Value

In Tip 75, "Using a Subquery in an UPDATE Statement to Change Values in Multiple Rows at Once," you learned how to UPDATE specific rows in a table based on the single value returned by the SELECT statement's aggregate function (AVG). (You will learn more about using an aggregate function in a subquery to return a single value in Tip 331, "Using an Aggregate Function in a Subquery to Return a Single Value.") You can also use a computed value to select rows you want the UPDATE statement to modify.

Suppose, for example, that you had an employee table defined by

```
CREATE TABLE employees
(employee_id       INTEGER,
 first_name        VARCHAR(25),
 last_name         VARCHAR(30),
 SSAN              CHAR(11),
 sales             INTEGER,
 status            VARCHAR(30),
 low_quota         INTEGER,
 medium_quota      INTEGER,
 high_quota        INTEGER,
 bonus             INTEGER,
 bonus_multiplier INTEGER DEFAULT 1)
```

and you want to reward employees whose SALES are greater than 150 percent of their high quota by doubling their bonuses. You could use the UPDATE statement:

```
UPDATE employees SET bonus_multiplier = 2
WHERE sales > high_quota * 1.5
```

In addition to using a computation on a column value, you can use the result of a computation using the value returned by an aggregate function as your selection criteria. Suppose, for example, that you want to double the bonus of all employees whose SALES exceed 150 percent of the average HIGH_QUOTA. You could use the UPDATE statement:

```
UPDATE employees SET bonus_multiplier = 2,
WHERE sales > (SELECT AVG(high_quota) FROM employees) * 1.5
```

When using computed values as selection criteria, the important thing to know is that the DBMS evaluates any expressions in the WHERE clause to a constant value and then uses that value to select the rows to be changed during the course of executing the UPDATE statement.

77 Using the UPDATE Statement to Change Values in One Table Based on Values in Another Table

Although the UPDATE statement lets you change only the column values in a single table (whose name appears immediately following the keyword UPDATE), you can use any table (or combination of tables) available to you in the UPDATE statement's WHERE clause. As such, you can decide which rows in the target table to update based on the values in columns of other tables.

For example, suppose you sell auto parts from various vendors, and one of them, XYZ Corp, has gone out of business. You can change the REORDER_STATUS column of all parts from XYZ Corp in your INVENTORY table using the UPDATE statement:

```
UPDATE INVENTORY SET reorder_status = 'Discontinued'
WHERE vendor_id IN (SELECT vendor_id FROM vendors
                    WHERE company_name = 'XYZ Corp')
```

Of course, this example may be a bit of a stretch since you would normally know the VENDOR_ID and use it in the WHERE clause in place of the subquery, writing the UPDATE statement as

```
UPDATE INVENTORY SET reorder_status = 'Discontinued'
WHERE vendor_id = 5
```

if XYZ Corp's VENDOR_ID were 5.

As another example suppose you wish to identify each salesperson with customers who have placed more than $1,000,000 worth of orders as a "Key Account Manager." Given tables created with the statements

```
CREATE TABLE employees
  (employee_id        INTEGER,
   first_name         VARCHAR(25),
   last_name          VARCHAR(30),
   SSAN               CHAR(11),
   total_sales        MONEY,
   status             VARCHAR(30))

CREATE table customers
  (customer_number INTEGER,
   company_name    VARCHAR(50),
   salesperson_id  INTEGER)

CREATE table orders
  (customer_id  INTEGER,
   order_number INTEGER,
   order_date   DATETIME,
   order_total  MONEY)
```

you can identify salespeople with individual customers whose orders total more than $1,000,000 using the UPDATE statement:

```
UPDATE employees SET status = 'Key Account Manager'
WHERE employee_id IN
  (SELECT salesperson_id FROM customers
   WHERE customer_number IN
     (SELECT customer_id FROM orders
      GROUP BY customer_ID
      HAVING SUM(order_total) > 1000000))
```

Note: *You did not use the value in the TOTAL_SALES column as the selection criteria because a salesperson can have more than $1,000,000 in TOTAL_SALES and still not have any customers that have made purchases totaling more than $1,000,0000. For example, if the salesperson had 100 accounts, each of which purchased $20,000 in goods, the TOTAL_SALES would be $2,000,000, but none of the customers would be "key accounts" since none made purchases totaling over $1,000,000.*

The important thing to understand is that you are not restricted to using only the target table in the UPDATE statement's WHERE clause. To the contrary, you can also use any other tables (to which you have SELECT access) whose columns you need to formulate the statement's selection criteria.

78 Using the UPDATE Statement to Change Table Data Through a View

As you learned in Tip 73, "Using the UPDATE Statement to Change Column Values," the UPDATE statement lets you change column values in a single *target* table. Using the syntax

```
UPDATE <target table name | view name>
SET <column name> = <expression>...
      [, <last column name> = <last expression>]
[WHERE <search condition>]
```

you can modify one or more values in one or more rows, and you can base row selection on values in any tables to which you have SELECT access. However, the UPDATE statement can have only one *target* table, meaning that the UPDATE statement can change values in only one table at a time.

In Tip 65, "Using the MS-SQL Server Enterprise Manager Create View Wizard to Create a View," you learned that a view is a virtual table—it does not contain any data, but it references data columns in one or more underlying tables. Since a view is a single, albeit virtual, table, it would seem that you could use a view based on multiple underlying tables to get the UPDATE statement to modify columns in multiple tables at once.

Unfortunately, the DBMS checks the view to make sure the view's SELECT statement includes only a single table. As such, if you attempt to execute the statement

```
UPDATE  cust_rep
SET employee_status ='Terminated', cust_sales_rep = 2
WHERE employee_id = 6
```

where CUST_REP is a view based on columns from multiple underlying tables, the DBMS will fail to execute the UPDATE statement and respond with an error message similar to:

```
Server: Msg 4405, Level 16, State 2, Line1
View 'CUST_REP' is not updateable because the FROM clause
  names multiple tables.
```

The two advantages for using a view in place of the underlying table in an UPDATE statement are that you can make column names more descriptive, and that you can limit the columns the user can update in the underlying table.

Suppose, for example, that you had a table created with the statement

```
CREATE TABLE employees
(emp_id      INTEGER PRIMARY KEY IDENTITY,
 fname       VARCHAR(25),
 lname       VARCHAR(30),
 addr        VARCHAR(30),
 SSAN        CHAR(11),
```

```
dept        VARCHAR(20),
badgno      INTEGER,
sales       INTEGER,
tot_sales   MONEY,
status      VARCHAR(30),
low_quota   INTEGER,
med_quota   INTEGER,
high_quota  INTEGER,
bonus       INTEGER,
bonus_mult  INTEGER DEFAULT 1)
```

and you only wanted a user to be able to update the name, address, Social Security number, and badge number for employees in the marketing department. You could use the CREATE VIEW statement:

```
CREATE VIEW vw_marketing_sup_emp_update
  (employee_number, first_name, last_name, address,
   social_security_number, badge_number)
AS SELECT emp_id, fname, lname, addr, ssan, badgno
FROM employees
WHERE dept = 'Marketing'
```

Given UPDATE access to the VW_MARKETING_SUP_EMP_UPDATE view, the user could then UPDATE a marketing employee's personal information and badge number without being able to change (or even display) the employee department, status, count, volume, quotas, and bonus information.

For example, to assign (or change) employee 123's badge number, the marketing supervisor could use the UPDATE statement:

```
UPDATE vw_marketing_sup_emp_update
SET badge_number = 1123
WHERE employee_number = 123
```

When the DBMS receives an UPDATE statement that uses a view as the target table, the DBMS builds the virtual table using the SELECT statement in the view definition. Thus, in the current example, the DBMS builds a temporary (virtual) table by selecting employees in the marketing department from the EMPLOYEES table. The virtual (view) table has only the columns listed in the view's SELECT statement, and the additional data in each row of the EMPLOYEE column is excluded.

After it builds the view table (VW_MARKETING_SUP_EMP_UPDATE in the current example), the DBMS uses the selection criteria in the UPDATE statement's WHERE clause to determine which row (or rows) in the virtual (view) table it is to UPDATE. (Thus, if employee 123 is in the EMPLOYEES table but not in the marketing department, the UPDATE command will fail because employee 123 does not exist in the target table, VW_MARKETING_SUP_EMP_UPDATE.)

Finally, the DBMS applies the updates specified in the UPDATE statement's SET clause to the columns in the underlying table, not the virtual (view) table. In the current example, the

DBMS will set the BADGNO column of the row where EMP_ID is 123 in the EMPLOYEES table to 1123.

You will learn all about creating views and how the DBMS handles them in Tips 206–215.

79 Using the DELETE Statement to Remove a Row from a Table

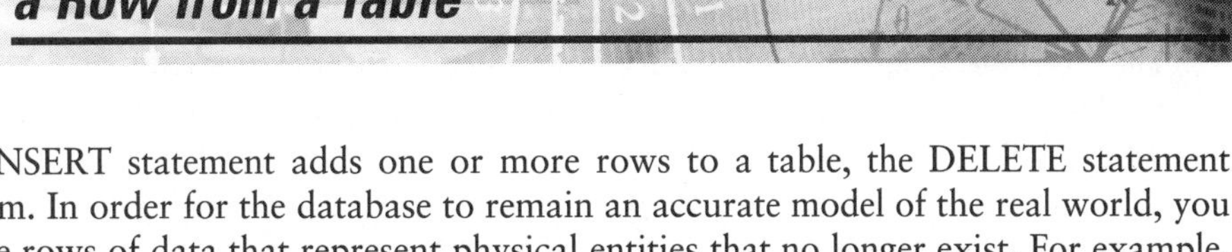

While the INSERT statement adds one or more rows to a table, the DELETE statement removes them. In order for the database to remain an accurate model of the real world, you must remove rows of data that represent physical entities that no longer exist. For example, if a customer cancels an order, you need to remove one or more rows from an ORDERS table. After you terminate an employee, you need to remove a row from the EMPLOYEES table. When you discontinue a product, you need to delete a row from the PRODUCTS table—and so on.

A single row is the smallest unit of data that the DELETE statement can remove from a table. (To remove a column from *all* of the rows in a table, use the ALTER TABLE statement with a DROP COLUMN clause, as you learned in Tip 58, "Using the MS-SQL Server ALTER TABLE, DROP COLUMN Clause to Remove a Table Column.")

Suppose, for example, that you have an e-mail database that has users and messages tables created by

```
CREATE TABLE hotmail_users
  (user_id      VARCHAR(25) PRIMARY KEY,
   name         VARCHAR(50),
   address      VARCHAR(50),
   phone_number VARCHAR(30),
   password     VARCHAR(20))

CREATE TABLE hotmail_messages
  (user_id            VARCHAR(25),
   date_time_received DATETIME,
   subject            VARCHAR (250),
   sent_by            VARCHAR(25),
   date_time_sent     DATETIME,
   priority           CHAR(1),
   message            TEXT
   CONSTRAINT recipient_account_id
     FOREIGN KEY (user_id) REFERENCES hotmail_users)
```

The syntax of the DELETE statement is:

```
DELETE from <table name> [WHERE <search condition>]
```

Therefore, if user KKI decides to discontinue use of his e-mail account, you could use the DELETE statements

```
DELETE FROM hotmail_messages WHERE user_id = 'KKI'
DELETE hotmail_users WHERE user_id = 'KKI'
```

to remove KKI from the HOTMAIL_USERS table and all of his e-mail messages from the HOTMAIL_MESSAGES table.

The WHERE clause in the DELETE statement identifies the row or set of rows that the DELETE statement is to remove from the table whose name appears immediately following the keyword DELETE.

As such, the first DELETE statement in the example will remove multiple rows from the HOTMAIL_MESSAGES table if user KKI has more than one e-mail message on file. Conversely, the second DELETE statement will DELETE a single row from the HOTMAIL_USERS table since USER_ID's are unique. (The PRIMARY KEY constraint on the USER_ID column of the HOTMAIL_USERS table specifies that all rows in the table must have a unique, non-NULL value in the USER_ID column.)

Note: *When removing rows from multiple tables, the order in which you execute the DELETE statements will be of consequence if the PRIMARY KEY in one of the tables is referenced by the FOREIGN KEY constraint in another table. In the current example, the PRIMARY KEY (USER_ID) in the HOTMAIL_USERS table is referenced by the FOREIGN KEY constraint (RECIPIENT_ACCOUNT_ID) in the HOTMAIL_MESSAGES table. As such, if you attempt to DELETE the HOTMAIL_USERS row with USER_ID KKI before you remove all of the e-mail messages stored for USER_ID KKI from the HOTMAIL_MESSAGES table, the DELETE statement will fail to execute and the DBMS will display messages similar to:*

```
Server: Msg 547, Level 16, State 1, Line 1
DELETE statement conflict with COLUMN REFERENCE constraint
  'recipient_account_id'.
The conflict occurred in database 'SQLTips', table
  hotmail_messages', column 'user_id'.
The statement has been terminated.
```

As you will learn in Tip 174, "Understanding Referential Integrity Checks and Foreign Keys," the FOREIGN KEY constraint specifies that the value in the column(s) defined as the FOREIGN KEY (USER_ID, in the current example) must exist as one of the PRIMARY KEY values in the table name in the FOREIGN KEY's REFERENCES clause (HOTMAIL_USERS, in the current example). Therefore, to successfully DELETE the user KKI and all of his messages, you must first DELETE the messages with USER_ID KKI from the HOTMAIL_MESSAGES table. Then you can DELETE the row with USER_ID KKI from the HOTMAIL_USERS table.

80 Using the DELETE Statement with a Conditional Clause to Remove Multiple Rows from a Table

In Tip 79, "Using the DELETE Statement to Remove a Row from a Table," you learned how to remove one or more rows from a table based on a column's contents being equal to a certain value. You can also use the DELETE statement to remove rows from a table based on column values being in a set of data values or satisfying the search condition based on conditional operators (such as <, >, <=).

Suppose, for example, that a group of the financial counselors left your brokerage firm and took all of their clients with them. You could use the DELETE statement

```
DELETE FROM clients WHERE fc_id IN (1001, 1005, 1010, 1015)
```

to remove all client records (table rows) taken to another firm by financial counselors with IDs 1001, 1005, 1010, and 1015.

To base row removal on a conditional operator, simply use the operator in the DELETE statement's WHERE clause. For example, to delete all back orders placed prior to January 2000, you could use the DELETE statement:

```
DELETE FROM orders
WHERE order_date < '01/01/2000' AND ship_date IS NULL
```

Although the syntax of the DELETE statement

```
DELETE from <table name> [WHERE <search condition>]
```

shows the WHERE clause as optional, you must omit the WHERE clause only if you want the DBMS to remove all of the rows from a table. Stated another way, if you omit the WHERE clause, the DBMS will, without warning, delete *all* of the rows from the table. As such, the DELETE statement

```
DELETE FROM clients
```

will delete all of the rows from the CLIENTS table. Therefore, be positive that you really want to remove all of the data in a table *before* you execute a DELETE statement without a WHERE clause.

Note: *If you are planning to remove all of the rows from a table, check to see if your DBMS has a special command for clearing a table while leaving its structure intact. MS-SQL Server, for example, provides the Transact-SQL TRUNCATE TABLE statement, which you will learn about in Tip 82, "Using the TRUNCATE Statement to Remove All Rows from an MS-SQL Server Table." Typically, specialized table-clearing facilities will complete their tasks more quickly (and efficiently) than using the DELETE statement to remove all of the data from a table one row at a time.*

As with the UPDATE statement, always reread your DELETE statement twice before you click your mouse on the Execute or Submit button. If you have some idea as to the number or rows you expect to remove, use the DELETE statement's WHERE clause in a SELECT COUNT (*) statement, such as:

```
SELECT COUNT (*) FROM orders
WHERE order_date > '01/01/2000' AND ship_date IS NULL
```

If you know there are very few old back orders on the system, but the count comes up as a large number, look at the WHERE clause again, and perhaps change the SELECT statement to display some of the columns in the rows it counted. Doing so may help you to avoid a possibly costly error in executing a DELETE statement based on an erroneous search condition.

(In the current example, the large row count returned by the **SELECT COUNT** (*) statement may have alerted you to the fact that you were about to delete all rows for unshipped orders placed *after* 01/01/2000 vs. *prior* to the beginning of the year.)

81 Using the DELETE Statement with a Subquery to Remove Multiple Rows from a Table

Tip 79, "Using the DELETE Statement to Remove a Row from a Table," and Tip 80, "Using the DELETE Statement with a Conditional Clause to Remove Multiple Rows from a Table," showed you how to select rows to DELETE based on column values in the target table's row. Sometimes, however, that you don't know the value in any of the columns in the row(s) you want to delete and must base the selection on values in columns of other tables. By adding a subquery to a DELETE statement, you can delete selected rows in one table based on values in another table.

Suppose, for example, that you wanted to remove all customer records for those customers who have not placed on order in over two years. You could use the DELETE statement

```
DELETE FROM customers
WHERE (SELECT COUNT (*) FROM orders
        WHERE customer_ID = ordered_by
        AND order_date > '05/30/1999') = 0
```

or, you could write the same DELETE statement as:

```
DELETE FROM customers
WHERE NOT EXISTS (SELECT * FROM ORDERS
                  WHERE customer_ID = ordered_by
                  AND order_date > '05/30/1999')
```

You can name only a single table in the DELETE statement's FROM clause. As such, the statement

```
DELETE FROM hotmail_messages, hotmail_users
WHERE hotmail_messages.user_id = hotmail_users.user_id
AND name = 'Konrad King'
```

is illegal since a multi-table join is not allowed in the FROM clause of a DELETE statement. If you want to remove all e-mail messages the username Konrad King has on file, use this DELETE statement instead:

```
DELETE FROM hotmail_messages
WHERE user_id = (SELECT user_id FROM hotmail_users
                 WHERE name = 'Konrad King').
```

When you include a subquery in a DELETE statement, the DBMS first executes the subquery to create a result set (of rows or columns values). The DBMS then uses the result set from the subquery in the search condition specified by the DELETE statement's WHERE clause. Thus, when executing the DELETE statement

```
DELETE FROM salesreps
WHERE 1000 >
  (SELECT SUM(order_total) FROM orders
      WHERE sold_by = salesrep_id))
```

the DBMS will evaluate the SELECT statement first. As such, it will use the SOLD_BY and ORDER_TOTAL columns of the ORDERS table to create a result set that contains a list of SALESREP_ID and total sales pairs. The DBMS will then work its way through the SALESREPS table one row at a time, deleting those rows where the total sales for the sales rep is less than $1,000.

82 Using the TRUNCATE Statement to Remove All Rows from an MS-SQL Server Table

Although you could use a DELETE statement without a WHERE clause to remove all rows from a table, the Transact-SQL TRUNCATE TABLE statement will execute the task more quickly and efficiently. The syntax of the TRUNCATE TABLE statement is:

```
TRUNCATE TABLE <table name>
```

If you use the DELETE statement

```
DELETE FROM employee
```

the DBMS will go through the EMPLOYEE table one row at a time, noting the row deletion and writing the values of the columns in the row to be deleted into the transaction log prior to removing the row from the table.

When you execute the TRUNCATE TABLE statement

```
TRUNCATE TABLE employee
```

the DBMS removes *pages* of information at once. Each page of data contains multiple rows. Thus, the TRUNCATE TABLE statement will remove multiple rows of data from the table at once (vs. one row at a time, the way the DELETE statement does). Moreover, the TRUNCATE TABLE statement does not update the transaction log. As such, if you remove rows from a table using the TRUNCATE TABLE statement, you will not be able to ROLLBACK (undo) the row deletions, even if you execute the TRUNCATE TABLE statement as part of a transaction.

Note: *The TRUNCATE TABLE statement is especially handy if your transaction log is full and the DBMS cannot expand it because there is no more room on the hard drive on which it is stored. If you try to use the DELETE statement to remove rows from a table to free up disk space, the statement will fail because the DBMS cannot write any more information to the transaction log. You can, however, use the TRUNCATE TABLE statement to remove all rows from a table to free up disk space, since it does not write any information to the transaction log as it permanently deletes table rows.*

83 Using the DELETE Statement to Remove Table Rows Based on a Computed Value

Tips 79–81 showed you how to use the DELETE statement to remove a row from a table based on a value stored in one or more of the row's columns. As you now know, you can select the rows to delete either by checking the value of the column(s) directly or by checking to see if the column value(s) in question are part of a result set returned by a subquery in the DELETE statement's WHERE clause.

In addition to using the value stored in a column, you can select rows to delete based on a computed value. Suppose, for example, that you had CUSTOMER TABLE defined as

```
CREATE TABLE customers
(cust_id             INTEGER PRIMARY KEY,
 first_name          VARCHAR(25),
 last_name           VARCHAR(35),
 address             VARCHAR(40),
 phone_number        VARCHAR(20),
 total_purchases     MONEY,
```

```
last_order_date    DATETIME,
order_count        INTEGER)
```

and you want to remove all customers who have not made a purchase within the year prior to 05/30/99, unless the customer's previous average purchase amount exceeds the overall average purchase amount by 75 percent. You could use a DELETE statement similar to the following:

```
DELETE FROM customers
WHERE last_order_date < CONVERT(DATETIME,'05/30/99'). - 365
AND total_purchases / order_count <
      (SELECT (SUM(total_purchases) / sum(order_count)) *
         1.75 FROM customers)
```

Notice that you can use computed values both inside and outside a subquery (if any) in the DELETE statement's WHERE clause.

Moreover, SQL-92 lets you use the target table in the subquery's FROM clause by evaluating the subquery as if none of the table's rows has been deleted. As such, although the DELETE in the current example changes the value of the overall average order as it removes customers from the table, the DBMS will use the same value for the average order for every row it checks—because it uses the overall average computed before any rows (TOTAL PURCHASES and ORDER_COUNTs) were removed from the table.

84 Using the DELETE Statement to Remove Table Rows Through a View

In addition to using a view to insert a row (as you learned to do in Tip 68, "Using the INSERT Statement to Insert Rows Through a View") or change the value of one or more columns in a row (as you learned to do in Tip 78, "Using the UPDATE Statement to Change Table Data Through a View"), you can also use a view to DELETE rows from a table. As you know, a view is a *virtual* table whose actual, physical data is stored in one or more underlying tables. As such, insertions, modifications, and deletions performed on a view are actually done to the underlying tables. As such, when you use a DELETE statement to remove a row from a view, you are actually removing a row from the table on which the view is based.

As was the case with the UPDATE statement, if you want to use a view as the target table in a DELETE statement, the view must be based on a single underlying table. The view need not display all of the columns in the underlying table, and it can display computed columns. The only restriction is that the view's SELECT statement must reference only a single table—the DELETE statement's target table.

Suppose, for example, that your company closed the Tulsa shipping department, and you want to remove all Tulsa shipping department personnel. Given a view named VW_TULSA_EMPLOYEES and created by

```
CREATE VIEW vw_tulsa_employees AS
SELECT employee_id, first_name, last_name, SSAN, department
FROM employees
WHERE location = 'Tulsa'
```

you can use the DELETE statement

```
DELETE FROM vw_tulsa_employees WHERE department = 'shipping'
```

to remove rows from the EMPLOYEES table where the value of the LOCATION column is Tulsa and the value of the DEPARTMENT column is shipping.

When you use a view as the target table for a DELETE statement, you can remove only rows that satisfy the search criteria in the view's SELECT clause. Thus, in the current example, the DELETE statement will remove rows where the location column has the value Tulsa, even though the location is not specified in the DELETE statement's WHERE clause. Thus, employees that work in the shipping department at other locations will remain in the table.

In short, you can DELETE only existing rows from the target table. (To restate the obvious, you cannot remove a row from a table if the row is not in the table.) As such, you can use a view to DELETE only rows that meet the view's selection criteria, since those are the only rows in the view.

Because a table row is the smallest unit of data that a DELETE statement can remove, a DELETE statement with a view as the target table will remove an entire row from the underlying table—even if the view displays only some of the table's columns. For example, suppose the EMPLOYEES table in the current example was created with:

```
CREATE TABLE employees
(employee_id      INTEGER,
 first_name       VARCHAR(25),
 last_name        VARCHAR(30),
 SSAN             CHAR(11),
 location         VARCHAR(20),
 department       VARCHAR(20),
 total_sales      MONEY)
```

Then, the DELETE statement

```
DELETE FROM vw_tulsa_employees
```

will remove all rows where the LOCATION column has a value of Tulsa, even though the VW_TULSA_EMPLOYEES view has only the columns EMPLOYEE_ID, FIRST_NAME, LAST_NAME, SSAN, and DEPARTMENT.

Although the DELETE statement will remove an entire table row (including columns not defined in the view), you can reference underlying only table columns that are part of the view's definition in the DELETE statement's WHERE clause. Thus, the DELETE statement

```
DELETE FROM vw_tulsa_employees WHERE total_sales < 1000
```

will fail because TOTAL_SALES is not a column in the VW_TULSA_EMPLOYEES view (virtual table). If you try to refer to an underlying table column that is not defined as a column in the DELETE statement's target table (the VW_TULSA_EMPLOYEES view, in the current example), the DBMS will respond with an error message similar to:

```
Server: Msg 207, Level 16, State 3, Line 1
Invalid column name 'total sales'.
```

85 Understanding What to Expect from a SELECT Statement

When executed, a SELECT statement always returns a table. The table may have only one column and no rows, but every SELECT statement returns its query results as a table. Moreover, when a SELECT statement appears within another SELECT statement as a subquery, the inner SELECT statement returns a results table that serves as the input table for the outer (or main) SELECT statement.

If you are using interactive SQL (such as the window-oriented MS-SQL Server Query Analyzer or the command-line MS-SQL Server ISQL application), the SELECT statement displays its query results in tabular form on your computer screen. If you are using a program (such as Visual Basic, C, or C++) to send a query (SELECT statement) to the DBMS, the DBMS will use a cursor (which you will learn about in Tip 415, "Understanding the Differences Between Buffers and Cursors") to hold the tabular query results while it passes the rows of column values to your application program's (host) variables.

The syntax of a SELECT statement is:

```
SELECT [ALL | DISTINCT] <select item list>
FROM <table list>
[WHERE <search conditions>]
[GROUP BY <grouping column list>
   [HAVING <having search conditions>]]
[ORDER BY <sort specification>]
```

You will explore each and every element of the SELECT statement in great detail as you read the next group of Tips. The important thing to know now is that a SELECT statement always returns its results in the form of a table.

Thus, the SELECT statement

```
SELECT employee_id, first_name, last_name, total_sales
FROM employees
```

will display the EMPLOYEE_ID, FIRST_NAME, LAST_NAME, and TOTAL_SALES column values in each row of the EMPLOYEES table, in a manner similar to:

```
employee_id  first_name  last_name  total_sales
===========  ==========  =========  ===========
1            Konrad      King       125258.2200
2            Sally       Fields     83478.2500
3            Wally       Wallberg   14258.1200
4            Sam         Kelleher   6012.5900
5            Sam         Walton     748252.2000
6            Helen       Eoff       45587.6600
7            NULL        Gomez      49258.7500
```

Note: *Since the SELECT statement in the example has no WHERE clause, the DBMS will display all of the rows in the EMPLOYEES table.*

A SELECT statement with a WHERE clause will still return a table, but the results table will include only those rows from the input table(s) (list in the FROM clause) that satisfy the search condition in the WHERE clause. Thus, in the current example, the SELECT statement

```
SELECT employee_id, first_name, last_name, total_sales
FROM employees
WHERE first_name = 'Sam'
```

will return a table of two rows:

```
employee_id  first_name  last_name  total_sales
===========  ==========  =========  ===========
4            Sam         Kelleher   6012.5900
5            Sam         Walton     748252.2000
```

If none of the rows in the underlying table(s) satisfies the search condition in its WHERE clause, a SELECT statement will return a table with headings and no rows. For example, the SELECT statement

```
SELECT employee_id, first_name, last_name, total_sales
FROM employees
WHERE first_name IS NULL
```

will display the results:

```
employee_id  first_name  last_name  total_sales
===========  ==========  =========  ===========
```

Note: *When a column has a NULL value, the DBMS must treat its value as "unknown." As such, the DBMS cannot make* any *assumptions about the value of the column—it cannot even assume that it is equal to another NULL value. As you will learn in Tip 317, "Understanding Why the Expression NULL = NULL Evaluates to False," the predicate NULL = NULL is always FALSE in SQL. To check for a NULL value in a column, use the predicate <column name> IS NULL.*

When you use an aggregate function in a SELECT statement to display a single value, the SELECT statement still returns its result as a table. For example, based on the sample data in the current example's EMPLOYEES table, the SELECT statement

```
SELECT SUM(total_sales) FROM employees
```

will return the table:

```
SUM(total_sales)
================
1072105.7900
```

The results table has only one column and one row, but it is a table nonetheless. (Note that the column heading you see may be "1," "Col1," or "Sum(total_sales)" as returned by MS-SQL Server in this example.)

Thus, the import thing to know now about the SELECT statement is that it *always* produces a table. Moreover, because they are always returned in a table, you can store SELECT statement results back into the database as a table; combine the results of one SELECT statement with another to produce a larger, composite table; and use the results of one SELECT statement as the target (or input) table for another SELECT statement.

86 Understanding the Structure of a SELECT Statement

A SELECT statement is often called a query because it tells the DBMS to answer a question about the data stored in one or more database tables. For example, if you want to query (or ask) the DBMS for a list of purchase dates, item descriptions, and costs on orders placed by Bruce Williams, you could execute the SELECT statement:

```
SELECT order_date, description, cost
FROM orders, customers
WHERE ordered_by = customer_id
AND   first_name = 'Bruce' AND last_name = 'Williams'
```

As you learned in Tip 85, "Understanding What to Expect from a SELECT Statement," the syntax of the SELECT statement is:

```
SELECT [ALL | DISTINCT] <select item list>
FROM <table list>
[WHERE <search conditions>]
[GROUP BY <grouping column list>
   [HAVING <having search conditions>]]
ORDER BY <sort specification>]
```

Thus, the parts of a SELECT statement are:

- The keyword SELECT followed by the list of items you want displayed in the SELECT statement's results table.
- The FROM clause, which lists the tables whose column data values are included in the item list for display or are part of the search criteria in the optional WHERE clause.
- An optional WHERE clause, which lists the search criteria to use in selecting the rows of data to display from the tables listed in the FROM clause. (If the SELECT statement has no WHERE clause, the DBMS assumes that all rows in the target table[s] [listed in the FROM clause] satisfy the selection criteria.)
- An optional GROUP BY clause, which tells the DBMS to combine subtotal query results based on the values in one or more columns listed in the <grouping column list>. (You will learn how to use the GROUP BY clause in Tip 270, "Using a GROUP BY Clause to Group Rows Based on a Single-Column Value," and Tip 271, "Using a GROUP BY Clause to Group Rows Based on Multiple Columns.")
- An optional HAVING clause, which lists additional row-selection criteria to filter out rows based on the results (subtotals) produced by the GROUP BY clause. (You will learn about the HAVING clause and how it differs from the WHERE clause in Tip 276, "Using a HAVING Clause to Filter the Rows Included in a Grouped Query's Results Table," and Tip 277, "Understanding the Difference Between a WHERE Clause and a HAVING Clause.")
- An optional ORDER BY clause, which tells the DBMS how to sort the rows in the SELECT statement's results table. (If there is no ORDER BY clause, the DBMS will display data in the order in which it finds it within the (unsorted) input table(s).)

Thus, the example SELECT statement

```
SELECT order_date, description, cost FROM orders, customers
WHERE ordered_by = customer_id
AND   first_name = 'Bruce' AND last_name = 'Williams'
```

tells the DBMS to list the values found in the ORDER_DATE, DESCRIPTION, and COST columns.

The FROM clause tells the DBMS that it will find columns listed in the SELECT clause in the ORDERS and/or CUSTOMERS tables.

Meanwhile, the WHERE clause tells the DBMS to return only those rows (from the virtual table formed by a CROSS JOIN of the ORDERS and CUSTOMERS tables) where the ORDERED_BY column (from the ORDERS table) contains the same value as the CUSTOMER_ID column (from the CUSTOMERS table), and where the FIRST_NAME column (from the CUSTOMERS table) contains the value Bruce and the LAST_NAME column (from the CUSTOMERS table) contains the value Williams. (You will learn about cross joins in Tip 298, "Using the CROSS JOIN to Create a Cartesian Product," and you will learn how the DBMS uses them to produce a virtual, composite table to which it applies the SELECT statement's selection criteria in Tip 87, "Understanding the Steps Involved in Processing an SQL SELECT Statement.")

87 Understanding the Steps Involved in Processing an SQL SELECT Statement

To have the DBMS display the values in a table, you need only execute a SELECT statement with a FROM clause, such as

```
SELECT * FROM employees
```

which displays all columns and all rows in the EMPLOYEES table.

In practice, almost all SELECT statements include a WHERE clause that forces output data to satisfy certain criteria. Moreover, many SELECT statements involve the selection of column data from multiple tables.

As you learned in Tip 85, "Understanding What to Expect from a SELECT Statement," and Tip 86, "Understanding the Structure of a SELECT Statement," the syntax of a SELECT statement is:

```
SELECT [ALL | DISTINCT] <select item list>
FROM <table list>
[WHERE <search conditions>]
[GROUP BY <grouping column list>
   [HAVING <having search conditions>]]
[ORDER BY <sort specification>]
```

When executing a SELECT statement, the DBMS performs the following steps:

1. Creates a working table based on the table or tables in the FROM clause. If there are two or more tables in the FROM clause, the DBMS will execute a CROSS JOIN to create a table that is a Cartesian product of the tables in the <table list> (in the SELECT statement's FROM clause). For example, if the SELECT statement lists two tables in its FROM clause, the DBMS will create a table that consists of each row of the first table concatenated with each row of the second table. After the DBMS builds it, the cross-joined working table contains all possible combination of rows that can result from combining a row from the first table with a row from the second.

Note: *No DBMS product actually uses a CROSS JOIN to construct the intermediate results table—the product table would be too large even when the <table list> in the FROM clause contains only a few rows. For example, if you have two 1,000-row tables, the resulting Cartesian product would be a table with 1,000,000 rows! The important thing to understand is that although it never really actually exists, the product table is a conceptual model that correctly describes the behavior of the DBMS when it executes a multi-table query.*

---

2. If there is a WHERE clause, the DBMS will apply its search condition to each row in the composite (Cartesian product) table generated in Step 1. The DBMS keeps those rows for

which the search condition tests TRUE and removes those for which the search condition tests NULL or FALSE. If the WHERE clause contains a subquery, the DBMS executes the subquery on each row that satisfies the selection criteria of the main query.

3. If there is a GROUP BY clause, the DBMS breaks the rows in the results table (from Step 2) into groups where columns in the <grouping column list> all have the same value. Next, the DBMS reduces each group to a single row, which is then added to a new results table that replaces the one at the beginning of this step.

Note: *All of the columns in the <grouping column list> in the GROUP BY clause must appear in the <select item list> in the SELECT clause.*

Note: *The DBMS treats NULL values is if they were equal and puts all of them into their own group.*

---

4. If there is a HAVING clause, the DBMS applies it to each of the rows in the "grouped" table produced in Step 3. The DBMS keeps those rows for which the <having search conditions> tests TRUE and removes those rows for which the <having search conditions> tests NULL (unknown) or FALSE. If the HAVING clause has a subquery, the DBMS performs the subquery on each row of the "grouped" table that satisfies the <having search conditions>.

Note: *You cannot have a HAVING clause in a SELECT statement without a GROUP BY clause because the HAVING clause filters the results of the GROUP BY clause. Moreover, any columns in the <having search conditions> must be included in the <grouping column list> of the GROUP BY clause.*

---

5. Apply the SELECT clause to the results table. If a column in the results table is not in the <select item list>, the DBMS drops the column from the results table. If the SELECT clause includes the DISTINCT option, the DBMS will remove duplicate rows from the results table.

Note: *The <select item list> in the SELECT clause can consist of constants (numeric or character string), calculations based on constants or table columns, columns, and functions.*

---

6. If there is an ORDER BY clause, sort the results table as specified in the <sort specification>.

7. Display the results table to the screen for an interactive SQL SELECT statement, or use a cursor to pass the results table to the calling (or host) program for programmatic SQL.

Suppose, for example, that you have two tables created with

```
CREATE TABLE employees
(emp_id    INTEGER PRIMARY KEY,
 last_name VARCHAR(25),
```

```
 trainer   VARCHAR(25),
 sales     INTEGER)

CREATE TABLE sales
(cust_id   INTEGER PRIMARY KEY,
 sold_by   INTEGER,
 sales_amt MONEY)
```

that have the following data:

```
EMPLOYEES table                   SALES table
id last_name trainer sales        cust_id sold_by sales_amt
-- --------- ------- -----        ------- ------- ---------
1  Hardy     Bob     3            1       1       $6,000
2  Wallace   Greg    3            2       1       $6,000
3  Green     Bob     2            3       4       $8,000
4  Marsh     Andy    2            4       2       $4,000
5  Brown     Greg    0            5       2       $6,000
                                  6       3       $7,000
                                  7       4       $4,000
                                  8       1       $6,000
                                  9       2       $7,000
                                  10      3       $9,000
```

To get a report on how well your trainers were doing in preparing your salesmen for the field, you could use a query similar to:

```
SELECT last_name trainer, COUNT(*) AS num_trainees,
       SUM(sales_amt) AS gross_sales, AVG(sales_amt)
FROM employees, sales
WHERE sales > 0
AND emp_id = sold_by
GROUP BY last_name, trainer
HAVING AVG(sales_amt) > 6000
```

After performing Step 1 of SELECT statement execution for the example query, the DBMS will create the following CROSS JOIN working table based on the data in the two tables (EMPLOYEES and ORDERS) listed in the example SELECT statement's FROM clause.

CROSS JOIN Working Table

```
EMPLOYEES                              ORDERS
emp_id last_name trainer sales         cust_id sold_by sales_amt
------ --------- ------- -----         ------- ------- ---------
1      Hardy     Bob     3             1       1       $6,000
1      Hardy     Bob     3             2       1       $6,000
1      Hardy     Bob     3             3       4       $8,000
1      Hardy     Bob     3             4       2       $4,000
1      Hardy     Bob     3             5       2       $6,000
1      Hardy     Bob     3             6       3       $7,000
1      Hardy     Bob     3             7       4       $4,000
```

```
1  Hardy    Bob   3  8   1  $6,000
1  Hardy    Bob   3  9   2  $7,000
1  Hardy    Bob   3  10  3  $9,000
2  Wallace  Greg  3  1   1  $6,000
2  Wallace  Greg  3  2   1  $6,000
2  Wallace  Greg  3  3   4  $8,000
2  Wallace  Greg  3  4   2  $4,000
2  Wallace  Greg  3  5   2  $6,000
2  Wallace  Greg  3  6   3  $7,000
2  Wallace  Greg  3  7   4  $4,000
2  Wallace  Greg  3  8   1  $6,000
2  Wallace  Greg  3  9   2  $7,000
2  Wallace  Greg  3  10  3  $9,000
3  Green    Bob   2  1   1  $6,000
3  Green    Bob   2  2   1  $6,000
3  Green    Bob   2  3   4  $8,000
3  Green    Bob   2  4   2  $4,000
3  Green    Bob   2  5   2  $6,000
3  Green    Bob   2  6   3  $7,000
3  Green    Bob   2  7   4  $4,000
3  Green    Bob   2  8   1  $6,000
3  Green    Bob   2  9   2  $7,000
3  Green    Bob   2  10  3  $9,000
4  Marsh    Andy  2  1   1  $6,000
4  Marsh    Andy  2  2   1  $6,000
4  Marsh    Andy  2  3   4  $8,000
4  Marsh    Andy  2  4   2  $4,000
4  Marsh    Andy  2  5   2  $6,000
4  Marsh    Andy  2  6   3  $7,000
4  Marsh    Andy  2  7   4  $4,000
4  Marsh    Andy  2  8   1  $6,000
4  Marsh    Andy  2  9   2  $7,000
4  Marsh    Andy  2  10  3  $9,000
5  Brown    Greg  0  1   1  $6,000
5  Brown    Greg  0  2   1  $6,000
5  Brown    Greg  0  3   4  $8,000
5  Brown    Greg  0  4   2  $4,000
5  Brown    Greg  0  5   2  $6,000
5  Brown    Greg  0  6   3  $7,000
5  Brown    Greg  0  7   4  $4,000
5  Brown    Greg  0  8   1  $6,000
5  Brown    Greg  0  9   2  $7,000
5  Brown    Greg  0  10  3  $9,000
```

In Step 2 of the procedure, the DBMS will apply the search criteria in the SELECT statement's WHERE clause, which includes two predicates in the current example. The first predicate, sales > 0, will remove rows with a zero in the SALES column from the working table; the second predicate, emp_id = sold_by, will remove rows where the value in the EMP_ID column is not equal to the value in the SOLD_BY column to produce the working table:

CROSS JOIN Working Table After WHERE Clause Filter

EMPLOYEES				ORDERS		
emp_id	last_name	trainer	sales	cust_id	sold_by	sales_amt
1	Hardy	Bob	3	1	1	$6,000
1	Hardy	Bob	3	2	1	$6,000
1	Hardy	Bob	3	8	1	$6,000
2	Wallace	Greg	3	4	2	$4,000
2	Wallace	Greg	3	5	2	$6,000
2	Wallace	Greg	3	9	2	$7,000
3	Green	Bob	2	6	3	$7,000
3	Green	Bob	2	10	3	$9,000
4	Marsh	Andy	2	3	4	$8,000
4	Marsh	Andy	2	7	4	$4,000

Note: *If any of the predicates in the WHERE clause use only one of the tables listed in the FROM clause, the DBMS optimizer will normally use the predicate to remove rows from the table prior to performing the CROSS JOIN. In the current example, the optimizer would have removed employee 5 from consideration since the employee has no sales, thereby eliminating 10 rows from the cross-joined working table.*

In Step 3, the DBMS will use the GROUP BY clause to group the working table by trainer and then compute values for the aggregate functions in the SELECT clause.

CROSS JOIN Working Table After WHERE Clause Filtering and Grouping

EMPLOYEES				ORDERS		
emp_id	last_name	trainer	sales	cust_id	sold_by	sales_amt
1	Hardy	Bob	3	1	1	$6,000
1	Hardy	Bob	3	2	1	$6,000
1	Hardy	Bob	3	8	1	$6,000
3	Green	Bob	2	6	3	$7,000
3	Green	Bob	2	10	3	$9,000
2	Wallace	Greg	3	4	2	$4,000
2	Wallace	Greg	3	5	2	$6,000
2	Wallace	Greg	3	9	2	$7,000
4	Marsh	Andy	2	3	4	$8,000
4	Marsh	Andy	2	7	4	$4,000

Aggregate Functions

trainer	num_trainees	gross_sales	AVG(sales_amt)
Bob	5	$34,000	$6,800.0000
Greg	3	$17,000	$5,666.6666
Andy	2	$12,000	$6,000.0000

Next, the DBMS will apply the search condition in the HAVING clause to eliminate working table rows with average sales of $6,000.00 or less.

Finally, the DBMS will apply the <select item list> in the SELECT clause to and display the query results in Step 7 as:

```
trainer  num_trainees  gross_sales  AVG(sales_amt)
-------  ------------  -----------  --------------
Bob      5             34000.00     6800.0000
(1 Row(s) affected)
```

Of course, the actual DBMS product will not create and drop actual, physical tables on disk as it works through the query—that would be very expensive in terms of system resources and processing time. The working tables in this tip model the way the DBMS executes a SELECT statement.

If you conceptualize the interim table data as you add WHERE, GROUP BY, and HAVING clauses to your SELECT statements, you will often avoid the frustration of having to say, "Well, it is syntactically correct and it looks right, but it just doesn't give me the results I know I should get!"

88 Using the SELECT Statement to Display Columns from Rows in One or More Tables

The simplest SQL query is a SELECT statement that displays the columns in a single table. For example, if you have a table created by

```
CREATE TABLE customer
  (customer_id  INTEGER PRIMARY KEY,
   first_name   VARCHAR(20),
   last_name    VARCHAR(30),
   address      VARCHAR(50),
   phone_number VARCHAR(20))
```

you can display its contents using the SELECT statement:

```
SELECT * FROM customer
```

The asterisk (*) in the query's SELECT clause tells the DBMS to display all of the columns in the table(s) list in the FROM clause. As you learned in Tip 87, "Understanding the Steps Involved in Processing an SQL SELECT Statement," the syntax of the SELECT statement is:

```
SELECT [ALL | DISTINCT] <select item list>
FROM <table list>
[WHERE <search conditions>]
[GROUP BY <grouping column list>
```

```
    [HAVING <having search conditions>]]
[ORDER BY <sort specification>]
```

Thus, in the current example, the DBMS treats the asterisk (*) in the SELECT clause as if it were the list of all of the columns in the FROM clause table. As such, the SELECT statement in the current example

```
SELECT * FROM customer
```

is equivalent to

```
SELECT customer_id, first_name, last_name, address,
       phone_number
FROM customer
```

If you want to display some (and not all) of the columns in a table, include only the columns you want to display in <select item list> in the query's SELECT clause. For example, if you want to display only the customer's ID, first name, and phone number, use the SELECT statement:

```
SELECT customer_id, first_name, phone_number FROM customer
```

The DBMS will go through the target table named in the FROM clause (CUSTOMER, in the current example) one row at a time. As it reads each row in the input table, the DBMS will take the columns listed in the <select item list> and use them to create a single row in a results table. Thus, the query

```
SELECT customer_id, first_name, last_name FROM customers
```

will produce a results table with four rows in the form:

```
customer_id    first_name    last_name
-----------    ----------    ---------
1              Wally         Cleaver
2              Dolly         Madison
3              Horace        Greely
4              Ben           Stepman
```

All of the column names in the <select item list> must be defined in the table (or tables) listed in the SELECT statement's FROM clause. For example, if you have two tables, CUSTOMERS and ORDERS, created by

```
CREATE TABLE customers
  (cust_id    INTEGER PRIMARY KEY,
   first_name VARCHAR(20)
   last_name  VARCHAR(30))

CREATE TABLE  ORDERS
  (order_number INTEGER PRIMARY KEY,
   order_date   DATETIME,
   cust_id      INTEGER,
   description  VARCHAR(25),
   order_total  MONEY)
```

and you want to query the database for a list of the IDs and names of all of the customers, and the date, description, and total amount of all of their orders, you can use the SELECT statement:

```
SELECT customers.cust_id, first_name, last_name,
       order_date, description, order_total
FROM customers, orders
WHERE customers.cust_id = orders.cust_id
```

Where the column values are unique to each table listed in the FROM clause, the DBMS will know which column value to display from which table—that is, the columns FIRST_NAME and LAST_NAME appear only in the CUSTOMERS table, so the DBMS knows to get the values for the FIRST_NAME and LAST_NAME columns from the CUSTOMERS table when it builds a row in the results table. Similarly, the ORDER_DATE, DESCRIPTION, and ORDER_TOTAL columns appear only in the ORDERS table, so the DBMS knows to retrieve these values from the ORDERS table when it adds them to a row in the results table.

When you want to display the value in columns that have the same name in more than one of the tables listed in the FROM clause, you must use the qualified column name (<table name>.<column name>) to tell the DBMS which table's data to use. In the current example, CUST_ID appears in both the CUSTOMERS and ORDERS tables. As such, to display the value of the CUST_ID column from the CUSTOMERS table, you must type the name of the column as CUSTOMERS.CUST_ID in the query's SELECT clause.

Similarly, if the WHERE clause contains ambiguous column names, you need to use qualified column names in the WHERE clause as well, as is shown by the WHERE clause in the current example.

```
WHERE customers.cust_id = orders.cust_id
```

89 Using the SELECT Statement to Display Column and Computed Values

In addition to using a SELECT statement to display column values, you can use it to display calculated columns and literals. Suppose, for example, that you managed a restaurant and wanted to get a feel for how your patrons felt about the service based on their tips. Since most people tip the customary 15 percent if the service is "okay," you are most interested in tips above and below the customary amount.

Given a sales table created by

```
CREATE TABLE sales
  (emp_id     INTEGER,
   meal_total MONEY,
   tip_rec    MONEY)
```

you can use the SELECT statement

```
SELECT emp_id, meal_total, '* 15% = ',
       meal_total * .15 AS standard_tip, tip_rec,
       tip_rec - (meal_total * .15) AS over_under
FROM sales
ORDER BY over_under
```

to produce a results table in the form:

```
emp_id meal_total              standard_tip tip_rec over_under
------ ---------- ------- ------------ ------- ----------
1       75.3300    * 15% = 11.2995      10.5000 -.799500
2       13.5700    * 15% = 2.0355       1.2500  -.785500
5       89.2500    * 15% = 13.3875      13.5000 .112500
7       110.4800   * 15% = 16.5720      17.2500 .678000
1       125.4400   * 15% = 18.8160      19.7500 .934000
3       271.2200   * 15% = 40.6830      47.5000 6.817000
```

Data items shown in the EMP_ID, MEAL_TOTAL, and TIP_REC columns are examples of using the SELECT statement to display column values (which you learned about in Tip 88, "Using the SELECT Statement to Display Columns from Rows in One or More Tables"). The * 15% = column, meanwhile, shows how you can include a literal string in a SELECT statement to have it displayed as a column value in each row of the SELECT statement's results table.

Note: *Although literal strings can make each row in the results table read more like a sentence, the DBMS treats them as a new column with a constant value (* 15% =, in the current example). This distinction is important when you are passing results table data back to a host program by column position—literal strings in a SELECT statement add new columns that the host program "knows about" and handles appropriately.*

Like the literal (constant) string column (* 15% =), the final two columns in the results table (STANDARD_TIP and OVER_UNDER) do not exist in the SALES table. The value of these columns in each results table row is the result of a computation on another column in the same row.

The example shows that you can both multiply a column value by a constant and use columns in place of all of the operands in mathematical expressions (such as subtraction and multiplication). In short, you can display the results of any mathematical operation or string manipulation function available in your DBMS implementation as a column value in the SELECT statement's results table.

Note: *When using column values in mathematical or string manipulation functions, you must pay careful attention to the column's data type. If you try to perform a mathematical operation (such as division) with a column of type CHAR or VARCHAR, the SELECT statement will fail to execute and the DBMS will display an error message.*

If you need to mix data types, such as appending a numeric column onto a literal string, use one of the type conversion functions available to your DBMS implementation. MS-SQL server, for example, has the STR function for converting numbers to character strings, and the CONVERT function to convert character strings (with only numbers and a plus [+] or minus [–] sign) to numbers.

90 Using the SELECT Statement to Display All Column Values

As a convenience, SQL lets you abbreviate an "all columns" list to use in a SELECT statement with an asterisk (*). The SELECT statement

```
SELECT * FROM <table name>
```

tells the DBMS to list all of the columns and data values in the table named in <table name>. As such, if you have the table created by

```
CREATE TABLE sales
  (emp_id      INTEGER,
   meal_total MONEY,
   tip_rec     MONEY)
```

then the SELECT statement

```
SELECT * FROM sales
```

will yield results in the form:

```
emp_id meal_total tip_rec
------ ---------- -------
1      75.3300    10.5000
2      13.5700    1.2500
5      89.2500    13.5000
7      110.4800   17.2500
1      125.4400   19.7500
3      271.2200   47.5000
```

Although SQL-92 specifies that a SELECT statement can use either the all columns abbreviation (*) or a selection list, but not both, most commercial SQL products let you combine the two. MS-SQL Server, for example, treats the asterisk (*) as another element in the select list. As such, the SELECT statement

```
SELECT *, meal_total * .15 AS expected_tip FROM sales
WHERE NULL = NULL
```

yields the results:

```
emp_id meal_total tip_rec expected_tip
------ ---------- ------- ------------
```

(The NULL = NULL in the WHERE clause is a convenient way to get a column list without displaying data because NULL = NULL always evaluates to FALSE.)

While the all columns list selection is convenient for interactive session, you should avoid using it in programmatic SQL.

When an application sends a query to the DBMS, it expects the results to be returned in a fixed number of columns of specific data types. If the structure of the table is changed by rearranging its columns or by adding a column, the DBMS takes care of the database-related details, but it cannot update the application program. As a result, the program will fail to function because the output from the DBMS is no longer in the exact format in which the program expects to receive it.

Therefore, if you are using a program to submit queries and process results, list the column names instead of using the all columns list selector (*). By listing the columns, you can keep the number of columns and their arrangement in the query results table constant even after changes to the structure of the input table.

91 Using the SELECT Statement with a WHERE Clause to Select Rows Based on Column Values

Although the WHERE clause is optional, most SELECT statements have one. Using SELECT without a WHERE clause is useful for browsing the data in database tables—and little else. If you are gathering information you need for a decision, or if you are producing a report, you normally want to retrieve only *some* of the rows in one or more tables—that is where the WHERE clause comes in.

The WHERE clause lets you specify which of the rows in the input table(s) you want included in the SELECT statement's results table. For example, suppose you want to get a list of all salespeople who are below their quota of sales for the month. You could use the SELECT statement

```
SELECT emp_id, first_name, last_name,
       quota - monthly_sales AS under_by
FROM employees
WHERE department = 'SALES' AND monthly_sales < quota
```

to produce a results table in the form:

```
emp_id  first_name  last_name  under_by
------  ----------  ---------  --------
1       Sally       Fields     6
7       Wally       Wells      9
9       Bret        Maverick   12
```

A WHERE clause consists of the keyword WHERE, followed by the search condition that specifies the rows to be retrieved. In the current example, the WHERE clause specifies that the DBMS is to retrieve those rows in which the value in the DEPARTMENT column is SALES and the value of the MONTHLY_SALES column is less than the value in the QUOTA column.

When processing a SELECT statement with a WHERE clause, the DBMS works its way through the input table, applying the search condition to each row. It substitutes the column values from the table row for the column names in the WHERE clause. In the current example, the DBMS substitutes the value in the DEPARTMENT column for "department" in the WHERE clause, the value in the MONTHLY_SALES column for "monthly_sales," and the value in the table row's QUOTA column for "quota" in the WHERE clause.

After performing the substitutions, the DBMS evaluates the WHERE clause. Rows with column values for which the WHERE clause evaluates TRUE are included in the results table. Those rows whose column values cause the WHERE clause to evaluate FALSE or NULL are excluded from the results table.

As such, you can think of the WHERE clause as a filter. Rows that satisfy the search condition in the WHERE clause pass through the filter. Conversely, rows that do not satisfy the search clause get "stuck" in the filter and are excluded from the results table.

92 Using a SELECT Statement with a WHERE Clause to Select Rows Based on a Computed Value

In addition to selecting rows by comparing column values to a literal string or number (as you learned to do in Tip 91, "Using the SELECT Statement with a WHERE Clause to Select Rows Based on Column Values"), you can also use a WHERE clause to select rows by comparing column contents to computed values. As you've learned, the general format of a SELECT statement with a WHERE clause is:

```
SELECT <column list> FROM <table name>
WHERE <search condition>
```

As such, to SELECT columns based on a computed value, simply use the computed value in the WHERE clause in search condition. For example, to list all salespeople whose sales are 20 percent or more below quota, you can use a SELECT statement similar to:

```
SELECT emp_id, first_name, last_name,
       quota - monthly_sales AS under_by
FROM employees
WHERE department = 'SALES'
AND monthly_sales < (quota * .80)
```

When formulating search conditions with computed values, you are not limited to performing mathematical operations on the columns in a single table. In fact, you can base the selection on a computed value using columns from different tables. Suppose, for example, that you want a list of customers who have exceeded their credit limit, and you have INVOICES and CUSTOMERS tables created by:

```
CREATE customers
  (customer_id  INTEGER PRIMARY KEY,
   first_name   VARCHAR(25),
   last_name    VARCHAR(30),
   credit_limit MONEY)

CREATE invoices
  (invoice_number INTEGER PRIMARY KEY,
   ordered_by     INTEGER,
   invoice_total  MONEY,
   total_paid     MONEY)
```

You can use the SELECT statement

```
SELECT customer_id, first_name, last_name, credit_limit
FROM customers, invoices
WHERE ordered_by = customer_id
AND credit_limit < (SELECT SUM(invoice_total - total_paid)
                    FROM invoices
                    WHERE ordered_by = customer_id)
```

to select customers who are currently over their credit limit.

In short, you can use a computed value in a WHERE clause as you would any other constant (literal string or number) or column value. The only restriction on using column values is that column names used to generate a computed value in a WHERE clause must appear in one of the tables named in the SELECT statement's FROM clause.

93 Using a SELECT Statement with a Comparison Predicate to Select Rows with Specific Column or Computed Values

You already learned how to use two of the six comparison operators to select rows when you used the equal to (=) and less than (<) comparison tests to select rows in Tip 91, "Using the SELECT Statement with a WHERE Clause to Select Rows Based on Column Values" and Tip 92, "Using a SELECT Statement with a WHERE Clause to Select Rows Based on a Computed Value." Table 93.1 lists the six SQL comparison operators. (There are seven entries in the table because some DBMS implementations use alternate forms for the "Not equal to" operator.)

Symbol	Meaning
=	Equal to
<>	Not equal to
!=	Not equal to
>	Greater than
<	Less than
>=	Greater than or equal to
<=	Less than or equal to

Table 93.1 SQL Comparison Operators

Note: *Table 93.1 includes only symbols that serve as operators. However, if you consider only the actions of a comparison operator, you could include the keyword LIKE to the list. As you will learn in Tip 261, "Using LIKE and NOT LIKE to Compare Two Character Strings," the LIKE keyword acts as a comparison operator when comparing character strings.*

The equal (=) comparison operator retrieves rows in which a column is equal to a specific value or another column. For example, if active employees have an A in the status column, you could use

```
SELECT * FROM employees WHERE status = 'A'
```

to display all columns for active employee rows in the EMPLOYEES table.

Use the not equal to (<>) comparison operator to retrieve all rows except those that contain a specific value. For example, to display student information for all students except seniors, you might use the select statement:

```
SELECT * FROM students WHERE class <> 'Senior'
```

You can use the greater than (>) comparison operator to display rows in which the value of a column is more than that specified to the right of the operator. For example, if you want to list citations in which the driver was traveling more than 50 percent over the speed limit, you could use a SELECT statement similar to:

```
SELECT *, (speed - posted_limit) AS mph_over_limit
FROM citation WHERE speed > 1.5 * posted_limit
```

To list those rows where a column value is less than a specific value, use the less than (<) comparison operator. For example, to list the department number and budget of those departments that have spent less than their allotted budgets for the current year, you could use the statement:

```
SELECT dept_no, budget, total_spent,
        budget - total_spent AS remaining
FROM dept_financials WHERE total_spent < budget
```

The greater than or equal to (>=) operator will return those rows with a column value at least as great as that listed in the WHERE clause. For example, to give the basketball recruiter a list of all seniors that are at least 6 feet, 6 inches tall (78 inches), you could use the SELECT statement:

```
SELECT student_id, first_name, last_name
FROM students WHERE class = 'Senior' AND height >= 78
```

Use the less than or equal to (<=) operator to select rows where a column's value is at most equal to that given in the WHERE clause. For example, suppose you want to give out "good attendance" awards to students who have never been absent and who have at most two tardies. You could use the SELECT statement:

```
SELECT student_id, first_name, last_name
FROM students WHERE absent_count = 0 AND late_count <= 2
```

***Note:** Although the examples in this tip used numeric values with the comparison operators >=, <=, >, and <, you can use them to compare literal strings as well. For example to display an alphabetical listing of all employees with last names greater than or equal to King, you could use the SELECT statement:*

```
SELECT employee_id, last_name
FROM employees WHERE last_name >= 'King' ORDER BY last_name
```

When performing a comparison operation on a column of type CHAR (or VARCHAR), the DBMS converts each letter in the strings to its binary representation. The DBMS then compares the bit strings to see which is greater. The binary value for the K (in King), for example, would be greater than the binary value of a name starting with J (and any letter appearing in the alphabet prior to J). As such, only names beginning with K through Z would appear in the list of employees.

If the first two letters of each string are the same, the DBMS compares the binary value of the next two letters, and then the next two until there are either no more letters to compare (in which case the strings are equal) or until a letter in one string has a different binary value than the letter in the other string (in which case one string will be either greater than or less than the other). (The case where one string is longer than the other is covered by the binary value of a letter from one string [a nonzero value] being compared to a different letter in a second string [the blank character whose binary value is less than all letters and numbers].)

94 Using Boolean Operators OR, AND, and NOT in a WHERE Clause

Boolean operators let you select rows using multiple search conditions in a single WHERE clause. When you want to select rows that satisfy any one of several search conditions, use an OR operator to combine the clauses into a compound search condition. Conversely, when you want to select rows that satisfy *all* of several search conditions, use an AND to combine search conditions in the WHERE clause. Finally, use the NOT operator to introduce a search condition in the WHERE clause when you want the DBMS to return rows that *do not* satisfy its criteria.

The general form of a SELECT statement including Boolean operator is:

```
SELECT <select item list> FROM <table name>
WHERE [NOT] <search condition>
  [<comparison operator>  [NOT] < search condition>]...
  [<last comparison operator> [NOT]
      <last search condition>]
```

Suppose, for example, that you are shopping for a car and would find any one of several models acceptable. You could use the SELECT statement

```
SELECT year, make, model, cost FROM auto_inventory
WHERE make = 'Jaguar' OR make = 'BMW' OR make = 'Corvette'
```

to return a list of Jaguars, BMWs, and Corvettes in the AUTO_INVENTORY table. The OR operators used to combine the search conditions in the WHERE clause tell the DBMS to display the columns in the selection list for each row where *any* one (or more) of the search conditions evaluates to TRUE.

Use the AND operator to combine search conditions in a WHERE clause, if you want the DBMS to display only rows in which *all* (vs. any, for the OR operator) of the search conditions are TRUE. As such, the SELECT statement

```
SELECT year, make, model, cost FROM auto_inventory
WHERE make = 'Corvette' AND year > 1990 AND color = 'Red'
```

tells the DBMS you are interested only in rows where the MAKE column has the value Corvette, the YEAR column has a value greater than 1990, and the COLOR column has the value Red. If any one (or more) of the search conditions evaluates to FALSE, the DBMS excludes the row from the results table. Said another way, the AND operator tells the DBMS to include a row in the results table only when *all* of the search conditions in the WHERE clause evaluate to TRUE.

The NOT operator lets you select rows based on values *not* found in their columns. Suppose, for example, that your son or daughter just turned 16 and will accept any car, as long as the cost to insure it is *not* more than $2,000 per year. To get a list of acceptable vehicles from the AUTO_INVENTORY table, you could use the select statement:

```
SELECT year, make, model, cost FROM auto_inventory
WHERE NOT cost_to_insure > 2000
```

Although the previous examples used a single type of Boolean operator in each WHERE clause, you can combine multiple, different Boolean operators in the same WHERE clause. For example, suppose that you will accept any Jaguar with a model year after 1998, or any Corvette, or any BMW, as long it is not blue. You could use the SELECT statement:

```
SELECT year, color, make, model, cost FROM auto_inventory
WHERE (make = 'Jaguar' AND year > 1998) OR
      (make = 'Corvette') OR
      (make = 'BMW' AND NOT color = 'blue')
```

Note: *You can normally replace the comparison operator in a search condition instead of using a negated search condition—a search condition introduced by the NOT operator. For example, if your search condition reads "not less than," you could simply use the greater than or equal to (>=) operator. Similarly, if the search condition reads "not greater than," use the less than or equal to (<=) operator instead. The main reason for using the NOT operator is if you feel that it is visually easier to understand than the equivalent comparison operator. Someone not used to mathematical symbols or working with sets may not be familiar with the not equal to (<> or !=) operator and would find a WHERE clause in the form*

```
WHERE NOT <column name> = <value>
```

easier to read than

```
WHERE <column name> != <value>
```

or

```
WHERE <column name> <> <value>
```

---

95 Using the ORDER BY Clause to Specify the Order of Rows Returned by a SELECT Statement

When the SELECT statement builds the results table in answer to a query, it does not arrange the rows displayed in any particular order. Normally, the DBMS displays query result in the order in which the selected rows were inserted into the input table. For efficiency, some DBMS products will use one of the indexes when reading through the rows in the input table. As such, the results table's rows may be arranged as they appear in the index used to traverse the input table.

If you want to control the order in which rows appear in the results table, add the ORDER BY clause to the SELECT statement.

The general form of a SELECT statement including an ORDER BY clause is:

```
SELECT <select item list> FROM <table name>
[WHERE <search condition>]
ORDER BY <sort specification>

where <sort specification> is defined as:

<column name | column number> [ASC | DESC]
   [,...<last column name | last column number>
     [ASC | DESC]}
```

You can use any of the columns from the <select item list> as part of the <sort specification>.

Suppose, for example, that you want to list student grades from lowest to highest. You could use a SELECT statement similar to

```
SELECT student_id, last_name, first_name, grade_received
FROM students
ORDER BY grade_received
```

that will yield a results table in the form:

```
student_id  last_name  first_name  grade_received
----------  ---------  ----------  --------------
1           Smith      Sally       65
8           Wells      Wally       70
9           Luema      Albert      75
12          Luema      Abner       75
90          Davis      Scott       96
```

If you omit the keywords ASC (ascending order) and DESC (descending order) from the sort specification, the DBMS will sort the rows in the results table in ascending order. As such, in the current example, the DBMS sorted the rows in the results table in ascending order based on the values stored in the GRADE_RECEIVED column.

To sort the results table by more than one column, simply include all of the columns you want to use for the sort in the <sort specification>. (Remember, the only restriction on the columns listed in the <sort specification> is that they must all appear as column names in the SELECT statement's <select item list>.)

Therefore, to sort the list of grades in descending order by GRADE_RECEIVED, then in ascending order by name, and finally in ascending order by STUDENT_ID, you could use the SELECT statement

```
SELECT student_id, last_name, first_name, grade_received
FROM students
ORDER BY grade_received DESC, last_name ASC, first_name,
         student_id
```

which will yield a results table in the form:

```
student_id  last_name  first_name  grade_received
----------  ---------  ----------  --------------
90          Davis      Scott       96
12          Luema      Abner       75
9           Luema      Albert      75
8           Wells      Wally       70
1           Smith      Sally       65
```

The second and subsequent columns listed in the ORDER BY clause act as "tie-breakers." If (as is the case in the current example) two rows have the same value in the first column listed in the ORDER BY clause (a 75 for GRADE_RECEIVED, in the current example), the DBMS will decide which of the two rows to display first by comparing the values in the column listed second in the ORDERED BY clause. If the second column is also identical (as is the case in the current example—both LAST_NAME columns have the value Luema), the DBMS will compare the values in the third column listed in the ORDER BY clause, and so on.

Notice that you can mix ascending and descending sort orders within the same ORDERED BY clause. Obviously, a single column must be arranged either in ascending or descending order—and not both. However, as is the case in the current example, if you list multiple columns in the ORDER BY clause, each of them can be displayed in either ascending (ASC) or descending (DESC) order without regard to the order (ASC or DESC) of the other columns in the clause.

In addition to using column names in the ORDER BY clause, you can refer to the <select item list> items by number. For example, to sort the results in the results table of the previous example by GRADE_RECEIVED, LAST_NAME, FIRST_NAME, and STUDENT_ID, you could have used the ORDER BY clause in the SELECT statement

```
SELECT student_id, last_name, first_name, grade_received
FROM students
ORDER BY 4 DESC, 2, 3, 1
```

instead of:

```
SELECT student_id, last_name, first_name, grade_received
FROM   students
```

```
ORDER BY grade_received DESC, last_name ASC, first_name,
         student_id
```

The number of the column in the ORDER BY clause is determined by its position in the <select item list>, not its position in the input table. As such, in the current example, you would refer to the GRADE_RECEIVED, the fourth item in the <select item list>, as column 4, whether GRADE_RECEIVED is defined as the first, tenth, or fiftieth column in the STUDENTS table.

You would use the column number in place of the column name in the ORDER BY clause when you want to sort by a computed column that does not exist in the input table and does not have a column name. For example, to display the list of salespeople in the EMPLOYEES table in order by the number of sales by which they exceeded (or missed) quota, you could use a SELECT statement similar to:

```
SELECT employee_id, first_name, last_name, quota,
       sales, sales - quota
FROM employees
ORDER BY 6 DESC, last_name, first_name, employee_id
```

The DBMS would return a results table in the form:

```
emp_id  first_name  last_name  quota  sales
------  ----------  ---------  -----  -----
1       Sally       Fields     3      7      4
7       Wally       Wells      8      9      1
9       Bret        Maverick   7      5      -2
```

Note: *If you add an AS clause to the sales-quota item in the select item list, you can use the name you give to the computed column in the ORDERED BY clause. For example, if you execute the select statement (that titles the SALES–QUOTA computed value as over_under)*

```
SELECT employee_id, first_name, last_name, quota,
       sales, sales - quota AS over_under
FROM employees
ORDER BY over_under DESC, last_name, first_name,
         employee_id
```

the DBMS will display the results table:

```
emp_id  first_name  last_name  quota  sales  over_under
------  ----------  ---------  -----  -----  ----------
1       Sally       Fields     3      7      4
7       Wally       Wells      8      9      1
9       Bret        Maverick   7      5      -2
```

Notice that the results table is still in the same order as before, but the computed column at the end of each row, now has a label: over_under.

96 Using Compound Conditions (AND, OR, and NOT) in a WHERE Clause to Select Rows Based on Multiple Column Values (or Computed Values)

Boolean operators AND and OR let you combine multiple, individual search conditions in a WHERE clause to form a compound search condition. The NOT operator, meanwhile, lets you negate the result of evaluating a search condition to tell the DBMS to select rows in which the search condition is FALSE (*not* TRUE).

Use the OR operator to combine search conditions when more than one may be TRUE but only one must be TRUE in order to SELECT the row for inclusion in the results table. For example, to generate a table of golfers eligible for the U.S. Open golf tournament, you could use the SELECT statement

```
SELECT first_name, last_name FROM golfers
WHERE previous_us_open_winner = 'Y' OR
      PGA_tournaments_won > 1 OR
      qual_school_ranking <= 10
```

to allow a golfer to play if the golfer were a previous U.S. Open winner *or* if the golfer won one of the other PGA tournaments, *or* if the golfer finished in the top 10 of the qualifying school.

When evaluating a compound search condition, the DBMS evaluates each individual search condition and then performs Boolean math to determine whether the overall WHERE clause evaluates to TRUE or FALSE. Thus, in the current example, the DBMS will evaluate each of the three search conditions (PREVIOUS_US_OPEN_WINNER='Y', PGA_TOURNAMENTS_WON > 1, and QUAL_SCHOOL_RANKING <= 10) and then use the OR Truth Table shown in Table 96.1 to determine whether the SELECT statement's WHERE clause is TRUE or FALSE.

OR	TRUE	FALSE	NULL
TRUE	TRUE	TRUE	TRUE
FALSE	TRUE	FALSE	NULL
NULL	TRUE	NULL	NULL

Table 96.1 OR Truth Table

(If the WHERE clause evaluates to TRUE, the DBMS includes the <select item list> values from the current row in the results table; if the WHERE clause evaluates to FALSE or NULL, the DBMS excludes the values.)

The AND operator lets you form a compound search condition by requiring that all of the individual search conditions listed in the WHERE clause be TRUE in order for the overall

WHERE clause to evaluate TRUE. For example, if you require that salespeople who have sold more than $75,000 in goods and services have a cancellation rate below 10 percent and make more than 30 sales in order to be eligible for a bonus, you can use the SELECT statement

```
SELECT employee_id, first_name, last_name, '$200' AS bonus
FROM employees
WHERE department = 'Sales' AND
      gross_sales > 75000 AND
      (cancellations / sales) < .1 AND
      sales > 30
```

to generate the bonus eligibility table.

As was the case with the OR operator, the DBMS will evaluate the individual search conditions (there are four in the current example) and then use the AND Truth Table shown in Table 96.2 to determine whether the WHERE clause is TRUE or FALSE.

AND	**TRUE**	**FALSE**	**NULL**
TRUE	TRUE	FALSE	NULL
FALSE	FALSE	FALSE	FALSE
NULL	NULL	FALSE	NULL

Table 96.2 AND Truth Table

(If the WHERE clause evaluates to TRUE, the DBMS includes the <select item list> values from the current row in the results table; if the WHERE clause evaluates FALSE or NULL, the DBMS excludes the values.)

Finally, you can use the NOT operator to negate the Boolean (TRUE or FALSE) value of a search condition. For example, if you wanted to get a list of salespeople who either did not have gross sales of more than $75,000 or did not have more than 30 sales, you could use the SELECT statement:

```
SELECT employee_id, first_name, last_name, gross_sales,
       sales
FROM employees
WHERE department = 'Sales' AND
      ((NOT gross_sales > 75000) OR
       (NOT sales > 30))
```

When determining the negated value of a search condition, the DBMS uses the logic given in the NOT Truth Table shown in Table 96.3.

NOT	**TRUE**	**FALSE**	**NULL**
	FALSE	TRUE	NULL

Table 96.3 NOT Truth Table

97 Understanding NULL Value Conditions When Selecting Rows Using Comparison Predicates

When writing a search condition, be sure to take into account the handling of NULL values. Since the results table will include only those rows for which a search condition is TRUE, some table rows will remain "hidden" even if you display the rows that satisfy the search criteria and then display the rows that satisfy the negated search criteria.

Suppose, for example, that you have an employees table with the following values:

```
first_name  last_name   sales  quota
----------  ---------   -----  -----
Sally       Fields      8      5
Wally       Wells       4      10
Sue         Smith       10     NULL
Kelly       Sutherland  7      7
```

The SELECT statement

```
SELECT first_name FROM employees WHERE sales < quota
```

would produce a results table with one name: Wally.

Conversely, the SELECT statement

```
SELECT first_name FROM employees WHERE sales >= quota
```

would produce a results table with two names: Sally and Kelly.

By adding the rows in the two results tables (employees with sales below quota and employees with sales equal to or above quota), you might come to the mistaken conclusion that there are three employees in the EMPLOYEES table, when there are, in fact, four.

The reason that one employee remains "hidden" from view is that no matter which of the comparison operators (=, >, <, <>, >=, <=) you use, if one of the columns being compared is NULL, the value of the entire expression will be NULL. As such, the row will be excluded from the results table because the results table includes rows for which the search condition evaluates TRUE—FALSE and NULL (unknown) valuations are excluded. Thus, in the current example, employee Sue will never show up in the results table generated from a search condition using a comparison operator with the quota column (which is NULL for Sue) as an operand.

Even the SELECT statement

```
SELECT first_name FROM employees WHERE quota = NULL
```

will produce a results table with zero rows! (If any operand in an expression using a comparison operator is NULL, the DBMS evaluates the overall expression as NULL and excludes the row in question from the results table.)

Note: To get a list of rows in which the value of a search condition is NULL, use the NULL value test IS NULL. As such, to get a list of employees with a NULL value in the QUOTA column, you could use the SELECT statement:

```
SELECT first_name FROM employees WHERE quota IS NULL
```

98 Using Row Value Expressions to Select Rows in a Table Based on Multiple Column Values

A row value constructor, as the name implies, is a list of literal values and expressions that, taken together, give the values for the columns in a single row in a table. You learned about row value constructors when you used them in INSERT statements to add rows to tables in Tip 67, "Using the INSERT Statement to Add Rows to a Table."

Similar to the row value constructor used in an INSERT statement, the row value constructor in a SELECT statement specifies the values in a row's columns. However, unlike the INSERT statement's row value constructor, the row value constructor in a SELECT statement is not used to add a row to a table. Rather, the row value constructor in a SELECT statement's WHERE clause is used to specify the value a row's columns must have in order for the row to be included in the SELECT statement's results table.

For example, to display active employees in the sales department, you could use a SELECT statement similar to:

```
SELECT employee_id, first_name, last_name, gross_sales
FROM employees
WHERE (status, department) = ('Active', 'Sales')
```

To process a select statement with a row value constructor, the DBMS goes through the input table one row at a time, substituting the value of each column named in the row value constructor for its column name on the left side of the equals (=) sign. The DBMS constructs a row from the substituted column values on the left side of the equals (=) sign and compares it to a row constructed from the literal values (or expressions) given in the value list on the right side of the row value constructor's equals (=) sign.

The comparison is accomplished by comparing each pair of columns in the two rows—that is, the first value in the list on the left side of the equals (=) sign is "paired" with and compared to the first value in the list on the right side of the equals (=) sign. The second value on the left side is compared to the second value on the right side, and so on.

A row value comparison for equality (such as that shown in the current example) is TRUE only if each of the "paired" columns has the same value.

Note: *Not all DBMS products support row value expressions in a SELECT statement's WHERE clause. If your DBMS does not, you can rewrite the row value expression using a WHERE clause with a compound search condition. For example, the SELECT statement in the current example can be rewritten as:*

```
SELECT employee_id, first_name, last_name, gross_sales
FROM employees
WHERE status = 'Active' AND department = 'Sales'
```

As you learned in this tip, each column value in the row value constructor in the value list on the left side of the equals sign is paired with and compared to each literal value or expression in the value list on the right side of the equals sign. As such, you can reconstruct the row value equality as a set of "paired" column-to-value equality search conditions combined with the AND operator, since *all* (and not some) of the search conditions must evaluate TRUE in order for the WHERE clause to evaluate TRUE.

99 Understanding Subqueries

A subquery is a SELECT statement within a SELECT statement and is often referred to as either an inner query or an inner SELECT statement. Conversely, the SELECT statement that contains the subquery is called the outer query, outer SELECT, or main SELECT statement.

Subqueries are most often used in a SELECT statement's WHERE clause to generate a single-column virtual table that the main SELECT statement will use in determining which of the input table's rows to include in the results table. Suppose, for example, that you want a list of all products in the PRODUCTS table where quantity on unshipped orders in the ORDERS table is greater than the amount currently in stock.

You can use a SELECT statement in the form

```
SELECT product_id, description, qty_in_stock FROM products
WHERE qty_in_stock < "total to ship"
```

to generate the list of back-ordered items once you know the value of the total to ship.

A query in the form

```
SELECT SUM(quantity) FROM orders
WHERE orders.item_number = "item to total" AND
      date_shipped IS NULL)
```

will return the quantity due to be shipped for each item whose item number you substitute for the item to total (given that unshipped orders have a NULL value in the DATE_SHIPPED column).

Adding the second SELECT statement as a subquery to the first, you get:

```
SELECT product_id, description, qty_in_stock FROM products
WHERE qty_in_stock < (SELECT SUM(quantity)
                      FROM orders
                      WHERE orders.item_number =
                              products.product_id AND
                            date_shipped IS NULL)
```

When executing the new SELECT statement with a subquery, the DBMS goes through each row in the PRODUCTS table and executes the subquery to determine the quantity of the product due to be shipped. Each subquery execution produces a virtual table containing a single value that the DBMS compares to the quantity of QTY_IN_STOCK. Whenever the quantity in stock (QTY_IN_STOCK) is less than the quantity due to be shipped (as returned by the subquery), the DBMS will include the values from the PRODUCT_ID, DESCRIPTION, and QTY_IN_STOCK columns of the current row of the PRODUCTS table in the results table.

The syntax of a subquery is:

```
(SELECT [ALL | DISTINCT] <select item list>
 FROM <table list>
 [WHERE <search condition>]
 [GROUP BY <group item list>
    [HAVING <group by search condition>]])
```

Thus, other than being enclosed in parenthesis (()), a subquery looks (and functions) exactly like any other SELECT statement. There are, however, a few rules a SELECT statement used as a subquery must follow:

- If the subquery is to provide a value to a comparison operator (=, <>, >, >=, <, <=) in a WHERE clause, the subquery most return a single value—that is, the subquery's results table must consist of a single column with at most one row. (A subquery with no rows evaluates to 0, vs. an error condition.)
- If the subquery is introduced by the keywords IN or NOT IN, the subquery must return a results table of one column; however, the results table may have more than one row.
- The subquery cannot have an ORDER BY clause. (Since the subquery results table is not displayed to the user and is used as the input table for its outer SELECT statement instead, ordering the rows in the subquery's results table is of no practical value.)
- Column names appearing in a subquery must be defined either in the tables listed in the subquery's FROM clause or in the tables listed in the outer SELECT statement's FROM.
- In most DBMS implementations, a subquery can consist of only a single SELECT statement and cannot consist of the UNION of several SELECT statements.

In this tip, you learned how to use a subquery to generate a (virtual) table of values that the DBMS used as the search criteria in the main SELECT statement's WHERE clause. Tip 336,

"Understanding the Role of Subqueries in a HAVING Clause," will show you how to use a subquery to generate the filter values in a SELECT statement's HAVING clause.

100 Using Row Value Subqueries to Select Rows in a Table Based on Multiple Column Values

Row value subqueries are inner SELECT statements whose results tables (like the row value expressions you learned about in Tip 98, "Using Row Value Expressions to Select Rows in a Table Based on Multiple Column Values") consist of more than one column. In Tip 99, "Understanding Subqueries," you learned that one of the restrictions on a subquery used to provide a value to a comparison operator is that it must return a single column. However, this is true only because the majority of DBMS products do not support SQL-92 row value expressions.

One of the row value operations included in the SQL-92 standard is a row value comparison. If your DBMS supports row value comparisons, a subquery can return multiple columns of data that the DBMS will compare to the values in a row value constructor.

Suppose, for example, that you want a list of customer IDs from people who purchased the highest-priced car in your automobile inventory. You first need to submit a query such as

```
SELECT manufacturer, make, model FROM auto_inventory
WHERE sticker_price = (SELECT MAX (sticker_price)
                       FROM auto_inventory)
```

to determine the manufacturer, make, and model of the highest-priced car in the inventory. Then have the DBMS compare the MANUFACTURER, MAKE, and MODEL of each car purchased to the MANUFACTURER, MAKE, and MODEL of the highest-priced car, include the example SELECT statement as the subquery in the SELECT statement:

```
SELECT customer_id, order_date, price_paid
FROM auto_purchases
WHERE (manufacturer, make, model) =
      (SELECT manufacturer, make, model FROM auto_inventory
       WHERE sticker_price = (SELECT MAX (sticker_price)
                              FROM auto_inventory))
```

In the current example, the right side of the equals (=) sign in the WHERE clause contains a subquery that, when executed, will return three columns: the MANUFACTURER, MAKE, and MODEL of the highest-priced car in the automobile inventory. By comparing the subquery's results to the values in the row value constructor on the left side of the equals (=) sign, the DBMS can decide whether or not to include the CUSTOMER_ID, ORDER_DATE, and PRICE_DATE values from the AUTO_PURCHASES (input) table in the outer query's results table.

If the column values returned by the subquery on the right side of the equals (=) sign are equal to the column values in the row value constructer on the left side of the equals (=) sign, the DBMS will include the CUSTOMER_ID, ORDER_DATE, and PRICE_PAID from the current row of the AUTO_PURCHASES table in the SELECT statement's results table.

If your DBMS does not support row value constructors as operands in a comparison, you can break the multiple-column comparison down into single-column search conditions joined by AND operators. In the current example, you can rewrite the SELECT statement with a row value subquery as the SELECT statement:

```
SELECT customer_id, order_date, price_paid
FROM auto_purchases
WHERE manufacturer = (SELECT DISTINCT manufacturer
                      FROM auto_inventory
                      WHERE sticker_price =
                           (SELECT MAX (sticker_price)
                            FROM auto_inventory))
AND make = (SELECT DISTINCT make FROM auto_inventory
             WHERE sticker_price =
                  (SELECT MAX (sticker_price)
                   FROM auto_inventory))
AND model = (SELECT DISTINCT model FROM auto_inventory
              WHERE sticker_price =
                   (SELECT MAX (sticker_price)
                    FROM auto_inventory))
```

The query in this example uses three *scalar* subqueries to produce the same results table as that produced by the previous SELECT statement, which used a single row value constructor to make the same query.

Note: *A "scalar" subquery is one that returns a single value (that is, the subquery's results table consists of a single column and, at most, a single row). If the scalar query's results table has no rows, then its value is 0. The current example assumes that the maximum sticker price of each car is unique by manufacturer, make, and model. If more than one model, for example, has a sticker price equal to the maximum sticker price, the SELECT DISTINCT MODEL subquery will no longer return a scalar value, and the SELECT statement will fail to execute.*

Comparing the length and structure of the last two SELECT statements in the current example, you can see that the SELECT statement with the row value subquery is more compact and easier to understand because it more closely follows the English-language description of the query.

101 Understanding Expressions

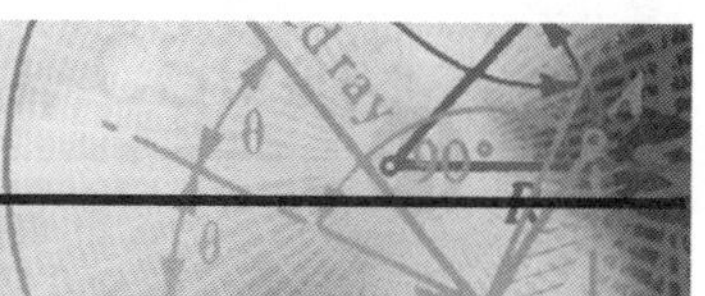

The SQL-92 standard defines four arithmetic operators you can use in expressions: addition (+), subtraction (–), multiplication (*), and division (/). Additionally, SQL-92 lets you use parenthesis (( )) to combine operators and operands into complex expressions.

The order or precedence for mathematical operations is familiar: multiplication and division in the order in which they are found, and then addition and subtraction in the order in which they occur. Thus, to evaluate the expression: A + B / C – D * E, the DBMS would:

1. Divide B by C
2. Multiply D by E
3. Add the result of Step 1 to A
4. Subtract the result of 2 to the result of Step 3

Reading the equation in the example from left to right, you might think the DBMS would add A to B first and then divide the sum by C. However, the mathematical order of precedence dictates that the division and multiplication operations be performed first, followed by the addition and subtraction operations.

If you want to change the order of the operations or make an expression easier to read, use parenthesis to group its operations. For example, if you rewrite the expression A + B / C – D * E as A + (B / C) – (D * E), it is easier to see which operands and results will be affected by which mathematical operations. Moreover, if you want to change the order of operations so they occur from left to right (as you would read them), rewrite the expression as ((A + B) / C – D) * E.

In SQL, expressions serve three main functions:

- To calculate values to be returned in a SELECT statement's results table. For example, to list employees and the revenues they generate per hour they work and per dollar they are paid, you could use the SELECT statement:

```
SELECT employee_id, first_name, last_name, gross_sales,
       gross_sales/ hours AS revenues_per_hour,
       gross_sales / amount_paid AS
          revenues_per_dollar_paid
FROM employees
```

- To calculate values used in search criteria. For example, to display those employees whose sales are more than 50 percent below quota, you could use the SELECT statement:

```
SELECT employee_id, first_name, last_name, quota, sales
FROM employees WHERE sales < .50 * quota
```

- To calculate values used to update data values in a table. For example, to increase the sales quota for all senior reps by 25 percent, you could use the UPDATE statement:

```
UPDATE employees SET quota = quota * .25
WHERE department = 'Marketing' and status = 'Senior'
```

Note: *Although SQL-92 specifies only four mathematical operators, your DBMS will most likely include trigonometric functions (SIN, COS, TAN, and so on), and other operators such as exponentiation, rounding, square roots, and so on. Check your system documentation for the full list of mathematical operations your DBMS supports.*

102 Understanding Numeric Value Expressions

Numeric value expressions are expressions that apply one of the four SQL standard arithmetic operators (+, – , /, *) or additional (implementation-specific) operators and functions to produce a numeric results. To be a numeric expression, the operands and result must be numeric.

Individual operands in a numeric expression may be of different numeric data types. As such, you can mix numeric literals (integers and real numbers) and columns of any of the numeric data types (INT, SMALLINT, NUMERIC, DOUBLE PRECISION, REAL, and so on) in a single expression. The SQL-92 standard does not specify the data type that results from the various combinations of operand data types. As such, you will need to check your system manual to determine whether you get a real number or an integer when multiplying a real number by an integer, for example.

Examples of numeric expressions include:

```
-37.89
378.95 + 458.3 - 37.9
(59.6 * 10) / (58.3 / 4)
quota * .10
gross_sales - costs
```

103 Understanding String Value Expressions

A string value expression is one in which all of the operands are either literal character strings or SQL objects such as columns of data type CHARACTER, CAST expressions, CASE expressions, set functions, or scalar subqueries that return a result of type CHARACTER. SQL-92 defines only a single operator for use in a string value expression—concatenation, which lets you combine two character string operands into a single character string result. The concatenation operator attaches the characters in a second character string to the end of the characters in the first string.

Note: *Your DBMS product may include additional data types that are equivalent to data type CHARACTER and can therefore be used as operands in string value expressions. MS-SQL Server, for example, lets you abbreviate the data type CHARACTER as CHAR and includes a variable-length CHARACTER string type named VARCHAR. Check your system documentation for a list of the string (CHARACTER) data types available to your DBMS.*

Thus, SQL-92 defines a string value expression as one or more operands of a character string data type concatenated together to produce a result that is also a character string. The simplest string value expression is a single string. More complex string value expressions involve concatenating operands of data type character using the concatenation operand—either a pair of vertical lines (||) or the plus (+) sign in some DBMS implementations.

Examples of string value expressions include:

```
'City'
'Peanut butter ' || 'and Jelly'
'Time' + 'shares'
first_name || ' ' || last_name
```

Note: *Although SQL-92 specifies concatenation as the only operation available for string value expressions, your DBMS product will most likely have additional functions and operators you can use for string manipulation. As an example, Table 103.1 lists some of the string functions provide by MS-SQL Server.*

String Function	***Description***
LOWER	Converts uppercase letters in a string to lower case
UPPER	Converts lowercase letters in a string to upper case
LTRIM	Removes leading spaces from a string
RTRIM	Removes trailing spaces from a string
CHARINDEX	Returns the starting position of the first character of one string in another
STR	Converts numeric data to a character string
STUFF	Inserts one character string into another
SUBSTRING	Returns a part of a character string

Table 103.1 Example MS-SQL Server String Manipulation Functions

Check your system documentation for the string manipulation functions available to your DBMS.

104 Understanding Datetime Value Expressions

Use datetime value expressions to work with operands of type DATE, TIME, TIMESTAMP, or INTERVAL to produce a result that is also of one of the datetime data types (DATE, TIME, or TIMESTAMP).

Before working with datetime data objects, you will need to determine the proper data type names used by your DBMS implementation. MS-SQL Server, for example, uses TIMESTAMP to data type a column you want the DBMS to update with the current system date and time each time a row is inserted into the table. Conversely, DATETIME is MS-SQL Server's solitary datetime data type, and consists of the date and time elements defined for the SQL-92 standard TIMESTAMP data type. Thus, while some DBMS implementations let you define datetime objects as data type DATE, TIME, or TIMESTAMP, MS-SQL Server reserves the TIMESTAMP keyword for "other" purposes (not to define objects you can use in datetime value expressions) and has only the single DATETIME data type for use in defining all columns that will hold either dates or times, or both dates and times.

In addition to unique datetime types, each vendor's DBMS product has unique functions you can use in datetime value expressions. The only rules that all must (and do) follow is that the functions in a datetime expression must accept operands that are either an interval (integer value) or one of the datetime data types, and evaluating the datetime value expression must yield a result of type datetime.

MS-SQL Server datetime expressions include:

```
'06/09/2000'
'06/09/2000 14:52:52'
start_date + 7
DATENAME(weekday, start_date)
DATEDIFF(stop_date, start_date)
GETDATE()
DATEPART(day,(GETDATE())
```

The bottom line is that you must check your system documentation to see which datetime data types and functions are available for datetime value expressions in your DBMS.

105 Understanding SQL Predicates

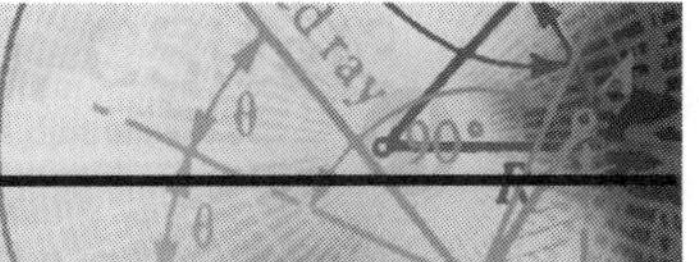

The ANSI/ISO standard refers to search conditions as predicates. As such, you already know what predicates are and how to use them since you've seen predicates in tip examples with SQL statements that have a WHERE clause.

For example, the SELECT statement

```
SELECT student_id, first_name, last_name FROM students
WHERE gpa = 4.0
```

uses the comparison predicate gpa = 40 to tell the DBMS to "filter out" or SELECT those rows in the STUDENTS table that have a value of 4.0 in the GPA column.

Predicates are the portion of the WHERE clause (or search condition) that describes the data values of interest to the DBMS. Because SQL is a data sublanguage designed to let you describe the data you want but not how to retrieve and store it, you will find SQL predicates (which describe data to the DBMS) in almost all SELECT, UPDATE, and DELETE statements.

There are seven basic SQL predicate classes:

- Comparison predicates (=, <>, >, >=, <, <=), used to compare the value of two expression or table columns.
- Range test predicate (BETWEEN), used to check if the value of an expression or table column falls between two values, the upper and lower bounds of the range. The range includes the end points.
- Set membership predicate (IN), tests to see if the value of an expression or table column is found within a list (or set) of values.
- Pattern-matching predicate (LIKE), used to check whether the value of a column of type CHARACTER has a character string that matches a specified pattern of characters.
- NULL value predicate (IS NULL), used to check whether a column contains a NULL or unknown value. (Some DBMS products use the keyword ISNULL in place of IS NULL.)
- Quantifier predicates (ALL, SOME, ANY), which let you use a comparison predicate to compare the value of a column or expression to the values found in a set or list of values.
- Existence predicate (EXISTS), used in conjunction with a subquery to determine if a table contains any rows that meet the subquery's search condition(s).

When executing an SQL statement with a predicate, the DBMS performs actions on those table rows where the predicate evaluates TRUE, and takes no action on rows for which the predicate evaluates to FALSE or unknown.

106 Understanding SQL Logical Connectives AND, OR, and NOT

In Tip 105, "Understanding SQL Predicates," you learned that an SQL predicate lets you specify the conditions under which the DBMS is to perform an action on a specific row or set of rows in a table. For example, the predicate in the DELETE statement

```
DELETE customers WHERE customer_since_date < '01/01/1995'
```

will remove the table rows for all customers added prior to 1 January 1995. If your intent in executing the DELETE statement in the example is to delete old, *inactive* customers, you certainly don't want to remove customers that currently making purchases—especially those that have been doing business with you for more than five years. As such, you need to limit the action of the DELETE statement by adding an additional condition to the predicate: Delete only inactive customers.

Unfortunately, a single, simple predicate will not let you specify multiple search conditions—that is where the logical connectives (AND, OR, NOT) come in. By using one or more logical connectives, you can combine two or more simple predicates into a compound predicate. A compound predicate can have as many search conditions as you need to identify the table rows on which you want the DBMS to act.

In the current example, you can add the logical connective AND to have the DBMS eliminate only those customers added to the database prior to 1995 who have not placed an order since 1997, as follows:

```
DELETE customers
WHERE customer_since_date < '01/01/1995' AND
      last_order_date < '12/31/1997'
```

The AND logical connective lets you specify multiple search conditions that must ALL evaluate TRUE in order for the DBMS to take action on the row being tested. In the current example, there are two search conditions, both of which must be true in order for the DBMS to DELETE the row being tested from the CUSTOMERS table.

If you have multiple search conditions and you want the DBMS to act on a row where any one or more of the search conditions evaluates to TRUE, use the logical connective OR to combine them. For example, if you want to remove all customers added to the system prior to 1995 and any who last ordered something prior to 1997 (regardless of when they were added to the database), you could use the DELETE statement:

```
DELETE customers
WHERE customer_since_date < '01/01/1995' OR
      last_order_date < '01/01/1997'
```

Use the NOT logical connective to negate the result of evaluating a search condition. For example, if you want to remove all customers added *after* 1/1/1995, you could use the DELETE statement:

```
DELETE customers
WHERE NOT customer_since_date < '01/01/1995'
```

Although the examples used thus far in this tip use a single logical connective, you can use multiple AND, OR, and NOT connectives in the same compound predicate. For example, the DELETE statement

```
DELETE customers
WHERE customer_since_date < '01/01/1995' AND
      last_order_date < '12/31/1997' OR
      total_paid = 0.00 AND
      NOT total_orders > 100000.00
```

will remove those rows where the customer was added prior to 1995, has not placed an order since 1997, or has never paid for an order—regardless of when the customer was added to the database as long as the total value of orders placed by the customer is less than $100,000.00.

Note: *The DELETE statement in the example will remove any customers added prior to 1995 who have not placed an order since 1997—even if the customers placed more than $100,000.00 in orders. The final AND in the example adds only the TOTAL_ORDERS > 100000.00 test to the TOTAL_PAID = 0.00 search condition.*

Logical connectives, like mathematical operators, have a specific order of precedence. The DBMS applies the NOT first, next it applies ANDs, finally, it uses the ORs. Use parenthesis (()) if you want to change the order of evaluation.

For example, if you want to keep *all* customers that have placed more than $100,000.00 in orders—regardless of the total amount they actually paid, when they were added to the system, or whether they placed an order since 1997— rewrite the example DELETE statement as:

```
DELETE customers
WHERE (customer_since_date < '01/01/1995' AND
       last_order_date < '12/31/1997' OR
       total_paid = 0.00) AND
      NOT total_orders > 100000.00
```

The parenthesis (()) tell the DBMS to evaluate the search conditions and apply the conditions inside the (innermost) parenthesis (()) first and work outward.

The reason why you would execute a DELETE statement based on the search conditions and logical connectives used in the example is not important. The important thing to know is that logical connectives let you combine multiple, simple (single search condition) predicates into one compound (multiple) search condition predicate that the DBMS will use to decide whether or not to take the action specified by the keyword at the start of the SQL statement.

107 Understanding Set (or Column) Functions

In addition to the data you can extract from the values in the individual rows of a table, you sometimes need information based on all of the values in a column taken as a set. SQL-92 has six *set* or *column* functions that let you do just that. (Set [or column] functions are sometimes called *aggregate* functions, since they "aggregate" or accumulate values stored in a column across multiple rows into a single value.)

The SQL Set (aggregate) functions are:

- COUNT(*), which returns the number of rows in a table that satisfy the search condition(s) in the WHERE clause
- COUNT(<column name>), which returns the number of (non-NULL) values in a column
- MAX, which returns the maximum value in a table column
- MIN, which returns the minimum value in a table column
- SUM, which returns the sum of the values in a column
- AVG, which returns the average of the values in a column

For example, to count the number of employees in an EMPLOYEE table, you could use the SELECT statement:

```
SELECT COUNT(*) FROM employees
```

Or, to display the count of employees who live in Nevada (state abbreviation NV), you could use the SELECT statement:

```
SELECT COUNT(*) FROM employees WHERE state = 'NV'
```

When you need the count of table rows that have non-NULL value in a particular column, use the SELECT (<column name>) aggregate function in place of the SELECT(*) function. For example, the SELECT statement

```
SELECT COUNT(quota) FROM employees WHERE state = 'NV'
```

will display the number of employees from Nevada who have a non-NULL value in the QUOTA column. The difference between

```
SELECT COUNT(*) FROM employees WHERE state = 'NV'
```

and

```
SELECT COUNT(quota) FROM employees WHERE state = 'NV'
```

is that the second statement does not count any rows that have a NULL value in the <QUOTA> field. As such, when you need a count of the rows in a table that meet a search criteria, use SELECT COUNT(*). When you want the count of only rows that meet a search criteria *and* that have a non-NULL value in a particular column, use a SELECT COUNT (<column name>) statement.

To determine the minimum or maximum value in a column, use the MIN or MAX function. For example, to display the employee ID and name of the oldest employees, you could use the SELECT statement:

```
SELECT employee_id, first_name, last_name, age
FROM employees
WHERE age = (SELECT MAX(age) FROM employees)
```

Conversely, if you want a list of the youngest employees, use the MIN function in a SELECT statement, similar to:

```
SELECT employee_id, first_name, last_name, age
FROM employees
WHERE age = (SELECT MIN(age) FROM employees)
```

When you need to add up the values in a column, use the SUM function. For example, to display the total sales made in May 2000, you could use the SELECT statement:

```
SELECT SUM (order_total) FROM sales
WHERE  date_sold >= '05/01/2000' AND
       date_sold <= '05/31/2000'
```

In order to SUM the values in a column, the column must, of course, be defined as one of the numeric data types. Moreover, the result from adding up all of the values in a column must fall within the range of the data type. As such, if you attempt to determine the SUM of a column of type SMALLINT, the resulting total cannot be any larger than the upper limit of the SMALLINT data type.

The AVG function returns the average of the values found in the rows of a numeric data type column. For example, to display the average order cost in addition to the total sold for May 2000, add the AVG function to the previous SELECT statement:

```
SELECT SUM (order_total), AVG (order_total) FROM sales
WHERE date_sold >= '05/01/2000' AND
        date_sold <= '05/31/2000'
```

Note: *NULLs have no determinable value—by definition, the value of a NULL column is "unknown." As such, any row with a NULL value is ignored by both the SUM and AVG functions and has no effect on the sum or average computed for a column.*

---

108 Understanding the CASE Expression

As you learned in Tip 17, "Understanding the Difference Between SQL and a Programming Language," SQL is a data sublanguage, not a full fledged programming language. Because SQL was designed to let you specify the data you want and not how to get at the data, the original SQL specification did not include block (BEGIN, END) statements, conditional (IF) statements, branch (GOTO) statements, or loop (DO, WHILE, FOR) statements. To reduce its reliance on external source programs to manipulate intermediate query results, many DBMS vendors have added block and statement flow control add-ons to SQL. (MS-SQL Server extensions are called Transact-SQL, and Oracle extensions are found in SQL*PLUS and PL/SQL.) One common "programming language" structure, the CASE expression, has even found its way into the SQL-92 specification.

CASE expressions are similar in function to the IF-THEN-ELSE statements found in almost all programming languages. The CASE expression reduces SQL's reliance on external programs for processing results table data by giving the data sublanguage limited decision-making capability. As such, you no longer have to retrieve data and run a separate, external program to modify the output data (results table) if the desired, modified results can be determined from current row or aggregate data values and as long as those changes are triggered by the value of a column in the current table row.

For example, if you have an employees table created with

```
CREATE TABLE employees
  (id           CHAR(3),
   name         VARCHAR(35),
   address      VARCHAR(45),
   phone_number CHAR(11),
   department   SMALLINT,
   commission   MONEY,
   bonus_level  VARCHAR(35),
   total_sales  MONEY,
   hourly_rate  MONEY,
   sales_calls  SMALLINT,
   sales_count  SMALLINT)
```

you could use the SELECT statement

```
SELECT id, name, department FROM employees
ORDER BY department
```

to display the table contents:

```
id name              department
-- ----------------- ----------
3  William Silverman 1
4  Walt Welinski     1
```

```
1   Carry Grant         2
2   Michael Lancer      2
5   Sally Fields        3
6   Walt Frazier        3
7   Melissa Gomez       4
```

If you wanted to convert department numbers to character (string) descriptions, you would have had to use an external program to convert the data prior to SQL-92. The SQL-92 CASE expression lets you modify the output on the fly based on the value of a column in a table row.

An SQL-92 CASE expression takes on one of two forms, depending on whether the CASE expression is *simple* or *searched*. A *simple* CASE expression is based on a straight equality between the value that follows the keyword CASE and the value that follows each keyword THEN in the CASE expression. Meanwhile, the *searched* CASE expression has a comparison operator in an expression right after the keyword CASE.

The syntax of a *simple* CASE expression based on the <value to test> (which follows the keyword CASE) being equal to the <value> that follows each WHEN keyword is:

```
CASE <value to test>
  WHEN <value> THEN <expression> | NULL
  [WHEN <value> THEN <expression> | NULL]...
    [WHEN <last value> THEN <last expression> | NULL]
  [ELSE <expression> | NULL]
END
```

Thus, to convert department numbers to literal strings in the results table of the current example, you could use the SELECT statement

```
SELECT id, name, CASE department
                   WHEN 1 THEN 'Marketing'
                   WHEN 2 THEN 'Customer Service'
                   WHEN 3 THEN 'Collections'
                   WHEN 4 THEN 'Customer Relations'
                 END AS dept_name
FROM employees
ORDER BY dept_name
```

to produce the results table:

```
id  name                dept_name
--  -----------------   ------------------
5   Sally Fields        Collections
6   Walt Frazier        Collections
7   Melissa Gomez       Customer Relations
1   Carry Grant         Customer Service
2   Michael Lancer      Customer Service
3   William Silverman   Marketing
4   Walt Welinski       Marketing
```

The syntax of a *searched* case expression is

```
CASE WHEN <search condition> THEN <expression> | NULL
     [WHEN <search condition> THEN <expression> | NULL]...
       [WHEN <last search condition> THEN
          <last expression> | NULL]
  [ELSE <expression> | NULL]
END
```

and you can rewrite the simple CASE expression in the current example as a searched CASE expression, as follows:

```
SELECT id, name,
       CASE WHEN department = 1 THEN 'Marketing'
            WHEN department = 2 THEN 'Customer Service'
            WHEN department = 3 THEN 'Collections'
            WHEN department = 4 THEN 'Customer Relations'
       END AS dept_name
FROM employees
ORDER BY dept_name
```

Although you can use a searched CASE expression to check for a column's contents being *equal* to a specific value, the real power of the searched CASE expression is that it lets you use subqueries and comparison operators in search conditions that test for something other than equality. Suppose, for example, that you assign your salespeople to bonus pools with increasing commission scales based on their total sales. You can use the SELECT statement with the searched CASE expression

```
SELECT id, name, total sales,
       CASE WHEN  total_sales <     10000) THEN 'Rookie'
            WHEN (total_sales >=    10000) AND
                 (total_sales <    100000) THEN 'Associate'
            WHEN (total_sales >=   100000) AND
                 (total_sales <   1000000) THEN 'Manager'
            WHEN (total_sales >= 1000000) THEN
                                                'Vice President'
       END
FROM employees
ORDER BY name, id
```

to display the ID, name, and bonus pool name based on the bonus range into which the salesperson's TOTAL_SALES falls.

109 Using the CASE Expression to Update Column Values

An SQL CASE expression differs from the CASE statements you find in most programming languages because it can be used only as part of an SQL statement and is not a statement in its own right. Said another way, SQL CASE expressions can appear in SQL statements almost anywhere a value is legal. However, SQL CASE expressions, unlike programming language CASE statements, cannot stand alone.

Tip 108 "Understanding the CASE Expression," showed you how to use the CASE expression in a SELECT statement to change the values in the results table based on the value of a column in one of the input tables. As you know, the "results table" is not a physical table on disk. Rather, it is a conceptual table that correctly models the way in which a SELECT statement returns the results of a query and how the DBMS can use those query results as an "input" or "target" table for another SQL statement.

In addition to altering the *virtual* results table, a CASE expression can modify the data stored in a *physical* table if the CASE expression appears in an UPDATE (vs. a SELECT) statement. For example, if you want to update the BONUS_LEVEL column in the employees record (vs. the values displayed in the virtual results table, as shown in Tip 108), you could use an UPDATE statement with a CASE expression similar to:

```
UPDATE employees
  SET bonus_level =
    CASE WHEN  total_sales <     10000  THEN 'Rookie'
         WHEN (total_sales >=    10000) AND
              (total_sales <    100000) THEN 'Associate'
      WHEN (total_sales >=  100000) AND
           (total_sales <  1000000) THEN 'Manager'
      WHEN (total_sales >= 1000000) THEN 'Vice President'
  END
```

When processing a CASE expression, the DBMS takes the column values in a row that satisfies the SQL statement's search condition and uses them to determine if the first condition in the CASE expression is TRUE. If so, the CASE expression receives the value in the first THEN part. If not TRUE, the DBMS evaluates the second WHEN (search) condition in the CASE expression. If TRUE, the CASE expression receives the value in the second THEN part. If not TRUE, the DBMS tests the third search condition, and so on.

If none of the CASE expression's search conditions evaluates to TRUE, the CASE expression receives the value given in the CASE expression's optional ELSE clause. A CASE expression that has no ELSE clause returns a NULL if none of its SEARCH conditions evaluate to TRUE.

When used in an UPDATE statement, the value returned by a CASE expression (and subsequently used to update a table column) must be of the same data type as the column to be updated. As such, if you have a literal (character) string in the CASE expression's THEN clause, the DBMS will return an error if you are attempting to update a numeric type data column.

In addition to using literal strings, you an use column names and mathematical expressions to compute the value returned by a CASE expression. For example, once the BONUS_LEVEL column in the EMPLOYEES table has a correct value, you can use the UPDATE statement

```
UPDATE employees
SET commission =
      CASE bonus_level
        WHEN 'Rookie'          THEN total_sales * .01
        WHEN 'Associate'       THEN total_sales * .05
        WHEN 'Manager'         THEN total_sales * .15
        WHEN 'Vice President'  THEN total_sales * .25
      END
```

to set the value of the COMMISSION column based on the commission level associated with the employee's BONUS_LEVEL and TOTAL_SALES.

110 Using the CASE Expression to Avoid Error Conditions

In addition to modifying results table values and updating data values in physical tables, you can use a CASE expression to avoid computations that are mathematically invalid or that would violate data type range constraints.

For example, if you want to display the percentage of times that a salesperson's calls result in a sale, you might use the SELECT statement:

```
SELECT id, name, (sales_calls / sales_count) * 100.00
         AS closing_percentage
FROM employees
WHERE department = 1
-
```

However, the DBMS will raise an error (and halt statement execution) if the value of SALES_COUNT is NULL or 0 (since dividing by zero is an illegal mathematical operation).

You can avoid the mathematical exception raised by dividing by zero or a NULL value by adding a CASE expression to the SELECT statement. For example, the SELECT statement

```
SELECT id, name, CASE WHEN sales_count > 0 THEN
                          sales_calls / sales_count * 100.00
                        ELSE 0
                 END AS closing_percentage
FROM employees
WHERE department = 1
```

will prevent the system from trying to divide SALES_COUNT by a zero or a NULL value. When SALES_COUNT is greater than 0, the DBMS will perform the division of the SALES_COUNT into the SALES_CALLS. Conversely, when the SALES_COUNT is 0 or unknown, the DBMS will skip the division and return a value of 0.

Sometimes mathematically legal computations can result in results that violate range constraints. Suppose, for example, that you deduct the cost of health insurance from an employee's GROSS_PAY using the UPDATE statement:

```
UPDATE payroll_records
SET net_pay = gross_pay - health_ins_deduction
```

You would violate a user-defined data range constraint if the amount of the HEALTH_INS_DEDUCTION is greater than the GROSS_PAY. After all, the NET_PAY amount on a check cannot be less than zero!

To avoid trying to write a check for a negative amount, you could add a CASE expression such as

```
UPDATE payroll_records
SET net_pay = CASE WHEN gross_pay >= health_ins_deduction
                     Then gross_pay - health_ins_deduction
                  ELSE gross_pay
              END
```

to the UPDATE statement. In the current example, the DBMS would "take" the HEALTH_INS_DEDUCTION out of the GROSS_PAY only if the employee earned at least the amount of money due to be deducted.

111 Understanding the NULLIF Expression

The NULLIF function is the inverse of the ISNULL function you learned about in Tip 31, "Understanding the MS-SQL Server ISNULL() Function." While the ISNULL function is used to replace a NULL with a non-NULL value, the NULLIF is used to replace a non-NULL value with a NULL.

Suppose, for example, that someone set the value of the SALES_QUOTA column in the EMPLOYEES table to –1 for new employees who have not yet been assigned a quota. The NULLIF expression in the SELECT statement

```
SELECT employee_id, first_name, last_name,
         NULLIF (SALES_QUOTA, -1) as Quota
FROM employees
```

lets you more accurately display the sales quotas in a virtual results table by replacing any values of –1 in the SALES_QUOTA column of the results table with a NULL

The syntax for the NULLIF expression is:

```
NULLIF (<expression 1>, <expression 2>)
```

When evaluating a NULLIF expression, the DBMS will return a value of NULL when <expression 1> and <expression 2> have the same value. If <expression 1> and <expression 2> have different values, the DBMS will return the value of <expression 1> as the value of the expression. Thus, in the current example, the NULLIF expression will evaluate to NULL whenever the value in the SALES_QUOTA column is equal to –1. Otherwise, the NULLIF expression will return the value in the SALES_QUOTA column of the current row.

Either one (or both) of the expressions in the NULLIF can be literals (numeric, datetime, or character constants); numeric, string, datetime or CASE expressions; or column names. However, using a literal for both <expression 1> and <expression 2> is of little practical value. For example, the SELECT statement

```
SELECT
  NULLIF ('match', 'match'), NULLIF ('no match', 'match')
```

which generates the results table

```
----- --------
NULL, no match
```

tells you only that the NULLIF expression for two identical literals evaluates to NULL, while the NULLIF expression for two different literals returns the value of the first literal.

Besides altering the contents of a SELECT statement's virtual results table, you can use a NULLIF expression in an UPDATE statement to change the values in an actual (physical) table. For example, suppose that you close one of your sales offices, office 6. You can use the UPDATE statement

```
UPDATE employees SET office = NULLIF (office, 6)
```

to put a NULL in the OFFICE column of all employees previously assigned to office 6.

112 Using the COALESCE Expression to Replace NULL Values

A COALESCE expression gives you a simple way to replace NULL (or missing) data with non-NULL values Although you can use a CASE expression to do the same job, the syntax of the COALESCE expression

```
COALESCE (<first expression>, <second expression>
          [,...<last expression>])
```

is compact and perhaps easier to read (and understand) than the equivalent CASE expression.

The DBMS sets the value of the COALESCE expression to the first non-NULL value in its expression list. As shown by the expression's syntax diagram, the COALESCE expression, unlike the ISNULL expression (which is also used to replace a chosen expression with NULL values) can more than two expressions in its expression list.

To compute the value of a COALESCE expression, the DBMS starts by evaluating the first expression in the list. If the first expression evaluates to a non-NULL result, the DBMS returns its value as the value of the COALESCE expression. If the first expression evaluates to NULL, the DBMS evaluates the second expression in the list. If the second expression evaluates to a non-NULL result, the DBMS returns the value of the second expression as the COALESCE expression's value. If the second expression also evaluates to NULL, the DBMS goes on to evaluate the third expression, and so on.

In the end, the DBMS returns the first non-NULL value in the list of expressions, reading from left to right, as the value of the COALESCE expression. If all of the expressions in the expression list evaluate to NULL, the COALESCE expression returns a NULL value.

As an example of how the DBMS computes the value of COALESCE expression, assume that you want to list the appointment quotas for your sales representatives. Moreover, assume that you want to use the minimum appointment quota in the employee table as the quota for any rep that has not yet been assigned an appointment quota. To produce the list, you could execute the SELECT statement:

```
SELECT employee_id, first_name, last_name,
  COALESCE (appt_quota,
    (SELECT MIN(appt_quota) FROM employees), 0) AS quota
FROM employees
WHERE department = 'Marketing'
```

After evaluating the COALESCE expression, the DBMS displays the value in the APPT_QUOTA column if it is not NULL. If the APPT_QUOTA is NULL, the DBMS evaluates the MIN aggregate function on the APPT_QUOTA column and displays the minimum appointment quota as the employee's quota—as long as at least one marketing representative has a quota. If all of the quotas are NULL, the MIN aggregate function will return a NULL and the DBMS will display the final value in the expression list, 0, as the employee's appointment quota.

113 Using the COUNT(*) Aggregate Function to Count the Number of Rows in a Table

COUNT(*) is an aggregate function that returns the number of rows that satisfy the search criteria in the SELECT statement's WHERE clause. As such, the SELECT statement

```
SELECT COUNT(*) FROM employees
```

will display the numbers of rows in the EMPLOYEES table. Similarly, the UPDATE statement

```
UPDATE managers SET employees_managed =
                    (SELECT COUNT(*) FROM employees
                     WHERE manager = managers.employee_id)
```

will set the EMPLOYEES_MANAGED column in the MANAGERS table to the number of rows in the employees table where the value of the MANAGER column (in the EMPLOYEES table) is equal to the value of the EMPLOYEE_ID column in the MANAGERS table. Thus, the UPDATE statement in the example tells the DBMS to set the EMPLOYEES_MANAGED column in each row of the MANAGERS table to the count of the employees that the manager manages.

Note: *If the COUNT(*) function's SELECT statement has no WHERE clause, then all of the rows in the table satisfy the "search condition." As such, the SELECT statement in the first example will return the count of* all *rows in the table because every row in the table satisfies the SELECT statement's omitted search condition.*

If the DBMS stores the number of table rows in its system tables, COUNT(*) will return the row count of even large tables very quickly because the DBMS can retrieve the row count directly from the system table (and doesn't have to read through and count the rows in the physical table). On those systems that do not maintain row counts in the system tables, you may be able to count table rows more quickly by using the COUNT() function with an indexed NOT NULL constrained column as a parameter.

When counting the rows in a table by using the COUNT() function instead of the COUNT(*) function, bear in mind that the value returned by the COUNT() function is equivalent only to the result of executing the COUNT(*) function if the column you pass to COUNT() has no NULL values in any of its rows.

For example, the COUNT() function in the SELECT statement

```
SELECT COUNT (employee_id) FROM employees
```

will return only the same value as the COUNT(*) function in the SELECT statement

```
SELECT COUNT(*) FROM employees
```

only if none of the rows in the EMPLOYEES table has a NULL value in the EMPLOYEE_ID column.

The value returned by the COUNT() function is best described as the count of non-NULL values in the column passed to the function. COUNT(*), on the other hand, is most accurately defined as an aggregate function that returns the count rows in a table. Therefore, since COUNT() returns the correct count of rows in a table only if none of the values in the column passed as a parameter is NULL, use COUNT() in place of COUNT(*) only if the column parameter is restricted by a NOT NULL constraint.

114 Using the COUNT(*) Aggregate Function to Count the Number of Data Values in a Column

While the purpose for using the COUNT(*) function is to count the number of rows in a table, the COUNT() function is used to count the number data values in a column. Unlike the COUNT(*) function, which ignores all column values, the COUNT() function checks the value of one (or more) columns and counts only those rows in which the value is not NULL.

For example, given the following data values in an EMPLOYEES table

```
employee_id  first_name  last_name  quota  manager
-----------  ----------  ---------  -----  -------
1            Lancer      Michael    5      NULL
2            Michael     Lancer     5      1
3            William     Silverman  NULL   2
4            Walt        Wellinski  8      1
5            William     Silverman  8      2
6            NULL        Gomez      10     2
7            Walt        Frazier    10     NULL
```

the SELECT statement

```
SELECT COUNT(*) AS Row_Count,
       COUNT(last_name) AS Last_Name_Count,
       COUNT(manager) AS Manager_Count
FROM employees
```

will return the results table:

```
Row_Count  Last_Name_Count  Manager_Count
---------  ---------------  -------------
7          7                5
```

Thus, in the current example, the COUNT(*) function returns the number of rows in the EMPLOYEES table—without regard for the values in any of the table's columns. Conversely, the two COUNT() functions return the number of rows with non-NULL values in columns passed (LAST_NAME and MANAGER) as the parameter to each function.

Since the LAST_NAME column has no NULL values, the COUNT(last_name) function returns the same value as the COUNT(*) function. Conversely, two of the table rows have a NULL in the MANAGER column, which causes the COUNT(manager) function to return the value 5, which is 2 less than the total number or rows in the EMPLOYEES table as reported by the COUNT(*) function.

The syntax of the COUNT() function is:

```
COUNT([ALL | DISTINCT] <expression>)
```

Because the DBMS defaults to ALL when neither ALL nor DISTINCT is specified, the ALL qualifier is normally omitted when using the COUNT() function. Tip 115, "Using the COUNT(*) Aggregate Function to Count the Number of Unique and Duplicate Values in a Column," will show you how to use the DISTINCT qualifier in the COUNT() function to count the number of unique data values in a column.

The important thing to understand is that the COUNT() function will accept a column name, a literal string, a numeric value, or an expression that combines column contents into a single value. As such, in the current example, you can use the SELECT statement

```
SELECT COUNT(first_name + last_name) FROM employees
```

to count the number of rows in which *both* the FIRST_NAME and LAST_NAME columns are not NULL.

Note: *If your DBMS implementation uses the double vertical lines (||) operator instead of the plus (+) operator for string concatenation, you would write the query as:*

```
SELECT COUNT(first_name || last_name) FROM employees
```

If you wanted to count only the number of non-NULL data values in a column based on rows that satisfy a search condition, add a WHERE clause to the SELECT statement. For example, if you want to know only the number of non-NULL values in the FIRST_NAME column for table rows with a 2 in the MANAGER column, you could use the SELECT statement:

```
SELECT COUNT(first_name) FROM employees WHERE manager = 2
```

Note: *The syntax of the COUNT() function lets you pass a character string or numeric literal (string or numeric constant) as the <expression>. Using a literal value (vs. a column name or expression involving a column) will always cause the COUNT() function* *to return the number of rows in the table. After all, a non-NULL constant value will never be NULL as the DBMS evaluates the function for each row of the table. As such, the DBMS will count each row as having a non-NULL value for the "column" (the constant value) it is to test. Thus, executing the SELECT statement*

```
SELECT COUNT('constant value') FROM employees
```

for example, will always return the number of rows in EMPLOYEES, since the literal string "constant value" will be non-NULL for each row in the table.

115 Using the COUNT(*) Aggregate Function to Count the Number of Unique and Duplicate Values in a Column

If you insert the DISTINCT constraint ahead of the expression passed as a parameter to the COUNT() function, the function will count the number of unique, non-NULL data values in a column. For example, given the following data values in an EMPLOYEES table

```
employee_ID  first_name  last_name  quota  manager
-----------  ----------  ---------  -----  -------
1            Lancer      Michael    5      NULL
2            Michael     Lancer     5      1
3            William     Silverman  NULL   2
4            Walt        Wellinski  8      1
5            William     Silverman  8      2
6            NULL        Gomez      10     2
7            Walt        Frazier    10     NULL
```

the SELECT statement

```
SELECT COUNT(first_name) AS Total_First_Names,
       COUNT(DISTINCT first_name) AS Unique_First_Names
FROM employees
```

will return the results table:

```
Total_First_Names  Unique_First_Names
-----------------  ------------------
6                  4
```

Note: *A simple way to display the number of unique rows in a table is to pass the table's PRIMARY KEY to the COUNT() function because the table's PRIMARY KEY column contains a unique, non-NULL value in every row of the table.*

You can also count the number of unique values across multiple columns by using the string concatenation function to combine column values into a single, composite value (which is then passed as the parameter to the COUNT() function).

Suppose, for example, that you want to count the number of unique employee names in the EMPLOYEES table. Executing the previous SELECT statement would yield inaccurate results since the COUNT() function in the statement checks for only unique values in the FIRST_NAME column. As such, the DBMS treats the second WALT as a duplicate name and does not count it, even though the full name Walt Wellinski is not the same as Walt Frazier.

To accurately count the number of unique employee names, then, you need to combine the contents of the FIRST_NAME and LAST_NAME columns into a single string and then pass that string as the parameter to the COUNT() function. In so doing, the SELECT statement

```
SELECT COUNT(first_name) AS Total_First_Names,
       COUNT(DISTINCT first_name) AS Unique_First_Names
       COUNT(DISTINCT first_name + last_name) AS
         Unique_Full_Names
FROM employees
```

will return the results table:

```
Total_First_Names  Unique_First_Names  Unique_Full_Names
-----------------  ------------------  -----------------
6                  4                   5
```

Note: *If any one of the concatenated columns has a NULL value, the result of the concatenation is NULL and the current row will not be counted by the COUNT() function. In the current example, the row in which the FIRST_NAME column is NULL and the LAST_NAME column is Gomez is not counted by the COUNT() function since the result of the expression (the concatenation of first and last names) passed as the parameter to the COUNT() function is NULL. Remember, the COUNT() function counts only those rows in which the parameter passed to the function is not NULL.*

SQL does not have a special function to count the number of nonunique (or duplicate) values in a column. You can, however compute the count of duplicate column values by subtracting the count of unique column values from the total count of column values, as shown in the SELECT statement:

```
SELECT COUNT(first_name + last_name) -
         COUNT(DISTINCT first_name + last_name)
  AS Dup_Name_Count
FROM employees
```

If you want to include the count of NULL values in the duplicate column data count, use the COUNT(*) function in place of the first COUNT() function in the SELECT statement. For example, the SELECT statement

```
SELECT COUNT(*) - COUNT(DISTINCT first_name + last_name)
  AS Dup_Name_And_NULL_Count
FROM employees
```

will display the count of duplicate and NULL data values in the composite FULL_NAME (FIRST_NAME + LAST_NAME) column.

116 Using MS-SQL Server CUBE and ROLLUP Operators to Summarize Table Data

The SQL GROUP BY clause lets you summarize table data based on one or more columns. MS-SQL Server provides two operators, CUBE and ROLLUP, which enhance the GROUP BY clause's totaling capabilities. By adding a WITH ROLLUP clause (or a WITH CUB clause) to a SELECT statement, you can tell MS-SQL Server to generate additional subtotals and grand totals for columns listed in the statement's GROUP BY clause.

Suppose, for example, that you have the following data in an INVOICES table:

```
inv_date    inv_no  cust_id  product_code  qty
----------  ------  -------  ------------  ---
2000-01-01  1       1        1             1
2000-01-01  1       1        6             1
2000-01-01  1       1        3             1
2000-01-01  1       1        5             6
2000-03-01  2       9        1             5
2000-03-01  2       9        2             4
2000-02-01  3       7        2             4
2000-05-01  4       7        5             1
2000-05-01  4       7        4             3
2000-05-01  4       7        2             8
2000-01-01  5       4        5             3
2000-01-01  5       4        6             3
2000-06-01  6       1        5             4
2000-06-01  7       5        5             4
```

To generate a summary report of products purchased by customers 4 and 5, use a SELECT statement with a GROUP BY clause similar to

```
SELECT cust_id, product_code, SUM(qty) AS quantity
FROM invoices WHERE cust_id IN (4, 5)
GROUP BY cust_id, product_code
ORDER BY cust_id
```

which, will produce the results table

```
cust_id  product_code  quantity
-------  ------------  --------
4        5             3
4        6             3
5        5             4
```

for the current example's data. Thus, the GROUP BY clause tells the DBMS to "group" (or summarize) the nongrouped items in the SELECT list into the "categories" (or columns) listed in the GROUP BY clause.

In the current example, the sum of the QTY column is the only nongrouped item. As such, the GROUP BY clause tells the DBMS to compute the sum of the QTY column's values for each unique combination of CUST_ID and PRODUCT_CODE in the INVOICES table. The WHERE clause tells the DBMS to display only the data for customers 4 and 5.

If you are using MS-SQL Server, you can tell the DBMS to display the total products each customer purchased (without regard to product code) and the total number of all products purchased by all customers by adding a WITH ROLLUP clause. For the current example data, the SELECT statement (WITH ROLLUP)

```
SELECT cust_id, product_code, sum(qty) AS quantity
FROM invoices WHERE cust_id IN (4, 5)
GROUP BY cust_id, product_code
WITH ROLLUP
ORDER BY cust_id
```

will generate the results table:

```
cust_id  product_code  quantity
-------  ------------  --------
NULL     NULL          10
4        5             3
4        6             3
4        NULL          6
5        5             4
5        NULL          4
```

Each additional results table row with a NULL value is a subtotal generated by the ROLLUP operator. The NULL denotes the column being subtotaled—or, said another way, a NULL value in a column means "for all values" of that column. For example, the first row, which has a NULL in both the CUST_ID and PRODUCT_CODE columns, tells you that the QUANTITY column contains the total purchases made by all customers for all product codes. Similarly, the fourth row in the results table has a NULL only in the PRODUCT_CODE column. As such, the QUANTITY column in the fourth row shows the total of all PRODUCT_CODEs purchased by customer 4.

Notice that the results table for a SELECT statement WITH ROLLUP has only one row with a NULL value in the CUST_ID column. The ROLLUP operator "rolls up" the subtotals for the first column in the GROUP BY clause based on the remaining columns listed in the clause into a single grand total, which represents the quantity in the nongrouped column for "all" values of all columns in the GROUP BY list.

If you want to display subtotals for the first column in the GROUP BY clause for each unique combination of column values listed in the remainder of the clause, use the WITH CUBE clause in place of the WITH ROLLUP clause. For the current example, the SELECT statement

```
SELECT cust_id, product_code, sum(qty) AS quantity
FROM invoices WHERE cust_id IN (4, 5)
GROUP BY cust_id, product_code
WITH CUBE
ORDER BY cust_id
```

will generate the results table

```
cust_id  product_code  quantity
-------  ------------  --------
NULL     NULL          10
NULL     5             7
NULL     6             3
4        5             3
4        6             3
4        NULL          6
5        5             4
5        NULL          4
```

which includes two additional rows (rows 2 and 3) that show the total of all product 5 and product 6 purchases made by all customers.

Note: *The examples in the current tip use SELECT statements with only two columns listed in the GROUP BY clause. This was done to reduce the size of the results table. The MS-SQL Server CUBE and ROLLUP operators will accept GROUP BY clause with up to 10 columns listed.*

---

117 Using the MAX() Aggregate Function to Find the Maximum Value in a Column

When you need to know the maximum or largest value in a column, use the MAX() aggregate (or set) function. The column passed to the MAX() function can be a numeric, a character string, or a datetime data type. As such, if you want to display the datetime of the most recent invoice for customer 1, you could use the SELECT statement

```
SELECT MAX(inv_date) AS 'Date Last Inv for Cust 1'
FROM invoices WHERE cust_id = 1
```

which will produce a results table similar to:

```
Date Last Inv for Cust 1
------------------------
2000-06-01 00:00:00.000
```

Similarly, if you want to display the highest ITEM_COST in the PRODUCTS table, you would use the SELECT statement

```
SELECT MAX(item_cost) AS 'Max Item Cost' FROM products
```

to produce a RESULTS table similar to:

```
MAX Item Cost
-------------
1844.5100
```

The MAX() function will return a single value of the same data type as the column it is passed. Thus, in the first example, the MAX() function scanned the values in the INV_DATE column (of type datetime) and returned its largest datetime value found in the column. Similarly, the MAX() function in the second example scanned a numeric column and returned the highest MONEY data type value in the ITEM_COST column.

Note: *When determining the maximum value in a column, the MAX() function ignores NULL values. However, if* all *rows in the column have a NULL value, the MAX() function will return a NULL value for that column.*

118 Using the MIN() Aggregate Function to Find the Minimum Value in a Column

When you need to know the minimum or smallest value in a column, use the MIN() aggregate (or set) function. The column passed to the MIN() function can be a numeric, a character string, or a datetime data type. As such, if you want to display the datetime of the oldest invoice for customer 1, you could use the SELECT statement

```
SELECT MIN(inv_date) AS 'Date First Inv for Cust 1'
FROM invoices WHERE cust_id = 1
```

which will produce a results table similar to:

```
Date First Inv for Cust 1
------------------------
2000-01-01 00:00:00.000
```

Similarly, if you want to display the least expensive ITEM_COST in the PRODUCTS table, you would use the SELECT statement

```
SELECT MIN(item_cost) AS 'Min Item Cost' FROM products
```

to produce a RESULTS table similar to:

```
Min Item Cost
-------------
258.2300
```

Note: *If you are working with a numeric column that contains negative values, the value returned by the MIN() function may not be the number closest to 0. For example, if a numeric column has the values 15, 5, 100, 0, –456, –10, and 200, the MIN() function will return the value –456. Remember, the* larger *the negative number, the* smaller *its value.*

The MIN() function will return a single value of the same data type as the column it is passed. Thus, in the first example, the MIN() function scanned the values in the INV_DATE column (of type datetime) and returned its smallest datetime value. Similarly, the MIN() function in the second example scanned a numeric column and returned the lowest MONEY data type value in the ITEM_COST column.

Note: *When determining the minimum value in a column, the MIN() function ignores NULL values. However, if* all *rows in the column have a NULL value, the MIN() function will return a NULL value for that column.*

119 Using the SUM() Aggregate Function to Find the Sum of the Values in a Column

The SUM() aggregate (or set) function returns the sum of the data values in a column. Because SUM() *adds* the values in the rows of a column together, the column passed to the SUM() function must be one of the numeric data types you learned about in Tip 21, "Understanding SQL Numeric Integer Data Types," and Tip 22, "Understanding SQL Numeric Floating-Point Data Types."

For example, to display the total sales commissions for all employees in the EMPLOYEES table, you could use a SELECT statement similar to

```
SELECT SUM(sales_commission) AS 'Total Commissions'
FROM employees
```

to produce a results table similar to:

```
Total Commissions
-----------------
1072105.7900
```

While the MIN() and MAX() functions each return a value that has exactly the same data type as the column passed to the function, the SUM() function returns a numeric data type that is either the same or a higher precision than the column passed. For example, to prevent an "overflow" error, the SUM() function may return a value of data type INTEGER when called upon to add up the values in a SMALLINT column—if the resulting sum is greater than 32,767.

Note: *The SUM() function ignores NULL values when adding up the numbers in a column. However, if all of the values in a column are NULL, the SUM() function will return NULL as its result for that column.*

The syntax of the SUM() function is:

```
SUM([DISTINCT] <expression>)
```

As such, you can have the SUM() function give you the sum of all unique (distinct) values in a column. For example, the SUM() function in the SELECT statement

```
SELECT SUM(DISTINCT quantity_on_hand) FROM products
```

will return 27 if the values in the QUANTITY_ON_HAND column are 1, 5, 9, 12, 9, and 5. Conversely, the SUM function in

```
SELECT SUM(quantity_on_hand) FROM products
```

will produce a sum of 41 for the same data values in rows of the column.

120 Using the AVG() Aggregate Function to Find the Average of the Values in a Column

The AVG() aggregate (or set) function returns the average of the data values in a column. Because the AVG() function adds up the data values in a column and divides the sum by the number of non-NULL values, the column being averaged must be one of the numeric data types you learned about in Tip 21, "Understanding SQL Numeric Integer Data Types," and Tip 22, "Understanding SQL Numeric Floating-Point Data Types."

To display the average cost of the items (ITEM_COST) in a PRODUCTS table, you would a SELECT statement similar to:

```
SELECT AVG(item_cost) FROM products
```

Like the SUM() function, the AVG() function may not return the exact data type of the column that it is passed. For example, if you use the AVG() function to determine the average age of the employees in an EMPLOYEE table, such as

```
SELECT AVG(age) FROM employees
```

the AVG() function may return a floating-point numeric value, even though the AGE column is of one of the integer data types (either INTEGER or SMALLINT).

Note: *Check the system documentation to determine the type of conversions that may occur on your specific DBMS. MS-SQL Server, for example, will round the result of an AVG() function executed on an INTEGER column so that it returns an INTEGER result, while other DBMS implementations will return the computed average as an unrounded floating-point number.*

When computing averages, the AVG() function ignores NULL values. As such,

```
SELECT SUM(sales_price) / COUNT(*) FROM products
```

is *not* equivalent to

```
SELECT AVG(sales_price) FROM products
```

if the SALES_PRICE for any product in the PRODUCT table has not yet been set and is set to NULL as a result. Although the SUM() function ignores NULL values, the COUNT(*) function does not.

Like the SUM() function the syntax of the AVG() function

```
AVG([DISTINCT] <expression>)
```

gives you the ability to average only unique (or distinct) values in a column. As such, if the AGE column in the EMPLOYEES table contains the values 26, 55, 34, 37, 34, and 55, the SELECT statement (for the average of unique values)

```
SELECT AVG(DISTINCT age) FROM employees
```

will display 38 as the average age, while the SELECT statement (for the average of all values)

```
SELECT AVG(age) FROM employees
```

would report an average age of 40.

Note: *As mentioned previously, the AVG() function ignores NULL values when computing a column's average value. However, if* all *rows in the column have a NULL value, the AVG() function will return a value of NULL for the column.*

---

121 Using the WHERE Clause with the AVG() Function to Determine an Average Value for Select Rows in a Table

As you learned in Tip 120, "Using the AVG() Aggregate Function to Find the Average of the Values in a Column," the AVG() aggregate (or column) function returns the average of the data values in a table column. If you do not want to average all of the values in a column, you can use the search condition in a WHERE clause to limit the rows (and, therefore, the data values) the DBMS will include in the computation of the aggregate function.

For example, to display the average gross sales for all salespeople in the company, you would use a SELECT statement similar to:

```
SELECT AVG(gross_sales) AS 'Avg Gross Sales' FROM salesreps
```

To compute the average gross sales for only those assigned to Nevada (vs. all salespeople companywide), you would limit the GROSS_SALES data values passed to the AVG() function to only Nevada salespeople by adding a WHERE clause such as the one in the SELECT statement:

```
SELECT AVG(gross_sales) AS 'Avg NV Gross Sales'
FROM salesreps
WHERE sales_territory = 'NV'
```

When executing a SELECT statement, the DBMS evaluates the search conditions in the WHERE clause for each row in the table. Only data values from those rows for which the search condition evaluates to TRUE are passed to the aggregate function. (By default, every row in the table satisfies the "search condition" if the SELECT statement has no WHERE clause.)

In the current example, only the GROSS_SALES from the rows in which the SALES_TERRITORY is equal to NV (the abbreviation for Nevada) are included in the average calculated by the AVG() function and displayed in the results table under the Avg NV Gross Sales heading.

In addition to displaying the average value in a column for some or all of the rows in a table, you can use the AVG() function as part of a search condition in the SELECT statement's WHERE clause. Suppose, for example, that you want to display the average QUOTA and GROSS_SALES for salespeople whose GROSS_SALES are above the average for all employees overall. The SELECT statement

```
SELECT AVG(quota) AS 'Avg Quota for Above Avg Sales',
       AVG(gross_sales) AS 'Avg Above Avg Sales'
FROM salesreps
WHERE gross_sales > (SELECT AVG(gross_sales)
                     FROM salesreps)
```

will determine the average of the GROSS_SALES for all salespeople and then compare each salesperson's GROSS_SALES against that average. Only QUOTA and GROSS_SALES values in those rows in which a salesperson's GROSS_SALES amount is above the overall average GROSS_SALES amount will be passed to the AVG(quota) and AVG(gross_sales) functions.

122 Understanding How Aggregate Functions in a SELECT Statement Produce a Single Row of Results

In Tips 113–120, you learned about the SQL aggregate functions COUNT(), MAX(), MIN(), SUM(), and AVG(). Although each performs a different function, all have the characteristic of *aggregating* (summarizing) a column's value from multiple table rows into a single value. The value returned by an aggregate function can then be used in a search condition or expression, or displayed as a column in a SELECT statement.

When executing a SELECT statement to display the values computed by one or more aggregate functions, the DBMS performs the following steps:

1. Generates a virtual interim table that represents the product (or CROSS JOIN) of the tables in the SELECT statement's FROM clause.
2. If there is a WHERE clause, evaluates its search condition(s) for each row in the interim table. Eliminates those rows for which the WHERE clause evaluates as FALSE or NULL (unknown)—that is, keeps only those rows for which the search condition evaluates to TRUE.
3. Uses the values in the updated interim table to calculate the value of the aggregate function(s) in the SELECT statement's select clause.
4. Displays the value computed by each aggregate function as a column value in a single-row results table.

Perhaps the best way to conceptualize the way in which the DBMS produces the results table for a summary query is think of the query's execution as having two distinct phases. In the first phase, the DBMS performs the steps in the detail query processing (which you learned about in Tip 87, "Understanding the Steps Involved in Processing an SQL SELECT Statement"). The resulting interim multi-row, multi-column input table has all of the columns from all of the tables in the SELECT statement's FROM clause, and all of the rows that satisfy the search criteria in the WHERE clause. In the second phase, the DBMS uses the aggregate functions in the query's select clause to summarize the multi-row interim input table into single values that it can display as columns in a single-row results table.

If you think of an aggregate function in a select clause as *directing* the DBMS to summarize data to produce a single line of results, you can understand why the SELECT statement

```
SELECT  dept, COUNT(*) FROM employees
```

is illegal. After all, the column reference DEPT tells the DBMS to provide a *multi*-row listing—one virtual table row showing the department number for every employee in the EMPLOYEES table. Unfortunately, this directly contradicts the direction of the second item in the select list. The aggregate function, COUNT(*) tells the DBMS to provide a *single*-row results table (with a column that displays the number of rows in the input table).

Thus, a SELECT statement with column and aggregate functions listed in the select clause is illegal when the columns listed tell the DBMS to perform a detailed query at the same time that the aggregate functions tell the DBMS to perform a summary query.

Note: *Mixing a column list and aggregate functions in a select clause is legal if all columns listed in the select clause also appear in the SELECT statement's GROUP BY clause. Thus, the SELECT statement*

```
SELECT dept, COUNT(*) FROM employees GROUP BY dept
```

is legal. (You will learn how single- and multiple-column GROUP BY clauses convert detailed queries into a summary queries in Tip 270, "Using a GROUP BY Clause to Group Rows Based on a Single-Column Value," and Tip 271, "Using a GROUP BY Clause to Group Rows Based on Multiple Columns.")

123 Understanding the Impact of Columns with NULL Values on Set Functions

The SQL-92 standard specifies that aggregate functions (COUNT(), MAX(), MIN(), SUM(), and AVG()) ignore NULL values. Thus, given an EMPLOYEES table with the values

```
emp_id  appt_quota  appt_count  sales_count  sales_amount
------  ----------  ----------  -----------  ------------
1       2           4           2            10725.0000
2       5           6           5            25625.0000
3       NULL        2           0            0.0000
4       NULL        5           0            0.0000
5       7           9           7            35259.0000
6       4           4           4            20748.0000
7       9           10          9            45589.0000
```

the SELECT statement

```
SELECT COUNT(*) AS 'Rows', COUNT(emp_id) AS 'Emps',
       COUNT(appt_quota) AS 'Quotas',
       SUM(appt_quota)   AS 'Sum Quotas',
       SUM(sales_count)  AS 'Sum Sales',
       AVG(appt_quota)   AS 'Avg Quota',
       AVG(sales_count)  AS 'Avg Sales'
FROM employees
```

produces the results table:

```
Rows Emps Quotas Sum Quotas Sum Sales Avg Quota Avg Sales
---- ---- ------ ---------- --------- --------- ---------
7    7    5      27         27        5         3
```

In Tip 113, "Using the COUNT(*) Aggregate Function to Count the Number of Rows in a Table," you learned that the row count function COUNT(*) is not affected by NULL values in any of the table's columns, while the COUNT() function counts only non-NULL values in a column. As such, the results table shows that the COUNT(emp_id) function returns the same value (7) as the COUNT(*) function since every row in the EMP_ID column has a non-NULL value. Conversely, the COUNT(appt_quota) function returns a value of 5 because two of the rows in the APPT_QUOTA column have NULL values. (Or, stated another way, only five of the rows in the APPT_QUOTA column have non-NULL values, and the COUNT() function includes only rows with non-NULL values in its count of values in a column).

The SUM() function ignores NULL values, too, hence the non-NULL result of computing the sum of column APPT_QUOTA, which has NULL values in two of its rows.

Note: *Be careful when using column values. With the exception of the SUM() function (which ignores NULL values), if a column used as an operand in an expression has a NULL value, the DBMS will evaluate the entire expression as NULL.*

While reviewing the value of the last two columns of the results table, you may have noticed what appears to be an error. Although the sum of the values in the APPT_QUOTA and SALES_COUNT columns comes to 27, the AVG() function returns a different average (5 vs. 3) for the two columns, even though the total is the same and the number of employees is the same for both columns.

The reason for the disparity is that the AVG() function, like the other aggregate functions, ignores NULL values. Thus, while the sum of the values in both columns is the same, the AVG(appt_quota) function has two fewer rows (5) to divide into the sum of the APPT_QUOTAs than the AVG(sales_count) function has to divide into the sum of the SALES_COUNTs. Thus, the AVG(appt_quota) is computed as 27 / 5, while the AVG(sales_count) is computed as 27 / 7 because rows with NULL values in the APPT_QUOTA column are omitted from the computation of the AVG(appt_quota).

Using the example data one last time, you would expect that the expressions

```
SUM (appt_count) - SUM(appt_quota)
```

and

```
SUM (appt_count - appt_quota)
```

to produce the same result—the number of appointments either above or below quota set by the employees.

Yet, the SELECT statement

```
SELECT
  SUM(appt_count) AS 'Sum Appts',
  SUM(appt_quota) AS 'Sum Quotas',
  SUM(appt_count - appt_quota) AS 'Sum of Difference'
  SUM(appt_count) - SUM(appt_quota) AS 'Difference of Sums'
FROM employees
```

produces the results table:

```
SUM Appts Sum Quotas  Sum of Difference  Difference of Sums
--------- ----------  -----------------  ------------------
40        27          6                  13
```

Comparing the sum of the appointments (40) to the sum of the appointment quotas (27), it would appear that the expression

```
SUM (appt_count - appt_quota)
```

yields the correct results, while

```
SUM (appt_count) - SUM(appt_quota)
```

does not. However, both results are correct—the difference is a matter of semantics.

The "sum of differences" takes the difference between the two columns in each row of the table. Unfortunately, two of the rows have a NULL value for one of the operands in the subtraction. As a result, two of the subtractions evaluate to NULL and are ignored by the SUM() function. Thus, the number in the Sum of the Differences column is best defined as "the number or appointments by which employees with quotas exceeded the quota for appointments."

Conversely, the "difference of sums" calculated the sum of each column first, thus increasing the total appointment count by 7 due to the inclusion of the APPT_COUNT values for employees 3 and 4. As a result, the number under the Difference of Sums heading can best be described as "the number of appointments by which all employees exceeded the quota for appointments."

(The APPT_COUNT for employees 3 and 4 was eliminated from the SUM(appt_count – appt_quota) expression because APPT_COUNT–APPT_QUOTA evaluates to NULL for both since the APPT_QUOTA operand in the subtraction is NULL in the two rows.)

124 Using the AND Logical Connective to Do Multiple Condition Selects of Rows in a Table

A WHERE clause in a SELECT statement lets you specify the search condition the DBMS is to use in selecting the data to display in its results table. While the WHERE clause is optional, almost every SELECT statement has one. After all, without a WHERE clause, the results table will include data from every row in the input table. Since database tables often grow to several million rows, displaying an entire table's contents is both impractical and of little use—especially since the answer to most nonacademic queries lies in the summary of a small portion of a table's data.

Suppose, for example, that you want a list of all employees currently working in the marketing department. You might use a query similar to:

```
SELECT emp_id, first_name, last_name FROM employees
WHERE dept = 'Marketing'
```

Without the WHERE clause, the SELECT statement will present a results table listing all employees in the company. If you are trying only to assign marketing personnel to floor supervisors, the "extra" nonmarketing employee names would just be in the way.

Even with its WHERE clause, the example SELECT statement does not narrow down the employee list enough. After all, you want to manage a list of only *active* marketing reps, while the employee table includes all marketing reps—including those no longer employed by your company. (For tax reporting purposes, most employee tables will include information for terminated employees, at least until the end of the calendar year.)

Since a single search condition in a WHERE clause can test only one data value, testing for multiple values (such as DEPT *and* EMPLOYMENT_STATUS) will require a multiple search condition (or compound) predicate. That's where the AND logical connective comes in.

The AND logical connective lets you specify an additional search condition that must also be true in order for the SELECT statement to display data values from the row the DBMS IS testing. For the current example, you would use the AND logical connective to add a second search condition to the WHERE clause, as follows:

```
SELECT emp_id, first_name, last_name FROM employees
WHERE dept = 'Marketing'
  AND employment_status = 'Active'
```

Now the DBMS will return the EMP_ID, FIRST_NAME, and LAST_NAME for only those rows in which the value in the DEPT column is Marketing *and* the value in the EMPLOYMENT_STATUS column is Active. As such, you will get a list of all marketing personnel currently working for your company.

You can use as many AND connectives in a WHERE clause as you need to specify all of the search conditions the input table's row must satisfy in order to have its select list values included in the results table. Each additional AND connective lets you add one more search condition. Thus, for the current example, if you wanted a list of only marketing personnel who were currently employed and not yet assigned to a supervisor, you would add a second AND connective to include a third search condition:

```
SELECT emp_id, first_name, last_name FROM employees
WHERE dept = 'Marketing'
  AND employment_status = 'Active'
  AND supervisor IS NULL
```

The important thing to know is that no matter how many ANDs you use to join search conditions in a WHERE clause, *all* of the search conditions connected by an AND must evaluate to TRUE in order for values from the current row in the input table to be included in the results table.

125 Using the NOT Logical Connective to Negate the Search Condition in a WHERE Clause

As you learned in Tip 124, "Using the AND Logical Connective to Do Multiple Condition Selects of Rows in a Table," the WHERE clause must evaluate to TRUE in order for the DBMS to perform the action prescribed by the SQL statement. A SELECT statement, for example, will display select list values for only those rows that satisfy the search criteria in the WHERE clause. Similarly, the UPDATE statement will change column values only in rows for which the search criteria evaluate to TRUE; and the DELETE statement will remove only rows whose data values satisfy the conditions set forth in the WHERE clause.

The NOT logical connective gives you a way to tell the DBMS to take action on those rows in which the search condition in the WHERE clause evaluates to FALSE instead of those in which it evaluates to TRUE.

Suppose, for example, that you want a list of all cars in the AUTO_INVENTORY table that were not red, green, or blue. If you do not know all of the possible colors for cars in your inventory, you cannot construct a WHERE clause for the select statement using:

```
SELECT vin_number, make, model, year, price, color
FROM AUTO_INVENTORY
WHERE color IN ('Orange', 'Brown', 'Chartreuse')
```

After all, if you fail to list the color of one of your (nonred, nongreen, or nonblue) cars in the set of all possible colors, the DBMS will omit the cars of that color from your inventory list. Moreover, since we already made the assumption that you do not know all of the possible automobile colors, your inventory list will most likely be incomplete and, therefore, inaccurate.

The NOT logical operator lets you avoid having to list all of the possible search conditions that could be TRUE by letting you tell the DBMS what must NOT be TRUE in order for the DBMS to include a row's data in the results table. For the current example, the SELECT statement

```
SELECT vin_number, make, model, year, price, color
FROM AUTO_INVENTORY
WHERE color NOT IN ('Red', 'Green', 'Blue')
```

will return a complete and accurate list of the cars in your AUTO_INVENTORY table that are not red, green, or blue in color.

When evaluating a search condition proceeded by the NOT logical connective, the DBMS changes the Boolean value of the search condition as follows:

```
NOT  TRUE     FALSE    NULL
     --------------------
     FALSE    TRUE     NULL
```

Thus, the NOT connective will change TRUE to FALSE, change FALSE to TRUE, and leave a NULL result unchanged.

Therefore, the SELECT statement

```
SELECT first_name, last_name FROM employees
WHERE NOT age > 50
```

will display the names of employees who are 50 years old or younger because the SELECT statement will include input from only table rows for which the WHERE clause evaluates TRUE. As such, when the inner search condition in the WHERE clause evaluates to TRUE for employees older than 50, the NOT logical connective changes the evaluation to FALSE. Thus, the overall WHERE clause evaluates to FALSE whenever AGE > 50 evaluates to TRUE—which means any row in which the AGE column is greater than 50 will be omitted from the results table.

Admittedly, the search condition in the previous example (which produced a list of employees under the age of 50) could be written more clearly as:

```
SELECT first_name, last_name FROM employees
WHERE age <= 50
```

However, the expression WHERE NOT age > 50 does illustrate how the NOT logical connective negates the Boolean value returned by the comparison operator and causes the DBMS to include the rows normally excluded while excluding those normally included.

The important thing to know now is that you can use the NOT logical connective in those instances in which telling the DBMS what rows *not* to include in the results table is more convenient or easier to understand than trying to test for all of the conditions under which a row is to be included.

126 Using the OR Logical Connective to Do Multiple Condition Selects of Rows in a Table

The WHERE clause in a SELECT statement tells the DBMS which rows from the input table to include in the query's results table. While executing a SELECT statement, the DBMS scans the rows in the input table, substituting column values from the current row into corresponding column name references in the search condition. If the search condition evaluates to TRUE, the DBMS adds values from the current row to the results table.

Each search condition in a WHERE clause can perform a conditional test on a single column. Thus, to query the STUDENTS table for a list of all chemistry majors, you might use a SELECT statement similar to:

```
SELECT student_id, first_name, last_name FROM students
WHERE major = 'Chemistry'
```

If the decision of whether or not to include a row's data in the results table involves checking more than one column or checking the same column multiple ways, you will need to add an additional search condition to the WHERE clause for each test the DBMS is to perform. In Tip 124, "Using the AND Logical Connective to Do Multiple Condition Selects of Rows in a Table," you learned how to use the logical connective AND to join multiple search conditions in a WHERE clause.

As you now know, the AND connective tells the DBMS that all search conditions it joins must be TRUE in order for the WHERE clause to evaluate TRUE. If you want the DBMS to include data from the current row if one or more of the search conditions in a WHERE clause is TRUE, use an OR (instead of an AND) to combine them.

Suppose, for example, that you want a list of students majoring in chemistry, biology, or mathematics. You could produce such a list by submitting a SELECT statement similar to:

```
SELECT student_id, first_name, last_name, major
FROM students
WHERE major = 'Chemistry' OR major = 'Biology'
OR major = 'Mathematics'
```

After the DBMS executes the SELECT statement, the results table will include student ID, name, and major information from rows in which the value in the MAJOR column is chemistry, biology, or mathematics—that is, if any one of the search conditions joined by an OR is TRUE, the WHERE clause evaluates to TRUE, and the DBMS will include data from row being checked in the results table.

127 Understanding SQL Transaction Processing

A database transaction is a sequence of one or more statements that must all be executed successfully in order to complete a specific task. SQL-92 specifies that the DBMS must provide a BEGIN TRANSACTION and an END TRANSACTION statement you can use to group commands that the DBMS is to execute atomically—either execute all of the statements in the group (bracketed by the BEGIN TRANSACTION and END TRANSACTION statements) or execute none of them.

If the DBMS has executed some of the statements in a transaction and the application program aborts or there is some other catastrophic hardware or software failure, the DBMS is responsible for undoing the tasks (statements) it has already executed and restoring the database tables back to their original, unmodified condition. In Tip 130, "Using the ROLLBACK Statement to Undo Changes Made to Database Objects," you will learn how use the ROLLBACK statement to take advantage of the ability of the DBMS to "undo" modifications if you change your mind and want to "back out" updates and deletes that executed successfully during a transaction.

SQL statements grouped together (between BEGIN TRANSACTION and END TRANSACTION statements) to form a transaction are typically interdependent and must all be executed in order to maintain database consistency. Suppose, for example, that you were changing the item number of a product in your inventory. To do so, you would have to:

- Check the PRODUCTS table to make sure the *new* PRODUCT_CODE does not belong to an existing product
- Update the PRODUCT_CODE in the INVENTORY table so that someone querying table with the new PRODUCT_CODE will be able to find out the quantity of the product that is in stock
- Update the PRODUCT_CODE in the ORDERS table so the warehouse personnel will know which item to pull from inventory (based on product code) and ship to the customer
- Update the PRODUCT_CODE in the INVOICES table so that the customer's bill will print the correct item cost and description on the customer's bill
- Update the product code in the PRODUCTS table so that the master item list will display the correct product description and cost when queried using the new PRODUCT_CODE

If any of the updates in the transaction are not done, the database will become inconsistent. For example, if the DBMS fails to change the PRODUCT_CODE value in the INVENTORY table, the SELECT statement

```
SELECT
  product_code, description, cost, vendor, serial_number
FROM inventory, products
WHERE inventory.product_code = products.product_code
```

will no longer produce correct results because the PRODUCT_CODE in the INVENTORY table would reference a nonexistent PRODUCT_CODE in the PRODUCTS table (which holds the DESCRIPTION, COST, and VENDOR for every product in the inventory).

From the current example, you can see that each statement in a transaction performs a part of a task, such as changing the PRODUCT_CODE code in one of several tables. Moreover, all of tasks must be completed in order to successfully finish the overall job at hand, such as changing the PRODUCT_CODE from one value to another throughout the entire database.

The important thing to understand about transaction processing is that the DBMS uses it to maintain the consistency of the database. Since the DBMS treats the statements in a transaction as an atomic unit of work, it will either execute all of the statements successfully or make it appear as if none of the statements was executed by restoring all data and database objects modified by statements in the transaction back to their original, unmodified states.

Tip 128, "Understanding the ANSI/ISO Transaction Model," will explain how most commercial database products automatically detect the start and end of an SQL transaction, and Tip 131, "Understanding the MS-SQL Server Transaction Model," will teach you how to group statements into transactions for MS-SQL Server using the BEGIN TRANSACTION and END TRANSACTION statements.

128 Understanding the ANSI/ISO Transaction Model

In Tip 127, "Understanding SQL Transaction Processing," you learned that a transaction is a sequence of SQL statements that the DBMS views as a single unit of work. Said another way, the statements in a transaction are considered an atomic unit of work—either all are executed successfully or any work performed is undone so that the database appears as if none of the statements in the transaction was executed.

The ANSI/ISO transaction model defines the roles of the COMMIT and ROLLBACK statements (which we will discuss in Tips 129 and 130, "Understanding When to Use the COMMIT Statement") and specifies that a transaction begins *automatically* with the first statement submitted to the DBMS by the user or application program. As such, a user working with a DBMS that follows the ANSI/ISO transaction model (DB2, for example) is always operating within a transaction.

An ANSI/ISO transaction begins automatically with the execution of an SQL statement and continues through subsequent statements until terminated in one of the four ways shown in Figure 128.1.

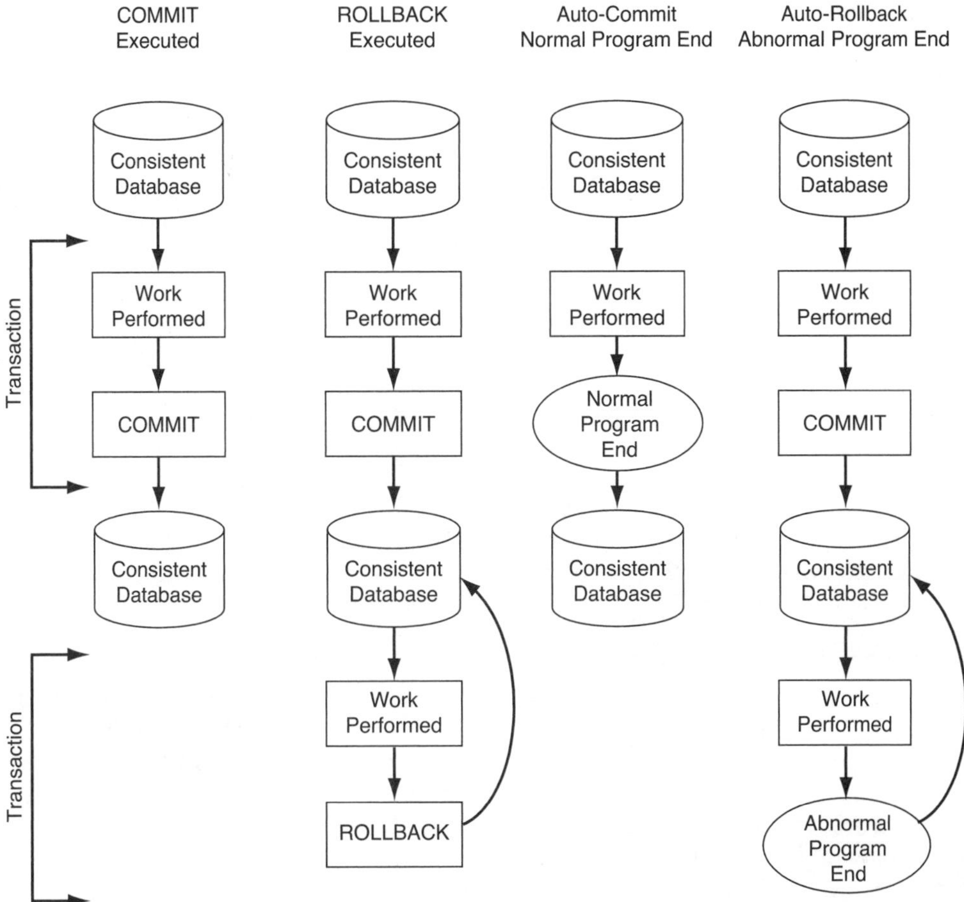

Figure 128.1 Database states after successful and unsuccessful transaction processing

Note that the defining characteristic of the ANSI/ISO Transaction model is that no explicit action is required to start a transaction. The user or application program is always in a transaction because a new transaction begins as soon as the current transaction ends with one of the following events:

- The user or application executes a COMMIT statement signaling that all of the transaction's statements executed successfully. The COMMIT statement makes the transaction's database changes permanent.
- The user or application executes a ROLLBACK statement that aborts the transaction and removes any work performed during the course of the transaction. (At the completion of the ROLLBACK, database objects and values are restored to their original pretransaction states, as if none of the transaction's statements were ever executed.)

- The application program terminates normally. When the application terminates normally, the DBMS issues an automatic COMMIT statement, which makes permanent any database updates performed while in the application program.
- The application program terminates abnormally. When the application terminates abnormally, the DBMS aborts the transaction and executes a ROLLBACK. As such, if the application terminates abnormally, the DBMS backs out any database updates the program performed, restoring the database to its state just prior to the start of the aborted programs execution.

Note: *You might consider hardware failure as the fifth way in which to terminate a transaction. If the hardware should fail, once the DBMS is restarted, it will back out any work from partially completed transactions before it lets any users or application programs access the database. In short, the DBMS automatically issues a ROLLBACK when it is restarted after a hardware failure such as a power outage.*

The ANSI/ISO transaction model does not lend itself to interactive multi-statement transaction processing. In fact, most DBMS products default their interactive sessions to *auto-commit* mode, in which the DBMS automatically starts a transaction when the user submits a Data Definition Language (DDL) or Data Manipulation Language (DML) statement, such as

```
UPDATE products SET sales_price = sales_price * 1.2
```

and then ends the transaction with a COMMIT as soon as the DBMS successfully performs its task. Because the DBMS issues a COMMIT as soon as the SQL statement finishes its execution, you cannot use a ROLLBACK to undo the work performed by a successfully executed statement during an interactive session in auto-commit mode. Moreover, as soon as you submit the next statement for processing, the DBMS starts a new transaction. As such, although you may want to undo both statements if the second statement fails to execute, the DBMS will roll back only the work from the failed second statement. (By the time the second statement executes, the DBMS already made the first statement's work permanent with a COMMIT.)

Tip 129 and Tip 130, "Using the ROLLBACK Statement to Undo Changes Made to Database Objects," will show you how to take an interactive session out of auto-commit mode. After you turn off the auto-commit, you will be able to execute multi-statement transactions and roll back the work performed by one or more statements you submit during an interactive session.

The important thing to know now is that the ANSI/ISO transaction model (which defines the roles of COMMIT and ROLLBACK statements) specifies that an SQL transaction begins *automatically* with the first statement executed by a user or application program. In Tip 131, "Understanding the MS-SQL Server Transaction Model," you will learn that the non-ANSI/ISO transaction model still defaults to auto-commit mode for an interactive session but requires programs to execute an explicit BEGIN TRANSACTION statement to start a transaction in programmatic SQL.

129 Understanding When to Use the COMMIT Statement

During SQL transaction processing, work performed by statements can be undone (with a ROLLBACK) until it is permanently written to the database. The COMMIT statement tells the DBMS to make database changes permanent.

As you learned in Tip 128, "Understanding the ANSI/ISO Transaction Model," most DBMS products default to auto-commit mode when accepting interactive queries and updates. As such, when you type the UPDATE statement

```
UPDATE products SET sales_price = sales_price * 1.2
```

into the MS-SQL Server Query Analyzer's (upper) input pane and then click on the Execute Query button, as shown in Figure 129.1, the DBMS will increase the SALES_PRICE of all products in the PRODUCTS table by 20 percent.

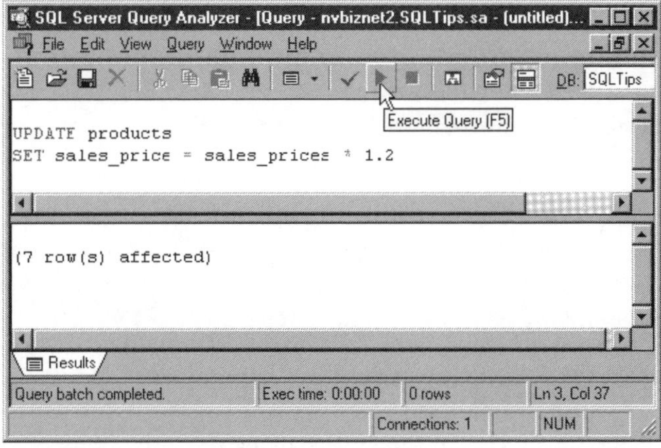

Figure 129.1 An MS-SQL Server's Query Analyzer interactive session

Since the Query Analyzer provides *interactive* connections to an MS-SQL Server database (SQL Tips, in the current example), the DBMS automatically issues a COMMIT statement after the UPDATE statement makes its last change and returns control to the Query Analyzer. Thus, when working in interactive auto-commit mode, you need not execute a COMMIT statement to have work permanently written to the database.

As with any transaction processing, if the transaction started by submitting an SQL statement to the DBMS during an interactive session does not run to a successful completion, the DBMS will roll back (undo) any work performed. Thus, in the current example, if the server loses power or locks up after updating the SALES_PRICE for half of the products in the PRODUCTS table, the DBMS will automatically set the SALES_PRICE of all products back to what it was prior to the 20 percent increase.

Note: *Obviously, you'll have to bring the server back online before it can roll back the partial update. After the server restarts the DBMS, the DBMS will check its transaction log for any partially executed and uncommitted transactions. Prior to letting any users or application programs connect to the database, the DBMS will reverse (ROLLBACK) any work done by* both *aborted and uncommitted transactions.*

The important thing to know is that when the DBMS executes a ROLLBACK, it undoes all work performed on the database subsequent to the last COMMIT. When executing SQL statements in interactive mode, the ROLLBACK reverses only the changes made by the most recent partially executed statement. (Remember, a fully executed statement is automatically *committed* during an interactive session in the default auto-commit mode.)

Executing an explicit COMMIT statement becomes important in programmatic SQL, in which you use an application program to send SQL statements to the DBMS. During a programmatic SQL session, you start a transaction with a BEGIN TRANSACTION statement.

Note: *As you learned in Tip 128, a DBMS that follows the ANSI/ISO transaction model will start a transaction automatically (without an explicit BEGIN TRANSACTION) as soon as the application program submits its first SQL statement.*

All statements submitted by the application program become part the transaction—which does not end until the application either submits a ROLLBACK or COMMIT statement, or ends (either normally or abnormally). Thus, if you have an application program that has the statement flow

```
BEGIN TRANSACTION
MOD 1...
MOD 2...
MOD 3...
MOD 4...
```

the four modifications are not *committed* (made permanent) until the application program ends normally. As such, an abnormal ending will cause the DBMS to roll back (undo) all modifications made by all four of the SQL statements in the body of the application. If you want the first two modifications to remain in the database without regard to the successful execution of modifications 3 and 4, have the application program execute a COMMIT statement after submitting MOD 2:

```
BEGIN TRANSACTION
MOD 1...
MOD 2...
COMMIT TRANSACTION

BEGIN TRANSACTION
MOD 3...
MOD 4...
```

Note: If you are using a DBMS that uses the ANSI/ISO transaction model, the program need not execute an explicit BEGIN TRANSACTION statement before MOD 1. As you learned in Tip 128, the ANSI/ISO transaction model DBMS automatically starts a new transaction with the first SQL statement following a COMMIT or a ROLLBACK.

The important thing to know now is that the COMMIT statement signals the successful completion of an SQL transaction and causes the DBMS to make permanent the work performed by statements in the transaction. Committed work cannot be reversed with a ROLLBACK and is not undone when the DBMS is restarted after either a normal or an abnormal shutdown.

130 Using the ROLLBACK Statement to Undo Changes Made to Database Objects

In Tip 129, "Understanding When to Use the COMMIT Statement," you learned how to make work performed as part of an SQL transaction permanent by executing a COMMIT statement. Prior to being written permanently to the database, you can use the ROLLBACK statement to reverse changes made by almost all SQL statements—including, in MS-SQL Server, bringing back a table and data removed from the database with a DROP TABLE statement!

During an interactive session, the DBMS defaults to *auto-commit* mode, which means that the DBMS automatically *commits* (makes permanent) the action of every SQL statement that it successfully executes. Therefore, if you execute the statement

```
DELETE FROM employees
```

which removes all rows from the EMPLOYEES table, you cannot bring the deleted data back with the statement:

```
ROLLBACK TRANSACTION
```

Remember, the DBMS starts the transaction when it receives the DELETE statement and then automatically executes a COMMIT TRANSACTION as soon is it has removed the last row from the EMPLOYEES table. As such, there is no uncommitted transaction to roll back, even if you execute the ROLLBACK TRANSACTION statement immediately after executing the DELETE statement.

If you want to be able to undo changes made by SQL statements you execute during an interactive session, you must first take the interactive session out of auto-commit mode.

MS-SQL Server, for example, lets you turn off auto-commit mode by executing the statement:

```
BEGIN TRANSACTION
```

Note: *You will need to check your system documentation for the specific statement your DBMS uses to turn off auto-commit mode. While MS-SQL Server uses BEGIN TRANSACTION, DB2 uses UPDATE COMMAND OPTIONS USING c OFF. Look in the index under "transaction," "commit," or "auto-commit."*

After you execute the BEGIN TRANSACTION statement, the DBMS treats subsequent SQL statements as being part of a multi-statement transaction. As such, if you execute the statement sequence

```
MOD 1

BEGIN TRANSACTION
MOD 2
MOD 3
MOD 4

ROLLBACK TRANSACTION
```

the DBMS will undo the work perform by the three SQL statements (MOD 2, MOD 3, MOD 4) that follow the BEGIN TRANSACTION statement. Therefore, after executing the ROLLBACK TRANSACTION statement, the database will look exactly like it did when it finished executing the SQL statement denoted as MOD 1 in the current example.

Note: *The ROLLBACK TRANSACTION did not undo the work performed by MOD 1 because MOD 1 was executed in auto-commit mode. As a result, changes made by MOD 1 were automatically committed (made permanent) upon the successful completion of the SQL statement MOD 1 represents.*

What may become a bit confusing is that if the DBMS follows the ANSI/ISO transaction model (which MS-SQL Server and Sybase do not), executing the example's SQL statements in an interactive session will have a different effect than using programmatic SQL to submit the same sequence of statements to the DBMS through an application program.

During an interactive session, the ROLLBACK TRANSACTION will have the same effect whether executed using interactive or programmatic SQL—the database will keep only changes performed by the SQL statement represented by MOD 1.

If the example statements are executed in an application program on a DBMS that follows the ANSI/ISO transaction model, the ROLLBACK TRANSACTION will undo changes made by MOD 1 along with those made by MOD 2, MOD 3, and MOD 4. However, if the example statements are executed in an application program on a DBMS that does not follow the ANSI/ISO transaction model (such as MS-SQL Server and Sybase), the ROLLBACK will not undo changes made by MOD 1, along with those made by MOD 2, MOD 3, and MOD 4.

The reason for the difference in behavior is that the ANSI/ISO transaction model automatically starts the transaction with the first statement submitted by the application program. Thus, MOD 1 is part of the transaction affected by the ROLLBACK TRANSACTION statement when submitted by an application program running on a DBMS that follows the ANSI/ISO transaction model.

When using a ROLLBACK to undo database changes, the important thing to understand is that the ROLLBACK statement reverses (undoes) all the work performed after the execution of the most recent COMMIT statement. Therefore, if you are executing SQL statements within an interactive session and want to be able to undo work by executing a ROLLBACK statement or want to execute multi-statement transactions, be sure to turn off the default auto-commit mode.

Note: *Consider using explicit BEGIN TRANSACTION and END TRANSACTION blocks (where possible) to make your SQL code transportable between DBMS servers that adhere to the ANSI/ISO transaction model (such as DB2) and those that do not (such as Sybase and MS-SQL Server).*

---

131 Understanding the MS-SQL Server Transaction Model

As you learned in Tip 127, "Understanding SQL Transaction Processing," and Tip 128, "Understanding the ANSI/ISO Transaction Model," an SQL transaction is a sequence of statements, all of which must be executed successfully in order to complete a task. All DBMS products perform the work specified by the statements in a transaction on an all-or-nothing basis—there is no partial execution. Either the DBMS successfully executes all statements in a transaction, or the system undoes any work performed and restores the database to its state prior to the start of the transaction. Moreover, all DBMS products support a ROLLBACK statement that will undo work performed in a transaction not yet made permanent by a COMMIT statement.

The MS-SQL Server transaction model is similar to the ANSI/ISO transaction model in that it:

- Executes the statements in a transaction atomically, on an all-or-nothing basis
- Ends a transaction and makes the work performed permanent when it receives a COMMIT statement
- Automatically executes a COMMIT statement when a programmatic SQL application ends normally
- Lets users execute a ROLLBACK to end a transaction and undo any uncommitted work performed in the transaction
- Automatically executes a ROLLBACK statement when a programmatic SQL application ends abnormally

In a departure from the ANSI/ISO transaction model, however, MS-SQL Server:

- Does not automatically start a transaction with the first statement in a programmatic SQL application. MS-SQL Server requires that the program explicitly group statements into a transaction by executing the BEGIN TRANSACTION statement before the first statement to be treated as part of a transaction.
- Includes a SAVE TRANSACTION statement you can use to establish savepoints in a transaction so users can undo the work performed by some (vs. all) of the transaction's statements.

MS-SQL Server savepoints are especially useful in transactions with a large number of statements in that they allow the application program to undo work and back up to specific points in a transaction. As such, the application program can use a ROLLBACK to a savepoint to redo statements in a portion of a transaction without having to start over from the beginning. For example, if you have MS-SQL Server execute the following statements

```
BEGIN TRANSACTION
CREATE TABLE trans_table
  (row_number SMALLINT, description VARCHAR(35))
INSERT INTO trans_table VALUES (1,'Inserted Row 1')
INSERT INTO trans_table VALUES (2,'Inserted Row 2')
SAVE TRANSACTION savepoint_1

DELETE FROM trans_table WHERE row_number = 2
INSERT INTO trans_table VALUES (3,'Inserted Row 3')
INSERT INTO trans_table VALUES (4,'Inserted Row 4')
SAVE TRANSACTION savepoint_2
DELETE FROM trans_table WHERE row_number = 1
DELETE FROM trans_table WHERE row_number = 3
INSERT INTO trans_table VALUES (5,'Inserted Row 5')
UPDATE trans_table SET description = 'All Rows Updated'

ROLLBACK TRANSACTION savepoint_2

UPDATE trans_table
  SET description = 'Row 1 After ROLLBACK to 2'
DELETE trans_table WHERE row_number = 4

COMMIT TRANSACTION
```

the results table for the SELECT statement

```
SELECT * FROM trans_table
```

is:

```
row_number  description
----------  -------------------------
1           Row 1 After ROLLBACK to 2
3           Inserted Row 3
```

Obviously, unlike the example, an actual application program will use some sort of decision mechanism such as the Transact-SQL statement IF @@ERROR or IF @@ROWCOUNT to determine whether to roll back (undo) work performed subsequent to a particular save-point. Moreover, the application (or stored procedure) will most likely be more complex and perform useful work. However, the example does demonstrate how a savepoint can be used to undo a portion of the work performed by statements in a transaction, as illustrated in Figure 131.1.

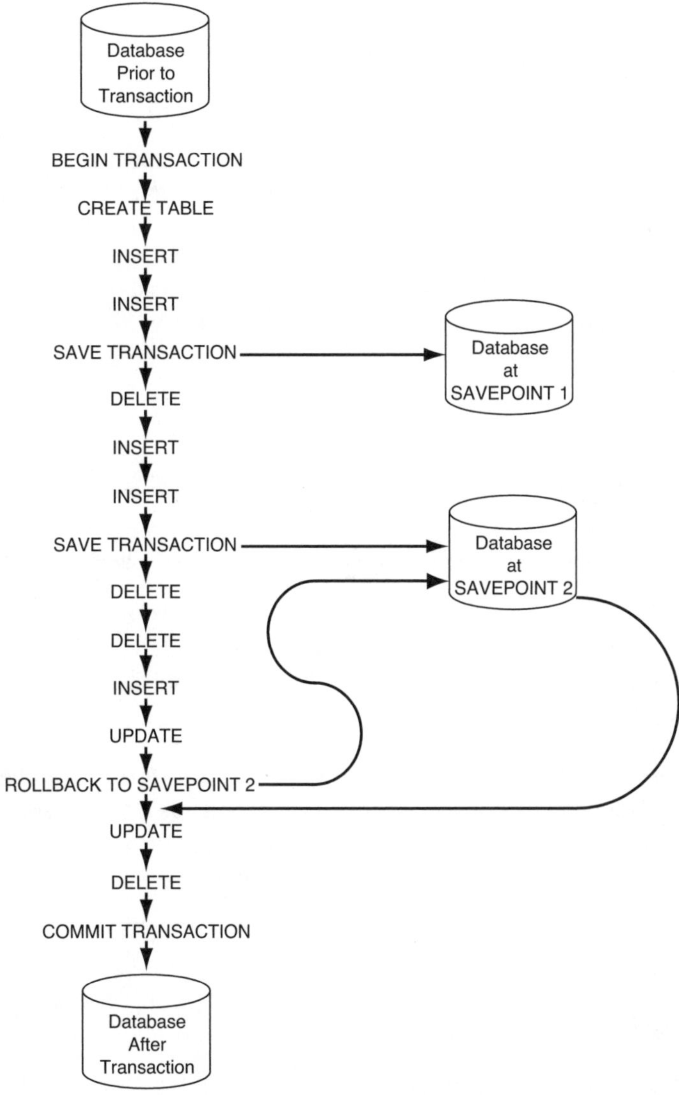

Figure 131.1 MS-SQL Server transaction processing using a savepoint

Notice that the ROLLBACK removes the effects of only the two DELETE statements, the INSERT statement, and the UPDATE statement executed after the statement:

```
SAVE TRANSACTION savepoint_2
```

The important thing to know is that the SAVE TRANSACTION statement lets you label savepoints within the sequence of statements that make up a transaction. You can then undo statements executed subsequent to a particular savepoint by using the ROLLBACK statement and naming the savepoint to which you want the database restored. In other words, you can do a ROLLBACK to any of the savepoints within a transaction and then continue execution of SQL statements from that point.

Note: *Although the SAVE TRANSACTION statement lets you name savepoints in a transaction, it does not COMMIT the work performed up to the savepoint. As such, the DBMS treats the entire sequence of statements following the BEGIN TRANSACTION statement as a single transaction. Therefore, if the program sending the statements aborts, or in the event of some other type of hardware or software failure, the DBMS will back out* all *statements within the transactions—including those before and after any savepoints.*

132 Using Named and Nested Transactions on MS-SQL Server

In Tip 131, "Understanding the MS-SQL Server Transaction Model," you learned how to use the SAVE TRANSACTION statement to create savepoints that let you roll back (undo) a portion of the work performed within a transaction. MS-SQL Server's capability to name and COMMIT named transactions serves an entirely different purpose. Named transactions and named commits should be used only to support transaction processing in stored procedures that may be called either as part of a transaction or outside of a transaction. The distinction of whether the stored procedure is called from within or outside of a transaction is important to the effect of named COMMIT executed statements within the stored procedure.

Suppose, for example, that you have a stored procedure created with

```
CREATE PROCEDURE SP_Insert_Row
  @row_number SMALLINT, @description CHAR(35)
AS BEGIN TRANSACTION insert_trans
     INSERT INTO trans_table
       VALUES (@row_number, @description)
   COMMIT TRANSACTION insert_trans
```

that starts a transaction, inserts the values passed into the TRANS_TABLE, and then makes the insertion permanent by ending the transaction by executing a named COMMIT statement.

If you execute the SQL statements

```
CREATE TABLE trans_table
  (row_number SMALLINT, description VARCHAR(35))

BEGIN TRANSACTION
  INSERT INTO trans_table VALUES (1, 'Inserted Row 1')
  INSERT INTO trans_table VALUES (2, 'Inserted Row 2')
  EXEC SP_Insert_Row 3, 'Inserted Row 3'
  EXEC SP_Insert_Row 4, 'Inserted Row 4'
ROLLBACK
```

the TRANS_TABLE will end up with no rows!

You might expect the rows inserted by the stored procedure to remain after the ROLLBACK, since the stored procedure executes the *named* COMMIT statement

```
    COMMIT TRANSACTION insert_trans
```

after each insertion. However, in the current example, the stored procedure is called from within another transaction, making the transaction in the stored procedure a *nested* or inner transaction. MS-SQL Server ignores named COMMIT statements executed on nested (inner) transactions.

Thus, when called from within another transaction, the final disposition of the work performed by the nested (inner) transaction in the procedure is determined by what happens to the outer transaction. In the current example, a ROLLBACK statement terminates the outer transaction. As a result, all work performed within the outer transaction, including the work performed by the executed procedure, is removed by the ROLLBACK.

On the other hand, if you call the same procedure outside a transaction, such as

```
EXEC SP_Insert_Row 3, 'Inserted Row 3'

BEGIN TRANSACTION
  INSERT INTO trans_table VALUES (1, 'Inserted Row 1')
  INSERT INTO trans_table VALUES (2, 'Inserted Row 2')
  EXEC SP_Insert_Row 4, 'Inserted Row 4'
ROLLBACK
```

the TRANS_TABLE will contain:

```
row_number  description
----------  --------------
3           Inserted Row 3
```

In this example, the work performed by the first call to the procedure

```
EXEC SP_Insert_Row 3, 'Inserted Row 3'
```

is permanently written to the TRANS_TABLE by the COMMIT statement at the end of the transaction. When the procedure is executed outside of a transaction, the transaction within the procedure is not nested, and its COMMIT statement makes permanent changes to the TRANS_TABLE.

Conversely, the work performed by the second execution of the stored procedure in the example is again undone by the ROLLBACK. When the procedure is executed within a transaction, the transaction within the procedure is nested, and the DBMS does not make permanent changes to the TRANS_TABLE when it sees the COMMIT statement (since a COMMIT executed on an inner transaction is ignored by MS-SQL Server).

The important thing to know now is that MS-SQL Server ignores named COMMIT statements executed on inner, or nested, procedures. This is true whether the nested transaction occurs within a stored procedure or within the application program itself.

Note: *The importance of using the named BEGIN TRANSACTION and named COMMIT TRANSACTION statements in the stored procedure may not, at first, be obvious. If you do not name the transaction in the stored procedure and end it with an unnamed COMMIT statement, the COMMIT TRANSACTION at the end of the procedure will COMMIT (make permanent) not only the work within the procedure but also end the outer transaction. As such, an unnamed COMMIT TRANSACTION statement at the end of the stored procedure SP_INSERT_ROW in either of the examples in this tip would have terminated both the inner and outer transactions and prevented the ROLLBACK at the end of the examples from undoing any work performed by making the INSERTs permanent prior to the ROLLBACK.*

---

133 Understanding Transaction Logs

The transaction log, created automatically when you create a database, makes it possible for the DBMS to undo work performed by statements in a transaction and to restore the database to a consistent state after recovery from a hardware or software failure. At first, undoing changes or making large amounts of deleted data "reappear" may seem like magic. However, the DBMS does it not with smoke and mirrors, but by maintaining copies of the data before and after changes in its transaction log.

Although the actual specifics of transaction log maintenance vary among the DBMS products, the basic concept is the same for all of them. Whenever the DBMS executes an SQL statement that updates the database, the DBMS adds a record to the transaction log. Each record in the transaction log contains two copies of every row being changed, removed, or inserted. One copy shows the table row *before* the change, and one copy shows the table row *after* the change. Maintenance of the transaction log is such an important and integral part of statement execution that the DBMS updates the actual table data only after it has finished updating the log.

In addition to storing before and after pictures of the table rows, the DBMS also notes transaction events (BEGIN TRANSACTION, SAVE TRANSACTION, and COMMIT statement execution) in the transaction log. Using transaction event markers in conjunction with premodification images of rows being modified, the DBMS is able to back out the work of partially executed transactions or satisfy a user's request to do a ROLLBACK (undo) of database updates made after a certain point.

To do a ROLLBACK of an uncommitted transaction, for example, the DBMS simply works its way backward through the transaction log, replacing the current table data with the *before* update image of the data until it reaches a BEGIN TRANSACTION marker. Restoring the table rows to their state prior to changes made by statements in the transaction effectively backs out (undoes) all work performed by the transaction. On DBMS products that support savepoints, the DBMS can undo a portion of the work performed in a transaction by stopping at a user-specified savepoint marker vs. restoring original data up to the BEGIN TRANSACTION marker.

If the DBMS needs to restore the database to a consistent state due to a failure in executing a statement in a transaction or after the DBMS is restarted due to an abnormal system shutdown, the transaction log makes it possible. In both cases, the DBMS reads backward through the transaction log, undoing the work performed by uncommitted transactions and substituting the *before* image of each table row for the current table row until the DBMS reaches the BEGIN TRANSACTION marker.

When there are no updates that can be undone, as is the case when all transactions have been committed, the DBMS finds a COMMIT marker at the end of the transaction log. Thus, if the COMMIT marker is the first thing the DBMS finds when reading backward through the transaction log on startup or when it receives a ROLLBACK statement, it makes no changes to the database since there are no uncommitted changes it can (or needs to) undo.

Note: *All updates noted in the transaction log are a part of a transaction. During an interactive session in auto-commit mode, the DBMS automatically writes a BEGIN TRANSACTION marker to the log at the start of statement execution, stores before and after pictures of each table row changed, and then automatically adds a COMMIT (end transaction) marker to the log after it makes the last change to the database. When it executes an explicit BEGIN TRANSACTION statement, the DBMS does not add the COMMIT marker to the transaction log until the application program interacting with the DBMS ends normally or until the program or user executes a COMMIT statement.*

---

134 Understanding How and Why to Limit Access to Various Database Objects

Over the course of time, the data in a company's database will grow to contain a complete description of the organization. It will hold information on past successes and failures, the current organization scheme, key customers and employees, proprietary processes, and what it costs to do businesses. In short, the database will have information on which the company relies to do businesses and which could definitely be damaging should it fall into the hands of a competitor. As such, a company has a fundamental need to keep its data secure from prying eyes of other companies vying for the same customers. In addition to forces outside the company, the database administrator (DBA) must also protect the database from employees within the company itself.

Not every table should be available to every user. Marketing employees, for example, should not have access to tables dealing with new products under development, lest they be tempted to promise customers products and capabilities the company is not yet ready to release. Moreover, in the interest of maintaining good morale among workers, you would not want to give all employees access to the payroll tables. In addition to causing contention among coworkers earning different salaries, the knowledge of what the company managers, supervisors, and officers make may unduly influence the employees' (or union's) demands during wage negations.

Finally, some users should be able to update particular tables or only certain columns in tables, while others should have only view access to the same data. Continuing with the payroll table example, employees in the human resources (HR) department or bookkeeping department need to be able to modify an employee's personal data and salary information. Meanwhile, the employee and perhaps his or her manager should be able to only view the information on file.

The SQL security scheme lets you not only protects your data from unauthorized, prying eyes, but it also lets you limit which tables (or portions of tables) authorized users can see and what actions they can take on database objects.

Implementing the security scheme set up by the DBA and enforcing its restrictions are the responsibilities of the DBMS. The SQL-92 standard defines an overall framework for database security, and all commercially available DBMS products support SQL statements the DBA can use to set up database security and GRANT and REVOKE user ID access and SQL statement execution privileges.

SQL security is based on three concepts:

- **Users.** Are the people who query and update the data in a database. All activities undertaken by the DBMS are initiated by a user request, either interactively or through an application program. The DBMS creates or drops objects and retrieves, inserts, removes, or updates data only in response to a user-submitted SQL statement. It is up to the DBMS to check the user's security profile and either permit or prohibit the action requested based on the ID of the user making the request.
- **Database objects.** Are the "things" in the database protected by the DBMS security scheme. Users will have permission to use certain objects such as tables, views, stored procedures, and application programs, and be prohibited from using others.
- **Privileges.** Are the types of statements a user is permitted to ask the DBMS to execute on database objects. A user might, for example, be allowed only to SELECT (or query) certain tables or views but not be able to DELETE or UPDATE existing table data. By using the GRANT and REVOKE statements, the DBA can permit or prevent a user from executing any SQL statement on any database object.

You will learn more about the GRANT and REVOKE statements in Tips 144–156. For now, the important thing to know is that setting up database security is a central part of a DBA's job. The DBA not only must protect the database from outside forces, but must also limit the actions users within the organization can perform on individual database objects. Every commercial SQL database supports the implementation of a security scheme and provides (at a minimum) the ability to set up user IDs and GRANT and REVOKE their access privileges.

135 Understanding Individual User IDs and Authentication

A single-user database, residing on a personal computer, will normally have only one user-ID—a short name that identifies the person that created and owns the database and (by extension) all of its objects. In a single-user environment, the one user ID normally has all privileges to access all database objects. After all, it doesn't make much sense to create database objects you then prevent yourself from using.

In a production environment, the database typically runs on a fileserver or networked personal computer and is used by many users. The database administrator (DBA) normally assigns user IDs, which are the heart of SQL security. As is the case for the single-user environment, each user ID is a short name that identifies the user to the DBMS software. The DBMS checks the user ID against the privileges given to that ID prior to carrying out an SQL statement. If the DBA assigned the necessary privileges to the user ID, the DBMS performs work specified by the SQL statement submitted by the user ID. Conversely, if the user ID does not have enough privilege, the DBMS prohibits the ID from executing the statement the user submitted.

Restrictions on the names the DBA can choose for user IDs vary from implementation to implementation. The SQL-89 standard specified that user IDs could be up to 18 characters and had to adhere to the database object-naming conventions you learned about in Tip 9, "Understanding Table Names," and Tip 10, "Understanding Column Names." MS-SQL Server and Sybase allow user IDs of up to 30 characters, while some mainframe databases limit user IDs to 8 characters or less. Check your system documentation for the specific limits on user IDs on your DBMS. (If you are concerned about portability, limit your user IDs to eight characters or less to ensure that they can be used across DBMS implementations.)

Although the name used to log on to a DBMS is most often called a user ID, the term authorization ID is more correct, since the DBA will sometimes assign the same ID to multiple users. Whether assigned to a single user or a group of users, the DBMS checks its system security tables to determine what the ID used to log on to the DBMS is *authorized* to do. However, a single ID assigned to all of the workers in a department such as the accounting, human resources, or payroll departments does not really identify an individual user as implied by the term *user ID*. (In fact, the ANSI/ISO specification uses the term authorization ID instead of user ID.)

While the SQL-92 standard specifies that the DBMS will provide authorization (user) IDs for database security, it is not specific as to the mechanism the DBMS will use for associating a specific user ID with the SQL statements the user submits to the database. It is left up to the DBMS to decide how to link a user ID to statements submitted in situations ranging from a user logon to the DBMS itself, to the use of forms-based data entry and query applications, and the running of report-generation programs that run against DBMS data at preprogrammed intervals, with no physical user present.

Most DBMS systems use *sessions* to associate user IDs with SQL statements submitted for execution. An interactive session begins when a user logs on to the DBMS and starts an interactive SQL program (such as the MS-SQL Server Query Analyzer). In the case of programmatic SQL (such as the report program running at a preset time), the session begins when the program connects to the DBMS and sends a user ID and password embedded within the application to gain access to the DBMS.

Whether started interactively or through an application program, the session ends when the user or application program terminates its connection to the DBMS by logging off. All SQL statements submitted to the DBMS during the session are associated with the user ID specified when the user or application program started the session by logging in.

To start an SQL session, the user or application program must supply both a user ID and a password. The user ID tells the DBMS what privileges the user (or application) has in accessing the database, and the DBMS uses the password to verify that the user (or application) is authorized to use the user ID specified.

Although the concept of using user ID/password pairs is common across database products, the specific way of supplying them to the DBMS varies from one DBMS to another. For example, to access the Oracle database using SQL Plus, you can start a session with

```
SQLPLUS KONRAD/KING
```

while MS-SQL Server lets you start an interactive session using the ISQL program and specifying the user name and password as:

```
ISQL /USER=KONRAD / PASSWORD=KING
```

Check your system manual to determine your system's requirements for specifying your user ID and password to connect to the DBMS and start an SQL session.

Note: *Some DBMS products use the user IDs defined on the host computer system's operating system as the user ID for connecting to the DBMS. MS-SQL Server, running on Windows NT, for example, lets you choose which authentication method you want to use on a per-session basis. If you are not already logged on to an MS-SQL Server when you start the MS-SQL Server Query Analyzer, the program will display a Connect to SQL Server dialog box similar to that shown in Figure 135.1.*

Figure 135.1 The MS-SQL Server's Query Analyzer Connect to SQL Server dialog box

If you click on the radio button to the left of Use SQL Server Authentication, you can supply the login name (user ID) and password that the Query Analyzer will send to the DBMS for authentication and logon to the DBMS. When using SQL Server Authentication, the user ID and password you supply need not match any defined for users on the NT Server itself. On the other hand, if you click on the radio button to the left of Use Windows NT Authentication, the Query Analyzer will use the user ID you used to log on to the NT server to start your DBMS session.

Whether your DBMS has its own user authentication method or uses that provided by the host operating system, the DBA must still define each individual user ID's access privileges in the DBMS. Thus, your network user ID may let you connect to the database, but the DBMS will permit you to execute only SQL statements to which the DBA has GRANTed your user ID execution privilege on database objects you are allowed to see.

136 Understanding MS-SQL Server Standard and Windows NT Integrated Security

As you learned in Tip 135, "Understanding Individual User IDs and Authentication," there are two ways for an SQL DBMS to manage user IDs. Some DBMS products use the user names defined in the host computer's operating system as database authorization IDs. Others, especially those that have versions available for several different operating systems, maintain their own internal list of user IDs and passwords. MS-SQL Server lets you manage user accounts using either of the two security methods.

The security method you choose controls how MS-SQL Server manages user accounts on the server and how the DBMS interacts with the Windows NT security system. In *standard* security mode, MS-SQL Server will accept Windows NT user names as authorization IDs and will also allow you to define additional user ID/password pairs within the DBMS itself.

Meanwhile, in *integrated* security mode, MS-SQL Server depends on Windows NT to manage user connections through the operating system's access control list (ACL).

Note: *MS-SQL Server integrated security (which lets the operating system manage user accounts) is available only if you are running MS-SQL Server on a Windows NT platform. If you are using any other operating system, MS-SQL Server must use standard security and manage its own user IDs and passwords.*

The most common way of configuring MS-SQL Server is to make the DBMS responsible for managing and maintaining database user accounts by starting MS-SQL Server in standard security mode. In standard security mode, the MS-SQL server authenticates the user login by checking the user ID/password pair against those stored in its internal system tables. As a result, if MS-SQL Server is running in standard security mode on a network server, starting a DBMS session requires two logins—one to log in to the server in order to gain network access and a second to log in to the database.

Integrated security mode, on the other hand, requires a single login to gain both network and database access. MS-SQL Server lets the NT operating system authenticate the user ID and password. It then creates a trusted connection to the DBMS—using the login name entered to gain access to the network as the user ID for the database session.

To use the MS-SQL Server Enterprise Manager to set the MS-SQL Server security mode, perform the following steps:

1. Start the Enterprise Manager by clicking your mouse on the Start button. When Windows displays the Start menu, move your mouse pointer to Programs, select Microsoft SQL Server 7.0, and then click your mouse on Enterprise Manager.
2. To display the list of SQL servers, click your mouse on the plus (+) to the left of SQL Server Group.
3. Click your mouse on the icon for the SQL server whose security system you wish to manage. For example, to work with the security system for the SQL server named NVBIZNET2, click your mouse on the icon for NVBIZNET2.
4. Select the Action menu Properties option.
5. Click your mouse on the Security tab. The Enterprise Manager will display the security tab for the SQL Server Properties dialog box similar to that shown in Figure 136.1.
6. To use *standard* security, which allows SQL server access by both user IDs maintained by MS-SQL Server and user names managed by Windows NT, click your mouse on the radio button to the left of SQL Server and Windows NT. To use *integrated* security, which allows only SQL server access to user names defined by Windows NT, click your mouse on the radio button to the left of Windows NT Only. For the current project, have MS-SQL Server use *standard* security by clicking your mouse on the SQL Server and Windows NT radio button.

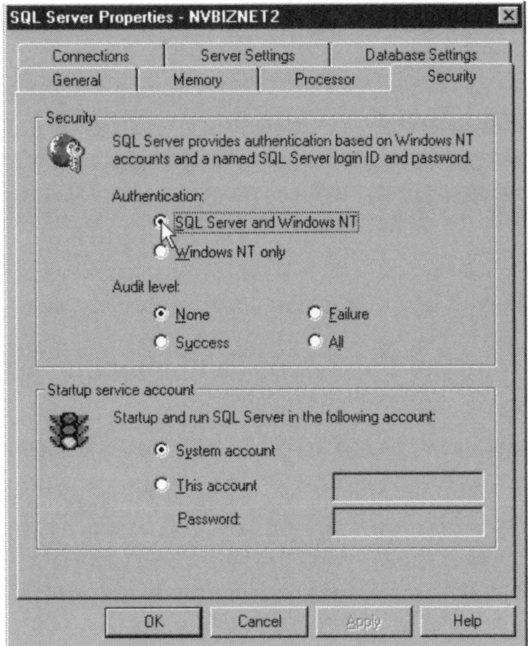

Figure 136.1 The Security tab of the MS-SQL Server SQL Server Properties dialog box

7. Click your mouse on the OK button to apply the security mode selection and close the SQL Server Properties dialog box.

Whether you use standard security to have MS-SQL Server handle user ID login and password authentication or you let the Windows NT operating system handle it by selecting integrated security mode, you must set up a user ID on the MS-SQL Server for every authorization ID (user name) allowed to start a database session. In Tip 137, "Using the MS-SQL Server Enterprise Manager to Add Logins and Users," you will learn how to use MS-SQL Server's Enterprise Manager to create and drop database login and user accounts.

137 Using the MS-SQL Server Enterprise Manager to Add Logins and Users

User IDs on an MS-SQL Server consists of two components: a *login*, which lets the user ID attach to the MS-SQL Server, and a *user*, which the MS-SQL Server uses to control the privileges a user ID has in a given database managed by the SQL Server. MS-SQL Server stores the login component of the user ID in the SYSLOGINS table of the MASTER database and stores the user component in the SYSUSERS table of each database in which the user ID has access privileges.

Each user ID allowed to attach to an MS-SQL Server will have a single login entry in the SQL server's SYSLOGINS table. Because a single MS-SQL Server normally manages several databases, a single user ID may have a user component in one or many databases. Splitting the user ID into login and user components lets a single user ID have different privileges in different databases while retaining a single password.

Thus, MS-SQL Server implements the SQL security scheme by authenticating the login component of the user ID with its password to let the user connect to the SQL Server and establish a session. The server then uses the user component of the user ID to determine whether to permit or prohibit SQL statement execution on objects in the databases managed by the server.

To use MS-SQL Server Enterprise Manager to add user ID login and user components, perform the following steps:

1. Start the Enterprise Manager by clicking your mouse on the Start button. When Windows displays the Start menu, move your mouse pointer to Programs, select Microsoft SQL Server 7.0, and then click your mouse on Enterprise Manager.
2. To display the list of SQL Servers, click your mouse on the plus (+) to the left of SQL Server Group.
3. Click your mouse on the plus (+) to the left of the icon for the SQL server on which you want to create the user ID. For example, if you want to manage user IDs on a server named NVBizNet2, click your mouse on the plus (+) to the left of the icon for NVBizNet2. The Enterprise Manager will display folders containing databases and services available on the MS-SQL Server you selected.
4. Click your mouse on the plus (+) to the left of the Security folder. The Enterprise Manager will display a list of security objects on the SQL Server you selected in Step 3, similar to that shown in Figure 137.1.
5. Click your mouse on the Logins icon.
6. Select the Action menu New Login option, or click on the New Login button (second button from right) on the Enterprise Manager Standard toolbar. Enterprise Manager will display an SQL Server Login Properties–New Login dialog box similar to that shown in Figure 137.2.
7. Enter the new user ID into the Name field. For the current example, enter **SQLTips**.

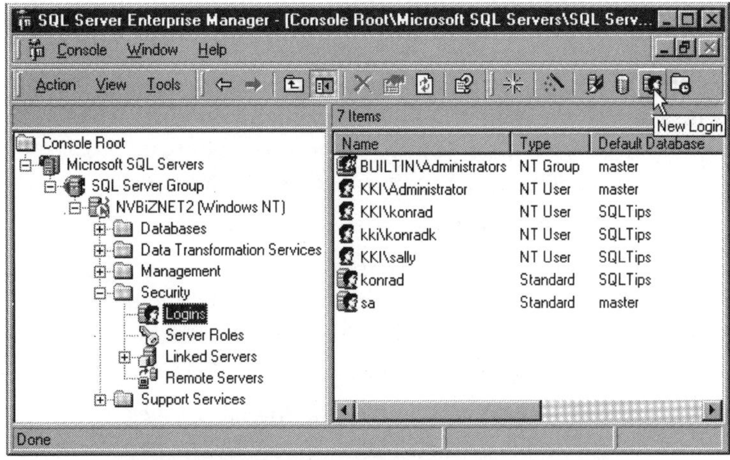

Figure 137.1 The MS-SQL Server's Enterprise Manager security object and login name list

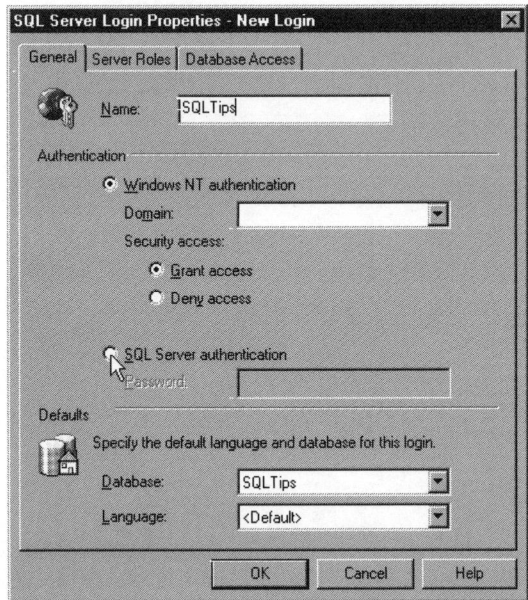

Figure 137.2 The General Tab of the MS-SQL Server's SQL Server Login Properties–New Login dialog box

8. If you want to use integrated Windows NT authentication to log in to the MS-SQL Server using the user ID you entered in Step 7, click your mouse on the radio button to the left of Windows NT Authentication. Then enter the name of the domain of the server on which the user name is defined in the Domain field. For the current example, use standard SQL Server authentication by clicking your mouse on the radio button to the left of SQL Server Authentication, and enter the password into the Password field. For the current example, enter **1001** for the password.

Note: *If you plan to use Windows NT authentication for a user ID, be sure to select Windows NT Authentication and enter the correct domain name into the Domain field. You cannot change the user name or authentication method for a user ID later without deleting the user ID and then re-entering it. If you select SQL Server Authentication, the user will have to enter the user ID and password prior to MS-SQL Server giving the user ID access to the database tables—even if Windows NT has the same user ID/password pair.*

---

9. To select the default database the user ID will use when a session is established, click on the drop-down button to the right of the Database field and select the default database from the list of databases managed by the SQL Server. For the current example, select SQLTips.

10. Click on the Database Access tab. Enterprise Manager will display the list of databases managed by the SQL Server, similar to that shown in Figure 137.3.

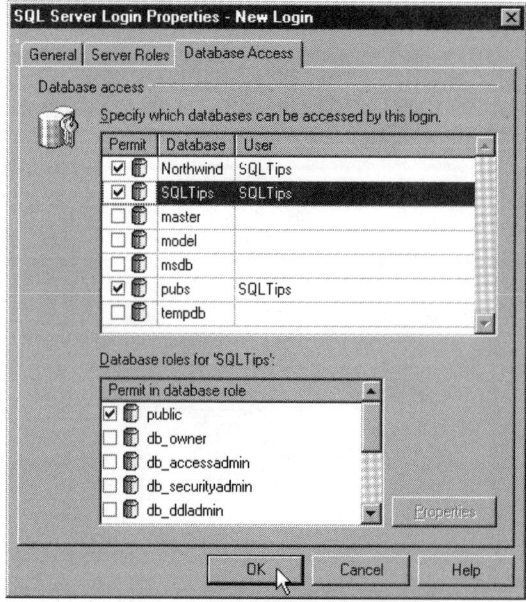

Figure 137.3 The Database Access tab of the MS-SQL Server SQL Server Login Properties–New Login dialog box

11. To give the user ID access to databases on the SQL Server, click on the check box to the left of each database to which the user ID is to have access. For the current example, click your mouse on the check boxes to the left of NORTHWIND, SQLTips, and PUBS until a check mark appears in each of the three check boxes.

12. Click your mouse on the OK button. The Enterprise Manager will display a Confirm Password dialog box if you selected SQL Server Authentication in Step 8. Re-enter the password you entered in Step 8. For the current example, enter **1001** and click on the OK button.

13. If you have additional user IDs to define, continue at Step 6. Otherwise, click your mouse on the Close button (the X) in the upper-right corner of the Enterprise Manager window to exit Enterprise Manager.

Steps 6–9 of the add new user-ID procedure setup the login component of the user-ID by specifying the login name the user or application program will use to connect to the SQL Server and the password the server can use to authenticate the login. (If you selected Windows NT Authentication in Step 8, MS-SQL Server will assume the operating system authenticated the login's password and will not ask the user to enter either the login name or the password again before establishing the connection the to the SQL Server.)

While Steps 6–9 establishes the login component of the user-ID, Steps 10 and 11 tell the server to add a user component for the "SQLTips" user-ID in the SYSUSERS tables of the NORTHWIND, SQLTips, and PUBS databases.

138 Using the MS-SQL Server Enterprise Manager to Drop Logins and Users

As you learned in Tip 137, "Using the MS-SQL Server Enterprise Manager to Add Logins and Users," MS-SQL Server creates a login and a user entry in its system tables for each user ID you add to the system. As such, you can prevent a user ID from working with objects in a particular database by removing the user ID's user record from the SYSUSERS table in that database. Or, if you want to prevent a user ID from accessing objects in all databases and stop the ID from connecting to the database server, remove the user ID's login record from the SYSLOGINS table in the MASTER database.

MS-SQL Server lets you remove logins and users either by executing the stored procedures sp_droplogin and sp_dropuser or with the Enterprise Manager by performing the following steps:

1. Start the Enterprise Manager and display the system login names by performing Steps 1–5 of the procedure in Tip 137.
2. If you want to remove login records, skip to Step 7. Otherwise, to remove user records, find the user ID whose user component you want to modify in the Enterprise Server window's right pane. Then right-click your mouse on the name (user ID). For the current project, right-click on SQLTips, the user ID you created in Tip 137.
3. When Enterprise Server displays the right-click pop-up menu, select the Properties option. Enterprise Server will display the SQL Server Login Properties dialog box you saw in Figure 137.2.

4. Click your mouse on the Database Access tab to display the list of databases managed by the MS-SQL Server. (You saw the Database Access tab in Figure 137.3.)

5. To prevent a user ID from accessing a database, clear the check box to the left of the database icon. For the current example, click your mouse on the check box to the left the NORTHWIND database icon until the check mark disappears.

Note: *You will not be able to remove the user component of the user ID from the SYSUSERS table of any database in which a user ID owns objects (such as tables, views, or stored procedures). To prevent the user ID from accessing the database, transfer ownership of the user ID's object to another user ID and then clear the check box in the Permit column.*

---

6. Click your mouse on the OK button to have Enterprise Server remove the user record from the SYSUSERS table (of the NORTHWIND database, in the current example).

7. To remove a login, find the user ID whose login component you want to drop in the Enterprise Server window's right pane. Then click your mouse on the name (user ID) to select it. Next, press the Delete key. (Or, you can right-click your mouse on the name and then select the Delete option from the right-click pop-up menu.) Enterprise Server will display an Are You Sure You Want to Remove This Login? message box.

Note: *You cannot remove the login record for any user ID that owns objects on the database server. Therefore, if you have a user ID that owns database objects (such as views, tables, or stored procedures), you can deny login access by:*

- *Transferring object ownership to another user ID and then repeating the delete login procedure*
- *Right-clicking your mouse on the login name, selecting the Properties option on the pop-up menu, and then changing the user ID's password on the General tab of the SQL Server Login Properties dialog box*
- *Right-clicking your mouse on the login name, selecting the Properties option on the pop-up menu, and then clicking on the radio button to the right of Deny Access on the General table of the SQL Server Login Properties dialog box*

---

8. Click your mouse on the Yes button to confirm your login delete request. Or, click on the No button if you do not want to remove the user name.

If you have additional user records you want to remove, continue at Step 2, or continue at Step 7 if you want to remove another login record. Otherwise, click your mouse on the Close button (the X) in the upper-right corner of the Enterprise Manager window to exit Enterprise Manager.

139 Understanding MS-SQL Server Security Roles and Group User Security

User groups simplify the administration of privileges by letting the database administrator (DBA) GRANT or REVOKE access to multiple database objects for several users at once. In a large organization, employees in the same department typically have the same database access needs. All of the employees in the human resources (HR) department, for example, will probably have the same privileges on a group of tables dealing with payroll and employee personal information. Likewise, all of the employees in the accounting department will most likely need a common set of access rights to tables dealing with the company's invoice and accounts payable data.

The ANSI/ISO security model lets you deal with setting up groups of users with similar access rights in one of two ways:

- Assign a single user ID to all of the people in the group. Granting the one user ID the privileges to database objects all of the users need lets you set up access for many users at once because the one user ID that you set up will be used by multiple users. However, when you let people share the same user ID, you cannot distinguish the work performed by one employee login from another. (So, you won't know which employee in HR accidentally deleted the EMPLOYEE table, for example.)
- Assign a different user ID for each person in the group. Using multiple user IDs lets you hold each user accountable for work performed. However, setting up the same privileges over and over again for each member of a group is tedious and (therefore) error-prone—especially if you nave a large number of users needing the same privileges to many database objects.

MS-SQL Server provides a third alternative—database roles, which let you set up a set of access privileges on one or many database objects. By assign a user ID to a role, you can GRANT access privileges to many database objects at once, thereby reducing the time spent (and tedious nature of) administering access rights on a server with many database objects and large groups of users needing the same access privileges on those objects.

There are two types of database roles, standard and application. A *standard* role is what most people would call a *group* because you assign user IDs to a standard role (group) and then grant the standard role privileges to access database objects.

An *application* role, on the other hand, is a password-protected set of privileges. Unlike a standard role, an application role has no user IDs assigned to it. Instead, an application program connects to the DBMS using the name of the application role as its user ID and the role's password for authentication. Once it has established the connection, the DBMS grants the privileges defined in the application role to the application program.

To use Enterprise Manager to assign a user ID to an MS-SQL Server database role, perform the following steps:

1. Start the Enterprise Manager by clicking your mouse on the Start button. When Windows displays the Start menu, move your mouse pointer to Programs, select Microsoft SQL Server 7.0, and then click your mouse on Enterprise Manager.
2. To display the list of SQL Servers, click your mouse on the plus (+) to the left of SQL Server Group.
3. Click your mouse on the plus (+) to the left of the icon for the SQL server on which you want to assign database roles. For example, if you want to assign roles on a server named NVBIZNET2, click your mouse on the plus (+) to the left of the icon for NVBIZNET2. The Enterprise Manager will display folders containing databases and services available on the MS-SQL Server you selected.
4. Click your mouse on the plus (+) to the left of the Databases folder. The Enterprise Manager will display a list of the databases managed by the server you selected in Step 3.
5. Select the database in which you want to assign roles. For the current project, select SQLTips by clicking your mouse on the plus (+) to the left of the SQLTips icon in the expanded Databases list. Enterprise Manager will display a list of database objects available in the database you selected.
6. To have Enterprise Manager display the list of database roles in its right pane, click your mouse on the Roles icon in the database objects list you expanded in Step 5.
7. Right-click on the role to which you wish to add a member, and select the Properties option from the pop-up menu. For the current example, right-click on the icon for the DB_OWNER role in the Enterprise Manager's right pane, and then select Properties on the pop-up menu. Enterprise Manager will display a Database Role Properties dialog box similar to that shown in Figure 139.1.
8. To add a user ID to the role, click your mouse on the Add button. Enterprise Manager will display the list of user IDs not yet assigned to the role.
9. Select the user IDs you want to add to the role, and then click your mouse on the OK button. For the current example, click your mouse on SQLTips and then the OK button. Enterprise Manager will add the user IDs you selected to the role and return to the Database Role Properties dialog box.
10. Click your mouse on the OK button to save your changes and return to the Enterprise Manager application window.
11. Click your mouse on the Close button (the X) in the upper-right corner of the Enterprise Manager window to exit Enterprise Manager.

You will learn how to create MS-SQL Server standard and application roles in Tip 142, "Using MS-SQL Server Enterprise Manager to Create Database Roles."

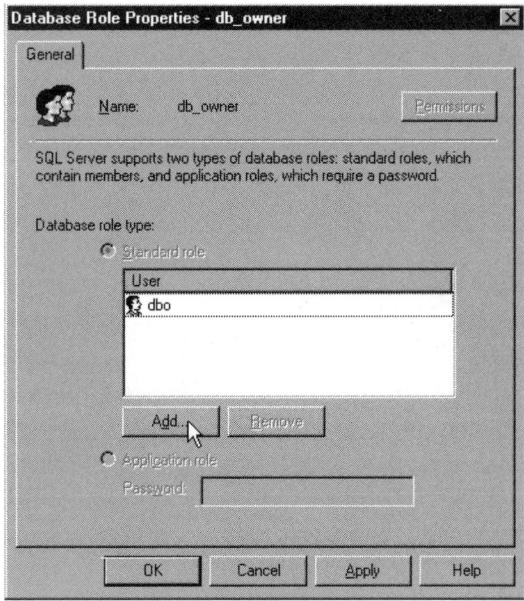

Figure 139.1 The MS-SQL Server Enterprise Manager Database Role Properties dialog box

140 Understanding MS-SQL Server Permissions

Permissions, or privileges, are the rights a user ID has to access a database object such as a table, view, domain, or stored procedure. The database administrator (DBA) controls user and application program interaction with the database by granting and revoking privileges (permissions) to user IDs and roles.

In addition to permissions *explicitly* granted by the DBA, the DBMS also *implicitly* (automatically) gives the full set of object privileges to the owner or creator of an object. As such, the database object owner (DBOO) automatically has SELECT, INSERT, UPDATE, DELETE, EXEC, DIR (foreign key references), and data definition language (DDL) privileges on the database objects the user or application program creates. Moreover, the DBOO can also GRANT and REVOKE privileges to other user IDs.

Note: *When a user ID creates a database (vs. a table, a view, or other objects within a database), the user ID becomes the database owner (DBO). MS-SQL Server automatically gives the DBO full permissions (all privileges) on all objects in the database. Moreover, the system administrator (SA) account, which is automatically created when you install MS-SQL Server, has full permissions (all privileges) to all objects in all databases on the SQL Server.*

The privileges, or permissions, available for database objects on MS-SQL Server are:

- **SELECT.** Lets a user-ID query or read data from a table or view. The SELECT privilege can be limited to individual columns within a table or view, or granted on the entire object as a whole.
- **INSERT.** Lets a user ID add rows to a table or view.
- **UPDATE.** Lets a user ID change data in a table or view. Similar to the SELECT privilege, the UPDATE privilege can be limited to individual columns within a table or view or granted on the entire objected as a whole.
- **DELETE.** Lets a user ID remove rows from a table or view.
- **EXEC.** (Execute.) Lets a user ID execute a stored procedure.
- **DRI.** (Declarative referential integrity.) Lets a user ID add FOREIGN KEY constraints on a table.
- **CREATE TABLE.** Lets the user ID add a new table to the database. As you already know, the user ID will become the DBOO of the table it creates and thus will have all privileges on that table.
- **ALTER TABLE.** Lets the user ID change the structure of a table.
- **DROP TABLE.** Lets the user ID DROP or delete a table.
- **CREATE.** Lets the user ID create the database object (such as a DEFAULT, PROCEDURE, RULE, or VIEW) to which it is granted the ALTER privilege. As was mentioned previously, the user ID will become the DBOO of the database object it creates, with all permissions (privileges) on the new database object.
- **ALTER.** Lets the user ID modify the structure of or the statements in (in the case of stored procedures) the database object (such as a DEFAULT, PROCEDURE, RULE, or VIEW) to which it is granted the ALTER privilege.
- **DROP.** Lets the user ID delete or remove the database object (such as a DEFAULT, PROCEDURE, RULE, or VIEW) to which it is granted the DROP privilege.
- **BACKUP DATABASE.** Lets the user ID back up an entire database to a backup device.
- **BACKUP LOG.** Lets the user ID back up a database transaction log to a backup device.
- **CREATE DATABASE.** Lets the user ID create a new database on the SQL Server. After creating the database, the user ID will become the DBO for the database and thus will have all permissions on all objects created in the new database by any user ID.

You will learn how to use the GRANT and REVOKE statements to give and remove permissions (privileges) from user IDs and roles in Tips 144–156.

141 Understanding SQL Security Objects and Privileges

An SQL database consists of objects such as tables, views, stored procedures, constraints, defaults, user-defined data types, indexes, and user IDs. The objects to which the DBMS applies security protections are further differentiated as *security* objects. Since tables and views are the two primary database objects, it was only logical that the first SQL standard (SQL-89) named both of them as security objects.

SQL-92 expanded the list of security objects beyond tables and views to include domains, data types, and character sets, and added external references protections for tables and views. In short, the SQL standards (both SQL-89 and SQL-92) specify that the DBMS be able to individually protect important objects found in all standard SQL database products. Protecting database security objects means letting a user ID have certain access privileges to some objects while prohibiting access to others.

Note: *Each DBMS product expands the list of standard security objects by affording security protections to data objects its developers feel are worth safeguarding. MS-SQL Server, for example, adds security protections for stored procedures. Meanwhile, DB2 includes protections for indexes, schemas, and packages. (Check the GRANT and REVOKE statements in your system manual for a complete list of security objects in your DBMS implementation.) The important thing to know now is that the underlying SQL security scheme is to use the GRANT and REVOKE statements to give or withhold specific SQL statement execution privileges for database objects on a user-ID-by-user-ID basis.*

The set of SQL statements the user ID can execute on a database object (that is, the things the user ID can do to a "thing" in the database) are the user ID's *privileges* on the security object. All commercial DBMS products support the four security privileges defined in the SQL-89 and in SQL-92 standards:

- **SELECT**. Lets the user ID retrieve data from a table or view by using the table or view name in the FROM clause of the SELECT statement. Although the SQL standard allows the SELECT privilege to be granted or withheld for an entire table, several DBMS products (including SYBASE and MS-SQL Server) let you GRANT SELECT on specific columns in a table or view (vs. the entire object).
- **INSERT.** Lets the user ID add new rows to a view or table by using the table or view name in the INTO clause of the INSERT statement. SQL-92 expanded the original SQL-89 INSERT security privilege by letting the DBMS limit it to only specific columns in each row. Thus, a user ID may be able to add new rows to a table, but it may be forced to leave some of the row's column values NULL.

- **DELETE.** Lets the user ID remove rows from a table or view by using the table or view name in the FROM clause of the DELETE statement.
- **UPDATE.** Lets the user ID change values in a table or view by using the table or view name as the target of an UPDATE statement. SQL-92 expanded the original SQL-89 UPDATE security privilege by letting the DBMS limit it to only specific columns in each row. As such, a user ID may be able to change values in some columns but not others.

Most DBMS products also support the two new privileges added in SQL-92:

- **REFERENCES.** Lets a user ID refer to a column in a table or view in a foreign key or check constraint (Tip 153 will show you how a user-ID can use a foreign key or check constraint to determine the values in a column-even if the user-ID is denied SELECT privilege on the column or the entire table.)
- **USAGE.** Lets the user ID use domains (named sets of legal column values), user-defined character sets, collating sequences, and translations. For example, without USAGE privilege on a domain, a user ID cannot CREATE a table with a column that uses the domain name as its data type.

Your DBMS product will likely support security privileges beyond the six specified by the SQL-92 standard. (In Tip 140, "Understanding MS-SQL Server Permissions," you learned about several additional privileges supported by MS-SQL Server.) The important thing to know is that the DBMS protects its objects by allowing a user ID to execute only those statements to which it has been granted the privilege. Check the your system's documentation on the GRANT and REVOKE statements for the list of security objects and privileges your DBMS supports.

142 Using MS-SQL Server Enterprise Manager to Create Database Roles

As you learned in Tip 139, "Understanding MS-SQL Server Security Roles and Group User Security," you can GRANT a user ID multiple privileges to one or several security objects by assigning the ID to a *role*. In effect, roles provide MS-SQL Server a group user security scheme. When you add a security permission to a role, that permission is granted to all of the members at once. Conversely, removing a privilege from a role causes every user ID in the group to lose the privilege. Thus, assigning a role to a user ID is the same as putting the ID into a group with the name of the role.

To use the MS-SQL Server Enterprise Manager to add a role to the database, perform the following steps:

1. Start the Enterprise Manager by clicking your mouse pointer on the Start button. When Windows displays the Start menu, move your mouse pointer to Programs, select Microsoft SQL Server 7.0, and then click your mouse pointer on Enterprise Manager.
2. To display the list of SQL servers, click your mouse pointer on the plus (+) to the left of SQL Server Group.
3. Click your mouse pointer on the plus (+) to the left of the icon for the SQL Server on which you want to create a database role. For example, if you want to create a role on a server named NVBIZNET2, click your mouse pointer on the plus (+) to the left of the icon for NVBIZNET2. The Enterprise Manager will display folders containing databases and services available on the MS-SQL Server you selected.
4. Click your mouse pointer on the plus (+) to the left of the Databases folder. The Enterprise Manager will display a list of the databases managed by the server you selected in Step 3.
5. Select the database in which you want to create the role. For the current project, click your mouse pointer on the SQLTips icon in the expanded Databases list.
6. Select the Action menu New option, and click your mouse pointer on Database role. Enterprise Manager will display a Database Role Properties–New Role dialog box similar to that shown in Figure 142.1.

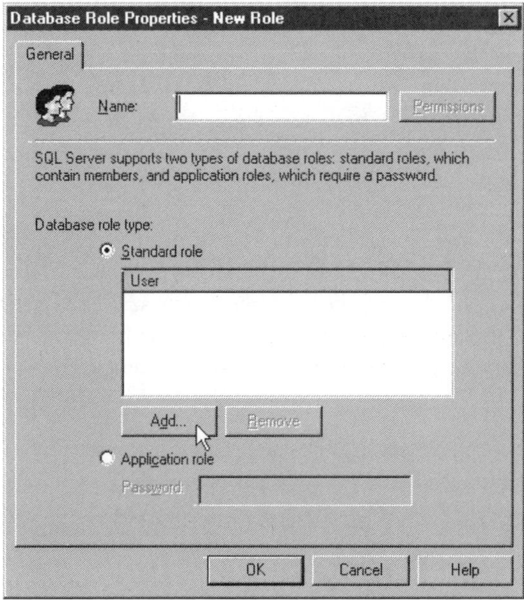

Figure 142.1 The MS-SQL Server's Enterprise Manager Database Role Properties–New Role dialog box

7. Enter the name of the new role in the Name field. For the current project, enter **SQLTips_Users.**
8. Select the type of role you want to create by clicking your mouse pointer on the radio button to the left of Standard Role to create a user ID group, or on the radio button to the

left of Application Role to create a privilege set for an application program. For the current project, click on the radio button to the left of Application Role.

9. If you are creating an application role, continue at Step 10. Otherwise, to assign a standard role to one or more user IDs, click your mouse pointer on the Add button. Enterprise Manager will display the Add Role Members dialog box showing the list of user IDs to which the role has not yet been assigned. Click your mouse pointer on the user IDs you want to include as role members, and then click your mouse pointer on the OK button. For the current project, click your mouse pointer on the user ID SQLTips (which you created in Tip 137, "Using the MS-SQL Server Enterprise Manager to Add Logins and Users"), and then click your mouse pointer on the OK button.
10. If you are creating a standard role, continue at Step 11. Otherwise, to finish creating an application role, enter the application role's password in the Password field.

Note: *Unless you want any user or application program that knows the name of the application role to have access to the database, be sure to put a nonblank password into the Password field.*

---

11. To add the new role to the database, click on the OK button.

Note: *MS-SQL Server roles are local to the database in which they are created. Therefore, if you create a role in one database (such as SQLTips, for example), the role is not available for assignment to user IDs in the PUBS database. As such, you must create the role in each database in which you need to use it—unless you create the role in the MODEL database. Roles, like other objects in the MODEL database, are added to each new database you tell MS-SQL Server to create.*

After you create a standard or application role, you must GRANT the role privileges, which you will learn to do in Tip 143, "Using MS-SQL Server Enterprise Manager to Assign Database Role Privileges." Remember, a role can bestow the set of privileges it is assigned only to the user IDs that are members of the standard role or the application programs or users that log on using the application role name as a user ID.

143 Using MS-SQL Server Enterprise Manager to Assign Database Role Privileges

You learned how to create standard and application roles in Tip 142, "Using MS-SQL Server Enterprise Manager to Create Database Roles," and how to assign a standard role to user IDs in Tip 139, "Understanding MS-SQL Server Security Roles and Group User Security." However, as was mentioned at the end of Tip 142, a role will give user IDs assigned to it only those privileges that make up the role's permissions set. There are two ways to give a role the set of privileges it can give to its members—either by using the GRANT statement (which you will learn about in Tip 144, "Understanding Ownership Privileges and the GRANT Statement") or by using the Enterprise Manager to edit role properties.

To give a role (and, by extension, the user IDs to which it is assigned) access privileges to database security objects, perform the following steps:

1. Start the Enterprise Manager and display the Database Role Properties dialog box by performing Steps 1 through 6 of the procedure in Tip 139.
2. Right-click your mouse pointer on the role whose privileges you want to assign. For the current project, right-click your mouse pointer on the icon for the SQLTips_USERS Role you created in Tip 142. Enterprise Manager will display the Database Role Properties dialog box.
3. To display the Permissions tab similar to that shown in Figure 143.1, click your mouse pointer on the Permissions button.

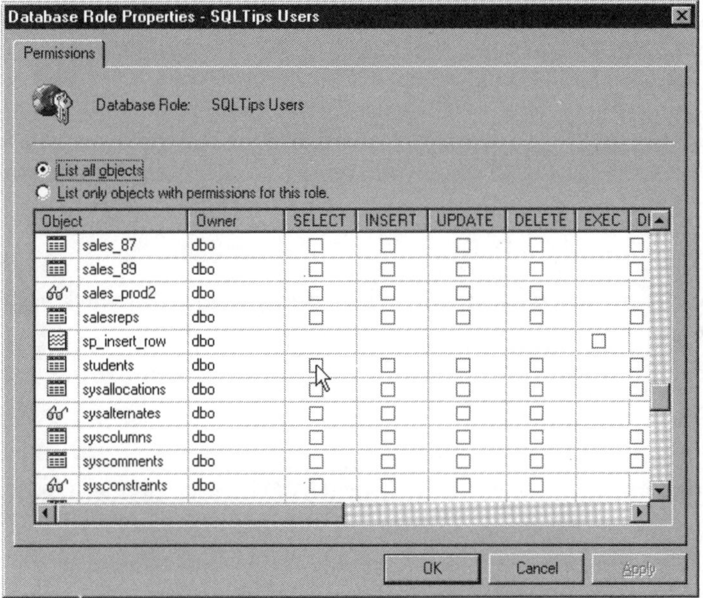

Figure 143.1 The Permissions tab of the MS-SQL Server Enterprise Manager Database Role Properties–New Role dialog box

---

Note: *If you are changing only some of the privileges on objects to which you gave the role permissions in the past, click your mouse pointer on the radio button to the left of List Only Objects with Permissions for This Role to reduce the number of database objects displayed in the object list area of the Permissions tab. When you want to give a role privileges (permissions) on additional database objects (as is the case in the current example), you want to see all database objects in the list area, which is the default.*

---

4. Use the scroll bar to the right of the database object list area to find the database object(s) on which you want the role to have SQL statement execution privileges. For the current example, find any one of the tables you created in previous tips. If you have not created any tables, use one of the views (denoted by the eyeglass icon in the Object column.)
5. To GRANT permissions (privileges), click your mouse pointer on the check box in the column of each permission you want user IDs or application programs assigned to the role to have on the database object. For example, to GRANT SELECT, INSERT, UPDATE, DELETE and DRI privileges on the STUDENTS table, you click your mouse pointer on the check boxes in column of the STUDENTS row of the list box until each one has a check mark in it.

***Note:** Not all privileges are available for all database objects, and the permissions check box is missing from the columns where the privilege is not applicable to the database object. For example, Figure 143 shows that you can GRANT EXEC (execute) privilege only on the SP_INSERT_ROW—which makes sense since SP_INSERT_ROW is a stored procedure and the other permissions are not applicable to it. Conversely, you cannot GRANT the role EXEC permission on the tables and rows listed in the object area. Finally, DIR (external FOREIGN KEY and CHECK reference privilege) is applicable only to database tables.*

---

6. Repeat Steps 4 and 5 until you have selected all of the privileges on each of the database objects you want the role (and its members or application program) to have.
7. Click your mouse pointer on the OK button to save your permission selections and return to the General tab of the Database Role Properties dialog box.
8. To update the role's definition in the database's system tables, click your mouse pointer on the OK button on the Database Role Properties dialog box.
9. To exit Enterprise Manager, click your mouse pointer on the Close button (the X) in the upper-right corner of the Enterprise Manager.

One minor problem in using Enterprise Manager to GRANT statement execution privilege to a role is that it allows you to GRANT or REVOKE each privilege only on the entire database object. As such, if you use Enterprise Manager to GRANT UPDATE privilege on the EMPLOYEES table to the SQLTips_USERS role, all of the role's members will be able to modify all of the columns in the EMPLOYEES table.

In Tips 145–156, you will learn how to use the GRANT statement to limit a role's privileges to specific columns in a table or view.

144 Understanding Ownership Privileges and the GRANT Statement

The user ID that successfully executes a CREATE TABLE or CREATE VIEW statement becomes the database object owner (DBOO) of the object created. Since the DBMS automatically assigns the full set of privileges on the object to its owner, the DBOO has SELECT, INSERT, DELETE, UPDATE, REFERENCES, and any other privilege supported by the DBMS to security objects he or she creates.

Other than the database administrator (DBA) (who has full privileges on all objects in all databases managed by the DBMS) and the database owner (DBO) (who has full privileges to all objects in the database he or she created), no one other than the DBOO has any rights to a newly created object. As such, in order for anyone (other than DBA and the DBO) to have access to a table, the table's DBOO must GRANT the user ID privileges to execute SQL statements with the table as their target.

Although a database view functions like a table in most SQL statements, creating a view to display a table's data does not give a user ID ownership privileges on the table. The user ID executing the CREATE VIEW command becomes the owner (DBOO) of the view and may exercise all privileges supported by the database on that view. However, the DBMS will disallow INSERT, UPDATE, or DELETE statements on the newly created view unless the user ID has the corresponding privilege on *both* the view *and* the view's base table. For example, if you have a view named NEW_EMPLOYEE_LIST based on the data in the EMPLOYEES table, you cannot UPDATE the view's HOURLY_RATE column unless you have UPDATE privilege on the EMPLOYEES table—even if you created the NEW_EMPLOYEE_LIST view yourself.

Note: *In order to execute a CREATE VIEW statement successfully, the user ID must have SELECT privilege on each of the source table columns the view is to display.*

A DBA (DBMS administrator), DBO (database operator), and DBOO (object operator) can use the GRANT statement to give a user ID or role privileges on a database object such as a table or view. The basic syntax of a GRANT statement is:

```
GRANT <privilege list> [(<column name list>)]
ON <object name>
TO <name list> [WITH GRANT OPTION]
```

Thus, to GRANT user ID KONRAD the privilege to retrieve employee data from and add new rows to the EMPLOYEES table, you would execute the GRANT statement:

```
GRANT SELECT, INSERT ON employees TO konrad
```

To give all members of the SQLTips_USERS role the ability to add rows to and remove rows from the TIPS table, you would execute the GRANT statement:

```
GRANT INSERT, DELETE ON tips TO sqltips_users
```

Finally, to give user ID SALLY the ability to modify only the FIRST_NAME, LAST_NAME, and ADDRESS columns of the rows in the EMPLOYEES table, you would use the GRANT statement:

```
GRANT UPDATE (first_name, last_name, address)
ON employees TO sally
```

You will learn more about using the GRANT statement to in Tips 149–156. For now, the important thing to know is that the owner of a database object (the DBOO) can use the GRANT statement to give other user IDs and roles permission to execute certain SQL statements on the object.

145 Using the GRANT Statement WITH GRANT OPTION to Allow Users to Give Database Object Access to Other Users

As the database object owner (DBOO), you have control over which user IDs can access objects you create and what those users can do to those objects. After you create an object such as a table or view, only your user ID can execute SQL statements on it until you use the GRANT statement to give another user access privileges.

Note: *The database administrator (DBA) and database owner (DBO) accounts have full privileges, including GRANT, on all objects in the database.*

For example, if you execute the GRANT statement

```
GRANT ALL PRIVILEGES ON employees TO sally
```

right after you create the EMPLOYEES table, only your user ID and user ID SALLY will be able to work with the EMPLOYEES table. Moreover, while the GRANT statement gives Sally all privileges on the EMPLOYEES table, she cannot give another user ID access privileges on the table because your GRANT statement did not include the WITH GRANT OPTION clause.

Suppose, for example, that you created a Las Vegas employees view named VW_VEGAS_EMPLOYEES. To give your Las Vegas office manager, Mary (user ID MARY), query access to the view, you can execute the GRANT statement:

```
GRANT SELECT ON vw_vegas_employees TO mary
```

After GRANTing her SELECT privilege, Mary is able to query the data in the underlying table(s) that "feed" the VW_VEGAS_EMPLOYEES view. However, she cannot give anyone else privilege to work with the view. Moreover, Mary cannot create another view based on the VW_VEGAS_EMPLOYEES view.

Note: *The DBOO has all privileges (including GRANT) on the objects he or she creates. However, letting Mary, in the current example, create an object that would let another user see VW_VEGAS_EMPLOYEES view data when Mary does not have WITH GRANT OPTION access to the view would violate DBMS access security. As such, the DBMS prevents a user ID from creating a view on any object (table or view) on which it does not have SELECT privilege and a WITH GRANT OPTION.*

If you want Mary to be able to GRANT other user IDs SELECT privilege on the VW_VEGAS_EMPLOYEES view, include the WITH GRANT OPTION. For example, the WITH GRANT OPTION in a GRANT statement such as

```
GRANT SELECT ON vw_vegas_employees
TO mary WITH GRANT OPTION
```

lets the user ID to which the privilege list is granted pass on any privilege(s) in the list to another user ID. Thus, the WITH GRANT OPTION in the current example will let Mary GRANT another user-ID SELECT access to the VW_VEGAS_EMPLOYEES view. Mary cannot, however, GRANT any privileges (such as INSERT, DELETE, UPDATE, or REFERENCES, in the current example) that she has not been granted WITH GRANT OPTION.

Be careful when including the WITH GRANT OPTION in a GRANT statement. By allowing another user to give access to your database objects, you are trusting that he or she will be as careful as you are in protecting the database object from other users. If you give WITH GRANT OPTION privilege to another user, that user not only can GRANT the privileges he or she has on the object, but also can pass along the privileges *and* the WITH GRANT OPTION privilege to another user ID.

146 Understanding the REVOKE Statement

In Tip 144, "Understanding Ownership Privileges and the GRANT Statement," you learned that the database object owner (DBOO) can use the GRANT statement to give other users access privileges to objects he or she owns. The REVOKE statement does the reverse. By executing a REVOKE statement, the DBOO takes away privileges he or she previously granted on a database object to other user IDs and/or roles.

The syntax of the REVOKE statement is:

```
REVOKE [GRANT OPTION FOR]<privilege list>[(<column list>)]
ON <object name>
FROM <name list> [CASCADE | RESTRICT]
```

If you previously granted SELECT, INSERT, and REFERENCES privileges on the EMPLOYEES table to user ID FRANK with a GRANT statement similar to

```
GRANT SELECT, INSERT, REFERENCES ON employees TO frank
```

and then executed the REVOKE statement

```
REVOKE INSERT, REFERENCES ON employees FROM frank
```

User ID FRANK will retain only the SELECT privilege on the EMPLOYEES table.

When you execute a REVOKE statement, bear in mind that you can rescind only privileges you previously granted. As such, if both you and another user GRANT the same privilege on an object to a user ID, the user ID will still have the privilege if you later REVOKE the privilege and the other user does not.

For example, suppose user ID CAROL executed the GRANT statement

```
GRANT SELECT, INSERT, UPDATE ON employees TO frank
```

and you executed the GRANT statement:

```
GRANT SELECT, INSERT, REFERENCES ON employees TO frank
```

If you later execute the REVOKE statement

```
REVOKE ALL PRIVILEGES ON employees FROM frank
```

User ID FRANK will still have SELECT, INSERT, and UPDATE privileges on the EMPLOYEES table because these privileges were granted by CAROL. Your REVOKE ALL PRIVILEGES command removed only all of the privileges on the EMPLOYEES table that *you* previously granted to FRANK.

147 Using the REVOKE Statement with the CASCADE Option to Remove Privileges

As you learned in Tip 145, "Using the GRANT Statement WITH GRANT OPTION to Allow Users to Give Database Object Access to Other Users," when the database object owner (DBOO) (or other grantor) adds WITH GRANT OPTION to a GRANT statement, the user ID receiving privileges on an object can GRANT those privileges to other users. Adding the CASCADE option to a REVOKE statement lets the original GRANTor take away the privilege(s) being revoked from the initial recipient and from any other user ID to which he or she passed the privilege.

For example, the GRANT statement

```
GRANT SELECT, INSERT ON employees TO frank
WITH GRANT OPTION
```

gives user ID FRANK SELECT and INSERT privilege on the EMPLOYEES table. The WITH GRANT OPTION gives FRANK the ability to GRANT his privileges (including the WITH GRANT OPTION) to another user ID with a GRANT statement such as:

```
GRANT SELECT, INSERT ON employees to SUE WITH GRANT OPTION.
```

Since user ID SUE received privileges and the WITH GRANT OPTION from FRANK, she, too, can execute a GRANT statement such as:

```
GRANT SELECT ON employees TO scott
```

If the a user wants to REVOKE one or more privileges previously granted to another user ID, the CASCADE option on the REVOKE statement tells the DBMS to remove all privilege(s) resulting from the original GRANT statement. Therefore, in the current example, the REVOKE statement

```
REVOKE INSERT ON employees FROM frank CASCADE
```

will take away the SELECT privilege on the EMPLOYEES table from user ID FRANK and then *cascades* through the security system removing the SELECT privilege on the EMPLOYEES table from SUE and SCOTT as well (because their SELECT privileges flowed from the original SELECT granted to FRANK).

SQL-92 requires that you tell the DBMS what to do when revoking privileges that have been granted to other users. MS-SQL Server implements the standard by requiring you to add the CASCADE option to any REVOKE statement that removes a privilege previously granted through the WITH GRANT OPTION. As such, if you are running MS-SQL Server, you cannot remove *only* the original user ID's privilege(s). Since the REVOKE statement must include the CASCADE option, MS-SQL Server requires that you take away the previously granted privilege(s) not only from the user ID to whom you granted the privilege(s) but also from all user IDs to which that user ID granted the privilege(s).

Because different implementations handle revoking privileges passed from one user to the next in different ways, you will need to check your system documentation on the REVOKE statement to see how your DBMS requires you to handle the removal of privileges granted with the WITH GRANT OPTION.

Some DBMS products let you issue the REVOKE statement without the CASCADE option if the user ID that granted the privilege has not yet passed it on to another user. Other products provide the RESTRICT option such that the REVOKE statement

```
REVOKE INSERT ON employees FROM frank RESTRICT
```

will execute successfully if FRANK has not granted INSERT privilege on the EMPLOYEES table to another user, and will fail (with an error message) if he has.

Protecting database objects (especially tables and views) from unauthorized access is very important to the DBMS. As such, you will want to maintain tight control over who can do what to the objects you own. Therefore, always add the CASCADE option when revoking a privilege previously granted with the WITH GRANT OPTION. If your DBMS lets you revoke only the original user's privilege(s), you lose control of who has what access privileges to the database objects you own. After all, you really do not know to whom the user (whose access rights you revoked) granted privileges by exercising the GRANT statement's WITH GRANT OPTION.

Note: *Almost all DBMS products automatically revoke all privileges derived from the original GRANT statement. As such, the CASCADE option in the REVOKE statement serves as a reminder that the effect of executing the REVOKE may have the effect of preventing database object access by more than just the user ID named in the statement.*

---

148 Using the REVOKE Statement GRANT OPTION FOR Clause to Remove GRANT Privilege

Executing a GRANT statement that includes the WITH GRANT OPTION, such as

```
GRANT SELECT, INSERT, UPDATE, DELETE ON invoices
TO konrad, mary WITH GRANT OPTION
```

gives the user IDs named in the statement the ability to pass any or all of the privileges they receive on to other users. Thus, in the current example, user IDs KONRAD and MARY can GRANT SELECT, INSERT, UPDATE, and DELETE on the INVOICES table to other user IDs or roles (groups of users).

In Tip 147, "Using the REVOKE Statement with the CASCADE Option to Remove Privileges," you learned how to use the REVOKE statement with the CASCADE option to remove a user IDs privilege(s) and those he or she granted to others by exercising the WITH GRANT OPTION. Sometimes, however, you want to remove only the user ID's GRANT privilege while leaving the actual access privileges to the object intact—that is where the GRANT OPTION FOR clause in the REVOKE statement comes in.

The GRANT OPTION FOR clause in the REVOKE statement lets you remove a user ID's ability to GRANT privileges on a database object to other users without taking away the user's access privileges on the database object.

For example, executing the REVOKE statement

```
REVOKE GRANT OPTION FOR INSERT ON invoices
FROM konrad CASCADE
```

on MS-SQL Server will allow user-ID KONRAD to keep SELECT, INSERT, UPDATE, and DELETE privileges on the INVOICES table but will REVOKE any INSERT privileges KONRAD granted to other users and prevent KONRAD from granting INSERT privilege in the future. As such, if KONRAD previously executed the GRANT statements

```
GRANT INSERT, UPDATE ON invoices TO sue
GRANT SELECT, INSERT, UPDATE ON invoices TO frank
```

SUE will retain UPDATE privilege on the INVOICES table, and FRANK will keep SELECT and UPDATE privileges after the database object owner (DBOO) executes the REVOKE (GRANT OPTION FOR) statement:

```
REVOKE GRANT OPTION FOR INSERT ON invoices
FROM konrad CASCADE
```

Although MS-SQL Server revokes the privilege(s) passed to other users when you REVOKE a user ID's GRANT privilege(s), not all DBMS products exhibit the same behavior.

Unlike revoking a privilege, which tells the DBMS to revoke the privilege from the user ID and from any users to whom he or she passed the privilege, revoking the WITH GRANT OPTION tells the DBMS only to disallow the user ID and any user to whom he passed the WITH GRANT OPTION from granting the privilege again. MS-SQL Server implements the revocation of the GRANT privilege by taking away the GRANT privilege from user ID named in the statement and REVOKING the privilege from all users to whom the user ID previously passed the privilege by exercising the GRANT option.

Check your system documentation on the REVOKE statement to see how your DBMS handles revoking a user ID's ability to GRANT access privileges to another user. All DBMS products let you use the REVOKE GRANT OPTION to take away a user ID's ability to GRANT privileges listed in the statement to others. (The user ID whose GRANT option is revoked still retains his own access privilege on the object.) Some products (unlike MS-SQL Server) will also let users previously granted the privilege (whose GRANT privilege is being revoked) to continue to exercise the privilege previously derived from the original GRANT WITH GRANT OPTION.

149 Using the GRANT SELECT (and REVOKE SELECT) Statement to Control Access to a Database Object

Granting SELECT privilege on a table or view to a user ID or role lets the user ID or role members "see" the data in a table. As you learned in Tip 144, "Understanding Ownership Privileges and the GRANT Statement," the database object owner (DBOO) has full privileges to objects he or she creates, while all other database users have no access rights at all. As such, the DBOO must execute a GRANT statement with SELECT as one of the privileges in the privilege list to let other user IDs and programs view data in a table.

The syntax of the GRANT statement used to give SELECT privilege is:

```
GRANT SELECT [(<column list>)]
ON <table name> | <view name>
TO <user and/or Role name list> [WITH GRANT OPTION]
```

Thus, to allow user ID KONRAD to execute SELECT or CREATE VIEW statements on the EMPLOYEES table, for example, the table's DBOO (or other user that has GRANT SELECT privilege) must execute a GRANT statement such as:

```
GRANT SELECT ON employees TO konrad
```

Or, to GRANT SELECT access on the VW_LV_EMPLOYEES view to MARY, SUE, and the PAYROLL_USERS role, the view's DBOO could execute the GRANT statement:

```
GRANT SELECT ON vw_lv_employees TO mary, sue, payroll_users
```

As a final example, to give SELECT access on the INVOICES table to FRANK and to allow FRANK to GRANT SELECT access to other users, a user ID with GRANT SELECT privileges on the INVOICE table would include the WITH GRANT OPTION in the GRANT statement, as follows:

```
GRANT SELECT ON invoices TO frank WITH GRANT OPTION
```

SELECT privilege (with or without the option to GRANT SELECT) to another user ID or role lets a user ID or program only query and view a table's data. It does not convey the ability to change column values, remove rows from, or add rows to a table.

When the person who granted SELECT access on an object to a user ID or role no longer wants the user ID or role members to view the data in a table, the grantor can execute a REVOKE statement to remove SELECT access. The syntax of a REVOKE statement that takes away SELECT access privilege is:

```
REVOKE [GRANT OPTION FOR] SELECT [(<column name list>)
ON <table name> | <view name>
FROM <user and/or Role name list> [CASCADE]
```

Thus, if the DBOO granted SELECT access on the VW_LV_EMPLOYEES view to MARY, SUE, and the members of the PAYROLL_USERS role and later wanted only SUE to have query access to the view, the DBOO could execute the REVOKE statement:

```
REVOKE SELECT ON vw_lv_employees FROM mary, payroll_users
```

One important thing to remember is that a user ID can REVOKE only access privilege that it granted. As such, if the DBOO granted SELECT access on the INVOICES table to user ID FRANK with the GRANT statement

```
GRANT SELECT ON invoices TO frank WITH GRANT OPTION
```

and FRANK subsequently exercised his GRANT option to GRANT SELECT access on the INVOICES table to SUE, the DBOO could not REVOKE SUE's SELECT access privileges with the REVOKE statement

```
REVOKE SELECT ON invoices FROM sue
```

since SUE's access was granted by FRANK.

To REVOKE SUE's SELECT access to the INVOICES table, either FRANK would have to execute the REVOKE statement or the user ID that granted FRANK SELECT access with the

WITH GRANT OPTION (the DBOO, in the current example) would have to either REVOKE FRANK's GRANT SELECT option using

```
REVOKE GRANT OPTION FOR SELECT ON invoices
FROM frank CASCADE
```

or REVOKE FRANK's SELECT privilege on the INVOICES table entirely using:

```
REVOKE SELECT ON invoices FROM frank CASCADE
```

As you learned in Tip 147, "Using the REVOKE Statement with the CASCADE Option to Remove Privileges," revoking a privilege or the GRANT OPTION for a privilege (on MS-SQL Server) removes the access privilege from all user IDs that derived the privilege on the object from the original GRANT statement. In the current example, SUE's SELECT privilege on the INVOICES table was derived from FRANK's GRANT statement. As such, revoking FRANK's SELECT privilege on the INVOICES table takes away SUE's *derived* SELECT privilege on the INVOICES table as well.

Note: *After the DBOO or another grantor uses the REVOKE statement to remove a user IDs SELECT privilege, the user ID will still have SELECT access on the database object if someone else* also *granted it the same privilege on the object. For example, if both WALTER and SCOTT granted SELECT on the INVOICES table to SUE, and SCOTT later executed the statement*

```
REVOKE SELECT ON invoices FROM sue
```

SUE would still have SELECT access on the INVOICES table because SCOTT's revocation of the SELECT privilege has no effect on the SELECT access that WALTER granted to SUE.

---

150 Understanding MS-SQL Server Column List Extension to the SELECT Privilege

The ANSI/ISO standard does not permit the inclusion of a column list when granting the SELECT privilege. As such, if a DBMS product strictly adheres to the standard, granting SELECT is an all-or-nothing proposition—either a user ID has SELECT access to *all* of the columns in a table or view, or the user ID has no SELECT access to any of them. By extending the standard, MS-SQL Server (as well as several other DBMS products) lets you specify a list of columns when you want to GRANT SELECT on some columns in a table or view and not others.

Suppose, for example, that you want to give the benefits coordinator, PAUL, access to the ID, name, insurance, and retirement plan information in the employee record. However, you do not want him to see any of the salary, ratings, and quota data. MS-SQL Server lets you specify the columns a user ID can query with a SELECT statement by including the column list in a GRANT statement similar to:

```
GRANT SELECT (id, name, health_plan_selection,
              health_plan_cost, dental_plan_selection,
              dental_plan_cost,
              retirement_plan_participation_pcnt,
              retirement_plan_vesting_date)
ON employees TO paul
```

In the current example, if PAUL executes the SELECT statement on a column in the EMPLOYEES table to which he does not have query access, such as

```
SELECT id, name, salary FROM employees
```

MS-SQL Server will respond with the error message similar to:

```
Server: Msg 230, Level 14, State 1, Line 1
SELECT permission denied on column 'salary' of object
'employees', database 'SQLTips', owner 'dbo'.
```

The important thing to remember is that granting SELECT privilege without a column list lets the user ID see data in all of the columns in the table or view on which the privilege is granted. Adding a column list to the GRANT SELECT statement limits the user ID's SELECT privilege to only displaying data in the listed columns.

Note: *If your DBMS product does not let you specify a column list in the GRANT SELECT statement, you can still limit the users to having only SELECT access on specific table columns by granting SELECT access on a view instead of on the base table itself. You will learn more about using a view to limit a user ID's SELECT access to specific table columns in Tip 157, "Using a View to Limit SELECT Privilege to Specific Columns in a Table."*

---

151 Using the GRANT INSERT (and REVOKE INSERT) Statement to Control Access to a Database Object

The INSERT privilege on a table or view lets a user ID or the members of a role add rows of data to a table. As you learned in Tip 150, "Understanding MS-SQL Server Column List Extension to the SELECT Privilege," a user with SELECT privilege can only "see" a table's data and is not able to modify its contents at all. Conversely, a user ID with only INSERT privilege is able to change a table's contents (by adding rows) but is not able to review any work performed—unless the ID also has SELECT privilege on the object. Moreover, without

DELETE privilege (which you will learn about in Tip 154, "Using the GRANT DELETE [and REVOKE DELETE] Statement to Control Access to Database Objects"), the user cannot remove a row just added or even change data values in the row without UPDATE access (which you will learn about in Tip 152, "Using the GRANT UPDATE [and REVOKE UPDATE] Statement to Control Access to Database Objects"). Thus, INSERT privilege is just that—the ability to add rows to a table (either directly or through a view). After insertion, the row becomes a part of the table, and the user ID that added it has no additional privileges on the row beyond those that the user has on the table or view.

The syntax of the GRANT statement used to give INSERT privilege is:

```
GRANT INSERT ON <table name> | <view name>
TO <user and/or Role name list> [WITH GRANT OPTION]
```

As such, to allow user ID SALLY to execute INSERT statements on the INVOICES table, for example, the table's owner (or other user with GRANT INSERT privilege) must execute a GRANT statement such as:

```
GRANT INSERT ON invoices TO sally
```

Or, to give INSERT access on the PRODUCTS table to GARY and to allow GARY to GRANT INSERT access to other users, someone with GRANT INSERT privilege on the PRODUCTS table must include the WITH GRANT OPTION in the GRANT statement, as follows:

```
GRANT INSERT ON products TO gary WITH GRANT OPTION
```

Finally, to GRANT INSERT access on the VW_KEY_CUST_ORDERS view to LEONARD, MARK, and the SALES_MANAGERS role, a user with GRANT INSERT access on the view must execute the GRANT statement:

```
GRANT INSERT ON vw_key_cust_orders
TO leonard, mark, sales_managers
```

Note: *In order to successfully GRANT INSERT access on a view, the owner (DBOO) of the view must also have GRANT INSERT on the underlying table on which the view is based. As you learned in Tip 11, "Understanding Views," a view is a virtual table in that it does not have any data (rows) of its own. Instead, a view simply displays data values found in an underlying "real" table. As such, when inserting a row into a view, the user is actually adding a row to the underlying table whose data the view displays.*

Since one needs only SELECT access on a table to create a view based on it, a user without INSERT access on the underlying table can create a view. Moreover, as the owner of the newly created view, the user can grant INSERT access on the view to another user. (Remember, the user ID creating a table or view has full privileges on the object as its owner—which includes the right to GRANT INSERT on the object to another user.) However, if the user that created the view does not have INSERT access on its underlying table, the DBMS will not allow the insertion of data into the underlying table through the view.

Conversely, when a user with GRANT INSERT access on the underlying table creates a view and then grants INSERT access on the view to another user, the user receiving INSERT access will be able to add rows to the underlying table through the view. For example, given a VW_KEY_CUST_ORDERS view based on an ORDERS table, a user with GRANT INSERT access on the view and on the ORDERS table can execute the GRANT statement

```
GRANT INSERT ON VW_KEY_CUST_ORDERS TO frank
```

to give user ID FRANK the access privilege to INSERT a row into the underlying (ORDERS) table by using the view in the INTO clause of an INSERT statement such as:

```
INSERT INTO vw_key_cust_orders
  VALUES ('1/1/2001', 1, 8, 6, 258.25, 20)
```

The DBMS will not, however, allow FRANK to add a row directly to the ORDERS table using the INSERT statement

```
INSERT INTO order VALUES ('1/1/2001', 1, 8, 6, 258.25, 20)
```

because FRANK has INSERT access only on the VW_KEY_CUST_ORDERS view and does not have INSERT access on the ORDERS table itself.

When you want to take away a user's ability to add rows to a table, execute a REVOKE INSERT statement to take away the INSERT privilege you previously granted. For example, if you granted INSERT access on the INVOICES table to SALLY, you can take away her ability to add rows to INVOICES by submitting the REVOKE statement:

```
REVOKE INSERT ON invoices FROM sally
```

After executing the REVOKE INSERT statement, any other privileges SALLY had on the INVOICES table remain in place. Moreover, as was the case with the SELECT privilege, SALLY will still have INSERT access on the INVOICES table if she received the privilege from another user in addition to the one executing the REVOKE INSERT statement. When you REVOKE a privilege, the DBMS takes away only the privilege *you* granted, and the REVOKE statement has no effect on the same privilege granted on the object by another user.

152 Using the GRANT UPDATE (and REVOKE UPDATE) Statement to Control Access to Database Objects

UPDATE privilege on a table or view lets a user or application program execute UPDATE statements to selectively change data values stored in existing rows. While users with UPDATE access can change a table's data, they cannot add new rows, remove rows, or even "see" existing data values stored in the table.

Note: *In some DBMS products (including MS-SQL Server), the user must have* both *UPDATE* and *SELECT access on an object to successfully execute an UPDATE statement on the table or view. When executing an UPDATE statement on MS-SQL Server, for example, the DBMS first selects the rows whose data values are to be updated and then executes the actual UPDATE on the selected rows. As such, if a user on an MS-SQL Server has UPDATE but not SELECT access on a table or view, the user will not be able to change the table's data because the DBMS will not allow the user to "select" the rows to be updated by the UPDATE statement. Therefore, to GRANT UPDATE access on MS-SQL Server, for example, you must GRANT both UPDATE and SELECT access on the object. Check your system documentation to see if your DBMS requires that a user ID have both UPDATE and SELECT access on an object to be able to change data values in it.*

The syntax of the GRANT statement used to give UPDATE privilege is:

```
GRANT UPDATE [(<column list>)]
ON <table name> | <view name>
TO <user and/or Role name list> [WITH GRANT OPTION]
```

Thus, to allow user ID KRIS to execute UPDATE statements on the INVOICES table, for example, the table's owner (or other user with GRANT UPDATE privilege) must execute a GRANT statement such as:

```
GRANT UPDATE ON invoices TO kris
```

Or, to give UPDATE access on the PRODUCTS table to FRANK and allow FRANK to GRANT UPDATE access to other users, someone with GRANT UPDATE privilege on the PRODUCTS table must include the WITH GRANT OPTION in the GRANT statement, as follows:

```
GRANT UPDATE ON products TO frank WITH GRANT OPTION
```

Finally, to GRANT UPDATE access on the VW_LV_INVENTORY view to SCOTT, HARMON, and the LV_STORE_MANAGERS role, a user with GRANT UPDATE permission on the view must execute the GRANT statement:

```
GRANT UPDATE ON vw_lv_inventory
TO scott, harmon, lv_store_managers
```

Note: *In order to successfully GRANT UPDATE access on an object through a view, the user granting UPDATE access on the view must also have GRANT UPDATE access on the underlying table on which the view is based. As you learned in Tip 11, a view is a virtual table without any physical data of its own. Rather, a view displays data values found in underlying "real" table(s). As such, when updating data values in a view, the user is actually changing the data in the columns of the view's underlying table.*

Since one needs only SELECT access on a table to create a view based on it, a user without UPDATE access on the underlying table can create a view. Moreover, the owner of the newly created view can GRANT UPDATE access on the view to another user. (Remember, the user

ID that creates a table or view has full privileges on the object—including the right to GRANT UPDATE on the object to another user.) However, if the user that created the view does not have UPDATE access on its underlying table, the DBMS will not allow the modification of data in the underlying table through the view.

Conversely, when a user with GRANT UPDATE access on the underlying table creates a view and then grants UPDATE access on the view to another user, the user receiving UPDATE access will be able to change data values in the underlying table through the view. For example, given a VW_KEY_CUST_ORDERS view based on an ORDERS table, a user with GRANT UPDATE access on the view and on the ORDERS table can execute the GRANT statement

```
GRANT UPDATE ON VW_KEY_CUST_ORDERS TO david
```

to give user ID DAVID permission to UPDATE values in the underlying (ORDERS) table by using the view as the target table in an UPDATE statement such as:

```
UPDATE vw_key_cust_orders SET ship_date = '07/11/2001'
WHERE invoice_date = '07/10/200' AND ship_date IS NULL
```

The DBMS will not, however, allow DAVID to change data values directly in the ORDERS table with the similar UPDATE statement

```
UPDATE ORDERS SET ship_date = '07/11/2001'
WHERE invoice_date = '07/10/200' AND ship_date IS NULL
```

that uses the ORDERS table instead of the view as the target of the UPDATE statement. David has UPDATE access only on the VW_KEY_CUST_ORDERS view but does not have UPDATE access on the ORDERS table itself.

Granting UPDATE access on a table or view is not an all-or-nothing proposition. If you want user ID KAREN, for example, to be able to modify data in only some of the columns in the INVENTORY table and not others, list the columns KAREN can modify in the GRANT UPDATE statement. For example, the GRANT statement

```
GRANT UPDATE ON inventory TO karen
```

gives user ID KAREN the ability to change data in any of the columns in the INVENTORY table, while the GRANT statement

```
GRANT UPDATE (item_description, item_cost) ON inventory
TO karen
```

lets KAREN modify only the values in the ITEM_DESCRIPTION and ITEM_COST columns of the INVENTORY table.

When you want to take away a user's ability to change data values in a table, execute a REVOKE UPDATE statement to remove the UPDATE privilege you previously granted to the user. For example, if you granted UPDATE access on the INVOICES table to SUE, you can take away her ability to change data values in the INVOICES table using the REVOKE statement:

```
REVOKE UPDATE ON invoices FROM sue
```

After the DBMS executes the REVOKE UPDATE statement, any other privileges the user ID has on the object remain in place. Moreover, as was the case with the SELECT and INSERT privileges, the user will still have UPDATE access on an object after you do a REVOKE UPDATE if the user also received UPDATE access on the object from another user. When you REVOKE a privilege, the DBMS takes away only the privilege *you* granted, and the REVOKE statement has no effect on the same privilege granted on the object by another user.

Just as granting UPDATE access on an object is not an all-or-nothing proposition, neither is revoking the privilege. To REVOKE UPDATE access on only specific columns in a table or view (vs. the entire object), list the columns the user is no longer allowed to UPDATE as part of the REVOKE statement. For example, while the REVOKE statement

```
REVOKE UPDATE ON invoices FROM sue
```

prevents user ID SUE from updating any of the columns in the INVOICES table, the REVOKE statement

```
REVOKE UPDATE (invoice_date, cust_id, item_cost)
ON invoices FROM sue
```

prevents user ID SUE only from updating the INVOICE_DATE, CUST_ID, and ITEM_COST columns of the INVOICES table.

153 Using the GRANT REFERENCES (and REVOKE REFERENCES) Statement to Control Access to Database Objects

The REFERENCES privilege allows a user to refer to the table's PRIMARY KEY and any other columns constrained by the UNIQUE constraint as the FOREIGN KEY in another table. (You will learn about the PRIMARY KEY constraint in Tip 171, "Understanding Primary Keys," and about the UNIQUE constraint in Tip 192, "Using the UNIQUE Column Constraint to Prevent Duplicate Values in a Column.") Although REFERENCES privilege does not give a user the ability to display a table's data directly, the access privilege was added to SQL-92 to deal with a subtle security issue posed by a user's ability to use a FOREIGN KEY to indirectly determine data values in a table's columns-without SELECT access on those columns. Suppose, for example, that a user does not have SELECT access to a table called TAKEOVER_STOCKS_LIST but knows that the STOCK_SYMBOL column is the PRIMARY KEY for the table. By creating a table with the definition

```
CREATE TABLE my_takeover_stocks
  (symbol VARCHAR(10)
   CONSTRAINT fk_takeover_targets FOREIGN KEY(symbol)
   REFERENCES takeover_stocks_list(stock_symbol))
```

My_TAKEOVER_STOCKS, the user will end up with a complete list of stocks in the TAKEOVER_STOCKS_LIST table.

As you learned in Tip 62, "Using the CREATE TABLE Statement to Assign Foreign Key Constraints," the value in each row of a FOREIGN KEY column must exist in one of the rows of the column in the table referenced by the FOREIGN KEY constraint. In the current example, the DBMS allows the user to INSERT a stock symbol into the MY_TAKEOVER_STOCKS table only if the stock symbol already exists in the TAKEOVER_STOCKS_LIST table. As such, attempts to insert symbols not in the TAKEOVER_STOCKS_LIST table into the MY_TAKEOVER_STOCKS will fail with an error message similar to:

```
Server: Msg 547, Level 16, State1, Line 1
INSERT statement conflicted with COLUMN FOREIGN KEY
  constraint 'fk_takeover_stocks'. The conflict occurred in
  database 'SQLTips', table 'takeover_stocks_list', column
  'stock_symbol'.

The statement has been terminated.
```

Since the DBMS will only allow the insertion of stock symbols already present in the TAKEOVER_STOCKS_LIST table, the MY_TAKEOVER_STOCKS table will have a list of all stocks in TAKEOVER_STOCKS_LIST after the user attempts to INSERT all possible stock symbols into MY_TAKEOVER_STOCKS.

The syntax of the GRANT statement used to give REFERENCES privilege is:

```
GRANT REFERENCES [(<column list>)] ON <table name>
TO <user and/or Role name list> [WITH GRANT OPTION]
```

Thus, to allow user ID ROB to CREATE a table with one or more FOREIGN KEY constraints that reference columns in the EMPLOYEES table, the table's owner (or other user with GRANT REFERENCES privilege) must execute a GRANT statement such as:

```
GRANT REFERENCES ON employees TO rob
```

Or, to give REFERENCES access on columns in the CUSTOMERS table to JAMES and to allow JAMES to GRANT REFERENCES access to other users, someone with GRANT REFERENCES privilege on the CUSTOMERS table must include the WITH GRANT OPTION in a GRANT statement such as:

```
GRANT REFERENCES ON customers TO james WITH GRANT OPTION
```

Granting REFERENCES access on a table is not an all-or-nothing proposition. If you want a user to be able to make FOREIGN KEY references only to some of the columns in a table, simply list the columns allowed as part of the GRANT statement. For example, the GRANT statement

```
GRANT REFERENCES (stock_symbol, security_cussip) ON
takeover_list_table TO karen
```

allows user ID KAREN to use only the columns STOCK_SYMBOL and SECURITY_CUSSIP as FOREIGN KEY references in tables she creates.

Note: *Although a FOREIGN KEY in one table is normally the PRIMARY KEY in another table, most DBMS products (including MS-SQL Server) let you use any column to which the UNIQUE constraint has been applied as the reference column for a FOREIGN KEY constraint. Therefore, if you have a table in which the only unique column is the PRIMARY KEY, you need not specify a column name when granting the REFERENCES privilege. However, if you have a table with multiple columns to which you have applied the UNIQUE constraint, use a column list in the GRANT REFERENCES statement, and be sure to exclude any columns whose values you want to remain hidden from the user to whom you are granting REFERENCES access.*

When you want to take away a user ID's ability to create FOREIGN KEY references to columns in a table, execute a REVOKE REFERENCES statement to remove the privilege you previously granted. For example, if you granted REFERENCES access on the EMPLOYEES table to JERRY, you can take away his ability to reference columns in the EMPLOYEES table by using the REVOKE statement:

```
REVOKE REFERENCES ON employees FROM jerry
```

After the DBMS executes the REVOKE REFERENCES statement, any other privileges a user has on the object remain in place. Moreover, as was the case with the SELECT, INSERT, and UPDATE privileges, the user will still have REFERENCES access on an object after you REVOKE REFERENCES if the user also received REFERENCES access on the same object from someone else. When you REVOKE a privilege, the DBMS takes away only the privilege *you* granted. The REVOKE statement has no effect on the same privilege granted on the object by another user.

As was the case with granting the privilege, revoking REFERENCES on an object need not be an all-or-nothing proposition. To REVOKE REFERENCES access on only specific columns in a table, list the columns the user is no longer allowed to reference as a FOREIGN KEY in the REVOKE statement. For example, while the REVOKE statement

```
REVOKE REFERENCES ON customers FROM sally
```

prevents user ID SALLY from referencing any of the columns in the CUSTOMERS table, the REVOKE statement

```
REVOKE REFERENCES (cust_ID, phone_number) ON  customers
FROM sally
```

prevents her only from referencing the CUST_ID and PHONE_NUMBER fields in a FOREIGN KEY.

Note: *If you granted REFERENCES access on an object to a user and the user created a table with FOREIGN KEY constraints referencing columns in the object, revoking REFERENCES access prevents the user ID only from defining subsequent FOREIGN KEY reference to the object. The FOREIGN KEY references in any tables created prior to the revocation of the REFERENCES privilege will continue to check for data values in the referenced column(s) even after REFERENCES is revoked.*

154 Using the GRANT DELETE (and REVOKE DELETE) Statement to Control Access to Database Objects

DELETE privilege on a table or view lets a user or application program remove one or more rows from a table. As you learned in Tip 151, "Using the GRANT INSERT (and REVOKE INSERT) Statement to Control Access to a Database Object," INSERT access lets a user add rows to a table. However, after adding a row, the user has no special access rights over it. In fact, as you learned in Tip 149, "Using the GRANT SELECT (and REVOKE SELECT) Statement to Control Access to a Database Object," the user that added a row cannot even ask the DBMS to display the data values in the row without SELECT access. DELETE access, like each of the other access privileges, gives the user ID a singular capability—to remove rows from a table (whether the user added the rows or not).

Note: *In some DBMS products (including MS-SQL Server), the user must have* both *DELETE* and *SELECT access on an object to successfully execute a searched DELETE statement such as:*

```
DELETE FROM invoices WHERE invoice_date < 01/01/1900
```

On MS-SQL Server, for example, the DELETE statement in the current example will fail with an error message similar to

```
Server: Msg 229, Level 14, State 5, Line 1
SELECT permission denied on object 'invoices', database
  'SQLTips', owner 'dbo'.
```

if the user ID executing it has DELETE access without SELECT privilege on the INVOICES table. Now, a user with only DELETE access can still execute a DELETE statement, just not a searched *DELETE.*

For example, a user needs only DELETE access to execute the DELETE statement

```
DELETE FROM employees
```

which will remove all rows from the employee table. Since removing all rows from a table is seldom (if ever) the desired outcome from executing a DELETE statement, be sure to GRANT SELECT access on the objects on which you are granting a user ID DELETE access.

The syntax of the GRANT statement used to give DELETE privilege is:

```
GRANT DELETE ON <table name> | <view name>
TO <user and/or Role name list> [WITH GRANT OPTION]
```

Thus, to allow user ID JERRY to execute DELETE statements on the INVOICES table, for example, the table's owner (or other user with GRANT DELETE privilege) must execute a GRANT statement such as:

```
GRANT DELETE ON invoices TO jerry
```

Or, to give DELETE access on the EMPLOYEES table to SCOTT and to allow SCOTT to GRANT DELETE access to other users, someone with GRANT DELETE privilege on the EMPLOYEES table must include the WITH GRANT OPTION in the GRANT statement, as follows:

```
GRANT DELETE ON employees TO scott WITH GRANT OPTION
```

Finally, to GRANT DELETE access on the VW_SHIPPED_ORDERS view to SALLY, SUSAN, and the SHIPPING_RECEIVING_CLERKS role, a user with GRANT DELETE permission on the view must execute the GRANT statement:

```
GRANT DELETE ON vw_shipped_orders
TO sally, susan, shipping_receiving_clerks
```

Note: *In order to successfully GRANT DELETE access on an object through a view, the user granting DELETE access on the view must also have GRANT DELETE access on the underlying table on which the view is based. As you learned in Tip 11, "Understanding Views," a view is a virtual table without any physical rows of its own. Rather, a view displays data values found in underlying "real" table(s). As such, when removing rows from a view, the user is actually deleting rows from the view's underlying table.*

Since one needs only SELECT access on a table to create a view based on it, a user without DELETE access on the underlying table can create a view. Moreover, the owner of the newly created view can GRANT DELETE access on the view to another user. (Remember, the user ID that creates a table or view has full privileges on the object—including the right to GRANT DELETE on the object to another user.) However, if the user that created the view does not have DELETE access on its underlying table, the DBMS will not allow the removal of rows from the underlying table through the view.

Conversely, when a user with GRANT DELETE access on the underlying table creates a view and then grants DELETE access on the view to another user, the user receiving DELETE access will be able to remove rows from the underlying table through the view.

For example, given a VW_SHIPPED_ORDERS view based on an ORDERS table, a user with GRANT UPDATE access on the view and on the ORDERS table can execute the GRANT statement

```
GRANT DELETE ON vw_shipped_orders TO david
```

to give user ID DAVID permission to DELETE values from the underlying (ORDERS) table by using the view as the target table in a DELETE statement such as:

```
DELETE FROM vw_shipped_orders
WHERE shipped_date < '01/01/1999'
```

The DBMS will not, however, permit DAVID to remove rows directly from the ORDERS table with the similar DELETE statement

```
DELETE FROM ORDERS WHERE shipped_date < '01/01/1999'
```

that uses the ORDERS table instead of the view as the target of the DELETE statement. David has DELETE access only on the VW_SHIPPED_ORDERS view but does not have DELETE access on the ORDERS table itself.

When you want to take away a user ID's ability to DELETE rows from a table or view, execute a REVOKE DELETE statement to remove the privilege you previously granted. For example, if you granted DELETE access on the CUSTOMERS table to WALTER, you can take away his ability to remove columns from the EMPLOYEES table by using the REVOKE statement:

```
REVOKE DELETE ON customers FROM walter
```

After the DBMS executes a REVOKE DELETE, any other privileges a user has on the object remain in place. Moreover, as was the case with the SELECT, INSERT, REFERENCES, and UPDATE privileges, the user will still have DELETE access on an object after you REVOKE the privilege if the user also received DELETE access on the object from someone else. When you REVOKE a privilege, you take away only the privilege *you* granted. The REVOKE statement has no effect on the same privilege granted on the object by another user.

155 Using the GRANT ALL (and REVOKE ALL) Statement to GRANT (or REVOKE) Privileges to Database Objects

SQL provides a convenient shortcut to use when you want to grant SELECT, INSERT, UPDATE, DELETE, and REFERENCES access on an object. Instead of enumerating the five privileges, you can simply execute a GRANT ALL statement.

The syntax of the GRANT statement to GRANT full access to an object is:

```
GRANT ALL [PRIVILEGES][(<column list>)] ON <table name>
TO <user and/or Role name list> [WITH GRANT OPTION]
```

Therefore, the GRANT statement

```
GRANT ALL ON employees TO sue
```

is equivalent to:

```
GRANT SELECT, INSERT, UPDATE, DELETE, REFERENCES
ON employees TO sue
```

In order to successfully execute the GRANT ALL statement, you must have the GRANT option for all security privileges available for the object. In the case of a table, you must have the access to GRANT: SELECT, INSERT, UPDATE, DELETE, and REFERENCES. If, on the other hand, you are granting all access privilege on a view, you must GRANT: SELECT,

INSERT, UPDATE, and DELETE access on the view and the view's underlying table—there is no REFERENCE access on a view.

As the database object owner (DBOO), you have all rights to the objects you create and thus can successfully execute the GRANT ALL statement on any of the objects you own. If you are not the DBOO, the DBOO (or another user with full access and GRANT option) will have to GRANT the five access rights (four, in the case of a view) along with the WITH GRANT OPTION to you so that you can GRANT ALL of the rights on the object to another user.

If you submit a GRANT ALL statement and are missing one or more of the available access rights or just the privilege to GRANT one or more of those privileges to another user, the DBMS will fail to execute the GRANT ALL statement and will return an error message similar to:

```
Server: Msg 4613, Level 16, State 1, Line 1
Grantor does not have GRANT permission.
```

Unfortunately, your DBMS (like MS-SQL Server, in the example), may not be specific as to which of the access privileges or GRANT option(s) you are missing.

Be careful when specifying a column list in a GRANT ALL statement. Because not all of the security privileges accept a column list, you will have to check your system documentation to see what your DBMS will do when presented with a column list in a GRANT ALL statement. MS-SQL Server, for example, will GRANT ALL privileges on the columns listed for those privileges that accept a column list (SELECT, UPDATE, and REFERENCES) and will ignore the column list for those privileges that do not accept a column list (DELETE and INSERT).

Thus, for MS-SQL Server, the GRANT ALL statement

```
GRANT ALL (employee_id, first_name, last_name)
ON employees TO rodger, sue, mary
```

is equivalent to the GRANT statements:

```
GRANT SELECT, UPDATE, REFERENCES
  (employee_id, first_name, last_name)
ON employees TO rodger, sue, mary
GRANT INSERT, DELETE ON employees TO rodger, sue, mary
```

The REVOKE ALL statement takes away all privileges granted on the object listed by the user executing the statement on the object listed in the ON clause from the user IDs or role(s) listed in the FROM clause. For example, to remove all privileges *you* granted to SUE on the EMPLOYEES table, execute the REVOKE statement:

```
REVOKE ALL ON employees FROM sue
```

Unlike the GRANT ALL statement, you do not have to have full access to WITH GRANT OPTION on an object to execute a REVOKE ALL statement. For example, if you have only GRANT SELECT, INSERT, UPDATE, and DELETE access on the INVOICES table and you execute the GRANT statements

```
GRANT SELECT, INSERT, UPDATE, DELETE ON invoices TO sue
GRANT SELECT, INSERT, DELETE ON invoices TO frank
GRANT SELECT ON invoices TO konrad
```

you could REVOKE ALL of the privileges you granted to SUE, FRANK, and KONRAD with a single REVOKE ALL statement, such as:

```
REVOKE ALL ON invoices FROM sue, frank, konrad
```

In the current example, in which you granted each user ID having a different set of access privileges, the REVOKE ALL statement is equivalent to the REVOKE statements:

```
REVOKE SELECT, INSERT, UPDATE, DELETE ON invoices FROM sue
REVOKE SELECT, INSERT, DELETE ON invoices FROM frank
REVOKE SELECT ON invoices FROM konrad
```

Note: *As was the case with the REVOKE statement, when you execute the REVOKE ALL statement, the DBMS takes away only the privileges* you *granted to the object from the user IDs listed in the statement's FROM clause. As such, if both you and another user granted user ID SUE all privileges on the CUSTOMERS table, SUE would still have all privileges on the CUSTOMERS table after you executed the REVOKE ALL statement:*

```
REVOKE ALL ON customers FROM sue
```

A REVOKE ALL statement, like a REVOKE statement, takes away only privileges *you* granted, and the user retains all privileges on the object received from someone else.

156 Using a View to Limit INSERT Privilege to Specific Columns in a Table

As you learned in Tip 151, "Using the GRANT INSERT (and REVOKE INSERT) Statement to Control Access to a Database Object," INSERT privilege lets you control who has the ability to add rows to a table or view. Those with INSERT privilege are allowed to add rows; those without it are not. SQL-92 extends the basic INSERT privilege by adding the ability to limit the INSERT privilege to one or more columns vs. having to grant INSERT access to all of the columns in a row (or none of them).

Suppose, for example, that you have an EMPLOYEES table created with

```
CREATE TABLE employees
  (id             INTEGER PRIMARY KEY,
   first_name     VARCHAR(25) NOT NULL,
   last_name      VARCHAR(30) NOT NULL,
```

```
    ssan            CHAR(11) NOT NULL,
    address         VARCHAR(50),
    manager         SMALLINT,
    quota           SMALLINT,
    hourly_rate     MONEY,
    commission_rate MONEY)
```

and you want let the marketing room manager, MIKE to add new employees, but you do not want MIKE to be able to specify an employee's MANAGER, QUOTA, HOURLY_RATE, and COMMISSION_RATE. If your DBMS supports a GRANT INSERT statement with a column list, you could accomplish your goal with:

```
GRANT INSERT (id, first_name, last_name, ssan, address)
ON employees TO mike
```

Unfortunately, not all DBMS products allow a column list in a GRANT INSERT statement. If your DBMS, like MS-SQL Server, does not, you can still limit the GRANT INSERT to specific columns by granting INSERT on a view with only some of the table's columns listed instead of granting INSERT on the table itself.

In the current example, you would CREATE a view with

```
CREATE VIEW vw_new_marketing_rep_template AS
(SELECT id, first_name, last_name, ssan, address
  FROM employees)
```

and then GRANT INSERT on the VW_NEW_MARKETING_REP_TEMPLATE view with:

```
GRANT INSERT ON vw_new_marketing_rep_template TO mike
```

Note: *When using a view to limit the INSERT privilege to specific columns, bear in mind that the DBMS will supply a NULL for those table columns not included in the view when the user uses the view to INSERT a row into the underlying table. As such, if the view does not include all of the columns to which you have applied a NOT NULL constraint, the user will not be able to INSERT any rows into the table through the view even after you GRANT INSERT on the view.*

In the current example, when MIKE adds a new employee with an INSERT statement similar to

```
INSERT INTO vw_new_marketing_rep_template VALUES
  (1, 'Konrad', 'King', 'SSAN', '765 E. Eldorado Lane')
```

the DBMS will add a row to the EMPLOYEES table using the specified column values for the ID, FIRST_NAME, LAST_NAME, SSAN, and ADDRESS columns, and place a NULL in the MANAGER, QUOTA, HOURLY_RATE, and COMMISSION_RATE columns. If the view's definition were changed to

```
CREATE VIEW vw_new_marketing_rep_template AS
(SELECT id, first_name, last_name, address FROM employees)
```

user ID MIKE could not use the view to add employees because each attempted INSERT statement into the VW_NEW_MARKETING_REP_TEMPLATE view would violate the NOT NULL constraint on the SSAN column.

157 Using a View to Limit SELECT Privilege to Specific Columns in a Table

Tip 149, "Using the GRANT SELECT (and REVOKE SELECT) Statement to Control Access to a Database Object," showed you how to use the GRANT SELECT statement to let a user display column values in a table or view. Unlike the INSERT, UPDATE, and REFERENCES privileges, the SQL-92 standard does not allow a column list in a SELECT statement. As such, if your DBMS implements the SELECT statement *exactly* as defined by the standard, you have to let a user ID see the data in either all of the columns of a table or none of its columns. Fortunately, as is the case with the GRANT INSERT statement, you can get around the SELECT statement's "no column list" limitation by granting SELECT on a view instead of on the underlying table itself.

Note: *Some DBMS products, including MS-SQL Server, extend the standard SELECT statement to allow a column list (as you learned in Tip 149). Check the GRANT statement syntax in your system manual for the list of privileges for which your DBMS supports a column list.*

To let a user see only some of the columns in a table, CREATE a view with only the columns you want the user to see defined, and GRANT SELECT on the view instead of on the underlying table. For example, given the EMPLOYEES table defined in Tip 156, "Using a View to Limit INSERT Privilege to Specific Columns in a Table," you could use the CREATE statement

```
CREATE VIEW vw_marketing_reps AS
(SELECT id, first_name, last_name, ssan, address, manager,
  quota FROM employees)
```

and then GRANT SELECT on the VW_MARKETING_REPS view to the MARKETING_EMPLOYEES role with:

```
GRANT SELECT ON vw_marketing_reps TO marketing_employees
```

The members of the MARKETING_EMPLOYEES role could then execute SELECT statements to display data in any (or all) of the columns in the VW_MARKETING_REPS view, which gets its data from the EMPLOYEES table. Since the two pay columns (HOURLY_RATE and COMMISSION_RATE) were omitted from the view's column list, the users would not be able to display data in these columns. In fact, they would not even know the columns existed.

158 Using Views to Extend SQL Security Privileges

As you learned in Tip 156, "Using a View to Limit INSERT Privilege to Specific Columns in a Table," and Tip 157, " Using a View to Limit SELECT Privilege to Specific Columns in a Table," you can use views to limit which columns in a table a user can display with a SELECT statement and the columns into which a user can place data when adding a row with an INSERT statement. Both of these tips show you ways in which you can use a view to limit the columns that a user can see and modify. You can also use a view to limit a user's access to specific rows within a table (in addition to specific columns within those rows).

Suppose, for example, that you have several sales offices, and each office is allowed to manage its employee records in a centralized EMPLOYEES table. By using a column list in a GRANT UPDATE statement, you can limit a manager's ability to make changes to specific columns such as:

```
GRANT UPDATE (first_name, last_name, address)
ON employees TO sales_office_managers
```

However, by granting UPDATE access on the EMPLOYEES table that contains employee information from all offices, a manager from one office could change the employee data on employees working at a different office. By granting the same UPDATE privilege on a view (instead of the underlying table) you can restrict the UPDATE privilege so that managers can change employee data only for employees working in their own offices.

For example, if you create a views such as

```
CREATE VIEW vw_office1_employees AS
  (SELECT * FROM employees WHERE office = 1)
CREATE VIEW wv_office1_employees AS
  (SELECT * FROM employees WHERE office = 2)
```

for each office, you can use GRANT statements such as

```
GRANT UPDATE (first_name, last_name, address)
ON vw_office1_employees TO office1_managers
GRANT UPDATE (first_name, last_name, address)
ON vw_office2_employees TO office2_managers
```

to limit each set of office managers to updating personal information only for its own employees.

The views created in the current example can also illustrate a way in which to limit SELECT access to only certain rows within a table. By granting SELECT privilege with the GRANT statements

```
GRANT SELECT ON vw_office1_employees TO office1_managers
GRANT SELECT ON vw_office2_employees TO office2_managers
```

you limit the members of the OFFICE1_MANAGERS role to displaying all EMPLOYEES table columns for employees working at office 1, and the members of the OFFICE2_MANAGERS role to seeing only the information on office 2 employees.

Note: *To further restrict SELECT access to specific columns within specific rows, modify the CREATE VIEW statements to SELECT only the columns and rows you want the user to see. For example, the CREATE VIEW statement*

```
CREATE VIEW vw_office1_employees AS
  (SELECT first_name, last_name, address
     FROM employees WHERE office = 1)
```

will allow only the members of the OFFICE1_MANAGERS role to display and modify the FIRST_NAME, LAST_NAME, and ADDRESS columns for office 1 employees after you execute the preceding GRANT UPDATE and GRANT SELECT statements in this tip.

Similar to limiting SELECT and UPDATE privileges, you can also use a view to limit DELETE access to specific rows in a table. Suppose, for example, that you wanted to let your shipping department manager, user ID FRANK, remove any back orders older than six months. You could create a view of old back orders using

```
CREATE VIEW vw_backorders_180 AS
  (SELECT * FROM orders WHERE date_shipped IS NULL AND
                         (GETDATE() - order_date) > 180)
```

and grant FRANK DELETE access to just those rows with:

```
GRANT DELETE ON vw_backorders_180 TO frank
```

User ID FRANK could then remove old back orders from the system using:

```
DELETE FROM vw_backorders_180
```

Note: *GETDATE() used in the current example is an MS-SQL Server built-in function that returns the current system date and time in DATETIME format.*

159 Understanding Indexes

Although not defined in the SQL-92 standard, most DBMS products automatically create an index based on a table's PRIMARY KEY and let you define additional indexes to speed up data access and retrieval. Do not confuse a PRIMARY KEY (see Tip 171, "Understanding Primary Keys") or a FOREIGN KEY (see Tip 173, "Understanding Foreign Keys") with an index. Database keys (which *are* defined in the SQL standard) are constraints that place limits on column data values. Indexes, meanwhile, are physical storage structures (like tables) that the DBMS can use to quickly find table rows with specific values in one or more columns.

While the rows in a table are not in any particular order, the values in an index are arranged in either ascending or descending order. The DBMS uses a table's index as you would an index in a book. When executing a query based on a data value in an indexed column, the database looks in the index to find the column value and then follows the index entry's pointer to the table row.

Note: *One exception to the unordered nature of rows in a relational table is MS-SQL Server's implementation of a clustered index, which you will learn about in Tip 165, "Understanding MS-SQL Server Clustered Indexes." For unclustered indexes, the DBMS sorts the values in the index but does not arrange a table's rows in any particular order. On MS-SQL Server, however, a table can have a single clustered index, and MS-SQL Server arranges the table's rows based on the data values that make up the columns in the clustered index.*

The presence of an index structure in an SQL database does not violate Codd's ninth rule, which specifies that a relational database must have "logical data independence," because the presence or absence of an index is completely transparent to the SQL user. (You learned about Codd's rules in Tip 6, "Understanding Codd's 12-Rule Relational Database Definition.")

Suppose, for example, that you wanted to display information on calls your marketing personnel made to 263-1052 using a SELECT statement similar to:

```
SELECT date_called, call_time, hangup_time, dispo,
  called_by
FROM call_history WHERE phone_number = 2631052
```

The statement itself does not indicate whether the CALL_HISTORY table has an index based on the PHONE_NUMBER column and will execute the query in either case. If there is no index, the DBMS will have to sequentially scan (read) every row in the table, displaying column values from those rows with a 2631052 in the PHONE_NUMBER column. If the CALL_HISTORY table has millions of rows, the process of retrieving and examining each and every row can take a long time.

If, on the other hand, the table has an index based on the PHONE_NUMBER column, as shown in Figure 159.1, the DBMS can use a search method to find the first index entry that satisfies the search criteria. Next, the DBMS needs to read sequential items in the index only until the "next" index value no longer satisfies the search condition.

The advantages of using an index are that:

- An index greatly speeds up a search because the index is sorted and the DBMS can use special access methods to find a particular data value in the index.

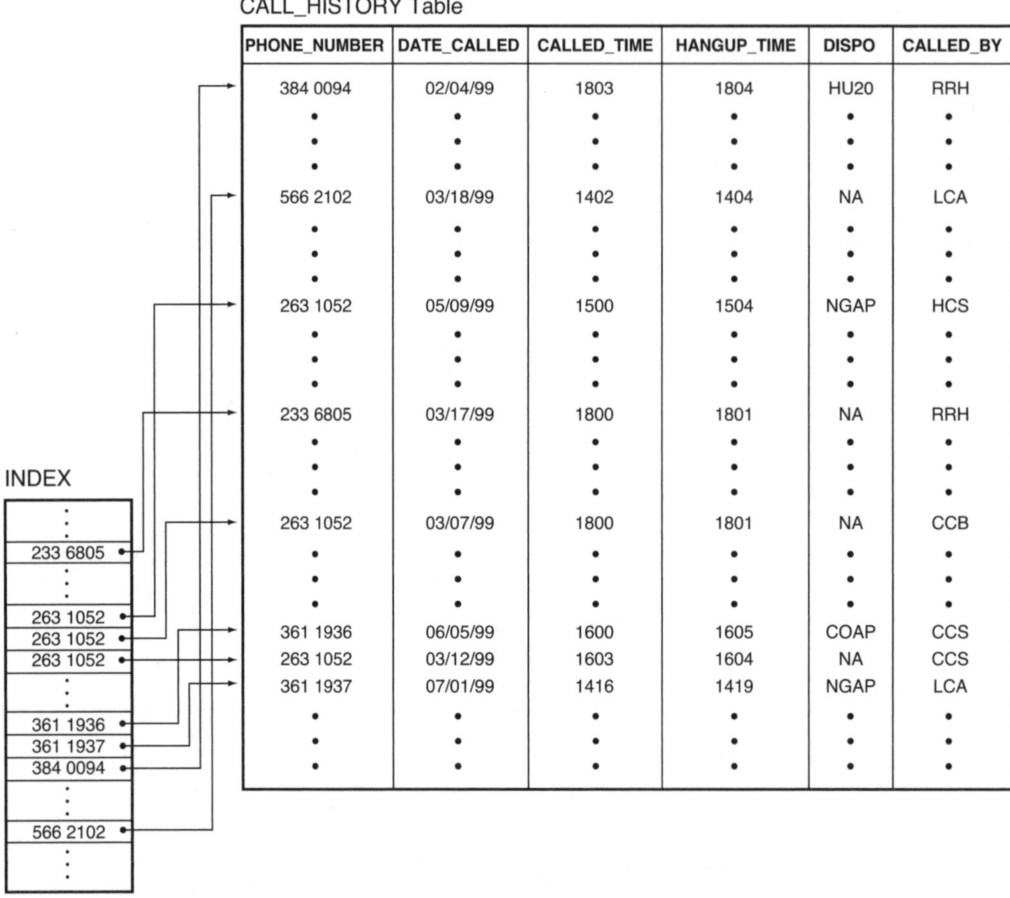

CALL_HISTORY Table
PHONE_NUMBER
DATE_CALLED
CALLED_TIME
HANGUP_TIME
DISPO
CALLED_BY
384 0094 02/04/99 1803 1804 HU20 RRH
566 2102 03/18/99 1402 1404 NA LCA
263 1052 05/09/99 1500 1504 NGAP HCS
233 6805 03/17/99 1800 1801 NA RRH
263 1052 03/07/99 1800 1801 NA CCB
361 1936 06/05/99 1600 1605 COAP CCS
263 1052 03/12/99 1603 1604 NA CCS
361 1937 07/01/99 1416 1419 NGAP LCA
INDEX
233 6805
263 1052
263 1052
263 1052
361 1936
361 1937
384 0094
566 2102

Figure 159.1 CALL_HISTORY Table with an index on the PHONE_NUMBER column

- The index adds little to the actual row retrieval overhead because each index row is small (typically a single data value and a pointer) and can, therefore, be retrieved quickly. Moreover, the index increases the speed of the physical row retrieval by providing a pointer value that tells the DBMS exactly where on disk it can find the row the user wants to see.
- The index drastically reduces the number of rows the DBMS must read during a query. In the current example, the DBMS can stop reading after three retrievals (given that there are only three 2631052 entries in the table) instead of scanning (reading) all of the perhaps millions of rows in the table.

Balanced against these advantages, the main disadvantages of using an index are that:

- The index uses disk space the DBMS could otherwise use to store table data or transaction logs.

- Each INSERT and DELETE requires additional overhead because the DBMS must add (INSERT) or remove (DELETE) a row not only in the table itself, but also in each of the indexes on the table. Moreover, each update on an indexed column requires that the DBMS change both the base table and the data stored in the index on the column being updated.

To maximize the advantages of using an index and minimize the disadvantages, add multiple indexes to tables that are more often used in queries than as targets of INSERT and UPDATE operations. Furthermore, in tables you index, base the index(es) on columns that are frequently found in search conditions your users use in queries on the table. As mentioned at the beginning of this tip, the DBMS always creates an index based on a table's PRIMARY KEY in anticipation that the table's rows will most often be queried with SELECT statements containing a range of PRIMARY KEY values in the WHERE clause.

160 Understanding How MS-SQL Server Selects an Index for a Query

MS-SQL Server has the ability to use multiple indexes per table within a single query. As a result, MS-SQL Server's 7.0 multiple search condition query execution is greatly improved over previous versions because the user can virtually eliminate table scans (in which the DBMS reads every row in a table) by creating indexes on the correct table columns. After creating one or more indexes on a table, you should typically let MS-SQL Server's query optimizer decide which index to use during query execution.

In order for MS-SQL Server to consider using an index, one of the columns in the SELECT statement's WHERE clause must be the first column in the index. For example, if you have a CALL_HISTORY table created with

```
CREATE call_history
  (phone_number INTEGER,
   date_called  DATETIME,
   call_time    SMALLINT,
   hangup_time  SMALLINT,
   disposition  VARCHAR(4),
   called_by    CHAR(3))
```

and create an index with

```
CREATE INDEX date_index
ON call_history (date_called, call_time, phone_number)
```

MS-SQL Server will never select the DATE_INDEX when executing the query

```
SELECT * FROM call_history WHERE phone_number = 2631070
```

because the column named in the search condition (PHONE_NUMBER) is not the first column in the index.

Note: *You will learn how to create indexes using the CREATE INDEX statement in Tip 161, "Using the CREATE INDEX Statement to Create an Index." For now, the important thing to know is that MS-SQL Server will choose to use an index only if its first column is one of the columns named in the SELECT statement's WHERE clause.*

Conversely, if you create another index by executing the CREATE statement

```
CREATE INDEX caller_index
ON call_history (called_by, date_called)
```

and submit the query

```
SELECT * FROM call_history
WHERE called_by = 'RRH' AND phone_number = 2631056
```

the MS-SQL Server optimizer will review the system tables that summarizes the distribution of information in the table being queried and decide whether a table scan or indexed query is the best way to retrieve the data requested by the SELECT statement. If the DBMS decides that an indexed query is best, it will use the second, CALLER_INDEX, as the only index available for selection (in the current example), since its first column (CALLED_BY) is one of the columns used in the SELECT statement's search criteria.

Instead of letting MS-SQL Server's optimizer choose the best index when it executes a query, you can tell the DBMS which index to use by including an INDEX = clause in the SELECT statement's FROM clause. For example, the SELECT statement

```
SELECT * FROM call_history INDEX=caller_index
WHERE date_called BETWEEN '01/01/2000' AND '01/31/2000'
```

forces the DBMS to use the CALLER_INDEX when MS-SQL Server would have chosen the DATE_INDEX to optimize the query.

Note: *Be very careful when forcing the DBMS to use a particular index vs. letting the optimizer select the best one for the job. In the current example, forcing the use of the CALLER_INDEX causes significant and unnecessary overhead in that the DBMS will have to read every entry in the index in order to satisfy the query. Had MS-SQL Server been allowed to use the DATE_INDEX instead, the DBMS would have used an efficient search algorithm to find the first index entry that satisfied the search criteria (DATE_CALLED BETWEEN '01/01/200' AND '01/31/2000') and could have stopped reading rows in the index as soon as it encountered the first date outside the acceptable date range.*

---

161 Using the CREATE INDEX Statement to Create an Index

As you learned in Tip 159, "Understanding Indexes," indexes let a DBMS answer queries without reading every row in each of the tables listed in a SELECT statement's FROM clause. For large tables, performing a full-table scan looking for rows whose column data values satisfy a query's search criteria can be very expensive in terms of processing time. Imagine reading a system manual from cover to cover each time you need help on a particular topic. Without an index, you (like the DBMS) would spend the majority of your time reading pages of information that have nothing to do with answering the question at hand. Just as using a system manual's alphabetized index lets you quickly zero in on the page(s) with the information you want, traversing the sorted values in database indexes lets the DBMS find and retrieve table rows that satisfy a query's search condition(s) with the least amount of system overhead.

When executing a CREATE INDEX statement, the DBMS reads through the table being indexed one row at a time. As it reads each row, the system creates a key (from the concatenation of the column[s] being indexed), and inserts the key into the index along with a pointer to the physical disk location of the row that produced it.

The basic syntax of the CREATE INDEX statement is:

```
CREATE [UNIQUE] INDEX <index name> ON <table name>
  (<column name> [ASC | DESC][,...<last column name>
   [ASC | DESC]])
```

Therefore, to create an index on the INV_DATE and INV_NO columns of an INVOICES table, you would use a CREATE INDEX statement similar to:

```
CREATE INDEX date_index ON INVOICES (inv_date, inv_no)
```

Note: *Some DBMS products let you specify whether the values in the index are sorted in ascending (ASC) or descending (DESC) order. Before using ASC or DESC in your CREATE INDEX statements, check your system manual to make sure that your DBMS product supports the selection of an index sort option. MS-SQL Server, for example, lets you add the ASC and DESC after the column name(s) in the CREATE INDEX statement, but it ignores both attributes and always sorts its indexes in ascending order.*

Adding the keyword UNIQUE to the CREATE INDEX statement tells the DBMS to create a *unique* index, which allows only nonduplicate entries. In the current example, if you change the CREATE INDEX statement to

```
CREATE UNIQUE INDEX date_index
ON INVOICES (inv_date, inv_no)
```

the DBMS will create the index DATE_INDEX only if *every* row in the INVOICES table has a unique pair of data values for INV_DATE and INV_NO—that is, only one row in a table could have an INV_DATE of 02/01/2000 and an INV_NO of 5. Moreover, after the DBMS creates a *unique* index, attempts to insert a row into the indexed table will fail with an error message similar to

```
Server: Msg 2601, Level 14, State 3, Line 1
Cannot insert duplicate key row in object 'invoices' with
  unique index 'date_index'.
The statement has been terminated.
```

if adding the row's key value requires the DBMS to INSERT a duplicate entry into a unique index.

Note: *When creating a unique index, make sure none of the columns being indexed allow NULL values. MS-SQL Server, for example, treats a NULL as a distinct value. As such, if you create a single-column unique index, MS-SQL Server will only allow users to add one row only to the table with a NULL in the indexed column. (Adding a second row would require a duplicate key entry [two NULLs] in the unique index.)*

---

162 Understanding MS-SQL Server CREATE INDEX Statement Options

Tip 161, "Using the CREATE INDEX Statement to Create an Index," refers to the statement syntax

```
CREATE [UNIQUE] INDEX <index name> ON <table name>
  (<column name> [ASC | DESC][,...<last column name>
   [ASC | DESC]])
```

as the *basic* syntax for a CREATE INDEX statement because every DBMS product provides its own set of additional options you can use to tell the system such things as the drive or location on the hard drive where it is to create the index, how much free space to leave for additional data on each index page, and how the index is to be maintained.

For example, the syntax of the CREATE INDEX statement on MS-SQL Server is:

```
CREATE [UNIQUE] [CLUSTERED | NONCLUSTERED]
INDEX <index name> ON <table name>
  (<column name>[,...<last column name>])
[WITH [DROP_EXISTING]
      [[,] FILLFACTOR = <% fill factor>]
      [[,] PAD_INDEX]
      [[,] IGNORE_DUP_KEY]
```

```
      [[,] STATISTICS_NONRECOMPUTE] ]
[ON <filegroup name>]
```

The remaining sections of this tip will explain the meaning of each of the options available when creating an index on an MS-SQL Server. If you are using an SQL server other than MS-SQL Server, familiarize yourself with the purpose of each option and then check your system manual to see which index options are available on your DBMS.

UNIQUE

In Tip 161, you learned that applying the UNIQUE option to an index prevents the insertion rows into the indexed table if the column values in the rows produce a key value that already exists in the table's unique index. In essence, creating an index based on two or more columns and specifying the UNIQUE option is a way to apply a non-PRIMARY KEY multi-column UNIQUE constraint to the table being indexed. Since every combination of the indexed column values must be unique in the INDEX, then the same combination of column values must also be unique in the table itself. You INSERT a row into a table without adding the key value for the row to each of the indexes on the table.

CLUSTERED/NONCLUSTERED

An MS-SQL Server *nonclustered* index works the way in which you would expect an index to work. The DBMS sorts the key values in the nonclustered index (in ascending order) while leaving the indexed table's rows unsorted. Conversely, when you create a *clustered* index, MS-SQL Server sorts not only the key values in the index, but also sorts the rows in the table to match the sort of the index. You will learn more about clustered indexes in Tip 165, "Understanding MS-SQL Server Clustered Indexes." By default, MS-SQL Server creates a nonclustered index if you specify neither the clustered nor the nonclustered option when creating an index.

DROP_EXISTING

Because a table can have only one clustered index, you must first DROP the existing clustered index if you want to re-create it or a new one based on a different set or order of indexed columns. Whenever you DROP a clustered index, MS-SQL Server automatically rebuilds each of the remaining nonclustered indexes on the table. The server also re-creates all nonclustered indexes on a table whenever it creates a clustered index for the table. Thus, dropping a clustered index and re-creating it using a DROP INDEX and then a CREATE CLUSTERED INDEX statement results in MS-SQL Server building each nonclustered index twice.

The DROP_EXISTING option lets you re-create a clustered index using a single statement. When the DBMS executes a CREATE CLUSTERED INDEX statement with the DROP_EXISTING option, it deletes the existing clustered index, re-creates it, and then rebuilds all of the nonclustered indexes.

FILLFACTOR

MS-SQL Sever stores table and index data in 2KB pages. Index pages are linked together in a tree arrangement such as that shown in Figure 162.1.

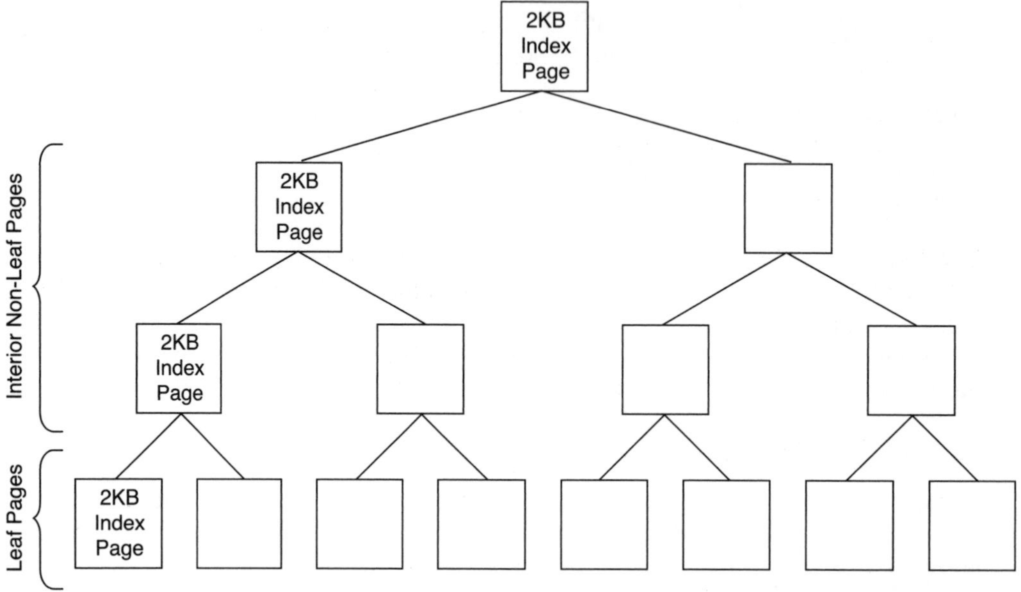

Figure 162.1 MS-SQL Server index page tree

The way in which MS-SQL Server uses a binary tree to find specific key values in an index is beyond the scope of this book. The important things to know are that index key values are stored in 2KB pages, and whenever an index page gets full, the DBMS must split the page in two to add additional nodes with space for more key values to its index page tree.

Page splits are very expensive in terms of system overhead and therefore should be avoided when possible. The FILLFACTOR tells the DBMS how much space to leave for additional key values on each of the leaf pages it creates while executing a CREATE INDEX statement.

Note: *Regardless of the value supplied for the FILLFACTOR, the DBMS always creates interior (nonleaf) pages with room for one additional entry in a clustered index and room for two additional entries in a nonclustered index.*

A FILLFACTOR of 100, for example, tells the DBMS to use 100 percent of the 2KB available in each leaf page for existing index values. While completely filling the leaf pages creates the smallest index possible, doing so also produces a large number of index page splits when rows are added to the table or indexed column values are changed. With a FILLFACTOR of 100 none of the leaf pages have room to hold additional key values and any row insertion or indexed column value change will cause a page split. Therefore, you should specify a FILLFACTOR of 100 percent (FILLFACTOR=100) only for "read-only" tables not subject to future insertions and updates.

Use a small FILLFACTOR such as 10 percent for indexes on tables that do not yet contain their complete datasets. When you specify a FILLFACTOR of 10, for example, the DBMS will fill leaf pages to only 10 percent of capacity. Therefore, if the sum of the column sizes that make up the index is such that 200 keys can fit on a 2KB page, the DBMS will build each leaf page with 20 key values—leaving the remaining 180 (90 percent) available to hold additional keys without requiring index page splits when adding new rows or updating indexed column values to the indexed table.

If you do not explicitly specify a FILLFACTOR (1 - 100), MS-SQL Server will set the FILLFACTOR to 100 and fill each leaf to 100% capacity.

PAD_INDEX

The PAD_INDEX option is useful only if you specify a nonzero FILLFACTOR. While the FILLFACTOR tells the DBMS what percentage of the 2KB leaf page space to use when building a new index, the PAD_INDEX option tells the DBMS to apply the FILLFACTOR usage percentage to the nonleaf, interior pages in the index tree. As such, if you specify FILLFACTOR=10 and also add the PAD_INDEX option to the CREATE INDEX statement, the DBMS will generate leaf and nonleaf index pages that contain only approximately 205 bytes of data (10 percent of 2KB).

Regardless of the FILLFACTOR specified, the DBMS always puts at least one key value on each interior page and leaves room for at least one additional key entry (two entries for nonclustered indexes).

IGNORE_DUP_KEY

Specifying the IGNORE_DUP_KEY option does not let you create a unique index on a column (or set of columns) if the table already contains duplicate values in the column (or combination of columns). IGNORE_DUP_KEY affects only the way in which MS-SQL Server handles future UPDATE and INSERT statements that attempt to add rows with duplicate key values into a unique index.

Whether you include the IGNORE_DUP_KEY option or not, the system will not allow you to add a row to a table if its column values would result in a duplicate key being added to a unique index. However, without the IGNORE_DUP_KEY option, the DBMS will abort a duplicate key insertion attempt with an error and will roll back all transaction processing up to that point. Conversely, if you include the IGNORE_DUP_KEY option in the CREATE UNIQUE INDEX statement, MS-SQL Server still aborts a duplicate key insertion attempt, but it issues a warning message (instead of raising an error) and continues transaction processing with the next statement.

STATISTICS_NONRECOMPUTE

During index creation, MS-SQL Server makes notes in a special statistics page regarding the distribution of data values in the indexed columns of the table. The DBMS later uses its statistics pages when deciding which of the indexes to use in minimizing the time it takes to answer a query. Adding the STATISTICS_NONRECOMPUTE option to the CREATE

INDEX statement tells MS-SQL Server not to automatically recompute the index statistics periodically when the statistics become outdated due to row insertions, deletions, and indexed column value changes.

Setting the STATISTICS_NONRECOMPUTE option eliminates the overhead involved in performing periodic table scans to update index statistics pages. However, out-of-date statistics may prevent the query optimizer from selecting the optimal index when executing a query. Using the "wrong" index reduces the speed at which the DBMS can return query results and may in fact wipe out any overhead reduction by forcing table scans for query results instead of allowing an efficient indexed search.

ON <filegroup name>

A FileGroup is the logical name MS-SQL Server uses to refer to a physical disk spaces the database uses to hold its objects. When you execute the CREATE DATABASE statement, MS-SQL Server creates the FileGroup PRIMARY and stores all tables, views, indexes, stored procedures, and so on in the disk space allocated to the PRIMARY FileGroup. You can create and add additional FileGroups (named physical disk areas) to the database at any time.

The advantage of having multiple FileGroups in a database is that you can spread them across multiple physical disk drives, which allows the system hardware to perform simultaneous I/O operations on database objects. Suppose, for example, that you let the DBMS create the PRIMARY FileGroup on the C drive and then created the FileGroup FILEGROUP2_D on the D drive and FILEGROUP3_E on the E drive. The CREATE INDEX statements

```
CREATE INDEX product_index ON invoices
  (product_code, inv_date, inv_no) ON FILEGROUP2_D
CREATE INDEX date_index ON invoices
  (inv_date, inv_no) ON FILEGROUP3_E
```

would place each of the two indexes on a different disk drive. As such, when you insert a new row into the INVOICES table, the DBMS could tell the system hardware to update the table on the C drive and then have it update both the indexes simultaneously. If both indexes were located in the same FileGroup, the operating system would have to update one index and then proceed to update the other.

163 Using the MS-SQL Server Enterprise Manager to Create an Index

In addition to the CREATE INDEX statement (which you learned about in Tip 161, "Using the CREATE INDEX Statement to Create an Index," and Tip 162, "Understanding MS-SQL Server CREATE INDEX Statement Options"), MS-SQL Server also provides a graphical method for index creation through the Enterprise Manager.

To use the MS-SQL Server Enterprise Manager to CREATE an index, perform the following steps:

1. Start the Enterprise Manager by clicking your mouse pointer on the Start button. When Windows displays the Start menu, move your mouse pointer to Programs, select Microsoft SQL Server 7.0, and then click your mouse pointer on Enterprise Manager.
2. To display the list of SQL servers, click your mouse pointer on the plus (+) to the left of SQL Server Group.
3. Click your mouse pointer on the plus (+) to the left of the icon for the SQL server on which you want to create the index. For example, if you want to create an index for a table on a server named NVBIZNET2, click your mouse pointer on the plus (+) to the left of the icon for NVBIZNET2. The Enterprise Manager will display folders containing databases and services available on the MS-SQL Server you selected.
4. Click your mouse pointer on the plus (+) to the left of the Databases folder. The Enterprise Manager will display a list of the databases managed by the server you selected in Step 3.
5. Select the database that contains the table on which you wish to create the index. For the current project, click your mouse pointer on the plus (+) to the left of the SQLTips icon in the expanded Databases list. Enterprise Manager will display the icons for the database objects types in the SQLTips database.
6. Click your mouse pointer on the icon for Tables. Enterprise Manager will display the list of tables in the SQLTips database in its right pane.
7. Click your mouse pointer on the table for which you wish to create an index. (Enterprise Manager sorts the list of tables alphabetically. If you do not see the one you want, use the scroll bar on the right side of the Enterprise Manager window to display additional database tables.) For the current example, click your mouse pointer on the icon for the INVOICES table.
8. Select the Action menu All Tasks option, and click your mouse pointer on Manage Indexes. Enterprise Manager will display the Manage Index dialog box.
9. To define a new index, click your mouse pointer on the New button. Enterprise Manager will display a Create New Index dialog box similar to that shown in Figure 163.1.
10. Enter a name for the index in the Index Name field. Although not any valid object name is permissible as an index name, use the name of the first column in the index as either part of or the beginning of the name to make it easier to figure out if MS-SQL Server will use the index to speed up a query. (In Tip 160, "Understanding How MS-SQL Server Selects an Index for a Query," you learned that MS-SQL Server will use an index for a query only if a column used in the SELECT statement's search criteria is the first column in the index.) Also, if you preface indexes on FOREIGN KEY columns with fk_ and the index on the PRIMARY KEY with pk_, you can easily keep track of which keys have indexes and which do not. For the current project, enter **product_code_index** into the Index Name field.

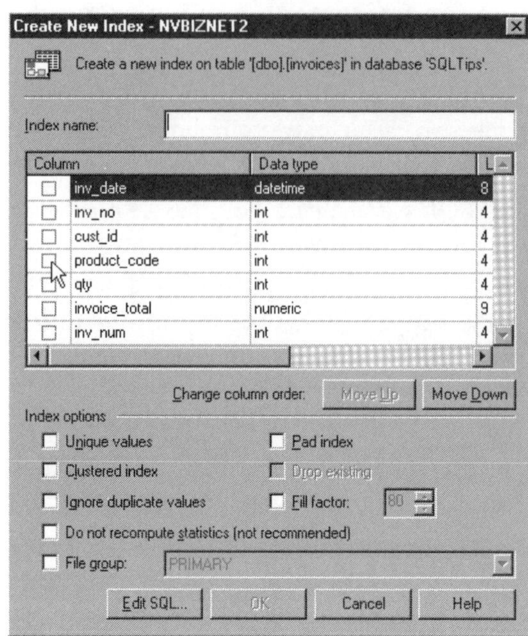

Figure 163.1 The MS-SQL Server Enterprise Manager Create New Index dialog box

11. To select the column(s) to index, click your mouse pointer on the check box to the left of each of the column names you want to include. For the current example, click your mouse pointer on the check box to the left of PRODUCT_CODE and on the check box to the left of INV_DATE until both contain check marks.

12. Use the Move Up and Move Down buttons to specify the order of the columns in the index. For the current project, move the INV_DATE column *down* so that it is the second column in the index. To do so, click you mouse pointer on the column name INV_DATE, and then click your mouse pointer on the Move Down button repeatedly until INV_DATE appears after PRODUCT_CODE in the column list area of the dialog box.

13. Select the additional options for the index by clicking your mouse pointer on the check boxes to the left of each index option you want to select in the Index options section of the dialog box. (You learned what each of the index options means in Tip 162.) For the current project, leave all of the index options check boxes blank.

14. To create the index and return to the Manage Index dialog box, click on the OK button.

15. Repeat Steps 9–14 for each new index you want to create. If you need to change the definition of an index, click your mouse pointer on the index you want to modify and then on the Edit button. Or, to remove (DROP) an index, click your mouse pointer on the Delete button.

16. When you are finished defining indexes for the table, click your mouse button on the Close button.

As you learned in Tip 160, the order of the columns in an index is very important. Therefore, be sure to arrange the columns in the index properly in Step 12. An index with the correct columns in an incorrect order is useless. For example, leaving the INV_DATE as the first column of the PRODUCT_CODE_INDEX will result in the DBMS having to perform a full-table scan to satisfy the query

```
SELECT SUM(qty) FROM invoices WHERE product_code = 4
```

whereas rearranging the index columns as PRODUCT_CODE followed by INV_DATE will let MS-SQL Server use the index PRODUCT_CODE_INDEX to reduce the number of table row retrievals to just those in which the value of the product code is 4.

164 Using the DROP INDEX Statement to Delete an Index

Although table indexes can greatly reduce the amount of time it takes the DBMS to return the results of a query by reducing the required number of read operations, indexes do take up disk space and can have a negative on performance if the indexed tables are often updated. Remember, updating the value in an indexed column is twice as expensive in terms of processing overhead as updating the same column if it is not part of an index.

When changing an indexed column value, the DBMS not only must change the value of the column in the table, but also must update each index that includes the column. Since the DBMS stores indexes as additional tables, updating a column that is also a part of three indexes results in four table updates vs. one for a table with no indexes. Similarly, each DELETE statement not only must remove a row from the main table, but also must delete a row from each index on the table. Moreover, INSERT statements add even more overhead since each one requires that the DBMS add data to the indexed table and to every one of the indexes on that table. (Unless you are updating a column that appears in every index on a table, the DBMS does not have to change every index when storing an updated indexed column value.)

To minimize the overhead and disk space usage of database indexes, use the DROP INDEX statement to remove indexes you no longer need. Like the CREATE INDEX statement, the syntax of the DROP INDEX statement will vary among database products. Some require only the name of the index, such as:

```
DROP INDEX <index name>
```

Others require both table name and index name, such as:

```
DROP INDEX <table name>.<index name>
```

MS-SQL Server, for example, requires both table name and index name. As such, you would execute the DROP INDEX statement

```
DROP INDEX invoices.product_code_index
```

to remove the index PRODUCT_CODE_INDEX from the INVOICES table.

165 Understanding MS-SQL Server Clustered Indexes

A *clustered* index is a special index on an MS-SQL Server table that forces the DBMS to store table data in the exact order of the index. The advantages of using a clustered index are:

- The table will use the minimum disk space required because the DBMS will automatically reuse space previously allocated to deleted rows when new rows are inserted.
- Queries with value range criteria based on the columns in a clustered index will execute more quickly because all of the values within a range are physically located next to each other on the disk.
- Queries in which data is to be displayed in ascending order based on the columns in the clustered index do not need an ORDERED BY clause since the table data is already in the desired output order.

When creating a clustered index, bear in mind that a table can have one and only one such index. After all, the table's rows must be arranged in the order of the clustered index, and a single table can have only one physical arrangement of records on disk.

To create a clustered index, add the keyword CLUSTERED to the CREATE INDEX statement you learned about in Tip 161, "Using the CREATE INDEX Statement to Create an Index," and Tip 162, "Understanding MS-SQL Server CREATE INDEX Statement Options." For example, to CREATE a clustered index based on the PRODUCT_CODE and INV_DATE columns of an INVOICES table, execute the CREATE INDEX statement:

```
CREATE CLUSTERED INDEX cl_product_code_index
ON invoices (product_code, inv_date)
```

Note: *The CL_ at the beginning of the index name CL_PRODUCT_CODE_INDEX, is optional. However, if you start every clustered index with CL_, you can easily distinguish the clustered index (if any) for a particular table from the nonclustered indexes on the table.*

If you define a clustered index for a table that contains data, MS-SQL Server will lock the table while creating the index. As such, make sure to create clustered indexes for tables with a lot of rows only during those times when it is most convenient for the table's data to be unavailable to DBMS users and application programs. While building the index, the DBMS not only inserts the clustered index column values into the index, but it also rebuilds the table itself, arranging the rows in the same order in which their key entries appear in the index.

After creating a clustered index on a table, the DBMS will automatically rearrange rows as necessary to keep the rows of the table in the same order as the keys in the index as you INSERT new rows or UPDATE values in columns that are part of the cluster. As such, it is not a good idea to CREATE a clustered index on a table that is subject to a high number of row insertions or updates to clustered index columns. The overhead involved in physically moving rows in the table as well as updating the index will quickly outweigh any performance gains resulting from the omission of ORDER BY clauses and the faster execution of value range searches.

Note: *When executing a CREATE INDEX statement that has neither the CLUSTERED nor the NONCLUSTERED keyword, the DBMS will create a NONCLUSTERED index.*

166 Using the MS-SQL Server Index Tuning Wizard to Optimize Database Indexes

In Tips 159–165, you learned that most DBMS products support indexes because indexes can greatly improve overall system performance by speeding up query execution and reducing the overhead resulting from unnecessary full table scans. However, you also learned that selecting the *wrong* columns to index can actually have a negative impact on system response time. If the majority of a system's queries are based on nonindexed columns while those columns that are indexed seldom appear in SELECT statement WHERE clauses, the DBMS not only fails to capitalize on the advantages of indexing, but it also incurs the additional overhead of maintaining indexes that serve no useful purpose.

MS-SQL Server provides the Server Profiler and Index Tuning Wizard to help you create the optimal set of indexes for your operating environment. After the Server Profiler captures a log of all queries submitted against a database to a trace file, the Index Tuning Wizard can analyze the statements within the log to determine the indexes that will result in the greatest improvement in query and overall DBMS performance. By using a trace file that lists a representative sample of system queries, the Index Tuning Wizard's suggestions are based on the server's actual workload vs. some theoretical database model.

To use the MS-SQL Server Index Tuning Wizard, perform the following steps:

1. Start the Enterprise Manager by clicking your mouse pointer on the Start button. When Windows displays the Start menu, move your mouse pointer to Programs, select Microsoft SQL Server 7.0, and then click your mouse pointer on Enterprise Manager.

2. To display the list of SQL servers, click your mouse pointer on the plus (+) to the left of SQL Server Group.
3. Select the SQL server that manages the database with the tables on which you want to run the Index Tuning Wizard by click your mouse pointer on the server's icon. For example, if you want to run the wizard on a server named NVBIZNET2, click your mouse pointer on the icon for NVBIZNET2.
4. Select the Tools menu Wizards option. Enterprise Manager will display the Select Wizard dialog box.
5. To display the list of database management wizards, click your mouse pointer on the plus (+) to the left of Management.
6. Click your mouse pointer on the Index Tuning Wizard entry in the expanded list of database management wizards, and then click on the OK button. Enterprise Manager will start the Index Tuning Wizard, which will display its Welcome to the Index Tuning Wizard message box.
7. Click your mouse pointer on the Next button to proceed to the Index Tuning Wizard–Select Server and Database dialog box shown in Figure 166.1.

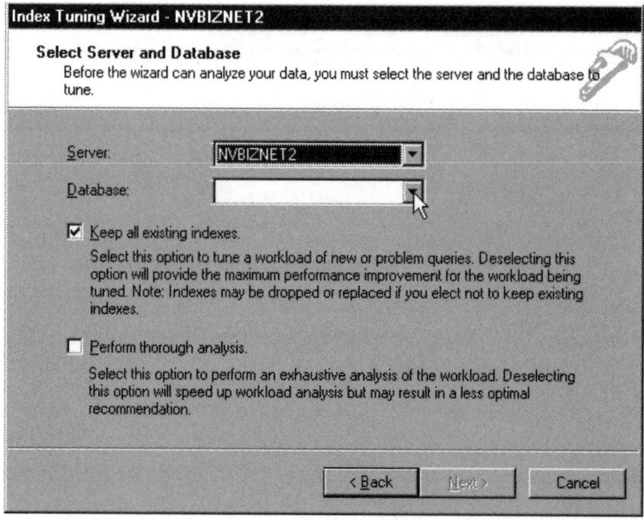

Figure 166.1 The MS-SQL Server Index Tuning Wizard Select Server and Database dialog box

8. To select the database with the tables you want to index, click your mouse pointer on the drop-down list button to the right of the Database field. After the Index Tuning Wizard displays the list of database names on the server you selected in Step 3, click your mouse pointer on the name of the database you want to use. For the current project, click your mouse pointer on SQLTips.

9. To have the Index Tuning Wizard remove existing indexes it finds to be unnecessary based on the system query workload, click your mouse button to the left of "Keep all existing indexes" to make the check mark disappear.

Note: *The Index Tuning Wizard may drop an index name in a SELECT statement's INDEX=<index name> clause. As a result, a previously functional query may stop working. Since the MS-SQL Server Query Optimizer almost always selects the most efficient index for a query, you should discourage the use of forcing the SQL Server to use a particular index by including an INDEX=<index name> clause in a SELECT statement.*

---

10. To have the Index Tuning Wizard suggest the indexes which will most improve system and query performance, click your mouse pointer on the check box to the left of "Perform thorough analysis" to make a check mark appear.

11. Click your mouse pointer on the Next button. The Wizard will display the Index Tuning Wizard–Identify Workload dialog box shown in Figure 166.2.

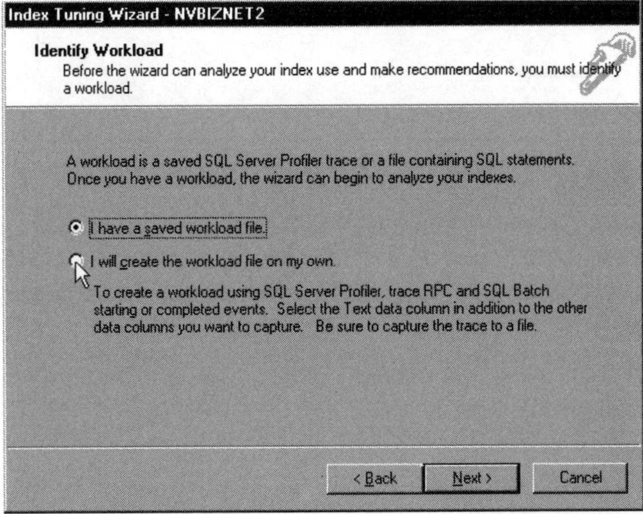

Figure 166.2 The MS-SQL Server Index Tuning Wizard Identify Workload dialog box

12. If you previously saved an MS-SQL Server Profiler trace to disk or have a file containing SQL statements on which you want the Index Tuning Wizard to base its analysis, click your mouse pointer on the I Have a Saved Workload File radio button; then click the Next button and continue at Step 21.

13. To create a new trace file of your system's workload, click your mouse pointer on the radio button to the left of I Will Create the Workload File on My Own, and then click on the Finish button. The Index Tuning Wizard will end, and the Enterprise Manager will start the MS-SQL Server Profiler.

14. In the MS-SQL Server Profiler application window, select the File menu Run Traces option (or click your mouse pointer on the Start Traces [the green triangle] button on the Standard toolbar). MS-SQL Server Profiler will display a list of traces in a Start Selected Traces dialog box, similar to that shown in Figure 166.3.

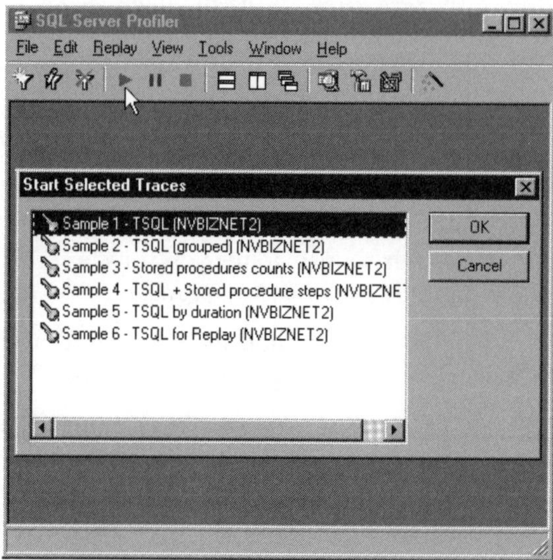

Figure 166.3 The MS-SQL Server Profiler Start Selected Traces dialog box

15. The Sample 1 trace (which comes standard with MS-SQL Server) will capture the events and data columns the Index Tuning Wizard needs for its analysis. As such, click your mouse pointer on Sample 1–TSQL (<database name>) to select the Sample 1 trace, and then click on the OK button.

    The MS-SQL Server Profiler will start logging SQL queries processed by the SQL server against the database you selected in Step 8. You need to let the profiler run for a while in order to build up a log with a representative sample of the database query workload on your DBMS. Depending on your system's usage patterns, capturing a representative sample workload may take several hours or several days. Capturing a good sample of the queries most often using during normal operations is important because the Index Tuning Wizard bases its recommendations on optimizing the SELECT statements in the log file. If the log is not representative of the queries that commonly occur in your DBMS, then the indexes the Index Tuning Wizard suggests may not be the ones that produce the best performance under your system's normal workload.

Note: *If you are running the Server Profiler over a long period of time, be sure to write the trace log's contents to your hard drive periodically by selecting the File menu Save option every couple of hours (at least). When presented with the Save As dialog box, enter a name for the trace file in the File Name field and then click your mouse pointer on the OK button. The one thing you want to avoid is creating a large, unsaved log* *file only to have your system reset or lock up for some reason before you save the trace log to a disk file.*

16. After the trace log contains a representative sample of your system's workload, click your mouse pointer on the Stop This Trace (the red square) button on the Standard toolbar.
17. To save the trace log to disk, select the File menu Save option. The MS-SQL Server Profiler will display the Save As dialog box.
18. Enter a filename for the log file in the File Name field, and then click your mouse pointer on the OK button. For the current project, enter **INDEX_TRACE-SQLTips** in the File Name field.
19. Select the File menu Exit option to exit the MS-SQL Server Profiler application.
20. Return to the MS-SQL Server Enterprise Manager window and repeat Steps 4–12. (If you closed the Enterprise Manager while running the Profiler, repeat Steps 1–12 instead.) Be sure to click the radio button to the left of I Have a Saved Workload File when you perform Step 12.
21. After you click your mouse pointer on the Next button in Step 12, the Index Tuning Wizard will display the Specify Workload dialog box shown in Figure 166.4. Click your mouse pointer on the My Workload File radio button. The wizard will display the Open dialog box.

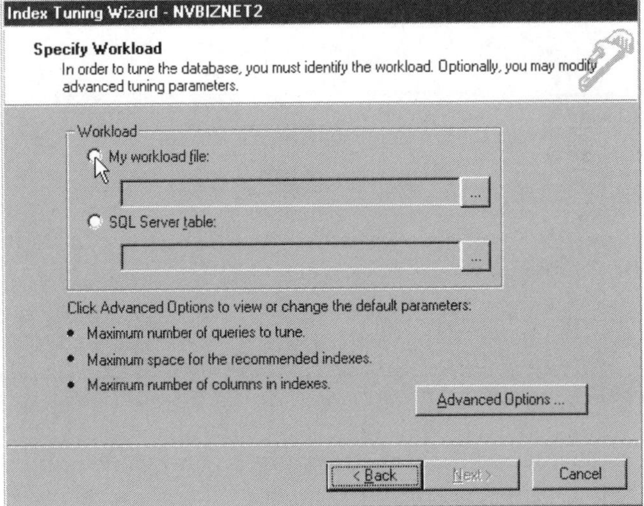

Figure 166.4 The MS-SQL Server Index Tuning Wizard Specify Workload dialog box

22. In the File Name field, enter the name of the trace (log) file you want the Index Tuning Wizard to analyze, and then click your mouse pointer on the OK button. For the current project, enter **INDEX_TRACE-SQLTips** in the File Name field.

23. If you want to specify the maximum number of queries to tune, the maximum space for the recommended indexes, or the maximum columns per index, click your mouse pointer on the Advanced Options button. The Index Tuning Wizard will display its Index Tuning Parameters dialog box, which has the fields you need to enter each of the three maximum value options. For the current project, accept the system defaults.

Note: *Of the three maximum options, you will want to increase the maximum space for the recommended indexes if your database tables have a large number or rows—which means each index will need to hold a large number of key values. The defaults for the maximum number of queries to tune and maximum columns per index will typically yield the optimal tuning results. If you are unsure of the settings you want, you can always try different settings by repeating Steps 23–25 and using the settings that yield the highest value for the percentage of estimated improvement shown near the bottom of the Index Recommendations dialog box (shown in Figure 166.6).*

24. Click your mouse pointer on the Next button to display the Index Tuning Wizard–Select Tables to Tune dialog box shown in Figure 166.5.

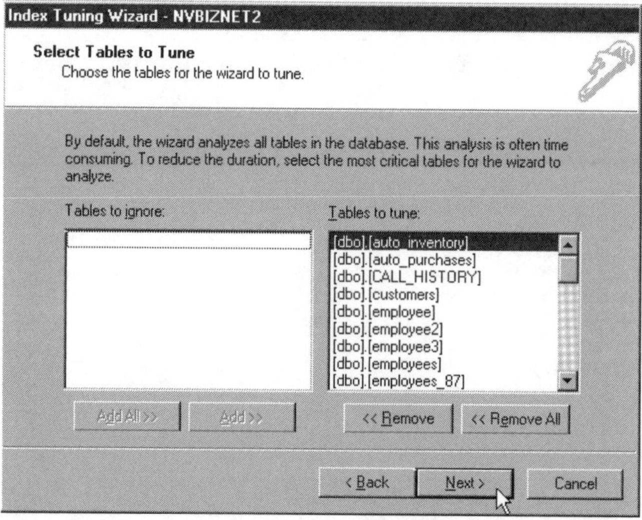

Figure 166.5 The MS-SQL Server Index Tuning Wizard Select Tables to Tune dialog box

The default is to have the wizard tune the indexes for all tables. If you want to work with only some of the tables, select the tables whose indexes you *do not* want to tune in Tables to Tune section of the dialog box, and then click your mouse pointer on the Remove button to exclude the tables you selected from the index tuning process. For the current project, accept the default and let the Index Tuning Wizard tune the indexes in all of the SQLTips database tables.

25. After you have the list of tables whose indexes you want to tune in the Tables to Tune section of the dialog box, click your mouse pointer on the Next button. The Index Tuning Wizard will read through the log file you entered in Step 22 and use the MS-SQL Server

Query Optimizer to asses the hypothetical performance of every query in the log based on using each of the possible combinations of indexes on columns used in the SELECT statements. After the wizard completes its analysis, it will display the list of indexes that produce the best overall performance for the entire set of queries in the log file, similar to that shown in Figure 166.6.

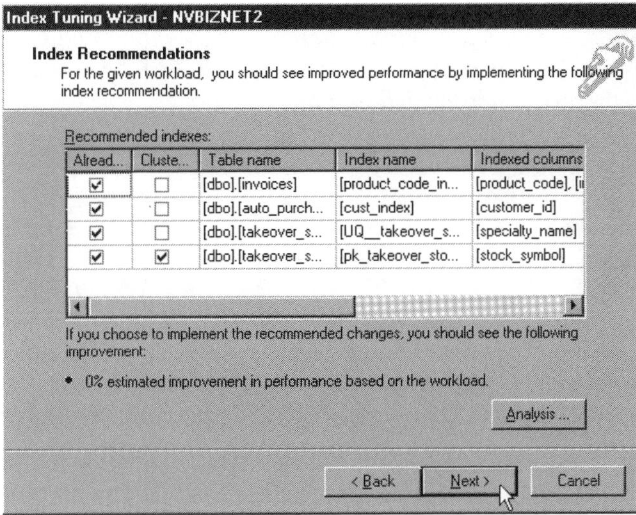

Figure 166.6 The MS-SQL Server Index Tuning Wizard Index Recommendations dialog box

26. Click your mouse pointer on the Next button. The wizard will display an Index Tuning Wizard–Schedule Index Update Job dialog box similar to that shown in Figure 166.7.

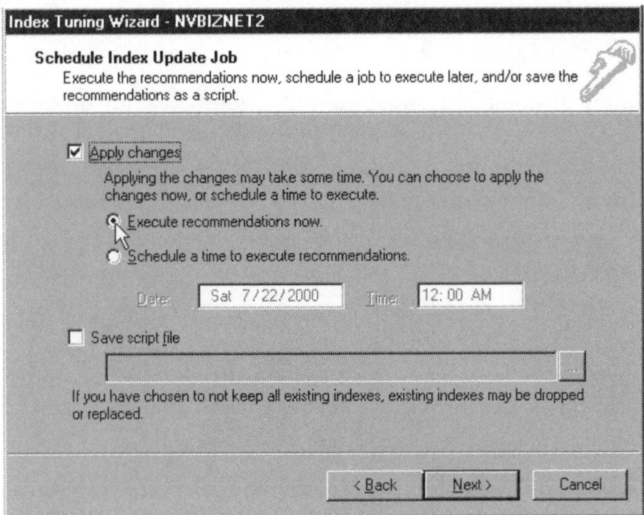

Figure 166.7 The MS-SQL Server Index Tuning Wizard Schedule Index Update Job dialog box

27. To have the Index Tuning Wizard apply the recommended changes to index structure of the database, click your mouse pointer on the "Apply changes" check box to make a check mark appear. Next, decide if you want the indexing process to happen now or if you want to schedule it for another time. For the current project, click your mouse pointer on the radio button to the left of Execute Recommendations Now.

Note: *Creating indexes on many and/or large database tables will have a significant impact on system performance, since the DBMS will spend the majority of its processing cycles on the task and users will find their statements executing much more slowly than normal. Moreover, when the DBMS creates a clustered index on an existing table, the table is unavailable for use while its index is being created. Therefore, carefully assess your system usage patterns and perform the index creation process at a time of low or (preferably) no system usage to have the least impact on database users and application programs.*

28. After making your selection of the timing of the index creation, click your mouse pointer on the Next button. The Index Tuning Wizard will display a Completing the Index Tuning Wizard message box. Click on the Finish button either to create the indexes now or to schedule their creation at a later time, depending on your selection in Step 27.

When the Index Tuning Wizard displays its successful completion message box after Step 28, click on the OK button to return to the Enterprise Manager application window.

167 Understanding the Importance of Database Keys

A key is a column or combination of columns whose values uniquely identify a row in a table. Because a table is an unordered collection of rows, there is no first row, fifth row, or last row. As such, when you want to access a particular row in a table, you must do so based on data values in the row's columns.

There are two types of database keys—a PRIMARY KEY and a FOREIGN KEY. A table can have only one PRIMARY KEY, and the combination of the values in the column or columns that make up a table's PRIMARY KEY must be unique in every row of the table. You will learn more about the restrictions on and the uses for a PRIMARY KEY in Tip 171, "Understanding Primary Keys." For now, the important thing to know is that since the PRIMARY KEY must be unique for every row in a table, you can use a PRIMARY KEY value in an SQL statement to target a specific row in a table.

Unlike a PRIMARY KEY, which has a unique value in each row of a table, the column or combination of columns that make up a FOREIGN KEY need not be unique within the table in which the FOREIGN KEY is defined. Allowing duplicate *key* values for a FOREIGN KEY seems to contradict the first statement in this tip—a key uniquely identifies a specific row in a table. However, the FOREIGN KEY definition does uniquely identify a row in a table—just not a row in the table in which the FOREIGN KEY is defined. Instead, a FOREIGN key "points to" the PRIMARY KEY (or other unique key) in another table. As such, the FOREIGN KEY uniquely identifies a row in *that* table.

Note: *Do not confuse a database key (PRIMARY KEY or FOREIGN KEY) with the key value in an index entry. A database key is actually one or more columns in a table that you have identified as being a key by applying either a PRIMARY KEY or a FOREIGN KEY constraint. The key value in an index, on the other hand, is a value computed from the column or columns being indexed and is stored in a separate database object—an index. While the DBMS will delete an index if you execute a DROP INDEX statement, the data values in the column (or columns) that make up a PRIMARY or FOREIGN KEY will remain unchanged if you DROP either of the two types of database key constraints. Thus, a key in an index is a separate data value in its own database object, while a database key (primary and foreign) is a label you put on the values in certain columns in a database table.*

---

168 Understanding Single-Column and Composite Keys

As you learned in Tip 167, "Understanding the Importance of Database Keys," a key is a column with a unique value in each row of the table. Therefore, if you know the key value and use it as the equality criterion in a SELECT statement in the form

```
SELECT * FROM <table name> WHERE <key column> = <key value>
```

the DBMS will display the contents of a single row in the table. If the DBMS returns more than one row, the column you chose is not the single-column key for the table named in the SELECT statement's FROM clause.

Suppose, for example, that you have an EMPLOYEE table created with:

```
CREATE TABLE employee
  (emp_num SMALLINT,
   name    VARCHAR(30),
   address VARCHAR(50),
   payrate MONEY)
```

Although any of the columns in the EMPLOYEE table is theoretically eligible for use as a key, using the NAME column, for example, would require that the company have only one employee named, John Smith. If the company hired a second John Smith, the DBMS could no longer use the single-column key based on the NAME column, because the DBMS would not be able to identify the first John Smith row from the second one in the EMPLOYEE table:

```
emp_num name         address               payrate
------- -----------  --------------------  -------
1       Konrad King  765 E. Eldorado Lane  10.25
2       Karen King   765 E. Eldorado Lane  25.75
3       John Smith   2234 State Street     12.35
4       Harry Smith  2258 Hilly Way        10.25
5       John Smith   589 Hillcrest Drive   32.58
```

Similarly, neither ADDRESS nor PAYRATE is a good key candidate because both have duplicate values in different rows of the table. If you used the ADDRESS column as the key, the DBMS cannot distinguish the first row in the table from the second; and if you used PAYRATE as the key, the DBMS cannot distinguish the first row from the fourth. Thus, EMP_NUM is the only suitable single column key for the EMPLOYEE table in the example because EMP_NUM has a unique value in each row of the table.

Whether you identify the EMP_NUM column as a PRIMARY_KEY or not, the SELECT statement

```
SELECT * FROM EMPLOYEE WHERE emp_num = 3
```

will display the contents of a single row in the EMPLOYEE table. Applying the PRIMARY KEY constraint to a column whose value is unique in every row of a table lets database users know which column they can use to find a particular row in a table, and also prevents anyone from adding a row with either a NULL or a duplicate value in the column.

Sometimes no single column in a table in a table has a unique value in each row. Suppose, for example, that your company has offices in more than one location—each with its own unique set of employee numbers. The EMP_NUM column in the EMPLOYEE table

```
emp_num Office name         address               payrate
------- ------ -----------  --------------------  -------
1       LV     Konrad King  765 E. Eldorado Lane  10.25
2       TX     Karen King   765 E. Eldorado Lane  25.75
3       LV     John Smith   2234 State Street     12.35
4       LV     Harry Smith  2258 Hilly Way        10.25
5       TX     John Smith   589 Hillcrest Drive   32.58
2       LV     Sally Field  215 State Street      25.75
4       TX     Wally Wells  7810 Greenwood Ave    17.58
3       TX     Harry Smith  258 Hilly Way         22.58
```

would not be a good key because there is more than one EMP_NUM 2, 3, and 4 in the table. Since no single column has a unique value in every row of the table, you must use a multiple-column or *composite* key.

In the current example, the composite key for the EMPLOYEE table would be EMP_NUM and OFFICE. If you know the values of the columns in a composite key, you can use them as the equality criteria in a SELECT statement in the form

```
SELECT * FROM <table name>
WHERE <first key column>  = <first column key value>  AND
      <second key column> = <second column key value>
```

to display one particular row in a table. (If the composite key has more than two columns, you would additional AND keywords to add equality criteria for the third and subsequent columns in the composite key.)

As was the case with a single-column key, the SELECT statement

```
SELECT * FROM EMPLOYEE WHERE emp_num = 3 AND office = 'TX'
```

will display the contents of a single row in the EMPLOYEE table—whether you've applied the PRIMARY KEY constraint to the columns or not. However, if you apply the PRIMARY KEY constraint, database users will know which combination of columns to use in order to find a specific row in a table. Moreover, the PRIMARY KEY constraint will prevent someone from adding a row with a NULL in either the EMP_NUM or the OFFICE column and adding a new employee row (record) with the same EMP_NUM and OFFICE as that of an existing employee.

169 Understanding MS-SQL Server Rules

A rule is an MS-SQL Server object that controls the data values that can be stored in a table column. Rules are similar to CHECK constraints (which you will learn about in Tip 193, "Using the CHECK Constraint to Validate a Column's Value"), in that the DBMS uses a rule (like a CHECK constraint) to determine if a data value is valid for a particular column. If the data value satisfies the rule's conditional expression, the DBMS will put the value in the target column. On the other hand, if the data value violates the rule (makes its conditional expression evaluate to FALSE), the DBMS aborts execution of the INSERT or UPDATE statement and returns an error message.

Applying a rule involves two steps. First, you must create the rule itself by using either the Transact-SQL CREATE RULE statement or the MS-SQL Server Enterprise Manager's Action menu New Rule option. Second, you must bind the rule to a table column or a user-defined data type either by using the MS-SQL Server Rules Properties, Bind Rules to Columns dialog box or by executing the stored procedure sp_bindrule. Once a rule is bound to a column or data type, the DBMS will apply the rule to every data value a user or application program tries to put into the column governed by the rule.

For example, to create a rule that the DBMS can use to validate grades to be placed in a COURSE_GRADE column, you could use the CREATE RULE statement

```
CREATE RULE validate_grades
AS @grade in ('A+', 'A', 'A-', 'B+', 'B', 'B-', 'C+', 'C',
              'C-', 'D+', 'D', 'D-', 'F', 'I', 'WD')
```

and then bind the rule to the COURSE GRADE column of the STUDENT_GRADES table created with

```
CREATE TABLE student_grades
  (student_id   SMALLINT,
   course_id    VARCHAR(20),
   course_grade CHAR(2))
```

by executing the sp_bindrule stored procedure:

```
EXEC sp_bindrule
       'validate_grades', 'student_grades.course_grade'
```

After a rule is bound to the table column, the DBMS will check future UPDATE and INSERT statements to make sure the data value given for the COURSE_GRADE is one of the values listed in the VALIDATE_GRADES rule. As such the DBMS will successfully execute the INSERT statement

```
INSERT INTO student_grades VALUES (1001, 'HIST-101', 'A+')
```

but will abort the INSERT statement

```
INSERT INTO student_grades VALUES (1001, 'HIST-101', 'NA')
```

with an error message similar to

```
Server: MSG 513, Level 16, State 1, Line 1
A column insert or update conflicts with a rule imposed by
  a previous CREATE RULE statement.
The statement was terminated.

The conflict occurred in database 'SQLTips', table
  'student_grades', column 'course_grade'.
The statement has been terminated.
```

because it violates the VALIDATE_GRADES rule on the column.

You will learn more about creating rules in Tip 195, "Using the Transact-SQL CREATE RULE Statement to Create an MS-SQL Server Rule." For now, the important thing to know is that MS-SQL Server lets you use rules to make sure a data value being placed in a table column either falls within a range of values, is one of a discrete set of values, or matches a specified character string pattern.

170 Using the CREATE DOMAIN Statement to Create Domains

A domain is a set of legal data values that a column can hold. When you define a column as being one of the standard SQL or SQL server-specific data types (INTEGER, NUMERIC, CHARACTER, DATETIME, and so on), you specify the set of legal values (the domain) for the column. MS-SQL Server, for example, has three INTEGER data types: INTEGER (or INT), SMALLINT, and TINYINT. When you define a column of type INTEGER, you set its domain as the set of whole numbers in the range –2,147,483,468 through 2,147,483,647. Columns of type SMALLINT have a domain of the whole numbers in the range –32,768 through 32,767. Meanwhile, TINYINT columns have a domain of whole numbers in the range 0 through 255.

Sometimes, however, you need to restrict a column's domain to a subset of all legal values for a particular data type—that is the purpose of CREATE DOMAIN. The SQL-92 CREATE DOMAIN statement lets you create a new data type by applying a CHECK constraint on a standard DBMS data type to limit its domain.

The syntax of the CREATE DOMAIN statement is

```
CREATE DOMAIN <domain name> AS <data type>
[DEFAULT <default value>]
[<first constraint definition>
  ...<last constraint definition>]
```

where:

```
<constraint definition> ::=
  [CONSTRAINT <constraint name>]
    CHECK (VALUE <conditional expression>)
```

Suppose, for example, that a company's employee numbers are four-digit numbers starting with the digit 1. The CREATE statement

```
CREATE TABLE employees
  (employee_num INTEGER,
   name         CHAR(30),
   address      CHAR(50))
```

would allow the insertion of invalid employee numbers—those outside the range 1000 through 1999. To limit the domain of the EMPLOYEE_NUM column to the range 1000 to 1999, you could create a domain using

```
CREATE DOMAIN valid_empnums
CHECK (VALUE BETWEEN 1000 AND 1999)
```

and then use the domain in place of the INTEGER type in the table definition:

```
CREATE TABLE employees
  (employee_num valid_empnums,
   name         CHAR(30),
   address      CHAR(50))
```

Note: *Not all DBMS products support the CREATE DOMAIN statement. If yours does not, check your system manual on CHECK constraints and user-defined data types. Many times you can create a named domain by creating a new data type and applying a CHECK constraint to it. MS-SQL Server, for example, does not have a CREATE DOMAIN statement. However, you can still limit the domain of the EMPLOYEE_NUM column in the current example on MS-SQL Server by executing the Transact-SQL statements:*

```
EXEC sp_addtype valid_empnums, 'SMALLINT'
CREATE RULE validate_empnum
AS @employee_number BETWEEN 1000 AND 1999
EXEC sp_bindrule 'validate_empnum', 'valid_empnums'
```

The net result of executing the three statements is the same as executing the CREATE DOMAIN statement—you end up with a VALID_EMPNUMS data type whose domain is whole numbers in the range 1000 through 1999.

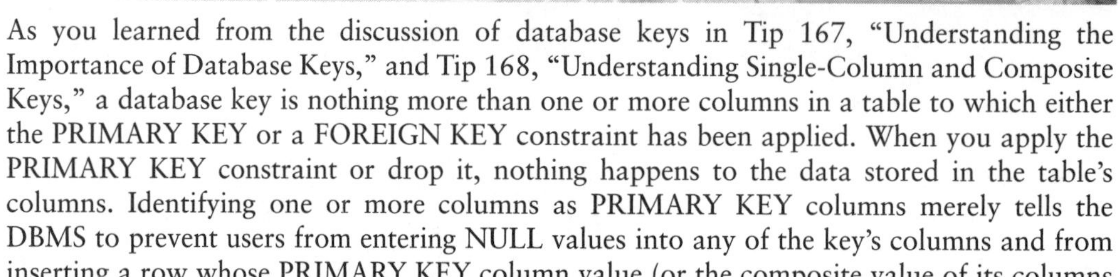

171 Understanding Primary Keys

As you learned from the discussion of database keys in Tip 167, "Understanding the Importance of Database Keys," and Tip 168, "Understanding Single-Column and Composite Keys," a database key is nothing more than one or more columns in a table to which either the PRIMARY KEY or a FOREIGN KEY constraint has been applied. When you apply the PRIMARY KEY constraint or drop it, nothing happens to the data stored in the table's columns. Identifying one or more columns as PRIMARY KEY columns merely tells the DBMS to prevent users from entering NULL values into any of the key's columns and from inserting a row whose PRIMARY KEY column value (or the composite value of its columns if it is a multi-column key) already exists in the table.

If a table has a single-column PRIMARY KEY, you can choose whether you want to use the PRIMARY KEY constraint or simply apply the UNIQUE and NOT NULL constraints to the *key* column. Suppose, for example, that you create an EMPLOYEES table in which the value in the employee number (EMP_NUM) column is unique and not NULL for all rows in the table. The table definition

```
CREATE TABLE employees
  (emp_num  SMALLINT UNIQUE NOT NULL,
   office   CHAR(2),
   name     VARCHAR(50),
   address  VARCHAR(50),
   payrate  MONEY)
```

is functionally equivalent to:

```
CREATE TABLE employees
  (emp_num      SMALLINT,
   office       CHAR(2),
   name         VARCHAR(50),
   address      VARCHAR(50),
   payrate      MONEY,
   PRIMARY KEY (emp_num))
```

The one difference between the two ways of defining a key in the current example is that on most DBMS products (including MS-SQL Server), the DBMS automatically creates an index on the columns explicitly identified as being part of the table's PRIMARY KEY. Thus, the DBMS will automatically create an EMP_NUM index on an EMPLOYEES table created by the second CREATE TABLE statement while leaving index creation to the database object owner (DBOO) when the same single column key is created by constraining a column's values as UNIQUE and NOT NULL.

When you have a composite (or multi-column) key in which the table's PRIMARY KEY constraint is applied to more than one column, you can no longer create an equivalent index using UNIQUE and NOT NULL constraints. Continuing with the current example,

```
CREATE TABLE employees
  (emp_num SMALLINT UNIQUE NOT NULL,
   office  CHAR(2) UNIQUE NOT NULL,
   name    VARCHAR(50),
   address VARCHAR(50),
   payrate MONEY)
```

is *not* equivalent to:

```
CREATE TABLE employees
  (emp_num      SMALLINT,
   office       CHAR(2),
   name         VARCHAR(30),
   address      VARCHAR(50),
   payrate      MONEY,
   PRIMARY KEY (emp_num, office))
```

A table created with UNIQUE and NOT NULL constraints on both key columns requires that both EMP_NUM and OFFICE must be unique (and not NULL) in all rows in of the EMPLOYEES table. As a result, an EMPLOYEES table with the values

```
emp_num Office  name         address               payrate
------- ------  -----------  --------------------  -------
1       LV      Konrad King  765 E. Eldorado Lane  10.25
2       TX      Karen King   765 E. Eldorado Lane  25.75
3       LV      John Smith   2234 State Street     12.35
4       LV      Harry Smith  2258 Hilly Way        10.25
5       TX      John Smith   589 Hillcrest Drive   32.58
2       LV      Sally Field  215 State Street      25.75
4       TX      Wally Wells  7810 Greenwood Ave    17.58
3       TX      Harry Smith  258 Hilly Way         22.58
```

would not be allowed because the EMP_NUM column has duplicate values, as does the OFFICE column. However, the combination of the EMP_NUM and OFFICE columns when taken together as a *composite* (or multi-column) PRIMARY KEY is unique in every row of the table. Thus, while neither EMP_NUM nor OFFICE alone is unique in each row of the table, the two taken together (as a composite key value) are and can therefore be the PRIMARY KEY for the table in the current example.

The important thing to understand from this discussion of primary keys is that a PRIMARY KEY is not a separate database object. Instead, a PRIMARY KEY is merely a constraint (or limit) on the values that can be placed in the column (or columns) defined as part of the key. In the case of a single-column PRIMARY KEY, the value in the key column must be unique and not NULL in every row of the table. Similarly, if the PRIMARY KEY consists of multiple columns, none of the columns that make up the key can have a NULL value, and the combination of the values in the key's columns must be unique for each row of the table.

172 Using the PRIMARY KEY Column Constraint to Uniquely Identify Rows in a Table

After reading about database keys in Tip 167, "Understanding the Importance of Database Keys"; Tip 168, "Understanding Single-Column and Composite Keys"; and Tip 171, "Understanding Primary Keys," you know that each row in a table is unique if the table has a PRIMARY KEY or has at least one column constrained as UNIQUE and not NULL. As such, it is possible to update columns in, display, or delete one particular row in a table by specifying the row's PRIMARY KEY value as an equality in an SQL statement's WHERE clause.

Suppose, for example, that you had a single column PRIMARY KEY in an EMPLOYEES table created by:

```
CREATE TABLE employees
  (emp_num       SMALLINT,
   office        CHAR(2),
   name          VARCHAR(50),
   address       VARCHAR(50),
   payrate       MONEY,
   PRIMARY KEY (emp_num))
```

The PRIMARY KEY constraint on the EMP_NUM column means that each and every row in the table has a different, non-NULL value for EMP_NUM. As such, executing the SELECT statement

```
SELECT * FROM employees WHERE emp_num = 1001
```

will display either 0 or 1 row. If there is no employee 1001, then the DBMS will display zero rows; if there is an employee 1001, the DBMS will display a single row because 1001 can appear in the EMP_NUM column of only one row in the table.

Similarly, if you have a two-column PRIMARY KEY such as the one defined in

```
CREATE TABLE employees
  (emp_num       SMALLINT,
   office        CHAR(2),
   name          VARCHAR(30),
   address       VARCHAR(50),
   payrate       MONEY,
   PRIMARY KEY (emp_num, office))
```

an SQL statement can target one particular row in the table by performing an equality test on each of the columns in the PRIMARY KEY and combining the two equalities using the Boolean operator AND. For example, the UPDATE statement

```
UPDATE employees SET payrate = payrate * 1.2
WHERE emp_num = 2 AND office = 'LV'
```

will give either zero or one employee a 20 percent pay rate increase. The PRIMARY KEY constraint on the two columns EMP_NUM and OFFICE guarantees that there will be at most one EMP_NUM/OFFICE pair. As you saw in Tip 171, there may be more than one row with a 2 in the EMP_NUM column and more than one row with an LV in the OFFICE column. However, the PRIMARY KEY constraint on the composite (multi-column)—in this case, two-column—key guarantees that the EMPLOYEES table will have no more than one row where the value in the EMP_NUM column is 2 *and* the value in the OFFICE column is LV.

As a third example, suppose you have a four-column PRIMARY KEY such as that defined in:

```
CREATE TABLE call_history
  (phone_number CHAR(7),
   called_by    CHAR(3),
```

```
    date_called  DATETIME,
    call_time    SMALLINT,
    hangup_time  SMALLINT,
    disposition  CHAR(4),
    PRIMARY KEY (phone_number, called_by, date_called,
                 hangup_time))
```

An SQL statement that performs four equality tests—one on each column of the PRIMARY KEY—joined by AND Boolean operators will uniquely target a single row in the CALL_HISTORY table. For example, the DELETE statement

```
DELETE FROM call_history
WHERE phone_number = '3610141'    AND called_by = 'KLK' AND
      date_called  = '07/24/2000' AND hangup_time = 2100
```

will remove either zero or one row from the CALL_HISTORY table. As was the case with the single- and two-column PRIMARY KEY constraints, the PRIMARY KEY constraint in the CALL_HISTORY table guarantees that, in this case, there is at most one row with a particular combination of PHONE_NUMBER *and* CALLED_BY *and* DATE_CALLED *and* HANGUP_TIME.

The specific values, columns, and tables used in this tip are not important. What you want to remember is that you can use a PRIMARY KEY to display or work with one particular row in a table by joining a WHERE clause equality test on each of the PRIMARY KEY's columns with Boolean AND operators.

173 Understanding Foreign Keys

Although its name may imply as much, a FOREIGN KEY is not a key with values written in a language other than your own. Instead, a FOREIGN KEY is a constraint in which the value of one column or the composite value of several columns in one table is equal to the PRIMARY KEY in another table. The word *foreign* in *FOREIGN KEY constraint* alludes to the fact that the FOREIGN KEY is not actually a key (or unique value) for the table in which it is defined. Rather, a FOREIGN KEY is a column in one table whose value matches the PRIMARY KEY in another table—hence, its moniker as a key that is *foreign* to the table it is stored.

As you learned from the discussion of the hierarchical, network, and relational database models (in Tip 3, "Understanding the Hierarchical Database Model"; Tip 4, "Understanding the Network Database Model"; and Tip 5, "Understanding the Relational Database Model), the relational model, unlike the other two, has no pointers to use in linking database records. Given the central role of pointers in establishing parent/child relationships in the hierarchical model, you might think that the relational model cannot represent them, since it has no pointers to link records (rows) in one table with those in another. However, parent/child relationships do exist in the relational model. Instead of using pointers, the DBMS represents relationships between tables through common data values stored in each of the two tables' columns.

Suppose, for example, that you have the CUSTOMERS, ORDERS, and ORDERS_ITEMS_DETAIL tables shown in Figure 173.1.

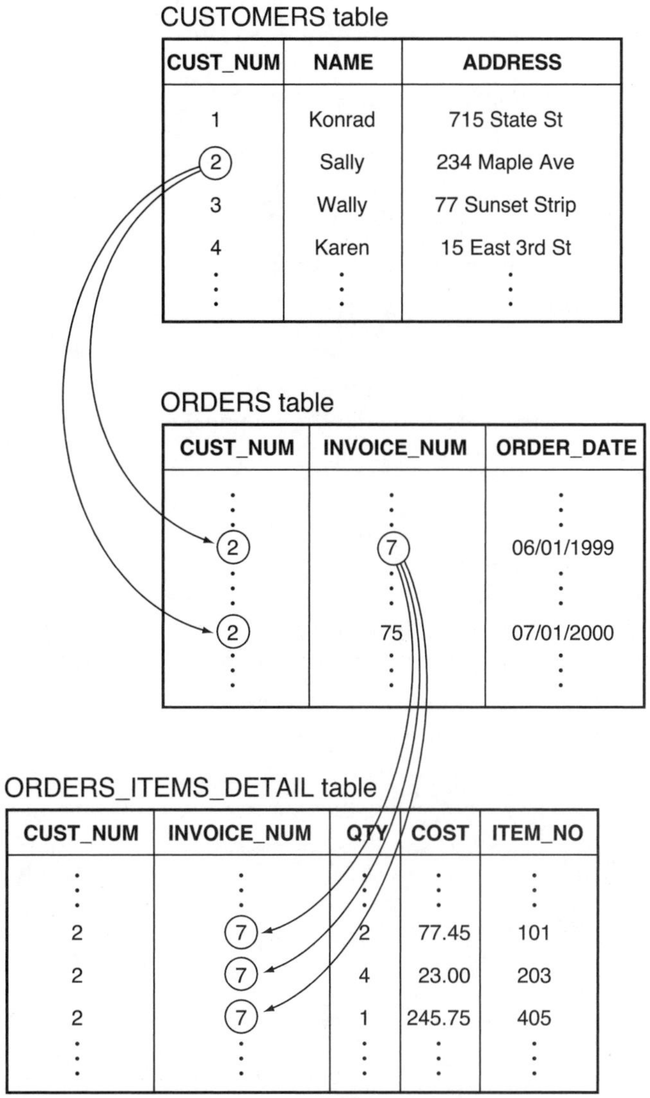

CUSTOMERS table

CUST_NUM	NAME	ADDRESS
1	Konrad	715 State St
2	Sally	234 Maple Ave
3	Wally	77 Sunset Strip
4	Karen	15 East 3rd St
⋮	⋮	⋮

ORDERS table

CUST_NUM	INVOICE_NUM	ORDER_DATE
⋮	⋮	⋮
2	7	06/01/1999
⋮	⋮	⋮
2	75	07/01/2000
⋮	⋮	⋮

ORDERS_ITEMS_DETAIL table

CUST_NUM	INVOICE_NUM	QTY	COST	ITEM_NO
⋮	⋮	⋮	⋮	⋮
2	7	2	77.45	101
2	7	4	23.00	203
2	7	1	245.75	405
⋮	⋮	⋮	⋮	⋮

Figure 173.1 CUSTOMERS parent with ORDERS child, and ORDERS parent with ORDERS_ITEMS_DETAIL child relationships

Given the CUSTOMERS table definition

```
CREATE TABLE customers
  (cust_no INTEGER,
   name    VARCHAR(30),
   address VARCHAR(50),
PRIMARY KEY (cust_no))
```

you can use the following FOREIGN KEY constraint in the ORDERS table to establish the parent/child relationship between an ORDERS row (the child record) and its parent row in the CUSTOMERS table:

```
CREATE TABLE orders
  (customer_number INTEGER,
   invoice_num     INTEGER,
   order_date      DATETIME,
   delivery_date   DATETIME,
PRIMARY KEY (customer_number, invoice_num)
CONSTRAINT fk_customers_orders
  FOREIGN KEY (customer_number)
  REFERENCES CUSTOMERS (cust_no))
```

A FOREIGN KEY constraint tells the DBMS that a user ID can INSERT a row in the table only if the composite value in the column (or columns) making up a FOREIGN KEY in the child table exists as a PRIMARY KEY value in the parent table.

In the current example, the DBMS will allow the insertion of a row into the ORDERS table only if the value the row's CUSTOMER_NUMBER column already exists in the CUST_NO column of one of the rows in the CUSTOMERS table. In effect, the FOREIGN KEY prevents the insertion of orphan (or parentless) child records (rows) into a database table. In the current example, every order inserted into the ORDERS table, must have a parent—a row that represents the customer that placed the order—in the CUSTOMERS table.

Similarly, a FOREIGN KEY in the ORDERS_ITEM_DETAIL table links the individual items on an order (the child rows) with the order "header" row (parent) in the ORDERS table:

```
CREATE TABLE orders_item_detail
  (cust_no     INTEGER,
   invoice_num INTEGER,
   qty         TINYINT,
   cost        MONEY,
   item_no     INTEGER
CONSTRAINT fk_orders_orders_item_detail
  FOREIGN KEY (cust_no, invoice_num)
  REFERENCES orders (customer_number, invoice_num))
```

Thus, the DBMS will allow an order item detail row to be added to the ORDERS_ITEM_DETAIL table only if the composite value of the FOREIGN KEY columns (CUST_NO + INVOICE_NUM) exists as a PRIMARY KEY value in one of the rows in the ORDERS (parent) table.

Note: *The names of the FOREIGN KEY column or columns need not match those in the PRIMARY KEY. The system uses the composite value in the column(s), not the column name(s), to match the child record (row) with its parent. Because the composite value of the FOREIGN KEY must match a PRIMARY KEY value in the table named in the FOREIGN KEY's REFERENCES clause, the column (or columns) making up the FOREIGN KEY (in the child table) must match column(s) that make up the PRIMARY KEY (in the parent table) both in number and in data type.*

174 Understanding Referential Integrity Checks and Foreign Keys

As you learned in Tip 173, "Understanding Foreign Keys," a FOREIGN KEY lets you set up a parent/child relationship between two tables. Instead of using a pointers to link a (parent) row in one table with one or more (child) rows in another table, the relational DBMS stores the PRIMARY KEY value of the *parent* row in the FOREIGN KEY column(s) of the *child* row. The relational database rule that dictates that every FOREIGN KEY value in the child table must exist as a PRIMARY KEY value in its parent table is known as the referential integrity constraint.

For example, if you have two tables, EMPLOYEES and TIMECARDS, created with

```
CREATE TABLE employees
  (employee_number  SMALLINT,
   name             VARCHAR(30),
   payrate          MONEY,
   PRIMARY KEY (employee_number))

CREATE TABLE timecard
  (emp_no     SMALLINT,
   card_date DATETIME,
   time_in    SMALLINT,
   time_out   SMALLINT,
   CONSTRAINT fk_employees_timecard FOREIGN KEY (emp_no)
     REFERENCES employees (employee_number)
```

the FOREIGN KEY constraint on the EMP_NO column in the TIMECARD table tells the DBMS to make sure that the value in the EMP_NO column in each row of the TIMECARD table has a matching value in the EMPLOYEE_NUMBER column (the PRIMARY KEY column) of one row in the EMPLOYEES table.

Maintaining the referential integrity of the FOREIGN KEY column(s) in one table with the PRIMARY KEY column(s) in another involves the performance of referential integrity checks on each of four types of table updates that could break parent/child relationships:

- **Inserting a row into the child table.** The DBMS must make sure that every new row inserted into the child table has a FOREIGN KEY that matches the PRIMARY KEY values in the parent table. If the FOREIGN KEY value in a new row does not match the value of one of the PRIMARY KEY values in the parent table, the DBMS aborts the INSERT statement. Inserting a nonmatching FOREIGN KEY value into the child table would corrupt referential integrity by creating an "orphan"—a child record (row) without a parent—and is therefore not allowed.
- **Deleting a row from the parent table.** The DBMS will abort any DELETE statement that attempts to remove a row from the parent table if the row's PRIMARY KEY value appears as the FOREIGN KEY value in a child table row. Removing the one matching PRIMARY KEY from the parent table would corrupt referential integrity by creating an "orphan"—a FOREIGN KEY value in a child record (row) without a matching value in the PRIMARY KEY of the parent table—and is therefore not allowed. (In Tip 183, "Understanding How Applying the CASCADE Rule to Updates and Deletes Helps Maintain Referential Integrity," you will learn how some DBMS products apply the CASCADE rule to the DELETE statement and remove both the parent row and all child rows to allow the DELETE statement to remove a parent table row that has children in other tables.)
- **Updating a FOREIGN KEY value in the child table.** Whether it is in a new row or an existing one, the FOREIGN KEY value in the row must match one of the PRIMARY KEY values in the parent table referenced by the FOREIGN KEY constraint. As such, the DBMS will abort any UPDATE statement that attempts to change the value of a FOREIGN KEY in a child row such that it no longer matches one of the PRIMARY KEY values in the parent table.
- **Updating a PRIMARY KEY value in the parent table.** Changing the PRIMARY KEY value in the parent table has the same effect as removing a row with the original PRIMARY KEY value and inserting another row with the new PRIMARY KEY. As such, the DBMS will abort any UPDATE statement that attempts to change a row's PRIMARY KEY if the current PRIMARY KEY value appears as the FOREIGN KEY value in a child table row. Changing the one matching PRIMARY KEY in the parent table to a new value would corrupt referential integrity by creating an "orphan"—a FOREIGN KEY value in a child record (row) without a matching value in the PRIMARY KEY column(s) of the parent table—and is therefore not allowed. (In Tip 183, you will learn how some DBMS products apply the CASCADE rule to the UPDATE statement and change both the PRIMARY KEY value in the parent row and the FOREIGN KEY value in each of the child rows to allow an UPDATE statement to change the PRIMARY KEY value in a parent table row that has children in other tables.)

The important thing about referential integrity checks is that the DBMS checks its system tables for FOREIGN KEY references to the PRIMARY KEY any time an UPDATE statement attempts to change a value in one or more columns in a table's PRIMARY KEY, or any time a DELETE statement attempts to REMOVE a row from a table that has a PRIMARY KEY constraint. Conversely, the DBMS checks the PRIMARY KEY index to make sure the value in the FOREIGN KEY column(s) exists in the PRIMARY KEY index before it executes an UPDATE to one or more column values in a FOREIGN KEY or executes an INSERT to add a new row to a table with a FOREIGN KEY constraint.

If executing an UPDATE, INSERT, or DELETE statement would create an "orphan"—a FOREIGN KEY value (in a child table) without a corresponding PRIMARY KEY value (in the parent table)—the DBMS will abort the statement in order to maintain referential data integrity.

175 Understanding How Referential Data Integrity Checks Can Jeopardize Security

In Tip 149, "Using the GRANT SELECT (and REVOKE SELECT) Statement to Control Access to a Database Object," you learned how to let some user IDs see information in a table by granting them SELECT access on the table. You also learned how to hide a table's contents from other user IDs either by never granting them SELECT access on the table or by revoking the SELECT access you previously granted. Unfortunately, a user ID without SELECT privileges on a table can exploit the referential data integrity checks you learned about in Tip 174, "Understanding Referential Integrity Checks and Foreign Keys," to deduce the values in a table's PRIMARY KEY column(s).

Suppose, for example, that you are a casino executive in charge of player relations, and you keep a list of your top players in a table created by:

```
CREATE TABLE high_rollers
  (player_ID       INTEGER,   name          VARCHAR(30),
   credit_limit    MONEY,
   average_action  MONEY,
   YTD_winnings    MONEY,
   YTD_losses      MONEY,
   PRIMARY KEY (player_ID))
```

Given the hotel tracks all players in a table created by:

```
CREATE TABLE big_gamblers
  (player_number INTEGER,
   name          VARCHAR(30),
   address       VARCHAR(50),
   phone_number  VARCHAR(20),
PRIMARY KEY (player_number))
```

An employee with only REFERENCES access to the HIGH_ROLLERS table and SELECT access to the PLAYER_CARDS table could make a list of high rollers by creating a table that references the PRIMARY KEY in the HIGH_ROLLERS table, such as

```
CREATE TABLE big_gamblers
  (player_number INTEGER,
   name          VARCHAR(30),
   address       VARCHAR(50),
   phone_number  VARCHAR(20),
CONSTRAINT fk_high_roller_id FOREIGN KEY (player_number)
  REFERENCES high_rollers (player_ID))
```

and then attempt an INSERT statement such as

```
INSERT INTO big_gamblers
VALUES (<customer_ID from players_cards table>, NULL, NULL,
        NULL)
```

for each of the CUSTOMER_IDs listed by the SELECT statement:

```
SELECT customer_ID FROM players_cards
```

Since the FOREIGN KEY constraint will allow the DBMS to INSERT a row into the BIG_GAMBLERS table only if the value in the row's PLAYER_NUMBER column exists in the PLAYER_ID column of one of the rows in the HIGH_ROLLERS table, the BIG_PLAYERS table will contain a list of all CUSTOMER_IDs from the PLAYERS_CARDS table that are also PLAYER_IDs in the HIGH_ROLLERS table.

Filling out the remaining information in the BIG_GAMBLERS table can be accomplished with the INSERT statement

```
INSERT INTO big_gamblers
  SELECT player_cards.customer_ID, player_cards.name,
         player_cards.address, player_cards.phone_number
  FROM big_gamblers, player_cards
  WHERE player_cards.customer_ID = big_gamblers.player_ID
```

and then by removing rows with only customer IDs using the DELETE statement:

```
DELETE FROM big_gamblers WHERE name IS NULL
```

The important thing to understanding from this example, is that a user can use the REFERENCES privilege and the referential integrity check on the INSERT statement to deduce the values in the table's PRIMARY KEY column(s) (and the values of any column with a UNIQUE constraint, on MS-SQL Server). Therefore, be sure to secure your table data from inadvertent disclosure by granting REFERENCES privilege only to those user IDs that are allowed to display the values in PRIMARY KEY and UNIQUE constrained columns.

176 Understanding How Referential Integrity Checks Can Limit the Ability to Delete Rows and Drop Tables

As you learned in Tip 174, "Understanding Referential Integrity Checks and Foreign Keys," referential integrity checks are actions taken by the SQL server to maintain the (parent/child) relationships between tables. A FOREIGN KEY, consisting of either the value in a single column or the composite value in multiple columns, matches the PRIMARY KEY VALUE in another table. In other words, you establish a link between two tables by adding one or more columns to one table and storing the PRIMARY KEY value of the "linked" row of another table in them. After you apply the FOREIGN KEY constraint to the columns you add, the DBMS makes sure that value in the columns always has a matching value in the PRIMARY KEY columns of the other table.

Note: *On MS-SQL Server, you can establish a FOREIGN KEY reference to table columns that have a UNIQUE constraint as well those with a PRIMARY KEY constraint.*

In order to maintain referential integrity, the DBMS checks each INSERT, UPDATE, DELETE, and DROP statement involving a table that has a PRIMARY KEY or one more FOREIGN KEY constraints. The DBMS aborts any statement that would result in the storage of a FOREIGN KEY value that references a nonexistent PRIMARY KEY value. For example, given the tables created by

```
CREATE TABLE item_master
  (product_code INTEGER,
   description  VARCHAR(30),
   bin_level    SMALLINT,
PRIMARY KEY (product_code))

CREATE TABLE inventory
  (item_number   INTEGER,
   supplier_code INTEGER,
   cost          MONEY,
   qty_on_hand   SMALLINT,
CONSTRAINT fk_item_master_inv FOREIGN KEY (item_number)
  REFERENCES item_master (product_code))
```

the DBMS will abort the execution of a DELETE statement that tries to remove an ITEM_MASTER row whose PRODUCT_CODE (PRIMARY KEY) value matches a value in the ITEM_NUMBER (FOREIGN_KEY) value in the INVENTORY table. As such, if the INVENTORY table has a row with 1001 in its ITEM_NUMBER column, the DBMS will abort the DELETE statement

```
DELETE item_master WHERE PRODUCT_CODE = 1001
```

and display an error message similar to:

```
Server: Msg 547, Level 16, State 1, Line 1
DELETE statement conflicted with COLUMN REFERENCE
  constraint 'fk_item_master_inv'. The conflict occurred in
  database 'SQLTips', tab 'inventory', column
  'item_number'.
The statement has been terminated.
```

To successfully execute the DELETE statement in the current example, you must first either DELETE all rows in the INVENTORY table with an ITEM_NUMBER of 1001 or use the ALTER TABLE statement to DROP the INVENTORY table's FK_ITEM_MASTER_INV FOREIGN KEY constraint.

Similarly, the DBMS will abort any DROP TABLE statement that attempts to remove a table referenced by a FOREIGN KEY constraint—even if the table making the FOREIGN KEY reference is empty. For example, given the tables in the current example, the DBMS will abort DROP TABLE statement

```
DROP TABLE item_master
```

with an error message similar to:

```
Server: Msg 3726, Level 16, State 1, Line 1
Could not drop object 'item_master' because it is
  referenced by a FOREIGN KEY constraint.
```

If you want to DROP the ITEM_MASTER table, you must first remove all FOREIGN KEY constraints that reference the table. Unfortunately, the error message generated when you try to DROP a table referenced by a FOREIGN KEY constraint may not be specific as to which tables contain the FOREIGN KEY references. (You need to know the table [or tables] with a FOREIGN KEY reference to the table you want to DROP so you can execute an ALTER TABLE statement to drop the FOREIGN KEY in those tables.) Check your data dictionary—it should document all table dependencies. Or, use one of your system tools to have the DBMS list the table references for you. On MS-SQL Server, for example, you can execute the stored procedure sp_help with

```
EXEC SP_HELP item_master
```

and then look in the "Table Is Referenced By" section of the output to see the names of all database objects and FOREIGN KEY constraints that reference the ITEM_MASTER table.

177 Understanding Referential Integrity Check INSERT Deadlock and How to Resolve It

Referential integrity checks ensure that each FOREIGN KEY value in one table has a matching PRIMARY KEY value in another table. Unfortunately, maintaining referential integrity can lead to INSERT statement deadlocks when the FOREIGN KEY in one table refers to the PRIMARY KEY of another table that has a FOREIGN KEY that references the PRIMARY KEY in the first table—such as that shown in Figure 177.1.

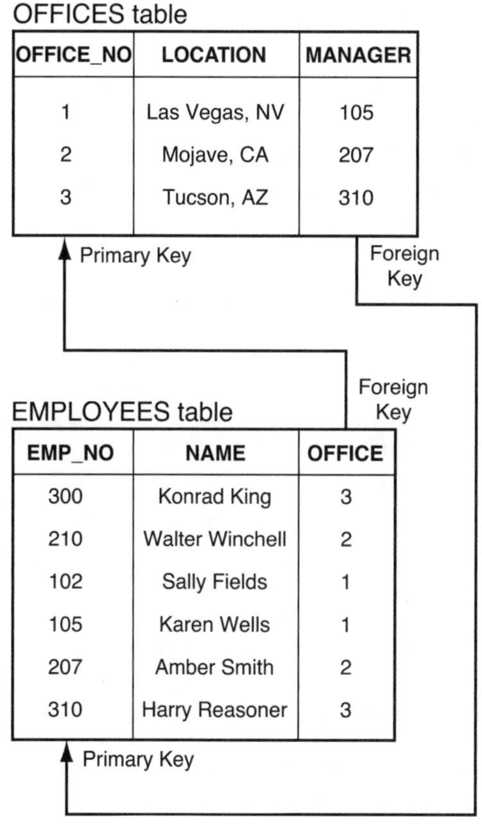

OFFICES table
OFFICE_NO
LOCATION
MANAGER
1
Las Vegas, NV
105
2
Mojave, CA
207
3
Tucson, AZ
310
Primary Key
Foreign Key
Foreign Key
EMPLOYEES table
EMP_NO
NAME
OFFICE
300
Konrad King
3
210
Walter Winchell
2
102
Sally Fields
1
105
Karen Wells
1
207
Amber Smith
2
310
Harry Reasoner
3
Primary Key

Figure 177.1 Circular FOREIGN KEY reference between two tables

Suppose, for example, that the company hires a new employee to open a new office, office 4, in Honolulu, Hawaii. An attempt to add the new employee with the INSERT statement

```
INSERT INTO employees VALUES (400, 'Debbie Jamsa', 4)
```

will fail because there is no office 4 in the OFFICE_NO column of the OFFICES table. Therefore, the INSERT statement fails the referential integrity check. However, if you try to add information on office 4 with the INSERT statement

```
INSERT INTO offices VALUES (4, 'Honolulu, HI', 400)
```

the DBMS will abort the INSERT statement because it violates the referential integrity check on the MANAGER column—there is no employee with EMP_NUM 400 in the EMPLOYEES table.

Thus, there appears to be no way to add a new office or manager for a new office to the database!

To prevent the INSERTION deadlock, make sure that at least one of the FOREIGN KEY constrained columns in tables the reference each other allows NULL values.

Thus, if the tables in the current example were created with

```
CREATE TABLE offices
  (office_no SMALLINT,
   location  VARCHAR(30),
   manager   SMALLINT,
PRIMARY KEY (office_no))

CREATE TABLE employees
  (emp_no SMALLINT,
   name   VARCHAR(30),
   office SMALLINT NOT NULL,
PRIMARY KEY (emp_no),
CONSTRAINT fk_offices_emp
  FOREIGN KEY (office) REFERENCES offices (office_no))

ALTER TABLE offices ADD CONSTRAINT fk_employees_ofce
  FOREIGN KEY (manager) REFERENCES employees (emp_no)
```

you still could not INSERT the employee information first, but you could execute the statement sequence

```
INSERT INTO offices VALUES (4, 'Honolulu, HI', NULL)
INSERT INTO employees VALUES (400, 'Debbie Jamsa', 4)
UPDATE offices SET manager = 400 WHERE office = 4
```

to create a new office, add the new employee record, and then designate the new employee as the office manager.

Note: *Unlike PRIMARY KEY columns, the DBMS allows FOREIGN KEY columns to contain NULL values. This may, at first, seem to violate referential integrity. After all, if a FOREIGN KEY is NULL and none of the PRIMARY KEY columns can have a NULL value, then a NULL FOREIGN KEY value can never have a matching value in the corresponding PRIMARY KEY, right? Well, the answer to the question depends on the "real" value of the NULL. Remember, NULL means missing or unknown. As such, the DBMS gives the NULL in FOREIGN KEY columns the benefit of the doubt by assuming that once the NULL's value is resolved, the non-NULL FOREIGN KEY will turn out to be one of the values in the PRIMARY KEY column(s).*

If all of the FOREIGN KEY columns in the tables involved in a circular referential reference are constrained as NOT NULL, you can still avoid the INSERT deadlock if your DBMS product allows you to suspend the referential integrity check temporarily. On MS-SQL Server, for example, you could execute the statement sequence:

```
ALTER TABLE employees NOCHECK CONSTRAINT fk_offices_emp
INSERT INTO employees VALUES (400, 'Debbie Jamsa', 4)
INSERT INTO offices VALUES (4, 'Honolulu, HI', NULL)
ALTER TABLE employees CHECK CONSTRAINT fk_offices_emp
```

The first ALTER TABLE statement suspends the referential integrity check on the FOREIGN KEY constraint (FK_OFFICES_EMP) on the OFFICES table. This allows the insertion of an employee with an OFFICE column value that does not yet exist in the PRIMARY KEY (OFFICE_NO) column of the OFFICES table. After you finish inserting the rows you want, be sure to reactivate the referential integrity, as is shown by the final ALTER TABLE statement in the current example.

178 Understanding and Maintaining Entity Integrity

In a relational database, a table has *entity integrity* if each of its rows is uniquely identifiable from every other row. Or, said another way, a table has entity integrity if it has no rows that are exact duplicates.

Each row in a table represents an entity (either a concept or a physical object or being) in the "real" world. If two (or more) rows in a table have the same value in every one of their columns, the table loses its integrity as a model of the outside world because no two "things" in the "real" world are absolutely identical to the last detail. (Even if two things are the same down to the subatomic level, two physical objects cannot occupy the same space at the same time—meaning their physical location makes for at least one difference in otherwise identical things.)

Because the PRIMARY KEY constraint requires that every row in the table has a unique, non-NULL value in the column or set of columns to which the constraint is applied, it follows that any table with a PRIMARY KEY has entity integrity. A table without a PRIMARY KEY may have entity integrity, but there is no guarantee that it does—unless at least one of the table's columns has UNIQUE and NOT NULL constraints.

Thus, the table created by

```
CREATE TABLE employees
  (emp_num  SMALLINT UNIQUE NOT NULL,
   office   CHAR(2),
   name     VARCHAR(50),
   address  VARCHAR(50),
   payrate  MONEY)
```

has entity integrity because the UNIQUE and NOT NULL constraints on the EMP_NUM column tell the DBMS to make sure that every row in the EMPLOYEES table has a different (unique) and non-NULL value in its EMP_NUM column. Similarly, the table created by

```
CREATE TABLE employees
  (emp_num       SMALLINT,
   office        CHAR(2),
   name          VARCHAR(30),
   address       VARCHAR(50),
   payrate       MONEY,
   PRIMARY KEY (emp_num, office))
```

has entity integrity because the PRIMARY KEY constraint tells the DBMS to make sure no row in the table has a NULL value in either the EMP_NUM or the OFFICE column, and that the combination of EMP_NUM and OFFICE values is unique (different) in every row of the table.

179 Understanding the Interaction of NULL Values and Uniqueness

Allowing NULL values to occur in PRIMARY KEY columns or in columns with a UNIQUE constraint poses a problem for the integrity-checking mechanisms in the DBMS. If one of the rows in a table has a NULL value in its PRIMARY KEY column, are the values in the PRIMARY KEY column truly unique for every row in the table? The answer depends on the "real" value of the missing (NULL) data.

As you learned in Tip 177, "Understanding Referential Integrity Check INSERT Deadlock and How to Resolve It," the DBMS will allows NULL values in FOREIGN KEY columns and satisfies the referential integrity requirement by assuming that the "real" value of the missing (NULL) data matches one of the values in the PRIMARY KEY referenced by the FOREIGN KEY. Applying this same reasoning to NULL values in a PRIMARY KEY means that a NULL value will be a duplicate of one of the other values in the key, thereby destroying the table's entity integrity (which you learned about in Tip 178, "Understanding and Maintaining Entity Integrity").

No DBMS product that supports primary keys allows any column named in the PRIMARY KEY constraint to hold a NULL value.

Some DBMS products do, however, allow you to insert a single NULL value into a column with a UNIQUE constraint or into an INDEX defined as UNIQUE. MS-SQL Server, for example, treats a NULL as a unique value when you add it to a UNIQUE column or index. As such, if you create a table with

```
CREATE TABLE test_null
  (row_id   INTEGER UNIQUE,
   row_name VARCHAR(30))
```

MS-SQL Server will let you store a single row with a NULL in the ROW_ID column of the TEST_NULL table. If you try to INSERT a second NULL value into the ROW_ID column, the INSERT statement will fail to execute with an error message similar to:

```
Server: Msg 2627, Level 14, State 2, Line1
Violation of UNIQUE KEY constraint
  'UQ__test_null__7720AD13'. Cannot insert duplicate key in
  object 'test_null'.
The statement has been terminated.
```

180 Understanding and Maintaining Domain Integrity

While the DBMS cannot determine whether or not a particular column value in a database is correct, it can make sure that the data item is valid by making sure its value falls within its defined domain. As you learned in Tip 170, "Using the CREATE DOMAIN Statement to Create Domains," a column's domain is the set of all valid values the column can hold. Preventing INSERT and UPDATE statements from storing a value in a column that falls outside of the column's domain (range of all legal values) is known as *maintaining domain integrity*.

Every DBMS automatically maintains the domain integrity of the columns in every table. For example, if you define a column as type INTEGER, the DBMS will automatically abort any UPDATE or INSERT statement that attempts to put non-numeric data or a nonwhole number into the column. In real life, however, the true domain of a column is often a subset of the values allowed for its data type.

For example, although the EMPLOYEE_ID column in the EMPLOYEES table created by

```
CREATE TABLE employees
  (employee_ID INTEGER,
   name        VARCHAR(30))
```

is of type INTEGER, your company might specify that all employee numbers be in the range 1000–9999. Therefore, an EMPLOYEE_ID of 123456, while well within the INTEGER domain, would not be a valid value for the EMPLOYEE_ID column of your EMPLOYEES table.

Some DBMS products let you use the CREATE DOMAIN statement to define data types that limit the range of data values a user can put into a column. For example, the statement

```
CREATE DOMAIN employee_id_type INTEGER
  CHECK (VALUE BETWEEN 1000 AND 9999)
```

will create a domain object you can use as a data type in a CREATE TABLE statement such as:

```
CREATE TABLE employees
  (employee_ID employee_id_type,
   name        VARCHAR(30))
```

After you create the EMPLOYEES table and declare the EMPLOYEE_ID column's data type as EMPLOYEE_ID_TYPE, the DBMS will execute only INSERT and UPDATE statements that have either a NULL or a non-NULL value that falls within the range specified in the CREATE DOMAIN statement (1000–1999, in the current example).

Not all DBMS products support the CREATE DOMAIN statement. MS-SQL Server, for example, does not. Instead of domains, MS-SQL Server lets you define "rules" (as you learned in Tip 169, "Understanding MS-SQL Server Rules"), which you can "bind" to columns and user-defined data types to limit the range of values users can put into those columns.

Either in addition to or in place of user-defined domains and rules, most DBMS products let you specify a column's domain using a CHECK constraint in a CREATE TABLE statement. For example, the CREATE TABLE statement

```
CREATE TABLE employees
  (employee_ID INTEGER
     CHECK (employee_ID BETWEEN 1000 AND 1999),
   name        VARCHAR(30))
```

will tell the DBMS to maintain the EMPLOYEE_ID's domain integrity by allowing INSERT and UPDATE statements to store only values ranging from 1000 to 1999 in the column.

181 Understanding and Maintaining Referential Integrity

As its name implies, a *relational* database consists of related data items and objects. Columns within a table are related in that column values are the attributes that describe a physical entity or concept. Moreover, the database tables themselves are interrelated in that rows representing purchases in an ORDERS table "belong to" to the customers (represented by rows in the CUSTOMERS table) that placed the orders. Similarly, rows representing hours worked in a TIMECARDS table "belong to" employees (represented by rows in an EMPLOYEES table) that worked those hours. The process of ensuring that the "links" between related rows in different tables remain intact is called *maintaining referential integrity.*

Every relational DBMS product uses one or more columns of matching data values to link rows in one table with those in another. Suppose, for example, that the database has two tables created with:

```
CREATE TABLE timecards
  (emp_num   SMALLINT,
   card_date DATETIME,
   time_in   SMALLINT,
   time_out  SMALLINT,
PRIMARY KEY (emp_num, card_date, time_in),
CONSTRAINT fk_employees_timecards FOREIGN KEY (emp_num)
  REFERENCES employees (emp_ID))

CREATE TABLE employees
  (emp_ID  SMALLINT,
   name    VARCHAR(30),
   address VARCHAR(50),
   payrate MONEY,
PRIMARY KEY (emp_ID))
```

To maintain the relationship between each timecard and the employee who worked the hours, each row in a TIMECARDS table will have an employee number column (EMP_NUM) whose value matches the value in the employee number column (EMP_ID) of one (and only one) of the rows of the EMPLOYEES table. The database, then, has referential integrity so long as every employee number in the EMP_NUM column of the TIMECARDS table matches the value in the EMP_ID column of exactly one row in the EMPLOYEES table.

A individual column value (or composite column value, for multi-column keys) that uniquely identifies a single row in a table (such as the EMP_ID column of the EMPLOYEES table) is called a PRIMARY KEY. A column or set of columns in a table used solely to store the PRIMARY KEY value of the corresponding row in another table (such as the EMP_NUM column in the TIMECARDS table) is called a FOREIGN KEY. As such, referential integrity dictates that every FOREIGN KEY value in one table has a matching PRIMARY KEY value in its related table. (The definition of the FOREIGN KEY constraint names the related table in its REFERENCES clause.)

As you learned in Tip 174, "Understanding Referential Integrity Checks and Foreign Keys," the DBMS maintains referential integrity by checking each INSERT, DELETE, and UPDATE statement on a table that has either a PRIMARY KEY or a FOREIGN KEY to make sure the link between a row in a child table and its parent row in another table remains intact. Whenever you INSERT a row in a table with a FOREIGN KEY (a child table), the *key* value in the FOREIGN KEY column(s) must exist as a PRIMARY KEY value in the corresponding (parent) table. If it does not, the DBMS will abort the INSERT statement. Conversely, if a table has a PRIMARY KEY, the DBMS will execute a DELETE statement on a row only if the row's PRIMARY KEY value is not a FOREIGN KEY value in a related (child) table.

The important thing to remember is that the DBMS represents the relationship between tables by storing matching key values in the FOREIGN KEY column(s) of one or more rows of a (child) table and in the PRIMARY KEY column(s) of one row in the related (parent) table. Maintaining referential integrity means preventing the execution of any statement that breaks the relationship between tables by leaving a child table with one or more FOREIGN KEY values that do not have a matching PRIMARY KEY in the parent table.

182 Understanding How Applying the RESTRICT Rule to Updates and Deletes Helps Maintain Referential Integrity

As you know, maintaining referential integrity means making sure that there is a matching PRIMARY KEY value in the parent table for every FOREIGN KEY value in a child table.

Since each row in a table with a PRIMARY KEY has a unique PRIMARY KEY value, removing a row with PRIMARY KEY value that matches one or more values in a FOREIGN KEY that references the PRIMARY KEY results in the loss of referential integrity. Removing the single matching PRIMARY KEY value causes the FOREIGN KEY value in one or more rows in the child table to refer to a nonexistent row (PRIMARY KEY) in the parent table. Similarly, changing a PRIMARY KEY value that matches one or more key values in a corresponding FOREIGN KEY—without changing those values to match the PRIMARY KEY's new value—also results in the loss of referential integrity in the database.

The RESTRICT rule applied to a FOREIGN KEY constraint tells the DBMS abort the execution of any DELETE statement that would remove a parent row (a row from a table with a PRIMARY KEY) if the row has any children. Thus, the RESTRICT rule tells the DBMS to preserve referential integrity when executing a DELETE statement by aborting statement execution (and to roll back any work performed within the current transaction) if the DELETE statement tries to remove a row with a PRIMARY KEY value that matches one or more values in a corresponding FOREIGN KEY.

Moreover, the RESTRICT rule also tells the DBMS to abort the execution of any UPDATE statement that changes the PRIMARY KEY value of a parent row that has child rows. Thus, the RESTRICT rule also tells the DBMS to preserve referential integrity when executing an UPDATE statement by aborting statement execution (and to roll back any work performed within the current transaction) if the UPDATE statement tries to change a PRIMARY KEY value that matches one or more values in a corresponding FOREIGN KEY.

Most DBMS products default to using the RESTRICT rule in determining what actions to take in processing an UPDATE or DELETE statement that tries to violate the referential integrity between tables. In fact, some DBMS products, including MS-SQL Server, not only default to the RESTRICT rule, but also prohibit the selection any one of the other possible rules—CASCADE, SET NULL, and SET DEFAULT.

Refer to the system manual for your DBMS to see which rule is the default for your system, to determine if the DBMS supports any of the other rules. Check the manual's index for "UPDATE_RULE" or "DELETE_RULE." Also look up the syntax for creating FOREIGN KEY constraints. If the DBMS lets you select the rule (the actions) the system will take when an UPDATE or DELETE statement attempts to violate referential integrity constraints, the FOREIGN KEY creation syntax will include optional ON UPDATE and ON DELETE clauses such as:

```
[ [ON UPDATE
     NO ACTION|CASCADE|RESTRICT|SET NULL|SET DEFAULT]
  [ON DELETE
     NO ACTION|CASCADE|RESTRICT|SET NULL|SET DEFAULT] ]
```

Note: *SQL-92 and MS-SQL Server refer to the rule for the actions described in this tip as NO ACTION vs. RESTRICT. MS-SQL Server's "Books Online" documentation states, "NO ACTION means that no action is performed and the Transact-SQL statement to perform changes does not execute." However, in addition to not executing the statement, the DBMS does raise an error condition and displays an error message. So, "RESTRICT" seems to more accurately describe what happens than does "NO ACTION." If your DBMS (like DB2) supports both rules, the only difference is in the timing of the application of each rule. The DBMS enforces the RESTRICT rule before any other column constraints and enforces the NO ACTION rule after enforcing other column constraints. In almost all cases, the two rules operate identically.*

183 Understanding How Applying the CASCADE Rule to Updates and Deletes Helps Maintain Referential Integrity

A database has referential integrity when every non-NULL key in the FOREIGN KEY column(s) of one table has one and only one matching entry its corresponding PRIMARY KEY.

By definition, the value of every key in a PRIMARY KEY is unique for each row in a table. As a result, if a DELETE statement removes a row with a PRIMARY KEY value that matches one or more key values in a corresponding FOREIGN KEY, the database loses its referential integrity. By removing the FOREIGN KEY's single matching PRIMARY KEY value, the DBMS creates an "orphan"—a child row whose FOREIGN KEY value refers to a nonexistent row (PRIMARY KEY) in the parent table. Similarly, referential integrity is destroyed if an UPDATE statement changes the PRIMARY KEY value in a parent row without also changing the matching FOREIGN KEY value in the child row.

The CASCADE rule applied to a FOREIGN KEY constraint tells the DBMS to automatically remove all of the row's children and then the parent row when executing a DELETE statement on a row in a parent table. By following the CASCADE rule, the DBMS ensures there are never any orphans because the system automatically removes child rows right along with the parent row.

Similarly, when executing an UPDATE statement that changes a PRIMARY KEY value, the CASCADE rule tells the DBMS to update the FOREIGN KEY value in all child rows to match the new PRIMARY KEY value. Thus, the CASCADE rule tells the DBMS to preserve referential integrity when executing an UPDATE statement by automatically changing the FOREIGN KEY values that matched the PRIMARY KEY's original value to the PRIMARY KEY's new value.

Many DBMS products apply only the RESTRICT rule (which you learned about in Tip 182, "Understanding How Applying the RESTRICT Rule to Updates and Deletes Helps Maintain Referential Integrity") when determining what actions to take in processing an UPDATE or DELETE statement that tries to violate the referential integrity between tables. Both DB2 and INFORMIX, however, support cascading DELETE statements.

Refer to the system manual for your DBMS to see which rule is the default for your DBMS product and to determine if your DBMS supports the CASCADE rule. Check the manual's index for "UPDATE_RULE" or "DELETE_RULE." Also review the syntax for creating FOREIGN KEY constraints. If the DBMS lets you select the rule (the actions) the system will take when an UPDATE or DELETE statement attempts to violate referential integrity constraints, the FOREIGN KEY creation syntax will include optional ON UPDATE and ON DELETE clauses such as:

```
[ [ON UPDATE
     NO ACTION|CASCADE|RESTRICT|SET NULL|SET DEFAULT]
  [ON DELETE
     NO ACTION|CASCADE|RESTRICT|SET NULL|SET DEFAULT] ]
```

184 Understanding How Applying the SET NULL Rule to Updates and Deletes Helps Maintain Referential Integrity

By definition, a database has referential integrity if each key in a FOREIGN KEY either is NULL or matches the value of one and only of the key values in its corresponding PRIMARY KEY.

The SET NULL rule applied to a FOREIGN KEY constraint tells the DBMS to set the FOREIGN KEY column(s) in all child rows to NULL when a DELETE statement removes the parent row or when an UPDATE statement changes the value(s) in the parent row's PRIMARY KEY column(s). Thus, the SET NULL rule tells the DBMS to maintain referential integrity when executing a DELETE statement that removes a row with children by changing the FOREIGN KEY value in each of the parent's child rows to NULL.

Note: *In Tip 177, "Understanding Referential Integrity Check INSERT Deadlock and How to Resolve It," you learned that a NULL FOREIGN KEY value does not violate referential integrity. The DBMS "assumes" that the FOREIGN KEY's NULL (missing or unknown) value will turn out to be one of the values in the parent table's PRIMARY KEY when a user or application program supplies the FOREIGN KEY's "real" value.*

While most DBMS products follow only the RESTRICT rule in determining what actions to take in processing an UPDATE or DELETE statement that tries to violate the referential integrity between tables, DB2 does support the SET NULL rule for DELETE statements.

Refer to the system manual for your DBMS to determine its default rule and to find out if your system supports the SET NULL rule. Check the manual's index for "UPDATE_RULE" or "DELETE_RULE." Also review the syntax for creating FOREIGN KEY constraints. If the DBMS lets you select the rule (the actions) the system will take when an UPDATE or DELETE statement attempts to violate referential integrity constraints, the FOREIGN KEY creation syntax will include optional ON UPDATE and ON DELETE clauses such as:

```
[ [ON UPDATE
    NO ACTION|CASCADE|RESTRICT|SET NULL|SET DEFAULT]
  [ON DELETE
    NO ACTION|CASCADE|RESTRICT|SET NULL|SET DEFAULT] ]
```

185 Understanding How Applying the SET DEFAULT Rule to Updates and Deletes Helps Maintain Referential Integrity

Referential integrity means that every non-NULL FOREIGN KEY value in a child row has a single matching value in the parent table's PRIMARY KEY.

The SET DEFAULT rule applied to a FOREIGN KEY constraint tells the DBMS to set the FOREIGN KEY column value in all of a parent row's child rows to the column's default value when executing a DELETE statement that removes a parent row and when an UPDATE statement changes the value in the parent row's PRIMARY KEY column. (For composite [multi-column] PRIMARY/FOREIGN KEY pairs, the DBMS sets each column in the

FOREIGN KEY its default value.) Thus, the SET DEFAULT rule tells the DBMS to maintain referential integrity when executing a DELETE or UPDATE statement that affects the PRIMARY KEY value in a parent row by changing the FOREIGN KEY value in each of the parent's child rows to the default value for the column(s) in the FOREIGN KEY.

Note: *It is up to the person that creates the table with the child rows to make sure that the default values for the column(s) in the FOREIGN KEY will generate a key value that is guaranteed to be present in the PRIMARY KEY of the parent table. Suppose, for example, that one of the rows in a SALESPERSON table's PRIMARY KEY column (EMP_ID) has a value of 999, meaning "House Lead." You could then set the default value for the related (SALESPERSON_ID) column in the CUSTOMERS table to 999 (either in the CREATE TABLE or the ALTER TABLE statement). Then, whenever you DELETE the row for a salesman that leaves the company from the SALESPERSONS table, the DBMS will automatically change the salesperson's customers to house accounts—SALESPERSON_ID 999.*

If the default value for the FOREIGN KEY column(s) produces a key value that does not match one of the values in the PRIMARY KEY, the DELETE or UPDATE statement will behave as if the RESTRICT rule applies—the statement will abort and the DBMS will roll back any work performed during the current transaction.

Although a part of the SQL-92 specification, no commercial DBMS product currently supports the SET DEFAULT rule for either an UPDATE or a DELETE statement that attempts to violate the referential integrity between tables.

Refer to the system manual for your DBMS to see which rule is the default for your system and to determine if your DBMS supports the SET DEFAULT rule. Check the manual's index for "UPDATE_RULE" or "DELETE_RULE." Also review the syntax for creating FOREIGN KEY constraints. If the DBMS supports the selection of the rule to apply when an UPDATE or a DELETE statement tries to violate referential integrity constraints, the FOREIGN KEY creation syntax will include optional ON UPDATE and ON DELETE clauses such as:

```
[ [ON UPDATE
      NO ACTION|CASCADE|RESTRICT|SET NULL|SET DEFAULT]
  [ON DELETE
      NO ACTION|CASCADE|RESTRICT|SET NULL|SET DEFAULT] ]
```

186 Understanding the Dangerous Nature of the Cascading Deletes Rule

In Tips 182–185, you learned about the eight rules a DBMS can follow when asked to execute an UPDATE or DELETE statement that violates referential integrity constraints. Of the eight rules, only the ON DELETE CASCADE rule can result in the loss of existing data beyond the values stored FOREIGN KEY columns. As such, be sure to review all FOREIGN KEY constraints that include an UPON DELETE CASCADE clause to make sure you really want to remove rows from the table when a row in the parent table is removed.

Suppose, for example, that your database includes the tables and data shown in Figure 186.1.

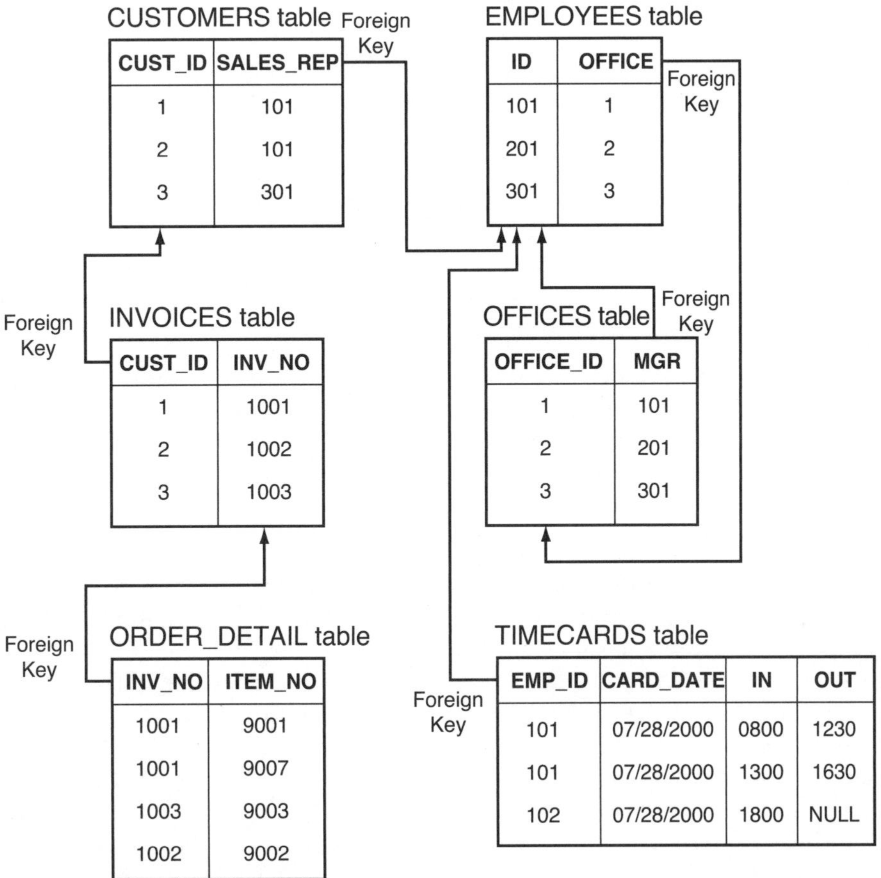

Figure 186.1 Multiple tables affected by a single DELETE due to the CASCADE DELETE rule

If your company closes office 1 (OFFICE_ID 1) and you remove its row from the OFFICES table with the DELETE statement

```
DELETE FROM offices WHERE office_ID = 1
```

you might think that the DELETE statement affects only a single row in the OFFICES table. After all, the statement's WHERE clause is based on an equality, and only one row in the target table, OFFICES, can have a value of 1 in its single-column PRIMARY KEY, OFFICE_ID. However, if the definition for each of the FOREIGN KEY constraints shown in Figure 186.1 specifies that the DBMS use the ON DELETE CASCADE rule for handling referential integrity violations, removing the row with OFFICE_ID 1 from the OFFICES table will result in the deletion of rows in each of the five other tables as well!

By virtue of its PRIMARY KEY/FOREIGN KEY relationship, each row in the OFFICE table is the parent of the child rows in the EMPLOYEES table in which the OFFICE_ID in the OFFICES table matches the value of the OFFICE column in the EMPLOYEES table. Each employee (row) in the EMPLOYEES table "owns" the rows in the TIMECARD table where the value in EMP_ID column in the TIMECARD table matches the ID column in the EMPLOYEES table.

In the current example, deleting OFFICE_ID 1 from the OFFICES table violates referential integrity by causing the value in the FOREIGN KEY (the OFFICE column) in the EMPLOYEES table to refer to a nonexistent row (1) in the OFFICES table. As a result, the DBMS will apply the ON DELETE CASCADE rule and remove the row with ID 101 from the EMPLOYEES table. However, removing the row with EMP_ID 101 violates referential integrity by causing the rows with the FOREIGN KEY (EMP_ID) value of 101 in the TIMECARDS table to refer to a (now) nonexistent row in the EMPLOYEES table. Therefore, the DBMS must again apply the UPON DELETE CASCADE rule and remove the rows with EMP_ID 101 from the TIMECARDS table.

Thus, executing the DELETE statement, which removes a single row from the OFFICES table, causes the deletion of rows in the EMPLOYEES and TIMECARDS tables as well. Moreover, the removal of rows to execute the DELETE statement in the current example does not end here because each row in the CUSTOMERS table is also related by the FOREIGN KEY (SALES_REP) to the salesperson with a matching ID in the EMPLOYEES table.

When the DBMS removes the row ID 101 from the EMPLOYEES table, the system violates referential integrity by leaving the rows of the CUSTOMERS table with a FOREIGN KEY value (SALES_REP 101) that refers to a nonexistent PRIMARY KEY (ID 101) in the EMPLOYEES table. As a result, the DBMS will apply the UPON DELETE CASCADE rule and delete CUSTOMERS table rows that have a 101 in the SALES_REP column. However, removing SALES_REP 101 rows from the CUSTOMERS column also violates referential integrity by leaving FOREIGN KEY (CUST_ID) values in INVOICES table that refer to nonexistent PRIMARY KEY (CUST_ID) values rows in the CUSTOMERS table. Thus, the DBMS must again follow the guidelines of the UPON DELETE CASCADE rule, and remove rows with CUST_ID 1 and rows with CUST_ID 2 from the INVOICES table. Unfortunately, removing these INVOICES table rows violates referential integrity by leaving rows with FOREIGN KEY (INV_NO) columns in the ORDER_DETAIL table that refer to nonexistent PRIMARY KEY values (1001 and 1002) in the INV_NO column of the INVOICES table. Therefore, the DBMS, following the UPON DELETE CASCADE rule, will remove those rows from the ORDER_DETAIL table.

The current example illustrates that applying the UPON DELETE CASCADE rule to all FOREIGN KEY constraints can cause a DELETE statement intended to remove a single row from one table to remove multiple rows from several related tables. As such, be very careful when specifying that the DBMS follow the ON DELETE CASCADE rule when a DELETE statement violates a particular FOREIGN KEY (referential integrity) constraint.

In the current example, you can limit the DELETE statement's row removal to a single row in the OFFICES table by specifying the ON DELETE SET NULL rule for the OFFICE column FOREIGN KEY constraint in the EMPLOYEES table.

The important thing to understand now is that the indiscriminate application of the ON DELETE CASCADE rule for FOREIGN KEY constraint violations can lead to an unintended loss of data. As such, be sure to analyze each FOREIGN KEY relationship and decide which of the eight rules (discussed in Tips 182–185) specify the actions most appropriate to the situation when the execution of an UPDATE or DELETE statement violates a FOREIGN KEY (referential integrity) constraint.

187 Using the Enterprise Manager to Add FOREIGN KEY Relationships Between Existing Tables

Tip 62, "Using the CREATE TABLE Statement to Assign Foreign Key Constraints," showed you how to define foreign key constraints when creating a new table using the CREATE TABLE statement; Tip 60, "Using the ALTER TABLE Statement to Change Primary and Foreign Keys," showed you how to use the ALTER TABLE statement to add a FOREIGN KEY constraint to an existing table. In addition to the two command-based tools, MS-SQL Server also provides a graphical method for creating FOREIGN KEY constraints through the MS-SQL Server Enterprise Manager.

To create FOREIGN KEY constraints using the MS-SQL Server Enterprise Manager, perform the following steps:

1. Start the Enterprise Manager by clicking your mouse pointer on the Start button. When Windows displays the Start menu, move your mouse pointer to Programs, select Microsoft SQL Server 7.0, and then click your mouse pointer on Enterprise Manager.
2. To display the list of SQL servers, click your mouse pointer on the plus (+) to the left of SQL Server Group.
3. Find the SQL server that manages the database with the tables in which you wish to setup one or more FOREIGN KEY constraints, and click you mouse pointer on the plus (+) to the left of SQL server's icon. Enterprise Manager will display the list of databases managed by the server. For example, if you want to work with a database managed by a server named NVBIZNET2, click your mouse pointer on the plus (+) to the left of the icon for NVBIZNET2.
4. Click your mouse pointer on the icon for the database with the tables you want to relate using a FOREIGN KEY constraint. For the current project, click your mouse pointer on the icon for the SQLTips database. Enterprise Manager will display the default database diagram. If you have not yet created a default database diagram, click your mouse pointer

on the Yes button when the Enterprise Manager asks if you want to create a database diagram. Enterprise Manager will start the Create Database Diagram Wizard.

5. If the database you selected in Step 4 already has a default database diagram (and Enterprise Manager did not prompt you to start the Create Database Diagram Wizard in Step 4), select the Action menu New option, and click your mouse pointer on Database Diagram. Enterprise Manager will start the Create Database Diagram Wizard.
6. On the Create Database Diagram Wizard welcome screen, click your mouse pointer on the Next button. The wizard will display a Select Tables to Be Added dialog box, similar to that shown in Figure 187.1.

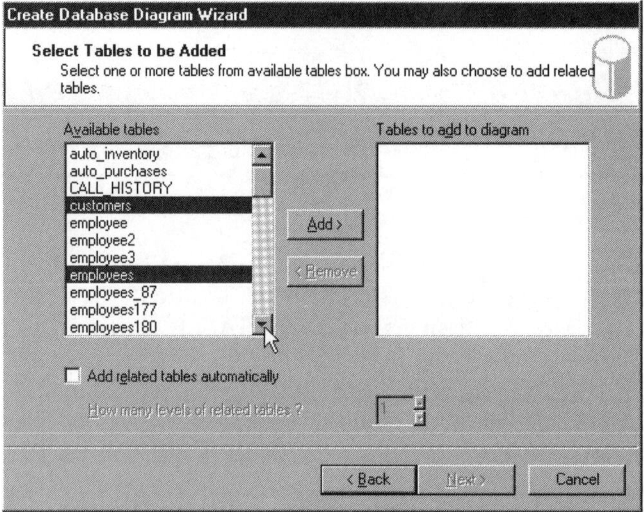

Figure 187.1 The Create Database Diagram Wizard's Select Tables to Be Added dialog box

7. From the list of tables in the Available Tables scroll window, select the tables in which you wish to set up FOREIGN KEY relationships. For the current project, hold down your Ctrl key and click your mouse pointer on CUSTOMERS, EMPLOYEES, and ORDERS. (The list of tables is alphabetized, and you may need to use the scroll bar to the right of the Available Tables scroll window do display additional table names.)
8. Release the Ctrl key and then click your mouse pointer on the Add button to move the tables you selected in Step 7 to the Tables to Add to Diagram scroll window.
9. Click your mouse pointer on the Next button. The Create Database Diagram Wizard will display the Completing the Create Database Diagram Wizard dialog box.
10. To create a database diagram based on the tables you selected in Step 7, click your mouse pointer on the Finish button.
11. After the wizard creates the database diagram, it will display a Tables Have Been Added and Arranged message box—click your mouse pointer on its OK button. Enterprise

Manager will display the tables in your database diagram in a window similar to that shown in Figure 187.2.

Figure 187.2 The Create Database Diagram Wizard New Diagram window

12. Move your mouse pointer over the column selection button to the left of the column you wish to use as a FOREIGN KEY, and then hold down the left mouse button. (If you want to create a multi-column FOREIGN KEY [to link with a multi-column PRIMARY KEY], hold down the Ctrl key on your keyboard as you click your mouse pointer on the column selection buttons to the left of the columns you want to include in the FOREIGN KEY. After you move your mouse pointer over select button for the final column in the FOREIGN KEY, hold down the left mouse button and then release the Ctrl key.) For the current project, move your mouse pointer over the select button to the left of the CUSTOMER_ID column in the ORDERS table, and then press and hold down your left mouse button.

13. While holding down your left mouse button, drag your mouse pointer until it is over the first column in the PRIMARY KEY of the table to which you wish to relate the FOREIGN KEY. For the current project, relate the ORDERS table to the CUSTOMERS table by holding down your left mouse button as you drag the mouse pointer until it points to the CUSTOMER_ID column in the CUSTOMERS table.

14. Release the left mouse button. Enterprise Manager will display a Create Relationship dialog box similar to that shown in Figure 187.3.

15. Click your mouse pointer on the OK button, and Enterprise Manager will create the FOREIGN KEY and display the link between the two tables graphically in the database diagram.

16. Repeat Steps 12–15 for each FOREIGN KEY relationship you want to create. For the current project, establish a second relationship by selecting the SALESMAN_ID column in the ORDERS table for Step 12 and dragging your mouse pointer over the EMPLOYEE_ID column of the EMPLOYEES table in Step 13.

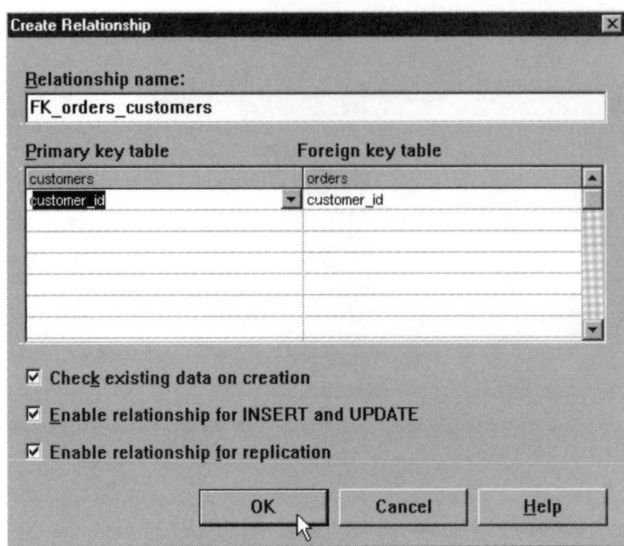

Figure 187.3 The Create Database Diagram Wizard Create Relationship dialog box

17. If the graphical representations of the FOREIGN KEY links overlap, click on the Arrange Tables button (the button at the right end) on the New Diagram window's Standard toolbar. Enterprise Manager will do its best to arrange the database diagram's tables without overlapping links, similar to that shown in Figure 187.4.

After you are finished creating new FOREIGN KEY relationships, exit the Database Diagram window by clicking your mouse pointer on the X in the window's upper-right corner. Enterprise Manager will ask you if you want to save your updated diagram as a disk file. Whether you save the diagram or not, the FOREIGN KEY relationships you created will remain in place. For the current project, click your mouse pointer on the No button to discard the new database diagram and return to the Enterprise Manager window.

Note: *If you answered Yes to create the default database diagram in Step 4, you do not have to exit the Database Diagram window. Instead, Enterprise Manager will continue to display the default database diagram in its right pane until you click your mouse pointer on another database object. When you choose to work with another database object or wizard, or exit Enterprise Manager, the Enterprise Manager will ask if you want to save the default database diagram.*

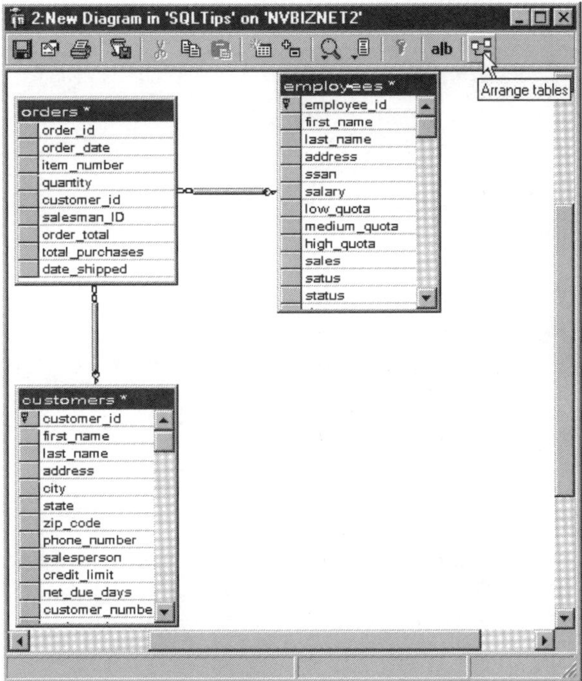

Figure 187.4 The Create Database Diagram Wizard New Diagram window, graphically depicting the FOREIGN KEY links between tables

188 Using the MATCH FULL Clause to Maintain Referential Integrity

In Tip 179 you learned a row with the value NULL in a FOREIGN KEY column does not violate referential integrity-the DBMS assumes that the "real" value of the missing data will turn out to be one of the PRIMARY KEY values in the related table. This "benefit of the doubt" rule seems clear enough in cases where a FOREIGN KEY consists of single column. However, when a table has a multi-column FOREIGN KEY, a NULL in any one of the columns that make up the key will cause the DBMS (by default) to skip the referential integrity check on the FOREIGN KEY and allow any NULL or valid (for the data type) non-NULL value in any of the key's remaining columns.

Suppose, for example, that you have two tables created with:

```
CREATE TABLE invoice
  (cust_ID      INTEGER,
   invoice_num INTEGER)

CREATE TABLE order_detail
  (cust_id      INTEGER,
   invoice_num INTEGER,
   order_date  DATETIME,
   item_number INTEGER,
CONSTRAINT fk_invoice_order_detail
  FOREIGN KEY (cust_ID, invoice_num)
  REFERENCES invoice (cust_ID, invoice_num))
```

If the invoice table contains a single row with CUST_ID 1 and INVOICE_NUM 1, the INSERT statement

```
INSERT INTO order_detail VALUES (1,1,07/30/2000,1000)
```

is obviously valid because both of the composite FOREIGN KEY values (1,1) in the new row exists as a PRIMARY KEY value in the related table. However, INSERT statements:

```
INSERT INTO order_detail VALUES (NULL,23,07/30/2000,1001)
INSERT INTO order_detail VALUES (77,NULL,07/30/2000,1002)
```

are also valid. Although the INVOICE table has no rows with a 23 in the INVOICE_NUM column or a 77 in the CUST_ID column, the NULL value in each INSERT statement's FOREIGN KEY (NULL, 23) and (27, NULL) tells the DBMS to suspend judgment on the referential integrity of the *entire* FOREIGN KEY—not just the column or columns with a NULL value.

To prevent the DBMS from allowing a non-NULL value in a FOREIGN KEY column that does not match any value in the corresponding column of the PRIMARY KEY, include the MATCH FULL clause in the definition of the FOREIGN KEY constraint. For example, if you create the ORDER_DETAIL table in the current example with

```
CREATE TABLE order_detail
  (cust_id INTEGER,
   invoice_num INTEGER,
   order_date DATETIME,
   item_number INTEGER,
CONSTRAINT fk_invoice_order_detail
  FOREIGN KEY (cust_ID, invoice_num)
  REFERENCES invoice (cust_ID, invoice_num) MATCH FULL)
```

the MATCH FULL option on a FOREIGN KEY constraint tells the DBMS that *all* of the columns in a multi-column FOREIGN KEY either must be NULL or must *all* be non-NULL. Thus, the DBMS will accept only a FOREIGN KEY that is completely NULL or whose non-NULL composite key value matches the composite value of a key in the PRIMARY KEY of the related table. (If the definition of the FOREIGN KEY constraint includes a MATCH

FULL clause, the DBMS will not allow the insertion of a row with a partially NULL FOREIGN KEY.)

Note: *Not all DBMS products, including MS-SQL Server, support a MATCH FULL clause in the definition of a FOREIGN KEY constraint. If your DBMS does not support the MATCH FULL option, you must place the NOT NULL constraint on each of the columns in a FOREIGN KEY in order to guarantee that all non-NULL values in the FOREIGN KEY columns match values in the corresponding columns of the related table's PRIMARY KEY.*

---

189 Understanding MATCH FULL, MATCH PARTIAL, and MATCH SIMPLE Clauses

As you learned from our discussion of referential integrity and FOREIGN KEY constraints in Tip 173, "Understanding Foreign Keys," and Tip 174, "Understanding Referential Integrity Checks and Foreign Keys," referential integrity requires that the FOREIGN KEY value in one table matches one and only one PRIMARY KEY value of the table referenced in the definition of the FOREIGN KEY. A referential integrity check, therefore, is relatively straightforward—check the PRIMARY KEY to make sure it has a value that matches the value of the FOREIGN KEY—except when dealing with a *partially* NULL FOREIGN KEY. As you learned in Tip 188, "Using the MATCH FULL Clause to Maintain Referential Integrity," the DBMS does not perform a referential integrity check on a FOREIGN KEY with a NULL in any one of its columns.

SQL-92 provides three MATCH clauses you can add to the definition of a FOREIGN KEY constraint to control the behavior of the DBMS when dealing with NULL values in a FOREIGN KEY:

- **MATCH FULL.** Tells the DBMS to require that all columns in a FOREIGN KEY be either NULL or not-NULL. For example, the definition of a two-column FOREIGN KEY constraint that includes a MATCH FULL clause tells the DBMS that the key value (NULL, NULL) is acceptable. However, key values such as (100, NULL) and (NULL, 100) always violate referential integrity because part of the key is NULL and part is non-NULL.
- **MATCH PARTIAL.** Tells the DBMS to allow partially NULL FOREIGN KEY values, so long as the value in each of the non-NULL columns in the FOREIGN KEY matches the value in the corresponding column of the PRIMARY KEY. Thus, the definition of a two-column FOREIGN KEY constraint that includes a MATCH PARTIAL clause tells the DBMS that the key value (NULL, NULL) is acceptable. However, key values such as (100, NULL) and (NULL, 100) pass the referential integrity check only if the corresponding column of the PRIMARY KEY has a value of 100 in one more of the rows in the table.

- **MATCH SIMPLE.** Tells the DBMS to skip the relational integrity check on partially NULL FOREIGN KEY values. Therefore, if the definition of a two-column FOREIGN KEY includes a MATCH SIMPLE clause (or has no MATCH clause at all), the DBMS will accept a FOREIGN KEY with the value (NULL, NULL), (NULL, 100), and (100, NULL)—whether or not the PRIMARY KEY has a value of 100 in the corresponding column of the rows in the table.

Not all DBMS products support a MATCH clause in the definition of a FOREIGN KEY constraint. As such, check your system manual to see if the syntax for defining a FOREIGN KEY constraint on your system includes:

```
[MATCH {FULL | PARTIAL | SIMPLE}]
```

If your DBMS, like MS-SQL Server, does not support the MATCH clause, the default (and only) handling of partially NULL FOREIGN KEY values will be as described by MATCH SIMPLE.

Note: *Some DBMS products may refer to MATCH SIMPLE as MATCH UNIQUE. While the names are different, the action of MATCH UNIQUE is the same as that described for MATCH SIMPLE.*

---

190 Understanding the Interaction of the SET NULL Rule and a MATCH Clause

In Tip 184, "Understanding How Applying the SET NULL Rule to Updates and Deletes Helps Maintain Referential Integrity," you learned that the ON DELETE SET NULL rule tells the DBMS to put a NULL in the FOREIGN KEY column(s) of child rows when it removes the PARENT row from the related table. Similarly, the ON UPDATE SET NULL rule tells the DBMS to change the value of the FOREIGN KEY columns in child rows to NULL when a user ID changes the PRIMARY KEY value in the parent row. If one or more of the columns in the FOREIGN KEY has a NOT NULL constraint, the DBMS does not report an error. Rather, it puts a NULL into only those FOREIGN KEY columns that will accept a NULL value.

For example, if you have two tables created with

```
CREATE TABLE customers
  (cust_ID       INTEGER,
   office        INTEGER,
   customer_name VARCHAR(30)
   CONSTRAINT PK_customers PRIMARY KEY (cust_ID, office))
```

```
CREATE TABLE invoices
  (cust_ID      INTEGER NOT NULL,
   office       INTEGER,
   invoice_num  INTEGER,
   order_date   DATETIME,
   item_number  INTEGER,
CONSTRAINT fk_customers_invoices
  FOREIGN KEY (cust_ID, office)
  REFERENCES customers (cust_ID, office)
  ON DELETE SET NULL ON UPDATE SET NULL)
```

and execute the DELETE statement

```
DELETE FROM customers WHERE cust_ID = 1 AND office = 5
```

the DBMS will set the OFFICE column to NULL and leave a 1 in the CUST_ID column for all rows with CUST_ID 1 and OFFICE 5 in the INVOICES table. As such, removing a parent row will cause the DBMS to create a partially NULL FOREIGN KEY value in each of its child rows where all the FOREIGN KEY columns do not have a NOT NULL constraint.

As you learned in Tip 188, creating partially NULL foreign keys is undesirable because the DBMS skips referential integrity checks on partially NULL key values and a column in the child row's FOREIGN KEY may hold a value that does not exist in the corresponding column of any row in the parent table.

For example, after executing the DELETE statement in the current example, all child rows in the INVOICES table (rows with CUST_ID 1 and OFFICE 5) will still show that customer 1 has invoices on the system (although the customer's OFFICE will be NULL). However, the CUSTOMERS table, which is supposed to have a row for every customer, will have no information on customer 1—if only OFFICE 5 had a customer with CUST_ID 1. Moreover, if other offices do have a customer with CUST_ID 1, each of these customers is now the parent row for the child rows with CUST_ID 1 and a NULL value in the OFFICE column.

You can add a MATCH clause to a FOREIGN KEY to tell the DBMS how to react to the creation of partially NULL FOREIGN KEY values when applying the ON DELETE NULL or ON UPDATE NULL rule for DELETE and UPDATE statements that violate referential integrity. If you do not include an explicit MATCH clause in the definition of a FOREIGN KEY constraint, the DBMS defaults the MATCH clause to MATCH SIMPLE. As a result, the DBMS is allowed to create a partially NULL FOREIGN KEY when following the ON DELETE or ON UPDATE SET NULL rule.

However, if you change the FOREIGN KEY constraint in the INVOICES table to

```
CONSTRAINT fk_customers_invoices
  FOREIGN KEY (cust_ID, office)
  REFERENCES customers (cust_ID, office)
  MATCH FULL ON DELETE SET NULL ON UPDATE SET NULL)
```

the MATCH FULL clause tells the DBMS it is not allowed to create partially NULL FOREIGN KEY values. Therefore, the DBMS will abort the DELETE statement

```
DELETE FROM customers WHERE cust_ID = 1 AND office = 5
```

because it violates a referential integrity constraint. The ON DELETE SET NULL rule would normally allow the DBMS to execute the DELETE statement successfully by setting the OFFICE column in the child rows to NULL and skipping the referential integrity check on the partially NULL FOREIGN KEY values created. However, the MATCH FULL clause tells the DBMS it cannot create partially NULL FOREIGN KEY values.

If you want to allow the DBMS to create partially NULL FOREIGN KEY values only if the non-NULL value(s) in each FOREIGN KEY column matches a value in the corresponding column of one of the rows in the parent table, include the MATCH PARTIAL clause in the FOREIGN KEY definition. For example, if you change the definition of the FOREIGN KEY in the INVOICES table to

```
CONSTRAINT fk_customers_invoices
  FOREIGN KEY (cust_ID, office)
  REFERENCES customers (cust_ID, office)
  MATCH PARTIAL ON DELETE SET NULL ON UPDATE SET NULL)
```

the MATCH PARTIAL clause tells the DBMS that it can successfully execute the DELETE statement

```
DELETE FROM customers WHERE cust_ID = 1 AND office = 5
```

by following the ON DELETE SET NULL rule to set the OFFICE column of the FOREIGN KEY in the INVOICES table to NULL while leaving the NOT NULL constrained CUST_ID column with a value of 1, so long as at least one row in the CUSTOMERS table has a value of 1 in its CUST_ID column.

191 Using the NOT NULL Column Constraint to Prevent NULL Values in a Column

As you know, a NULL value in a column indicates that the actual value of the column is either unknown or missing. Rule 3 of Codd's 12-rule relational database definition requires that NULL is included in the domain (range of valid values) for every data type. However, there are occasions when you want to prevent users from entering a NULL into certain columns in a table. By adding the NULL constraint to a column's definition, you can tell the DBMS to abort any INSERT or UPDATE statement that attempts to put NULL into the column. (A NULL constraint in a FOREIGN KEY column also prevents the DBMS from changing the column's value to NULL if it must apply the ON DELETE SET NULL rule or ON

UPDATE SET NULL rule when executing a DELETE or UPDATE statement that violates referential integrity).

To place a NOT NULL constraint on a column when creating a new table, simply add the constraint after the column's data type. For example, the CREATE TABLE statement

```
CREATE TABLE customer
  (cust_ID     INTEGER NOT NULL,
   first_name VARCHAR(30),
   last_name  VARCHAR(30) NOT NULL,
   address    VARCHAR(50) NOT NULL)
```

creates a CUSTOMER table in which the DBMS will not allow a user to put a NULL into the CUST_ID, LAST_NAME, or ADDRESS columns. As such, the INSERT statement

```
INSERT INTO customer VALUES (0,'','','')
```

will execute successfully—remember that neither the value 0 nor a zero-length string is NULL. However, the INSERT statement

```
INSERT INTO customer
VALUES (1,'Konrad',NULL,'765 E. Eldorado Lane')
```

will fail with an error message similar to

```
Server: Msg 515, Level 16, State 2, Line 1
Cannot insert the value NULL into column 'last_name', table
  'SQLTips.dbo.customer'; column does not allow nulls.
  INSERT fails.
The statement has been terminated.
```

because the INSERT statement attempts to add a row with a NULL in the LAST_NAME column—which is constrained and has a NOT NULL in the table definition. Similarly, the DBMS will abort an UPDATE statement such as

```
UPDATE customer SET address = NULL WHERE cust_ID = 0
```

because it attempts to put a NULL into a NOT NULL constrained column of an existing row in the table.

Some DBMS products allow you to specify the NOT NULL constraint for a column only when you first create a table. MS-SQL Server, however, lets you use the ALTER TABLE statement to add the NOT NULL constraint to a column in an existing table—even if the table has data. For example, the ALTER TABLE statement

```
ALTER TABLE customer
ALTER COLUMN first_name VARCHAR(30) NOT NULL
```

will add the NOT NULL constraint to the FIRST_NAME column of the CUSTOMER table. If any of the existing rows in the CUSTOMER table have a NULL in the FIRST_NAME column, the ALTER TABLE statement will abort with an error message similar to the one the DBMS displayed when the INSERT statement tried to add a row with a NULL value for a column constrained as NOT NULL. To get around this problem, change the NULL values in the column to a non-NULL value with an UPDATE statement such as

```
UPDATE customer SET first_name = ''
WHERE first_name IS NULL
```

and then execute the ALTER TABLE statement again.

192 Using the UNIQUE Column Constraint to Prevent Duplicate Values in a Column

As you learned in Tip 172, "Using the PRIMARY KEY Column Constraint to Uniquely Identify Rows in a Table," you can use a PRIMARY KEY constraint to tell the DBMS to force the value in a column to be different (unique) for every row in a table. Unfortunately, a table can have only one PRIMARY KEY, and you may want more than one column to contain a unique value in every row.

Suppose, for example, that every employee must have a unique ID (for identification purposes) and that your security officer requires each employee to have a unique password as well. You can create a table with multiple UNIQUE column constraints using a CREATE TABLE statement similar to:

```
CREATE TABLE employees
  (ID       INTEGER PRIMARY KEY,
   name     VARCHAR(30),
   SSAN     INTEGER UNIQUE,
   password VARCHAR(15) UNIQUE)
```

In the current example, the PRIMARY KEY constraint specifies that the ID column must contain unique, non-NULL values. Moreover, the UNIQUE constraints on the SSAN and password columns tell the DBMS to prevent the entry of duplicate values in to these columns as well.

```
INSERT into employees
VALUES (1, 'Konrad King', 123456789, 'SECRET')
```

will succeed as long as no existing row in the EMPLOYEES table has an ID of 1 or an SSAN with the value 123456789 or a PASSWORD of SECRET. If an INSERT statement attempts to add a duplicate value to any one or more of the table's UNIQUE columns, the DBMS will abort the error message with:

```
Server: Msg 2627, Level 14, State 2, Line 1
Violation of UNIQUE KEY constraint 'UQ_employees_1D4655FB'.
  cannot insert duplicate key in object 'employees'.
The statement has been terminated.
```

The DBMS also enforces the UNIQUE constraint when executing an UPDATE statement. For example, the UPDATE statement

```
UPDATE employees SET password = 'NEW PASSWORD' WHERE ID = 1
```

will execute successfully only if no rows in the EMPLOYEES table have the value NEW PASSWORD in the PASSWORD column. Otherwise, the DBMS will abort the UPDATE statement with an error message similar to that shown when attempting to INSERT a row with a duplicate value in a UNIQUE column.

Note: *There is an important difference between a column defined with the PRIMARY KEY constraint and a column constrained as UNIQUE. The DBMS will allow the insertion of a single NULL value into a UNIQUE column. Conversely, no NULL values are allowed in a PRIMARY KEY column.*

---

193 Using the CHECK Constraint to Validate a Column's Value

A CHECK constraint is a tool you can use to limit the domain (or valid range of values), for one or more columns in a table, to a subset of the full range of values allowed for the data type. Each CHECK constraint consists of the word *CHECK* followed by a search condition that the DBMS evaluates each time a DELETE, INSERT, or UPDATE statement changes the contents of the table. If the search condition evaluates to TRUE after the modification, the DBMS allows the change; if the search condition evaluates to FALSE, the system undoes the work performed and returns an error.

The syntax of a CHECK constraint is:

```
[CONSTRAINT <constraint name>] CHECK (<search condition>)
```

Therefore, you can use the CHECK constraint in the CREATE TABLE statement

```
CREATE TABLE employees
  (ID             INTEGER PRIMARY KEY,
   name           VARCHAR(30) NOT NULL,
   SSAN           INTEGER UNIQUE NOT NULL,
   department     VARCHAR(15) CONSTRAINT valid_department
     CHECK (department IN ('MARKETING','SALES','ADMIN',
                           'EXECUTIVE','SERVICE',
                           'COLLECTIONS', 'WAREHOUSE')),
   hourly_rate    MONEY,
   monthly_salary MONEY,
   commission     MONEY)
```

to create an EMPLOYEES for which the DBMS will check the DEPARTMENT value supplied by an INSERT or UPDATE statement to make sure that it is one of those listed in the CHECK constraint's search condition. In the current example, the DBMS will add the row inserted with the INSERT statement

```
INSERT INTO employees VALUES
  (1,'Konrad King',123456789,'Executive',NULL,3000.00,NULL)
```

to the table but will reject the change attempted by the UPDATE statement

```
UPDATE employees SET department = 'MIS' WHERE ID = 1
```

and will display an error message similar to:

```
Server: Msg 547, Level 16, State 1, Line 1
UPDATE statement conflicted with COLUMN CHECK constraint
  'valid_department'. The conflict occurred in database
  'SQLTips', table 'employees'.
The statement has been terminated
```

In addition to checking to make sure the data in a single column falls within a range or is one of a discrete set of values, you can use a CHECK constraint to check the validity of data in multiple columns and even use the value in one column to define the domain for another column. For example, the CREATE TABLE statement

```
CREATE TABLE employees
  (ID             INTEGER PRIMARY KEY,
   name           VARCHAR(30) NOT NULL,
   SSAN           INTEGER UNIQUE NOT NULL,
   department     VARCHAR(15) CONSTRAINT valid_department
     CHECK (department IN ('MARKETING','SALES','ADMIN',
                           'EXECUTIVE','SERVICE',
                           'COLLECTIONS', 'WAREHOUSE')),
   hourly_rate    MONEY,
   monthly_salary MONEY,
   commission     MONEY,
CONSTRAINT valid_pay CHECK(
 (department IN ('MARKETING','SALES') AND
    (hourly_rate IS NULL) AND (monthly_salary IS NULL) AND
    (commission BETWEEN 100.00 and 500.00)) OR
 (department IN ('ADMIN','EXECUTIVE') AND
    (hourly_rate IS NULL) AND (monthly_salary BETWEEN
     1000.00 AND 10000.00) AND (commission IS NULL)) OR
 (department IN ('SERVICE','COLLECTIONS','WAREHOUSE') AND
    (hourly_rate BETWEEN 10.00 AND 45.00) AND
    (monthly_salary IS NULL) AND (COMMISSION IS NULL)))
```

tells the DBMS to make sure that EMPLOYEES table rows for:

- Employees in MARKETING and SALES are assigned a commission (per sale) between \$100.00 and \$500.00, and no monthly salary or hourly pay

- Employees in ADMIN and EXECUTIVE are assigned a monthly salary between $1,000.00 and $10,000.00, and no hourly pay or commissions
- Employees in SERVICE, COLLECTIONS, and WAREHOUSE receive an hourly rate between $10.00 and $45.00 and no monthly salary or commission

194 Using the MS-SQL Server Enterprise Manager to Bind a Rule to a Data Type or Column

As you learned in Tip 169, "Understanding MS-SQL Server Rules," a *rule* is an MS-SQL Server object you can use to specify the domain (or valid range of values) for a column or data type. MS-SQL Server uses rules as it does CHECK constraints. Each time an SQL statement puts a value in a column governed by a rule, the DBMS evaluates the rule's conditional expression. If the expression evaluates to TRUE, the DBMS allows the update; if the rule's conditional expression evaluates to FALSE, the MS-SQL Server undoes the work performed and reports an error.

Unlike a CHECK constraint, a rule is a database object and not a part of a table or column definition. As such, before the DBMS can apply the rule to check the validity of data being placed in a column, you must first bind the rule to the column or user-defined data type used to define the column. To bind a rule to a column or user-defined data type, you can either execute the stored procedure sp_bindrule (which you will learn about in Tip 593) or use the MS-SQL Server Enterprise Manager by performing the following steps:

1. Start the Enterprise Manager by clicking your mouse pointer on the Start button. When Windows displays the Start menu, move your mouse pointer to Programs, select Microsoft SQL Server 7.0, and then click your mouse pointer on Enterprise Manager.
2. To display the list of SQL servers, click your mouse pointer on the plus (+) to the left of SQL Server Group.
3. Find the SQL server that manages the database with the rule(s) you want to bind to table columns or data types, and click your mouse pointer on the plus (+) to the left of SQL server's icon. For example, if you want to work with a database managed by a server named NVBIZNET2, click your mouse pointer on the plus (+) to the left of the icon for NVBIZNET2. Enterprise Manager will display the list of databases managed by the server.
4. Click your mouse pointer on the plus (+) to the left of the icon of the database in which the rules are defined. For the current project, click your mouse pointer on the plus (+) to the left of the icon for the SQLTips database. The Enterprise Manager will display an icon for each class of objects in the database.

5. Click your mouse pointer on Rules in the expanded list of database objects. Enterprise Manager will use its right pane to display the list of rules defined in the database.
6. Double-click your mouse pointer on the rule you wish to bind. For the current project, double-click your mouse pointer on the VALIDATE_EMPNUM rule. Enterprise Manager will display a Rule Properties dialog box similar to that shown in Figure 194.1.

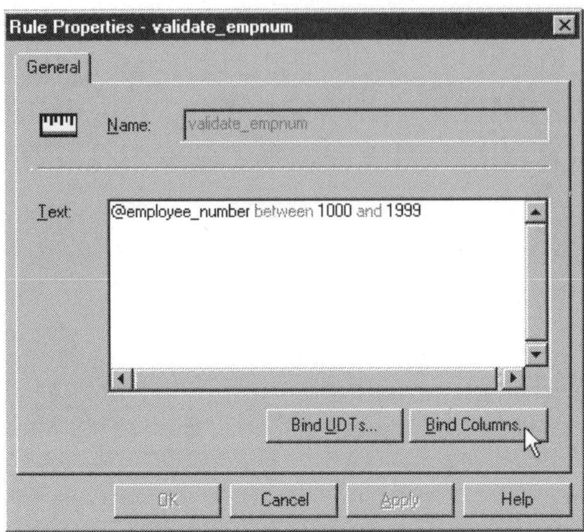

Figure 194.1 The Enterprise Manager Rule Properties dialog box

7. If you want to bind the rule you selected in Step 6 to a user-defined data type, continue at Step 11; otherwise, to bind the rule to a column, click your mouse pointer on the Bind Columns button. The Enterprise Manager will display a Bind Rule to Columns dialog box similar to that shown in Figure 194.2.
8. To select the table with the column(s) to which you wish to bind the rule, click your mouse pointer on the drop-down button to the right of the Table field in the dialog box. Then select the table you want from the drop-down list of database tables. For the current project, click your mouse pointer on [dbo].[employees] in the database list to select the EMPLOYEES table. Enterprise Manager will display the table columns not yet bound by a rule in the Unbound Columns box and the columns bound to a rule in the Bound Columns box.
9. To bind the rule to a column, look in the Unbound Columns box and click your mouse pointer on the name of the column you want to bind. Next, click your mouse pointer on the Add button. For the current project, click your mouse pointer on EMPLOYEE_ID in the Unbound columns box, and then click your mouse pointer on the Add button. Enterprise Manager will transfer the name of the column you selected from the Unbound Columns list to the Bound Columns list.
10. If you wish to bind the rule to additional columns, repeat Steps 8 and 9. When you are finished binding rules to table columns, click your mouse pointer on the OK button. The Enterprise Manager, in turn, will display the Rule Properties dialog box.

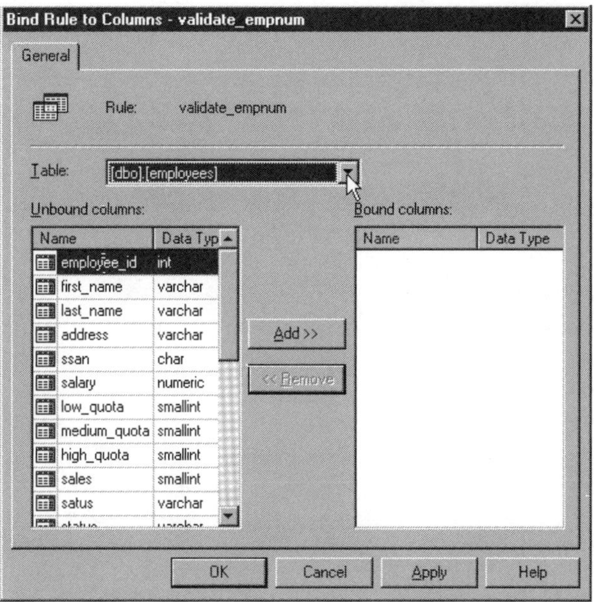

Figure 194.2 The Enterprise Manager Bind Rule to Columns dialog box

11. If you want to bind the rule to a user-defined data type, click your mouse pointer on the Bind UDTs button. The Enterprise Manager will display a Bind Rule to User-Defined Data Types dialog box similar to that shown in Figure 194.3. If you do not want to bind the rule to a user-defined data type, continue at Step 15.

12. To bind the rule to the data type, click your mouse pointer in the Bind check box of the row that lists the data type you want to bind. For the current project, bind the rule to the VALID_EMPNUMS data type by clicking your mouse pointer on the Bind check box to the right of the VALID_EMPNUMS data type until a check mark appears. If you want the rule to apply only to columns defined using the data type from this point on, click your mouse pointer on the Future Only check box; otherwise, clear the Future Only check box, and the DBMS will apply the rule to all columns created using the data type. For the current project, clear the Future Only check box.

13. If you want to bind the rule to additional user-defined data types, repeat Step 12 until you are done.

14. To exit the dialog box, click your mouse pointer on the OK button. Enterprise Manager will return to the Rule Properties dialog box.

15. To exit the Rule Properties dialog box and return to the Enterprise Manager window, click on the OK button.

Figure 194.3 The Enterprise Manager Bind Rule to User-Defined Data Types dialog box

MS-SQL Server lets you bind only a single rule to each column in a database table. You can, however, bind a rule and one or more CHECK constraints to the same column. Also, the DBMS will apply the rule only when making changes to the value in bound column (or to the columns defined using the data type to which the rule is bound). The DBMS does not check the existing values in a rule-bound column to make sure none of them violates the rule.

195 Using the Transact-SQL CREATE RULE Statement to Create an MS-SQL Server Rule

In Tip 169, "Understanding MS-SQL Server Rules," you learned that an MS-SQL Server rule lets you define the domain (the valid range of values) for a column or user-defined data type, and in Tip 194, "Using the MS-SQL Server Enterprise Manager to Bind a Rule to a Data Type or Column," you learned how to bind the rule to a column or user-defined data type. To create the rule itself, you can use either the Enterprise Manager or the Transact-SQL CREATE RULE statement.

The syntax of the CREATE RULE statement is:

```
CREATE RULE <rule name>

AS @<parameter> <conditional predicate>
```

Therefore, to create a rule that the value placed in a column is in the range 1000.00–10000.00, execute a CREATE RULE statement such as:

```
CREATE RULE validate_salary

AS @salary BETWEEN 1000.00 AND 10000.00
```

Or, to create a rule that tells the DBMS to make sure the value placed in a column is one of the values in a list of values, execute a CREATE RULE statement such as:

```
CREATE RULE validate_freshman_classes

AS @class IN ('English','History','Math','Science')
```

As you learned in Tip 169, the CREATE RULE statement creates a rule object only in the database. Before the DBMS will use the rule to check column values being changed or added, you must bind the rule to the column or its user-defined data type by using the Enterprise Manager (as you learned in Tip 194) or by executing the stored procedure sp_bindrule.

The syntax for executing sp_bindrule is:

```
EXEC '<rule name>',
   '<table name>.<column name>',['FUTUREONLY']
```

Thus, to bind the VALIDATE_SALARY rule to the MONTHLY_SALARY column of an EMPLOYEES table, you would enter the Transact-SQL statement:

```
EXEC sp_bindrule
   'validate_salary','employees.monthly_salary'
```

196 Using the MS-SQL Server Enterprise Manager Rule Properties Screen to Change a Rule

As you learned in Tip 169, "Understanding MS-SQL Server Rules," and Tips 193–195, MS-SQL Server rules and SQL CHECK constraints let the DBMS perform validity tests on values a user or application tries to place into a column in a table row. While a CHECK constraint exists as only one of the elements in the definition of a table, each MS-SQL Server rule is a separate database object and not part of a column or user-defined data type definition. Consequently, clauses in CREATE TABLE and ALTER TABLE statements manage CHECK constraints, and MS-SQL Server provides a set of stored procedures and the Enterprise Manager to manage rules, as it does other database objects.

To use the MS-SQL Server Enterprise Manager to work with a rule's properties, perform the following steps:

1. Start the Enterprise Manager by clicking your mouse pointer on the Windows Start button. After Windows displays the Start menu, move your mouse pointer to Programs, select Microsoft SQL Server 7.0, and then click your mouse pointer on Enterprise Manager.
2. To display the list of SQL servers, click your mouse pointer on the plus (+) to the left of SQL Server Group.
3. Find the SQL Server that manages the database with the rule(s) you want to change, and click your mouse pointer on the plus (+) to the left of the SQL server's icon. For example, if you want to work with a database managed by a server named NVBIZNET2, click your mouse pointer on the plus (+) to the left of the icon for NVBIZNET2. Enterprise Manager will display the list of databases managed by the server.
4. Click your mouse pointer on the plus (+) to the left of the icon of the database in which the rules you want to change are defined. For the current project, click your mouse pointer on the plus (+) to the left of the icon for the SQLTips database. The Enterprise Manager will display an icon for each class of objects in the database.
5. Click your mouse pointer on Rules in the expanded list of database objects. Enterprise Manager will use its right pane to display the list of rules defined in the database.
6. To work with a rule's properties, right-click your mouse pointer on the name of the rule (or its icon). For the current project, right-click your mouse pointer on the rule VALIDATE_FRESHMAN_CLASSES. Enterprise Manager will display a Rule properties dialog box similar to that shown in Figure 196.1.
7. To change the range of values a rule allows the DBMS to put into a column, modify the rule's search condition in the Text field of the Rule Properties dialog box. For the current project, assume that freshman class titles now include a –101 suffix and that an engineering course has been added to the curriculum. As such, replace the contents of the Text box with: **@class(English-101,'History-101','Math-101','Science-101','Engineering-101')**.
8. Click your mouse pointer on the OK button. Enterprise manager will store the new rule definition and close the Rule Properties dialog box.

One of the main advantages of using a rule over using a CHECK constraint is that while a CHECK constraint can validate updates to only a single column, each rule can validate data being put into multiple columns in one or more tables. As such, if the same CHECK constraint is used in several tables, you must execute an ALTER TABLE statement on each of them to reflect a domain change (such as the one in Step 7 of the preceding procedure). Conversely, if you bind a single rule to multiple columns (either directly or indirectly by binding the rule to the user-defined data type used to define a column), a single change to the rule's search condition (as you performed in Step 7) will alter the validity test for updates to all of the columns bound by the rule.

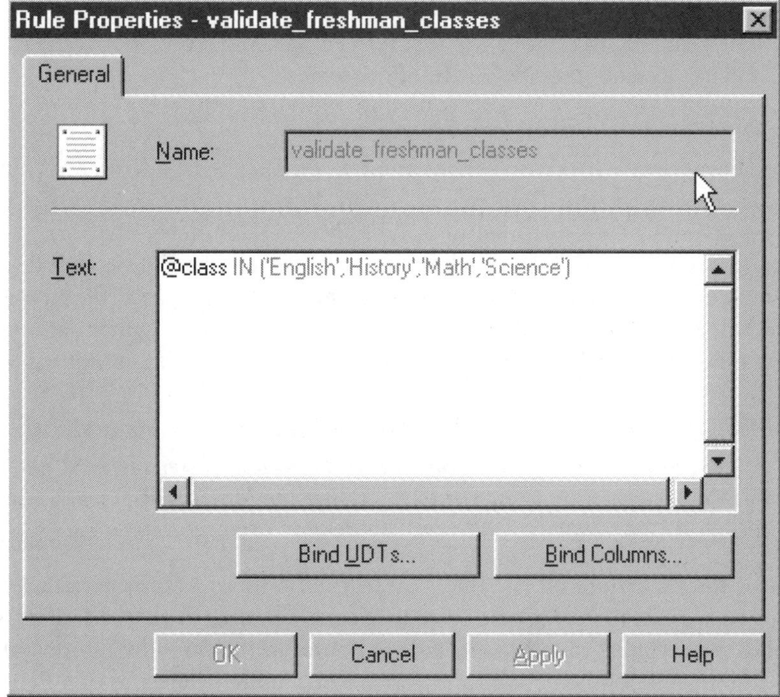

Figure 196.1 The Enterprise Manager Rule Properties dialog box

197 Using the Transact-SQL DROP RULE Statement to Permanently Remove a Rule from a Database

While they perform the same basic function, MS-SQL Server rules, unlike SQL CHECK constraints, exist as separate database objects. Because each CHECK constraint is part of a table's definition, you use the ALTER TABLE statement with a DROP <constraint> clause statement to remove a CHECK constraint. Conversely, because a rule is a database object in its own right, you use a DROP statement to delete a rule—just as you would to remove any other object form the database.

The syntax of the DROP RULE statement is:

```
DROP RULE <rule name> [,...<last rule name>]
```

As such, you can use a single DROP RULE statement to remove one or more rules from the database. For example, to remove the VALIDATE_GRADES and VALIDATE_SALARY rules from a database, execute the DROP RULE statement:

```
DROP RULE validate_grades, validate_salary
```

Before you can delete a database rule, you must *unbind* the rule from the column(s) or user-defined data type(s) to which the rule is bound. If you attempt to DROP a rule that is still bound to a column or user-defined data type, MS-SQL Server will abort the DROP RULE statement with an error. Unfortunately, the error message the DBMS will display as a result of the error condition will not tell you the columns or user-defined data types to which the rule is bound. As such, you must refer to your data dictionary, which, among other things, should list all database objects and dependencies (including rule bindings).

Note: *If the data dictionary is not available or is out-of-date, you can also use the Enterprise Manager's Bind Rule to Columns and Bind Rule to User-Defined Data types screens (which you learned about in Tip 194, "Using the MS-SQL Enterprise Manager to Bind a Rule to a Data Type or Column") to display (and remove) a rule's bindings.*

In Step 8 of the procedure in Tip 194, you learned how to select the table with the column to which you were binding the rule. If you select each table in turn, the Enterprise Manager will display the columns to which the rule is bound in the Bound Columns field of the Bind Rule to Columns dialog box each time you select a table where the rule is bound to one or more of the columns. To unbind the rule from the column(s), click your mouse pointer on the column name in the Bound Columns field and then on the Remove button. If you unbind the rule from a column, be sure to click your mouse button on the Apply button before moving on to the next table.

Similarly, when you perform Step 11 of the procedure in Tip 194, Enterprise Manager will use the Bind Rule to User-Defined Data Types screen to list all user-defined data types. Each user-defined data type to which the rule is bound will have a check mark in its Bind check box. To unbind the rule from the data type, simply clear the check box by clicking your mouse pointer on the check box until the check mark disappears. Be sure to click your mouse pointer on the OK button (vs. the Cancel button) to exit the screen if you clear any Bind check boxes.

198 Using the MS-SQL Server Enterprise Manager to List and Edit Views

A view is a *virtual* table. Although it has the look and feel of a "real" table and can be used in most SQL statements wherever a table reference is allowed, a view has no rows and columns of data of its own. Instead, a view consists of a SELECT statement that extracts and displays data from columns and rows in other tables (or views). Although not a "real" table, a view is, however, a "real" database object that exists apart from the tables on which the view is based.

To use MS-SQL Server Enterprise Manager to list and edit views, perform the following steps:

1. Start the Enterprise Manager by clicking your mouse pointer on the Windows Start button. After Windows displays the Start menu, move your mouse pointer to Programs, select Microsoft SQL Server 7.0, and then click your mouse pointer on Enterprise Manager.
2. To display the list of SQL Servers, click your mouse pointer on the plus (+) to the left of SQL Server Group.
3. Find the SQL Server that manages the database with the views on which you wish to work, and click your mouse pointer on the plus (+) to the left of the SQL Server's icon. For example, if you want to work with a database managed by a server named NVBIZNET2, click your mouse pointer on the plus (+) to the left of the icon for NVBIZNET2. Enterprise Manager will display the list of databases managed by the server.
4. Click your mouse pointer on the plus (+) to the left of the icon of the database that contains the views you want. For the current project, click your mouse pointer on the plus (+) to the left of the icon for the SQLTips database. The Enterprise Manager will display an icon for each class of objects in the database.
5. Click your mouse pointer on Views in the expanded list of database objects. Enterprise Manager will display a list of the database's views in its right pane.
6. To work with a view, double-click your mouse pointer on the view's name (in the Enterprise Manager's right pane). For the current project double-click your mouse pointer on the view: name: CONSTRAINT_COLUMN_USAGE. Enterprise Manager will display the View Properties dialog box shown in Figure 198.1.
7. To change the data displayed by the view you selected in Step 6, edit the contents of the Text field in the lower half of the View Properties dialog box. Be sure to click your mouse pointer on the Check Syntax button to have Enterprise Manager check the syntax of the views before you save the view's new definition to disk by clicking your mouse pointer on the View Properties dialog box OK button.
8. To specify the access privileges user IDs and roles have on the view, click your mouse pointer on the PERMISSIONS button near the top right-hand corner of the dialog box. Enterprise Manager will list the database user IDs and roles along with check boxes showing the privileges each one has on the view, similar to that shown in Figure 198.2.

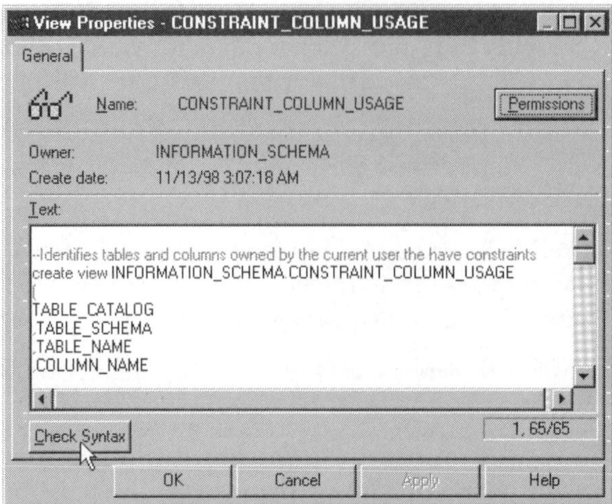

Figure 198.1 The Enterprise Manager View Properties dialog box

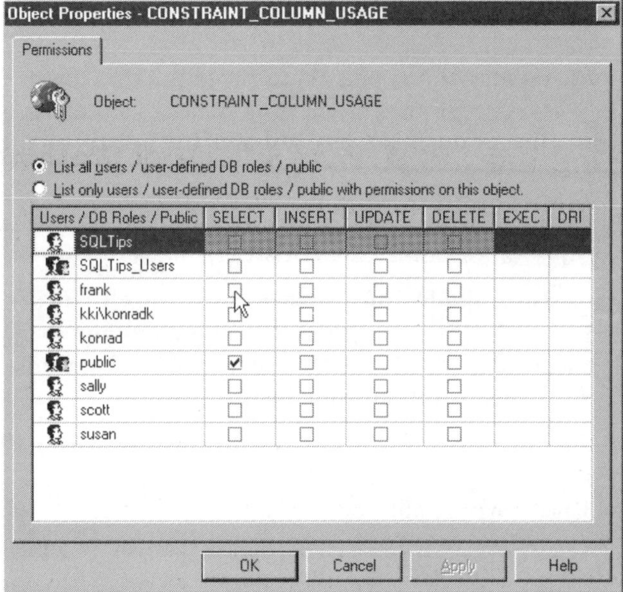

Figure 198.2 The Enterprise Manager Object Properties screen

9. To give a user ID or role the privileges, click your mouse pointer on the check box for the privilege in the row of the user ID or role to which you wish to GRANT the privilege. For example, to GRANT SELECT privilege to user ID FRANK, you click your mouse pointer on the check box in the SELECT column of the FRANK row until the check mark appears.

10. Similarly, to REVOKE a privilege on the view, clear the contents of the check box of the privilege you want to REVOKE in the row of the user ID or role that is no longer to have the privilege.
11. After you finish granting and revoking privileges on the view, click your mouse pointer on the OK button. Enterprise Manager will update the system privilege tables and return to the View Properties dialog box.
12. To save changes you made to the view and return to the Enterprise Manger application window, click your mouse pointer on the OK button near the bottom left corner of the View Properties dialog box.

In addition to the Enterprise Manager, you can also use SQL statements to change a view and the permissions user IDs and roles have on it. While the GRANT and REVOKE statements are as convenient to use as Enterprise Manager for assigning privileges on the view, the ALTER VIEW statement requires that you retype the entire definition of the view—even if you want to modify only a portion of the view. Enterprise Manager, on the other hand, lets you edit just the parts of the view's definition that you want to change. As such, Enterprise Manager is clearly the best choice when you want to make a small change to a long view definition.

199 Using the CREATE ASSERTION Statement to Create Multi-table Constraints

CHECK constraints and MS-SQL Server rules limit the values an SQL statement can place into a column in a table. An *assertion*, meanwhile, places a limit (a restriction) on the values the DBMS can store in the database as a whole.

CHECK constraints, when present, are included in table definitions. Rules, though separate from database objects, must be bound to specific table columns or user-defined data types before the DBMS will use them to validate the actions of UPDATE and INSERT statements.

An assertion, like a rule, is a separate database object. However, unlike a rule, it is not bound to a specific data type or column. Instead, the DBMS is required to evaluate the search condition in an assertion any time there is an attempt to change the contents of any one of the tables used in the assertion's CHECK clause.

For example, given the syntax of the CREATE ASSERTION statement

```
CREATE ASSERTION <assertion name>
CHECK (<search condition>)
```

you would create an assertion to make sure the sum of all outstanding orders for a product does not exceed the quantity of the item in inventory by executing the CREATE ASSERT statement:

```
CREATE ASSERTION item_in_stock
CHECK((orders.item_number = inventory.item_number) AND
      (SUM (orders.qty) <= inventory.qty_on_hand))
```

After you add the ITEM_IN_STOCK assertion to the database definition (by executing the CREATE ASSERTION statement in the current example), the DBMS is required to evaluate the search condition in the assertion whenever an SQL statement attempts to change either the ORDERS or the INVENTORY table. If the update causes the assertion to evaluate to FALSE, the DBMS undoes the work performed, raises an error, and displays an error message indicating that the statement could not be executed due to the violation of the assertion.

Note: *Although included in the SQL-92 specification, most database products do not support assertions. Therefore, be sure to check your system manual for the CREATE ASSERTION statement before you include assertions in your database design.*

---

200 Understanding Database Normalization

In general, database normalization involves splitting tables with columns that have different types of data (and perhaps even unrelated data) into multiple tables, each with fewer columns that describe the attributes of a single concept or physical object or being. The goal of normalization is to prevent the problems (called modification anomalies) that plague a poorly designed relation (table). Suppose, for example, that you have a table with resort guest ID numbers, activities the guests have signed up to do, and the cost of each activity—all together in the following GUEST_ACTIVITY_COST table:

```
guest_ID  activity          cost
--------  ----------------  ------
2587      Scuba Diving      250.00
2564      Deep Sea Fishing  750.00
4589      Massage Therapy   150.00
1247      Golf              225.00
1269      Aromatherapy      75.00
```

Each row in the table represents a guest that has signed up for the named activity and paid the specified cost. Assuming that the cost depends only on the activity—that is, a specific activity costs the same for all guests—if you delete the row for GUEST_ID 2587, you lose not only the fact that guest 2587 signed up for scuba diving, but also the fact that scuba diving costs $250.00 per outing. This is called a *deletion anomaly*—when you delete a row, you lose more information than you intended to remove. In the current example, a single deletion resulted in the loss of information on two entities—what activity a guest signed up to do and how much a particular activity costs.

Now, suppose the resort adds a new activity such as horseback riding. You cannot enter the activity name (horseback riding) or cost ($190.00) into the table until a guest decides to sign up for it. The unnecessary restriction of having to wait until someone signs up for an activity before you can record its name and cost is called an *insertion anomaly*.

In the current example, each insertion adds facts about two entities. Therefore, you cannot INSERT a fact about one entity until you have an additional fact about the other entity. Conversely, each deletion removes facts about two entities. Thus, you cannot DELETE the information about one entity while leaving the information about the other in the table.

You can eliminate modification anomalies through normalization—that is, splitting the single table with rows that have attributes about two entities into two tables, each of which has rows with attributes that describe a single entity. For example, by splitting the GUEST_ACTIVITY_COST table in the current example into a GUEST_ACTIVITY table

```
guest_ID  activity
--------  ----------------
2587      Scuba Diving
2564      Deep Sea Fishing
4589      Massage Therapy
1247      Golf
1269      Aromatherapy
```

and an ACTIVITY_COST table

```
activity          cost
----------------  ------
Scuba Diving      250.00
Deep Sea Fishing  750.00
Massage Therapy   150.00
Golf              225.00
Aromatherapy       75.00
```

you will be able to remove the aromatherapy appointment for guest 1269 without losing the fact that an aromatherapy session costs $75.00. Similarly, you can now add the fact that horseback riding costs $190.00 per day to the ACTIVITY_COST table without having to wait for a guest to sign up for the activity.

During the development of relational database systems in the 1970s, relational theorists kept discovering new modification anomalies. Someone would find an anomaly, classify it, and then figure out a way to prevent it by adding additional design criteria to the definition of a "well-formed" relation. These design criteria are known as *normal forms*. Not surprisingly E. F. Codd (of the 12-rule database definition fame), defined the first, second, and third normal forms (1NF, 2NF, and 3NF). (Tips 201–203 discuss 1NF, 2NF, and 3NF.)

After Codd postulated 3NF, relational theorists formulated Boyce-Codd normal form (BCNF) and then fourth normal form (4NF) and fifth normal form (5NF). However, all normal forms had a serious flaw—no theory (or theorist) could guarantee that any of the normal forms could eliminate all modification anomalies. The nagging feeling that there would be seventh, eighth, and ninth (and so on) normal forms as people discovered and figured out criteria to prevent new anomalies lasted until 1981, when Ronald Fagin defined *domain/key* normal form (DK/NF) and proved it to be free of all modification anomalies.

Since a relation (a relational table) in DK/NF is guaranteed to exhibit no modification anomalies, finding ways to put all database relations in DK/NF is *the* design goal. Unfortunately, unlike 1NF, 2NF, and 3NF, there are no software design tools that will (or can) split a relational table into relations that are in domain/key normal form. Moreover, there is no guarantee that *every* relation can even be put into DK/NF. As a result, while a database with all tables (relations) in DK/NF is theoretically possible, most designers strive for 3NF, which removes most anomalies and thus provides a high degree of integrity.

201 Understanding First Normal Form (1NF)

In Tip 200, "Understanding Database Normalization," you learned that normalization is a processes by which database designers attempt to eliminate modification anomalies such as the:

- **Deletion anomaly.** The inability to remove a single fact from a table without removing other (unrelated) facts you want to keep.
- **Insertion anomaly.** The inability to insert one fact without inserting another (and sometimes, unrelated) fact.
- **Update anomaly.** Changing a fact in one column creates a false fact in another set of columns.

Modification anomalies are a result of functional dependencies among the columns in a row (or tuple, to use the precise relational database term). A functional dependency means that if you know the value in one column or set of columns, you can always determine the value of another. For example, given the data in the table

```
CLASS SECTION TEACHER  DEPARTMENT STUDENTS
----- ------- -------- ---------- --------------
H100  1       Smith    HISTORY    1005,2110,3115
CS100 1       Bowls    COMP-SCI   4001,4515,8978
M200  3       Rawlins  MATH       2002,4587,2358
```

if you know the CLASS and SECTION, you know the TEACHER. Similarly, if you know the TEACHER, you know the DEPARTMENT. Thus, the value in the TEACHER column is functionally dependant on the combination of the values in the CLASS and SECTION columns. Also, the value in the DEPARTMENT column is functionally dependent on the value in the TEACHER column.

In addition to the single-value functional dependencies where A determines B or A + B determines C, the preceding table also exhibits a multi-valued dependency in which the value of one attribute (column) determines the values in a set of another attribute (column). In the current example, the value of TEACHER determines the list of students (in the STUDENTS column).

First normal form (1NF), the most basic form for relational tables, requires that the table has no duplicate rows and that none of the rows has repeating groups. This means that every row must have a unique value in at least one of its columns, and each column of a row must have an *atomic* (scalar) value. As such, the table in the current example is not in 1NF because the value in the STUDENTS column is a repeating group—it consists of a list of values and not a single valued (*atomic*) value.

To put the table in first normal form (1NF), you could break up the student number list in the STUDENTS column of each row such that each row had only one of the student IDs in the STUDENTS column. Doing so would change the table's structure and rows to:

```
CLASS SECTION TEACHER  DEPARTMENT STUDENT
----- ------- -------- ---------- -------
H100  1       Smith    HISTORY    1005
H100  1       Smith    HISTORY    2110
H100  1       Smith    HISTORY    3115
CS100 1       Bowls    COMP-SCI   4001
CS100 1       Bowls    COMP-SCI   4515
CS100 1       Bowls    COMP-SCI   8978
M200  3       Rawlins  MATH       2002
M200  3       Rawlins  MATH       4587
M200  3       Rawlins  MATH       2358
```

The value given by the combination (CLASS,SECTION,STUDENT) is the *composite key* for the table because it makes each row unique and all columns atomic. Now that each the table in the current example is in 1NF; each column has a single, scalar value. Unfortunately, the table still exhibits modification anomalies:

- **Deletion anomaly.** If professor SMITH goes to another school and you remove his rows from the table, you also lose the fact that STUDENTs 1005, 2110, and 3115 are enrolled in a history class.
- **Insertion anomaly.** If the school wants to add an English class (E100), it cannot do so until a student signs up for the course. (Remember, no part of a primary key can have a NULL value.)
- **Update anomaly.** If STUDENT 4587 decides to sign up for the SECTION 1, CS100 CLASS instead of his math class, updating the CLASS and SECTION columns in the row for STUDENT 4587 to reflect the change will cause the table to show TEACHER RAWLINS as being in both the MATH and the COMP-SCI departments.

Thus, "flattening" a table's columns to put it into first normal form (1NF) does not solve any of the modification anomalies. All it does is guarantee that the table satisfies the requirements for a table defined as "relational" and that there are no multi-valued dependencies between the columns in each row.

202 Understanding Second Normal Form (2NF)

As you learned in Tip 200, "Understanding Database Normalization," and 201, "Understanding First Normal Form (1NF)," the process of normalization involves removing functional dependencies between columns in order to eliminate the modification anomalies caused by these dependencies. In Tip 201, you learned that putting a table in first normal form (1NF) requires removing all multi-valued dependencies. When a table is in second normal form, it must be in first normal form (no multi-valued dependencies) and have no *partial key* dependencies.

A partial key dependency is a situation in which the value in part of a key can be used to determine the value of another attribute (column). Thus, a table is in 2NF when the value in all nonkey columns depends on the entire key. Or, said another way, you cannot determine the value of any of the columns by using part of the key.

Suppose, for example, that you have the data in the table

```
CLASS SECTION TEACHER  DEPARTMENT  STUDENT MAJOR
----- ------- -------  ----------- ------- -----------
H100  1       Smith    HISTORY     1005    ENGLISH
H100  2       Riley    HISTORY     2110    ENGLISH
H100  1       Smith    HISTORY     2358    MATH
CS100 1       Bowls    COMP-SCI    4001    COMP-SCI
CS100 1       Bowls    COMP-SCI    2110    ENGLISH
CS100 1       Bowls    COMP-SCI    8978    ENGINEERING
M200  3       Rawlins  MATH        4001    COMP-SCI
M200  2       Brown    MATH        2110    ENGLISH
M200  4       Riley    MATH        2358    MATH
E100  1       Jones    ENGINEERING 8978    ENGINEERING
```

with (CLASS,SECTION,STUDENT) as its primary key. If the university has two rules about taking classes—no student can sign up for more than one section of the same class, and a student can have only one major—then the table, while in 1NF, is not in 2NF.

Given the value of (STUDENT,COURSE) you can determine the value of the SECTION, since no student can sign up for two sections of the same course. Similarly, since students can sign up for only one major, knowing STUDENT determines the value of MAJOR. In both instances, the value of a third column can be deduced (or is determined) by the value in a portion of the key (CLASS,SECTION,STUDENT) that makes each row unique.

To put the table in the current example in 2NF will require that it be split into three tables described by:

```
courses (class, section, teacher, department)
PRIMARY KEY (class,section)

enrollment (student, class, section)
```

```
PRIMARY KEY (student, class)

students (student, major)
PRIMARY KEY (student)
```

Unfortunately, putting a table in 2NF does not eliminate modification anomalies. Suppose, for example, that professor Jones leaves the university. Removing his row from the COURSES table would eliminate the entire ENGINEERING department, since he is currently the only professor in the department. Similarly, if the university wants to add a music department, it cannot do so until it hires a professor to teach in the department.

203 Understanding Third Normal Form (3NF)

To be in third normal form (3NF) a table must satisfy the requirements for 1NF (no multivalued dependencies) and 2NF (all nonkey attributes must depend on the entire key). In addition, a table in 3NF has no *transitive* dependencies between nonkey columns.

Given a table with columns (A, B, C), a transitive dependency is one in which A determines B, and B determines C, therefore, A determines C. Or, expressed using relational theory notation: If A→B and B→C then A→C.

When a table is in 3NF, the value in every nonkey column of the table can be determined by using the entire key and only the entire key. Therefore, given a table in 3NF with columns (A, B, C), if A is the PRIMARY KEY, you could not use the value of B (a nonkey column) to determine the value of C (another nonkey column). As such, A determines B (A→B), and A determines C (→C). However, knowing the value of column B does not tell you the value in column C—that is, it is *not* the case that B→C.

Suppose, for example, that you have a COURSES table with columns and PRIMARY KEY described by

```
courses (class, section, teacher, department, dept_head)
PRIMARY KEY (class,section)
```

that contains the data:

```
(<---- A ---->)   (B)        (C)          (D)
 CLASS SECTION  TEACHER  DEPARTMENT  DEPT_HEAD
 ----- -------  -------  ----------- ---------
 H100   1       Smith    HISTORY     SMITH
 H100   2       Riley    HISTORY     SMITH
 CS100  1       Bowls    COMP-SCI    PEROIT
 M200   3       Rawlins  MATH        HASTINGS
 M200   2       Brown    MATH        HASTINGS
 M200   4       Riley    MATH        HASTINGS
 E100   1       Jones    ENGINEERING JONES
```

Given that a TEACHER can be assigned to only one DEPARTMENT and that a DEPARTMENT can have only one department head, the table has multiple transitive dependencies.

For example, the value of TEACHER is dependant on the PRIMARY KEY (CLASS,SECTION), since a particular SECTION of a particular CLASS can have only one teacher—that is, A→B. Moreover, since a TEACHER can be in only one DEPARTMENT, the value in DEPARTMENT is dependant on the value in TEACHER—that is, B→C. However, since the PRIMARY KEY (CLASS,SECTION) determines the value of TEACHER, it also determines the value of DEPARTMENT—that is, A→C. Thus, the table exhibits the transitive dependency in which A→B and B→C, therefore A→C.

The problem with a transitive dependency is that it makes the table subject to the deletion anomaly. When Smith retires and we remove his row from the table, we lose not only the fact that Smith taught SECTION 1 of H100, but also the fact that SECTION 1 of H100 was a class that belonged to the HISTORY department.

To put a table with transitive dependencies between nonkey columns into 3NF requires that the table be split into multiple tables. To do so for the table in the current example, we would need split it into tables described by:

```
courses (class, section, teacher)
PRIMARY KEY (class,section)
teachers (teacher, department)

PRIMARY KEY (teacher)
departments (department, dept_head)
PRIMARY KEY (department)
```

204 Denormalizing a Database to Improve Performance

From Tips 201–203 you learned that the process of normalization involves changing the structure of a table (sometimes by splitting it into more than one table) in order to eliminate functional dependencies between pairs of its nonkey columns. You also learned that the goal of normalization is to eliminate modification anomalies.

Unfortunately, splitting a table into two or more tables has a downside—if you need a "complete" picture in answer to a query, the DBMS must perform a multi-table join, which is very expensive in terms of time and memory resources. As such, if you have several normalized tables with related historical information, you should considering combining them into one denormalized table. After all, if it is purely historical information, it is not subject to change and therefore is not subject to modification anomalies—even in its denormalized state.

Suppose, for example, that you have historical data in tables created by:

```
CREATE TABLE customers
  (cust_id     INTEGER,
   name        VARCHAR(30),
   address     VARCHAR(50),
   salesrep_ID INTEGER)

CREATE TABLE invoices
  (invoice_no    INTEGER,
   invoice_date DATETIME,
   date_shipped DATETIME)

CREATE TABLE invoice_detail
  (invoice_no  INTEGER,
   item_number INTEGER,
   price        MONEY)

CREATE TABLE item_master
  (item_number INTEGER,
   description VARCHAR(30),
   cost        MONEY)

CREATE TABLE employees
  (salesrep_ID INTEGER,
   name        VARCHAR(30),
   SSAN        CHAR(11),
   OFFICE      SMALLINT)
```

Each time you want a list of customer orders complete with customer name, address, salesperson name, and invoice detail including a one-line description of each item on each invoice, the DBMS must perform a multi-table join of all of the data in five tables. If the tables are large (have many rows) and you often produce individual customer reports, you will end up wasting a significant amount of processor time by performing the same joins over and over again.

Denormalizing the database into a single table created by

```
CREATE TABLE customer_histories
  (cust_id          INTEGER,
   name             VARCHAR(30),
   address          VARCHAR(50),
   salesrep_name    VARCHAR(30),
   salesrep_office  SMALLINT,
   invoice_number   INTEGER,
   invoice_date     DATETIME,
   date_shipped     DATETIME,
   item_number      INTEGER,
   item_description VARCHAR(30),
   item_cost        MONEY,
   item_price       MONEY)
```

will let the DBMS perform a single table search whether printing a complete list of a customer's orders including the salesman, a description of the product, the price paid and the actual item cost, or printing the detail of orders by salesperson and office number.

205 Using a SELECT Statement with a FROM Clause for Multi-table Selections

In Tip 85, "Understanding What to Expect from a SELECT Statement," you learned that a SELECT statement tells the DBMS to display the values stored in the rows and columns of a table. For example, to display the values in all columns of all rows in a table, you would use a SELECT statement in the form:

```
SELECT * FROM <table name>
```

To display only the data from certain columns and rows within a table, you would execute a SELECT statement with a column list and a WHERE clause in the form:

```
SELECT <column list> FROM <table name>
WHERE <search condition>
```

In addition to displaying information from a single table, you can use a SELECT statement to combine and display information from multiple tables. A multi-table SELECT statement, like a single-table SELECT statement, lets you list the columns you want to see in the SELECT clause and requires that you list the table(s) from which the DBMS is to extract the column values in the statement's FROM clause. However, while a single-table SELECT statement without a WHERE clause will display the selected column values for all rows in a table, a multi-table SELECT clause requires a WHERE clause to produce the same results.

When the DBMS is to extract data from two (or more) tables, you must include a WHERE clause with an equality conditional expression that tells the DBMS which rows in one table to match up with which rows in another table for each pair of tables listed in the SELECT statement's FROM clause. For example, given the tables created by

```
CREATE customers
  (cust_ID  INTEGER,
   name     VARCHAR(30),
   address  VARCHAR(50),
   salesrep INTEGER)

CREATE employees
  (salesrep_ID INTEGER,
   name        VARCHAR(30))
```

you must execute a SELECT statement such as

```
SELECT * FROM customers, employees
WHERE salesrep = salesrep_ID
```

to produce a results table with the name and ID of the customer's salesperson listed next to the information on each customer in the CUSTOMERS table.

After you tell the DBMS which rows from one table to combine with which rows from the other, you can include additional conditional expressions to specify exactly which rows you want to display. For example, to display information from both the CUSTOMERS and the EMPLOYEES tables only for specific customers, you could use a SELECT statement such as

```
SELECT cust_ID AS 'ID', customers.name, address,
  employees.name AS 'salesperson'
FROM customers, employees
WHERE salesrep = salesrep_ID AND customers.name = 'Jones'
```

which includes CUSTOMERS table selection criteria in addition to the multi-table row match (equality) conditional expression. Similarly, if you want to limit the rows in the results table based on the "other" table in the SELECT statement's FROM clause, you can execute a SELECT statement such as

```
SELECT cust_ID AS 'ID', customers.name, address,
  employees.name AS 'salesperson'
FROM customers, employees
WHERE salesrep = salesrep_ID AND employees.name = 'Smith'
```

that decides which rows to display based on the name of the salesperson vs. the name of the customer.

The important things to remember about executing a multi-table SELECT statement are that the FROM clause must list the names of all tables from which column values are to be displayed. And, unless you want to produce a Cartesian product (or CROSS JOIN), which you will learn about in Tip 298, "Using the CROSS JOIN to Create a Cartesian Product," the multi-table SELECT statement must include a WHERE clause with an equality conditional expression for each pair of tables listed in the FROM clause. (The equality conditional expression tells the DBMS which column's value[s] to use in matching a row in one table with its corresponding row in the another table.)

206 Using a View to Display Columns in One or More Tables or Views

As you learned in Tip 11, "Understanding Views," views are *virtual* tables. Although you can use a view almost anywhere a table reference is allowed, a view is not a physical table that resides on the hard drive along with the other tables and indexes in a database. Instead, a view consists of a SELECT statement that extracts rows and columns from one or more base tables (or other views). The results table for the SELECT statement the DBMS executes when an SQL statement references a view is an in-memory table that can be used as the target of other SQL statements.

The syntax for creating a view is:

```
CREATE VIEW <view name>
  [(<column name>[,...<last column name>])]
AS <SELECT statement>
```

Thus, to create a view of student information based on a table created by

```
CREATE TABLE students
  (SID               INTEGER,
   first_name        VARCHAR(15),
   last_name         VARCHAR(20),
   SSAN              CHAR(11),
   home_address      VARCHAR(50),
   home_city         VARCHAR(20),
   home_state        CHAR(2),
   home_phone_number CHAR(14),
   major             VARCHAR(20))
```

you could execute a CREATE VIEW statement similar to

```
CREATE VIEW vw_student_list AS SELECT * FROM students
```

and the view could then be used to display student information in a SELECT statement such as:

```
SELECT SID AS 'student ID', first_name, last_name
FROM vw_student_list
```

Given the additional overhead required in having the DBMS query an underlying table to create an in-memory virtual table, you will find few (if any) single table views define solely as SELECT * without a WHERE clause. After all, if why create a view to display all of the columns and rows of a single table? If a user is to have access to all of the data in a table, avoid the overhead of making the DBMS generate the view, and let the user execute SQL statements against the table (STUDENTS in the current example) instead.

One of the real advantages of using a view is its ability to hide portions of a table you do not want a user to see. Suppose, for example, that you wanted users to be able to work with values only in the SID, FIRST_NAME, and LAST_NAME columns of the STUDENTS table. By creating a view with a CREATE VIEW statement similar to

```
CREATE VIEW vw_student_name_list
  (student_ID, first_name, last_name)
AS SELECT SID, first_name, last_name FROM students
```

the SELECT statement

```
SELECT * FROM vw_student_name_list
```

will display only those columns you wanted the user to see, not all of the columns in the underlying table. By granting the user access to the view and not the base table(s), you limit the user to working in and displaying only some of the columns in a table.

207 Using a View to Display Columns from Specific Rows in One or More Tables

In Tip 206, "Using a View to Display Columns in One or More Tables or Views," you learned how to hide columns in a table by creating a view with only the columns you want the user to see. By granting the user access to the view and not its underlying table(s), you limit what the user sees after executing a SELECT * statement to data in only those columns included in the view.

A view that displays only some of the columns in an underlying table is called a *vertical* view. The term *vertical* is used in the name because when you view data in a table column, you proceed vertically (up or down) from one row to the next. Since a table consists of both vertical columns and horizontal rows, you might correctly surmise that if there is a *vertical* view, there should also be a *horizontal* view.

A *horizontal* view is a view that lets the user display and work with only specific rows in a table. For example, the view created by

```
CREATE VIEW vw_LVNV_student_list
AS SELECT * FROM students
WHERE home_city = 'Las Vegas' AND home_state = 'NV'
```

is a horizontal view because it lets the user work with only some of the rows in the STUDENTS table—those for students from Las Vegas, Nevada. The current example shows that you can create a horizontal view by including a WHERE clause in the view's SELECT statement.

Moreover, you can combine vertical and horizontal limits on a view to allow a user to see only certain columns in current rows of one or more tables. For example, to limit a user to working only with student ID and name information for students from Las Vegas, Nevada, you could execute a CREATE VIEW statement similar to:

```
CREATE VIEW vw_LVNV_student_name_list
  (student_ID, first_name, last_name)
AS SELECT SID, first_name, last_name FROM students
WHERE home_city = 'Las Vegas' AND home_state = 'NV'
```

In addition to limiting a user to displaying (and perhaps updating) only specific columns or rows, a view can also be used to simplify the SELECT statement a user must execute to display information from a combination of several tables. Suppose, for example, that in addition to the STUDENTS table in Tip 206, you have tables created by:

```
CREATE TABLE grades
  (class         VARCHAR(15),
   section       SMALLINT,
   grade         VARCHAR(4),
   student_ID    INTEGER,
   professor_ID INTEGER)

CREATE TABLE teachers
  (PID         INTEGER,
   professor  VARCHAR(30),
   department VARCHAR(20))
```

You can then create a view that combines data from all three tables using:

```
CREATE VIEW vw_students_grades_teachers AS
SELECT * FROM students, grades, teachers
WHERE (grades.student_id = students.SID) AND
      (grades.professor_ID = teachers.PID)
```

After you GRANT SELECT access to the view, a user can execute single-table SELECT statements to answer multi-table queries, such as:

"How many of professor Rawlins' students received an A in his M200 (math) class?"

```
SELECT COUNT (*) FROM vw_students_grades_teachers
WHERE professor = 'Rawlins' AND class = 'M200' AND
      grade = 'A'
```

"What grades did student 2110 receive in her classes, and who were the instructors?"

```
SELECT first_name,last_name,class,section,grade,professor
FROM vw_students_grades_teachers WHERE SID = 2110
```

"What students took classes from the history department, and what were their grades?"

```
SELECT first_name,last_name,class,section,grade,professor
FROM vw_students_grades_teachers
WHERE department = 'History'
```

Notice that in each query, the view takes care of joining (matching) parent/child rows in related tables. As such, a multi-table view lets a user execute simple (single table) SELECT statements to extract information that is really available only through queries based on multi-table joins.

208 Understanding How the DBMS Handles Views

When a DBMS parses an SQL statement and encounters a reference to a view, the DBMS retrieves the definition of the view from its system tables. It then uses the definition of the view to translate the action making the view reference into the equivalent action on the view's underlying table(s). By performing SELECT, UPDATE, and DELETE statement actions on the base table(s) (from which the view's SELECT statement extracts its data), the DBMS maintains database integrity while allowing the user to act on the view as if it were "real" physical table.

For example, if you execute the UPDATE statement

```
UPDATE vw_students_grades_teachers SET grade='B+'
WHERE SID = 1005 AND class = 'H100'
```

on the view created in Tip 207, "Using a View to Display Columns from Specific Rows in One or More Tables," the DBMS translates the UPDATE statement to

```
UPDATE grades SET grade='B+'
WHERE student_ID = 1005 AND class = 'H100'
```

and updates the GRADES table, which is the source (or base) table for the letter grade "stored" in the view's GRADE column.

For views created with a simple SELECT statement, the DBMS will construct each row of the view "on the fly" by retrieving columns of data from a row in the underlying table(s) as it displays the data to the user. For views consisting of complex multi-table joins and sub-queries, the DBMS will actually *materialize* the view—that is to say, the DBMS will execute the SELECT statement that defines the view and will create a temporary data with the view's data. The DBMS will then satisfy query requests against the view by retrieving data from the temporary table. (When the DBMS no longer needs it to satisfy SQL queries on the view, it automatically discards the temporary table.)

Whether the DBMS materializes a view or creates the view's rows "on the fly" is transparent to the user. In either case, the view behaves is if it is a "real" table. Moreover, whether the view exists only in memory or as a temporary table, any updates performed on the view are reflected as changes in its base table(s).

209 Using a View to Display the Results of an Expression

Views can display not only values stored in tables, but also the results of expressions and functions. For example, given a table created by

```
CREATE TABLE invoice_detail
  (invoice_number INTEGER,
   item_number    INTEGER,
   sales_price    MONEY,
   qty            INTEGER)
```

the view created by

```
CREATE VIEW vw_item_sales
  (item, order_ct, sold_ct, avg_sales_price) AS
SELECT item_number, COUNT(*), SUM(qty), AVG(sales_price)
FROM invoice_detail
GROUP BY item_number
```

will display the results of SQL aggregate functions on a base table called INVOICE_DETAIL.

Note: *The view definition for views that display function or expression results must include a column name list, while the column name list is optional in the definition of views that display only data from columns in one or more underlying tables.*

In order for the DBMS to be able to treat a view as if it were a physical table, all of the view's columns (like those in a physical table) must have names. When a view displays only data from underlying tables, the DBMS can use the name of the base table column for name of the view column that displays its data. However, when a column in a view displays the result of a function or expression, the DBMS cannot determine the column's name because the view column is not simply displaying data on one of a base table's columns. As a result, you must supply a column name when defining views with (otherwise nameless) columns that display function or expression results.

To display expression (vs. SQL aggregate function) results, simply include the expressions in the SELECT clause in the view's definition, as with any other column from a base table. For example, given the a table created by

```
CREATE TABLE item_master
  (item_number INTEGER,
   description VARCHAR(30),
   item_cost   MONEY)
```

and the preceding INVOICE_DETAIL table and VW_ITEM_SALES view, the view created by

```
CREATE VIEW vw_item_sales_profits
  (item_number, description, order_ct, sold_ct,
   avg_sales_price, total_cost, total_sales, profit,
   pct_profit) AS

SELECT vw_item_sales_profits.item_number, description,
  order_ct, sold_ct, avg_sales_price, sold_ct * item_cost,
  sold_ct * avg_sales_price,
  (avg_sales_price * sold_ct) - (sold_ct * item_cost),
  (((avg_sales_price * sold_ct) - (sold_ct * item_cost)) /
       (sold_ct * item_cost)) * 100
FROM item_master, vw_item_sales_profits
WHERE item_master.item_number = vw_item_sales.item_number
```

will display not only the results of aggregate functions, but also the computed values of total cost, net profit, and percent profit based on those values.

210 Using an UPDATE Statement to Change Data in Multiple Tables Through a View

As you learned in Tip 73, "Using the UPDATE Statement to Change Column Values," an UPDATE statement lets you change the value of one or more columns in one and only one target table. However, the syntax of the UPDATE statement

```
UPDATE <table name|view name> SET <column name> =
  <expression>[,...<last column name> = <last expression>]
WHERE <search condition>
```

seems to indicate that one could update columns in multiple tables by specifying a view based on multiple tables as the target "table" for the UPDATE statement. Using the view as the one and only target table, you could reference view columns derived from different tables in set clauses following the target table name in the UPDATE statement.

Unfortunately, the DBMS will allow you to include columns from only a single underlying (base) table in the SET clause(s) following the target table name in an UPDATE statement. As such, if you have a view created by

```
CREATE VIEW vw_customer_invoices AS
SELECT * FROM customers, invoices
WHERE cust_ID = purchased_by
```

based on tables created with

```
CREATE TABLE customers
  (cust_ID  INTEGER,
   name     VARCHAR(30),
   address  VARCHAR(50))

CREATE TABLE invoices
  (invoice_number INTEGER,
   invoice_date   DATETIME,
   purchased_by   INTEGER,
   ship_to        VARCHAR(50)
```

then the statement statements

```
UPDATE vw_customer_invoices SET address = 'New Address'
  WHERE CUST_ID = 1
UPDATE VW_customer_invoices SET ship_to = 'New Address'
  WHERE CUST_ID = 1
```

are acceptable to the DBMS because each statement updates a column in only one table—even though the view itself consists of data from more than one table. However, the DBMS will not accept the UPDATE statement

```
UPDATE vw_customer_invoices SET address = 'New Address',
  ship_to = 'New Address'
WHERE CUST_ID = 1
```

because it attempts to update columns in more than on table.

Remember, the DBMS handles an SQL statement that references a view by generating the equivalent statement on the column(s) of the base table(s) involved. Therefore, in order for the DBMS to execute the UPDATE statement that references both ADDRESS (from the CUSTOMERS table) and SHIP_TO (from the INVOICES table), the DBMS would have to construct an invalid UPDATE statement—one that lists two tables and not one as its target.

Note: *MS-SQL Server provides a special type of stored procedure called a "trigger" that you can use to cause an update of a column in one table to result in updates to columns in other tables. You will learn all about triggers in Tip 448 and how to use them to perform multi-table updates using a single UPDATE statement in Tip 453.*

---

211 Using the CHECK OPTION Clause in a CREATE VIEW Statement to Apply View Constraints to INSERT and UPDATE Statements

As you learned in Tip 207, "Using a View to Display Columns from Specific Rows in One or More Tables," a *horizontal* view is a virtual table that displays only some of the rows from one or more underlying tables or views. Because a vertical view does not display all of the rows in its base table(s), a user with INSERT privilege on a vertical view could use the view to INSERT rows into the base table that are not visible in the view itself. Similarly, a user with UPDATE could change column values in such as way as to make rows "disappear" from the view.

Suppose, for example, that you have the vertical view created by

```
CREATE VIEW vw_nv_employees AS
SELECT * FROM employees WHERE office = 'NV'
```

which has rows from an (underlying) EMPLOYEES table with the data

```
id  name    ssan         office
--  ------  -----------  ------
1   Konrad  555-55-5555  TX
10  Sally   222-22-2222  NV
15  Wally   111-11-1111  NV
28  Walter  333-33-3333  CA
```

and you execute the SELECT statement:

```
SELECT * FROM vw_nv_employees
```

The DBMS will display data in the rows for employee ID 10 and 15, since these are the only two EMPLOYEES table rows whose OFFICE column has the value NV.

If you execute the INSERT statement

```
INSERT INTO vw_nv_employees
VALUES (2,'Kris','777-77-7777','TX')
```

the DBMS will add the new row to the EMPLOYEES table. However, if you then execute

```
SELECT * FROM vw_nv_employees
```

again, the DBMS will still display information on only employees 10 and 15 because the new row you inserted into the EMPLOYEES table does not satisfy the view's search condition (OFFICE = 'NV').

Similarly, if you execute the UPDATE statement

```
UPDATE vw_nv_employees SET office = 'LA' WHERE id = 10
```

employee ID 10 will "disappear" from the view. Although the UPDATE statement did not DELETE the row from the underlying EMPLOYEES table, the row no longer satisfies the view's search criteria and is therefore no longer included in the view.

To prevent a user from using a view to INSERT rows the view will not display and from changing data in a view's columns so that rows are dropped from the view, add the WITH CHECK OPTION clause to the view definition. In the current example, if you create the VW_NV_EMPLOYEES view with

```
CREATE VIEW vw_nv_employees AS
SELECT * FROM employees WHERE office = 'NV'
WITH CHECK OPTION
```

the DBMS will allow a user to INSERT only rows that have a value of NV in the OFFICE column. Moreover, the DBMS will not allow the user to execute an UPDATE statement that attempts to change the value in the OFFICE column in an existing row to something other than NV.

For example, while the UPDATE statement

```
UPDATE vw_nv_employees SET office = 'LA' WHERE id = 10
```

was perfectly acceptable when the definition of the VW_NV_EMPLOYEES view lacked a WITH CHECK OPTION clause, the DBMS will now abort execution of the UPDATE statement and return an error message similar to:

```
Server: Msg 550, Level 16, State 1, Line 1
The attempted insert or update failed because the target
  view either specifies WITH CHECK OPTION or spans a view
  that specifies WITH CHECK OPTION and one or more row
  resulting from the operation did not qualify under the
  CHECK OPTION constraint.
The statement has been terminated.
```

212 Using a View to Allow a User to See Only Certain Rows in a Table

When you have a source table that contains data for various organizations or groups of users, you can use a *horizontal* view to give each department or set of users its own virtual table with only the rows of data it needs or to which it should have access. Suppose, for example, that a salesperson, BOB (employee ID 101), is allowed to view information on only his own customers, while the sales manager, SUE (employee ID 302), is allowed to generate reports on all customers belonging to salespeople she manages. You could create a VW_BOB_CUSTOMERS view for user ID BOB that displays only his customers with:

```
CREATE VIEW vw_bob_customers AS
SELECT * FROM customers WHERE salesperson_ID = 101
```

Similarly, you can execute the CREATE VIEW statement

```
CREATE VIEW vw_sue_subordinate_customers AS
SELECT * FROM customers
WHERE cust_ID IN (SELECT cust_ID FROM customers, employees
                  WHERE
                    customers.salesperson_ID = employees.ID
                  AND employees.manager = 'SUE')
```

to create a virtual table that SUE can use to review information on her salespersons' customer accounts.

The SELECT * in the view's definition tells the DBMS to include all of the source table's columns in the view. Meanwhile, the WHERE limits the view to displaying only some (and not all) of the underlying table's rows.

By granting SELECT, UPDATE, or DELETE privilege on a horizontal view and not on the base table, you can limit a user's ability to SELECT (display), DELETE, and UPDATE data to only certain rows within the view's underlying table. However, as you learned in Tip 211, you must include the WITH CHECK OPTION clause in a horizontal view's definition if you want to prevent the user with INSERT and/or UPDATE privilege from using the view to add data not visible in the view to the base table.

213 Using a View to Allow a User to See Only Certain Columns in a Table

In addition to limiting a user's access to only specific rows in a table (as you learned to do in Tip 212, "Using a View to Allow a User to See Only Certain Rows in a Table"), you can also use a view to limit a user to working with only specific columns within a row. As you already know, a view is a *virtual* table with no data of its own. The view displays data from one or more underlying tables, and any work done on its rows or column values is actually performed on the view's source table(s). While a view's WHERE clause (if any) limits the underlying table rows that a user can access through the view, the view's column list determines the column values a user can display and (perhaps) change.

For example, if you have a table created with

```
CREATE TABLE students
  (SID                INTEGER,
   first_name         VARCHAR(15),
   last_name          VARCHAR(20),
   SSAN               CHAR(11),
   home_address       VARCHAR(50),
   home_city          VARCHAR(20),
   home_state         CHAR(2),
   home_phone_number  CHAR(14),
   major              VARCHAR(20))
```

you can limit students to seeing only name and major information by granting them SELECT access to a VW_STUDENT_NAME_MAJOR view created by:

```
CREATE VIEW vw_student_name_major AS
SELECT first_name, last_name, major FROM students
```

Note: *Since its CREATE VIEW statement has no WHERE clause, the view in the current example (VW_STUDENT_NAME_MAJOR) will display all of the rows from the STUDENTS table. To limit a view's access to specific columns* and *specific rows, include both a column list and a WHERE clause in the definition of the view. For example, to limit the VW_STUDENT_NAME_MAJOR view to displaying only name and major information for Nevada students, change the view definition to:*

```
CREATE VIEW vw_student_name_major AS
SELECT first_name, last_name, major FROM students
WHERE home_state = 'NV'
```

214 Using a GROUP BY Clause in a CREATE VIEW Statement to Create a View That Displays Summary Data

If you create a view using a SELECT statement that has no GROUP BY clause, there is a one-to-one correspondence between the rows in the view and the rows in the underlying table(s) whose data the view displays. Thus, an (ungrouped) SELECT statement in a view makes the view act as a filter on the data in the source table, screening out certain rows and columns and letting others pass through unchanged. Conversely, when you use a *grouped* SELECT (a SELECT statement with a GROUP BY clause) to define a view, the DBMS groups related rows of data, and the view will display one row of results for each group or rows from the base table. As such, there is no one-to-one relationship between the rows in a *grouped* view (a view created with a grouped SELECT statement) and the rows in its underlying table(s).

The syntax used to create a grouped view is:

```
CREATE VIEW <view column name list>
AS SELECT <source table column name list>
FROM <source table list> [<WHERE clause>]
GROUP BY <group by column list>
```

Thus, to create a grouped view summarizing a customer's orders, you would use a CREATE VIEW statement similar to:

```
CREATE VIEW vw_customer_orders
  (customer_number, orders_placed_ct, orders_shipped_ct,
   total_amt_purchased, total_amt_paid, total_amt_due,
   high_order_amt, avg_order_amt, low_order_amt)
AS SELECT
  cust_ID, COUNT(*), COUNT(date_shipped),
  SUM(invoice_total), SUM(amt_paid), SUM(invoice_total) -
  SUM(amt_paid), MAX(invoice_total), AVG(invoice_total),
  MIN(invoice_total)
FROM invoices
GROUP BY cust_ID
```

The main disadvantage of using a grouped view is that it is read-only. Since there is not a one-to-one correspondence between the rows in a view and its source table(s), the DBMS cannot translated UPDATE or DELETE statements into equivalent statements that perform work on specific rows in the view's underlying table(s).

On the other hand, the main advantage of using a grouped view is that it simplifies queries on summarized data. For example, you can execute a simple select statement such as

```
SELECT TOP 10 customer_number, name, total_amt_due
FROM customers, vw_customer_orders
WHERE cust_ID = customer_number
ORDERED BY total_amt_due DESC
```

on a grouped view to get a list of the 10 customers with the highest outstanding balances due.

215 Using the CREATE VIEW Statement to Display the Results of Joining Two or More Tables

In addition to providing security by limiting a user's access to data in specific rows and columns, a view provides a way to consolidate related data from the many tables in a normalized database into a single, comprehensive virtual table. As you learned from the discussion of database normalization in Tips 200–203, designers normalize a database (to at least

3NF) in order to prevent modification anomalies that can destroy database integrity as users make changes to database contents over time.

However, even simple queries such as "List each salesperson's customers" normally require joining at least two tables when executed on a normalized database because customer data will be in one table while employee (salesperson) data will be in another. If you further complicate the query by adding ". . . and list the total and average amount of each customer's orders," the person writing the SQL statement must know how to write a SELECT statement that will properly join three tables and perform a grouped query.

Fortunately, views provide a way to continue storing data in multiple tables—to maintain database integrity through normalization—while at the same time letting users access database information by executing simple, single-table SELECT statements. In other words, the DBA and programming staff can write complex SELECT statements that join rows from multiple related tables and store them in view definitions. The user can then use the views to execute a complex query involving the joining of several tables by referencing the columns in a view as if all of the related data were in a single table with a lot of columns.

For example, with views similar to those created by

```
CREATE VIEW vw_cust_invoices
  (cust_id, total_purchased, avg_purchase)
AS SELECT
  customers.cust_id, SUM(invoice_total), AVG(invoice_total)
FROM customers, invoices
WHERE customers.cust_id = invoices.cust_ID

CREATE VIEW vw_salesperson_customers
  (salesperson_ID, salesperson_name, customer_ID,
   customer_name, total_purchased, avg_purchase)
AS SELECT
  employees.ID, employees.name, customers.cust_ID,
  customers.name, total_purchased, avg_purchase
FROM customers, employees, vw_cust_invoices
WHERE customers.salesperson_ID = employees.ID AND
      vw_cust_invoices.cust_ID = customers.cust_id
```

a user can execute the simple SELECT statement

```
SELECT * FROM vw_salesperson_customers
ORDER BY salesperson_ID, customer_ID
```

to perform the complex query: "List each salesperson's customers and the total and average amount sold to each customer."

The important thing to learn from the current example is that referencing a view that consolidates data from multiple tables lets a user execute a single-table SELECT statement to pose a query that requires the joining of data in rows from several tables.

216 Using the UNION Operator to Select All Rows That Appear in Any or All of Two or More Tables

The UNION operator provides a convenient way to combine the results of two or more queries. Each time the DBMS performs a UNION operation, the final results table contains all of the rows produced by each query in the UNION, with duplicate rows eliminated. In order to be union-compatible, queries must exhibit the following characteristics:

- All queries must have the same number of columns.
- The data type of corresponding columns in each query results table must be the same data type. (That is, if the first column in one results table is of type CHAR, then the data type of the first column in all results tables must be CHAR; if the data type of the second column of one results table is INTEGER, then the data type of the second column in all results tables must be INTEGER, and so on.)
- None of the SELECT statements can have an ORDER BY clause. (In Tip 220, "Using the ORDER BY Clause to Sort the Results of a Union Operation," you will learn how to sort the final results table produced by the UNION operator by placing an ORDER BY clause *after* the final SELECT statement.)

To use the UNION operator, place it between SELECT statements whose results tables you want to join. Suppose, for example, that your company resells products for three vendors, each with its own products table, such as:

```
ABC_Products table
item_no  item_desc  price   count_on_hand
-------  ---------  ------  -------------
1        Widget     254.00  5
2        Gidget     123.00  7
3        Gadget     249.00  10

DEF_Products table
item_number  description  cost    qty_on_hand
-----------  -----------  ------  -----------
1            Sprocket     243.00  15
2            Gadget       100.00  7

GHI_Products table
item_number  description  cost    qty_on_hand
-----------  -----------  ------  -----------
7            Laser        575.00  12
10           Phaser       625.00  5
15           Taser         75.00  7
```

You can produce a complete product list of everything available for sale by using UNION operators in a query similar to:

```
  SELECT 'ABC' as 'vendor', item_no, item_desc, price,
    count_on_hand FROM abc_products
UNION
  SELECT 'DEF' as 'vendor', item_number, description, cost,
    qty_on_hand FROM def_products
UNION
  SELECT 'GHI' as 'vendor', item_number, description, cost,
    qty_on_hand FROM ghi_products
```

After executing the query in the current example, the DBMS will display a single results table (similar to that shown in Figure 216.1), which contains all of the rows returned by the each of the SELECT statements joined by the UNION operator.

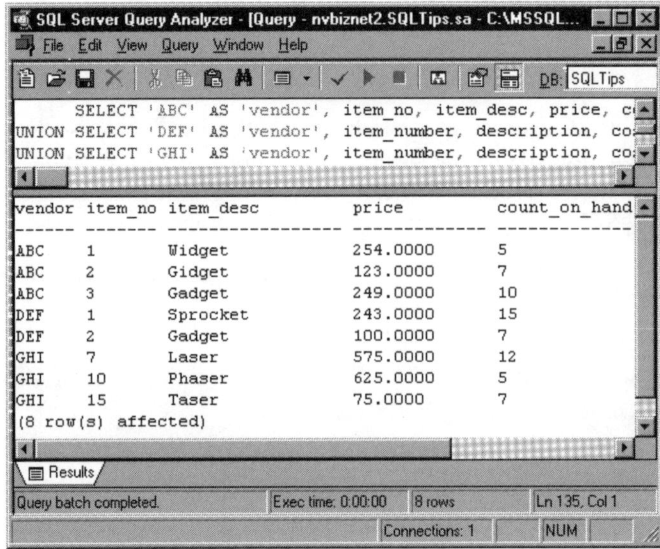

Figure 216.1 MS-SQL Server Query Analyzer showing the results table produced by a UNION of three queries

---

Note: *As shown in the current example, the UNION operator requires only that the SELECT statements it is combining have matching corresponding column types—the names of corresponding columns may differ. Unfortunately, some DBMS products will produce a results table with unnamed columns for each corresponding pair of SELECT statement columns with different names (such as ITEM_NO vs. ITEM_NUMBER, ITEM_DESC vs. DESCRIPTION, PRICE vs. COST, and COUNT_ON_HAND vs. QTY_ON_HAND, in the current example). Other DBMS products, such as MS-SQL Server, will use the column names from the first SELECT statement in the UNION as the headings for the columns in the final results table.*

---

217 Using the UNION ALL Operator to Select All Rows That Appear in Any or All of Two or More Tables, Including Duplicate Rows

As mentioned in Tip 216, "Using the UNION Operator to Select All Rows That Appear in Any or All of Two or More Tables," one of the features of the UNION operator is that it eliminates duplicate rows from the final results table. The default behavior of the UNION operator contrasts with that of the SELECT statement, which (by default) displays any duplicate rows it finds. As such, to prevent a query from returning duplicate rows, you must add the keyword DISTINCT to the SELECT clause (as in SELECT DISTINCT * FROM <table name>). Conversely, since the UNION operator returns only unique (distinct) rows in its results table, you must use the UNION ALL operator to combine queries for which you want the DBMS to display *all* rows (including duplicates).

For example, suppose you have a house inventory table created by

```
CREATE table house_inventory
  (address          VARCHAR(50),
   sales_price      MONEY,
   pool             CHAR(1),
   gated_community  CHAR(1),
   acreage          NUMERIC,
   bedrooms         SMALLINT,
   square_footage   INTEGER,
   realtor_ID       SMALLINT)
```

and you want to get a list of houses that satisfy a buyer's criteria for an ideal home. You could execute a SELECT statement such as

```
SELECT * FROM house_inventory
WHERE acreage > 2 OR bedrooms >= 4 OR gated_community = 'Y'
```

to get a list of properties that fulfill at list one of the buyer's expectations. However, given that some properties might satisfy only one of the criteria, some two, and others perhaps all three, it would be handy to put the houses in the list such that those that satisfy the most criteria are at the top, and those that satisfy the least are at the bottom.

To create a list of houses sorted in order by the number of buyer criteria satisfied, first create a temporary table (such as HOUSE_PROSPECTS) with the same structure as HOUSE_INVENTORY. Next, use an INSERT statement such as

```
  INSERT INTO house_prospects
     SELECT * FROM house_inventory WHERE acreage > 2
   UNION ALL
     SELECT * FROM house_inventory WHERE bedrooms >= 4
   UNION ALL
     SELECT * FROM house_inventory WHERE gated_community = 'Y'
```

to populate the table with the rows from the HOUSE_INVENTORY table that meet at least one of the buyer's expectations.

The UNION ALL operators create a final results table by combining all of the rows from each SELECT statement's (interim) results table—without filtering out duplicate rows. As such, if a house sits on 3 acres and has four bedrooms, the UNION ALL operator will put property into the final results table twice (once from the first SELECT statement's results table and once again from the second SELECT statement's results table). The INSERT statement retrieves the rows from the final results table and inserts them into the HOUSE_PROSPECTS (temporary) table.

Finally, execute a SELECT statement similar to

```
SELECT COUNT(*) AS 'Score', address, sales_price, acreage,
  bedrooms, gated_community FROM house_prospects
GROUP BY address, acreage, bedrooms, gated_community
  sales_price
ORDER BY score DESC, sales_price ASC
```

and the DBMS will display a report, sorted in descending order by the "score," that represents the number of times each property appears in the HOUSE_PROSPECTS table. (In effect, the score (or duplicate row count) tells you how many search conditions a property satisfied because the UNION ALL operator added the same row each time one of the SELECT statements in the UNION included the row in its interim results table.

218 Using the UNION CORRESPONDING Operator to Combine Rows in Two or More Tables That Are Not Union-Compatible

Two tables are *union-compatible* if both have the same number of columns and if the data type of each column in one table is the same as the data type of its corresponding column (by ordinal position) in the other table. For example, the tables created by

```
CREATE TABLE table_a            CREATE TABLE table_b
  (ID          SMALLINT,          (emp_ID          SMALLINT,
   office      INTEGER,            office          INTEGER,
   address     VARCHAR(30),        home_address    VARCHAR(30),
   department  CHAR(5))            emp_department  CHAR(5))
```

are union-compatible because both have the same number of columns and because the first column in TABLE_A is the same data type as the first column in TABLE_B, the second column in TABLE A is the same data type as the second column in TABLE_B, and so on.

When two tables are union-compatible, you use the UNION operator with SELECT statements such as

```
  SELECT * FROM table_a
UNION
  SELECT * FROM table_b
```

to display a results table that has a combination of all columns from all rows in TABLE_A and all columns from all rows in TABLE_B—with duplicate rows removed. If two (or more) tables are not union-compatible (either because corresponding columns are not in the same ordinal positions or because one table has columns not found in the other table), you can use the UNION CORRESPONDING operator to tell the DBMS to create a results table by merging data in columns with matching names in both tables, regardless of their ordinal position in each table.

For example, if you have the (non–union-compatible) tables created by

```
CREATE TABLE table_c             CREATE TABLE table_d
  (ID          SMALLINT,           (office          INTEGER,
   office      INTEGER,             ID              SMALLINT,
   address     VARCHAR(30),         address         VARCHAR(30),
   department  CHAR(5),             emp_department  CHAR(5))
   pay_rate    MONEY)
```

you can use the UNION CORRESPONDING operator with SELECT statements such as

```
  SELECT * FROM table_c
UNION CORRESPONDING
  SELECT * FROM table_b
```

to display a results table with the data in columns that the two tables have in common (namely, ID, OFFICE, and ADDRESS, in the current example).

Note: *Not all DBMS products, including MS-SQL Server, support the UNION CORRESPONDING operator. Do not despair. As you will learn in Tip 219, "Using the UNION Operator to Combine the Results of Two Queries," if your DBMS does not support the UNION CORRESPONDING operator, you can still display the union of tables that are not union-compatible by explicitly listing the columns (vs. using SELECT *) that the DBMS is to merge into the final results table.*

219 Using the UNION Operator to Combine the Results of Two Queries

In Tip 216, "Using the UNION Operator to Select All Rows That Appear in Any or All of Two or More Tables," you learned how to use the UNION operator to combine the results of two or more queries into a single results table. If the tables are union-compatible (that is, all of the tables to be combined have the same number of columns in the same order), you can use the UNION operator to merge results from "select all columns" queries such as

```
  SELECT * FROM innvoices_99 WHERE invoices_99.cust_ID =
    (SELECT cust_ID FROM CUSTOMERS WHERE name = 'XYZ Corp')
UNION
  SELECT * FROM innvoices_00 WHERE invoices_00.cust_ID =
    (SELECT cust_ID FROM CUSTOMERS WHERE name = 'XYZ Corp')
```

which lists all orders placed by XYZ CORP during the past two years.

On the other hand, if you are working with tables that are not union-compatible, you can still use the UNION operator to combine query results if you explicitly list the columns the operator is to merge. Suppose, for example, that the Ford Motor Company announces an enhancement for the Ford Explorer (all model years), and you want a complete list of both Explorers waiting to be sold and those you already sold.

Given that the AUTO_INVENTORY and AUTO_SALES tables have different structures, you could use the UNION operator to combine queries that list the columns to merge into the final results table, such as:

```
  SELECT store_name AS 'sold_to', address, phone, make,
         model, vehicle_ID, 'Inventory' AS 'location',
         date_received
  FROM auto_inventory, dealerships
  WHERE dealerships.store_ID = auto_inventory.dealership_ID
    AND make = 'Ford' AND model = 'Explorer'
UNION
  SELECT first_name + ' ' + last_name AS 'sold_to',
         address, home_phone, make, model, vehicle_ID,
         'Customer' AS 'location', date_sold
  FROM customers, auto_sales
  WHERE customers.customer_ID = auto_sales.cust_ID
    AND make = 'FORD' AND model = 'Explorer'
```

Although each SELECT statement's tables have a different structure, you can use the UNION operator (vs. having to use the UNION CORRESPONDING operator) to merge their (interim) results tables, as long as the columns returned by each SELECT statement match the columns returned by the every other SELECT statement both in number and in type (by ordinal position).

Note: *Some DBMS products only allow either a column name list or the asterisk (*) (meaning all columns) in the SELECT clause of queries to be combined by UNION operators. Other products, such as MS-SQL Server, allow both aggregate functions, simple expressions (such as concatenation (FIRST_NAME + ' ' + LAST_NAME), and the use of literal strings ('Inventory', 'Customer'), as shown in the current example. Be sure to check your system manual for the specific restrictions your DBMS product imposes on SELECT statements joined by a UNION operator.*

---

220 Using the ORDER BY Clause to Sort the Results of a Union Operation

None of the SELECT statements combined by a UNION operator can have an ORDER BY clause. (Sorting the interim results tables the UNION operator merges into the final results table would be inefficient anyway. After all, the user never sees the interim results tables.) You can, however, place an ORDER BY clause *after* the final SELECT statement in the UNION to sort the final (merged) results table.

For example, to sort the final results table for a query similar to that in Tip 216, "Using the UNION Operator to Select All Rows That Appear in Any or All of Two or More Tables," you would add an ORDER BY clause after the final SELECT statement, as follows:

```
  SELECT 'ABC', item_no, item_desc, price, count_on_hand
  FROM abc_products
UNION
  SELECT 'DEF'' item_number, description, cost, qty_on_hand
  FROM def_products
UNION
  SELECT 'GHI', item_number, description, cost, qty_on_hand
  FROM ghi_products
ORDER BY item_no
```

The ORDER BY clause can specify a sort by any column name from the *final* results table.

In the current example, the DBMS will sort the final results table in ascending order by the values in its ITEM_NO column because MS-SQL Server (conveniently) named the third column in the final results table ITEM_DESC. Unfortunately, some DBMS products will not name columns that combine queries on tables that use different names for corresponding columns. If you are using one of these DBMS products, your system will leave all of the columns in the final results table for the current example unnamed because the first column is a literal string and has no column name to start with and because the remaining columns have different names in one of the three tables used in the query.

To use an ORDER BY clause to sort the contents of a final results table by an unnamed column, refer to the column's ordinal position in the results table. For example, to sort the final results table in the current example by ITEM_NO, you would write the ORDER BY clause as

```
ORDER BY 2
```

since ITEM_NO is the second column in the final results table. Similarly, to sort the final results table in the current example by the literal string (which happens to be the vendor ID) and item description, you can use the ORDER BY clause

```
ORDER BY 1, 3
```

since the literal string (vendor ID) is the first column and the item description is the third column in the results table.

221 Using the UNION Operator to Combine Three or More Tables

As you learned in Tips 216–219, UNION operators are used to combine the results from multiple SELECT statements into a single composite results table. Whether you use a single UNION operator to combine the output of 2 SELECT statements or use 10 UNION operators to combine results from 11 SELECT statements, the unions of queries are always executed 2 results tables at a time.

Suppose, for example, that you were to EXECUTE the statements:

```
SELECT * FROM table_a UNION
SELECT * FROM table_b UNION
SELECT * FROM table c
```

The DBMS will execute the unions according to the workflow shown in Figure 221.1.

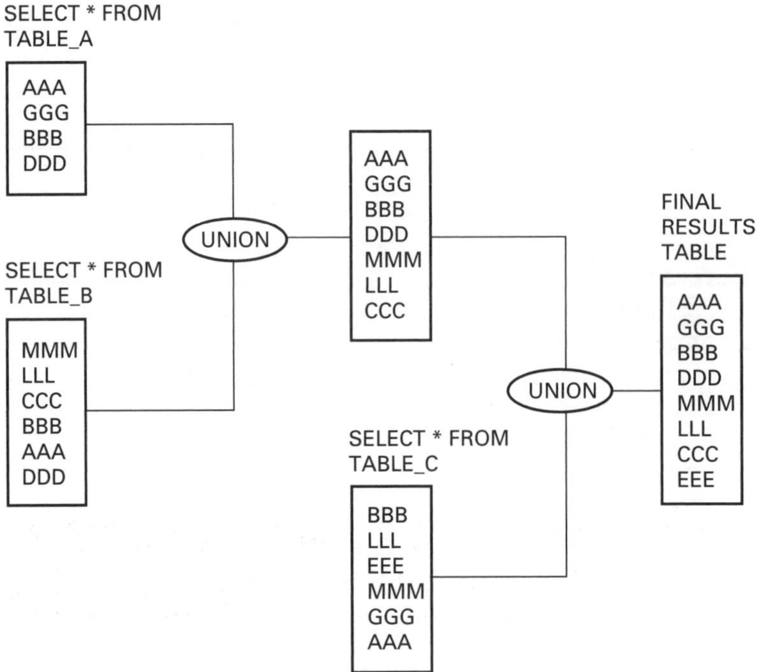

Figure 221.1 The UNION of three query results tables

You can uses parenthesis (()) to tell the DBMS the order in which to combine SELECT statement results. However, the final results table will be the same regardless of the order in which the unions take place if all SELECT statements are combined using UNION operators or if all SELECT statements are combined using all UNION ALL operators.

When you have a mix of UNION and UNION ALL operators, the order of execution becomes important. For example, given the table data shown in Figure 221,

```
 table_a UNION (table_b UNION table_c)
(table_a UNION table_b) UNION table_c
(table_a UNION table_c) UNION table_b
```

will all produce the same final results table with eight nonduplicate rows. Similarly, executing the UNION ALL statements grouped as

```
 table_a UNION ALL (table_b UNION ALL table_c)
(table_a UNION ALL table_b) UNION ALL table_c
(table_a UNION ALL table_c) UNION ALL table_b
```

will all produce the same final results table with 16 rows. (Remember, the UNION ALL operator does not eliminate duplicate rows.) However, if you want the DBMS to execute

```
table_a UNION ALL table_b UNION table_c
```

the results are different if the system orders the execution as

```
table_a UNION ALL (table_b UNION table_c)
```

which will produce 13 rows (9 nonduplicate rows from the inner UNION of table_b and table_c, plus the outer UNION ALL of all 4 rows in table_a) vs.

```
(table_a UNION ALL table_b) UNION table_c
```

which will produce only 8 rows (after the inner UNION ALL of table_a and table_b produces 10 rows, the outer UNION adds its UNIQUE row EEE and eliminates the duplicate rows—AAA and DDD, in the current example).

The important thing to understand is that if you combine query results using only UNION or using only UNION ALL operators, you do not have to tell the DBMS the order in which to perform the unions. However, if you use a mix of UNION and UNION ALL operators to combine query results, you should always use parenthesis to specify the order of execution so that the system will discard only those duplicate rows you want to eliminate.

222 Understanding Where to Place the MS-SQL Server Transaction Log to Improve Performance

In Tip 133, "Understanding Transaction Logs," you learned that the DBMS uses the transaction log to

- Undo uncommitted work performed when the user executes a ROLLBACK statement
- Redo (roll forward) work performed by completed transactions if you restore a backup version of the database and apply a more recent transaction log

- Redo (roll forward) work committed but not yet written to the database files when the DBMS is restarted after a system failure
- Roll back (undo) an uncommitted transaction when the DBMS is restarted after a system failure

In order to use the transaction log for these purposes, the DBMS must use it to maintain a serial list of all work performed on the database, along with a copy of each value in the database both before and after it is modified. In fact, most DBMS products write the original and updated data values to the transaction log before changing the database tables themselves. As such, the physical location of the transaction log has a significant impact on overall database performance.

When possible, locate the transaction log on a fast, physically separate disk drive or RAID array. Since the DBMS maintains the transaction log by appending new information to the end of the log file, placing the log on a dedicated drive will allow the disk heads to stay in place for the next write operation. As a result, the DBMS will not have to wait for the system hardware to reseek the end of the log prior to updating it. Although a few milliseconds does not seem like a lot of time, it does add up when you consider that every command and two copies of every modified data value must be written to the transaction log *before* the DBMS can update the database and process another SQL statement.

Tip 41, "Using the CREATE DATABASE Statement to Create an MS-SQL Server Database and Transaction Log," shows you how to specify the location (file name and physical disk storage device) for the transaction log as part of the CREATE DATABASE statement, and Tip 42, "Using the MS-SQL Server Enterprise Manager to Create a Database and Transaction Log," explains how to do the same thing using the MS-SQL Server Enterprise Manager instead. Please refer to these tips for the specific steps involved in creating a transaction log.

For now, the important thing to understand is that you should create a large transaction log on a separate (dedicated) drive. Doing so will improve DBMS performance because the system will not have to extend the size of the log or wait for the hardware to find the end of the file before it records commands and data values in the log prior to updating the database and continuing statement execution.

223 Understanding Multicolumn UNIQUE Constraints

In Tip 192, "Using the UNIQUE Column Constraint to Prevent Duplicate Values in a Column," you learned how to apply the UNIQUE constraint to a column definition to ensure that the DBMS will prevent duplicate data values from being stored in the column. A *single* column UNIQUE constraint is appropriate when creating a table such as

```
CREATE TABLE employees
  (employee_ID SMALLINT,
   office      SMALLINT,
   emp_name    VARCHAR(30),
   SSAN        CHAR(11) UNIQUE)
```

where the value in the SSAN (Social Security account number) column must be unique for every row in the table, since no two employees can have the same Social Security number. However, suppose that the company has multiple offices and each office has its own employee number sequence. As such, although OFFICE 1 can have only one EMPLOYEE_ID 101, OFFICE 2 can also have one and only one EMPLOYEE_ID 101; likewise the same goes for OFFICE 3, and so on.

When the combination of values in two or more columns must be unique, you cannot use multiple, single-column UNIQUE constraints such as:

```
CREATE TABLE employees
  (employee_ID SMALLINT UNIQUE,
   office      SMALLINT UNIQUE,
   emp_name    VARCHAR(30),
   SSAN        CHAR(11) UNIQUE)
```

If you add the UNIQUE constraint to each column definition, as shown in the current example, the DBMS will allow the insertion of only one employee row for each office, since an office number, such as "1", can appear in the OFFICE column of only one row in the table. Conversely, if you apply the UNIQUE constraint only to the EMPLOYEE_ID column, the DBMS will not allow duplicate EMPLOYEE_ID's for different offices.

To apply a multicolumn UNIQUE constraint (in which each set of values from two or columns must be unique throughout the table), define the constraint apart from the column definitions. For example, to constrain the EMPLOYEES table in the current example such that employee numbers must be unique within each office, but can be repeated from one office to the next, use a CREATE TABLE statement such as:

```
CREATE TABLE employees
 (employee_ID SMALLINT,
  office      SMALLINT,
  emp_name    VARCHAR(30),
  SSAN        CHAR(11) UNIQUE,
  CONSTRAINT unique_by_office UNIQUE (employee_ID, office))
```

The UNIQUE_BY_OFFICE constraint will allow the insertion of rows with (EMPLOYEE_ID,OFFICE) pairs of (101,1), (101,2), (102,2), (102,3), and so on, but will prevent the insertion of more than one row where the OFFICE is 1 and the EMPLOYEE_ID is 101 (101,1).

224 Understanding Literal Values

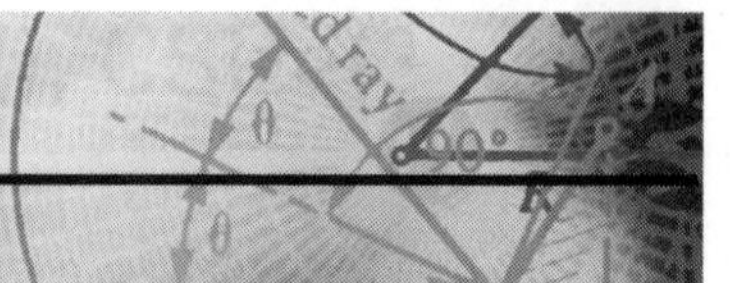

A literal value is a constant used to place values into table columns with statements such as:

```
INSERT INTO employees (emp_ID, name, hire_date, hourly_rate)
  VALUES (1, 'Konrad King', '08/20/2000', 52.75)
```

(which tells the DBMS to insert a row with the literal values listed in the VALUES clause into the EMPLOYEES table) and in expressions such as:

```
UPDATE employees SET hourly_rate = 10.0 + hourly_rate * 1.2
```

(which tells the DBMS to multiply the value in the HOURLY_RATE column by the numeric literal value "1.2", add the numeric literal value "10.0" to the product, and store the new value back in the HOURLY_RATE column).

Every DBMS product has a type of literal value that can be used in expressions and column value assignments for each of the standard SQL data types supported by the DBMS. Table 224.1 shows examples of literal values for some of the data types supported by MS-SQL Server.

Data Type	***Example Literal Values***
BINARY, VARBINARY, UNIQUEIDENTIFIER	0xab, 0x451245, 0x2586AB
CHAR, VARCHAR, NCHAR, NTEXT, NVARCHAR, TEXT, SYSNAME	'Konrad King', 'Konrad's Tips', 'Hello'
DATETIME, SMALLDATETIME	'April 15, 2000 05:25pm', '08/20/2000'
DECIMAL, MONEY, SMALLMONEY	458.878, 789.5698, -58.78, -785.12
FLOAT, NUMERIC, REAL	258.5E10, -258.45E5, -237E-5, 78.59
INT, INTEGER, SMALLINT	–258, 32767, –15789, –987, 478
TINYINT	1, 0, 255, 200, 75

Table 224.1 MS-SQL Server Data Types and Example Literal Values

Note: *Single quotes are used to denote non-numeric literal values such as character strings and dates. To use a character string literal value that itself contains a single quote mark, write two single quotes in a row. For example, the INSERT statement*

```
INSERT INTO books (author, title)
  VALUES ('Konrad King', 'Konrad''s Tips')
```

adds a row to the BOOKS table with "Konrad King" in the AUTHOR column and "Konrad's Tips" in the TITLE column.

225 Understanding Variables

A variable is a named memory location you can use to store a value temporarily. Unlike the constants used as literal values that you learned about in Tip 224, "Understanding Literal Values," the values in variables can change. MS-SQL Server supports two types of variables: *local* and *global*.

Local variables are created by a DECLARE statement and can be used only within the statement batch or stored procedure in which they are declared. Suppose, for example, that you wanted to display information about an INVENTORY table in a more readable format than that provide by a standard SELECT statement. You could execute the statement batch

```
DECLARE @item_count INTEGER, @avg_value MONEY,
  @total_value MONEY

SELECT @item_count = COUNT(*), @avg_value = AVG(cost),
  @total_value = SUM(cost) FROM inventory

PRINT 'There are ' + RTRIM(CONVERT(CHAR(6), @item_count)) +
  ' items in inventory.'
PRINT 'The total value of the inventory is $' +
  RTRIM(LTRIM(CONVERT(CHAR(8), @total_value))) + '.'
PRINT 'Each item has an average value of $' +
  RTRIM(LTRIM(CONVERT(CHAR(8), @avg_value))) + '.'
```

which will display three lines of output similar to:

```
There are 16 items in inventory.
The total value of the inventory is $8020.62.
Each item has an average value of $501.29.
```

At this point, the important things to know are that:

- You use the DECLARE statement to create a local variable.
- Each local variable name must start with an at sign (@).
- You use a SELECT statement to place a value into a local variable.

Global variables are useful when you need to use the same value in multiple stored procedures or in several SQL statement batches. Suppose, for example, that you run a store and want to base the sales price of your goods on your cost plus a fixed percentage based on the type of customer making a purchase. If you have a three-tier price schedule where your best customers pay 10 percent over your cost, the next best pay 20 percent, and the remainder pay 30 percent over cost, you could use the UPDATE statement

```
UPDATE cost_sheet SET wholesale = cost * 1.1,
  discount = cost * 1.2, retail = cost * 1.3
```

to set your prices. Now, suppose it is holiday season or that new competition comes into town, and you want to reduce your margins by 5 percent to be more competitive. You could search your code and change all instances if * 1.1 to * 1.05, all instances of * 1.20 to * 1.15, and all instances of * 1.3 to * 1.25. However, the more places you use the same value and the more often you change your target profit margins, the more tedious and error-prone the process becomes.

A better alternative is to declare three global variables, such as @@wholesale_margin, @@discount_margin, and @@retail_margin. You then need only execute three SET statements, such as

```
SET @@wholesale_margin = 1.05
SET @@discount_margin = 1.15
SET @@retail_margin = 1.25
```

to change the values in the three global variables. After you change the values in the global variables, the DBMS will automatically use the new values wherever you reference the variables in your code. As such, statements such as

```
UPDATE cost_sheet SET wholesale = cost * @wholesale_margin,
  discount = cost * @@retail_margin,
  retail = cost * @@list_margin
```

can remain unchanged, no matter how often you change your price structure.

226 Understanding Parameters

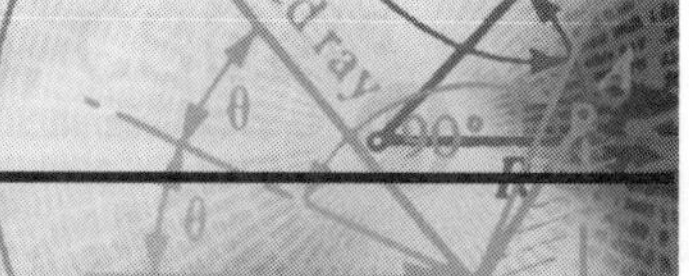

Parameters are variables (named memory locations) you can use to pass values to and from stored procedures. By using parameters, you can create a general-purpose stored procedure and execute its statements using different values in clauses, without having to rewrite the procedure's SQL code.

Suppose, for example, that you have a stored procedure such as:

```
CREATE PROCEDURE sp_call_history (@phone_number INTEGER,
  @start_date DATETIME, @stop_date DATETIME,
  @message VARCHAR(90) OUTPUT) AS

IF @phone_number = 0 AND
   (@stop_date = '' OR @start_date = '')
  SET @message = 'Call this routine with either ' +
    '(<phone number>,'''',''''') or '+
    '(0,<first date>,<last_date>)'
```

```
ELSE
  BEGIN
    IF @phone_number = 0
      SELECT * FROM oldcalls
      WHERE date_called >= @start_date
        AND date_called <= @stop_date
      ORDER BY date_called, call_time, hangup_time
    ELSE
      SELECT * FROM oldcalls
      WHERE phone_number = @phone_number
      ORDER BY date_called, call_time, hangup_time
  END
```

To get a list of calls made to a particular phone number, execute a statement batch similar to:

```
DECLARE @msg_ret VARCHAR(255)
EXEC sp_call_history 3320144,'','',@message=@msg_ret OUTPUT
PRINT @msg_ret
```

which uses the @PHONE_NUMBER parameter to pass the phone number 3320144 and the @START_DATE and @STOP_DATE parameters to pass blank dates to the stored procedure. The stored procedure uses 3320144 in statement references to @PHONE_NUMBER and blank dates for @START_DATE and @STOP_DATE.

You can also use the same stored procedure to get a list of calls made to all phone numbers within a date range by executing a statement batch similar to

```
DECLARE @msg_ret VARCHAR(255)
EXEC sp_call_history 0,'08/01/2000','08/05/2000',
      @message=@msg_ret OUTPUT
PRINT @msg_ret
```

which passes a zero (0) to the stored procedure through the @PHONE_NUMBER parameter and uses the @START_DATE and @STOP_DATE parameters to pass the first and last date in the date range. The stored procedure uses 08/01/2000 in statement references to @START_DATE, 08/05/2000 in statement references to @STOP_DATE, and zero (0) for @PHONE_NUMBER references.

If you supply neither a phone number nor a date range, the stored procedure uses the @MESSAGE parameter to put a message prompting you to specify one or the other when calling the procedure into the variable @MSG_RET. The DBMS uses the PRINT statement to display the value of the @MSG_RET parameter to the screen. Notice that the keyword OUTPUT must follow the name of the parameter (both in the stored procedure declaration and the EXEC statement that executes it) if the stored procedure is to use the parameter to pass a value back to the host (calling) program.

Note: *The current example shows how to declare a stored procedure and how to pass values to and from the procedure using MS-SQL Server Transact-SQL. Each DBMS product will have its own methods for creating procedures, declaring variables, and passing parameter values to and from stored procedures. Check your system manual for the* *specific statement syntax for your DBMS. The important thing to understand now is that you can use parameters to pass values between the host program (such as MS-SQL Server Query Analyzer or an application written in a programming language such as C or Visual Basic) and the SQL statements in a stored procedure.*

227 Understanding User/Session and Date/Time Functions and Variables

Each SQL Server either provides functions you can call or maintains several variables (*registers* on DB2) you can reference to determine user ID/session and date/time information. The SQL-92 specification codifies the requirement for the system to make the data available but (as with many things) leaves the specific mechanics of retrieving the information up to each DBMS vendor. As a result, each DBMS has its own way of letting you retrieve user, session, date, and time information.

Commonly implemented user/session functions and values include:

- **USER.** (System-supplied value.) The username used to connect to the database. The username used to connect to the database may be different than the login name used to log in to the network fileserver.
- **USER_ID([<username>]).** Returns the INTEGER database user identification number for the CHARACTER string username (value from USER or returned by USER_NAME()) passed to the function as a parameter. If called without a parameter, the USER_ID() function returns the database identification number of the current user.
- **USER_NAME([<user_ID>]).** Returns the CHARACTER string username for the INTEGER database identification number passed as a parameter. When called without a parameter, the USER_NAME() function returns the CHARACTER string username of the current user—the same as that maintained in the USER variable.
- **CURRENT_USER.** The CHARACTER string username of the current user. (Equivalent to USER_NAME().)
- **SUSER_ID([<login name>]).** Returns the INTEGER login ID number for the CHARACTER string login (vs. user) name passed to the function as a parameter. If called without a parameter, the SUSER_ID() function returns the login ID number of the current user.
- **SUSER_NAME([<login ID number>]).** Returns the CHARACTER string login name for the INTEGER login ID number passed as a parameter. When called without a parameter, the SUSER_NAME() function turns the login name for the current user.

- **SUSER_SID([<login name>]).** Returns the BINARY security identification number (SID) for the CHARACTER string login name passed as a parameter. When called without a parameter, the SUSER_ID() function returns the SID current user. (The SID is *not* the binary representation of the login ID number.)
- **SUSER_SNAME([<SID>]).** Returns the CHARACTER string login name for the BINARY SID number passed as a parameter. When called without a parameter, the SUSER_SNAME() function returns the login name of the current user.
- **SESSION_USER.** Niladic function that returns the current session's username as a value of type NCHAR. You can use the value returned by the SESSION_USER function as a column's DEFAULT constraint, or as an item in a SELECT clause, WHERE clause, or PRINT statement, and so on.
- **SYSTEM_USER.** Niladic function that returns the login name (vs. the username found in SESSION_USER) as a value of type CHAR. You can use the value returned by the SYSTEM_USER function as a column's DEFAULT constraint, or as an item in a SELECT clause, WHERE clause, or PRINT statement, and so on.
- **APP_NAME().** Returns the NVARCHAR(128) string application name if one was set by the current session.

Commonly implemented date/time functions and values include:

- **CURRENT_DATE.** (SQL) System-maintained variable with the value of the date on which the current statement was executed. Implemented as the CURRENT DATE register, which holds a DATE data type value on IBM DB2.
- **GETDATE().** Function that returns the current date and time in DATETIME format on MS-SQL Server.
- **CURRENT_TIME.** (SQL) System-maintained variable that contains the time of day at which the current SQL statement was executed. Implemented as the CURRENT TIME register, which holds a TIME data type value on IBM DB2.
- **CURRENT_TIMESTAMP.** Niladic function that returns the current date and time as a DATETIME data type value. Implemented as the CURRENT TIMESTAMP register with a TIMESTAMP data type on IBM DB2.
- **CURRENT TIMEZONE.** Register value of data type DECIMAL(6,0) on IBM DB2, which contains the difference between Coordinated Universal Time (also known as Greenwich Mean Time [GMT]) and the local time on the server. The difference is expressed as a signed six-digit number with the first two digits signifying hours, the next two signifying minutes, and the final two digits signifying seconds.

Please check your system manual for the specific calling syntax and usage restrictions for user/session and date/time functions and values on your DBMS implementation.

228 Understanding Column References

In an SQL database, the data values are stored in table columns, with each column holding one value in each row of a table. To use a column's values in SQL statements, simply type the column names whose values you want the DBMS to use.

If an SQL statement references a single table in its FROM clause, such as

```
SELECT employee_ID, first_name, last_name, office_ID
FROM employees WHERE office_ID = 1
```

you need only use the column names. The DBMS will assume that the column names in the statement refer to the values in columns from the table in the FROM clause—even if more than one table in the DBMS has columns with the same names. As such, in the current example, the DBMS will display the values in the EMPLOYEE_ID, FIRST_NAME, LAST_NAME, and OFFICE number columns from the rows in the EMPLOYEES table in which the value in the OFFICE column is 1.

If you are working with a single table, you can also use fully qualified column references that consist of the table name a period (.) and the name of the column. For example, the SELECT statement

```
SELECT employees.employee_ID, employees.first_name,
  employees.last_name, employees.office_ID
FROM employees WHERE employees.office_ID = 1
```

is equivalent to the previous example SELECT statement using only (unqualified) column names.

When combining data from two or more tables, use fully qualified column names to tell the DBMS which values to use from which table. For example, the SELECT statement

```
SELECT employees.employee_ID, employees.first_name,
  employees.last_name, employees.manager,
  offices.office_ID, offices.location, offices.manager,
  customers.customer_ID, customers.company_name
FROM customers, employees, offices
WHERE  employees.office_ID   = 1
  AND (employees.office_ID   = offices.office_ID)
  AND (customers.employee_ID = employees.employee_ID
```

combines data from the CUSTOMERS, EMPLOYEES, and OFFICES tables. Although the SELECT statement in the example makes it easy for a person reading the statement to see which column values are coming from which tables, the DBMS really requires only that you use fully qualified names for columns whose names appear in more than one of the tables in the statement's FROM clause. In the current example, the SELECT statement

```
SELECT employees.employee_ID, first_name, last_name,
  employees.manager, offices.office_ID, location,
```

```
  offices.manager, customer_ID, company_name
FROM customers, employees, offices
WHERE  employees.office_ID   = 1
  AND (employees.office_ID   = offices.office_ID)
  AND (customers.employee_ID = employees.employee_ID
```

will generate the same results table as the previous SELECT statement. Only the EMPLOYEE_ID, MANAGER, OFFICE_ID, and EMPLOYEE_ID columns need fully qualified column references because the remainder of the columns appear in only one of the tables listed in the statement's FROM clause and the DBMS.

229 Using the SUBSTRING Function to Retrieve a Portion of a String

Use the SUBSTRING function when you need to extract a portion of the characters from a binary string, a character string value in a table column, or a character string expression. For example, to extract characters 7–12 from a character string, use the SUBSTRING function syntax

```
SUBSTRING(<target string>, <start>, <length>)
```

in a SELECT statement such as:

```
SELECT SUBSTRING ('King, Konrad',7, 6)
```

which will display six characters from the string literal "King, Konrad" starting at character 7:

```
------
Konrad
```

Although extracting a portion of a string literal (such as "King, Konrad," in the current example), makes for an easy example, the real power of the SUBSTRING function becomes evident when you use it to extract a portion of a string found in a table column and use the resulting string as a conditional in a WHERE clause. Suppose, for example, that you want a list of all employees with last names starting with KIN; you could produce the list using the SUBSTRING function in the WHERE clause of a SELECT statement such as:

```
 SELECT last_name, SUBSTRING(last_name,1,3) AS 'First_Three',
   SUBSTRING(last_name,4,15) AS 'Remainder'
 FROM employees WHERE SUBSTRING(last_name,1,3) = 'KIN'
```

If you do not know the actual length of a string, simply specify the maximum number of characters you want the SUBSTRING function to return. When the SUBSTRING function finds that the <target string> has less than <length> characters from the <start> character to the end of the string, the function simply returns the characters from <start> to the end of the string (without reporting an error or warning). As such, the SELECT statement in the current example will produce the results table

```
Last_name First Three Remainder
--------- ----------- ---------
King      Kin         g
Kingsly   Kin         gsly
Kingston  Kin         gston
```

if the EMPLOYEES table has three employee with last names KING, KINGSLY, and KINGSTON—even though the longest last name has only eight characters and the SUBSTRING parameters specify that the function return characters 4–18.

Note: *If the <target string> is NULL, the SUBSTRING function will return a NULL value. Similarly, if you specify a <start> character that is higher than the length of the <target string>, some DBMS products will return a NULL result. Others, such as MS-SQL Server, will return an empty string (a string of length 0).*

230 Using the UPPER Function to Convert All of a String's Characters to Uppercase

The UPPER function converts the lowercase letters in a string to uppercase letters. For example, the SELECT statement

```
SELECT UPPER('konrad '+'king''s'),
  UPPER(SUBSTRING('1001 SQL Tips Book',1,14))
```

will display the output:

```
------------ -------------
KONRAD KING'S 1001 SQL TIPS
```

Notice that the UPPER function has no effect on any symbols, numbers, and uppercase letters in the target character string.

In addition to string literal expressions and function results, you can use the UPPER function to convert lowercase letters to upper case in table columns of data type CHARACTER (or VARCHAR) with statements such as

```
SELECT UPPER(first_name), UPPER(last_name),
  UPPER(first_name+' '+last_name), first_name, last_name
FROM employees
```

which will display

```
                              first_name  last_name
------  ----  -----------  ----------  ---------
KONRAD  KING  KONRAD KING  konrad      king
```

if the EMPLOYEES table has a single row with konrad in the FIRST_NAME column and king in the LAST_NAME column.

As was the case with the SUBSTRING function, the UPPER function returns an object of data type character. As such, you can use the UPPER function not only in SELECT statements to display uppercase strings, but also in UPDATE statements such as

```
UPDATE employees SET first_name = UPPER(first_name),
  last_name = UPPER(last_name)
```

which converts all FIRST_NAME and LAST_NAME column values in the EMPLOYEES table to upper case.

231 Using the DISTINCT Clause to Eliminate Duplicates from a Set of Rows

Individual columns not constrained by a PRIMARY KEY or UNIQUE constraint can have duplicate values in two or more rows in a table. By adding the DISTINCT clause to a query, you can tell the DBMS to eliminate duplicate rows from the SELECT statement's results table. Suppose, for example, that you want to know how many customers placed orders during the past 90 days. Executing the query

```
SELECT COUNT(customer_ID) FROM orders
WHERE order_date >= GETDATE() - 90
```

will give you an incorrect customer count if any customers placed more than one order during the period. However, if you add the DISTINCT clause to the same query

```
SELECT COUNT(DISTINCT customer_ID) FROM orders
WHERE order_date >= GETDATE() - 90
```

the DBMS will eliminate duplicate customer_IDs from the results table and give you an accurate count of unique customer_IDs (and, therefore, customers) that placed orders during the past 90 days.

In addition to COUNT(<column name>), you can use the DISTINCT clause with the SUM, AVG, and COUNT(*) aggregate functions. For example, given the ITEM_COUNT values

```
item_count
----------
4
5
6
4
4
5
```

executing the query shown in the top pane of Figure 231.1 will produce the results table shown in the figure's bottom pane.

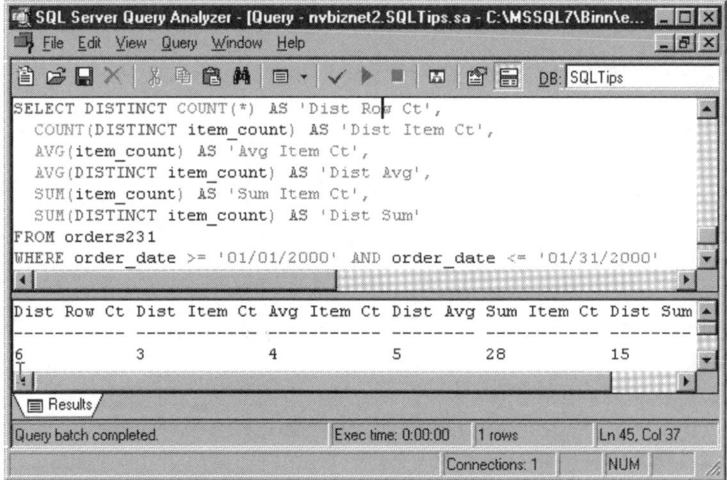

Figure 231.1 The MS-SQL Server Query Analyzer window showing a query using DISTINCT clauses in the upper (input) pane and the query's results table in the lower (output) pane

Notice that the DISTINCT COUNT(*) function produces what may at first appear to be an incorrect result. After all, there are only three unique ITEM_COUNT values (4, 5, 6), yet the DISTINCT COUNT(*) function returns a value of 6.

The reason for the disparity is that when you precede a column name list with a DISTINCT clause, the DBMS will eliminate only rows with duplicate values in the combined columns. For example, executing the query

```
SELECT DISTINCT customer_ID, item_count FROM orders
WHERE order_date >= '01/01/2000'
  AND order_date <= '01/31/2000'
```

can produce a results table similar to:

```
customer_ID item_count
----------- ----------
101         4
102         4
102         5
102         6
103         5
```

Although each of the two output columns (CUSTOMER_ID and ITEM_COUNT) contains duplicate values, the results table has no duplicate values for the combination of both columns (CUSTOMER_ID,ITEM_COUNT). Similarly, in the previous example, the DBMS expanded the COUNT(*) to mean "all columns." As such, the DISTINCT clause in DISTINCT COUNT(*) will eliminate only rows in which *all* columns values in one row are exact duplicates of *all* column values in another row.

232 Using the LOWER Function to Convert All of a String's Characters to Lowercase

In Tip 230, "Using the UPPER Function to Convert All of a String's Characters to Uppercase," you learned how to use the UPPER function to convert all lowercase letters in a character string to upper case. The LOWER function is the converse of the UPPER function in that the LOWER function converts all of the uppercase letters in a character string to lower case. For example, the SELECT statement

```
SELECT LOWER('KONRAD '+'KING''S'),
  LOWER(SUBSTRING('601 SQL Tips Book',1,14))
```

will display the output:

```
------------- -------------
konrad king's 601 sql tips
```

Notice that the LOWER function has no effect on any symbols, numbers, and lowercase letters in the target character string.

In addition to character string literal expressions and string function results, you can use the LOWER function to convert uppercase letters to lower case in table columns of data type CHARACTER (or VARCHAR). For example, the SELECT statement

```
SELECT LOWER(first_name), LOWER(last_name),
  LOWER(first_name+' ' +last_name), first_name, last_name
FROM employees
```

will display the results table

```
                                first_name  last_name
------  ----  -----------  ----------  ---------
konrad  king  konrad king  KONRAD      KING
```

if the EMPLOYEES table has a single row with KONRAD in the FIRST_NAME column and KING in the LAST_NAME column.

As was the case with the SUBSTRING and UPPER functions, the LOWER function returns an object of data type CHARACTER when passed a target string of data type CHARACTER (or VARCHAR when the target string is of data type VARCHAR). As such, you can use the LOWER function not only in SELECT statements to display lowercase strings, but also in UPDATE statements such as

```
UPDATE employees SET first_name = LOWER(first_name),
  last_name = LOWER(last_name)
```

which changes the values in the FIRST_NAME and LAST_NAME columns of rows in the EMPLOYEES table to lower case.

233 Using the TRIM Function to Remove Leading and Trailing Blanks

The TRIM function lets you remove leading or trailing blanks (or other characters) from a character string. Table 233.1 shows the results of using the TRIM function on various example character literals.

TRIM Function Call	***Returns***
TRIM (LEADING 'SQL Tips')	'SQL Tips'
TRIM (TRAILING 'SQL Tips')	'SQL Tips'
TRIM (BOTH 'SQL Tips')	'SQL Tips'
TRIM ('SQL Tips')	'' (empty string)
TRIM (BOTH 'S' FROM 'SQL Tips')	'QL Tips'
TRIM (LEADING 'S' FROM 'SSQL TIPS'	'SQL TIPS'
TRIM (BOTH 'S' FROM 'SSQL TIPS'	'SQL TIP'

Table 233.1 Example TRIM Function Calls and Results

As is the case with the SUBSTRING, UPPER, and LOWER functions (which you learned about in Tip 229, "Using the SUBSTRING Function to Retrieve a Portion of a String"; Tip 230, "Using the UPPER Function to Convert All of a String's Characters to Uppercase"; and Tip 232, "Using the LOWER Function to Convert All of a String's Characters to Lowercase," respectively), you can use CHARACTER (and VARCHAR) data type column references as the target string parameter for the TRIM function. For example, the SELECT statement

```
SELECT '>' + TRIM(last_name) + ', ' + TRIM(first_name)
FROM employees
```

will display the results table

```
------------
KING, KONRAD
```

if the EMPLOYEES table has a single row with KONRAD in the FIRST_NAME column and KING in the LAST_NAME column.

By the way, the calls to the TRIM function in the current example show the most abbreviated form of the TRIM function call syntax:

```
TRIM ([LEADING|TRAILING|BOTH] [<character to trim>][FROM]
  <target string>)
```

When you omit the <character to trim>, the TRIM function assumes you want to remove spaces. Moreover, if you do not specify LEADING, TRAILING, or BOTH, the function defaults to BOTH. As such, in the current example, the TRIM function calls in the form of TRIM(<target string>) tell the DBMS to remove BOTH leading and trailing spaces (blanks) on either side of the <target string>.

Note: *Some DBMS products, such as MS-SQL Server, implement the RTRIM and LTRIM functions instead of the TRIM function. Table 233.2 shows the RTRIM and LTRIM function call equivalents of the TRIM function used to remove leading, trailing, and both leading and trailing spaces.*

TRIM Function Call	***RTRIM or LTRIM Function Call***
TRIM (LEADING <target_string>)	LTRIM (<target_string>)
TRIM (TRAILING <target_string>)	RTRIM (<target_string>)
TRIM (BOTH <target_string>)	LTRIM(RTRIM(<target_string>))

Table 233.2 The TRIM Function Call Syntax and Equivalent LTRIM and RTRIM Function Call Syntax

Unlike the TRIM function, the syntax of the LTRIM and RTRIM function calls does not include a <character to trim> parameter. As such, you can use only LTRIM and RTRIM to strip blanks from the <target string> (while the TRIM function lets you specify the character to remove).

234 Using the Transact-SQL STUFF Function to Insert One Character String into Another

MS-SQL Server lets you use the STUFF function to insert one character string into another. The syntax of the STUFF function call is:

```
STUFF(<string 1>, <starting position>,
      <length to delete from string 1>, <string 2>)
```

As such, the PRINT statement

```
PRINT STUFF('**Konrad King''s Tips**',16,0,' 1001 SQL')
```

will display the results

```
**Konrad King's 1001 SQL Tips**
```

after the STUFF function inserts <character string 2> ("1001 SQL") into <string 1> ("**Konrad King's Tips**") after the 16th character in <string 1>.

If you want MS-SQL Server to remove a portion of <string 1> before inserting <string 2>, set the <length to delete from string 1> to something other than 0. For example, the PRINT statement

```
PRINT STUFF('**Konrad King''s Tips**',9,7,'''s 1001 SQL')
```

will display the results

```
**Konrad's 1001 SQL Tips**
```

after the STUFF function removes seven characters from <string 1> starting with character 9, (the space after "**Konrad") and then inserts <string 2> in <string 1> at the same character position (7).

Note: *If the <starting position> or <length to delete from string 1> is negative, or if the <starting position> is a number larger than the length of <string 1>, the STUFF function will return a NULL result.*

As is the case with the other character string functions you learned about in Tips 229–230 and 232–233, you can use variables and columns of data type CHARACTER (or VARCHAR) as parameters to the STUFF function. For example, to display the first letter of the FIRST_NAME followed by the LAST_NAME you can use a SELECT statement similar to

```
SELECT STUFF(first_name,2,40,'. ' + last_name)
  AS 'First Initial & Last Name' FROM employees
```

to produce output such as:

```
First Initial & Last Name
-------------------------
K. KING
S. FIELDS
D. JAMSA

(3 row(s) affected)
```

Note: *If you specify a <length to delete from string 1> that is longer than the number of characters from <starting position> to the end of <string 1>, the STUFF function will not report an error or warning. Instead, the function will simply truncate <string 1> with the character at <starting position –1>, as illustrated in the current example.*

235 Using the Transact-SQL Concatenation Operator "+" to Add One String to the End of Another String

MS-SQL Server lets you use the plus (+) operator to append the results of one character or binary string expression onto the results of another character or binary string expression using the syntax:

```
<string expression> + <string expression>
   [...+ <last string expression>]
```

For example, the PRINT statement

```
SELECT 'He' + 'llo' + ' ' + world!'
```

will display the results table:

```
------------
Hello world!
```

As usual, the real value of the concatenation operator is its ability to concatenate string literals, other character string function results, and CHARACTER (and VARCHAR) data type column values. For example, the SELECT statement

```
SELECT first_name + ' ' + last_name + ' wrote: "' + title +
  '" for ' + publisher + ' circa ' +
  CONVERT(VARCHAR(11),publish_date) + '.'
FROM authors, titles
WHERE author_ID = author
ORDER BY last_name, first_name
```

can be used to combine literal strings and column values from the AUTHORS and TITLES tables to form English sentences such as those in the results table:

```
---------------------------------------------------------
Kris Jamsa wrote: "Java Programmer's Library" for Jamsa
  Press circa Jun  1 1996.
Kris Jamsa wrote: "1001 Windows 98 Tips" for Jamsa Press
  circa Jun  1 1998.
Konrad King wrote: "SQL Tips & Techniques" for Prima
  Publishing circa Feb  1 2002.
Konrad King wrote: "Hands on PowerPoint 2000" for Jamsa
  Press circa Aug  1 1999.
```

236 Understanding the Transact-SQL CONVERT Function

SQL requires that all operands in each expression and data values in each table column be of the same data type. You may not have noticed this restriction, however, because many DBMS products, like MS-SQL Server, perform most data type conversions automatically. On MS-SQL Server, for example, you can place a character string such as "'–123'" into an INTEGER or NUMERIC column because the system automatically changes the string literal into the equivalent INTEGER or NUMERIC value before inserting it into the table. (The only restriction is that the string literal must consist entirely of numbers, and optionally, a single decimal point and a minus sign (–). Similarly, MS-SQL Server lets you compare a CHARACTER string data type object or expression with a DATETIME data type object or expression without first performing a data type conversion.

For those instances in which MS-SQL Server will not perform an automatic data type conversion, you can use the Transact-SQL CONVERT function. You can also use the CONVERT function to specify the format of DATETIME, FLOATING and REAL, and MONEY and SMALLMONEY data type values when you want any of them displayed or stored in CHARACTER (or VARCHAR) columns in other than the default format.

The syntax of the CONVERT function call is

```
CONVERT (<data type> [(<length>)], <data to convert>
  [, <style>])
```

where:

- **<data type>** is the data type you want the CONVERT function to return.
- **<length>** is the maximum number of characters (letters, symbols, numbers) in the returned value. If you omitted, the system defaults the length to 30.

- **<data to convert>** can be a literal value, expression, function call, or database object such as a column name or variable.
- **<style>** specifies scientific notation when converting FLOAT and REAL values; comma placement and decimal precision when converting MONEY and SMALLMONEY values; or the date and time format when converting DATETIME values.

When using the CONVERT function, you can either store its results in a variable or table column or display the results to the screen using a PRINT statement or a SELECT statement, such as

```
SELECT 'There are ' + CONVERT(VARCHAR(COUNT(*))) +
  ' invoices on file.
The oldest is dated ' +
  CONVERT(VARCHAR,MIN(invoice_date),1) +
' and the most recent is ' +
  CONVERT(VARCHAR,MAX(invoice_date),1) + '.'
FROM invoices
```

which uses the CONVERT function to change the INTEGER result of the COUNT(*) function and the two DATETIME values returned by the MIN() and MAX() functions to VARCHAR strings to produce the results table similar to:

```
----------------------------------------------------------
There are 24 invoices on file.
The oldest is dated 06/30/99 and the most recent is 9/15/00
```

As mentioned previously and shown in the current example, you can use the <style> argument in the CONVERT function to select the format you want the system to use for displaying a DATETIME value. Table 236.1 shows the different <style> values CONVERT will accept.

Note: *If you add 100 to any numeric <style> value shown in Table 236.1, the CONVERT function will return a four-digit year instead of a two-digit year. For example, a <style> of 1 will return a date in the form mm/dd/yy, while a <style> of 101 will return a date in the form mm/dd/yyyy. (Styles 0, 9, 13, 20, and 21 are exceptions to the rule because they already return the year as a four-digit value.)*

When converting REAL or FLOAT data types, you can omit the <style> value or use it to specify the use of scientific notation as outlined in Table 236.2.

Finally, when converting MONEY or SMALLMONEY data types, you can omit the <style> value or use it to specify the use commas as outlined in Table 236.3.

<style>	*Format*	*Example*
(blank), 0	mmm dd yyyy hh:mmAM/PM	Jun 30 1999 10:13AM
1	mm/dd/yy	06/30/99
2	yy.mm.dd	99.06.30
3	dd/mm/yy	30/06/99
4	dd.mm.yy	30.06.99
5	dd-mm-yy	30-06-99
6	dd mmm yy	30 Jun 99
7	mmm dd, yy	Jun 30, 99
8	hh:mm:ss	10:13:23
9	mmm dd yyyy hh:mm:ss:sssAM/PM	Jun 30 1999 10:13:23:060AM
10	mm-dd-yy	06-30-99
11	yy/dd/mm	99/06/30
12	yymmdd	990630
13	dd mmm yyyy hh:mm:ss:sss	30 Jun 1999 10:13:23:060
14	hh:mm:ss:sss	10:13:23:060
20	yyyy-dd-mm hh:mm:ss	1999-06-30 10:13:23
21	yyyy-dd-mm hh:mm:ss.sss	1999-06-30 10:13:23.060

Table 236.1 CONVERT Function <style> Values and Date Formats for Converting DATETIME Data

<style>	*Format*
(blank)	No scientific notation
0	Use scientific notation if the value has more than six digits to the left of the decimal
1	Always use scientific notation and display as eight digits
2	Always use scientific notation and display as 16 digits

Table 236.2 CONVERT Function <style> Values for Converting FLOAT and REAL Data

<style>	*Format*
(blank), 0	No commas
1	Commas every three digits to the left of the decimal and two digits to the right of the decimal.
2	Commas every three digits to the left of the decimal and four digits to the right of the decimal

Table 236.3 CONVERT Function <style> Values for Converting MONEY and SMALLMONEY Data

237 Understanding the UNION, INTERSECT, and EXCEPT Operators

The UNION, INTERSECT, and EXCEPT operators let you perform mathematical set operations on database tables (or query results tables) to combine two union-compatible results tables into a single results table. For example, if you use the UNION operator to combine two tables, the results table will consist of all of the rows from the first table together with all of the rows from the second table. (By default, the DBMS will eliminate any duplicate rows from the results table.) As an example, suppose you have two tables with the following data:

```
TABLE A                        TABLE B
Make     Model                 Make  Model
-------  ----------            ----  --------
Ford     Explorer              Ford  Mustang
Lincoln  Navigator             Ford  Explorer
Chevy    Vega                  Ford  Jaguar
Ford     Expedition
```

The statement

```
(SELECT * FROM a) UNION (SELECT * FROM b)
```

will produce the results table:

```
Make     Model
-------  ----------
Ford     Explorer
Lincoln  Navigator
Chevy    Vega
Ford     Expedition
Ford     Mustang
Ford     Jaguar
```

While the UNION operator produces a results table by merging the rows in two tables and eliminating any duplicate rows, the INTERSECT operator creates a results table consisting of rows in one table that are duplicated in the other. For example, given the same tables and data as those used in the previous example, the statement

```
(SELECT * FROM a) INTERSECT (SELECT * FROM b)
```

will produce the results table:

```
Make   Model
----   ----------
Ford   Explorer
```

The EXCEPT operator, meanwhile, is the converse of the INTERSECT operator in that it creates a results table consisting of the rows from the first table that are not duplicated in the second table. Again given the same table A and table B values, the statement

```
(SELECT * FROM a) EXCEPT (SELECT * FROM b)
```

will produce the results table

```
Make      Model
-------   ----------
Lincoln   Navigator
Chevy     Vega
Ford      Expedition
```

because these three row values are found in the first table (A) and not in the second table (B). Notice that the two rows found only in table B (and one in table A) are not included in the results table.

Note: *Some DBMS products do not support all three of the set operators. MS-SQL Server, for example, supports only the UNION operator. If your DBMS does not support the INTERSECT operator, you can generate the INTERSECT results table using a SELECT statement with a WHERE clause that tests for the equality of each of the corresponding columns in the two tables. For example, given tables A and B from the current example, the SELECT statement*

```
SELECT DISTINCT a.make, a.model FROM a, b
WHERE a.make = b.make
  AND a.model = b.model
```

will produce the same results table as

```
(SELECT * FROM a) INTERSECT (SELECT * FROM b)
```

Similarly, you can generate the EXCEPT results table by using a SELECT statement with a WHERE clause that excludes rows in which the composite value of the columns in the first table are the same as the composite value of the columns in a second table. For example, given tables A and B from the current example, the SELECT statement

```
SELECT DISTINCT a.make, a.model FROM a
WHERE (a.make + a.model)
  NOT IN (SELECT b.make + b.model FROM b)
```

will produce the same results table as

```
(SELECT * FROM a) EXCEPT (SELECT * FROM b)
```

238 Using the INTERSECT Operator to Select Rows That Appear in All of Two or More Source Tables

As you learned in Tip 237, "Understanding the UNION, INTERSECT, and EXCEPT Operators," the INTERSECT operator creates a results table that includes only those rows included in both database tables (or query results tables) joined by the operator. For example, executing the statement

```
(SELECT * FROM a) INTERSECT (SELECT * FROM b)
```

will create a results table that includes all of the rows from table A that are also in table B.

You can use the INTERSECT (or UNION, or EXCEPT) operator to combine two SELECT statements that use the asterisk (*) in the SELECT clause to specify "all columns" only if the tables are union-compatible. (As you learned in Tip 216, "Using the UNION Operator to Select All Rows That Appear in Any or All of Two or More Tables," two tables are union-compatible when they have the same number of columns, the corresponding columns are of the same data type, and the corresponding columns are in the same order in two tables.) As such, two tables created by

```
CREATE TABLE a                  CREATE TABLE b
  (make,        VARCHAR(15),      (model        VARCHAR(15),
   model,       VARCHAR(15),       make         VARCHAR(15),
   sales_price MONEY)              sales_price MONEY)
```

are not union-compatible because the corresponding columns (MAKE in table A and MAKE in table B, and MODEL in table A and MODEL in table B) are not in the same order in both tables.

You can still use the INTERSECT operator to combine query results from two tables that are not union-compatible by explicitly naming the columns from each table that the operator is to match up. For example, given the two tables described in the preceding paragraph, you could use the INTERSECT operator to combine queries on each the two tables by executing the statement:

```
  (SELECT  make, model FROM a)
INTERSECT
  (SELECT make, model FROM b)
```

Note: *When you explicitly name the columns to be combined, the INTERSECT operator looks for only duplicates in the combination of columns listed. As such, in the current example, the results table will include rows in which the combination of (MAKE,MODEL) is the same in both table A and table B—even if none of the values in the SALES_PRICE column in table A matches those from the SALES_PRICE column of table B.*

In effect, the INTERSECT operator combines two queries using an "and" operator vs. the UNION operator, which combines two queries using an "or" operator. For example, if you want to know "What products are supplied by vendor A *or* vendor B *or* vendor C?" you would use the UNION operator to join SELECT statements such as:

```
  (SELECT vendor_ID, product, price FROM product_list_A)
UNION
  (SELECT vendor_ID, product, price FROM product_list_B)
UNION
  (SELECT vendor_ID, product, price FROM product_list_C)
```

On the other hand, if you want to know "What products are supplied by vendor A *and* vendor B *and* vendor C?" you would use the INTERSECT operator to join the queries such as:

```
  (SELECT vendor_ID, product, price FROM product_list_A)
INTERSECT
  (SELECT vendor_ID, product, price FROM product_list_B)
INTERSECT
  (SELECT vendor_ID, product, price FROM product_list_C)
```

239 Using the EXCEPT Operator to Select Rows in One Table That Do Not Appear in a Second Table

In Tip 237, "Understanding the UNION, INTERSECT, and EXCEPT Operators," you learned that the EXCEPT operator is one of the three mathematical *set* operators (along with UNION and INTERSECT) that you can use to combine the results tables from two or more queries. While "a INTERSECT b" (which you learned about in Tip 238, "Using the INTERSECT Operator to Select Rows That Appear in All of Two or More Source Tables") generates a results table with rows from table A that *are* duplicated in table B, the expression "a EXCEPT b" generates a results table with rows from table A that *are not* duplicated in table B.

The EXCEPT operator is useful for queries such as:

"Give me a list of products provided only by vendor A":

```
((SELECT description FROM vendor_a_products)  EXCEPT
 (SELECT description FROM vendor_b_products)) EXCEPT
(SELECT description FROM vendor_c_products)
```

"Give me a list of customers that have not purchased a Widget yet":

```
(SELECT customer_ID FROM customers) EXCEPT
(SELECT (customer_ID FROM orders WHERE item = 'Widget')
```

"Give me a list of freshmen that have not yet taken Chemistry 101":

```
(SELECT student_ID FROM students
 WHERE class = 'freshman') EXCEPT
(SELECT student_ID FROM classes WHERE class_ID = 'CHEM 101')
```

If two tables are union-compatible (meaning that both tables have the same number of columns with corresponding columns that are of the same data type and in the same order) you can use the "all columns" operator (*) in the SELECT clause of the queries to produce a results table that includes all of the columns from the rows in the first table that are not duplicated in the second table. For example, if the you have two sales offices and want a list of inventory items stored only at office 1, you could execute the SELECT statement

```
(SELECT * FROM inventory_o1) EXCEPT
(SELECT * FROM inventory_o2)
```

if both office inventory tables, INVENTORY_O1 (the inventory table for office 1) and INVENTORY_O2 (the inventory table for office 2), have the same structure.

Note: *As shown by the three example queries at the beginning of this tip, you can use the EXCEPT operator to combine queries on tables that are not union-compatible by listing the corresponding columns in the SELECT clause of each query instead of using the all columns operator (*).*

---

240 Using the POSITION Function to Return the Location of a Letter or Substring in a Character String

The POSITION function lets you search for a target string within a source string and return the (INTEGER) character position where the first occurrence of the target string begins in the source string. For example, the statement

```
PRINT POSITION ('k' IN 'My name is Konrad')
```

will display the INTEGER value 12 because, as dictated by the syntax of the POSITION function call

```
POSITION (<target string> IN <source string>)
```

the DBMS will search the <source string> "My name is Konrad" for the first occurrence of the <target string> k, and return the character position (12) where the <target string> starts in the <source string>.

Note: *Whether the POSITION function performs a case-sensitive or case-insensitive search depends on the sort order settings on your SQL server. If the server's sort order is case-insensitive, than an uppercase letter has the same value as a lowercase letter. As such, K = k for any comparison tests and substring searches. The current example assumes the server's sort order is case-insensitive. If the sort order were case-sensitive, the statement*

```
PRINT POSITION ('k' IN 'My name is Konrad')
```

would display the INTEGER value 0 because, on a case-sensitive system, K has a different value than k, and there is no lowercase k in the <source string> "My name is Konrad."

If the <target string> consists of more than one character, the POSITION function searches the <source string> for the first matching sequence of characters in the <source string>. For example, the statement

```
PRINT
POSITION ('Kingsly' IN 'My last name is king, not kingsly')
```

will display the INTEGER value 27 because the first character of the substring that matches the <target string> "Kingsly" starts at character position 27 of the <source string>.

Note: *The SQL-92 specification calls for a POSITION function. However, your DBMS product may have a different name (and syntax) for the function. On MS-SQL Server, for example, the POSITION function is implemented as CHARINDEX with the syntax*

```
CHARINDEX(<target_string>,
  <source string>[, <start location>])
```

which lets specify the <start location> in the <source string> that the CHARINDEX function is to begin its search. As such, the PRINT statement

```
PRINT
CHARINDEX('King','My last name is king, not kingsly', 18)
```

will display the INTEGER value 27 and not 17 (the starting position of the first occurrence of king in the <source string>) because CHARINDEX started its search at character position 18 and therefore found the "king" in kingsly to be the first occurrence of the <target string> in the portion of the <source string> it was told to search.

As is the case with the other string functions, the real power of POSITION (or CHARINDEX, on MS-SQL Server) is its ability to accept any CHARACTER (or VARCHAR) data type objects or expressions as the <source string> or <target string>. For example, the CHARINDEX function in the SELECT statement

```
SELECT employee_name AS 'Full Name',
  SUBSTRING(LTRIM(employee_name),1,
    CHARINDEX(' ',LTRIM(employee_name))-1) AS 'First Name',
  SUBSTRING(LTRIM(employee_name),
    CHARINDEX(' ',LTRIM(employee_name))+1,30)
  AS 'Last Name'
FROM employees
```

uses the result returned by the LTRIM function (executed on a table column), and the SUBSTRING function uses the results of the CHARINDEX function in an expression to extract character strings from the EMPLOYEE_NAME column, which the SELECT statement then uses to produce a results table similar to:

```
Full Name      First Name   Last Name
------------   ----------   ---------
Konrad King    Konrad       King
Sally Fields   Sally        Fields
```

241 Using the CHAR_LENGTH Function to Return the Length of a String Variable

The CHAR_LENGTH function returns the number of characters in a character string. For example, the statement

```
PRINT CHAR_LENGTH('Captain Kirk')
```

will display the INTEGER value 12. Although the SQL standard specifies the CHAR_LENGTH function with the syntax

```
CHAR_LENGTH (<string expression>)
```

your DBMS product may use CHARACTER_LENGTH, LENGTH, or LEN as the function's name. MS-SQL Server, for example, uses LEN to return the number of characters in a string expression, excluding trailing blanks.

As is the case with the other string functions, using the CHAR_LENGTH function on a string literal is useful for illustrative purposes. However, the true value of the CHAR_LENGTH function lies in its ability to return the length of any string expression, including a column reference. For example, on MS-SQL Server, the statement

```
SELECT MAX (LEN(CONVERT(VARCHAR,qty))) AS 'MAX Digits Qty'
  MAX (LEN(description = units))  AS 'MAX Len Des + Units'
  MAX (LEN(CONVERT(VARCHAR,unit_cost)))AS 'MAX Len Unit Cost'
```

will produce a results table similar to:

```
MAX Digits Qty  MAX Len Desc + Units  MAX Len Unit Cost
--------------  --------------------  -----------------
2               31                    5
```

You can then use the results to format output such as that shown in Figure 241.1 into a more readable format, as shown in Figure 241.2.

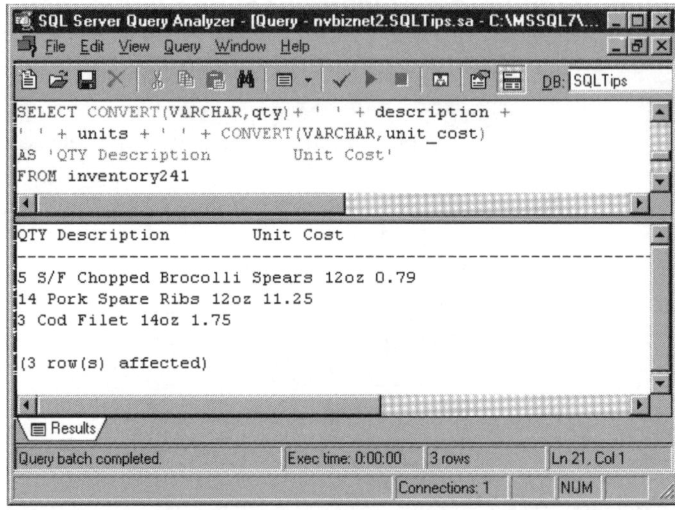

Figure 241.1 SELECT statement combining INTEGER, MONEY, and variable character string data

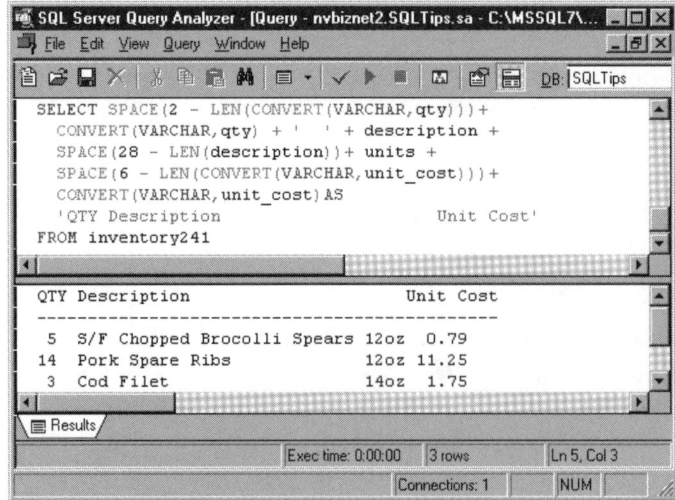

Figure 241.2 SELECT statement using the LEN function to convert variable-length strings into fixed-length strings

242 Using the OCTET_LENGTH Function to Determine the Number of Bytes Required to Hold a String Variable or Literal

Computers use bits—individual 1s and 0s—to store data in memory or on disk. The minimum number of bits required to store a character (such as a letter, symbol, or number) is called a byte. In the past, many computer systems used 8 bits to represent a character. As a result, 8 bits was (for a time) simply referred to as a byte of data. Unfortunately, the term "byte" does not indicate a number of bites. To correct this inadequacy, SQL's designers decided to borrow the musical term *octet* (meaning an ensemble of eight voices) when naming the function OCTET_LENGTH, which returns the number of 8-bit bytes required to store the value passed to the function as a parameter.

For example, on systems with 8-bit bytes, the statement

```
PRINT OCTET_LENGTH ('Yellow Brick Road')
```

will display the INTEGER value 17 because the system will use 8 bytes (one octet) to represent each character. Similarly, the statement

```
PRINT OCTET_LENGTH (0x1001000110011101)
```

will display the INTEGER value 2 because it takes two 8-bit bytes (16 bits) to store the binary value of 268,505,345.

Note: *Not all DBMS products support the OCTET_LENGTH function. MS-SQL Server, for example, defines OCTET_LENGTH as a Reserved Word, but has no function for returning the number of 8-bit sequences required to store a value or image. (The LEN function returns the number of characters required to store a value, not the number of bytes [or octets].) The important thing to remember is that if the DBMS supports the OCTET_FUNCTION, the system will compute the result by dividing 8 into the number of bits required to store a value or an image and rounding up to the nearest whole number.*

243 Using the BIT_LENGTH Function to Determine the Number of Bits Required to Hold a String Variable or Literal

While the OCTET_LENGTH function returns the number of octets (or sets of 8 bits) needed to hold a data value or image, the BIT_LENGTH function returns the number of bits (individual 1s and 0s) required. As such, the statement

```
PRINT BIT_LENGTH (0x100111011111)
```

will display the INTEGER value 12, since the BINARY value contains twelve 1s and 0s. As such, it will take 12 bits to store them on the system. Similarly, the statement

```
PRINT BIT_LENGTH ('Yellow Brick Road')
```

will display the INTEGER value 136 on those systems that use 8 bits to store a character.

Note: *As was the case with the OCTET_FUNCTION, many DBMS products do not support the BIT_LENGTH function. MS-SQL Server, for example, defines BIT_LENGTH as a Reserved Word but has no function for determining the number of bits required to store a data value or image. Therefore, check your system manual to make sure the BIT_LENGTH function is available on your DBMS before attempting to use it in your code. Most DBMS products do support a LEN (CHAR_LENGTH or CHARACTER_LENGTH) function that will return the number of characters in an object. As such, if your DBMS does not support the BIT_LENGTH function, you can use the LEN function to compute the number of bits in an object (such as a picture stored in a column of data type IMAGE) by multiplying the character length of an object (returned by the LEN function) by the number of bits per byte on your system.*

244 Using the EXTRACT Function to Extract a Single Field from a DATETIME Value

Although a DBMS normally stores date and time as a single value such as 2000-09-04 17:03:35.640, you sometimes need only one of the fields, such as the month, day, or year. The SQL EXTRACT function provides a way to extract or separate a DATETIME value into its component parts. For example, the statement

```
PRINT EXTRACT(DAY FROM '2000-09-04 17:03:35.640')
```

will display the value 4. Similarly, the statement

```
PRINT EXTRACT(MINUTE FROM '2000-09-04 17:03:35.640')
```

will display the value 3.

Unfortunately, some DBMS products do not support the EXTRACT function. For those that do, the syntax function is

```
EXTRACT(<datetime field> FROM <datetime value>)
```

Where:

```
<datetime field> is either YEAR, MONTH, DAY, HOUR, MINUTE,
SECOND, TIMEZONE_HOUR or TIMEZONE_MINUTE

<datetime value> is a column, literal, variable, or
expression with a value of data type DATETIME
```

If your DBMS product does not support the EXTRACT function, you may have to convert the DATETIME value into a CHARACTER string using either the CONVERT function (which you learned about in Tip 236, "Understanding the Transact-SQL CONVERT Function") or CAST function (which you will learn about in Tip 249, "Using the CAST Function to Convert a Value from One Data Type to Another)". After you have the DATETIME in an object of data type CHARACTER, you can use the SUBSTRING function (which you learned about in Tip 229, "Using the SUBSTRING Function to Retrieve a Portion of a String") to extract the portion of the DATETIME value you want.

For example, executing the statement batch

```
DECLARE @date_string VARCHAR(19), @month INTEGER
SELECT @date_string = CONVERT(VARCHAR,GETDATE(),120)
SELECT @month = SUBSTRING(@date_string,5,2)
PRINT @month
```

on MS-SQL Server will retrieve the system date, convert it to a character string, and display the value of the month.

245 Using the CURRENT_TIME Function to Read the Current System Time

Every DBMS provides a way for you to retrieve the current system time. The SQL standard specifies a CURRENT_TIME function that will return the system time as a TIME data type when called using the syntax:

```
CURRENT_TIME (<decimal second precision>)
```

As such,

```
PRINT CURRENT_TIME(2)
```

will display a current system time such as:

```
20:08:01.22
```

Some DBMS products, such as DB2, implement the CURRENT_TIME as a register (named memory location) of data type TIME. Other products, such as MS-SQL Server, will return the system time as part of a function call, such as GETDATE(). Therefore, you need to check your system manual for the exact variable or function call the DBMS provides to retrieve the current time from the operating system. On MS-SQL Server for example, the statement

```
PRINT GETDATE()
```

will display the current system time along with the current date, such as:

```
May  9 2000  8:15PM
```

You can then either use the SUBSTRING function to extract the time portion of the DATE-TIME value returned by the GETDATE() function, or use the CONVERT function you learned about in Tip 236 to have the GETDATE() function return a time-only value. For example, the statement

```
PRINT CONVERT(VARCHAR,GETDATE(),14)
```

will display a current system time alone in the form:

```
20:21:56:450
```

Note: *If you are using MS-SQL Server, review Tip 236 on the CONVERT function for additional date and time formats available.*

246 Using the CURRENT_DATE Function to Read the Current System Date

Each DBMS gives you a way to retrieve the current system date, such as the SQL CURRENT_DATE function, which, when you execute a statement such as

```
PRINT CURRENT_DATE
```

will display a system date such as:

```
2000-09-04
```

Some DBMS products, such as DB2, implement CURRENT_DATE as a register (named memory location) of data type DATE. Other products, such as MS-SQL Server, will return the system date as part of a function call, such as GETDATE(). Therefore, you must check your system manual for the exact variable or function call that will retrieve the current date on your system. On MS-SQL Server for example, the statement

```
PRINT GETDATE()
```

will display the current system time along with the current date, such as:

```
Sep  4 2000  9:19PM
```

After using the GETDATE() function to retrieve the system date, you can use the SUBSTRING function to extract the date portion of the DATETIME value, or you can use the CONVERT function you learned about in Tip 236, "Understanding the Transact-SQL CONVERT Function," to have the GETDATE() function return a date-only value. For example, the statement

```
PRINT CONVERT(VARCHAR,GETDATE(),106)
```

will display a current date alone, such as:

```
04 Sep 2000
```

Note: *If you are using MS-SQL Server, review Tip 236, on the CONVERT function, for additional date and time formats available.*

247 Using the CURRENT_TIMESTAMP Function to Read the Current System Date and Time

Most DBMS products support the CURRENT_TIMESTAMP function, which lets you retrieve the current system date and time together as a single value of data type TIMESTAMP. According to the SQL standard, the TIMESTAMP data type is defined as:

```
<date value><space><time value>
```

As such, the statement

```
PRINT CURRENT_TIMESTAMP
```

will retrieve and display the current system date and time (its timestamp) in the form:

```
2000-09-05 05:40:01:547
```

Some DBMS products, such as DB2, implement the CURRENT_TIMESTAMP as a register (named memory location) of data type TIMESTAMP. On MS-SQL Server, the CURRENT_TIMESTAMP function is equivalent to the GETDATE() function and returns a value of data type DATETIME instead of TIMESTAMP. For example, executing the statement

```
PRINT 'The current TIMESTAMP is: ' +
  CONVERT(VARCHAR, CURRENT_TIMESTAMP) +
  ' and  the GETDATE() value is: ' +
  CONVERT(VARCHAR,CURRENT_TIMESTAMP) + '.'
```

on MS-SQL Server will display:

```
The current TIMESTAMP is: Sep  5 2000  6:54AM and the
  GETDATE() value is: Sep  5 2000  6:54AM
```

Note: The DATETIME data type is the MS-SQL Server equivalent of the SQL TIMESTAMP data type. Both are used to define columns and variables that will hold a date and time value separated by a space.

248 Understanding MS-SQL Server Date and Time Functions

Unlike some DBMS products, MS-SQL Server does not support separate data types for TIME, DATE, and TIMESTAMP data. Instead, MS-SQL Server supports a single data type, DATETIME, for use in defining columns and variables to hold composite date and time values. In fact, MS-SQL Server does not even support separate functions for retrieving the current system time or the current system date. Instead, the Transact-SQL GETDATE() function always returns both the system date and time as a DATETIME data type value.

You can, however, use the CONVERT function to change the current system date-time value into a character string that contains only the current date or only the current time. As such, the CONVERT function used in conjunction with GETDATE() can be used to produce the same results as both the CURRENT_TIME and CURRENT_DATE functions. Keep in mind, however, that when used to extract a date or time from a date-time value, the CONVERT function must return a value of data type CHARACTER, not DATE or TIME (since the DATE and TIME data types are not defined on MS-SQL Server).

Table 248.1 shows the formats you can tell MS-SQL Server to use when displaying or storing the current system time. For example, the MS-SQL Server equivalent of the statement

```
INSERT INTO orders (time_order_placed)
  VALUES (CURRENT_TIME)
```

which uses the CURRENT_TIME function to place a TIME value of the form 15:25:23 into the TIME_ORDER_PLACED_COLUMN of the ORDERS table, is the statement

```
INSERT INTO orders (time_order_placed)
  VALUES(CONVERT(VARCHAR,GETDATE(),8))
```

which uses the GETDATE() function to retrieve the current system date and time (as a value of data type DATETIME) and then uses the CONVERT function to extract the time portion of the date-time value into a character string that it then places in the TIME_ORDER_PLACED column.

<style>	Format	Example
8	hh:mm:ss	10:13:23
14	hh:mm:ss:sss	10:13:23:060

Table 248.1 CONVERT Function <style> Values That Let the GETDATE() Function Approximate the CURRENT_TIME Function

Although MS-SQL Server does not support the CURRENT_DATE function, you can specify one of the styles shown in Table 248.2 to the CONVERT function and have the function convert the date portion of a date-time expression to a character string representing the current system date. For example, the MS-SQL Server equivalent of the INSERT statement

```
INSERT INTO orders (date_order_placed)
  VALUES (CURRENT_DATE)
```

which uses the CURRENT_DATE value to place the current system date in the form 09/05/2000 into the DATE_ORDER_PLACED column of the ORDERS table, is the statement

```
INSERT INTO orders (date_order_placed)
  VALUES (CONVERT(VARCHAR,GETDATE(),101)
```

which uses the GETDATE() function to retrieve the current system date and time (as a value of type DATETIME) and then uses the CONVERT function to extract the date portion of the system date-time value into a character string that it then places in the DATE_ORDER_PLACED column in the ORDERS table.

<style>	Format	Example
1	mm/dd/yy	06/30/99
2	yy.mm.dd	99.06.30
3	dd/mm/yy	30/06/99
4	dd.mm.yy	30.06.99
5	dd-mm-yy	30-06-99
6	dd mmm yy	30 Jun 99
7	mmm dd, yy	Jun 30, 99
10	mm-dd-yy	06-30-99
11	yy/dd/mm	99/06/30
12	yymmdd	990630

Table 248.2 CONVERT Function <style> Values That Let the GETDATE() Function Approximate the CURRENT_DATE Function

---

Note: *As you learned in Tip 236, "Understanding the Transact-SQL CONVERT Function," adding 100 to any of the style values listed tells MS-SQL Server to return the year as a four-digit value vs. a two-digit value. For example, CONVERT(VARCHAR, GETDATE(),6) will return the date a: 30 Jun 99. Meanwhile, CONVERT(VARCHAR,GETDATE(),106) will return the same date as 30 Jun 1999.*

Finally, as shown in Table 248.3, you can use the style value parameter in the CONVERT function call to control how MS-SQL Server provides the current system timestamp (date and time together as a single value). For example to place a timestamp in the format: 2000-09-05 15:23:32:015 into the ORDER_TIMESTAMP column of the ORDERS table, execute a statement similar to:

```
INSERT INTO orders (order_timestamp)
  VALUES (CONVERT(VARCHAR,CURRENT_TIMESTAMP,21))
```

Or, you can use the GETDATE() function in place of the CURRENT_TIMESTAMP function as

```
INSERT INTO orders (order_timestamp)
  VALUES (CONVERT(VARCHAR,GETDATE(),21))
```

to place the same current system date-time value into the ORDER_TIMESTAMP column of a row in the ORDERS table.

<style>	***Format***	***Example***
(blank), 0	mmm dd yyyy hh:mmAM/PM	Jun 30 1999 10:13AM
9	mmm dd yyyy hh:mm:ss:sssAM/PM	Jun 30 1999 10:13:23:060AM
13	dd mmm yyyy hh:mm:ss:sss	30 Jun 1999 10:13:23:060
20	yyyy-dd-mm hh:mm:ss	1999-06-30 10:13:23
21	yyyy-dd-mm hh:mm:ss.sss	1999-06-30 10:13:23.060

Table 248.3 CONVERT Function <style> Values and Date Formats for Converting DATETIME Data

---

Note: *If you are transporting code from a system with DATE and TIME data types, you will have to use a column of type CHARACTER if you want to store only a date or only a time on MS-SQL Server. If you place either only a date or only a time into a column of data type DATETIME, MS-SQL Server will still store both a date and a time value in the column. (If you omit the time, MS-SQL Server sets the time portion of the DATETIME data type column to 00:00:00.000; if you omit the date, MS-SQL Server sets the date portion of the DATETIME data type column to 1900-01-01.)*

---

249 Using the CAST Function to Convert a Value from One Data Type to Another

As mentioned in Tip 236, "Understanding the Transact-SQL CONVERT Function," MS-SQL Server, unlike the SQL-92 specification, is very forgiving when it comes to mixing values of different data types in an expression. According to the SQL standard, the DBMS should convert automatically only values of similar data types. As such, if you were to compare a SMALLINT value with an INTEGER value, for example, the DBMS should perform the operation. However, if you tried to compare a character string to a NUMERIC value, the DBMS should disallow the comparison and generate an error.

If your DBMS adheres to the SQL standard's restrictive rules about combining data of different types in expressions, you can use the CAST function to convert data from one type to another so that the DBMS can execute your mixed data type expressions without error. Suppose, for example, that you stored the CUSTOMER_ID as a CHARACTER string in the ORDERS table, but you stored CUSTOMER_NUM as an INTEGER in the CUSTOMERS table. So long as all of the CHARACTER data type values in the CUSTOMER_ID column of the ORDERS table either were NULL or contained all numeric digits, you can use the CAST function to convert the CHARACTER, CUSTOMER_ID into an INTEGER in the SELECT statement

```
SELECT customer_name, product_code, qty, amount
FROM customers, orders
WHERE CUSTOMER_NUM = CAST (customer_ID INTEGER)
ORDER BY customer_name
```

so the DBMS will be able to compare an INTEGER value to another INTEGER value in the query's WHERE clause, vs. aborting on an error as it tried to compare the INTEGER CUSTOMER_NUM with the CHARACTER CUSTOMER_ID.

Because most DBMS products do not strictly adhere to the SQL standard's tight data type checking rules, you will use the CAST function most often when you need to pass a value from the DBMS back to an application program that does not support the value's data type. For example, most programming languages do not support a DATETIME data type. As such, you must use the CAST function to convert values of data type DATETIME into CHARACTER strings so that the host program can work with them. The SELECT statement

```
SELECT customer_ID, CAST (order_date AS CHAR(11)),
  CAST(date_shipped as CHAR(11)), order_total FROM Orders
```

for example, will convert DATETIME data type values in the ORDER_DATE and DATE_SHIPPED columns to 10-letter character strings. (If the SELECT statement puts its results into a cursor, which you will learn about in Tip 379, " Using the SQLFetch Function to Retrieve a Row of Data From an SQL Database," you can then pass the ORDER_DATE and DATE_SHIPPED to the host program variables as CHARACTER strings instead of DATETIME values, which the host program does not support.)

As shown by the current example, the syntax of the CAST function call is

```
CAST (<value expression> AS <data type>)
```

and you can use it almost anywhere a value of <data type> can appear in an SQL statement (similar to the way in which you use other functions such as CONVERT or GETDATE()). Keep in mind that you can use the CAST function only to perform *valid* data type conversions. For example, the DBMS cannot execute the statement

```
PRINT CAST('Hello' AS INTEGER)
```

because the CHARACTER literal contains non-numeric characters. However, the statement

```
PRINT CAST('-12.35' AS INTEGER)
```

will execute successfully since the character literal contains all numbers, zero or one decimal point, and zero or one plus (+) sign or zero or one minus sign (-). In short, if the DBMS will allow you to enter a specific literal value into a column of the data type given by <data type> column, then you can use the CAST function in the form

```
CAST (<value expression> AS <data type>)
```

to convert the value from <value expression> into an equivalent value of data type <data type>.

Note: *When converting a numeric data type value into a CHARACTER string, make sure your string is large enough to hold all of the digits, the decimal point (.), if any, and sign, if the number is negative. If the string into which the system is to CAST (convert) the number is too small to hold all of its value, some DBMS products will truncate the number to fit the string, while others, like MS-SQL Server, will abort the statement with an error message such as:*

```
Server: Msg 8115, Level 16, State 5, Line 1
Arithmetic overflow error converting numeric to data type
  varchar.
```

250 Using the CASE Expression to Select a Literal Based on the Value of a Column

A CASE expression provides SQL with limited decision-making capabilities. As mentioned previously, SQL is a data sublanguage, not a full procedural or object-oriented programming language. SQL lets you tell the DBMS only *what* to find or do, but not *how* to find it or do it. Most DBMS products provide extensions to standard SQL that let you *program* the order of execution of the statements an SQL statement batch. The CASE expression, meanwhile, is a part of SQL itself and gives the data sublanguage an IF-THEN-ELSE control structure it can use to decide what an SQL statement will do based on the data it finds in the table column(s) on which it operates.

When the DBMS encounters a CASE statement in the form

```
CASE WHEN <search condition> THEN <expression>
 [...WHEN <last search condition>
      THEN <last expression>]
[ELSE <expression>]
END
```

the system checks the first <search condition>, and if it evaluates to TRUE, then the CASE statement takes on the value of the first <expression>. If the first <search condition> evaluates to FALSE, then the DBMS goes on to the second <search condition>. If the second <search condition> evaluates to TRUE, then the CASE statement takes on the value of the <second expression>; if, FALSE, the DBMS goes on to check the third <search condition>, and so on. If none of the CASE expression's search conditions evaluate to TRUE, then the CASE expression takes on the VALUE of the expression in its (optional) ELSE clause—or if there is no ELSE clause, the CASE expressions evaluates to NULL.

For example, the CASE expression in the SELECT statement

```
SELECT first_name, last_name,
  CASE WHEN pts_accumulated >= 100000 THEN 'High Roller'
       WHEN pts_accumulated >= 50000 THEN 'Premium Player'
       WHEN pts_accumulated >= 25000 THEN 'Preferred Guest'
       WHEN pts_accumulated >= 12500 THEN 'Regular'
       ELSE 'Patron'
  END AS 'Rating',
  pts_accumulated
FROM casino_guests
```

can be used to display casino guest names and player ratings in a results table similar to:

```
first_name last_name Rating          pts_accumulated
---------- --------- --------------- ---------------
Sally      Fields    Patron          1300
Lenny      Hall      Premium Player  50000
Wally      Wells     Regular         13000
Brent      McCoy     Preferred Guest 25000
Erwin      Shiff     Preferred Guest 45000
Bruce      Wayne     Premium Player  75000
James      Bond      High Roller     107500
```

As shown in the example, the DBMS evaluates the first search condition pts_accumulated >= 100000 and, if TRUE, sets the value of the RATING column in the results table to High Roller. If a search condition evaluates to FALSE, the DBMS moves on to the next search condition until it finds one that evaluates to TRUE. If none of the search conditions evaluates to TRUE, as is the case for Sally Fields in the current example, the DBMS sets the value of the RATING column in the results table to the value of the expression in the ELSE clause.

251 Using a Subquery in a Searched CASE Expression

In Tip 250, "Using the CASE Expression to Select a Literal Based on the Value of a Column," you leaned how to use a simple form of the CASE expression in which the WHEN clauses consist of a column reference and all of the THEN clause values (the result expressions) are literals. However, in addition to column names and literals, you can use any valid SQL expression in a CASE expression's clauses. Suppose, for example, the you are a scrap metal dealer and will pay a 25% premium above the base price of a metal if the quantity on hand is less then the amount you want. By including a subquery in a CASE expression such as the one in the query

```
SELECT metal, desired_lbs,
   (SELECT SUM(lbs) FROM scrap_inv
      WHERE scrap_inv.metal = scrap_master.metal) AS
     'lbs_on_hand',
   base_price,
   CASE WHEN (SELECT SUM(lbs) FROM scrap_inv
              WHERE scrap_inv.metal = scrap_master.metal) <=
          desired_lbs THEN base_price * 1.25
        ELSE base_price
   END AS 'current_price'
FROM scrap_master
```

you can use the SUM aggregate function in the WHEN clause to find out the amount of the metal currently on hand. The result of the subquery then determines the value of the CURRENT_PRICE in the results table. If the poundage is at or below the desired level, the THEN clause sets the current price at 125% of the base price in the SCRAP_MASTER to produce a results table similar to:

```
metal     desired_lbs lbs_on_hand base_price current_price
--------  ----------- ----------- ---------- -------------
Tin       1000        1625        .7500      .750000
Iron      1500        625         .2500      .312500
Aluminum  2000        850         .4500      .562500
```

In addition to using a subquery in a CASE expression's WHEN clause, you can use a subquery in its THEN clause. Suppose, for example, that you want to set the current price you will pay for a metal at 25 percent above the average price you paid in the past if you have less in inventory than you want. The CASE expression SELECT statement similar to

```
SELECT metal, desired_lbs,
   (SELECT SUM(lbs) FROM scrap_inv
      WHERE scrap_inv.metal = scrap_master.metal) AS
     'lbs_on_hand',
   base_price,
   CASE WHEN (SELECT SUM(lbs) FROM scrap_inv
              WHERE scrap_inv.metal = scrap_master.metal) <=
```

```
            desired_lbs
      THEN CASE WHEN (SELECT SUM(lbs) FROM scrap_inv
                      WHERE scrap_inv.metal =
                        scrap_master.metal) > 0
                THEN (SELECT AVG(purchase_price) * 1.25
                      FROM scrap_inv
                      WHERE scrap_inv.metal =
                              scrap_master.metal)
                ELSE base_price * 1.25
           END
      ELSE base_price
  END AS 'current_price'
FROM scrap_master
```

will produce a results table in which the CURRENT_PRICE is based on the average cost of the metal instead of its base price when the quantity on hand is low.

252 Using the NULLIF Function to Set the Value of a Column to NULL

The NULLIF function is a special form of the CASE expression that lets you set the value of a column to NULL if the two expressions passed as parameters to the function have the same value. When the DBMS encounters a NULLIF function in the form

```
NULLIF (<first expression>,<second expression>)
```

it evaluates the <first expression> (usually a column value) and compares its value to the value of the <second expression> (usually a numeric or character literal value). If the two expressions evaluate to the same (equal) value, then the NULLIF function returns a NULL. Otherwise, the function returns the value of the <first expression>.

You would use the NULLIF function if an attribute of the physical entity or concept represented by the column's value goes from a known to an unknown or missing state. Suppose, for example, that you have an EMPLOYEES table in which the MANAGER column contains the ID (EMP_ID) of the employee's manager. If the manager, Susan (EMP_ID, 101), leaves your company, the employees she managed no longer have a manager. You could execute an UPDATE statement with a CASE expression such as

```
UPDATE employees SET manager =
  CASE WHEN manager = 101 THEN NULL
       ELSE manager
  END
```

to set the MANAGER column for all of Susan's employees to NULL. Or, you can execute an UPDATE statement with a NULLIF function such as

```
UPDATE employees SET manager = NULLIF(manager,101)
```

which accomplishes the same purpose. In the current example, if the value of a row's MANAGER column is 101, then the NULLIF function returns the value NULL, which the UPDATE function puts into the MANAGER column. Otherwise, the NULLIF function returns the value in the MANAGER column—meaning that the UPDATE statement will leave unchanged any rows in which the value in the MANAGER column is not 101.

The NULLIF function is particularly useful when importing data previously maintained by one of the standard programming languages. NULL values, for example, are not allowed such languages as COBOL, Pascal, and FORTRAN. As a result, the programmers may have use a special code such as a –1 in a field such as SALARY, for example, to indicate a NULL salary for those employees that are paid hourly. To convert the –1 values in the SALARY column to NULL, you could execute an UPDATE statement with a CASE expression such as:

```
UPDATE employees SET salary = CASE salary WHEN -1 then NULL
                                           ELSE salary
                              END
```

Or, you could execute an UPDATE statement with a more compact NULLIF function, such as:

```
UPDATE employees SET salary = NULLIF(salary,-1)
```

253 Using the CAST Function to Compare Values in Columns of Different Data Types

You learned about the different SQL data types in Tips 21–28, and as mentioned in Tip 249, DBMS products that strictly follow the SQL-92 standard will not allow you to mix values of different data types in single expression. As such, a DBMS adhering to SQL-92 guidelines would abort the SELECT statement

```
SELECT employees WHERE hire_date = 'Aug 20 2000'
```

because the BOOLEAN expression in the WHERE clause attempts to compare a column value of data type DATETIME to a character literal.

Fortunately, many DBMS products, such MS-SQL Server, will automatically convert the two values in the WHERE clause of the current example to a common data type and then will execute the statement without error. However, if you have a DBMS that will perform type conversions only when the operands involved have similar data types (such as INTEGER and

SMALLINT, or FLOAT and NUMERIC, or CHAR and VARCHAR), you can use the CAST function to perform the conversions manually.

For example, if your DBMS will not let you compare a character literal (character string) to a column of data type DATETIME, you can use the CAST function in the form

```
CAST (<value expression> AS <data type>)
```

to convert the DATETIME data type value to a character string. As such, your DBMS will find the query

```
SELECT * FROM employees
WHERE CAST(hire_date AS CHARACTER(11)) = 'Aug 20 2000'
```

acceptable because both values in the WHERE clause are character strings. Similarly, if you have an EMPLOYEE table in which the EMP_ID column is of data type INTEGER and a CUSTOMER table in which the SALESPERSON_ID is of type VARCHAR(6), the CAST function in the query

```
SELECT customer_name, employee_name AS 'sold_by'
FROM   employees, customers
WHERE  emp_ID = CAST(salesperson_ID AS INTEGER)
```

will convert the SALESPERSON_ID to an INTEGER value, so the DBMS will compare it to the value in the EMP_ID column without error. In short, you can use the CAST expression to convert a data type in an SQL statement anywhere an expression or value can appear.

There are, of course, some restrictions on what you can do with the CAST expression. You cannot, for example, use CAST to convert the character string Konrad into a value of data type MONEY. After all Konrad has no numeric value. Similarly, you cannot use CAST to convert 09/19/2000 into an INTEGER value.

Basically, you can use CAST to convert a value of any data type into a CHARACTER or VARCHAR data type. However, you can convert values of a non-numeric data type into a numeric data type only if the non-numeric data type value contains all digits (numbers 0–9), (optionally) a single decimal point, and (optionally) a single dash (–) or plus (+) at the beginning of the string to indicate whether the number is negative or positive.

254 Using the CAST Function to Pass Values from SQL to a Host Language

Host variables let you pass values from an application program written in a *host* programming language (such as C, FORTRAN, Pascal, or Visual Basic) to the DBMS and to pass values from the DBMS back to the host program. Unfortunately, no host programming language supports all of the SQL data types. The CAST function lets you convert a value of an SQL data type not supported by the host language into an equivalent value in data type that is.

The DATETIME data type, for example, lets you store a combination date and time value in a column of an SQL table. However, none of the host programming languages supports the DATETIME date type. As such, you must convert values of data type DATETIME that you want to pass from the DBMS to an external application into a data type the program supports. That is where the CAST function comes in.

Suppose you want to pass an employee's hire date to a C program. Because C does not have a DATETIME, you would use the CAST function in a statement such as

```
SET :date_hired = (SELECT CAST(hire_date AS CHAR(19))
                   FROM employees
                   WHERE employee_id = 101)
```

to convert the combination date and time information into a character string value. (In the current example, string-parsing subroutines in the C program will extract the employee's date of hire from a combination date and time string for display on the screen using standard C I/O functions.)

You will learn how to embed SQL commands in a host (procedural) language application in Tips 372 through 389. For now, the important thing to know is that the CAST function gives you a way to pass values of data types unique to SQL from the DBMS to the host application through host variables.

255 Understanding How to Use Modifying Clauses in a Select Statement

The SELECT statement is used to read and display data values in SQL table columns. Modifying clauses FROM, WHERE, HAVING, GROUP BY, and ORDER BY let you specify the table to query what data to display and how to order the rows of results. Table 255.1 summarizes the purpose of each of the modifying clauses you can use in a SELECT statement.

Clause	**Purpose**
FROM	Specifies the table(s) whose column data values the SELECT statement is to display.
WHERE	Specifies the search condition(s) to be used in filtering out those rows the query is *not* to display.
GROUP BY	Combines rows into groups based on the values in the grouping columns.

Clause	*Purpose*
HAVING	Filters out groups that do not meet one or more search conditions. (HAVING can appear only in conjunction with a GROUP BY clause.)
ORDER BY	Sorts the rows in the results table (prior to display) based on the values in specified columns (can reference only columns listed in the SELECT clause).

Table 255.1 Select Statement Modifying Clauses

At a minimum, every SELECT statement must have a FROM clause. (After all, you must always tell the DBMS which table[s] to query.) In addition to the FROM clause, the query can include any or all of the modifying clauses in the following order:

```
SELECT <column list>
FROM <table list>
[WHERE <search condition(s)>]
[GROUP BY <grouping column list>]
[HAVING <search condition(s)>]
[ORDER BY <column list>]
```

With the exception of the FROM clause (which specifies the table(s) on which the SELECT statement operates), the DBMS processes the results of each of the clauses it finds in a query in a sequential manner. Said another way, the results table from one clause serves as the input table for the next.

For example, the query

```
SELECT customers.cust_ID, cust_name, inv_total
FROM customers, invoices
```

creates a results table that consists of a Cartesian product of the rows in the CUSTOMERS table and the rows in the INVOICES table. (In Tip 281, "Understanding Cartesian Products," you will learn about Cartesian products—tables consisting of all the rows from one table combined with all of the rows from another table.)

Adding the WHERE clause

```
SELECT customers.cust_ID, cust_name, inv_total
FROM customers, invoices
WHERE customers.cust_ID = invoices.cust_ID
```

tells the DBMS take to filter out those rows in which the value in the CUST_ID column from the CUSTOMERS table is not equal to the value in the CUST_ID column from the INVOICES table.

Adding the GROUP BY clause

```
SELECT customers.cust_ID, cust_name, SUM(inv_total)
FROM customers, invoices
WHERE customers.cust_ID = invoices.cust_ID
GROUP BY customers.cust_ID, cust_name
```

tells the DBMS to take the rows in the results table generated by the WHERE clause and combine all rows with the same composite (CUST_ID,CUST_NAME) value into a single row.

Adding the HAVING clause

```
SELECT customers.cust_ID, cust_name, SUM(inv_total)
FROM customers, invoices
WHERE customers.cust_ID = invoices.cust_ID
GROUP BY customers.cust_ID, cust_name
HAVING customers.cust_ID > 500
```

tells the DBMS to take the results table from the GROUP BY clause and filter out any rows in which the value in the CUST_ID column is less than 500.

Finally, adding the ORDER BY clause

```
SELECT customers.cust_ID, cust_name, SUM(inv_total)
FROM customers, invoices
WHERE customers.cust_ID = invoices.cust_ID
GROUP BY customers.cust_ID, cust_name
HAVING customers.cust_ID > 500
ORDER BY cust_name
```

tells the DBMS to arrange the rows in the results table generated by the HAVING clause in ascending order according to the value in each row's CUST_NAME column.

256 Understanding Comparison Predicates

An SQL predicate is an expression (often referred to as search condition) in a WHERE clause that asserts a fact. If the assertion is TRUE for a given row in a table, the DBMS performs the action specified by the SQL statement; if the assertion is FALSE, the DBMS goes on to check the predicate against the column values in the next row of the input table. In short, a predicate acts as a filter, allowing only rows that meet its specifications to pass through for further processing.

Table 256.1 shows the six comparison operators you can use to write a comparison predicate.

Operator	Usage	Meaning
=	A = B	Process when A is equal to B
<	A < B	Process when A is less than B
<=	A<= B	Process when A is less than or equal to B
>	A > B	Process when A is greater than "B"
>=	A >= B	Process when A is greater than or equal to B
<>	A <> B	Process when A is not equal to B

Table 256.1 SQL Comparison Operators

Although you can use a comparison operator to compare any two values—even two literals (constants)—the true value of a comparison predicate is that it lets you identify rows you want based on the value stored in each of one or more columns. For example, the comparison predicate in the WHERE clause of the statement

```
SELECT * FROM customers WHERE 5 = 5
```

is of no use as a filter, since 5 is equal to 5 for all rows in the table. As such, the query will display every row in the EMPLOYEE table and could have been written more efficiently without the WHERE clause as:

```
SELECT * FROM customers
```

Conversely, the statement

```
DELETE FROM invoices WHERE invoice_date < '01/01/1900'
```

tells the DBMS to remove only those rows for invoices dated prior to 01/01/1900 from the INVOICES table. Similarly the comparison predicate in the statement

```
SELECT cust_ID, cust_name, last_paid, amt_paid, still_due
FROM   customers
WHERE (GETDATE() - last_paid) > 30
AND    total_due > 500
```

tells the DBMS to display only those customers who have outstanding balances greater than $500 and who have not made a payment within the last 30 days. Finally, the UPDATE statement

```
UPDATE customers
SET salesperson = 'Konrad' WHERE salesperson = 'Kris'
```

tells the DBMS to change the value in the SALESPERSON column to Konrad only in those rows that currently have Kris as the SALESPERSON.

Note: *Each comparison operator always works with two values. However, you can test for as many column values as you like (two at a time) by joining multiple comparison predicates using the Boolean operators (OR, AND, and NOT) that you learned about in Tip 94, "Using Boolean Operators OR, AND, and NOT in a WHERE Clause."*

---

257 Using the BETWEEN Keyword in a WHERE Clause to Select Rows

When you want to work with a set of rows with a column value that lies within a specified range of values, use the keyword BETWEEN in the statement's WHERE clause. For example, to get a list of employees hired during the month of March 2000, you can use a SELECT statement similar to that shown in the MS-SQL Server Query Analyzer input pane near the top of Figure 257.1 to produce a results table similar to that shown at the bottom of the figure.

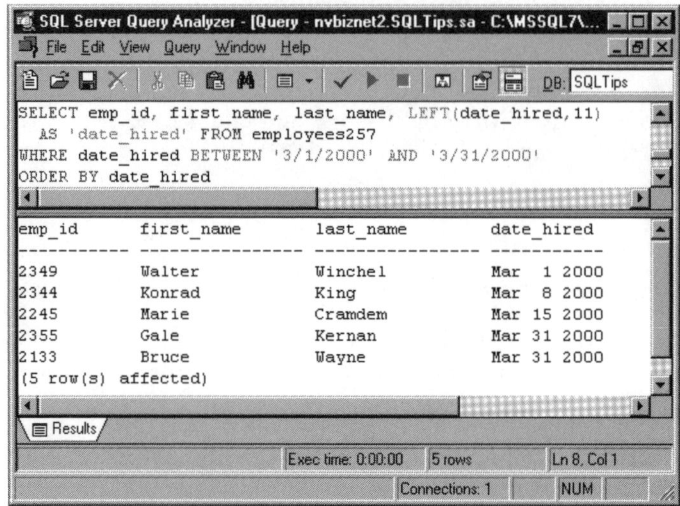
```
SELECT emp_id, first_name, last_name, LEFT(date_hired,11)
  AS 'date_hired' FROM employees257
WHERE date_hired BETWEEN '3/1/2000' AND '3/31/2000'
ORDER BY date_hired

emp_id      first_name       last_name        date_hired
----------- ---------------- ---------------- -----------
2349        Walter           Winchel          Mar  1 2000
2344        Konrad           King             Mar  8 2000
2245        Marie            Cramdem          Mar 15 2000
2355        Gale             Kernan           Mar 31 2000
2133        Bruce            Wayne            Mar 31 2000
(5 row(s) affected)
```

Figure 257.1 MS-SQL Server Query Analyzer query and results table using the BETWEEN keyword

Although the SELECT statement in the current example shows a query in which the upper and lower bounds of the range are literal values, the BETWEEN predicate can actually consist of any three valid SQL expressions with compatible data types, using the syntax:

```
<test expression>
   BETWEEN <low expression> AND <high expression>
```

For example, you can use the SELECT statement

```
SELECT * FROM employees
WHERE (total_sales - 25000)
  BETWEEN (SELECT AVG(total_sales) FROM employees)
    AND   (SELECT AVG(total_sales) * 1.2 FROM employees)
```

to list those employees whose total sales volume minus $25,000, is between the average sales volume and 120 percent of the average.

The BETWEEN predicate evaluates to TRUE whenever the value of <test expression> is greater than or equal to the value of <low expression> and less than or equal to the value of <high expression>. Therefore, the query

```
SELECT first_name, last_name FROM employees
WHERE last_name BETWEEN 'J' and 'Qz'
```

is equivalent to:

```
SELECT first_name, last_name FROM employees
WHERE last_name >= 'J' and last_name <= 'Qz'
```

One thing to keep in mind is that the value of the low end of the range (<low expression>) must be less than or equal to the value of the high end of the range (<high expression>). While query

```
SELECT * FROM employees WHERE date_hired
BETWEEN '01/01/2000' AND '01/31/2000'
```

may appear to be equivalent to

```
SELECT * FROM employees WHERE date_hired
BETWEEN '01/31/2000' AND '01/01/2000'
```

it is not. The first query lists employees hired in January 2000, while the second query will never list any employees because it can never be the case that the DATE_HIRED is greater than or equal to 01/31/2000 (the <low expression>) while at the same time being less than or equal to 01/01/2000 (the <high expression>).

258 Using the IN or NOT IN Predicate in a WHERE Clause to Select Rows

IN and NOT IN predicates let you select a row based on whether or not the row has a column value that is a member of (included in) a set of values. Suppose, for example, that your company has offices in Nevada, California, Utah, and Texas. Since you have to collect sales tax for customers living in those states, you could use the IN predicate in an UPDATE statement such as

```
UPDATE invoices SET sales_tax = invoice_total * 0.07
WHERE ship_to_state IN ('NV', 'CA', 'UT', 'TX')
```

to compute the sales tax (given that each state charges the same 7 percent sales tax rate). Conversely, the NOT IN predicate in an UPDATE statement such as

```
UPDATE invoices SET sales_tax = 0.00
WHERE ship_to_state NOT IN ('NV', 'CA', 'UT', 'TX')
```

will set sales tax due to 0.00 for customers that do not live any of the states in which your company has offices.

The syntax for the IN and NOT IN predicates is:

```
<test expression>
   [NOT] IN (<first value> [... , <last value>])
```

While the IN predicate evaluates to TRUE if the <test expression> is a member of the set of values listed between the parenthesis (()), the NOT IN predicate evaluates to TRUE if the <test expression> is not a member of the set.

As was the case with the BETWEEN predicate (which you learned about in Tip 257, "Using the BETWEEN Keyword in a WHERE Clause to Select Rows"), the IN and NOT IN predicates do not really add to the expressive power of SQL. In the current example, you could have written the UPDATE statement by testing for multiple equalities (joined with OR operators) such as:

```
UPDATE invoices SET sales_tax = invoice_total * 0.07
WHERE ship_to_state = 'NV' OR ship_to_state = 'CA' OR
      ship_to_state = 'UT' OR ship_to_state = 'TX'
```

However, the IN (and NOT IN) predicate does save you some typing if there are a large number of values in the set you are testing for membership (or exclusion) of the value of the <test expression>.

259 Using Wildcard Characters in the LIKE Predicate

You can use the LIKE predicate to query the database for a character string value when you know only a portion of the string you want. As such, the keyword LIKE when used in a WHERE clause lets you compare two character strings for a partial match and is especially valuable when you have some idea of the string's contents but do not know its exact form.

The LIKE predicate has two wildcard characters you can use to write the search string when you know only its general form and not all of its characters. The percent sign (%) can stand for any string of zero or more characters in length, and underscore (_) can stand for any single character. To search for a character string using one or more wildcard characters in a LIKE query, simply include the wildcard(s) in a string literal along with the portion of the string you know.

For example, to search for all teachers whose last names begin with the letters "Ki," you could execute a SELECT statement similar to

```
SELECT first_name, last_name FROM faculty
WHERE last_name LIKE 'Ki%'
```

which will produce a results table similar to:

```
first_name  last_name
----------  ---------
Konrad      King
Wally       Kingsly
Sam         Kingston
```

Each of the rows selected from the FACULTY table has a LAST_NAME value staring with the two letters "Ki" and followed by any number of other characters.

Similarly, if you want to match any *single* character vs. any *multiple* characters, you would use the underscore (_) instead of the percent sign (%). For example, if you know that the letter S was the second character of any class in the Sciences curriculum, and you wanted a list of 100-level courses, you could execute a SELECT statement similar to

```
SELECT course_ID, description FROM curriculum
WHERE course_ID LIKE '_S10_'
```

to produce a results table similar to:

```
course_ID   description
---------   ----------------------------------------
CS101       Introduction to Computer Science
BS109       Biological Sciences - Anatomy & Physiology
MS107       Beginning Quadratic Equations
```

Each of the rows the DBMS selects from the CURRICULUM table has COURSE_ID value with S as the second character, followed by 10, and ending with one and only one additional character. Unlike the percent sign (%) wildcard, which can match *zero* or more characters, the underscore (_) wildcard can match one and only one character. As such, in the current example, the course_IDs S101 and CS101H would not be included in the query's results table. The S in S101 is the first and not the second character, and two characters instead of one follow the 10 in CS101H.

260 Using Escape Characters in the LIKE Predicate

In Tip 259, "Using Wildcard Characters in the LIKE Predicate," you learned how to use wildcard characters in a LIKE predicate to query the database for string values when you know only a portion of the string you want. However, what do you do when you want to search for a string that includes one of the wildcard characters?

To check for the existence of a percent sign (%) in a character data type column, for example, you need a way to tell the DBMS to treat a percent sign (%) in the LIKE predicate as a literal value instead of a wildcard. The keyword ESCAPE lets you identify a character that tells the DBMS to treat the character immediately following the *escape* character in the search string as a literal value. For example, the query

```
SELECT cust_ID, cust_name, discount FROM customers
WHERE discount LIKE "%S%" ESCAPE 'S'
```

uses the *escape* character S to tell the DBMS to treat the second percent sign (%) in the search string %S% as a literal value (and not a wildcard). As a result, the query will return the CUST_ID, CUST_NAME, and DISCOUNT column values for any rows in which the last character in the DISCOUNT column is a percent sign (%).

Similarly, if you want to search for the underscore (_) character in a data type column, you would use the keyword ESCAPE in a query such as

```
SELECT product_code, description FROM inventory
WHERE product_code LIKE "XY$_%" ESCAPE '$'
```

to tell the DBMS to treat the character following the dollar sign ($) as a literal character instead of a wildcard. As a result, of the query in the current example, the DBMS will display the PRODUCT_CODE and DESCRIPTION of all INVENTORY items in which the product code starts with "XY_".

261 Using LIKE and NOT LIKE to Compare Two Character Strings

SQL has two predicates that let you search the contents of a CHARACTER, VARCHAR, or TEXT data type column for a pattern of characters. The LIKE predicate will return the set of rows in which the target column contains the pattern of characters in the search string. Conversely, the NOT LIKE predicate will return those rows in which the pattern is not found in the target column.

For example, the query

```
SELECT * FROM customers WHERE cust_name LIKE 'KING'
```

will display rows in the CUSTOMERS table in which the value in the target column (CUST_NAME) is KING. Meanwhile, the query

```
SELECT * FROM customers WHERE cust_name NOT LIKE 'SMITH'
```

will display the rows in the CUSTOMERS table that do not have SMITH in the CUST_NAME column.

The LIKE and NOT LIKE predicates are of little value if not used with the wildcard characters you learned about in Tip 259, "Using Wildcard Characters in the LIKE Predicate." After all, you could have written the two example queries using the equality (=) and not equal to (<>) comparison operators, as follows:

```
SELECT * FROM customers WHERE cust_name = 'KING'
SELECT * FROM customers WHERE cust_name <> 'SMITH'
```

In short, the LIKE predicate is useful when you "know" only some of the characters in the target column, or if you want to work with all rows that contain a certain pattern of characters. For example, if you "know" the name of the customer is something *like* KING, but you are not sure if it is KINGSLY, KING, or KINGSTON, you could query the database using a SELECT statement similar to:

```
SELECT * FROM customers WHERE cust_name LIKE 'KING%'
```

The percent sign (%) wildcard character tells the DBMS to match any zero of more characters. As such, the query in the current example tells the DBMS to display the columns in a CUSTOMERS table rows in which the value of the target column (CUST_NAME) starts with the letters KING followed by any zero or more additional characters.

Similarly, if you precede the search string with a percent sign (%) you can search for a pattern of characters within a string. For example, the query

```
SELECT * FROM customers WHERE notes LIKE "%give%discount%"
```

will display the rows in the CUSTOMERS table in which the value in the target column (NOTES) includes the word GIVE followed by at least one occurrence of the word DISCOUNT. Therefore, the DBMS would display the columns in a row in which the NOTES column contained the string: "Excellent customer. Make sure to give a 5% discount with next order."

Conversely, the NOT LIKE predicate, when used in conjunction with one or more wildcard characters, will display those rows that do not contain the pattern of characters given by the search string. Thus, the query

```
SELECT * FROM customers WHERE notes NOT LIKE "%discount%"
```

will display a list of customer rows whose NOTES column does not include the pattern of letters that make up the word *discount*.

262 Understanding the MS-SQL Server Extensions to the LIKE Predicate Wildcard Characters

In Tip 259, "Using Wildcard Characters in the LIKE Predicate," you learned how to use the percent sign (%) and underscore (_) wildcard characters in LIKE predicates to compare character strings for a partial match. While the underscore lets you match any single character and the percent sign (%) lets you match any pattern of zero or more characters, neither wildcard lets you specify the *range* in which the unknown character(s) must fall. For example, the query

```
SELECT * FROM employees WHERE badge LIKE '1___'
```

with three underscores after the 1 tells the DBMS to display any employees whose four-character badge number starts with a 1. If you want to limit the results to badge numbers in which the first character is a 1 and the second character is an a, A, b, B, c, or C, for example, MS-SQL Server lets you use brackets ([]) to provide specify a set of characters the wildcard underscore (_) can match. As such, the query

```
SELECT * FROM employees WHERE badge LIKE '1[a-cA-C]__'
```

tells the DBMS to display four character badge numbers in which the first character is a "1", the second character is an uppercase or lower case letter "A", "B", or "C", and is followed by any to other characters (represented by the final two wildcard underscores in the search string).

Conversely, if you want to exclude a range of characters from those matched by the wildcard, insert a caret (^) between the left bracket ([) and the first value in the range of characters that can be substituted for the wildcard character.. For example, if you want a list of badge numbers in which the first character is a number 1–9 and the three remaining characters are not letters of the alphabet, MS-SQL Server lets you execute a query similar to:

```
SELECT * FROM employees
WHERE badge LIKE '[1-9][^a-zA-Z][^a-zA-Z][^a-zA-Z]'
```

263 Using the NULL Predicate to Find All Rows in Which a Selected Column Has a NULL Value

As you learned in Tip 30, "Understanding the Value of NULL," a NULL value in a column indicates unknown or missing data. Because the actual value in the column is not known, the DBMS cannot make any assumptions about its value. As a result, the SELECT statement

```
SELECT * FROM employees WHERE manager = NULL
```

will never display any rows—even if several rows in the EMPLOYEES table have a NULL value in the MANAGER column.

The reason for the seemingly incorrect behavior in which the WHERE clause test

```
NULL = NULL
```

does not return TRUE when the value in the MANAGER column is NULL is that NULL really means "not known." As such, the DBMS cannot make a determination whether the unknown value on the left side of the equality operator is the same as the unknown value on the right side. Therefore, the DBMS must return the value NULL for

```
NULL = NULL
```

instead of TRUE.

To find out if a table column's value is NULL, use the IS NULL predicate. Unlike the equality operator (=), which evaluates to TRUE only if the items on both sides of the operator are equal, the IS NULL operator simply tests for a state of being—that is, "is the value in the column NULL?" which can be either TRUE or FALSE without making any assumptions as to the actual value of the column. Thus, the query

```
SELECT * FROM employees WHERE manager IS NULL
```

will display those rows in the EMPLOYEES table in which the value in the MANAGER column has a NULL (unknown or missing) value.

SQL also provides a special predicate you can use to find those rows that do not have a NULL value in a specific column. After all, if the test

```
NULL = NULL
```

evaluates NULL (and not TRUE), the test

```
NULL <> NULL
```

must evaluate NULL as well, since the DBMS cannot make *any* assumptions as to the actual value of the NULL (unknown) value on either side of the not equal to (<>) comparison operator.

To query the DBMS for rows in which the value in the MANAGER column is not NULL, use IS NOT NULL. For example, the SELECT statement

```
SELECT * FROM employees WHERE manager IS NOT NULL
```

will display the columns in the rows of the EMPLOYEES table in which the value in the MANAGER column is not NULL.

264 Understanding the ALL Qualifier in a WHERE Clause

The ALL qualifier uses the syntax

```
<scalar expression> <comparison operator> ALL <subquery>
```

to let you use a <comparison operator> (such as =, <>, >, and <) to compare the (single) value of the <scalar expression> to each of the values in the results table returned by the single column <subquery> that follows the keyword ALL. If *every* comparison evaluates to TRUE, the WHERE clause returns TRUE. On the other hand, if *any* comparison evaluates to FALSE, or if the <subquery> returns no rows, the WHERE clause returns FALSE.

For example, if you want a list of salespeople from OFFICE 1 that had more sales than all of the salespeople in your company's other offices, you can execute a SELECT statement with an ALL qualified WHERE clause similar to:

```
SELECT * FROM employees
WHERE sales > ALL (SELECT sales FROM employees
                   WHERE OFFICE <> 1)
```

When evaluating an ALL qualifier in a WHERE clause, the DBMS uses the <comparison operator> to compare each value of the <scalar expression> to each of the column values returned by the <subquery>. In the current example, the WHERE clause evaluates TRUE only when the value of the SALES column (the <scalar value>) is greater than (the <comparison operator>) *every* value in the results table returned by the <subquery> (the single column SELECT statement that follows the keyword ALL). The WHERE clause evaluates to FALSE if any comparison of the <scalar value> to a <subquery> results table value is FALSE or if the subquery returns no rows.

In addition to using a column reference as the <scalar value>, you can also use any literal value (constant) or SELECT statement that returns a single value. (While the <subquery> to the right of the keyword ALL can return more the one value, the query used to generate the <scalar value> must return, by definition, a single value.)

For example, if you are a publisher and want to see if any one title sold more copies than all of the other titles you published combined, you could execute a SELECT statement with an ALL qualifier similar to the following:

```
SELECT * FROM titles
WHERE (SELECT SUM(qty_sold)
       FROM sales WHERE sales.isbn = titles.isbn)
  > ALL (SELECT SUM(qty_sold)
         FROM sales WHERE sales.isbn <> titles.isbn)
```

In the current example, the SELECT clause used as the <scalar expression> computes the total sales volume for each of the books in the SALES table. The DBMS uses the greater than comparison operator to compare each sales volume figure to the value returned by the <subquery>. If the comparison evaluates to TRUE for a given row in the TITLES table, the WHERE clause returns TRUE, and the DBMS displays the row's columns in the SELECT statement's results table.

265 Understanding the SOME and ANY Qualifiers in a WHERE Clause

Similar to the ALL qualifier you learned about in Tip 264, "Understanding the ALL Qualifier in a WHERE Clause," the SOME and ANY qualifiers use the syntax

```
<scalar expression>
  <comparison operator> {SOME|ANY} <subquery>
```

to let you use a <comparison operator> to compare the (single) value of the <scalar expression> to each of the values in the results table returned by the single-column <subquery>. If *any one* of comparisons evaluates to TRUE, the WHERE clause returns TRUE. Conversely, if *all* comparisons evaluate to FALSE, or if the <subquery> returns no rows, the WHERE clause returns FALSE.

Suppose, for example, that you want a list of salespeople from OFFICE 1 that have more sales than at least one of the salespeople in your company's other offices, you can execute a SELECT statement with either a SOME (or an ANY) qualified WHERE clause similar to:

```
SELECT * FROM employees
WHERE sales > SOME (SELECT sales FROM employees
                    WHERE OFFICE <> 1)
```

When evaluating a SOME qualifier in a WHERE clause, the DBMS uses the <comparison operator> to compare each value of the <scalar expression> to each of the column values returned by the <subquery>. In the current example, the WHERE clause evaluates to TRUE whenever a value in the SALES column of a row from the EMPLOYEES table (the <scalar value>) is greater than (the <comparison operator> of) *one or more* values in the results table returned by the <subquery> (the single-column SELECT statement that follows the keyword ALL). The WHERE clause evaluates to FALSE if *every* comparison of the <scalar value> to <subquery> results table value is FALSE or if the subquery returns no rows.

As was true with the ALL qualifier, the <scalar expression> can be a column reference, a literal value (constant), or a subquery that returns a single value—so long as the data type of the <scalar value> is compatible with the data type of values returned by the single-column <subquery> that follows the keyword ALL.

For example, if you are a publisher and want to see if any one title sold more copies than any one of the other titles you published, you could execute a SELECT statement with an ANY (or a SOME) qualifier similar to the following:

```
SELECT * FROM titles
WHERE (SELECT SUM(qty_sold)
       FROM sales WHERE sales.isbn = titles.isbn)
  > ANY (SELECT qty_sold
         FROM sales WHERE sales.isbn <> titles.isbn)
```

In the current example, the SELECT clause, used as the <scalar expression>, takes the number of books sold for each title, and uses the greater than (>) comparison operator to compare the count sold to the sales counts of all of the other books in the results table returned by the <subquery>. If any of the comparisons evaluates to TRUE for a given row in the TITLES table, the WHERE clause returns TRUE, and the DBMS displays the row's columns in the SELECT statement's results table.

Note: *The reason SQL-92 includes both the ANY and a synonymous SOME qualifier is due to the ambiguity of the word* any. *If I ask, "Do any of you know how to write an SQL SELECT statement with a WHERE clause?" I am using* any *as an existential quantifier to mean "at least one" or "some." On the other hand, if I say, "I can type faster than any of you," I am using* any *as a universal quantifier meaning "all." As such, when you write a WHERE in a SELECT statement such as*

```
SELECT * FROM <table a>
WHERE b > ANY <subquery results table values>
```

should the DBMS interpret any as an existential quantifier to mean "Display the columns in the row from <table a> if b is greater than at least one of the values in <subquery results table values>"? Or, should the DBMS treat any as a universal quantifier meaning "Display the columns in the row from <table a> if b is greater than all of the values in the <subquery results table values>"?

To clear up the confusion, SQL-92's designers added SOME (which has only one meaning—"one or more") to the SQL-92 standard and retained the existential ANY as a synonym for backward compatibility.

266 Understanding the UNIQUE Predicate

A UNIQUE predicate in a WHERE clause lets you execute a DELETE, INSERT, SELECT, or UPDATE statement based on whether or not the subquery in the UNIQUE predicate produces a results table in which all of the rows are nonduplicates (that is, all rows in the results table are unique). If the subquery's results table's rows are unique, the DBMS executes the SQL statement on the row being tested. Conversely, if the results table has at least one set of duplicate rows, the DBMS skips execution of the SQL command and goes on to check the next row in the table.

For example, to get a list of salespeople who either had no sales or made only one sale during the month of September 2000, you can execute a query similar to:

```
SELECT emp_ID, first_name, last_name FROM employees
WHERE UNIQUE (SELECT salesperson FROM invoices
              WHERE invoice_date >= '9/1/2000' AND
                    invoice_date <= '9/30/2000' AND
                    invoices.salesperson = employees.emp_ID)
```

Always used in conjunction with a subquery, the syntax of the UNIQUE is:

```
[NOT] UNIQUE <subquery>
```

If the results table produced by the subquery in the UNIQUE predicate either has no rows or has no duplicate rows, the UNIQUE predicate returns TRUE. In the current example, the subquery's results table has a single column, SALESPERSON. Therefore, if a salesperson's ID appears in no more than one row in the results table (meaning the person made at most one sale during the period), the outer SELECT statement will display the employee's ID and name. On the other hand, if the subquery's results table has one or more sets of duplicate rows, the UNIQUE predicate evaluates to FALSE, and the DBMS will go on to test the next row in the EMPLOYEES table.

Note: *When checking for duplicate values in a subquery's results table, the UNIQUE predicate ignores any NULL values. As such, if the subquery in a UNIQUE predicate produces the results table*

```
Salesperson  cust_ID  sales_total
-----------  -------  -----------
101          NULL     100.00
101          1000     NULL
101          NULL     NULL
101          1000     100.00
```

the predicate will evaluate to TRUE, because no two rows have columns with all of the same non-NULL values.

Few DBMS products support the UNIQUE predicate. Therefore, be sure to check your system manual before using it in your SQL code. If your DBMS does not support the predicate, you can always use the COUNT aggregate function in a WHERE clause to accomplish the same purpose. For example, the query

```
SELECT emp_ID, first_name, last_name FROM employees
WHERE (SELECT count(salesperson) FROM invoices
       WHERE invoice_date >= '9/1/2000' AND
             invoice_date <= '9/30/2000' AND
             invoices.salesperson = employees.emp_ID) <= 1
```

will produce the same results as the previous example query that used the UNIQUE predicate to list salespeople with zero or one sale for the month of September 2000.

267 Using the OVERLAPS Predicate to Determine If One DATETIME Overlaps Another

The OVERLAPS predicate uses the syntax

```
 (<temporal value 1>,
    {<temporal value 2>|<temporal argument>}) OVERLAPS
(<temporal value 3>,
    {<temporal value 4>|<temporal argument>})
```

where

```
<temporal value>::
   {DATE <date>}|{TIME <time>}|{TIMESTAMP <datetime>}

<temporal argument>::
   {DATE <date>}|[TIME <time>}|{TIMESTAMP <datetime>}|
```

```
   {INTERVAL <interval>}

<interval>::
   '<integer value>' {YEAR|MONTH|DAY|HOUR|MINUTE|SECOND}
```

to let you test two chronological periods of time for an overlap.

For example, the OVERLAPS predicate

```
(DATE '01-01-2000', INTERVAL '03' MONTHS) OVERLAPS
(DATE '03-15-2000', INTERVAL '10' DAYS)
```

evaluates to TRUE because a portion of the second date range (03-15-200 to 03-25-2000) lies within (or overlaps) a portion of the first date range (01-01-2000 to 04-01-2000). Similarly, the OVERLAPS predicate

```
(TIME '09:23:00', TIME '13:45:00') OVERLAPS
(TIME '14:00:00', TIME '14:25:00')
```

evaluates to FALSE because no portion of the second time period lies within (or overlaps) a portion of the first time period.

Many DBMS products do not support the OVERLAPS predicate. If yours does, you will most likely use the OVERLAPS predicate in a stored procedure that accepts dates, times, and intervals as CHARACTER data type parameters. The CHARACTER parameters used to hold the dates or time intervals will appear in the OVERLAPS predicate in place of the literal values shown in the current examples. The important things to know now are that the OVERLAPS predicate returns TRUE if any portion of the second time span falls within the first, and you can specify either of the two time spans as a start date/time and end date/time, or a start date/time and a duration (or interval).

268 Understanding the GROUP BY Clause and Grouped Queries

In Tip 122, "Understanding How Aggregate Functions in a SELECT Statement Produce a Single Row of Results," you learned how the SQL aggregate functions (AVG(), COUNT(), MAX(), and MIN()) summarize data from one or more tables to produce a single row of results. Like the aggregate functions, the GROUP BY clause summarizes data. However, instead of generating a single, grand total row of results, the GROUP BY clause produces multiple subtotals—one for each group of rows in a table.

For example, if you want to know the total value of the purchases made by customers during the previous year, you can use the SUM() aggregate function in a SELECT statement similar to

```
SELECT SUM(invoice_total) AS 'Total Sales' FROM invoices
WHERE invoice_date >= (GETDATE() - 365)
```

which will produce a results table with a single (grand total) row similar to:

```
Total Sales
-----------
47369
```

On the other hand, if you want a breakdown of the total sales volume by customer, add a GROUP BY clause such as the one in the query

```
SELECT cust_ID, SUM(invoice_total) AS 'Total Sales'
FROM invoices
WHERE invoice_date >= (GETDATE() - 365)
GROUP BY cust_ID
```

to tell the DBMS to produce a results table with a subtotal of sales volume for each customer, similar to:

```
cust_ID   Total Sales
-------   -----------
1         7378
5         7378
7         22654
8         1290
9         8669
```

A query that includes a GROUP BY clause (such as that shown in the current example) is called a *grouped query* because the DBMS *groups* (or summarizes) rows selected from the source table(s) as one row of values for each group. The columns named in the GROUP BY clause (CUST_ID, in the current example) are known as the *grouping columns* because the DBMS uses the values of these columns to decide which rows from the source table belong in which groups in the interim table.

After the DBMS arranges the interim results table into groups of rows in which every row in a group has identical values for all of the grouping columns, the system computes the value of the aggregate functions (listed in the SELECT clause) for the rows in the group. Finally, the aggregate function results, along with the values of other items listed in the SELECT clause, are added to the final results table as one row for each group.

269 Understanding the Restrictions on Grouped Queries

A *grouped query* (defined as any SELECT statement that includes a GROUP BY clause) is subject to restrictions on both the columns listed in the GROUP BY clause and the output value expressions listed in the SELECT clause.

All of the *grouping columns* (the columns listed in the GROUP BY clause) must be columns from the tables listed in the FROM clause. As such, you cannot group rows based on literal values, aggregate function results, or the value of any other calculated expression.

The items in a grouped query's select list (column references, aggregate functions, literals, and other expressions in the SELECT clause) must have a single (scalar) value for each group of rows. As such, each item in a grouped query's SELECT clause can be:

- A grouping column
- A literal (constant)
- An aggregate function that the DBMS will apply to the rows in a group to produce a single value representing the row count (COUNT(), COUNT(*)) or aggregate column value (MAX(), MIN(), AVG()) for each group
- An expression involving a combination of one or more of the other (three) valid SELECT clause items

Because grouped queries are used to summarize (or subtotal) data in groups (as defined by grouping columns listed in the GROUP BY clause), the SELECT clause of a grouped query will (almost) always include at least one of the grouping columns and one or more aggregate (column) function. After all, a grouped query such as

```
SELECT cust_ID FROM invoices
WHERE inv_date >= (GETDATE() - 365)
GROUP BY cust_ID
```

which has only column references in its SELECT clause, can be expressed more simply as a SELECT DISTINCT statement such as:

```
SELECT DISTINCT cust_ID FROM INVOICES
WHERE inv_date >= (GETDATE() - 365)
```

Conversely, if a SELECT clause has only aggregate functions, such as the query

```
SELECT SUM(invoice_total) AS 'Total Sales',
  AVG(invoice_total) AS 'Average Invoice'
FROM invoices
WHERE invoice_date >= (GETDATE() - 365)
GROUP BY cust_ID
```

one cannot tell which row of query results came from which group. For example, the results table for the current example

```
Total Sales  Average Invoice
-----------  ---------------
7378         7378.000000
7378         7378.000000
22654        663.5000000
1290         258.000000
8669         4334.500000
```

gives you the total sales and average invoice for each customer. However, after reviewing the data in the results table, you cannot determine which total sales and average invoice belongs to what customer.

270 Using a GROUP BY Clause to Group Rows Based on a Single-Column Value

As you learned in Tip 88, "Using the SELECT Statement to Display Columns from Rows in One or More Tables," a SELECT statement lets you display all of the rows in a table that satisfy the search criteria specified in the query's WHERE clause. (If there is no WHERE clause, the SELECT statement will display column data values from all of the rows in the table.) To divide the rows returned by a SELECT statement into groups and display only one row of data values per group, execute a grouped query by adding a GROUP BY clause to a SELECT statement.

When executing a grouped query, the DBMS performs the following steps:

1. Generates an interim table based on the Cartesian product (see Tip 281, "Understanding Cartesian Products") of the tables listed in the query's FROM clause.
2. Applies the search criteria in the WHERE clause (if any) by eliminating any rows from the interim table (produced in Step 1) for which the WHERE clause evaluates to FALSE.
3. Arranges the remaining rows in the interim table into groups such that the value in the grouping column (listed in the GROUP BY clause) is the same for every row in a group.
4. Calculates the value of each item in the SELECT clause for each group of rows and produces one row of query results for each group.
5. If the query includes a HAVING clause, applies the search condition to rows in the results table and eliminates those summary rows for which the HAVING clause evaluates to FALSE.
6. If the SELECT statement includes a DISTINCT clause (which you learned about in Tip 231, "Using the DISTINCT Clause to Eliminate Duplicates from a Set of Rows"), eliminates any duplicate rows from the results table.
7. If there is an ORDER BY clause, sorts the rows remaining in the RESULTS table according to the columns listed in the ORDER BY clause. (You learned about the ORDER BY clause in Tip 95, "Using the ORDER BY Clause to Specify the Order of Rows Returned by a SELECT Statement.")

For example, when you execute a grouped query such as

```
SELECT state, COUNT(*) AS 'Customer Count' FROM customers
GROUP BY state
```

the DBMS will produce a results table showing the number of customers you have in each state. Since the FROM clause has only one table (CUSTOMERS), the interim table produced by Step 1 consists of all of the rows in the CUSTOMERS table. Because there is no WHERE clause, the DBMS will not eliminate any rows from the interim table. In Step 3, the DBMS will arrange the rows in the interim table into groups in which the value of the grouping column (STATE) is the same for every row in each of the groups.

Next, the DBMS applies the COUNT(*) column function to each group in order to produce a results table row that contains the state code and the count of customers (rows) in the group for each group in the table. Since there is neither a HAVING nor a DISTINCT clause, the DBMS will not eliminate any of the rows from the results table similar to that shown in the lower pane of the MS-SQL Server application window shown in Figure 270.1.

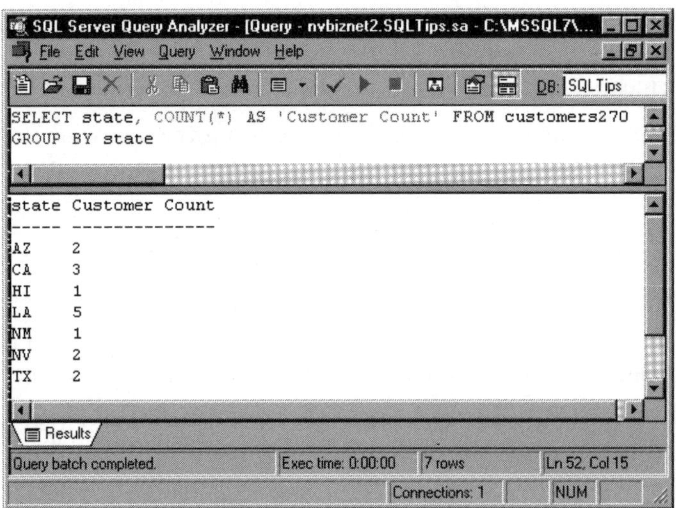

Figure 270.1 MS-SQL Server Query Analyzer query and results table for a single-column grouped query

---

Note: *Because there is no ORDER BY clause, the arrangement of the rows in the results table in ascending order by the grouping column (STATE) is coincidental. The DBMS will display the rows in the results table in the order in which it happens to arrange the groups in the interim table. As such, be sure to include an ORDER BY clause if you want the DBMS to sort rows in the results table in ascending or descending order according to the values in one or more of its columns.*

---

271 Using a GROUP BY Clause to Group Rows Based on Multiple Columns

In Tip 270, "Using a GROUP BY Clause to Group Rows Based on a Single-Column Value," you learned how to use a GROUP BY clause to generate a results table with summary (subtotal) rows based on grouping source table rows based on values in a single grouping column. A SELECT statement with one column in its GROUP BY clause is the simplest form of a grouped query. If the groups of rows in a table is dependant on the values in multiple columns, simply list all of the columns needed define the groups in the query's GROUP BY clause. There is no upper limit on the number of columns you can list in a SELECT statement's GROUP BY clause, and the only restriction on the grouping columns is that each must be a column in one of the tables listed in the query's FROM clause. Bear in mind, however, that no matter how many columns you list in the GROUP BY clause, standard SQL will display only one level of group subtotals in a query's results table.

For example, in Tip 270, you learned you could use the grouped query

```
SELECT state, COUNT(*) AS 'Customer Count' FROM customers
GROUP BY state
```

to produce a results table showing the number of customers you had in each state. If you now want to break down the state customer counts by salesperson within each state, you can execute a query similar to

```
SELECT state, salesperson, COUNT(*) AS 'Customer Count'
FROM customers
GROUP BY state, salesperson
```

to produce a results table such as

```
state  salesperson  Customer Count
-----  -----------  --------------
AZ     101          1
CA     101          3
LA     101          2
HI     102          1
LA     102          2
NV     102          2
TX     102          1
AZ     103          1
LA     103          1
NM     103          1
TX     103          1
```

which groups the customer counts by SALESPERSON and within STATE. Notice, however, that the new query produces only a subtotal line for each (STATE,SALESPERSON) pair. Standard SQL will not give you *both* a subtotal based on SALESPERSON and a subtotal based on STATE in the same results table, even though you listed both columns in the GROUP BY clause.

Note: *Since standard SQL gives you only one level of subtotals for each unique combination of all of the grouping columns (columns listed in the GROUP BY clause), you will have to use programmatic SQL to pass the results table to an application program, which can produce as many levels of subtotals as you like. Another option is to change the order of the rows in the results table using an ORDER BY clause (which you will learn to do in Tip 272, "Using the ORDER BY Clause to Reorder the Rows in Groups Returned by the GROUP BY Clause"). Although the ORDER BY clause does not itself produce any subtotals, it does make it easier for you to manually compute a second level of subtotals by grouping rows with identical column values together. A final way to get multiple subtotals directly from a single SQL statement is to use the MS-SQL Server Transact-SQL COMPUTE clause (which you will learn about in Tip 273, "Using the MS-SQL Transact-SQL COMPUTE Clause to Display Detail and Total Lines in the Same Results Table"). Unfortunately, the COMPUTE clause is not part of the SQL-92 standard, and you will be able to use it only on the MS-SQL Server DBMS.*

---

272 Using the ORDER BY Clause to Reorder the Rows in Groups Returned by the GROUP BY Clause

In Tip 95, "Using the ORDER BY Clause to Specify the Order of Rows Returned by a SELECT Statement," you learned how to use an ORDER BY clause to sort the results table rows returned by an ungrouped query. An ORDER BY clause in a grouped query works like an ORDERED BY clause in an ungrouped query. For example, to sort the results table from the grouped query

```
SELECT state, COUNT(*) AS 'Customer Count' FROM customers
GROUP BY state
```

in descending order of the customer count in each state, rewrite the SELECT statement to include an ORDER BY clause:

```
SELECT state, COUNT(*) AS 'Customer Count' FROM customers
GROUP BY state
ORDER BY "Customer Count" DESC
```

Notice that you are not limited to sorting query results based on any of the columns listed in the GROUP BY clause. As is the case in all queries, the columns listed in an ORDER BY clause are limited only to the columns or headings named in the query's SELECT clause. Therefore, each of the following ORDER BY clauses is valid for the SELECT statement in the current example:

```
ORDER BY state
ORDER BY state "Customer Count"
ORDER BY "Customer Count" state
ORDER BY "Customer Count"
```

As mentioned in Tip 271, "Using a GROUP BY Clause to Group Rows Based on Multiple Columns," you can use an ORDER BY clause to make it easier to manually compute a second (or third, or fourth, or so on) level of subtotals when reviewing the results table from a grouped query with multiple grouping columns. For example, the arrangement of the rows in the results table from the (STATE,SALESPERSON) grouped query in Tip 271 makes it easy to manually subtotal the customer count for each salesperson, even though the query provides only a subtotal for each (STATE,SALESPERSON) pair. Simply draw a horizontal line across the page at each change of SALESPERSON and add up the CUSTOMER COUNT values in the block (group) of rows.

Conversely, if you wanted to compute subtotals for the customer counts by state, the task is more difficult because identical state abbreviations are not grouped together in the results table. However, if you change the ORDER BY clause in the grouped query as follows

```
SELECT state, salesperson, COUNT(*) AS 'Customer Count'
FROM customers
GROUP BY state, salesperson
ORDER BY state, "Customer Count"
```

you can produce a results table similar to

```
state  salesperson  Customer Count
-----  -----------  --------------
AZ     101          1
AZ     103          1
CA     101          3
HI     102          1
LA     101          2
LA     102          2
LA     103          1
NM     103          1
NV     102          2
TX     102          1
TX     103          1
```

which makes it easier to manually subtotal state customer counts by listing group customer counts for identical state codes next to each other.

273 Using the MS-SQL Transact-SQL COMPUTE Clause to Display Detail and Total Lines in the Same Results Table

The MS-SQL Server Transact-SQL COMPUTE clause lets you perform aggregate (column) functions (SUM(), AVG(), MIN(), MAX(), COUNT()) on the rows in a results table. As such, you can use a COMPUTE clause in a SELECT statement to generate a results table with *both* detail and summary information.

For example, the COMPUTE clause in the SELECT statement

```
SELECT * FROM customers WHERE state IN ('CA','NV')
COMPUTE SUM(total_purchases), AVG(total_purchases,
  COUNT(cust_ID)
```

will produce a results table similar to

```
cust_id  cust_name      state  salesperson  total_purchases
-------  -------------  -----  -----------  ---------------
1        CA Customer 1  CA     101          78252.0000
2        CA Customer 2  CA     101          45852.0000
6        NV Customer 1  NV     102          12589.0000
7        CA Customer 3  CA     101          75489.0000
12       NV Customer 2  NV     102          56789.0000

                                            sum
                                            ===============
                                            268971.0000

                                            avg
                                            ===============
                                            53794.2000

cnt
==========
5
```

which has rows of detail information on the company's California and Nevada customers, and ends with summary lines showing the count of customers on the report along with the overall grand total and average sales for the group as a whole.

Note: *Strictly speaking, a SELECT statement with a COMPUTE clause violates a basic rule of relational queries because its result is not a table. Because MS-SQL Sever adds two heading lines and a total line for each aggregate function in the COMPUTE clause, the query returns a combination of different types of rows.*

Although it is extremely useful for counting rows and summarizing numeric values in a results table, use of a COMPUTE BY clause in a SELECT statement is restricted by the following rules:

- Only columns from the SELECT clause can be used in the COMPUTE clause.
- Aggregate functions in the COMPUTE clause cannot be constrained as DISTINCT.
- A COMPUTE clause cannot be used in a SELECT INTO statement.
- Only column names (and no column headings) are allowed in a COMPUTE clause.

274 Using the MS-SQL Transact-SQL COMPUTE and COMPUTE BY Clauses to Display Multi-level Subtotals

In Tip 271, "Using a GROUP BY Clause to Group Rows Based on Multiple Columns," you learned how to use a grouped query (a SELECT statement with a GROUP BY clause) to group source table data and display it in a results table as one summary row per group. You also found out that a grouped query will only display a single level of subtotals. Therefore, you cannot use a standard grouped query to display both group subtotals and overall grand totals in the same results table. If you use a COMPUTE BY and a COMPUTE clause in a single *ungrouped* query, however, you can generate a results table that has both subtotals and grand totals. (In other words, you can generate multi-level subtotals by adding a COMPUTE BY clause and a COMPUTE clause to a SELECT statement that has no GROUP BY clause.)

For example, the COMPUTE BY and COMPUTE clauses in the query

```
SELECT state, salesperson, total_purchases FROM customers
WHERE state IN ('LA','CA')
ORDER BY state, salesperson
COMPUTE SUM(total_purchases) BY state, salesperson
COMPUTE SUM(total_purchases)
```

will display subtotals and grand totals in a results table similar to:

```
state  salesperson  total_purchases
-----  -----------  ---------------
CA     101          78252.0000
CA     101          45852.0000
CA     101          75489.0000

                    sum
                    ===============
                    199593.0000
```

```
LA      101         74815.0000
LA      101         15823.0000

                    sum
                    ===============
                     90638.0000

LA      102         96385.0000
LA      102         85247.0000

                    sum
                    ===============
                    181632.0000

LA      103         45612.0000

                    sum
                    ===============
                    45612.0000

                    sum
                    ===============
                     517475.0000
```

In addition to the COMPUTE clause restrictions (which you learned about in Tip 273, "Using the MS-SQL Transact-SQL COMPUTE Clause to Display Detail and Total Lines in the Same Results Table"), a query with a COMPUTE BY must also adhere to the following rules:

- In order to include a COMPUTE BY clause, the SELECT statement must have an ORDER BY clause.
- Columns listed in the COMPUTE BY clause must either match or be a subset of the columns listed in the ORDER BY clause. Moreover, the columns in the two clauses (ORDER BY and COMPUTE BY) must be in the same order, left to right, must start with the same column, and must not skip any columns.
- The COMPUTE BY clause cannot contain any heading names—only column names.

The final "no headings" restriction would seem to imply that it is not possible to execute a query that uses a COMPUTE BY clause to "total up" the subtotals from the aggregate function(s) in a grouped query such as:

```
SELECT state, salesperson,
       SUM(total_purchases) AS 'Tot_Purchases"
FROM customers
GROUP BY state, salesperson
ORDER BY state, salesperson
```

After all, TOT_PURCHASES in the results table is a heading and not a column name. As such, the column with the subtotal of purchases for each (STATE,SALESPERSON) pair is not eligible for use in a COMPUTE BY clause.

However, if you execute a CREATE VIEW statement such as

```
CREATE VIEW vw_state_emp_tot_purchases AS
SELECT state, salesperson,
  SUM(total_purchases) AS 'Tot_Purchases)
```

that creates a *virtual* table that uses the aggregate function's heading (TOT_PURCHASES, in the current example) as a column, you can use a COMPUTE BY clause to subtotal the aggregate column's subtotals. In the current example, TOT_PURCHASES is a column in the VW_STATE_EMP_TOT_PURCHASES view. Therefore, if you reference the view as a (virtual) table in the SELECT statement's FROM clause, you can use a COMPUTE BY clause in a query such as

```
SELECT state, salesperson, tot_purchases
FROM vw_state_emp_tot_purchases
ORDER BY state, salesperson
COMPUTE SUM(tot_purchases) BY state
```

to both display the subtotal of sales for each SALESPERSON by STATE (the aggregate subtotals from the grouped query) as well as "total up" and display sales by STATE in the same results table.

275 Understanding How NULL Values Are Treated by a GROUP BY Clause

The problem NULL values pose when they occur in one (or more) of the grouping columns in a grouped query is similar to the problem these values pose for aggregate functions and search criteria. Since a group is defined as a set of rows in which the composite value of the grouping columns is the same, which group should include a row in which the value of one or more of the columns that define the group is unknown (NULL)?

If the DBMS were to follow the rule used for search criteria in a WHERE clause, then the GROUP BY would make a separate group for each row with a NULL value in any of the grouping columns. After all, the result from an equality test of two NULL values in a WHERE clause is always FALSE because NULL is not equal to NULL according to the SQL standard. Therefore, if a row has a grouping column with a NULL value, it cannot be placed in the same group with another row that has a NULL value in the same grouping column because all rows in the same group must have matching grouping column values (and NULL <> NULL)

Because they found creating a separate group for every row with a NULL in a grouping column both confusing and of no useful value, SQL's designers wrote the SQL standard such that NULL values are considered equal for the purposes of a GROUP BY clause. Therefore, if two rows have NULL values in the same grouping columns and matching values in the remaining non-NULL grouping columns, the DBMS will group the rows together.

For example, the grouped query

```
SELECT state, salesperson,
  SUM(amount_purchased) AS 'Total Purchases'
FROM customers
GROUP BY state, salesperson
ORDER BY state, salesperson
```

will display a results table similar to

```
state  salesperson  Total Purchases
-----  -----------  ---------------
NULL   NULL         61438.0000
NULL   101          196156.0000
AZ     NULL         75815.0000
AZ     103          36958.0000
CA     101          78252.0000
LA     NULL         181632.0000
```

for CUSTOMERS that contain the following rows:

```
state  salesperson  amount_purchased
-----  -----------  ----------------
NULL   NULL         45612.0000
NULL   NULL         15826.0000
NULL   101          45852.0000
NULL   101          74815.0000
NULL   101          75489.0000
AZ     NULL         75815.0000
AZ     103          36958.0000
CA     101          78252.0000
LA     NULL         96385.0000
LA     NULL         85247.0000
```

276 Using a HAVING Clause to Filter the Rows Included in a Grouped Query's Results Table

The HAVING clause, like the WHERE clause you learned about in Tip 91, "Using the SELECT Statement with a WHERE Clause to Select Rows Based on Column Values," is used to filter out rows with attributes (column values) that do not satisfy the clause's search criteria. When executing a query, the DBMS uses the search criteria in a WHERE as a filter by going through the table listed in the query's FROM clause (or the Cartesian product of the tables, if the FROM clause has multiple tables) one row at a time. The system keeps, for further processing, only those rows whose column values meet the search condition(s) in the WHERE clause. After the WHERE clause (if any) weeds out unwanted rows, the DBMS uses the HAVING clause as a filter to remove groups of rows (vs. individual rows) whose aggregate or individual column values that fail to satisfy the search condition in the HAVING clause.

For example, the WHERE clause in the query

```
SELECT RTRIM(first_name)+' '+last_name AS 'Employee Name',
  SUM(amt_purchased) AS 'Total Sales'
FROM customers, employees
WHERE customers.salesperson = employees.emp_ID
GROUP BY RTRIM(first_name)+' '+last_name
HAVING SUM(amt_purchased) > 250000
ORDER BY "Total Sales"
```

tells the DBMS to go through the interim table created from the Cartesian product of the CUSTOMERS and EMPLOYEES tables one row at a time and eliminate any rows in which the value in the EMP_ID column is not equal to the value in the SALESPERSON column.

Next, the DBMS groups the remaining rows by employee name (as specified by the GROUP BY clause). Then the DBMS checks each group of rows using the search criteria in the HAVING clause. In the current example, the system computes the sum of the AMT_PURCHASED column for each group of rows, and eliminates the rows in any group where the aggregate function (SUM(AMT_PURCHASED)) returns a value equal to or less than 250,000.

Although the search criteria in a HAVING clause can test for individual column values as well as aggregate function results, it is more efficient to put individual column value tests in the query's WHERE clause (vs. its HAVING clause). For example, the query

```
SELECT emp_ID, RTRIM(first_name)+' '+last_name
  AS 'Employee Name', SUM(amt_purchased) AS 'Total Sales'
FROM customers, employees
WHERE customers.salesperson = employees.emp_ID
GROUP BY RTRIM(first_name)+' '+last_name
HAVING (SUM(amt_purchased) < 250000) AND (emp_ID >= 102)
ORDER BY "Total Sales"
```

which tests the EMP_ID column value in the HAVING clause to eliminate any employees with total sales equal to or over 250,000 that have an EMP_ID value less than 102 from the final results table is less efficient than the query:

```
SELECT emp_ID, RTRIM(first_name)+' '+last_name
  AS 'Employee Name', SUM(amt_purchased) AS 'Total Sales'
FROM customers, employees
```

```
WHERE (customers.salesperson = employees.emp_ID)
AND (emp_ID >= 102)
GROUP BY RTRIM(first_name)+' '+last_name
HAVING (SUM(amt_purchased) < 250000)
ORDER BY "Total Sales"
```

which tests the EMP_ID value in the WHERE clause (to produce the same results table).

In the first query (with the EMP_ID column test in the HAVING clause), the DBMS will compute the sum of the AMT_PURCHASED column for several groups of employees (those with EMP_ID column values in the range 001–101) to eliminate only these rows in these groups when the system checks the group's EMP_ID value. The second query avoids arranging rows with EMP_ID column values less than 102 into groups and calculating total sales for these groups by eliminating the rows from the interim results table before the DBMS arranges rows into groups and applies the aggregate function (SUM()) in the HAVING clause to each group.

277 Understanding the Difference Between a WHERE Clause and a HAVING Clause

The DBMS uses the search criteria in both the WHERE and HAVING clauses to filter out unwanted rows from interim tables produced when executing a query. However, each clause affects a different set of rows. While the WHERE clause filters individual rows in the Cartesian product of the tables listed in the SELECT statement's FROM clause, the HAVING clause screens unwanted groups (of rows) out of the groups created by the query's GROUP BY statement. As such, you can use a WHERE clause in any SELECT statement, while a HAVING clause should be used only in a grouped query (a SELECT statement that has a GROUP BY clause).

If you use a HAVING clause without a GROUP BY clause, the DBMS considers all of the rows in a source table as a single group. As such, the aggregate functions in the HAVING clause are applied to one and only one group (all of the rows in the input table) to determine whether the group's rows are to be included in or excluded from the query's results.

For example, the query

```
SELECT SUM(amt_purchased) FROM customers
HAVING SUM(amt_purchased) < 250000
```

will put the sum of the values in the AMT_PURCHASED column in the results table only if the grand total of the AMT_PURCHASED column for the entire CUSTOMERS table is less than 250,000.

In practice, you almost never see a HAVING clause in a SELECT statement without a GROUP BY clause. After all, what is the point of displaying an aggregate value for a table column only if it satisfies one more search criteria? Moreover, if you try to limit the aggregate to a subset of rows in the input table, such as "show me the total purchases for any customer from California, Nevada, or Louisiana that has total purchases under $250,000" by changing the query in the current example to

```
SELECT SUM(amt_purchased) FROM customers
HAVING (SUM(amt_purchased) < 250000)
AND (state IN ('CA','NV','LA'))
```

Then the DBMS will abort execution of the query and display an error message similar to:

```
Server: Msg 8119, Level 16, State 1, Line 1
Column 'customers.state' is invalid in the having clause
  because it is not contained in an aggregate function and
  there is no GROUP BY clause.
```

As a result, you would end up rewriting the SELECT statement (correctly) as a grouped query

```
SELECT state, SUM(amt_purchased) FROM customers
WHERE STATE IN ('CA','NV','LA')
GROUP BY state
HAVING SUM(amt_purchased) < 250000
```

in which the HAVING clause immediately follows a GROUP BY clause.

The important thing to know now is that a WHERE clause is useful in both grouped and ungrouped queries, while a HAVING clause should appear only immediately after the GROUP BY clause in a grouped query.

278 Understanding SQL Rules for Using a HAVING Clause in a Grouped Query

As you learned in Tip 276, "Using a HAVING Clause to Filter the Rows Included in a Grouped Query's Results Table," and Tip 277, "Understanding the Difference Between a WHERE Clause and a HAVING Clause," you can use a WHERE clause or a HAVING clause to exclude rows from or include rows in query results. Because the DBMS uses the search criteria in a WHERE clause to filter one row of data at a time, the expressions in a WHERE clause must be computable for individual rows. The expression(s) in the search criteria in a HAVING clause, meanwhile, must evaluate to a single value for a group of rows. As such, search conditions in a WHERE clause consist of expressions that use column references and literal values (constants). Search conditions in a HAVING clause, on the other hand, normally consist of expressions with one or more aggregate (column) functions (such as COUNT(), COUNT(*), MIN(), MAX(), AVG(), or SUM()).

When executing a grouped query with a HAVING clause, the DBMS performs the following steps:

1. Creates an interim table from the Cartesian product of the tables listed in the SELECT statement's FROM clause. If the FROM clause has only one table, then the interim table will be a copy of the one source table.
2. If there is a WHERE clause, applies its search condition(s) to filter out unwanted rows from the interim table.
3. Arranges the rows in the interim table into groups of rows in which all of the grouping columns have identical values.
4. Applies each search condition in the HAVING clause to each group of rows. If a group of rows fails to satisfy one or more search criteria, removes the group's rows from the interim table.
5. Calculates the value of each item in the query's SELECT clause and generates a single (summary) row for each group of rows. If a SELECT clause item references a column, uses the column's value from any row in the group in the summary row. If the SELECT clause item is an aggregate function, computes the function's value for the group of rows being summarized and adds the value to the group's summary row.
6. If the query includes the keyword DISTINCT (as in SELECT DISTINCT), eliminates any duplicate rows from the results table.
7. If there is an ORDER BY clause, sorts the results table by the values in the columns listed in the ORDER BY clause.

279 Understanding How SQL Handles a NULL Result from a HAVING Clause

A HAVING clause, like a WHERE clause, can have one of three values, TRUE, FALSE, or NULL. If the HAVING clause evaluates to TRUE for a group of rows, the DBMS uses the values in the group's rows to produce a summary line in the results table. Conversely, if the HAVING clause evaluates to FALSE or NULL for a group of rows, the DBMS does not summarize the group's rows in the results table. Thus, the DBMS handles a NULL-valued HAVING clause in the same way it handles a NULL-valued WHERE clause—it omits the rows that produced NULL value from the results table.

Bear in mind that NULL values in a group's columns do not always cause the search condition in a HAVING clause to evaluate NULL. For example, the query

```
SELECT state, COUNT(*) AS 'Customer Count',
  (COUNT(*) - COUNT(amt_purchased)) AS 'NULL Sales Count'
  SUM(amt_purchased) AS 'Sales' FROM Customers
GROUP BY state
HAVING SUM(amt_purchased) < 50000
```

will produce a results table similar to that shown in the results pane in the bottom half of the MS-SQL Server Query Analyzer Window shown in Figure 279.1 even through three of four AMT_PURCHASED values are NULL in the group of California customer rows.

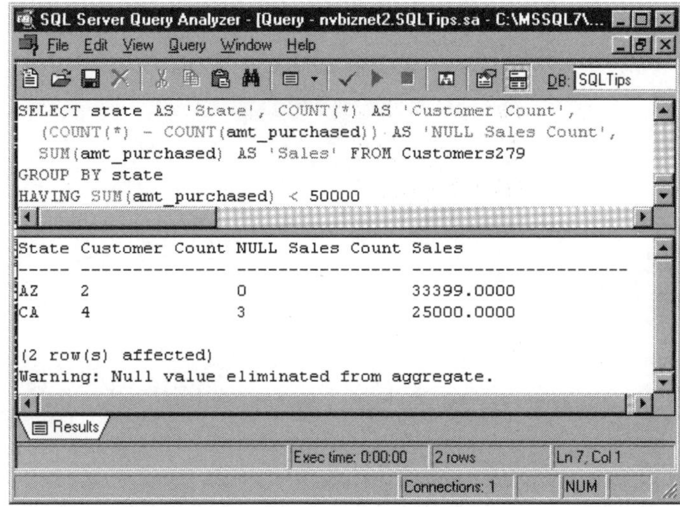

Figure 279.1 MS-SQL Server Query Analyzer query and results table for a grouped query with a HAVING clause

As you learned in Tip 119, "Using the SUM() Aggregate Function to Find the Sum of the Values in a Column," the SUM() aggregate function omits NULLs when totaling a column's values. Therefore, in the current example, the search condition in the HAVING clause evaluates to TRUE for California customers because the SUM() aggregate ignores the three NULL AMT_PURCHASED values in the group and returns the aggregate non-NULL result (25,000).

On the other hand, if *all* of the values in the AMT_PURCHASED column are NULL for a group of rows (such as the California customers, for example), the SUM() function will return a NULL. As a result, the HAVING clause will evaluate to NULL, and the SELECT statement will not summarize the group's rows in its results table. For the current example, if all California customer rows have a NULL value in AMT_PURCHASED column, the SELECT statement will produce a results table similar to

```
State  Customer Count  NULL Sales Count  Sales
-----  --------------  ----------------  ----------
AZ     2               0                 33399.0000
```

which makes no mention of California customers.

However, if you change the example query by adding an IS NULL search condition, as follows:

```
SELECT state, COUNT(*) AS 'Customer Count',
  (COUNT(*) - COUNT(amt_purchased)) AS 'NULL Sales Count'
  SUM(amt_purchased) AS 'Sales' FROM Customers
GROUP BY state
HAVING (SUM(amt_purchased) < 50000)
OR (SUM(amt_purchased) IS NULL)
```

the HAVING clause will evaluate to TRUE for California customers (*because* the SUM() aggregate function returns a NULL value), and the SELECT statement will display a results table similar to:

```
State  Customer Count  NULL Sales Count  Sales
-----  --------------  ----------------  ----------
AZ     2               0                 33399.0000
CA     4               4                 NULL
```

The important thing to understand now is that any group of rows for which a HAVING clause evaluates to NULL (or FALSE) will be omitted from a grouped query's results table.

280 Working with Tables from Multiple MS-SQL Server Databases

Although the example SELECT statements in all of the previous Tips reference tables in single database (SQLTips), MS-SQL Server lets you execute SQL statements that work with tables from multiple databases.

If you refer to a table using only its name, the DBMS assumes that you want to use a table you own in the current database. For example, if you log in to the SQLTips database as username FRANK and execute the query

```
SELECT * FROM customers
```

the DBMS will show you the contents of the CUSTOMERS table if CUSTOMERS exists in the SQLTips database and is owned by FRANK.

If you want to work with a table that exists in the current database but is owned by a different username, your table reference must include the name of the table's owner using the syntax:

```
<owner name>.<table name>
```

As such, if you log in to the SQLTips database as username FRANK and want to query the CUSTOMERS table owned by MARY, for example, you would execute a SELECT statement similar to:

```
SELECT * FROM mary.customers
```

To work with a table in another database, the table reference must use the syntax

```
<database name>.<owner name>.<table name>
```

to specify the name of the database in which the table is located, the username of the table's owner, and the name of the table.

For example, if you are logged into the SQLTips database and want to query the AUTHORS table, owned by DBO in the PUBS database, you would execute a SELECT statement similar to:

```
SELECT * FROM pubs.dbo.authors
```

As mentioned at the beginning of this tip, you can use tables from multiple databases in the same SQL statement—simply use the syntax necessary to tell the DBMS where it can find the table you want to use. For example, if you want to cross-reference the EMPLOYEES table in the current database (SQLTips) with the AUTHORS table in the PUBS database (to see if you have any published authors working for you), execute a SELECT statement similar to:

```
SELECT emp_ID, au_lname, au_fname
FROM employees, pubs.dbo.authors
WHERE employees.SSAN = pubs.dbo.authors.au_ID
```

Because the query omits the database name and owner name in its reference to the CUSTOMERS table, the DBMS knows the table must exist in the current (SQLTips) database. Conversely, because the query's reference to the AUTHORS table includes *both* the database name and the owner's name, the DBMS knows to work with the AUTHORS table owned by DBO in the PUBS database.

Note: *The DBMS will, of course, check its system tables to ensure that your username has the access rights necessary to execute the SQL statement you submit for processing. If you do not, the DBMS will abort execution of the statement with an error message similar to:*

```
Server: Msg 229, Level 14, State 5, Line 1
SELECT permission denied on object 'authors', database
  'pubs', owner 'dbo'.
```

In short, DBMS will not allow you to circumvent system security by using a fully qualified table name (<database name>.<owner name>.<table name>).

---

281 Understanding Cartesian Products

The *Cartesian product* of two tables is a (third) table that contains all of the possible pairs of rows from the two source tables. Each row in the table produced by a Cartesian product consists of the columns from the first table followed by columns from the second table.

Understanding Cartesian products is important because whenever you execute an SQL query that has multiple tables in its FROM clause, the DBMS creates the Cartesian product of the source tables as an interim virtual table. The system then uses the interim table as the single source table for the column data values referenced by column name in the query's expressions.

Suppose, for example, that you have a CUSTOMERS table and an INVOICES table with the following data:

```
CUSTOMERS table       INVOICES table
====================  ===================================
cust_ID cust_name     inv_date   inv_no cust_ID inv_total
------- ------------  ---------- ------ ------- ---------
101     Customer 101  01/02/2000 1      101     15874
202     Customer 202  01/05/2000 2      202     6859
205     Customer 205  03/05/2000 3      101     20225
                      09/05/2000 4      101     30228
                      09/27/2000 5      202     7400
```

If you execute the SELECT statement

```
SELECT * FROM customers, invoices
```

the DBMS will produce a results table similar to:

```
cust_ID cust_name    inv_date   inv_no cust_ID inv_total
------- ------------ ---------- ------ ------- ---------
101     Customer 101 01/02/2000 1      101     15874.0000
101     Customer 101 01/05/2000 2      202     6859.0000
101     Customer 101 03/05/2000 3      101     20225.0000
101     Customer 101 09/05/2000 4      101     30228.0000
101     Customer 101 09/27/2000 5      202     7400.0000
202     Customer 202 01/02/2000 1      101     15874.0000
202     Customer 202 01/05/2000 2      202     6859.0000
202     Customer 202 03/05/2000 3      101     20225.0000
202     Customer 202 09/05/2000 4      101     30228.0000
202     Customer 202 09/27/2000 5      202     7400.0000
205     Customer 205 01/02/2000 1      101     15874.0000
205     Customer 205 01/05/2000 2      202     6859.0000
205     Customer 205 03/05/2000 3      101     20225.0000
205     Customer 205 09/05/2000 4      101     30228.0000
205     Customer 205 09/27/2000 5      202     7400.0000
```

Because the SELECT statement in the current example has no WHERE clause, its final results table includes all of the rows produced by the Cartesian product of the CUSTOMERS table and the INVOICES table in the query's FROM clause. (The "display all column values," [that is, the asterisk "*"] within the query's select clause tells the DBMS to include all the Cartesian product's columns in the results table as well.)

When you review the contents of the results table in the current example, you will see that computing the Cartesian product of the tables in a query's FROM clause produces a lot of unwanted rows. For example, customer 205 has no invoices in the INVOICES table, yet the results table has five invoice detail lines for customer 205. Similarly, customer 202 made two purchases (INV_NO 2 and INV_NO 5), yet the results table has detail lines showing that customer 202 is also responsible for INV_NO 1 and 4.

The Cartesian product of the tables in a SELECT statement's FROM clause is normally used as an interim table (albeit virtual) and is almost never intended as a query's final results table. Real-world multi-table SELECT statements almost always include a WHERE clause with search criteria that filter out the unwanted (nonsense) rows in the interim (Cartesian product) table. (You will learn all about using WHERE clause filters in multi-table queries in Tips 284–287.)

Note: *Although the query in the current example shows the Cartesian product from a SELECT statement with two tables in its FROM clause, the DBMS will also generate a Cartesian product when executing a query involving three (or more) tables. For example, if you submit the SELECT statement*

```
SELECT * FROM table_a, table_b, table_c
```

the DBMS will create the Cartesian product of TABLE_A and TABLE_B as a product table (TABLE_AB). It then creates the Cartesian product of the product table (TABLE_AB) and TABLE_C as a product table (TABLE_ABC). (If there were a fourth table (TABLE_D), the DBMS would create the Cartesian product of TABLE_ABC and TABLE_D to produce a product table [TABLE_ABCD], and so on.) As is the case with a two-table query, the DBMS uses the final Cartesian product (such as TABLE_ABC, in a three-table query) as the source table for the column data values referenced by column name in the query's expressions.

---

282 Using the FROM Clause to Perform a Multi-table Query

A FROM clause, as its name implies, lists the tables *from* which the DBMS is to get the data values to use in a query. For example, a query with a single table in its FROM clause, such as

```
SELECT * FROM customers
```

is easy to understand—retrieve each row *from* the CUSTOMERS table and supply its column values to the "display all column values" (the asterisk (*)) expression in the query's SELECT clause.

If a query needs data from columns in multiple tables, the FROM clause (which always lists all of the sources of a query's data), will have more than one table. However, whether the FROM clause lists a single table or several tables, the various clauses in a SELECT statement act on data one row at a time. Therefore, if a FROM clause has multiple tables, the DBMS will compute the Cartesian product of the tables listed in the FROM clause to create a single table from which it can draw data one row at a time.

As you learned in Tip 281, "Understanding Cartesian Products," the interim (Cartesian product) table consists of all of the possible combinations of rows in the FROM clause tables. Each row is made up of all of the columns from all of the tables listed in the FROM clause.

For example, suppose that you have a STUDENTS table with 12,000 rows, each of which has 15 columns (attributes), and a CLASSES table with 1,000 rows with 5 columns per row. When you execute the query

```
SELECT * FROM students, classes
```

the DBMS creates a virtual table with 12,000,000 rows (12,000 × 1,000) and 20 columns per row (15 from STUDENTS plus 5 from CLASSES). If you add a third table, TEACHERS, which has 1,000 rows of 10 columns each, the DBMS will combine the three tables in the FROM clause of the query

```
SELECT * FROM students, classes, teachers
```

to produce an interim virtual table with 12,000,000,000 rows (12,000 × 1,000 × 1,000) and 30 columns (15 + 5 + 10) per row. As you can see, the Cartesian product of the tables listed in the FROM clause of a multi-table SELECT can become very large.

Of course, no DBMS product actually creates a *physical* table from the Cartesian product of the tables listed a query's FROM clause. However, multi-table queries involving large tables will sometimes take hours to run because the DBMS creates and stores in memory the portions of the *virtual* interim table that it needs to process data from multiple tables one composite row at a time.

The important thing to understand is that a multi-table query actually works with a single (albeit large) virtual table that the DBMS creates by taking the Cartesian product of the tables listed in the SELECT statement's FROM clause. This concept is important because it helps to explain why a multi-table query needs a WHERE clause to filter out unwanted rows.

283 Understanding Joins and Multi-table Queries

In Tip 281, "Understanding Cartesian Products," and Tip 282, "Using the FROM Clause to Perform a Multi-table Query," you learned that the DBMS *joins* multiple tables listed in a SELECT statement's FROM clause by generating the Cartesian product of the tables.

SQL-92 refers to a Cartesian product as a CROSS JOIN. As such, the SELECT statement

```
SELECT * FROM students, classes
```

is equivalent to:

```
SELECT * FROM students CROSS JOIN classes
```

Each of the two example queries joins two tables (STUDENTS and CLASSES) to produce a third table that contains all of the possible pairs or rows from each of the original tables. As you learned in Tip 281, a CROSS JOIN (or Cartesian product) is seldom (if ever) the desired result when you pose a query—there are simply too many unwanted (and perhaps nonsensical) rows. Therefore, multi-table queries almost always include a WHERE clause to filter out rows whose column values do not represent the attributes of valid physical objects or concepts—such as the invoice detail rows for CUST_ID 205 in the interim source table of the example in Tip 281.

When executing a multi-table query, you normally want the DBMS to perform a *natural join* (or *equi-join*) instead of a cross join of the source tables. In an equi-join the DBMS filters out interim (joint) table rows that do not have matching values in one (or more) columns common to both tables. You learned how to set up a shared column relationship between tables when you read about the FOREIGN KEY constraint in Tip 173, "Understanding Foreign Keys."

In short, a FOREIGN KEY lets you set up a parent/child relationship between tables by duplicating the PRIMARY KEY (see Tip 171, "Understanding Primary Keys") column value from the parent table in a FOREIGN KEY (see Tip 173) column of the child table. Then you can use the syntax

```
SELECT {<column name list> | *}
FROM <table 1>, <table 2>
WHERE <PRIMARY KEY column name> = <FOREIGN KEY column name>
```

to write a two-table query that joins the row with the attributes (column values) from <table 1> that partially describe an object or concept to the row(s) in <table 2> with additional attributes (column values) pertaining to the same object or concept.

You will learn more about the various SQL joins (CROSS JOIN, NATURAL JOIN, INNER JOIN, LEFT OUTER JOIN, RIGHT OUTER JOIN, FULL OUTER JOIN, and UNION JOIN) in Tips 296–309. For now, the important thing to understand is that a *join* is used by a multi-table SELECT statement to combine related rows of values from different tables into a single virtual table. The DBMS then works with the joined rows in a single interim virtual table to produce the final query results table.

284 Using a WHERE Clause to Join Two Tables Related by a Single-Column PRIMARY KEY/FOREIGN KEY Pair

As you learned in Tip 283, "Understanding Joins and Multi-table Queries," when executing a multi-table query, the DBMS joins the rows in one table with the rows in another table to create an interim virtual table that has all of the data values from both of the source tables. Then the system uses the SELECT statement's clauses to filter and display the data values in the interim (joined) table.

The simplest form of a multi-table query is an equi-join (or natural join) based on a parent/child relationship between pairs of rows in two tables. The DBMS joins rows in the parent table with rows in the child table by matching PRIMARY KEY column values in the parent table with FOREIGN KEY column values in the child table. Figure 284.1 shows the relationship between a CUSTOMERS (parent) table and an INVOICES (child) table as defined by the values in the parent table's PRIMARY KEY column and the child table's FOREIGN KEY column.

To display a list of invoices and the name of the customer that placed each order, the DBMS must join each child row in the INVOICES table to its parent row in the CUSTOMERS table. For example, a query similar to

```
SELECT f_name, l_name, inv_num, inv_date,
  (inv_total - amt_paid) AS 'Balance Due'
FROM invoices, customers
WHERE CID = ID
```

will perform an equi-join of the CUSTOMERS and INVOICES table. The query's FROM clause tells the DBMS to create an interim virtual table by joining the rows in the INVOICES table with the rows in the CUSTOMERS table. Next, the system uses the search criteria in the WHERE clause to filter out unwanted interim table rows. In an equi-join involving a parent and a child table, the DBMS passes to the SELECT clause only those interim (joined) table rows in which the FOREIGN KEY column matches the value of the PRIMARY KEY column. The equi-join query in the current example will produce a results table similar to:

```
f_name l_name   inv_num inv_date                Balance Due
------ -------- ------- ----------------------- -----------
Walter Winchell 2001    2000-01-01 00:00:00.000 .0000
Konrad King     3010    2000-07-01 00:00:00.000 3200.0000
Walter Winchell 2730    2000-05-01 00:00:00.000 23750.0000
Walter Winchell 9050    2000-09-29 00:00:00.000 19300.0000
```

CUSTOMERS table

ID	F_NAME	L_NAME	ADDRESS
1001	Konrad	King	765 E. Eldorado Lane
1003	Walter	Winchell	214 State Street
1009	Sally	Springer	77 Sunset Strip
⋮	⋮	⋮	⋮

Primary Key

INVOICES table

INV_NUM	CID	INV_DATE	SHIP_DATE	INV_TOTAL	AMT_PAID
2001	1003	01/01/2000	02/05/2000	4500	4500
⋮	⋮	⋮	⋮	⋮	⋮
3010	1001	07/01/2000	08/15/2000	17500	14300
⋮	⋮	⋮	⋮	⋮	⋮
2730	1003	05/01/2000	07/05/2000	23750	0
⋮	⋮	⋮	⋮	⋮	⋮
9050	1003	09/29/2000	NULL	19300	0
⋮	⋮	⋮	⋮	⋮	⋮

Foreign Key

Figure 284.1 CUSTOMERS (parent) table and INVOICES (child) table related by common columns—ID in CUSTOMERS and INV_NUM in INVOICES

SQL does not require that the SELECT clause include columns referenced in WHERE clause expressions. In fact, key columns (used to set up parent/child relationships between tables) are often ID numbers. Although numeric key values make it easy for computers to uniquely identify and pair related rows, they are of little value in a results table. After all, a person (vs. a machine) using query results is more likely to know and refer to a customer, employee, inventory item, and so on by name or description rather than by number.

285 Using a WHERE Clause to Join Two Tables Related by a Composite PRIMARY KEY/FOREIGN KEY Pair

In Tip 174, "Understanding Referential Integrity Checks and Foreign Keys," you learned that the DBMS lets you INSERT a row in a child table only if the row's FOREIGN KEY column value matches the value in the PRIMARY KEY column of an existing row in a parent table. However, as you learned in Tip 284, "Using a WHERE Clause to Join Two Tables Related by a Single-Column PRIMARY KEY/FOREIGN KEY Pair," the system does not automatically use the matching PRIMARY KEY/FOREIGN KEY column value requirement to filter out unwanted rows in a query involving a parent/child table pair.

To exploit the parent/child relationship between two tables, you must perform an equi-join query. The search condition in the SELECT statement's WHERE clause tells the DBMS you want to work with only joined rows in which the PRIMARY KEY column value from the row in the parent table matches the FOREIGN KEY column value in the row from the child table.

For example, if you have an INVENTORY (child) table with a single-column FOREIGN KEY and an ITEM_MASTER (parent) table with a single-column PRIMARY KEY, you can use a SELECT statement similar to

```
SELECT inventory.item_number, description, qty_on_hand
FROM inventory, item_master
WHERE inventory.item_number = item_master.item_number
ORDER BY description
```

to display an item's description (from the ITEM_MASTER table) along with the quantity of the item you have in inventory (from the INVENTORY table) as a single, joined row in a results table.

As you learned in Tip 168, "Understanding Single-Column and Composite Keys," you sometimes have composite key values—tables in which the PRIMARY KEY (or FOREIGN KEY) value consists of multiple-column values. For example, suppose you purchase items with the same item number from different vendors and want to find out the quantity of each vendor's products you have on hand. If you use a composite PRIMARY KEY consisting of (ITEM_NUMBER,VENDOR_CODE), the preceding query with a single search criterion will produce an incorrect results table similar to

```
item_number  description           qty_on_hand
-----------  --------------------  -----------
1            Item 1 from Vendor 1  111
2            Item 2 from Vendor 1  222
2            Item 2 from Vendor 1  111
2            Item 2 from Vendor 1  111
```

```
2           Item 2 from Vendor 2  222
2           Item 2 from Vendor 2  111
2           Item 2 from Vendor 2  111
3           Item 3 from Vendor 1  333
3           Item 3 from Vendor 3  333
```

when you *actually* have in inventory:

```
item_number  description           qty_on_hand
-----------  --------------------  -----------
1            Item 1 from Vendor 1  111
2            Item 2 from Vendor 1  111
3            Item 3 from Vendor 1  111
2            Item 2 from Vendor 2  222
3            Item 3 from Vendor 3  333
```

To perform an equi-join query using the parent/child relationships defined by matching composite (multi-column) FOREIGN KEY/PRIMARY KEY values in related tables, the SELECT statement's WHERE clause must have a search condition that matches each pair of columns that make up the composite key. For example, if you have two tables related by a composite key such as (ITEM_NUMBER,VENDOR_CODE), execute a query similar to

```
SELECT inventory.item_number, description, qty_on_hand
FROM inventory, item_master
WHERE (inventory.item_number = item_master.item_number)
AND   (inventory.vendor_code = item_master.vendor_code)
ORDER BY description
```

in which the WHERE clause search condition tells the DBMS to filter out all joined rows except those in which both pairs of columns that make up the composite FOREIGN KEY and PRIMARY KEY values have matching values. (If the composite keys consisted of three columns each, the WHERE clause would have three equality expressions [one for each matching column pair] joined by AND operators.)

286 Using a WHERE Clause to Join Three or More Tables Based on Parent/Child Relationships

As you learned in Tip 284, "Using a WHERE Clause to Join Two Tables Related by a Single-Column PRIMARY KEY/FOREIGN KEY Pair," and Tip 285, "Using a WHERE Clause to Join Two Tables Related by a Composite PRIMARY KEY/FOREIGN KEY Pair," the DBMS generates the Cartesian product of the tables listed in the SELECT statement's FROM clause each time the system executes a two table query. (You learned about Cartesian products in Tip 281, "Understanding Cartesian Products.") The DBMS then uses one or more search conditions in the query's WHERE clause to filter out joined yet unrelated pairs of rows. If you increase the number of tables joined in the query from two to three (or more), the DBMS still goes through the same process of generating the Cartesian product of the tables and then filtering out the joined yet unrelated rows from the interim virtual (Cartesian product) table.

Each search condition in the WHERE clause that is used to filter out unrelated joined rows must identify a pair of columns (one column from each pair of related tables) whose values must match if the joined row in the interim table expresses a valid parent/child relationship. For example, the WHERE clause in the two-table query

```
SELECT f_name, l_name, inv_num, inv_date,
  (inv_total - amt_paid) AS 'Balance Due'
FROM invoices, customers
WHERE invoices.CID = customers.ID
```

filters out invoice detail rows joined to unrelated customer detail rows (and vice versa).

A parent/child relationship between two tables requires that a child's FOREIGN KEY value (INVOICES.CID) must match the parent's PRIMARY KEY value (CUTOMERS.ID). Therefore, the WHERE clause filter in the current example removes all joined rows in which the values in the PRIMARY KEY/FOREIGN KEY column pair do not match because these rows do not express a valid parent/child relationship between the two tables.

Similarly, to filter unwanted "garbage" rows out of the Cartesian product in a query on three (or more) tables, the WHERE clause must test pairs of column values that include at least one column from each of the source tables. For example, to get a list of customers including the invoice balances and salesperson's name, you can submit a three table query similar to:

```
SELECT f_name, l_name, inv_no, inv_date,
  (inv_total - amt_paid) AS 'Balance Due',
  RTRIM(first_name)+' '+last_name AS 'Salesperson'
FROM invoices, customers, employees
WHERE (customers.ID = invoices.CID)
AND   (invoices.salesrep = employees.emp_ID)
```

The search condition in the WHERE clause filters out joined rows in which the ID (the PRIMARY KEY) from the CUSTOMERS (parent) table does not match the CID (the FOREIGN KEY) from the INVOICES (child) table, and joined rows in which the SALESREP (the FOREIGN KEY) from the INVOICES (child) table does not match the EMP_ID (the PRIMARY KEY) from the EMPLOYEES (parent) table.

As shown by the current example, the WHERE clause in a query on three (or more) tables does not have to test the same matching pair of column values for each table. The only requirement is that the WHERE clause must check the equality of at least one pair of FOREIGN KEY/PRIMARY KEY values from each set of parent/child tables listed in the query's FROM clause.

287 Using a WHERE Clause to Join Tables Based on Nonkey Columns

All of the WHERE clauses in the example multi-table queries in Tips 284–286 filtered out joined rows in which the FOREIGN KEY value from a child table did not match the PRIMARY KEY value from a parent table. However, SQL also lets you join rows based on matching values in other than PRIMARY KEY and FOREIGN KEY columns. Suppose, for example, that your company has a different set of training manuals for employees in each if its departments. The WHERE clause in the query

```
SELECT first_name, last_name, title
FROM manuals, employees
WHERE manuals.for_dept = employees.dept
```

will filter out those rows that join employees in one department with manuals for another department and will produce a results table similar to:

```
first_name  last_name  title
----------  ---------  ----------------------------
Richard     Kimbal     Handling Complaints
Richard     Kimbal     Efficient Order Taking
Richard     Kimbal     Frequently Asked Questions
Hellen      Waters     Handling Complaints
Hellen      Waters     Efficient Order Taking
Hellen      Waters     Frequently Asked Questions
Ed          Norton     Prospecting
Ed          Norton     Working Callbacks
Ed          Norton     Making Referral Calls
Steve       Forbes     Prospecting
Steve       Forbes     Working Callbacks
Steve       Forbes     Making Referral Calls
Charles     Coulter    Mechanics of the Pre-Close
Charles     Coulter    Successful Closing Strategies
Charles     Coulter    Proper Menu Planning
Ralph       Cramden    Mechanics of the Pre-Close
Ralph       Cramden    Successful Closing Strategies
Ralph       Cramden    Proper Menu Planning
```

Joining tables based on matching nonkey column values generates a results table with joined rows that show many-to-many relationships between the two tables. For example, the results table in the current example shows that based on matching department values, each row from the MANUALS table is related to several rows from the EMPLOYEES table. Moreover, each row from the EMPLOYEES table has the same department as (and is therefore related to) several rows from the MANUALS table.

Joining tables based on matching pairs of PRIMARY KEY/FOREIGN KEY values, on the other hand, generates a results table that shows the one-to-many relationship between each row from the parent table and its children (related rows) in the child table. Or, looking at the relationships in reverse, the results table shows the many-to-one relationship between children (rows in the child table) related by a matching key value to a single (parent) row in the parent table.

Suppose, for example, that you have an EMPLOYEES parent table and a TIMECARDS child table. The SELECT statement

```
SELECT first_name, last_name, card_date, start_time,
  stop time
FROM employees, timecards
WHERE employees.emp_ID = timecards.emp_ID
```

will join parent rows (from the EMPLOYEES table) with related child rows (from the TIMECARDS table, based on matching pairs of PRIMARY KEY (EMPLOYEES.EMP_ID) and FOREIGN KEY (TIMECARDS.EMP_ID) values. After the WHERE clause filters out joined, unrelated rows, the results table will show each row from the EMPLOYEES table (parent) joined (by a matching pair of key column values) to zero or more rows from the TIMECARDS (child) table. Or, said another way, the results table will show one or more rows from the TIMECARDS (child) table joined (by a matching pair of key column values) to one and only one of the rows from the EMPLOYEES (parent) table.

The important thing to understand from the preceding discussion of many-to-one and one-to-many relationships is that you write the SELECT statement's WHERE clause the same way whether you are joining tables based on matching pairs of key column values or matching pairs of nonkey column values. In both cases, the WHERE clause includes a comparison test that filters out joined rows in which the values in the pair of columns that join related rows in the two tables do not match.

288 Understanding Non–Equi-Joins

Although all of the example multi-table queries in Tips 284–287 joined tables based on the equality of pairs of columns common to both tables, SQL also lets you join tables based on nonequality relationships between pairs of columns. Suppose, for example, that you want to generate a list of employees and the company benefits to which each is entitled based on length of employment. Given an EMPLOYEES table and an unrelated BENEFITS table, you can execute the SELECT statement

```
SELECT first_name, last_name,
  CAST((GETDATE() - date_hired) AS INTEGER)
    AS 'Days Employed',
  description AS 'Eligible For'
FROM employees, benefits
WHERE CAST((GETDATE() - date_hired) AS INTEGER) >=
  days_on_job_required
ORDER BY emp_ID
```

to produce a results table similar to:

```
first_name  last_name   Days Employed  Eligible For
----------  ----------  -------------  ---------------
Robert      Cunningham  3440           Retirement Plan
Robert      Cunningham  3440           Paid Vacation
Robert      Cunningham  3440           Paid Sick Days
Robert      Cunningham  3440           Paid Dental
Robert      Cunningham  3440           Paid Medical
Lori        Swenson     153            Paid Dental
Lori        Swenson     153            Paid Medical
Richard     Kimbal      93             Paid Dental
Richard     Kimbal      93             Paid Medical
Glenda      Widmark     32             Paid Medical
```

Each row in the results table joins an employee's name and length of employment (from the EMPLOYEES table) with each of the benefits to which the employee is entitled (from the BENEFITS table) based on length of employment.

Whether the multi-table query is based on an equi-join or a non–equi-join, a comparison test in the query's WHERE clause filters out the joined rows in which values in the pair of columns used to relate the two tables fail to satisfy the condition that defines the relationship between the tables.

In an equi-join, the WHERE clause uses the equality operator to compare values in the pair of columns used to relate the tables and filters out joined rows in which the paired columns have different values. Similarly, in the non–equi-join shown in the current example, the WHERE clauses uses the greater than or equal to (>=) comparison operator to filter out joined rows in which the value of the "Days Employed" expression is less than the value of the DAYS_ON_JOB_REQUIRED column (from the BENEFITS table).

The important thing to understand is that when executing a multi-table query, the DBMS always generates the Cartesian product of the tables listed in the SELECT statement's FROM clause. It then uses one or more search conditions in the WHERE clause to filter out the rows with values in related (paired) columns that do not satisfy the conditions of the comparison operator used to define the relationship between the two tables.

289 Using Qualified Column Names in Multi-table Queries That Join Tables That Have the Same Names for One or More Columns

When writing a multi-table query, you can retrieve data from a table by using the name of the column in the SELECT statement if the name of the column with the data you want is unique to one of the tables joined in the query. For example, if you have a CUSTOMERS table and an EMPLOYEES as defined by the CREATE statements

```
CREATE TABLE customers       CREATE TABLE employees
(cust_ID      INTEGER,       (emp_ID      INTEGER,
 cust_f_name VARCHAR(30),     emp_f_name VARCHAR(30),
 cust_l_name VARCHAR(30),     emp_l_name VARCHAR(30))
 salesperson INTEGER)
```

you can execute a SELECT that retrieves column data values by name alone, such as:

```
SELECT RTRIM(cust_f_name)+' '+cust_l_name AS 'Customer',
  RTRIM(emp_f_name)+' '+emp_l_name AS 'Salesperson'
FROM customers, employees
WHERE salesperson = emp_ID
```

The DBMS automatically *knows* to retrieve the customer's first and last names (CUST_F_NAME and CUST_L_NAME) from the CUSTOMERS table, and the employee's first and last names (EMP_F_NAME and EMP_L_NAME) from the EMPLOYEES table. After all, the DBMS can find each of the column names used in the query in one and only one of the query's source tables.

If, on the other hand, you execute a multi-table query in which you need data from a column that has the same name in more than one of the tables joined in the query, you must use a *qualified* column name in the SELECT statement. A qualified column name, as you learned in Tip 228, "Understanding Column References," tells the DBMS both the name of the table and the name of the column from which it is to retrieve a data value.

For example, if the CUSTOMERS and EMPLOYEES tables were created with the CREATE statements

```
CREATE TABLE customers          CREATE TABLE employees
(cust_ID      INTEGER,          (emp_ID      INTEGER,
 cust_f_name VARCHAR(30),         f_name VARCHAR(30),
 cust_l_name VARCHAR(30),         l_name VARCHAR(30))
 emp_ID       INTEGER)
```

the DBMS would abort the execution of the SELECT statement

```
SELECT RTRIM(cust_f_name)+' '+cust_l_name AS 'Customer',
  RTRIM(f_name)+' '+l_name AS 'Salesperson'
FROM customers, employees
WHERE emp_ID = emp_ID
```

and display an error message similar to

```
Server:  Msg 209, Level 16 State 1, Line 1
Ambiguous column name 'emp_ID'.
Server:  Msg 209, Level 16 State 1, Line 1
Ambiguous column name 'emp_ID'.
```

because the system cannot determine whether you want to use data values from the EMP_ID column of the CUSTOMERS table, or from the EMP_ID column of the EMPLOYEES table, or both in the query's WHERE clause.

To use data from a column whose name appears in more than one of the query's source tables, you must use a *qualified* column in the form:

```
<table name>.<column name>
```

Therefore, to correct the ambiguous reference to the EMP_ID column in the preceding example, rewrite the query as:

```
SELECT RTRIM(cust_f_name)+' '+cust_l_name AS 'Customer',
  RTRIM(f_name)+' '+l_name AS 'Salesperson'
FROM customers, employees
WHERE customers.emp_ID = employees.emp_ID
```

When executing the revised (corrected) query, the DBMS knows to retrieve the EMP_ID value from the CUSTOMERS table for the expression on the left side of the equals (=) sign and to retrieve the EMP_ID value from the EMPLOYEES table for the expression on the right side of the equals (=) sign.

290 Using the ALL Keyword with an INTERSECT Operator to Include Duplicate Rows in the Query Results Table

As you learned in Tip 237, "Understanding the UNION, INTERSECT, and EXCEPT Operators," and Tip 238, "Using the INTERSECT Operator to Select Rows That Appear in All of Two or More Source Tables," you can use the INTERSECT operator to get a list of rows that appear in all of the results tables from two or more queries. For example, if you keep the list of your auto insurance customers in a table named AUTO_INS_CUSTOMERS and you keep the list of your home insurance customers in a union-compatible table named HOME_INS_CUSTOMERS, executing the query

```
  (SELECT * FROM auto_ins_customers)
INTERSECT
  (SELECT * FROM home_ins_customers)
```

will produce a results table that lists all customers that have *both* an auto insurance and a home insurance policy.

The INTERSECT operator, like the UNION operator, eliminates duplicate rows from its results table. As such, if you want to get a list of 18- to 21-year-old auto insurance customers who have had an accident and a traffic ticket within the past year, execute a query similar to:

```
  (SELECT cust_ID FROM auto_ins_customers
   WHERE age BETWEEN 18 AND 21)
INTERSECT
  (SELECT cust_ID FROM traffic_violations
   WHERE date_of_infraction >= (GETDATE() - 365))
INTERSECT
  (SELECT cust_ID FROM auto_claims
   WHERE date_of_claim >= (GETDATE() - 365))
```

Because the DBMS eliminates duplicate rows of query results, the results table for the current query will list a particular CUST_ID once and only once—whether the 18- to 21-year-old customer has had one ticket and one claim or five tickets and three claims within the past year.

If you do not want the DBMS to eliminate duplicate rows from the results table generated from the INTERSECT of two or more sets of query results, use the ALL keyword in conjunction with the INTERSECT operator. For example, to list the CUST_ID in the results table once for each traffic violation or auto claim for 18- to 21-year-old customers who have had both a traffic violation and an accident claim within the past year, execute the INTERSECT query:

```
  (SELECT cust_ID FROM auto_ins_customers
   WHERE age BETWEEN 18 AND 21)
INTERSECT ALL
  (SELECT cust_ID FROM traffic_violations
   WHERE date_of_infraction >= (GETDATE() - 365))
INTERSECT ALL
  (SELECT cust_ID FROM auto_claims
   WHERE date_of_claim >= (GETDATE() - 365))
```

Note: *If your DBMS, like MS-SQL Server, does not support the INTERSECT operator, you can use an AND Boolean operator to add a subquery that tests set membership to the query's WHERE clause in place of each INTERSECT <query> pair. For example, the SELECT statement*

```
SELECT cust_ID FROM auto_ins_customers
WHERE age BETWEEN 18 and 21
```

```
AND cust_ID IN (SELECT cust_ID FROM traffic_violations
                WHERE date_of_infraction >=
                        (GETDATE() - 365))
AND cust_ID IN (SELECT cust_ID FROM auto_claims
                WHERE date_of_claim >= (GETDATE() - 365)
```

will generate the list of 18- to 21-year-old customers who have had both a traffic citation and an auto insurance claim within the past year—just like the second INTERSECT query in the current tip.

Generating the results table from the INTERSECT ALL query in the current tip requires the UNION of two non-INTERSECT queries such as:

```
  SELECT cust_ID FROM traffic_violations
  WHERE date_of_infraction >= (GETDATE() - 365)
  AND cust_ID IN (SELECT cust_ID FROM auto_ins_customers
                  WHERE age BETWEEN 18 and 21)
  AND cust_ID IN (SELECT cust_ID FROM auto_claims
                  WHERE date_of_claim >= (GETDATE() - 365)
UNION ALL
  SELECT cust_ID FROM auto_claims
  WHERE date_of_claim >= (GETDATE() - 365)
  AND cust_ID IN (SELECT cust_ID FROM auto_ins_customers
                  WHERE age BETWEEN 18 and 21)
  AND cust_ID IN (SELECT cust_ID FROM traffic_violations
                  WHERE date_of_infraction >=
                         (GETDATE() - 365)
ORDER BY cust_ID
```

291 Using the CORRESPONDING Keyword in an INTERSECT Query on Non-union–Compatible Tables

By definition, two tables are *union-compatible* if both have the same number of columns and if the data type of each column in one table is the same as the data type of its corresponding column (by ordinal position) in the other table. If two tables are union-compatible, you can use the INTERSECT operator (which you learned about in Tip 238, "Using the INTERSECT Operator to Select Rows That Appear in All of Two or More Source Tables") on the rows returned by two SELECT statements such as

```
  SELECT * FROM table_a
INTERSECT
  SELECT * FROM table_b
```

to generate a results table that has all of the rows from TABLE_A that are also in TABLE_B.

If, on the other hand, you have two tables that are not union-compatible, you can still use the INTERSECT operator to find sets of data values common to both tables by adding the CORRESPONDING keyword to the INTERSECT query. Suppose, for example, that you want a list of your vendors that contribute to *both* the Republican and Democratic parties. As long as each of the columns with the same name in all of the tables also has an identical data type across the tables, a query such as

```
  SELECT * FROM vendors
INTERSECT CORRESPONDING
  SELECT * FROM republican_contributors
INTERSECT CORRESPONDING
  SELECT * FROM democrat_contributors
```

will produce a results table similar to:

```
tax_ID       vendor_name         phone_number
----------   -----------------   --------------
88-5481815   'ABC Corporation'   (748)-254-5565
88-5107204   'XYZ Corporation'   (754)-875-5648
```

In the current example, the three tables have three columns with the same name (TAX_ID, VENDOR_NAME, PHONE_NUMBER), and only two rows have matching values in the three columns across the three tables. (When you execute an INTERSECT CORRESPONDING query, the DBMS checks for matching data values in [and displays] only the columns with identical names in all of the tables.)

When you want to display the data values from only some of the matching columns while still requiring that all matching corresponding columns have the same value, list the columns you want to display after one of the CORRESPONDING keywords in the INTERSECT CORRESPONDING query. For example, if you want to display only the VENDOR_NAME, change the query in the current example to:

```
  SELECT * FROM vendors
INTERSECT CORRESPONDING
  SELECT * FROM republican_contributors
INTERSECT CORRESPONDING (vendor_name)
  SELECT * FROM democrat_contributors
```

The DBMS will then display only the VENDOR_NAME for those rows with the same combination of TAX_ID, VENDOR_NAME, and PHONE_NUMBER.

292 Using a Multi-table JOIN Without a WHERE Clause to Generate a Cartesian Product

Whenever you tell the DBMS to execute a multi-table query, the system first generates the Cartesian product of the source tables listed in the SELECT statement's FROM clause. It then uses the search condition in the WHERE clause to filter out unwanted rows. Therefore, if you want to generate the Cartesian product of two or more tables, simply omit the WHERE clause normally present in a multi-table query.

For example, if you want to get a list of teachers and the classes they teach, execute a query similar to

```
SELECT class_ID,
  RTRIM(first_name)+' '+last_name AS 'Instructor'
FROM classes, teachers
WHERE classes.instructor = teachers.ID
```

which joins each row of class information from the CLASSES table with the name of the instructor for the class from the TEACHERS table to produce a results table similar to:

```
class_ID          Instructor
---------------   --------------
English 101       Ishud Reedmour
Composition 101   Wanda Wright
Math 101          Mathew Mattick
```

If you want the list of all possible combinations of classes and teachers (that is, the Cartesian product of selected columns from the CLASSES table and the TEACHERS table) instead, rewrite the query as

```
SELECT class_ID,
  RTRIM(first_name)+' '+last_name AS 'Instructor'
FROM classes, teachers
```

to produce a (Cartesian product) results table similar to:

```
class_ID          Instructor
---------------   --------------
English 101       Ishud Reedmour
Composition 101   Ishud Reedmour
Math 101          Ishud Reedmour
English 101       Wanda Wright
Composition 101   Wanda Wright
Math 101          Wanda Wright
English 101       Mathew Mattick
Composition 101   Mathew Mattick
Math 101          Mathew Mattick
```

Moreover, if you have a third table—STUDENTS, for example—simply add its name to the list of source tables in the query's FROM clause, and add the STUDENTS columns you want to see in the results table to the query's SELECT clause. For example, when the DBMS executes the query

```
SELECT class_ID,
  RTRIM(first_name)+' '+last_name AS 'Instructor',
  RTRIM(students.f_name)+' '+students.l_name AS 'Student'
FROM classes, teachers, students
```

it will first generate the Cartesian product of the CLASSES table and the TEACHERS table. Next, the system will generate the Cartesian product of that (Cartesian) product table and the STUDENTS table, to produce a results table similar to

```
class_ID          Instructor       Student
---------------   --------------   -------------
English 101       Ishud Reedmour   Ima Pupil
Composition 101   Ishud Reedmour   Ima Pupil
Math 101          Ishud Reedmour   Ima Pupil
English 101       Wanda Wright     Ima Pupil
Composition 101   Wanda Wright     Ima Pupil
Math 101          Wanda Wright     Ima Pupil
English 101       Mathew Mattick   Ima Pupil
Composition 101   Mathew Mattick   Ima Pupil
Math 101          Mathew Mattick   Ima Pupil
English 101       Ishud Reedmour   Uhara Student
Composition 101   Ishud Reedmour   Uhara Student
Math 101          Ishud Reedmour   Uhara Student
English 101       Wanda Wright     Uhara Student
Composition 101   Wanda Wright     Uhara Student
Math 101          Wanda Wright     Uhara Student
English 101       Mathew Mattick   Uhara Student
Composition 101   Mathew Mattick   Uhara Student
Math 101          Mathew Mattick   Uhara Student
```

given that Ima Pupil and Uhara Student are the only two names in the STUDENTS table.

Note: *The Cartesian product of two (or more) tables actually consists of all possible combinations of rows from all of the tables with each row made up of the columns from all of the tables as well. Therefore, the preceding examples do not generate a* true *Cartesian product, since they show all possible combinations of rows but not the combination of all of the columns from all of the tables in each row. To get a* true *Cartesian product, use the "all columns" operator (the asterisk (*)) or list* all *(vs. some) of the column names in the query's SELECT clause. For example, rewrite the preceding example query as*

```
SELECT * FROM classes, teachers, students
```

to generate the true Cartesian product of the CLASSES, TEACHERS, and STUDENTS tables.

---

293 Using Aliases (Correlation Names) as Shorthand for Table Names

If a column name used in an SQL statement has the same name in two or more of the statement's source tables, you must use a *qualified* column name. As you learned in Tip 289, "Using Qualified Column Names in Multi-table Queries That Join Tables That Have the Same Names for One or More Columns," a qualified column name includes both the name of the column and the name of the table whose data the query is to use.

Moreover, to reference a table owned by another user, you must use a *fully* qualified column name, which means your column reference must include the column name, the table name, and the username of the table's owner. Therefore, if you want to generate a list of birthdays and anniversaries using tables owned by another user (such ANNIVERSARY_BIRTHDAY owned by KONRAD, and EMPLOYEES owned by HR_ADMIN, for example), the column references in the query will be rather long:

```
SELECT
  CONVERT(CHAR(12,konrad.anniversary_birthday.next_date,107)
    AS 'Date', hr_admin.employees.emp_ID,
  RTRIM(hr_admin.employees.first_name)+
    ' '+hr_admin.employees.last_name AS 'Employee Name',
  konrad.anniversary_birthday.relationship,
  RTRIM(konrad.anniversary_birthday.first_name)+' '+
    konrad.anniversary_birthday.last_name AS
    'Family Member', konrad.anniversary_birthday.event,
  CONVERT(INTEGER,DATENAME(year,
    konrad.anniversary_birthday.next_date)) -
    CONVERT(INTEGER,DATENAME(year,
      konrad.anniversary_birthday.first_date)) AS 'Years'
FROM hr_admin.employees, konrad.anniversary_birthday
WHERE konrad.anniversary_birthday.next_date
        BETWEEN GETDATE() AND (GETDATE() + 30)
AND   hr_admin.employees.emp_ID =
        konrad.anniversary_birthday.emp_ID
ORDER BY konrad.anniversary_birthday.next_date,
           hr_admin.employees.emp_ID
```

Because typing a query with long qualified column names or several references to columns common to multiple tables can get quite tedious, SQL lets you use an alias (or correlation name) in place of any or all of the table names used in a statement. To define an alias you can use in place of a table name, simply type the alias after the name of the table in the statement's FROM clause. Thus, in the current example you would replace the FROM clause

```
FROM hr_admin.employees, konrad.anniversary_birthday
```

with the FROM clause

```
FROM hr_admin.employees e, konrad.anniversary_birthday ab
```

if you want to use the letter *e* as an alias for HR_ADMIN.EMPLOYEES table and the letters *ab* to mean KONRAD.ANNIVERSARY_BIRTHDAY table in the query. You could then rewrite the query in the current example as:

```
SELECT
  CONVERT(CHAR(12,ab.next_date,107) AS 'Date', e.emp_ID,
  RTRIM(e.first_name)+' '+e.last_name AS 'Employee Name',
  ab.relationship,
  RTRIM(ab.first_name)+' '+ab.last_name AS 'Family Member',
  ab.event, CONVERT(INTEGER,DATENAME(year,ab.next_date)) -
    CONVERT(INTEGER,DATENAME(year,ab.first_date)) AS 'Years'
FROM hr_admin.employees e, konrad.anniversary_birthday ab
WHERE ab.next_date BETWEEN GETDATE() AND (GETDATE() + 30)
AND   e.emp_ID = ab.emp_ID
ORDER BY ab.next_date, e.emp_ID
```

The only restrictions on correlation names (aliases) are that you cannot use the same alias to refer to more than one of the tables listed in the FROM clause, and you cannot use both an alias and the table's long (full) name in the same statement.

294 Understanding One-to-Many and Many-to-One Joins

In a relational database, a one-to-many relationship is most often called a parent-child relationship because one parent can have many children, while a child can have only one parent. Arguably (in the real world), a child has two parents. However, only one of the parents brings the child into the world. Similarly, think of child rows as being the offspring from a single parent row. Figure 294.1 illustrates the one-to-many relationship (parent-to-children) between a row in the EMPLOYEES (parent) table and several rows in the TIMECARDS (child) table.

The relationship between parent and child is represented by the value of a column (or set of columns) common to both tables. In the current example, a parent-child relationship exists between those rows in which the value in the EMP_ID column of the EMPLOYEES table matches the value in the EMP_ID column of the TIMECARDS table.

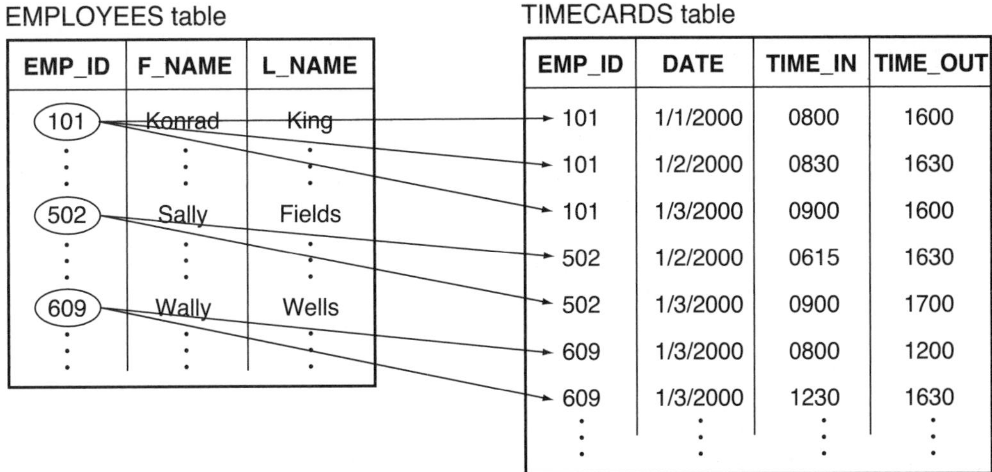

Figure 294.1 One-to-many relationships between (parent) rows in an EMPLOYEES table and (child) rows in a TIMECARDS table

---

Note: *SQL does not require that the column used to create the one-to-many relationship between parent and child tables have the same name in both tables. In the current example, the EMP_ID column in the EMPLOYEES table could have had another name (such as EMP_NUM, for example). The value in the column, not its name, defines the relational link between rows in one table and rows in another.*

To exploit (or exercise) the one-to-many relationship, execute a query that equates the related column in one table with its counterpart in the other table. For example, the query

```
SELECT * FROM employees, timecards
WHERE employees.emp_ID = timecards.emp_ID
```

will produce a results table that joins each row in the parent table (EMPLOYEES) with one or more rows from the child table (TIMECARDS) based on a matching value in the pair of EMP_ID columns-one from each table.

Actually, as you learned in Tip 283, "Understanding Joins and Multi-table Queries," the DBMS first generates the Cartesian product of the TIMECARDS table and the EMPLOYEES table. It then filters out all rows except those in which the value in the EMP_ID column from EMPLOYEES matches the value in the EMP_ID column from TIMECARDS.

The end result of a one-to-many query is a results table similar to

```
emp_ID f_name l_name emp_ID date       time_in time_out
------ ------ ------ ------ ---------- ------- --------
101    Konrad King   101    2000-01-01 800     1600
101    Konrad King   101    2000-01-02 830     1630
101    Konrad King   101    2000-01-03 900     1600
502    Sally  Fields 502    2000-01-02 615     1630
```

```
502    Sally  Fields 502    2000-01-03 700     1700
609    Wally  Wells  609    2000-01-03 800     1200
609    Wally  Wells  609    2000-01-03 1230    1630
```

which has only parent rows joined with one or more child rows. Therefore, you may find it easier to conceptualize a multi-table query as joining parent and child rows versus generating all possible combinations of joins and then filtering out unwanted rows that combine a parent row with a child row that belongs to a different parent.

If you reverse the links in Figure 294.1 (from TIMECARDS to EMPLOYEES), you can see that the child-to-parent relationship is many-to-one. Many (that is, one or more) rows in the child table relate (again by matching column value) to one and only one row in the parent table.

Note: *Figure 294.1 shows the one-to-many relationship between EMPLOYEES and TIMECARDS rows by relating the PRIMARY KEY value in the parent table (EMPLOYEES) with a FOREIGN KEY value in the child table (TIMECARDS). However, SQL does not require that you use a pair of key columns to relate to tables. As long as one of the columns in the two related tables is constrained as UNIQUE or has no duplicate values, performing an equi-join on the source tables will produce a results table showing one-to-many relationships. If both tables have duplicate values in the column used to relate rows in an equi-join, the results table will show many-to-many relationships—which you will learn about in Tip 295, "Understanding Many-to-Many Joins."*

---

295 Understanding Many-to-Many Joins

As you learned in Tip 294, "Understanding One-to-Many and Many-to-One Joins," a *join* (or multi-table query) is a two-step process. First, generate all possible pairs of rows from two related tables. Second, use the Boolean expression in the statement's WHERE clause to filter out the "garbage" rows. (Garbage rows are interim [virtual] table rows that join a row from one table with an unrelated row from the other table.)

In a one-to-many join, the WHERE clause filters out joined rows such that only those that join each row from the first table with one or more rows from the second table are left. Or, looking at the relationship in reverse, the WHERE clause filter leaves only joined rows in which each row from the second table is joined with one (and only one) row from the first table.

In a many-to-many join, on the other hand, the WHERE clause filter leaves not only rows in which each row from the first table is joined with one or more rows from the second table, but also rows in which each row from the second table is joined with one or more rows from the first table.

The decision whether or not to include a joined row from the interim (virtual) table in the final results table is based on the values in one or more pairs of columns common to both tables. When the DBMS executes either an *equi-join* (which you learned about in Tip 283, "Understanding Joins and Multi-table Queries") or a *non–equi-join* (which you learned about in Tip 288, "Understanding Non–Equi-Joins), the system filters out joined rows in which the values in the matching pair (or pairs) of columns used to relate the tables fails to satisfy the condition of the relational operator in the query's WHERE clause.

For example, when executing an equi-join such as

```
SELECT * FROM customers, autos_sold
WHERE customers.cust_ID = autos_sold.sold_to
```

the DBMS will generate an interim (virtual) table that has all possible pairs of rows from the CUSTOMERS table and the AUTOS_SOLD table. Then the system will use the WHERE clause to filter out all joined rows that do not have matching values in the CUST_ID and SOLD_TO columns.

Similarly, when executing a non–equi-join such as

```
SELECT * FROM customers, auto_inventory
WHERE customers.max_price >= auto_inventory.price
```

the DBMS will generate an interim (virtual) table that has all possible pairs of rows from the CUSTOMERS table and the AUTO_INVENTORY table. Next, the system will use the WHERE clause to filter out all joined rows in which the value in the MAX_PRICE column is less than the value in the PRICE column.

In both of these queries (or joins), the DBMS uses the value in a pair of columns (one column from each of the related tables) to decide which of the joined rows to keep in the results table. (In the first example, an equi-join, the pair of columns has to have matching values; in the second example, a non–equi-join, the value in one column has to be greater than or equal to the value in the other.)

Non–equi-joins (queries in which the Boolean operator in the WHERE clause is other than an equals [=] sign) always produce a results table with many-to-many relationships. For example, Figure 295.1 shows some of the joined rows that will pass through the WHERE clause filter into the results table of the second query in the current tip.

As shown in Figure 295.1, the results table will have rows in which each row from the CUSTOMERS table is joined with one or more rows from the AUTO_INVENTORY table. Moreover, the results table will also have rows in which each row from the AUTO_INVENTORY table is joined with one or more rows from the CUSTOMERS table.

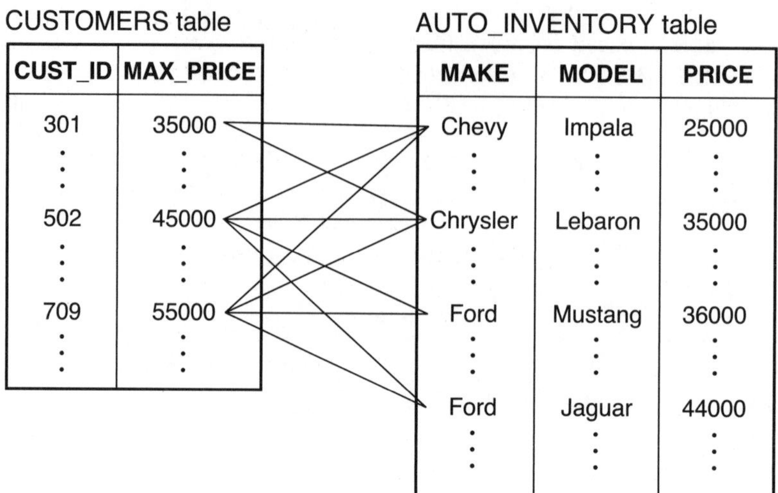

Figure 295.1 Many-to-many relationships between rows in a CUSTOMERS table and rows in an AUTO_INVENTORY table

---

Note: *The equi-join used as the first example in the current tip will perform a one-to-many join of the CUSTOMERS table and the AUTOS_SOLD table only if the values in either the CUST_ID column or the SOLD_TO column are unique. If you allow the user to add duplicate CUST_ID and SOLD_TO values, the equi-join query*

```
SELECT * FROM customers, autos_sold
WHERE customers.cust_ID = autos_sold.sold_to
```

like the non–equi-join query

```
SELECT * FROM customers, auto_inventory
WHERE customers.max_price >= auto_inventory.price
```

will generate a results table that shows many-to-many join relationships in the joined rows.

---

296 Understanding the NATURAL JOIN

A NATURAL JOIN is a special type of equi-join with an implied WHERE clause that compares all columns in one table with corresponding columns that have the same name in another table for equality. Therefore, after the DBMS filters the product of the source tables through the natural join's implied WHERE clause, the final results table will have only joined rows in which all pairs of columns that have the same name in both two tables also have matching values.

Suppose, for example, that you have an EMPLOYEES table and a SALES table created by:

```
CREATE TABLE employees        CREATE TABLE sales
(emp_ID INTEGER,              (sales_date  DATETIME,
 f_name VARCHAR(30),           amount_sold MONEY,
 l_name VARCHAR(30))           emp_ID      INTEGER,
                               office_ID   INTEGER)
```

To get a list of employees and their sales for each office, you can submit a NATURAL JOIN similar to:

```
SELECT employees.emp_ID, sales.office_ID, f_name, l_name,
  sales_date, amount_sold
FROM employees NATURAL JOIN sales
```

When the DBMS executes the query, it will join rows from the EMPLOYEES table with rows from the SALES table that have matching values in the pair of EMP_ID columns—the two columns that have the same name in both tables. Similarly, if the EMPLOYEES table also had an OFFICE_ID column, the NATURAL JOIN query in the current example would join rows in which both pairs of same name columns (EMP_ID and OFFICE_ID) had matching values in the two tables.

In effect, a NATURAL JOIN is equivalent to an equi-join with a WHERE clause that equates each pair of columns with the same name in both source tables. As such, you can rewrite the NATURAL JOIN in the current example as:

```
SELECT employees.emp_ID, sales.office_ID, f_name, l_name,
  sales_date, amount_sold
FROM employees, sales
WHERE employees.emp_ID = sales.emp_ID
```

Or, if the EMPLOYEES table also had an OFFICE_ID column, you could rewrite the NATURAL JOIN of EMPLOYEES and SALES in the current example as:

```
SELECT employees.emp_ID, sales.office_ID, f_name, l_name,
  sales_date, amount_sold
FROM employees, sales
WHERE employees.emp_ID    = sales.emp_ID
AND   employees.office_ID = sales.office_ID
```

Note: *If your DBMS product, like MS-SQL Server, does not support the NATURAL JOIN operator, simply use an equi-join with a WHERE clause that uses AND operators to combine search conditions that equate each pair or columns with the same names in both tables. Whatever its form, the important thing to remember is that a NATURAL JOIN is a query that joins rows only if* all *pairs of columns with the same name in both source tables have matching values. Therefore, if you use a NATURAL JOIN, make sure that all related (joinable) columns have the same name in both tables and that all unrelated columns have names unique to each table.*

297 Understanding the Condition JOIN

A *condition join* is a multi-table query that can use any of the relational operators (>, <, >=, <=, <>, and =) to relate a column in one table with the column value of a corresponding (related) column in another table. In short, a condition join is like an equi-join, except you can use any relational operator in a condition join, while you can use only the equality operator (=) in an equi-join. The only difference between a condition join and a multi-table query with a WHERE clause is that you will find the search condition used to relate the tables in the condition join's ON clause instead of a WHERE clause.

For example, the condition join

```
SELECT * FROM employees JOIN customers
ON (salesperson_ID = emp_ID)
```

will generate a results table with each row from the CUSTOMERS table joined to the row in the EMPLOYEES table in which the value in the EMP_ID column (from the row in the EMPLOYEES table) matches the SALESPERSON_ID (from the row in the CUSTOMERS table). As such, the condition join in the current example is functionally equivalent to the multi-table join:

```
SELECT * FROM employees, customers
WHERE salesperson_ID = emp_ID
```

Similarly, you can use a condition join such as

```
SELECT DISTINCT e.emp_ID e.f_name, e.l_name, e.total_sales
FROM NV_employees e JOIN AZ_employees
ON (e.total_sales > AZ_employees.total_sales)
```

to generate a list of Nevada office salespeople (from rows in the NV_EMPLOYEES table) whose TOTAL_SALES are greater than the TOTAL_SALES of at least one of the Arizona office salespeople (found in the AZ_EMPLOYEES table). Or, you could use the multi-table query

```
SELECT DISTINCT e.emp_ID e.f_name, e.l_name, total_sales
FROM NV_employees e, AZ_employees
WHERE e.total_sales > AZ_employees.total_sales
```

to produce the same result.

Note: *If your DBMS product does not support a condition join, simply rewrite the condition join as a multi-table query with a WHERE clause. Put the search condition from the condition join's ON clause into the query's WHERE clause. The important thing to remember is that a condition join, like every other multi-table query or join, uses the search condition (whether in a WHERE clause or in an ON clause) to filter out any joined yet unrelated rows. The DBMS rejects joined, unrelated rows because their column values fail to satisfy the search condition in the WHERE clause (or in the ON clause).*

298 Using the CROSS JOIN to Create a Cartesian Product

A *CROSS JOIN* (also called a cross product or a Cartesian product) of two tables is a third table that contains all possible pairs of rows from the two cross joined source tables. For example, if you have two tables, TABLE_1 and TABLE_2, each of which has two columns and three rows, the CROSS JOIN

```
SELECT * FROM table_1 CROSS JOIN table_2
```

will pair each of the rows in TABLE_1 with each of the rows in TABLE_2 to produce a results table with four columns and nine rows, as shown in Figure 298.1.

Note: *You can determine the number of columns in a CROSS JOIN (or Cartesian product) of two tables by adding the number of columns in the first table to the number of columns in the second table. Moreover, the number of rows in a CROSS JOINs results table will always be the number of rows in the first table multiplied by the number of rows in the second table.*

If your DBMS product does not support the CROSS JOIN operator, you can still generate the Cartesian product of two tables by executing a multi-table query without a WHERE clause. Suppose, for example, that you have an ATHLETES table and want to pair each athlete with each row of events in a DECATHLON_EVENTS table. If your DBMS supports the CROSS JOIN operator, you can write the query as:

```
SELECT * FROM athletes CROSS JOIN decathlon_events
```

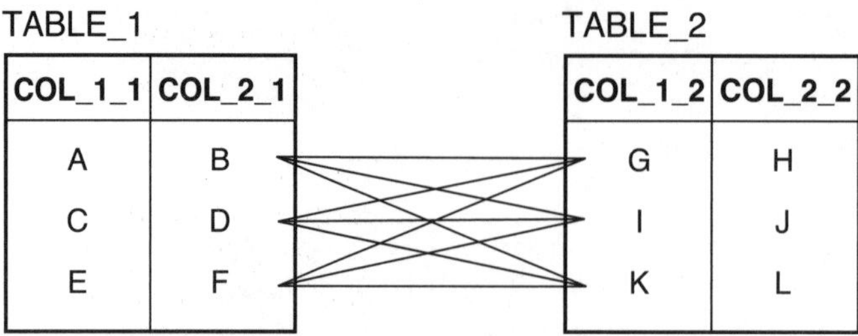

RESULTS_TABLE

COL_1_1	COL_2_1	COL_1_2	COL_2_2
A	B	G	H
A	B	I	J
A	B	K	L
C	D	G	H
C	D	I	J
C	D	K	L
E	F	G	H
E	F	I	J
E	F	K	L

Figure 298.1 The CROSS JOIN of TABLE_1 and TABLE_2

Or, you can generate the same results table with the multi-table query:

```
SELECT * FROM athletes, decathlon_events
```

As you learned from the multi-table queries in Tips 282–289, the CROSS JOIN (or Cartesian product) is rarely the final result you want from a query. However, the DBMS normally generates the CROSS JOIN of the tables in a SELECT statement's FROM clause as a first step in every query. The system then performs a sequence of steps that manipulate and filter the interim (virtual) Cartesian product table (of the source tables) to produce the joined rows in the final results table.

299 Understanding the Column Name JOIN

A *column name join* is very much like the NATURAL JOIN you learned about in Tip 296, "Understanding the NATURAL JOIN." While a NATURAL JOIN requires that *all* pairs of columns with the same name in both tables have matching values, a column name join lets you specify the pairs of same-name column values the DBMS is to compare. As a result, you can use the column name join to join not only tables that are joinable with a NATURAL JOIN, but also tables that are not. After all, if you write a column name join that requires a match of all pairs of columns with the same name in both tables, the column name join is in effect, a NATURAL JOIN. However, if you have a CUSTOMERS table and an EMPLOYEES table created by

```
CREATE TABLE customers      CREATE TABLE employees
(cust_ID INTEGER,           (emp_ID INTEGER,
 f_name  VARCHAR(30),        f_name VARCHAR(30),
 l_name  VARCHAR(30))        l_name VARCHAR(30))
 emp_ID  INTEGER)
```

you cannot use the NATURAL JOIN

```
SELECT RTRIM(c.f_name)+' '+c.l_name AS 'Customer',
  RTRIM(e.f_name)+' '+e.l_name AS 'Salesperson'
FROM customers c NATURAL JOIN employees e
```

to get a combined list showing each customer's name and the name of the customer's salesperson. As you learned in Tip 296, the NATURAL JOIN requires that *all* pairs of same-name columns have matching values in joined rows. Therefore, the NATURAL JOIN of CUSTOMERS and EMPLOYEES in the current example will show only the customers that happen to have a salesperson whose first and last names match the customer's first and last name, respectively.

However, you can use a column name join such as

```
SELECT RTRIM(c.f_name)+' '+c.l_name AS 'Customer',
  RTRIM(e.f_name)+' '+e.l_name AS 'Salesperson'
FROM customers c JOIN employees e
USING (emp_ID)
```

to join the CUSTOMERS and EMPLOYEES tables in the current example. Instead of requiring matching values in all pairs of same-name columns, the USING clause in the current example query tells the DBMS to join rows that have matching values in the EMP_ID column (from each table)—whether the F_NAME and L_NAME column values match or not.

Note: *If your DBMS, like MS-SQL Server, does not support the USING clause, use a condition join instead of a column name join. The only difference between the two types of joins is that the column name join implicitly specifies that the same name column(s) named in the USING clause must have matching values, while the condition join* *explicitly equates the pair of columns in an ON clause. As such, to convert the column name join in the current example to a condition join, simply rewrite the query as:*

```
SELECT RTRIM(c.f_name)+' '+c.l_name AS 'Customer',
  RTRIM(e.f_name)+' '+e.l_name AS 'Salesperson'
FROM customers c JOIN employees e
ON (c.emp_ID = e.emp_ID)
```

300 Using an INNER JOIN to Select All Rows in One Table That Relate to Rows in Another Table

An *INNER JOIN* is a multi-table query in which the DBMS returns only related pairs of rows from the source tables—that is, the query's results table will contain only joined rows that satisfy the search condition in the query's ON clause. Conversely, if a row in either source table does not have a corresponding (related) row in the other table, the row is filtered out and therefore not included in the results table.

Suppose, for example, that you have stocks lists from two analysts, and you want to create a list of the stock recommendations they have in common. If one analyst's list is in table STOCK_LIST_A and the other analyst's list is in table STOCK_LIST_B, then an INNER JOIN of the two tables, such as

```
SELECT a.symbol,
  a.buy_at AS 'Buy Price A', a.sell_at AS 'Sell Price A',
  b.buy_at AS 'Buy Price B', b.sell_at AS 'Sell Price B'
FROM stock_list_a a INNER JOIN stock_list_b b
ON (a.symbol = b.symbol)
```

will display a results table similar to

```
symbol Buy Price  A Sell Price  A Buy Price  B Sell Price B
------ ---------  ------------  -----------  --------------
CSCO   50         60            55           70
LU     32         40            30           45
F      26         32            27           40
GM     60         69            58           63
VTSS   86         92            82           89
LEN    28         32            30           34
```

which lists only stock symbols and price information for those stocks in *both* STOCK_LIST_A and STOCK_LIST_B. Therefore, any row with a SYMBOL column value in either table that does not match the value in the SYMBOL column of a row in the other table will be filtered out and therefore not included as one of the joined rows in the final results table.

If you rewrite the INNER JOIN in the current example as an equivalent multi-table query such as

```
SELECT a.symbol,
  a.buy_at AS 'Buy Price A', a.sell_at AS 'Sell Price A',
  b.buy_at AS 'Buy Price B', b.sell_at AS 'Sell Price B'
FROM stock_list_a a, stock_list_b b
WHERE a.symbol = b.symbol
```

you can see that an INNER JOIN is just another syntax (or way of writing) the multi-table equi-join queries you learned about in Tips 282–289.

Note: *By default, the DBMS will execute a multi-table query as an INNER JOIN unless you specify one of the OUTER JOIN queries you will learn about in Tips 302–305. Therefore, the query*

```
SELECT * FROM table_a JOIN table_b
ON (table_a.column_to_relate = table_b.column_to_relate)
```

is equivalent to:

```
SELECT * FROM table_a INNER JOIN table_b
ON (table_a.column_to_relate = table_b.column_to_relate)
```

301 Understanding the Role of the USING Clause in an INNER JOIN

The *USING* clause in an INNER JOIN lists the pairs of same name columns whose values must match in order for the DBMS to include a joined row in the query's results table. In other words, the system generates the Cartesian product of the tables listed in the SELECT statement's FROM clause and then filters out any joined rows in which the pairs of same name columns listed in the USING clause do not have matching values.

For example, the USING clause in the query

```
SELECT class, section, description, title
FROM curriculum INNER JOIN book_list
USING (class)
```

tells the DBMS to generate a results table with only joined rows in which the value in the CLASS column from the CURRICULUM table matches the value in the CLASS column from the BOOK_LIST table.

Note: The column name(s) listed in a USING clause must appear in both of the tables listed in the FROM clause. Moreover, the column(s) must be defined as either of the same data type or of compatible data types.

If the relationship between the tables in a query is based on matching values in multiple same-name columns, the USING clause will have more than one column name. For example, if the required reading list for each section of a class is unique, then the query in the current example must be rewritten as

```
SELECT class, section, description, title
FROM curriculum INNER JOIN book_list
USING (class, section)
```

to indicate that both the SECTION column pair and the CLASS column pair must have matching values in order for the DBMS to include the joined row in the results table.

The important thing to remember is that the USING clause can specify table row relationships based only on the equality of values in same name column pairs. Therefore, the USING clause in the preceding query is equivalent to the ON clause in

```
SELECT class, section, description, title
FROM curriculum INNER JOIN book_list
ON ((curriculum.class = book_list.class) AND
   (curriculum.section = book_list.section)
```

and the WHERE clause in:

```
SELECT class, section, description, title
FROM curriculum, book_list
WHERE (curriculum.class = book_list.class)
AND   (curriculum.section = book_list.section)
```

Note: The USING clause really does not add any functionality to SQL. As a result, many DBMS products, such as MS-SQL Server, do not support it. After all, as you can see from the final two example queries in the current tip, you can use an ON clause or a WHERE clause to perform the same function as a USING clause. However, if your DBMS supports it, you may want to use the USING clause because it lets you write queries that are more compact and (perhaps) easier to understand.

302 Understanding the OUTER JOIN

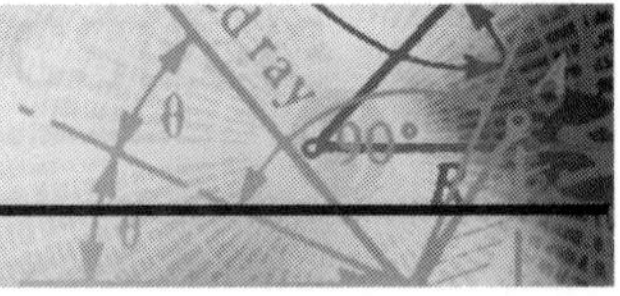

Both inner joins and multi-table queries with a WHERE clause combine rows from multiple tables (two tables at a time) and generate results tables that contain only *pairs* of rows. In other words, if a row in either of the source tables does not have a match (or related row) in the other source table, the DBMS will not place the row in the final results table. As a result, unmatched rows from both tables appear to "vanish" when you execute a multi-table query or INNER JOIN.

An OUTER JOIN, on the other hand, tells the DBMS to generate a results table with not only pairs of related rows, but also unmatched rows from either of the two source tables. For example, if you have a STUDENTS table and a FACULTY table with the following data

```
STUDENTS table                  FACULTY table
f_name l_name   major           f_name l_name   dept_head
------ -------- -----------     ------ -------- ---------
Sally  Smith    English         Lori   Raines   English
Allen  Winchell Mathematics     Marcus Elliot   Engineering
Bruce  Dern     Business        Kelly  Wells    Mathematics
Susan  Smith    NULL            Kris   Matthews NULL
Howard Baker    NULL            Linda  Price    NULL
```

then the single-table queries

```
SELECT * FROM students
SELECT * FROM faculty
```

will generate results tables with five rows of data. However if you join rows from the STUDENTS table with rows from the FACULTY table using a multi-table query such as

```
SELECT RTRIM(s.f_name+' '+s.l_name AS 'Student', major,
  dept_head, RTRIM(f.f_name)+' '+f.l_name AS 'Professor'
FROM students s, faculty f
WHERE major = dept_head
ORDER BY major, dept_head
```

then the DBMS will generate a results table with only two rows:

```
Student         major        dept_head    Professor
--------------  -----------  -----------  -----------
Sally Smith     English      English      Lori Raines
Allen Winchell  Mathematics  Mathematics  Kelly Wells
```

The remaining three rows in the STUDENTS table seem to "vanish" because the DBMS cannot pair with rows in the FACULTY table by finding a matching DEPT_HEAD column value (from the FACULTY table) for the MAJOR column value (from the STUDENTS table). Similarly, the system filters out three unmatched rows from the FACULTY table for the same reason—no matching value in the MAJOR column (from the STUDENTS table) for the value in the DEPT_HEAD column (from the FACULTY table).

Note: *The SQL standard specifies that the predicate NULL = NULL is FALSE. As a result, the WHERE clause filters out any rows that join a student without a major (that is, a row from the STUDENTS table with a NULL in the MAJOR column) with a faculty member who is not the head of a department (that is, a row from the FACULTY table with a NULL in the DEPT_HEAD column).*

To list not only paired (related) rows but also unmatched rows from either table, rewrite the multi-table query (which is, in effect, an INNER JOIN based on the columns listed in the WHERE clause) with a FULL OUTER JOIN such as

```
SELECT RTRIM(s.f_name+' '+s.l_name AS 'Student', major,
  dept_head, RTRIM(f.f_name)+' '+f.l_name AS 'Professor'
FROM students s FULL OUTER JOIN faculty f
ON (major = dept_head)
ORDER BY major, dept_head
```

to generate a results table similar to:

```
Student         major        dept_head    Professor
--------------  -----------  -----------  -------------
NULL            NULL         NULL         Kris Mathews
NULL            NULL         NULL         Linda Price
Susan Smith     NULL         NULL         NULL
Howard Baker    NULL         NULL         NULL
NULL            NULL         Engineering  Marcus Elliot
Bruce Dern      Business     NULL         NULL
Sally Smith     English      English      Lori Raines
Allen Winchell  Mathematics  Mahtematics  Kelly Wells
```

The results table from the FULL OUTER JOIN has eight rows:

- Two joined (related) rows (Sally Smith and Allen Winchell) produced by the multi-table query (the INNER JOIN)
- Two unmatched rows (from the STUDENTS table) for students without a major (Susan Smith and Howard Baker)
- One unmatched row (from the STUDENTS table) for a student (Bruce Dern) with a MAJOR (Business) without a department head in the FACULTY table
- Two unmatched rows (from the FACULTY) table for professors who are not department heads (Kris Mathews and Linda Price)
- One unmatched row (from the FACULTY table) for a professor (Marcus Elliot) who is head of a department (Engineering) in which no students are majoring

Notice that the DBMS fills the remaining results table columns from the "other" table with NULL values in each of the unmatched rows. For example, Bruce Dern is a business major. However, since there is no DEPT_HEAD for the business department in the FACULTY table, the DBMS puts a NULL into the DEPT_HEAD and PROFESSOR columns (from the FACULTY table) in the joined row in the results table. Similarly, Kris Mathews is not the head of a department, so the DBMS puts a NULL in the STUDENT and MAJOR columns (from the STUDENTS table) in the joined row in the results table.

303 Understanding the LEFT OUTER JOIN

As you learned in Tip 302, "Understanding the OUTER JOIN," the results table from an INNER JOIN includes only pairs of related rows, while the results table from an OUTER JOIN includes both matched (related) rows and unmatched rows. The FULL OUTER JOIN in Tip 302 included unmatched rows from both tables in the final results table. If you want to include unmatched rows from only one of the two source tables involved in a join (or multi-table query), use either a LEFT OUTER JOIN or a RIGHT OUTER JOIN instead of a FULL OUTER JOIN.

A *LEFT OUTER JOIN* tells the DBMS to generate a results table that includes joined rows and any unmatched rows from the table listed to the *left* (that is, listed before) the keyword JOIN in the query's FROM clause.

Suppose, for example, that you want to join the list of all customer names and total purchases from a CUSTOMERS table with the name of salesperson to whom each customer is assigned from the EMPLOYEES table. However, since you want a list of *all* customers, you want the DBMS to include any customers not currently assigned to an active salesperson as well.

If you execute an INNER JOIN such as

```
SELECT cust_ID, RTRIM(c.f_name)+' '+c.l_name AS 'Customer',
  total_purchases, emp_ID,
  RTRIM(e.f_name)+' '+e.l_name AS 'Salesperson'
FROM customers c JOIN employees e
ON (salesperson = emp_ID)
ORDER BY emp_ID DESC
```

the results table will display only the name, total purchases, and salesperson's name for customers currently assigned to a salesperson (that is, rows from the CUSTOMERS customer table with a SALESPERSON value that the DBMS can find in the EMP_ID column of the EMPLOYEES table). As a result, any CUSTOMERS table rows with a NULL SALESPERSON or an invalid SALESPERSON will not appear in the SELECT statement's results table.

However, if you execute the same basic query as a LEFT OUTER JOIN

```
SELECT cust_ID, RTRIM(c.f_name)+' '+c.l_name AS 'Customer',
  total_purchases, emp_ID,
  RTRIM(e.f_name)+' '+e.l_name AS 'Salesperson'
FROM customers c LEFT OUTER JOIN employees e
ON (salesperson = emp_ID)
ORDER BY emp_ID DESC
```

the DBMS will generate a results table similar to

```
cust_ID Customer        total_purchases emp_ID Salesperson
------- --------------- --------------- ------ -----------
6753    Sally Brown     95658.0000      NULL   NULL
3758    Richard Stewart 15425.0000      NULL   NULL
1001    Linda Reed      158112.0000     101    Konrad King
7159    Walter Fields   96835.0000      101    Konrad King
4859    Sue Coulter     45412.0000      101    Konrad King
2158    Jimmy Tyson     754515.0000     201    Kris Jamsa
5159    James Herrera   74856.0000      201    Kris Jamsa
```

which includes not only joined rows showing each customer and the customer's salesperson's name, but also any customers not yet assigned to a salesperson or that have values in the SALESPERSON column (from the CUSTOMERS table) that do not match any values in the EMP_ID column (from the EMPLOYEES table). Notice that the DBMS puts NULL values into the results table EMP_ID and SALESPERSON columns (from the EMPLOYEES table) in each of the unmatched rows from the CUSTOMERS table.

Note: *The keyword LEFT in a LEFT OUTER JOIN tells you that the results table will include unmatched rows from the table to the LEFT of the keyword JOIN in the query's FROM clause. As such, if you changed the FROM clause in the current example to*

```
FROM (employees e JOIN customers c)
```

you would get a different results table. The new results table, like the one in the current example, would still have the same pairs of joined rows. However, instead of unmatched CUSTOMERS table rows, the results table would include all unmatched from the EMPLOYEES table and no unmatched rows from the CUSTOMERS table.

304 Understanding the RIGHT OUTER JOIN

In Tip 303, "Understanding the LEFT OUTER JOIN," you learned that a LEFT OUTER JOIN tells the DBMS to generate a results table that includes all related rows from the query's source tables, and any unmatched rows from the table to the *left* of the keyword JOIN. Conversely, a *RIGHT OUTER JOIN* tells the DBMS to generate a results table that includes all related rows and any unmatched rows from the table to the *right* (that is, the table that follows) the keyword JOIN in the SELECT statement's FROM clause.

For example, if you work for a food delivery service that lends freezers to its customers, you can get a complete list of freezers the company owns along with the names of customers who have the freezer currently out on loan by executing a RIGHT OUTER JOIN such as

```
SELECT RTRIM(f_name)+' '+l_name AS 'Customers Name'
  freezer_inventory.freezer_ID, date_purchased AS
  'Purchased', cost, amt_repairs AS 'Repairs'
FROM customers RIGHT OUTER JOIN freezer_inventory
ON (customers.freezer_ID = freezer_inventory.freezer_ID)
ORDER BY freezer_inventory.freezer_ID
```

which will generate a results table similar to:

```
Customer Name   freezer_ID Purchased   Cost     Repairs
--------------- ---------- ---------- -------- -------
NULL            11111      2000-10-11 155.9900 10.0000
Richard Stewart 15425      1999-01-01 179.9400 .0000
NULL            15915      1998-05-05 133.4500 .0000
NULL            16426      1998-07-05 100.4500 12.7500
NULL            21345      1996-09-09 100.4500 12.2300
NULL            22222      2000-04-07 255.5800 .0000
Sue Coulter     45412      1995-03-05 179.9400 45.8900
NULL            45413      1999-01-01 255.2800 .0000
NULL            74845      1997-04-01 99.9900  .0000
James Herrera   74856      1999-05-09 185.2500 12.2500
Sally Brown     95658      2000-06-01 188.8500 15.5500
Walter Fields   96835      2000-10-15 155.9900 75.5500
NULL            97999      1996-09-03 75.9800  44.2500
```

Notice that the DBMS places a NULL in the results table Customer Name column for each unmatched row from the FREEZER_INVENTORY table. Moreover, the system filters out any unmatched rows from the CUSTOMERS table. (Unmatched CUSTOMERS table rows in the results table would have a customer name and NULL values for the results table columns from the FREEZER_INVENTORY table (FREEZER_ID, PURCHASED, COST, and REPAIRS).

Note: *If you are doing a RIGHT OUTER JOIN and the results table includes the column used to match (join) related rows in the query's source tables, be sure to use the column from the table listed to the* right *of the keyword JOIN in the SELECT statement's FROM clause. If you use the column from the table listed to the left of the JOIN instead, results table rows for unmatched rows from the right table will have a NULL value in the matching column. For example, if the SELECT clause in the preceding query listed CUSTOMERS.FREEZER_ID (the matching column from the left table) instead of FREEZER_INVENTORY.FREEZER_ID (the matching column from the right table) results table would show a NULL value for the freezer_ID column for freezers 11111, 15915, 16426, 21345, 22222, 45413, 74845, and 97999. As a result, you would not know the serial numbers for the freezers that should be in your warehouse. Moreover, you would not know the purchase date, initial cost, and cost of repairs for a particular freezer not currently on loan.*

---

305 Understanding the FULL OUTER JOIN

The *FULL OUTER JOIN* combines the results of the LEFT OUTER JOIN (which you learned about in Tip 303, "Understanding the LEFT OUTER JOIN") and the RIGHT OUTER JOIN (which you learned about in Tip 304, "Understanding the RIGHT OUTER JOIN"). When the DBMS executes a FULL OUTER JOIN, it generates a results table that contains joined (related) rows along with any unmatched rows from both the table to the *left* and the table to the *right* of the keyword JOIN in the SELECT statement's FROM clause.

For example, to list all customer names from the CUSTOMERS table along with all freezers from the FREEZER_INVENTORY table, you could execute the FULL OUTER JOIN

```
SELECT RTRIM(f_name)+' '+l_name AS 'Customers Name'
  customers.freezer_ID AS 'Cust_FID',
  freezer_inventory.freezer_ID AS 'Inv_FID',
  date_purchased AS 'Purchased', cost,
  amt_repairs AS 'Repairs'
FROM customers FULL OUTER JOIN freezer_inventory
ON (customers.freezer_ID = freezer_inventory.freezer_ID)
ORDER BY freezer_inventory.freezer_ID
```

which will produce a results table similar to:

```
Customer Name   Cust_FID Inv_FID  Purchased  Cost     Repairs
--------------- -------- -------  ---------- -------- ------
Jimmy Tyson     754515   NULL     NULL       NULL     NULL
Linda Reed      158112   NULL     NULL       NULL     NULL
NULL            NULL     11111    2000-10-11 155.9900 10.0000
Richard Stewart 15425    15425    1999-01-01 179.9400 .0000
NULL            NULL     15915    1998-05-05 133.4500 .0000
NULL            NULL     16426    1998-07-05 100.4500 12.7500
NULL            NULL     21345    1996-09-09 100.4500 12.2300
NULL            NULL     22222    2000-04-07 255.5800 .0000
Sue Coulter     45412    45412    1995-03-05 179.9400 45.8900
NULL            NULL     45413    1999-01-01 255.2800 .0000
NULL            NULL     74845    1997-04-01 99.9900  .0000
James Herrera   74856    74856    1999-05-09 185.2500 12.2500
Sally Brown     95658    95658    2000-06-01 188.8500 15.5500
Walter Fields   96835    96835    2000-10-15 155.9900 75.5500
NULL            NULL     97999    1996-09-03 75.9800  44.2500
```

If you are using a FULL OUTER JOIN not only to display all rows in both tables (both matched and unmatched) but also to look for inconsistencies in related tables, be sure the results table includes *all* of the columns in the pair(s) of columns used to relate the tables.

For example, if the results table in the current example displayed only the FREEZER_ID from the FREEZER_INVENTORY table, it would not show that CUSTOMERS table rows for Jimmy Tyson and Linda Reed have invalid freezer ID numbers in the FREEZER_ID column. A results table without the CUST_FID column (the FREEZER_ID from the CUSTOMERS table) would tell you only that the two customers did not have a freezer with a FREEZER_ID that matched one of the FREEZER_ID values in the FREEZER_INVENTORY table.

Conversely, if the results table had only the CUST_FID (the FREEZER_ID from the CUSTOMERS table) and not the INV_FID (the FREEZER_ID column from the FREEZER_INVENTORY table), you could still tell that Jimmy and Linda had invalid freezer ID numbers. (Unmatched rows from the CUSTOMERS table with an invalid FREEZER_ID in the CUSTOMERS table would have a non-NULL value in the CUST_FID column NULL values for the PURCHASED, COSTS, and REPAIRS columns in the results table.) However, without an INV_FID column, the results table would show only the FREEZER_ID values for the freezers currently on loan, since the DBMS would put a NULL in the CUST_FID column for each unmatched row from the FREEZER_INVENTORY table.

306 Understanding MS-SQL Server OUTER JOIN Notation

When you learned how to write LEFT OUTER JOIN, RIGHT OUTER JOIN, and FULL OUTER JOIN queries in Tips 303–305, all of the examples used an ON clause to specify the relationship for joining matching pairs of rows. However, MS-SQL Server also lets you write LEFT and RIGHT OUTER JOIN queries as multi-table SELECT statements with a WHERE clause.

If you attach an asterisk (*) to the comparison operator in a SELECT statement's WHERE clause, the DBMS treats the multi-table query as an OUTER JOIN. As shown in Table 306.1, the position of the asterisk (*) (to the left or to the right of the comparison operator) tells the DBMS the type of OUTER JOIN you want to perform.

Type of OUTER JOIN	***WHERE Clause Operators***
LEFT OUTER JOIN	*=, *<, *>, *<=, *>=, *<>
RIGHT OUTER JOIN	=*, <*, >*, <=*, >=*, <>*

Table 306.1 MS-SQL Server WHERE Clause OUTER JOIN Notation

For example, you can write the LEFT OUTER JOIN used as an example in Tip 303, "Understanding the LEFT OUTER JOIN," as a multi-table SELECT statement by attaching an asterisk (*) to the left of the equality (=) comparison operator in the query's WHERE clause:

```
SELECT cust_ID, RTRIM(c.f_name)+' '+c.l_name AS 'Customer',
  total_purchases, emp_ID,
  RTRIM(e.f_name)+' '+e.l_name AS 'Salesperson'
FROM customers c, employees e
WHERE salesperson *= emp_ID
ORDER BY emp_ID DESC
```

Similarly, if you attach an asterisk (*) to the right of an equality operator (=) operator in a SELECT statement's WHERE, MS-SQL Server will execute a RIGHT OUTER JOIN. Therefore, you can write the RIGHT OUTER JOIN used as an example in Tip 304, "Understanding the RIGHT OUTER JOIN," as:

```
SELECT RTRIM(f_name)+' '+l_name AS 'Customers Name'
  freezer_inventory.freezer_ID, date_purchased AS
  'Purchased', cost, amt_repairs AS 'Repairs'
FROM customers, freezer_inventory
WHERE customers.freezer_ID =* freezer_inventory.freezer_ID
ORDER BY freezer_inventory.freezer_ID
```

You may be surprised to find (as I was) that MS-SQL Server does not have a WHERE clause operator for a FULL OUTER JOIN. I fully expected the DBMS to use an asterisk (*) on both sides of the comparison operator in the WHERE clause to specify a FULL OUTER JOIN. After all, the FULL OUTER JOIN is a combination of the LEFT OUTER JOIN and the RIGHT OUTER JOIN. Therefore, one would think that the "combination" FULL OUTER JOIN notation would be an asterisk (*) on *both* sides of the comparison operator in the query's WHERE clause. (After all, the LEFT OUTER JOIN has an asterisk [*] to the left of the comparison operator [*=], and the RIGHT OUTER JOIN has an asterisk [*] to the right of the comparison operator [=*]).

307 Joining More Than Two Tables in a Single Query

Whether executing an OUTER JOIN or an INNER JOIN, the DBMS always performs its joins two tables at a time. Therefore, to JOIN three or more tables in a single query will require multiple JOIN clauses that combine pairs of source tables, pairs of (interim) joined tables, or a single source table with an interim joined table.

Suppose, for example, that you keep information on the stocks you own in a PORTFOLIO table, and you want to know if insider trading activity (noted in an INSIDER_TRADES table) is at all related to the analyst recommendations (stored in an ANALYST_RECOMMENDATIONS) table. To answer your question, the DBMS must join the three tables, two tables at a time. First, write a two-table INNER JOIN such as

```
SELECT p.symbol, trade_type, share_ct, position
FROM portfolio p INNER JOIN insider_trades it
ON p.symbol = it.symbol
ORDER BY p.symbol
```

to get a list of stocks in the PORTFOLIO table that also have insider trading activity in the INSIDER_TRADES table. The INNER JOIN tells the DBMS to filter out any rows from the PORTFOLIO table that do not have a related row (by matching SYMBOL column values) in the INSIDER_TRADES table, and vice versa. Next, add a LEFT OUTER JOIN that will relate the joined (PORTFOLIO/INSIDER_TRADES) rows in the interim table (by matching SYMBOL column values) with rows in the ANALYST_RECOMMENDATIONS table:

```
SELECT p.symbol, trade_type, share_ct, position,
  recommendation
FROM portfolio p INNER JOIN insider_trades it
ON p.symbol = it.symbol
LEFT OUTER JOIN analyst_recommendations ar
ON p.symbol = ar.symbol
ORDER BY p.symbol
```

Note: *The LEFT OUTER JOIN in current example tells the DBMS that you want the query results to include all matched rows from the ANALYST_RECOMMENDATIONS table and any unmatched joined rows from the INNER JOIN of the PORTFOLIO table and the INSIDER_TRADES table. If you used an INNER JOIN instead of the LEFT OUTER JOIN, the final results table would include only stocks from the PORTFOLIO table that had* both *insider trades (from the INSIDER_TRADES table) and analyst recommendations (from the ANALYST_RECOMMENDATIONS table). However, the original query was "Are analyst recommendations related to insider trades?" Therefore, you really need a final results table that includes not only your insider-traded stocks with (matching) analyst recommendations, but also all of your insider-traded stocks without (matching) analyst recommendations.*

After the DBMS puts all of your insider-traded stocks in the final results table, you can compare the number of insider trades matched with analyst recommendations to the number that are not.

Now, suppose you want to submit a query that can be answered only by joining multiple joined tables instead of by joining a source table to a joined table (as shown in the preceding example). For example, to get a list of stocks in your PORTFOLIO table that have matching rows in the INSIDER_TRADES table *or* matching rows in the ANALYST_RECOMMENDATIONS, submit a query similar to

```
SELECT (CASE WHEN p1.symbol IS NULL THEN p2.symbol
             ELSE p1.symbol
        END) AS 'Stock',
  trade_type, share_ct, position, recommendation
FROM (portfolio p1 INNER JOIN insider_trades it
      ON p1.symbol = it.symbol)
```

```
FULL OUTER JOIN
     (portfolio p2 INNER JOIN analyst_recommendations ar
      ON p2.symbol = ar.symbol)
ON p1.symbol = p2.symbol
ORDER BY Stock
```

which performs a FULL OUTER JOIN of the joined rows from the INNER JOIN of rows from the PORTFOLIO table with rows from the INSIDER_TRADES table, and the joined rows from the INNER JOIN of rows from the PORTFOLIO table with rows from the ANALYST_RECOMMENDATIONS table.

The important thing to understand is that the DBMS always executes a JOIN two tables at a time. However, the two tables you tell the DBMS to join can be two individual source tables, an individual source table and a joined table, or two joined tables. As such, your query can join any number of tables—just be aware that the DBMS works its way through joining them, two tables at a time.

308 Understanding Non-equality INNER and OUTER JOIN Statements

All of the INNER JOIN and OUTER JOIN examples in Tips 300–305 used the equality (=) comparison operator to join rows in one table with related rows in another based on matching pairs of column values. However, both INNER JOIN and OUTER JOIN queries also let you join pairs of rows based on column value relationships other than equality.

Suppose, for example, that an airline wants to generate a list of customers and the rewards they have earned based on the balance in each customer's frequent flier account. An INNER JOIN such as

```
SELECT member_ID,
  RTRIM(f_name)+' '+l_name AS 'Member Name', miles_earned,
  miles_required, description AS 'Reward Earned'
FROM frequent_fliers INNER JOIN rewards
ON miles_earned >= miles_required
ORDER BY l_name, f_name, member_ID, miles_required
```

will generate a results table that lists customer IDs, names, account balances, and rewards earned for all customers eligible for at least one reward.

In the current example, the relationship between a row in the FREQUENT_FLIER table and a row in the REWARDS table is not based on matching MILES_EARNED and MILES_REQUIRED column values alone. Rather, the final results table will include not only rows in which the two columns have matching values, but also rows in which the value in the MILES_EARNED column is greater than the value in the MILES_REQUIRED column.

You can also use nonequality comparison operators in OUTER JOIN queries. For example, if a real estate firm wants to prepare a list of its listed properties and prospective buyers, the FULL OUTER JOIN query

```
SELECT address, RTRIM(f_name)+' '+l_name AS 'Buyer',
  min_sales_price AS 'Seller Minimum',
  max_purchase_price AS 'Buyer Maximum',
  (max_purchase_price - min_sales_price) AS 'Spread'
FROM listings FULL OUTER JOIN buyers
ON  (max_purchase_price >= min_sales_price)
AND (size_required <= square_footage)
AND (bedrooms_required <= num_bedrooms)
ORDER BY address DESC, buyer
```

will generate a results table that not only matches each potential buyer with listings within the buyer's price range and specifications, but also lists properties with no prospects and buyers with requirements not satisfied by any of the listed properties.

The important thing to understand is that you can use any of the comparison operators (=, <, >, <=, >=, and <>) in the ON clause of an INNER and an OUTER join to express the relationship between pairs of columns in related rows.

309 Understanding the UNION JOIN

The UNION JOIN, unlike the other joins you learned about in Tips 296–305, makes no attempt to match and actually *join* a row from one source table with one or more rows from the other source table. Instead, the UNION join simply creates a results table that contains the rows of columns from the first table *plus* the rows of columns from the second table.

For example, the UNION JOIN

```
SELECT * FROM portfolio_a a UNION JOIN portfolio_b b
```

will generate a single results table with all of the rows and columns from both the PORTFOLIO A table and the PORTFOLIO_B table, as shown in Figure 309.1.

While an OUTER JOIN supplies only NULL values for the *other* table's columns in unmatched rows, every row in a UNION JOIN consists of the column values from one table joined to NULL column values for the other table. In the current example of a UNION JOIN, the DBMS inserts all of the rows from PORTFOLIO_A—joined to a row with a NULL value for each of the columns in PORTFOLIO_B—into the results table. Then the system inserts each of the rows from PORTFOLIO_B—joined to a row with a NULL value for each of the columns in PORTFOLIO_A into the results table.

PORTFOLIO_A

SYM	SHARES	AVG_COST
BAC	200	64 5/8
CMB	400	50 7/8
HCA	1000	35 5/8

PORTFOLIO_B

SYM	SHARES	AVG_COST
ADP	500	21 3/4
BAC	440	53 7/8
CDN	500	33 3/4
CMB	400	50 7/8

PORTFOLIO_A UNION JOIN PORTFOLIO_B

A. SYM	A. SHARES	A. AVG_COST	B. SYM	B. SHARES	B. AVG_COST
BAC	200	64 5/8	NULL	NULL	NULL
CMB	400	50 7/8	NULL	NULL	NULL
HCA	1000	35 5/8	NULL	NULL	NULL
NULL	NULL	NULL	ADP	500	21 3/4
NULL	NULL	NULL	BAC	440	53 7/8
NULL	NULL	NULL	CDN	500	33 3/4
NULL	NULL	NULL	CMB	400	50 7/8

Figure 309.1 The source and results tables for a two-table UNION JOIN

A UNION JOIN is handy when you want to work with all of the rows from two or more (perhaps union-incompatible) tables as if they were a single table—without losing the ability to tell which rows came from which table.

Note: *The results table from a UNION JOIN of two tables is* not *the same the results table generated by the DBMS when you use the UNION operator to SELECT all rows that appear in either or both of the same two tables. (You learned about the UNION operator in Tip 216, "Using the UNION Operator to Select All Rows That Appear in Any or All of Two or More Tables.") Unlike the results table for the UNION JOIN shown in Figure 309, a UNION query of the same two tables*

```
  SELECT * FROM portfolio_a
UNION
  SELECT * FROM portfolio_b
```

generates a results table similar to:

```
SYM   SHARES  AVG_COST
---   ------  --------
BAC   200     64 5/16
CMB   400     50 7/8
HCA   1000    33 5/8
ADP   500     21 3/4
BAC   440     53 7/16
CDN   500     33 3/4
```

While the results table from the UNION JOIN has seven rows of six columns each, the DBMS generates a results table with six rows of three columns each when you use the UNION operator to combine the rows in the two tables instead.

---

310 Using the COALESCE Expression to Refine the Results of a UNION JOIN

In Tip 309, "Understanding the UNION JOIN," you learned that the UNION JOIN of two (or more) tables creates a results table with the rows and columns from *all* of the source tables. Each row in the results table contains the column values from one of the rows in the source table joined with NULL column values for each of the columns in each of the query's other source tables. As such, the UNION JOIN generates a final results table with a lot of null values.

For example, the UNION JOIN query

```
SELECT * FROM
  joint_acct j UNION JOIN SEP_acct s UNION JOIN IRA_acct i
```

will generate a results table similar to:

```
 sym  shares avg_cst sym  shares avg_cst  sym   shares avg_cst
 ---- ------ ------- ---- ------ -------  ----  ------ -------
 BAC  200    64.625  NULL NULL   NULL     NULL  NULL   NULL
 CMB  400    50.875  NULL NULL   NULL     NULL  NULL   NULL
 HCA  1000   35.625  NULL NULL   NULL     NULL  NULL   NULL
 NULL NULL   NULL    ADP  500    21.75    NULL  NULL   NULL
 NULL NULL   NULL    BAC  440    53.875   NULL  NULL   NULL
 NULL NULL   NULL    CDN  500    33.75    NULL  NULL   NULL
 NULL NULL   NULL    NULL NULL   NULL     F     500    41.125
 NULL NULL   NULL    NULL NULL   NULL     HCA   300    27.375
 NULL NULL   NULL    NULL NULL   NULL     CMB   400    50.875
```

The large number of NULL values in the final results table makes it hard to discern any meaningful information from its contents. The expression "can't see the forest for the trees" comes to mind.

Fortunately, you can use the COALESCE expression (which you learned about in Tip 112, "Using the COALESCE Expression to Replace NULL Values") to filter out the NULL values from the final results table. For example, if you rewrite the preceding UNION JOIN as

```
SELECT
  COALESCE (j.symbol,  s.symbol,  i.symbol)  AS 'Symbol',
  COALESCE (j.account, s.account, i.account) AS 'Account',
  COALESCE (j.shares,  s.shares,  i.shares)  AS 'Shares',
  COALESCE (j.avg_cst, s.avg_cst, i.avg_cst) AS 'Avg Cost'
FROM          (SELECT 'Joint Acct' AS 'Account', j.*) j,
  UNION JOIN (SELECT 'SEP Acct'   AS 'Account', s.*) s,
  UNION JOIN (SELECT 'IRA Acct'   AS 'Account', i.*) i
ORDER BY symbol, account
```

the query's COALESCE expressions will select the one non-NULL value from each set of columns—thereby filtering out the NULL values from the (now) interim results table from the UNION JOIN clauses to generate a final results table similar to:

```
Symbol  Account     Shares  Avg Cost
------  ----------  ------  --------
ADP     SEP Acct    500     21.7500
BAC     Joint Acct  200     64.6250
BAC     SEP Acct    440     53.8750
CDN     SEP Acct    500     33.7500
CMB     IRA Acct    400     50.8750
CMB     Joint Acct  400     50.8750
F       IRA Acct    500     41.1250
HCA     IRA Acct    300     27.3750
HCA     Joint Acct  1000    35.6250
```

Moreover, you need only change the ORDER BY clause to

```
ORDER BY account, symbol
```

to sort the list of stocks in order by account—thereby making it easier to see which stocks you are holding in which account.

311 Understanding the Role of the FROM Clause in a JOIN Statement

The FROM clause in a JOIN, or multi-table SELECT statement, is the virtual table from which the DBMS retrieves the rows of column values it uses as input for the remaining clauses in the query. Suppose, for example, that you have a GRADES table and a STUDENTS table created by:

```
CREATE TABLE grades              CREATE TABLE students
course_ID      VARCHAR(15),      (SID     INTEGER,
section        SMALLINT,          f_name VARCHAR(20),
student_ID     INTEGER,           l_name VARCHAR(20))
professor_ID   INTEGER,
grade          NUMERIC)
```

If you submit an INNER JOIN query such as

```
SELECT  RTRIM(f_name)+' '+l_name AS 'Student', course_ID,
  section, grade
FROM grades JOIN students ON student_ID = SID
```

the DBMS will generate a results table that lists student names, classes, and grades.

When executing a query, the BMS first creates a virtual table by joining the rows from the tables listed in the FROM clause that satisfy the search condition(s) in the ON clause. In the current example, the DBMS creates a virtual table consisting of rows from the GRADES table joined with rows from the STUDENTS table in which the value in the STUDENT_ID column from the GRADES table matches the value in the SID column of the STUDENTS table.

Next, the system passes column values from each joined row in the virtual table (and not each of the physical source tables) to the SELECT clause, which filters out unwanted columns and displays the rest in the results table. In the current example, the SELECT clause filters out all but the F_NAME, L_NAME, COURSE_ID, SECTION, and GRADE column values from the joined rows in the GRADES+STUDENTS virtual table.

Similarly, if you have the names of the school's teachers in a PROFESSORS table, you can use a query similar to

```
SELECT RRIM(s.f_name)+' '+s.l_name AS 'Student', course_ID,
  section, grade, RTRIM(p.f_name)+' '+p.l_name AS 'Teacher'
FROM (grades JOIN students s ON student_ID = SID)
JOIN professors p ON professor_ID = PID
```

to display the name of the professor who taught the class next to the class ID, student name, and grade.

In the current example, the FROM clause tells the DBMS to create a virtual table with joined rows from the STUDENTS and GRADES table, as it did in the preceding example. Next, the DBMS creates another virtual table by joining rows from the PROFESSORS table with joined rows in the STUDENTS+GRADES virtual table in which the value in the PID column from a row in the PROFESSOR table matches the value in the PROFESSOR_ID column from a joined row in the (virtual) STUDENTS+GRADES table.

Therefore, although the FROM clause in a query such as

```
SELECT * FROM students, grades
WHERE student_ID = SID
ORDER BY student_ID
```

might give you the impression that a FROM clause simply lists the names of source table(s) used by a SELECT statement, the FROM is actually the *virtual* table with the joined rows that serve as the data source for the query. The DBMS first creates a virtual table either from the Cartesian product of the tables listed in the FROM clause or by joining matching rows from related tables as specified in each JOIN statement in the FROM clause. Next the system uses the other clauses in the SELECT statement to filter unwanted rows and columns out of the virtual table and adds the remaining column values as rows to the final results table.

312 Using the "*" Operator to Specify All Columns in All or Only in Some Tables in a Multiple Table JOIN

As you learned in Tip 90, "Using the SELECT Statement to Display All Column Values," the asterisk (*) "all columns" operator gives you a shortcut way to tell the DBMS to that you want to include all of a table's columns in the query's results table. For example, the results table for the SELECT statement

```
SELECT * FROM students
```

includes all of the columns in the STUDENTS table. Similarly, the results table for the query

```
SELECT * FROM students, grades
WHERE SID = student_ID
```

includes all of the columns from the STUDENTS table followed by all of the columns from the GRADES table. If you execute a query for three (or more) tables with only the asterisk (*) all columns operator in the SELECT clause, the results table will include all of the columns from the first table listed in the FROM clause, followed by all of the columns from the second table listed in the FROM clause, followed by all of the columns from the third table listed in the FROM clause, and so on.

To display all of the columns from only some of the tables listed in the FROM clause, use a *qualified* all columns operator. As you learned in Tip 289, "Using Qualified Column Names in Multi-table Queries That Join Tables That Have the Same Names for One or More Columns," a *qualified* column name is a column name that includes the name of the table in which the column is located. Similarly, a *qualified* all columns operator includes the name of the table from which the DBMS is to display all column values. Thus, to display all columns from the STUDENTS table, you could execute a SELECT statement such as:

```
SELECT students.* FROM students
```

which uses the qualified all columns operator STUDENTS.* to tell the DBMS to display all of the column values in the STUDENTS table. Similarly, if you want to display all of the columns in the STUDENTS table while displaying only two of the columns from the GRADES table, you can execute a query similar to

```
SELECT students.*, grade FROM students, grades
WHERE SID = student_ID
```

which uses the qualified all columns operator to tell the DBMS to display all columns from the STUDENTS table along with only the COURSE_ID and GRADE columns from the GRADES table.

313 Using a Table Alias to a Single-table JOIN (i.e. Self-JOIN)

Strange as it sounds, some multi-table queries (or joins) involve a relationship a table has with itself (vs. with another table). Suppose, for example, that you offer your customers an incentive to recommend your company to people they know. If you keep track of the referring customer's ID number in a column of the CUSTOMERS table (such as REFERRER, for example), you can submit a query similar to

```
SELECT cust_ID, RTRIM(f_name)+' '+l_name AS 'Customer',
  referrer AS 'Referred By'
FROM customers
WHERE referrer IS NOT NULL
ORDER BY "Referred By"
```

to generate a results table that displays the CUST_ID of the referrer next to the name of each customer that was referred by another customer. However, to list the name of each referrer instead of the CUST_ID number, you will need to join each row in the CUSTOMERS table that has a non-NULL value in the REFERRER column with the row in the CUSTOMERS table that has a matching value in the CUST_ID column. In other words, you need to JOIN rows in the CUSTOMERS table with other rows in the CUSTOMERS table based on matching REFERRER and CUST_ID column values.

Based on what you learned (in Tip 282, "Using the FROM Clause to Perform a Multi-table Query," and Tip 311, "Understanding the Role of the FROM Clause in a JOIN Statement") about the role of the FROM clause in multi-table queries and JOIN statements, you might assume you can join rows in a table with other rows in the same table by simply including the same table name twice in the FROM clause of a SELECT statement such as:

```
SELECT cust_ID, RTRIM(f_name)+' '+l_name AS 'Customer',
  RTRIM(f_name)+' '+l_name AS 'Referred By'
FROM customers, customers
WHERE referrer = cust_ID
ORDER BY "Referred BY"
```

When executing the query, the DBMS should first CROSS JOIN the rows in the table with itself. Then the system should use the search condition in the WHERE clause to filter out unwanted joined rows from the (virtual) interim table—those in which the value in the CUST_ID column does not match the value in the REFERRER column.

Unfortunately, SQL will not let you list the *same* table name more than once in a single FROM clause. As a result, when you submit the preceding example query to the DBMS for execution, the system will display an error message similar to:

```
Server: Msg 1013, Level 15, State 1, Line 4
Tables 'customers' and 'customers' have the same exposed
  names. Use correlation names to distinguish them.
```

Moreover, if you simply drop the second CUSTOMERS reference from the FROM clause, the DBMS will execute the query. However, as the system goes through the CUSTOMERS table one row at a time, it will display the names from CUSTOMERS table rows in which the REFERRER is the same as the CUST_ID. Since a customer cannot referrer himself (or herself), the query (with only a single reference to CUSTOMERS in the FROM clause) will execute successfully, but will not provide the desired customer names.

To join a table with itself, SQL requires that you use an *alias* or correlation name for the second reference to the same table. In this way, the DBMS can join two tables with *different* names when processing the query's FROM clause. Thus, a SELECT statement such as

```
SELECT customers.cust_ID, RTRIM(customers.f_name)+
  ' '+customers.l_name AS 'Customer',
  RTRIM(referrers.f_name)+' '+referrers.l_name
    AS 'Referred By'
FROM customers, customers referrers
WHERE customers.referrer = referrers.CUST_ID
ORDER BY "Referred By"
```

which defines the REFERRERS alias for the CUSTOMERS table, will display referrer's name next to the name of each customer your company now has as a result of the referrer's recommendation.

In the current example, the DBMS generates the Cartesian product of the CUSTOMERS table and the (imaginary, duplicate) REFERRERS table. Then the system filters out those joined rows from the interim (virtual) CUSTOMERS+REFERRERS table in which the value of the REFERRER column from the CUSTOMERS table is not equal to the CUST_ID from the (imaginary) REFERRERS table.

Similarly, you can use a query such as

```
SELECT c.cust_ID, RTRIM(c.f_name)+' '+c.l_name
  AS 'Customer',
  (SELECT count(*) FROM customers r
   WHERE r.referrer = c.cust_ID) AS 'Referral Count'
FROM customers c
WHERE c.cust_ID IN (SELECT referrer FROM customers)
ORDER BY "Referral Count" DESC
```

to get a count of customer referrals you received from each referrer. (The WHERE clause in the example eliminates from the results table those customers who have not given you any referrals.)

314 Understanding Table Aliases

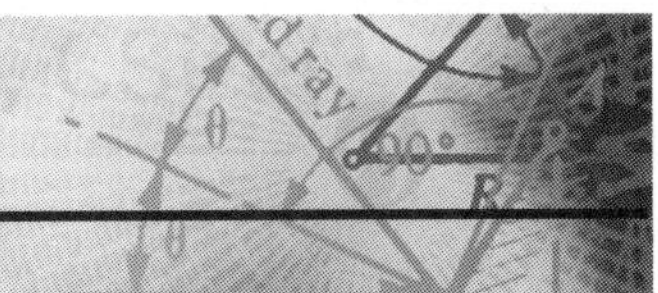

In Tip 313, "Using a Table Alias to a Single-table JOIN," you learned that SQL requires that you use a second name, or *alias,* whenever you want to perform a self-join that relates rows in a table to other rows in the same table. You can, however, use an alias (also called a *correlation name*) for a table name in any query—whether SQL requires it or not.

Suppose, for example, that you want to list the names and phone numbers from the rows in a PROSPECTS table owned by another user, SUSAN. You can execute a query similar to

```
SELECT RTRIM(susan.prospects.f_name)+
  ' '+susan.prospects.l_name AS 'Prospect'
  susan.prospects.phone_number
FROM susan.prospects
ORDER BY 'Prospect'
```

in which you type the fully qualified column reference throughout the query. (As you learned in Tip 228, "Understanding Column References," you have to specify the fully qualified column name [which includes the username of the table owner, the table name, and the column name] when referencing a column in a table owned by another user.)

Alternatively, you can shorten the column name references in the query to

```
SELECT RTRIM(sp.f_name)+' '+sp.l_name AS 'Prospect',
  sp.phone_number
FROM susan.prospects sp
ORDER BY 'Prospect'
```

by defining an alias for the table name in the SELECT statement's FROM clause. To define a table alias (or correlation name), type the alias you want to use immediately after the name of the table in the SELECT statement's FROM clause. You can then use the alias in place of the table name (or the fully qualified table name, such as SUSAN.PROSPECTS, in the current example), throughout the query.

The benefit of using table aliases is more readily apparent when you write a query that displays several columns from the JOIN of two or more tables (especially if the tables have long names or are owned by other usernames). Suppose, for example, that you are the sales manager and want to generate a list of the duplicate phone numbers among the PROSPECTS tables belonging to the three salespeople (FRANK, SUSAN, and RODGER) you manage. If you execute a query such as

```
SELECT RTRIM(COALESCE(frank.prospects.f_name,
    rodger.prospects.f_name,susan.prospects.f_name))+' '+
  COALESCE(frank.prospects.l_name,rodger.prospects.l_name,
           susan.prospects.l_name) AS 'Prospect',
  COALESCE(frank.prospects.phone_number,
           rodger.prospects.phone_number,
           susan.prospects.phone_number) AS 'Phone Number',
  (CASE WHEN frank.prospects.phone_number IS NOT NULL
          THEN 'Frank ' ELSE '' END)+
  (CASE WHEN rodger.prospects.phone_number IS NOT NULL
          THEN 'Rodger ' ELSE '' END)+
  (CASE WHEN susan.prospects.phone_number IS NOT NULL
          THEN 'Susan' ELSE '' END) AS 'Being Called By'
FROM ((frank.prospects FULL JOIN rodger.prospects ON
       frank.prospects.phone_number =
         rodger.prospects.phone_number)
FULL JOIN susan.prospects ON
       frank.prospects.phone_number =
         susan.prospects.phone_number
       OR rodger.prospects.phone_number =
            susan.prospects.phone_number)
WHERE frank.prospects.phone_number =
        rodger.prospects.phone_number
   OR frank.prospects.phone_number =
        susan.prospects.phone_number
   OR rodger.prospects.phone_number =
        susan.prospects.phone_number
ORDER BY "Being Called By", 'Prospect'
```

the DBMS will display a results table similar to:

```
Prospect        Phone Number    Called By
--------------  --------------  ------------------
Bill Barteroma  (222)-222-2222  Frank Rodger Susan
Steve Kernin    (555)-555-5555  Frank Rodger Susan
Frank Burns     (111)-222-1111  Frank Susan
Hawkeye Morgan  (333)-222-3333  Frank Susan
Steve Pierce    (444)-222-4444  Frank Susan
Walter Phorbes  (666)-666-6666  Rodger Susan
```

You can use aliases for each of the three table names and then shorten the query to:

```
SELECT RTRIM(COALESCE(fp.f_name,rp.f_name,sp.f_name))+' '+
  COALESCE(fp.l_name,rp.l_name,sp.l_name) AS 'Prospect',
  COALESCE(fp.phone_number,rp.phone_number,sp.phone_number)
    AS 'Phone Number',
  (CASE WHEN fp.phone_number IS NOT NULL
          THEN 'Frank ' ELSE '' END)+
```

```
  (CASE WHEN rp.phone_number IS NOT NULL
          THEN 'Rodger ' ELSE '' END)+
  (CASE WHEN sp.phone_number IS NOT NULL
          THEN 'Susan' ELSE '' END) AS 'Being Called By'
FROM ((frank.prospects fp FULL JOIN rodger.prospects rp
  ON fp.phone_number = rp.phone_number)
FULL JOIN susan.prospects sp
  ON fp.phone_number = sp.phone_number
  OR rp.phone_number = sp.phone_number)
WHERE fp.phone_number = rp.phone_number
   OR fp.phone_number = sp.phone_number
   OR rp.phone_number = sp.phone_number
ORDER BY "Being Called By", 'Prospect'
```

As you can see, using FP, RP, and SP (as aliases) in place of the fully qualified table names in the query not only makes the column name references shorter and less tedious to type, but also makes the query easier to read.

315 Understanding the Ambiguous Nature of ANY and How SQL Implements It to Mean SOME

In the English language, the word *any* can have one of two different meanings depending on the context in which it is used.

For example, if you ask, "Do any of you know how to write an SQL query?" you are using *any* as an existential quantifier, in that you want to know if there is at least one person (among those you are addressing) who knows how to write an SQL query. Conversely, if you say, "I have more fun writing SQL statements than any of you," you are using *any* as a universal quantifier to mean that you have more fun writing SQL statements than every person in your audience.

SQL lets you use the existential connotation of the keyword *ANY* in conjunction with one of the six comparison operators (=, <>, <, <=, >, and >=) to compare a single value to a column of data values generated by a subquery. If at least one of the comparisons of the single value to a data value in the set data values from the subquery evaluates to TRUE, then the entire ANY test evaluates to TRUE.

For example, if you have a list of stock symbols and prices in a PORTFOLIO table, and a list of symbols and historical price information in a PRICE_HISTORY table, you could execute a query such as

```
SELECT symbol, current_price FROM portfolio
WHERE current_price >= ANY
  (SELECT closing_price 1.5 FROM price_history
```

```
WHERE price_history.symbol = portfolio.symbol
  AND price_history.trade_date >= (GETDATE() - 180))
```

to get a list of stock symbols and current prices for stocks with a current price that is greater by 50 percent or more than at least one of the same stock's closing prices during the past 6 months (180 days).

When executing the query, the DBMS tests the data values in the CURRENT_PRICE column of the PORTFOLIO one row at a time. The system retrieves a stock symbol from the SYMBOL column and its price from the CURRENT_PRICE column of a row in the PORTFOLIO table. Then the subquery generates a list with the stock's CLOSING_PRICE values multiplied by 1.5 (150 percent) for each day during the past 6 months (180 days). If there is *any* (that is, at least one) CURRENT_PRICE value that is greater than or equal to a computed value in the CLOSING_PRICE list (generated by the subquery), the DBMS includes the stock SYMBOL and its CURRENT_PRICE in the results table. If the CURRENT_PRICE is less than *all* of the computed CLOSING PRICE * 150% values in the list generated by the subquery, then the system does not include the stock's SYMBOL and CURRENT_PRICE in the results table.

Another way to write the same query is

```
SELECT symbol, current_price FROM portfolio
WHERE current_price >= SOME
  (SELECT closing_price * 1.5 FROM price_history
   WHERE price_history.symbol = portfolio.symbol AND
         price_history.date >= (GETDATE() - 180))
```

which reads: "List the stock SYMBOL and CURRENT_PRICE of each stock whose CURRENT_PRICE is 150 percent or more of some of the values in the list of CLOSING_PRICE values for the same stock the stock during the past 6 months (180 days)."

Note: *Although the SQL-92 standard specifies the keyword SOME as an alternative to the keyword ANY, some DBMS products do not yet support the use of SOME. Check your system documentation. If your DBMS product lets you do so, use the keyword SOME in place of the keyword ANY because SOME is less confusing—unlike "any" it can never mean "all."*

316 Using EXISTS Instead of COUNT(*) to Check Whether a Subquery Returns at Least One Row

The COUNT(*) function, as its name implies, returns the *count* of the rows in a table that satisfy the search condition(s) in a WHERE clause. The EXISTS predicate, meanwhile, is a

BOOLEAN expression that evaluates to TRUE if a subquery generates at least one row of query results. As such, the predicate

```
WHERE 0 < (SELECT COUNT(*) FROM <table name>
           WHERE <search condition(s)>)
```

is equivalent to:

```
WHERE EXISTS (SELECT * FROM <table name>
              WHERE <search condition>)
```

When the subquery in the first WHERE clause returns no rows, its COUNT(*) function returns 0 and the WHERE clause evaluates to FALSE. Similarly, if an identical subquery used in the second WHERE clause returns no rows, EXISTS will (by definition) evaluate to FALSE, which will, in turn, cause the WHERE clause to evaluate to FALSE.

Conversely, if the subquery in the first WHERE clause returns one or more rows, its COUNT(*) function will return a value greater than 0, which, in turn, will cause the WHERE clause to evaluate to TRUE. Similarly, if an identical subquery used in the second WHERE clause returns one or more rows, EXISTS will (by definition) evaluate to TRUE; in turn, this will cause the WHERE clause to evaluate to TRUE.

Therefore, if you want a list of policy holders that have had a least one accident during the past year, you can use the COUNT(*) function in a query similar to:

```
SELECT cust_ID, f_name, l_name FROM customers
WHERE 0 < (SELECT COUNT(*) FROM claims
           WHERE claims.date_of_claim >= (GETDATE() - 365)
             AND claims.cust_ID = customers.cust_ID)
```

Or, you can use a similar query with an EXISTS predicate instead of the COUNT(*) > 0 comparison test:

```
SELECT cust_ID, f_name, l_name FROM customers
WHERE
  EXISTS (SELECT * FROM claims
          WHERE claims.date_of_claim >= (GETDATE() - 365)
          AND claims.cust_ID = customers.cust_ID)
```

After you submit either query to the DBMS, the system goes through the CUSTOMERS table one row at a time and executes the subquery in the WHERE clause for each row in the CUSTOMERS table.

When executing the subquery in the first SELECT statement, the system counts the number of rows in the CLAIMS table that have both a DATE_OF_CLAIM within the past year and a CUST_ID column value matching the value in the CUST_ID column of the row from the CUSTOMERS table being processed. If the COUNT(*) function returns a value greater than 0, the WHERE clause evaluates to TRUE and the DBMS adds the customer's CUST_ID and name to the results table.

When processing the second SELECT statement, the DBMS can abort execution of the subquery as soon as it finds the first row in the CLAIMS table that satisfies the search conditions in the subquery's WHERE clause. If the subquery returns any rows at all, the EXISTS predicate evaluates to TRUE and the system adds the customer's CUST_ID and name from the CUSTOMERS table to the query's results table.

So, should you use EXISTS or COUNT to determine whether at least one row in a table satisfies the search condition in the subquery's WHERE clause? The simple answer is: If you need the COUNT(*) of rows that satisfy the search criteria, use COUNT(*). Otherwise, use EXISTS.

Arguably, using EXISTS to check for the *existence* of a row that satisfies the WHERE clause search criteria makes the query easier to read than using the comparison of 0 < COUNT(*). Moreover, depending on the strength of the optimizer that your DBMS uses, EXISTS may actually execute faster than COUNT(*), especially if the table in the subquery has a lot of rows.

Remember, the purpose of the COUNT(*) function is to *count* the number of rows in a table that satisfy the search condition in the (sub)query's WHERE clause. As such, when you use COUNT(*) to check for the existence of at least one row that satisfies the WHERE clause search criteria, some DBMS products will read every row in the (sub)query's table, counting those that satisfy the search criteria in the WHERE clause. Only after it completes its (time-consuming) full-table scan does COUNT(*) return the number of rows that satisfy the WHERE clause search criteria. (If COUNT(*) returns a value of 0, then the WHERE clause evaluates FALSE, and vice versa.)

The EXISTS predicate, on the other hand, does not use any data values returned by the subquery's SELECT * clause. Moreover, the DBMS does not care about the exact number of rows in the subquery's table that satisfy the search condition in its WHERE clause. As such, the DBMS can stop retrieving and filtering rows from the subquery's source table as soon as it finds the first row whose column values satisfy the search conditions in the subquery's WHERE clause.

In short EXISTS, may outperform the COUNT(*) function when used to determine whether at least one row satisfies the criteria in a subquery's WHERE clause. EXISTS needs to process only 2 rows in a 10,000,000-row table if the second row satisfies the search condition in the WHERE clause. The COUNT(*) function, on the other hand, must read all 10,000,000 rows and then compare the count of rows that satisfy the search condition(s) to 0.

317 Understanding Why the Expression NULL = NULL Evaluates to FALSE

As you learned in Tip 30, "Understanding the Value of NULL," the value of NULL is not 0. In fact, NULL really has no specific value because a NULL in a column (or expression) represents a missing or unknown quantity. Moreover, whenever an expression uses one of the six SQL comparison operators (=,<>,>,>=,<,<=) to compare a NULL value with any other value (including another NULL), the expression always evaluates to NULL.

For example, the results table for the query

```
SELECT * FROM customers
WHERE salesperson = NULL
```

will always have no rows because the expression in the WHERE clause will never evaluate to TRUE. (Because the WHERE clause search condition uses the equality (=) comparison operator to compare a NULL value to another value, the WHERE clause will always evaluate to NULL, not to TRUE.)

The WHERE clause in the current example evaluates to NULL even if the DBMS encounters a row *from* the CUSTOMERS table that has a NULL value in its SALESPERSON column. That's strange behavior, considering that the search condition in the WHERE clause becomes

```
NULL = NULL
```

when the value in the SALESPERSON column is NULL. However, because the values on both sides of the equals (=) sign are unknown, the system cannot tell whether one NULL (unknown) value is equal to the other. As such, the expression

```
NULL = NULL
```

evaluates neither to TRUE nor to FALSE, but to NULL.

Note: *To query a table for rows with a NULL value in a specific column, you must use the IS NULL value test that you learned about in Tip 97, "Understanding NULL Value Conditions When Selecting Rows Using Comparison Predicates." For example, to get a list of CUSTOMERS table rows with a NULL in the SALESPERSON column, rewrite the query in the current example as:*

```
SELECT * FROM customers
WHERE salesperson IS NULL
```

---

318 Understanding When to Use the ON Clause and When to Use the WHERE Clause

An ON clause is always used as a filter for one of the JOIN clauses that you learned about in Tips 300–305. A WHERE clause, meanwhile, is used to filter unwanted rows returned by both single-table and multi-table queries. Therefore, an ON clause (if present) must always follow a JOIN clause. A WHERE clause, on the other hand, can be used in both queries with a JOIN clause and those without.

The ON clause in an INNER JOIN query is functionally equivalent to a WHERE clause with an identical search condition. Therefore, if you want to generate a results table listing the name of each instructor (from a TEACHERS table) next to the description of the class(es) (from the CLASSES table) that each professor teaches, this INNER JOIN (with an ON clause)

```
SELECT course_ID, description,
  RTRIM(f_name)+' '+l_name AS Instructor
FROM classes JOIN teachers
ON classes.professor_ID = teachers.PID
```

and this multi-table SELECT statement (with a WHERE clause)

```
SELECT course_ID, description,
  RTRIM(f_name)+' '+l_name AS Instructor
FROM classes, teachers
WHERE classes.professor_ID = teachers.PID
```

will produce the same results table.

Conversely, when executing one of the OUTER JOIN queries (LEFT, RIGHT, or FULL OUTER JOIN) using a WHERE clause with identical search conditions instead of an ON clause will not produce the same results table. In an OUTER JOIN, both the ON clause and the WHERE clause filter out rows that do not satisfy one or more of the search conditions in the WHERE clause. However, rows filtered out (that is, rejected) by a WHERE clause in an OUTER JOIN are not included in the results table. Meanwhile, the ON clause in an OUTER JOIN first filters out unwanted rows and then includes some or all of the rejected rows as NULL-valued columns in the results table.

For example, suppose that some professors in the TEACHERS table have not yet been assigned to teach a class. The LEFT OUTER JOIN (without a WHERE clause) shown in the top pane of the MS-SQL Server Query Analyzer window shown in Figure 318.1 will produce the results table shown in Figure 318.1's lower pane.

Conversely, this LEFT OUTER JOIN (with a WHERE clause)

```
SELECT course_ID, description,
  RTRIM(f_name)+' '+l_name AS Instructor
FROM teachers LEFT JOIN classes
ON    teachers.PID = classes.professor_ID
WHERE teachers.PID = classes.professor_ID
```

will produce a results table similar to this:

```
course_ID  description                       Instructor
---------  --------------------------------  -----------
CS-101     Introduction To Computer Science  Kris Jamsa
COMP101    Beginning Composition             Grady Booch
```

This results table has no NULL values in any of its columns.

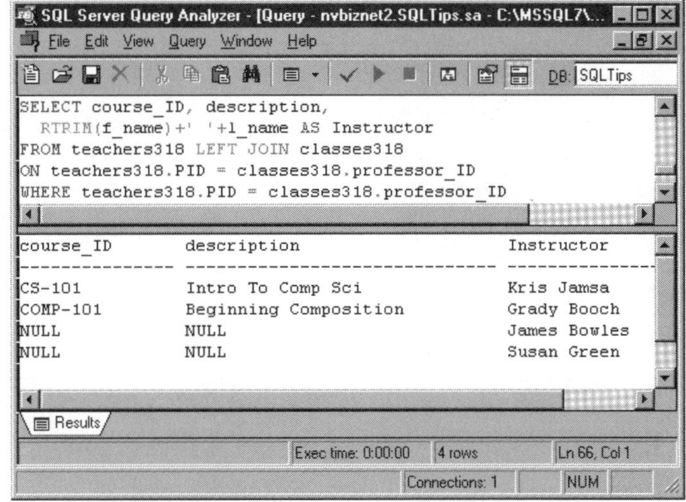

Figure 318.1 The MS-SQL Server Query Analyzer Window for a LEFT OUTER JOIN of two tables

319 Understanding How to Use Nested Queries to Work with Multiple Tables at Once

A subquery or *nested* query is a SELECT statement within another SQL statement. Although a nested query is always a SELECT statement, the enclosing SQL statement (which contains the nested SELECT statement (or subquery) may be a DELETE, an INSERT, an UPDATE, or another SELECT statement. In fact, a nested query may even be a subquery within another subquery.

Because the enclosing SQL statement and its subquery can each work on different tables, you can sometimes use a (single-table) query that contains a (single table) subquery in place of a (two-table) JOIN. For example, you can use a nested query instead of a JOIN to relate information in two tables when you want to include data values from only one of the tables in the query results. As an example, this nested query

```
SELECT CID AS 'Cust ID',
  RTRIM(f_name)+' '+l_name AS 'Customer'
FROM customers
WHERE EXISTS (SELECT * FROM trades
              WHERE trade_date >= GETDATE() - 365
                AND cust_ID = CID
```

will list the names of all customers that made at least one stock trade during the past year.

Conversely, when you need to generate a results table with values from more than one table, you will often have to execute either a JOIN or a multi-table query with a WHERE clause. For example, you would use a query such as

```
SELECT trade_date, symbol, shares * price AS 'Total Trade',
  CID, RTRIM(f_name)+' '+l_name AS 'Customer'
FROM customers JOIN trades
  ON CID = cust_ID
WHERE shares * price > 100000
  AND trade_date >= GETDATE() -365
ORDER BY Customer
```

to join rows from the CUSTOMERS table with rows from the TRADES table to generate a list of customer names and trade dollar values of any trades of $100,000 or more made within the past year.

Multi-table queries and nested subqueries are not, however, mutually exclusive. Suppose, for example, that you want to include aggregate totals such as a SUM() of the dollar amount and a COUNT() of the number of trades, along with the other information in the preceding example. A query such as

```
SELECT trade_date, symbol, shares * price AS 'Total Trade',
   (SELECT COUNT(*) FROM trades
    WHERE trade_date > GETDATE() - 365
      AND cust_ID = CID) AS 'Count'
   (SELECT SUM(price) * SUM(shares),
    FROM trades
    WHERE trades.trade_date >= GETDATE() - 365
      AND cust_ID = CID) AS 'Total $ Volume),
    CID AS 'Cust ID'-, TRIM(f_name)+' '+l_name AS 'Customer'
FROM customers JOIN trades
ON CID = cust_CID
WHERE shares * price >= 100000
  AND trade_date >= GETDATE() -365
ORDER BY Customer
```

will execute the same two-table JOIN found in the preceding example. However, the query's results table includes the values returned by the two aggregate function subqueries (in the SELECT cause).

In short, a nested query works independent of the enclosing SQL statement and can make use of any of the column values from the tables listed in the enclosing statement's FROM clause. You can use nested queries to perform multi-table operations without having to JOIN rows in multiple related tables. However, if you need data values from multiple tables, or if you want individual column values *and* aggregate function values in the same row in the results table, you can nest a subquery with the aggregate function that you need in the SELECT clause of a multi-table query or JOIN.

320 Understanding Nested Queries That Return Sets of Rows

Although all of the example nested queries in Tip 319, "Understanding How to Use Nested Queries to Work with Multiple Tables at Once," return a single column of data values, a subquery's SELECT clause can contain multiple column references or expressions instead. Your DBMS, however, may restrict your ability to work with multiple-column subquery results. Suppose, for example, that you want to generate a list of customers waiting for a specific make and model of car that you now have in inventory. If your DBMS product lets you use row value constructors in an IN set membership test, you can execute a query similar to this

```
SELECT * FROM customers
WHERE (model_year, make, model)
   IN (SELECT model_year, make, model
       FROM auto_inventory)
```

to generate a list of customers whose "dream" cars you now have on hand. However, if your DBMS, like MS-SQL Server, allows you to test for a set membership only one value at a time, you can rewrite the query as:

```
SELECT * FROM customers
WHERE (model_year+make+model)
   IN (SELECT model_year+make+model FROM auto_inventory)
```

Here, the subquery's SELECT clause returns a single, composite value. The most important thing to understand now is that SQL does not limit the number of columns that a subquery can return. Each DBMS product imposes its own rules on which SQL statements and clauses are allowed to work with multiple column values at once.

A nested query that returns sets of rows with multiple columns is especially useful when you want to execute an INSERT statement that copies either some or all of the column data values from rows in one table into another table. Suppose, for example, that you want to consolidate customer and "dream car" inventory information into a single table named: CUST_CARS_INVENTORY. First, execute the TRUNCATE statement

```
TRUNCATE TABLE cust_cars_inventory
```

to remove any rows previously added to the table. Next, execute an INSERT statement similar to this:

```
INSERT INTO cust_cars_inventory
  SELECT c.*, VIN, price
  FROM customers c, auto_inventory I
  WHERE (c.model_year+c.make+c.model) =
          (i.model_year+i.make+i.model)
```

The subquery (the nested SELECT statement) sends the INSERT clause joined rows consisting of all of the columns from rows in the CUSTOMERS table joined to the vehicle ID number (VIN) and price column data values from related rows in the AUTO_INVENTORY table.

Note: *You can avoid taking up disk space for a CUST_CARS_INVENTORY table by using the CREATE VIEW statement (which you learned about in Tip 215, "Using the CREATE VIEW Statement to Display the Results of Joining Two or More Tables") to create a virtual instead of a physical table. For the current example, the CREATE VIEW statement*

```
CREATE VIEW vw_cust_cars_inventory AS
  SELECT c.*, VIN, price
  FROM customers c, auto_inventory I
  WHERE (c.model_year+c.make+c.model) =
            (i.model_year+i.make+i.model)
```

will create a virtual table named VW_CUST_CARS_INVENTORY whose contents are identical to the (physical) CUST_CARS_INVENTORY table filled by the INSERT statement with joined rows from the CUSTOMERS and AUTO_INVENTORY tables.

The most important thing to understand now is that a nested query (or subquery) can return either rows with a single column value or rows with multiple column values. The DBMS product that you are using determines whether you must tell the subquery to return values one column at a time or one row (of column values) at a time.

321 Understanding Subqueries

A *subquery* is a SELECT statement within another SQL statement. In general, you can use a subquery in a statement anywhere an expression can appear. Moreover, a subquery can retrieve data from any table to which you have the correct access rights. As such, by nesting a subquery within a query or even within another subquery, you can combine information from two or more tables without writing complex JOIN statements that combine entire tables and then filter out many unwanted and unrelated joined rows.

For example, to generate a results table that shows the names of a company's managers, the names of the employees they manage, and the total sales for each employee, you can use a grouped query with a self-JOIN and an INNER JOIN similar to:

```
SELECT RTRIM(m.f_name)+' '+m.l_name AS 'Manager',
  RTRIM(e.f_name)+' '+e.l_name AS 'Employee',
  SUM(invoice_total) AS 'Total Sales'
FROM employees m JOIN employees e
ON m.emp_ID = e.emp_ID
JOIN invoices ON salesperson = e.emp_ID
GROUP BY m.f_name, l.f_name, e.f_name, e.l_name
ORDER BY manager, employee
```

Or, you can use a single-table query with two subqueries such as:

```
SELECT (SELECT RTRIM(f_name)+' '+l_name FROM employees
        WHERE emp_ID = e.manager_ID) AS 'Manager',
  RTRIM(f_name)+' '+l_name AS 'Employee',
  (SELECT SUM(invoice_total) FROM invoices
   WHERE salesperson = emp_ID) AS 'Total Sales'
FROM employees e
WHERE manager_ID IS NOT NULL
ORDER BY manager, employee
```

In the current example, the main query retrieves the name of each employee assigned to a manager from the EMPLOYEES table and then uses a subquery to get the manager's name from the same table and a second subquery to retrieve the total sales for each employee from the INVOICES table.

Aside from always being enclosed in parentheses (()) the subquery appears otherwise identical to all other SELECT statements. There are, however, a few differences between a subquery and other SQL statements:

- While a SELECT statement can use only columns from the tables listed in its FROM clause, a subquery can use not only columns from tables listed in the subquery's FROM clause, but also any columns from tables listed in the FROM clause of the enclosing SQL statement.
- A subquery in a SELECT statement must return a single column of data. Moreover, depending on its use in the query (such as using subquery results as an item in the enclosing query's SELECT clause), the enclosing query may require that the subquery return a single value (vs. multiple rows of values from single column).
- A subquery cannot have an ORDER BY clause. (Since the user never sees a results table from a subquery that returns multiple data values, it does not make any sense to sort the rows in the hidden interim results table anyway.)
- A subquery must consist of only one SELECT statement—meaning that you cannot write an SQL statement that uses the UNION of multiple SELECT statements as a subquery.

You will learn everything you ever wanted to know about subqueries in Tips 322–343. For now, the important thing to understand is that a subquery is a SELECT statement you can use as an expression in an SQL statement.

322 Understanding the Value of a Main Query Column When Referenced in a Subquery

A feature critical to the operation of a subquery is its ability to reference column values from the *current* row in the *main* (or enclosing) query.

```
SELECT emp_ID, RTRIM(f_name)+' +l_name AS 'Name',
  (SELECT SUM(invoice_total) FROM invoices
   WHERE salesperson = emp_ID) AS 'Sales Volume'
FROM employees WHERE dept = 'Sales'
```

will list the EMP_ID, name, and total sales for each employee in the sales department. As such, the query gives both summary and detail information in each row of the results table. The main (or enclosing) query provides the employee detail (EMP_ID and name) from the EMPLOYEES table, while the subquery (or inner query) provides the sales volume (summary/aggregate total) from the INVOICES table.

To generate the query's results table, the DBMS executes the main (enclosing) query

```
SELECT emp_ID, RTRIM(f_name)+' +l_name AS 'Name'
FROM employees WHERE dept = 'Sales'
```

by reading the rows of employee data in the EMPLOYEES table one row at a time. After retrieving a row of employee information, the system checks the DEPT column of the *current* row (that is, the row just read and now being processed) to see of the employee is in the sales department. If the employee is in the sales department, the DBMS adds the EMP_ID and name from the current row to the results table and then executes the subquery

```
(SELECT SUM(invoice_total) FROM invoices
 WHERE salesperson = emp_ID)
```

to get the employee's total sales volume from the INVOICES table.

Notice that in the current example, SALESPERSON in the subquery's WHERE clause references a column in the subquery's INVOICES table, while EMP_ID in the subquery's WHERE clause references a column in the main (enclosing) query's EMPLOYEES table. After the DBMS reads a row from the EMPLOYEES table, the system uses the value in the EMP_ID column of the current row (the row just read) when it executes the subquery.

The EMP_ID column referenced in the WHERE clause of the subquery in the current example is an *outer reference*—a reference to a column name that does not appear in any of the tables listed in the subquery's FROM clause. Instead, an outer reference refers to a column from one of the tables listed in the main (outer) query's FROM clause. Moreover, the DBMS takes the value of the outer reference (EMP_ID, in the current example) from the column in the row currently being processed in the main (outer) query.

323 Understanding Subquery Comparison Tests

If a subquery generates a results table with a single value (that is, a results table with one column and no more than one row), you can use the subquery as one (or both) of the expressions in a *subquery* comparison test. As you can see from the syntax of a subquery comparison test,

```
{<expression>|<subquery>| {=|<>|>|>=|<|<=}
  {<expression>|<subquery>
```

the only difference between it and any other comparison test is that the subquery comparison test (as its name implies) includes at least one subquery. The six comparison operators work exactly the same way whether comparing the values of two nonsubquery expressions, the value of a nonsubquery expression with a subquery result, or the results from two subqueries.

When present in SQL statements, you will find subquery comparison tests in a WHERE clause. For example, you can use a subquery comparison in the WHERE clause of a SELECT statement similar to

```
SELECT emp_ID, RTRIM(f_name)+' '+l_name) AS 'Name',
  (SELECT sum(invoice_total) FROM invoices
   WHERE salesperson = emp_ID) AS 'Sales Volume'
FROM employees
WHERE dept = 'Sales'
  AND (SELECT SUM(invoice_total) FROM invoices
       WHERE salesperson = emp_ID) > 5000.00
```

to get a list of salespeople with total sales above $5,000.00.

Note: *In order for a subquery comparison to evaluate to a valid value of TRUE or FALSE, the subquery (or subqueries) in the comparison test must generate a results table with* exactly *one row and one column. If the results table returns more than one column or more than one row, the DBMS will abort execution of the query and display an error message similar to:*

```
Server: Msg 512, Level 16, State 1, Line 1
Subquery returned more than 1 value. This is not permitted
  when the subquery follows =, !=, <, <=, >, >= or when the
  subquery is used as an expression.
```

On the other hand, if a subquery in a comparison test returns zero rows, the comparison test will evaluate to NULL (and not FALSE). As you learned in Tip 317, "Understanding Why the Expression NULL = NULL Evaluates to FALSE," when the comparison test evaluates NULL, the query will not abort processing. However, the final results table will have no rows because the WHERE clause did not evaluate to TRUE.

The EMP_ID column used in the subquery comparison test

```
(SELECT SUM(invoice_total) FROM invoices
 WHERE salesperson = emp_ID) > 5000.00
```

is an outer reference to an EMP_ID column in one of the tables listed in the enclosing query's FROM clause. As you learned in Tip 322, "Understanding the Value of a Main Query Column When Referenced in a Subquery," the DBMS uses the column value from the row currently being processed by the enclosing query when it encounters an outer (column) reference in a subquery.

Therefore, in the current example, the DBMS works its way through the EMPLOYEES table, one row at a time. When the DBMS encounters an EMPLOYEES table row that contains "sales" in the DEPT column, the system executes the subquery in the SELECT statement. The subquery generates a single-value results table with the total dollar volume of sales on invoices whose SALESPERSON column has the same value as the EMP_ID column in the current row of the EMPLOYEES table. If the total sales volume generated by the subquery is greater than $5,000.00, the DBMS adds the EMP_ID, employee name, and total sales volume to the main query's results table.

Note: *You do not have to include a subquery in the enclosing query's SELECT clause to use it in a subquery comparison test. Moreover, you can use a subquery as either of the two expressions or as both of the expressions in a comparison. As such, if you want to know only the EMP_ID and name of each employee whose average invoice total is less than the overall average order for all salespeople, you can submit a query similar to*

```
SELECT emp_ID, RTRIM(f_name)+' '+l_name) AS 'Name',
FROM employees
WHERE dept = 'Sales'
  AND (SELECT AVG(invoice_total) FROM invoices
       WHERE salesperson = emp_ID) <
      (SELECT AVG(invoice_total) FROM invoices)
```

to the DBMS for processing.

---

324 Using the EXISTS Predicate in a Subquery to Determine If Any Rows Have a Column Value That Satisfies the Search Criteria

The EXISTS predicate lets you check a table to see if at least one row satisfies a set of search conditions. In practice, EXISTS is always used in conjunction with a subquery and evaluates to TRUE whenever the subquery returns at least one value. If the subquery's results table has no values (meaning that no rows in the table satisfied the search criteria in the subquery's WHERE clause), then the EXISTS predicate evaluates to FALSE.

Suppose, for example, that you want a list of salespeople who have a single customer that purchased more than $100,000 worth of merchandise or whose customers (taken as a whole) have made purchases of more than $500,000. Stated another way, you might say, "List the salespeople for whom there EXISTS at least one customer with total orders of more than $100,000, or for whom there EXISTS a set of customers that have made purchases or more than $5000.00." A query similar to

```
SELECT emp_ID, f_name, l_name
FROM employees
WHERE EXISTS (SELECT * FROM customers
              WHERE salesperson = emp_ID
                AND (total_purchases > 100000
                 OR (SELECT SUM(total_purchases)
                     FROM customers
                     WHERE salesperson = emp_ID) > 500000))
```

will generate the list of employees you want. To execute the query, the DBMS goes through the EMPLOYEES table one row at a time. When passed the EMP_ID column value from the row currently being processed in the main query, the subquery generates an interim (virtual) table with a value from one of the columns in the CUSTOMERS table for each row in the CUSTOMERS table that satisfies the search conditions in the subquery's WHERE clause.

If the subquery's interim (virtual) table has no values after the subquery executes, then the EXISTS predicate evaluates to FALSE, and the DBMS goes on to the next row in the EMPLOYEES table. On the other hand, if the subquery's interim (virtual) table has at least one value, the EXISTS predicate evaluates to TRUE and the DBMS will (in the current example) add the employee ID name to the main query's results table before going on to process the next row in the EMPLOYEES table.

Note: *As you learned in Tip 321, "Understanding Subqueries," a subquery must produce a single column of results. Given a CUSTOMERS table with more than one column, the SELECT * in the subquery of the EXISTS test seems to violate this rule. However, since the EXISTS predicate really does not use any of the data values generated by subquery (the EXISTS predicate needs to know only if any values are generated), SQL treats the SELECT * in the subquery's SELECT clause as meaning "select any one column" vs. the usual "select all columns."*

In addition to the EXISTS predicate, which evaluates to TRUE if its subquery produces at least one row, you can use the NOT EXISTS, which evaluates to TRUE if its subquery produces no rows. For example, to get a list of salespeople who have not yet generated any revenue, you can submit a query similar to:

```
SELECT emp_ID, RTRIM(f_name)+' '+l_name AS 'Employee Name'
FROM employees
```

```
WHERE NOT EXISTS (SELECT * FROM customers
                  WHERE salesperson = emp_ID
                    AND total_purchases > 0)
```

If a salesperson has no customers or if none of the customers assigned to the salesperson has made a purchase (in which case TOTAL_PURCHASES will be 0.00), then the subquery in the EXISTS predicate will produce no rows. The absence of rows returned by its subquery will cause the EXISTS predicate to evaluate to FALSE. However, the keyword NOT will reverse the value of the EXISTS predicate, thereby causing it—and, consequently, the WHERE clause as well—to evaluate to TRUE. The DBMS will add the ID and name of the employee with zero sales to the main query's results table.

325 Understanding the Relationship Between Subqueries and Joins

When writing a SELECT statement that uses data from more than one table, you can often write the query as either a single-table SELECT statement with one or more subqueries or as a multi-table SELECT (or JOIN). For example, to get a list of customers whose orders are shipped to Arizona, California, Nevada, Oregon, or Washington, you can execute a multi-table query such as

```
SELECT DISTINCT c.cust_ID, f_name, l_name
FROM customers c, orders o
WHERE c.cust_ID = o.cust_ID
  AND ship_to_state IN ('AZ','CA','NV','OR','WA')
```

which first cross joins the rows in the CUSTOMER table with the rows in the ORDERS table and then filters out unrelated joined rows (where CUST_ID from CUSTOMERS does not equal CUST_ID from ORDERS) and rows with SHIP_TO_STATE abbreviations for states other than one of the five states of interest.

Alternatively, you can generate the same results table using a single-table query with a subquery similar to:

```
SELECT cust_ID, f_name, l_name FROM customers
WHERE cust_ID IN
        (SELECT cust_ID FROM orders
         WHERE ship_to_state IN ('AZ','CA','NV','OR','WA')
```

When executing the query that has a subquery, the DBMS does not CROSS JOIN the rows of the table in the enclosing query with the rows of the table in the subquery. Instead, the DBMS retrieves the table in the main query, one row at a time. Then the DBMS executes the subquery for each of the rows in the main query.

In the current example, the DBMS retrieves a row from the CUSTOMERS table. Then the system executes the subquery to generate an interim results table with the CUST_ID value for each row in the ORDERS table that has a SHIP_TO_STATE that matches one of the five listed in the subquery's WHERE clause. If the value of the CUST_ID column from the current row being processed in the main query appears in the subquery's interim results table, the DBMS adds the customer name and ID to the main query's final results table.

Thus, a multi-table SELECT statement (or JOIN) involves the DBMS generating the CROSS JOIN of the tables list in the SELECT statement's FROM clause and filtering out the unwanted joined rows from the interim (virtual) Cartesian product. Conversely, the DBMS does not CROSS JOIN the main query table with the subquery table in a single-table SELECT with one or more subqueries. Instead, the DBMS goes through the rows in the main table and uses the subquery results to decide which rows from the main query's table to include in the SELECT statement's results table.

While *most* queries can be written either way, do not be surprised if you find that some queries can be written only as joins while others can be written only as single-table queries with subqueries. For example, if you want a list of customer names from the CUSTOMERS table along with each customer's total purchases from the ORDERS table, you can do this only with a grouped multi-table query similar to:

```
SELECT c.cust_ID, f_name, l_name,
  SUM(order_total) AS 'Total Purchases'
FROM customers c, orders o
WHERE c.cust_ID = o.cust_ID
GROUP BY cust_ID, f_name, l_name
```

On the other hand, if you want to select rows from one table based on summary information from another table, only a query with subqueries will do. For example, there is no multi-table query (JOIN) only equivalent for a query such as

```
SELECT SID, f_name, l_name FROM students s
WHERE (SELECT AVG(grade_received) FROM grades g
       WHERE g.student_ID = s.SID)
    > (SELECT AVG(grade_received) FROM grades)
```

which generates a list of student names from the STUDENTS who have above-average grades.

326 Using the Keyword IN with a Subquery to SELECT Rows in One Table Based on Values Stored in a Column in Another Table

The keyword IN lets you test whether or not a literal, the value of an expression, or the (single-value) result from a subquery that precedes the keyword matches one of the values in the set of values that follows it. For example, if you want to make a list of customers from California, Nevada, or Oregon, you can submit a query similar to:

```
SELECT cust_ID, f_name, l_name, phone_number
FROM customers
WHERE state IN ('CA','NV','OR')
```

The DBMS will test the value of the STATE column in each row of the CUSTOMERS table for a matching value in the set literals that follows the keyword IN. If the system finds a matching value, the WHERE clause evaluates to TRUE, and the DBMS adds the customer's CUST_ID, name, and PHONE_NUMBER to the SELECT statement's results table. Conversely, if the value in the STATE column has no match in the set of state abbreviations that follows the keyword IN, then the WHERE clause evaluates to FALSE, and the DBMS does not insert any column values from the current row being tested into the query results table.

If used to introduce a subquery, the keyword IN lets the DBMS use the single column of values returned by the subquery as the *set* of values in which it is to find a match for the data value that precedes the keyword. For example, suppose you want to get a list of all customers (from the CUSTOMERS table) that live in the same state as one of your company's offices (from the OFFICES table). The query

```
SELECT cust_ID, f_name, l_name, state
FROM customers
WHERE state IN (SELECT state FROM offices)
```

will go through the CUSTOMERS table one row at a time, checking to see if the value in each row's STATE column matches one of values in the STATE column from the OFFICES table (returned by the subquery). If the state abbreviation in the STATE column from the CUSTOMERS table matches one of the values in the STATE column from the OFFICES table, the WHERE clause evaluates to TRUE, and the DBMS will insert the customer's CUST_ID, name, and STATE in the query's final results table.

You will learn more about using IN and NOT IN to introduce subqueries in Tips 327–328. For now, the important thing to understand is that the subquery introduced by the keyword IN can retrieve a column of data values from *any* database table—not just those used in the main query. As such, the keyword IN, used in conjunction with a subquery, often makes it possible to extract from multiple tables information that is not available in a single table.

For example, in the current example, the CUSTOMERS table does not have a list of states in which your company has offices. Conversely, the OFFICES table does not have any customer details. The keyword IN, used to introduce the subquery in the WHERE clause, lets the DBMS SELECT rows from the CUSTOMERS table based on values stored in the STATE column of the OFFICES table.

327 Using the Keyword IN to Introduce a Subquery

When you use the keyword IN to introduce a subquery, you tell the DBMS to perform a *subquery set membership test*. In other words, you tell the DBMS to compare a single data value (that precedes the keyword IN) to a column of data values in the results table generated by the subquery (that follows the keyword). If the single data value matches one of the data values in the column of data values returned by the subquery, then the IN predicate evaluates to TRUE.

The syntax used to generate a results table based on a subquery set membership test is

```
SELECT <column name list> FROM <table list>
WHERE <test expression> IN <subquery>
```

where <test expression> can be a literal value, a column name, an expression, or another subquery that returns a single value.

For example, if student information is stored in a STUDENTS table, and the classes each student is taking are listed in an ENROLLMENT table, then you can use a SELECT statement similar to

```
SELECT SID, f_name, l_name FROM students
WHERE SID IN (SELECT student_ID FROM enrollment
              WHERE course_ID = 'ENGLISH-101')
```

to get a list of students enrolled in ENGLISH-101.

In executing a query, the DBMS processes the innermost subquery first. Thus, in the current example, the system first generates a list of all STUDENT_ID values from rows in the ENROLLMENT table that have ENGLISH-101 in the COURSE_ID column. Next, the DBMS goes through the STUDENTS table one row at a time and compares the value in the SID column of each row to the list of student IDs in the subquery's results table.

If the system finds a matching STUDENT_ID value (in the subquery results table) for the value in the SID column of the STUDENTS row it is processing, then the WHERE clause evaluates to TRUE, and the system inserts the student's ID and name into the main query's results table before going on to process the next row in the STUDENTS table. If, on the other hand, the DBMS finds no match for SID in the subquery results, then the WHERE clause evaluates to FALSE and the DBMS goes on to the next row in the STUDENTS table—without inserting the student ID and name from the current row being processed into the query's results table.

Note: *The column of values returned by a subquery introduced by the keyword IN can be from either one of the tables used in the main query or another table altogether. The only requirement SQL places on the subquery is that it must return a single column of data values whose data type is compatible with the data type of the expression that precedes the keyword IN.*

---

328 Using the Keywords NOT IN to Introduce a Subquery

As you learned in Tip 327, "Using the Keyword IN to Introduce a Subquery," the keyword IN, when used to introduce a subquery in a WHERE clause, lets you test whether or not a value (from a row in the main query) matches one of the values in the column of values returned by the subquery. If the DBMS finds a matching value, the WHERE clause evaluates to TRUE, and the DBMS takes the action specified by the SQL statement before going on to process the next row in the table. If, on the other hand, there is no matching value in the subquery's single-column results table, then the DBMS takes no action on the current row being processed before going on to the next row.

The NOT keyword reverses the effect of the IN test. As such, if you introduce a subquery with the keywords NOT IN (vs. the keyword IN), the DBMS takes the action specified by the SQL statement if there is *no* matching value in the subquery's results table.

For example, using the same general syntax as the subquery set membership test (which you learned about in Tip 327), you submit a query such as

```
SELECT class_ID, title, instructor_ID
FROM classes
WHERE class_ID NOT IN (SELECT course_ID FROM enrollment)
```

and get a list of classes for which no students have registered—similar to the one in the lower pane of the MS-SQL Server Query Analyzer Window shown in Figure 328.1.

When executing a query, the DBMS processes the innermost subquery first. Thus, in the current example, the system first generates a list of all CLASS_ID values from rows in the ENROLLMENT table. Next, the DBMS goes through the CLASSES table one row at a time and compares the value in the CLASS_ID column of each row to each of the values in the list of class IDs in the subquery's results table.

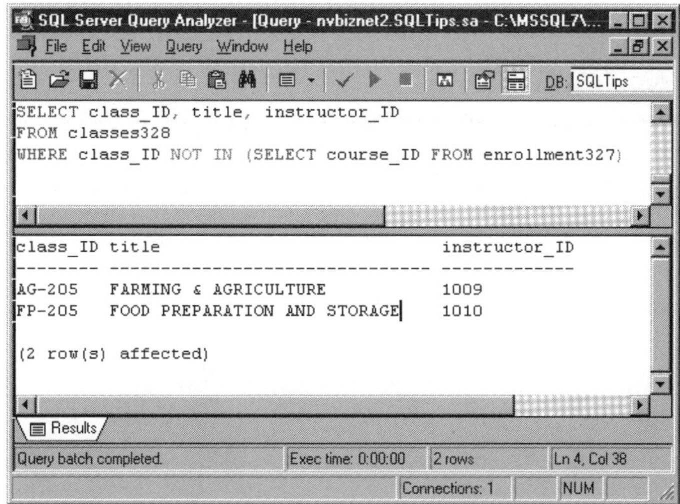

Figure 328.1 The MS-SQL Server Query Analyzer window with the results table from a NOT IN subquery set membership test

If the system finds *no* matching CLASS_ID value (in the subquery results table) for the value in the CLASS_ID column of the CLASSES row it is processing, then the IN predicate evaluates to FALSE. However, the NOT keyword then reverses the result of the predicate such that the WHERE clause evaluates to TRUE. The system inserts the CLASS_ID, TILE, and INSTRUCTOR_ID column values from the current row being tested into the main query's results table before going on to process the next row in the CLASSES table. If, on the other hand, the DBMS *does* find a matching value for CLASS_ID in the single-column subquery results table, then the IN predicate evaluates to TRUE. After the NOT modifier reverses the predicate's value, the WHERE clause evaluates to FALSE, and DBMS goes on to the next row in the CLASSES table—without inserting column values from the current row being processed into the main query's results table.

Note: *The IN and NOT IN subquery set membership tests are not limited to being used only in the WHERE clause of a SELECT statement. Although always found in a WHERE clause, the WHERE clause itself may be part of any SQL statement (such as DELETE, INSERT, SELECT, or UPDATE) that accepts a WHERE clause. For example, if you want to remove all classes in which no students have enrolled during the past five years, you can use NOT IN to introduce the subquery in a DELETE statement such as:*

```
DELETE FROM classes
WHERE date_class_added < GETDATE() - 1825
  AND class_ID
      NOT IN (SELECT course_ID FROM enrollment
              WHERE date_enrolled >= GETDATE() - 1825)
```

329 Using ALL to Introduce a Subquery That Returns Multiple Values

If you are going to use only one of the six SQL comparison operators (=, <>, >, >=, <, or <=) to compare the values of two expressions, then the expression that precedes the operator and the expression that follows it must each evaluate to a single value. Therefore, you can use a subquery as one of the expressions in a comparison predicate only if the subquery produces a single value for the comparison test.

For example, if you have an AUTO_POLICIES table and an ACCIDENTS table, you can submit a query similar to

```
SELECT policy_number, make, model FROM auto_policies p
WHERE (SELECT COUNT(*) FROM accidents a
       WHERE (description LIKE '%rollover%' AND mph <= 35)
         AND a.make  = p.make
         AND a.model = p.model) > 0
```

and the DBMS will generate a list of insurance policies written on cars that have had at least one rollover accident at or below 35 miles per hour. If the ACCIDENTS table has more than one row detailing a ROLLOVER at under 35 MPH for the make and model of car being tested in the main query, the subquery will generate an interim results table with more than one row. However, the subquery is still a valid expression for the comparison predicate because the COUNT(*) aggregate function reduces the results table generated by the subquery to a single value.

Now, suppose you want to get a list of the policies written on the make and model of automobile with the highest incident of rollover accidents at or below 35 MPH. The single value for an entire table returned by an aggregate function, such as COUNT(*), will not suffice in this type of query. Instead, you need the DBMS to subtotal the count of rollover accidents by make and model of automobile, and then you need the system to compare the rollover count for each make and model of automobile against the maximum rollover count from the other makes and models of automobiles.

The quantifiers ALL, SOME, and ANY let you use a comparison operator to compare a single value to each of the values returned by a subquery. For example, a query such as

```
SELECT policy_number, f_name, l_name, make, model
FROM auto_policies p
WHERE (SELECT COUNT(*) FROM accidents a
       WHERE (description LIKE '%rollover%' AND mph <= 35)
         AND a.make  = p.make
         AND a.model = p.model)
     > ALL
```

```
(SELECT COUNT(*) FROM accidents a
 WHERE (description LIKE '%rollover%' AND mph <= 35)
   AND (a.make <> p.make OR a.model <> p.model)
 GROUP BY make, model)
```

will list the make and model of car in the POLICIES table that has more rollover accidents than any other make and model of car in the ACCIDENTS table.

The first subquery (on the left side of the > ALL comparison) returns a single value—the number of rollover accidents experienced by the make and model of car being tested in the main query. Meanwhile, the second subquery (on the right side of the > ALL comparison) returns the rollover accident count for each of the other makes and models of cars from the ACCIDENTS table.

Although the subquery to the right to the greater than (>) comparison operator has more than one value, the ALL quantifier lets you use it in the comparison by telling the DBMS to compare the multiple values in the list of values with the single value, one value at a time. In other words, the ALL quantifier changes the comparison from one in which a single value is compared to a set of multiple values into multiple single value comparisons—one for each row in the subquery's results table.

If *all* of the comparison tests evaluate to TRUE, then the WHERE clause evaluates to TRUE, and the main query adds column values from the current row in the AUTO_POLICIES table to the SELECT statement's final results table. If, on the other hand, any of the comparisons evaluates to FALSE, the WHERE clauses evaluates to FALSE, and the DBMS goes on to test the next row in the AUTO_POLICIES table—without adding any column data values to the query's final results table.

You will learn how to use the SOME and ANY quantifiers to introduce a multi-valued subquery in Tip 330, "Using SOME or ANY to Introduce a Subquery That Returns Multiple Values." For now, the important thing to know is that the ALL qualifier lets you compare a single value that precedes a comparison operator with each of the values in the set of values returned by a subquery that follows it. Moreover, the comparison predicate (and subsequently the WHERE clause) evaluates to TRUE only if *all* of the comparisons between the single value to the left of the comparison operator and each of the values in the subquery's results table evaluates to TRUE.

330 Using SOME or ANY to Introduce a Subquery That Returns Multiple Values

As you learned in Tip 329, "Using ALL to Introduce a Subquery That Returns Multiple Values," ALL, SOME, and ANY are quantifiers that let you compare a single value to the left of a comparison operator with a subquery (to the right of the comparison operator) that generates a single-column results table with multiple rows. Remember, the DBMS will abort a query of the form

```
SELECT <column name list> FROM <table>
WHERE <expression> {=|<>|>|>=|<|<=} <subquery>
```

with an error message similar to

```
Server: Msg 512, Level 16, State 1, Line 1
Subquery returned more than 1 value. This is not permitted
  when the subquery follows =, !=, <, <=, >, >= or when the
  subquery is used as an expression.
```

if the subquery in the WHERE clause generates a single-column results with multiple values.

If you rewrite the query by introducing the subquery with one of the three quantifiers (ALL, SOME, ANY, or any), such as:

```
SELECT <column name list> FROM <table>
WHERE <expression> {=|<>|>|>=|<|<=} {SOME|ANY|ALL}
         <subquery>
```

the DBMS will not abort the query if the subquery's single-column results table has more than one row of data. Instead, the DBMS will compare the value of <expression> (left of the comparison operator) to each of the values returned by the subquery that follows the comparison operator.

As you learned in Tip 329, if you use the ALL quantifier, every one of the comparisons of the <expression> value with one of the <subquery> values must evaluate to TRUE in order for the WHERE clause to evaluate to TRUE. The SOME and ANY quantifiers, on the other hand, let the WHERE clause evaluate to TRUE so long as at least one of the comparisons between the value of <expression> and one of the values returned by the subquery evaluates to TRUE.

For example, if you want a list of salespeople that have exceeded their daily sales quota by 50% or more at least once during the past two weeks, you can submit a query similar to:

```
SELECT emp_ID, f_name, l_name, sales_quota
FROM employees
WHERE dept = 'SALES'
  AND (sales_quota * 1.50) <= ANY
        (SELECT SUM(order_total) FROM orders
         WHERE salesperson = emp_ID
           AND order_date >= GETDATE() - 14
         GROUP BY order_date)
```

Although the subquery to the right of the less than or equal to (<=) comparison operator has more than one value, the ANY quantifier lets you use it as one of the expressions in a comparison.

Then ANY quantifier tells the DBMS to compare the single value to the left of the comparison operator with each of the values returned by the subquery, one at a time. If the operation evaluates to TRUE for *any* (that is, at least one) of the comparisons performed, then the WHERE clause evaluates to TRUE. When the WHERE clause evaluates to TRUE, the DBMS adds column data values from the current row being tested as a row to the main query's results table.

The important thing to understand about the ANY (or SOME) quantifier is that it lets you compare a single value that precedes a comparison operator with each of the values in the set of values returned by a subquery that follows it. If *any* of the comparisons between the single value to the left of the comparison operator and each of the values in the subquery's results table evaluates to TRUE, then the predicate (and the WHERE clause) evaluates to TRUE.

Note: *The quantifiers SOME and ANY are synonymous. As you learned in Tip 315, "Understanding the Ambiguous Nature of ANY and How SQL Implements It to Mean SOME," the ambiguous nature of ANY prompted the SQL standards committee to add the quantifier SOME to the SQL-92 standard. Some DBMS products support only the original quantifier ANY. However, most now support both SOME and ANY. If your DBMS supports both, the one you choose is a matter of personal preference since both will produce a TRUE result if any one of the comparisons of the test value to each of the subquery data values evaluates to TRUE.*

331 Using an Aggregate Function in a Subquery to Return a Single Value

When you read about aggregate functions in Tips 113–120, you learned how to use each of the functions to display a table attribute in summary form in the query's results table. For example, when you wanted to know the number of rows in the EMPLOYEES table in Tip 113, "Using the COUNT(*) Aggregate Function to Count the Number of Rows in a Table," you submitted the query:

```
SELECT COUNT(*) FROM employees
```

And when you wanted to know the cost of the highest-priced item the PRODUCTS table in Tip 117, "Using the MAX() Aggregate Function to Find the Maximum Value in a Column," you submitted the query:

```
SELECT MAX(item_cost) AS 'Max Item Cost' FROM products
```

In addition to including aggregate function results in a query's results table, you can also get the value returned by an aggregate function as part of a search condition in a subquery's

WHERE clause. For example, if you want to display the PRODUCT_ID, DESCRIPTION, and ITEM_COST of the highest-priced item in your PRODUCTS table, you can submit a query similar to:

```
SELECT product_ID, description, item_cost
FROM products
WHERE item_cost = (SELECT MAX(item_cost) FROM products)
```

Note: *An aggregate function, such as MAX(),* always *returns a single value. Therefore, a subquery with only an aggregate function in its SELECT statement will always return a single value. Bear in mind, however, that just because the subquery returns a single value does not mean that the enclosing query, too, will return a single row. In the current example, if more than one product has the same price as the highest-priced item in the PRODUCTS table, the subquery will sill return one value—the largest value in the ITEM_COST column in the PRODUCTS table. However, the main query will display the PRODUCT_ID, DESCRIPTION, and ITEM_COST for each of the items in the PRODUCTS table that has the same ITEM_COST as the maximum ITEM_COST in the PRODUCTS table. Thus, the results table in the current example will have more than one row if more than one product has an ITEM_COST equal to the highest ITEM_COST in the PRODUCTS table.*

Because an aggregate function always returns a single value, you can use a subquery whose SELECT clause has only aggregate function as either of the two expressions in a comparison predicate. After all, a subquery with only one column (the aggregate function) in its SELECT clause is guaranteed to *always* return one an only one value—the single value returned by the aggregate function. Therefore, to get a list of employees whose average total order is larger than the overall average order total, you can submit a query similar to:

```
SELECT emp_ID, f_name, l_name FROM employees e
WHERE (SELECT AVG(order_total) FROM orders o
      WHERE o.salesperson = e.emp_ID) >
  (SELECT AVG(order_total) FROM orders)
```

Notice that the SELECT clause in each of the two subqueries contains a single aggregate function: AVG(ORDER_TOTAL). As such, each subquery is a single valued expression the DBMS can compare using one of the six comparison operators (such as the greater than [>], in the current example) in a comparison predicate.

332 Understanding Nested Subqueries

With the exception of the enclosing parenthesis (()), a subquery looks and functions exactly the same as any other SELECT statement. Therefore, since a SELECT statement can have a subquery, a subquery, which is (arguably) nothing more than a SELECT statement within another SQL statement, can itself have a subquery. Although the examples in Tips 321–331 show a two-level nesting of queries with a first-level subquery inside a main query, SQL also allows three-level (and higher) queries.

For example, the SELECT statement

```
SELECT f_name, l_name, ticker, rating_date, rating,
  employer AS 'underwriter' FROM stock_picks sp, analysts a
WHERE sp.analyst_ID = a.analyst_ID
  AND a.analyst_ID IN
        (SELECT analyst_ID FROM analysts
         WHERE employer IN (SELECT underwriter
                            FROM IPO_list i
                            WHERE i.ticker = sp.ticker))
```

is a three-level query designed to display ratings for stock purchases made by the analysts who work for the companies that brought a stock public.

The DBMS executes subqueries starting with the innermost subquery and then working its way outward through the subqueries. Thus, in the current example, the DBMS retrieves a stock symbol from a row in the CROSS JOIN of the rows in the STOCK_PICKS table and the ANALYSTS table. The system then uses the stock symbol in the innermost (second-level) subquery

```
WHERE employer IN (SELECT underwriter FROM IPO_list i
                   WHERE i.ticker = sp.ticker)
```

to generate a column that lists the names of the firms that brought the company with ticker symbol TICKER public. Next, the DBMS uses the second-level subquery's results table for the IN predicate of the first-level subquery

```
(SELECT analyst_ID FROM analysts
 WHERE employer IN (<second-level subquery>)
```

which generates the list of analysts who work for the firms that underwrote the stock with ticker symbol TICKER. The system then uses the results of the first-level subquery to filter out unwanted joined rows in the CROSS JOIN of STOCK_PICKS and ANALYSTS in the main query:

```
SELECT f_name, l_name, symbol, rating_date, rating,
  employer AS 'underwriter' FROM stock_picks sp, analysts a
WHERE sp.analyst_ID = a.analyst_ID
AND analyst_ID IN (<first-level> subquery)
```

The DBMS uses the same methodology to process fourth-level, fifth-level, and so on (through *n*th-level) queries. (It works it way from the innermost [highest-level] subquery outward.)

SQL-92 does not specify a maximum number of nesting levels for subqueries. However, most DBMS implementations restrict the number of subquery levels to a small number. A query quickly becomes too time consuming to process (and often too difficult to understand and maintain) as its level of subquery nesting increases.

333 Understanding the Role of Subqueries in a WHERE Clause

A subquery in a WHERE clause acts as a filter for the row-selection process of the enclosing query (or subquery). For example, if you want to know the names of the salespeople with above-average GROSS_SALES_YTD, you can execute a query such as:

```
SELECT f_name, l_name FROM employees
WHERE dept = 'Sales'
  AND gross_sales_ytd > (SELECT AVG(gross_sales_ytd)
                         FROM employees WHERE dept='Sales')
```

The DBMS will execute the inner query to get the average GROSS_SALES_YTD for all employees in the sales department. It then uses this number to filter out rows of sales department employees from the EMPLOYEES table who have GROSS_SALES_YTD below the average (returned by the AVG aggregate function in the subquery).

In the current simple example, you could execute the subquery on its own to get the average GROSS_SALES_YTD. Then, when you know the average, you can use it in place of the subquery in the SELECT statement. For example, suppose the average value in GROSS_SALES_YTD column is $227,500.50. You could then rewrite the query as:

```
SELECT f_name, l_name FROM employees
WHERE dept = 'Sales' AND gross_sales_ytd > 227500.50
```

However, if you "hard-code" the average GROSS_SALES_YTD figure into the query, you will have to execute the (sub)query and rewrite the query again the next time you want the list of above-average salespeople. A subquery lets you avoid this duplication of effort by letting you filter out unwanted rows based on values that change over time-without your having to know that the "filter" values are beforehand.

Moreover, using a subquery in a WHERE clause to filter out unwanted rows is much less time-consuming than writing and executing multiple queries when there are a large number of computations to perform. Suppose, for example, that the EMPLOYEES table does not have a GROSS_SALES_YTD column. Rather, to get the gross sales figure for each employee, you have to compute the sum of the values in the ORDER_TOTAL column of the ORDERS table for each salesperson's customers' orders. If the company has a large number of salespeople, executing a query such as

```
SELECT SUM(order_total) FROM orders WHERE salesperson = 11
```

repeatedly (substituting each salesperson's EMP_ID for 11 in the example) to get the total sales for each employee can be quite time-consuming—especially if you have to complete the report on a monthly, weekly, or even daily basis.

If you use a subquery (or multiple subqueries) in a WHERE clause instead, you can have the DBMS compute the average order (YTD) for each salesperson, determine the average sales

(YTD) for all salespeople, and report the names of salespeople with above-average sales—all in one query similar to:

```
SELECT f_name, l_name FROM employees
WHERE dept = 'Sales'
  AND (SELECT AVG(order_total) FROM orders
       WHERE salesperson = emp_ID
         AND order_date >= '01/01/2000')
    > (SELECT AVG(order_total) FROM orders
       WHERE order_date >= '01/01/2000')
```

The important thing to understand is that the subquery in a WHERE clause is used to compute the value (or set of values) that the DBMS can use in a search condition—just like any other literal value of column reference. As always, the DBMS inserts into the final results table column values from only those (joined) rows for which the WHERE clause search condition evaluates to TRUE.

334 Using Nested Queries to Return a TRUE or FALSE Value

In Tip 333, "Understanding the Role of Subqueries in a WHERE Clause," you learned that you can use a subquery to compute a value for use with a comparison operator in a WHERE clause. Sometimes, however, you want to take an action based on whether or not a table has *any* rows that satisfy a search condition vs. whether or not a column or set of columns has a specific value. A WHERE clause subquery introduced with the keyword EXISTS will return a simple TRUE or FALSE Boolean value that the DBMS can use in deciding whether or not to take the action specified by the SQL statement.

For example, if an insurance company wants to impose a 10 percent surcharge on any auto policy on which it has paid a claim during the past year, you can submit a query similar to

```
SELECT policy_number, RTRIM(f_name)+' '+l_name AS 'Name',
  cost * .10 AS 'Surcharge'
FROM auto_policies ap
WHERE EXISTS (SELECT * FROM claims_paid c
              WHERE c.policy_number = ap.policy_number
                AND claim_date > GETDATE() - 365)
```

which will list the POLICY_NUMBER, insured's name, and SURCHARGE for each policy listed in the CLAIMS_PAID table. Conversely, if the POLICY_NUMBER from the AUTO_POLICIES table in the main query is not found in the CLAIMS_PAID table by the subquery, the EXISTS predicate returns FALSE, and the system will not add the column data values from the row currently being processed to the final results table.

Similarly, a subquery introduced by NOT EXISTS will return the Boolean value TRUE when the table(s) in the subquery have no rows that satisfy the search condition(s) in its WHERE clause. For example, suppose the AUTO_POLICIES table in the preceding example were altered to include a SURCHARGE and DISCOUNT column. If you wanted to record the 10 percent claims surcharge in the SURCHARGE column of policies on which the company paid claims, you could use an UPDATE statement similar to:

```
UPDATE auto_policies
  SET surcharge = .1 * cost, discount = 0.00
WHERE EXISTS (SELECT * FROM claims_paid c
              WHERE c.policy_number =
                        auto_policies.policy_number
                AND claim_date > GETDATE() - 365)
```

Similarly, to record a 10 percent discount in the DISCOUNT column of policies that were claims-free during the past year, you could execute an UPDATE statements such as:

```
UPDATE auto_policies ap
  SET discount = .1 * cost, discount = 0.00
WHERE NOT EXISTS (SELECT * FROM claims_paid c
                  WHERE c.policy_number =
                            auto_policies.policy_number
                  AND claim_date > GETDATE() - 365)
```

When the DBMS executes the second UPDATE statement in the current example, the NOT EXISTS predicate will return TRUE if its subquery returns no rows. Therefore, if none of the rows in the ACCIDENTS table in the subquery has the same POLICY_NUMBER as the current row being processed from the AUTO_POLICIES table in the main query, then the subquery results table will contain no rows. EXISTS will evaluate to FALSE. However, the NOT keyword will reverse the value of EXISTS, and the NOT EXISTS predicate (and overall WHERE clause) will evaluate to TRUE. When the WHERE clause evaluates to TRUE in the second UPDATE statement of the current example, the DBMS will set the value of DISCOUNT column to 10 percent of the policy's cost and will set the value of the SURCHARGE column to 0.

335 Understanding Correlated Subqueries

As you learned in Tip 321, "Understanding Subqueries," and Tip 332, "Understanding Nested Subqueries," the DBMS executes the SELECT statement in a subquery over and over again—once each time it processes a (joined) row from the source table(s) in the main query. Sometimes, however, a subquery produces the same results table for every row processed by the main query. For example, if there are 10 salespeople in the sales department and you submit the query

```
SELECT RTRIM(f_name)+' 'l_name AS 'Employee', sales_YTD
FROM employees
WHERE dept = 'Sales'
  AND sales_YTD > (SELECT AVG(sales_YTD) FROM employees)
```

to list the name and SALES_YTD for each employee with an above-average amount of sales in the year, it is very inefficient to have the DBMS repeat the subquery 10 times. After all, the average of the SALES_YTD column values will be the same every time the system computes it.

Fortunately, the DBMS optimizer recognizes subqueries that make no outer column references and executes them only once. After determining the constant value (or set of values) the subquery will return (each time it is executed), the DBMS uses this constant value (or constant set of values) when processing each row of the main query.

Therefore, if the average SALES_YTD in the current example is $50,000.00, then the DBMS optimizer will convert the SELECT statement in the current example to

```
SELECT RTRIM(f_name)+' 'l_name AS 'Employee', sales_YTD
FROM employees WHERE sales_YTD > 50000.00
```

to reduce the amount of processing required by the query. In its new form, the SELECT statement will produce the same results table, but the shortcut makes it possible for the DBMS to process the subquery once instead of 10 times.

The optimizer cannot use this shortcut, however, if the subquery contains an outer column reference. For example, if you submit a query such as

```
SELECT c.cust_ID, f_name, l_name, inv_date,
  SUM(amt_due) AS 'Total Due'
FROM customers c, invoices i
WHERE amt_due <> 0 AND c.cust_ID = i.cust_ID
  AND (
    (SELECT SUM(amt_due) FROM invoices
     WHERE invoices.cust_ID = c.cust_ID) > 5000.00
   OR
     EXISTS (SELECT inv_date FROM invoices
             WHERE invoices.cust_ID = c.cust_id
               AND amt_due > 0
               AND inv_date < GETDATE() - 30)
      )
GROUP BY c.cust_ID, f_name, l_name, inv_date
ORDER by "Total Due"
```

to get the list of customers who currently owe over $5,000.00 total on invoices or have an invoice with a balance on an invoice dated more than 30 days in the past, the DBMS must execute the subquery

```
(SELECT SUM(amt_due) FROM invoices
 WHERE invoices.cust_ID = c.cust_ID) > 5000.00
```

and the subquery

```
EXISTS (SELECT inv_date FROM invoices
        WHERE invoices.cust_ID = c.cust_id AND amt_due > 0
          AND inv_date < GETDATE() - 30)
```

once for each row in the customers table, because the "sum" of the outstanding balances will be different for each of the customer rows in the CUSTOMERS table.

A subquery (such as the two in the current example) that references a column value from an enclosing (or outer) query, is called a correlated subquery because the subquery's results are correlated with each of the rows in the enclosing (outer) query. In the current example, the C.CUST_ID in each of the two subqueries is an outer reference to the CUST_ID column of the row currently being tested in an enclosing (and, in this instance, main) query. Because the value of the CUST_ID is unique to each row in the CUSTOMERS table, the two subqueries in the SELECT statement will be working with a different set of invoices for each joined row from the CROSS JOIN of the rows in the CUSTOMERS table and the rows in the INVOICES table. As a result, the DBMS cannot execute either query only once and use the results of that execution when it processes each of the joined rows in turn.

The important thing to understand now is that a correlated subquery is a subquery that makes an outer reference to at least one column in the row being tested by an enclosing query. Whenever the DBMS "sees" an outer reference in a subquery, it "knows" that it is working with a correlated subquery and must therefore execute the subquery once for each (joined) row it processes from the source table(s) in the enclosing query.

336 Understanding the Role of Subqueries in a HAVING Clause

In Tip 333, "Understanding the Role of Subqueries in a WHERE Clause," you learned that you can use a subquery in a WHERE clause to filter out individual unwanted rows. A subquery in HAVING clause can also be used in the filtering process. However, instead of using subquery results in a HAVING clause to filter out *individual* rows, the subquery's results table filters out *groups* of rows at a time

While a WHERE clause can appear in both grouped and ungrouped queries, a HAVING clause, if present, almost always follows the GROUP BY clause in a grouped query. For example, the HAVING clause in the grouped query

```
SELECT f_name, l_name, SUM(order_total) AS 'Total Orders'
FROM employees, orders
WHERE employees.emp_ID = orders.salesperson
  AND order_date BETWEEN '10/01/2000' AND '10/31/2000'
GROUP BY f_name, l_name
```

```
HAVING SUM(order_total) > .25 *
  (SELECT SUM(order_total) FROM orders
   WHERE order_date BETWEEN '10/01/2000' AND '10/31/2000')
```

tells the DBMS to list each salesperson whose total sales for October 2000 represented more than 25 percent of the sales made during the month by all of the salespeople combined.

Because the subquery in the HAVING clause makes no outer column references, the DBMS can calculate the product of the total orders multiplied by .25 once, and then use the product repeatedly (as a constant) in the HAVING clause as it tests each group of rows for inclusion in the final results table. (After all, 25 percent of the ORDER_TOTAL for October 2000 will be the same whether the DBMS is comparing it to the ORDER_TOTAL for the group of orders sold by the first, tenth, or *n*th salesperson.)

When executing the main query, the system goes through joined (EMPLOYEES/ORDERS) rows one row at a time, grouping (and totaling) the orders by salesperson. The DBMS then uses the search condition in the HAVING clause to filter out unwanted groups of rows. In the current example, the system removes any groups of rows in which the sum of the ORDER_TOTAL column values in the group is less than or equal to 25 percent of the grand total of all of the values in the ORDER_TOTAL column for the month of October 2000.

In addition to noncorrelated subqueries (that is, subqueries without outer references), you can also use correlated subqueries in a HAVING clause. Suppose, for example, that you want a list showing the name and total sales for each salesperson whose sales during October 2000 exceeded the person's total sales for the prior month by 50 percent or more. Because the subquery contains an outer reference (to the EMP_ID in the group of rows being processed in the main query), the DBMS must execute the correlated subquery in HAVING clause of the query

```
SELECT f_name, l_name, SUM(order_total) AS 'Total Orders'
FROM employees, orders, emp_ID
WHERE employees.emp_ID = orders.salesperson
  AND order_date BETWEEN '10/01/2000' AND '10/31/2000'
GROUP BY f_name, l_name, emp_ID
HAVING SUM(order_total) >= 1.5 *
   (SELECT SUM(order_total) FROM orders
    WHERE salesperson = emp_ID
      AND order_date BETWEEN '09/01/2000' AND '09/30/2000')
```

multiple times—one time for each salesperson with sales during the month of October 2000.

To execute the SELECT statement in the current example, the DBMS goes through the joined rows in the (EMPLOYEES/ORDERS) table one group of rows at a time, totaling orders by salesperson. Instead of using a constant value (computed once before applying the HAVING clause filter), the DBMS must compute the total September 2000 sales for a salesperson before going on to test the group of orders from the next salesperson. If the sum of the values in the ORDER_TOTAL column of the group of rows being tested does not exceed the value in the subquery's results table by 50 percent or more, the DBMS filters the group of rows out of the final results table.

The important thing to understand now is that a subquery in a HAVING clause serves the same purpose as a subquery in a WHERE clause. After executing the subquery either once or multiple times (once for each group or rows being processed if the HAVING clauses has a correlated subquery), the system uses the value returned by the subquery to filter unwanted (joined) rows from the enclosing query's results table.

337 Understanding the Execution Order of Correlated and Noncorrelated Subqueries in JOIN Statements

When executing a JOIN statement that has a noncorrelated subquery, the DBMS joins related rows in the main query's tables first. Next, the system uses any nonsubquery search criteria in main query's WHERE clause to filter out unwanted rows. Then the DBMS executes the subquery to filter out the remaining unwanted rows from the interim (virtual) results table. Finally, the DBMS sends column values from the remaining joined rows to the SELECT clause for output in the query's final results table.

Suppose, for example, that you submit the JOIN statement

```
SELECT RTRIM(c.f_name)+' '+c.l_name AS 'Customer',
  RTRIM(e.f_name)+' '+e.l_name AS 'Salesperson'
FROM customers c JOIN employees e
ON salesperson = emp_ID
WHERE cust_ID IN
  (SELECT cust_ID FROM orders
   WHERE order_date BETWEEN '01/01/2000' AND '12/31/2000'
   GROUP BY cust_ID
   HAVING SUM(order_total) > 100000.00)
```

to generate a list showing the customer and salesperson for each account that purchased more than $100,000 in products during the year 2000. The DBMS first generates the CROSS JOIN of the CUSTOMERS and EMPLOYEES tables. Next, it uses the nonsubquery conditions in the WHERE clause to filter out rows in which the SALESPERSON (from the CUSTOMERS table) does not match the EMP_ID (from the EMPLOYEES table). The system also filters out any rows with an order date before 01/01/200 or after 12/31/2000. Then the DBMS executes the subquery to generate a table of CUST_ID values from customers with orders totaling more than $100,000.00. Finally, the system works its way through the joined rows in the in the interim (virtual) main query table one row at a time, checking for the existence of the CUST_ID from the joined row in the list of CUST_ID values returned by the subquery. If the CUST_ID from the joined row is in the list returned by the subquery, the DBMS sends the customer and employee name column values to the SELECT clause for output in the final results table.

If the subquery in the JOIN statement is a noncorrelated subquery—meaning that it makes no outer references to column values in an enclosing query—the DBMS needs to execute the subquery only once. For example, in the current example, the DBMS needs to generate the list of CUST_ID values only one time because the list of customers that purchased over $100,000.000 in products will be the same whether the DBMS is testing the first row or the 200th row for inclusion in the final results table. However, if the JOIN statement uses a correlated subquery instead, the DBMS must execute the subquery repeatedly—once for each of the rows not yet filtered out of the interim results table.

For example, if you rewrite the query in the preceding example as

```
SELECT RTRIM(c.f_name)+' '+c.l_name AS 'Customer',
  RTRIM(e.f_name)+' '+e.l_name AS 'Salesperson'
FROM customers c JOIN employees e
ON salesperson = emp_ID
WHERE (SELECT SUM(order_total) FROM orders o
        WHERE o.cust_ID = c.cust_ID
          AND order_date
                 BETWEEN '01/01/2000' AND '12/31/2000')
     > 100000.00
```

the subquery in the WHERE clause is now correlated, since it makes an outer reference to the CUST_ID column value from the enclosing (main) query. Because the sum of each customer's orders is different, the DBMS must execute the subquery repeatedly—once for each joined row in the interim (CUSTOMERS/EMPLOYEES) table it is testing for inclusion in the final results table.

338 Using the Keyword IN to Introduce a Correlated Subquery to Determine the Existence of a Table Column Having a Specific Value

A correlated subquery can be used in an SQL statement anywhere a noncorrelated subquery can appear. Therefore, while the example queries in Tips 326 and 327 used the keyword IN to produce non-correlated subqueries, you can also use IN to produce correlated subqueries. For example, the query

```
SELECT cust_ID, f_name, l_name, street_address, state,
  zip_code
FROM customers
WHERE 'NV' IN (SELECT ship_to_state FROM orders o
               WHERE o.cust_ID = c.cust_ID)
```

will display the rows in the CUSTOMERS table that have NV in the SHIP_TO_STATE column.

Note: *Due to the heavy processing requirements of correlated subqueries, use them only when there is no alternative. In the current example, the DBMS will execute the subquery repeatedly, generating the list of states to which orders were sent once for each customer. A more efficient alternative is to rewrite the query in the current example either as a JOIN, such as:*

```
SELECT DISTINCT c.cust_ID, f_name, l_name, street_address,
  state, zip_code
FROM customers c JOIN orders o
ON o.cust_ID = c.cust_ID
WHERE ship_to_state = 'NV'
```

or as a multi-table SELECT statement with a WHERE clause similar to:

```
SELECT DISTINCT cust_ID, f_name, l_name, street_address,
  state, zip_code
FROM customers c, orders o
WHERE c.cust_ID = o.cust_ID
  AND ship_to_state = 'NV'
```

---

339 Understanding Correlated Subqueries Introduced with Comparison Operators

As is the case with a noncorrelated subquery, you can use a correlated subquery in an SQL statement almost anywhere an expression can appear. However, depending on the context in which a subquery is used, SQL places certain restrictions on the subquery's results. For example, if you use a correlated subquery as the expression following one of the six SQL comparison operators (=, <>, >, >=, <, or <=), the subquery must return a single value.

Suppose, for example, that you give your customers a discount of up to 6 percent off their next orders based on the amount they purchased from your company during the past 30 days according to the following schedule:

```
lower_limit  upper_limit  discount
-----------  -----------  --------
       0.00     9,999.99        0%
  10,000.00    19,999.99        1%
  20,000.00    29,999.99        2%
  30,000.00    39,999.99        3%
  40,000.00    49,999.99        4%
```

```
50,000.00     59,999.99       5%
60,000.00    999,999.99       6%
```

The query

```
SELECT cust_ID, RTRIM(f_name)+' '+l_name AS 'Customer',
  (SELECT discount FROM discount_schedule
   WHERE lower_limit <= (SELECT SUM(order_total) FROM orders
                         WHERE orders.cust_ID = c.cust_ID
                           AND order_date >= GETDATE() - 30
                           AND order_date < GETDATE())
     AND upper_limit >= (SELECT SUM(order_total) FROM orders
                         WHERE orders.cust_ID = c.cust_ID
                           AND order_date >= GETDATE() - 30
                           AND order_date < GETDATE()))
  AS 'Pct_Discount'
FROM customers c
WHERE c.cust_ID IN (SELECT cust_ID FROM orders
                    WHERE order_date >= GETDATE() - 30
                      AND order_date < GETDATE())
```

will display the CUST_ID, name, and discount percentage for all customers who have placed at least one order during the past 30 days.

In the current example, the correlated subquery introduced by each of the two comparison operators (<= and >=) produces a single value—the sum of the ORDER_TOTAL column for the orders placed by the customer with the CUST_ID from the row being tested in the main query. Because a correlated subquery makes an outer reference to a column in the row being tested in an enclosing query, the DBMS must execute the subquery repeatedly. Therefore, in the current example, the system will sum the ORDER_TOTAL column in the orders table each time it tests another customer row (from the CUSTOMERS table) for inclusion in the final results table.

The DBMS optimizer should pick up the fact that the two correlated subqueries are identical and should sum up each customer's ORDER_TOTAL only once (per customer). Another way to write the query is

```
SELECT cust_ID, RTRIM(f_name)+' '+l_name AS 'Customer',
  (SELECT discount FROM discount_schedule
   WHERE (SELECT SUM(order_total) FROM orders
          WHERE orders.cust_ID = c.cust_ID
            AND order_date >= GETDATE() - 30
            AND order_date < GETDATE())
     BETWEEN lower_limit AND upper_limit) AS 'Pct_Discount'
FROM customers c
WHERE c.cust_ID IN (SELECT cust_ID FROM orders
                    WHERE order_date >= GETDATE() - 30
                      AND order_date < GETDATE())
```

which has only one correlated subquery. The keyword BETWEEN performs the greater than or equal to (>=) and less than or equal to (<=) tests on the LOWER_LIMIT and UPPER_LIMIT values in the DISCOUNT_SCHEDULE table.

Note: *The correlated subquery in the current example is itself the subquery of another subquery that puts the customer's discount percentage into the PCT_DISCOUNT column of the main query's final results table. Notice, too, that a correlated subquery can make an outer column reference to any query (or subquery) that encloses it. In the current example, the correlated sub-subquery makes an outer column reference not to the subquery in which it is enclosed, but rather to the CUST_ID column of the row being tested in the main query (which encloses both the subquery and the subquery's correlated subquery).*

---

340 Using a Correlated Subquery as a Filter in a HAVING Clause

While the DBMS uses the search conditions in a WHERE clause to filter *individual* unwanted rows out of the query's results table, the system uses search conditions in a HAVING clause to remove *groups* of rows for which the search conditions evaluate to FALSE. In Tip 336, "Understanding the Role of Subqueries in a HAVING Clause," you learned that you can use a subquery as one of the expressions in a HAVING clause search condition. It should come as no surprise, then, that you can use a correlated subquery as one of the expressions in a HAVING clause search condition as well.

Suppose, for example, that you want to see if an organization is a bit "top heavy" in its management ranks because it has more managers than workers in any department. A query similar to

```
SELECT dept FROM employees e
GROUP BY dept
HAVING (SELECT COUNT(*) FROM employees cs_e
        WHERE e.dept = cs_e.dept
          AND(position LIKE '%Manager%' OR
              position LIKE '%Supervisor%' OR
              position LIKE '%President%')) >
       (SELECT COUNT(*) FROM employees cs_e
        WHERE e.dept = cs_e.dept
          AND(position NOT LIKE '%Manager%' AND
              position NOT LIKE '%Supervisor%' AND
              position NOT LIKE 'President%'))
ORDER BY dept
```

will display the names of the departments that have more employees with job titles such as manger, assistant manger, supervisor, vice president, or president than not.

In executing the SELECT statement, the DBMS first groups all rows from the EMPLOYEES table in an interim (virtual) table by department—conceptually similar to that shown in Figure 340.1.

EMP_ID	F_NAME	L_NAME	DEPT	POSITION
13	Clint	Rutberg	HR	Manager
14	Linda	Eastwood	HR	Clerk
5	Sally	Lauren	Marketing	Floor Supervisor
6	Hillary	Rafer	Marketing	Floor Supervisor
7	Jessica	Lewinski	Marketing	Day Manager
8	Chris	Hahn	Marketing	Telemarketer
9	Walter	Mathews	Marketing	Telemarketer
10	James	Mondale	Marketing	Night Manager
11	Clide	Dean	Marketing	Floor Supervisor
15	George	Tyson	Office	Manager
16	Michele	Harrison	Office	Receptionist
⋮	⋮	⋮	⋮	⋮

Figure 340.1 The rows in grouped query's interim (virtual) EMPLOYEES table grouped by DEPT

Next, the system goes through the virtual table one department at a time, executing the correlated subqueries in the HAVING clause for each department, and using the subquery results to filter out the groups of rows from departments that have a "management" count that is less than or equal to the "worker" count. Finally, the DBMS sends the value in the DEPT column from each of the remaining groups to the SELECT clause for output in the final results table.

341 Using a Correlated Subquery to Select Rows for an UPDATE Statement

If you submit an UPDATE statement without a WHERE clause, the DBMS will change the values stored in the column(s) specified in the UPDATE statement's SET clause throughout every row of a table. For example, if you submit the UPDATE statement

```
UPDATE inventory SET price = price * .75
```

the DBMS will reduce the PRICE of every item in the inventory by 25 percent. Although this may make your salespeople and customers very happy, you may have to answer to your stockholders for reducing the company's profit margin on high-demand items that are already in short supply.

To confine the changes an UPDATE statement will make to specific rows in a table, add a WHERE clause to the UPDATE statement. For example, to discount only those items that have had no sales within the past 30 days, rewrite the UPDATE statement in the preceding example as:

```
UPDATE inventory SET price = price * .75
WHERE NOT EXISTS
            (SELECT * FROM invoice_details i
             WHERE inventory.item_no = i.item_number
               AND inv_no IN
                     (SELECT inv_no FROM invoices
                      WHERE inv_date >= GETDATE() - 30))
```

When processing the revised UPDATE statement, the DBMS first executes the sub-subquery (the noncorrelated subquery within the correlated subquery in the WHERE clause) to generate the list of invoice numbers from invoices for sales made during the past 30 days. The system then goes through the INVENTORY table one item (row) at a time, testing the UPDATE requirement for each row by executing the correlated subquery for each item_number (ITEM_NO) in the INVENTORY table.

Each time it is executed, the correlated subquery builds a list of INVOICE_DETAILS rows from invoices entered within the last 30 days in which the ITEM_NUMBER (from the INVOICE_DETAILS table) matches the value in the ITEM_NO column of the INVENTORY table row being tested. If the item number was not included on any invoice detail records (rows) generated during the past 30 days, then the subquery returns no rows—which causes the EXISTS clause to evaluate to FALSE. However, the keyword NOT (which introduces the EXISTS clause) changes the FALSE to TRUE, thereby causing the WHERE clause to evaluate to TRUE. As such, the WHERE clause causes the DBMS to reduce the item's price by 25 percent whenever there are no invoices that show the item number (ITEM_NO) as being sold within the past 30 days.

The important thing to understand is that the outer column reference in an UPDATE statement's correlated subquery lets you implement a JOIN between the table(s) in the subquery and the target table in the UPDATE statement. While the SQL-89 specification prohibited subqueries in an UPDATE statement from making outer references to columns in the table being updated, the SQL-92 specification has no such restriction. As such, an UPDATE statement such as

```
UPDATE orders SET shipping_and_handling = 0
WHERE (SELECT SUM(order_total) FROM orders o
       WHERE o.order_number = orders.order_number)
     > 1000.00
```

(which waives the shipping and handling charge on all orders over $1,000.00) was unacceptable under the SQL-89 specification but is perfectly legal in SQL-92.

Note: *If a correlated subquery in the WHERE clause of an UPDATE statement makes outer references to columns being changed by the statement itself, the DBMS uses the values in the columns prior to any changes throughout the execution of the UPDATE statement.*

342 Understanding the Necessity of Cascading Deletes and Updates

Whenever you DELETE, INSERT, or UPDATE rows in a table, you run the risk of making the table's data inconsistent with other tables in the database. Consider for a moment the parent/child relationships between tables shown in Figure 342.1.

Each row in the group of rows in INVOICE_DETAILS with the same value in the INV_NO column is the child of the row in the INVOICES table with a matching value in its INV_NO column. Similarly, each row in the INVOICE_DETAILS table is related to the row in the ITEM_MASTER table that has a matching value in the ITEM_NO column. Thus, the three tables are consistent with each other when there are no rows in the INVOICE_DETAILS table that have INV_NO values not found in the INVOICES_TABLE; and when there are no rows in the INVOICE_DETAILS table that have ITEM_NO values not found in the ITEM_MASTER table.

If you change the item number (ITEM_NO) of an item by executing an UPDATE statement such as

```
UPDATE item_master SET item_no = 17002
WHERE item_no = 7002
```

INVOICES table

CUST_ID	INV_NO	INV_DATE	INV_TOTAL
101	1001	10/25/00	5000.00
202	1002	10/26/00	450.00
303	1003	10/27/00	3200.00
⋮	⋮	⋮	⋮

INVOICE_DETAILS table

INV_NO	ITEM_NO	QTY	COST
1001	7002	5	2500.00
1001	7005	5	2500.00
1002	6500	2	1500.00
1002	5500	5	2500.00
1002	5300	10	500.00
⋮	⋮	⋮	⋮

ITEM_MASTER table

ITEM_NO	DESCRIPTION	PRICE
7002	Widget	500.00
7005	Gidget	500.00
6500	Gadget	750.00
5500	Fiber Relay	500.00
5300	Sonic Coupler	50.00
⋮	⋮	⋮

Figure 342.1 INVOICES table related to INVOICE_DETAILS by INV_NO, and INVOICE_DETAILS related to ITEM_MASTER by ITEM_NO

the ITEM_MASTER and INVOICE_DETAILS tables become inconsistent with each other because ITEM_NO 7002 is now an *orphan* since it no longer has a parent (a row with a matching value for ITEM_NO) in the ITEM_MASTER table. Similarly, if you execute a DELETE statement such as

```
DELETE FROM invoices WHERE inv_no = 1002
```

or an INSERT statement such as

```
INSERT INTO INVOICE_DETAILS VALUES (1009,7005,5,2500)
```

you destroy the referential integrity between the INVOICE_DETAILS and INVOICES table because the INVOICE_DETAILS table will have rows with INV_NO values that have no parent (a row with a matching value for INV_NO) in the INVOICES table.

To avoid creating orphan rows in child tables, you must *cascade* any updates and deletes performed on rows in a parent table to corresponding rows in the child table. Thus, in the current example, rather than simply changing ITEM_NO 7002 to 17002 in the ITEM_MASTER table, to maintain referential integrity, you would execute the following SQL statement batch:

```
INSERT INTO item_master VALUES(17002,'Widget',500.00)
UPDATE invoice_details SET item_no = 17002
  WHERE item_no = 7002
DELETE FROM item_master WHERE item_no = 7002
```

Similarly, if you want to DELETE the invoice "header" row for the invoice with INV_NO 1002 from the INVOICES table, to maintain referential integrity in the database, you must execute a DELETE statement such as

```
DELETE FROM invoice_details WHERE inv_no = 1002
```

to remove any child rows for INV_NO 1002 from the INVOICE_DETAILS table prior to executing the DELETE statement that removes the parent row.

Unfortunately, most SQL products, like MS-SQL Server, do not support cascading deletes and updates. As such, to maintain database integrity, you must execute the appropriate sequence of statements (in the proper order) to avoid creating orphan rows in a child table when you execute a DELETE, INSERT, or UPDATE statement.

Note: *The DBMS will assist you in maintaining referential database integrity if you apply FOREIGN KEY constraints (which you learned about in Tip 173, "Understanding Foreign Keys") to columns used in parent/child relationships between tables. For example, if you attempt to INSERT a row in a child table with a FOREIGN KEY value that has no matching value in the corresponding key column in the parent table, the DBMS will abort the INSERT and display an error message. Similarly, the DBMS will abort any UPDATE or DELETE statements attempted on rows in the parent table that have key values that match the corresponding FOREIGN KEY values in child tables.*

---

343 Using an INSERT Statement with a Correlated Subquery to Create a Snapshot Table

You can uses a subquery in an INSERT statement to return not only multiple rows, but also multiple columns of data. (When you used the keyword IN, ANY, SOME, or ALL to introduce each subquery in Tips 327–330, the subquery could return multiple rows but only a single column.) Therefore, to transfer the entire contents of one table into another, you can execute an INSERT statement similar to

```
INSERT INTO table2 (SELECT * FROM table1)
```

as long as TABLE1 and TABLE2 have exactly the same structure (the same number and type of columns and in the same order).

If you want to copy data in only some of the columns from TABLE1 into TABLE2, simply modify the INSERT statement and subquery to include the list of columns to copy. For example, suppose you want to create a PRICE_LIST table for your salespeople based on data values stored in the ITEM_MASTER table. An INSERT statement with a subquery such as

```
INSERT INTO price_list (product_code, description, price)
  (SELECT item_number, description, ROUND(cost * 1.20,2)
   FROM item_master)
```

will copy the ITEM_NUMBER and DESCRIPTION from ITEM_MASTER and build a 20 percent profit margin into the PRICE stored in PRICE_LIST vs. the actual COST stored in ITEM_MASTER.

A *snapshot* table, as its name implies, is a table with a copy (or picture) of the data in another table at a particular moment in time. Suppose, for example, that you want to store a snapshot of your month-end inventory. (Having a copy of the inventory as of the month end will let you run various reports on the inventory as of a specific date, such as total value, item quantities, and a comparison of item quantities from one month to the next without interrupting the fulfillment of customer orders.) If you create a table such as INVENTORY_10_31_2000, for example, with the same structure as the inventory table (INVENTORY), you can submit the INSERT statement

```
INSERT INTO inventory_10_31_2000 (SELECT * FROM inventory)
```

to store a "snapshot" of the contents of the INVENTORY table as of 10/31/2000 in the INVENTORY_10_ 31_2000 table.

If you want a snapshot of only some of the data in a table, simply add a WHERE clause to the subquery. For example, to store a snapshot of all orders recorded in the ORDERS table during October 2000, submit an INSERT statement similar to:

```
INSERT INTO orders_Oct_2000
  (SELECT * FROM orders
   WHERE order_date BETWEEN '10/01/2000' AND '10/31/2000')
```

Or, to take a snapshot of only orders for product XYZ taken during the month of October 2000, submit an INSERT statement such as:

```
INSERT INTO XYZ_orders_Oct_2000
  (SELECT * FROM orders
   WHERE order_date BETWEEN '10/01/2000' AND '10/31/2000'
     AND product_code = 'XYZ')
```

344 Understanding the Role of the Database Administrator (DBA)

As soon as your DBMS installation has more than a few users, someone will be drafted into the job of *database administrator* (DBA). The DBA has all usage, execution, and access rights to all database objects. Moreover, the DBA has the ability to add and remove user accounts and to GRANT and REVOKE access rights on any object to other users. In short, the DBA is the supreme authority for a database.

While being assigned the role of DBA can give one a rush of power, the job also carries with it a great deal of responsibility. In short, the DBA is responsible for:

- Installing DBMS upgrades and service packs (maintenance releases), which includes having a working plan for restoring the DBMS (and its data) to a preupdate state in case of an unsuccessful upgrade
- Monitoring and tuning DBMS performance
- Managing system resources by increasing the size of the transaction log as necessary and adding new hard drives before the DBMS storage requirements exceed the available physical disk space
- Backing up and recovering data by scheduling (daily) database backups, making sure backups are successful, and testing the ability to restore from backup—before doing so is necessary due to the inevitable system failure
- Managing database security by GRANTING and REVOKING privileges and adding and removing user accounts
- Importing data into and exporting data from the DBMS
- Working with developers to implement a data warehouse
- Setting up and maintaining data replication (for a distributed database)

Perhaps the best way to sum up the DBA's job is that he or she is the one person responsible for protecting all database objects and equipment so that the database server is up and its data is accessible 24 hours a day, 7 days a week.

Note: *The easiest way to become the DBA is to be the person who installs the DBMS. When you install a DBMS, the installation process creates a "superuser" account such as* DBO *(database owner),* SA *(system administrator), or DBA, depending on the DBMS product you are installing. The first thing you should do after installing the DBMS is to log in to the DBA account and change its password. After all, you do not want an unauthorized user who happens to read the installation manual to have DBA privileges. (The system manual documents the DBA account login name and its default password.) After you change the DBA account's password, be sure to write it down* *and put it in a safe, but accessible place—just in case you win the lottery or get vested with millions in stock options, and your colleagues have to carry on without you while you sit on the beach of your own tropical island.*

345 Understanding the Role of the Database Object Owner (DBOO)

Whenever you create a database object (such as a table, index, view, trigger, or stored procedure), you become the owner of that database object—that is, you are the object's *database object owner* (DBOO). Therefore, the only thing required to be a DBOO is the right to execute the CREATE TABLE, CREATE VIEW, or CREATE PROCEDURE statement.

As the DBOO, you have all applicable rights to the objects you create. Moreover, you can GRANT and REVOKE access rights to objects you own to other users. In fact, after you create an object, *only* you and the database owner (DBA) (normally the system administrator or SA account on MS-SQL Server) have any rights to the object. While the DBMS implicitly GRANTs the DBOO all rights to objects he or she creates, the DBOO must explicitly GRANT others permission to use the objects before they can access them.

If you create a stored procedure, then, no one but you (or the DBO) can execute it until you GRANT others EXECUTE rights to the routine. Similarly, if you are the DBOO of a table or view, you must GRANT DELETE, INSERT, REFERENCES, SELECT, or UPDATE before another can execute a DELETE, INSERT, SELECT, or UPDATE statement on the database object you own. Moreover, to even use a column in one of your tables or views as the target of a FOREIGN KEY reference, you must GRANT the user desiring to do so REFERENCES privilege on the table or view.

In short, as the DBOO, you become the database administrator for the set of database objects you create. While you will still rely on the actual DBA to take care of such things as backup and recovery of the database objects, as the DBOO you have the responsibility for ensuring that you give DELETE access, for example, only to someone who will not wipe out another person's work. Moreover, once you give other users access to your database objects (tables and views), you must be careful in the statements you execute. After all, you will turn friends into enemies very quickly if you execute a TRUNCATE TABLE or DROP TABLE statement that destroys the data it took another user (perhaps) hundreds of hours to create.

Note: *Every object in a database must have an owner (a DBOO). As such, before the DBA (or DBO/system administrator) can remove a username from the DBMS, the ownership of all objects for which the username is the DBOO must be transferred to another user (or other users).*

346 Using the GRANT Statement to Give Someone DELETE Privilege

In Tip 345, "Understanding the Role of the Database Object Owner (DBOO)," you learned that as a database object owner (DBOO), you have all privileges (INSERT, UPDATE, and DELETE) on the database objects you create. Moreover, you can GRANT any one or all of these privileges to other users. Therefore, if you create an EMPLOYEES table and a TIMECARDS table, for example, you will probably give the people in Personnel (or Human Resources) the ability to remove (DELETE) rows of employee information and timecards when employees leave the company. Similarly, if you create a CUSTOMERS table, you may GRANT DELETE privilege to your sales managers so they can remove customers who have not made purchases for an extended period of time.

The syntax of the GRANT DELETE statement is:

```
GRANT DELETE ON <table name>|<view_name> TO <username|role>
  [...,<last username|role>][WITH GRANT OPTION]
```

Thus, to allow usernames MARY, SUE, and FRANK to remove rows from the EMPLOYEES table, execute the GRANT DELETE statement:

```
GRANT DELETE ON employees TO mary, sue, frank
```

Similarly, if users TOM, HELEN, SUSAN, and RODGER are members of the PERSONNEL role (group), you can grant all of them DELETE privilege on the TIMECARDS table with a GRANT DELETE statement such as:

```
GRANT DELETE ON timecards TO personnel
```

(You learned about group security (i.e. Database Roles) in Tips 139, 142, and 143.)

If you include the WITH GRANT OPTION in the GRANT DELETE statement, you allow the usernames to whom you are granting the DELETE privilege to grant it to other users as well. As such, be careful whenever you use the WITH GRANT OPTION. In so doing, you must trust the person to whom you GRANT the DELETE privilege not only to remove only table rows that are no longer needed, but also to show judgment as good as yours in GRANTING the DELETE privilege to other users. Therefore, if SUE and BILL are your sales department managers, for example, you can allow the two of them and *anyone* else they choose to remove rows from the CUSTOMERS table by executing the GRANT DELETE statement:

```
GRANT DELETE ON customers TO sue, bill WITH GRANT OPTION
```

Note: *When you GRANT DELETE privilege to a user, you should also use GRANT SELECT. If you use only GRANT DELETE, then the user cannot be selective as to which rows the DBMS is to remove from the table. For example, if you use only*

GRANT DELETE on the TIMECARDS table to username SUE, then SUE can execute the DELETE statement

```
DELETE timecards
```

which removes all rows from the TIMECARDS file. However, if SUE wants to remove only timecards that are more than 4 years old by executing the DELETE statement

```
DELETE timecards WHERE card_date < GETDATE() - 1460
```

the DBMS will abort the DELETE statement and display an error message similar to:

```
Server: Msg229, level 14, State 5, Line 1
SELECT permission denied on object 'timecards', database
  'SQLTips', owner 'dbo'.
```

Therefore, since you seldom (if ever) want a user to whom you GRANT DELETE privilege to be able to DELETE all of the rows from a table, be sure to GRANT both SELECT and DELETE privileges when you want a user to be able to remove specific rows from a table.

347 Understanding the Security Implications of Granting USAGE on Domains Used as Constraints

As you learned in Tip 15, "Understanding Constraints," a constraint is a restriction on the values that a user can store in a column. For example, if you define a column as being of type INTEGER, the DBMS will constrain (or prevent) a user from putting letters, symbols, non-whole numbers, and whole numbers outside the range 2**–31 to 2**31 –1 into the column. A *domain* lets you further limit the values a user can place in a column by specifying that the column's values must be from a subrange of all values allowed for a particular SQL data type.

For example, if you know that you will never carry more than 500 of any one item in your inventory, you can execute a CREATE DOMAIN statement such as:

```
CREATE DOMAIN qty_on_hand_domain AS INTEGER
  CONSTRAINT value_range CHECK (VALUE BETWEEN 0 AND 500)
```

The DBMS will allow users to insert only INTEGERS in the range 0–500 (inclusive) into any column defined as being of data type QTY_ON_HAND. Similarly, if you want the PRODUCT_CODE for each of the items in the INVENTORY table to be of data type CHARACTER(5) and start with a letter (A–Z), and end with a digit 5, 7, or 9, then you could execute a CREATE DOMAIN statement such as

```
CREATE DOMAIN product_code_domain AS CHARACTER(5)
  CONSTRAINT first_character
    CHECK (SUBSTRING (VALUE, 1, 1) BETWEEN 'A' AND 'Z')
  CONSTRAINT last_character
    CHECK (SUBSTRING (VALUE IN ('5','7','9'))
```

to set up the constraint.

To apply a domain, simply use it instead of the standard SQL data type definition for the columns to which the domain applies. For example, the CREATE statement for an INVENTORY table using the QTY_ON_HAND_DOMAIN and PRODUCT_CODE_DOMAIN used as examples in the current tip might be:

```
CREATE TABLE inventory
  (product_code      product_code_domain,
   qty_on_hand       qty_on_hand_domain,
   qty_on_backorder INTEGER)
```

As is the case with other database objects, after you create a domain, only you (as the DBOO) and the database owner (DBO) have access to the domain. If you want others to be able to create table using a domain you define, GRANT them the privilege to use the domain by executing a GRANT statement such as

```
GRANT USAGE ON qty_on_hand_domain TO warehouse_staff
```

which allows every username in the WAREHOUSE_STAFF group (role) to use the QTY_ON_HAND_DOMAIN as a column data type.

Granting usage on a domain becomes a security issue when you use a domain to limit the values in a column, and you do not want users to know the actual limits of the domain. Suppose, for example, that you define an EXECUTIVE_SALARY domain constraints as:

```
CREATE DOMAIN executive_salary AS REAL
  CONSTRAINT salary_range
    CHECK (VALUE BETWEEN 10000.00 AND 25000.00)
```

If you GRANT USAGE on the EXECUTIVE SALARY domain to username FRANK, for example (who has CREATE TABLE privilege as well), then FRANK could execute a CREATE table statement such as:

```
CREATE TABLE find_executive_salary_range
(executive_pay executive_salary)
```

He could then INSERT increasing values into the EXECUTIVE_PAY column until the DBMS accepted the value he inserted (once the value he inserted reached the lower end of the EXECUTIVE_SALARY range). If FRANK then continued to INSERT increasing values for EXECUTIVE_PAY into the table until the DBMS aborted the INSERT statement with an error message, FRANK would know both the upper and lower boundaries of the EXECUTIVE_SALARY domain.

348 Understanding the Effects of Revoking GRANT Privilege (CASCADE and Non-CASCADE)

As you learned in Tip 146, "Understanding the REVOKE Statement," the REVOKE statement lets you remove a privilege you previously granted to a user. Moreover, since the ability to GRANT a privilege is itself a privilege, you can use the REVOKE statement syntax

```
REVOKE [GRANT OPTION FOR] <privilege list> ON <object>
  FROM <username|role>[..., <last username|role>]
    [RESTRICT|CASCADE]
```

to remove a user's ability to GRANT a privilege to others, while leaving the original privilege in place. For example, if you execute the GRANT statement

```
GRANT INSERT ON employees TO sue WITH GRANT OPTION
```

username SUE will have the privilege to INSERT new rows into the EMPLOYEES table *and* the privilege to GRANT INSERT privilege on the employees table to other users. If SUE then executes the GRANT statement

```
GRANT INSERT ON employees TO frank, mary WITH GRANT OPTION
```

FRANK and MARY, too, will be able to INSERT rows into the EMPLOYEES table. Moreover, both of these users can themselves GRANT the INSERT privilege on the EMPLOYEES table to other users.

If you later decide the REVOKE SUE's ability to GRANT INSERT privilege on the EMPLOYEES table to other users, you can do so either with or without the CASCADE option. By executing the REVOKE statement

```
REVOKE GRANT OPTION FOR INSERT ON employees FROM sue
```

you allow SUE, any users to whom SUE has granted INSERT privilege (FRANK and MARY, in the current example), and any users to whom those users have granted INSERT privilege (since SUE granted INSERT on the EMPLOYEES table WITH GRANT OPTION) to continue adding rows to the EMPLOYEES table. On the other hand, if you include the CASCADE option when you execute the REVOKE statement

```
REVOKE GRANT OPTION FOR INSERT ON employees FROM sue
  CASCADE
```

SUE will still be able to INSERT rows *into* the EMPLOYEES table. However, SUE will no longer be able to GRANT INSERT privilege on the EMPLOYEES table to other users, *and* any users to whom she granted INSERT privilege on the EMPLOYEES table (and any users to whom they granted INSERT privilege on the EMPLOYEES table) will no longer be able to INSERT rows into the EMPLOYEES table—unless they also received the same INSERT privilege from someone else. Therefore, after executing the REVOKE statement in the current example, SUE will be able to INSERT rows into the EMPLOYEES table, but FRANK and MARY will no longer be able to do so, since they received their ability to INSERT rows into the EMPLOYEES table from SUE's GRANT INSERT privilege (which you revoked).

Note: *Some DBMS products, such as MS-SQL Server, will not allow you to REVOKE a privilege or the GRANT OPTION for a privilege without including the CASCADE option. If you attempt to do so, MS-SQL Server, for example, will abort the REVOKE statement with an error message similar to:*

```
Server: Msg 4611, Level 16, State 1, Line 1
To revoke grantable privileges, specify the CASCADE option
  with REVOKE.
```

Therefore, be sure to check your system manual to see if your DBMS product allows you to omit the CASCADE option when executing a REVOKE statement to remove the GRANT OPTION for a privilege you previously granted.

349 Understanding How to Use GRANT and REVOKE Statements Together to Save Time When Granting Privileges

When you need to grant privileges on multiple columns in a table (or several tables) to several users, you can sometimes save yourself some typing by granting a broad range of privileges to all users and then revoking the few that only some of them should have. Suppose, for example, that you have an EMPLOYEES table and you want everyone to have SELECT privilege on it. However, only the department managers (ROBERT, RICHARD, LINDA, and JULIE) should be able to update the pay columns, and only human resources (HR) personnel (LINDA, DOREEN, and FRED) should be able to UPDATE the personal information, DELETE rows (to remove terminated employees), or INSERT information on new employees. Finally, no one should be able to change the employee ID in the EMP_ID column.

To set up the security on the EMPLOYEES table, you could execute a series of GRANT statements such as:

```
GRANT INSERT, DELETE, SELECT ON employees
  TO linda, doreen, fred
GRANT UPDATE ON employees
  (f_name, l_name, address, city, SSAN, state, zip_code,
   phone1, phone2, email_address, emergency_contact,
   sheriff_card, bond_amount, bond_number)
  TO linda, doreen, fred
GRANT UPDATE ON employees
  (quota, bonus_rate, weekly_salary)
```

```
  TO robert, richard, linda, julie
GRANT SELECT ON employees
  TO lori, samantha, helen, william, james, joyce, nick,
     donna, karen, amber, vivian, george
```

Or, you can achieve the same result with a little less typing by combining GRANT and REVOKE statements, as follows:

```
GRANT SELECT ON employees TO public
GRANT INSERT, DELETE, UPDATE ON employees
  TO linda, doreen, fred
REVOKE UPDATE ON employees
  (emp_ID, quota, bonus_rate, weekly_salary)
  FROM doreen, linda, fred
GRANT UPDATE ON employees
  (quota, bonus_rate, weekly_salary)
  TO robert, richard, linda, Julie
```

Notice that using the PUBLIC role to GRANT the SELECT privilege to all users with DBMS access eliminated the need for typing each and every username into a GRANT SELECT statement. Meanwhile, granting UPDATE to all columns in the EMPLOYEES table to the HR personnel and then using the REVOKE statement to remove UPDATE privilege from the few columns that they should not update eliminated having to type the full list of column names in the EMPLOYEES table in the GRANT UPDATE statement for the HR users.

350 Understanding Concurrent Transaction Processing Problems and Isolation Levels

When multiple users access and update a database at the same time, the DBMS must ensure that work performed while processing a transaction for one user does not supply inconsistent database values to statements in another user's transaction. Ideally, every user should be able to work with the database without being concerned about the concurrent actions of others.

In general, there are four fundamental problems that can occur if the DBMS does not handle concurrent transaction processing properly:

- **The lost update.** Suppose that Rob and Lori each go to a different automated teller machine (ATM) at the same time and attempt to withdraw $150 from a single joint checking account that has a $200 balance. Rob starts his transaction by entering his account number and requesting a withdrawal of $150. The ATM responds with the current balance in the account and asks Rob to confirm the withdrawal. In the meantime, Lori starts her transaction and is also given the balance of $200 and asked to confirm her $150 withdrawal request. If each then confirms the withdrawal, Rob's ATM dispenses $150 and updates the balance in the account to be $50. In the meantime, Lori's ATM, too, dispenses $150 and updates the account balance to be $50. Depending on which transaction the DBMS completed first, the effect of the other transaction on the account balance is lost. Both Rob and Lori are happy since each was able to withdraw $150 ($300 in total) from the joint account, and the account shows a credit balance of $50 instead of being overdrawn by $100.

- **The uncommitted data/dirty read.** Suppose that Rob and Lori are shopping in separate stores for anniversary gifts for each other. They each find the "right" gift and take it to a register and attempt to use a credit card for the same account, which has $750 available credit remaining. Lori starts the checkout transaction as the clerk swipes her card in the machine and enters the purchase price of $500. While Lori thinks about her purchase while waiting for the clerk to complete the sales transaction, Rob hands another clerk his charge card (for the same account), and the clerk starts the transaction by swiping the card in the machine and entering the $400 purchase price. However, because Lori's transaction already reduced the available credit in the account by $500 (leaving only $250 available), Rob's transaction is declined. Moments later, Lori changes her mind about the gift and has the clerk cancel the charge. Thus, Rob now thinks there is less than $400 available on the credit card, while there is really $750 remaining because his transaction was able to "see" the uncommitted update from Lori's transaction.
- **The inconsistent data/nonrepeatable read.** Rob decides that he really wants the anniversary gift he selected, so he goes to an ATM to transfer money from savings into the joint checking account. He begins the transaction by requesting the balance in the savings account, which shows $2,000. Rob then requests the balance in the checking account, which shows $50. In the meantime, Lori is at the bank withdrawing money from savings to pay the electric bill of $250. As the teller finishes Lori's withdrawal transaction, Rob continues his transaction of transferring $750 from savings into checking, only this time, when the ATM shows him the savings account balance again, it reads $1,750 and not $2,000. Thus, the balance shown in the savings account was always a correct reflection of reality. However, "something" happened during the course of Rob's savings-to-checking transfer transaction that caused the program at the ATM to show him first one balance in the savings account and then another. In other words, a "read" of the BALANCE column was nonrepeatable because it produced two different results at different times during Rob's transaction.
- **The phantom insert/delete.** Now Rob, confused by the changing balances in the savings and checking accounts, cancels the transaction and starts over. He requests the balance in the savings account and the ATM displays $1,750—so far so good. Rob then requests the balance in the checking account and is told it is still $50. He then continues the transfer transaction by entering $750 as the amount to move from savings to checking. In the meantime, Lori deposits her net pay of $1,500 into the checking account. When the teller completes the deposit transaction just before Rob completes his transfer transaction by requesting a balance in both accounts, Rob's transaction falls victim to the *phantom insert* problem. The balance in the checking account at the beginning of the transaction ($50) plus the $750 he transferred into the checking account should have made the new account

balance $800. However, there is now $2,300 in the account because, as far as Rob's transaction is concerned, the $1,500 showed up "out of nowhere" the second time it queried the checking account balance. (A *phantom delete* occurs if, for example, Lori deposits her check just before Rob starts his transaction and then withdraws the cash during Rob's funds transfer.)

Isolation levels are advanced DBMS locking techniques that attempt to maintain the fiction of each user's exclusive use of the database in a multi-user environment, while still trying to give as many users as possible simultaneous access to the data in the database. Although a transaction can prevent the four concurrent transaction processing problems by locking the set of tables it uses, doing so will make the DBMS appear sluggish as users have to wait for multiple transactions to finish before they get any response from the system. You will learn all about isolation levels in Tips 351–360. For now, the important thing to understand is that isolation levels give you a way to tell the DBMS that a program (or batch of SQL statements in a transaction) will not re-retrieve data, which allows the DBMS to release locks before the transaction ends.

351 Understanding READ UNCOMMITTED and Dirty Reads

READ UNCOMMITTED is the weakest of the four transaction isolation levels. In fact, READ UNCOMMITTED is the same as having no locks on the database at all. If you submit the statement:

```
SET TRANSACTION ISOLATION LEVEL READ UNCOMMITTED
```

the DBMS will set your session's environment so that your transactions will not issue any shared (or exclusive) locks on the data they process. Moreover, statements in your transactions will not observe any locks held by others. Therefore, if another user submits a transaction that makes changes to the database, your query will see these changes before they are committed. In fact, transactions executed at the READ UNCOMMITTED isolation level are subject to all four of the concurrent transaction processing problems you learned about in Tip 350, "Understanding Concurrent Transaction Processing Problems and Isolation Levels."

Performing a *dirty read* (that is, reading updated but as yet uncommitted data) is problematic because users updating the database may roll back uncommitted transactions and undo any changes. As a result, the data values retrieved and being used by transactions working at the READ UNCOMMITTED isolation-level environment may not match those that exist in the actual database tables.

The main advantage of setting the isolation level to READ UNCOMMITTED is that statements processed in a READ UNCOMMITTED environment avoid the overhead involved in concurrency control. The DBMS does not have to issue locks (which reduces database management overhead), the statements do not have to wait for other transactions to finish (which lets you retrieve information more quickly), and others do not have to wait for your transaction to complete its work (which makes the overall system appear more responsive). Unfortunately, the performance gains come at a price—transaction results in a READ UNCOMMITTED environment are based on inaccurate input values when dirty (uncommitted) data is rolled back (undone) and not finalized (written permanently into the database).

Use the READ UNCOMMITTED isolation level only for applications such as reports that are statistically unaffected by the average change that might occur while the DBMS is processing your transaction—for example, if you want to know the average, minimum, or maximum delay in filling orders, or if you want to know the average amount of an employee's sales or a customer's purchases during the past three months.

Note: *Most DBMS products (like MS-SQL Server) set the transaction isolation level for the entire time a session is connected to the database. As such, if you have an application that sets the isolation level to READ UNCOMMITTED, make sure that the program sets the isolation level back to the default (READ COMMITTED) prior to exiting or executing a section of code that requires a higher (more protective) isolation level.*

352 Understanding READ COMMITTED and Nonrepeatable Reads

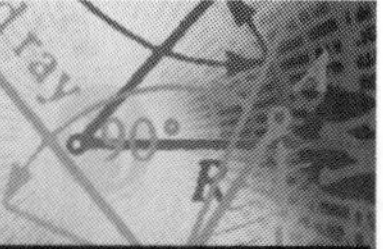

The isolation level READ COMMITTED solves the dirty read concurrent transaction processing problems by hiding any uncommitted changes. Thus, if your application executes the SET statement

```
SET TRANSACTION ISOLATION LEVEL READ COMMITTED
```

any statements executed during the session will see (work with) only data values committed (permanently written) to the database. Therefore, if SUE, for example, is taking a customer order for 10 of the 20 hammers you currently have in inventory and her program executes the UPDATE statement

```
UPDATE inventory SET qty = qty - 10
WHERE description = 'hammer'
```

your query

```
SELECT qty FROM inventory WHERE description = 'hammer'
```

will return the QTY as 20 (and not 10) until such time as SUE's application either terminates or executes a COMMIT statement and the DBMS commits (permanently writes) SUE's UPDATE to the INVENTORY table.

An interesting side effect of the READ COMMITTED isolation level is that a transaction may end up working with data no longer found in the database. Suppose, for example, that MARY in the payroll department is performing a period end closing procedure that executes the DELETE statement

```
DELETE FROM timecards
WHERE card_date BETWEEN @period_start and @period_end
```

to remove TIMECARDS rows inserted during the pay period she is closing. If you are running queries and reports that involve TIMECARDS rows with CARD_DATE values between @PERIOD_START and @PERIOD_END, your application will continue to "see" these rows even though SUE's DELETE statement has removed them from the TIMECARDS table.

Now, after SUE's application executes a COMMIT to finalize the DELETE statement's actions, the deleted TIMECARDS rows will "disappear" as far as your application is concerned. Thus, the READ COMMITTED isolation level does not prevent the phantom INSERT or phantom DELETE concurrent transaction processing problems.

Moreover, while READ COMMITTED eliminates dirty reads to prevent the inconsistent data problem, it does not prevent nonrepeatable reads. Suppose, for example, that MARY and SUE are each taking an order from a customer. MARY queries to INVENTORY table to find that she has 25 copies of *1001 FrontPage 2000 Tips* and lets her customer know. In the meantime, SUE completes her order for 20 copies of the book, and the DBMS commits her work to the INVENTORY table. When MARY's customer says, "I'll take all 25 copies," she finds that she is unable to process the order because a second query as to the number of copies available shows there are now only 5. As such, the same query executed at two different points in the one sales transaction produced two different results, with the results of the first read (query) being nonrepeatable.

353 Understanding REPEATABLE READ and Phantom Inserts

REPEATABLE READ, which is one step above READ COMMITTED in the four isolation-level hierarchy, prevents both the dirty read problem and (as its name implies) the nonrepeatable read problem. Instead of simply ignoring any uncommitted updates and deletes, the DBMS issues a lock that prevents other users from changing any data read by a transaction executed at the REPEATABLE READ isolation level. Moreover, if a transaction running at the REPEATABLE READ isolation level is unable to lock the portion of the database it needs to query (because another user's transaction already has a lock on it), the DBMS waits until the lock is released before executing the transaction.

Thus, in the previous tip's example where both MARY and SUE were taking orders for the same 25 copies of the *1001 FrontPage 2000 Tips* book, the repeatable read problem occurred because both MARY and SUE were able to access the same rows of data in the INVENTORY table at the same time. If the order entry program is executed at the REPEATABLE READ isolation level (instead of the READ COMMITTED isolation level), then only one of the two operators will be able to work with a specific portion of the INVENTORY table at a time.

Therefore, if the order entry program operates at the REPEATABLE READ isolation level, MARY's request for a count of the copies of the book locks a portion of the INVENTORY table from modification and query requests in other transactions operating at the same or higher isolation level. As such, when SUE later starts a transaction for the same book (which will involve reading the same section of the INVENTORY table on which MARY's transaction has a lock), the DBMS refuses the lock requested by SUE's transaction. As a result, SUE's transaction must wait until MARY's transaction completes its work and releases its lock on the portion of the INVENTORY table that SUES's transaction wants to read.

Because the REPEATABLE READ isolation level prevents other users from modifying only data an open transaction has read, transactions running at the REPEATABLE READ isolation level are still subject to the phantom INSERT (and DELETE) problem. Suppose, for example, that you execute the statement batch:

```
SET TRANSACTION ISOLATION LEVEL REPEATABLE READ
SELECT SUM(order_total) FROM orders WHERE cust_ID = 101
SELECT * FROM orders WHERE cust_ID = 101
```

It is possible for the value returned by the aggregate function, SUM(ORDER_TOTAL), to be different than the total you get if you were to add up the values in the ORDER_TOTAL column of the rows returned by the SELECT statement (the third statement in the batch). This error, or anomaly, occurs if users INSERT additional orders for CUST_ID 101 into the ORDERS table between the time the DBMS computes the SUM of the ORDER_TOTAL column and the SELECT statement displays the rows of ORDERS for CUST_ID 101.

354 Understanding Table-, Page-, and Row-Level Locking

Although you can set the isolation level of your DBMS session to insulate you from the concurrent actions of other users (as discussed in Tips 351–353), you should not write applications that access the database without regard for others that may need to work with its data. Suppose, for example, that you write a program that sets its isolation level to REPEATABLE READ and then executes a series of large queries and requests for user input. Executing the program without a COMMIT statement after each query and before each prompt for user interaction will prevent everyone else from updating (and perhaps even reading) an ever-increasing portion of the database for an extended period of time.

Even if a program makes no changes to the data in the database, the DBMS automatically starts a transaction when it executes the first statement in the application. Without a COMMIT statement, the transaction will not end until the application terminates. In the meantime, the DBMS prevents others from modifying data read during a transaction (while the program is running) in order to keep the data self-consistent. (As you learned in Tip 353, "Understanding REPEATABLE READ and Phantom Inserts," the REPEATABLE READ isolation level requires that the system keep data read during a transaction unaffected by transactions executed concurrently on behalf of other users.) Locking the data against changes from other users is the only way the DBMS has to ensure that data values read at the start of a transaction will be the same if the program reads the same rows again later in the transaction.

The physical mechanism used for locking and unlocking portions of the database is automatically controlled by the DBMS and is transparent to the user. Therefore, you do not have to understand database locks to use SQL transactions. However, if you write your transactions with an understanding that a lock gives you exclusive access to a portion of the database, you will use COMMIT statements to break a single, large transaction into a group of smaller transactions—thereby preventing other users' transactions from waiting for a long time while parts of the database they need are locked by your application.

There are basically four levels of locking available to the DBMS. The crudest and easiest to implement is database-level locking. In *database-level locking*, the DBMS locks the entire database at the start of a transaction, and all other transactions must wait for the transaction to complete before they can start. No commercial DBMS products use database-level locking because processing one transaction at a time leads to unacceptably slow performance in a multi-user environment.

The next step up in the lock-level hierarchy is *table-level locking,* in which the DBMS locks only those tables accessed by a transaction. Therefore, if Transaction A uses data in the OFFICES and CUSTOMERS tables, for example, then Transaction B needs to wait only for Transaction A to complete if it uses one or both of these tables. If Transaction B uses other tables such as EMPLOYEES and TIMECARDS, for example, the DBMS will execute the statements in Transaction A and Transaction B concurrently. Unfortunately, table-level locking leads to unacceptably slow DBMS performance in applications such as online order processing, where many users need simultaneous access to the same tables.

Currently, many DBMS products use *page-level locking* by segregating tables into 2KB, 4KB, 8KB, and 16KB blocks. Since most large tables may span hundreds or even thousands of pages, two transactions trying to access data in the same table will often use data from different segments (or pages) of the file. Therefore, with page-level locking, if Transaction A and Transaction B both need to work with data in the ORDERS table, the system will process the transactions concurrently, as long as the ORDERS data needed by Transaction A is on different pages than that being used by Transaction B.

Some DBMS products (such as MS-SQL Server) use *row-level locking* to allow an even greater amount of concurrent processing. In row-level locking, the DBMS locks only the specific rows used by a transaction. Row-level locking fixes a shortcoming of page-level locking in processing small tables (such as an EMPLOYEES table) where different EMPLOYEE rows needed by separate transactions happen to reside in the same 2KB, 4KB, 8KB, or 16KB disk block. In row-level locking, the DBMS will process Transaction A and Transaction B concurrently even if both use the same tables—as long as each transaction is working with different rows in the tables.

In theory, it is possible to increase lock granularity beyond the row level and implement attribute-level locking, in which the DBMS locks only specific columns in a row. Unfortunately, while each level of locking (from table level to page level to row level) increases database concurrency, it also increases the overhead necessary to manage the locks. As a result, no commercial DBMS products currently implement attribute-level locking because the overhead involved in managing locks on individual columns in a row outweighs the potential advantages of doing so.

355 Understanding MS-SQL Server Lock Escalation

As mentioned in Tip 354, "Understanding Table-, Page-, and Row-Level Locking," maintaining row-level locking requires more overhead than maintaining page-level locking, which requires more overhead than managing table-level locking. By default, MS-SQL Server will lock data at the row level. Therefore, any query executed by the system will hold locks on at least one row in a table. As the system executes the statement(s) in a transaction, the DBMS keeps track of the number of locks it holds on each 8KB page of data. At a certain point, based on the percentage of rows locked per page, the DBMS will *escalate* the lock level so that it will begin using page-level locking instead of row-level locking.

For example, if a transaction executes an UPDATE statement such as

```
UPDATE employees SET hourly_rate = hourly_rate * 1.2
WHERE office = 1
```

the DBMS will lock individual EMPLOYEES table rows given that there are only a few rows per 8KB page in the EMPLOYEES table that have a value of 1 in the OFFICE column. If, on the other hand, the transaction executes a query such as

```
SELECT * FROM orders
WHERE order_date BETWEEN '01/01/2000' AND '12/31/2000'
```

which reads (and locks) a large number of rows on a page, the DBMS will lock the ORDERS table an 8KB page at a time instead of a single row at a time. Moreover, if a transaction exceeds the table-level escalation threshold with a statement such as

```
SELECT * FROM customers
```

which will eventually lock every row and page in a table, the DBMS will begin using table-level locking on the CUSTOMERS table.

Lock escalation, then, is the process of converting a large number of highly granular row-level locks into fewer, coarser page-level locks and, if necessary, table-level locks—all in an effort to reduce system overhead. MS-SQL Server dynamically sets the lock escalation thresholds, so you need not configure them. For example, when a transaction requests rows from a table, MS-SQL Server locks rows used by statements in the transaction and places page-level *intent* locks on pages that contain the locked rows. If the transaction later exceeds the page-level threshold, the DBMS attempts to change the higher-level intent locks to actual locks. After acquiring the (fewer) page-level locks, the DBMS drops the (many) row-level locks, thereby reducing the system's lock overhead. (The DBMS follows the same procedure when escalating from page-level locking to table-level locking.)

Thus, when an SQL statement references a small number of rows scattered throughout a large table, the MS-SQL Server maximizes concurrent access to the data with row-level locks. However, if a statement references most or all of the rows in a table, the system maximizes concurrent access (and reduces lock overhead) by switching to table-level locking. Because MS-SQL Server dynamically adjusts its lock granularity by table, a single statement may use row-level locking on one table, page-level locking on another, and table-level locking on a third table.

356 Understanding Deadlocks and How the DBMS Resolves Them

Deadlock is a situation in which two users (or sessions) have a lock on separate objects, and each user's transaction is waiting for a lock on an object held by the other user. Figure 356.1 illustrates a deadlock condition in which Transaction A has a lock on the ORDERS table and needs a lock on the CUSTOMERS table to proceed. Transaction B, meanwhile, has a lock on the CUSTOMERS table and is waiting on Transaction A to complete and release its lock on the ORDERS table.

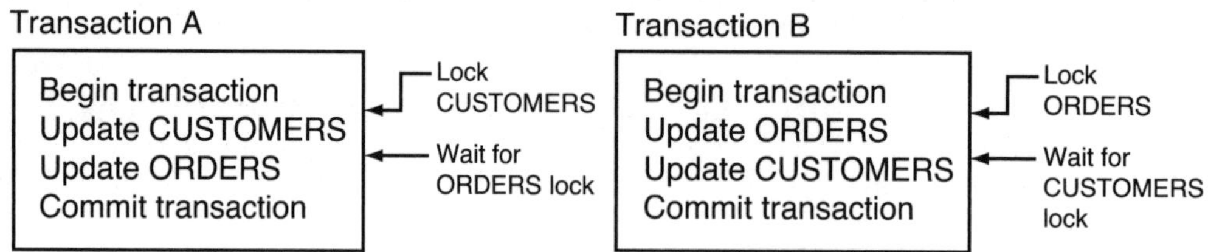

Figure 356.1 Transaction A and Transaction B, deadlocked with each transaction waiting for the other to release a table before proceeding

Without intervention by the DBMS, each session will wait forever for the other to COMMIT (or ROLLBACK) its transaction and unlock the portion of the data file the transaction in the session needs to continue. While Figure 356 depicts a simple situation in which two transactions are deadlocked, in real life, the situation is often more complex, with three or more sessions stuck in a cycle of locks, each waiting for data locked by one or more of the other sessions.

To deal with deadlocks, the DBMS will choose one of the sessions as the "deadlock victim," terminate it, ROLLBACK (undo) any changes made by the transaction running in the session, and release its lock(s) so that the transaction(s) in the other session(s) can continue.

Each DBMS product has its own methodology for detecting deadlocks and selecting which of the sessions will be the deadlock victim. MS-SQL Server, for example, periodically scans for and flags sessions waiting on a lock request. If a flagged session is still waiting for a lock during the next periodic scan for locks, the DBMS begins a recursive deadlock search. (After all, the session may just be blocked, waiting for a large query or other long-running SQL statement to complete its work.) If the recursive search detects a circular chain of lock requests, MS-SQL Server selects the transaction with the least amount of work to undo and terminates it.

Not only does MS-SQL Server roll back the deadlock victim's transaction, but the DBMS also notifies the user's application of the transaction's failure by sending an error message 1205. The server then cancels the terminated transaction's locks and lock requests, and allows the nonterminated transaction(s) to continue.

Due to the way in which the DBMS handles deadlocks, any SQL statement is a potential deadlock victim. As such, an application program executing an SQL statement batch must check for and be able to handle the deadlock victim error code in any transaction that works with multiple tables. If a deadlock victim error code is returned in an interactive session, the user can simply retype and resubmit the SQL statements. In programmatic SQL, an application that receives the deadlock victim error code may either alert the user and terminate or automatically restart the transaction.

357 Understanding the SERIALIZABLE Isolation Level

Serializable is a DBMS concept that means that each database user can access the database as if there were no other users accessing the same data concurrently. In short, serializability requires that a user's application will see a completely consistent view of the data during a transaction, and neither uncommitted nor committed actions of other users will have any effect on data values seen by the transaction's statements. Or, said another way, SERIALIZABLE implies that if two transactions (Transaction A and Transaction B) are executing concurrently, the DBMS will ensure that the results will be the same whether Transaction A is executed first, followed by Transaction B, or whether Transaction B is executed first, followed by Transaction A.

As shown in Table 357.1, if you execute the SET statement

```
SET TRANSACTION ISOLATION LEVEL SERIALIZABLE
```

the DBMS will ensure that transactions executed during the session are not subject to *any* of the four concurrent transaction processing problems you learned about in Tip 350, "Understanding Concurrent Transaction Processing Problems and Isolation Levels."

Isolation Level	***Lost Update***	***Uncommitted Data/ Dirty Read***	***Inconsistent Data/ Nonrepeatable Read***	***Phantom Insert***
Serializable	Prevented	Prevented	Prevented	Prevented

Table 357.1 SERIALIZABLE Isolation Level and Concurrent Transaction Update Problems

In short, the SERIALIZABLE isolation level completely insulates a transaction from the actions of all SQL statements concurrently executed by the DBMS on behalf of other users.

When a session is at the SERIALIZABLE isolation level, the DBMS will maintain each transaction's exclusive lock on updates to the portion of the database tables it uses throughout the transaction's lifespan. After starting the execution of a transaction at the SERIALIZABLE isolation level, the DBMS will not allow any other user(s) to make any changes to data read or modified by the statements in the transaction. Moreover, the DBMS will also prevent users from inserting new rows of data that would be included in the results set of any of the executed WHERE clauses in the transaction's statements, nor will they be able to execute DELETE statements that would remove any such rows.

358 Understanding the REPEATABLE READ Isolation Level

The REPEATABLE READ isolation level is the second-highest isolation level (just below SERIALIZABLE). At the REPEATABLE READ isolation level, the DBMS prevents a second transaction from modifying data read by the first transaction until the first transaction ends (and releases its shared locks on the data read). However, another user can INSERT additional rows into the table(s) queried by the first transaction. As a result, a query such as

```
SELECT * FROM orders WHERE cust_ID = 2002
```

may generate a different results table when executed at the beginning of Transaction A than it does when executed again later in the same transaction—even if the transaction itself makes no changes to the ORDERS table. The inconsistent query results, due to the phantom insert problem, occur if another user executes an INSERT statement that adds an additional row (or additional rows) with CUST_ID 2002 into the ORDERS table between the times at which Transaction A executes the two identical queries on the ORDERS table.

Most applications do not need the capability to repeat a multi-row query during a single transaction. As such, leave sessions at the (MS-SQL Server default) READ COMMITTED isolation level whenever possible because the explicit locking of data from other users at the REPEATABLE READ isolation level reduces the concurrency of the database. In most instances, an application will never "see" the newly inserted rows (because they do not execute the same query at multiple points in the same transaction), and the DBMS will remain self-consistent as long as data values read at some point during a transaction remain unchanged by other users throughout the transaction.

As shown in Table 358.1, the REPEATABLE READ isolation level prevents three of the four concurrent (multi-user) update problems.

Isolation Level	Lost Update	Uncommitted Data/ Dirty Read	Inconsistent Data/ Nonrepeatable Read	Phantom Insert
Serializable	Prevented	Prevented	Prevented	Prevented
Repeatable Read	Prevented	Prevented	Prevented	Possible

Table 358.1 SERIALIZABLE and REPEATABLE READ Isolation Levels and Concurrent Transaction Update Problems

The main advantage of executing at the REPEATABLE READ isolation level over the SERIALIZATION isolation level is the improvement in overall system performance. If Transaction A is executing at the REPEATABLE READ isolation level and other users submit INSERT statements to add rows to tables used in the transaction, the DBMS will add the rows while continuing to process the statements in Transaction A. If, on the other hand, Transaction A is running at the SERIALIZABLE isolation level, any INSERT statement that adds rows to a results table returned by a WHERE clause in any of the executed statements in Transaction A will have to wait until the DBMS finishes processing Transaction A.

359 Understanding the READ COMMITTED Isolation Level

While the READ COMMITTED isolation level prevents only two of the four concurrent transaction processing problems (as shown by Table 359.1), the third-highest level in the isolation-level hierarchy improves database concurrency by releasing shared locks as soon as data is read.

Isolation Level	Lost Update	Uncommitted Data/ Dirty Read	Inconsistent Data/ Nonrepeatable Read	Phantom Insert
Serializable	Prevented	Prevented	Prevented	Prevented
Repeatable Read	Prevented	Prevented	Prevented	Possible
Read Committed	Prevented	Prevented	Possible	Possible

Table 359.1 SERIALIZABLE, REPEATABLE READ, and READ COMMITTED Isolation Levels and Concurrent Transaction Update Problems

The DBMS prevents the uncommitted data/dirty read problem by not allowing statements in a transaction executed at the READ COMMITTED isolation level to see uncommitted updates made by other concurrently executed transactions. However, the nonrepeatable read and phantom insert problems can occur because committed changes made by other transactions may become visible during the course of the transaction. As a result, a transaction that repeats a query such as

```
SELECT cust_ID, total_orders FROM customers
WHERE cust_ID = 3003
```

may return a different value for TOTAL_ORDERS each time, as transactions executed concurrently on behalf of other users change the values in the CUST_ID 3003 row of the CUSTOMERS table and execute COMMIT statements to write the changes permanently to the table. Similarly, a transaction that executes a SELECT statement such as

```
SELECT COUNT(*) FROM orders WHERE cust_ID = 4004
```

more than once may find that the aggregate COUNT(*) returns a different value each time the DBMS executes the query because other transactions such as COMMIT, INSERT, and/or DELETE statements add or remove ORDERS table rows for CUST_ID 4004.

In addition to avoiding dirty reads by hiding uncommitted changes, the READ COMMITTED isolation level prevents lost updates. If a statement in Transaction A, for example, attempts to update a row already changed by Transaction B, the DBMS will automatically ROLLBACK (undo) *all* changes made by Transaction A. As such, if you write an application that executes several UPDATE statements, be sure to execute a COMMIT statement after each one. Otherwise, the DBMS will undo all changes made since the application started, if the program happens to attempt an UPDATE on a row already updated by another concurrently executing transaction.

360 Understanding the READ UNCOMMITTED Isolation Level

READ UNCOMMITTED is the lowest isolation level defined by the SQL-92 standard and (as shown in Table 360.1) prevents only the lost update problem. In fact, on some DBMS products (such as MS-SQL Server, for example), the READ UNCOMMITTED isolation level does not even prevent the lost updates. Therefore, be sure to check your system documentation to see if READ UNCOMMITTED, as specified by the SQL-92 specification, implies "READ ONLY" and therefore disallows updates by transactions executed at the READ UNCOMMITTED isolation level.

If READ UNCOMMITTED implies "READ ONLY" mode on your DBMS product, then the DBMS will protect you from lost updates at the READ UNCOMMITTED isolation level, since a transaction cannot execute updates of any kind when executed in READ UNCOMMITTED mode. However, if your DBMS product, like MS-SQL Server, allows updates at the READ UNCOMMITTED isolation level, the lost update problem can (and will) occur if two concurrently running transactions execute UPDATE statements that change data values in the same rows and column(s) of a table. Since neither transaction requests or holds shared nor exclusive locks on the data it modifies to prevent concurrent changes by the other transaction, data values changed by one UPDATE statement can be immediately changed by a second UPDATE statement—even before the DBMS completes the execution of the first UPDATE statement.

Isolation Level	***Lost Update***	***Uncommitted Data/ Dirty Read***	***Inconsistent Data/ Nonrepeatable Read***	***Phantom Insert***
Serializable	Prevented	Prevented	Prevented	Prevented
Repeatable Read	Prevented	Prevented	Prevented	Possible
Read Committed	Prevented	Prevented	Possible	Possible
Read Uncommitted	Prevented	Possible	Possible	Possible

Table 360.1 SERIALIZABLE, REPEATABLE READ, READ COMMITTED, and READ UNCOMMITTED Isolation Levels and Concurrent Transaction Update Problems

The main advantage of executing SELECT statements at the READ UNCOMMITTED isolation level is that doing so allows the highest degree of database concurrency because queries executed in READ UNCOMMITTED mode not only do not lock the data they read, but also ignore any existing shared or exclusive locks held by other transaction. However, by circumventing the system's concurrent processing protections, a SELECT statement such as

```
SELECT item_number, qty_on_hand inventory
```

may report inaccurate results when the query performs "dirty reads" of updated but as yet uncommitted data values in the INVENTORY table. If, for example, the DBMS executes a ROLLBACK of uncommitted and subsequently aborted inventory update or online order entry transactions concurrent with the execution of the SELECT statement, the query's results table will contain values that never really existed in the database.

Therefore, use the READ UNCOMMITTED isolation level only for queries whose results do not have to be 100 percent accurate, such as a COUNT(*) of orders processed over an extended period or time, or for a report where the user is looking for general trends in the data and is not concerned about the actual values in specific rows or sets of rows. Moreover, to avoid the lost update problem, *never* execute an UPDATE statement at the READ UNCOMMITTED isolation level, even if your DBMS product allows you to do so.

361 Using the MS-SQL Server Enterprise Manager to Display Blocking and Blocked Sessions

As you learned in Tip 356, "Understanding Deadlocks and How the DBMS Resolves Them," MS-SQL Server automatically resolves deadlocks by terminating one of the deadlocked transactions to release locks so that the other(s) can continue running. However, a session can block other applications from reading or updating one or more tables for an extended period of time without creating a deadlock the DBMS will clear. Suppose, for example, that FRANK starts an MS-SQL Server Query Analyzer session and executes the statement batch:

```
BEGIN TRANSACTION
SELECT * FROM auto_inventory
UPDATE auto_inventory SET MODEL = 'Model 2'
  WHERE year = 1999 AND make = 'Camero'
```

MS-SQL Server will grant FRANK's transaction exclusive locks on the AUTO_INVENTORY table rows modified by his UPDATE statement. Moreover, FRANK's process will retain these locks until he terminates the transaction by ending his session or by executing a ROLLBACK or a COMMIT statement.

If another process attempts to query or update the AUTO_INVENTORY table, the transaction will "hang" waiting for FRANK's session to release its exclusive locks. Furthermore, the DBMS will not terminate either FRANK's transaction or the other query (or UPDATE) transaction because the two processes are not deadlocked. Rather, FRANK's process is simply *blocking* the other's request for a shared or exclusive lock on rows in the AUTO_INVENTORY table.

You can use the MS-SQL Server Enterprise Manager to display blocking and blocked sessions by performing the following steps:

1. To start the MS-SQL Server Enterprise Manager, click your mouse pointer on the Start button. When Windows displays the Start menu, move your mouse pointer to Programs, select Microsoft SQL Server 7.0, and then click your mouse pointer on Enterprise Manager.
2. To display the list of SQL servers, click your mouse pointer on the plus (+) to the left of SQL Server Group.
3. Click your mouse pointer on the plus (+) to the left of the icon for the SQL server whose sessions you want to display. For example, if you want to display sessions running on a server named NVBIZNET2, click your mouse pointer on the plus (+) to the left of the icon for NVBIZNET2. The Enterprise Manager will display folders containing databases and services available on the MS-SQL Server you selected.
4. Click your mouse pointer on the plus (+) to the left of the Management folder. The Enterprise Manager will display icons for various database management activities and status reports.
5. Click your mouse pointer on the plus (+) to the left of the Current Activity icon. The Enterprise Manager will display icons you can use to display process information and locks (by process ID and by object ID).
6. Double-click your mouse pointer on icon to the left of Locks/Process ID. The Enterprise manager, in turn, will display the currently running system process ID's (SPID's), similar to that shown in Figure 361.1.

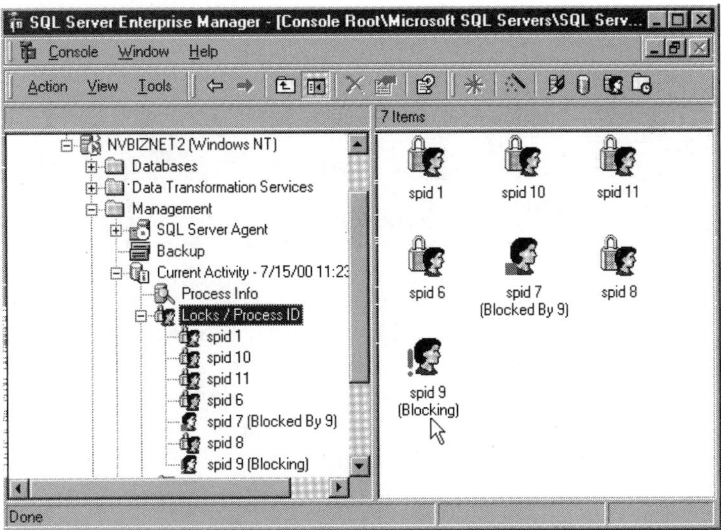

Figure 361.1 The MS-SQL Server Enterprise Manager Locks/Process ID window

Notice that the right pane of the Enterprise Manager window shows which of the sessions is blocking the transaction processing in other sessions. In the current example, the Enterprise Manager shows that the SA's session (SPID 7) is blocked by FRANK's session (SPID 9).

To display the display the last statement batch executed by a session, right-click your mouse pointer on the icon of the session whose last statement batch you want to see, and then select Properties from the Enterprise Manager pop-up menu. The Enterprise manger, in turn, will display a Process Details dialog box similar to that shown in Figure 361.2.

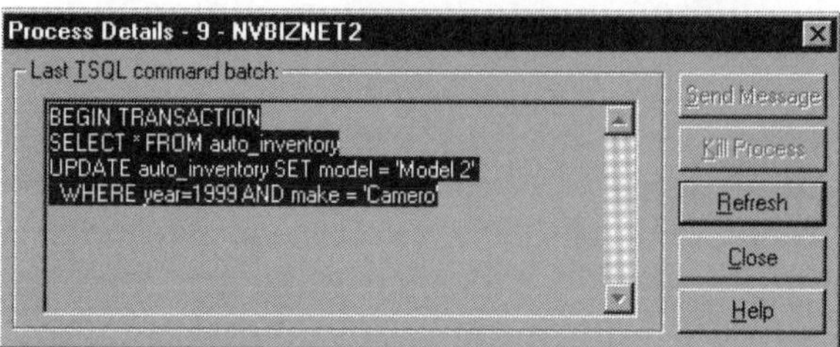

Figure 361.2 The MS-SQL Server Process Details dialog box

Review the last statement(s) executed by the blocking session to determine whether the user is just executing a process that will take a long time to complete, or (as is the case in the current example) if the user inadvertently failed to execute a COMMIT statement to close an open transaction and release its locks on database objects. After you find out why a session is blocking another, you can wait patiently for the blocking process to finish, contact the owner of the blocking session, and ask the user to complete or abort the open transaction, or you can terminate the blocking session (as you will learn to do in Tip 362, "Using the MS-SQL Server Enterprise Manager to Kill Processes Holding Locks on Database Objects").

To exit the Process Details dialog box, click your mouse pointer on the Close button.

362 Using the MS-SQL Server Enterprise Manager to Kill Processes Holding Locks on Database Objects

In Tip 361, "Using the MS-SQL Server Enterprise Manager to Display Blocking and Blocked Sessions," you learned how to use the MS-SQL Server Enterprise Manager to determine the system process ID (SPID) of the session(s) that are blocking (or being blocked by) other sessions. If you decide that a transaction will not complete its work within a reasonable period of time, you can use the Enterprise Manager to terminate it. (Suppose, for example, that FRANK starts a transaction that makes updates to the AUTO_INVENTORY table and then goes to lunch before executing a COMMIT statement to close the transaction, make the changes permanent, and release locks held by the transaction.)

To use the MS-SQL Server Enterprise Manager to terminate the open transaction running in a session, perform the following steps:

1. Follow the six-step procedure in Tip 361 to display the list of sessions running on the MS-SQL Server and to determine which sessions are blocking other sessions.

2. Click your mouse pointer on the icon to the left of Process Info to display the information on the processes running on the MS-SQL Server you selected in Step 1. (You will find the Process Info icon immediately above the Locks/Process ID icon in the MS-SQL Server Enterprise Manager's left pane, as shown in Figure 362.1.)

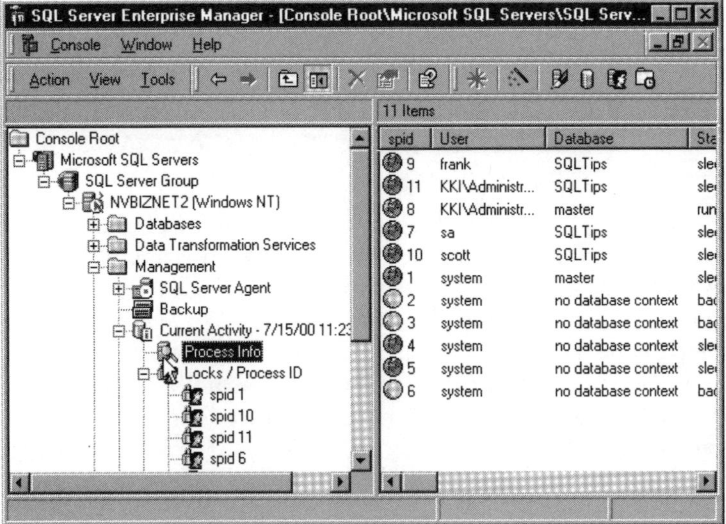

Figure 362.1 The MS-SQL Server Enterprise Manager Process Info window

3. Right-click your mouse pointer on the icon to the left of the SPID running the process you want to terminate (KILL). For the current example in which FRANK's transaction (SPID 9) is blocking SA's query (SPID 7), you would right-click your mouse pointer on the globe icon to the left of 9 in the SPID column in the Enterprise Manager's right pane.

4. Select the Kill Process option from the pop-up menu. Enterprise Manager will display a Kill Process message box prompting you to confirm your intent to kill (terminate) the process running in the SPID you selected in Step 3.

5. To kill the process, click your mouse pointer on the Yes button.

After you complete Step 5, MS-SQL Server will abort the transaction running in the session with the SPID you selected in Step 3 and ROLLBACK (undo) any uncommitted work the session has done.

Note: *In addition to the Enterprise Manager's graphical user interface (GUI), MS-SQL Server provides stored procedures and an SQL statement you can execute from the command line to find a blocking SPID and terminate it. If you execute the stored procedure* ***sp_lock****, MS-SQL Server will display the list of SPID's with locks and those requesting locks (i.e. the blocked SPID's). After you determine the SPID of the session* *running the transaction you want to terminate, you can abort the transaction the SPID is running by executing the statement*

```
KILL <SPID>
```

(where <SPID>) is the number of the SPID with the process you want to kill.)

363 Understanding Locking and Transaction Isolation on MS-SQL Server versus Oracle

From a review of the intricate locking mechanisms and isolation levels described in Tips 350–360, you can see that DBMS products make every reasonable effort to process queries and updates for multiple users concurrently while isolating each user from the actions of others. In fact, one of the primary functions of the DBMS is to make sure that multiple users can query and update the database without receiving inconsistent information from in-progress transactions and without inadvertently overwriting each others' updates. However, while the goal of all DBMS products is the same, the method each uses to protect users from each other may differ greatly.

For example, Oracle and MS-SQL Server take a very different approach to database locks and isolation strategies. On Oracle, statements that read data neither acquire locks nor wait for locks to be released before reading rows of data. As such, the eternally blocked process in Tip 361, "Using the MS-SQL Server Enterprise Manager to Display Blocking and Blocked Sessions," could not occur as described in that tip. On an Oracle DBMS, the UPDATE statement in FRANK's transaction would still acquire an exclusive lock on a row (or perhaps a page) in the AUTO_INVENTORY table. However, the query in the system administrator's (SA's) session would not "hang." Instead, in an Oracle environment, the SA's query would read a copy of the data that contains data values prior to FRANK's uncommitted changes vs. waiting for READ COMMITTED access to the most current data values once FRANK's session commits its work.

Therefore, on an Oracle DBMS, when a SELECT statement requests data that has been changed but not yet committed by another transaction, the system supplies the query with the last set of values already committed (permanently written) to the database at the start of the query. The session executing INSERT, DELETE, or UPDATE statements acquires exclusive locks on all modifications and holds these locks until the end of the transaction to prevent others from overwriting uncommitted changes.

MS-SQL Server, on the other hand, uses shared locks to ensure that queries see only committed data (unless, of course, you set the transaction isolation level to READ UNCOMMITTED). As such, a SELECT statement executed on MS-SQL Server acquires and releases shared locks as it retrieves data for its results table. Although these shared locks have no effect on other SELECT statements, the DBMS does require that a query wait for a transaction to COMMIT any pending changes prior to reading updated but as yet uncommitted data. As such, releasing locks quickly and reducing the length of transactions that modify data is more important on MS-SQL Server than on an Oracle server.

The important thing to understand is that you must check the lock and isolation philosophy of your DBMS product to ensure that you are writing applications that will support what will be an ever-increasing number of concurrent users. A code review is especially important when moving SQL code from one DBMS product do another. As you learned from the comparison of MS-SQL Server and Oracle locking strategies in the current tip, an SQL statement batch that runs perfectly fine on an Oracle DBMS can cause multiple lockups (and unhappy users) when run without modification on MS-SQL Server.

364 Using the SET TRANSACTION Statement to Set a Transaction's Isolation Level

A transaction's isolation level tells the DBMS the extent to which you want the system to insulate your work from interaction with work the DBMS performs concurrently on behalf of other users. Each DBMS product has a default isolation level at which it executes the statements in a transaction. MS-SQL Server, for example, uses a default isolation level of READ COMMITTED. The SET TRANSACTION statement lets you change a session's isolation level.

In Tip 350, "Understanding Concurrent Transaction Processing Problems and Isolation Levels," you learned that concurrently processing multiple transactions subjects database data to four main problems. The way in which the DBMS implements its locking mechanism at each of the four isolation levels prevents one or more of these problems, as shown in Table 364.1.

Isolation Level	Lost Update	Uncommitted Data/ Dirty Read	Inconsistent Data/ Nonrepeatable Read	Phantom Insert
Serializable	Prevented	Prevented	Prevented	Prevented
Repeatable Read	Prevented	Prevented	Prevented	Possible
Read Committed	Prevented	Prevented	Possible	Possible
Read Uncommitted	Prevented	Possible	Possible	Possible

Table 364.1 Isolation Levels and Concurrent Transaction Processing Problems

The syntax of the SET TRANSACTION statement is:

```
SET TRANSACTION [{READ ONLY|READ WRITE}]
  ISOLATION LEVEL {READ UNCOMMITED|READ COMMITTED|
                  REPEATABLE READ|SERIALIZABLE}
  [DIAGNOSTICS SIZE <number of error messages>]
```

Therefore, to tell the DBMS that you want the statements in a transaction that makes no changes to the database protected only from lost update problems, you would execute a SET TRANSACTION statement such as:

```
SET TRANSACTION READ ONLY ISOLATION LEVEL READ UNCOMMITTED
```

Similarly, to protect a transaction that updates the database from all four of the update concurrency problems and return at most three error messages (if necessary), you would execute a SET TRANSACTION statement similar to:

```
SET TRANSACTION READ WRITE ISOLATION LEVEL SERIALIZABLE
  DIAGNOSTICS SIZE 3
```

Note: *Like many other statements defined in the SQL-92 standard, some DBMS products support the SET TRANSACTION in ways that do not adhere strictly to the letter of the specification. MS-SQL Server, for example, gives the syntax of the SET TRANSACTION statement as*

```
SET TRANSACTION ISOLATION LEVEL {READ UNCOMMITTED|
  READ COMMITTED|REPEATABLE READ|SERIALIZABLE}
```

which eliminates both the statement's ability to set the transaction's access mode as READ ONLY or READ WRITE and to control the number of error messages the server can return if it encounters errors while executing the statements in a transaction.

Be sure to check your system documentation to determine your DBMS product's rules for the use of the SET TRANSACTION statement. Some DBMS products, like the SQL-92 specification, require that you execute the SET TRANSACTION statement as the first statement in a transaction. In addition, these DBMS products use the statement's clause(s) to change the default transaction settings for only the one transaction in which the statement appears. MS-SQL Server, on the other hand, lets you execute the SET TRANSACTION anywhere in a transaction and uses the value that follows the TRANSACTION ISOLATION LEVEL clause to set the isolation level for statements executed during the remainder of the *session*—not just those executed in a single *transaction.*

Note: *MS-SQL Server, unlike most other DBMS products, does not revert the transaction isolation level back to the system's default (READ COMMITTED) after a user (or application) changes it by executing a SET TRANSACTION statement during the session. Therefore, if you lower the isolation level to READ UNCOMMITTED, for example, MS-SQL Server will process transactions at the READ UNCOMMITTED* *isolation level for the remainder of the session—unless you execute another SET TRANSACTION statement that raises the isolation to the session's initial default (READ ONLY) or above.*

365 Using the COMMIT Statement to Make Database Updates Permanent

The SQL-92 specification defines two statements you can use to terminate a transaction: COMMIT and ROLLBACK. While executing a ROLLBACK statement undoes any work performed in a transaction, submitting a COMMIT statement makes all data modifications (the actions of all UPDATE, INSERT, and DELETE statements) performed since the start the transaction a permanent part of the database. Moreover, after committing a transaction, the DBMS frees resources (such as table, page, and row locks) held by the session.

Up to the point at which you execute a COMMIT statement, you can undo the actions taken by the statements submitted to the DBMS in a transaction by executing a ROLLBACK statement. Suppose, for example, that you start an MS-SQL Server Query Analyzer session and execute the statement sequence:

```
BEGIN TRAN
  UPDATE employees SET salary = salary * 1.5
  DELETE employees WHERE office = 1
  UPDATE employees SET manager = NULL WHERE manager = 102
```

If you then execute the statement

```
ROLLBACK
```

the DBMS will make the EMPLOYEES table look like it did before you executed the first UPDATE statement that follows BEGIN TRAN—including "bringing back" all of the rows removed from the table by the DELETE statement. However, if you follow the initial sequence of statements with

```
COMMIT
ROLLBACK
```

the COMMIT statement closes the transaction and makes your updates and the row removal permanent, and the subsequent ROLLBACK will not be able to undo the work performed by the committed (and now closed) transaction.

If your DBMS product lets you nest transactions, COMMIT statements executed to close inner (nested) transactions do not release resources or make permanent changes to the database. Only the COMMIT statement executed to terminate the outermost transaction makes actual changes to the DBMS that cannot be rolled back. Suppose, for example, that you execute the statement batch:

```
BEGIN TRAN outermost_tran
  UPDATE employees SET salary = salary * 1.5

  BEGIN TRAN nested_tran1
    DELETE employees WHERE office = 1
      BEGIN TRAN nested_tran2
        UPDATE employees SET manager = NULL
        WHERE manager = 102
      COMMIT TRAN nested_tran2  – the DBMS commits no work

  COMMIT TRAN nested_tran1 – the DBMS commits no work

COMMIT outermost_tran – the DBMS commits ALL work
```

Only the final COMMIT statement (on the outer transaction) actually makes work performed by the outer and inner (nested) transactions a permanent part of the database. As such, nested transactions provide a convenient way to create groups of statements whose work you can undo (on a statement-group-by-statement-group basis), while reserving a decision as to whether or not to COMMIT the entire body of work performed until you either COMMIT or ROLLBACK the outermost transaction.

Note: *Interactive DBMS tools, such as the MS-SQL Server Query Analyzer, normally treat statements you enter and execute (by pressing F5 or by selecting the Query menu Execute option, for example) as implicit transactions. As such, if you type*

```
DELETE employees
```

and then tell the Query Analyzer to execute the statement, you cannot then type

```
ROLLBACK
```

and press F5 to undo the work performed by the DELETE statement.

The Query Analyzer executes an implicit COMMIT statement after each sequence of statements (or each individual statement) you tell it to execute. To prevent interactive DBMS tools (such as the MS-SQL Server Query Analyzer) from committing your work each time you tell them to execute one or more statements, you must explicitly mark the start of each transaction by executing a BEGIN TRAN (or BEGIN TRANSACTION) statement. After you do, the Query Analyzer will treat all individual statements and groups of statements you tell it to execute as part of a single, open transaction. You can then either undo all work performed since the most recent BEGIN TRAN statement executing a ROLLBACK statement, or make the work a permanent part of the database by executing a COMMIT statement. (If you close the Query Analyzer session normally prior to executing a COMMIT for each open transaction, the Query Analyzer will execute implicit COMMIT statements to close all open transactions and make any work they performed permanent.)

---

366 Understanding When Constraints Are DEFERRABLE and When They Are Not

In Tip 15, "Understanding Constraints," you learned that a constraint is a limitation you can place on a table column or group of columns to prevent users from inserting data values that violate business rules or database integrity. For example a PRIMARY KEY constraint in the table definition

```
CREATE TABLE offices
  (office_ID       INTEGER PRIMARY KEY,
   manager_ID      INTEGER,
   manager_count   INTEGER,
   employee_count  INTEGER
   sales_quota     MONEY)
```

prevents any UPDATE or INSERT statement from placing a nonunique or NULL value into the OFFICE_ID column of the OFFICES table. While many DBMS products force the system to check all relevant constraints every time a user executes an INSERT, UPDATE, or DELETE statement, the SQL-92 standard includes the capability to *defer* constraint checking.

If a user tells the DBMS to defer constraint checking, the system will not validate modified or newly inserted data values after executing each of the statements in a transaction. Instead, the DBMS will hold its constraint checks in abeyance until the user submits a COMMIT statement to mark the completion of the transaction. At that point, the DBMS will check all deferred constraints. If none of the modified or newly inserted data violates any of the deferred constraints, the DBMS will execute the COMMIT statement and make the transaction's work a permanent part of the database. On the other hand, if proposed changes violate one or more constraints, the DBMS will execute a ROLLBACK and undo any work performed by the transaction.

The ability to defer constraint checking is important when you need to make two or more updates to the database simultaneously in order to maintain its integrity. Suppose, for example, that the database is constrained by the assertion

```
CREATE ASSERTION office_employee_count
  CHECK ((offices.employee_count = COUNT(employees.emp_ID))
    AND  (employees.office_ID = offices.office_ID)
    AND  (employees.status = 'A'))
```

which holds that the value in the EMPLOYEE_COUNT column of each row in the OFFICES table is equal to the number of active employees assigned to the office. Without deferred constraint checking, the OFFICE_EMPLOYEE_COUNT constraint would prevent you from adding a new employee or from changing a terminated employee's STATUS to T. In order to satisfy the constraint at all times, you must add the employee (or change the employee's status) in the EMPLOYEES table at the same time you change the EMPLOYEE_COUNT in the OFFICES table.

Unfortunately, the DBMS can execute only one statement at a time. As a result, if you INSERT a new EMPLOYEES row or UPDATE an employee's STATUS first, the EMPLOYEE_COUNT in the OFFICES table will be wrong. Similarly, if you UPDATE the OFFICES table first, the EMPLOYEE_COUNT for the OFFICE will no longer match the actual count of active employees assigned to the office in the EMPLOYEES table. The obvious way to resolve the problem is to defer constraint checking until the DBMS has executed both statements. At that point, the DBMS can check to make sure that the work of both statements (when taken as a whole) maintains database integrity.

When defining a constraint (in a table or in an ASSERTION), SQL-92 lets you identify the constraint as either DEFERRABLE or NON DEFERRABLE. If a constraint is defined as DEFERRABLE, a user can execute a SET CONSTRAINTS statement (which you will learn about in Tip 367, "Using the SET CONSTRAINTS Statement to Defer DEFERRABLE Constraints Prior to Committing a Transaction") and have the DBMS check the constraint at the completion of a transaction (that is, after executing a set of SQL statements) instead of checking the constraint after each SQL statement the system executes that updates data governed by the constraint. Conversely, checking a constraint defined as NON DEFERRABLE cannot be put off and must be done right after each SQL statement that modifies data in or adds data to any of columns referenced in the constraint.

By default, the DBMS treats each constraint as NON DEFERRABLE unless you explicitly set specify that the constraint is DEFERRABLE when you create or alter it. Moreover, the system sets each constraint as INITIALLY IMMEDIATE, meaning that the system must check the constraint immediately after an SQL statement modifies columns referenced in the constraint. Obviously, a NON DEFERRABLE constraint must also be INITIALLY IMMEDIATE. However, if you define a constraint as DEFERRABLE, you can also set it to INITIALLY DEFERRED, meaning that the constraint will be checked only when a transaction that modifies data it governs executes a COMMIT statement.

In the current example, the OFFICE_EMPLOYEE_COUNT assertion is NON DEFERRABLE and INITIALLY IMMEDIATE by default. In Tip 369, "Adding the Data Control Component to a Visual Basic (VB) Form to Retrieve SQL Table Data," you will learn how to use the SET CONSTRAINTS statement to defer constraint checking for DEFERRABLE constraints.

367 Using the SET CONSTRAINTS Statement to Defer DEFERRABLE Constraints Prior to Committing a Transaction

You can use the SET CONSTRAINTS statement to tell the DBMS to check DEFERRABLE constraints after the system executes all of the statements in a transaction vs. each time it executes one of the statements in the transaction. Suppose, for example, that you have an INVENTORY table created with the CREATE TABLE statement

```
CREATE TABLE inventory
  (item_number INTEGER UNIQUE DEFERRABLE,
   item_cost   MONEY,
   description VARCHAR(30),
   CONSTRAINT non_zero_cost
     CHECK (item_cost > 0) DEFERRABLE)
```

which specifies the UNIQUE constraint on the ITEM_NUMBER column as DEFERRABLE. If you want to make sure that there is a numeric gap of at least 500 between each item number, you might execute and UPDATE statement similar to:

```
UPDATE inventory SET item_number = item_number + 500
```

However, the DBMS will abort the execution of the statement if adding 500 to any of the current values in the ITEM_NUMBER column would cause the insertion of a duplicate value into the column (as would be the case if there is an existing ITEM_NUMBER 101 and an ITEM_NUMBER 601). However, if the DBMS were to check the UNIQUE constraint after updating *all* item numbers, there would be no duplicate values.

If you execute the SET CONSTRAINTS statement

```
SET CONSTRAINTS ALL DEFERRED
```

the DBMS will set all DEFERRABLE constraints to DEFERRED for the remainder of your session. As a result, the UPDATE statement:

```
UPDATE inventory SET item_number = item_number + 500
```

will execute without error because the DBMS will not check the UNIQUE constraint on the ITEM_NUMBER column until it executes the implicit COMMIT statement after updating all rows in the INVENTORY table.

The important thing to understand is that you can defer constraints only until such time as you COMMIT a transaction. At that point, the DBMS always checks all deferred constraints to make sure none of the transaction's work violates database integrity. If the work you want to do requires that the system defer constraint checks for more than a single SQL statement, either submit the statements together as a single batch, or explicitly execute a BEGIN TRANSACTION (or BEGIN TRAN) statement, which you then have to end either by ending your session normally or by executing a COMMIT statement.

In addition to letting you defer the timing of the system's constraint checks for all DEFERRABLE constraints at once, the syntax of the SET CONSTRAINTS statement

```
SET CONSTRAINTS
  {<constraint_name>|ALL} {DEFERRED|IMMEDIATE}
```

also lets you specify individual, named constraints whose constraint checks you want to be IMMEDIATE vs. those whose checks you want to defer. For example, if you want to defer only the NON_ZERO_COST constraint and not UNIQUE constraint on the ITEM_NUMBER column, you would execute the SET CONSTRAINTS statement

```
SET CONSTRAINTS non_zero_cost DEFERRED
```

which names the NON_ZERO_COST constraint as the one you want checked when the transaction is committed.

Note: *Since the SET CONSTRAINTS statement changes the timing of constraints checking for the remainder of your session, be sure to execute the statement*

```
SET CONSTRAINTS ALL IMMEDIATE
```

after you COMMIT the transaction whose work required that you defer constraint checking.

---

368 Creating a Data Source Name (DSN) for an SQL Open Database Connectivity (ODBC) Connection

A *data source name* (DSN), as its name implies, is a name by which a data source is known to the programs running on your computer. After you attach a DSN to a DBMS (like MS-SQL Server, Oracle, or DB2, for example), your applications can use the Open Database Connectivity (ODBC) driver to connect with the DBMS by name and send SQL statements to it. The ODBC driver not only passes your SQL commands to the DBMS for execution, but also returns query results back to your program.

After you install and start an SQL server on an accessible network workstation, server, or standalone personal computer, you can create a DSN for the DBMS by performing the following steps:

1. Open the Control Panel by selecting the Windows Start menu Settings option and clicking your mouse pointer on Control Panel.
2. Double-click your mouse pointer on the ODBC Data Sources icon. Windows will start the ODBC administrator, which will display an ODBC Data Source Administrator dialog box similar to that shown in Figure 368.1.
3. Click your mouse pointer on the Add button. The ODBC administrator will start the Create a New Data Source Wizard, which will prompt you to select the driver to use in communicating with the database.

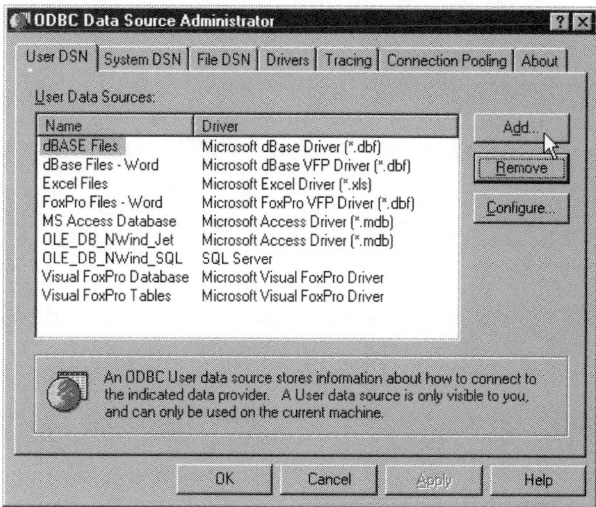

Figure 368.1 The User DSN tab of the ODBC Data Source Administrator dialog box

4. To work with the ODBC driver that communicates with an SQL server, click your mouse pointer on SQL Server in the scroll box on the wizard's Create New Data Source dialog box. Then click your mouse pointer on the Finish button. The wizard will prompt you to describe the SQL server with a dialog box similar to that shown in Figure 368.2.

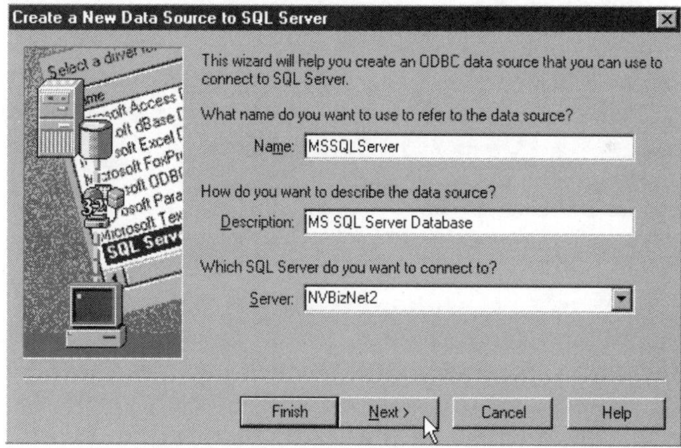

Figure 368.2 The Create a New Data Source Wizard's database description (second) screen

5. Enter the name (the DSN) that you want your applications to use when they need to communicate with the SQL server in the Name field. The DSN you enter does not have to be any particular name. For example, you could use the name of the SQL server or the name of the DSN's default database base on the server. For the current project, enter **MSSQLServer**.

Note: If you plan to set up DSNs for multiple SQL servers, you may want to include the name of the server in each DSN. If you do so, each name will tell you which DSN to use when you want a program to communicate with a specific server. For example, if you have an MS-SQL Server running on an NT server named NVBIZNET2, enter a descriptive DSN similar to ***MSSQLServer_NVBizNet2*** *in the Name field.*

6. Enter a description of the data source data source in the Description field. For the current example, enter **Microsoft SQL Server Database.**
7. Enter the name of the server on which the DBMS is running in the Server field. If the DBMS is running on the computer on which you are defining the DSN, you can click your mouse pointer on the drop-down list button to the right of the Server field and select "(local)".
8. Click your mouse pointer on the Next button. ODBC will prompt you for username and password information as shown in Figure 368.3.

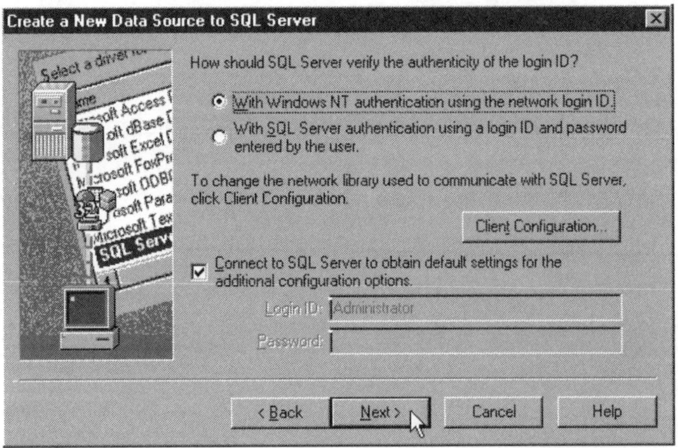

Figure 368.3 The Create a New Data Source Wizard's username/password (third) screen

9. If your MS-SQL Server uses Windows NT Integrated Security (which you learned about in Tip 136, "Understanding MS-SQL Server Standard and Windows NT Integrated Security") you can accept the defaults shown in Figure 368.3. SQL Server will assume that Windows NT authenticated the username/password pair at login. To have the SQL Server authenticate the username/password pair instead, click your mouse pointer on the radio button to the left of With SQL Server Authentication Using a Login ID and Password Entered by the User, and then enter your username and password for the MS-SQL Server in the Login ID and Password fields, respectively.
10. Click your mouse pointer on the Next button. The wizard will try to make a connection to the SQL server you specified in Step 7. If you do not have an SQL server running or if the DBMS does not recognize the username/password pair you entered in Step 9, ODBC will hang momentarily (less than a minute) and then display an error message that explains why the connection attempt failed. To create a DSN, your session must be able

to connect to the DBMS you are trying to name. Therefore, take the necessary corrective actions and then repeat Step 10.

11. After using the username/password pair specified in Step 9 to connect to the DBMS selected in Step 7, the wizard will prompt you for the SQL database defaults with a dialog box similar to that shown in Figure 368.4.

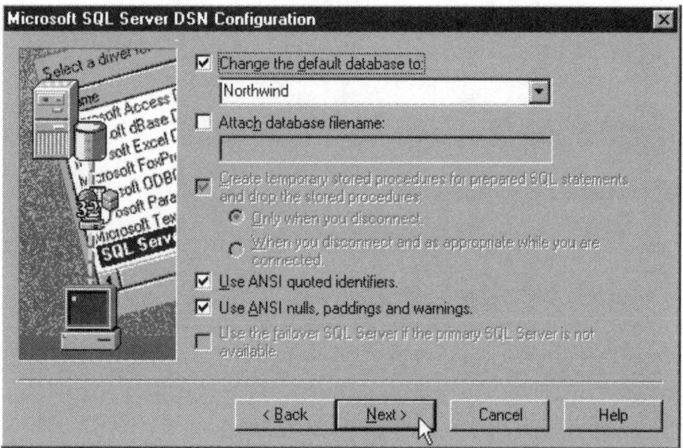

Figure 368.4 The Create a New Data Source Wizard's database defaults (fourth) screen

12. To select the default database for applications using the DSN you are creating to connect to the DBMS, click your mouse pointer on the check box to the left of the Change the Default Database To label until a check mark appears.

13. Click your mouse on the drop-down list button to the right of the default database name field and select the default database from the drop-down list. For the current example, click your mouse pointer on Northwind. Then click your mouse pointer on the Next button.

14. Depending on the version of ODBC running on your computer, the wizard will display one or two more setup screens. Simply click your mouse pointer on the Next button to accept the defaults on each screen until you reach the wizard's final screen, where you will click your mouse pointer on the Finish button. The wizard, in turn, will display an ODBC Microsoft SQL Server Setup dialog box similar to that shown in Figure 368.5.

15. Click your mouse pointer on the Test Data Source button. The wizard will attempt to connect to the DBMS using the settings you entered in Steps 5–13. If the test is unsuccessful, go back through the DSN setup procedure and make any changes called for by the wizard's error dialog boxes, and then repeat Step 15. After the wizard indicates it successfully completed its data source tests, click your mouse pointer on the OK button on the Test Results dialog box.

16. Click your mouse pointer on the OK button near the bottom-right corner of the ODBC Microsoft SQL Server Setup dialog box.

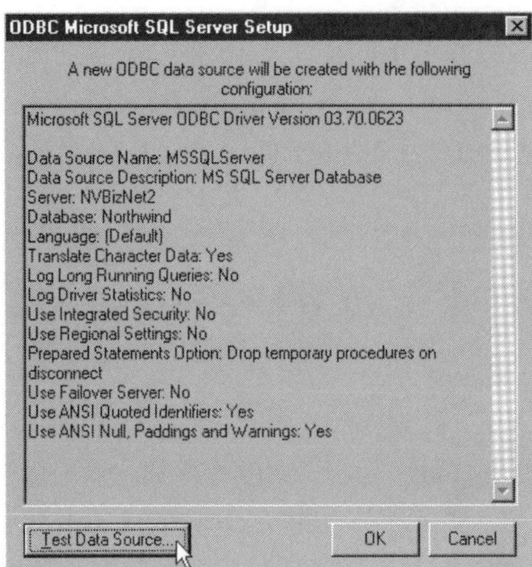

Figure 368.5 The Create a New Data Source Wizard's test ODBC settings (final) screen

After you complete Step 16, the Create a New Data Source Wizard will register the new DSN on your computer and display its name and description in the User Data Sources list box on the ODBC Data Source Administrator dialog box. To exit the ODBC Data Source administrator application, click your mouse pointer on the OK button (first button on the left) in the row of buttons at the bottom of the ODBC Data Source Administrator dialog box.

Note: *To make a DSN that is visible to all users who connect to the machine (vs. only to the username logged in when you create the DSN), add the DSN to the System DSN tab instead of the User DSN tab on the Data Source Administrator dialog box.*

369 Adding the Data Control Component to a Visual Basic (VB) Form to Retrieve SQL Table Data

The Visual Basic (VB) Data Control component supplies subroutines (*methods*) a VB application can use to work with data stored in an SQL database. In fact, after adding the Data Control component to a VB form, your application will be able to perform most data access operations without you having to write any code at all. Moreover, if you bind an MSFlexGrid Control to the Data Control (which you will learn to do in Tip 370, "Adding the MSFlexGrid Control to a Visual Basic (VB) Form to Display SQL Table Data"), your VB program will have all of the tools it needs to retrieve, manipulate, and display data from one or more tables on SQL servers to which you have access rights.

To add a Data Control component to a VB form, perform the following steps:

1. If you have not already done so, start MS-Visual Basic (VB) and open a Standard.EXE project.
2. Double-click your mouse pointer on the Data icon on the VB toolbox along the left-hand side of the VB application window shown in Figure 369.1. VB will add the Data Control component to the currently active form (Form1, in the current example).

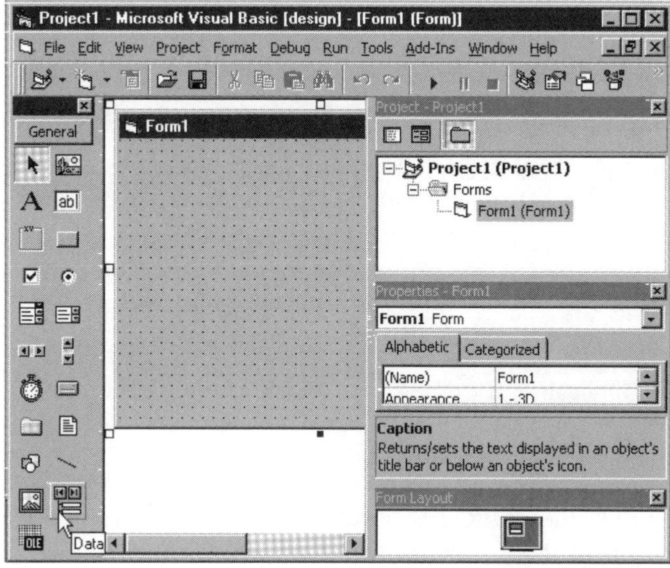

Figure 369.1 The Microsoft Visual Basic 5.0 application window

3. Use your mouse pointer to drag the Data Control toward the lower-left corner of your form. (By the time you finish the current project, which spans Tips 369 and Tip 370, you will have positioned and sized the Data Control below an MSFlexGrid Control as shown in Figure 370.2.)
4. To work with the Data Control properties, select the View menu Properties Window option (or press F4).
5. Click your mouse pointer on the Caption property label. (The Data Control's property labels [and properties] are listed alphabetically on the Alphabetic tab of the Properties window.)
6. Click your mouse pointer in the Caption property field (immediately to the right of the Caption property label), and enter the label you want VB to display on the Data Control. For the current project enter: Product/Supplier in the Caption property field.
7. Click your mouse pointer on the DatabaseName property label. Then click your mouse pointer in the DatabaseName property field and enter the data source name (DSN) for the SQL server with the database you want to access. If the database you want is located on

the SQL Server whose DSN you created (registered) in Tip 368, "Creating a Data Source Name (DSN) for an SQL Open Database Connectivity (ODBC) Connection," enter **MSSQLServer** in the DatabaseName property field.

8. Click your mouse pointer on the Connect property label. Then click your mouse pointer in the Connect property field and enter the information that the ODBC Driver Manager needs to connect with your SQL server in the form:

```
ODBC;UID=<username>;PWD=<password>;DATABASE=<database name>
```

For example, to connect to an SQL server as user KONRAD with password KING and use the NORTHWIND database, you would type

```
ODBC;UID=KONRAD;PWD=KING;DATABASE=NORTHWIND
```

in the Connect properties field. (Be sure to enter you own username and password in place of username KONRAD and password KING shown in the current example.)

Note: *You can omit the DATABASE=<database name> portion of the connect string if the DSN defaults to the database you want to use, or if the DBA has assigned it as the default database for your username.*

When your VB application uses the Data Control component's methods to access the database, Windows will combine the Data Control's connection properties and the DSN connection settings, and attempt to establish a connection with the SQL server. If you omit the username or password (or if the username/password pair you entered in the Connect property field is invalid), the ODBC driver will prompt you to enter the proper username/password pair to log in to the SQL server with the DSN you entered in Step 7.

(Tip 370 will show you how to bind an MSFlexGrid Control to the Data Control so you can display data you retrieve, and Tip 371, "Adding Text and Button Controls to a Visual Basic (VB) Form to Create an Application That Sends a Query to an SQL Server," will show you how to add a text field and Search button for interactive queries to the VB form.)

370 Adding the MSFlexGrid Control to a Visual Basic (VB) Form to Display SQL Table Data

The MSFlexGrid Control gives a VB application the ability to display and work with tabular data. Using the MSFlexGrid Control methods (subroutines), the VB program can sort, merge, and format tables that contain text or graphics images. If you bind the MSFlexGrid Control to the Data Control (you added to a VB form in Tip 369, "Adding the Data Control Component to a Visual Basic (VB) Form to Retrieve SQL Table Data"), you can use it to display read-only data that the Data Control retrieves from SQL server tables.

To add an MSFlexGrid Control to a Visual Basic form, perform the following steps:

1. If you have not already done so, start MS-Visual Basic (VB), open a Standard.EXE project and add a Data Control to the form (by following the procedure in Tip 369).
2. To add the MSFlexGrid Control component to your project, right-click your mouse pointer on the project toolbox (along the left-hand side of the VB application window) and select Components from the pop-up menu. VB, in turn, will display a Components dialog box similar to that shown in Figure 370.1.

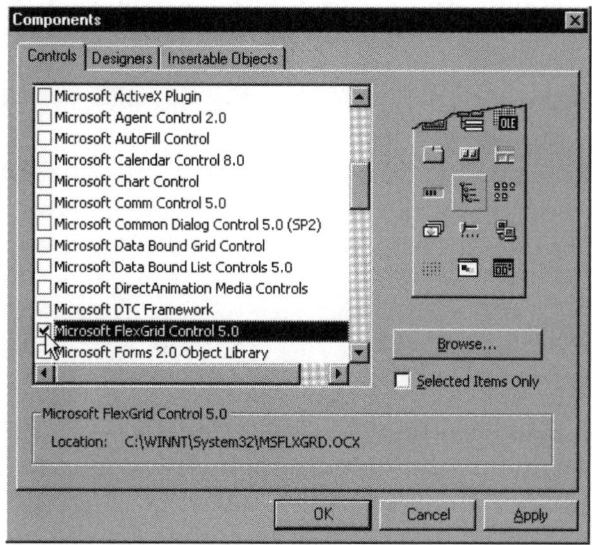

Figure 370.1 The Microsoft Visual Basic 5.0 Components dialog box

3. Use the scroll bar to the right of the Components list box on the Controls tab to scroll the Control Components list until you see the Microsoft FlexGrid Control. Then click your mouse pointer on the check box to the left of Microsoft FlexGrid Control 5.0 until the check mark appears. (Select the latest version of the MSFlexGrid Control available on your system.)
4. Click your mouse pointer on the OK button near the bottom center of the Components dialog box. VB will return to the VB application window and add the MSFlexGrid Control as the last control component in the VB toolbox.
5. Double-click your mouse pointer on the MSFlexGrid icon to add an MSFlexGrid Control to your VB form.
6. To work with the MSFlexGrid Control properties, select the View menu Properties Window option (or press F4).
7. Click your mouse pointer on the DataSource property label. (The MSFlexGrid Control's property labels [and properties] are listed alphabetically on the Alphabetic tab of the Properties window.)

8. Click your mouse pointer on the drop-down list button to the right of the DataSource property field (immediately to the right of the DataSource property label) and select the name of the Data Control that will supply data to the MSFlexGrid. For the current project, you added a single Data Control named Data1 to the VB form in Tip 369. As such, select Data1 from the drop-down list.
9. Right-click your mouse pointer on the MSFlexGrid Control (on your VB form) and select Properties from the pop-up menu. VB will display the Properties Pages dialog box.
10. Set the number of rows and columns of data you want the MSFlexGrid Control to display. Make the number of columns equal to the number of columns you expect the SQL query (which you will learn how to enter and execute in Tip 371) to return. For the current project, enter **6** in the Rows field and **4** in the Columns field on the General tab of the Properties Pages dialog box.
11. Enter the number of (fixed) headings columns and rows the MSFlexGrid is to display in the Fixed Cols field. For the current project, enter **1** in the Fixed Rows field and **0** in the Fixed Cols field. (You don't have to enter the column headings; VB will fill them in at run time.)
12. To let the user resize the columns while the VB application is running, click your mouse pointer on the drop-down list box to the right of the AllowUserResizing field and select 1-Columns from the drop-down list.
13. Click your mouse pointer on the OK button at the bottom left of the Properties Pages dialog box. VB will return to the VB design application window.

After you complete Step 13, your VB form will contain an MSFlexGrid control bound to a Data Control (named Data1, which you added to the VB form in Tip 369).

Now, use your mouse pointer to arrange the controls and size them (by using the mouse pointer on the each control's sizing handles), such that your VB form appears similar to that shown in Figure 370.2.

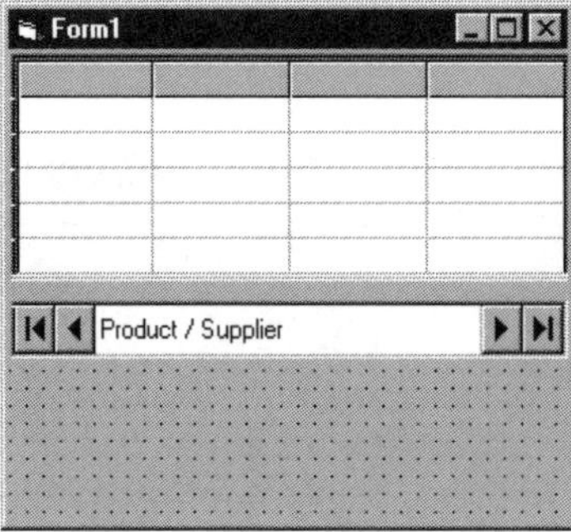

Figure 370.2 A VB form with an MSFlexGrid Control (at the top) and Data Control (near the bottom)

You will learn how to add a text field and a Search button for interactive queries to the VB form in Tip 371.

371 Adding Text and Button Controls to a Visual Basic (VB) Form to Create an Application That Sends a Query to an SQL Server

In Tip 369, "Adding the Data Control Component to a Visual Basic (VB) Form to Retrieve SQL Table Data," you learned how to place a Data Control on a VB form to give your application the methods (subroutine calls) it needs to retrieve data from an SQL Server. Then Tip 370, "Adding the MSFlexGrid Control to a Visual Basic (VB) Form to Display SQL Table Data," showed you how to add an MSFlexGrid Control to display the data retrieved. Now you need only add a Text Control that lets a user enter an SQL query and Button Controls that tell VB to send the query to the SQL Server, and you will have a VB application that can query an SQL DBMS and display its data.

Note: *The remainder of this tip assumes that you currently have VB open in design mode with a single-form project that has a Data Control from the procedure in Tip 369 and an MSFlexGrid Control from the procedure in Tip 370.*

To add Text and Button Controls to a VB form, perform the following steps:

1. Double-click your mouse pointer on the TextBox icon in the VB toolbox along the left side of the VB application window. (If you do not recognize the TextBox icon, move your mouse pointer over each icon in the VB toolbox and let VB display the name of the control the icon represents.)
2. To work with the TextBox Control properties, select the View menu Properties Window option (or press F4).
3. Click your mouse pointer on the "(Name)" property label. (The TextBox Control's property labels [and properties] are listed alphabetically on the Alphabetic tab of the Properties window.)
4. Click your mouse pointer in the "(Name)" property field (immediately to the right of the "(Name)" property label) and enter the name you want to use when referring to the contents of the form's text box. For the current project, enter **SupplierName** in the "(Name)" property field.
5. Click your mouse pointer on the Text property label. Then click your mouse pointer in the Text property field, and delete its contents.
6. To add a CommandButton Control to the VB form, double-click your mouse pointer on the CommandButton icon in the VB toolbox along the left side of the VB application window.
7. To work with the CommandButton Control properties, select the View menu Properties Window option (or press F4).

8. Click your mouse pointer on the "(Name)" property label. Then click your mouse pointer in the "(Name)" property field and enter the name you want to use when referring to a mouse pointer click on the button. For the current project, enter **SearchButton** in the "(Name)" property field.
9. Click your mouse pointer on the Caption property label. Then click your mouse pointer in the Caption property field, and enter the label you want VB to put on the button. For the current project, enter **Search** in the Caption property field.
10. Repeat Steps 6–9, only this time, enter **CloseButton** in the "(Name)" property field in Step 8, and enter **Close** in the Caption property field in Step 9.

After you complete Step 10 (for the second time), position and size the two CommandButton Controls and the TextBox control on the VB form as shown in Figure 371.1.

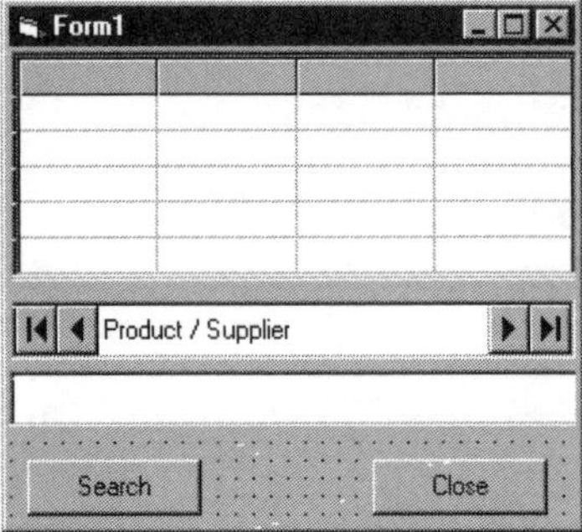

Figure 371.1 A VB SQL query form with a Data Control, an MSFlexGrid Control, a TextBox Control, and two CommandButton Controls

Now that you have all of the controls on the VB form, all that is left to do is to write the code you want the computer to execute when a user clicks the mouse pointer on each of the command buttons. Suppose, for example, that you want the Search button to send the SELECT statement

```
SELECT productid 'Product ID', productname 'Description',
  companyname 'Supplier', s.supplierid 'ID'
FROM products p, suppliers s
WHERE p.supplierid = s.supplierid
AND companyname LIKE '%:SupplierName%'
ORDER BY supplier, description
```

which lists all products (in the PRODUCTS table) supplied by the supplier whose name (or partial name) the user entered in the form's SupplierName field (its TextBox Control) to the SQL server.

To add code to the SEARCH button, double-click your mouse pointer on the CommandButton Control with the "Search" label to open the VB code panel to the SearchButton method (subroutine), and enter the VB code as shown in Figure 371.2. To add code to the Search button, double-click your mouse pointer on the CommandButton Control with the Search label to open the VB code panel to the SearchButton method (subroutine), and enter the VB code as shown in Figure 371.2.

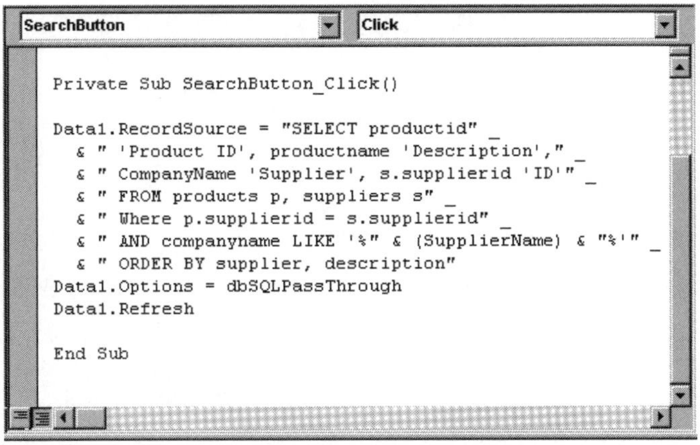

```
SearchButton                    Click

Private Sub SearchButton_Click()

Data1.RecordSource = "SELECT productid" _
  & " 'Product ID', productname 'Description'," _
  & " CompanyName 'Supplier', s.supplierid 'ID'" _
  & " FROM products p, suppliers s" _
  & " Where p.supplierid = s.supplierid" _
  & " AND companyname LIKE '%" & (SupplierName) & "%'" _
  & " ORDER BY supplier, description"
Data1.Options = dbSQLPassThrough
Data1.Refresh

End Sub
```

Figure 371.2 The code pane of the VB application window with the code for the CommandButton Control named SearchButton

As a quick explanation of the Search button's code, consider the following:

- Data1 is the name you gave the Data Control in Tip 369.
- The SQL statement you want the SQL server to execute must be placed in the Data Control's RecordSource property.
- Placing the enumerated constant dbSQLPassThrough in the Data Control's Options property tells the Jet database engine not to parse the query or check its syntax, and simply to pass it on to the SQL server for processing.
- The Data Control's Refresh method call sends the query in the RecordSource property to the SQL server and then accepts and displays the query results in the rows and columns that make up the MSFlexGrid Control.

Select the View menu Object option to redisplay the VB form in the VB application window. Then double-click your mouse pointer on the CommandButton Control with the Close label to edit the code VB will execute when the user clicks the mouse pointer on the Close button. For the current project, enter

```
Private Sub CloseButton_Click()
Unload Me
End Sub
```

in the VB Code pane of the VB application window. Then select the View menu Object option to redisplay the VB form you created.

Finally, take your new VB application for a test drive by selecting the Run menu Start option! After the VB interpreter displays your form on the screen, enter a supplier's name into the form's text box and then click your mouse pointer on the Search button. For example, to display all products supplied by companies with "new" in their names, enter "new" into the text box and click your mouse pointer on the Search button. The VB application (you wrote) will respond by displaying products and suppliers as shown in Figure 371.3.

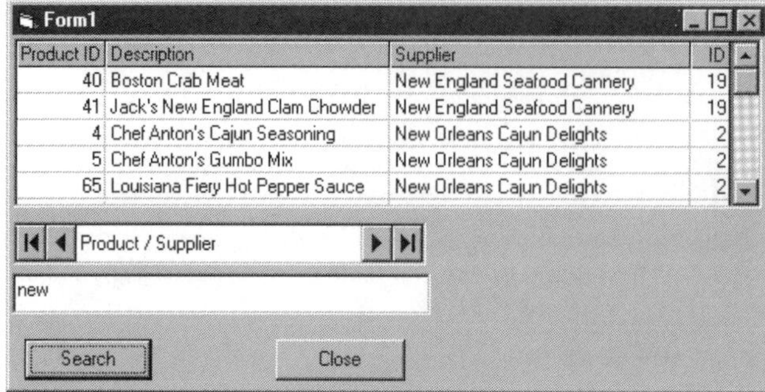

Figure 371.3 VB application window with the results of an SQL query of the Northwind database for suppliers with "new" in the company name

To end the VB application gracefully, click your mouse pointer on its Close button.

372 Creating a Simple C++ Shell for Use in Communicating with an SQL Server

As of this writing, C is still the language of choice when writing Windows applications, especially those that communicate with MS-SQL Server and other DBMS products. However, as you saw in Tips 369–371, Visual Basic's (almost) seamless interface with data sources (such as SQL servers) and ease of use are bound to give C some serious competition in the near future. This tip shows you how to write a C main program shell that you will use to connect to and communicate with an SQL server in Tips 373–383.

If you are at all like me, the first thing that you want to do when learning a new programming language is to print something to the screen. After you get over the hurdle of writing that "first program," you know that any future development is just a matter of looking up the proper function calls that you need and adding what you need to a "working" program shell that you wrote previously. Therefore, let us start with the "Hello World!" example that you have most likely seen and perhaps written several times before.

When written for a Windows environment, the MS-DOS "Hello World!" program

```
#include <stdio.h>
void main()
{  printf ("Hello world!\n");
   return;  }
```

becomes:

```
#include <windows.h>
int WINAPI WinMain(HINSTANCE hInstance,
                   HINSTANCE hPrevInstance,
                   LPSTR     lpCmdLine,
                   int       iCmdShow)
{
 MessageBox (0,"Hello World!","1001 SQL Tips - Tip 372",
     MB_OK)
 return 0;
}
```

The first statement in the program (#include <windows.h>) tells the compiler to include the WINDOWS.H header file that comes with every C programming environment for Windows. WINDOWS.H, in turn, has #INCLUDE statements (in the form #include <filename>.h) that tell the compiler to include additional header files that contain declarations of Windows functions, structures, data types, and numeric constants.

Every C program has a "main" entry point at which the program begins execution. When Windows starts the compiled program (the .EXE file), the system first executes a few lines of "startup" code inserted by the compiler. The compiler's startup code, in turn, calls the *main* function written by the programmer. For MS-DOS programs, the main entry point is the function main(); for Windows programs, the main entry point is always called WinMain.

In the current example, the "Hello World!" program uses the WINAPI calling sequence and returns a value of data type integer (int) to the Windows operating system when the program ends. (The last statement in the program [return 0;] tells the main function [WinMain] to return the value 0 to Windows after the program completes its execution.)

The first parameter that Windows passes to the "Hello World!" program, hInstance, is the *instance handle*, a number that uniquely identifies the program to the Windows operating system. Think of hInstance as the program's process ID (or PID), a unique number that a multitasking operating system such as Windows NT assigns to each of the programs (or tasks) that it is running concurrently. If you start multiple copies (or instances) of the same program, Windows assigns each instance a unique instance handle and then uses the hInstance parameter to pass the value of the handle to the application's WinMain routine.

The second parameter, hPrevInstance, became obsolete with Windows 95 and is retained for backward compatibility. If Microsoft were to eliminate the second parameter, all C programs running on a Windows/NT platform would have to be recompiled and redistributed. (Can you imagine the logistics of such an undertaking?). hPrevInstance *was* the instance handle of the most recent copy of the program started prior to the current instance that was still active. If no other copies of the program were running, Windows set hPrevInstance to either 0 or NULL. Windows versions starting with Windows 95 and NT currently set hPrevInstance NULL, regardless of the number of copies of the program currently running in sessions under the operating system.

lpCmdLine is a long (32-bit) pointer to a NULL-terminated character string that contains any command-line arguments that Windows wants passed to the program. For example, if you start the program TIP372.EXE by typing

```
TIP372 Parameters for startup
```

at the MS-DOS command line or in the Start menu Run option's dialog box, Windows will pass a pointer to the memory location in which it has stored the character string "Parameters for startup" to the program.

The final parameter, iCmdShow, tells the application how the user wants Windows to display the window for the session in which the program is running. The different values for the iCmdShow parameter are listed in the ShowWindow() Commands section of the WINRESRC.H header file (which is included in the "Hello World!" program by an #INCLUDE statement in the WINDOWS.H header file). Typically, iCmdShow will have a value of 1 (SW_SHOWNORMAL), to run the program in an active, normal window displayed on the Windows desktop, or 7 (SW_SHOWMINNOACTIVE), to run the application minimized as an icon on the taskbar.

Do not worry too much about the only statement in the example program that does any work:

```
MessageBox (0,"Hello World!","1001 SQL Tips - Tip 372",
     MB_OK)
```

The Windows MessageBox function simply displays the message "Hello World!" on the screen in a (you guessed it!) Windows message box. As you write more C programs, you cannot help but memorize the required parameters for many functions that you often use. In (almost) all cases, when you call a function, you will not concern yourself with knowing *how* the function does what it does. Instead, you will need to know only what the function does (instead of how it does it) and what parameters you need to pass when you call the function.

If you work the project in Tips 373–383, you will build on the basic C program shell used as an example in this tip so that you end up with a working application that you can use to access any SQL DBMS with an ODBC driver and a defined Data Source Name (DSN).

Note: *C is case-sensitive. As such, the function WinMain is not the same as winmain or WINMAIN. Similarly, MessageBox is not the same as MESSAGEBOX or messagebox. Therefore, be very careful when you declare types, variables, functions, and so on, and when you make function calls. For example, if you attempt to compile the "Hello World!" program in the current example using WINMAIN instead of WinMain as the main entry point, the compiler will abort with an error because it did not find the entry point WinMain, which is the main function for all Windows C programs.*

---

373 Using SQLAllocEnv and SQLFreeEnv to Allocate and Release ODBC Environment Resources

Open Database Connectivity (ODBC) is a set of functions (applications program interface [API] calls) that your programs can use to work with data in any database for which there is an ODBC driver. Because you have to know only which function calls perform what tasks, the ODBC call-level interface frees you from having the know the specifics of how each DBMS that you want to use retrieves, updates, and stores its data. You need specify only the function (or work) that you want the DBMS to perform by calling the appropriate ODBC function. The function then lets the specific ODBC driver for the DBMS that you want to access take care of the "details" involved in executing your requests.

Prior to calling any other ODBC function, an application must call SQLAllocEnv to allocate memory for an ODBC environment handle and initialize the ODBC call-level interface. Note that the parameter passed to SQLAllocEnv in the following example program is the memory address in which the function is to store the actual physical address (the handle) of the program's ODBC environment.

```
#INCLUDE <stdio.h>
#include <windows.h>
#INCLUDE <sqlext.h>
int WINAPI WinMain(HINSTANCE hInstance,
                   HINSTANCE hPrevInstance,
                   LPSTR     lpCmdLine,
                   int       iCmdShow)
{
 HENV    henv;                //pointer to a memory location
 RETCODE retcode;             //signed short (16-Bit) integer
 LPSTR retcode_text = " ";    //character string

 retcode = SQLAllocEnv(&henv);//allocate environment handle
 if (retcode == SQL_SUCCESS)
   {
     /* CONNECT TO SQL SERVER & PERFORM WORK HERE */

    SQLFreeEnv(henv);//free environment handle & its memory
    }
 else
   sprintf(retcode_text,"Error on SQLAllocEnv = %d",
     retcode);

/* display any error messages */
 if (strcmp(retcode_text," ") != 0)
   MessageBox (0, retcode_text, "Connect to MSSQLServer",
     MB_OK|MB_ICONERROR);

 return 0;
}
```

In the current example, if SQLAllocEnv is successful in allocating and initializing a memory area for the ODBC environment, the pointer henv will contain for use by the application's functions the memory address (or handle) of the the application's ODBC environment. (For example, in Tip 374, "Using SQLAllocConnect and SQLFreeConnect to Allocate and Release Connection Handles and Memory Resources," you will pass the ODBC environment handle to the SQLAllocConnect function when you call it to initialize the connection parameter portion of the ODBC environment.)

Notice that the C program in the example tells the compiler to include the header file, SQLEXT.H (in addition to STDIO.H and WINDOWS.H). The SQLEXT.H header file, in turn, contains type definitions and #INCLUDE statements that tell the compiler to include the header files SQL.H, SQLTYPES.H, and SQLUCODE.H. Taken together, the four header files provide your C applications with the data types, function calls, structures, and constants they need to access data on SQL servers.

374 Using SQLAllocConnect and SQLFreeConnect to Allocate and Release Connection Handles and Memory Resources

SQLAllocConnect and SQLFreeConnect are similar in function to SQLAllocEnv and SQLFreeEnv, respectively. When your program establishes a connection to an SQL server, the ODBC driver must keep track of several details about your session. For example, because each command sent to the SQL server must be validated by the DBMS security mechanism, the ODBC driver keeps each connection's username and password on file. That way, the driver can pass the username/password pair along to the DBMS when its sends your statement to the server for execution. Similarly, the ODBC driver must keep track of any statements the DBMS is currently executing for a session and whether the session has any open transactions.

The ODBC driver stores all of the information it needs about each connection within a portion of the ODBC environment space (the area in memory) that you allocated by calling the SQLAllocEnv function (in Tip 373, "Using SQLAllocEnv and SQLFreeEnv to Allocate and Release ODBC Environment Resources"). While the SQLAllocEnv function maps out a portion of the computer's total memory for use by the ODBC driver interface between your application and the DBMS, the SQLAllocConnect function maps out a portion of the memory allocated by SQLAllocEnv to use as storage for details about each of the ODBC connections that the program makes to a DBMS. When you call SQLAllocConnect, the function not only maps out a portion of the ODBC environment (memory) space, but the function also returns a pointer (called the connection handle) that gives your program the starting memory address at which it can find the connection settings area within the ODBC environment area in memory.

The syntax of the SQLAllocConnect function call is

```
RETCODE SQLAllocConnect(henv, phdbc)
```

where:

- **henv** is the environment handle—that is, the pointer to the memory location where the program can find the memory allocated for use as the ODBC environment by the SQLAllocEnv function (which you learned about in Tip 373).
- **phdbc** is the database connection handle—that is, the pointer to the memory location where the program can find the settings and information on a particular connection with the DBMS.

In the example program from Tip 373, you would call SQLAllocConnect to establish a connection handle with a statement similar to this:

```
retcode = SQLAllocConnect(henv, &hdbc);
```

Notice that (as was the case with SQLAllocEnv) the second parameter is the memory address of the hdbc (pointer) variable (defined in the program with the statement: HDBC hdbc;). The SQLAllocConnect function will place the actual memory location of the connection area (the connection handle) in the hdbc variable.

Just as your application should call the SQLFreeEnv function to release memory allocated by the SQLAllocEnv function when it no longer needs it, your program should call the SQLFreeConnect function to release memory allocated by SQLAllocConnect when you no longer need the memory to hold connection information.

The syntax of the SQLFreeConnect function call is

```
RETCODE SQLFreeConnect(hdbc)
```

where:

- **hdbc** is the connection handle (the pointer to the starting memory location) of the connection area allocated by calling the SQLAllocConnect function.

If you add the SQLAllocConnect and SQLFreeConnect functions, the C program started in Tip 373 will look like:

```
#INCLUDE <stdio.h>
#include <windows.h>
#INCLUDE <sqlext.h>
int WINAPI WinMain(HINSTANCE hInstance,
                   HINSTANCE hPrevInstance,
                   LPSTR     lpCmdLine,
                   int       iCmdShow)
{
 HENV     henv;                 //HENV is data type: void*
 HDBC     hdbc;                 //HDBC is data type: void*
```

```
 RETCODE retcode;            //signed short (16-Bit) integer
 LPSTR retcode_text = " "; //character string

 retcode = SQLAllocEnv(&henv);
 if (retcode == SQL_SUCCESS)
   {                            //allocate connection handle
    retcode = SQLAllocConnect(henv,&hdbc);
    If (retcode == SQL_SUCCESS)
      {
       /* CONNECT TO SQL SERVER & PERFORM WORK HERE */

       SQLFreeConnect(hdbc);
      }
    else
      sprintf(retcode_text,"Error on SQLAllocConnect = %d",
        retcode);

    SQLFreeEnv(henv);
    }
 else
   sprintf(retcode_text,"Error on SQLAllocEnv = %d",
     retcode);

/* display any error messages */
 if (strcmp(retcode_text," ") != 0)
   MessageBox (0, retcode_text, "Connect to MSSQLServer",
     MB_OK|MB_ICONERROR);

 return 0;
}
```

375 Using SQLSetConnectOption to Set a Session Option for an ODBC Connection with an SQL Server

After you call the SQLAllocConnect function to allocate a connection handle and a memory area for a DBMS connection, you can use the SQLSetConnectOption function to set the connection's options summarized in Table 375. The syntax of the SQLSetConnectOption function call is:

```
RETCODE SQLSetConnectOption(hdbc, wOption, dwOpVal)
```

Where:

- **hdbc** is the connection handle (the pointer for the starting memory location) of the connection area of the ODBC environment (memory) space returned by SQLAllocConnect.
- **wOption** is one of the connection options shown in Table 375.1.
- **dwOpVal** is the value setting for wOption. Depending on which option you are calling SQLSetConnectOption to set, dwOpVal will be either a 32-bit integer or a null-terminated character string.

Your program must call the SQLConnectOption function once for each of the session's connection options that you want to set.

wOption (Connection Options)	***dwOpVal (Connection Option Settings)***
SQL_ACCESS_MODE	SQL_MODE_READ_ONLY, SQL_MODE_READ_WRITE.
SQL_AUTOCOMMIT	SQL_AUTO_COMMIT_OFF, SQL_AUTO_COMMIT_ON.
SQL_CURRENT_QUALIFIER	A null-terminated character string that contains the data source qualifier. On MS-SQL Server, data source qualifiers are the database names. Therefore, the driver will send a USE <database> statement to the DBMS, where <database> is the string supplied in dwOpVal.
SQL_LOGIN_TIMEOUT	The number of seconds to wait for the DBMS to complete a login request. A value of 0 disables the timeout, and the driver will wait indefinitely for the DBMS to complete the login request.
SQL_ODBC_CURSORS	SQL_CUR_USE_IF_NEEDED, SQL_CUR_USE_ODBC, SQL_CUR_USE_DRIVER.
SQL_OPT_TRACE	SQL_OPT_TRACE_OFF, SQL_OPT_TRACE_ON.
SQL_OPT_TRACEFILE	The name of the trace file in a null-terminated character string.
SQL_PACKET_SIZE	The network packet size, in bytes.
SQL_QUIET_MODE	The handle of the window in which the ODBC driver is to display dialog boxes. If set equal to a NULL pointer, the ODBC driver will not display any dialog boxes.

wOption (Connection Options)	*dwOpVal (Connection Option Settings)*
SQL_TRANSLATE_DLL	A null-terminated character string with the name of the DLL that contains the functions SQLDriverToDataSource and SQLDataSourceToDriver that the ODBC driver is to load and use to perform tasks such as character set translation.
SQL_TRANSLATE_OPTION	A 32-bit integer value that the ODBC driver is to pass to the translation DLL.
SQL_TXN_ISOLATION	SQL_TXN_READ_UNCOMMITTED, SQL_TXN_READ_COMMITTED, SQL_TXN_REPEATABLE_READ, SQL_TXN_SERIALIZABLE, SQL_TXN_VERSIONING.

Table 375.1 SQLSetConnectionOption Function Options and Option Values

When you call the SQLSetConnectOption by executing the statement

```
retcode = SQLSetConnectOption(hdbc, SQL_AUTOCOMMIT,
            SQL_AUTOCOMMIT_ON);
```

the ODBC driver sets the option for all active statements and for all subsequent statements that you send to the DBMS for processing using ODBC function calls. (The code sample in Tip 376, "Using SQLConnect and SQLDisconnect to Establish and Terminate a DBMS Session," uses SQLSetConnectionOption to set the connection timeout value to 15 seconds.)

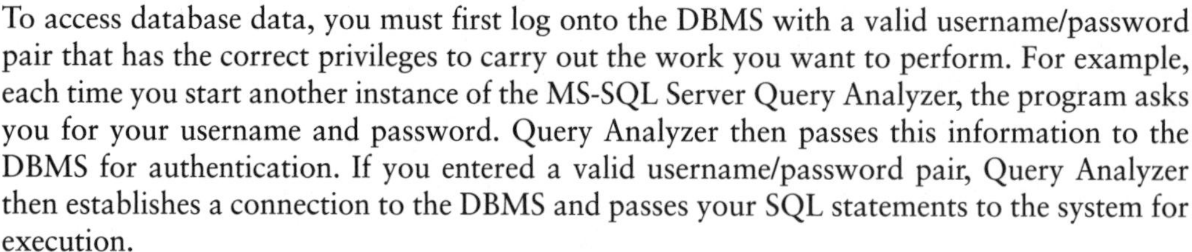

376 Using SQLConnect and SQLDisconnect to Establish and Terminate a DBMS Session

To access database data, you must first log onto the DBMS with a valid username/password pair that has the correct privileges to carry out the work you want to perform. For example, each time you start another instance of the MS-SQL Server Query Analyzer, the program asks you for your username and password. Query Analyzer then passes this information to the DBMS for authentication. If you entered a valid username/password pair, Query Analyzer then establishes a connection to the DBMS and passes your SQL statements to the system for execution.

The SQLConnect function lets your C program establish a connection with the DBMS. After establishing a connection with an SQL server, your application can send SQL statements to the DBMS for execution.

The syntax of the SQLConnect function call is

```
RETCODE SQLConnect(hdbc, szDSN, cbDSN, szUID, cbUID,
         szAUthStr, cbAuthStr)
```

where:

- **hdbc** is the connection handle (pointer value) returned by the SQLAllocConnect function.
- **szDSN** is a null-terminated string with the Data Source Name (DSN) that the ODBC driver is to use when connecting to the DBMS.
- **cbDSN** is the length of the DSN in the szDSN parameter.
- **szUID** is a null-terminated string with the username to use when logging onto the DBMS.
- **cbUID** is the length of the username in the cbDSN parameter.
- **szAuthStr** is the user's authentication string (password).
- **cbAuthStr** is the length of the password in the szAuthStr parameter.

Therefore, to log into the default database associated with the DSN MSSQLServer as username konrad with password king, you would first place the parameter values (other than hdbc) into appropriately typed variables such as

```
unsigned char data_source_name[]="MSSQLServer";
unsigned char user_ID[]="konrad";
unsigned char password[]="king";
```

and then call the SQLConnect function as:

```
retcode = SQLConnect(hdbc, data_source_name, SQL_NTS,
            user_ID, SQL_NTS, password, SQL_NTS);
```

Note: *The value of SQL_NTS (or SQL Null Terminated String) is defined as the constant –3 in the SQL.H. If you set any (or all) of the character string length parameters (cbDSN, cbUID, cbAuthStr) to SQL_NTS, the system will determine the length of characters in the strings that you passed in the other parameters for you.*

To terminate a session on the DBMS, call the SQLDisconnect function and pass it the connection handle of the session that you want to end. For example, in the current example, you would have the program execute the statement

```
SQLDisconnect (hdbc);
```

when the application completes the work that you want it to perform.

After adding function calls SQLConnect and SQLDisconnect to create and break a connection to a DBMS to the example program started in Tip 373, "Using SQLAllocEnv and SQLFreeEnv to Allocate and Release ODBC Environment Resources," the application will be able to take all of the steps necessary to connect to a DBMS and then to disconnect and free all handles and memory allocated to the ODBC driver:

```
#INCLUDE <stdio.h>
#include <windows.h>
#INCLUDE <sqlext.h>
int WINAPI WinMain(HINSTANCE hInstance,
                   HINSTANCE hPrevInstance,
                   LPSTR     lpCmdLine,
                   int       iCmdShow)
{
 HENV    henv;              //HENV is data type: void*
 HDBC    hdbc;              //HDBC is data type: void*
 RETCODE retcode;           //signed short (16-Bit) integer
 LPSTR retcode_text = " "; //character string
 unsigned char data_source_name[]="MSSQLServer";
 unsigned char user_ID[]="konrad";
 unsigned char password[]="king";

 retcode = SQLAllocEnv(&henv);
 if (retcode == SQL_SUCCESS)
   {
    retcode = SQLAllocConnect(henv, &hdbc);
    If (retcode == SQL_SUCCESS)
      {                                  //connect to a DBMS
       retcode = SQLConnect(hdbc,data_source_name,SQL_NTS,
                   user_ID,SQL_NTS,password,SQL_NTS);

       if (retcode == SQL_SUCCESS ||
           retcode == SQL_SUCCESS_WITH_INFO)
          {
  /* SEND STATEMENTS FOR EXECUTION BY DBMS HERE(Tip 377) */

          MessageBox(0,"Connection to MSSQLServer, OK!",
            "Connect to MSSQLServer", MB_OK);

          SQLDisconnect(hdbc); //disconnect from DBMS
          }
       else
         sprintf(retcode_text,"Error on SQLConnect = %d",
           retcode)

       SQLFreeConnect(hdbc);
      }
    else
      sprintf(retcode_text,"Error on SQLAllocConnect = %d",
        retcode);

    SQLFreeEnv(henv);
```

```
    }
  else
    sprintf(retcode_text,"Error on SQLAllocEnv = %d",
      retcode);

/* display any error messages */
  if (strcmp(retcode_text," ") != 0)
    MessageBox (0, retcode_text, "Connect to MSSQLServer",
      MB_OK|MB_ICONERROR);

  return 0;
}
```

In this tip, you completed the C program that lets you connect to any DBMS that has a defined Data Source Name (DSN) and an ODBC driver. In Tip 377, "Using SQLAllocStmt and SQLFreeStmt to Allocate and Release SQL Statement Handles and Memory Resources," you will learn how to send statements to the DBMS for execution.

377 Using SQLAllocStmt and SQLFreeStmt to Allocate and Release SQL Statement Handles and Memory Resources

After you make the necessary function calls in your C program to establish a connection with an SQL server (as you learned to do in Tips 373–376), you can use the connection to send SQL statements to the DBMS for execution. However, before you can call SQLExecDirect to send a command to the SQL server, you must call the SQLAllocStmt function to reserve a memory area for SQL statement information and a statement handle that points to the area.

The syntax of the SQLAllocStmt function header is

```
RETCODE SQLAllocStmt (hdbc, phstmt)
```

where:

- **hdbc** is the handle of the connection through which you plan to send SQL statements to the DBMS. (You learned how to call the SQLAllocConnect function to allocate a connection handle in Tip 374, "Using SQLAllocConnect and SQLFreeConnect to Allocate and Release Connection Handles and Memory Resources.")
- **phstmt** is a pointer to the memory address in which the system is to store the statement handle. (The statement handle is a pointer to the memory location where the program can find information about the statement such as its current processing status, error codes and messages, the name of the statement's cursor, and the number of columns it contains.)

The value of the RETCODE returned by the function can be SQL_SUCCESS, SQL_SUCCESS_WITH_INFO, SQL_INVALID_HANDLE, or SQL_ERROR.

As such, when your application calls the SQLAllocStmt function with a statement such as

```
retcode = SQLAllocStmt (hdbc, &hstmt);
```

the ODBC driver allocates memory for statement information and stores the value of the statement handle (the pointer to the statement memory area) in the variable hstmt.

Note: *Before calling the SQLAllocStmt function, your program must call SQLAllocConnect to allocate a connection handle (hdbc in the current example) and then use the connection handle to establish a connection to the DBMS by calling SQLConnect.*

When your program is finished sending SQL statements to the DBMS, call SQLFreeStmt to release the statement handle and its memory resources. The syntax of the SQLFreeStmt function header is

```
SQLFreeStmt(hstmt,uiOption)
```

where:

- **hstmt** is the statement handle (which you called with the SQLAllocStmt function call).
- **uiOption** is one of the following options:

  SQL_CLOSE—Closes the cursor associated with the statement handle hstmt and discards all pending results.

  SQL_DROP—Releases the hstmt statement handle, closes the cursor (discards all of its pending results), and frees all memory resources associated with the handle.

  SQL_UNBIND—Releases all column buffers bound to the hstmt statement handle by an SQLBindCol function call.

  SQL_RESET_PARAMS—Releases all parameter buffers bound to the hstmt statement handle by an SQLBindParameter function call.

Review the C source code in Tip 378, "Using SQLExecDirect to Send an SQL Statement to a DBMS for Execution," for an example of how to use both the SQLAllocStmt and the SQLFreeStmt functions. The important thing to understand now is that your program must make an SQLAllocStmt call to allocate a statement handle and an area in memory through which the ODBC driver can pass SQL statements to the DBMS. Moreover, the program can allocate the statement handle (and memory resources) only *after* the application successfully allocates a connection handle (see Tip 373, "Using SQLAllocEnv and SQLFreeEnv to Allocate and Release ODBC Environment Resources") and uses it to establish a connection with the DBMS (see Tip 376, "Using SQLConnect and SQLDisconnect to Establish and Terminate a DBMS Session").

378 Using SQLExecDirect to Send an SQL Statement to a DBMS for Execution

After you allocate a statement handle by calling SQLAllocStmt, you can call the SQLExecDirect function to send an SQL statement to the data source (that is, the DBMS to which you already have a connection). The advantage of using the ODBC interface is that you only have to make sure that your SQL statement is syntactically correct. The ODBC driver will modify the statement to conform to the particular form of SQL used by the data source before it sends it to the target DBMS for execution.

The syntax of the SQLExecDirect function is

```
RETCODE SQLExecDirect(hstmt, szSQLStmt, cbSQLStmt)
```

where:

- **hstmt** is the statement handle that you allocated by calling the SQLAllocStmt function (in Tip 377, "Using SQLAllocStmt and SQLFreeStmt to Allocate and Release SQL Statement Handles and Memory Resources").
- **szSQLStmt** is the character string that contains the SQL statement you want the DBMS to execute.
- **cbSQLStmt** is the length of the character string (the SQL statement) in szSQLStmt.

The value of the RETCODE returned by the function can be SQL_SUCCESS, SQL_SUCCESS_WITH_INFO, SQL_NEED_DATA, SQL_STILL_EXECUTING, SQL_ERROR, or SQL_INVALID_HANDLE.

Suppose, for example, that you want the DBMS to execute the UPDATE statement

```
UPDATE products SET unitprice = unitprice * 1.20
```

on the PRODUCTS table in the NORTHWIND (sample) database. Assuming that other parts of the C program called the function to connect to the DBMS using a Data Source Name (DSN) that specifies NORTHWIND as the default database, you can execute the UPDATE command by calling a function similar to:

```
void Raise_Prices(HDBC hDb_connection_handle)
{HSTMT hStatement_handle;  //data type void*
 RETCODE retcode;          //signed short (16-Bit Integer)
 LPSTR retcode_text = " "; //character string
 retcode = SQLAllocStmt(hDb_connection_handle,
                        &hStatement_handle);
 if (retcode == SQL_SUCCESS)
 {retcode = SQLExecDirect(hStatement_handle,(UCHAR *)
    "UPDATE products SET unitprice = unitprice "
    "* 1.20",SQL_NTS);
```

```
  if (retcode !=SQL_SUCCESS &&
      retcode != SQL_SUCCESS_WITH_INFO)
    sprintf(retcode_text,"Error on SQLExecDirect = %d",
            retcode);
  else
    MessageBox (0,"Sucessful action",
      "Send statements to MSSQLServer in Raise_Prices",
              MB_OK);

  SQLFreeStmt (hStatement_handle, SQL_DROP);}
 else
   sprintf(retcode_text,"Error on SQLAllocStmt = %d",
           retcode);
if (strcmp(retcode_text, " ") != 0)
  MessageBox (0,retcode_text,"In Raise_Prices",
              MB_OK|MB_ICONERROR);}
```

Note: *The entire C++ program, including the functions to establish the connection with a DBMS through the MSSQLServer DSN, is on the book's companion Web site at www.premierpressbooks.com/downloads.asp as Tip378.cpp. Before running the program, be sure to replace the username and password in the iConnect_SQL_Data_Source function with your username and password. Also, you must create a DSN name MSSQLServer, as you learned to do in Tip 368, "Creating a Data Source Name (DSN) for an SQL Open Database Connectivity (ODBC) Connection."*

379 Using the SQLFetch Function to Retrieve a Row of Data from an SQL Database

In Tips 372–377, you learned how to write a C program to connect with an SQL database. Then, in Tip 378, "Using SQLExecDirect to Send an SQL Statement to a DBMS for Execution," you learned how to use the SQLExecDirect function to send SQL statements to an SQL server for execution. Although the example only sent an UPDATE statement to the DBMS, any valid SQL statement is fair game—including SELECT statements that let you extract data from the database for use in your C program.

Extracting data from an SQL database into your C application involves four steps. First, you must establish a connection with the SQL server (as you learned to do in Tips 372–377). Second, you must call the SQLExecDirect statement (which you learned about in Tip 378) to send the SELECT statement to the DBMS. Third, you must call the SQLBindCol function to tell the ODBC driver which variables in your program it is to use when transferring data from table columns. Finally, you must call the SQLFetch or the SQLExtendedFetch functions to retrieve the SQL database data from the ODBC statement buffer into the C variables that you created to receive it.

The syntax of the SQLFetch function header is

```
RETCODE SQLFetch(hstmt)
```

where:

- **hstmt** is the statement handle.

The value of the RETCODE returned by the function can be SQL_SUCCESS, SQL_SUCCESS_WITH_INFO, SQL_NO_DATA_FOUND, SQL_STILL_EXECUTING, SQL_ERROR, or SQL_INVALID_HANDLE.

The important thing to understand is that you must call the function once for each column of data that you want to retrieve into a C variable. For example, to extract COMPANYNAME, CONTACTNAME, and PHONE from columns in the CUSTOMERS table in the NORTHWIND database into your C program, you would the three SQLBindCol statements and SQLFetch in the Get_Cust_Info function:

```
void Get_Cust_Info(HDBC hDb_connection_handle)
{#define COMPANYNAME_LEN 40
 #define CONTACTNAME_LEN 30
 #define PHONE_LEN       24
 UCHAR  szCompanyName[COMPANYNAME_LEN],
        szContactName[CONTACTNAME_LEN],
        szPhoneNumber[PHONE_LEN];
 SDWORD cbCompanyName, cbContactName, cbPhoneNumber;
 HSTMT hStatement_handle;  //data type void*
 RETCODE retcode;          //signed short (16-Bit Integer)
 LPSTR retcode_text = " "; //character string
 LPSTR szCustomerString = " ";

 retcode = SQLAllocStmt(hDb_connection_handle,
                        &hStatement_handle);
 if (retcode == SQL_SUCCESS)
 {retcode = SQLExecDirect(hStatement_handle,(UCHAR *)
    "SELECT companyname, contactname, phone FROM customers"
    " WHERE customerid LIKE 'B%'"
    " ORDER BY companyname",SQL_NTS);

  if (retcode !=SQL_SUCCESS && retcode !=
      SQL_SUCCESS_WITH_INFO)
    sprintf(retcode_text,"Error on SQLExecDirect = %d",
            retcode);
  else
  {/* Bind columns CompanyName (SELECT statement column 1),
      ContactName(SELECT statement column 2), and
      Phone(SELECT statement column 3) */
```

```
   SQLBindCol(hStatement_handle,  1, SQL_C_CHAR,
           szCompanyName, COMPANYNAME_LEN, &cbCompanyName);
   SQLBindCol(hStatement_handle,  2, SQL_C_CHAR,
           szContactName, CONTACTNAME_LEN, &cbContactName);
   SQLBindCol(hStatement_handle,  3, SQL_C_CHAR,
           szPhoneNumber, PHONE_LEN, &cbPhoneNumber);
    /* Fetch and display each row of data.
       On an error, display a message and exit. */
   while (TRUE)
   {retcode = SQLFetch(hStatement_handle);

    if (retcode == SQL_ERROR || retcode ==
        SQL_SUCCESS_WITH_INFO)
      sprintf(retcode_text,"Error on SQLExecDirect = %d",
              retcode);
     if (retcode == SQL_SUCCESS || retcode ==
        SQL_SUCCESS_WITH_INFO)
    {strcpy(szCustomerString,"Company: ");
     strcat(szCustomerString,(const char *)szCompanyName);
     strcat(szCustomerString,"\nContact: ");
     strcat(szCustomerString,(const char *)szContactName);
     strcat(szCustomerString,"\nPhone:    ");
     strcat(szCustomerString,(const char *)szPhoneNumber);
     MessageBox (0,(const char *)szCustomerString,
                 "In Get_Cust_Info",MB_OK);}
    else break;}}

 SQLFreeStmt (hStatement_handle, SQL_DROP);}
else
  sprintf(retcode_text,"Error on SQLAllocStmt = %d",
          retcode);

if (strcmp(retcode_text, " ") != 0)
  MessageBox (0,retcode_text,"In Raise_Prices",
              MB_OK|MB_ICONERROR);}
```

Note: *Review Tip379.cpp on the book's companion Web site at www.premierpressbooks.com/downloads.asp for a copy of the C++ program of which the Get_Cust_Info function is a part.*

380 Using the SQLExtendedFetch Function to Create an Updateable Cursor

Tip 379, "Using the SQLFetch Function to Retrieve a Row of Data from an SQL Database," used the SQLExecDirect function to send a SELECT statement to the DBMS that would most likely return more than one row of data. The ODBC driver handles multiple rows returned from a query by creating a *cursor*, a buffer area, on your local hard drive in which it stores the data values retrieved. When the application that sent the query to the DBMS calls the SQLFetch function, the ODBC driver advances the cursor's pointer to the next row of data retrieved from the database and sends data values to bound variables in the program. A second SQLFetch function call retrieves data from the second row in the cursor; the third call retrieves data from the third row, and so on.

If you only need to retrieve column data values and you are not planning to update the database by deleting rows in the cursor or updating their contents, use the SQLFetch function. On the other hand, if your program needs to update cursor values and have those changes reflected in the database, use the SQLExtendedFetch function instead.

The syntax of the SQLExtendedFetch function header is

```
RETCODE SQLExtendedFetch(hstmt,fFetchType,irow,pcrow,
                         rgfRowStatus
```

where:

- **hstmt** is the statement handle.
- **fFetchType** is the type of fetch, either SQL_FETCH_NEXT, SQL_FETCH_FIRST, SQL_FETCH_LAST, SQL_FETCH_PRIOR, SQL_FETCH_ABSOLUTE, SQL_FETCH_RELATIVE, or SQL_FETCH_BOOKMARK.
- **irow** is the number of rows to retrieve from the DBMS.
- **pcrow** is the number of rows actually retrieved from the DBMS.
- **rgfRowStatus** is an array of status values regarding changes in status of the row since it was last retrieved from the data source (the DBMS). Possible values are SQL_ROW_SUCCESS (meaning that the row is unchanged), SQL_ROW_UPDATED, SQL_ROW_DELETED, SQL_ROW_ADDED, SQL_ROW_ERROR, or SQL_ROW_NOWROW (for each row where the irow exceeds the actual number of rows retrieved [pcrow]).

The value of the RETCODE returned by the function can be SQL_SUCCESS, SQL_SUCCESS_WITH_INFO, SQL_NO_DATA_FOUND, SQL_STILL_EXECUTING, SQL_ERROR, or SQL_INVALID_HANDLE.

Note: *The SQLExtendedFetch function retrieves data from the cursor on a rowset vs. a row-by-row basis. A rowset is a group (or set of rows) defined by calling the*

SQLSetStmtOption function) and setting the SQL_ROWSET_SIZE option. For example, if you call the SQLSetStmtOption function and set the rowset size to 10, then each rowset will consist of 10 cursor rows. Consequently, each SQLExtendedFetch function call will retrieve the column values from 10 rows of data from the cursor into bound program variables.

Unlike the SQLFetch function call, which can only move forward one row at a time through the cursor, the SQLExtendedFetch function lets you specify both the direction (forward or backward) in which you want to move through the cursor and the number of rows at a time you want to move.

For example, given the type definitions

```
RETCODE retcode  //signed short  (defined in SQLTypes.h)
HSTMT   hstmt    //void*  (defined in SQLTypes.h)
UDWORD  pcrow
UWORD   rgfRowStatus
```

the SQLExtendedFetch function call

```
retcode = SQLExtendedFetch(hstmt, SQL_FETCH_LAST, 1,
                           &pcrow,rgfRowStatus)
```

will fetch column values from the last rowset in the cursor. Alternatively, this call

```
retcode = SQLExtendedFetch(hstmt, SQL_FETCH_FIRST, 1,
                           &pcrow,rgfRowStatus)
```

will fetch columns values from the first rowset. Meanwhile, the function call

```
retcode = SQLExtendedFetch(hstmt, SQL_FETCH_ABSOLUTE, 10,
                           &pcrow,rgfRowStatus)
```

will fetch the rowset that contains the tenth row in the cursor. The function call

```
retcode = SQLExtendedFetch(hstmt, SQL_FETCH_RELATIVE, -4,
                           &pcrow,rgfRowStatus)
```

will retrieve column values from the rowset that contains the row that is four rows before the first row in the current rowset.

Review the C++ source code in Tip380.cpp on the book's companion Web site at www.premierpressbooks.com/downloads.asp for a fully functional application using the SQLExtendedFetch function. In Tips 383–385, you will learn how to use the SQLSetPos function call subsequent to an SQLExtendedFetch function call to update, delete, or add rows of data through the cursors created by the SQLExtendedFetch function.

381 Understanding the Difference Between Row-wise and Column-wise Binding

When retrieving data values from an SQL database for use in an application written in a programming language such as C, the ODBC driver first takes the data generated by a query and stores it temporarily on your hard disk. As you learned in Tip 380, "Using the SQLExtendedFetch Function to Create an Updateable Cursor," this temporary storage area (or buffer) is called a cursor. To use the database data in a program, you must fetch the data from the cursor into the application's declared variables. The processes of telling the ODBC driver which variables in the program are to receive data from which columns in the cursor is called binding.

In *column-wise* binding, you call the SQLBindCol function to establish the link between a variable declared in the program and a column in the cursor. In *row-wise* binding, you call the same SQLBindCol function, but you use the function to establish a link between one of the members (or fields) in a structure and a column in a cursor.

If you plan to use column-wise binding, there is no need to call the SQLStmtOption function—unless you previously called the SQLStmtOption function to request row-wise binding. As such, because you have already established a database connection and have allocated a statement handle (hStatementHandle, in the current example), your application could execute the following code to set up column-wise binding:

```
#define TEN_ROWS         10
#define CMPNY_LEN        40
#define CONTACTNAME_LEN 30
#define PHONE_LEN        24
UCHAR  szCmpnyName[CMPNY_LEN],
       szContactName[CONTACTNAME_LEN],
       szPhoneNumber[PHONE_LEN];
SDWORD cbCmpyName, cbContactName,cbPhoneNumber;

SQLBindCol(hStatementHandle,  1, SQL_C_CHAR,
         szCmpnyName, CMPNY_LEN, &cbCmpnyName);
SQLBindCol(hStatementHandle,  2, SQL_C_CHAR,
         szContactName, CONTACTNAME_LEN, &cbContactName);
SQLBindCol(hStatementHandle,  3, SQL_C_CHAR,
         szPhoneNumber, PHONE_LEN, &cbPhoneNumber);
```

After executing the three SQLBindCol function calls, any subsequent calls to either SQLFetch or SQLExtendedFetch would result in the ODBC driver copy the data values in the first column in the cursor to the variable CmpnyName and noting the number of bytes of data used to hold the data in the variable cbCmpnyName. The driver would copy data in the second cursor column to ContactName and would note the number of bytes copied in cbContactName. Finally, the ODBC driver would copy data from the cursor's third column to the PhoneNumber variable and would note the number of bytes copied in the cbPhoneNumber variable.

Because column-wise binding is the default, you must call the SQLStmtOption function and request row-wise binding if you want to use either SQLFetch or SQLExtendedFetch function calls to transfer cursor data into the members of structure instead of into individual variables. Again, assuming that you have already established a connection to the database and have allocated a statement handle (hStatementHandle, as in the last example), your application could execute the following code to set up row-wise binding:

```
#define CMPNYNAME_LEN   40
#define CONTACTNAME_LEN 30
#define PHONE_LEN       24

typedef struct{UCHAR  szCmpnyName[CMPNYNAME_LEN],
               SDWORD cbCmpnyName;
               UCHAR  szContactName[CONTACTNAME_LEN],
               SDWORD cbContactName;
               UCHAR  szPhoneNumber[PHONE_LEN];
               SDWORD cbPhoneNumber;}
        CustInfoTable;

CustInfoTable citCustInfo;

SQLSetStmtOption(hStatementHandle, SQL_BIND_TYPE,
                 sizeof(CustInfoTable));

SQLBindCol(hStatement_handle,  1, SQL_C_CHAR,
          citCustInfo.szCmpnyName, CMPNYNAME_LEN,
          &citCustInfo.cbCmpnyName);
SQLBindCol(hStatement_handle,  2, SQL_C_CHAR,
          citCustInfo.szContactName, CONTACTNAME_LEN,
          citCustInfo.&cbContactName);
SQLBindCol(hStatement_handle,  3, SQL_C_CHAR,
          citCustInfo.szPhoneNumber, PHONE_LEN,
          citCustInfo.&cbPhoneNumber);
```

After executing the three SQLBindCol function calls, any subsequent calls to either SQLFetch or SQLExtendedFetch would result in the ODBC driver copying the data values stored in the first column in the cursor to the structure memory CmpnyName and then noting the number of bytes of data used to hold the data in the structure member cbCmpnyName. The driver would copy data in the second cursor column to the structure memory ContactName and would note the number of bytes copied in the structure member cbContactName. Finally, the ODBC driver would copy data from the third cursor column to the structure member PhoneNumber variable and would note the number of bytes copied in the structure member cbPhoneNumber variable.

To switch from row-wise binding back to column-wise binding, call the SQLSetStmtOption function with the defined constant SQL_BIND_BY_COLUMN as the third parameter

```
SQLSetStmtOption(hStatementHandle, SQL_BIND_TYPE,
                 SQL_BIND_BY_COLUMN));
```

instead of passing the size of the structure that will hold the data as the third parameter:

```
SQLSetStmtOption(hStatementHandle, SQL_BIND_TYPE,
                 sizeof(name_of_structure));
```

Note: *Review the C++ source code in Tip380.cpp on the book's companion Web site at www.premierpressbooks.com/downloads.asp for a working example of column-wise binding, and in Tip381.cpp, in which the same application uses row-wise binding instead.*

---

382 Using the SQLSetConnectOption Function to Select the Database to Use When Executing SQL Statements

In Tip 378, "Using SQLExecDirect to Send an SQL Statement to a DBMS for Execution," you learned how to call the SQLExecDirect function to send an SQL statement to a data source (a DBMS) for execution. Then, in Tips 379–381 you learned how to use the SQLFetch and SQLExtendedFetch functions to retrieve data from an SQL database into a C application's variables. The examples in Tips 378–381 assumed that the programs needed data from the default database selected when the Data Source Name (DSN) was created. (You learned how to create a DSN for an SQL server in Tip 368, "Creating a Data Source Name (DSN) for an SQL Open Database Connectivity (ODBC) Connection.") To find out the name of the database for a particular connection handle, call the SQLGetConnectOption function.

The syntax of the SQLGetConnectOption function header is

```
RETCODE SQLGetConnectOption(hdbc, fOption, vParam)
```

where:

- **HDBC hdbc.** Is the connection handle used to connect the C program to an SQL server.
- **UWORD fOption.** Is the connection option whose value you want to retrieve. (For a list of option values, see Table 375 in Tip 375, "Using SQLSetConnectOption to Set a Session Option for an ODBC Connection with an SQL Server.")
- **UDWORD vParam.** Is either a 32-bit integer value or a pointer to a null terminated character string, depending on the type of connection option (as determined by the "fOption" value) the function is to retrieve.

Therefore, given that the program previously established a connection with an SQL server and made the variable declarations

```
HDBC     hdbc;
LPSTR    szDatabaseToUse = " ";
RETCODE retcode;
```

the function call

```
retcode = SQLGetConnectOption(hDb_connection_handle,
            SQL_CURRENT_QUALIFIER, szDatabaseToUse);
```

will place the name of the database that statements sent to the DBMS through the connection handle hDb_connection_handle will use into the variable szDatabaseToUse.

To change the database used by a connection handle, call the SQLSetConnectOption function. The SQLSetConnectOption function header has the same syntax as the SQLGetConnectOption function. However, in an SQLSetConnectOption function call, the vParam parameter is an *input* parameter. Therefore, to have the DBMS use the SQLTips database when executing statements sent through the connection handle hDb_connection_handle, execute the SQLSetConnectOption function call:

```
retcode = SQLSetConnectOption(hDb_connection_handle,
            SQL_CURRENT_QUALIFIER, (UDWORD) "SQLTips");
```

Tip 382.cpp on the companion CD contains the source code for an application that uses the SQLGetConnectOption function to retrieve the name of the database used by a connection handle and then selects a new database for the handle to use by calling the SQLSetConnectionHandle function.

383 Using the SQLSetPos Function to Set the Cursor Position in a Rowset

SQLSetPos is a multipurpose function in that it not only lets you set the pointer in a cursor to a particular row in a rowset of query results, but also lets you refresh and/or change the cursor's contents. Bear in mind that when you call the SQLSetPos function to modify a cursor's contents (by specifying SQL_UPDATE, SQL_DELETE, or SQL_ADD in the function call), the ODBC driver will send SQL statements to the DBMS to make the same changes on the cursor's underlying data on the SQL server.

The syntax of the SQLSetPos function header is

```
RETCODE SQLSetPos(hstmt, irow, fOption, fLock)
```

where:

- **HSTMT hstmt.** Is the statement handle.
- **UWORD irow.** Is the number of the row in the rowset on which to perform the operation specified in the fOption parameter.
- **UWORD fOption.** Is the operation to perform in the cursor and in the database on the data source (the database) to which the statement handle is connected through its connection handle. The possible fOption operations are SQL_POSITION, SQL_REFRESH, SQL_UPDATE, SQL_DELETE, and SQL_ADD.
- **fLock.** Is used to control database concurrency by simulating transactions on data sources that do not support them. Although fLock can be set to SQL_LOCK_NO_CHANGE, SQL_LOCK_EXCLUSIVE, or SQL_LOCK_UNLOCK, only the SQL_LOCK_NO_CHANGE option is supported for SQL server cursors because the DBMS has its own isolation level (concurrency) and transaction support.

The value of the RETCODE returned by the function can be SQL_SUCCESS, SQL_SUCCESS_WITH_INFO, SQL_NEED_DATA, SQL_STILL_EXECUTING, SQL_ERROR, or SQL_INVALID_HANDLE.

For example, to position the cursor's pointer to the fifth row in a rowset, execute the statement:

```
retcode = SQLSetPos(hstmt, 5, SQL_POSITION,
                    SQL_LOCK_NO_CHANGE)
```

After you position the cursor pointer (often referred to as "positioning the cursor"), the SQL_POSITION option tells the ODBC driver to take no further action. As you will learn in Tips 384–385, you can have the ODBC driver update or delete a row in a database table by substituting SQL_UPDATE or SQL_DELETE for SQL_POSITION in the SQLSetPos function call.

384 Using the SQLSetPos Function SQL_UPDATE Option to Perform a Positioned UPDATE

If the ODBC driver for the data source allows it, a program can use the SQLSetPos function's SQL_UPDATE option to modify data values in a cursor and have those changes reflected in the database row from which the cursor row's data was retrieved. When an application calls the SQLSetPos function with the SQL_UPDATE option, the ODBC driver positions the cursor's pointer to the row in the rowset passed to the function as the value of irow parameter. Next, the driver and updates the underlying row of data in the database by sending data values from the cursor row's buffers (its columns) to the columns in the table row from which the row in the cursor retrieved its data.

Suppose, for example, that a program calls the SQLSetStmtOption function to set its rowset size to 10 and then calls the SQLExecDirect function (see Tip 378, "Using SQLExecDirect to Send an SQL Statement to a DBMS for Execution") to send the query

```
SELECT cust_ID, f_name, l_name, phone_number
FROM customers384
```

to the DBMS. After calling the SQLBindCol function to bind the buffers in the cursor to variables in the program (as you learned to do in Tips 379–381), the application can update the table columns bound to szFirstName and szLastName from the 12th row of data retrieved by executing the following code:

```
retcode = SQLExtendedFetch(hStatementHandle,
            SQL_FETCH_ABSOLUTE, 12, &pcrow, rgfRowStatus);

if (rgfRowStatus[0] != SQL_ROW_DELETED &&
    rgfRowStatus[0] != SQL_ROW_ERROR)
{
  strcpy(citCustInfoRecord[0].szFirstName,"Konrad");
  strcpy(citCustInfoRecord[0].szLastName,"King");
  SQLSetPos(hStatementHandle, 1, SQL_UPDATE,
            SQL_LOCK_NO_CHANGE)
}
```

In the current example, the SQLExtendedFetch function call retrieves rows from the second rowset in the cursor starting with row 12. Because the array of citCustInfoRecord structures was bound to the cursor buffers by SQLBindCol function calls (not shown), the first element in the array (index 0) contains the values from the 12th row in the cursor after the SQLExtendedFetch function call. Next, the strcpy function calls update the cursor buffers in the first row of the current rowset (the 12th row in the cursor) by changing the values of the structure elements szFirstName and szLastName in the first row of the structure array. Finally, the SQLSetPos function call tells the ODBC driver to copy the values in the buffers of the first row in the current rowset (the 12th row in the cursor) into the underlying table columns in the row from which they were originally retrieved by the SQLExtendedFetch function call.

Please review the C source code in Tip384.cpp on the companion CD to see a program that creates a database connection, retrieves database table values into the cursor, and then uses SQLSetPos to perform a positioned update to the underlying data in the database.

Note: *Many ODBC drivers do not support positioned updates using the SQLSetPos function's SQL_UPDATE option. If the ODBC driver for the data source you are using is one of those that does not, your application can still update column values in a database. However, you will have to use a function such as SQLExecDirect instead of the SQLSetPos, SQL_UPDATE option. Tip 387, "Using the SQLExecDirect Function to UPDATE Column Values in a Database When an ODBC Driver Does Not Support Positioned Updates," will show you how to use the SQLExecDirect function to send a UPDATE statement to the DBMS while you have a cursor open.*

---

385 Using the SQLSetPos Function SQL_DELETE Option to Perform a Positioned DELETE

As you learned in Tip 384, "Using the SQLSetPos Function SQL_UPDATE Option to Perform a Positioned UPDATE," when you use the SQLSetPos function to update the values in a cursor's buffers, the ODBC driver sends commands to the DBMS to make the same changes to the data values in the columns of the underlying row from which the updated cursor row was derived. Similarly, when you use the SQLSetPos function's SQL_DELETE option, the ODBC driver positions the cursor to the row specified by the irow parameter, tells the DBMS to delete the underlying row in the database table, and changes the cursor row's status flag (in the rgfRowStatus array) to SQL_ROW_DELETED.

As you learned in Tip 383, "Using the SQLSetPos Function to Set the Cursor Position in a Rowset," the syntax of the SQLSetPos function header is:

```
RETCODE SQLSetPos(hstmt, irow, fOption, fLock)
```

Therefore, to remove the row in the database underlying the ninth row in the cursor, your application would execute code similar to:

```
retcode = SQLExtendedFetch(hStatementHandle,
            SQL_FETCH_ABSOLUTE, 9, &pcrow, rgfRowStatus);

if (rgfRowStatus[0] != SQL_ROW_DELETED &&
    rgfRowStatus[0] != SQL_ROW_ERROR)
  SQLSetPos(hStatementHandle, 1, SQL_DELETE,
            SQL_LOCK_NO_CHANGE)
```

Notice that the value of the irow parameter in the SQLSetPos function call is set to 1, not 9. As you learned in Tip 380, "Using the SQLExtendedFetch Function to Create an Updateable Cursor," the SQLExtendedFetch function retrieves data from the cursor one rowset of data at a time. The first row in the set of rows retrieved by the SQLExtendedFetch function call is the row passed as its irow parameter—9, in the current example. Therefore, to work with the ninth row in the cursor, the application must tell the driver to work with first row in the rowset.

When using the SQLSetPos function's SQL_DELETE option, be sure to set the value of the irow parameter to something other than zero (0) unless you want the ODBC driver to delete the underlying rows for all of the rows in the rowset. For example, while the function call

```
  SQLSetPos(hstmt, 2, SQL_DELETE, SQL_LOCK_NO_CHANGE)
```

will delete the underlying row for the second row in the cursor's rowset, the function call

```
  SQLSetPos(hstmt, 0, SQL_DELETE, SQL_LOCK_NO_CHANGE)
```

will delete all rows in the rowset. Therefore, if the rowset contains 10 rows, the first SQLSetPos function call will delete a single row, while the second SQLSetPos function call will delete 10 rows.

Please review the contents of Tip384.cpp on the companion CD for the source code of a C++ application that connects with a DBMS, executes a query to create a cursor and fill it with data, and then uses the SQLSetPos function to delete a row of data in the cursor's underlying table.

Note: *As was the case with the SQL_UPDATE option, some ODBC drivers do not support positioned deletes using the SQLSetPos function's SQL_DELETE option. If the ODBC driver for the data source you are using is one of those that does not, your program can still delete rows in the database by calling the SQLExecDirect function, as you will learn to do in Tip 386, "Using the SQLExecDirect Function to DELETE Rows in the Database When an ODBC Driver Does Not Support Positioned Deletes."*

---

386 Using the SQLExecDirect Function to DELETE Rows in the Database When an ODBC Driver Does Not Support Positioned Deletes

A SQL DELETE statement such as

```
DELETE FROM customers WHERE cust_id = 9
```

is called a *searched* DELETE because the DBMS searches the target table for rows that satisfy the search criteria in the WHERE clause and then deletes them. The term *positioned* DELETE, on the other hand, applies only to a programmatic SQL statement that deletes the single underlying row in the database table referenced by the "current" row in a cursor. Similarly, an SQL UPDATE statement such as

```
UPDATE customers SET f_name = 'Konrad', l_name = 'king'
WHERE cust_id = 9
```

is a *searched* UPDATE because the DBMS uses the search criteria in the WHERE clause to determine which row(s) to update as it scans the rows in the CUSTOMERS table. Like a positioned DELETE statement, a *positioned* UPDATE statement changes the data values in columns of the single underlying row referenced by the "current" row in a cursor.

If your ODBC driver does not support them using the SQLSetPos function, you can simulate both positioned updates and positioned deletes by calling the SQLExecDirect function with an UPDATE or DELETE statement string in which the WHERE clause links the "current" cursor row with its underlying row in the database table. For example, if the underlying table includes a TIMESTAMP column named TSTAMP, your program can execute a "positioned" delete of the database table row underlying the fifth row in the cursor by executing code such as:

```
strcpy(szSQLStatement,
       "DELETE FROM customers WHERE tstamp = 0x");
strcat(szStatementString, citCustInfoRecord[0].szTimeStamp
retcode = SQLExecDirect(hDeleteStmtHandle,
            (UCHAR *)szSQLStatement,SQL_NTS)
```

Notice that although the DELETE statement sent to the DBMS by the SQLExecDirect function in the current example "acts like" a positioned DELETE in that it tells the DBMS to remove the one row in the table from which the cursor row was retrieved, it is really a searched DELETE. Since the value in each row of a column of type TIMESTAMP is guaranteed to be unique across the entire database, the searched DELETE in the current example will always delete at most one row from the underlying table. (It is possible to delete zero rows if another user has already deleted the cursor's underlying row.)

If the underlying table does not have a column of type TIMESTAMP, you can still simulate a positioned DELETE. Simply change the search condition in the WHERE clause to look for a value in one of the underlying table's PRIMARY KEY column(s) in any column constrained as UNIQUE, or values in some other combination of columns whose composite value is unique for each row in the underlying table.

Please review the source code for Tip386.ccp on the companion CD for a complete listing of the source code necessary to use SQLExecDirect to simulate a positioned DELETE.

Note: *If you want to call the SQLExecDirect function while you have a cursor open, you must allocate a second statement handle first. Otherwise, the SQLExecDirect function call will abort with an error code indicating "Invalid Cursor State." Tip386.ccp on the companion CD uses the statement handle hQueryStmtHandle when working with the cursor data and a second statement handle hDeleteStmtHandle to send SQL statements to the DBMS by calling the SQLExecDirect function.*

---

387 Using the SQLExecDirect Function to UPDATE Column Values in a Database When an ODBC Driver Does Not Support Positioned Updates

In Tip 384, "Using the SQLSetPos Function SQL_UPDATE Option to Perform a Positioned UPDATE," you learned that you can use the SQLSetPos function's SQL_UPDATE option to perform a positioned UPDATE on a cursor row's underlying row in the database. When performing a positioned UPDATE, the ODBC driver tells the DBMS to UPDATE the values in the table row from that the current row in the cursor was derived to match the values in the cursor row's buffers. In short, a positioned UPDATE is nothing more than a searched UPDATE in which the search condition in the WHERE clause uniquely identifies the underlying row for the current row in the cursor.

Unfortunately, many ODBC drivers do not support positioned updates (or positioned deletes). As a result, you may have to use the SQLExecDirect function to simulate a positioned UPDATE just as you used the function to simulate a positioned DELETE in Tip 385, "Using the SQLSetPos Function SQL_DELETE Option to Perform a Positioned DELETE." For example, suppose you have a cursor with rows produced by calling the SQLExecDirect function with the query:

```
retcode = SQLExecDirect(hQueryStmtHandle, (UCHAR *)
  "SELECT tstamp, cust_ID, f_name, l_name, phone_number"
  " FROM customers", SQL_NTS);
```

After you make the SQLBindCol function calls that bind the buffers in the cursor to variables your C application, you can execute the statements

```
retcode = SQLExtendedFetch(hQueryStmtHandle, SQL_FETCH_ABSOLUTE, 5,
&pcrow, rgfRowStatus);
strcpy(citCustInfoRecord[0].szFirstName,"Sally");
strcpy(citCustInfoRecord[0].szLastName,"Wells");
```

to update the values in the fifth row of the cursor. Then you would execute the statements

```
strcpy(szStmtString,"UPDATE customers SET f_name = '");
strcat(szStmtString,citCustInfoRecord[0].szFirstName);
strcat(szStmtString,"', l_name = '"
strcat(szStmtString,citCustInfoRecord[0].szLastName);
strcat(szStmtString,"' WHERE tstamp = 0x");
strcat(szStmtString, citCustInfoRecord[0].szTimeStamp);

retcode = SQLExecDirect(hUpdateStmtHandle,
                        (UCHAR *)szStmtString,SQLNTS);
```

to have the DBMS make the same changes to the cursor's underlying row in the CUSTOMERS table.

Although the WHERE clause search criteria in the examples in both Tip 385 and the current tip used a value in a TIMESTAMP column (TSTAMP) to uniquely identify the cursor row's underlying row in the database, the value in any column constrained as UNIQUE will do just as well. For example, if the CUST_ID column in the current example is unique for each row cursor's underlying table, then the executing the statements

```
strcpy(szStmtString,"UPDATE customers SET f_name = '");
strcat(szStmtString,citCustInfoRecord[0].szFirstName);
strcat(szStmtString,"', l_name = '"
strcat(szStmtString,citCustInfoRecord[0].szLastName);
strcat(szStmtString,"' WHERE cust_ID = ");
strcat(szStmtString, citCustInfoRecord[0].szCust_ID);
```

```
retcode = SQLExecDirect(hUpdateStmtHandle,
                        (UCHAR *)szStmtString,SQLNTS);
```

will have the same effect as calling the SQLExecDirect function using the value of the TSTAMP column as the search criteria in the preceding example.

Review the contents of Tip387.ccp on the book's companion Web site at www.premierpressbooks.com/downloads.asp for a complete listing of the source code necessary to use SQLExecDirect to simulate a positioned UPDATE.

Note: *If you want to call the SQLExecDirect function to send an UPDATE statement to the DBMS after you open a cursor by sending a SELECT statement to the DBMS for execution, you must allocate a second statement handle first. Otherwise, the SQLExecDirect function call will abort with an error code indicating "Invalid Cursor State." Tip387.ccp on the book's companion Web site at www.premierpressbooks.com/downloads.asp uses the statement handle hQueryStmtHandle to send the query (which creates the cursor) to the DBMS and uses a second statement handle, hUpdateStmtHandle, when calling the SQLExecDirect function to send SQL statements that UPDATE the cursor's underlying rows in the database.*

388 Using the SQLError Function to Retrieve and Display ODBC Error Codes and Error Messages

When you call an ODBC function, the ODBC driver communicates with a data source using one or more communication handles. The SQLConnect function, for example, creates and uses a connection handle (data type HDBC). Meanwhile, the SQLAllocEnvironment function uses values in the database connection handle and creates the environment handle (data type HENV). Finally, the SQLAllocStmt function uses values in the connection handle and creates the statement handle (data type HSTMT). Any ODBC function call can post zero or more error, warning, or information messages in the handles it creates or uses. Moreover, whenever a function returns a return code (RETCODE) of SQL_ERROR or SQL_SUCCESS_WITH_INFO, you will definitely find at least one message in the communications handle used by the function. The SQLError function lets you retrieve a message from the data structure of its rightmost non-null handle parameter, and it removes the message from the stack of up to 64 messages that each handle can hold.

The syntax of the SQLError function header is

```
RETCODE SQLError(henv, hdbc, hstmt, szSQLState,
        pfNativeError, szErrorMessage, cbErrorMsgMax,
        pcbErrorMsg);
```

where:

- **HENV henv** is an environment handle or SQL_NULL_HENV.
- **HDBC hdbc** is a database handle or SQL_NULL_HDBC.
- **HSTMT hstmt** is a statement handle or SQL_NULL_HSTMT.
- **UCHAR SQLState** is the numeric ODBC driver-mapped error code cast as a null-terminated string.
- **SDWORD FAR* pfNativeError** is a pointer to 32-bit numeric variable (memory location) that will hold the data native (data source–specific) error code that is mapped into an ODBC driver error code, as specified in the ANSI SQL specification.
- **UCHAR FAR* szErrorMessage** is a pointer to the memory location for the null-terminated character string that will hold the error message.
- **SWORD cbErrorMsgMax** is the maximum length of the error message storage area szErrorMessage. The value must be less than or equal to SQL_MAX_MESSAGE_LENGTH – 1 (or 511, as of this writing).
- **SWORD FAR* pcbErrorMsg** is a pointer to a 16-bit numeric variable (memory location) that will hold the number of non-null bytes placed in the error message area szErrorMessage.

The value of the RETCODE returned by the function can be SQL_SUCCESS, SQL_SUCCESS_WITH_INFO, SQL_NO_DATA_FOUND, SQL_ERROR, or SQL_INVALID_HANDLE.

Therefore, to retrieve an error message stored in an environment handle, call the SQLError function with a valid environment handle (henv) and the hdbc and hstmt parameters set to null, as in:

```
retcode = SQLError(henv, SQL_NULL_HDBC, SQL_NULL_HSTMT,
            szSQLState, &pfNativeError, szErrorMessage,
            MSG_BUFF_SIZE, &cbErrorMsg);
```

Similarly, to retrieve an error associated with a connection handle, call the SQLError function with a valid connection handle (hdbc) and null parameters for henv and hstmt, as in:

```
retcode = SQLError(SQL_NULL_HENV, henv, SQL_NULL_HSTMT,
            szSQLState, &pfNativeError, szErrorMessage,
            MSG_BUFF_SIZE, &cbErrorMsg);
```

Finally, to retrieve an error message posted in a statement handle, call the SQLError function with a valid statement handle (hdbc) and null parameters for henv and hdbc, as in:

```
retcode = SQLError(SQL_NULL_HENV, SQL_NULL_ENV, hstmt,
            szSQLState, &pfNativeError, szErrorMessage,
            MSG_BUFF_SIZE, &cbErrorMsg);
```

Review the source code in Tip388.cpp to see how an application can make a call to the SQLError function to retrieve error information and then call the MessageBox routine to display it as shown in Figure 388.1.

Figure 388.1 MessageBox displaying the results of an SQLError function call

As mentioned previously, each SQLError function call retrieves one error code (and message) from the rightmost non-null handle. To display multiple errors posted in any of the three handle structures, call the SQLError function multiple times. If you call the SQLError function and there are no (additional) error messages in the handle structure, SQLError will return a retcode value of SQL_NO_DATA_FOUND, szSQLState will equal 00000, pfNativeError will be undefined, and szErrorMsg will contain only a single null termination byte.

389 Handling NULL Values in Host Program Variables

Most programming languages do not support SQL NULL values. In C, for example, a variable declared as

```
SWORD sSalespersonID
```

can hold a 16-bit integer value. However, while the value of sSalespersonID can be negative, 0, or positive, it cannot have an unknown or missing value. In short, sSalespersonID cannot be NULL. As such, when you retrieve data from an SQL table column that may contain one or more NULL values, you must check the number of bytes retrieved into the variable passed as the pcbValue parameter of the SQLBindCol function.

For example, given the syntax of the SQLBindCol

```
SQLBindCol(hstmt, icol, fCType, rgbvalue, cbValueMax,
           pcbValue)
```

the program statement

```
SQLBindCol(hStatementHandle, 4, SQL_C_SSHORT,
           &sSalespersonID, 0, &cbSalespersonID);
```

will bind the fourth buffer column in the ODBC cursor to the variable sSalespersonID. Each time the application calls the SQLFetch (see Tip 379, "Using the SQLFetch Function to Retrieve a Row of Data from an SQL Database") or the SQLExtendedFetch (see Tip 380, "Using the SQLExtendedFetch Function to Create an Updateable Cursor") function, the ODBC driver will place the value from the fourth column in the cursor into the variable sSalespersonID and store the number of bytes transferred in the variable cbSalespersonID—unless the value in the fourth column is NULL. If the value in a cursor column is NULL and the program calls the SQLFetch or SQLExtendedFetch functions, the ODBC driver does not change the value in the program variable to which the cursor buffer is bound. The driver does, however, set the value of the pcbvalue parameter—cbSalespersonID, in the current example—to SQL_NULL_DATA, which is –1 as of this writing.

Therefore, before using the value from an SQL column that may contain NULL data values, have your program check the value of the number of bytes retrieved from the cursor (the pcbValue value). For example, the IF statement

```
if (cbSalespersonID != SQL_NULL_DATA)
  sprintf((char *)szSalerspersonID,
          "\nSalesperson ID: %d",sSalespersonID);
else
  strcpy((char *)szSalespersonID,
         "\nSalesperson ID: **UNASSIGNED **");
```

will place the salesperson ID from the fourth column in the cursor into the szSalespersonID character string if the column has a non-NULL value. Otherwise, the string will show the salesperson ID as ** UNASSIGNED **.

Review the code in Tip389.cpp on the book's companion Web site at www.premierpress-books.com/downloads.asp for a complete listing of the variable definitions and function calls necessary to retrieve data from an SQL table and handle NULL values appropriately.

390 Understanding the Role of APIs in a Client/Server Environment

Before the development of the Open Database Connectivity (ODBC) standard, the only way for an application to work with the data in a database was through *embedded* SQL. In embedded SQL, SQL statements are intermixed with other non-SQL language statements.

The embedded SQL statements serve as the program's interface with the DBMS by retrieving data from it, updating the data in the database, and manipulating its objects.

When creating an executable program using embedded SQL with a programming language such as C, COBOL, PL/I, FORTRAN, Pascal, and so on, the source code is first submitted to an SQL precompiler that is unique for each programming language and SQL server. The SQL precompiler parses, validates, optimizes, and converts the SQL statements into their binary forms. The code is then sent through the native language compiler, which converts the non-SQL statements into their executable (binary) form and links them with the binary SQL statements to produce an executable program.

While the embedded SQL approach combines SQL and non-SQL statements in a program's source code, the application program interface (API) approach keeps the two separate. The API approach (which you learned about as you worked with the ODBC API in Tips 373–389) is to provide the procedural language (C, COBOL, Visual Basic, Pascal, and so on) a set of function calls that it can use to work with the data and objects in a database. Because most programmers already have some experience in using function libraries for such things as string manipulation, mathematical functions, and file and screen I/O, the SQL APIs are a straightforward and easy way to use SQL.

As shown in Figure 390.1, in a client/server environment, an application makes one or more API calls that connect the program with a DBMS. The application then allocates a memory (and perhaps hard-disk) buffer area at the workstation for use in passing commands and data back and forth between the DBMS running on the server and the application running on the client (workstation). After creating SQL statements as text strings and placing them in the buffer along with any necessary data values, the program calls API functions that send the buffer's contents to the DBMS for processing. The program then makes API calls that check the status of the commands/statements sent to the DBMS and handles any errors.

The DBMS, for its part, analyzes the buffer contents it receives from the client (the program running at the workstation) and executes the SQL statement batch in it. If the statements include a query, the DBMS generates the query's results table and sends the requested data to buffers on the client workstation for further processing. (You learned about the process of retrieving (and sending) rows of data through cursors in Tips 379–387.)

When a program is finished working with the DBMS, it ends its database access by making API calls that disconnect it from the DBMS and free up the resources allocated both at the server and at the client for the session's communication's processes.

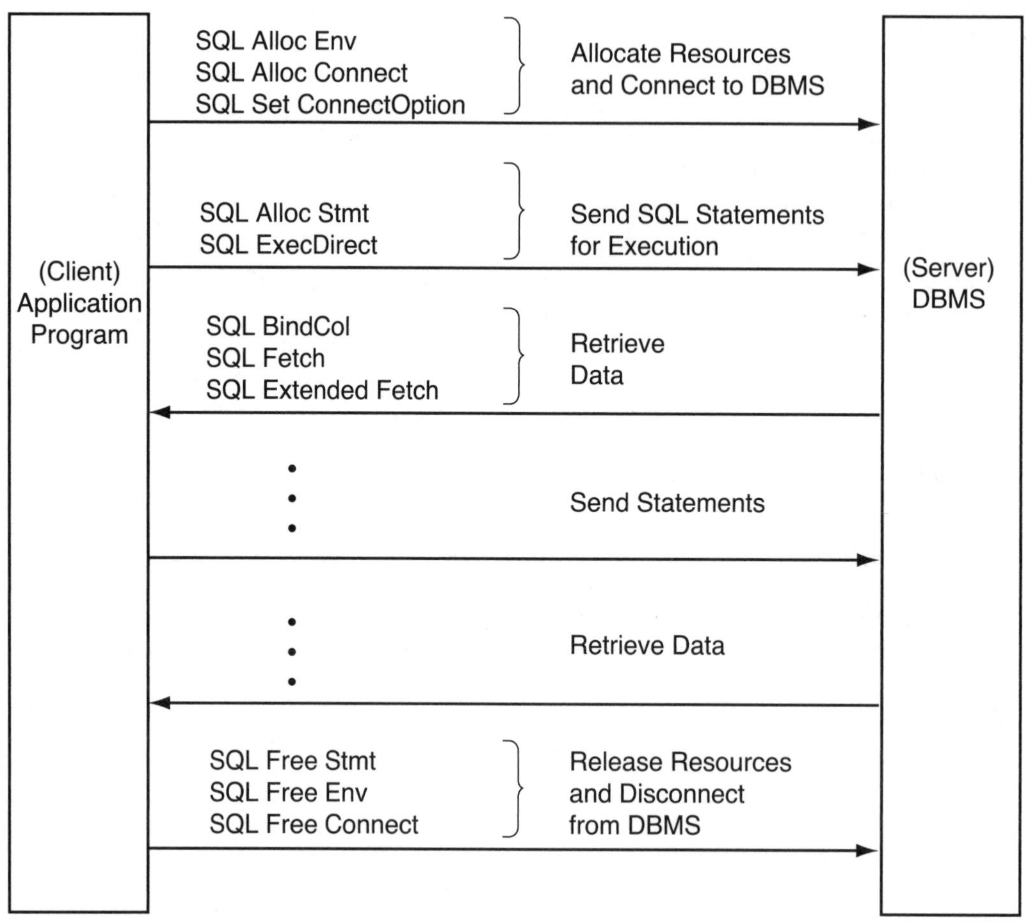

Figure 390.1 The API approach to DBMS access

391 Adding DB-Library (DBLIB) Functionality to Visual Basic (VB)

Tips 372–389 showed you how to use an Open Database Connectivity (ODBC) driver to work with SQL server data. Using the data source name (DSN) you created in Tip 368, "Creating a Data Source Name (DSN) for an SQL Open Database Connectivity (ODBC)

Connection," the ODBC applications program interface (API) lets you work with a variety of different data sources, one of which happens to be MS-SQL Server. The DB-Library (DBLIB), on the other hand, is a native MS-SQL Server data access technology provided by Microsoft and can be used only to access data on an MS-SQL Server.

DBLIB for Visual Basic (VB) is a subset of the DBLIB for C. Both are included with MS-SQL Server. However, neither the C nor the VB DBLIB is installed as part of the default MS-SQL Server client installation process. To install DBLIB, run MS-SQL Server's Custom installation and select the Development Tools option. After you install the VB DBLIB on your hard drive, you can use its functions in your VB projects to allow them to make API calls that work with MS-SQL Server data, much like those you learned about when using the ODBC API.

Because a DBLIB-enabled VB application makes calls to various DBLIB functions defined in the VBSQL.OCX dynamic link library (DLL), you will need to add the VBSQL.OCX component to your VB toolbox by performing the following steps:

1. If you have not already done so, start MS-Visual Basic (VB) and open a Standard.EXE project.
2. Right-click your mouse pointer on the project toolbox (along the left side of the VB application window) and select Components from the pop-up menu. VB will display a Components dialog box (similar to the one you saw in Figure 370.1 in Tip 370, "Adding the MSFlexGrid Control to a Visual Basic (VB) Form to Display SQL Table Data").
3. Use the scroll bar to the right of the Components list box on the Controls tab to scroll through the Control Components list until you see the Vbsql Control. Then click your mouse pointer on the check box to the left of Vbsql OLE Custom Control Module until the check mark appears. (The controls are listed in alphabetical order, so the control that you want will be near the end of the list because its name starts with a *V*.)

Note: *VB will try to find the Vbsql Control in the folder in which it was installed when installed you the MS-SQL Server development tools. For MS-SQL Server 7.0, the default folder is C:\MSSQL7\DevTools\Lib\. If you moved to VBSQL.OCX file to another folder, you will need to click your mouse pointer on the Browse button and search for or enter the full pathname of the folder in which you placed VBSQL.OCX.*

4. Click your mouse pointer on the OK button near the bottom center of the Components dialog box. VB will return to the VB application window and add the Vbsql Control as the last control component in the VB toolbox.

Before you can use any of the functions in the Vbsql Control that you added to the VB toolbox, you must declare the function headers (their names and parameters) in a .BAS or .CLS module. Fortunately, Microsoft provides the VBSQL.BAS module for the Vbsql Control, and you can add it to your VB environment by performing the following additional steps:

1. Right-click your mouse pointer in the Project window near the upper-right side of your VB application window. Then move your mouse pointer over the Add option on the pop-up menu and select the Module option. VB will display an Add Module dialog box similar to that shown in Figure 391.1.

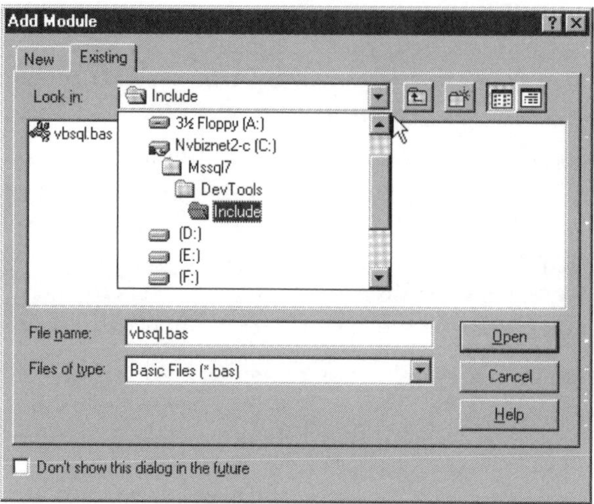

Figure 391.1 The Visual Basic (VB) Add Module dialog box

2. Click your mouse pointer on the Existing tab and enter the full pathname for the VBSQL.BAS module into the File_name field. If you installed the MS-SQL Server development tools to the C:\MSSQL7 folder, for example, enter **C:\MSSQL7\DEVTOOLS\VBSQL.BAS** into the File_name field.
3. Click your mouse pointer on the Open button. VB will add the VBSQL.BAS module to your current project and return to the VB application window.

Now that you have both the Vbsql Control and the VBSQL.BAS modules available in your project, you can use the DBLIB function to work with MS-SQL Server data, as you will learn to do in Tips 392–417.

392 Starting a Visual Basic (VB) Program Without Displaying a Form

As you learned in Tips 369–371 (when you wrote a Visual Basic [VB] program to display SQL DBMS data), VB is forms-oriented. In fact, when you started VB and chose to work on a Standard.EXE project in Tip 391, "Adding DB-Library (DBLIB) Functionality to Visual Basic (VB)," VB automatically added the form named Form1 to your project. Sometimes, however, you may want to perform some work in a VB program before displaying a form on the screen. Fortunately, VB lets you do just that—as long as you define a function named MAIN() in one of the modules in your application.

If you have not done so already, execute the procedure in Tip 391 to start a VB project that includes the VBSQL.BAS module and has the Vbsql.ocx control in the VB Toolbox. Next, add a module that contains the MAIN() function that your VB application will execute on startup by performing the following steps:

1. Right-click your mouse pointer in the project window, select Add from the pop-up menu, and then select Module from the Add submenu. VB will display the Add Module dialog box.
2. Click your mouse pointer on the New tab and then on the Open button. VB will add a module named Module1 to your project.
3. Double-click your mouse pointer on the name (Module1) in the "(Name)" field of the Module1 properties window to select the module's name. Enter a more descriptive name for the module. For the current project, replace Module1 with **MainRoutine**.

Note: *Renaming Module1 is optional. However, changing default object names such as Module1, Form1, and so on will make your VB source code easier to read. Moreover, you do not have to name the module in which you place the MAIN() routine MainRoutine—or any specific name, for that matter. You cannot, however, name the module itself MAIN. If you do so, VB will generate an error indicating that you cannot have a module named MAIN when you attempt to compile your program.*

4. Select the Project menu Properties option. VB will display a Project Properties dialog box similar to that shown in Figure 392.1. (If you have not yet changed the name of the project, the Properties option will be Project1 Properties on the Project menu.)

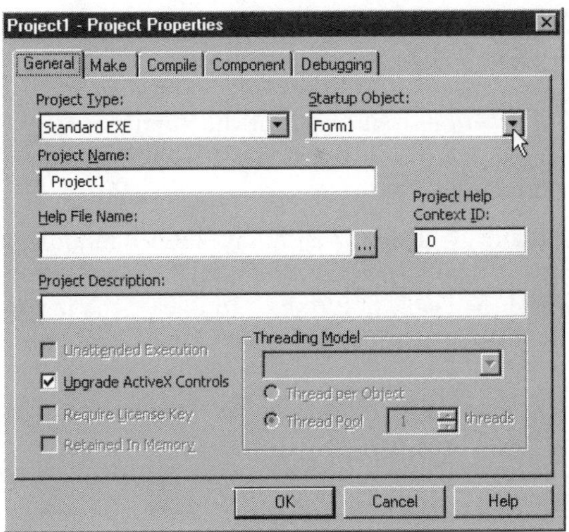

Figure 392.1 The Visual Basic (VB) Project Properties dialog box

5. Click your mouse pointer on the General tab.

6. Click your mouse pointer on the drop-down list button to the right of the Startup Object field, and select Sub Main from the drop-down list of startup objects.
7. Click your mouse pointer on the OK button.

After you complete Step 7, you are ready to enter the code for the MAIN() routine that your application will execute at startup into the code window of the MainRoutine module you added to your project. Tip 393, "Using the SqlInit() Function to Initialize the DB-Library and the SqlWinExit Routine to Release Memory Allocated by SqlInit()," will have you write the code for a MAIN() routine that initializes the DB-Library for use in a VB application.

Be sure to save your work to disk periodically so you do not lose it due to a computer lockup or power failure. To save your work to disk now, select the File menu Save Project option. VB will prompt you for the file names and folder in which you want to store your project's modules and forms. For the current project, store your VB application's files in a folder such as C:\SQL Projects\Tip392.

393 Using the SqlInit() Function to Initialize the DB-Library and the SqlWinExit Routine to Release Memory Allocated by SqlInit()

The DB-Library (DBLIB) contains functions and subroutines that let your VB application work with data in an MS-SQL Server database. However, before you can call any other routine in the DBLIB, you must call SqlInit. When running in a Windows environment, the DBLIB maintains information about each of the applications that reference it. Calling the SqlInit function allocates the memory and initializes the variables DBLIB uses to keep track of its use by a particular application.

The following code (which you should enter into the VB module [MainRoutine] you created in Tip 392, "Starting a Visual Basic (VB) Program Without Displaying a Form") calls SqlInit to initialize DBLIB and then calls SqlWinExit to release the memory resources allocated for the application by DBLIB:

```
Sub main()

DIM sDBLIBVersion AS String

sDBLIBVersion = SqlInit()
If sDBLIBVersion = vbNULLString Then
  MsgBox "Error!  Failed to initialize the DB-Library!"
  Exit Sub
Else
  'Make subroutine calls and start the main program
```

```
    'loop here
    MsgBox sDBLIBVersion

    'Exit the DB-Library and free its memory resources
    SqlWinExit
End If

End Sub
```

After reviewing the example VB code, you are probably thinking, "Hey! This program doesn't do anything other than let me know whether or not it was able to initialize the DBLIB successfully!"—and you are right! As you work the projects in Tips 394–419 you will add code to the "Else" part of the "If-Then-Else" structure in the MAIN() routine.

For now, the important thing to understand is that a VB application must call the SqlInit function before calling any other routine in the DBLIB. The SqlInit function has no parameters and returns a NULL character string if it is unable to initialize the DBLIB for your VB application. If successful, SqlInit returns a character string with the DBLIB's version identification. Be sure that you *do not* call other DBLIB routines if SqlInit returns an empty string because doing so will cause unpredictable results.

As is the case with any well-behaved program, the application in the example releases the memory resources allocated to it prior to exiting. In this case, the SqlWinExit function call tells the DBLIB to release the memory allocated by SqlInit. SqlWinExit has no parameters and does not return any values.

After calling the SqlWinExit routine, an application must call SqlInit again before any subsequent calls to other routines or functions in the DBLIB.

Note: *Before you can compile and execute the example program you must add the Vbsql Control to a form (such as Form1) in your VB program. Otherwise, the VB compiler will abort with an error message stating, "File not found: VBSQL.OCX." To add the Vbsql Control to Form1, perform the following steps:*

1. *Double-click your mouse pointer on Form1 in the project window. VB will display Form1 in its Design window.*
2. *Click your mouse pointer on the Vbsql Control button near the bottom of the VB Toolbox.*
3. *Use your mouse pointer to draw a Vbsql Control area on Form1. (The size and placement of the control you draw is not important at this point since the VB application does not display Form1 to the screen.)*

---

394 Using the SqlOpenConnection() Function to Log On to an MS-SQL Server

After your application initializes the DB-Library (DBLIB) by making a successful call to the SqlInit function, the program must log on to an MS-SQL Server before working with its data. The logon process is fairly straightforward in that it involves a single function call, SqlOpenConnection, whose syntax is

```
hConnHandle = SqlOpenConnection(sServerName, sLoginID,
              sPassword, sWsName, sAppName)
```

where:

- **Long hConnHandle.** Is the connection handle returned by the SqlOpenConnection function. The application will use the value of hConnHandle in subsequent DBLIB function calls that send commands to the MS-SQL Server over the connection opened by the SqlOpenConnection function.
- **String sServerName.** Is the name of the MS-SQL Server to which the program wishes to connect.
- **String sLoginID.** Is the program's login ID, its username, on the MS-SQL Server. The sLoginID can be up to 30 characters in length, and the application must provide a valid sLoginID/sPassword (username/password) pair to open a connection (logon) to an MS-SQL Server.
- **String sPassword.** Is the password associated with the username (login ID) in sLoginID. The sPassword can be up to 30 characters in length, and the application must provide a valid sLoginID/sPassword (username/password) pair to open a connection (logon) to an MS-SQL Server.
- **String sWsName.** The name of the workstation on which the application is running. Although sWsName can be up to 30 characters in length, MS-SQL Server stores only the first 10 characters. (MS-SQL Server displays the sWsName as the HOSTNAME when you execute the stored procedure SP_WHO.)
- **String sAppName.** The name the MS-SQL Server is to place in its SYSPROCESSES table to help identify the connection. Although sAppName can be up to 30 characters, MS-SQL Server stores only the first 16. (sAppName is an option and can be left blank.)

The value of the connection handle (hConnHandle) will be nonzero if SqlOpenConnection was successful in its effort to open a connection with the DBMS sServerName. If unsuccessful, the SqlOpenConnection function will return a connection handle of zero (0), so be sure to test the value of hConnHandle before using it access DBMS data in subsequent DBLIB function calls.

For example, to open a connection with an MS-SQL Server named NVBizNet2 by logging on as username konrad with password king, a program would make an SqlOpenConnection function call similar to:

```
hConnHandle = SqlOpenConnection("NVBizNet2", _
                "konrad", "king","myworkstation", _
                App.EXEName)
```

Tip394.bas on the companion CD contains Visual Basic (VB) source code that includes the preceding function call and displays the connection handle value in a message box. Although the example program (in Tip394.bas) displays the value of the 32-bit (Long) integer connection handle, the handle's value is of little use to the person using your program. However, the application will need to pass the connection handle to other DBLIB functions that need to communicate with the MS-SQL Server using the open connection.

395 Using the SqlClose() Routine to Close a Single MS-SQL Server Connection, or Calling SqlExit to Close All Open Connections

As you learned in Tip 394, "Using the SqlOpenConnection() Function to Log On to an MS-SQL Server," you can call the SqlOpenConnection function to log on to an MS-SQL Server. The SqlClose function has the opposite effect—it ends (closes) a single connection with an MS-SQL Server. Because a program can open multiple connections with one or more MS-SQL Servers, the syntax of the SqlClose routine

```
SqlClose (hConnHandle)
```

includes one parameter—the connection handle (hConnHandle) of the connection the routine is to close.

For example, if the application executed the function calls

```
hConnHandle1 = SqlOpenConnection("NVBizNet2", _
                 "konrad", "king","my_ws-1", App.EXEName)
hConnHandle2 = SqlOpenConnection("NVBizNet2", _
                 "konrad", "king","my_ws-2", App.EXEName)
hConnHandle3 = SqlOpenConnection("NVBizNet2", _
                 "konrad", "king","my_ws-3", App.EXEName)
```

you would make the subroutine call

```
SqlClose(hConnHandle2)
```

to close the second connection while leaving the first and third connections open for use in subsequent DBLIB function calls.

As an alternative to closing each connection, your application can call the SqlExit routine as

```
SqlExit
```

to close all open connections. Notice that SqlExit has no parameters. Thus, in the current example, calling SqlExit once will close both of the remaining open connections (hConnHandle1 and hConnHandle2) if executed after calling SqlClose(hConnHandle2). (Of course, if the program had not called SqlClose at all, then the calling SqlExit would have closed all three of the open connections.)

396 Using the SqlSendCmd Function to Send an SQL Statement to an MS-SQL Server for Execution

The DB-Library (DBLIB) provides two methods for sending SQL statements to an MS-SQL Server for execution. SqlSendCmd lets you send individual commands. On the other hand, calls to the SqlCmd function let you put multiple SQL statements into a batch that you can then tell the DBMS to execute by calling the SqlExec function. (You will learn how to use SqlExec in conjunction with SqlCmd in Tip 398, "Using the SqlColName() Function to Retrieve the Names of the Columns in the Results Set Generated by a Query.")

To send an SQL statement to the MS-SQL Server using the SqlSendCmd function, use the syntax

```
nRetCode = SqlSendCmd(hConnHandle, sSQLStatement)
```

where:

- **Long nRetCode.** Is the integer result returned by the SqlSendCmd function call. After the function call, the value of nRetCode will be either SUCCEED (1) or FAIL (0).
- **Long hConnHandle.** Is the connection handle returned by the SqlOpenConnection function.
- **sSQLStatement.** Is the string (variable) containing the SQL statement the MS-SQL Server is to execute.

For example, to execute a USE statement to switch the default database to NORTHWIND and then execute an UPDATE statement to increase the values UNITPRICE column of the PRODUCTS table, execute the following (2) SqlSendCmd function calls:

```
nRetCode = SqlSendCmd(hConnHandle, "USE Northwind")
nRetCode = SqlSendCmd(hConnHandle, _
  "UPDATE PRODUCTS SET unitprice = unitprice * 1.20")
```

Before calling the SqlSendCmd function, the application must, of course, call SqlOpenConnection to open a connection with the target MS-SQL Server (as you learned to do in Tip 394, "Using the SqlOpenConnection() Function to Log On to an MS-SQL Server"). Please review the contents of Tip396.BAS on the companion CD for a complete listing of the Visual Basic program that updates the UNITPRICE column and displays the value of nRetCode in a message box after executing each of two function calls in the current example.

397 Using the SqlNumCols() Function to Determine the Number of Columns in the Results Set Generated by a Query

As you learned in Tip 396, "Using the SqlSendCmd Function to Send an SQL Statement to an MS-SQL Server for Execution," you can use the SqlSendCmd() function to send SQL statements (in the form of character strings) to the DBMS for execution. Any valid SQL statement that the program used to open a connection with the server, provided that the username/login ID has enough privilege to execute is fair game. Therefore, in addition to statements that modify data values or objects in the database, an application can send queries that return zero, one, or several rows of data for the program to display or modify.

When an application sends a SELECT statement to an MS-SQL Server, the DBMS automatically creates a cursor and fills it with the query's results table. The application can then retrieve data values from the cursor into program variables or forms fields for display or modification. By using the SqlNumCols() function in conjunction with the SqlColName() function (see Tip 398, "Using the SqlColName() Function to Retrieve the Names of the Columns in the Results Set Generated by a Query"), you can build a general-purpose subroutine that will fill an MSFlexGrid (which you learned about in Tip 370, "Adding the MSFlexGrid Control to a Visual Basic (VB) Form to Display SQL Table Data") with the names of the columns returned by the query. Then (as you will learn in Tip 399, "Using the SqlData() Function to Retrieve Query Results from a Cursor into an Application") you can use the SqlData() function to retrieve the cursor's data into the MSFlexGrid's columns as you move forward through the rows in the cursor by calling SqlNextRow().

The syntax of the SqlNumCols() function call is

```
SqlNumCols (nConnHandle)
```

where Long nConnHandle is the connection handle (returned by the SqlOpenConnection() or the SqlOpen() function) that was used by SqlSendCmd() (or SqlSend()) to send an SQL statement (or set of set statements) to the MS-SQL Server for execution.

The function returns the number of columns in the nConnHandle cursor's current set of results.

For example, the SqlNumCols() function near the end of the Visual Basic program

```
Sub main()

Dim sDBLIBVersion As String
Dim nConnHandle As Long
Dim nRetCode As Long
sDBLIBVersion = SqlInit()
nConnHandle = SqlOpenConnection("NVBizNet2", "konrad", _
                "king", "my_ws-1", App.EXEName)
nRetCode = SqlSendCmd(nConnHandle, "USE Northwind")
nRetCode = SqlSendCmd(nConnHandle,"SELECT * FROM products")

MsgBox "Cursor column count = " & SqlNumCols(nConnHandle)

SqlExit
SqlWinExit
End Sub
```

will display the number of columns in the cursor created by the DBMS when it executed the query:

```
SELECT * FROM products
```

The usefulness of being able to retrieve the number of columns in a cursor will become apparent when you learn how to write a general-purpose subroutine that displays cursor column names in an MSFlexGrid in Tip 398.

Note: *For clarity, the example VB program in the current Tip has no error handler that checks for errors-such as making sure that the SqlInit() function returns a non-null string (indicating a successful DBLIB initialization) and making sure that nConnHandle is not zero (indicating a successful connection with the MS-SQL Server). Tip397.bas on the companion CD performs the same work as the example but also includes statements that check for and handle errors returned by the DBLIB function calls.*

---

398 Using the SqlColName() Function to Retrieve the Names of the Columns in the Results Set Generated by a Query

In Tip 397, "Using the SqlNumCols() Function to Determine the Number of Columns in the Results Set Generated by a Query," you learned how to use the SqlNumCols() function to determine the number of columns of data the DBMS put into the results set for a query you sent to the MS-SQL Server by calling the SqlSendCmd() function. Being able to determine the number of columns in a cursor while the program is running makes it possible to write a single subroutine that retrieves and displays the names of the columns returned by various queries—even if each query's SELECT clause contains a different number of columns.

The syntax of the SqlColName() function call is

```
SqlColName(nConnHandle, iColNo)
```

where:

- **Long nConnHandle** is the connection handle (returned by the SqlOpenConnection() or the SqlOpen() function) that was used by SqlSendCmd() (or SqlSend()) to send an SQL statement (or set of set statements) to the MS-SQL Server for execution.
- **Integer iColNo** is the number of the column whose name the function is to retrieve. The first column in the cursor is number 1 (vs. 0).

The function returns a character string that contains the name of the results table column referenced by the iColNo value. (If the column has no name or if the value of iColNo is greater than the number of columns in the cursor, the function will return an empty string.)

Therefore, the subroutine

```
Private Sub GetColumnNames _
  (nConnHandle As Long, FlexGrid As MSFlexGrid)
Dim i As Integer

FlexGrid.Cols = SqlNumCols(nConnHandle)
FlexGrid.Rows = 1
FlexGrid.Row = 0
FlexGrid.Col = 0

For i = 1 To FlexGrid.Cols
  FlexGrid.Text = SqlColName(nConnHandle, i)
  FlexGrid.ColWidth(FlexGrid.Col) = _
    Form1.TextWidth(FlexGrid.Text) + 120
  If FlexGrid.Col < FlexGrid.Cols - 1 Then
    FlexGrid.Col = FlexGrid.Col + 1
  End If
Next i

FlexGrid.Redraw = True
End Sub
```

will fill the first row in an MSFlexGrid object (which you learned about in Tip 370, "Adding the MSFlexGrid Control to a Visual Basic [VB] Form to Display SQL Table Data") with the names of the columns in the query results set in cursor for the connection handle passed to the subroutine as the nConnHandle parameter.

Please review Tip398.bas on the companion CD to see an example application that opens a connection with an MS-SQL Server, uses the connection to send a query to the DBMS, and then displays the column names in the query's results table.

399 Using the SqlData() Function to Retrieve Query Results from a Cursor into an Application

The MSFlexGrid is a "flexible" data grid that a Visual Basic (VB) application can use to display DBMS data without knowing the number of rows and columns of data values to be displayed until run time. As you learned in Tip 398, "Using the SqlColName() Function to Retrieve the Names of the Columns in the Results Set Generated by a Query," a program can change the number of columns in an MSFlexGrid on the fly. For example, an application might use an MSFlexGrid to display a query results set with 5 columns and 300 rows at one point during the program's execution, and later resize the same grid to display 250 rows of data with 15 columns per row.

After adding an MSFlexGrid to a VB form (see Tip 370, "Adding the MSFlexGrid Control to a Visual Basic (VB) Form to Display SQL Table Data") and filling in its column headings (see Tip 398), you can use the SqlData() function to retrieve query results from the connection handle's cursor into the cells that make up the MSFlexGrid. The syntax of the SqlData() function call is

```
SqlData(nConnHandle, iColNo)
```

where:

- **Long nConnHandle** is the connection handle (returned by the SqlOpenConnection() or the SqlOpen() function) that was used by SqlSendCmd() (or SqlSend()) to send an SQL statement (or set of set statements) to the MS-SQL Server for execution.
- **Integer iColNo** is the number of the column whose value the function is to retrieve. The first column in the cursor is number 1 (vs. 0).

The function returns a character string containing the data value in the results column given by the value of iColNo. If the cursor column is of data type binary, varbinary, or image, the SqlData() function will return a string of binary data with one character per byte of data in the cursor column. For all other data types (both character string and numeric), the SqlData() function will return a character string of readable characters. (If the column number to be retrieved [iColNo] is greater than the highest-numbered cursor column, or if the cursor's column value is blank or NULL, the SqlData() function will return an empty string.)

Because each SqlData() function call returns the character string representation of the data value in only a single column of a row in the cursor, your program must call the function multiple times to retrieve the data values from a row of query results that has several columns. For example, to retrieve the data value in the sixth column in the nConnHandle cursor into the sUnitPrice character string, use the VB expression:

```
sUnitPrice = SqlData(nConnHandle,6)
```

To retrieve all of the column values from the "nConnHandle" cursor into the cells of the MSFlexGrid "FlexGrid", use a VB For-Next loop such as:

```
FlexGrid.col = 0
For i = 1 to SqlNumCols(nConnHandle)
  FlexGrid.text = SqlData(nConnHandle,i)

  If FlexGrid.col < FlexGrid.cols - 1 Then
    FlexGrid.col = FlexGrid.col + 1
  End If
Next i
```

400 Using the SqlNextRow() Function to Move Forward Through the Rows in a Cursor

As you learned in Tip 399 the SqlData() function retrieves the value from one of the columns in the *current* row of the cursor. The SqlNextRow() function lets you change the cursor's current row by moving the cursor pointer forward one row at a time. Because the DBLIB positions the cursor pointer prior to the first row in the cursor after the DBMS fills the cursor with query results, be sure to call the SqlNextRow() before the first SqlData() function call to retrieve data from a column in the first row of query results. By calling the SqlNextRow() function repeatedly until it returns the value NOMOREROWS, an application can move forward (one row at a time) through all of the rows of query results that the DBMS placed into the cursor.

The syntax of the SqlNextRow() function call is

```
SqlNextRow (nConnHandle)
```

where Long nConnHandle is the connection handle (returned by the SqlOpenConnection() or the SqlOpen() function) that was used by SqlSendCmd() (or SqlSend()) to send an SQL statement (or set of set statements) to the MS-SQL Server for execution.

The function returns one of five integer values:

- **REGROW (–1).** If the current row in the cursor contains SELECT statement results.
- **<COMPUTE clause ID number>.** If the current row in the cursor contains the results from a COMPUTE statement.
- **FAIL (0).** If the SqlNextRow() function was unsuccessful.

- **NOMOREROWS (–2).** If there are no more rows in the cursor—whether the SELECT statement returned no rows or the DBMS was unable to execute the query due to a deadlock, for example.
- **BUFFULL (–3).** If row buffering is turned on and the buffer is full.

For example, the Visual Basic subroutine

```
Private Sub GetResultsSet _
  (nConnHandle As Long, FlexGrid As MSFlexGrid)
Dim i As Integer

FlexGrid.Redraw = False
FlexGrid.AllowUserResizing = FlexResizeColumns
FlexGrid.FixedCols = 0
FlexGrid.Row = 0
Do Until NOMOREROWS = SqlNextRow(nConnHandle)
  FlexGrid.Col = 0
  FlexGrid.Rows = FlexGrid.Rows + 1
  FlexGrid.Row = FlexGrid.Row - 1

  For i = 1 To FlexGrid.Cols
    FlexGrid.Text = SqlData(nConnHandle,i)
    If FlexGrid.Col < (FlexGrid.Cols - 1) Then
      FlexGrid.Col = FlexGrid.Col + 1
    End If
  Next i
Loop

FlexGrid.Redraw = True
End Sub
```

will fill the rows of cells in an MSFlexGrid object (which you learned about in Tip 370, "Adding the MSFlexGrid Control to a Visual Basic (VB) Form to Display SQL Table Data") with the data values from each of the columns in the rows of query results of the nConnHandle cursor.

Note: *The subroutine in the current example assumes that the program calls it after making a call to the GetColumNames subroutine (see Tip 398, "Using the SqlColName() Function to Retrieve the Names of the Columns in the Results Set Generated by a Query,") which set the number of columns (FlexGrid.Cols) property of the MSFlexGrid and set its number of rows property (FlexGrid.Rows) at 1 (to account for the row of column headings in the grid).*

Please review Tip400.bas on the companion CD for an example program that opens a connection to an MS-SQL Server, uses the connection to send a query to the DBMS, and then uses an MSFlexGrid to display the column names and data values in the query's results table.

401 Using the SqlCmd() Function to Build an SQL Statement Batch

While the SqlSendCmd() function (which you learned about in Tip 396, "Using the SqlSendCmd Function to Send an SQL Statement to an MS-SQL Server for Execution") lets you send individual SQL statements to an MS-SQL Server for execution, the SqlCmd() function lets you build a statement batch. After you finish adding statements to the batch, the SqlExec() and SqlSend() functions let you send the entire set of statements to the MS-SQL Server for execution as a single transaction.

The syntax of the SqlCmd() function call is

```
nRetCode = SqlCmd(nConnHandle, sSQLStatement)
```

where:

- **Long nRetCode** is the integer result returned by the SqlCmd() function call. After the function call, the value of nRetCode will be either SUCCEED (1) or FAIL (0).
- **Long nConnHandle** is a connection handle returned by the SqlOpenConnection() (or SqlOpen()) function.
- **String sSQLStatement** is a character string the function is to append onto the existing contents of the nConnHandle command buffer. The sSQLStatement parameter in an SqlCmd() function call can contain a complete SQL statement or a portion of one or more statements.

For example the Visual Basic code

```
nRetCode = SqlCmd(nConnHandle, "USE Northwind")
nRetCode = SqlCmd(nConnHandle, " SELECT * FROM products")
nRetCode = SqlCmd(nConnHandle, " USE Pubs")
nRetCode = SqlCmd(nConnHandle, " SELECT * FROM authors")
```

builds an SQL statement batch that consists of two USE statements and two queries. Each SqlCmd() function call appends the contents of its sSQLStatement parameter onto the existing contents of the nConnHandle statement buffer (vs. deleting or overwriting any existing text). (A connection handle's statement buffer is not cleared until the program makes an SqlExec() or SqlSend() function call that sends the buffer's contents [the SQL statement batch] to the DBMS for execution.)

Note: *Each SqlCmd() function call concatenates the contents of the statement buffer and the character string passed in its sSQLStatement parameter. As such, be sure to add at least one blank (space) either at the end of each statement or prior to the first character in the second and subsequent statements you add to the SQL statement batch. For example, notice that the second, third, and fourth statements in the current tip's example each begin with a blank (space).*

402 Using the SqlExec() Function to Submit an SQL Statement Batch to an MS-SQL Server for Execution

As you learned in Tip 401, "Using the SqlCmd() Function to Build an SQL Statement Batch," the SqlCmd() function calls let you create an SQL statement batch by appending character strings onto the existing text in a connection handle's command buffer. Calling the SqlExec() function sends the contents of the command buffer (the SQL statement batch) as a single (and perhaps lengthy) character string to the DBMS for execution.

The syntax of the SqlExec() function call is

```
nRetCode = SqlExec(nConnHandle)
```

where:

- **Long nRetCode** is the integer result returned by the SqlExec() function call. After the function call, the value of nRetCode will be either SUCCEED (1) or FAIL (0).
- **Long nConnHandle** is the connection handle returned by an SqlOpenConnection() (or SqlOpen()) function.

For example, if the Visual Basic expression

```
nRetCode = SqlExec(nConnHandle)
```

follows the SqlCmd() function calls in Tip 401, the SqlExec() function will send the character string

```
USE Northwind SELECT * FROM products USE Pubs SELECT * FROM authors
```

to an MS-SQL Server, clear the command buffer, and wait for the DBMS to finish executing all of the statements in the batch. If the command buffer is empty, or if any of its statements contain syntax errors or attempt actions that exceed the connection's privileges on the server, the SqlExec() function will return a value of FAIL (0). Conversely, if the DBMS successfully executes all of the statements in the SQL statement batch, the SqlExec() function will return a value of SUCCEED (1), and each statement's results will be available for retrieval into the connection handle's cursor by calling the SqlResults() function (which you will learn about in Tip 403, "Using the SqlResults() Function to Retrieve an SqlExec() Submitted Query's Results Set").

Note: *The set of SQL statements in the statement batch sent to the MS-SQL Server by an SqlExec() function call are treated as a single transaction. Therefore, if the DBMS is unable to execute any of the statements in the batch successfully, the system will roll back (undo) any work performed by prior statements in the batch and will not return any rows of query results.*

403 Using the SqlResults() Function to Retrieve an SqlExec() Submitted Query's Results Set

After calling the SqlExec() function to send an SQL statement batch to an MS-SQL Server for execution, your application must call the SqlResults() function once for each statement in the batch to tell the DBLIB to prepare each statement's results set for retrieval by function calls in the application program. Moreover, if you neglect to call the SqlResults() function until there are no more unprepared results sets, any subsequent SqlExec() function call will fail because previous results were not completely processed. Although you do not have to call SqlData() to retrieve all of the data values returned by SELECT statements (if any) in an SqlExec() (or SqlSend()) transmitted statement batch, you do have to flag each results set as prepared and processed by calling the SqlResults() function until there are no more results sets for it to process.

Note: *An application must call the SqlResults() function once for each statement in the SQL statement batch sent by the SqlExec() (or SqlSend()) function to the DBMS for processing—whether or not the statement returns any rows of data. For example, although the statement batch created in Tip 401, "Using the SqlCmd() Function to Build an SQL Statement Batch," and sent to an MS-SQL Server in Tip 402, "Using the SqlExec() Function to Submit an SQL Statement Batch to an MS-SQL Server for Execution," includes two USE statements (which return no rows of data when executed) and two SELECT statements (which may return rows of data), the program must call the SqlResults() function four times after sending the SQL statement batch in the example to the MS-SQL Server for processing.*

The syntax of the SqlResults() function call is

```
nRetCode = SqlResults(nConnHandle)
```

where:

- **Long nRetCode** is the integer result returned by the SqlResults() function call. After the function call, the value of nRetCode will be SUCCEED (1), FAIL (0), NOMORERESULTS (2), or NOMORERPCRESULTS (3).
- **Long nConnHandle** is the connection handle (returned by the SqlOpenConnection() or the SqlOpen() function) that was used by SqlSend() to send an SQL statement batch to the MS-SQL Server for execution.

To avoid having to keep track of the number of statements in the command buffer so you know how may times to call the SqlResults() function, simply use a Do-Until loop, such as

```
Do Until NOMORERESULTS = SqlResults(nConnHandle)
  If SqlNumCols(nConnHandle) > 0 Then
'Routines that retrieve and work with query results
```

```
    GetColumnNames nConnHandle, Form1.QueryResults
    GetResultsSet nConnHandle, Form1.QueryResults

    MsgBox "Click your mouse pointer on the OK button " _
      & "to process the next set of results."
  End If
Loop
```

which will continue making SqlResults() function calls until there are no more results sets to process (at which point the SqlResults() function will return the value NOMORERESULTS).

Because the SqlResults() function only *prepares* a results set for processing, your application must still call the SqlNextRow() function to work its way through the rows in a query results set's cursor and the SqlData() function to retrieve the value in a column of the cursor's current row. For example, the Do-Until loop in the preceding example checks to see if the results set from an executed statement in the SQL statement batch returned any columns of data (in which case SqlNumCols(nConnHandle) > 0). If so, then the program calls the subroutines (which you developed in Tip 398, "Using the SqlColName() Function to Retrieve the Names of the Columns in the Results Set Generated by a Query," and Tip 400, "Using the SqlNextRow() Function to Move Forward Through the Rows in a Cursor") to retrieve the cursor's column names and data values.

Please review the contents of Tip402.bas on the companion CD to see an example Visual Basic (VB) program that connects with an MS-SQL Server, uses the SqlExec() function to send two USE statements and two queries to the DBMS for execution, and then displays the results of each query in an MSFlexGrid on a VB form.

404 Using SqlSend() to Submit a Statement Batch Without Waiting for the DBMS to Finish Executing All of Its Statements

As mentioned in Tip 402, "Using the SqlExec() Function to Submit an SQL Statement Batch to an MS-SQL Server for Execution," an SqlExec() function call halts further program execution while the SqlExec() function waits for the DBMS to finish processing the SQL statement batch. Consequently, if one (or more) of the statements in the batch retrieves or sorts a large amount of data, or has to wait for another DBMS user to release required resources, the application may appear to "hang" for an unacceptable length of time. If you want the program to perform other tasks while the DBMS executes the SQL statements in a batch, submit the batch by calling the SqlSend() function instead of calling the SqlExec() function.

The syntax of the SqlSend() function call is

```
nRetCode = SqlSend(nConnHandle)
```

where:

- **Long nRetCode** is the integer result returned by the SqlSend() function call. After the function call, the value of nRetCode will be either SUCCEED (1) or FAIL (0).
- **Long nConnHandle** is a connection handle returned by the SqlOpenConnection() (or SqlOpen()) function.

After executing an expression such as

```
nRetCode = SqlSend(nConnHandle)
```

(which tells the DBLIB to send the SQL statements in the nConnHandle command buffer to the MS-SQL Server for processing), the system will execute the next statement in the program—without waiting for the DBMS to finish processing the statements in the batch. However, before making another SqlSend() or SqlExec() function call, the program must call the SqlOk() function to find out whether or not the DBMS finished processing the statements in the batch. In fact, the function call

```
nRetCode = SqlExec(nConnHandle)
```

is equivalent to

```
nRetCode = SqlSend(nConnHandle)
nRetCode = SqlOk(nConnHandle)
```

because SqlOk() (like the SqlExec()) will wait for the DBMS to finish processing the statements in the nConnHandle command buffer before returning control to the application program.

Fortunately, the DBLIB lets you use the SqlDataReady() function (which you will learn about in Tip 405, "Using the SqlDataReady() Function to Determine If an MS-SQL Server Has Finished Processing an SQL Statement Batch") to check whether or not the DBMS has finished processing the SQL statement batch (submitted by SqlSend()) without waiting for the system to actually finish executing all of the statements in the batch.

Therefore, a Visual Basic (VB) command sequence that would allow an application to perform other tasks while waiting for the DBMS to process an SQL statement batch would be similar to:

```
'SqlCmd() function calls to build the SQL batch
SqlSend(nConnHandle)

Do Until SUCCEED = SqlDataReady(nConnHandle)
  'VB statements that perform work you want the application
  'to do while waiting for the DBMS to finish processing
  'the SQL statements in the "nConnHandle" command buffer
Loop
```

```
If SqlOk(nConnHandle) = SUCCESS Then
  'VB statements that process the results sets (one for
  'each statement in the batch) for the SQL statement batch
  'submitted to the MS-SQL Server by the SqlSend() function
  'call
End If
```

After you learn how to use the SqlDataReady() function in Tip 405, review the contents of Tip405.bas on the companion CD for an example of a program that submits a statement batch to the DBMS for execution and performs other work while waiting for the DBMS to finish processing the batch.

405 Using the SqlDataReady() Function to Determine If an MS-SQL Server Has Finished Processing an SQL Statement Batch

In Tip 404, "Using SqlSend() to Submit a Statement Batch Without Waiting for the DBMS to Finish Executing All of Its Statements," you learned how to use the SqlSend() function to submit the contents of a connection handle's command buffer to an MS-SQL Server for processing. The main advantage gained by calling SqlSend() instead of SqlExec() is that the SqlSend() function submits the contents of the command buffer to an MS-SQL Server for processing and lets your application continue on with other work while the DBMS executes the statements in the batch. (As you learned in Tip 402, "Using the SqlExec() Function to Submit an SQL Statement Batch to an MS-SQL Server for Execution," after an application calls it, the SqlExec() function sends the contents of the connection's command buffer to the MS-SQL Server for processing and halts further program execution while it waits for the DBMS execute all of the statements in the statements batch.)

The SqlDataReady() function lets you check whether or not the DBMS is finished processing a batch of statements submitted to an MS-SQL Server by calling the SqlSend() function. After an application calls SqlSend() (and the DBLIB sends the contents of the command buffer to the DBMS), the program must call SqlOk() to find out whether or not the DBMS successfully executed all of the statements in the batch. Unfortunately, SqlOk(), like SqlExec(), will not return control to an application until the DBMS finishes processing the entire batch.

SqlDataReady(), on the other hand, does not wait for the DBMS to finish processing the contents of the command buffer. Instead, the function simply just checks whether or not the DBMS is finished with the batch. Therefore, if SqlDataReady() returns SUCCEED (1), calling SqlOk() will not cause the program to "hang" because the DBMS is finished with the batch. As a result, SqlOk() can retrieve the batch-processing result code without having to wait. On the other hand, if SqlDataReady() returns FAIL (0), the DBMS has not yet finished processing the batch and the application should call SqlOk() at a later time, to give the DBMS a chance to finish executing the remaining (unexecuted) statements in the batch.

The syntax of the SqlDataReady() function call is

```
nRetCode = SqlSend(nConnHandle)
```

where:

- **Long nRetCode** is the integer result returned by the SqlDataReady() function call. After the function call, the value of nRetCode will be either SUCCEED (1) (meaning the DBMS has finished processing the statement batch) or FAIL (0) (meaning the DBMS is still executing statements in the batch).
- **Long nConnHandle** is the connection handle (returned by the SqlOpenConnection() or the SqlOpen() function) that was used by SqlSend() to send an SQL statement batch to the MS-SQL Server for execution.

For example, the following code for the Check if Done button on Form1 of the Visual Basic PROJECT405.VBP on the companion CD

```
Private Sub DataReady_Click()
If SqlDataReady(nConnHandle) = SUCCEED Then
  If SqlOk(nConnHandle) = SUCCEED Then
    GetBatchResults (nConnHandle)
  Else
    MsgBox "The statement batch failed to execute."
  End If
Else
  MsgBox "The DBMS is still processing the batch."
End If
End Sub
```

lets the user check the progress of the statement batch and calls the SqlOk() function only after the DBMS is finished processing the batch, thus allowing the user to do other work while the DBMS executes the batch of SQL statements submitted to it by the SqlSend() function call.

406 Using SqlCancel() to Stop the Execution of a Statement Batch Sent to an MS-SQL Server and Clear the Batch Results Buffer

The SqlCancel() function lets an application tell an MS-SQL Server to stop processing a statement batch. When the DBMS receives the SqlCancel() function's cancel request, it aborts the execution of the current statement in the batch, undoes any work performed by a partially executed statement batch, and clears the batch's results buffer.

The syntax of the SqlCancel() function call is

```
nRetCode = SqlCancel(nConnHandle)
```

where:

- **Long nRetCode** is the integer result returned by the SqlCancel() function call. After the function call, the value of nRetCode will be either SUCCEED (1) (meaning the DBMS was able to respond to the cancel request) or FAIL (0).
- **Long nConnHandle** is the connection handle (returned by the SqlOpenConnection() or the SqlOpen() function) that was used by SqlSend(), SqlExec(), or SqlSendCmd() to send one or more SQL statements to the MS-SQL Server for execution.

Therefore, the expression

```
nRetCode = SqlCancel(nConnNVBizNet2)
```

in a Visual Basic (VB) program will tell the MS-SQL Server to which the application is connected by the nConnNVBizNet2 connection handle to stop processing the connection's statement batch and clear any pending results from the connection's results buffer.

In addition to aborting the execution of a statement batch (by calling the SqlCancel() after calling SqlSend()), an application can use SqlCancel() to clear pending results from an executed statement batch by calling the function after calling SqlOk(), SqlExec(), or SqlSendCmd(). As you learned in Tip 403, "Using the SqlResults() Function to Retrieve an SqlExec() Submitted Query's Results Set," a program must call the SqlResults() function repeatedly (once for each statement in a statement batch) until there are no more sets of results to process. However, if you do not want the data produced by the statements in a batch, or if the statements did not produce any query results, you can skip making SqlResults() function calls by calling the SqlCancel() function, which clears all pending results.

The VB project in PROJECT406.VBP on the companion CD adds a Cancel Batch button (which calls the SqlCancel() function) to the project you reviewed in Tip 405, "Using the SqlDataReady() Function to Determine If an MS-SQL Server Has Finished Processing an SQL Statement Batch" (PROJECT405.VBP).

407 Using the SqlCanQuery() Function to Remove the Remaining (Unprocessed) Rows in the Current Set of Results

While the SqlCancel() function lets you stop the processing of a statement batch and discard *all* sets of results, the SqlCanQuery() function lets you discard the remaining rows of unprocessed results in the *current* results set. Suppose, for example, that your Visual Basic (VB) program executes the expression

```
nRetCode = SqlSendCmd(nConnHandle, "USE Northwind" _
  & " SELECT * FROM products USE Pubs " _
  & " SELECT * FROM authors "
```

which sends four SQL statements to an MS-SQL Server for execution. As you learned in Tip 403, "Using the SqlResults() Function to Retrieve an SqlExec() Submitted Query's Results Set," the program must call the SqlResults() function four times (once for each SQL statement sent to the MS-SQL Server) before calling the SqlSendCmd(), SqlSend(), or SqlExec() function again. Moreover, as you learned in Tip 400, "Using the SqlNextRow() Function to Move Forward Through the Rows in a Cursor," the program must call the SqlNextRow() function once for each row returned by the two queries in the current example. If the application does not call the SqlNextRow() function until the function returns the value NOMOREROWS, a subsequent call to the SqlResults() function will fail because all of the rows in the current results set (retrieved by calling SqlResults()) were not processed (by calling SqlNextRow()).

If you want to stop processing rows in the results set generated when the DBMS executes the query

```
SELECT * FROM products
```

without calling the SqlNextRow() function once for each row of PRODUCTS in the query's results table, call the SqlCanQuery() function as

```
nRetCode = SqlCanQuery(nConnHandle)
```

where:

- **Long nRetCode** is the integer result returned by the SqlCanQuery() function call. After the function call, the value of nRetCode will be either SUCCEED (1) (meaning the DBLIB was able to clear the remaining, unprocessed rows of query results) or FAIL (0).
- **Long nConnHandle** is the connection handle (returned by the SqlOpenConnection() or the SqlOpen() function) that was used by SqlSend(), SqlExec(), or SqlSendCmd() to send one or more SQL statements to the MS-SQL Server for execution.

The DBLIB will then discard any unprocessed rows of query results from the SELECT * FROM products query. However, the rows of results from the second query, SELECT * FROM authors, will still be available for retrieval (by calling the SqlNextRow() function) after calling the SqlResults() function twice more—once to prepare the results set for the USE Pubs statement, and a second time to prepare the results set for the SELECT * FROM authors statement.

Note: *If the VB application calls the SqlCancel() function (instead of calling the SqlCanQuery() function) while processing the results set from the first query (SELECT * FROM products), the DBLIB not only will discard the remaining rows of results from the query,* *but it also will discard the results set from each of the remaining two SQL statements (USE Pubs and SELECT * FROM authors).*

408 Using the SqlUse() Function to Set the Current Database for an MS-SQL Server Connection

The SqlUse() function lets you select the *current* database for a connection with an MS-SQL Server. When executing an SQL statement, the MS-SQL Server assumes that it will find the tables referenced in the FROM clause in the session's current database. As such, if you log in to an MS-SQL Server and your initial default database is NORTHWIND, for example, you can execute the statement

```
SELECT * FROM products
```

because PRODUCTS is one of the tables in the NORTHWIND database. On the other hand, if you attempt to execute the statement

```
SELECT * FROM authors
```

while your current database is still NORTHWIND, the DBMS will abort your query and display an error message similar to:

```
Server: Msg 208, Level 16, State 1, Line1
Invalid object name 'authors'.
```

You can correct the error either by typing in the fully qualified object name for the AUTHORS table, as

```
SELECT * FROM pubs.dbo.authors
```

or by selecting a new default/current database and then submitting the query again using the table's unqualified name:

```
USE pubs
SELECT * from authors
```

In the SqlUse() function call syntax

```
nRetCode = SqlUse(nConnHandle)
```

the following is true:

- **Long nRetCode** is the integer result returned by the SqlUse() function call. After the function call, the value of nRetCode will be either SUCCEED (1) or FAIL (0).
- **Long nConnHandle** is the connection handle (returned by the SqlOpenConnection() or the SqlOpen() function).

This call performs the same work as the Transact-SQL USE statement. Therefore, your Visual Basic application can select the PUBS database and query its AUTHORS table by executing the following statements:

```
nRetCode = (nConnHandle, "PUBS")
nRetCode = SqlSendCmd(nConnHandle, "SELECT * FROM authors")
```

Note: *When calling the SqlUse() function, bear in mind that the DBLIB implements the function by filling the connection handle's statement buffer with the USE <database name> string and then calling the SqlExec() and SqlResults() functions to send the USE statement to the DBMS for execution. As such, if you call the SqlCmd() function to place statements in the connection handle's command buffer, be sure to call SqlExec() (or SqlSend()) to send the statement batch to the MS-SQL Server for execution before calling the SqlUse() function, which will overwrite the current contents of the command buffer with a USE statement. Moreover, the SqlUse() function call will return a result code of FAIL (0) if there are unprocessed result sets or unprocessed rows in the current result set because it uses the SqlExec() function to send the USE statement to the DBMS. (As you learned in Tip 400, "Using the SqlNextRow() Function to Move Forward Through the Rows in a Cursor," and Tip 403, "Using the SqlResults() Function to Retrieve an SqlExec() Submitted Query's Results Set," an application cannot call the SqlExec() function until there are no more result sets that have not been processed and there are no more unprocessed rows in the current result set.)*

409 Using the Vbsql1_Error() Routine to Display DBLIB-Generated Error Messages

After you include the Visual Basic (VB) SQL control (VBSQL.OCX) on one of the forms in your VB project (as you learned to do in Tip 391, "Adding DB-Library [DBLIB] Functionality to Visual Basic [VB]"), you can define an error-handling routine that the DBLIB will execute if it encounters an error during run time. Although a DBLIB function typically returns a value of FAIL (0) when it is unable to complete its work successfully, the error code does not tell you *why* the function failed to execute. Fortunately, you can use the DBLIB error handler Vbsql1_Error() to display not only the error number and the severity of the error, but also a text message that tells you want went wrong.

To add the DBLIB error handler to your VB project, perform the following steps:

1. Click your mouse pointer on the form to which you added the VBSQL.OCX control. For example, if you worked on the project in Tip 391, you added the VBSQL.OCX control to Form1. Therefore, click your mouse pointer on Form1.frm in the project window near the upper-right corner of the VB application window.

2. Select the View menu Code option from the Standard toolbar. VB will display the code for the subroutines and functions defined for Form1, similar to that shown in Figure 409.1.

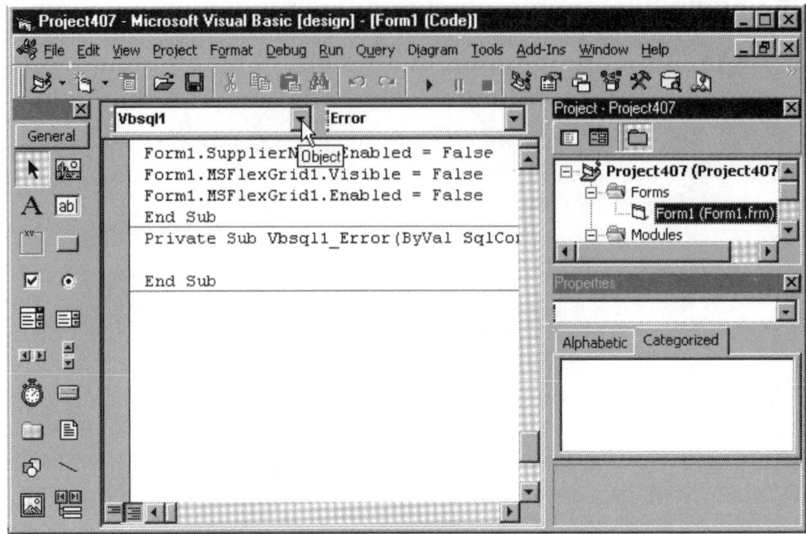

Figure 409.1 The Visual Basic (VB) application window with the Code pane for Form1 of a VB project

3. Click your mouse pointer on the drop-down list button to the right of the Object field (at the top of the Code pane), and select Vbsql1 from the drop-down list.
4. Click your mouse pointer on the drop-down list button to the right of the Procedure field (immediately to the right of the Object field at the top of the Code pane), and select Error from the drop-down list. VB will add the declaration for the Vbsql1_Error() routine to the Code pane for Form1.

Next, add the code you want the application to execute in case of a DBLIB error at run time. For example, to display the error code, severity, and error description, add a MsgBox call to the body of the Vbsql1_Error() subroutine definition as:

```
Private Sub Vbsql1_Error(ByVal SqlConn As Long, _
  ByVal Severity As Long, ByVal ErrorNum As Long, _
  ByVal ErrorStr As String, ByVal OSErrorNum As Long, _
  ByVal OSErrorStr As String, RetCode As Long)

Select Case ErrorNum
  Case 10007: 'Do not display non-error (info) messages
  Case Else
    MsgBox "Error Code: " & ErrorNum & vbCrLf & _
        "Severity: " & Severity & vbCrLf & _
        "Message: " & ErrorStr, vbOKOnly, _
        "DBLib Error In - " & App.EXEName
End Select
End Sub
```

After you add the code in the current example to the body of the Vbsql1_Error() routine, your VB application will use a Windows message box to display the error code and description of any DBLIB error encountered during run time.

410 Using the Vbsql1_Message() Routine to Display MS-SQL Server-generated Error Messages

In addition to defining an error handler for errors encountered by the DBLIB during run time (as you learned to do in Tip 409, "Using the Vbsql1_Error() Routine to Display DBLIB-Generated Error Messages"), you can also create an error handler for errors reported to the DBLIB by an MS-SQL Server. DBLIB errors include such things as attempting to call the SqlExec() function a second time without calling the SqlResults() function until it returns NOMORERESULTS, or calling the SqlResults() function to retrieve a second results set before calling the SqlNextRow() function until it returns NOMOREROWS first. MS-SQL Server reported errors, on the other hand, would include such things as a SELECT statement that includes an undefined object name in its SELECT clause or an UPDATE statement that attempts to modify the contents of an object when the connection does not have the correct set of privileges to do so. In short, the Vbsql1_Error() routine reports errors that occur within the DBLIB, while the Vbsql_Message() routine reports errors that occur on the MS-SQL Server.

To add the MS-SQL Server error message handler to your Visual Basic (VB) project, perform the following steps:

1. Click your mouse pointer on the form to which you added the VBSQL.OCX control. For example, if you worked on the project in Tip 391, "Adding DB-Library (DBLIB) Functionality to Visual Basic (VB)," you added the VBSQL.OCX control to Form1, so you would click your mouse pointer on Form1.frm in the project window near the upper-right corner of the VB application window.
2. Select the View menu Code option from the Standard toolbar. VB will display the code for the subroutines and functions defined for Form1.
3. Click your mouse pointer on the drop-down list button to the right of the Object field (at the top of the Code pane), and select Vbsql1 from the drop-down list.
4. Click your mouse pointer on the drop-down list button to the right of the Procedure field (immediately to the right of the Object field at the top of the Code pane), and select Message from the drop-down list. VB will add the declaration for the Vbsql1_Message() routine to the Code pane for Form1.frm.

Next, add the code you want the application to execute whenever an MS-SQL Server reports an error to the DBLIB error at run time. For example, to display the message number, error state, severity, and description, add a MsgBox() call to the Vbsql1_Message() subroutine as:

```
Private Sub Vbsql1_Error(ByVal SqlConn As Long, _
  ByVal Message As Long, ByVal State As Long, _
  ByVal Severity As Long, ByVal MsgStr As String, _
  ByVal ServerNameStr As String, ProcNameStr As String, _
  ByVal Line As Long)

Select Case Message
  Case 5701: 'Do not display non-error (info) messages
  Case Else
    MsgBox "Error reported by MS-SQL Server: " & _
      ServerNameStr & "." & vbCrLf & "Msg: " & _
      Message & ", Severity: " & Severity & _
      ", State: " & State & ", Line: " & _
      Line & vbCrLf & "Message: " & MsgStr, vbOKOnly, _
      "MS-SQL Server Reported Error In - " & App.EXEName
End Select
End Sub
```

After you add the code in the current example to the body of the Vbsql1_Message() routine, your VB application will use a Windows message box to display the error code and description of any error that an MS-SQL Server reports to the DBLIB during run time.

411 Using the SqlColType() Function to Determine the Data Type of a Column

As you learned in Tip 399, "Using the SqlData() Function to Retrieve Query Results from a Cursor into an Application," the SqlData() function lets you retrieve a data value from a column in a DBLIB buffer into program an object (such as a variable, field in a structure, field in a form, or an MSFlexGrid) in your application. If the DBLIB buffer column contains data of type BINARY, VARBINARY, or IMAGE, the SqlData() function returns a string of binary data that consists of one character per byte of data from the (DBLIB buffer) results column. For all other data types (both numeric and character/text) the SqlData() function will return a character string of readable characters. While the SqlData() function returns a column's data value as either a bit string or a character string, the SqlColType() function lets you determine the actual data type of the columns data.

The syntax of the SqlColType() function call is

```
iColType = SqlColType(nConnHandle, iColNo)
```

where:

- **Integer iColType** is the integer value constant from the list in Table 411.1 that represents the data type of the results table column specified by the value of iColNo.
- **Long nConnHandle** is the connection handle (returned by the SqlOpenConnection() or the SqlOpen() function) that was used by SqlSendCmd(), SqlExec(), or SqlSend() to send an SQL statement (or set of set statements) to the MS-SQL Server for execution.
- **Integer iColNo** is the number of the DBLIB buffer column whose data type the function is to retrieve. The first column in the DBLIB buffer is number 1 (vs. 0).

Therefore, to find out if the third column of query results in the DBLIB buffer is of data type IMAGE, a Visual Basic program could execute a statement such as:

```
If SqlColType (nConnHandle, 3) = SQLIMAGE
  MsgBox "Use Image App. to display image in Col 3."
End If
```

SQL Column Data Type	Numeric Value Returned	SQL Column Data Type	Numeric Value Returned
binary	SQLBINARY	varbinary	SQLBINARY
char	SQLCHAR	varchar	SQLCHAR
datetime	SQLDATETIME	smalldatetime	SQLDATATIME4
decimal	SQLDECIMAL	numeric	SQLNUMERIC
float	SQLFLOAT8	real	SQLFLT4
image	SQLIMAGE	text	SQLTEXT
int	SQLINT4	smallint	SQLINT2
		tinyint	SQLINT1
money	SQLMONEY	smallmoney	SQLMONEY4

Table 411.1 Visual Basic (VB) INTEGER Constants That Represent Each of the Valid VB and SQL Data Types

412 Using the SqlDatLen() Function to Determine the Number of Bytes of Data Stored in a DBLIB Buffer Column

For non-numeric data types (such as TEXT, CHAR, and VARCHAR), the SqlDatLen() function will return the number of characters the SqlData() function can retrieve from a particular column of a row in a DBLIB buffer. If a buffer column contains numeric data (such as SMALL-INT, FLOAT, or MONEY), the SqlDatLen() function will return the maximum printable width (the storage size) for the data type instead of the actual number of digits currently stored in the DBLIB buffer column. (To determine the number of digits stored in a numeric DBLIB buffer column, use the Visual Basic LEN() function instead of calling SqlDatLen().)

The syntax of the SqlDatLen() function call is

```
iColLen = SqlDatLen(nConnHandle, iColNo)
```

where:

- **Integer iColLen** is the number of characters the SqlData() function will return if called to retrieve data from a non-numeric iColNo DBLIB buffer column, or the maximum number of bytes used to store the iColNo column if the data value in column iColNo is one of the numeric data types.
- **Long nConnHandle** is the connection handle (returned by the SqlOpenConnection() or the SqlOpen() function) that was used by SqlSendCmd(), SqlExec(), or SqlSend() to send an SQL statement (or set of statements) to the MS-SQL Server for execution.
- **Integer iColNo** is the number of the column whose contents' byte size the function is to determine. The first column in the DBLIB buffer is number 1 (vs. 0).

For example, to display the number of characters in the first column in the DBLIB buffer for the nConnHandle server connection, you would execute a Visual Basic (VB) statement similar to:

```
MsgBox "The number of letters in""" & _
  SqlData(nConnHandle,1) & """""" & _
  " is " & SqlDatLen(nConnHandle, 1) & "."
```

Conversely, to determine the number of digits stored in a numeric column, you would use the VB LEN() function instead of the SqlDatLen() function, as in

```
MsgBox "The number of bytes used to store the decimal" & _
  " DISCOUNT value: " & SqlData(nConnHandle, 5) & _
  " is " & SqlDatLen(nConnHandle, 5) & "." & vbCrLf & _
  "The number of digits retrieved by SqlData() is " & _
  Len (SqlData(nConnHandle, 5)) & ".", vbOKOnly, _
  "SqlDatLen() Value vs. Len() Value for Numeric Data"
```

which will display a message box similar to that shown in Figure 412.1.

Note: *If the DBLIB buffer column whose length you are trying to determine contains a NULL value, then the SqlDatLen() function will return 0 as the number of bytes SqlData() can retrieve from the column.*

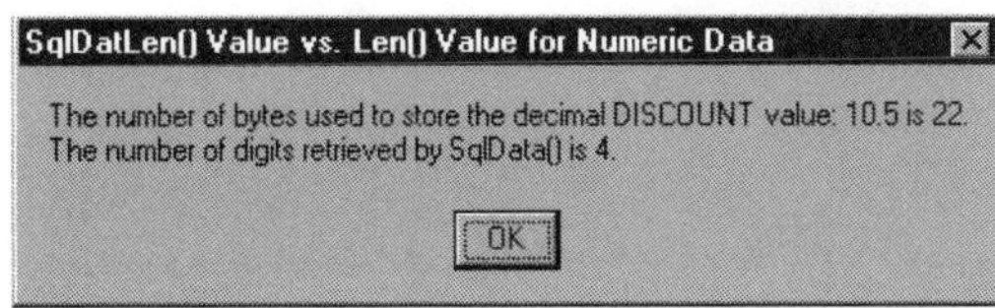

Figure 412.1 A Windows message box displaying the results of the SqlDatLen() and Len() function calls for numeric (decimal) data retrieved by an SqlData() function call

413 Assigning NULL Values to Host Variables in a Visual Basic Application

When a Visual Basic (VB) variable definition, such as

```
DIM iHighQty
```

does not include a data type, VB will type the variable as data type *variant*—meaning that the variable may hold different types of data at different times during a program's execution. In fact, a VB application can use a variable of data type variant to hold a value of any standard data type or one of three special values: *Empty*, *Null* or *Error*.

When you first declare a variable of data type variant in a VB program (by omitting the type definition from the variables declaration), the system assigns the Empty value to it. The value Empty is not the same is NULL. Empty indicates that a variable of data type variant has not yet been assigned a value. A VB variant variable will be NULL only if you assign the NULL value to by executing a statement such as:

```
iHighQty = Null
```

As you learned in Tip 399, "Using the SqlData() Function to Retrieve Query Results from a Cursor into an Application," the SqlData() function returns the value from any column in a connection's DBLIB buffer as a character string. If the DBLIB buffer column has a NULL value, the SqlData() function will return an empty character string (that is, the character string returned will contain no characters). However, the character string will not be NULL. Therefore, to copy a NULL value from a DBLIB buffer column into a host program variable of data type variant, your application must call the SqlDatLen() function to check the number of bytes of data stored in the DBLIB buffer column whose contents you want to retrieve. If the SqlDatLen() function returns a value of zero (0), set the target variant variable's value to NULL.

For example, the VB code

```
If SqlDataLen(nConnHandle,3) = 0 Then
  iHighQty = NULL
End If

If IsNull(iHighQty) Then
  MsgBox "The HIGHQTY column for the discount type " & _
    SqlData(nConnHandle,3) & " is NULL."
End If
```

will display the text "NULL" whenever the value of third column in the nConnHandle results set has a NULL value. Notice that VB, like SQL, requires that you use a special function, IsNull(), to check whether or not the value of a variable is NULL. As you learned in Tip 317, "Understanding Why the Expression NULL = NULL Evaluates to FALSE," performing an equality (or nonequality) test in which one of the operands is NULL (If NULL = NULL) is never TRUE because the logical test will always evaluate to NULL.

A VB application can assign a NULL value only to variables of data type variant. As such, the cells in an MSFlexGrid (which are, by definition, data type TEXT), cannot hold NULL values. However, a program can put the character string such as NULL into an MSFlexGrid cell to indicate that the value of the cell's underlying DBLIB buffer column is NULL. For example, the VB code

```
For i = 1 To FlexGrid.Cols
  If SqlDataLen(nConnHandle, I) <> 0 Then
    FlexGrid.Text = SqlData(nConnHandle, i)
  Else
    FlexGrid.Text = "** NULL **"
  End If
Next i
```

(extracted from the GetResultsSet() subroutine in Tip413.BAS on the companion CD) assigns the character string ** NULL ** to any cell in the MSFlexGrid when the SqlDatLen() function returns a value of 0 (which indicates that the cell's underlying DBLIB buffer column contains a NULL value).

414 Using SqlSetOpt() to Set the Size of the Row Buffer in Order to Allow Random Row Retrieval Using SqlGetRow()

In Tip 400, "Using the SqlNextRow() Function to Move Forward Through the Rows in a Cursor," you learned how to use the SqlNextRow() function to move forward (one row at a time) through the rows in the DBLIB buffer that holds the query results set from an MS-SQL Server. By default, the DBLIB allows only forward movement through its buffer. In order to keep its buffer as small as possible, the DBLIB discards the current row in the buffer when the program moves on to the next row by calling the SqlNextRow() function. After all, since the application cannot move backward in a forward-only buffer, there is no reason to keep a row in the buffer after the program has left it to move on to the next row.

The SqlSetOpt() function's SQLBUFFER option tells the DBLIB to maintain a fixed number of rows in its buffer until the application calls the SqlClrBuff() function to delete rows from the buffer. After calling the SqlSetOpt() function with the SQLBUFFER option, the DBLIB will allow an application to call the SqlGetRow() function, which lets the program move to any row in the buffer. You will learn all about the SqlGetRow() function in Tip 416, "Using the SqlGetRow() Function to Select the Current Row in a DBLIB Query Results Buffer." For now, the important thing to understand is that SqlGetRow() lets you make any one of the rows in the DBLIB's buffer the *current* row—whether the target row is prior to or after the row you are currently on. After calling the SqlGetRow() function to move to a specific row in the DBLIB buffer, you can call the SqlNextRow() function to move forward sequentially through the buffer, or call the SqlGetRow() function again to move to another row (either before or after the current row).

The syntax of the SqlSetOpt() function to set the number of rows the DBLIB is to maintain in its query results buffer is

```
nRetCode = SqlSetOpt(nConnHandle,SQLBUFFER,iBuffRowCt)
```

where:

- **Long nRetCode** is the integer result returned by the SqlSetOpt() function call. After the function call, the value of nRetCode will be either SUCCEED (1) or FAIL (0).
- **Long nConnHandle** is the connection handle (returned by the SqlOpenConnection() or the SqlOpen() function) that was used by SqlSendCmd(), SqlExec(), or SqlSend() to send the query (or queries) to the MS-SQL Server for execution.
- **Integer iBuffRowCt** is the number of rows of query results the DBLIB is to maintain in its buffer. The value of iBuffRowCt must be either 0 (meaning no buffering) or in the range 2–32, 767.

Thus, to have the DBLIB maintain a 10-row buffer area for a query's results set, a program would execute a statement similar to:

```
NRetCode = SqlSetOpt (nConnHandle, SQLBUFFER, 10)
```

As mentioned previously, after the application calls the SqlSetOpt() function with the SQL-BUFFER option, it can still call the SqlNextRow() function to retrieve data from the "next" row in the buffer. Moreover, the application can also call the SqlGetRow() function any number of times to move to any row in the DBLIB buffer. For example, the following Visual Basic code moves sequentially through the first 3 rows of the current example's 10-row DBLIB buffer.

```
For iRow = 1 To 3
  nRetCode = SqlNextRow(nConnHandle)

  If (nRetCode <> NOMOREROWS) And
     (nRetCode <> BUFFULL) Then

     'Call SqlData() to retrieve specific data value from
     'columns in the "current" row of the query results set
  End If
Loop
```

If the program were to call the SqlNextRow() function a fourth time, the DBLIB would make the fourth row in the buffer the current row, and the application could call the SqlData() function to retrieve a column value from the DBLIB buffer's fourth (current) row. However, if the program were to call the SqlGetRow() function as

```
NRetCode = SqlGetRow(nConnHandle, 7)
```

instead, the DBLIB would make the seventh row in the buffer the current row, and a subsequent SqlNextRow() function call would move the current row pointer on to the buffer's eighth row.

Please review the code for the Next 5 Authors button and the five Row buttons in Tip 414. BAS on the companion CD. Each of the Row buttons calls the SqlGetRow() function to move to a specific row in the application's six-row DBLIB buffer. The Next 5 Authors button, meanwhile, calls the SqlClrBuff() function (which you will learn about in Tip 417, "Using the SqlClrBuf() Function to Make Room for Additional Rows in the DBLIB Query Results Buffer") to clear the DBLIB buffer and then makes SqlNextRow() function calls to refill the buffer with another set of five rows from the query's results set.

415 Understanding the Differences Between Buffers and Cursors

Depending on the DBMS implementation, a cursor consists of either a set of pointers to the rows returned by a query or a copy of the data in the query's results set. When working with a cursor, an application does not have to know whether the cursor contains pointers to its underlying rows of query results or a copy of the data itself. As far as an application is concerned, the cursor contains the data it needs to display or modify because the cursor's *methods* (the subroutines and function calls the program uses to display or modify the cursor's underlying data) pass column values to the application and accept data values from the application for storage in the database.

A buffer, on the other hand, is a client-side memory-based (and perhaps hard drive-based) storage area where query results data is stored temporarily until a portion (or all) of it is moved into an application's objects (variables, structures, fields on forms, and so on) for display or modification. Unlike a cursor, a buffer is simply a copy of the data extracted from an SQL server (by executing a query), and any changes made on the server after the query's data is extracted to a buffer are not reflected in buffer's data. Conversely, unless an application is using a *static* cursor, any changes made to a cursor's underlying rows on the server are automatically reflected in the cursor's data.

To work with the data in a buffer, an application must use the available functions and subroutines in an interface program such as the DBLIB. Since a buffer is an RAM (or combination RAM/hard drive) based storage area, there is only one "type" of buffer, and the interface program's options settings determine the way in which an application can "move" among the buffers rows. Cursors, by contrast, are maintained by the DBMS itself and can be any one of three different types, depending on how they store information. The three types of cursors are: static, keyset-driven, and dynamic.

A *static* cursor contains a query results set based on data values present in the DBMS when the cursor is created. Subsequent changes made to database data after the cursor was created are not reflected in the cursor. However, it is possible to update the database itself through changes made to a static cursor.

The DBMS creates a *keyset-driven* cursor by placing a pointer to the underlying row for each row in a query's results set into the cursor. Whenever an application requests data from one of the rows in the cursor, the DBMS uses the pointer to retrieve the current data values from the underlying row in the database table(s). As such, a keyset-driven cursor's data will contain any changes made to the cursor's underlying rows even if those changes occur after the cursor was created. As is the case with the two other types of cursors, changes made to a keyset-driven cursor's data will update the underlying data values in the DBMS.

Finally, when maintaining a *dynamic* cursor, the DBMS not only keeps track of changes made to data values in underlying rows that existed when the cursor was created, but also makes sure that the cursors reflects database row deletions and insertions. As such, the number of rows in a dynamic cursor will change as rows that satisfy the search criteria in the cursor query's results set are inserted into or deleted from the database.

You will learn more about cursors in Tips 426–443. For now, the important thing to understand is that a buffer is a "staging area" for a one-way flow of data values from the DBMS to an application program. A cursor, meanwhile, is a database object that not only allows an application to retrieve database data, but also lets the program change the data on the server by updating the cursor's contents.

416 Using the SqlGetRow() Function to Select the Current Row in a DBLIB Query Results Buffer

While the SqlNextRow() function lets an application move forward through a DBLIB buffer one row at a time, the SqlGetRow() function lets the program access any row in the buffer at random. Before calling SqlGetRow(), a program must call both the SqlSetOpt() function to set the number of rows of query results that the DBLIB is to maintain in its buffer and the SqlNextRow() function to retrieve rows of query results from the DBMS into the DBLIB buffer.

The syntax of the SqlGetRow() function call is

```
nRetCode = SqlGetRow (nConnHandle, iRowNo)
```

where:

- **nRetCode (Long)** is the integer result code returned by the SqlGetRow() function call. After the function call, the value of nRetCode will be one of the following:
  - REGROW (–1) if buffer row iRowNo is a regular row of query results
  - The ID of the COMPUTE clause if buffer row iRowNo is a COMPUTE row
  - FAIL (0)
  - NOMOREROWS (–2) if row number iRowNo is not currently a row in the DBLIB buffer
- **nConnHandle (Long)** is the connection handle (returned by the SqlOpenConnection() or SqlOpen() functions) that was used by SqlSendCmd(), SqlSend(), or SqlExec() to send the query (or queries) to the MS-SQL Server for execution.
- **iRowNo (Integer)** is the number of the row of query results that the function is to select. For example, if iRowNo is 5, then the function will try to find the fifth row from the query results set in the DBLIB buffer.

Therefore, after making the function calls

```
   'Set the DBLIB buffer to 6 rows
nRetCode = SqlSetOpt(nConnHandle, SQLBUFFER, 6)
   'Read 6 rows of data from the query results set into the
   'DBLIB buffer
For i = 1 to 6
  nRetCode = SqlNextRow(nConnHandle, i)
Next i
```

an application can make the SqlGetRow() function call

```
nRetCode = SqlGetRow(nConnHandle, 4)
```

to select the fourth row from the query results set as the DBLIB's *current* row. Remember, the SqlGetRow() function tells the DBLIB only which row to treat as its current row. To retrieve the data values from the current row into its variables or fields on forms, an application must call the SqlData() function.

You can call the SqlGetRow() function to move to any one of the rows of query results stored in the DBLIB buffer. However, if the buffer is full and the row that you want to select is not currently in the buffer, you must call the SqlClrBuf() routine (which you will learn about in Tip 417, "Using the SqlClrBuf() Function to Make Room for Additional Rows in the DBLIB Query Results Buffer") to discard some of the rows in the buffer and then call the SqlNextRow() routine to refill the buffer until the query result set row that you want to select is in the DBLIB buffer.

For example, if you are using a 6-row DBLIB buffer and you have executed a query that produced 15 rows of results, you can move to the 12th row of query results by executing the following code:

```
    'Read 6 rows of query results into the DBLIB buffer
For i = 1 to 6
  nRetCode = SqlNextRow(nConnHandle, i)
Next i
    'Clear the DBLIB buffer to make room for more results
SqlClrBuf nConnHandle,6
    'Read rows 7 - 12 of query results into the DBLIB buffer
For i = 1 to 6
  nRetCode = SqlNextRow(nConnHandle, i)
Next i
    'Select the 12th row of query results
nRetCode = SqlGetRow(nConnHandle,12)
```

Notice that the row number (iRowNo) supplied as a parameter to the SqlGetRow() function refers to a row's position in the set of rows that make up the query's results set, not its position among the rows stored in the DBLIB's buffer.

417 Using the SqlClrBuf() Function to Make Room for Additional Rows in the DBLIB Query Results Buffer

As you saw in first example in Tip 416, "Using the SqlGetRow() Function to Select the Current Row in a DBLIB Query Results Buffer," the SqlSetOpt() function's SQLBUFFER option lets you specify the number of rows of query results that the DBLIB is to maintain in its buffer. For example, if a program executes the statement

```
nRetCode = SqlSetOpt(nConnHandle, SQLBUFFER, 10)
```

the DBLIB will allow the application to retrieve 10 rows of data from the query's results set into the DBLIB buffer by calling the SqlNextRow() function 10 times. If called an 11th time, in the current example, the SqlNextRow() function will be unable to add another row to the DBLIB buffer. As a result, the function will not retrieve a row of query results and will return an error code of BUFFULL (–3) instead. The SqlClrBuf() function lets you tell the DBLIB to discard one or more rows from its buffer to make room for additional rows of query results (which you can then call the SqlNextRow() function to retrieve).

The syntax of the SqlClrBuf() function call is

```
SqlClrBuf nConnHandle, iRowCt
```

where:

- **nConnHandle (Long)** is the connection handle (returned by the SqlOpenConnection() or the SqlOpen() functions) that was used by SqlSendCmd(), SqlSend(), or SqlExec() to send the query (or queries) to the MS-SQL Server for execution.
- **iRowCt (Integer)** is the number of rows of query results to clear from the buffer. If the value of iRowCt is less than 1, the DBLIB ignores the SqlClrBuf() function call. On the other hand, if the value of iRowCt is greater than or equal to the number of rows in the buffer, the DBLIB discards all of the rows in the buffer.

The DBLIB clears the rows in its buffer on a first-in/first-out basis. Therefore, if you have a 10-row buffer and you have called the SqlNextRow() function 10 times to fill it with the first 10 rows of query results, executing the statement

```
SqlClrBuf nConnHandle, 5
```

will tell the DBLIB to discard the first 5 rows added to the buffer (by calling the SqlNextRow() function).

Review the code for the Next 5 Authors button on Form1 of Tip417.bas on the book's companion Web site at www.premierpressbooks.com/downloads.asp. Each time the user clicks the mouse pointer on the Next 5 Authors button, the application calls the NextAuthors_Click() routine. NextAuthors_Click() uses the SqlClrBuf() function to discard all rows of query results from the DBLIB buffer. Then NextAuthors_Click() calls GetResultsSet(), which uses the SqlNextRow() function to refill the DBLIB buffer with an additional five rows of query results.

418 Understanding the MS-SQL Server FOR BROWSE Clause in a SELECT Statement

When added to a SELECT statement, the FOR BROWSE clause lets you read rows from a table in which another user is inserting, updating, or deleting rows. Normally, the MS-SQL Server's locking mechanisms will prevent you from reading the pages of a table for which there are pending (uncommitted) UPDATE, DELETE, or INSERT statements.

A SELECT statement without a FOR BROWSE clause that tries to read a row with a pending (uncommitted) UPDATE, for example, will "hang," waiting for the user modifying the table's contents to execute either a COMMIT or a ROLLBACK statement. If the user commits (or rolls back) the pending UPDATE before the expiration of the query's timeout interval, the SELECT statement will return its results table. Otherwise, the SELECT statement will abort without retrieving any rows of results. The FOR BROWSE clause tells the DBMS to let the query proceed without waiting for the other user to COMMIT or ROLLBACK a pending UPDATE, INSERT, or DELETE.

In other words, the statement

```
SELECT * FROM employees
```

will wait for other users to COMMIT (or ROLLBACK) pending transactions that modify the contents of the EMPLOYEES table. The statement

```
SELECT * FROM employees FOR BROWSE
```

will generate a results table without waiting, as long as the EMPLOYEES table has both a TIMESTAMP field and a UNIQUE INDEX.

To use the FOR BROWSE clause in a SELECT statement, the query must contain a single table that has both a TIMESTAMP column and a UNIQUE INDEX. Moreover, as shown in the current example, the FOR BROWSE clause should be the last clause in the SELECT statement. If a SELECT statement with the FOR BROWSE clause does not satisfy these requirements, the DBMS will execute the query as if it did not have a FOR BROWSE clause.

Note: *If the table you want to query has no UNIQUE INDEX or has no column of data type TIMESTAMP, you can approximate the effects of a SELECT statement's FOR BROWSE clause by setting the session's TRANSACTION ISOLATION LEVEL to READ UNCOMMITTED. Bear in mind that reading updated or inserted data before it is committed will result in a nonrepeatable read anomaly if the user who is making a change decides to undo it by executing a ROLLBACK statement.*

---

419 Understanding Why the DBLIB Does Not Support Positioned UPDATE and DELETE Statements

Unlike the ODBC interface, the DBLIB does not support positioned UPDATE and DELETE statements (which you learned about in Tips 384, "Using the SQLSetPos Function SQL_UPDATE Option to Perform a Positioned UPDATE," and 385, "Using the SQLSetPos Function SQL_DELETE Option to Perform a Positioned DELETE"). When an application calls the ODBC driver's SQLFetch() function to retrieve a row of data from a single database table into a cursor, the DBMS maintains a direct correspondence between the current row of query results and its corresponding row in the underlying table. Using this correspondence, an application can build and execute an UPDATE or DELETE statement with a WHERE CURRENT OF <cursor name> clause. When submitted to the DBMS for execution, the system will UPDATE or DELETE the table row that corresponds to the current row in the cursor named in the WHERE CURRENT OF clause. When using the DBLIB interface, an applications calls SqlSendCmd(), SqlSend(), or SqlExec() to send a SELECT statement to the DBMS for execution. The server sends the query's results set the DBLIB, which uses its buffer area to store the data. When a program using calls SqlNextRow(), the function retrieves a row of query results from the DBLIB buffer, not from the database itself. As a result, there is no DBMS-maintained correspondence between the row of query results retrieved into an application from the DBLIB buffer and the row in the database table from which its column values were copied.

The inability to relate the current row retrieved from the DBLIB buffer with a specific row in a database table makes it impossible for the DBLIB to tell the DBMS to execute a positioned UPDATE or DELETE. Because the lack of positioned updates and deletes is a real disadvantage when a user is allowed to browse a set of query results and wants to UPDATE (or DELETE) the data currently being displayed on the screen, the DBLIB provides a set of browse mode functions that an application can use to execute a searched UPDATE (or DELETE) that targets the database row from which the DBLIB's current row was derived.

You will learn about the DBLIB browse mode functions in Tips 420–422.

420 Understanding the DBLIB Browse Mode Functions

To get around the inability to relate the current DBLIB buffer row with its underlying row in a database table, the DBLIB API includes a set of *browse mode* functions that a program can use to create a pseudo-*positioned* update capability (which you will learn about in Tip 422, "Using the SqlQual() Function to Generate the WHERE Clause for a DBLIB Browse Mode UPDATE or DELETE"). The DBLIB browse mode functions are:

- **SqlTabCount(nConnHandle)**, which returns the number of tables, including server work tables, used in the SELECT statement sent to the server using the connection handle passed as the function's only parameter.
- **SqlTabBrowse(nConnHandle,iTabNum)**, which returns the value SUCCEED(1) if the iTabNum table used by the query sent to the DBMS using the connection handle nConnHandle can be updated using DBLIB browse mode procedures, or FAIL (0), if not. The first table in a DBLIB query is table 1 (vs. 0). Thus, after executing the statement

```
iCanBeUpdated = SqlTabBrowse(nConnHandle,1)
```

  the value of iCanBeUpdated will be 1 (SUCCEED) if the first table used in the query can be updated by the DBLIB browse mode routines.

- **SqlTabName(nConnHandle,iTabNum)**, which returns the name of the iTabNum table used in the query sent to the DBMS using the connection handle nConnHandle. The first table in a DBLIB query is table 1 (vs. 0). Therefore, the statement

```
sTableName = SqlTabName(nConnHandle,2)
```

  will place the name of the second table used in a query into the character string sTableName.

- **SqlColBrowse(nConnHandle,iColNum)**, which returns the value SUCCEED(1) if the iColNum column in the query results set can be updated using DBLIB browse mode procedures, or FAIL (0), if not. The first column in the DBLIB results set is column 1 (vs. 0).
- **SqlTabSource(nConnHandle,iColNum,iTabNum)**, which returns the name from which the result set column iColNum was derived and places the table number in the iTabNum parameter. Therefore, after executing the statement

```
sTableName = SqlTabSource(nConnHandle,4,iTabNum)
```

  the variable sTableName will contain the name of the table from which the fourth column in the query was derived, and the value of iTabNum will contain its table number.

- **SqlColSource(nConnHandle,iColNum)**, which returns the name of the table column from which the iColNum column in the query results set was derived.
- **SqlQual(nConnHandle,iTabNum,sTabName)**, which returns a character string WHERE clause that can be used in an UPDATE or DELETE statement to change or remove the current row of query results from the database table identified either by number as iTabNum or by name as sTabName.

421 Preparing the DBLIB to Perform a Browse Mode UPDATE or DELETE

Before calling any of the DBLIB browse mode functions, an application must open a connection with an MS-SQL Server and send a SELECT statement that includes a FOR BROWSE clause to the DBMS. As you learned in Tip 418, "Understanding the MS-SQL Server FOR BROWSE Clause in a SELECT Statement," only tables that have both a UNIQUE INDEX and a TIMESTAMP column may appear in the FROM clause of a SELECT statement with a FOR BROWSE clause. Therefore, the DBLIB browse mode functions can be used only on tables with both a UNIQUE INDEX and a TIMESTAMP column.

Because the DBLIB browse mode UPDATE or DELETE is actually a searched UPDATE or DELETE, the DBLIB must have a way of identifying the particular row in the table that corresponds with the *current* row in its buffer. The UNIQUE INDEX ensures that the DBLIB can find the row in the table from which each of the rows in its query results buffer was derived. The table's TIMESTAMP column provides a way of determining whether the underlying row was updated since its contents were copied into the DBLIB's buffer.

When executing a DBLIB browse mode UPDATE or DELETE, you will need two connections to the MS-SQL Server. The application will use one connection to send the SELECT statement (with the BROWSE MODE clause) to the server and then to retrieve the query results set into the DBLIB buffer. Then the program uses the second connection to send UPDATE or DELETE statements to the server.

Tip 423, "Executing a DBLIB Browse Mode DELETE," will show you a sample of code that you can use to execute a DBLIB browse mode DELETE; Tip 424, "Executing a DBLIB Browse Mode UPDATE," goes through the process of executing a DBLIB browse mode UPDATE. The important things to understand now are that target tables for DBLIB browse mode functions must have both a column of data type TIMESTAMP and a UNIQUE INDEX. Moreover, the application must open two connections with the same MS-SQL Server—one to send and retrieve query results, and the other to use when sending UPDATE or DELETE statements to the server.

422 Using the SqlQual() Function to Generate the WHERE Clause for a DBLIB Browse Mode UPDATE or DELETE

As mentioned in Tip 421, "Preparing the DBLIB to Perform a Browse Mode UPDATE or DELETE," the DBLIB can simulate positioned UPDATE and DELETE statements only because neither the DBLIB nor the DBMS really knows which row in the database table corresponds with the current row in the DBLIB buffer. The DBLIB can, however, call the SqlQual() function to generate a WHERE clause that you can use in an UPDATE or DELETE statement to perform a searched update that will find the DBLIB's current row in the database table from which it was derived.

The syntax of the SqlQual() function is

```
sWhereClause = SqlQual(nConnHandle,iTabNum,sTabName)
```

where:

- **sWhereClause (String)** is the WHERE clause returned by the SqlQual() function. The WHERE clause will include the column name and value for both the UNIQUE INDEX column and the TIMESTAMP column in the table numbered iTabNum or named sTabName that corresponds to the current row in the DBLIB.
- **nConnHandle (Long)** is the connection handle (returned by the SqlOpenConnection() or SqlOpen() functions) that was used by SqlSendCmd(), SqlSend() or SqlExec() to send the query (or queries) to the MS-SQL Server for execution.
- **iTabNum (Integer)** is the number of the table in the SELECT statement's FROM clause that is to be the target of the browse mode UPDATE or DELETE. (Tables are numbered starting with 1 as the first table from the left in the FROM clause.) If iTabNum is –1, then the SqlQual() function will use the string in sTabName to identify the table.
- **sTabName (String)** is the name of the table to be updated by a DBLIB browse mode UPDATE or DELETE. If sTabName is an empty string, then the SqlQual() function will use the value of iTabNum to identify the table.

Therefore, if you call the SqlGetRow() function as

```
SqlGetRow(nQueryConnHandle,5)
```

to select the fifth row of results returned by the query as the DBLIB's current row and then you call SqlQual() function as

```
sWhereClause = SqlQual(nQueryConnHandle,-1,"employees422")
```

the (String) variable sWhereClause will contain a WHERE clause similar to:

```
where (emp_ID=5) and tsequal(tstamp,0x00000000000006fc)
```

You can then add this WHERE clause to a DELETE statement (as you will learn to do in Tip 423, "Executing a DBLIB Browse Mode DELETE") or an UPDATE statement (which you will learn about in Tip 424, "Executing a DBLIB Browse Mode UPDATE") to DELETE or UPDATE the DBLIB's current row in the database.

Review the code in the ShowEmployee() routine in Form1.frm of Project422 on the book's Web site at www.premierpressbooks.com/downloads.asp. When called, the routine uses a Windows message box similar to that shown in Figure 422.1 to display the WHERE clause that the DBMS can use to find the underlying table row from which the current row in the DBLIB buffer was derived.

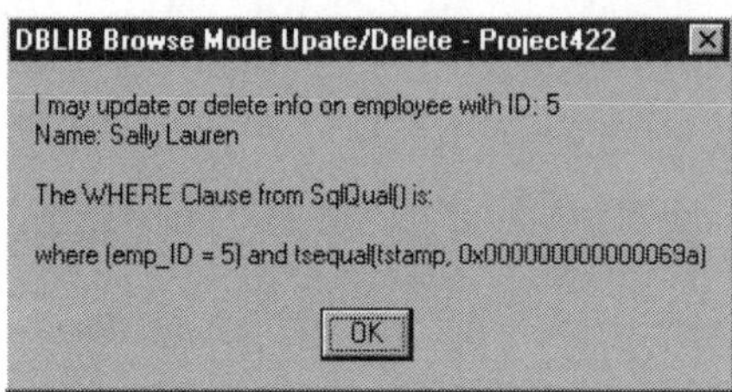

Figure 422.1 Windows message box with a WHERE clause returned by an SqlQual() function call

423 Executing a DBLIB Browse Mode DELETE

Before attempting a DBLIB browse mode DELETE, bear in mind that the table from which the current DBLIB buffer row is to be deleted must have both a column of data type TIMESTAMP and a UNIQUE INDEX. After selecting an eligible table, open two connections to the MS-SQL Server—one through which to send a query to the DBMS (and retrieve its results set) and the second for use in sending a browse mode DELETE statement. For example, the Visual Basic (VB) code

```
Dim sDelStmt As String
Dim nRetCode As Long
Dim nQueryConnHandle As Long
Dim nDelConnHandle As Long
nQueryConnHandle=SqlOpenConnection("NVBizNet2","konrad",_
  "king","ws-query",App.EXEName)
nDelConnHandle=SqlOpenConnection("NVBizNet2","konrad",_
  "king","ws-delete",App.EXEName)
```

will establish two connections with the MS-SQL Server NVBizNet2.

Next, select the database that contains the table with the row you want to DELETE. Then use the query connection handle to send a SELECT statement with a FOR BROWSE clause to the DBMS:

```
nRetCode = SqlCmd(nQueryConnHandle," USE SQLTips")
nRetCode = SqlCmd(nQueryConnHandle,
  " SELECT * FROM employees423 FOR BROWSE")
nRetCode = SqlSend(nQueryConnHandle)
```

After the DBMS executes the FOR BROWSE SELECT statement, retrieve the query's results set by executing VB code similar to:

```
nRetCode = SqlOk(nQueryConnHandle)
nRetCode = SqlResults(nQueryConnHandle) 'Get USE results
nRetCode = SqlResults(nQueryConnHandle) 'Get SELECT results
nRetCode = SqlSetOpt(nQueryConnHandle, SQLBUFFER, 100)
Do Until NOMOREROWS = SqlNextRow(nQueryConnHandle)
Loop
```

Now, suppose that you want to DELETE the EMPLOYEES423 table row that corresponds with the 10th row in the query results set. First, use the SqlGetRow() function to select the query's 10th row of results as the DBLIB's current row:

```
nRetCode = SqlGetRow(nQueryConnHandle,10)
```

Then call the SqlQual() function to create the WHERE clause that a searched DELETE can use to find and remove the row from the EMPLOYEES423 table:

```
sDelStmt = "DELETE FROM employees423 " & _
             SqlQual(nQueryConnHandle,-1,"employees423")
```

Finally, use the DELETE connection handle in nDelConnHandle to send the DELETE statement to the MS-SQL Server for execution:

```
nRetCode = SqlSendCmd(nDelConnHandle,sDelStmt)
```

Review the source code for Project423.vbp on the book's Web site at www.premierpressbooks.com/downloads.asp. The VB program first queries the employees data in the EMPLOYEES423 table and then lets you DELETE individual employees from the table by clicking on one of the five Del Row buttons.

424 Executing a DBLIB Browse Mode UPDATE

As is the case with a DBLIB browse mode DELETE, you can perform a DBLIB browse mode UPDATE only on a table that has both a column of data type TIMESTAMP and a UNIQUE INDEX. To perform a DBLIB browse mode UPDATE, first open two connections to the

MS-SQL Server—one through which to send a query and the second to use when sending an UPDATE statement. For example, the Visual Basic (VB) code

```
Dim sUpdtStmt As String
Dim nRetCode As Long
Dim nQueryConnHandle As Long
Dim nUpdtConnHandle As Long
nQueryConnHandle=SqlOpenConnection("NVBizNet2","konrad",_
  "king","ws-query",App.EXEName)
nUpdtConnHandle=SqlOpenConnection("NVBizNet2","konrad",_
  "king","ws-update",App.EXEName)
```

will establish two connections with the MS-SQL Server NVBizNet2.

Next, select the database with the table that has the row you want to UPDATE. Then use the connection with the query connection handle to send a SELECT statement with a FOR BROWSE clause to the DBMS:

```
nRetCode = SqlCmd(nQueryConnHandle," USE SQLTips")
nRetCode = SqlCmd(nQueryConnHandle,
  " SELECT * FROM employees424 FOR BROWSE")
nRetCode = SqlSend(nQueryConnHandle)
```

After sending the FOR BROWSE SELECT statement to the DBMS for execution, retrieve the query's results set by executing the VB code similar to:

```
nRetCode = SqlOk(nQueryConnHandle)
nRetCode = SqlResults(nQueryConnHandle) 'Get USE results
nRetCode = SqlResults(nQueryConnHandle) 'Get SELECT results
nRetCode = SqlSetOpt(nQueryConnHandle, SQLBUFFER, 100)
Do Until NOMOREROWS = SqlNextRow(nQueryConnHandle)
Loop
```

Now suppose that you want to UPDATE the EMPLOYEES423 table row that corresponds with the seventh row in the query results buffer. First, use the SqlGetRow() function to select the query's seventh row of results as the current row in the DBLIB buffer:

```
nRetCode = SqlGetRow(nQueryConnHandle,7)
```

Then call the SqlQual() function to create the WHERE clause that a searched UPDATE can use to find the underlying row (in the EMPLOYEES423 table) from which the current row in the DBLIB was derived. For example, to set the POSITION column in the underlying row that corresponds with the DBLIB's current row to NULL, execute VB statements similar to:

```
sUpdtStmt = "UPDATE employees423 SET position = NULL " & _
              SqlQual(nQueryConnHandle,-1,"employees423")
nRetCode = SqlSendCmd(nUpdtConnHandle,sUpdtStmt)
```

Review the source code for Project424.vbp on the book's companion Web site at www.premierpressbooks.com/downloads.asp. The VB program first queries the employees data in the EMPLOYEES424 table and then lets you UPDATE individual rows in the table by transferring the content of the fields on the input form to columns in a table row when you click your mouse pointer on one of the five Update Row buttons.

425 Performing Dynamic SQL Queries Using the DBLIB API

Although the SELECT statements used in the projects for Tips 417–424 are "hard-coded" in each of the example Visual Basic (VB) programs, the DBLIB functions also let you write applications that let users formulate queries at runtime. This *dynamic* SQL query capability works especially well with the MSFlexGrid, which lets you define its column names and set its column and row counts on the fly.

For example, if you design a VB form with text field (named Text1) similar to that shown in Figure 425.1, you can call the SqlSendCmd() functions as

```
nRetCode = SqlSendCmd(nQueryConnHandle,Form1.text1.Text)
```

to place the contents of the Text1 field into the nQueryConnHandle command buffer and send the buffer's contents to the DBMS for execution.

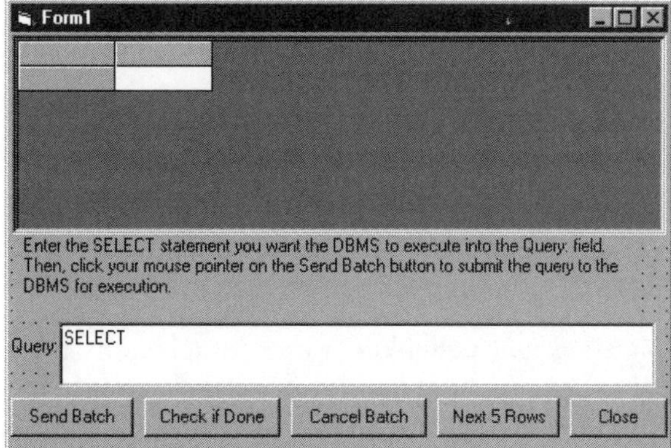

Figure 425.1 Visual Basic form with a text field to accept a user's dynamic SQL statement during runtime

Assuming that the Text1 field on Form1 contains a valid SELECT statement that queries a table to which the VB program's connection has SELECT access, the VB code

```
Dim i As Integer
FlexGrid.Cols = SqlNumCols(nQueryConnHandle)
FlexGrid.Rows = 1
FlexGrid.Row = 0
FlexGrid.Col = 0
```

```
For i = 1 To FlexGrid.Cols
  FlexGrid.Text = SqlColName(nQueryConnHandle,i)
  If FlexGrid.Col < FlexGrid.Cols - 1 Then
    FlexGrid.Col = FlexGrid.Col + 1
  End If
Next i
```

will retrieve the count of columns and their names from the query's results table.

If you then pass the MSFlexGrid with the column names and column count set by the preceding VB code along with the query connection handle to the VB routine

```
Sub GetResultsSet (nConnHandle As Long, _
                     FlexGrid As MSFlexGrid)
Dim iCol As Integer
Dim nRetCode As Long

Do Until NOMOREROWS = SqlNextRow(nConnHandle)
  FlexGrid.Col = 0
  FlexGrid.Rows = FlexGrid.Rows + 1
  FlexGrid.Row = FlexGrid.Rows - 1

  For iCol = 1 To FlexGrid.Cols
    If SqlDatLen(nConnHandle, iCol) <> 0 Then
      FlexGrid.Text = SqlData(nConnHandle, iCol)
    Else
      FlexGrid.Text = "** NULL **"
    End If

    If FlexGrid.Col < (FlexGrid.Cols - 1) Then
      FlexGrid.Col = FlexGrid.Col + 1
    End If
  Next iCol
Loop
End Sub
```

you have a VB application that will allow a user to query any table to which the VB application's connection has the proper access. Moreover, the program's MSFlexGrid object will display the query results with the correct column names, even though the columns selected, number of columns, and number of rows may change with each new dynamic SQL query that the user enters into the Text1 field and sends to the MS-SQL Server for execution.

Review Project425.frm and Project425.bas on the book's companion Web site at www.premierpressbooks.com/downloads.asp for a complete listing of a VB program that lets the user write, submit, and display the results from dynamic SQL queries.

426 Understanding the Purpose of a Cursor

The first time I heard that most SQL servers let you store and work with results set data in cursors, I wondered how much information could fit into a $\frac{1}{8}$-inch vertical (or horizontal) flashing line—and how one could possible view its contents. However, unlike a Windows or DOS cursor (which shows you the current insertion point for text in a document, field, or DOS command line), an SQL cursor is a temporary database object that either holds a copy of, or pointers to, rows of data stored in the system's permanent tables. A cursor gives you way to manipulate table data on a row-by-row basis instead of a result-set-at-a-time basis.

For example, if you want to give your customers a 1 percent rebate of their total orders placed during the period 12/01/00 to 12/31/00, you can execute an UPDATE statement similar to:

```
UPDATE customers SET rebate =
  (SELECT SUM(order_total) FROM orders
   WHERE order_date BETWEEN '12/01/2000' AND '12/31/2000'
   GROUP BY cust_no
   HAVING cust_no = cust_ID) * .01
```

The subquery in the current example generates a results set that lists the total amount purchased by each customer during the month of December 2000. The UPDATE statement then applies the 1 percent rebate to the orders as a group and places the REBATE due each customer into the customer's row in the CUSTOMERS table. Thus, SQL's standard way of working with data (in this case, each customer's December 2000 orders) a results set at a time is an efficient way of computing a rebate when the same percentage applies to each row of orders in the group.

Now, suppose you want to give rebates ranging from 1 percent to 2 percent, depending on how much a customer purchased during the same period. A customer is to receive a 1 percent rebate on the first $1,000.00 in purchases, 1.5 percent on the next $1,000.00 worth of orders, and 2 percent on additional purchase made after the customer's cumulative order total reaches $2,000.00. Although you still need to work with the group of orders each customer placed in December 2000, you can no longer apply the same percentage rebate to each row of orders in the results set. As such, a cursor is useful because it will let you work your way through each customer's orders one order at time. By keeping track of the cumulative amount purchased as you move from one order to the next, you can apply a different (higher) rebate percentage to orders placed as the pervious order total moves from one tier in the rebate table to the next.

You will learn how to create and work with cursors in Tips 427–444. For now, the important thing to understand is that a cursor is a temporary database object that lets you work with the data in its underlying table(s) one row at a time. When you need to perform multiple actions on the same set of data, using a cursor to hold the data while you work with it is more efficient than executing the same query multiple times—once for each of the actions you need to take on the results set.

427 Using the DECLARE CURSOR Statement to Define a Cursor

An SQL DECLARE CURSOR statement lets you specify not only the query that will be used to generate the results set (the set of rows) that the DBMS will store in a cursor, but also the actions a user (or an application) can take while working with the cursor. When you declare a cursor by executing a DECLARE CURSOR statement such as

```
DECLARE cur_payroll_work CURSOR
FOR SELECT emp_num, dept, hourly_rate, ot_rate,
           monthly_salary, time_in, time_out, project,
           tcard_hourly_rate, tcard_labor_cost
    FROM timecards, employees
    WHERE timecards.emp_ID = employees.emp_num
```

the SQL server validates the cursor's query, making sure it is syntactically correct and that tables or views listed in the SELECT statement's FROM clause do indeed exist in the database.

The syntax of the DECLARE CURSOR statement is

```
DECLARE <cursor name> [INSENSITIVE][SCROLL] CURSOR
FOR <SELECT statement>
[FOR {READ ONLY|UPDATE[OF <column list>]}]
```

where:

- **INSENSITIVE** tells the DBMS to make a temporary copy of the query results set data (vs. using pointers that reference columns in rows of "live" data in permanent database tables). If you are using an (UPDATE and DELETE) INSENSITIVE cursor, any changes made to the underlying tables will not be reflected in the cursor's data. Moreover, an INSENSITIVE cursor is READ ONLY, which means you cannot modify its contents or use an INSENSITIVE cursor to modify the contents of its underlying (base) tables. If the INSENSITIVE option is omitted from the DECLARE CURSOR statement, the DBMS will create an UPDATE and DELETE sensitive cursor that reflects any changes made to its underlying rows in the permanent database table(s).
- **SCROLL** specifies that the cursor is to support the selection of any of its rows as the current row by using any of the FETCH options (FIRST, LAST, PRIOR, NEXT, RELATIVE, and ABSOLUTE). If the SCROLL option is omitted from the DECLARE CURSOR statement, the cursor will support only single-row forward movement through its rows (that is, it will support only the FETCH NEXT option for moving through the cursor).

- **READ ONLY** prevents the user (or application) using the cursor from changing the cursor's contents by updating data values or deleting rows. Consequently, you cannot use a READ ONLY cursor to modify data in the cursor's underlying table(s). If READ ONLY is omitted from the DECLARE CURSOR statement, the DBMS will create a cursor that can be used to modify its base table(s).
- **UPDATE** is the UPDATE clause that tells the DBMS to create an updateable cursor and (optionally) lists the cursor columns whose values can be updated. If any columns are listed in the UPDATE, *only* the columns listed are updateable. On the other hand, if the DECLARE CURSOR statement specifies only the UPDATE option (without a column list), then the cursor will allow updates to any or all of its columns.

Therefore, the DECLARE CURSOR statement at the beginning of this tip defines (declares) a "forward only" cursor named PAYROLL_WORK, which displays all of the columns and rows in the TIMECARDS table and some of the columns values from rows in the EMPLOYEES table.

428 Using an OPEN Statement to Create a Cursor

When executing a DECLARE CURSOR statement, the DBMS only *validates* the cursor's SELECT statement. Conversely, when executing an OPEN statement, the DBMS not only creates the cursor, but it also populates (fills) it with data by *executing* the cursor's SELECT statement. If the DECLARE CURSOR statement includes the INSENSITIVE option, the OPEN statement will cause the DBMS to create a temporary table to hold the query's results set. Otherwise, the DBMS will place the row ID for each of the rows in the cursor query's results set into a temporary workspace managed by the cursor.

They syntax of the (cursor) OPEN statement is:

```
OPEN <cursor name>
```

As such, to create and populate the cursor created at the beginning of Tip 427, "Using the DECLARE CURSOR Statement to Define a Cursor," execute the OPEN statement:

```
OPEN cur_payroll_work
```

Because the declaration for the cursor in the current example does not include the INSENSITIVE option, the DBMS will fill the cursor's storage structure with the row ID of each of the rows in the underlying table(s) (listed in the cursor query's FROM clause) that satisfy the search criteria in the cursor query's WHERE clause. (If the DECLARE CURSOR statement had included the INSENSITIVE option, the DBMS would have created a table and filled it with a copy of the data from the corresponding rows in the cursor's underlying table[s].)

Note: *After you execute the OPEN statement to create and populate the cursor, you can use the @@CURSOR_ROWS function to retrieve the number of rows in the most recently opened cursor.*

429 Using the ORDER BY Clause to Change the Order of the Rows in a Cursor

If you need to process cursor data in a particular order, you can have the DBMS sort the cursor data for you by adding an ORDER BY clause to the query in the DECLARE CURSOR statement. For example, if you are working on a payroll system and have a cursor that contains weekly timecard data, you will want the time cards sorted in order by date within employee number. By grouping all of the timecards for the same employee together in date order, you can make one pass through the rows in the cursor to total the number of hours the employee worked during the period and compute the employee's rate of pay for each timecard. As soon as the total hours worked exceeds 40 for the week, you know to switch to the overtime rate as you compute the hourly wage for the employee's remaining timecards. Then, as soon as you FETCH a timecard that has a different employee number than the one you just processed, you know to reset the total hours to the number of hours in the new timecard since you have moved on to the next employee.

The syntax of the ORDER BY clause used to set the order of the rows in a cursor is the same as the ORDER BY clause in a normal query:

```
ORDER BY <column name> [ASC | DESC]
  [,...<last column name> [ASC | DESC]]
```

Thus, to sort the TIMECARDS in the CUR_PAYROLL_WORK cursor (declared in Tip 427, "Using the DECLARE CURSOR Statement to Define a Cursor") in ascending order by date and time within employee ID, change the cursor's definition to:

```
DECLARE cur_payroll_work CURSOR
FOR SELECT emp_num, dept, hourly_rate, ot_rate,
           monthly_salary, time_in, time_out, project,
           tcard_hourly_rate, tcard_labor_cost
    FROM timecards, employees
    WHERE timecards.emp_ID = employees.emp_num
    ORDER BY emp_ID, time_in, time_out
```

Since the default sort order is *ascending*, you do not have to include the ASC option after any of the columns listed in the ORDER BY clause to sort the query results table in ascending order. However, if you want the rows sorted in descending order by any of the columns named in the column list, you must include the DESC option after the column name.

Note: Unlike the ORDER BY clause in noncursor SELECT statements, only the columns listed for display in the query's SELECT clause can appear as columns in the ORDER BY clause. (In noncursor SELECT statements, any column in the table[s] listed in the query's FROM clause may appear in the ORDER BY clause—even if the columns are not listed [for display] in the statement's SELECT clause.)

430 Including Calculated Values as Columns in a Cursor

In addition to columns from tables and views listed in the cursor SELECT statement's FROM clause, a cursor can include computed columns. Suppose, for example, that some of the employees in a company are paid a monthly salary instead of an hourly wage. However, for the purposes of computing a labor cost for each of the company's projects, the salaried employees submit timesheets showing the time worked on each project, and an "hourly rate" is computed according to the formula:

```
(<monthly salary> * 12) / (40 hours * 52 weeks)
```

If the HOURLY_RATE column is NULL for salaried employees and the MONTHLY_SALARY column is NULL for hourly employees, then you can use the COALESCE function to add a computed HRLY_PAYRATE column to the CUR_PAYROLL_WORK cursor by changing the DECLARE CURSOR statement to:

```
DECLARE cur_payroll_work CURSOR
FOR SELECT emp_num, dept, ot_rate, monthly_salary,
           time_in, time_out, project,
           tcard_hourly_rate, tcard_labor_cost,
           COALESCE(hourly_rate,
             (monthly_salary * 12) / 2080) hrly_rate
           (CONVERT(REAL,(time_out - time_in),8) * 24)
             hours_worked
    FROM timecards, employees
    WHERE timecards.emp_ID = employees.emp_num
    ORDER BY emp_ID, time_in, time_out
```

(In addition to the HRLY_RATE column, the cursor in the current example includes the computed column HOURS_WORKED, to avoid having to compute the amount of time worked on each timecard when processing the cursor's data.)

Note: Be sure to name each of the computed columns so that it will be easy to refer to all of the columns in the cursor as necessary when you process the data in the cursor.

431 Using the FOR UPDATE Clause to Specify Which Underlying Table Columns a Cursor Can Modify

By default, an updateable cursor will let you UPDATE the values in all of the columns listed in the SELECT clause of the query used to define the cursor. Moreover, the cursor will let you use it to DELETE one row at a time any of its underlying tables. If you want to prevent a user from being able to use a cursor to modify column values in or remove rows from its underlying (base) table(s), add the READ ONLY clause to the DECLARE CURSOR statement, as in:

```
DECLARE <cursor name> CURSOR
FOR <SELECT statement> READ ONLY
```

Conversely, if you omit both the READ ONLY clause and the FOR UPDATE clause from a DECLARE CURSOR statement, or include a FOR UPDATE clause without a column list, the user will be able to use the cursor to UPDATE the value of any column listed in the cursor's SELECT statement. Then, by executing an UPDATE or DELETE statement with a WHERE CURRENT OF <cursor name> clause, the user can use the cursor to make changes in or remove a row from the cursor's underlying table. (You will learn about positioned updates and deletes in Tip 434, "Understanding Cursor-based Positioned DELETE Statements," and Tip 435, "Understanding Cursor-based Positioned UPDATE Statements.")

Thus, the DECLARE CURSOR statements

```
DECLARE <cursor name> CURSOR
FOR <SELECT statement>
```

and

```
DECLARE <cursor name> CURSOR
FOR <SELECT statement> FOR UPDATE
```

will allow the user to UPDATE any column listed the SELECT clause of the cursor's SELECT statement. To limit the user to being able to update values in only some of the cursor's columns, list the columns eligible for update in the FOR UPDATE clause of the DECLARE CURSOR statement.

For example, listing the two columns in the FOR UPDATE clause of the DECLARE CURSOR statement

```
DECLARE cur_payroll_work CURSOR
FOR SELECT emp_num, dept, ot_rate, monthly_salary,
           time_in, time_out, project,
           tcard_hourly_rate, tcard_labor_cost,
           COALESCE(hourly_rate,
             (monthly_salary * 12) / 2080) hrly_rate
           (CONVERT(REAL,(time_out - time_in),8) * 24)
             hours_worked
```

```
    FROM timecards, employees
    WHERE timecards.emp_ID = employees.emp_num
    FOR UPDATE OF tcard_hourly_rate, tcard_labor_cost
```

will let a user use the cursor to UPDATE values in only the TCARD_HOURLY_RATE and TCARD_LABOR_COST columns of the cursor and the TIMECARDS table.

Note: *If you add an ORDER BY clause to the cursor's SELECT statement, the DBMS will restrict the cursor as READ ONLY. As such, you cannot have both an ORDER BY clause and a FOR UPDATE clause in the same cursor SELECT statement.*

432 Using a FETCH Statement to Retrieve Column Values from a Row in the Cursor

A FETCH statement lets you retrieve or display data values from the *next* row in the cursor. When you execute an OPEN (cursor) statement, the DBMS opens the cursor whose name follows the keyword OPEN by populating (filling) the cursor with the results set from the cursor's SELECT statement and positioning the cursor's current row pointer prior to the first row in the cursor. Therefore, when the first FETCH statement you execute after opening a cursor retrieves data from the "next" row in the cursor, it will return the data values in the cursor's first row.

The syntax of the FETCH statement is:

```
FETCH [NEXT|PRIOR|FIRST|LAST|
      {ABSOLUTE <row number>}|{RELATIVE <row number>}]
      FROM <cursor name>
      [INTO <variable name>[,...<last variable name>]]
```

Therefore, to display the IDs and names of the first two authors in the CU_AUTH cursor declared by

```
USE pubs
DECLARE cur_authors CURSOR
FOR SELECT au_ID, au_fname, au_lname FROM authors
```

you could execute the Transact-SQL code

```
DECLARE @au_ID CHAR(11),
        @au_fname VARCHAR(30), @au_lname VARCHAR(30)
OPEN cur_authors
FETCH cur_authors INTO @au_ID, @au_fname, @au_lname
PRINT 'ID: '+ @au_ID+'  Name: '+@au_fname +' '+@au_lname
```

which will produce output similar to:

```
ID: 172-32-1176  Name: Johnson White
ID: 213-46-8915  Name: Marjorie Green
```

Each time you execute a FETCH statement, the DBMS moves to the next row in the cursor and fetches (copies) the values in the cursor's columns into the temporary variables listed in the statement's INTO clause. The FETCH statement works its way through the cursor columns and the variables in its INTO clause from left to right, copying the value in the cursor column into the corresponding variable in the variable list. As such, the variable list in the FETCH statement's INTO clause must match the column list in the cursor's SELECT statement both in number and in data type. (If a FETCH statement has no INTO clause, then the DBMS will display the values in all of the columns of the cursor's current row to the screen.)

Notice that if the FETCH statement does not include a row selection (ABSOLUTE, RELATIVE, FIRST, LAST) or movement direction (NEXT, PRIOR), the DBMS executes the statement as FETCH NEXT.

433 Orienting the Cursor's Current Row Pointer Prior to Fetching Column Values from the Current Row

As you saw in Tip 432, "Using a FETCH Statement to Retrieve Column Values from a Row in the Cursor," if you execute a FETCH statement that does not include a direction for movement through the cursor, such as

```
FETCH FROM <cursor name> INTO <variable list>
```

the DBMS assumes you want to execute a FETCH NEXT. As such, the system moves the cursor's row pointer from its current location forward one row in the cursor and then has the FETCH statement retrieve the column values from that row into the variables in the statement's INTO clause—or display them to the screen, if there is no INTO clause. If you do not include the SCROLL option when declaring a cursor, the DBMS will allow you only to move forward one row at a time through the cursor, using the FETCH NEXT statement.

You can use the FETCH statement's row positioning options (other than NEXT) only if you are working with a SCROLL cursor. To declare a SCROLL cursor, include the keyword SCROLL in the cursor's declaration, as in:

```
DECLARE <cursor name> SCROLL CURSOR
FOR <SELECT statement>
```

When working with a SCROLL cursor, you can use any of the FETCH statement's cursor row pointer positioning options to move to a specific row in the cursor prior to retrieving its column values into temporary variables (or to the screen). The FETCH statement's row positioning options are:

- **NEXT.** Move forward one row.
- **PRIOR.** Move backward one row.
- **FIRST.** Move to the first row in the results set.
- **LAST.** Move to the last row in the results set.
- **ABSOLUTE *n*.** Move to the *n*th row in the results set. If *n* is a positive number, the DBMS moves forward to the *n*th row from the top of the cursor. If *n* is negative, the DBMS moves to the *n*th from the bottom of the results set.
- **RELATIVE *n*.** Move *n* rows from the current position of the row pointer. If *n* is positive, the DBMS moves the row pointer *n* rows forward. If *n* is negative, the DBMS moves the row pointer *n* rows backward (toward the top of the cursor).

Therefore, if you are working with a cursor declared as

```
DECLARE cur_authors SCROLL CURSOR
FOR SELECT au_fname, au_lname FROM authors
```

executing the FETCH statement

```
FETCH RELATIVE 1 FROM cur_authors INTO @au_fname, @au_lname
```

has the same effect as

```
FETCH NEXT FROM cur_authors INTO @au_fname, @au_lname
```

in that both statements move the cursor's current row pointer forward one row before retrieving the column values in the cursor's (new) current row. Similarly, the FETCH statement

```
FETCH RELATIVE -1 FROM cur_authors
INTO @au_fname, @au_lname
```

has the same effect as

```
FETCH PRIOR FROM cur_authors INTO @au_fname, @au_lname
```

in that both statements move the cursor's current row pointer backward (toward the first row in the cursor) one row from the current row.

Now, suppose the cursor's current row pointer is on row 5 of a 20-row cursor. The FETCH statement

```
FETCH RELATIVE 10 FROM cur_authors
INTO @au_fname, @au_lname
```

will move the current row pointer forward 10 rows to row 15, while the FETCH statement

```
FETCH ABSOLUTE 10 FROM cur_authors
INTO @au_fname, @au_lname
```

will move the current row pointer to cursor row 10. Similarly, the FETCH statement

```
FETCH RELATIVE -3 FROM cur_authors
INTO @au_fname, @au_lname
```

will move the cursor's current row pointer to cursor row 2 (which is three rows up [toward the top of the cursor]) from current row 5; the FETCH statement

```
FETCH ABSOLUTE -3 FROM cur_authors
INTO @au_fname, @au_lname
```

will move the cursor's current row pointer to cursor row 17, which is three rows back from the bottom of the cursor (row 20).

434 Understanding Cursor-based Positioned DELETE Statements

If a cursor is updateable (that is, the DECLARE CURSOR statement used to declare the cursor does not include a READ ONLY clause), you can use the cursor to DELETE a row from the table from which the cursor's data was derived. A cursor-based DELETE is called a *positioned* DELETE because you tell the DBMS to remove a row from the table based on the current position of the cursor's row pointer.

The WHERE clause in a standard (searched) DELETE statement describes the rows to be deleted based on the value in one or more of their columns. For example, the searched DELETE statement

```
DELETE FROM orders
WHERE date_shipped = NULL AND order_date < GetDate() - 30
```

tells the DBMS to search for and DELETE any rows in which the DATE_SHIPPED is NULL and the ORDER_DATE is more than 30 days prior to the current date.

A positioned DELETE, on the other hand, tells the server to DELETE the row in the underlying (base) table associated with the cursor's current row, as in:

```
DELETE FROM <table name> WHERE CURRENT OF <cursor name>
```

Thus, to remove the third row in the cursor and DELETE the row from the cursor's underlying table, you would first execute a FETCH statement to make the third row the cursor's current row, and then execute a positioned DELETE. For example, to remove the third row from the cursor CU_TIMECARDS and the row from which the third row in the cursor was derived, you would execute a statement batch similar to:

```
OPEN cur_timecards CURSOR
FETCH FROM cur_timecards
```

```
FETCH FROM cur_timecards
FETCH FROM cur_timecards
DELETE FROM timecards WHERE CURRENT OF cur_timecards
```

Note: *Be sure to check the effect of the various DECLARE CURSOR clauses on a cursor's READ ONLY status for your DBMS. MS-SQL Server, for example, forces a SCROLL cursor to be READ ONLY. MS-SQL Server does, however, allow you to add a DYNAMIC clause to the DECLARE cursor statement to create a scrollable cursor that is also updateable.*

435 Understanding Cursor-based Positioned UPDATE Statements

In addition to executing positioned DELETE statements, you can use an updateable cursor to perform positioned updates. A positioned UPDATE lets you set column values in the underlying (base) table row from which the current row in the cursor was derived. Thus, a positioned UPDATE is similar to a positioned DELETE because the search criteria in its WHERE clause is based on the position of a cursor's current row pointer instead of the value in one or more of the columns in a row.

The WHERE clause in a standard (searched) UPDATE statement describes the rows to be modified based on the value in one or more columns. For example, the searched UPDATE statement

```
UPDATE employees SET ot_payrate = 1.5
WHERE monthly_salary IS NULL
```

tells the DBMS to search the EMPLOYEES table for rows in which the MONTHLY_SALARY column is NULL, and then set the value of the OT_PAYRATE column in those rows to 1.5.

A positioned update, meanwhile, uses the syntax

```
UPDATE <table name> SET <column name> = <value>
  [,...<last column name> = <last value>]
WHERE CURRENT OF <cursor name>
```

to tell the DBMS to UPDATE values in one or more columns of the row in the underlying (base) table that corresponds with the current row in the cursor. For example, the SQL statement batch

```
OPEN cur_payroll_work CURSOR
FETCH FROM cur_payroll_work
FETCH FROM cur_payroll_work INTO @emp_num, @dept, @ot_rate,
```

```
  @time_in, @time_out, @project, @tcard_hourly_rate,
  @tcard_labor_cost, @hrly_payrate, @hours_worked
UPDATE timecards SET tcard_hourly_rate = @hrly_payrate,
  tcard_labor_cost = @hrly_payrate * @hours_worked
WHERE CURRENT OF cur_timecards
```

will set the value of the columns TCARD_HOURLY_RATE and TCARD_LABOR_COST in the TIMECARDS table row that generated the second (current) row in the CUR_PAYROLL_WORK cursor.

436 Using an Index to Change the Order of the Rows in a Cursor

In Tip 429, "Using the ORDER BY Clause to Change the Order of the Rows in a Cursor," you learned that you can add an ORDER BY clause to a cursor's SELECT statement to sort the rows in a cursor by the value in one or more of its columns. Unfortunately, some DBMS implementations, including MS-SQL Server, allow you to use an ORDER BY clause only in the SELECT statement of a READ ONLY cursor. Therefore, if you add an ORDER BY clause to the SELECT statement of a cursor on an MS-SQL Server, you will not be able to use the cursor to execute positioned DELETE or positioned UPDATE statements.

If you need an updateable cursor with sorted data, create an index on the cursor's base table(s) and tell the DBMS to use the index when populating the cursor. For example, suppose you have a set of timecards you want sorted by date and time within the employee ID. If you use the CREATE INDEX statement syntax

```
CREATE [UNIQUE][CLUSTERED|NONCLUSTERED] INDEX <index name>
ON <table name|view name>
(<column name>[,...<last column name>])
```

to create an index such as

```
CREATE INDEX tc_emp_ID_date
ON timecards (emp_ID, time_in, time_out)
```

on the TIMECARDS table, you can add a WITH INDEX clause to the FROM clause in the cursor's SELECT statement

```
DECLARE cur_payroll_work CURSOR
FOR SELECT emp_num, dept, ot_rate, time_in, time_out,
  project, tcard_hourly_rate, tcard_labor_cost,
  COALESCE(hourly_rate, (monthly_salary * 12) / 2080)
  hrly_payrate, (CONVERT(REAL(time_out - time_in),8)* 24)
  hours_worked
FROM timecards WITH (INDEX(tc_emp_ID_date)), employees
```

```
WHERE timecards.emp_ID = employees.emp_ID
FOR UPDATE OF tccard_hourly_rate, tcard.labor_cost
```

to create an updateable cursor whose rows are sorted (in the order of the index TC_EMP_ID_DATE).

Without an ORDER BY clause in its DECLARE CURSOR statement, the DBMS will leave the rows in a cursor arranged in the order in which the system added them when it populated the cursor (in response to an OPEN [cursor] statement). The WITH INDEX clause in the SELECT statement's FROM clause tells the DBMS to retrieve TIMECARD rows for the cursor in order by EMP_ID/TIME_IN/TIME_OUT.

437 Using @@FETCH_STATUS to Work Through the Rows in a Cursor with a WHILE Loop

@@FETCH_STATUS is an MS-SQL Server system-defined global variable that contains the execution status (the result code) of the most recently executed FETCH statement. An @@FETCH_STATUS value of zero (0) indicates that the DBMS successfully executed the most recent FETCH statement. Any other value indicates that the FETCH was unsuccessful. As such, you can use the value of @@FETCH_STATUS as the termination test in a Transact-SQL WHILE loop to work your way through the rows in a cursor.

For example, if you execute the statement batch

```
SET NOCOUNT ON
DECLARE cur_authors CURSOR
FOR SELECT * FROM pubs.dbo.authors
-DECLARE temporary variables here

OPEN cur_authors

FETCH FROM cur_authors
WHILE @@FETCH_STATUS = 0
BEGIN

-Add statements to process individual rows of the cursor
-here

-A FETCH statement without an INTO clause tells the DBMS
-to display the contents of the cursor row's columns to
-the screen.
-If you are processing the rows in a cursor, you will
-normally FETCH cursor row column values INTO temporary
-variables vs. just displaying them.
```

```
  FETCH FROM cur_authors
END

DEALLOCATE cur_authors
SET NOCOUNT OFF
```

the MS-SQL Server will populate the CUR_AUTHORS cursor with rows from the AUTHORS table in the PUBS database. Then the DBMS will FETCH and display the column values in each row of the cursor until the @@FETCH_STATUS is no longer zero (0). A nonzero @@FETCH_STATUS indicates that the DBMS was not able to FETCH another row from the cursor, which terminates the loop under the assumption that there are no more rows left to retrieve.

Notice that the current example includes a FETCH statement prior to the WHILE loop. This is because the value of @@FETCH_STATUS is undefined before the connection has executed its first FETCH statement. Moreover, the system does not set the value of @@FETCH_STATUS to zero (0) when you populate a cursor by executing an OPEN statement. As such, you must execute one FETCH to set the value of @@FETCH_STATUS before testing its value in a WHILE loop.

Note: *@@FETCH_STATUS is global to all cursors used by a connection. As such, if you execute a FETCH statement on one cursor and then call a stored procedure that opens and fetches rows from another cursor, the value of @@FETCH_STATUS will reflect the execution status of the last FETCH executed in the stored procedure, not the FETCH executed before the stored procedure was called.*

438 Understanding How to Set Cursor Sensitivity to Changes in Underlying Tables

As you learned from the discussion of cursors in Tips 426–436, a cursor's SELECT statement determines which table rows (and columns) to include in the cursor. Even if you declare a cursor as READ ONLY, the contents of its underlying table(s) may change between the time the cursor is populated (by executing its OPEN statement) and the time it is closed (by executing a CLOSE or a DEALLOCATE statement). When working with cursors, you must decide whether or not you want the actions of other users to change the contents of the cursor after the DBMS populates it by executing the cursor's SELECT statement.

Suppose, for example, that you DECLARE and OPEN a cursor as:

```
DECLARE cur_employees CURSOR
FOR SELECT * FROM employees
```

```
WHERE hrly_rate < 10.00 AND status = 'Active'
OPEN cur_employees
```

If someone changes the hourly rate of one of the employees from $9.50 to $9.75, should the cursor continue to display the row's contents as if nothing had happened? Now, suppose someone deletes an active employee making $8.75 per hour from the EMPLOYEES table, changes an employee's status from active to terminated, or changes an HRLY_RATE from $9.50 to $10.25. Should the cursor continue to display a row if the corresponding row has been deleted from the underlying table or if the underlying row's column values no longer satisfy the search criteria in the cursor's SELECT statement?

The answer to both questions is a definite "Maybe"—depending on the purpose of the cursor. If you need a "snapshot" of the average salary and count of employees making less than $10 per hour at a particular point in time, you would want the cursor to remain static and ignore any changes made to its underlying table(s). On the other hand, if you are trying to generate an "up-to-the-minute" report of existing employees, you will want the cursor to reflect new additions and to remove rows that no longer meet your criteria as you work your way through the rows in the cursor.

Fortunately, SQL lets you decide whether or not a cursor is to reflect changes made after the DBMS opens and populates it. To make a cursor insensitive to modifications made to its underlying (base) table(s), add the INSENSITIVE clause to the cursor's definition, as in:

```
DECLARE cur_employees INSENSITIVE CURSOR
FOR SELECT * FROM employees
WHERE hrly_rate < 10.00 AND status = 'Active'
OPEN cur_employees
```

If a cursor is INSENSITIVE, the DBMS will store a copy of the cursor's underlying data in a temporary table. Any changes made to the underlying (base) table will not be reflected in the cursor because the cursor will FETCH data values from the temporary, static table. On the other hand, if you omit the INSENSITIVE clause (as shown in the current tip's first example), the cursor will reflect the results of any committed DELETE and UPDATE statements that modify the contents of the cursor's underlying (base) table(s).

439 Using the CLOSE Statement to Close a Cursor

After you finish working with a cursor, CLOSE the cursor to free up the system resources (such as hard disk space and server memory) used by the cursor and to release any locks on rows (or memory pages) currently held by the cursor. The syntax of the CLOSE (cursor) statement is

```
CLOSE <cursor name>
```

and executing it will, conceptually, DROP the table of query results created when the DBMS opened the cursor with:

```
OPEN <cursor name>
```

Unlike the DBLIB buffer, you do not have to FETCH and process all of the rows in a cursor before you CLOSE it. Just bear in mind that any rows left unprocessed when you close a cursor are no longer available to any DBMS user, external application, or stored procedure.

As mentioned at the beginning of the current tip, the CLOSE statement frees up the storage space used by the cursor's pointers to rows in its underlying (base) table(s) or by the temporary table that holds a copy of the underlying data for INSENSITIVE and STATIC cursors. However, the CLOSE statement does not remove the cursor's structure from the database. As such, the cursor itself still exists as a database object—even after you CLOSE the cursor. After closing a cursor, you need only execute another OPEN statement to repopulate it. Then you can begin processing the rows in the cursor rows from the beginning again. (You need not [and, indeed, cannot] redeclare the same cursor if you have only closed [vs. deallocated] it.)

Note: *If you declare an INSENSITIVE or (MS-SQL Server) STATIC cursor, you can CLOSE and then OPEN the cursor again to have the cursor's contents reflect any changes made to its underlying tables since the cursor was opened the first time. Closing a cursor discards all of the rows of data values (or pointers) from the cursor. Reopening the cursor tells the DBMS to re-execute the cursor's SELECT statement to repopulate (refill) the cursor with data that now meets the cursor's search criteria.*

440 Using the DEALLOCATE Statement to Drop a Cursor and Free Its Server Resources

If you are finished using a cursor and do not plan to repopulate it by reopening it during the current session, execute a DEALLOCATE statement to both CLOSE the cursor and remove its structure and definition from the database. Unlike the CLOSE statement, which leaves the cursor's definition and structure in the DBMS system tables, the DEALLOCATE statement not removes any data in the cursor (by closing the cursor), but also removes the cursor as an object from the database. As such, if you do plan to reuse the cursor, execute a CLOSE statement instead of a DEALLOCATE (cursor) statement to avoid the overhead of having to execute another DECLARE CURSOR statement before executing an OPEN statement to reopen the same cursor later.

The syntax of a DEALLOCATE statement is

```
DEALLOCATE <cursor name>
```

and the cursor need not be closed prior to being deallocated—the DEALLOCATE will take care of both actions, closing the cursor (if it is still open) and removing the cursor as a database object.

Note: *Deallocating a SCROLL cursor frees any scroll locks the cursor holds to protect its data in underlying tables from UPDATE or DELETE statements executed by other users. However, if the cursor was declared and opened within a transaction, deallocating the cursor does not release any locks the (still) open transaction has on the cursor's underlying table(s). Open transaction locks are released only when you close the transaction by executing a COMMIT statement (to keep the changes made) or a ROLLBACK (to undo any work performed by the transaction).*

441 Understanding the Transact-SQL Extended Syntax for the DECLARE CURSOR Statement

MS-SQL Server supports two forms of the DECLARE CURSOR statement. You can declare a cursor using the standard SQL syntax

```
DECLARE <cursor name> [INSENSITIVE][SCROLL] CURSOR
FOR <SELECT statement>
[FOR {READ ONLY|UPDATE[OF <column list>]}]
```

(which you learned about in Tip 427, "Using the DECLARE CURSOR Statement to Define a Cursor"), or you can use the Transact-SQL Extended syntax

```
DECLARE <cursor name> CURSOR [GLOBAL|LOCAL]
[FORWARD_ONLY|SCROLL][STATIC|KEYSET|DYNAMIC|FAST_FORWARD]
[READ_ONLY|SCROLL_LOCKS|OPTOMISTIC][TYPE_WARNING]
FOR <SELECT statement>
[FOR UPDATE[OF <column list>]}]
```

where:

- **GLOBAL.** Specifies that the scope of a cursor is global to the connection. If a cursor has a *global* scope, it can be referenced in any SQL statement on the connection after the cursor is declared. (By default, a cursor normally has a *local* scope, which means it exists as a database object only with the statement batch, stored procedure, or trigger in which it is declared.) The DBMS will automatically DEALLOCATE a GLOBAL cursor only when the connection on which it was created disconnects from the server.
- **LOCAL.** Specifies that a cursor can be referenced only by statements within the same statement batch, stored procedure, or trigger in which the cursor was defined. (You will learn about triggers in Tip 448, "Understanding Triggers.") The DBMS automatically

deallocates a LOCAL cursor after it executes the last statement in a statement batch, trigger, or stored procedure—unless the stored procedure passes the cursor to the caller in an OUTPUT parameter. If passed as an OUTPUT parameter, the system will DEALLOCATE the cursor when the last variable that references the cursor goes out of scope.

- **FORWARD_ONLY.** Specifies that you can use the FETCH NEXT statement only to move forward through the cursor, one row at a time.
- **STATIC.** Is the Transact-SQL equivalent of the standard DECLARE CURSOR statement's INSENSITIVE setting. If a cursor is STATIC (or INSENSITIVE), the DBMS makes a temporary copy of the data in the cursor's underlying rows in a table in the TEMPDB database. A STATIC cursor cannot be used with a WHERE CURRENT OF clause to execute a positioned UPDATE or DELETE. Moreover, a STATIC cursor will not reflect any changes made to its underlying table(s) after the DBMS populates the cursor.
- **KEYSET.** Specifies that the rows and the order of the rows in a cursor are set when the DBMS opens the cursor and populates it. The *KEYSET* is a table in the TEMPDB database that contains a set of keys that uniquely identify each row in the cursor. A KEYSET cursor will reflect any committed changes made to nonkey column values. Moreover, if a row referenced is removed from the cursor's underlying table, a subsequent FETCH of the same row in the cursor will return an @@FETCH_STATUS of –2.

Any row inserted into a KEYSET cursor's underlying table will not be added to the cursor—even if the new row's column values satisfy the search criteria in the cursor's SELECT statement.

Any changes made to key columns in the KEYSET cursor's underlying table(s) are treated as a DELETE of the original row followed by an INSERT of a new row. As such, UPDATE statements that change the values in key columns in the underlying table will cause the corresponding row in the KEYSET cursor to "disappear" as if it had been deleted. Any changes to key (and nonkey columns) made through the cursor (with a positioned UPDATE) remain visible in the cursor.

- **DYNAMIC.** Specifies that the cursor is to reflect any changes made to its underlying table(s) by committed UPDATE, DELETE, and INSERT statements. As such, the DBMS will add new row pointers to the cursor as rows that satisfy the cursor's search criteria are added to the cursor's underlying table(s). Conversely, the DBMS will remove row pointers from the cursor as corresponding rows are deleted from the underlying table or if their column values are changed such that they no longer satisfy the cursor's search criteria. Because the rows in a DYNAMIC cursor can change prior to each FETCH, a DYNAMIC cursor does not support the FETCH ABSOLUTE statement.
- **FAST_FORWARD.** Specifies that the DBMS is to optimize the cursor for performance as a READ_ONLY, FORWARD_ONLY cursor.
- **SCROLL_LOCKS.** Tells the DBMS to place a lock on each row in the underlying table(s) as the server adds the row to the cursor. The SCROLL_LOCKS option is used to guarantee that positioned UPDATE and DELETE statements made through the cursor will succeed.

- **OPTIMISTIC.** Specifies that any positioned UPDATE or DELETE made through the cursor will fail if the target row was updated after it was added to the cursor. Unlike the SCROLL_LOCKS option, the OPTIMISTIC option does not tell the DBMS to place a lock on each underlying table row it puts into the cursor. Instead, when determining whether or not to allow a positioned UPDATE or DELETE, the DBMS checks the value of the underlying row's TIMESTAMP column (or its checksum, if the row has no column of data type TIMESTAMP) to determine if the row was changed after it was added to the cursor.
- **TYPE_WARNING.** Specifies that the DBMS is to send a warning message to the client if the cursor's declaration contains conflicting options that will implicitly convert the cursor from the requested type to another.

442 Understanding Asynchronous KEYSET Cursor Population

When you use the Transact-SQL DECLARE CURSOR syntax (which you learned about in Tip 441, "Understanding the Transact-SQL Extended Syntax for the DECLARE CURSOR Statement") to declare a STATIC or KEYSET cursor, you can tell the MS-SQL Server to populate the cursor asynchronously.

Both STATIC and KEYSET cursors create a work table in the TEMPDB database. While a KEYSET cursor uses the work table to store the keys that identify the cursor's rows in its underlying table(s), a STATIC cursor stores a copy of its underlying rows in the table. When the DBMS populates a STATIC or KEYSET cursor synchronously, the server takes control of the session until it has filled the cursor's work table with all of the rows or keys returned by the cursor's SELECT statement.

If the query optimizer estimates that a STATIC or KEYSET cursor's query will return more rows than the value in the server's CURSOR THRESHOLD setting, the server will partially populate the work table, start another thread to finish generating the cursor's result set, and return control to the user or application that submitted the cursor's OPEN statement. As a result, the user (or application) can start fetching the first rows in an asynchronously populated cursor without having to wait until the DBMS retrieves the entire results set into the cursor before performing the first FETCH.

To set the value of the CURSOR THRESHOLD, use the SP_CONFIGURE system stored procedure. Then use the Transact-SQL RECONFIGURE command to tell the query optimizer to start using the new value. For example, to have the optimizer populate cursors with more than 500 rows asynchronously, execute the statement batch:

```
EXEC SP_CONFIGURE 'CURSOR THRESHOLD',500
RECONFIGURE
```

When you set the CURSOR THRESHOLD to –1, the DBMS will populate all cursors synchronously. Conversely, a CURSOR THRESHOLD of 0 tells the server to populate all cursors asynchronously. Set the CURSOR THRESHOLD to any other value, and the optimizer will compare the number of rows it expects the cursor's query to return to the value of CURSOR THRESHOLD. If the number of expected rows exceeds the value of CURSOR THRESHOLD, the DBMS will populate the cursor asynchronously. Otherwise, the server will populate it synchronously.

Note: *There is extra overhead associated with populating a cursor asynchronously. As such, it is more efficient to populate small cursors synchronously. Therefore, make the value of the CURSOR THRESHOLD parameter large enough that the server will use asynchronous cursor population only for cursors with a SELECT statement that returns a large number of rows.*

443 Using the @@CURSOR_ROWS System Variable to Determine the Number of Rows in a Cursor

When an MS-SQL Server populates any type of cursor other than a DYNAMIC cursor, the DBMS sets the value of @@CURSOR_ROWS to the number of rows in the results table generated by the cursor's SELECT statement. For example, if the SELECT statement

```
SELECT * FROM pubs.dbo.authors
```

generates a results set with 23 rows of data, then executing the statement batch

```
DECLARE cur_authors SCROLL CURSOR
FOR SELECT * FROM pubs.dbo.authors
PRINT 'There are ' + CAST(@@CURSOR_ROWS AS VARCHAR(6) +
      ' rows in the cursor.'
```

will display the message:

```
There are 23 rows in the cursor.
```

Bear in mind that @@CURSOR_ROWS is a global system variable whose value is set by the last cursor opened on a connection as defined in Table 443.1.

@@CURSOR_ROWS	Description
-<row count>	If the cursor is populated asynchronously, the value of @@CURSOR_ROWS will be a negative number that represents the number of rows currently in the work table. For example, an @@CURSOR_ROWS value of –758 tells you that the system is still populating an asynchronous cursor that contains 758 rows thus far. Whether populated asynchronously or synchronously, @@CURSOR_ROWS will contain the number of rows in the cursor as a positive value as soon as the DBMS is finished populating the cursor.
–1	If the cursor is DYNAMIC, then the number of rows in the cursor may change after the DBMS opens it. As such, the cursor's row count is set to –1 because the server never knows for sure that it has retrieved all qualified rows into the cursor.
0	Either no cursors have been opened yet, the cursor's SELECT statement returned no rows, or the last cursor opened on the connection has since been closed or deallocated.
<row count>	After the DBMS fully populates a cursor, the value of @@CURSOR_ROWS will be the number of rows in the cursor.

Table 443.1 @@CURSOR_ROWS Values and Descriptions

444 Understanding When to Use a CHECK Constraint Instead of a Trigger

As you will learn in Tip 448, "Understanding Triggers," a trigger is a set of one or more SQL statements the DBMS is to execute when a user attempts to INSERT, DELETE, or UPDATE one or more rows in a table. If you are trying to use the DBMS to enforce a business rule such as "Do not accept any orders of more than $100,000," you could use a trigger similar to

```
CREATE trigger order_total_over_100000
ON orders
FOR INSERT, UPDATE
AS IF ((SELECT order_total FROM inserted) > 100000)
     BEGIN
       PRINT 'Order rejected. Total order > 100000.'
       ROLLBACK
     END
```

which will display an error message and undo (ROLLBACK) any INSERT or UPDATE of the ORDERS table row in which the ORDER_TOTAL column is greater than $100,000.

One of the problems with triggers is that they exist as separate database objects, and someone looking at the definition if the ORDERS table has no idea that the system will reject any order that exceeds $100,000. Therefore, you may find it more straightforward and convenient (from a documentation standpoint) to enforce simple business rules using a CHECK constraint instead of a trigger.

For example, to implement the business rule in the current example as a CHECK constraint, add the constraint to the CREATE TABLE statement as:

```
CREATE TABLE orders
  (cust_ID INTEGER,
   order_date DATETIME,
   shipped_date DATETIME,
   salesperson_ID INTEGER,
   order_total MONEY,
   total_paid MONEY,
   CONSTRAINT order_total_over_100000
     CHECK (order_total <= 100000))
```

You will learn all about triggers in Tips 448–461. For now, the important thing to understand is that if the trigger's only purpose is to prevent the insertion of a row with a column value that violates a business rule, you should consider replacing the trigger with a CHECK constraint in the CREATE TABLE statement used to define the table.

445 Understanding Nested Cursors

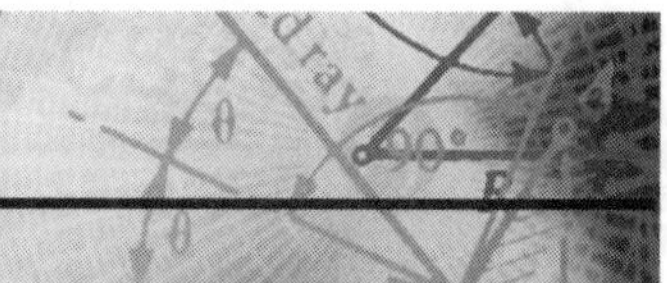

A connection can have multiple cursors open simultaneously. Moreover, you can nest one cursor within another. However, as you work your way through the outer cursor, you will incur the additional overhead of declaring, opening, and deallocating each inner cursor multiple times. Therefore, you should nest one cursor declaration within another only if you need to use one or more column values from the current row in the outer cursor in the inner (nested) cursor's SELECT statement.

Suppose, for example, that you want to create a stored procedure that will list your sales offices in order from the lowest to highest amount of total sales and will show the manager and top salesperson for each office. The following code creates a stored procedure using nested cursors to produce output similar to that shown in Figure 445.1.

```
CREATE PROCEDURE Show_Sales AS
DECLARE @avg_sale  MONEY,        @emp_fname    VARCHAR(20),
        @emp_lname VARCHAR(20), @manager      INT,
```

```
        @max_sale  MONEY         @manager_name VARCHAR(50),
        @office_ID INT,          @total_sales  MONEY

/* cursor used to display the office cursor information,
   arranged in ascending order by total sales */
DECLARE cur_office_sales CURSOR
FOR SELECT office, SUM(order_total) total_sales,
           AVG(order_total) avg_sale
    FROM orders GROUP BY office ORDER BY total_sales DESC
OPEN cur_office_sales

/* work through the office cursor fetching rows until there
   are no more rows to display (@@FETCH_STATUS <> 0) */

FETCH cur_office_sales INTO @office_ID, @total_sales,
      @avg_sale
WHILE @@FETCH_STATUS = 0
BEGIN
  PRINT 'Office ' + CAST(@office_ID AS CHAR(1)) +
    ' Total sales: ' + CAST(@total_sales AS VARCHAR(11)) +
    ' Avg sale: ' + CAST(@avg_sale AS VARCHAR(11))

/* the cursor used to list managers for each office is
   nested, because it uses the value of @office_ID from the
   outer cursor in its SELECT statement */

  DECLARE cur_office_manager CURSOR
  FOR SELECT emp_ID,office, f_name+' 'l_name office_manager
      FROM employees, offices
      WHERE emp_ID = manager AND office = @office_ID
  OPEN cur_office_manager

/* the cursor used to list the top employee for each office
   is also nested, because it too uses the @office_ID value
   from the outer cursor */
  DECLARE cur_office_employees CURSOR
  FOR SELECT f_name, l_name, MAX(order_total) max_order,
             AVG(order_total) avg_order
      FROM orders, employees
      WHERE orders.office = @office_ID AND
            salesperson = emp_ID
      GROUP BY f_name, l_name ORDER BY max_order DESC
  OPEN cur_office_employees

/*work through the (embedded) office manager cursor,
  displaying the name and ID of the managers for the
  office in the current row in the (outer) office cursor*/
```

```
  FETCH cur_office_manager INTO @manager, @office_ID,
        @manager_name
  WHILE @@FETCH_STATUS = 0
  BEGIN
    PRINT '  Manager: ' + @manager_name +
        ' (ID: ' + CAST(@manager AS VARCHAR(4)) + ')'

/* retrieve and display the "top" employee from the
  (embedded) office employees cursor for the office in the
  current (outer) row of the offices cursor */

    FETCH cur_office_employees INTO @emp_fname, @emp_lname,
        @max_sale, @avg_sale
    PRINT '    Top Salesperson: ' @emp_fname + ' ' +
        @emp_lname + ' Avg sale: ' +
        CAST(@avg_sale AS VARCHAR(11))
    PRINT ' '
    FETCH cur_office_manager INTO @manager, @office_ID,
        @manager_name
  END

  DEALLOCATE cur_office_manager
  DEALLOCATE cur_office_employees

  FETCH cur_office_sales INTO @office_ID, @total_sales,
      @avg_sales
END

DEALLOCATE cur_office_sales
RETURN 0
```

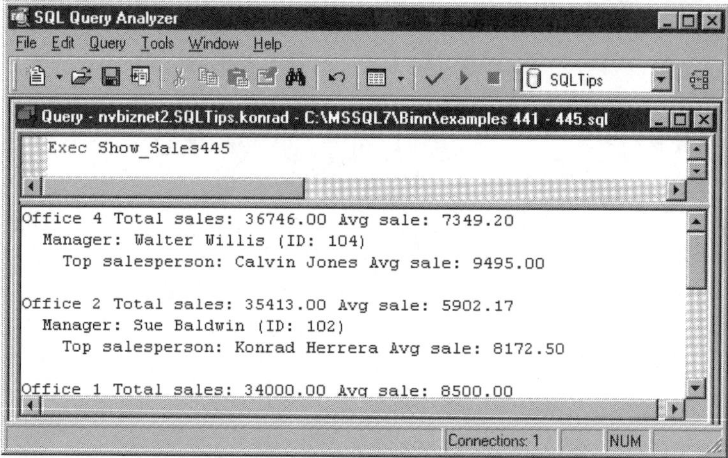

Figure 445.1 Composite office report produced using embedded and multiple open cursors

Note: The reason you have to DEALLOCATE the embedded (managers and employees) cursors while working through the offices cursor is because the value of the @OFFICE_ID variable is set for the cursor's SELECT statement when the cursor is declared. As such, to change the value of @OFFICE_ID in each cursor's WHERE clause to match the value of the office ID in the current row of the outer (offices) cursor, you must DEALLOCATE and re-create the embedded cursors.

446 Using the @@ERROR Function to Determine the Error Status of the Last Transact-SQL Statement Executed

When an MS-SQL Server successfully executes a Transact-SQL statement, the @@ERROR function returns zero (0). If an error occurs during statement execution, the DBMS returns a text error message, and @ERROR returns the error code (number) associated it. You can display all of the server's error codes and messages by querying the SYSMESSAGES system table with a query such as:

```
SELECT * FROM master.dbo.sysmessages
```

Or, to display the error message generated by the last Transact-SQL statement executed, submit the query:

```
SELECT * FROM master.dbo.sysmessages
WHERE error = @@ERROR
```

Note: The system clears and resets the last statement execution status each time it executes a statement—including the query to display the text of the error message in the previous example. As such, either check and use the value returned by @@ERROR to decide on an action immediately after the statement in question, or save the value returned by @@ERROR to a local variable for use later.

Common uses for the @@ERROR function are to display customized error messages and to return an error code from a stored procedure. For example, the following procedure attempts to INSERT a new title into the TITLES table and uses @@ERROR to select and display an error message to the screen, if necessary. The stored procedure also returns a result code to the calling program, which if 0 = success and if <>0 indicates failure.

```
CREATE PROCEDURE add_title @ISBN CHAR(13), @auth_ID INT,
                           @title VARCHAR(40) AS
DECLARE @result_code INT
```

```
INSERT INTO titles VALUES (@ISBN, @auth_ID, @title)

SET @result_code = @@ERROR
IF @result_code <> 0
  BEGIN
    IF @result_code = 515
      PRINT 'ERROR!  ISBN, author ID, or title is NULL.'
    ELSE IF @result_code = 547
      PRINT 'ERROR!  Author ID is not in AUTHORS table.'
    ELSE IF @result_code = 2627
      PRINT 'ERROR!  Duplicate ISBN is not allowed.'
    ELSE PRINT 'ERROR! Unable to add new title.'
  END

RETURN @result_code
```

447 Understanding That the Value of the Current Date and Time Is Set at the Start of Statement Execution

The GETDATE() function returns the current system date and time (down to the millisecond, if stored into a table column of data type DATETIME). If you use GETDATE() in an SQL statement, the DBMS calls the function only once, regardless of the amount of time it takes the system to finish executing the statement.

Suppose, for example, that you submit the UPDATE statement

```
UPDATE orders
  SET late_fee = (late_fee +
                  ((order_total - amount_paid) * 0.10)),
      date_fee_assessed = GETDATE()
WHERE CONVERT(CHAR(9),date_due,6) =
        CONVERT(CHAR(9),GETDATE() - 1,6) AND
      (order_total - amount_paid) > 0
```

at 1 minute before midnight on 01/12/2001, and due to the large number or rows in the ORDERS table, the system does not finish executing the UPDATE until 10 minutes after midnight. The DBMS will assess a late fee only on orders with a DUE_DATE of 01/11/2001—even though the "current date" changed from 01/12/2001 to 01/13/2001 while the server was in the process of executing the UPDATE statement. Moreover, the DATE_FEE_ASSESSED column in each of the updated rows will have the same date and time value (down to the millisecond)—even though each successive update occurred at a later time during the 11 minutes it took the DBMS to work its way through the ORDERS table.

448 Understanding Triggers

A trigger is a special type of stored procedure that the DBMS executes in response to an INSERT, UPDATE, or DELETE operation against a specific table or column. Triggers are most often used to enforce business rules such as:

- Notify the branch manager if any account is given a credit line of $75,000 or more.
- No customer is allowed to make charges that would exceed the customer's credit limit by 10 percent.
- Place a 14-day hold on the funds available from any check for $2,500.00 or more deposited into an account.

In addition, many triggers are used to maintain the integrity of totals, counts, and other amounts such as:

- When an office hires a new salesperson, increase the office sales quota by the amount of the new hire's sales quota.
- After adding a new order to the system, increase the customer's total purchases, and the salesperson and sales office's total sales by the amount of the order.
- When a customer makes a credit card charge, increase the account's rewards credit by 1 percent of the amount charged.

The DBMS takes responsibility for maintaining entity integrity with PRIMARY KEY and UNIQUE constraints, domain integrity through CHECK constraints, and referential integrity with FOREIGN KEY constraints. However, with the exception of FOREIGN KEY constraints, each of these integrity checks is confined to a single table. Even each FOREIGN KEY constraint can validate data only by looking for an exact match in a column or combination of columns in one other table. Thus, enforcing business rules and maintaining totals across multiple tables go beyond the scope of standard SQL constraints and have therefore been the responsibility of the application programs that access the database. Triggers are an attempt to give the DBMS the capability to check all necessary constraints so that the application programmer need worry about only designing the *best* interface that allows users to enter data and displays information in the most efficient manner possible.

While all of the major database products (MS-SQL Server, Sybase, Informix, Oracle, DB2, and so on) support triggers, neither the SQL-86 nor the SQL-92 specification mentions them. As a result, each DBMS product has a different syntax for creating a trigger and places its own limitations on the statements a trigger can execute. Tips 449–461 will detail the MS-SQL Server trigger syntax and capabilities.

While the specific syntax for creating a trigger and its capabilities will differ from one DBMS product to another, the basic concept of triggers and their general purpose is the same for all SQL servers that support them. A trigger is a set of statements the DBMS is to execute when a user attempts the triggering action—an UPDATE, INSERT, or DELETE (as defined by the trigger). You can associate a trigger with a table, in which case any DELETE, INSERT, or UPDATE on the table will cause the DBMS to execute its code. Or, you can attach a trigger to a specific column or group of columns within a table, in which case the DBMS will activate the trigger only when an INSERT or UPDATE supplies a NULL or non-NULL value for the column to which the trigger is attached.

449 Using the CREATE TRIGGER Statement to Create a Trigger

Only a table's owner (the DBOO) or the database owner (the DBO) can create a trigger on a table (or on one or more of its columns). Creating a trigger is very similar to creating a stored procedure in that a trigger, like a stored procedure, has a name and a set of statements the DBMS is to execute when the trigger (or stored procedure) is called. The syntax for the CREATE TRIGGER statement is

```
CREATE TRIGGER <trigger name>
ON {<table name>|<view name>}
[WITH ENCRYPTION]
{{FOR|AFTER|INSTEAD OF}{[INSERT],[UPDATE],[INSERT]}
 [NOT FOR REPLICATION]
 AS [{IF UPDATE (<column name>)
           [{AND|OR} UPDATE (...<last column name>)]
      |IF (COLUMNS_UPDATED()
            {<bitwise operator>}<column bitmask>)
               {...<last comparison operator>
                      <last column bitmask>}
     }]
 <SQL statements>
}
```

where:

- **trigger name** is the name of the trigger. Since triggers are global to the database, each trigger must have a unique name within the database, not just among the trigger owner's database objects.
- **table name | view name** is the name of the table or view to which the trigger is attached.
- **WITH ENCRYPTION** is the DBMS that stores the text of each trigger in the SYSCOMMENTS table. If the CREATE TRIGGER statement includes the WITH ENCRYPTION clause, the DBMS will encrypt the text of the trigger, which prevents users from displaying the trigger's code by querying the SYSCOMMENTS table. However, encrypting the trigger also prevents the DBMS from publishing the trigger to other MS-SQL Servers during MS-SQL Server replication.

- **FOR** or **AFTER** specifies that the DBMS is to execute the trigger *after* the DBMS executes the triggering INSERT, UPDATE, or DELETE statement on the table listed in the ON clause.

AFTER is the default if FOR is the only keyword specified.

You cannot define an AFTER trigger on a view.

- **INSTEAD OF.** Tells the DBMS to execute the trigger instead of (in place of) the INSERT, UPDATE, or DELETE on the table or view name in the CREATE TRIGGER statement's ON clause.

Each table and view can have at most one INSTEAD OF (INSERT, UPDATE, and DELETE) trigger. However, you can create multiple views of the same table and a different INSTEAD OF (INSERT, UPDATE, or DELETE) for each view.

You cannot create an INSTEAD OF trigger on a view whose definition includes a WITH CHECK OPTION.

- **DELETE, INSERT, UPDATE.** The SQL statement that, when attempted against the table or view listed in the ON clause, activates the trigger. Each CREATE TRIGGER statement must include at least one of the three statement types and may include any combination of the three. If you want more than one of the three actions to activate the trigger, list the desired triggering actions separated by commas.

You cannot create an INSTEAD OF DELETE trigger on a table with an ON DELETE CASCADE option defined. Similarly, you cannot create an INSTEAD OF UPDATE trigger on a table with an ON UPDATE CASCADE option.

- **NOT FOR REPLICATION.** Tells the DBMS not to activate the trigger when the table is modified during a replication process.

- **IF UPDATE (<column name>).** Tells the DBMS to activate the trigger only if an INSERT or UPDATE action modifies the value in the column named by <column name>. To test for an INSERT or UPDATE action on more than one column, use an AND or an OR logical connective to add the desired additional column name(s) to the IF UPDATE clause.

- **IF COLUMNS_UPDATED().** The COLUMNS_UPDATED() function returns a VARBINARY bit pattern indicating which of the columns have been updated due to an INSERT or UPDATE action on the table. The leftmost bit is the least significant bit and represents the first column in the table or view, second from the left represents the second column, third from the left represents the third column, and so on. To check if column 2, 4, *or* 6 was updated, for example, write the IF COLUMNS_UPDATED() clause as:

```
IF (COLUMNS)_UPDATED() & 42) > 0
```

Or, to test if all three of the columns (2, 4, *and* 6) were updated, write the AS IF COLUMNS_UPDATED() clause as:

```
IF (COLUMNS)_UPDATED() & 42) = 42
```

- **AS <SQL statements>.** Details the actions that the trigger is to perform when activated.

Whenever the DBMS activates a trigger (that is, executes the SQL statements in a trigger's AS clause) in response to an INSERT, UPDATE, or DELETE action on the trigger's table or view, the DBMS creates two virtual tables: INSERTED and DELETED. Both tables are structurally identical to the table or view on which the trigger is defined and hold the original and new value for all of the rows the DBMS will change in response to the trigger action.

For an INSERT trigger, the INSERTED table holds all of the new values to be inserted into the table to which the trigger is attached. For an UPDATE trigger, the INSERTED table holds the new (updated) values to be placed in the trigger's table, while the DELETED table holds the column values prior to the UPDATE. Finally, for a DELETE trigger, the DELETED table holds the values (rows) to be removed from the table on which the trigger is created.

Tip 450, "Understanding INSERT Triggers"; Tip 451, "Understanding DELETE Triggers"; and Tip 453, "Understanding UPDATE Triggers," will show you how to use the CREATE TRIGGER statement to create INSERT, DELETE, and UPDATE triggers.

450 Understanding INSERT Triggers

An INSERT trigger is a stored procedure you want the DBMS to execute either AFTER or INSTEAD OF executing an INSERT statement on a particular table or view. Suppose, for example, that you want to UPDATE the TOTAL_SALES column in the OFFICES table and the TOTAL_SALES column in the EMPLOYEES table whenever a salesperson inserts a new order into the ORDERS table. The CREATE TRIGGER statement

```
CREATE TRIGGER tri_ins_order ON orders
AFTER INSERT AS
  SET NOCOUNT ON
  UPDATE offices SET total_sales = total_sales +
                     (SELECT order_total FROM INSERTED)
    WHERE offices.office_ID =
            (SELECT office_ID FROM INSERTED)
  UPDATE employees SET total_sales = total_sales +
                       (SELECT order_total FROM INSERTED)
    WHERE employees.emp_ID =
            (SELECT salesperson FROM INSERTED)
```

tells the DBMS to UPDATE the totals in each of the two tables *after* it successfully executes the INSERT statement that adds the new order to the ORDERS table.

As mentioned in Tip 449, "Using the CREATE TRIGGER Statement to Create a Trigger," the DBMS automatically creates a virtual table named INSERTED when it activates an INSERT trigger. The INSERTED table has all of the columns from the table in the trigger's ON clause and contains a copy of every row the DBMS will INSERT into the trigger table if the system is allowed to complete the current INSERT statement. Notice that you can use any of the column values in the INSERTED table in statements within the trigger. For example, the trigger in the current example uses the ORDER_TOTAL column from the row to be inserted to increase the value in the TOTAL_SALES column in the EMPLOYEES and OFFICES tables. Moreover, the trigger uses the OFFICE_ID and SALESPERSON values from the inserted row in each UPDATE statement's WHERE clause to specify which rows in the two tables are to be updated.

In addition to updating totals in multiple tables, you might use an INSERT trigger to enforce a business rule such as "All orders must be entered into the system at least three days prior to the EXPECTED_DEL_DATE." The trigger created with

```
CREATE TRIGGER tri_check_delivery_date ON orders
FOR INSERT AS
SET NOCOUNT ON
IF (SELECT expected_del_date FROM INSERTED) <
      (GETDATE() + 3)
BEGIN
  ROLLBACK TRAN
  RAISERROR('You cannot take an order to be delivered less
than three days from now.',16,1)
END
```

will enforce the "delivery in three or more days" business rule.

As shown by the examples in this tip, you can create more than one INSERT trigger on the same table. The DBMS considers the INSERT statement and *all* of the triggers it activates to be part of the same transaction. Therefore, the end result is the same whether or not the DBMS executes the TRI_INS_ORDER trigger before the TRI_CHECK_DELIVERY_DATE trigger. Any work performed by the current open transaction (including actions taken within any activated triggers) will be undone (rolled back) by the ROLLBACK TRAN statement in the TRI_CHECK_DELIVERY_DATE trigger if the EXPECTED_DEL_DATE on the new order is less than three days in the future.

Note: *When an activated trigger executes a ROLLBACK, the DBMS undoes any work performed. Therefore, any additional triggers on the table will not be activated, since the DBMS will return the table to the condition it was in prior to the execution of any triggering (INSERT, UPDATE, or DELETE) statement.*

---

451 Understanding DELETE Triggers

A DELETE trigger is a stored procedure that the DBMS executes either after or instead of executing a DELETE statement on a specific table or view. For example, if you create the INSERT trigger you learned about in Tip 450, "Understanding INSERT Triggers," on an

ORDERS table to maintain the TOTAL_SALES value in the EMPLOYEES and OFFICES tables, you also need to create a DELETE trigger such as:

```
CREATE TRIGGER tri_del_order ON orders AFTER DELETE AS
IF @@ROWCOUNT > 1
  BEGIN
    ROLLBACK TRAN
    RAISERROR('Each DELETE statement must remove only a single
order.',16,2)
  END
ELSE BEGIN
  SET NOCOUNT ON
  UPDATE offices SET total_sales = total_sales -
                       (SELECT order_total FROM DELETED)
    WHERE offices.office_ID =
            (SELECT office_ID FROM INSERTED)
  UPDATE employees SET total_sales = total_sales -
                         (SELECT order_total FROM DELETED)
    WHERE employees.emp_ID =
            (SELECT salesperson FROM DELETED)
END
```

Each time a user (or application) executes a DELETE statement that removes a row from the ORDERS table, the DBMS activates the DELETE trigger, which reduces the TOTAL_SALES in the OFFICES and EMPLOYEES tables by the ORDER_TOTAL value of the order removed.

Notice that unlike the INSERT trigger in Tip 450, the DELETE trigger must take into consideration that a single DELETE statement can remove more than one row from the trigger table. The DELETE trigger in the current example uses the @@ROWCOUNT variable to determine the number of rows affected by the triggering (DELETE) statement. If the DELETE statement attempts to remove more than one row from the ORDERS table, the DELETE trigger undoes the deletion by executing a ROLLBACK.

Although the current example does not allow it, you could modify the DELETE trigger to allow for multiple-row deletions. Remember, the DBMS creates a virtual DELETED table and fills it with a copy of each of the rows removed by the DELETE statement that activated the trigger. Therefore, the trigger could create a cursor, populate it with the rows from the DELETED table, and then work through the cursor one row at a time—reducing the TOTAL_SALES from the EMPLOYEES and OFFICES tables by the value in the ORDER_TOTAL column in each row of the cursor.

Note: *Executing a Transact-SQL TRUNCATE TABLE statement will delete all rows from a table without activating a DELETE trigger created on the table being truncated. As such, be careful when executing a TRUNCATE TABLE statement in a production environment. After truncating a table that has a DELETE trigger designed to summarize the table's data in another table, you must execute an UPDATE statement that zeroes out the totals maintained by the trigger.*

452 Understanding Cascading Triggers

Because a trigger can execute INSERT, UPDATE, and DELETE statements, work performed by one trigger can cause the DBMS to activate another trigger, which may execute a statement that activates a third trigger, and so on. In short, a single triggering (INSERT, UPDATE, or DELETE) statement can cause the DBMS to activate a cascade of triggers, each trigger executing statements that activate other triggers.

Suppose, for example, that you wanted to remove a customer (from the CUSTOMERS table) and all of the customer's orders (from the ORDERS table), while still maintaining accurate TOTAL_SALES figures in the EMPLOYEES and OFFICES tables for the remaining orders (for other customers) in the ORDERS table. If you create a trigger such as

```
CREATE TRIGGER tri_del_customer ON customers
INSTEAD OF DELETE AS
IF @@ROWCOUNT > 1
  BEGIN
    ROLLBACK TRAN
    RAISERROR('You can DELETE only one customer at a time.',16,3)
  END
ELSE BEGIN
  SET NOCOUNT ON
  DECLARE @timestamp AS TIMESTAMP

/* Create a cursor and populate it with all of the
   customer's orders */

  DECLARE cur_del_orders CURSOR
  FOR SELECT order_timestamp FROM orders
      WHERE cust_ID = (SELECT cust_ID FROM DELETED)
  OPEN cur_del_orders

/* Go through the cursor one row at a time, deleting each
   of the customer's orders in turn */

  FETCH NEXT FROM cur_del_orders INTO @timestamp
  WHILE @@FETCH_STATUS = 0
  BEGIN
    DELETE FROM orders WHERE order_timestamp = @timestamp
    FETCH NEXT FROM cur_del_orders
  END

  DEALLOCATE cur_del_orders

/* Remove the customer record from the CUSTOMERS table */
```

```
  DELETE FROM customers
  WHERE cust_ID = (SELECT cust_ID FROM DELETED)
END
```

and then DELETE a customer from the CUSTOMERS table, the DBMS will create a cursor, populate it with the customer's orders, and then delete one order at a time from the ORDERS table. Given that the database owner (DBO) or the owner of the ORDERS table created the DELETE trigger in Tip 451, "Understanding DELETE Triggers," each DELETE statement in the TRI_DEL_CUSTOMERS trigger that removes a row from the ORDERS table will activate that TRI_DEL_ORDER trigger.

Note: *In the current example, the CUST_ID column of the CUSTOMERS table is a FOREIGN KEY for the ORDERS table. As a result the DBMS will abort any DELETE statement that tries to remove a customer (from the CUSTOMERS table) who still has orders (in the ORDERS table). To get around this problem, the DELETE trigger includes an INSTEAD OF clause that tells the DBMS to substitute the actions of the trigger in place of the DELETE statement that activated it. After the trigger in the current example removes all of the customer's orders from the ORDERS table, the DBMS allows it to DELETE the customer row from the CUSTOMERS table because doing so no longer violates the ORDERS table's FOREIGN KEY (referential integrity) constraint. Notice that deleting a row from the table on which the DELETE trigger is declared does not itself activate the DELETE trigger recursively—unless you use the system stored procedure SP_DBOPTION to enable RECURSIVE TRIGGERS.*

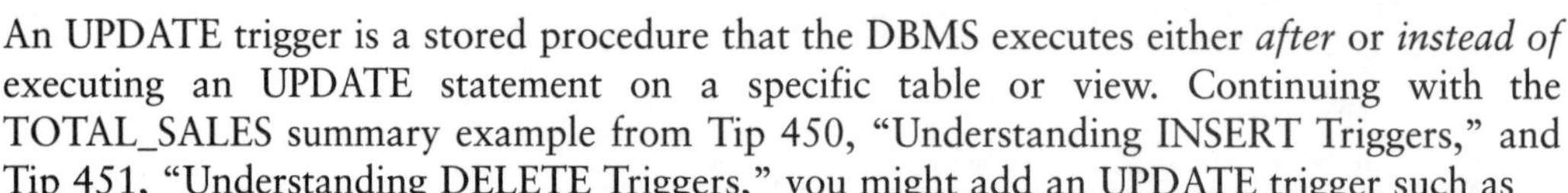

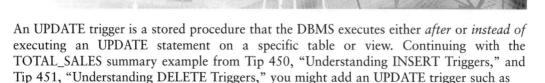

453 Understanding UPDATE Triggers

An UPDATE trigger is a stored procedure that the DBMS executes either *after* or *instead of* executing an UPDATE statement on a specific table or view. Continuing with the TOTAL_SALES summary example from Tip 450, "Understanding INSERT Triggers," and Tip 451, "Understanding DELETE Triggers," you might add an UPDATE trigger such as

```
CREATE TRIGGER tri_update_order ON orders AFTER UPDATE AS
DECLARE @rowcount INT
SET @rowcount = @@rowcount

IF UPDATE (order_total) OR UPDATE (office_ID) OR
     UPDATE(salesperson) BEGIN
  IF @@ROWCOUNT > 1
    BEGIN
      ROLLBACK TRAN
      RAISERROR('Each UPDATE must change only one order at a time.',16,2)
    END
```

```
  ELSE BEGIN
    SET NOCOUNT ON
    UPDATE offices SET total_sales = total_sales -
                      (SELECT order_total FROM DELETED)
      WHERE offices.office_ID =
              (SELECT office_ID FROM DELETED)
    UPDATE offices SET total_sales = total_sales +
                      (SELECT order_total FROM INSERTED)
      WHERE offices.office_ID =
              (SELECT office_ID FROM INSERTED)

    UPDATE employees SET total_sales = total_sales -
                      (SELECT order_total FROM DELETED)
      WHERE employees.emp_ID =
              (SELECT salesperson FROM DELETED)
    UPDATE employees SET total_sales = total_sales +
                      (SELECT order_total FROM INSERTED)
      WHERE employees.emp_ID =
              (SELECT salesperson FROM INSERTED)
  END
END
```

to maintain the correct value for TOTAL_SALES in the OFFICES and EMPLOYEES tables when a user (or application) changes the amount of an order, its salesperson, or the office from which it was purchased.

The first IF statement in the UPDATE trigger in the current example determines if the updated row's ORDER_TOTAL, OFFICE_ID, or SALESPERSON column value was included in the UPDATE statement's SET clause. If the UPDATE statement did not set the value in any one of the three columns, then the change made to the row in the ORDERS table has no effect on the TOTAL_SALES values maintained by the trigger. Therefore, the trigger will execute its UPDATE statements only if the value in one or more of the three columns (ORDER_TOTAL, OFFICE_ID, or SALESPERSON) was set by the UPDATE statement that activated the trigger.

Notice that an UPDATE trigger can take advantage of both the INSERTED and the DELETED virtual tables that the DBMS creates when it activates the trigger. For an UPDATE trigger, the DELETED table contains a copy of the original column values from each row that satisfied the search criteria in the UPDATE statement's WHERE clause. The INSERTED table, meanwhile, contains a copy of the same rows, but the column values in each row of the INSERTED table reflect the changes made by in the UPDATE statement's SET clause.

Note: *If the UPDATE trigger's IF UPDATE (column) clause appears in the UPDATE statement's SET clause, the IF UPDATE clause returns TRUE—whether the UPDATE statement changed the value in the column or not. For example, the DBMS will execute the UPDATE trigger in the current example if you execute the UPDATE statement*

```
UPDATE orders Set salesperson = salesperson
WHERE customer_ID = 1001 AND order_date = '01/06/2001'
```

so long as the column values in at least one row in the ORDERS table satisfy search criteria in the UPDATE statement's WHERE clause. (Bear in mind that some application programs submit an UPDATE with a SET clause that contains all updateable fields when the user clicks the mouse pointer on the OK button, whether any changes were made or not.) If the trigger performs a significant amount of work when column values change, you can improve its performance by checking the original column values in the DELETED table against the updated column values in the INSERTED table to see if the user (or application) actually made any changes. The trigger needs to perform its work only if the column values actually changed, and not just because the trigger columns appeared in the UPDATE statement's SET clause.

Like the DELETE trigger in Tip 451, an UPDATE trigger must allow for the possibility that a single UPDATE statement will set column values in more than one row in the trigger table. The UPDATE trigger in the current example uses the @@ROWCOUNT variable to determine the number of rows affected by the triggering (UPDATE) statement. If the UPDATE statement sets values in more than one row within the ORDERS table, the UPDATE trigger undoes the work performed by executing a ROLLBACK and returns an error message and status codes.

Although the current example does not allow it, you could modify the UPDATE trigger to allow for multiple-row updates. Remember, the DELETED table contains a copy of each of the original column values from every ORDERS table row that satisfies the search criteria in the UPDATE statement's WHERE clause. Similarly, the INSERTED table contains the same rows with the column values as they would be if the UPDATE statement is allowed to complete its work. Therefore, the trigger could create two cursors, populate one with the rows from the INSERTED table and the other with the rows from the DELETED table, and then work its way through each cursor, one row at a time, reducing the TOTAL_SALES figure by the ORDER_TOTAL column value from each row in the DELETED cursor and increasing the TOTAL_SALES figure by the value of the ORDER_TOTAL column value from each row in the INSERTED cursor.

454 Using an UPDATE Trigger to Change the Value of a PRIMARY KEY/FOREIGN KEY Pair

In Tip 173, "Understanding Foreign Keys," you learned how to use FOREIGN KEY constraints to maintain referential integrity. By matching the FOREIGN KEY value in a child table with the PRIMARY KEY value in a parent table, the DBMS maintains referential integrity by preventing users (and applications) from deleting a row in the parent table if doing so will create an orphan row in the child table. However, the FOREIGN KEY constraint prevents you not only from deleting a row that has a PRIMARY KEY that matches the FOREIGN KEY in one or more rows in the child table, but also from updating the PRIMARY KEY.

Suppose, for example, that you are using the customer's phone number (in the PHONE_NUMBER column) as the PRIMARY KEY in the CUSTOMERS table. The DBMS will ensure that no orders or payments for nonexistent customers are inserted in the ORDERS and PAYMENTS tables by requiring that the FOREIGN KEY in each new row has a matching value in the PRIMARY KEY column of one (and only one) of the rows in the CUSTOMERS table.

Now, suppose you need to change the customer's phone number. The DBMS will not allow you to change the phone number in either the ORDERS or the PAYMENTS table because the new phone number does not exist in the CUSTOMERS table. Similarly, the system will not let you change the phone number in the CUSTOMERS table because doing so will create FOREIGN KEY values (with the old phone number) in the ORDERS and PAYMENTS tables that have no matching phone number in the PRIMARY KEY column of the CUSTOMERS table.

Fortunately, you can use an UPDATE trigger (with an INSTEAD OF clause) to let the user execute a single UPDATE statement that changes both PRIMARY KEY and FOREIGN KEY values in a single transaction. For example, the UPDATE trigger

```
CREATE TRIGGER tri_change_phone_number ON customers
INSTEAD OF UPDATE AS
IF @@ROWCOUNT > 1
  BEGIN
    ROLLBACK
    RAISERROR('You must UPDATE customer columns one row at a time.',16,4)
  END
ELSE BEGIN
  SET NOCOUNT ON
  DECLARE @new_phone_num CHAR(7), @old_phone_num CHAR(7)
  SET @new_phone_num = (SELECT phone_number FROM INSERTED)
  SET @old_phone_num = (SELECT phone_number FROM DELETED)

  IF @new_phone_num <> @old_phone_num
    BEGIN

/*INSERT duplicate customer record with new phone number*/

      INSERT INTO customers SELECT * FROM INSERTED

/*Change phone number in child rows*/

      UPDATE payments SET phone_number = @new_phone_num
      WHERE phone_number = @old_phone_num

      UPDATE orders SET phone_number = @new_phone_num
      WHERE phone_number = @old_phone_num
```

```
/*DELETE original customer record*/

      DELETE FROM customers
      WHERE phone_number = @old_phone_num
    END

/*If not changing the primary key then update the remaining
  columns in the customers table as normal*/

  ELSE BEGIN
    UPDATE customers SET
      f_name = (SELECT f_name FROM INSERTED),
      l_name = (SELECT l_name FROM INSERTED)
    WHERE customers.phone_number = @old_phone_num
  END
END
```

first inserts a duplicate customer row with the new phone number into the CUSTOMERS table. Then the trigger changes the FOREIGN KEY value in each of the child rows in the ORDERS and PAYMENTS tables from the old phone number to the new phone number. Finally, the UPDATE trigger deletes the original (now childless) customer row with the old phone number from the CUSTOMERS table.

455 Using Triggers to Enhance Referential Integrity

In Tip 454, "Using an UPDATE Trigger to Change the Value of a PRIMARY KEY/FOREIGN KEY Pair," you learned that you can use an UPDATE trigger to work around FOREIGN KEY referential integrity constraints that prevent you from changing the PRIMARY KEY value in parent table rows that have children (related rows) in one more related tables. Meanwhile, Tip 452, "Understanding Cascading Triggers," showed you how to use a DELETE trigger to remove related (child) rows prior to deleting a parent row in response to a user's request to DELETE a row from the parent table that has related (child) rows in one or more child tables. In addition to letting you work around referential integrity constraints (while still maintaining database referential integrity), triggers provide an alternative means to implement the referential integrity constraints normally provided by the DBMS through PRIMARY KEY/FOREIGN KEY pairs.

The main reason to implement referential integrity using triggers instead of primary and foreign keys is that triggers can display customized, descriptive messages as to why a statement failed to execute. For example, if you attempt to DELETE a parent row with child rows in one ore more related tables, the DBMS will display an error message similar to:

```
Server: Msg 547, Level 16, State 1, Line 1
DELETE statement conflicted with COLUMN REFERENCE
  constraint fk_pay_cust. The conflict occurred in database
  'SQLTips', table 'payments', column 'cust_ID'.
The statement has been terminated
```

Moreover, the DBMS will display a nearly identical error message (substituting only the word INSERT for DELETE) if you attempt to INSERT a child row with a FOREIGN KEY value that has no matching PRIMARY KEY in the parent table.

To maintain referential integrity using triggers that provide more descriptive error messages when aborting statements that attempt to create orphans (one or more rows in a child table that have no related row in the parent table), create an INSERT/UPDATE trigger such as the following for each FOREIGN KEY in each of the child tables

```
CREATE TRIGGER tri_order_ins_updt ON payments
FOR INSERT, UPDATE AS
IF ((SELECT COUNT(*) FROM customers, INSERTED
     WHERE customers.cust_ID = INSERTED.cust_ID) = 0)
  BEGIN
    ROLLBACK

    PRINT 'The customer ID (CUST_ID) is invalid.'
    PRINT 'The CUST_ID in a payment record must match one
of the CUST_ID values in the CUSTOMERS table.'

    RAISERROR('The statement has been terminated.',16,547)
  END
```

Then create a DELETE trigger such as that shown here in conjunction with an UPDATE (like the one shown in Tip 454) on the parent table

```
CREATE TRIGGER tri_cust_del ON customers FOR DELETE AS
DECLARE @child_count INT
SET @child_count = 0
IF ((SELECT COUNT(*) FROM payments, DELETED
     WHERE payments.cust_ID = DELETED.cust_ID) > 0)
  BEGIN
    PRINT 'You must DELETE the customer''s payments from
the PAYMENTS table before deleting the customer.'

    SET @child_count = 1
  END

IF ((SELECT COUNT(*) FROM orders, DELETED
     WHERE orders.cust_ID = DELETED.cust_ID) > 0)
  BEGIN
    PRINT 'You must DELETE the customer''s orders from the
ORDERS table before deleting the customer.'
    SET @child_count = 1
```

```
  END

IF @child_count > 0
  BEGIN
    ROLLBACK

    RAISERROR('The DELETE statement has been terminated
without deleting any rows.',16,547)
  END
```

456 Using a Trigger to Send an E-mail Message

Each MS-SQL Server installation includes a set of extended procedures which enable the DBMS to execute command strings in external operating system shells and to send and receive e-mail messages. Moreover, the system stored procedure SP_ADDEXTENDEDPROC lets you make additional extended procedures (function calls in Dynamic Link Library [DLL] files) available to the server as well. A trigger can call any of the extended procedures available on the MS-SQL Server.

For example, to send an e-mail message to the SALESMANAGER e-mail box and to the members of the SALESPEOPLE e-mail group when a new item is inserted into the PRODUCTS table, create an INSERT trigger similar to:

```
CREATE TRIGGER tri_email_re_new_item ON products
FOR INSERT AS
DECLARE @product_code  VARCHAR(10),
        @description   VARCHAR(30),
        @email_message VARCHAR(75)
SET NOCOUNT ON

/* Get the product code and description of the new product
   from the row being inserted into the PRODUCTS table */

SELECT @product_code = INSERTED.product_code,
       @description = INSERTED.description
FROM INSERTED

/* Form the e-mail message to send */

SELECT @email_message = 'PRODUCT CODE: (' + @product_code +
         ')  DESCRIPTION: ' + @description

/* Formulate and send the e-mail message */
```

```
EXEC master.dbo.xp_sendmail
      @recipients = 'SalesManager, SalesPeople',
      @message = @email_message,
      @subject = 'NEW PRODUCT Availability Alert'
```

You will learn more about the syntax (and capabilities) of the extended procedure XP_SENDMAIL, how to use other extended procedures to start and stop MS-SQL Server e-mail processes, and how to read and delete e-mail message in Tips 588–590. For now, the important thing to understand is that you can use triggers to call an extended procedure that lets you send e-mail messages.

457 Understanding Nested Triggers

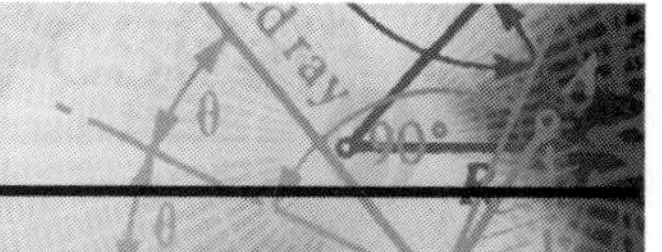

A *nested* (or cascading) trigger is a trigger that executes a statement that activates another trigger (which may execute a statement that activates a third trigger, and so on.) You learned how to use nested DELETE triggers in Tip 452, "Understanding Cascading Triggers," and how to use nested UPDATE triggers in Tip 454, "Using an UPDATE Trigger to Change the Value of a PRIMARY KEY/FOREIGN KEY Pair." In addition to giving the DBMS the ability to execute cascading deletes and updates, nested triggers are also useful for such housekeeping functions as making a backup copy of rows being deleted or updated by another trigger.

For example, if you implement the DELETE trigger in Tip 452

```
CREATE TRIGGER tri_del_customer ON customers
INSTEAD OF DELETE AS
IF @@ROWCOUNT > 1 BEGIN
    ROLLBACK TRAN
    RAISERROR('You can DELETE only one customer at a time.',16,3)
  END
ELSE BEGIN

/*                      .
   Statements which remove PAYMENTS and ORDERS table
   rows go here-- see Tip 454 for details --
                        .                          */

/* Remove the customer record from the CUSTOMERS table */

  DELETE FROM customers
  WHERE cust_ID = (SELECT cust_ID FROM DELETED)
END
```

and you want to make a backup copy of the row being deleted from the CUSTOMERS table, create a nested DELETE trigger such as:

```
CREATE TRIGGER tri_archive_del_cust ON customers FOR DELETE
AS INSERT archive_customers SELECT * FROM DELETED
```

As a result of the INSTEAD OF DELETE trigger and the nested DELETE trigger on the CUSTOMERS table, if a user executes a DELETE statement on the CUSTOMERS table, the DBMS will activate the INSTEAD OF DELETE trigger. When the INSTEAD OF DELETE executes the DELETE statement that attempts to DELETE a row from the CUSTOMERS table, the DBMS will activate the nested DELETE trigger, which will INSERT a copy of the deleted row from the CUSTOMERS table into the ARCHIVE_CUSTOMERS table.

When nesting triggers, keep in mind that the MS-SQL Server cannot determine whether the nesting you set up will start an infinite loop of cascading triggers until it activates the triggers at run time. For example, the DBMS will let you create an UPDATE trigger on table A that updates table B, and also let you create an UPDATE trigger on table B that updates table A. (Of course, when you later execute an UPDATE statement on either table, the triggers will execute and activate each other until the trigger execution nesting exceeds the maximum of 32 levels and the DBMS terminates the trigger. Note that the maximum level of nesting varies among DBMS products.)

Note: *Nested triggers execute within a single transaction. Therefore, if the DBMS terminates a trigger because it exceeds the maximum nesting level, or if a trigger terminates due to some other error, the DBMS will execute a ROLLBACK to undo all work performed by all nested triggers and the UPDATE, DELETE, or INSERT statement that activated the first trigger in the chain.*

458 Using the MS-SQL Server Enterprise Manager to Display or Modify a Trigger

The MS-SQL Server system stored procedure SP_HELPTEXT lets you use the syntax

```
SP_HELPTEXT <object name>
```

to display the text contents of a rule, default, unencrypted stored procedure, trigger, user-defined function, or view. Therefore, to display the code the governs the behavior of the TRI_DEL_CUSTOMER trigger created in Tip 457, "Understanding Nested Triggers," call the SP_HELPTEXT stored procedure as:

```
SP_HELPTEXT TRI_DEL_CUSTOMER
```

If you want to modify (as well as view) the contents of a trigger, use the MS-SQL Server Enterprise manager to display the trigger by performing the following steps:

1. Click your mouse pointer on the Start button. Windows will display the Start menu.
2. Move your mouse pointer to Programs on the Start menu, select the Microsoft SQL Server 2000 option, and click your mouse pointer on Enterprise Manager. Windows will start the Enterprise Manager in a new application window.
3. Click your mouse pointer on the plus (+) to the left of SQL Server Group to display the list of MS-SQL Servers available on your network.
4. Click your mouse pointer on the plus (+) to the left of the SQL server that has the table with the trigger you want to display (and perhaps modify). Enterprise Manager will display the Databases, Data Transformation, Management, Security, and Support Services folders for the SQL Server you selected.
5. Click your mouse pointer on the plus (+) to the left of the Databases folder to display the list of databases currently on the SQL server, and then on the plus (+) to the left of the database that has the table with trigger you want to display. For the current project, click on the plus (+) to the left of the SQLTips folder.
6. To display the list of tables in the database you selected in Step 5, click your mouse pointer on the Tables icon. The Enterprise Manager will use its right pane to display the list of the tables in the database you selected.
7. Right-click your mouse pointer on the table whose trigger you want to view. For the current project, right-click your mouse pointer on the icon to the left of CUSTOMER457. The Enterprise Manager will display a context-sensitive pop-up menu.
8. Move your mouse pointer to All Tasks on the pop-up menu, and then select Manage Triggers. The Enterprise Manager will display the Trigger Properties dialog box.
9. Click your mouse pointer on the drop-down list button to the right of the Name field, and select the name of the trigger you want to display from the drop-down list of trigger names. For the current project, click your mouse pointer on TRI_DEL_CUSTOMER457. The Enterprise Manager will display the trigger's code in the Text field of the Trigger Properties dialog box, as shown in Figure 458.1.
10. If you want to modify the trigger's behavior, make the desired changes, deletions, and additions in the Text window of the Trigger Properties dialog box, and then click your mouse pointer on the Check Syntax button.
11. Repeat Step 10 as necessary to correct any errors reported by the Enterprise Manager's syntax check of the trigger in the Text window.
12. To save your changes and make the updated trigger available to the DBMS, click your mouse pointer on the OK button.

After you complete Step 12, the Enterprise Manager will save the trigger as a database object, INSERT the trigger's text into the server's system tables, and exit the Trigger Properties dialog box.

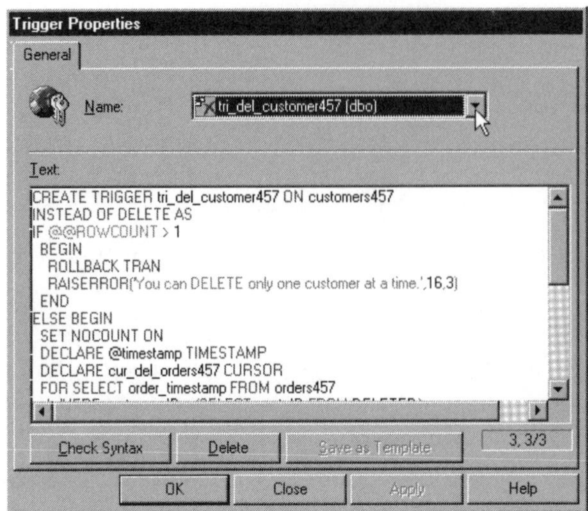

Figure 458.1 The MS-SQL Server Enterprise Manager Trigger Properties dialog box

---

Note: *If you included the WITH ENCRYPTION clause when you used the CREATE TRIGGER statement to create a trigger, neither SP_HELPTEXT nor the Enterprise Manager will be able to display the trigger's source code. Moreover, you will not be able to use the Enterprise Manager to change the trigger's behavior by editing its text on the Trigger Properties dialog box.*

---

459 Using the DROP TRIGGER Statement to Delete a Trigger

When you no longer want a trigger to perform a set of actions in response to an INSERT, DELETE, or UPDATE on a particular table, execute a DROP TRIGGER statement using the syntax

```
DROP TRIGGER <trigger name>[...,<last trigger name>]
```

to delete the trigger. For example, to delete the TRI_ARCHIVE_DEL_CUST and TRI_ARCHIVE_DEL_ORDER triggers created in Tip 457, "Understanding Nested Triggers," execute the DROP TRIGGER statement:

```
DROP TRIGGER tri_archive_del_cust, tri_archive_del_order
```

The MS-SQL Server will delete the triggers from the database and remove each trigger's text from the SYSOBJECTS and SYSCOMMENTS system tables.

Only the table owner, the database owner (DBO), or a member of the system administrator (SA) role can DROP a trigger on a particular table. To list a table's triggers and the username of the owner, execute the SP_HELPTRIGGER system stored procedure (which you will learn about in Tip 572, "Using the MS-SQL Server Stored Procedure sp_helptrigger to Display Information about Triggers on Tables") as:

```
SP_HELPTRIGGER <table name>
```

For example, to display the list of triggers on CUSTOMERS table, execute the statement:

```
SP_HELPTRIGGER customers
```

The MS-SQL Server will display the names, types, and owner of the triggers on the CUSTOMERS table. If you do not have the rights to DROP the trigger you want to remove from the table, either log in to the account that owns the trigger or ask the SA, the DBO, or the table's owner to execute the DROP TRIGGER statement for you.

Note: *If you execute a DROP TABLE statement to remove a table from the database or a DROP VIEW statement to delete a view, the DBMS will automatically DROP (delete) all triggers on the table or view. Therefore, you do not have to DROP triggers on a table or view before or after you delete the table or view—the DBMS automatically drops the triggers on a database object when it removes the object from the database.*

460 Using the ALTER VIEW Statement to Modify a View

Unlike the ALTER TABLE statement (which you will learn about in Tip 461, "Using the ALTER TABLE Statement to Change the Data Type of a Column"), you cannot write an ALTER VIEW statement that adds, removes, or changes the type of one or more individual columns in an existing view. As a result, other than substituting the word ALTER for CREATE, the syntax of an ALTER VIEW statement

```
ALTER VIEW [<database name>.][<view owner>.]<view name>
  [(<column name>[...,<last column name>])]
[WITH ENCRYPTION|SCHEMABINDING|VIEW_METADATA]
AS <SELECT statement>
[WITH CHECK OPTION]
```

is identical to the CREATE VIEW statements you learned about in Tips 206–215. Therefore, if you execute the CREATE VIEW statement

```
CREATE VIEW vw_student_name_list
  (student_ID, first_name, last_name)
AS SELECT SID, first_name, last_name FROM students
```

and later want to add the MAJOR column in the STUDENTS table to the view, you would use and ALTER VIEW statement such as

```
ALTER VIEW vw_student_name_list
  (student_ID, first_name, last_name, major)
AS SELECT SID, first_name, last_name, major FROM students
```

which includes all of the elements from the original view definition, plus the new column you want to add to the view.

At first glance, the ALTER VIEW statement seems to add no functionality to the DBMS data definition language. After all, an ALTER VIEW statement does not provide a shortcut way to change the definition of a view. As mentioned at the beginning of the current tip, the ALTER VIEW statement used to define a view must be identical in all but its name (ALTER vs. CREATE) to the CREATE VIEW statement used to create the same view. Therefore, it seems to be the case that when you want to change a view, you may as well use a DROP VIEW statement to remove the existing view and then execute a CREATE VIEW statement to re-create the view with its new structure.

However, the ALTER VIEW statement does provide one major advantage (over the DROP VIEW/CREATE VIEW sequence) in that it lets you change a view while leaving all access privileges and triggers created on the view in place. When you DROP a view, the DBMS automatically drops any triggers created on the view. Then, when you re-create the view, the system not only does not reinstate the triggers on the view, but it also does not GRANT any access privileges to the usernames (and roles) that had privileges on the original view.

As such, if you modify a view by executing a DROP VIEW statement followed by executing a CREATE VIEW statement to re-create the view (in its new form), you must also re-enter the code for all TRIGGERS on the original view, and GRANT access privileges on the view to users, roles, and accounts that were allowed to use the original view. Conversely, if you execute an ALTER VIEW statement to make the same change to the view's definition, you need not execute a DROP VIEW statement, and all triggers and access privileges granted on the original view remain in place on the new (modified) view.

461 Using the ALTER TABLE Statement to Change the Data Type of a Column

The ALTER TABLE statement's ALTER COLUMN clause lets you change a column's data type by using the syntax

```
ALTER TABLE <table name>
  ALTER COLUMN <new data type>[(precision[,scale])]
```

where:

- **table name.** Is the name of the table with the column whose type you want to change.
- **new data type.** Is a valid data type (INTEGER, NUMERIC, VARCHAR, CHAR, and so on). If the column whose data type you are changing has non-NULL data values, the existing data type must be implicitly convertible to the new data type. For example, you can convert a column of data type CHAR to NUMERIC, so long as all of the data values in the column (of data CHAR) are numbers.
- **precision.** Is the total number of digits in a number.
- **scale.** Is the number of digits to the right of the decimal point in a number.

Suppose, for example, that you created a CUSTOMERS table with a PHONE_NUMBER column that you defined as data type CHAR(14). As long as all phone numbers were inserted as numbers (that is, without dashes [–] and parentheses [()]), you can change the data type of the PHONE_NUMBER column to NUMERIC by executing the ALTER TABLE statement:

```
ALTER TABLE customers ALTER COLUMN phone_number NUMERIC
```

Before using the ALTER TABLE statement to change a column's data type, check your system manual to see if your DBMS imposes any limitations on the old or new data type of the target column. On an MS-SQL Server, for example, some of the limitations on the target column are that it cannot be:

- Of data type TEXT, IMAGE, or TIMESTAMP
- A computed column, or used in a computed column
- A replicated column
- Used in an INDEX—unless the column's data type is VARCHAR, NVARCHAR, or VARBINARY and the new data type increases the columns' current maximum length
- Used in a PRIMARY KEY or referenced by a FOREIGN KEY
- Used in a CHECK or UNIQUE constraint, or have a DEFAULT value—unless the new data type changes only a column's length, precision, or scale

462 Understanding the Challenges Presented by Binary and Character Large Object (BLOB) Processing

Because the majority of SQL servers are installed to support business data processing, columns in SQL tables are most often used to store such things as names; addresses; units of sales or inventory; money amounts due, sold, or paid; dates and times; and so on. Columns that hold data of these data types require a small amount of storage space—a few bytes for INTEGER, MONEY, and DATETIME values and perhaps 50–100 bytes each for (CHAR or VARCHAR) names, addresses, and product descriptions.

Due to the (typically) minimal data storage requirements of individual columns, DBMS products have been optimized to work with short rows (in terms of byte length), even though each table's rows may have dozens of columns. The SQL server assumes that rows will occupy at most a few thousand bytes when managing disk storage space, and indexes table data for speedy retrieval. Similarly, applications written to work with SQL database data assume that they will be able to retrieve a large number of rows of data into available (free) memory at the workstation or into temporary storage on a local hard drive through the workstations memory buffer. As you saw when you worked with Visual Basic applications and the DBLIB in Tips 391–425, row-at-a-time processing techniques for handling query results are relatively easy to understand and use.

Over the past few years, character-oriented business applications have been replaced by programs that take advantage of the Windows graphical user interface. The requirement on applications not only to display high-resolution graphics and animations but also to play sound files and video clips has caused the average size of "business" data items to grow exponentially. Consequently, with multimedia applications now an integral part of employee training programs, sales presentations, statistical analysis at company board meetings, and customer support services, business users need the DBMS to manage these new, large-size data type items along with other (more traditional and smaller-size) character and numeric data.

The challenge for the DBMS is that a single high-resolution graphic image may require hundreds of thousands of bytes of storage, a short audio file will occupy millions of bytes disk space, and video clips typically take up several megabytes of storage. Therefore, placing just one of these "new" (multimedia) data type items in a single column of one row in a table may require more storage space than an entire table that contains thousands of rows with dozens of columns of numeric and character data per row. While the disk space required to store a video clip, for example, is the same whether the clip is stored in a separate file on disk or in a column in a table row, using normal DBMS methods to work with exceptionally large rows may cause a few problems.

For example, when a user creates and populates a static cursor with rows that have a video clip column, 10 rows of data could easily take up 100MB of storage space (or server memory). Although 100MB per user is no problem if you have only a few users, in a more typical environment with 100 or more active connections, user queries might easily consume hundreds of gigabytes of storage on the server. Moreover, after waiting for the server to copy (perhaps) hundreds of megabytes of data from one disk location to another, the user will be able to work with the data on a workstation with only an inordinately large amount of memory available to buffer the data retrieved by a FETCH statement on a row-at-a-time basis.

Initial DBMS attempts to support *binary large objects*, or BLOBs (as items of data type TEXT, NTEXT, and IMAGE are often called), involved storing BLOB data outside the database in individual external files. Instead of the BLOB data itself, the DBMS stored the name of the BLOB file in a CHARACTER (or VARCHAR) data type column. When an application needed BLOB data, it would retrieve the name of the BLOB file from the DBMS and then communicate with the operating system to open and work with the file's contents.

Unfortunately, this approach required that the programmer understand both the DBMS and the file system interfaces. Furthermore, because application programs were responsible for managing the contents of the external BLOB files, users could not, for example, ask the DBMS to compare two BLOB items (in a search condition). Moreover, the DBMS could not provide even a simple BLOB text search capability.

Today, most commercial DBMS products store and manage at least two types of BLOB data within the database (vs. in external files). MS-SQL Server, for example, supports TEXT, NTEXT, and IMAGE data type columns. Oracle, meanwhile, supports these same BLOB data items but calls its data types for these CLOB, NCLOB, and BLOB.

463 Understanding MS-SQL Server BLOB (TEXT, NTEXT, and IMAGE) Processing

MS-SQL Server lets you store up to 2GB of data as a single item in a column. A TEXT column, as its name implies, is used to store character string data such as that stored in columns of data type CHAR and VARCHAR. Therefore, use a column of data type TEXT when you have a character string longer than 8,000 characters—which is the maximum number of characters a column of CHAR or VARCHAR can hold. Similarly, an IMAGE column lets you store binary data that exceeds the 8,000-byte maximum length imposed on columns of data type BINARY and VARBINARY. Typical items stored in columns of data type IMAGE are MS-Word documents, MS-Excel spreadsheets, bitmaps (BMP files), Graphics Interchange Format (GIF) pictures, and Joint Photographic Experts Group (JPEG or JPG) images.

If the data in a TEXT or IMAGE column is less than or equal to 8,000 bytes in length, you can use standard INSERT, SELECT, and UPDATE statements to work with the column. For example, to display the contents of a NOTES column of data type TEXT in the EMPLOYEES table, execute the SELECT statement

```
SELECT notes FROM EMPLOYEES
```

if the NOTES column has up to 8,000 characters. Bear in mind that although you can use a SELECT statement to show the contents of an IMAGE column, online query tools (such as MS-Query Analyzer) will display column's binary code as 1s and 0s (and not as a graphics image, sound file, or video clip). To interpret and convert the binary 1s and 0s into a document or image, you will need to send the column's contents to an application such as MS-Word, MS-Excel, or WinJPEG.

To optimize storage space usage and data retrieval performance, the MS-SQL Server, like other DBMS products, organizes table data in 8K pages. If the DBMS were to store BLOB items (TEXT, NTEXT, and IMAGE data) intermixed with data from the row's other columns, the BLOB data would make it impossible for the DBMS to fit rows of data into 8K pages. After all, a single BLOB data item may require hundreds of pages of storage. To keep tables optimized, the MS-SQL Server stores any BLOB data that is larger than 256 bytes in a separate area on disk. The server then places a pointer to the first page of BLOB data into the TEXT, NTEXT, or IMAGE column in the table.

As mentioned in Tip 462, "Understanding the Challenges Presented by Binary and Character Large Object (BLOB) Processing," most application programs that work with database data cannot hold an entire BLOB in a memory buffer at once. Instead, the programs must process the BLOB in sections. However, the APIs that the programs use to retrieve and store table data work on a row-at-a-time basis. To get around this problem, you use the Active Data Object (ADO) APPENDCHUNK and GETCHUNK methods, which let you store and retrieve data in BLOB columns a piece-at-a-time. (Tip 601, "Displaying Image Data Stored within an SQL Table," discusses how to retrieve image data from a table and write it to a disk file using the GETCHUNK method.)

One final issue to address in handling BLOB data is what to do about transaction logging. When logging work performed in a transaction, the DBMS normally maintains a "before" and "after" image of all modified data. Since each BLOB data item can be very large, making multiple "before" and "after" copies of it as it is modified can cause unacceptable delays in waiting for the DBMS to copy the data, and may fill up the transaction log while doing so. As such, DBMS products either do not support the logging of BLOB data or let you control the logging by providing a stored procedure (or other utility) you can use to turn it on and off. MS-SQL Server, for example, lets you use the WRITETEXT and UPDATETEXT statements to modify the contents of a BLOB without logging "before" and "after" images of the BLOB in the transaction log.

464 Using an INSERT or UPDATE Statement to Place Data into a BLOB Data Type Column

As you learned in Tip 462, "Understanding the Challenges Presented by Binary and Character Large Object (BLOB) Processing," and Tip 463, "Understanding MS-SQL Server BLOB (TEXT, NTEXT, and IMAGE) Processing," the MS-SQL Server lets you define table columns that can hold up to 2GB of binary or character string data. These columns of data type TEXT, NTEXT, and IMAGE are often called BLOBs (or bulk data, on MS-SQL Server). You can use an INSERT statement to place data into a BLOB.

For example, if you have a CUSTOMERS table created by

```
CREATE TABLE customers
  (cust_ID INTEGER,
   f_name  VARCHAR(15),
   l_name  VARCHAR(20),
   notes   TEXT,
   remarks TEXT,
   photo   IMAGE)
```

you can use an INSERT statement such as

```
INSERT INTO customers VALUES (1,'Konrad','King','
  'Notes on the customer','No Photo as yet','010')
```

to place data into the CUSTOMER table's BLOB columns (NOTES, REMARKS, PHOTO).

Similarly, you can use an UPDATE statement such as

```
UPDATE customers SET remarks = 'The PHOTO column has no
photo. It has only example data used to show the binary
conversion of character string data placed into an IMAGE
column.

WHERE cust_ID = 1
```

to change the contents of a BLOB column, just as you would change the contents of a column of any other data type.

Bear in mind that the DBMS logs all work performed by INSERT and UPDATE statements in the database transaction log. Since the amount of data in a BLOB column can be very large (up to 2GB in length), you may want to use a WRITETEXT statement (see Tip 465, "Using the Transact-SQL WRITETEXT Statement to Place Data into a TEXT, NTEXT, or IMAGE Column") or UPDATETEXT statement (see Tip 466, "Using the Transact-SQL UPDATETEXT Statement to Change the Contents of a TEXT, NTEXT, or IMAGE Column") in place of INSERT and UPDATE statements when working with BLOB data. Work performed by WRITETEXT and UPDATEXT statements is (by default) not written to the transaction log.

Note: *As mentioned by the text of the "remarks" placed into the REMARKS column of the current example, if you store a character string in a column of data type IMAGE, the server will treat the character string as a binary value. For example, if you execute the SELECT statement*

```
SELECT photo FROM customers
```

to display the result of placing the character string 010 into the IMAGE data type column PHOTO in the current example, the MS-SQL Server will display the column's contents as

```
photo
----------------------------
0x303130
```

which is the hexadecimal representation of (0 [ASCII value 48] 1 [ASCII value 49], and 0 [ASCII value 48]). Obviously, you want to store character strings in TEXT columns and reserve binary columns for binary data such as MS-Word documents, MS-Excel Spreadsheets, graphics images, sound files, and video clips.

---

465 Using the Transact-SQL WRITETEXT Statement to Place Data into a TEXT, NTEXT, or IMAGE Column

When you use an UPDATE statement to change the contents of a BLOB (TEXT, NTEXT, or IMAGE data type) column, the DBMS must write "before" and "after" copies of the column's contents into the transaction log. To avoid the overhead of logging changes to BLOB data, execute a Transact-SQL WRITETEXT instead of an UPDATE statement.

The WRITETEXT statement uses the syntax

```
WRITETEXT <table.column> <text pointer> <data>
```

where:

- **table.column** is the name of the table and column to update.
- **text pointer** is a local variable of data type BINARY(16), which contains a pointer to the first page of the WRITETEXT statement's target BLOB data.
- **data** is the data the DBMS is to store in the TEXT, NTEXT, or IMAGE column.

Use WRITETEXT to replace the current contents of a BLOB (TEXT, NTEXT, or IMAGE data type) column. If you want to modify (vs. replace) the contents of a BLOB, execute a Transact-SQL UPDATETEXT statement (which you will learn about in Tip 466, "Using the Transact-SQL UPDATETEXT Statement to Change the Contents of a TEXT, NTEXT, or IMAGE Column") instead.

In order for the DBMS to execute a WRITETEXT statement successfully, the system needs a valid pointer to the first 8K page that the DBMS has allocated to hold its BLOB data. If the target column contains a non-NULL BLOB, then the text pointer value is already valid. Otherwise, set the value of the BLOB's text pointer by executing an INSERT statement or an UPDATE statement to write either a zero-length character string or a portion of the BLOB data to the target column.

For example, to place a character string into the REMARKS column of the row for the customer with CUST_ID 1 in the CUSTOMERS table created in Tip 464, "Using an INSERT or UPDATE Statement to Place Data into a BLOB Data Type Column," use a statement batch similar to the following:

```
UPDATE customers SET remarks = '' WHERE cust_ID = 1

DECLARE @text_pointer BINARY(16)

SELECT @text_pointer = TEXTPTR(remarks)
FROM customers WHERE cust_ID = 1

WRITETEXT customers.remarks @text_pointer
  'These are the remarks to write into the REMARKS column'
```

466 Using the Transact-SQL UPDATETEXT Statement to Change the Contents of a TEXT, NTEXT, or IMAGE Column

As mentioned in Tip 465 "Using the Transact-SQL WRITETEXT Statement to Place Data into a TEXT, NTEXT, or IMAGE Column," both the Transact-SQL WRITETEXT and UPDATETEXT statements tell the DBMS to modify the contents of a TEXT, NTEXT, or IMAGE column (a BLOB) without writing "before" and "after" copies of the column's contents into the transaction log. The WRITETEXT statement can be used only to replace one BLOB with another. An UPDATETEXT statement, meanwhile, is more flexible in that it not only lets you replace one BLOB with another, but it also lets you modify (vs. overwrite) a BLOB, delete some or all of the BLOB's data, and add additional data to a BLOB.

The syntax of the UPDATETEXT statement is

```
UPDATETEXT <target table.column> <target text pointer>
  {NULL|<insert offset>} {NULL|<data length>}
  {<data>|{<source table.column> <source text pointer>}}
```

where:

- **target table.column** is the name of the table and column whose contents the UPDATE-TEXT statement is to modify.
- **target text pointer** is a local variable of data type BINARY(16), which contains a pointer to the first page of the UPDATETEXT statement's target BLOB data.
- **insert offset** is the number of bytes to skip from the start of the existing data in the TEXT or IMAGE column before inserting new data. (For columns of data type NTEXT, <insert offset> is the number of 2-byte characters to skip.) To insert new data at the beginning of the existing data, set <insert offset> to 0. To append new data onto the column's existing contents, set <insert offset> to NULL.

- **delete length** is the number of bytes of TEXT and IMAGE data or (2-byte) characters of NTEXT data to delete from the BLOB starting at the <insert offset>. To delete no data, set <delete length> to 0. To delete all data from <insert offset> to the end of the BLOB set <delete length> to NULL.
- **data** is a literal or variable with the CHAR, NCHAR, VARCHAR, NVARCHAR, BINARY, VARBINARY, TEXT, NTEXT, or IMAGE data the DBMS is to insert into the <target table.column> at the <insert offset>.
- **source table.column** is the name of the table and column whose data is to be inserted into the <target table.column> at the <insert offset>.
- **source text pointer** is a local variable of data type BINARY(16), which contains a pointer to the first page of the BLOB in the <source table.column> that the DBMS is to insert into the <target table.column> at the <inserted offset>.

In order for the DBMS to execute an UPDATETEXT statement successfully, the system needs a valid pointer to the first page of the BLOB data to be updated. If the target column is not NULL, the text pointer to its BLOB data is already valid. Conversely, if the BLOB data column is NULL, you must set the value of the BLOB's text pointer by executing an INSERT statement or an UPDATE statement to write either a zero-length character string or a portion of the BLOB data to the target column.

For example, to insert a character string at the beginning of the current BLOB in the REMARKS column for customer 1, use a statement batch similar to:

```
DECLARE @dest_text_pointer BINARY(16)
SELECT @dest_text_pointer = TEXTPTR(remarks)
FROM customers WHERE cust_ID = 1

IF @dest_text_pointer IS NULL
  BEGIN
    UPDATE customers SET remarks = '' WHERE cust_ID = 1
    SELECT @dest_text_pointer = TEXTPTR(remarks)
    FROM customers WHERE cust_ID = 1
  END

IF @dest_text_pointer IS NOT NULL
  UPDATETEXT customers.remarks @dest_text_pointer 0 0
    '  This is an additional remark.'
```

467 Using the READTEXT() Function to Read a Portion (or ALL) of the Data in a TEXT, NTEXT, or IMAGE Column

The Transact-SQL READTEXT() function is to a BLOB (TEXT, NTEXT, or IMAGE data) as the SUBSTRING() function is to a character string. While the SUBSTRING() function returns a portion of the characters in a character string, the READTEXT() function returns a specified number of bytes from a BLOB.

If you want to display the first @@TEXTSIZE bytes in a BLOB, you can use a SELECT statement that lists the BLOB column in its SELECT clause. (You will learn how to set the number of bytes in the TEXTSIZE option in Tip 471, "Understanding the TEXTSIZE Option and the @@TEXTSIZE() Function.") However, if you want to read some number of bytes other than the @@TEXTSIZE or starting with other than the first byte in the BLOB, use a READTEXT instead of a SELECT statement.

The syntax of the READTEXT statement is

```
READTEXT <table.column> <text pointer> <offset> <size>
  [HOLDLOCK]
```

where:

- **table.column** is the table and column in which has the TEXT, NTEXT, or IMAGE data to be displayed.
- **text pointer** is a local variable of data type BINARY(16), which contains a pointer to the first page of the BLOB in the <table.column> the DBMS is to display.
- **offset** is the number of bytes of TEXT or IMAGE data to skip before starting the read operation. (If you are working with an NTEXT BLOB, offset is the number of 2-byte characters to skip.)
- **size** is the number of bytes of TEXT or IMAGE data to read, or the number of (2-byte) NTEXT characters to read.
- **HOLDLOCK** tells the DBMS to LOCK the BLOB for reads until the end of the transaction. If you place a HOLDLOCK on a BLOB, other users can still "read" the data in the BLOB, but they cannot modify it until you either COMMIT or ROLLBACK the transaction in which you executed the READTEXT statement.

Therefore, to display 21 bytes of data starting with the 15th byte in the REMARKS column of the CUSTOMERS table row for CUST_ID 1, execute the statement batch:

```
DECLARE @text_pointer BINARY(16)

SELECT @text_pointer = TEXTPTR(remarks)
```

```
FROM customers WHERE cust_ID = 1

IF @text_pointer IS NOT NULL
  READTEXT customers.remarks @text_pointer 14 21
```

468 Using the MS-SQL Server TEXTVALID() Function to Determine If a Text Pointer Is Valid

As you saw in Tip 464, "Using an INSERT or UPDATE Statement to Place Data into a BLOB Data Type Column," and Tip 467, "Using the READTEXT() Function to Read a Portion (or ALL) of the Data in a TEXT, NTEXT, or IMAGE Column," the WRITETEXT, UPDATETEXT, and READTEXT statements require that you provide the address of the first 8K page of the target TEXT, NTEXT, or IMAGE data. The TEXTVALID() function lets you check to see if the TEXTPTR() function will return a valid text pointer to the BLOB data for a particular column in a row of the target table.

The TEXTVALID() function uses the syntax

```
TEXTVALID('<table.column>',<text pointer>)
```

where:

- **table.column** is the TEXT, NTEXT, or IMAGE data type table and column whose text pointer value the TEXTVALID() function is to check.
- **text pointe** is the pointer to the first 8K page of data in the TEXT, NTEXT, or IMAGE stored in <table.column>.

TEXVALID() will return an INTEGER value of 1 if the <text pointer> for <table.column> is valid, or an INTEGER value of 0 if the <text pointer> is invalid. As such, the UPDATE statement

```
UPDATE customers SET remarks = ''
WHERE TEXTVALID('customers.remarks', TEXTPTR(remarks)) <> 1
```

uses the TEXTVALID() function to check the validity of the text pointer to the REMARKS BLOB for each row in the CUSTOMERS table and initializes the text pointer for those rows with a NULL value in the REMARKS column.

Note: *When you INSERT a row with a NULL value in a TEXT, NTEXT, or IMAGE (BLOB) data type column, the DBMS does not preallocate an 8K page to hold the first 8K of BLOB data. As a result, if the BLOB column value is NULL, the text pointer to its first 8K storage page is invalid (or NULL). As soon as you place a value (even a zero-length string) into the BLOB column, the DBMS allocates an 8K page and initializes the value of the text pointer that points to it. The text pointer for a BLOB data* *item remains valid until a user or application deletes the row in which the BLOB is stored.*

469 Using the PATINDEX() Function to Return the Location of the First Occurrence of a Character String in a BLOB

The PATINDEX() function lets you search the contents of a TEXT or NTEXT column for a character string. If PATINDEX() finds the character string in the column's data, it returns the byte offset (that is, the location) of the first occurrence of the first letter in the character string. Conversely, if the function does not find the pattern of characters in the column, it returns 0. PATINDEX()returns a NULL value only if the either the TEXT or the NTEXT column is NULL, or if you tell the function to search for a NULL value.

The syntax of a PATINDEX() function call is that shown here:

```
PATINDEX('<pattern>',<expression>)
```

where:

- **pattern** is the character string literal the DBMS is to find in the CHAR, VARCHAR, TEXT or NTEXT <expression>. <pattern> can include the wildcard percent (%) wildcard character, which matches any number of characters, or the underscore (_), which matches any single character.
- **expression** is an expression (usually a column name) of data type CHAR, VARCHAR, TEXT, or NTEXT to be searched for the first occurrence of the character string given by <pattern>.

For example to get a list of all customers who complained about the "chicken" products, use the PATINDEX() function in the WHERE clause of a query, such as:

```
SELECT cust_ID, f_name + ' ' + l_name 'Customer Name',
  complaints
FROM customers WHERE PATINDEX('%chicken%', complaints) >= 1
```

The percent (%) characters that surround the <pattern> (the character string to find in the BLOB) tell the DBMS to treat as "matching" any number of characters that precede or follow the <pattern>. If you only want to display those rows that start with the <pattern>, omit the leading percent (%) character, as in:

```
SELECT cust_ID, f_name + ' ' + l_name 'Customer Name',
  complaints
FROM customers WHERE PATINDEX('chicken%', complaints) >= 1
```

To display only those rows with a COMPLAINTS column that ends in the <pattern>, omit the trailing percent (%) character, as in:

```
SELECT cust_ID, f_name + ' ' + l_name 'Customer Name',
  complaints
FROM customers WHERE PATINDEX('%chicken', complaints) >= 1
```

470 Using the DATALENGTH() Function to Return the Number of Bytes in a BLOB

The DATALENGTH() function, syntax

```
DATALENGTH(<expression>)
```

will return the number of bytes in an <expression> of any data type as an INTEGER value. If the <expression> has a NULL value, the DATALENGTH() function will return NULL.

DATALENGTH() lets you determine the size of the BLOB in a TEXT, NTEXT, or IMAGE column. For example, to display the number of bytes in the LOGO and PR_INFO columns (data type IMAGE and TEXT, respectively) in the PUB_INFO table of the PUBS database, execute a query such as

```
USE pubs
SET TEXTSIZE 45
SELECT DATALENGTH(logo) 'Logo Size',
  DATALENGTH(pr_info) 'PR Info Size',
  pr_info 'Public Relations Info Text' FROM pub_info
```

and MS-SQL Server will display a results similar to that shown in Figure 470.1.

Note: *The TEXTSIZE option (which you will learn about in Tip 471, "Understanding the TEXTSIZE Option and the @@TEXTSIZE() Function") sets the maximum number of characters the SELECT statement will return when it is told to display the contents of a TEXT, NTEXT, or IMAGE column.*

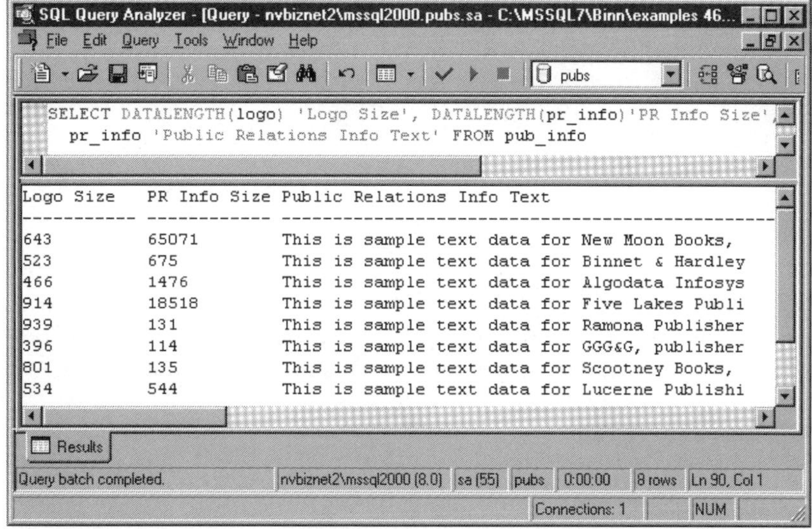

Figure 470.1 The MS-SQL Server Query Analyzer window displaying query results that use the DATALENGTH() function to show the byte length of an IMAGE and a TEXT column

471 Understanding the TEXTSIZE Option and the @@TEXTSIZE() Function

When using an interactive program such as MS-SQL Server's Query Analyzer, you may want to prevent a TEXT column's data from "wrapping" around from one line to the next so that each row in the query's results table fits on a single line on the screen. Or, suppose that you write an application that works with data in a table that has a column of data type TEXT, and you are interested in only the first 250 characters in the column. In both cases, you can execute a SET statement to specify the number of bytes that a SELECT statement (executed either interactively or by an application program) will return from a column of data type TEXT, NTEXT, or IMAGE (for example, a column that contains a BLOB).

The SET statement's TEXTSIZE option lets you tell the MS-SQL Server the number of bytes of data that it is to return when told to display a BLOB. Each time a user logs in, the server sets the connection's initial TEXTSIZE to 64,512—meaning that a SELECT statement on a BLOB will return, at most, 64,512 bytes of data. To tell the server to return only the first 20 bytes of data instead, execute the SET statement:

```
SET TEXTSIZE 20
```

You can use either a PRINT or a SELECT statement to display the value of the TEXTSIZE option for a session. For example, the PRINT statement

```
PRINT @@TEXTSIZE
```

will display the number 64512—if you have not yet use the SET statement to change the initial value of the connection's TEXTSIZE option.

Note: *When setting the value of TEXTSIZE to specify the number of* characters *you want a SELECT statement to display from a column of data type TEXT or NTEXT, bear in mind that each NTEXT (or UNICODE) character occupies 2 bytes of storage. As such, if you set the TEXTSIZE to 20, for example, a SELECT statement will display the first 20 characters in a column of data type TEXT and only the first 10 characters of in a column of data type NTEXT.*

472 Understanding the Information Schema

A database consists of *data* and *metadata*. Data, as the name implies, is the collection of values (including TEXT, NTEXT, and IMAGE items) stored in the columns that make up each row in the tables within the database. Metadata is a description of the database objects and is used to store and manage the data items in the database. The system stores database metadata in a set of tables known collectively as the *system catalog*. If you were to query the tables in the system catalog, you could display metadata that describes the database tables, columns, views, constraints, domains, privileges, and so on. In short, the DBMS system catalog's tables contain metadata data that describe every object in the database.

Although the DBMS maintains the system catalog for its own internal use, you can use standard SQL queries (SELECT statements) to access the system tables as well. As a matter of fact, you used the system catalog when you called the SQLColName() function to retrieve the names of the columns in a query's results set in Tip 398, "Using the SqlColName() Function to Retrieve the Names of the Columns in the Results Set Generated by a Query," and when you called the SQLNumCols() function to retrieve the number of columns returned by a query in Tip 397, "Using the SqlNumCols() Function to Determine the Number of Columns in the Results Set Generated by a Query." In short, a user-accessible system catalog makes a relational DBMS self-describing and lets you design general-purpose "front ends" such as query tools like the MS-SQL Server's Query Analyzer.

While all of the major DBMS products use system catalogs to store metadata, neither SQL-89 nor the current SQL-92 standard requires that they do so. As a result, the structure of the system catalog tables and the metadata contained in them varies greatly from one DBMS product to another. Rather than taking on the impossible task of trying to get DBMS vendors to change their products and agree on a standard structure (and physical implementation) for the system catalog, the SQL standards committee defined a series of views of the system catalog tables instead. These *views* of the system catalog are called the *information schema* in the SQL-92 standard.

The system catalog table views that make up the information schema give each user a standardized way to get a description of the database objects available on the user's database connection. Tips 473–492 describe the 20 information schema views available on MS-SQL Server. The important thing to understand now is that if your DBMS product is compliant with the SQL-92 standard, it, too, will have information schema views similar to those found on the MS-SQL Server. However, the SQL-92 standard allows DBMS vendors to add additional views and to add additional columns to the standard-defined information schema views. Therefore, use the following 20 tips (Tips 473–492) as a guide to the type of information available in the various information schema views, and check your system manual for the information schema definition specific to your DBMS product.

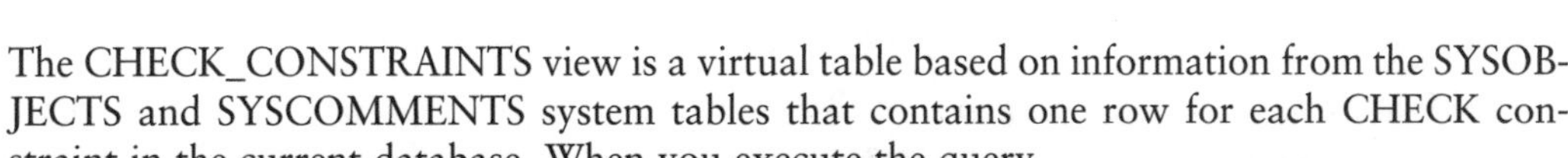

473 Understanding the Information Schema CHECK_CONSTRAINTS View

The CHECK_CONSTRAINTS view is a virtual table based on information from the SYSOBJECTS and SYSCOMMENTS system tables that contains one row for each CHECK constraint in the current database. When you execute the query

```
SELECT * FROM INFORMATION_SCHEMA.CHECK_CONSTRAINTS
```

the DBMS will return the information shown in Table 473.1 about the CHECK constraints on objects in the current database to which the login ID you used to connect with the server has at least one of the access privileges.

Column Name	Data Type	Description
CONSTRAINT_CATALOG	NVARCHAR(128)	Database in which the constraint is defined
CONSTRAINT_SCHEMA	NVARCHAR(128)	Owner of the constraint
CONSTRAINT_NAME	SYSNAME	Name of the constraint
CHECK CLAUSE	NVARCHAR(4000)	Text of the CHECK constraint

Table 473.1 The Columns in the Information Schema CHECK_CONSTRAINTS View

To display the information schema CHECK_CONTRAINTS view column information for all tables in the current database (even those to which you do not have any access privileges), execute a SELECT statement such as:

```
SELECT db_name()                    'Database/Catalog',
       user_name(sysobjects.UID)  'Constraint Owner',
       sysobjects.name             'Constraint Name',
       syscomments.text            'Constraint Text'
FROM sysobjects, syscomments
WHERE sysobjects.ID = syscomments.ID
  AND sysobjects.xtype = 'C'
```

474 Understanding the Information Schema COLUMN_DOMAIN_USAGE View

The COLUMN_DOMAIN_USAGE view is a virtual table based on information from the SYSOBJECTS, SYSCOLUMNS, and SYSTYPES system tables that contains one row for each column in the current database that has a user-defined data type. When you execute the query

```
SELECT * FROM INFORMATION_SCHEMA.COLUMN_DOMAIN_USAGE
```

the DBMS will return the information shown in Table 474.1 about the columns defined using user-defined data types in tables in the current database to which the login ID that you used to connect with the server has at least one of the access privileges.

Column Name	Data Type	Description
DOMAIN_CATALOG	NVARCHAR(128)	Database in which the user-defined data type was created
DOMAIN_SCHEMA	NVARCHAR(128)	The username that created the user-defined data type
DOMAIN_NAME	SYSNAME	The name of the user-defined data type
TABLE_CATALOG	NVARCHAR(128)	The database that contains the table with the column that has a user-defined data type
TABLE_SCHEMA	NVARCHAR(128)	The user ID of the owner of the table with the column that has a user-defined data type

Column Name	Data Type	Description
TABLE_NAME	SYSNAME	The name of the table with the column that has a user-defined data type
COLUMN_NAME	SYSNAME	The name of the column with the user-defined data type

Table 474.1 The Columns in the Information Schema COLUMN_DOMAIN_USAGE View

To display the information schema, COLUMN_DOMAIN_USAGE view column information for all tables in the current database (even those to which you do not have any access privileges), execute a SELECT statement such as:

```
SELECT db_name()                    'Domain Database/Catalog',
       user_name(systypes.UID)      'Domain Owner',
       systypes.name                'Domain Name',
       db_name()                    'Table Database/Catalog'
       user_name(sysobjects.UID)    'Table Owner',
       sysobjects.name              'Table Name',
       syscolumns.name              'Column Name'
FROM sysobjects, syscolumns, systypes
WHERE sysobjects.ID = syscolumns.ID
  AND syscolumns.xusertype = systypes.xusertype
  AND systypes.xusertype > 256
```

475 Understanding the Information Schema COLUMN_PRIVILEGES View

The COLUMN_PRIVILEGES view is a virtual table based on information from the SYSPROTECTS, SYSOBJECTS, and SYSCOLUMNS system tables that contains one row for each privilege on a column granted to or granted by a database user. When you execute the query

```
SELECT * FROM INFORMATION_SCHEMA.COLUMN_PRIVILEGES
```

the DBMS will return the information shown in Table 475.1 about the privileges on table columns in the current database granted by or granted to the login ID you used to connect with the server.

Column Name	Data Type	Description
GRANTOR	NVARCHAR(128)	ID of the account that granted the privilege
GRANTEE	NVARCHAR(128)	ID of the account to which the privilege was granted
TABLE_CATALOG	NVARCHAR(128)	The name of the database that contains the table column on which the privilege was granted
TABLE_SCHEMA	NVARCHAR(128)	ID of the user that owns the table that contains the column on which the privilege was granted
TABLE_NAME	SYSNAME	The name of the table that contains the column on which the privilege was granted
COLUMN_NAME	SYSNAME	The name of the column on which the privilege was granted
PRIVILEGE_TYPE	VARCHAR(10)	The access privilege (permission) granted on the column
IS_GRANTABLE	VARCHAR(3)	YES if the privilege grantee has the right to grant the privilege (permission) to others, or NO if the grantee does not

Table 475.1 The Columns in the Information Schema COLUMN_PRIVILEGES View

To review the Transact-SQL code that defines the information schema COLUMN_PRIVILEGES view, perform the procedure outlined in Tip 493, "Using the MS-SQL Server Enterprise Manager to View the Contents of an Information Schema View."

476 Understanding the Information Schema COLUMNS View

The COLUMNS view is a virtual table based on information from the SYSOBJECTS, MASTER.DBO.SPT_DATATYPE_INFO, SYSTYPES, SYSCOLUMNS, SYSCOMMENTS, and MASTER.DBO.SYSCHARSETS system tables that contains one row for each privilege on a column granted to or granted by a database user. When you execute the query

```
SELECT * FROM INFORMATION_SCHEMA.COLUMNS
```

the DBMS will return the information shown in Table 476.1 about the table columns in the current database available to the login ID you used to connect with the server.

Column Name/Data Type	***Description***
TABLE_CATALOG NVARCHAR(128)	The name of the database that contains the column
TABLE_SCHEMA NVARCHAR(128)	The ID of the user that owns the table that contains the column
TABLE_NAME NVARCHAR(128)	The name of the table that contains the column
COLUMN_NAME NVARCHAR(128)	The name of the column
ORDINAL_POSITION SMALLINT	The position of the column in its table definition, counting from left to right (\\ with the first column on the left \ having an ordinal position of 1)
COLUMN_DEFAULT NVARCHAR(4000)	The column's default value
IS_NULLABLE VARCHAR(3)	YES if the column allows a NULL value, or NO if not
DATA_TYPE NVARCHAR(128)	The column's data type
CHARACTER_MAXIMUM_LENGTH SMALLINT	Maximum length in characters for BINARY, CHARACTER, TEXT, and IMAGE data; NULL for columns of other data types
CHARACTER_OCTET_LENGTH SMALLINT	Maximum length in bytes for BINARY, CHARACTER, TEXT, and IMAGE data; NULL for columns of other data types
NUMERIC_PRECISION TINYINT	Precision for INTEGER data, precise and approximate numeric data, and MONEY data; NULL for columns of other data types
NUMERIC_PRECISION_RADIX SMALLINT	Precision radix for INTEGER data, precise and approximate numeric data, and MONEY data; NULL for columns of other data types
NUMERIC_SCALE TINYINT	The scale for INTEGER data, precise and approximate numeric data, and MONEY data; NULL for columns of other data types
DATETIME_PRECISION SMALLINT	Subtype code for DATETIME and INTERVAL data; NULL for columns of other data types

Column Name/Data Type	*Description*
CHARACTER_SET_CATALOG VARCHAR(6)	The name of the database (normally MASTER) in which the character set for character and TEXT data is located; NULL for columns of other data types
CHARACTER_SET_SCHEMA VARCHAR(3)	The ID (normally DBO) of the owner of the character set for character and TEXT data; NULL for columns of other data types
CHARACTER_SET_NAME NVARCHAR(128)	The name of the character set for character and TEXT columns; NULL for columns of other data types
COLLATION_CATALOG VARCHAR(6)	The name of the database (normally MASTER) in which the sort order for the column's character or TEXT data is defined; NULL for columns of other data types
COLLATION_SCHEMA VARCHAR(3)	The ID (normally DBO) of the owner of the collation for a column with character or TEXT data; NULL for columns of other data types
COLLATION_NAME NVARCHAR(128)	The name of the sort order for columns with character or TEXT data; NULL for columns of other data types
DOMAIN_CATALOG NVARCHAR(128)	The name of the database in which the user-defined data type was created if the column has a user-defined data type; NULL for columns of other data types
DOMAIN_SCHEMA NVARCHAR(128)	The ID of the user that created the user-defined data type if the column has a user-defined data type; NULL for columns of other data types
DOMAIN_NAME NVARCHAR(128)	The name of the user-defined data type if the column has a user-defined data type; NULL for columns of other data types

Table 476.1 The Columns in the Information Schema COLUMNS View

To review the Transact-SQL code that defines the information schema COLUMNS view, perform the procedure outlined in Tip 493, "Using the MS-SQL Server Enterprise Manager to View the Contents of an Information Schema View."

477 Understanding the Information Schema CONSTRAINT_COLUMN_USAGE View

The CONSTRAINT_COLUMN_USAGE view is a virtual table based on information from the SYSOBJECTS, SYSCOLUMNS, and SYSTYPES system tables that contains one row for each column with a constraint defined on it. When you execute the query

```
SELECT * FROM INFORMATION_SCHEMA.CONSTRAINT_COLUMN_USAGE
```

the DBMS will return the information shown in Table 477.1 about the table, column, and constraints on each of the columns in the current database that is defined with a constraint and to which the login ID you used to connect with the server has at least one of the access privileges.

Column Name/Data Type	Description
TABLE_CATALOG NVARCHAR(128)	The name of the database in which the table with the constrained column is defined
TABLE_SCHEMA NVARCHAR(128)	The ID of the owner of the table with the constrained column
TABLE_NAME NVARCHAR(128)	The name of the table with the constrained column
COLUMN_NAME NVARCHAR(128)	The name of the column on which the constraint is defined
CONSTRAINT_CATALOG NVARCHAR(128)	The name of the database in which the constraint is defined
CONSTRAINT_SCHEMA NVARCHAR(128)	The ID of the constraint's owner
CONSTRAINT_NAME NVARCHAR(128)	The name of the constraint

Table 477.1 The Columns in the Information Schema CONSTRAINT_COLUMN_USAGE View

To display the information schema CONSTRAINT_COLUMN_USAGE view information for all columns in the current database that have constraints (even those to which you do not have any access privileges), execute a SELECT statement such as:

```
SELECT iskcu.table_catalog        'Table Database',
       iskcu.table_schema         'Table Owner ID',
       iskcu.table_name           'Table Name',
       iskcu.column_name          'Column Name',
       iskcu.constraint_catalog   'Constraint Database',
       iskcu.constraint_schema    'Constraint Owner ID',
```

```
        iskcu.constraint_name      'Constraint Name'
  FROM information_schema.key_column_usage iskcu
UNION
  SELECT db_name(),
         user_name(tableobj.UID),
         tableobj.name,
         syscolumns.name,
         db_name(),
         user_name(constraintobj.UID),
         constraintobj.name
  FROM sysobjects tableobj, sysobjects constraintobj,
       syscolumns
  WHERE tableobj.ID          = constraintobj.parent_obj
    AND constraintobj.xtype = 'C'
    AND constraintobj.info  = syscolumns.colid
    AND syscolumns.ID       = constraintobj.parent_obj
UNION
  SELECT db_name(),
         user_name(tableobj.UID),
         tableobj.name,
         syscolumns.name,
         db_name(),
         user_name(constraintobj.UID),
         constraintobj.name
  FROM sysobjects tableobj, sysobjects constraintobj,
       syscolumns, systypes
  WHERE tableobj.ID            = syscolumns.ID
    AND syscolumns.xusertype = systypes.xusertype
    AND systypes.xusertype   > 256
    AND systypes.domain      = constraintobj.ID
    AND constraintobj.xtype  = 'R'
```

478 Understanding the Information Schema CONSTRAINT_TABLE_USAGE View

The CONSTRAINT_TABLE_USAGE view is a virtual table based on information from the SYSOBJECTS system table that contains one row for each table with a constraint defined on it. When you execute the query

```
SELECT * FROM INFORMATION_SCHEMA.CONSTRAINT_TABLE_USAGE
```

the DBMS will return the information shown in Table 478.1 about each table in the current database that is defined with a constraint and to which the login ID you used to connect with the server has at least one of the access privileges.

Column Name	Data Type	Description
TABLE_CATALOG	NVARCHAR(128)	The name of the database in which the constrained table is defined
TABLE_SCHEMA	NVARCHAR(128)	The ID of the owner of the constrained table
TABLE_NAME	SYSNAME	The name of the constrained table
CONSTRAINT_CATALOG	NVARCHAR(128)	The name of the database in which the table constraint is defined
CONSTRAINT_SCHEMA	NVARCHAR(128)	The ID of the constraint's owner
CONSTRAINT_NAME	SYSNAME	The name of the table constraint

Table 478.1 The Columns in the Information Schema CONSTRAINT_TABLE_USAGE View

To display the information schema CONSTRAINT_TABLE_USAGE view information for all tables in the current database that have constraints (even those to which you do not have any access privileges), execute a SELECT statement such as:

```
SELECT db_name()                       'Table Database',
       user_name(tableobj.UID)         'Table Owner',
       tableobj.name                   'Table Name',
       db_name()                       'Constraint Database',
       user_name(constraintobj.UID) 'Constraint Owner',
       constraintobj.name              'Constraint Name'
FROM sysobjects tableobj, sysobjects constraintobj
WHERE tableobj.ID          =  constraintobj.parent_obj
  AND constraintobj.xtype IN ('C','UQ','PK','F')
```

479 Understanding the Information Schema DOMAIN_CONSTRAINTS View

The DOMAIN_CONSTRAINTS view is a virtual table based on information from the SYSOBJECTS and SYSTYPES system tables that contains one row for each user-defined data type in the current database with a RULE bound to it. When you execute the query

```
SELECT * FROM INFORMATION_SCHEMA.DOMAIN_CONSTRAINTS
```

the DBMS will return the information shown in Table 479.1 about each RULE-bound user-defined data type in the current database to which the login ID you used to connect with the server has access.

Column Name	Data Type	Description
CONSTRAINT_CATALOG	NVARCHAR(128)	The name of the database in which the RULE is defined
CONSTRAINT_SCHEMA	NVARCHAR(128)	The ID of the RULE's owner
CONSTRAINT_NAME	SYSNAME	The name of the RULE
DOMAIN_CATALOG	SYSNAME	The name of the database in which the user-defined data type is defined
DOMAIN_SCHEMA	NVARCHAR(128)	The ID of the user that created the user-defined data type
DOMAIN_NAME	SYSNAME	The name of the user-defined data type
IS_DEFERRABLE	VARCHAR(2)	Whether constraint checking is deferrable; always NO
INITIALLY_DEFERRED	VARCHAR(2)	Whether constraint checking is initially deferred; always NO

Table 479.1 The Columns in the Information Schema DOMAIN_CONSTRAINTS View

To display the information schema DOMAIN_CONSTRAINTS view information for all RULE-bound user-defined data types (even those to which you do not have access), execute a SELECT statement such as:

```
SELECT db_name()                    'Rule Database/Catalog',
       user_name(sysobjects.UID) 'Rule Owner',
       sysobjects.name              'Rule Name',
       db_name()                    'User Data Type Database',
       user_name(systypes.UID)      'User Data Type Owner',
       systypes.name                'User Data Type Name',
       'NO'                         'Is Deferrable',
       'NO'                         'Initially Deferred'
FROM sysobjects, systypes
WHERE sysobjects.xtype    = 'R'
  AND sysobjects.ID       = systypes.domain
  AND systypes.xusertype > 256
```

480 Understanding the Information Schema DOMAINS View

The DOMAINS view is a virtual table based on information from the MASTER.DBO.SPT_DATATYPE_INFO, SYSTYPES, SYSCOMMENTS, and MASTER.DBO.SYSCHARSETS system tables that contains one row for each user-defined data type, in the current database. When you execute the query

```
SELECT * FROM INFORMATION_SCHEMA.DOMAINS
```

the DBMS will return the information shown in Table 480.1 about each user-defined data type in the current database to which the login ID you used to connect with the server has access.

Column Name/Data Type	*Description*
DOMAIN_CATALOG NVARCHAR(128)	The name of the database in which the user-define data type is defined
DOMAIN_SCHEMA NVARCHAR(128)	The ID of the user that created the user-defined data type
DOMAIN_NAME SYSNAME	The name of the user-defined data type
DATA_TYPE SYSNAME	The system-supplied (SQL) data type
CHARACTER_MAXIMUM_LENGTH SMALLINT	The column's maximum length in characters for columns with character, BINARY, TEXT, and IMAGE data; NULL for columns of other data types
CHARACTER_OCTET_LENGTH SMALLINT	The column's maximum length in bytes for columns with character, BINARY, TEXT, and IMAGE data; NULL for columns of other data types
COLLATION_CATALOG VARCHAR(6)	The name of the database (normally MASTER) in which the sort order for columns with character or TEXT data; NULL for columns of other data types
COLLATION_SCHEMA VARCHAR(3)	The name of the database (normally the ID of the owner of the sort order) for columns with character or TEXT data—always DBO or NULL for columns of other data types

Column Name/Data Type	Description
COLLATION_NAME NVARCHAR(128)	The name of the sort order for columns with character or TEXT data; NULL for columns of other data types
CHARACTER_SET_CATALOG VARCHAR(6)	The name of the database in which the sort order is defined for columns with character or TEXT data—always MASTER or NULL for columns of other data types
CHARACTER_SET_SCHEMA VARCHAR(3)	The ID of the owner of the character set for columns with character or TEXT data—always DBO or NULL for columns of other data types
CHARACTER_SET_NAME NVARCHAR(128)	The name of the character set for columns with character or TEXT data; NULL for columns of other data types
NUMERIC_PRECISION TINYINT	Precision for columns with numeric data; NULL for columns of other data types
NUMERIC_PRECISION_RADIX SMALLINT	Precision radix for columns with numeric data; NULL for columns of other data types
NUMERIC_SCALE TINYINT	Scale for columns with numeric data; NULL for columns of other data types
DATETIME_PRECISION SMALLINT	Subtype code for DATETIME and INTERVAL data; NULL for columns of other data types
DOMAIN_DEFAULT NVARCHAR(4000)	Transact-SQL definition of the domain

Table 480.1 The Columns in the Information Schema DOMAINS View

To review the Transact-SQL code that defines the information schema DOMAINS view, perform the procedure outlined in Tip 493, "Using the MS-SQL Server Enterprise Manager to View the Contents of an Information Schema View."

481 Understanding the Information Schema KEY_COLUMN_USAGE View

The KEY_COLUMN_USAGE view is a virtual table based on information from the SYSOBJECTS, SYSCOLUMNS, SYSREFERENCES, MASTER.DBO.SPT_VALUES, and SYSIN-

DEXES system tables that contains one row for each column used in either a PRIMARY KEY or a FOREIGN KEY constraint. When you execute the query

```
SELECT * FROM INFORMATION_SCHEMA.KEY_COLUMN_USAGE
```

the DBMS will return the information shown in Table 481.1 about the columns in the current database that are part of either a PRIMARY KEY or a FOREIGN KEY in tables to which the login ID you used to connect with the server has at least one of the access privileges.

Column Name/Data Type	***Description***
CONSTRAINT_CATALOG NVARCHAR(128)	The name of the database that contains the PRIMARY KEY or FOREIGN KEY constraint that uses the column
CONSTRAINT_SCHEMA NVARCHAR(128)	The ID of the user that owns the key constraint that uses the column
CONSTRAINT_NAME NVARCHAR(128)	The name of the key constraint that uses the column
TABLE_CATALOG NVARCHAR(128)	The name of the database that contains the table with the key that uses the column
TABLE_SCHEMA NVARCHAR(128)	The ID of the user that owns the table with the key constraint that uses the column
TABLE_NAME NVARCHAR(128)	The name of the table with the key constraint that uses the column
COLUMN_NAME NVARCHAR(128)	The name of the column that is in a FOREIGN KEY or PRIMARY key constraint
ORDINAL_POSITION INTEGER	The position of the column in the table in which it is defined

Table 481.1 The Columns in the Information Schema KEY_COLUMN_USAGE View

To review the Transact-SQL code that defines the information schema KEY_COLUMN_USAGE view, perform the procedure outlined in Tip 493, "Using the MS-SQL Server Enterprise Manager to View the Contents of an Information Schema View."

482 Understanding the Information Schema PARAMETERS View

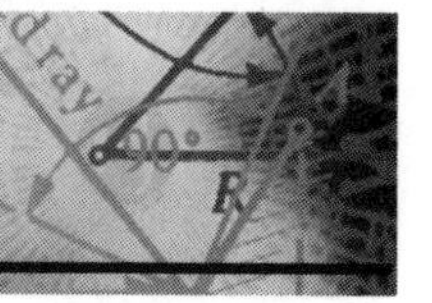

The PARAMETERS view is a virtual table based on information from the SYSOBJECTS, SYSCOLUMNS, and MASTER.DBO.SYSCHARSETS system tables that contains one row for each parameter passed to a user-defined function or stored procedure. Moreover, the view contains an additional row with return value information for each user-defined function. When you execute the query

```
SELECT * FROM INFORMATION_SCHEMA.PARAMETERS
```

the DBMS will return the information shown in Table 482.1 about the parameters for user-defined functions and stored procedures, and the return value for each function available to the login ID you used to connect with the server.

Column Name/Data Type	***Description***
SPECIFIC_CATALOG NVARCHAR(128)	The name of the database that contains the function or stored procedure (the routine) that uses the parameter or returns the value described in the current row of the PARAMETERS view
SPECIFIC_SCHEMA NVARCHAR(128)	The ID of the owner of the of the routine that uses the parameter returns the value
SPECIFIC_NAME NVARCHAR(128)	The name of the routine that uses the parameter or returns the value
ORDINAL_POSITION SMALLINT	The position of the parameter in the routine's parameter list (starting at 1), or 0 for the return value for a function
PARAMETER_MODE NVARCHAR(10)	IN for an input parameter; OUT for an output parameter; INOUT for an input/output parameter
IS_RESULT NVARCHAR(10)	YES if the parameter is the return value from a function, or NO if it is not
AS_LOCATOR NVARCHAR(10)	YES if the parameter is declared as a locator, or NO if it is not
PARAMETER_NAME NVARCHAR(128)	The name of the parameter, or NULL if the parameter is the return value for a function
DATA_TYPE NVARCHAR(128)	The parameter's data type
CHARACTER_MAXIMUM_LENGTH INTEGER	The maximum length in characters for character and TEXT data; NULL for parameters of other data types
CHARACTER_OCTET_LENGTH INTEGER	The maximum length in bytes for columns that contain character or TEXT data; NULL for columns of other data types

Column Name/Data Type	Description
COLLATION_CATALOG NVARCHAR(128)	The name of the database that contains the sort order for parameters of one of the character data types; NULL for parameters of other data types
COLLATION_SCHEMA NVARCHAR(128)	The name of the schema that contains the collation (sort order) for parameters of one of the character data types; NULL for parameters of other data types
COLLATION_NAME NVARCHAR(128)	The name of the collation (sort order) for parameters of one of the character data types; NULL for parameters of other data types
CHARACTER_SET_CATALOG NVARCHAR(128)	The name of the database that contains the character set for parameters of one of the character data types; NULL for parameters of other data types
CHARACTER_SET_SCHEMA NVARCHAR(128)	The user ID of the owner of the character set for parameters of one of the character data types; NULL for parameters of other data types
CHARACTER_SET_NAME NVARCHAR(128)	The name of the character set for parameters of one of the character data types; NULL for parameters of other data types
NUMERIC_PRECISION TINYINT	Precision for columns with numeric data; NULL for columns of other data types
NUMERIC_PRECISION_RADIX SMALLINT	Precision radix for columns with numeric data; NULL for columns of other data types
NUMERIC_SCALE TINYINT	Scale for columns with numeric data; NULL for columns of other data types
DATETIME_PRECISION SMALLINT	Subtype code for DATETIME and INTERVAL data; NULL for columns of other data types
INTERVAL_TYPE NVARCHAR(30)	NULL (reserved for future use)
INTERVAL_PRECISION SMALLINT	NULL (reserved for future use)
USER_DEFINED_TYPE_CATALOG NVARCHAR(128)	NULL (reserved for future use)
USER_DEFINED_TYPE_SCHEMA NVARCHAR(128)	NULL (reserved for future use)
USER_DEFINED_TYPE_NAME NVARCHAR(128)	NULL (reserved for future use)

Column Name/Data Type	Description
SCOPE_CATALOG NVARCHAR(128)	NULL (reserved for future use)
SCOPE_SCHEMA NVARCHAR(128)	NULL (reserved for future use)
SCOPE_NAME NVARCHAR(128)	NULL (reserved for future use)

Table 482.1 The Columns in the Information Schema PARAMETERS View

To review the Transact-SQL code that defines the information schema PARAMETERS view, perform the procedure outlined in Tip 493, "Using the MS-SQL Server Enterprise Manager to View the Contents of an Information Schema View."

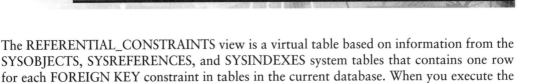

483 Understanding the Information Schema REFERENTIAL_CONSTRAINTS View

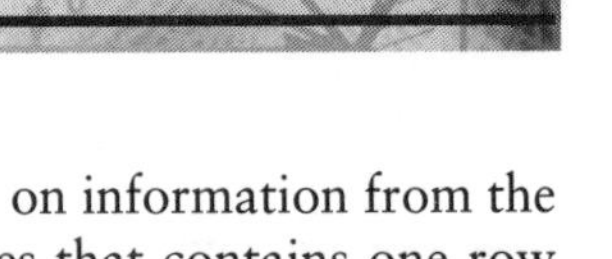

The REFERENTIAL_CONSTRAINTS view is a virtual table based on information from the SYSOBJECTS, SYSREFERENCES, and SYSINDEXES system tables that contains one row for each FOREIGN KEY constraint in tables in the current database. When you execute the query

```
SELECT * FROM INFORMATION_SCHEMA.REFERENTIAL_CONSTRAINTS
```

the DBMS will return the information shown in Table 483.1 about each FOREIGN KEY constraint in tables to which the login ID you used to connect with the server has at least one of the access privileges.

Column Name/Data Type	Description
CONSTRAINT_CATALOG NVARCHAR(128)	The name of the database in which the FOREIGN KEY is defined
CONSTRAINT_SCHEMA NVARCHAR(128)	The user ID of the FOREIGN KEY constraint's owner
CONSTRAINT_NAME SYSNAME	The name of the FOREIGN KEY constraint
UNIQUE_CONSTRAINT_CATALOG NVARCHAR(128)	The name of the database in which the FOREIGN KEY is defined
UNIQUE_CONSTRAINT_SCHEMA NVARCHAR(128)	The user ID of the owner of the FOREIGN KEY

Column Name/Data Type	Description
UNIQUE_CONSTRAINT_NAME SYSNAME	The name of the FOREIGN KEY constraint—from the SYSREFERENCES table
MATCH_OPTION VARCHAR(7)	Always NONE
UPDATE_RULE VARCHAR(9)	Either CASCADE or NO ACTION, depending on whether the DBMS is to change the value of the FOREIGN KEY to match the new value of the PRIMARY KEY that it references if the PRIMARY KEY is changed
DELETE_RULE VARCHAR(9)	Either CASCADE or NO ACTION, depending on whether the DBMS is to remove the row with the FOREIGN KEY if the row with the PRIMARY KEY referenced by the FOREIGN key is deleted

Table 483.1 The Columns in the Information Schema REFERENTIAL_CONSTRAINTS View

To display the information schema REFERENTIAL_CONSTRAINTS view information for foreign keys in the current database (even those in tables on which you have no access privileges), execute a SELECT statement such as:

```
SELECT db_name()                          'FOREIGN KEY Database',
       user_name(foreignkey_obj.UID)'FOREIGN KEY Owner',
       foreign_obj.name                   'FOREIGN KEY Table',
       db_name()                          'PRIMARY KEY Database',
       user_name(primarykey_obj.UID)'PRIMARY KEY Owner',
       sysindexes.name                    'FK INDEX Name',
       'NONE'                             'Match',
       CASE WHEN (OBJECTPROPERTY
         (sysreferences.constid,'CnstIsUpdateCascade')=1)
       THEN 'CASCADE'
       ELSE 'NO ACTION' END               'UPDATE Rule',
       CASE WHEN (OBJECTPROPERTY
         (sysreferences.constid,'CnstIsDeleteCascade')=1)
         THEN 'CASCADE'
       ELSE 'NO ACTION' END               'DELETE Rule'
FROM sysobjects foreignkey_obj, sysreferences, sysindexes,
     sysobjects primarykey_obj
WHERE foreignkey_obj.xtype     = 'F'
  AND sysreferences.constID    = foreignkey_obj.ID
  AND sysreferences.rkeyID     = sysindexes.ID
  AND sysreferences.rkeyindID = sysindexes.indID
  AND sysreferences.rkeyID     = primarykey_obj.ID
```

484 Understanding the Information Schema ROUTINES View

The ROUTINES view is a virtual table based on information from the SYSOBJECTS, SYSCOLUMNS, MASTER.DBO.SPT_DATATYPE_INFO, and MASTER.DBO.SYSCHARSETS system tables that contains one row for each stored procedure and function in the current database. When you execute the query

```
SELECT * FROM INFORMATION_SCHEMA.ROUTINES
```

the DBMS will return the information shown in Table 484.1 about the stored procedures and functions in the current database that are accessible by the login ID you used to connect with the server.

Column Name/Data Type	***Description***
SPECIFIC_CATALOG NVARCHAR(128)	The name of the database in which the stored procedure or function is defined
SPECIFIC_SCHEMA	The user ID of the owner of the stored procedure or function
SPECIFIC_NAME NVARCHAR(128)	The name of the stored procedure or function
ROUTINE_CATALOG NVARCHAR(128)	Same as SPECIFIC_CATALOG
ROUTINE_SCHEMA NVARCHAR(128)	Same as SPECIFIC_SCHEMA
ROUTINE_NAME NVARCHAR(128)	Same as SPECIFIC_NAME
ROUTINE_TYPE NVARCHAR(20)	PROCEDURE for stored procedures, and FUNCTION for functions
MODULE_CATALOG NVARCHAR(128)	NULL (reserved for future use)
MODULE_SCHEMA NVARCHAR(128)	NULL (reserved for future use)
UDT_CATALOG NVARCHAR(128)	NULL (reserved for future use)
UDT_SCHEMA NVARCHAR(128)	NULL (reserved for future use)

Column Name/Data Type	Description
UDT_NAME NVARCHAR(128)	NULL (reserved for future use)
DATA_TYPE NVARCHAR(128)	Data type returned by a function, or TABLE for table valued functions; NULL for stored procedures
CHARACTER_MAXIMUM_LENGTH INTEGER	The maximum length in characters for functions that return character type data; otherwise, NULL
CHARACTER_OCTET_LENGTH INTEGER	The maximum length in bytes for functions that return character type data; otherwise, NULL
COLLATION_CATALOG NVARCHAR(128)	The name of the database that contains the collation (sort order) for functions that return character type data; otherwise, NULL
COLLATION_SCHEMA NVARCHAR(128)	The ID of the user that owns the collation (sort order) for functions that return character type data; otherwise, NULL
COLLATION_NAME NVARCHAR(128)	The name of the collation (sort order) for functions that return character type data; otherwise, NULL
CHARACTER_SET_CATALOG NVARCHAR(128)	The name of the database that contains the character set for functions that return character type data; otherwise, NULL
CHARACTER_SET_SCHEMA NVARCHAR(128)	The ID of the owner (normally DBO) of the database that contains the character set for functions that return character type data; otherwise, NULL
CHARACTER_SET_NAME NVARCHAR(128)	The name of the character set for functions that return character type data; otherwise, NULL
NUMERIC_PRECISION SMALLINT	The precision of the value returned by functions that return numeric data; otherwise, NULL
NUMERIC_PRECISION_RADIX SMALLINT	The precision radix of the value returned by functions that return numeric data; otherwise, NULL
NUMERIC_SCALE SMALLINT	The scale of the value returned by functions that return numeric data; otherwise, NULL

Column Name/Data Type	Description
DATETIME_PRECISION SMALLINT	The fractional precision of the seconds in a DATETIME value for functions that return a DATETIME value; otherwise, NULL
INTERVAL_TYPE NVARCHAR(30)	NULL (reserved for future use)
INTERVAL_PRECISION SMALLINT	NULL (reserved for future use)
TYPE_UDT_CATALOG NVARCHAR(128)	NULL (reserved for future use)
TYPE_UDT_SCHEMA NVARCHAR(128)	NULL (reserved for future use)
TYPE_UDT_NAME NVARCHAR(128)	NULL (reserved for future use)
SCOPE_CATALOG NVARCHAR(128)	NULL (reserved for future use)
SCOPE_SCHEMA NVARCHAR(128)	NULL (reserved for future use)
SCOPE_NAME NVARCHAR(128)	NULL (reserved for future use)
MAXIMUM_CARDINALITY BIGINT	NULL (reserved for future use)
DTD_IDENTIFIER NVARCHAR(128)	NULL (reserved for future use)
ROUTINE_BODY NVARCHAR(30)	Always SQL
ROUTINE_DEFINITION NVARCHAR(4000)	The text of the Transact-SQL statements that define the stored procedure or function—if unencrypted; otherwise, NULL
EXTERNAL_NAME NVARCHAR(128)	NULL (reserved for future use)
EXTERNAL_LANGUAGE NVARCHAR(30)	NULL (reserved for future use)
PARAMETER_STYLE NVARCHAR(30)	NULL (reserved for future use)
IS_DETERMINISTIC NVARCHAR(10)	YES for deterministic functions; NO for for nondeterministic functions and stored procedures

Column Name/Data Type	Description
SQL_DATA_ACCESS NVARCHAR(30)	READS for all functions and MODIFIES for all stored procedures
IS_NULL_CALL NVARCHAR(10)	Always YES
SQL_PATH NVARCHAR(128)	NULL (reserved for future use)
SCHEMA_LEVEL_ROUTINE NVARCHAR(10)	Always YES
MAX_DYNAMIC_RESULT_SETS SMALLINT	0 for functions and –1 for stored procedures
IS_USER_DEFINED_CAST NVARCHAR(10)	Always NO
IS_IMPLICITLY_INVOCABLE NVARCHAR(10)	Always NO
CREATED DATETIME	The date and time that the function or stored procedure was created
LAST_ALTERED INTEGER	The date and time that the function or stored procedure was last modified

Table 484.1 The Columns in the Information Schema ROUTINES View

To review the Transact-SQL code that defines the information schema ROUTINES view, perform the procedure outlined in Tip 493, "Using the MS-SQL Server Enterprise Manager to View the Contents of an Information Schema View."

485 Understanding the Information Schema SCHEMATA View

The SCHEMATA view is a virtual table based on information from the MASTER.DBO.SYSDATABASES and MASTER.DBO.SYSCHARSETS system tables that contains one row for each database accessible on the current MS-SQL Server. For example, if you execute the SELECT statement

```
SELECT * FROM INFORMATION_SCHEMA.SCHEMATA
```

the DBMS will return the information shown in Table 485.1 about each of the database managed by the DBMS:

Column Name	Data Type	Description
CATALOG_NAME	NVARCHAR(128)	The name of the database
SCHEMA_NAME	NVARCHAR(128)	The user ID of the database owner—normally DBO
SCHEMA_OWNER	NVARCHAR(128)	Same as SCHEMA_NAME
DEFAULT_CHARACTER_SET_CATALOG	VARCHAR(6)	Always NULL
DEFAULT_CHARACTER_SET_SCHEMA	VARCHAR(3)	Always NULL
DEFAULT_CHARACTER_SET_NAME	SYSNAME	The name of the default character set

Table 485.1 The Columns in the Information Schema SCHEMATA View

486 Understanding the Information Schema TABLE_CONSTRAINTS View

The TABLE_CONSTRAINTS view is a virtual table based on information from the SYSOBJECTS system table that contains one row for each table constraint in the current database. When you execute the query

```
SELECT * FROM INFORMATION_SCHEMA.TABLE_CONSTRAINTS
```

the DBMS will return the information shown in Table 486.1 about the table constraints on tables in the current database to which the login ID you used to connect with the server has at least one of the access privileges.

Column Name/Data Type	Description
CONSTRAINT_CATALOG NVARCHAR(128)	The name of the database that contains the CHECK, FOREIGN KEY, PRIMARY KEY, or UNIQUE constraint (for example, the name of the database that contains the table constraint)
CONSTRAINT_SCHEMA NVARCHAR(128)	The ID of the user that owns the table constraint

Column Name/Data Type	Description
CONSTRAINT_NAME SYSNAME	The name of the table constraint
TABLE_CATALOG NVARCHAR(128)	The name of the database that contains the table on which the table constraint is defined
TABLE_SCHEMA NVARCHAR(128)	The ID of the user that owns the table with the table constraint
TABLE_NAME SYSNAME	The name of the table whose contents are constrained by the table constraint
CONSTRAINT_TYPE VARCHAR(11)	The type of table constraint: CHECK, FOREIGN KEY, PRIMARY KEY, or UNIQUE constraint
IS_DEFERRABLE VARCHAR(2)	Always NO
INITIALLY_DEFERRED VARCHAR(2)	Always NO

Table 486.1 The Columns in the Information Schema TABLE_CONSTRAINTS View

To display the information schema TABLE_CONSTRAINTS view information for all table constraints in the current database (even those on tables to which you have no access privileges), execute a SELECT statement such as:

```
SELECT db_name()                        'Constraint Database',
       user_name(constraintobj.UID) 'Constraint Owner',
       constraintobj.name               'Constraint Name',
       db_name()                        'Table Database',
       user_name(tableobj.UID)          'Table Owner',
       tableobj.name                    'Table Name',
       CASE constraintobj.xtype
         WHEN 'C'  THEN 'CHECK'
         WHEN 'UQ' THEN 'UNIQUE'
         WHEN 'PK' THEN 'PRIMARY KEY'
         WHEN 'F'  THEN 'FOREIGN KEY'
       END                              'Constraint Type',
       'NO'                             'Is Deferrable',
       'NO'                             'Initially Deferred'
FROM sysobjects constraintobj, sysobjects tableobj
WHERE tableobj.ID = constraintobj.parent_obj
  AND constraintobj.xtype IN ('C','UQ','PK','F')
```

487 Understanding the Information Schema TABLE_PRIVILEGES View

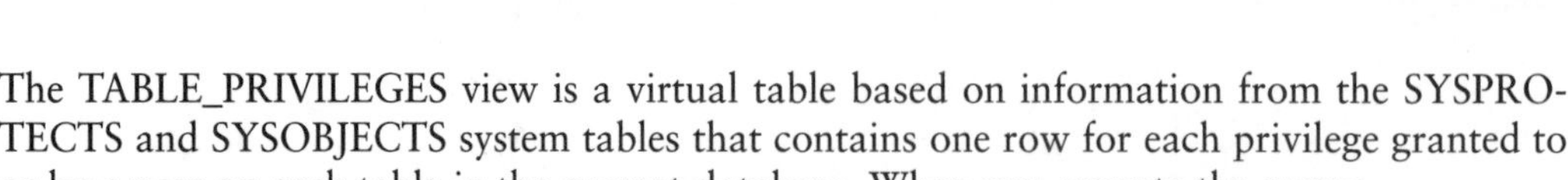

The TABLE_PRIVILEGES view is a virtual table based on information from the SYSPROTECTS and SYSOBJECTS system tables that contains one row for each privilege granted to or by a user on each table in the current database. When you execute the query

```
SELECT * FROM INFORMATION_SCHEMA.TABLE_PRIVILEGES
```

the DBMS will return the information shown in Table 487.1 about the privileges on each table either granted by or granted to the login ID you used to connect with the server.

Column Name	Data Type	Description
GRANTOR	NVARCHAR(128)	The user ID of the account granting the privilege
GRANTEE	NVARCHAR(128)	The user ID of the account to which the privilege was granted
TABLE_CATALOG	NVARCHAR(128)	The name of the table on which the privilege was granted
TABLE_SCHEMA	NVARCHAR(128)	The user ID of the table owner
TABLE_NAME	SYSNAME	The name of the table
PRIVILEGE_TYPE	VARCHAR(10)	The type of privilege granted
IS_GRANTABLE	VARCHAR(3)	YES if the grantee can grant the privilege to another user; NO if not

Table 487.1 The Columns in the Information Schema TABLE_PRIVILEGES View

To review the Transact-SQL code that defines the information schema TABLE_PRIVILEGES view, perform the procedure outlined in Tip 493, "Using the MS-SQL Server Enterprise Manager to View the Contents of an Information Schema View."

488 Understanding the Information Schema TABLES View

The TABLES view is a virtual table based on information from the SYSOBJECTS system table that contains one row for each table in the current database. When you execute the query

```
SELECT * FROM INFORMATION_SCHEMA.TABLES
```

the DBMS will return the information shown in Table 488.1 about each table in the current database to which the login ID you used to connect with the server has at least one of the access privileges.

Column Name	Data Type	Description
TABLE_CATALOG	NVARCHAR(128)	The name of the database in which the table is defined
TABLE_SCHEMA	NVARCHAR(128)	The ID of the user that owns the table
TABLE_NAME	SYSNAME	The name of the table
TABLE_TYPE	VARCHAR(10)	The table type: either VIEW or BASE TABLE

Table 488.1 The Columns in the Information Schema TABLES View

To display the information schema TABLES view information for all tables in the current database (including those in tables on which you have no access privileges), execute a SELECT statement such as:

```
SELECT db_name()                    'Database/Catalog Name',
       user_name(sysobjects.UID) 'Table Owner',
       sysobjects.name              'Table Name',
       CASE sysobjects.xtype
         WHEN 'U' THEN 'BASE TABLE'
         WHEN 'V' THEN 'VIEW'
       END                          'Table Type'
FROM sysobjects
WHERE sysobjects.xtype IN ('U','V')
```

489 Understanding the Information Schema VIEW_COLUMN_USAGE View

The VIEW_COLUMN_USAGE view is a virtual table based on information from the SYSOBJECTS, SYSDEPENDS, and SYSCOLUMNS system tables that contains one row for each column used in a view definition. When you execute the query

```
SELECT * FROM INFORMATION_SCHEMA.VIEW_COLUMN_USAGE
```

the DBMS will return the information shown in Table 489.1 about each column in the current database that is used in a view definition to which the login ID you used to connect with the server has at least one of the access privileges.

Column Name	Data Type	Description
VIEW_CATALOG	NVARCHAR(128)	The name of the database in which the view that uses the column is defined
VIEW_SCHEMA	NVARCHAR(128)	The ID of the user that owns the view that uses the column
VIEW_NAME	SYSNAME	The name of the view that uses the column
TABLE_CATALOG	NVARCHAR(128)	The name of the database in which the table that contains the column is defined
TABLE_SCHEMA	NVARCHAR(128)	The ID of the user that owns the table that contains the column
TABLE_NAME	SYSNAME	The name of the table that contains the column
COLUMN_NAME	SYSNAME	The name of the column used in the view

Table 489.1 The Columns in the Information Schema VIEW_COLUMN_USAGE View

To display the information schema VIEW_COLUMN_USAGE view information on columns used in any of the views in the current database (including columns used in views on which you have no access privileges), execute a SELECT statement such as:

```
SELECT db_name()                'View Database/Catalog',
       user_name(viewobj.UID)   'View Owner',
       viewobj.name             'View Name',
       db_name()                'Table Database/Catalog',
       user_name(tableobj.UID)  'Table Owner',
       tableobj.name            'Table Name',
       syscolumns.name          'Column Name'
FROM sysobjects viewobj, sysobjects tableobj, sysdepends,
     syscolumns
WHERE viewobj.xtype          = 'V'
  AND sysdepends.ID          = viewobj.ID
  AND sysdepends.depID       = tableobj.ID
  AND tableobj.ID            = syscolumns.ID
  AND sysdepends.depnumber = syscolumns.colID
```

490 Understanding the Information Schema VIEW_TABLE_USAGE View

The VIEW_TABLE_USAGE view is a virtual table based on information from the SYSOBJECTS and SYSDEPENDS system tables that contains one row for each table used in a view definition. When you execute the query

```
SELECT * FROM INFORMATION_SCHEMA.VIEW_TABLE_USAGE
```

the DBMS will return the information shown in Table 490.1 about each table in the current database that is used in a view definition to which the login ID you used to connect with the server has at least one of the access privileges.

Column Name	Data Type	Description
VIEW_CATALOG	NVARCHAR(128)	The name of the database in which the view based on the table is defined
VIEW_SCHEMA	NVARCHAR(128)	The ID of the user that owns the view based on the table
VIEW_NAME	SYSNAME	The name of the view based on the table
TABLE_CATALOG	NVARCHAR(128)	The name of the database in which the table is defined
TABLE_SCHEMA	NVARCHAR(128)	The ID of the user that owns the table
TABLE_NAME	SYSNAME	The name of the table

Table 490.1 The Columns in the Information Schema VIEW_TABLE_USAGE View

To display the information schema VIEW_TABLE_USAGE view information on tables used in any of the views in the current database (including tables used in views on which you have no access privileges), execute a SELECT statement such as:

```
SELECT db_name()                  'View Database/Catalog',
       user_name(viewobj.UID)     'View Owner',
       viewobj.name               'View Name',
       db_name()                  'Table Database/Catalog',
       user_name(tableobj.UID)    'Table Owner',
       tableobj.name              'Table Name'
FROM sysobjects viewobj, sysobjects tableobj, sysdepends
WHERE viewobj.xtype      = 'V'
  AND sysdepends.ID      = viewobj.ID
  AND sysdepends.depID = tableobj.ID
```

491 Understanding the Information Schema ROUTINE_COLUMNS View

The ROUTINE_COLUMNS view is a virtual table based on information from the SYSOBJECTS, SYSCOLUMNS, and MASTER.DBO.SYSCHARSETS system tables that contains one row for each column returned by a table-valued function. (Table-valued functions include FN_VIRTUALFILESTATS, which returns the I/O statistics for database files [including the log file], and FN_HELPCOLLATIONS, which lists each collation [sort order] supported by the MS-SQL Server.) When you execute the query

```
SELECT * FROM INFORMATION_SCHEMA.ROUTINE_COLUMNS
```

the DBMS will return the information shown in Table 491.1 about the columns returned by table-valued functions in the current database available to the login ID you used to connect with the server.

Column Name/Data Type	*Description*
TABLE_CATALOG NVARCHAR(128)	The name of the database that contains the table-valued function
TABLE_SCHEMA NVARCHAR(128)	The ID of the user that owns the table-valued function
TABLE_NAME NVARCHAR(128)	The name of the table-valued function
COLUMN_NAME NVARCHAR(128)	The name of the column returned by the table-valued function
ORDINAL_POSITION SMALLINT	The column's unique identification number within the table-valued function. ORDINAL_POSITION values are unique within each function but not across all functions.
COLUMN_DEFAULT NVARCHAR(4000)	The default value for a column
IS_NULLABLE VARCHAR(3)	YES if the column is allowed to hold a NULL value; NO if not
DATA_TYPE NVARCHAR(128)	The column's SQL data type
CHARACTER_MAXIMUM_ LENGTH SMALLINT	The maximum length in characters for columns with binary, character, TEXT, or IMAGE data; otherwise, NULL

Column Name/Data Type	Description
CHARACTER_OCTET_LENGTH SMALLINT	The maximum length in bytes for columns with binary, character, TEXT, and IMAGE data; otherwise, NULL
NUMERIC_PRECISION TINYINT	The precision for columns with numeric type data; otherwise, NULL
NUMERIC_PRECISION_RADIX SMALLINT	The precision radix for columns with numeric type data; otherwise, NULL
NUMERIC_SCALE TINYINT	The scale for columns with numeric type data; otherwise, NULL
DATETIME_PRECISION SMALLINT	The subtype code for columns with DATETIME and INTEGER data; otherwise, NULL
CHARACTER_SET_CATALOG VARCHAR(6)	Always MASTER
CHARACTER_SET_SCHEMA VARCHAR(3)	Always DBO
CHARACTER_SET_NAME NVARCHAR(128)	The name of the character set for columns with TEXT or character type data; otherwise, NULL
COLLATION_CATALOG VARCHAR(6)	Always MASTER
COLLATION_SCHEMA VARCHAR(3)	Always DBO
COLLATION_NAME NVARCHAR(128)	The name of the sort order for columns with TEXT or character type data; otherwise, NULL
DOMAIN_CATALOG NVARCHAR(128)	The name of the database in which the user-defined data type was created if the column contains data of a user-defined data type; otherwise, NULL
DOMAIN_SCHEMA NVARCHAR(128)	The ID of the user that created the user-defined data type for columns that contain data of a user-defined data type; otherwise, NULL
DOMAIN_NAME NVARCHAR(128)	The name of the user-defined data type if the column contains data of a user-defined data type; otherwise, NULL

Table 491.1 The Columns in the Information Schema ROUTINE_COLUMNS View

To review the Transact-SQL code that defines the information schema ROUTINE_COLUMNS view, perform the procedure outlined in Tip 493, "Using the MS-SQL Server Enterprise Manager to View the Contents of an Information Schema View."

492 Understanding the Information Schema VIEWS View

The VIEWS view is a virtual table based on information from the SYSOBJECTS and SYSCOMMENTS system tables that contains one row for each view in the current database. When you execute the query

```
SELECT * FROM INFORMATION_SCHEMA.VIEWS
```

the DBMS will return the information shown in Table 492.1 about the views in the current database accessible to the login ID you used to connect with the server.

Column Name/Data Type	Description
TABLE_CATALOG NVARCHAR(128)	The name of the database in which the view is defined
TABLE_SCHEMA NVARCHAR(128)	The user ID of the account that owns the view
TABLE_NAME NVARCHAR(128)	The name of the view
VIEW_DEFINITION NVARCHAR(4000)	The text of the view definition if the length of the view definition's text is less than or equal to 4,000 characters; otherwise, NULL
CHECK_OPTION VARCHAR(7)	CASCADE if the statement used to create the view included the WITH CHECK OPTION; otherwise, NONE
IS_UPDATABLE VARCHAR(2)	Always NO

Table 492.1 The Columns in the Information Schema VIEWS View

To display the information schema VIEWS view information for all views in the current database (including those views on which you have no access privileges), execute a SELECT statement such as:

```
SELECT db_name()                    'Database/Catalog Name',
       user_name(sysobjects.UID) 'View Owner',
       sysobjects.name              'View Name',
       CASE WHEN EXISTS
                  (SELECT * FROM syscomments
                   WHERE syscomments.ID = sysobjects.ID
                     AND syscomments.colID > 1) THEN
         CONVERT(NVARCHAR(4000),NULL)
       ELSE syscomments.text
       END                          'View Definition',
       CASE WHEN EXISTS
                (SELECT * FROM syscomments
                 WHERE syscomments.ID = sysobjects.ID
                   AND CHARINDEX('WITH CHECK OPTION',
                         UPPER(syscomments.text)) > 0 THEN
         'CASCADE'
       ELSE 'NONE'
       END                          'Check Option',
       'NO'                         'Is Updateable'
FROM sysobjects, syscomments
WHERE sysobjects.xtype = 'V'
  AND sysobjects.ID = syscomments.ID
  AND syscomments.colID = 1
```

493 Using the MS-SQL Server Enterprise Manager to View the Contents of an Information Schema View

As you learned from the sample code at the end of Tip 492, "Understanding the Information Schema VIEWS View," the MS-SQL Server stores the definition of a view the SELECT statement that returns the view's results set) in the TEXT column of the SYSOBJECTS table. Therefore, you can use a query (such as the one shown at the end of Tip 492) to display a view's definition. Alternatively, you can use the MS-SQL Server Enterprise manager to view the definition of a view by performing the following steps:

1. Click your mouse pointer on the Start button. Windows will display the Start menu.
2. Move your mouse pointer to Programs on the Start menu, select the Microsoft SQL Server 2000 option, and click your mouse pointer on Enterprise Manager. Windows will start Enterprise Manager in the SQL Server Enterprise Manager application window.
3. Click your mouse pointer on the plus (+) to the left of SQL Server Group to display the list of MS-SQL Servers available on your network.

4. Click your mouse pointer on the plus (+) to the left of the SQL server that has the view whose definition you want to display (and perhaps modify). Enterprise Manager will display the Databases, Data Transformation, Management, Security, and Support Services folders for the SQL Server you selected.

5. Click your mouse pointer on the plus (+) to the left of the Databases folder to display the list of databases currently on the SQL server, and then click on the plus (+) to the left of the database that has the view whose definition you wish to display. For the current project, click on the plus (+) to the left of the Master folder.

6. To display the list of views in the database that you expanded in Tip 5, "Understanding the Relational Database Model," click your mouse pointer on the Views icon. Enterprise Manager will use its right pane to display the list of the views in the database similar to that shown in Figure 493.1.

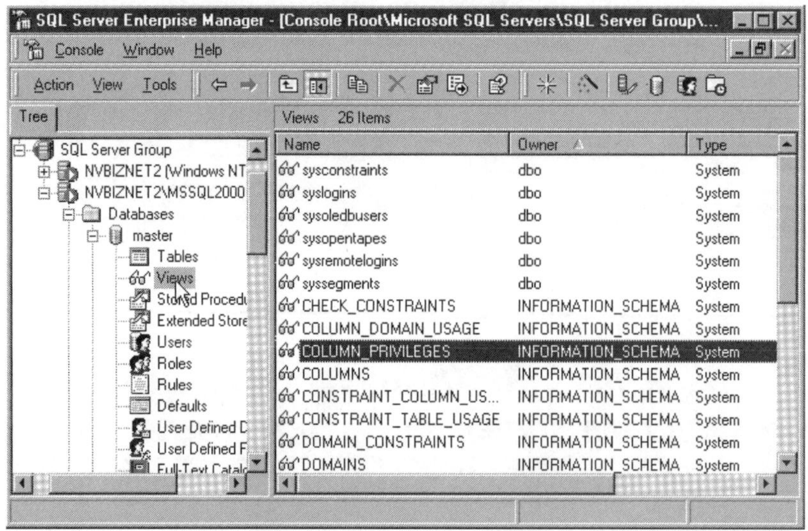

Figure 493.1 The MS-SQL Server Enterprise Manager listing views in the MASTER database

7. Double-click your mouse pointer on the view whose definition you want to display. For the current project, double-click your mouse pointer on COLUMN_PRIVILEGES (in the right pane). Enterprise Manager will display the text of the view definition in a View Properties dialog box similar to that shown in Figure 493.2.

8. To exit the View Properties dialog box (and return to Enterprise Manager's main window, press the Esc (Escape) key on your keyboard (or click your mouse pointer on the OK button or the Cancel button at the bottom of the View Properties dialog box).

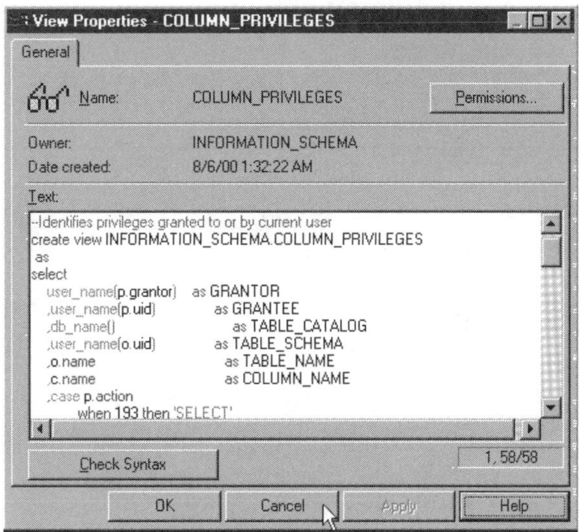

Figure 493.2 The View Properties dialog box

In addition to displaying the text of view, you can also use the Enterprise Manger to edit a view's definition. To edit a view, make any changes that you want in the Text area of the View Properties dialog box after you complete Step 7 of the preceding procedure. Then, instead of pressing the Esc key (or clicking your mouse pointer on the Cancel button), exit the View Properties dialog box by clicking your mouse pointer on the OK button. The Enterprise Manager will check the syntax of the view definition and (if the syntax is correct) store the updated view. (If the syntax is incorrect, the Enterprise Manager will display a message, which gives the source of the problem, so you can make the necessary corrections.)

494 Understanding the MS-SQL Server System Database Tables

When you need information about a database managed by MS-SQL Server, you should use one or more of the Information Schema views (discussed in Tips 472–492), system stored procedures, and Transact-SQL statements and functions. By not working directly with the system tables, you avoid having to rewrite SQL code and prevent introducing errors when Microsoft changes the structure of a system table or the meaning of one or more of its columns from one version of MS-SQL Server to the next. However, MS-SQL Server does let you work directly with the system tables it uses to manage tables, indexes, foreign keys, users, permissions, and so on.

Table 494.1 describes each of the system tables that MS-SQL Server places in each database you create on an MS-SQL Server.

Table Name	*Description*
SYSCOLUMNS	Contains one row for each column in every table and view in the database. Each row's columns give the target column's attributes (such as name, location, and data type) and describe its behavior.
SYSCOMMENTS	Contains one or more rows for each CHECK constraint, DEFAULT constraint, rule, stored procedure, trigger, and view in the database. The table's TEXT column contains the SQL or Transact-SQL statement that defines the constraint, rule, stored procedure, trigger, or view. Since definitions can be up to 4MB in size while the TEXT column can hold only 4,000 bytes (characters), a single object may be described by more than one row in the SYSCOMMENTS table.
SYSCONSTRAINTS	Contains one row that describes the name, ID, and type for each constraint in the database. The table's ID column gives the name of the table that owns the constraint.
SYSDEPENDS	Describes the dependencies between objects (stored procedures, views, and triggers) and the objects (stored procedures, stored procedures, and views) they contain in their definitions.
SYSFILEGROUPS	Contains one row for each filegroup in the database.
SYSFILES	Contains one row for each physical disk file combined into filegroups and used to store the objects in a database. Each row's columns describe such things as the file's physical location on disk, its file name, its current size, the maximum size, and its growth rate.
SYSFOREIGNKEYS	Contains one row for each FOREIGN KEY constraint used in a table definition.
SYSFULLTEXTCATALOGS	Contains one row for each full-text index created in the database.
SYSINDEXES	Contains one row for each index, table, and BLOB in the database. The columns in each row describe such things as the location of the object's first page of data, the row size, the number of keys, row count, the name of the table, and the name of the key columns.
SYSINDEXKEYS	Contains one row with the table ID, index ID, column ID, and ordinal position of the column in the index for each column in every index in a database.

Table Name	Description
SYSMEMBERS	Contains one row that gives the user ID, (Windows) group ID, and role ID for each member of every role and (Windows) group in the database.
SYSOBJECTS	Contains one row for each object (constraint, default, index, log, rule, stored procedure, table, and so on) in the database.
SYSPERMISSIONS	Contains one row with the object ID, grantor, and grantee for each permission granted or denied each user or role on a database object.
SYSPROTECTS	Contains one row for each permission granted or denied on database objects by executing GRANT and DENY statements. The columns in each row describe the type of privilege granted or denied, the user or role ID, the object ID, the grantor, and (for SELECT and UPDATE permissions) a bitmap to the columns to which the permission (or denial) applies.
SYSREFERENCES	Contains one row for each FOREIGN KEY constraint in every table in the database.
SYSTYPES	Contains one row for each system-supplied and user-defined data type in the database.
SYSUSERS	Contains one row for each Windows user, Windows group, MS-SQL Server user, and MS-SQL Server role in the database.

Table 494.1 The System Database Table That MS-SQL Server Maintains in Each Database It Manages

495 Defining the Physical Location of the Database

When you used the CREATE DATABASE statement in Tip 41, "Using the CREATE DATABASE Statement to Create an MS-SQL Server Database and Transaction Log," you specified the physical location for the file in which the DBMS is to place all database objects in the FILENAME clause as:

```
CREATE DATABASE SQLTips
ON     (NAME       = SQLTips_data,
        FILENAME   = 'c:\mssql7\data\SQLTips_data.mdf',
        SIZE       = 10, FILEGROWTH = 1MB)
LOG ON (NAME = 'SQLTips_log',
```

```
        FILENAME = 'c:\mssql7\data\SQLTips_log.ldf',
        SIZE = 3, FILEGROWTH = 1MB)
```

Thus, in the current example, the DBMS will place each table you create in the file named SQLTIPS_DATA.MDF in the \MSSQL7\DATA\ folder on the server's C drive. (The server will expand the size of the SQLTIPS_DATA.MDF beyond the 10MB initial size, 1MB at a time, as necessary, to accommodate the storage space required to hold the data in the tables you create and fill.)

To split the single large database (MDF) file into multiple smaller files or to allow it to span disk volumes, the MS-SQL Server lets you define one more physical data files in *filegroups*. The MS-SQL Server will then grow the individual, physical files in each filegroup as necessary to store its table data and will let you specify the filegroup in which to place the table (and its data) as part of the CREATE TABLE statement you use to create the table.

For example, the CREATE DATABASE statement

```
CREATE DATABASE company_db
ON PRIMARY (NAME        = company_data,
            FILENAME    = 'c:\mssql\data\co_data.mdf',
            SIZE        = 10, FILEGROWTH = 1MB),
FILEGROUP marketing (NAME    = marketing_data,
                   FILENAME = 'c:\mssql\data\mkt_data.mdf',
                   SIZE     = 10, FILEGROWTH = 1MB),
FILEGROUP office (NAME      = office_data,
                  FILENAME = 'd:\mssql\data\ofce_data.mdf',
                  SIZE     = 10, FILEGROWTH = 1MB)
LOG ON (NAME     = 'co_db_log',
        FILENAME = 'c:\mssql\data\db_log.ldf',
        SIZE     = 3, FILEGROWTH = 1MB)
```

will create three filegroups: PRIMARY, MARKETING, and OFFICE. You can then use a CREATE TABLE statement such as

```
CREATE TABLE call_history
(call_time   DATETIME,
 hangup_time DATETIME,
 called_by   VARCHAR(3),
 disposition VARCHAR(4)) ON marketing
```

to place the CALL_HISTORY table in the MARKETING filegroup on the C drive, and a CREATE TABLE statement such as

```
CREATE TABLE orders
(customer_ID  INTEGER,
 order_date   DATETIME,
 order_total  MONEY,
 date_shipped DATETIME) ON office
```

to place the ORDERS table in the OFFICE filegroup on the D drive.

Distributing tables within a database across two or more drives lets you take advantage of parallel disk I/O operations. With the CALL_HISTORY table on one drive and the ORDERS table on another, the DBMS can issue simultaneous writes to add a row to the CALL_HISTORY table while adding a row to the ORDERS table. If both tables are on the same drive, the system must complete one I/O operation before starting the other.

Note: *Each DBMS product has its own way for specifying the physical location of database files and of the tables within each database. As such, check your system manual for the statement syntax required by your DBMS. The important thing to understand now is that all DBMS products allow the DBA to manage the physical location of the database file(s) and to select the file in which the DBMS is to place individual database tables.*

496 Adding Files and Filegroups to an Existing Database

In Tip 41, "Using the CREATE DATABASE Statement to Create an MS-SQL Server Database and Transaction Log," you learned how to use the CREATE DATABASE statement to create an MS-SQL Server database with multiple filegroups and multiple files distributed across two physical disk drives. If you are managing an SQL server in a typical business environment, database storage requirements will eventually exceed the initial available storage capacity as the company collects and retains marketing, sales, and customer data. Moreover, advances in technology and additional funds available to your department will make it possible for you to bring new, larger-capacity, and faster storage solutions online. Fortunately, the MS-SQL Server provides the Transact-SQL ALTER DATABASE command, which lets you add additional drives to those already in use to hold DBMS files.

For example, if you created the SQLTips database in Tip 41 and you later add a new hard drive (or RAID disk array) with the logical drive letter D, you can use an ALTER DATABASE statement such as

```
ALTER DATABASE SQLTips
  ADD FILE (NAME     = SQLTips_data2,
            FILENAME = 'd:\mssql\data\SQLTips_data2.mdf',
            SIZE     = 30, FILEGROWTH = 5MB)
ALTER DATABASE SQLTips
  ADD LOG FILE (NAME     = 'SQLTips_log2',
                FILENAME = 'd:\mssql\data\SQLTips_log2.ldf',
                SIZE     = 3, FILEGROWTH = 1MB)
```

to allow the database and its log file to grow on the D drive. (After executing the ALTER DATABASE statement, which adds a new drive, the DBMS will automatically start using the new [disk] file space and will split data in individual tables across the two disk files as necessary.)

In addition to adding new files to the database, you can also use the ALTER DATABASE statement to add new filegroups and add files to existing filegroups. Suppose, for example, that you created the COMPANY_DB database in Tip 495, "Defining the Physical Location of the Database." If you execute an ALTER DATABASE statements such as

```
ALTER DATABASE company_db
  ADD FILE (NAME     = marketing_data2,
            FILENAME = 'e:\mssql\data\mkt_data.mdf',
            SIZE     = 10, FILEGROWTH = 1MB)
    TO FILEGROUP marketing
ALTER DATABASE company_db ADD FILEGROUP multimedia
ALTER DATABASE company_db
  ADD FILE (NAME     = blobs,
            FILENAME = 'i:\mssql\data\blob_data.mdf',
            SIZE     = 100, FILEGROWTH = 25MB)
    TO FILEGROUP multimedia
```

then the MS-SQL Server will begin using a second file (MARKETING_DATA2, in the current example) to store tables created in the MARKETING filegroup. Moreover, you can create tables with TEXT and IMAGE (BLOB) data on the I drive in the new filegroup MULTIMEDIA.

Note: *By placing tables with BLOB data on a separate drive, you can reduce bottlenecks that occur when users execute queries that return a small amount of data and have to wait for the hardware to return the data in a BLOB being retrieved by another user. Remember, BLOB (TEXT and IMAGE) data can be exceptionally large—hundreds of megabytes or several gigabytes in length. Therefore, BLOB data can take much longer to retrieve than a result set for a typical query, which will normally run a few thousand or a few tens of thousands of bytes.*

---

497 Using the MS-SQL Server Enterprise Manager to Add Files and Filegroups to an Existing Database

When you need to change the files or filegroups in a database, you can use the ALTER DATABASE statement (as you learned to do in Tip 496, "Adding Files and Filegroups to an Existing Database"), or you can use the MS-SQL Server Enterprise Manager. For example, to add the file BLOBS in the filegroup MULTIMEDIA to the SQLTips database, perform the following steps:

1. Click your mouse pointer on the Start button. Windows will display the Start menu.
2. Move your mouse pointer to Programs on the Start menu, select the Microsoft SQL Server 2000 option, and click your mouse pointer on Enterprise Manager. Windows will start Enterprise Manager in the SQL Server Enterprise Manager application window.
3. Click your mouse pointer on the plus (+) to the left of Microsoft SQL Servers, and then click on the plus (+) to the left of SQL Server Group to display the list of MS-SQL Servers available on your network.
4. Click your mouse pointer on the plus (+) to the left of the SQL server that has the database whose files or filegroups you want to modify. Enterprise Manager will display the Databases, Data Transformation, Management, Security, and Support Services folders for the SQL Server you selected.
5. Click your mouse pointer on the folder to the left of Databases. Enterprise Manager will display the databases being managed by the SQL server (which you selected in Step 4) in Enterprise Manager's right pane.
6. Double-click your mouse pointer on the icon of the database whose files or filegroups you want to change. For the current project, double-click your mouse pointer on the SQLTips database icon. Enterprise Manager will display the SQL Properties dialog box.
7. Click your mouse pointer on the Data Files tab to display the current list of files and filegroups in the database, similar to that shown in Figure 497.1.

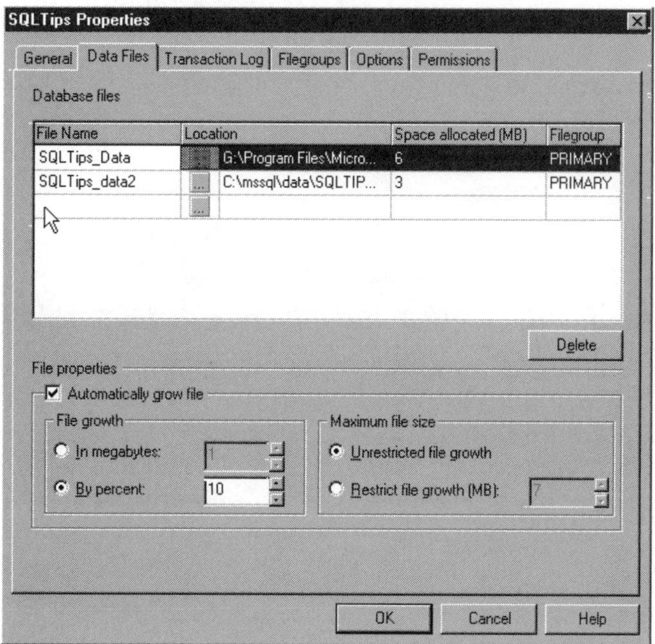

Figure 497.1 The MS-SQL Server Enterprise Manager database Properties Dialog box, Data Files tab

8. To add a new file, click your mouse pointer in the blank field at the bottom of the File Name column, and type the name of the new *logical* file name into the field. For the current project, enter **BLOBS** into the File Name field.
9. After you complete Step 8, Enterprise Manager will enter a default *physical* file location (and name) into the Location field. For the current project, accept the default. However, you can change the physical file name or its location by clicking your mouse pointer on the Location column and then changing the pathname in the Location field.

Note: *The folders in the pathname you enter into the Location field must already exist—Enterprise Manager will not create them for you. Therefore, if you want to place the physical database file into a new folder, use the MS-DOS MD command or Windows Explorer to create the new folder before entering its pathname into the Location field.*

10. By default, Enterprise Manager will set the initial space allocation for the file to 1MB. To change the initial database file size, click your mouse pointer in the Space Allocated (MB) column and enter the initial size of the database file in megabytes. For the current project, click your mouse pointer on the Space Allocated (MB) column and then enter **5** into the Space Allocated (MB) field.
11. By default, Enterprise Manager assigns new files to the default filegroup (normally PRIMARY). To assign the new file to another filegroup, click your mouse pointer on the Filegroup column, and then enter the name of the filegroup into the Filegroup field. For the current project, enter **MULTIMEDIA** into the filegroup field.

After you complete Step 11, click your mouse pointer on the OK button. Enterprise Manager will create the new database file and filegroup, and then return to the main application window.

498 Understanding the Advantages and Disadvantages of Using Single- and Multi-database Architectures

In a single-database architecture (such as that used by a DB2 or ORACLE SQL Server), the DBMS supports (and manages) a single database. (The database may consist of multiple *physical* files, but all database objects exist in a single *logical* database file.) As shown in Figure 498.1, sets of individual tables in the database are often owned by the user ID of the person or the group ID (role) responsible for the application used to enter and maintain the data in a given group of tables.

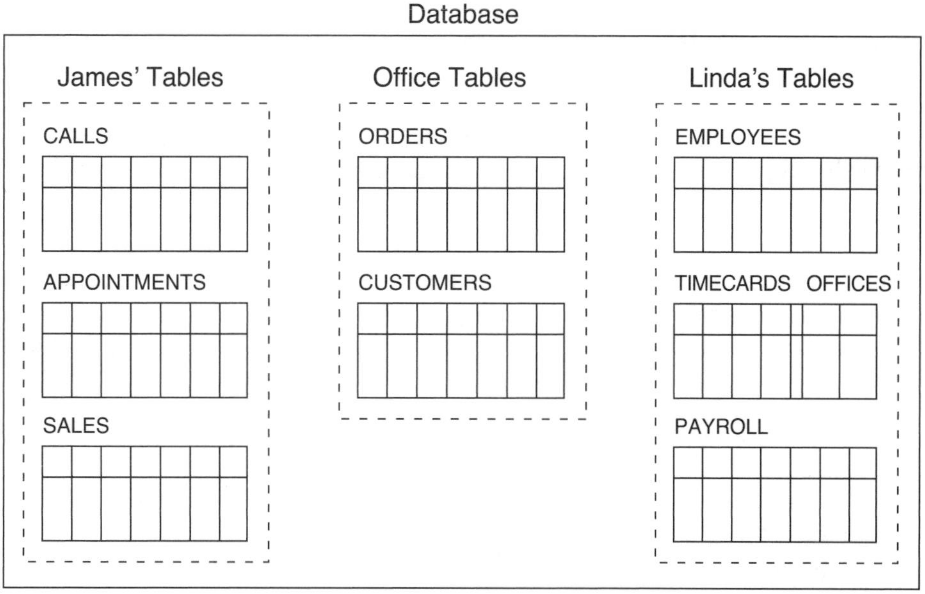

Database

James' Tables: CALLS, APPOINTMENTS, SALES

Office Tables: ORDERS, CUSTOMERS

Linda's Tables: EMPLOYEES, TIMECARDS, OFFICES, PAYROLL

Figure 498.1 Single-database SQL server architecture

In the current example, user ID JAMES owns the CALLS, APPOINTMENTS, and SALES tables. The OFFICE role (or user group) owns the ORDERS and CUSTOMERS tables. User ID LINDA owns the EMPLOYEES, TIMECARDS, OFFICES, and PAYROLL tables.

The main advantage of a single-database architecture is that all tables reside in the same database and can therefore easily reference each other. For example, both the SQL-89 and SQL-92 standards require the DBMS to support FOREIGN KEY references in the CUSTOMERS table (in Figure 498.1) that relate CUSTOMERS rows with rows in the EMPLOYEES and OFFICES tables. In short, relating tables within a single-database (even those owned by different IDs) is a standard SQL feature. Therefore, in a single-database system, you will have no problems linking a customer (in the CUSTOMERS table) with the salesperson (in the EMPLOYEES table) that made the sale and the office (in the OFFICES table) responsible for servicing the customer. Moreover, after the owners of the various tables GRANT the necessary privileges, users and applications can easily run queries that combine data from tables maintained by various applications (and departments).

Gaining access to database tables on a single-database server is a simple process. After you log in to the SQL server, you need not select a database, since there is only one. For example, if JAMES wants to display data from the CUSTOMERS table (owned by OFFICE) and EMPLOYEES table (owned by LINDA), he needs to specify only the table owner along with the table name in a SELECT statement such as:

```
SELECT c.f_name, c.l_name, c.salesperson, e.f_name, e.l_name
FROM office.customers c, linda.employees e
WHERE c.salesperson = e.emp_ID
```

The main disadvantage of using the single-database architecture is that the database will grow very large with many complex relationships in a short amount of time. In addition to the data file size expanding as applications and users fill tables with data, the number of tables will also increase at an exponential rate as each user adds the tables the user needs to support applications. Then, as the number of tables and the database file size grows, performing backups, recovering data, and analyzing and tuning performance will require a full-time DBA.

A multi-database architecture, as shown in Figure 498.2, lets you group tables (by owner) within multiple database files. Instead of keeping tables for multiple applications in the same database file (as is the case in a single-database architecture), each database will normally support a single (or set of related) applications. When you add a new, different application, you will typically create a new database to hold that tables used to support it.

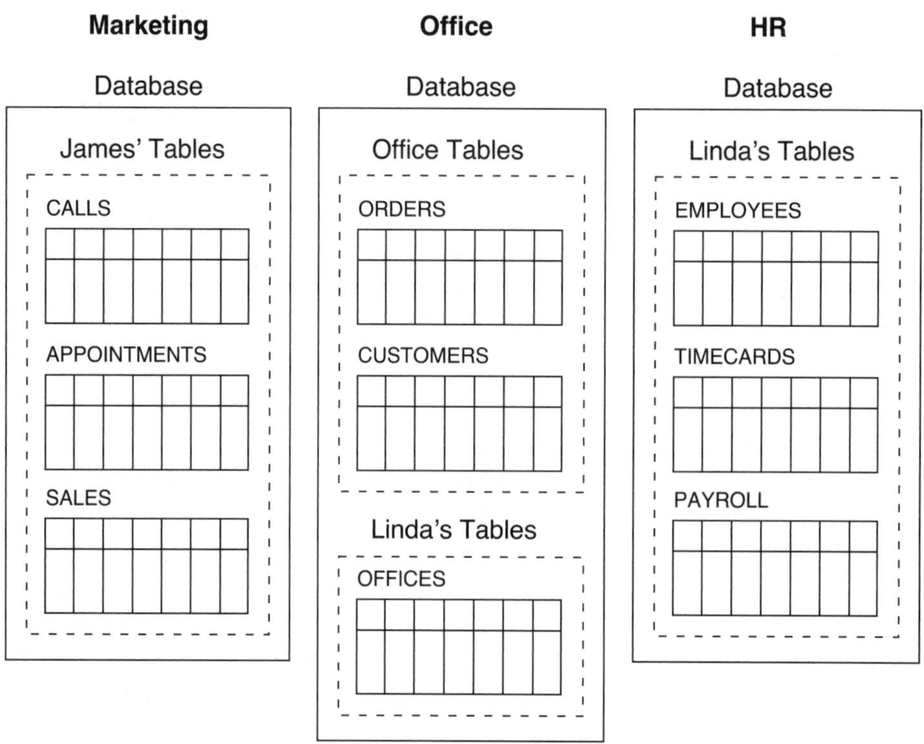

Figure 498.2 Multi-database SQL server architecture

The main advantage of a multi-database architecture (over the single-database architecture) is that the multi-database architecture lets you divide the "database" management tasks into smaller pieces. Instead of having a single DBA, each person responsible for an application will be responsible for acting as the DBA for the department's database. Then, when the organization adds a new department, the department's programmers can deploy a new database to support their applications without having to restructure or change existing databases.

Moreover, the number of tables and the size of the database file for each database will remain small (as compared to the table count and database file size in a single-database architecture).

Gaining access to database tables on a multi-database server is slightly more complex than on single-database server. After you log in to the SQL server, you must either select a database you want to use or (if the server supports it) include the database name as well as the object owner's ID in each fully qualified name. For example, if JAMES wants to display data from the CUSTOMERS table (owned by OFFICE) and the EMPLOYEES table (owned by LINDA), he must specify both the database and the table owner's ID in a SELECT statement such as:

```
SELECT c.f_name, c.l_name, c.salesperson, e.f_name, e.l_name
FROM office.office.customers c, hr.linda.employees e
WHERE c.salesperson = e.emp_ID
```

Unfortunately, many SQL servers that support the multi-database architecture do not let you set up relationships and do not support queries among tables in different databases. As a result, it may become necessary to duplicate tables in multiple databases or to combine several databases (with related data) into a single database, thereby incurring the disadvantages of a single-database architecture.

499 Simplifying Multi-table Queries by Creating a Joined Table View

After working with SQL for a while, writing multi-table joins will become second nature, since almost all queries involve extracting and relating data from two or more tables. When you find that you need the same combination of data from several tables on an ongoing basis, creating and using a joined table view is more convenient than retyping the same complex query repeatedly. Moreover, many managers who are unfamiliar with SQL and who don't have the time to learn it thoroughly may know how to write only simple, single-table queries. As such, you will often get requests to de-normalize the database so that the information management needs resides in a single table instead of being spread across multiple related tables which managers must join to get the summary reports they need.

Rather than denormalize the database and risk database corruption due to the modification anomalies you learned about in Tips 200–203, create a view or virtual table instead. By using a view to combine data from multiple tables, the manager will have a single (albeit virtual) table with data from several tables and will be able to use a single-table SELECT statement to get the desired information from the database.

Suppose, for example, that the marketing manager needs to generate a productivity report for each phone representative in the sales department. The manager will need the employee name from the EMPLOYEES table, the count of appointments and order volume from the

APPOINTMENTS table, and the number and volume of delivered sales from the CUSTOMERS table. After you create a view to join the three tables (EMPLOYEES, SALES, and CUSTOMERS), such as

```
CREATE VIEW vw_productivity (ID, Phone_Rep_Name,
    Appointments, Sales, Sales_Volume, Deliveries,
    Total_Revenue) AS
SELECT emp_ID, f_name + ' ' + l_name,
  (SELECT COUNT(*) FROM appointments
   WHERE phone_rep = emp_ID),
  (SELECT COUNT(*) FROM appointments
   WHERE phone_rep = emp_ID AND disposition = 'Sold')
  COALESCE((SELECT SUM(order_total)
   FROM appointments WHERE phone_rep = emp_ID),0),
  (SELECT COUNT(*)
   FROM customers WHERE phone_rep = emp_ID),
  COALESCE((SELECT SUM(contract_total)
   FROM customers WHERE phone_rep = emp_ID),0)
FROM employees
WHERE department = 'Marketing' AND status = 'A'
```

the marketing manager can execute a single-table query

```
SELECT * FROM vw_productivity ORDER BY total_revenue DESC
```

to get a list of active phone representatives in descending order by the amount of revenue each has generated for the company.

500 Understanding the WITH SCHEMABINDING Clause in a CREATE VIEW Statement

One of the problems with creating a view based on columns from one or more tables is that a table's owner may alter the table definition and drop a column used in the view, or perhaps drop the table altogether. Unfortunately, neither the ALTER TABLE statement nor the DROP TABLE statement will generate any errors or warnings to let you know when you are dropping a column or table used in a view. As such, if you execute the ALTER TABLE statement

```
ALTER TABLE customers DROP COLUMN contract_total
```

the DBMS will remove the CONTRACT_TOTAL column from the CUSTOMERS table used in Tip 499, "Simplifying Multi-table Queries by Creating a Joined Table View," without warning or error. However, when the marketing manager attempts to execute a SELECT statement on the VW_PRODUCTIVITY view, the DBMS will abort the query with error messages similar to:

```
Server: Msg 207, Level 16, State 3, Procedure Productivity,
  Line 4.
Invalid column name 'contract total'.
Server: Msg 4413, Level 16, State 1, Line1
Could not use view or function 'vw_productivity' because of
  binding errors.
```

The manager will most likely fire off an unpleasant e-mail to the DBA, who will have to figure out who dropped the column, why, and what can be done to fix the problem. For infrequently used views, the errors caused by table modifications may not manifest themselves for several months.

Fortunately, the CREATE VIEW statement lets you use the WITH SCHEMABINDING clause to prevent a table owner (or other user with the proper privilege) from dropping a table used in a schema-bound view and to abort any ALTER TABLE statements that affect the view definition. For example, if you create the view

```
CREATE VIEW vw_sales (ID, Phone_Rep_Name, Appointments,
    Sales, Sales_Volume) WITH SCHEMABINDING AS
SELECT emp_ID, f_name + ' ' + l_name,
  (SELECT COUNT(*) FROM frank.appointments
   WHERE phone_rep = emp_ID),
  (SELECT COUNT(*) FROM frank.appointments
   WHERE phone_rep = emp_ID AND disposition = 'Sold')
  COALESCE((SELECT SUM(order_total)
    FROM frank.appointments WHERE phone_rep = emp_ID),0)
FROM linda.employees
WHERE department = 'Marketing' AND status = 'A'
```

the DBMS will not allow FRANK to DROP the APPOINTMENTS table or LINDA to DROP the EMPLOYEES table without first dropping the VW_SALES view or changing the view definition so that it does not include the table to be dropped. Moreover, no user will be able to execute an ALTER TABLE statement on either table that drops a column used in the view.

Note: *When using the WITH SCHEMABINDING clause, the SELECT statement(s) used in the view must include two-part names <owner.object> for tables, views, and user-defined functions.*

---

501 Understanding MS-SQL Server Multi-tasking and Multi-threading on a Multi-processor Windows NT System

When considering the scalability and performance of an MS-SQL Server running in a Windows NT environment, it is important to understand the differences among the impacts of multi-tasking, multi-threading, and multi-processing on MS-SQL Server performance.

Multi-tasking refers to the operating system's ability to run multiple programs at the same time. Although only one application can have control of the central processing unit (CPU) at a time, the operating system creates the illusion that several programs are executing simultaneously, by letting each of them use the CPU for a period of time. At the end of the program's CPU time slice, the system notes where the program left off so that it can restart the program at the same point the next time it gives the application control of the CPU. Then the system switches to another application and lets that program control use the CPU for a time, and so on. It takes the operating system only a few hundred milliseconds to switch from one application to another. However, each of the programs will appear to run more slowly when the time between CPU time slices allotted to the program increases as the server shares the CPU among an increasing number of programs.

Each program running on an NT Server is called a *process*. Figure 501.1 shows statistics on several of the 35 processes (including 2 instances of MS-SQL Server) running on a Windows NT Server.

The operating system assigns each process a priority from 1 to 31 (which increases the longer the process waits for its CPU time slice) and grants use of the CPU to the process with the highest priority. Each instance of MS-SQL Server, for example, defaults to an initial (base) priority of 7. (Processes that run at a base priority of 7 are said to run at *normal* priority because the majority of applications start themselves at a base priority of 7.) In Tip 502, "Using the MS-SQL Server PRIORITY BOOST Configuration Option to Increase Server Thread Priority from 7 to 13," you will learn how to use the PRIORITY BOOST configuration option to increase the MS-SQL Server's base priority to 13, which will cause the MS-SQL Server process to run at *high* priority.

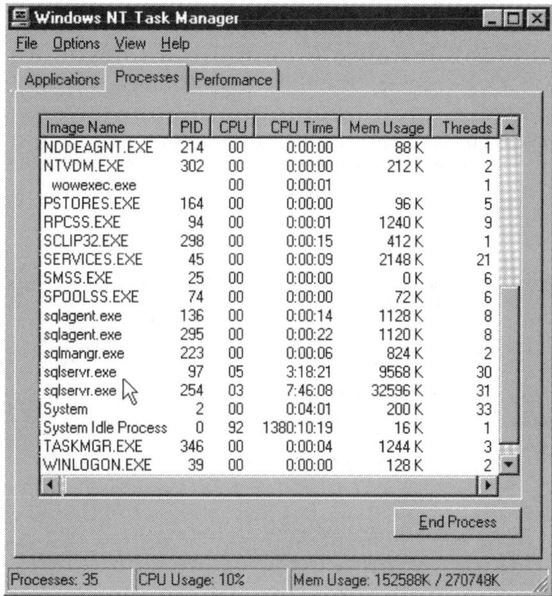

Figure 501.1 The Windows NT Task Manager showing statistics on processes running on an NT Server

Multi-threading relates to multi-processing in that each program running on an NT Server may be written in sections so that each section or *thread* in an application can operate on the CPU independently. Thus, when the NT operating system gives a CPU time slice to a multi-threaded process, the system actually starts (or restarts) the highest-priority thread (or section of code within the process) at the point at which the thread halted the last time it had to give up the CPU to another process or thread. One of the instances of MS-SQL Server (shown in Figure 501), for example, has 30 threads, while the other has 31. Therefore, when Windows NT gives control of the CPU to one of the two instances of MS-SQL Server, it is actually giving the CPU time slice to the MS-SQL Server thread with the highest priority that is waiting to execute.

Each instance of the MS-SQL Server always runs several threads: one for each network protocol used to communicate with workstations and other servers, one to handle login requests, another to communicate with the server's service control manager, and several others to execute the individual SQL and Transact-SQL statements and statement batches users send to the MS-SQL Server for execution. Multi-tasking with multiple threads is most advantageous when the NT Server has multiple processors because a single CPU (or processor) can execute only one thread at a time.

Multi-processing refers to the Windows NT operating system's ability to spread processes and threads across multiple CPUs located in a single server. Thus, a Windows NT Server with five CPUs can execute five threads or processes simultaneously. A multi-CPU NT Server is particularly advantageous when used to host an MS-SQL Server because the MS-SQL Server can use one of the CPUs to execute database I/O requests while at the same time using another CPU to execute a login thread to allow another user to open a connection to the SQL server and executing a query for another user on a third CPU, and so on.

502 Using the MS-SQL Server PRIORITY BOOST Configuration Option to Increase Server Thread Priority from 7 to 13

As you learned in Tip 501, "Understanding MS-SQL Server Multi-tasking and Multi-threading on a Multi-processor Windows NT System," Windows NT assigns a priority from 1 to 31 to each process and thread waiting to execute on one of the server's CPUs. If more than one process or thread is waiting to execute, the operating system will give the available CPU time slice to the thread with the highest priority. Each MS-SQL Server thread defaults to the normal priority of 7. However, you can use the PRIORITY BOOST option to increase the thread base priority to 13. Since doing so will give MS-SQL Server threads a higher priority than other processes and threads waiting to execute on the server, MS-SQL Server will tend to execute queries and other DBMS commands more quickly. In fact, at a (high) base priority of 13, the NT Server will tend to execute its threads whenever they are ready to run (since they will tend to have a higher priority than other threads and processes). Moreover, the high-priority MS-SQL Server threads will not be preempted by threads from other processes—again because they will tend to have a higher priority than other processes and threads waiting to use the CPU. (A thread is *preempted* when it is forced to relinquish control of the CPU to another waiting thread with a higher priority.)

To boost the base priority of MS-SQL Server threads from 7 (normal) to 13 (high), perform the following steps:

1. Click your mouse pointer on the Start button. Windows will display the Start menu.
2. Move your mouse pointer to Programs on the Start menu. Select the Microsoft SQL Server 2000 option, and click your mouse pointer on Enterprise Manager. Windows will start Enterprise Manager in the SQL Server Enterprise Manager application window.
3. Click your mouse pointer on the plus (+) to the left of Microsoft SQL Servers and then on the plus (+) to the left of SQL Server Group to display the list of MS-SQL Servers available on your network.
4. Right-click your mouse pointer on the name of the SQL server whose base priority you want to boost, and then select Properties from the pop-up menu. The Enterprise manager will display the SQL Server Properties (Configure) dialog box.

5. Click your mouse pointer on the Processor tab.
6. Click your mouse pointer on the check box to the left of Boost SQL Server Priority on Windows until a check mark appears.
7. Click your mouse pointer on the OK button to update the MS-SQL Server configuration and return to the Enterprise Manager main application window.

After you complete Step 7, you must stop and restart the MS-SQL Server in order for the priority boost to take effect.

Note: *Running the MS-SQL Server with PRIORITY BOOST can greatly improve the SQL server's performance. However, if MS-SQL Server is executing a memory-intensive operation (such as a sort) that takes a long time to complete, other applications are unlikely to have a high enough priority to preempt the MS-SQL Server thread. As a result, the performance of other applications or other instances of the MS-SQL Server running at normal priority (priority 7) will be adversely affected because these threads and processes are forced to wait for the priority-boosted thread to finish executing before they get a CPU time slice.*

---

503 Understanding the NT Server Performance Monitor Chart View

Windows NT Server includes a Performance Monitor that you can use to check the performance of one or more computers (both workstations and servers) on a network. Items that the Performance Monitor can monitor (referred to as *objects* by the application) include processors (CPUs), executing programs (processes), threads, hard drives, network resources, Internet services, and memory. To start the Windows NT Performance Monitor and generate a graphical display of MS-SQL Server statistics, perform the following steps:

1. Click your mouse pointer on the Windows NT Start button. Windows will display the Start menu.
2. Move your mouse pointer to Programs on the Start menu. Select the Administrative Tools (Common) option, and click your mouse pointer on Performance Monitor. Windows will start the Performance Monitor in Chart View similar to that shown in Figure 503.1.
3. To add objects (items to monitor) to the chart displayed in Chart View, select the Edit menu Add to Chart option, or click your mouse pointer on the Add counter button (the button with the plus [+]) on the Standard toolbar. The Performance Monitor will display an Add to Chart dialog box similar to that shown in Figure 503.2.

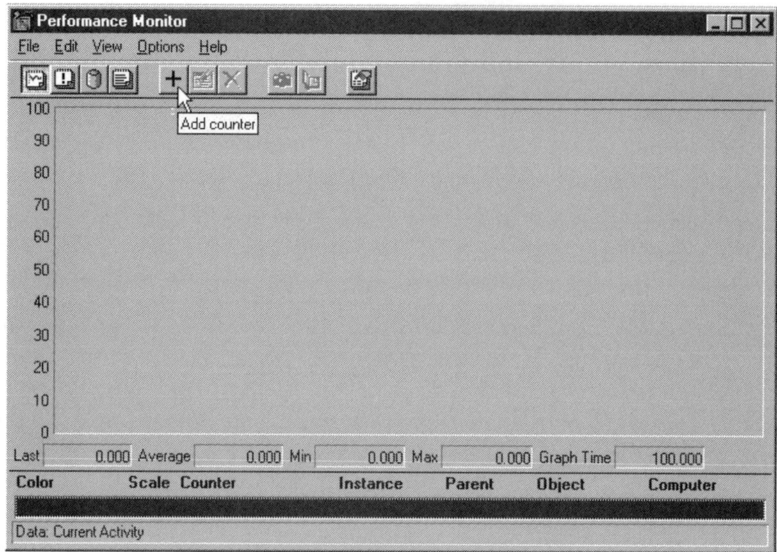

Figure 503.1 The Windows NT Performance Monitor Chart View

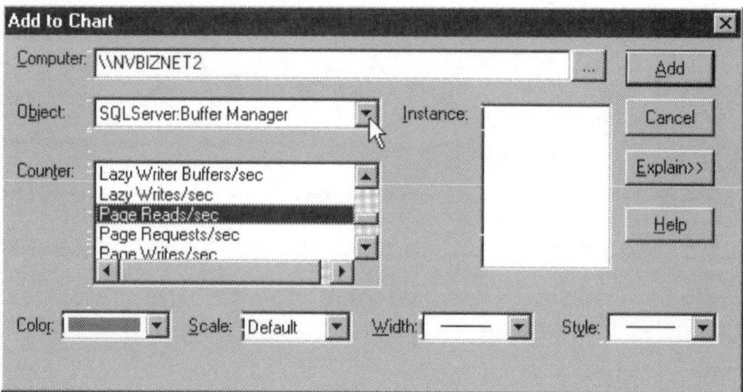

Figure 503.2 The Windows NT Performance Monitor Add to Chart dialog box

4. Enter the network path of the NT Server on which the SQL Server you wish to monitor is running into the Computer field. If you started Performance Monitor on the NT Server running the SQL Server you want to monitor, you can accept the default. If you do not know the server's path, click your mouse pointer on the Search button (labeled with the three dots [. . .]) to the right of the Computer field, and then select the NT Server you want from the drop-down list in the Select Computer dialog box.

5. To select the type of resource you want to monitor, click your mouse pointer on the drop-down list button to the right of the Object field, and then select one of the objects from the drop-down list. For the current project, select SQLServer:Buffer Manager from the drop-down list of objects you can monitor.

Note: *The name of the MS-SQL Server may be something other than SQLServer on your system. For example, MS-SQL Server 2000 will be labeled as MSSQL$<folder name>. Therefore, if you installed MS-SQL Server 2000 into the MSSQL2000 folder, you would select MSSQL$MSSQL2000:Buffer Manager in Step 5.*

6. Click your mouse pointer on the scroll bar to the right of the Counter list box to find the specific counter value you want to display for the object you selected in Step 5. For the current project, select Page Reads/sec in the Counter list box.
7. Click your mouse pointer on the Add button to add the Counter you selected in Step 6 for the Object you selected in Step 5 to the Performance Monitor Chart View display.
8. Repeat Steps 4 through 7 for each Object/Counter you want to add to the Performance Monitor real-time chart. Each time you add a new Object/Counter, Performance Monitor will automatically change the line color it will use to draw the selected counter's statistics on the chart.
9. To exit the Add to Chart dialog box and return to the Performance Monitor Chart View of the Object/Counter items you selected (in Steps 4–8), click your mouse pointer on the Done button.

If you decide that you want to add additional items to the chart, you can repeat the preceding procedure from Step 3. Conversely, to remove an Object/Counter, click your mouse pointer on the item you no longer want displayed in the list of Object/Counter items at the bottom of the Performance Monitor application window, and then select the Edit menu's Delete from Chart option, or click your mouse pointer on the Delete Selected Counter button (labeled with an X) on the Standard toolbar.

To clear all Object/Counter items, select the File menu's New Chart option.

504 Understanding the NT Server Performance Monitor Report View

In Tip 503, "Understanding the NT Server Performance Monitor Chart View," you learned how to use Performance Monitor to display Object/Counter information in graphical form. Charts work well when you want to view the change in an Object/Counter item's value over time and when you want to compare the values of two or more Object/Counter items. However, there are times when you want to see the Performance Monitor statistics in tabular (vs. graphical) form. The Performance Monitor's Report View will display the numeric values for the Object/Counter items you select. In Chart View, you must interpret the values of the items by the position of the line(s) on the graphic relative to the data point's height on the chart's vertical axis.

To display Performance Monitor Object/Counter items in Report View, perform the following steps:

1. Click your mouse pointer on the Windows Start button. Windows will display the Start menu.
2. Move your mouse pointer to Programs on the Start menu. Select the Administrative Tools (Common) option, and click your mouse pointer on Performance Monitor. Windows will start the Performance Monitor in Chart View similar to that you saw in Figure 503.1 in Tip 503.
3. Select the View menu Report option, or click your mouse pointer on the View Report data button (fourth button from the left) on the Standard toolbar.
4. To add objects (items to monitor) to the report, select the Edit menu's Add to Report option, or click your mouse pointer on the Add counter button (the button with the plus [+]) on the Standard toolbar. Performance Monitor will display the Add to Report dialog box (similar to the Add to Chart dialog box you saw in Figure 503.2 in Tip 503).
5. Enter the network path of the NT Server on which the SQL Server you wish to monitor is running into the Computer field.
6. To select the type of resource you want to monitor, click your mouse pointer on the drop-down list button to the right of the Object field. Then select one of the objects from the drop-down list. For the current project, select SQLServer:Databases.
7. Click your mouse pointer on the scroll bar to the right of the Counter list box to find the specific fact (or counter) you want to display about the object you selected in Step 6. For the current project, select Data File(s) Size (KB) in the Counter list box.
8. Select the database whose file size(s) you want to monitor in the for those listed in the Instance list box. For the current project, select SQLTips. (If you do not have the SQLTips database on your MS-SQL Server, select any one of the databases listed in the Instance list box.)

Note: *Performance Monitor will display items in the Instance list box whenever you select a counter that pertains to more than one object (or "instance"). Conversely, if you select an Object/Counter item such as the Cache Size (pages) counter of the SQLServer:Buffer Manager object, the Performance Monitor does give you a choice of Instance selections, since the Object/Counter can pertain to only a single item—the MS-SQL Server.*

---

9. Click your mouse pointer on the Add button to add the Counter you selected in Steps 7 and 8 about the Object you selected in Step 6 to the Performance Monitor Report View display.

10. Repeat Steps 5 through 9 for each Object/Counter/Instance you want to add to the Performance Monitor tabular report. For the current project, perform Steps 5 through 9 once more, selecting Log File(s) Size (KB) in Step 7 the second time through.

11. To exit the Add to Report dialog box and view the Performance Monitor Report View of the Object/Counter/Instance items you selected (in Steps 5–10), click your mouse pointer on the Done button. Performance Monitor will display a tabular report similar to that shown in Figure 504.1.

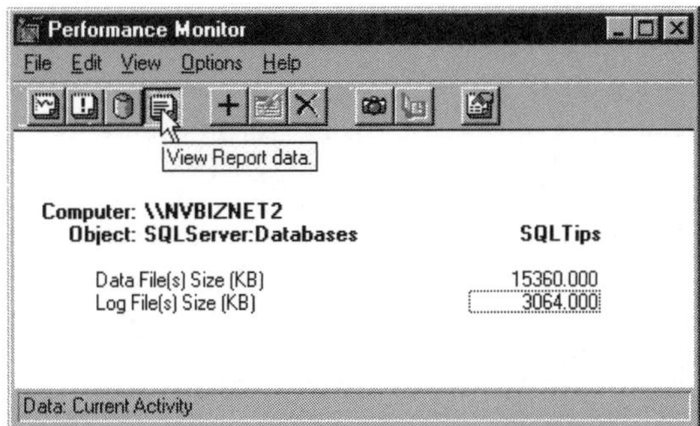

Figure 504.1 The Windows NT Performance Monitor Report View

If you decide you want to add additional items to the tabular report, you can repeat the preceding procedure from Step 4. Conversely, to remove an Object/Counter/Instance item, click your mouse pointer on the item (in the body of the report) that you want to remove, and then select the Edit menu's Delete from Report option, or click your mouse pointer on the Delete Selected Counter button (labeled with an X) on the Standard toolbar.

To clear all Object/Counter/Instance items, select the File menu's New Report Settings option.

505 Understanding the NT Server Performance Monitor Alert View

Tip 503, "Understanding the NT Server Performance Monitor Chart View," and Tip 504, "Understanding the NT Server Performance Monitor Report View," showed you how to use Performance Monitor to display MS-SQL Server data on an ongoing basis. However, there are certain conditions you hope will never or rarely occur. Rather than watch a graphical or tabular display for a spike or dip in a counter value that corresponds to one or more of these events, you can tell Performance Monitor to display an alert only when a specific event occurs.

To have Performance Monitor display an alert whenever an Object/Counter item value or Object/Counter/Instance item value falls below or exceeds a specific threshold, perform the following steps:

1. Click your mouse pointer on the Windows Start button. Windows will display the Start menu.
2. Move your mouse pointer to Programs on the Start menu. Select the Administrative Tools (Common) option, and click your mouse pointer on Performance Monitor. Windows will start Performance Monitor in Chart View, similar to what you saw in Figure 503.1 in Tip 503.
3. Select the View menu Alert option, or click your mouse pointer on the View the Alerts button (second button from the left) on the Standard toolbar.
4. To add objects (items to monitor) to the alerts report, select the Edit menu's Add to Alert option, or click your mouse pointer on the Add counter button (the button with the plus [+]) on the Standard Toolbar. The Performance Monitor will display an Add to Alert dialog box similar to that shown in Figure 505.1.

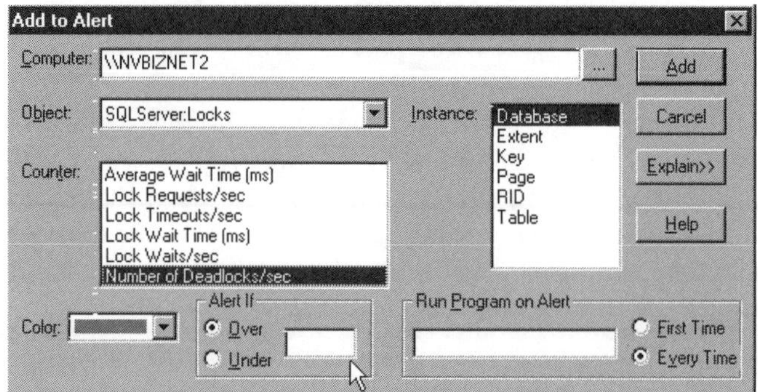

Figure 505.1 The Windows NT Performance Monitor Add to Alert dialog box

5. Enter the network path of the NT Server on which the SQL Server you wish to monitor is running into the Computer field.
6. To select the type of resource you want to monitor, click your mouse pointer on the drop-down list button to the right of the Object field, and then select one of the objects from the drop-down list. For the current project, select SQLServer:Locks.
7. Click your mouse pointer on the scroll bar to the right of the Counter list box to find the specific fact (or counter) you want to watch about the object you selected in Step 6. For the current project, select Number of Deadlocks/Sec in the Counter list box.
8. When the same counter is used for more than one item, Performance Monitor will list the available items (instances of the counter) in the Instance list box. As such, whenever it is not empty, select the instance of the counter you want to monitor in the Instance list box. For the current project, select Database in the Instance list box.

9. Into the Alert If field, enter the value against which you wish Performance Monitor to test the current value of the Object/Counter/Instance item you selected in Steps 6 through 9. For the current project, enter 0 in the Alert If field.
10. If you want Performance Monitor to alert you if the value of the Object/Counter/Instance value is above the value you entered in the Alert If field, click your mouse pointer on the radio button to the left of Over. Otherwise, click your mouse pointer on the radio button to the left of Under. For the current project, click your mouse pointer on the radio button to the left of Over.
11. If you want Performance Monitor to execute a program whenever it raises the alert (by displaying a notification message in the Alert View display), enter the name of the program into the Run Program on Alert field. Then click your mouse pointer on the radio button the left of First Time if you want Performance Monitor to execute the program only the first time it raises the alert, or click on the radio button the left of Every Time if you want the program executed every time Performance Monitor raises the alert.
12. Click your mouse pointer on the Add button to add the alert for the Counter you selected in Steps 7 and 8 about the Object you selected in Step 6 to the Performance Monitor Alert View.
13. Repeat Steps 5 through 12 for each Object/Counter/Instance about which you want Performance Monitor to post an alert (and, optionally, execute a program) if its value satisfies the alert criteria you specified in Steps 9 and 10. Each time you add a new alert, Performance Monitor will change the color of the "next" alert, so you will be able to distinguish one alert from another easily on the Performance Monitor Alert View display.
14. To exit the Add to Alert dialog box and, click your mouse pointer on the Done button.

The Performance Monitor Alert View display will remain empty until one of the Object/Counter/Instance values satisfies the alert criteria. Thereafter, Performance Monitor will add each alert raised to the display similar to that shown in Figure 505.2.

If you decide that you want to add additional alerts, repeat the preceding procedure from Step 4. Conversely, to remove an alert, click your mouse pointer on the alert that you no longer want in the list of alerts at the bottom of the Performance Monitor application window, and then select the Edit menu's Delete Alert option, or click your mouse pointer on the Delete Selected Counter button (labeled with an X) on the Standard toolbar.

To clear all alerts, select the File menu's New Alert Settings option.

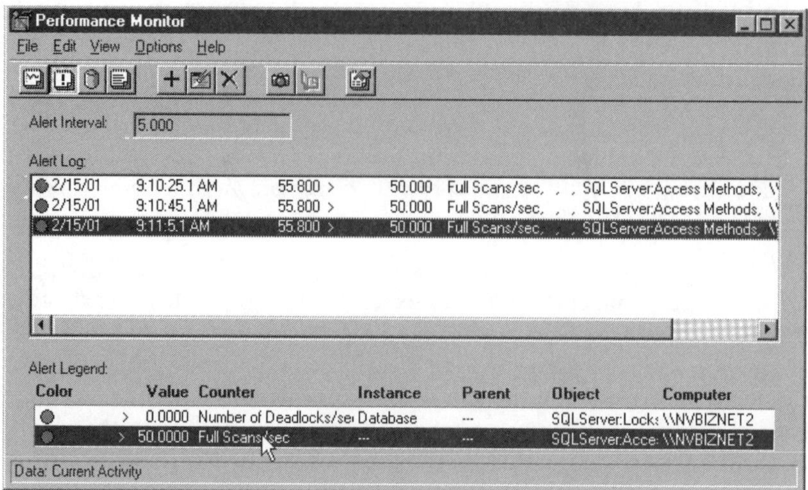

Figure 505.2 The Windows NT Performance Monitor Alert View

506 Using the CREATE SCHEMA Statement to Create Tables and Grant Access to Those Tables

The SQL-89 standard made a strong distinction between the SQL data manipulation language (DML) statements and data definition language (DDL) statements. While the standard required that the DBMS be able to execute DML statements during its normal operation, it made no such demand with regard to the ability to execute DML statements. In fact, the SQL-89 standard permits an SQL database to have a static structure like that used by the older hierarchical and network database models (which you learned about in Tip 3, "Understanding the Hierarchical Database Model," and Tip 4, "Understanding the Network Database Model").

If an SQL-89–compliant DBMS were implemented using a static database structure, the database administrator (DBA) would use DDL statements to create a *database schema*—a map of the database that shows its structure including tables, views, users, and access privileges. The DBA would then submit the database schema to a "builder" utility that creates the database according to the specifications in the schema. Once created (by the "builder" utility), the database objects and security scheme could not be changed. DML statements could add, change, remove, and retrieve data. However, to add a new table or user to the database—which requires the execution of DDL statements—the DBA would have to stop all access to the database, unload all of its data, use the DDL to create a revised schema, submit the new schema to the "builder" utility, and then reload the database data.

Although allowed by the SQL-89 standard, no database product actually used a static database structure. In fact, the later SQL-92 standard includes DROP (TABLE, VIEW, USER, and so on) and ALTER (TABLE, VIEW, USER, and so on) statements that effectively require an SQL-92–compliant database to support dynamic database object definition and modification. However, the concept of using a *database schema* to create a set of tables, views, and permissions (in effect, a database) is still supported by many DBMS products—despite their ability to create, drop, and alter individual database objects on the fly.

The CREATE SCHEMA statement lets you create a conceptual database object that contains the definitions of tables and views and to grant access privileges on those tables and views to DBMS users and roles. The syntax of the CREATE SCHEMA statement is:

```
CREATE SCHEMA AUTHORIZATION <account ID>
[<table definition(s)>|<view definition(s)>|
 <grant statement(s)>]
```

Note: *Although the AUTHORIZATION <account ID> is required, it is not actually used when the DBMS assigns ownership of the tables and views it creates. All tables and views created by executing the CREATE SCHEMA statement are owned by the user ID executing the statement.*

To create a set of tables and views, you can execute a CREATE SCHEMA statement such as:

```
CREATE SCHEMA AUTHORIZATION frank
  CREATE VIEW vw_offices AS
    SELECT offices.office_ID, manager_ID,
           f_name + l_name manager_name
    FROM offices, employees
    WHERE manager_ID = emp_ID

  CREATE TABLE employees
  (emp_ID       INTEGER,
   f_name       VARCHAR(15),
   l_name       VARCHAR(15),
   total_sales MONEY,
   office_ID    SMALLINT)

  CREATE TABLE offices
  (office_ID       SMALLINT,
   street_address VARCHAR(30),
   manager_ID      INTEGER)

  GRANT SELECT ON vw_offices        TO PUBLIC
  GRANT ALL PRIVILEGES ON offices   TO sally
  GRANT ALL PRIVILEGES ON employees TO sally
```

In short, the CREATE SCHEMA does not add any real functionality to the DDL. However, the CREATE SCHEMA statement does give you a single SQL statement that you can use to create one or more tables and views and to grant access permissions to those tables and views.

With the exception of views that are dependant on other views, the objects created in the CREATE SCHEMA statement need not appear in any specific order. As such, you can grant permissions or create a view based on a table created later in the CREATE SCHEMA statement. Moreover, view definitions and foreign keys created in one part of the statement can refer to columns in tables created later in the CREATE SCHEMA statement. However, if a view definition references columns in another view (vs. columns in a table), the view whose columns are being referenced must be created before the view that references its columns.

As is the case with any single SQL statement, the DBMS will roll back (undo) the CREATE SCHEMA statement's work if any part of the statement fails to execute successfully. Therefore, if any one of the CREATE SCHEMA statement's CREATE or GRANT statements fails, the DBMS will not create any of schema's tables or views, nor will the DBMS grant any of the privileges specified in the schema.

507 Setting Up the NT Server Performance Monitor Log to Help in Optimizing the MS-SQL Server

Tip 503, "Understanding the NT Server Performance Monitor Chart View," and Tip 504, "Understanding the NT Server Performance Monitor Report View," showed you how to use Performance Monitor to display real-time object/counter values in chart and tabular form, respectively. If you want to store the values of the counters for one or more Performance Monitor objects so that you can display the counter values and analyze them later, use the Performance Monitor Log View. The Performance Monitor's Log View will write counter values to a disk file at set intervals. As you will learn in Tip 508, "Using the NT Performance Monitor to View a Performance Log File," you can tell the Performance Monitor to retrieve object/counter values from its log files and display them in chart or graphical form.

To have Performance Monitor log the values of the counters for one or more objects for later review, perform the following steps:

1. Click your mouse pointer on the Start button. Windows will display the Start menu.
2. Move your mouse pointer to Programs on the Start menu. Select the Administrative Tools (Common) option, and click your mouse pointer on Performance Monitor. Windows will start the Performance Monitor in Chart View similar to that you saw in Figure 503.1 in Tip 503.

3. Select the View menu's Log option, or click your mouse pointer on the View output Log file status button (third button from the left) on the Standard toolbar.

4. To add objects (sets of counters) whose values you want recorded in a Performance Monitor log file, select the Edit menu's Add to Log option, or click your mouse pointer on the Add counter button (the button with the plus [+] on the Standard toolbar). Performance Monitor will display an Add to Log dialog box similar to that shown in Figure 507.1.

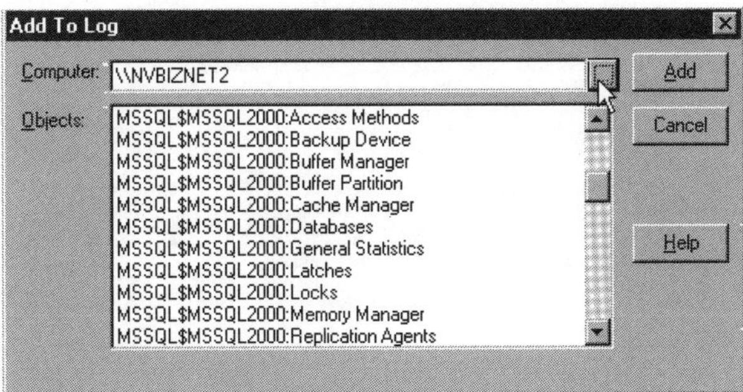

Figure 507.1 The Windows NT Performance Monitor Add to Log dialog box

5. Enter the network path of the NT Server on which the SQL Server you wish to monitor is running into the Computer field. (If you do not know the server's path, click your mouse pointer on the Select button to the right of the Computer field so that you can select the computer you want from the list of servers in a Select Computer dialog box.)

6. Click your mouse pointer on the category of counters you want to log in the list of objects in the Objects section of the Add to Log dialog box. For example, if you plan to generate a chart of page reads/sec values (as you did for the project in Tip 503), select the Buffer Manager object, which includes the page reads/sec counter.

7. Click your mouse pointer on the Add button, to add the object you selected in Step 6 to the list of objects whose sets of counter values Performance Monitor will write its log file.

8. Repeat Steps 6 and 7 until you've selected all of the objects whose counter values you want to review later. Then click your mouse pointer on the Done button. Performance Monitor will close the Add to Log dialog box and return to its Log View. (If you selected any object you no longer want, click your mouse pointer on it and then press the Delete key on your keyboard.)

9. Select the Options menu's Log option. Performance Monitor will display a Log Options dialog box similar to that shown in Figure 507.2.

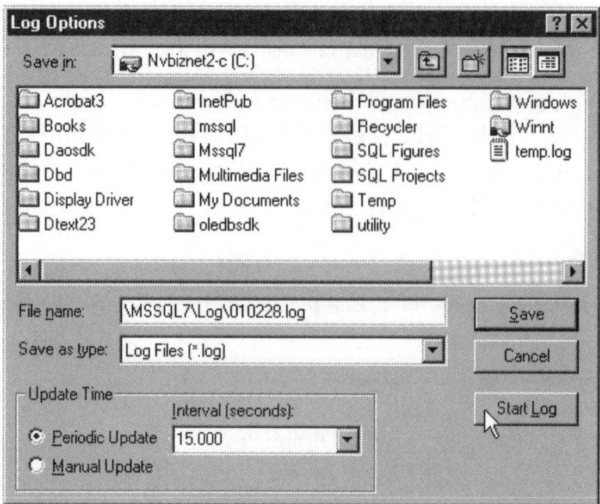

Figure 507.2 The Windows NT Performance Monitor Log Options dialog box

10. Enter the pathname of the file into which you want Performance Monitor to store the objects' counter values into the File Name field.
11. In the Periodic Update field (near the bottom-left corner of the dialog box), enter how often, in seconds, you want Performance Monitor to record values in its log file.
12. Click your mouse pointer on the Start Log button.

When you complete Step 12, Performance Monitor will close the Log Options dialog box and begin writing the object/counter values (which you selected in Steps 6–8) into the log file (which you specified in Step 10), at the interval you entered in Step 11. Click your mouse pointer on the dash (–) (third button from the right in the upper-right corner of the Performance Monitor application window), and shrink the application to an icon on the task bar at the bottom of your computer screen.

After Performance Monitor (running as a background task on your computer) has collected data for a desired time period, click you mouse pointer on its icon on the task bar at the bottom of your screen to display its application window. Next, select the Options menu's Log option to again display the Log Options dialog box. To stop the application from logging counter values, click your mouse pointer on the Stop Log button (in the lower-right corner of the dialog box).

You will learn how to use Performance Monitor to display the contents of its log files in Tip 508.

508 Using the NT Performance Monitor to View a Performance Log File

After you create Performance Monitor log files (by performing the steps in the procedure in Tip 507, "Setting Up the NT Server Performance Monitor Log to Help in Optimizing the MS-SQL Server"), you can use Performance Monitor to display the contents of the log files in chart (graphical) or tabular form. The process is very simple. Instead of having Performance Monitor retrieve the counter values it is to display directly from the NT Server hosting the MS-SQL Server, you tell the program to use the counter values in the log file (as if they were coming directly from the server).

For example, to use Performance Monitor to display previously logged counter values in chart form, perform the following steps:

1. Click your mouse pointer on the Start button. Windows will display the Start menu.
2. Move your mouse pointer to Programs on the Start menu. Select the Administrative Tools (Common) option, and click your mouse pointer on Performance Monitor. Windows will start Performance Monitor in Chart View similar to that you saw in Figure 503.1 (see Tip 503, "Understanding the NT Server Performance Monitor Chart View").
3. Select the View menu's Chart option.
4. Select the Options menu's Data From option. Performance Monitor will display a Data From dialog box similar to that shown in Figure 508.1.

Figure 508.1 The Windows NT Performance Monitor Data From dialog box

5. To have Performance Monitor collect and display counter values from a log file, click your mouse pointer on the Log File radio button, and then enter the pathname of the log file in the field at the bottom of the Data From dialog box. (If you click your mouse pointer on the Current Activity radio button, Performance Monitor will collect the counter values it is to display directly from the server.)
6. Click your mouse pointer on the OK button.
7. To select objects/counter values you want to display in Chart View, select the Edit menu's Add to Chart option, or click your mouse pointer on the Add counter button (the button with the plus [+]) on the Standard toolbar. Performance Monitor will display an Add to Chart dialog box similar to the one you saw in Figure 503.2, in Tip 503.

8. Use the Select button (labeled with the three dots [. . .]) to the right of the Computer field, and then select the NT Server whose data values you want to display. (Only servers with data in the log file that you selected in Steps 5 and 6 will appear in the Search button's drop-down list of servers.)
9. To select the object whose logged counter values you want to display, click your mouse pointer on the drop-down list button to the right of the Object field, and then select one of the objects from the drop-down list. Only those objects whose counter values were written to the current log file will appear on the drop-down list of objects you can select.
10. Click your mouse pointer on the scroll bar to the right of the Counter list box to find the specific counter value that you want to display for the object you selected in Step 9.
11. Click your mouse pointer on the Add button to add the counter you selected in Step 10 for the object you selected in Step 9 to the Performance Monitor Chart View display.
12. Repeat Steps 8 through 11 for each Object/Counter you want to add to the Performance Monitor chart. Each time you add a new object/counter, Performance Monitor will automatically change the line color that it will use to draw the selected counter's statistics on the chart.
13. To exit the Add to Chart dialog box and return to the Performance Monitor Chart View, click your mouse pointer on the Done button.

After you complete Step 13, Performance Monitor will display the entire contents of the log file on a single chart. To view, "zoom in" on the values logged during a specific period of time, select the Edit menu's Time Window, and specify the time period of interest on the Input Log File Timeframe dialog box.

509 Configuring the Windows NT Application Event Log

In Tip 505, "Understanding the NT Server Performance Monitor Alert View," you learned how to use Performance Monitor to alert you to potential problems with the MS-SQL Server's operation by displaying a message in Alert View whenever object/counter values either exceeded or fell below certain limits. The Performance Monitor, however, is not the only tool you can use to monitor the health of your MS-SQL Server. Windows NT includes an integrated logging tool that maintains a log of application, security, and system operations called *events*. By reviewing the *application* log events generated by your MS-SQL Server, you can learn how often the SQL Server/Agent was stopped and started, see how often it encounters file (table, log, and index) errors, and review warnings and error messages generated by various other database operations such as transaction rollbacks and roll-forwards executed when the SQL server is restarted after an abnormal shutdown.

Windows NT enables the event-logging service automatically when you start the server. To avoid losing event notifications due to a full event log, you should use the Event Viewer to configure the event logs after you install the MS-SQL Server on the server. To use the Event Viewer to set the maximum log file size in kilobytes, the length of time events remain in the log, and whether or not the event logging service will overwrite events if the log file is full, perform the following steps:

1. Click your mouse pointer on the Start button. Windows will display the Start menu.
2. Move your mouse pointer to Programs on the Start menu. Select the Administrative Tools (Common) option, and click your mouse pointer on Event Viewer.
3. Select the Log menu's Log Settings option. The Event Viewer will display an Event Log Settings dialog box similar to that shown in Figure 509.1.

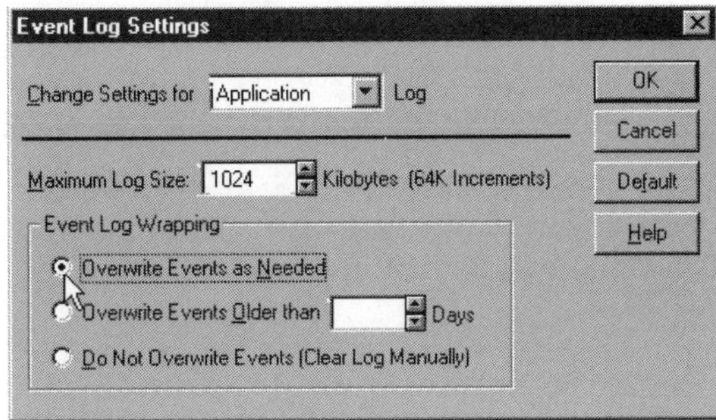

Figure 509.1 The Windows NT Event Viewer Event Log settings

4. Click your mouse pointer on the drop-down list button to the right of the Change Setting For field (near the top of the dialog box), and select Application from the drop-down list.
5. Enter the maximum size for the event log into the Maximum Log Size field. If you increase the maximum size of the log file beyond the 512Kb default, you will be able to keep more events in the log file for a longer time in order to see a trend among the events reported by the MS-SQL Server.
6. Choose the action you want the event-logging service to take if the log file gets full. To avoid losing new events, click your mouse pointer on the Overwrite Events as Needed radio button. By doing so, the event-logging service will overwrite the oldest events as new events are added to a full log. (Selecting either of the other two settings could cause the loss of new event notifications.)
7. Click your mouse pointer on the OK button to save your configuration changes and return to the Event Viewer application window.

While you are still in the Event View, you should go ahead and set the configuration settings for the system and security logs as well. To do so, start at Step 3 of the preceding procedure and select System in Step 4. Then, after completing Steps 5 and 6, repeat the procedure again, starting at Step 3, and select Security at Step 4 the third time through.

510 Displaying Windows NT Application Event Details and Clearing the Application Event Log

The Event Viewer lets you view application (system and security) log information recorded by the Windows NT server's event-logging service. As shown in Figure 510.1, each line in an event log shows the date and time the event occurred, the source of the event, and the event's category, ID number, and username (if applicable) of the user that launched the transaction.

Event Viewer - Application Log on \\NVBIZNET2

Log View Options Help

Date	Time	Source	Category	Event	User
3/1/01	12:20:04 AM	SQLServerAgent	Alert Engine	312	N/A
3/1/01	12:20:04 AM	SQLServerAgent	Alert Engine	311	N/A
3/1/01	12:20:04 AM	SQLServerAgent	Alert Engine	318	N/A
3/1/01	12:19:44 AM	SQLAgent$MSS(	Alert Engine	312	N/A
3/1/01	12:19:44 AM	SQLAgent$MSS(	Alert Engine	311	N/A
3/1/01	12:19:44 AM	SQLAgent$MSS(	Alert Engine	318	N/A

Figure 510.1 A Windows NT Event Viewer application event log

To display more detailed information on an event, double-click your mouse pointer on the event (or click your mouse pointer on the event, and then select the View menu's Detail option). The Event Viewer will display an Event Detail message box similar to that shown in Figure 510.2.

After you invoke the Event Detail dialog box to display the detail for one event, you can click your mouse pointer on its Next button to display the next event (toward the bottom of the event list) or on the Previous button to display event detail for the next event toward the top of the list. When you are finished viewing event detail, click your mouse pointer on the Close button to close the Event Detail dialog box and return to the Event View application window.

If you noticed a trend in the application log's event messages, made a correction to the application's settings or hardware, and now want to monitor the server for the reoccurrence of the trend, you will want start with an empty event log. To clear all events from a log, select the Log menu's Clear All Events option. The Event Monitor will display a Clear Event Log confirmation textbox. Click your mouse pointer on the Yes button if you want to write the event log to a disk file before clearing it, click on the No button to clear the event log before saving its contents to another file on disk, or click on the Cancel button to leave the event log unchanged.

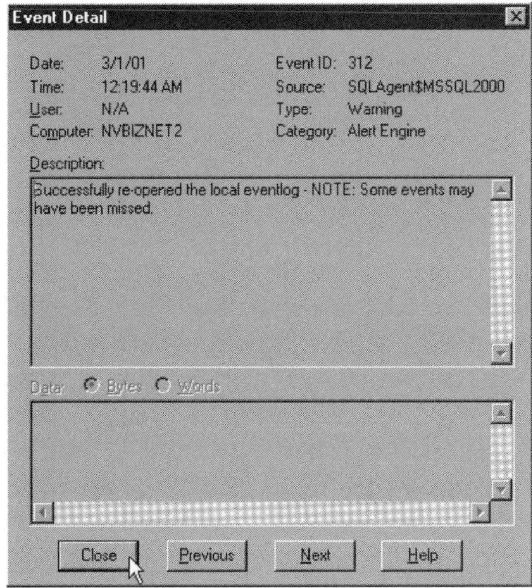

Figure 510.2 The Windows NT Event Viewer Event Detail message box

511 Using the MS-SQL Server Service Manager to Start the MS-SQL Server

There are several ways you can start the MS-SQL Server on a Windows NT Server. When you install the MS-SQL Server (as you will learn to do in Tip 527, "Installing the MS-SQL Server"), you can select an option on one of the setup screens to have Windows NT start the MS-SQL Server as a service automatically whenever you boot the operating system. Conversely, you can choose to start the MS-SQL Server manually with the MS-SQL Server Service Manager or by entering a command at the command prompt in the MS-SQL Server's BINN directory.

To start the MS-SQL Server using the MS-SQL Server Service Manager, perform the following steps:

1. Click your mouse pointer on the Start button on the Windows NT Server on which you installed the MS-SQL Server. Windows will display the Start menu.
2. Move your mouse pointer to Programs on the Start menu. Select the Microsoft SQL Server program group, and click your mouse on Service Manager. Windows NT will start the MS-SQL Server Service Manager which will display a dialog box similar to that shown in Figure 511.1.

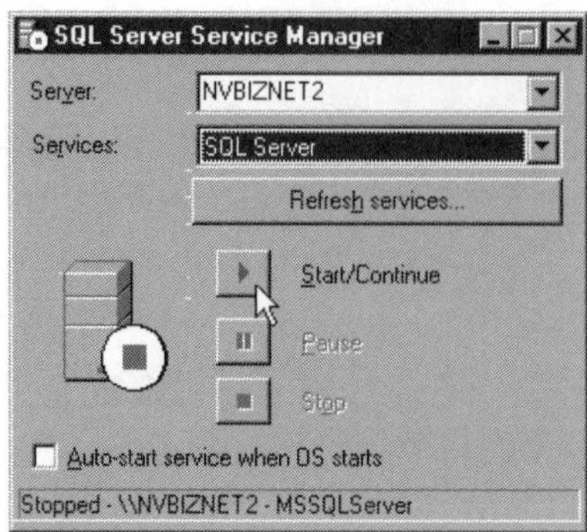

Figure 511.1 The MS-SQL Server Service Manager dialog box

3. If you have more than one MS-SQL Server installed on your system, click your mouse pointer on the drop-down list button to the right of the Server field to display the list of installed MS-SQL Servers, and then select the MS-SQL Server that you want to start.
4. Click your mouse pointer on the drop-down list button to the right of the Services field to display the list of services that the MS-SQL Service Manager controls, and select SQL Server.
5. To start the MS-SQL Server you selected in Step 3, click your mouse pointer on the Start/Continue button in the lower half of the dialog box. The MS-SQL Server Service Manager will attempt to start the MS-SQL Server. If successful, the Server Service Manager will change the red block on the server icon in the dialog box to a green arrow to indicate a running service, the MS-SQL Server.

Note: *If you want the Windows NT Server to start the MS-SQL Server (service) automatically each time you boot the operating system, click your mouse pointer on the check box to the left of Auto-start Service When OS Starts until a check mark appears.*

---

6. To exit the MS-SQL Server Service Manager, click your mouse pointer on the close button (the X) in the upper-right corner of the dialog box.

In addition to starting the MS-SQL Server, you can use the MS-SQL Server Service Manager to start four other SQL related services:

- **Microsoft Search**—Service that builds indexes for and supports advanced queries on character and text based columns
- **Microsoft Distributed Transaction Coordinator** (MSDTC)—Service that manages transactions to allow applications to combine data from several different data sources (including multiple instances of MS-SQL Server) running on the same or different Windows NT servers

- **MSSQLServerOLAPService**—Online analytical processing services used to maintain data warehouse data cubes and provide rapid analytical access to data warehouse data
- **SQL Server Agent**—Application that runs scheduled MS-SQL Server administrative tasks such as backups, index updates, and stored procedures scheduled for execution at specific dates and times

To start any of these MS-SQL Server support services, select the service you want to start instead of SQL Server in Step 4 of the preceding procedure.

512 Starting the MS-SQL Server from a Command Prompt

As mentioned in Tip 511, "Using the MS-SQL Server Service Manager to Start the MS-SQL Server," you can start the MS-SQL Server from the command prompt. To start the MS-SQL Server from a command prompt, perform the following steps:

1. Click your mouse pointer on the Start button. Windows will display the Start menu.
2. Move your mouse pointer to Programs on the Start menu, and select Command Prompt.
3. At the command prompt, enter the **CD** (change directory) command and move to the MS-SQL Server BINN directory. For example, if you are starting MS-SQL Server Version 7 installed to the default directories, you enter **CD \MSSQL7\BINN** at the command prompt and then press the Enter key.
4. Enter the command to start the MS-SQL Server as:

```
 sqlservr -<master database>
<drive>:\<directory>\master.mdf
```

   For example, if you are starting MS-SQL Server Version 7 installed to the default directories, with database files in the C:\MSSQL7\DATA directory, enter **sqlserver -master c:\mssql7\data\master.mdf** at the command prompt and then press the Enter key.
5. Type **EXIT** at the command prompt and then press the Enter key to return to the Windows desktop.

If you used something other than MASTER for the name of the master database when you installed the MS-SQL Server, substitute that name for <master database> and for the "master" in master.mdf in Step 4.

513 Using the Windows Control Panel to Enable Automatic MS-SQL Server Startup

In Tip 527, "Installing the MS-SQL Server," you will learn how to install the MS-SQL Server on a Windows NT server. As mentioned in Tip 511, "Using the MS-SQL Server Service Manager to Start the MS-SQL Server," the installation process gives you the option of having the operating system (OS) start the MS-SQL Server automatically during the OS boot process. If you select the installation option to force a manual restart of the MS-SQL Server each time you restart the Windows NT server, you can change the "manual" MS-SQL Server startup election later.

As you learned from Tip 511, you can make the election to automatically start the server in the future by clicking a check mark into the Auto-start Services When OS Starts check box on the MS-SQL Server Service Manager dialog box. Alternatively, to tell Windows NT to start the MS-SQL Server automatically as part of the boot process (vs. manually after the Windows NT server is running), through the Windows NT server's Control Panel, perform the following steps:

1. Double-click your mouse pointer on the My Computer icon on the Windows NT server desktop.
2. In the My Computer window, double-click your mouse pointer on Control Panel.
3. In the Control Panel window, double-click your mouse pointer on Services. Windows NT will display the Services dialog box, which shows all services (both running and stopped) defined to the operating system.
4. To select the MS-SQL Server whose startup option you want to change from manual to automatic (or from automatic to manual), click your mouse pointer on its name in the Service list box of the Services dialog box. For example, if you accepted the defaults when you installed MS-SQL Server Version 7, look for the MSSQLServer entry in the Service list box of the Services dialog box. Similarly, if you assigned the name MSSQL2000 to the SQL server during the MS-SQL Server 2000 installation process, click your mouse pointer on the MSSQL$MSSQL2000 entry in the Service list box.
5. Click your mouse pointer on the Startup button. Windows NT will display a Service (startup) dialog box similar to that shown in Figure 513.1.
6. To have Windows NT start the MS-SQL Server service automatically at startup, click your mouse pointer on the Automatic radio button in the Startup Type section of the dialog box.
7. Click your mouse pointer on the OK button. Windows NT will close the Service dialog box and change the value in the MS-SQL Server Startup column from manual to automatic.

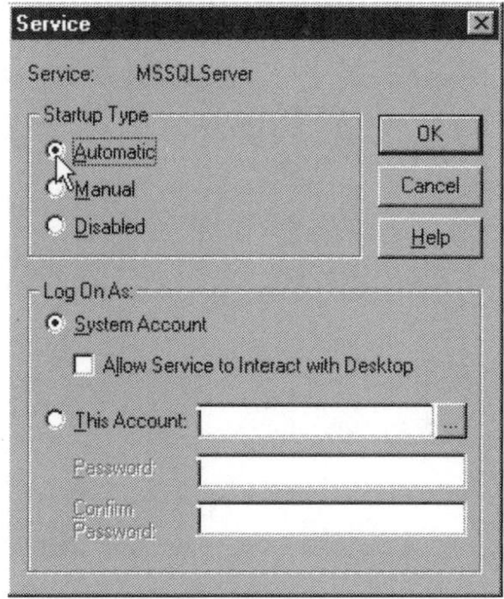

Figure 513.1 The Windows NT Control Panel Services window's Service (startup) dialog box

8. Click your mouse pointer on the Close button to exit the Services dialog box and return to the Control Panel.

In addition to enabling (or disabling) automatic startup of the MS-SQL Server, you can manually start (or stop) the MS-SQL Server on the Control Panel's Services dialog box. If the MS-SQL Server is not running at Step 4 (or after Step 7), you will see nothing in the MS-SQL Server's Status column. To start the MS-SQL Server, click your mouse pointer on the Start button in Step 5 (vs. the Startup button). Windows NT will start the MS-SQL Server and display Started in the Status column of the line for the MS-SQL Server that you selected in Step 4. Conversely, if you want to shut down a running MS-SQL Server, at Step 4 (or after Step 7), click your mouse pointer on the Stop button. Windows NT will stop the MS-SQL Server and remove Started from the Status column of the affected MS-SQL Server's line in the Service list box of the Services dialog box.

514 Understanding MS-SQL Server Client Software

When you run the MS-SQL Server installation program, the application will install both the MS-SQL Server and the tools you need to manage it and to modify and query its data. As such, if the computer on which you installed the MS-SQL Server is also the workstation you are using to work with the SQL server, you need not install any additional client software. However, as is most likely the case, when you are using one computer to manage or work with data on the MS-SQL Server installed on another computer, you need to install some (if not all) of the MS-SQL Server client software shown in Table 514.1 on your workstation.

Component	***Space***	***Subcomponent***	***Space***
Management Tools	28,672K	Enterprise Manager	25,024K
		Profiler	640K
		Query Analyzer	1,696K
		DTC Client Support	0K
		Conflict Viewer	1,024K
Client Connectivity	288K		
Books Online	32,512K		
Development Tools	16,800K	Headers and Libraries	6,400K
		MDAC SDKs	9,600K
		Backup/Restore API	512K
		Debugger Interface	288K
Code Samples	6,944	Active-X Data Objects (ADO)	192K
		DB-Library (DBLIB)	160K
		Desktop	3,424K
		Data Transformation Services (DTS)	576K
		Embedded SQL for C (ESQLC)	160K
		Miscellaneous	224K
		Microsoft Distributed Transaction Coordinator (MSDTC)	160K
		Open Database Connectivity (ODBC)	160K
		Open Data Services (ODS)	160K
		Object Linking and Embedding (OLE) Automation	160K
		Replication	160K
		SQL Distributed Management Objects (SQLDMO)	192K
		SQL Namespace (SQLNS)	160K
		Utils	288K
		XML	288K

Table 514.1 MS-SQL Server Client Utilities List and Disk Space Requirements

If you want to install all of the client software, books online (documentation), development tools, and code samples, you will need approximately 180MB of free space on your computer. At a minimum, you will need to install the management tools (which let you manage the MS-SQL Server and work with its data) and the client connectivity tools (which allow the clients to communicate with the server through DBLIB, ODBC, and OLEDB drivers). If you plan to write applications, you will also need the headers and libraries, MDAC SDK's subcomponents of the development tools component, and the subcomponents of the code samples component relevant to your planned development environment.

In Tip 515, "Installing MS-SQL Server Client Software," you will learn how to install the MS-SQL Server client software. For now, the important thing to understand is that the MS-SQL Server client software lets you use any workstation on the network to manage the MS-SQL Server and work with its data—as long as the DBA and the network administrator have given your user ID the required access rights. Although there are still some 16-bit clients available, the latest clients (released with MS-SQL Server 7.0 and above) require that you install and run them on a 32-bit operating system (such as Windows 95, 98, ME, NT, 2000, UNIX, Apple Macintosh, OS/2, and so on).

515 Installing MS-SQL Server Client Software

As mentioned in Tip 514, "Understanding MS-SQL Server Client Software," you will need to install MS-SQL Server client software on a workstation when you want to work with the data or manage the MS-SQL Server installed on another computer on the network. You will find the MS-SQL Server client software on the MS-SQL Server installation CD. Please refer to table 514 in Tip 514 for a complete list of the client applications, documentation, and code samples available for installation.

Before starting the installation process, close all applications running on your workstation (be sure to save any unsaved work first) because you will be prompted to reboot your computer to finish the setup process. Then, to install the MS-SQL Server client software, documentation, or code samples on your workstation, perform the following steps:

1. Insert the MS-SQL Server installation CD in your CD-ROM drive. Windows will start the MS-SQL Server setup program. (If the MS-SQL Server installation does not begin momentarily after you insert the CD, double-click your mouse pointer on CD-ROM drive in the My Computer window.
2. After the MS-SQL Server installation program displays the initial installation screen, click your mouse pointer on SQL Server 2000 Components. The installation program will display the Install Components screen.

3. Click your mouse pointer on Install Database Server. The setup program will check your system hardware and operating system to see if the MS-SQL Server will run on your system. If your system does not meet the requirements to run MS-SQL Server, the installation program will display a warning message in a textbox, indicating that setup will only make the MS-SQL Server client components available for installation, since the MS-SQL Server is not supported for your operating system/hardware setup. If you see the warning message, do not worry; just click your mouse pointer on the OK button.
4. After the installation program displays its Welcome screen, click your mouse pointer on the Next button.
5. On the Computer Name screen, click your mouse pointer on the Local Computer radio button and then on the Next button.
6. On the Installation Selection screen, click your mouse pointer on the Create a New Instance of SQL Server, or Install Client Tools radio button and then click on the Next button. The setup program will display the User Information dialog box.
7. Enter your name into the Name field and your company's name into the Company field, and then click your mouse pointer on the Next button.
8. When the setup program displays the Software License Agreement, read it and, if you agree to its terms, click your mouse pointer on the Yes button near the bottom-right corner of the dialog box.
9. On the Installation Definition screen, click your mouse pointer on the Client Tools Only radio button and then on the Next button. The installation program, will display the Select Components dialog box.
10. To select a component and all of its subcomponents for installation, click your mouse pointer on the checkbox to the left of the component name until a check mark appears. (If you want to install only some of the subcomponents for a component, clear the check box next to the component, and click your mouse pointer on the check box to the left of each subcomponent you want to install until a checkmark appears.)
11. Click your mouse pointer on the Next button (in the lower-right corner of the Select Components dialog box). The Installer will display the Start Copying Files screen.
12. To have the setup program start copying files from the MS-SQL Server CD-ROM onto your workstation, click your mouse pointer on the Next button.

After you complete Step 12, the MS-SQL Server installation program will begin copying the documentation and code sample files, and will install the client software applications that you selected in Step 10. Once it has finished the installation process, the setup program will display the Setup Complete screen. When you see it, click your mouse pointer on the Finish button to restart your computer.

To use an MS-SQL Server client, select the client from those listed in the MS-SQL Server group under Programs on the Windows start menu. If you installed code samples as well, you can find them in folders subordinate to the C:\PROGRAM FILES\MICROSOFT SQL SERVER\ folder.

516 Understanding the MS-SQL Server System Catalog

MS-SQL Server uses tables to store both data and metadata. (Metadata consists of the fields and the value of the fields that describe the overall structure of the database and the objects such as tables, views, constraints, indexes, and keys, in it.) While users create and maintain the data tables that model real-world objects or events, the server's installation program creates the tables in the System Catalog and the SQL server maintains the metadata stored in the tables. Thus, the System Catalog consists of a set of tables whose data values describe everything about the database itself. By querying the System Catalogs, then, you can retrieve information such as:

- The number and names of all database tables and views
- The number of columns in a table or view, along with the name, data type, scale, and precision of each column
- The constraints defined on each table in the database
- The indexes and keys created for each table

Tables 516.1–516.4 provide the name, database location, and a brief description for each of tables in the MS-SQL Server system catalog. Although you can query the tables in the System Catalog directly, Microsoft recommends against this practice because the structure of the tables in the System Catalog changes from one version of the MS-SQL Server to another. Therefore, issue SELECT statements against System Catalog tables only if you cannot retrieve the information you need by using an information schema view (discussed in Tips 472–493), metadata function, or system stored procedure (discussed in Tips 606–640).

The following System Catalog tables are stored only in the MS-SQL Server's MASTER database.

Table Name	*Description*
sysaltfiles	Contains information about the physical files in which the database and its transaction log are stored on the hard drive(s). The logical name and physical pathname of each file, along with its initial size, maximum size, and growth rate, are stored in this table. (These are the parameters you entered on tabs in the <database> Properties dialog box in Tips 495–497.)
syscacheobjects	Contains information about MS-SQL Server's system cached usage.

Table Name	***Description***
syscharsets	Contains one row of information about each of the character sets and sort orders available on MS-SQL Server. The character set and sort order marked as the default sort order in the SYSCONFIGURES table is the only one the server is actually using.
sysconfigures	Contains the saved values of MS-SQL Server's user settable configuration options. These are the configurations settings currently in effect when you first start MS-SQL Server.
syscurconfigs	Contains the system configuration settings currently in effect for any configuration options you change while the MS-SQL Server is running. The SYSCURCONFIGS table is empty each time you start the MS-SQL Server because it contains only the configuration settings you change during the server's operation.
sysdatabases	Contains the logical name, physical filename, creator, creation date, status, and other information on each of the databases managed by MS-SQL Server.
sysdevices	Contains one row of information on each disk-based backup file, tape-based backup file, and physical database file for the databases managed by MS-SQL Server. (Provided for backward compatibility with versions of MS-SQL Server prior to version 7.0.)
syslanguages	Contains one row of information about the date and numeric data format for each language available to the MS-SQL Server. Although not listed in SYSLANGUAGES, U.S. English is always available to the MS-SQL Server.
syslockinfo	Contains information about each lock request currently active on the system. The information includes the ID of user requesting the lock, its current status, the type of lock requested, and the object that is (or is to be) locked.
syslogins	Contains one row of information for each login to MS-SQL Server. The information includes the login name, whether the login ID is an individual or group name, and indicators that show whether the user is a member of an administration group or a DBCREATOR.
sysmessages	Contains one row with the error number, message group ID, severity, and description for each system error, alert, or warning message MS-SQL Server can issue.
sysoledbusers	Contains one row of information for each username/password pair that can be used to log in to and use a remote server (whose ID is also specified in the same row) as an OLE DB data source.
sysperfinfo	The MS-SQL Server's performance counters that can be displayed using the Windows NT Performance Monitor.

Table Name	Description
sysprocesses	Built dynamically when you query the table. Contains one row of information on each of the processes (both client and system) running on the MS-SQL Server at the time of the query.
sysremotelogins	Contains one row of information for each user allowed to run stored procedures on the current MS-SQL Server while logged in on a remote MS-SQL Server.
sysservers	Contains one row of information on each remote server that a user logged into the current server can access as an OLE DB data source.

Table 516.1 System Catalog Tables Found Only in the MASTER Database

The following System Catalog tables are stored in each of the databases managed by MS-SQL Server.

Table Name	Description
syscolumns	Contains one row with the name, data type, scale, precision, and length for each column in every table and view, and a row with the same information plus the behavior of each parameter in a stored procedure.
syscomments	Contains one or more rows of information about each view, rule, default, trigger, CHECK constraint, DEFAULT constraint, and stored procedure. The number of rows used to define an object depends on the length of the SQL statements that define it. Each row's TEXT column (which holds the object's SQL statements) can hold a maximum of 4,000 characters.
sysconstraints	Contains a row with the mapping of each constraint to the table and column (where applicable) whose values it limits.
sysdepends	Contains rows that define the dependencies between database objects such as views, stored procedures, and triggers, and the database objects (tables, views, and stored procedures) used in the definition of each object.
sysfilegroups	Contains one row for each filegroup in the database. Each row contains a filegroup's ID, name, and status.
sysfiles	Contains one row for each physical disk file used to store database data. The row's columns hold the file's ID, the ID of the filegroup to which it belongs, and the physical pathname, logical (database) name, status, size, maximum size, and growth rate.
sysforeignkeys	Contains one row for each FOREIGN KEY constraint on table definitions.
sysfulltextcatalogs	Lists information about each full-text index created in the database.

Table Name	Description
sysindexes	Contains one row of information for each index and table in the database.
sysindexkeys	Contains one row of mapping information for each column used in an index.
sysmembers	Contains one row with the user ID and group (role) ID for each member of a database role.
sysobjects	Contains one row with the name, ID, object type, and owner ID for each object in the database.
syspermissions	Contains one row for each permission granted or denied to users, groups, and roles for each object in the database.
sysprotects	Contains one row with the user ID, object ID, and permission granted or denied using a GRANT or DENY statement.
sysreferences	Contains one row listing the referenced columns for each FOREIGN KEY constraint.
systypes	Contains one row of information about each system-supplied and user-defined data type.
sysusers	Contains one row of information on each user, group, and role allowed to access the database.

Table 516.2 System Catalog Tables Found in Each Database

The following System Catalog tables are stored in the MSDB database for use by the SQL Server Agent.

Table Name	Description
sysalerts	Contains one row describing the alert event that causes it, users to be alerted, and the delivery method for each alert defined to the MS-SQL Server.
syscategories	List of categories used by the MS-SQL Server Enterprise Manager to organize jobs, alerts, and operators.
sysdownloadlist	Contains the list of queued download instructions for all target servers.
sysjobhistory	Contains one row with the execution results for each job executed by the MS-SQL Server Agent.
sysjobs	Contains one row with the description of each job in the MS-SQL Server Agent's job queue.
sysjobschedules	Contains one row with the scheduling information for each job to be executed by the MS-SQL Server Agent.

Table Name	Description
sysjobservers	Contains one row that defines the target server on which to run the job for each job in the MS-SQL Server Agent's job queue.
sysjobsteps	Contains one row of description information for each step in each job to be executed by the MS-SQL Server Agent.
sysnotifications	Contains one row with the alert ID, user ID to receive the alert, and delivery method for each job status notification defined on MS-SQL Server.
sysoperators	Contains one row of information about each database operator.
systargetserver-groupmembers	Contains one row with the server ID and server group ID for each target server in a multi-server group.
systargetservergroups	Contains one row with the server ID and server group ID for each target server in a multi-server group.
systargetservers	Contains one row with the name, status, and lasting poll date, time, and status for each of the target servers in each multi-server group.
systaskids	Contains one row with information that maps each task created in an earlier version of MS-SQL Server to MS-SQL Server Enterprise Manager jobs in the current version.

Table 516.3 SQL Server Agent–Specific System Catalog Tables Found Only in the MSDB Database

The following System Catalog tables are stored in the MSDB database for use by backup and restore operations.

Table Name	Description
backupfile	Contains one row of information for each file in the database and transaction log file that is backed up.
backupmediafamily	Contains one row of information about each media family used to back up data and log files. Each media family is a part of a backup set.
backupmediaset	Contains one row of information about each media set.
backupset	Contains one row of information about each backup set. Backup sets contain one or more media families.
restorefile	Contains one row for each file restored from backup, including the individual files restored when restoring all of the files in a file-group.
restorefilegroup	Contains one row for each filegroup restored from backup.
restorehistory	Contains one row of information about each restore operation executed on the MS-SQL Server.

Table 516.4 System Catalog Tables Used by Backup Operations and Found Only in the MSDB Database

517 Understanding SQL Server Backups

If you have not backed up your computer in a while, the last question you want to hear when you call the support department for an application you are running is, "When was your last backup?" While painful when it happens to you at home on your personal computer, being caught without a recent backup for a database used by multiple departments in a company can cause severe repercussions. Having to reenter a huge amount of data can be costly in terms of employee time and salaries, and it also could cost the company business as customers unable to place orders or access accurate account information take their business elsewhere.

Fortunately, all commercially available SQL servers provide several different methods you can use to protect against (or at least minimize) data loss and downtime due to equipment failure or user/application program error. These techniques range from "hot backups" that duplicate the information in the database on mirrored disks, to manual or scheduled backups that copy both database data files and transaction log files to a named backup device (either a tape drive or a disk drive file) at specific intervals during the day.

When implementing an SQL server backup scheme, keep in mind that you need to back up two different (and equally important) components of the database. First, you need to back up the database data and its objects—that is, you need to back up the physical disk file(s) in which the SQL server stores its tables, views, stored procedures, indexes, defaults, constraints, and so on. Second, you need to back up the transaction log file(s) that contains the "before" and "after" pictures of the database, stored by the SQL server as it executes transactions that change the structure of database objects or the data stored in them.

The most important things to understand when designing a backup strategy are that a backup is a snapshot of the database taken at a specific point in time, and the database's transaction log contains all of the changes made after the snapshot was taken since the last backup. Therefore, if the physical database file (the file with all of the database objects) is that large and you cannot back it up on a daily basis, then, at a minimum, back up the database file once per week and back up the transaction logs daily. In doing so, you can restore the database exactly as it was as on a specific date and time, and then restore and apply the transaction logs from the backup device, one at a time, for each day between the last backup and the day of the system failure that required you to restore the database.

One other consideration to keep in mind is that not all restore operations follow a catastrophic hardware failure. Sometimes a new program or stored procedure installed on the system causes data loss or stores invalid data values. In such instances, the problem may go unnoticed for several days (or weeks). As a result, you may want to restore the database to the way it was just before a user executed the erroneous program or stored procedure for the first time, instead of as it was when the data loss was detected. Therefore, a good backup system keeps a month (or at least two weeks) of backup sets available for restoration. By selecting the appropriate full backup and associated transaction log backups, you can then restore the database as it was at any point during the month (or the past two weeks).

518 Creating an MS-SQL Server Backup (Dump) Device

When you *back up* a database file or its transaction log file, you copy its contents to a dump device. The dump device can be either a disk file on the local system, a disk file in a folder on a network drive, or a tape device. If you use a disk file as the dump device for the backup operation, you then set up the system-wide non-SQL server backup program to copy the database dump file to tape, to another hard drive, or to whatever location you use to store and manage your system backups.

When creating a backup file for SQL server data, the most important thing to understand is that you must let the SQL server create the backup file if you want the SQL server to be able to restore the data from the backup file later. If you simply rely on your system-wide backup program to back up the SQL server files (along with the other files it backs up), you must shut down the SQL server while the backup is running. (If you run an external backup program without shutting down the SQL server, the database and transaction log files will remain "in use" and the backup file will not be able to save them to the backup device. Moreover, if you use a non-SQL server backup program to create a backup, you cannot restore the backup and apply changes from the transaction log—you will have to use the snapshot of the database as is.)

To set up an MS-SQL Server backup (dump) device, perform the following steps:

1. Start Enterprise Manager by clicking your mouse on the Windows Start button. When Windows displays the Start menu, select Programs, move your mouse pointer to the Microsoft SQL Server program group, and then click your mouse on Enterprise Manager.
2. To display the list of SQL servers, click your mouse pointer on the plus (+) to the left of Microsoft SQL Servers and then on the plus (+) to the left of SQL Server Group.
3. Click your mouse on the plus (+) to the left of the icon for the SQL server for which you want to create the backup device. For example, if you want to create a dump device for a server named MSSQL2000 running on an NT server name NVBIZNET2, click your mouse on the plus (+) to the left of the icon for NVBIZNET2\MSSQL2000. Enterprise Manager will display folders containing databases and services available on the MS-SQL Server you selected.
4. Click your mouse on the plus (+) to the left of the Management folder.

5. Right-click your mouse pointer on Backup and select New Backup Device from the pop-up menu. Enterprise Manager will display a Backup Device Properties–New Device dialog box similar to that shown in Figure 518.1

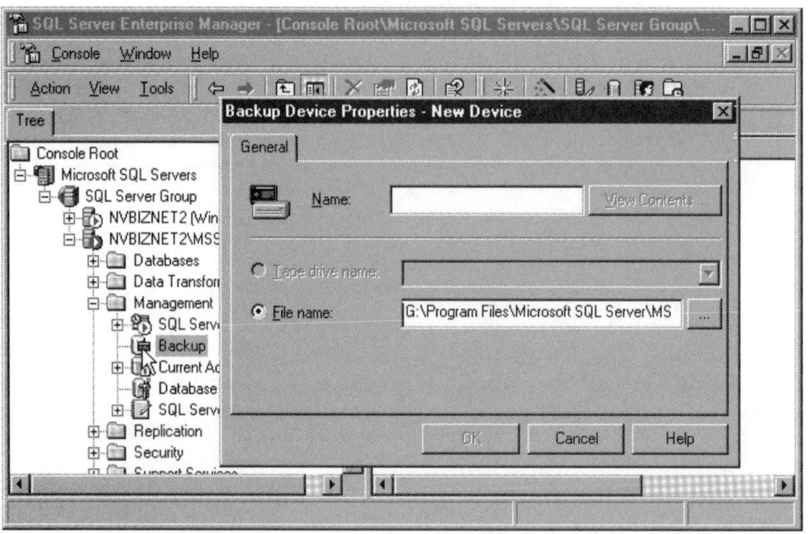

Figure 518.1 The MS-SQL Server Enterprise Manager Backup Device Properties–New Device dialog box

6. In the Name field, enter a name for the backup device. For example, if you are creating a dump device on disk so that you can use it to back up the SQLTips database every Monday, enter a file name such as **SQLTIPS-MONDAY** into the Name field.

7. To back up the database to a tape drive, click the mouse pointer on the Tape Drive Name radio button and enter the name of the tape device in the field to the right of the button. (If you do not know the name of the tape device installed on your system, click the mouse pointer on the drop-down list button to the right of the Tape Drive Name field and select the tape drive you want to use from the drop-down list of available tape drives.) Otherwise, click the mouse pointer on the File Name radio button, and enter the full pathname of the file to which you want MS-SQL Server to copy the database data during the backup operation. For example, to tell MS-SQL Server to create the SQLTIPS-MONDAY.BAK SQL Server backup file in the BACKUP subfolder of the MSSQL2000 folder on the G: drive, enter **G:\MSSQL2000\BACKUP\SQLTIPS-MONDAY.BAK** in the File Name field.

Note: *If any of the folders listed in the backup file's path name do not exist, Enterprise Manager will display a warning message box similar to that shown in Figure 518.2 when you click the mouse pointer on the OK button in Step 8.*

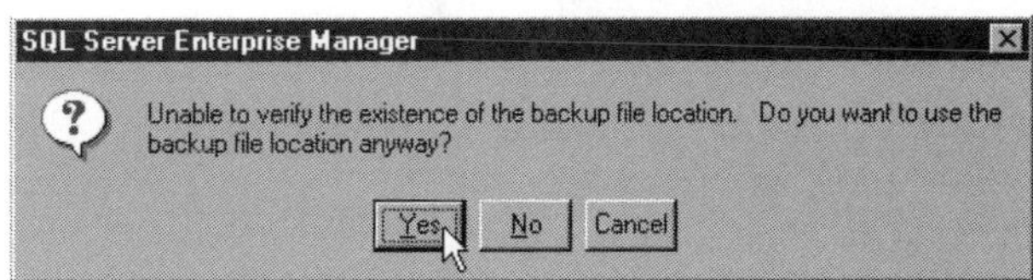

Figure 518.2 The MS-SQL Server Enterprise Manager message warning that folders in the backup device pathname do not exist or are not currently accessible

---

Note: *If you receive this error message, verify the path name that you entered. If the path name is correct, click the mouse pointer on the Yes button near the bottom center of the message box. Enterprise Manager will then go ahead and create the backup device. However, before you back up the database to the device (as you will learn to do in the next tip), you must create the folder path that you entered in Step 7. If you do not, the backup will fail and MS-SQL Server will display an error message similar to that shown in Figure 518.3.*

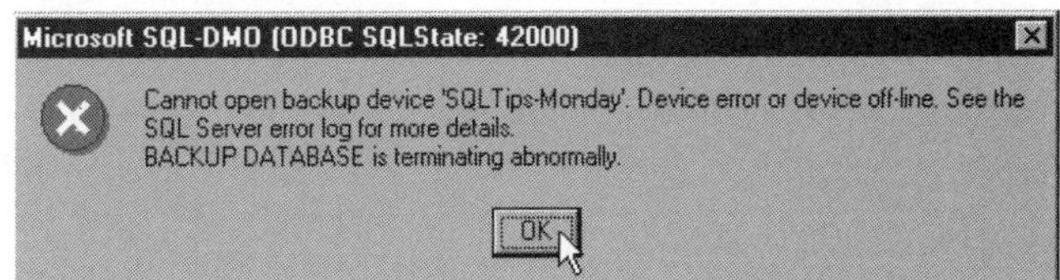

Figure 518.3 The MS-SQL Server error message displayed if the folders in the backup device is not accessible when attempting to execute an SQL file backup

---

Note: *If you receive this error message during the backup process, click the mouse pointer on the OK button at the bottom of the message box, use the Windows Explorer (or DOS command prompt) to create the folder structure you need, and then repeat the backup procedure (in the next tip).*

---

8. Click your mouse pointer on the OK button near the bottom center of the Backup Device Properties–New Device dialog box. Enterprise Manager will create and display an icon along with the name and physical location of the backup device in the right pane of the Enterprise Manager application window.

The important thing to understand now is that you must perform the steps in the preceding procedure to create a named backup (dump) device. To perform the actual SQL server backup operation, you will select the dump device that you learned to create in this tip while performing a manual SQL server backup (as you will learn in the next tip) or scheduling an automated backup (as you will learn to do in Tip 520, "Scheduling Automatic Backups of an MS-SQL Server"). As such, if you plan to make weekly full backups and daily transaction log backups, repeat the preceding procedure and then create a separate backup device for each backup that you plan to perform. For example, you would create the transaction log backup devices SQLTIPS-LOG-TUESDAY, SQLTIPS-LOG-WEDNESDAY, SQLTIPS-LOG-THURSDAY, SQLTIPS-LOG-FRIDAY, SQLTIPS-LOG-SATURDAY, and SQLTIPS-LOG-SUNDAY to be used in conjunction with the SQLTIPS-MONDAY full backup. You would then be able to back up to a different device (backup file) each day of the week.

519 Executing a Manual Backup of an MS-SQL Server Database

After you create the backup (dump) devices needed to support your backups (as you learned to do in Tip 518, "Creating an MS-SQL Server Backup [Dump] Device"), you can use the devices to perform either manual or automatic/scheduled backups. However, because business emergencies, unexpected meetings, and the demands of life in general have a way of making even the most conscientious worker forget to perform a manual backup now and again, use the manual backup process as a "backup on demand." For example, prior to installing a new application or upgrade to an existing one, perform a manual backup so that you can restore the database to the state it was in immediately before problems caused by the new software. To protect database data against accidental loss on an ongoing basis, implement an automated backup scheme (which you will learn about in Tip 520, "Scheduling Automatic Backups of an MS-SQL Server").

To execute a manual backup, perform the following steps:

1. Start the Enterprise Manager by clicking the mouse pointer on the Windows Start button and selecting Programs from the Start menu. Then move your mouse pointer onto the Microsoft SQL Server programs group, and click the mouse pointer on Enterprise Manager.
2. To display the list of SQL Servers under the Enterprise Manager's control, click your mouse pointer on the plus (+) to the left of Microsoft SQL Servers and then on the plus (+) to the left of SQL Server Group.
3. Click the mouse pointer on the icon for the SQL server with the database (or transaction log) that you want to back up. For example, if you want to back up a database on an SQL server named MSSQL2000 running on an NT Server named NVBIZNET2, click your mouse pointer on the icon to the left of NVBIZNET2\MSSQL2000. The Enterprise Manager will use its right pane to display icons for folders that contain databases and services available on the MS-SQL Server you selected.
4. Select the Tools menu Backup Database option. The Enterprise Manager will display an SQL Server Backup dialog box similar to that shown in Figure 519.1.

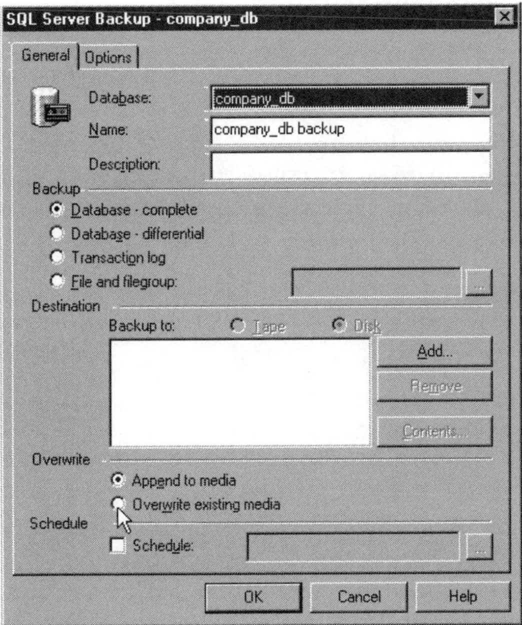

Figure 519.1 The MS-SQL Server Enterprise Manager SQL Server Backup dialog box

5. Click your mouse pointer on the drop-down list button to the right of the Database field, and select the database that you want to back up from the drop-down list. The Enterprise Manager will enter the name of the database you selected, followed by the word Backup, into the Name field. For example, if you select SQLTips from the drop-down list box below the Database field, the Enterprise Manager will enter SQLTips Backup into the Name field.
6. If you do not like the system-generated name for the backup setup, enter a new name into the Name field.
7. In the Description field, enter a description of the backup. For example, if you plan to perform a complete database backup, you might enter **Complete Backup** into the Description field. Conversely, if you are planning to back up only the database transaction log, enter a description such as **Transaction Log Backup**.
8. Click the mouse pointer on the radio button for the type of backup you want to perform. The backup options are:
   - **Database—complete:** To back up the entire database file and enough of the transaction log file to produce a consistent database if you were to restore the database from the complete backup
   - **Database—differential:** To back up only the parts of the database that have changed since the last complete backup and enough of the transaction log file to produce a consistent database if you were to restore the database using the differential backup

- **Transaction log:** To back up only the transaction log
- **File and file group:** To use the Browse button to the right of the File and Filegroup field to select the logical filegroup(s) or physical database file(s) that you want to back up

9. Use the Add and Remove buttons to the right of the Backup To list box to select the backup (dump) device that you want use. For example, if the Backup To list box contains undesired backup device(s), click the mouse pointer on the device(s) and then on the Remove button. To select the backup device that you want to use, click the mouse pointer on the Add button. The Enterprise Manager will display a Select Backup Destination dialog box similar to that shown in Figure 519.2.

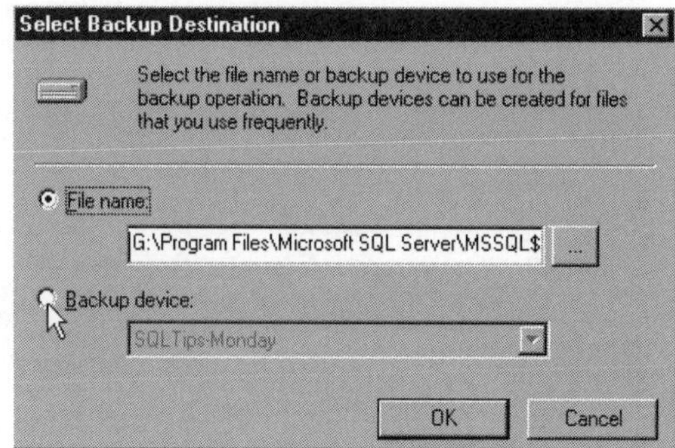

Figure 519.2 The MS-SQL Server Enterprise Manager Select Backup Destination dialog box

Either click the mouse pointer on the File Name radio button and enter that pathname of the disk file to which you want the Enterprise Manager to back up the database, or click your mouse pointer on the Backup Device radio button and select a backup (dump) device that you defined previously.

Then, click your mouse pointer on the OK button near the bottom-right corner of the Select Backup Destination dialog box.

10. If you want to keep the current contents on the backup device intact and add the new backup data to it, click the mouse pointer on the Append to Media radio button. Conversely, if you want to overwrite the existing contents on the backup device (if any) with the new backup, click the mouse pointer on the Overwrite Existing Media radio button.

Note: *Only use the "Append to media" option if you are performing a multiple database backup during a single backup session. For example, if you start the backup session with a backup of the SQLTips database, select the "Overwrite existing media" option. If you then decide to backup the MASTER database and the MSDB database to the same backup device, select the "Append to media" option when you perform the manual backup procedure for the second and third time.*

---

11. When you are satisfied with the backup specifications on the General tab, click the mouse pointer on the OK button near the bottom center of the SQL Server Backup dialog box to start the backup process.

After you complete Step 11, the Enterprise Manager will display a Backup Progress message box with a status bar that shows you how close the backup process is to completion. When the Enterprise Manager completes the backup process, it will display a "Backup operation completed successfully" message box. Click the mouse pointer on the OK button at the bottom center of the message box to return to the Enterprise Manager application window.

A manual backup provides a convenient way to see how the MS-SQL Server backup process works, how long it takes to back up a particular database (or transaction log), and the impact on performance of executing a backup while users are logged in and using the database. For a greater degree of protection from accidental data loss (because someone forgot to run the backup the day before you need it for a database restore), set up a schedule of automatic backups, as you will learn to do in the next tip.

520 Scheduling Automatic Backups of an MS-SQL Server

As mentioned in Tip 519, "Executing a Manual Backup of an MS-SQL Server Database," scheduled/automatic backups are your strongest defense against data loss due to equipment failure or the actions of errant applications or stored procedures. While the manual backup process is simple to execute, it is too often forgotten or put off "until tomorrow" because hardware has become so reliable. However, you need only experience the loss of several months worth of data one time to understand the importance of implementing a comprehensive and reliable database backup plan.

Fortunately, MS-SQL Server provides an easy way to make database backups occur automatically. After you schedule the backup jobs that you want done on a daily basis, you can rely on the server not to forget to execute a backup due to an upheaval in its "normal" workday.

Before you create the schedule of automatic backups, perform the procedure that you learned in Tip 518, "Creating an MS-SQL Server Backup [Dump] Device," as many times as necessary to create a different backup (dump) device for each of the backups that you want to schedule. If you plan to perform backups to tape, you need only a single backup device, since all backups will use to the same tape drive. (You can have the backup program vary the backup set's name to indicate the day of the week on which the MS-SQL Server Agent started it.) If you plan to perform backups to disk, however, you will want to use a different disk file for each backup session. As such, create at least seven backup (dump) devices similar to those shown in the right pane of the Enterprise Manager application window in Figure 520.1.

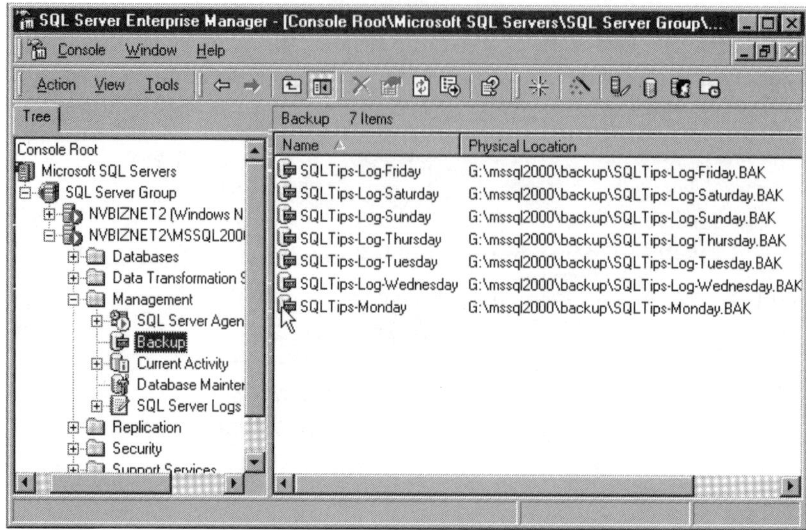

Figure 520.1 The MS-SQL Server Enterprise Manager application window with seven (daily) backup devices shown in its right pane

To create a queue of scheduled/automatic backups, perform the following steps:

1. Perform Steps 1–10 of the procedure for performing a manual backup (as detailed in Tip 519, "Executing a Manual Backup of an MS-SQL Server Database").
2. Click your mouse pointer on the Schedule check box in the Schedule section at the bottom of the SQL Server Backup dialog box until a check mark appears. Then click the mouse pointer on the Browse button to the right of the check box to display an Edit Schedule dialog box similar to that shown in Figure 520.2.

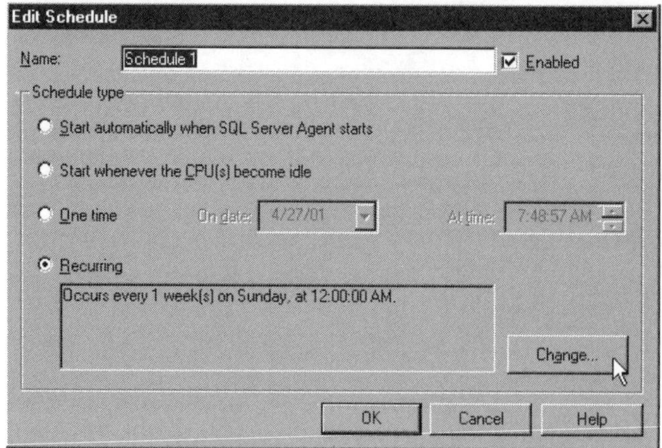

Figure 520.2 The MS-SQL Server Enterprise Manager Edit Schedule dialog box

3. Into the Name field at the top of the Edit Schedule dialog box, enter a descriptive name for the backup job. For example, if you selected the SQLTIPS-MONDAY backup device (in Step 9 of the procedure in Tip 519, "Executing a Manual Backup of an MS-SQL Server Database") and are scheduling a complete backup of the SQLTips database and transaction log files to start every Tuesday morning at 12:00 a.m., enter **Monday SQLTips Full Backup to Disk** into the Name field. Similarly, if you selected SQLTIPS-LOG-TUESDAY as the backup device (in Step 9 of the procedure in Tip 519) and are scheduling a backup of the SQLTips transaction log file(s) to start every Wednesday morning at 12:00 a.m., you might enter **Tuesday SQLTips Transaction Log Backup to Disk** into the Name field.
4. Click your mouse pointer on the Recurring radio button and then on the Change button at the lower-right corner of the Schedule Type area of the dialog box. The Enterprise Manager will display the Edit Recurring Job Schedule dialog box shown in Figure 520.3.

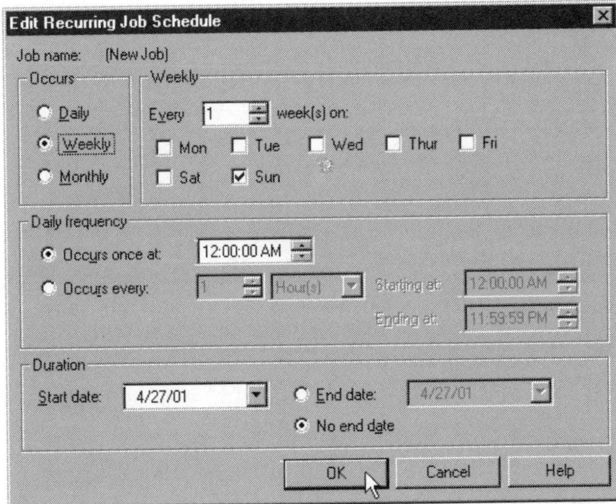

Figure 520.3 The MS-SQL Server Enterprise Manager Edit Recurring Job Schedule dialog box

5. To have the MS-SQL Server Agent execute the backup job each week, click your mouse pointer on the Weekly radio button and enter **1** into the Every Week(s) field (in the Weekly section at the top of the dialog box and to the right of the Occurs section).
6. Click the mouse pointer on the day of week that you want the backup to occur. For example, to schedule a backup to occur at 12:00 a.m. on Sunday each week, click your mouse pointer on the Sun check box until a check mark appears.
7. Click your mouse pointer on the OK button near the bottom center of the Edit Recurring Job Schedule dialog box to save the recurring schedule settings you entered and return to the Edit Schedule dialog box.
8. Click your mouse pointer on the OK button near the bottom center of the Edit Schedule dialog box to return to the SQL Server Backup dialog box.

9. Click your mouse pointer on the OK button near the bottom center of the SQL Server Backup dialog box to schedule the automatic backup by adding it to the MS-SQL Server Agent's Jobs queue and return to the Enterprise Manager's application window.

Repeat Steps 1–9 six additional times to create weekly backup jobs for each of the remaining days of the week. Each time you perform the steps in the procedure, select a different day's backup (dump) device (in Step 9 of the procedure in Tip 519) and enter an appropriate description of the backup performed into the Name field in Step 3. Be sure to click the mouse pointer on the check box next to the correct day of the week in Step 6.

Note: *If your scheduled backups use a tape device, either you or another very trustworthy person on your staff must change the backup tape in the tape drive on a daily basis. Since each day's backup will overwrite the tape's contents, the backup scheme will fail if, for example, you leave Monday's backup tape in the drive and Tuesday's transaction log backup overwrites Monday's full database backup. If you are using a disk file as the backup device, your backup scheme will work as long as you do not run out of space on the hard drive on which you told MS-SQL Server to store the backup data.*

521 Understanding How to Restore an MS-SQL Server Database

No one looks forward to a hardware or software failure. However, failures are bound to occur. Fortunately, having designed and implemented a comprehensive backup plan, you will be able to restore your SQL data and get the database back online in the shortest time possible.

Typically, restoring an MS-SQL Server to full functionality involves the following steps:

1. In case of a hard drive failure, you may have to reinstall the MS-SQL Server itself. (If you do have to install the MS-SQL Server again, you do not have to re-create its database(s)—let MS-SQL Server's Restore Database process do it for you.)

2. If it is damaged or lost, restore the Master database, which contains information about all of the other databases and database objects available on MS-SQL Server at the time of the backup.

3. If it is damaged or lost, restore the MSDB database, which contains information about alerts, backups, tasks, and the database replication scheme (if any).

4. For each database lost or damaged, restore the last complete (full) backup.

5. For each database restored in Step 4, restore the transaction log backups made since the last full backup, in sequential order.

Prior to starting a database restore operation, you must have a functional MS-SQL Server installed and running on your fileserver. Therefore, execute the MS-SQL Server installation procedure (detailed in Tip 527, "Installing the MS-SQL Server"), if necessary.

Note: *If you are restoring database data after a hard drive failure, you have to reinstall MS-SQL Server only if its program files were somehow damaged or deleted. You do not have to reinstall MS-SQL Server in order to restore a damaged or lost database file. Therefore, before reinstalling the MS-SQL Server software, check the fileserver's task list to see if MS-SQL Server is already installed and running. If MS-SQL Server is not shown in the fileserver's task list, or if its status is not Running, check with the network administrator to make sure that the MS-SQL Server that you want to use was not moved to another fileserver or taken offline for some other reason. If the MS-SQL Server is simply Stopped, you can use the MS-SQL Server Service Manager to restart it (as you learned to do in Tip 511, "Using the MS-SQL Server Service Manager to Start the MS-SQL Server").*

Next, make sure that the most recent complete (full) database backup file and any subsequent transaction log backup files are available. If you used a disk-based backup scheme to back up the MS-SQL Server to disk, restore the server's backup files from the network-wide backup system's disks as necessary. Conversely, if you used a tape-based backup scheme for MS-SQL Server backups, make sure that the tape device is available, and retrieve the MS-SQL Server backup tapes you need from storage.

After MS-SQL Server is up and running and you have the full database backup file and transaction log backup file(s) that you want to restore either on disk or on tape, perform the following steps to restore a database from a complete (full) backup file:

1. Start the Enterprise Manager by clicking the mouse pointer on the Windows Start button and selecting Programs from the Start menu. Then move your mouse pointer onto the Microsoft SQL Server programs group and click the mouse pointer on Enterprise Manager.
2. To display the list of SQL servers, click your mouse pointer on the plus (+) to the left of Microsoft SQL Servers and then on the plus (+) to the left of SQL Server Group.
3. Click the mouse pointer on the icon for the SQL server whose database(s) you want to restore. For example, if you want to restore the COMPANY_DB database on an SQL server named MSSQL2000 running on an NT server named NVBIZNET2, click your mouse pointer on the icon to the left of NVBIZNET2\MSSQL2000 in the Enterprise Manager's left pane. The Enterprise Manager will use its right pane to display icons of folders that contain a list of the databases and services available on the MS-SQL Server you selected.
4. Select the Tools menu Restore Database option. The Enterprise Manager will display a Restore Database dialog box similar to that shown in Figure 521.1.

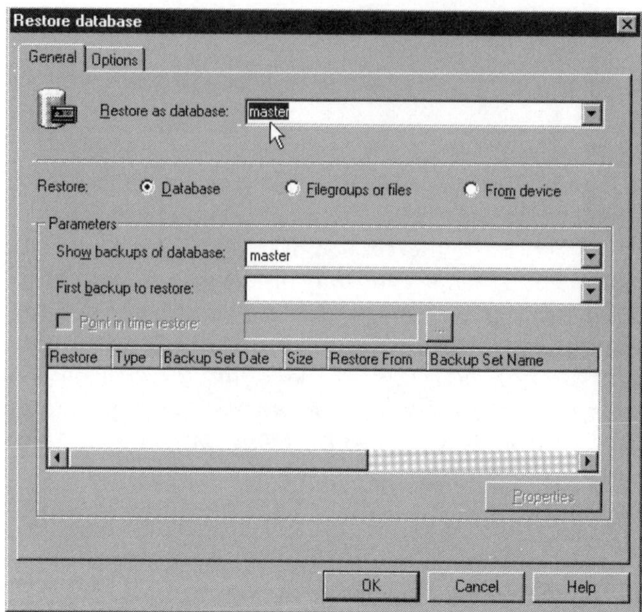

Figure 521.1 The MS-SQL Server Enterprise Manager Restore Database dialog box's General tab

5. Into the Restore As database: field, enter the logical name of the database you want to restore. Alternatively, if the database that you are planning to restore is already present on the MS-SQL Server, click the mouse pointer on the drop-down list button to the right of the Restore as Database field, and select the name of the database from the drop-down list.

Note: *If you are restoring* all *of the databases on an MS-SQL Server, make sure that you restore the MASTER database first. Next, repeat the steps in the current full backup restore procedure to restore the MSDB database. Then install any user-created databases. Be careful that you do not restore a user-created database such as SQLTips or COMPANY_DB as the MASTER database by accepting the default database name in the Restore to Database field.*

---

6. Click the mouse pointer on the From Device radio button in the Restore section of the dialog box. The Enterprise Manager will display the Restore from Device options in the Parameters section of the dialog box, similar to that shown in Figure 521.2.

7. Click the mouse pointer on the Select Devices button to the right of the Device scroll box in the middle of the dialog box. The Enterprise Manager will display a Choose Restore Devices dialog box similar to that shown in Figure 521.3.

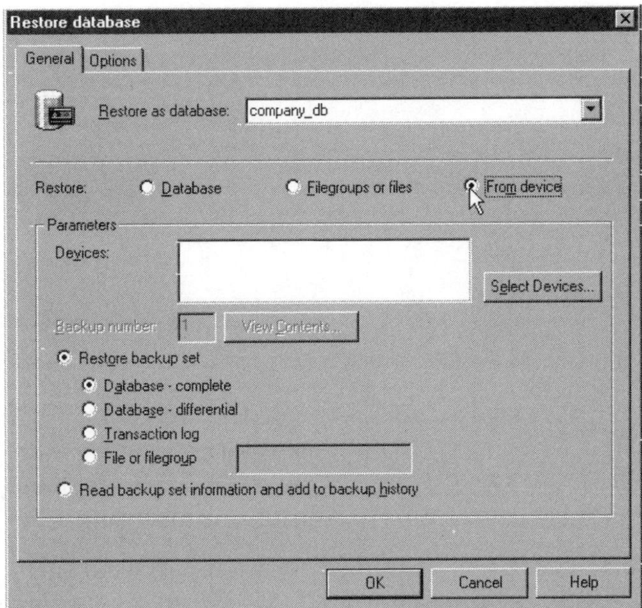

Figure 521.2 The MS-SQL Server Enterprise Manager Restore Database dialog box's General tab, with Restore from Device options displayed

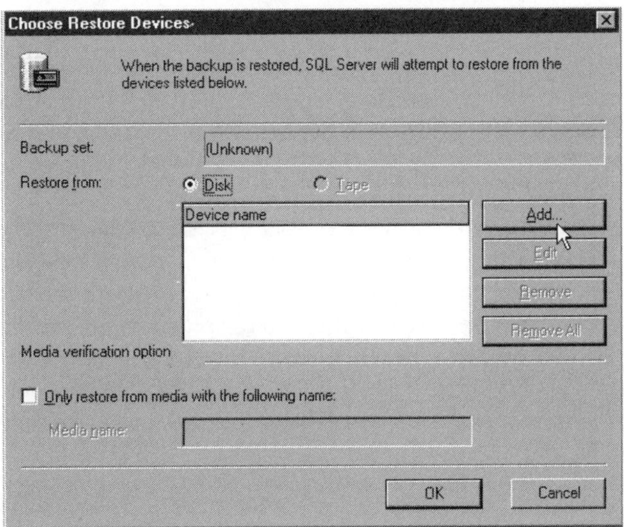

Figure 521.3 The MS-SQL Server Enterprise Manager Choose Restore Devices dialog box

8. Click your mouse pointer on the Disk radio button and then on the Add button in the Restore from Set section in the middle of the dialog box. The Enterprise Manager will display a Choose Restore Destination dialog box similar to that shown in Figure 521.4.

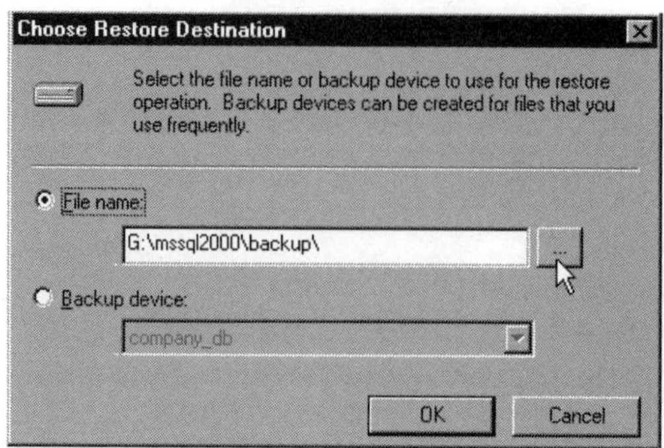

Figure 521.4 The MS-SQL Server Enterprise Manager Choose Restore Destination dialog box

9. Click your mouse pointer on the File Name radio button. Then enter the full pathname of the MS-SQL Server backup file into the File Name field. Alternatively, use the Browse button to the right of the File Name field to navigate to the folder with the backup file and then double-click the mouse pointer on the backup file's name.
10. Click the mouse pointer on the OK button near the bottom-right corner of the Choose Restore Destination dialog box to return to the Choose Restore Devices dialog box.
11. If the backup that you want to restore is stored in multiple files, repeat Steps 8–10 as necessary.
12. Click your mouse pointer on the OK button near the bottom-right side of the Choose Restore Devices dialog box to return to the Restore Database dialog box.
13. Click your mouse pointer on the Restore Backup Set radio button and then on the Database—Complete radio button in the lower half of the dialog box.
14. Click your mouse pointer on the Options tab to expose the fields shown in Figure 521.5.
15. Review the file locations to which the restore process will write the physical database base and transaction log files in the Restore Database Files As scroll box in the center of the Options tab. By default, the Enterprise Manager will restore the backup file's contents to the same folders they were in when the Enterprise Manager executed the complete (full) database backup procedure. If you need to change the physical location of any of the files in the database, click your mouse pointer on the file's current location in the Move to Physical File Name column of the scroll box, and replace the existing file location with the one you want to use.
16. If you have transaction log files that you need to restore after you restore the full backup file, click your mouse pointer on the Leave Database Nonoperational but Able to Restore Additional Transaction Logs radio button. This will prevent users from logging into the database before you have finished restoring it from the full backup file and the transaction log file backup file(s) made subsequent to the full backup.

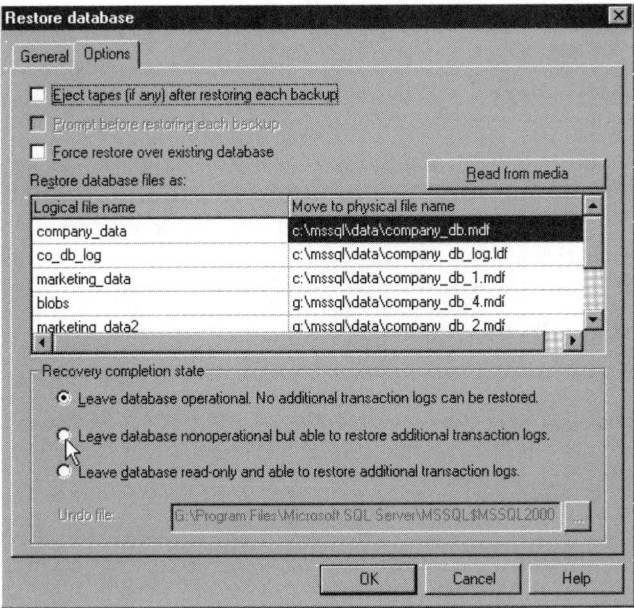

Figure 521.5 The MS-SQL Server Enterprise Manager Restore Database dialog box's Options tab

17. Click your mouse pointer on the OK button near the bottom center of the Restore Database dialog box. The Enterprise Manager will start the complete database backup file restoration process and display a Restore Progress message box shown in Figure 521.6 to keep you informed as to the status of the restore operation.

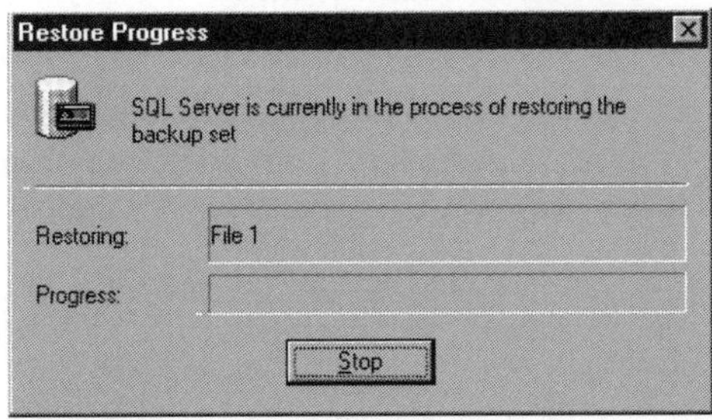

Figure 521.6 The MS-SQL Server Enterprise Manager Restore Progress message box

When the Enterprise manager is finished restoring the database from the backup file, the program will display a "Restore Completed Successfully" message box. When you see the message box, click the mouse pointer on its OK button.

After you restore the database from the complete (full) backup file, you need to apply the changes to the database stored in the transaction log backup files created subsequent to the full database backup file. To restore and apply changes from a transaction log backup file, perform the following steps:

1. Click the mouse pointer on the icon for the SQL server with the database whose transaction log file backup(s) you want to restore. For example, if you want to restore transaction log backup files for the COMPANY_DB database on an SQL server named MSSQL2000 running on an NT server named NVBIZNET2, click your mouse pointer on the icon to the left of NVBIZNET2\MSSQL2000 in the Enterprise Manager's left pane. The Enterprise Manager will use its right pane to display folders containing databases and services available on the MS-SQL Server that you selected.
2. Select the Tools menu's Restore Database option. The Enterprise Manager will display a Restore Database dialog box similar to that shown (previously) in Figure 521.1.
3. Click the mouse pointer on the drop-down list button to the right of the Restore as Database field, and select the name of the database whose transaction log you want to restore from drop-down list.
4. Click the mouse pointer on the From Device radio button in the Restore section of the dialog box. The Enterprise Manager will display the Restore from Device options in the Parameters section of the dialog box, similar to that shown (previously) in Figure 521.2.
5. Click the mouse pointer on the Select Devices button to the right of the Device scroll box in the middle of the dialog box. The Enterprise Manager will display a Choose Restore Devices dialog box similar to that shown (previously) in Figure 521.3.
6. Click your mouse pointer on the Disk radio button and then on the Add button in the Restore from Set section in the middle of the dialog box. The Enterprise Manager will display a Choose Restore Destination dialog box similar to that shown (previously) in Figure 521.4.
7. Click your mouse pointer on the Backup Device radio button. Then click the mouse pointer on the drop-down list button to the right of the Backup Device field, and select the backup (dump) device that you used to create the transaction log backup file.
8. Click the mouse pointer on the OK button near the bottom-right corner of the Choose Restore Destination dialog box to return to the Choose Restore Devices dialog box.
9. If the transaction log backup that you want to restore is stored in multiple files, repeat Steps 6–8 as necessary.
10. Click your mouse pointer on the OK button near the bottom-right side of the Choose Restore Devices dialog box to return to the Restore Database dialog box.
11. Click your mouse pointer on the Restore Backup Set radio button and then on the Transaction Log radio button in the lower half of the dialog box.
12. Click your mouse pointer on the Options tab to expose the fields shown (previously) in Figure 521.5.

13. Look at the contents of the Restore Database Files As scroll box in the center of the Options tab to verify the validity of the file locations in which the restore process will look for the existing physical database and transaction log files that it is to update. By default, the Enterprise Manager will restore the transaction log backup file(s) to the same folder(s) they were in when the Enterprise Manager executed the transaction log backup. If you changed the physical location of the database or transaction log files when you restored the complete database backup file, make the same changes in the Move to Physical File Name column now.
14. If you have additional transaction log files that you need to restore after restoring the current transaction log backup file, click the mouse pointer on the Leave Database Nonoperational but Able to Restore Additional Transaction Logs radio button.
15. Click your mouse pointer on the OK button near the bottom center of the Restore Database dialog box. The Enterprise Manager will start the transaction log backup file restoration process and display a Restore Progress message box shown (previously) in Figure 521.6 to keep you informed as to the status of the restore operation.

After the Enterprise Manager has finished restoring the transaction log from the backup file, it will display a "Restore completed successfully" message box. When you see the message box, click the mouse pointer on its OK button.

In addition to restoring the physical transaction log file, the restore process updates the database by executing the transactions stored in the transaction log file. As such, when you finish the transaction log backup file-restoration process, the database will look as it did when MS-SQL Server performed the transaction log backup.

Repeat the transaction log restore procedure as often as necessary in order to restore all of the transaction log backup files created subsequent to the full database backup. When you perform the steps in the procedure to restore the final transaction log backup file, be sure to select the Leave Database Operational, No Additional Transaction Logs Can Be Restored radio button in Step 14.

522 Understanding MS-SQL Server Optimizer Hints

When you submit an SQL statement to the MS-SQL Server for execution, the database management system (DBMS) sends the statement to its query optimizer. The query optimizer analyzes the statement and generates the execution plan (i.e., the sequence of steps) the DBMS will perform in order to execute the statement. By adding one or more *optimizer hints* to an SQL statement, you can change the data retrieval methods and locking mechanisms the query optimizer will include in the statement's execution plan. In short, when you add optimizer hints to a statement, you are doing a portion of the query optimizer's job by deciding the most efficient way to retrieve data from the database or to issue locks in order to prevent deletion and modification anomalies.

For example, without optimizer hints, the query optimizer might decide against using an index when executing a SELECT statement, because the query only returns a small number of rows. It would be faster to retrieve the data only from the table (vs. the table and the index). Similarly, if a table has more than one index and the query optimizer decides it should use one of them when retrieving data from the table, the optimizer will select the index that it thinks will result in the fastest retrieval of data to satisfy the query. In both cases, you could add an optimizer hint to the query to force the query optimizer to use a particular index in its execution plan, thereby return a set of rows sorted in ascending order by the columns in the index you select.

You can also use optimizer hints to control the system's lock behavior when executing a DELETE, INSERT, SELECT, or UPDATE statement. For example, adding the WITH NOLOCK hint to a SELECT statement tells the DBMS to read data currently locked by other users (including inserted or updated and yet uncommitted data). Similarly, adding the WITH HOLDLOCK optimizer hint tells the DBMS to prevent others from modifying data in rows returned by your SELECT statement until the end of the current transaction.

Table 522.1 lists the optimizer hints available on an MS-SQL Server and a description of each hint.

Optimizer Hint	***Description***
FAST x	Optimize the query for fast retrieval of "x" rows. After returning the first "x" rows, query execution will continue to produce a full-results set.
HOLDLOCK	Hold a shared lock until the end of a transaction instead of releasing the lock on the row, table, or data page after reading its data. Using HOLDLOCK is similar to setting the transaction isolation level to SERIALIZABLE (Tip 357).
INDEX = x	Use INDEX "x" when selecting rows.
INDEX (<index number list>)	Use the indexes in the order specified when selecting rows.
NOLOCK	Do not issue shared locks and do not honor exclusive locks. NOLOCK is only applicable to the SELECT statement, and makes it possible for the query to read data from uncommitted UPDATE and DELETE statements that might be rolled back before the end of the query.
PAGLOCK	Use page-level locks to lock data in a table a page at a time instead of using a row-level lock or a table-level lock.

Optimizer Hint	***Description***
READCOMMITTED	Scan the rows in a table using the semantics of the READ COMMITTED transaction isolation level (Tip 360).
READPAST	Skip rows locked by other transactions instead of waiting for those transactions to release their locks before completing the query. READPAST is only applicable to a SELECT statement operating at the READ COMMITTED transaction isolation level (Tip 359), and will only skip over row level locks.
READUNCOMITTED	Equivalent to executing a SELECT statement with the NOLOCK optimizer hint or at the READ UNCOMMITTED transaction isolation level (Tip 360).
REPEATABLEREAD	Scan the rows in a table using the semantics of the REPEATABLE READ transaction isolation level (Tip 358).
ROWLOCK	Use row-level locks to lock data in a table a row at a time instead of using a page-level lock or a table-level lock.
SERIALIZABLE	Equivalent to executing a statement at the SERIALIZABLE transaction isolation level (Tip 357).
TABLOCK	Issue a table-level lock that locks the entire table instead of using a row-level lock or a page-level lock.
TABLOCKX	Issue an exclusive (vs. the default, shared) table-level lock, that locks the entire table instead of using a row-level lock or a page-level lock. Executing a statement with the TABLOCKX optimizer hint prevents other transactions from reading or updating the data in an entire table.
UPDLOCK	Use update locks instead of shared locks when reading the data in a table. An update lock lets others read data read by your transaction, but prevents them from updating the data until your transaction ends and releases its update locks.
XLOCK	Issue-exclusive (vs. shared or update) locks. Exclusive locks prevent others from accessing data read by your transaction until your transaction ends and releases the exclusive locks it issued.

Table 522.1 MS-SQL Server Optimizer Hints

Use a WITH or OPTION clause to introduce one or more optimizer hints into SQL statements as follows:

```
DELETE [FROM] <table name> WITH (<optimizer hints>) ...
          or
DELETE [FROM] <table name>
       [<WHERE clause>] OPTION (<optimizer hints>)

INSERT [INTO] <table name> WITH (<optimizer hints>) ...

SELECT <query expression> [<ORDER BY clause>]
       [<COMPUTE clause>] [<FOR clause>]
       OPTION (<optimizer hints>)

UPDATE <table name> WITH (<optimizer hints>) ...
          or
UPDATE <table name> [<FROM clause>]
       OPTION (<optimizer hints>)
```

When choosing optimizer hints in an effort to increase the efficiency of a query, you will find it helpful to review the list of instructions in the execution plan that the query optimizer generates. If you find a costly step such as full table scans, you can create new INDEXES or perhaps use an optimizer hint that directs the optimizer to use an existing index to eliminate the step.

If you execute a query after turning on the MS-SQL Server's SHOWPLAN_TEXT option (which you will learn about in Tip 523), the DBMS will display the steps that the query optimizer generated for the SELECT statement's execution plan. After you look through the plan, you can try executing the same query with different sets of optimizer hints until the query optimizer generates an execution plan more to your liking.

523 Using the MS-SQL Server SHOWPLAN_TEXT Option to Display a Statement's Execution Plan

As mentioned in Tip 522 "Understanding MS-SQL Server Optimizer Hints," when you submit an SQL statement to the MS-SQL Server for execution, the DBMS sends the statement to the query optimizer, which, in turn, generates the statement's execution plan. (An *execution plan* is the sequence of steps the query optimizer tells the DBMS is to perform in order to execute a statement.)

When you tell the MS-SQL Server to execute a statement, you are normally interested only in the statement's results and not in *how* the DBMS produced them. For example, when you submit the query

```
SELECT a.au_lname, a.au_fname, t.title, t.ytd_sales
FROM authors a, titles t, titleauthor ta
WHERE a.au_id = t.au_ID AND t.title_ID = ta.title_ID
```

to the DBMS, you want the SQL server to return a list of author names, book titles, and sales figures. However, you really do not care how the DBMS retrieves the information from its tables. As such, the DBMS hides the execution plan from view.

However, if you are trying to improve a statement's performance, you will want to see the steps the DBMS must perform in order to execute it. When optimizing a SELECT statement, for example, you definitely want to know if the DBMS must perform a full-table scan when executing the query. Because reading every row in a large table usually makes executing a query take an unacceptably long time, the DBMS only performs a full-table scan if it cannot use any existing indexes to retrieve the data in the manner requested. Therefore, seeing a full-table scan in the query's execution plan would tell you that it might be possible to create an INDEX that will reduce the query's execution time.

You can use the MS-SQL Server's SHOWPLAN_TEXT option (and the SHOWPLAN_ALL option discussed in Tip 524), to tell the DBMS to show you what it plans to do "behind the scenes" when executing the SQL statements in a statement batch. One important thing to understand is that after you turn on the SHOWPLAN_TEXT option by submitting the SET statement

```
SET SHOWPLAN_TEXT ON
```

to the MS-SQL Server for execution, the DBMS will display the execution plan for each of the statements you submit to the DBMS. However, the DBMS will not actually *execute* any of the statements you submit until you turn off the SHOWPLAN_TEXT option by executing the SET statement

```
SET SHOWPLAN_TEXT OFF
```

For example, if you execute the SET statement

```
SET SHOWPLAN_TEXT ON
```

and then submit the statement batch shown in the upper pane in Figure 523.1, the DBMS will return a results set with the text of the statements in the batch, followed by the results set shown in the results (lower) pane in Figure 523.1.

When you are finished reviewing execution plans for SQL statements you are trying to optimize, execute the SET statement

```
SET SHOWPLAN_TEXT OFF
```

to tell the DBMS to stop displaying execution plans and resume the normal execution of statements you submit to the server.

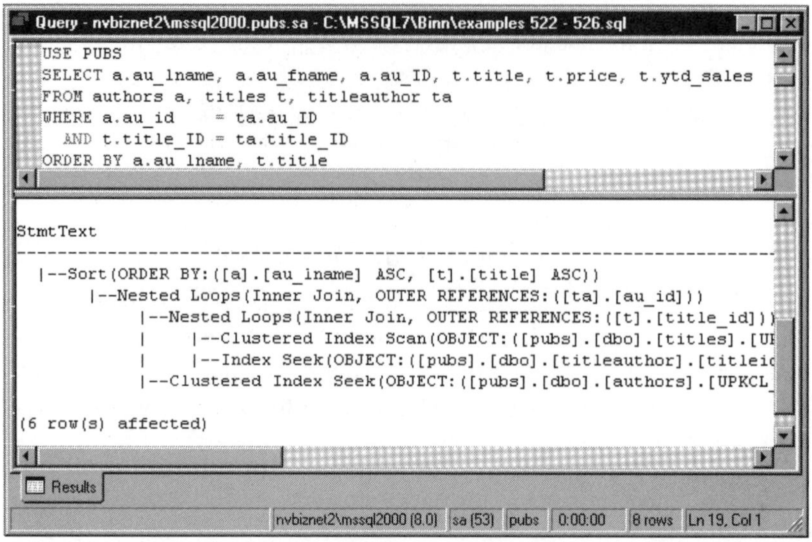

Query - nvbiznet2\mssql2000.pubs.sa - C:\MSSQL7\Binn\examples 522 - 526.sql

```
USE PUBS
SELECT a.au_lname, a.au_fname, a.au_ID, t.title, t.price, t.ytd_sales
FROM authors a, titles t, titleauthor ta
WHERE a.au_id    = ta.au_ID
  AND t.title_ID = ta.title_ID
ORDER BY a.au_lname, t.title
```

```
StmtText
---------------------------------------------------------------------------
  |--Sort(ORDER BY:([a].[au_lname] ASC, [t].[title] ASC))
       |--Nested Loops(Inner Join, OUTER REFERENCES:([ta].[au_id]))
            |--Nested Loops(Inner Join, OUTER REFERENCES:([t].[title_id]))
            |    |--Clustered Index Scan(OBJECT:([pubs].[dbo].[titles].[UF
            |    |--Index Seek(OBJECT:([pubs].[dbo].[titleauthor].[titleic
            |--Clustered Index Seek(OBJECT:([pubs].[dbo].[authors].[UPKCL_

(6 row(s) affected)
```

Results | nvbiznet2\mssql2000 (8.0) | sa (53) | pubs | 0:00:00 | 8 rows | Ln 19, Col 1

Figure 523.1 The MS-SQL Server SQL Query Analyzer results after submitting a query with SHOWPLAN_TEXT set on

524 Understanding the MS-SQL Server SHOWPLAN_ALL Option for Displaying Statement Execution Plans and Statistics

To construct a statement's execution plan, the MS-SQL Server's query optimizer uses statistical information that the server stores with database tables and indexes to evaluate alternative ways in which to execute the statement. For example, when you submit a SELECT statement with an ORDER BY clause, the query optimizer will check to see if the database has an index it can use to satisfy the sort requirements of the clause, or if it must add the step of physically sorting the rows it retrieves them from the table(s) involved in the query. In short, the query optimizer attempts to create a "least cost" (i.e., most efficient) execution plan for each SQL statement you submit to the MS-SQL Server for execution.

In Tip 523 "Using the MS-SQL Server SHOWPLAN_TEXT Option to Display a Statement's Execution Plan," you learned how to set the SHOWPLAN_TEXT option to "on" so that the DBMS would show you the execution plan for statements you told it to execute. Setting the MS-SQL Server's SHOWPLAN_ALL option to "on" also tells the DBMS to display statement execution plans rather than actually executing the statements. However, in addition to displaying the steps in an execution plan, the SHOWPLAN_ALL option also provides the data shown in Table 524.1 (as applicable) for each step.

Column Name	***Description***
StmtText	Contains the text of the Transact-SQL statement for rows that are **not** of type PLAN_ROW. For rows of type PLAN_ROW, this contains a description of the operation involved that includes a physical operator (such as "Index Seek" or "Clustered Index Scan"), and perhaps a logical operator, such as "Compute Scalar" or "Stream Aggregate."
StmtID	The number of the statement in the current connection. For example, if you are using the SQL Query Analyzer to execute SQL statements and this is the fifteenth statement you have submitted to the server, StmtID will have a value of 15.
NodeID	ID of the node in the current step. (A single step may consist of multiple physical database operations or nodes.)
ParentID	Node ID of the current step's parent step.
PhysicalOp	Physical database operation performed in the node.
LogicalOp	The logical and relational algebraic operation represented by the physical operation performed in the node.
Argument	Additional information about the physical database operation performed in the node.
DefinedValues	Contains a comma-separated list of values introduced by the operation that is performed in this node. The values may be computed expressions or internal values the query operator needs to process the query. Once introduced, defined values may be referenced elsewhere within the statement.
EstimateRows	An estimate of the number of rows of output the current operator will generate.
EstimateIO	Estimated input/output cost of the current operation.
EstimateCPU	Estimated CPU cost of the current operation.
AvgRowSize	Estimated average number of bytes of data in each row passed through the current operator.
TotalSubtreeCost	Estimated total cost of the current operation and all of its child operations.
OutputList	Contains a comma-separated list of columns projected by the current operation.
Warnings	Contains a comma-separated list of warning messages relating to the current operation. The query optimizer issues a warning message each time it has to make a decision based on a column for which it has no data.
Type	Contains the Transact-SQL statement type for a parent node and PLAN_ROW for nodes in the execution plan.

Column Name	Description
Parallel	Zero (0) if the operator is not running in parallel or one (1) if it is.
Estimated Executions	Estimated number of times this operation will be executed in the current statement.

Table 524.1 Columns in each row of the SHOWPLAN_ALL execution plan results set

As was the case with the SHOWPLAN_TEXT option, you must execute the SET statement:

```
SET SHOWPLAN_TEXT OFF
```

when you are finished reviewing execution plans for SQL statements and want the DBMS to stop displaying execution plans and resume the normal execution of SQL statements you submit.

525 Using MS-SQL Server SQL Query Analyzer SHOWPLAN Options

In addition to generating a text-based results sets with execution-plan information, the MS-SQL Server SQL Query Analyzer also lets you display execution plans graphically. In Tips 523 and 524, you learned how to use the statements SET SHOWPLAN_TEXT ON and SET SHOWPLAN_ALL ON. These statements are used so the DBMS returns the query optimizer-generated execution plans for SQL statements instead of executing the statements and returning their results sets.

When you submit an SQL statement with SHOWPLAN_TEXT ON or SHOWPLAN_ALL ON to the MS-SQL Server for execution, the DBMS returns an execution plan which lists the steps it *would* perform if it were to execute the statement. The DBMS returns the execution plan as rows of column values in a table—just like it would return the results set generated by a statement executed by the server. As such, with SHOWPLAN_TEXT or SHOWPLAN_ALL set to on, you can type an SQL statement batch in the SQL Query Analyzer's query (top) pane, select the Query menu Execute option, and review the statement's execution plan in the SQL Query Analyzer's results (bottom) pane.

You can also use the MS-SQL Server's SQL Query Analyzer to display a statement's execution plan graphically by performing the following steps:

1. Start the SQL Query Analyzer by clicking your mouse pointer on the Windows Start button. When Windows displays the Start menu, move your mouse pointer to Programs, select Microsoft SQL Server 2000, then click your mouse pointer on Query Analyzer. Windows, in turn, will start the SQL Query Analyzer, which will display the Connect to SQL Server dialog box.

2. Use the drop-down list button to the right of the SQL Server field at the top of the dialog box to select the SQL Server that you wish to login. Enter your username and password into the Login name and Password fields. Then, click the mouse pointer on the OK button near the bottom center of the dialog box to complete the login process.

3. Use the drop-down list button (sixth button from the right) on the SQL Query Analyzer's Standard toolbar to select the database with which you wish to work. For the current project, select **PUBS**.

4. Enter the SQL statement whose execution plan you want to see into the query pane at the top of the SQL Query Analyzer's application window. For the current project, enter **SELECT * FROM authors ORDER BY au_lname.**

Note: *If you type more than one statement into the query pane, you can generate an execution plan for all of the statements as a "statement batch." Conversely, if you only want to generate the execution plan for one of several statements in the query pane, use the mouse pointer to select the statement whose execution plan you want to see before you perform Step 6.*

---

5. To display the execution plan for the statement (or statement batch) in the SQL Query Analyzer's query pane without executing the statement, select the Query menu Display Estimated Execution Plan option. The SQL Query Analyzer will use its results (bottom) pane to display the execution plan for the statement (or statement batch) in query (top) pane, similar to that shown in Figure 525.1.

Note: *If you want the SQL Query Analyzer to submit both the statement (or statement batch) in the query pane to the DBMS for execution and display the execution plan, select the Query menu Show Execution Plan option. Unfortunately, the SQL Query Analyzer will not open a second results pane so you can see query results as well as the execution plan. Therefore, if you enter a SELECT statement into the query pane and select the Query menu Show Execution Plan option, the SQL Query Analyzer will ask the DBMS to execute the query. Keep in mind, however, that you will only see an execution plan (and not the query's results set) onscreen.*

Each of the icons displayed in the graphics-execution plan in the results pane represents a step in the plan. When you move your mouse pointer over an icon, the SQL Query Analyzer will display the values for several of the SHOWPLAN_ALL columns (explained in Table 524.1) for that step in the plan, similar to that shown in Figure 525.2.

Similarly, if you move the mouse pointer over an arrow between icons, the SQL Query Analyzer will display the estimated number or rows passed from one step to the next along with the estimated average byte length of each row passed.

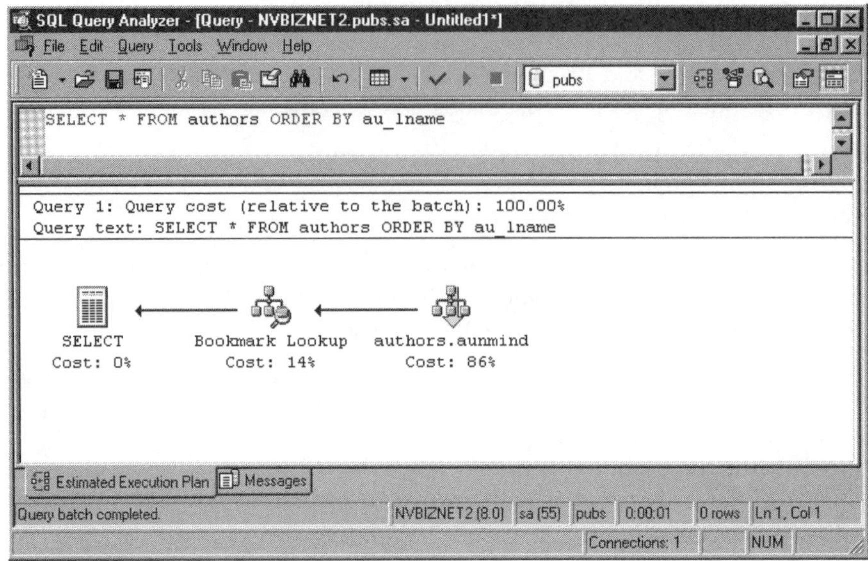

Figure 525.1 The SQL Query Analyzer's graphical display of a statement execution plan

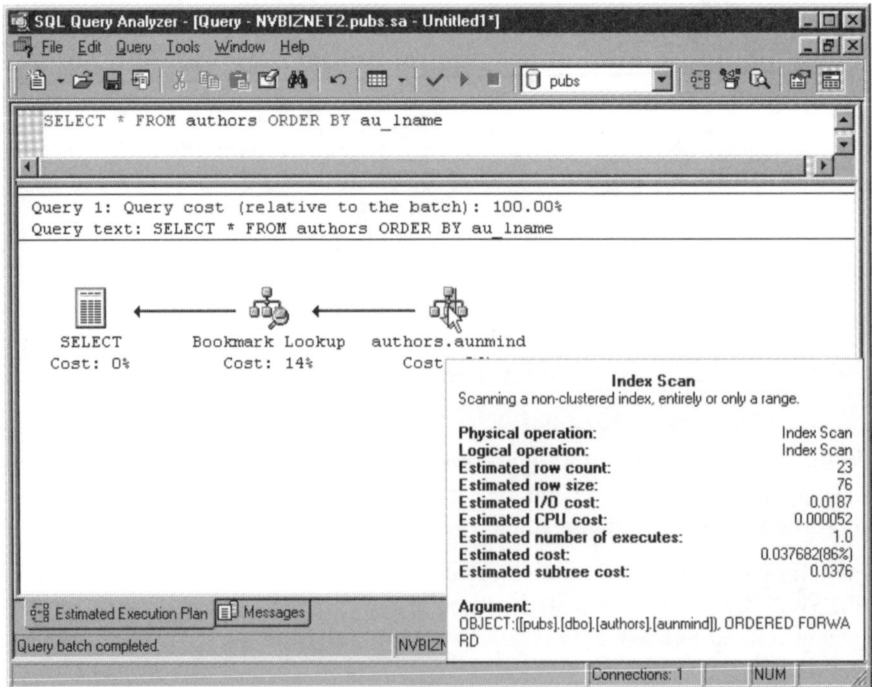

Figure 525.2 The SQL Query Analyzer's graphical execution plan detail

526 Understanding MS-SQL Server 2000 Hardware and Operating System Requirements

Before you install the MS-SQL Server 2000 on your computer, make sure your system meets the minimum hardware requirements for the edition of the MS-SQL Server you are about to install.

At a minimum, to install and run the MS-SQL Server 2000, you need:

- A personal computer (PC) with an Intel Pentium or compatible processor running at 166-Megahertz (or higher).
- 64 megabytes of memory (minimum); 128 megabytes of memory (recommended). You will need a minimum of 32 megabytes to run the Personal Edition or Desktop Engine under any version of Windows other than Windows 2000, which requires at least 64 megabytes of memory.
- 95 to 270 megabytes of available disk space for the core MS-SQL Server software with a typical installation using 250 megabytes. If you are installing the Desktop Engine, you will need 44 megabytes of available disk space.
- 50 megabytes of available disk space for the Analysis Services with a typical installation using 130 megabytes. Installing the Analysis Services is optional.
- 80 megabytes of available disk space for the Microsoft English Query support. Installing the Microsoft English Query support is optional.
- A CD-ROM drive.
- VGA or higher resolution monitor.
- You can run the MS-SQL Server 2000 Enterprise Edition and Standard Edition under Windows NT Server version 4.0 with Service Pack 5 (SP5) or later; Windows NT Server 4.0 Enterprise Edition with Service Pack 5 (SP5) or later; Windows 2000 Server; Windows 2000 Advanced Server; or Windows 2000 Datacenter Server.
- You can run the MS-SQL Server 2000 Evaluation Edition and Developer Edition under the same operating systems as the Enterprise and Standard Editions plus Windows 2000 Professional and Windows NT Workstation 4.0 with Service Pack 5 (SP5) or later.
- You can run the MS-SQL Server 2000 Personal Edition and the Desktop Engine under the same operating systems as the Enterprise and Standard Editions plus Windows 98, Windows ME, Windows 2000 Professional, and Windows NT Workstation 4.0 with Service Pack (SP5) or later.
- To install and use the MS-SQL Server 2000's Internet tools, you will need to install Microsoft Internet Explorer (IE) version 5.0 or later

Note: The MS-SQL is available in several editions: Enterprise Edition, Standard Edition, Evaluation Edition, Developer Edition, Personal Edition, and Desktop Engine. Please visit the MS-SQL Server 2000 area on the Microsoft Web site (www.microsoft.com/sql) for detailed product information about each edition. Then you can select the one that best satisfies your needs.

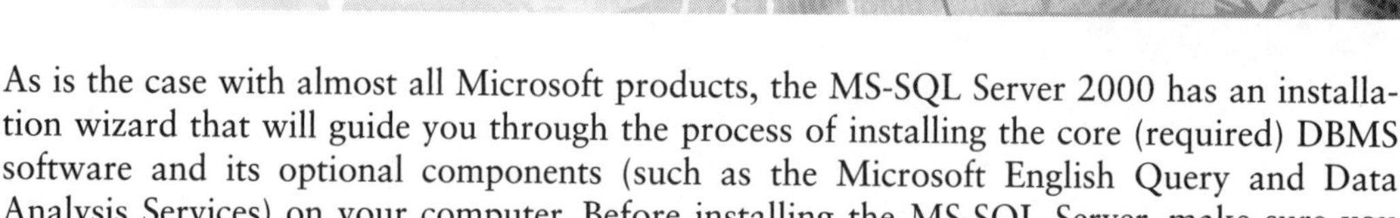

527 Installing the MS-SQL Server

As is the case with almost all Microsoft products, the MS-SQL Server 2000 has an installation wizard that will guide you through the process of installing the core (required) DBMS software and its optional components (such as the Microsoft English Query and Data Analysis Services) on your computer. Before installing the MS-SQL Server, make sure you computer meets the minimum requirements (detailed in Tip 526).

To install the MS-SQL Server, perform the following steps:

1. Insert the MS-SQL Server 2000 installation CD-ROM. Windows starts the installation program, which displays a Welcome screen, similar to that shown in Figure 527.1. If you do not have the CD-ROM AutoPlay enabled on your system, use the Windows explorer to navigate to your CD-ROM drive and double-click the mouse pointer on AUTORUN.EXE.
2. Click the mouse pointer on SQL Server 2000 Prerequisites. The installation program checks for operating system (OS) patches, external support programs (such as Internet Explorer), and other DLL files you need to install before MS-SQL Server will run successfully on your computer. Follow the installation program's instructions for installing any required software or OS patches. The install program may ask you to reboot the computer before allowing you to continue at Step 3.
3. Click the mouse pointer on Select SQL Server 2000 Components. The installation program will ask you which of three MS-SQL Server components you want to install. Your choices are:
   - **Install Database Server**—The MS-SQL Server 2000 DBMS.
   - **Install Analysis Services**—OLAP (online analytical processing) and data mining tools.
   - **Install English Query**—Tools to develop applications that let users query by posing questions in English instead of putting the questions in the form of SQL statements.
4. Click the mouse pointer on Install Database Server to install the MS-SQL Server 2000 DBMS. The installation program will start the MS-SQL Server 2000 installation wizard, which displays a Welcome screen.

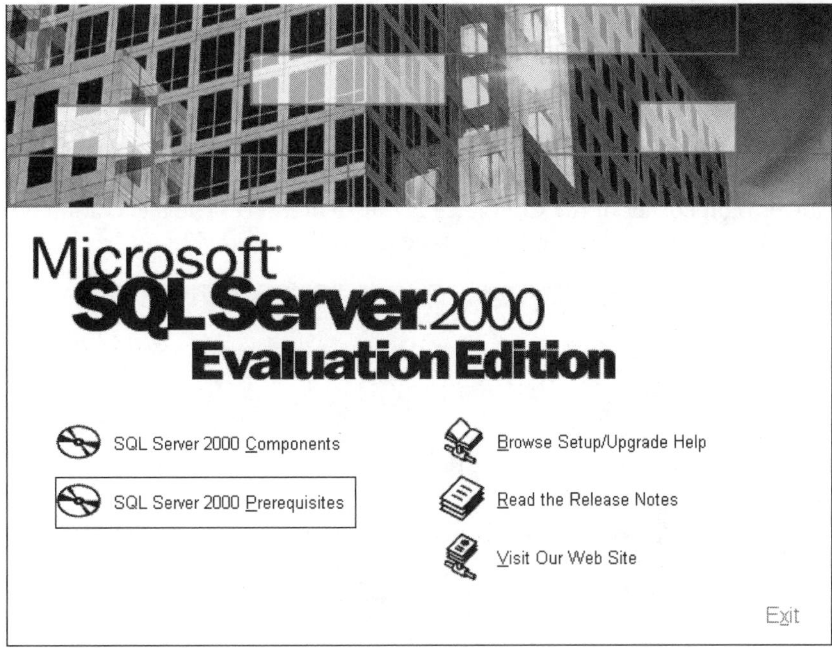

Figure 527.1 The MS-SQL Server Installation Welcome screen

5. Click the mouse pointer on the Next button near the lower right corner of the installation wizard's Welcome screen. The installation wizard displays a Computer Name dialog box similar to that shown in Figure 527.2.

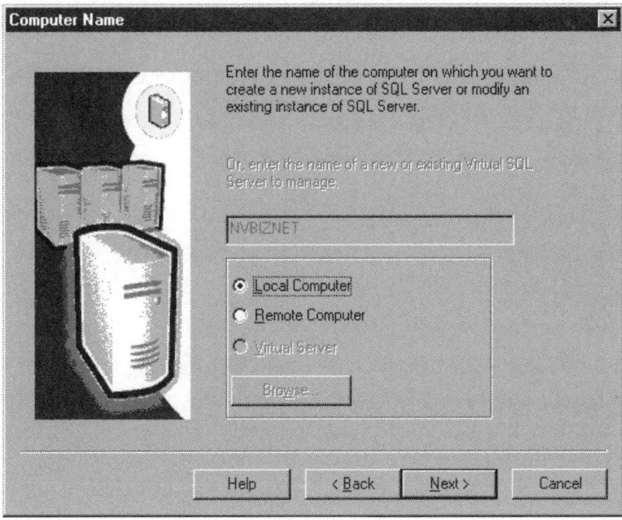

Figure 527.2 The MS-SQL Server 2000 installation wizard Computer Name dialog box

6. If you want to install the MS-SQL Server 2000 on the local computer, click the mouse pointer on the Local Computer radio button and then on the Next button near the lower right corner of the Computer Name dialog box. Conversely, if you want to install the DBMS on another computer connected to your local area network, click the mouse pointer on the Remote Computer radio button and enter the name of the computer into the field above the radio buttons. Then, click the mouse pointer on the Next button near the lower right corner of the Computer Name dialog box. The installation wizard will display the Installation Selection dialog box shown in Figure 527.3.

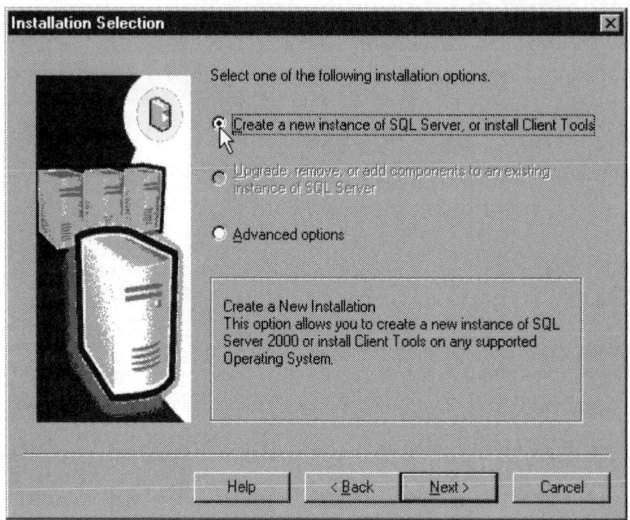

Figure 527.3 The MS-SQL Server 2000 installation wizard Installation Selection dialog box

7. Click the mouse pointer on the Create a new instance of SQL Server, or install Client Tools radio button and then on the Next button near the lower right corner of the dialog box. The installation wizard will display the User Information dialog box.

8. Into the Name field of the User Information dialog box, enter your first and last name. Then, into the Company field, enter the name of the company for whom you are installing the MS-SQL Server. If there is no company name, leave the Company field blank. Next, click the mouse pointer on the Next button near the lower right corner of the dialog box. The installation wizard will display the MS-SQL Server 2000 Software License Agreement dialog box.

9. After you read through DBMS software license agreement, click the mouse pointer on the Yes button (near the lower right corner of the dialog box) to accept the terms of the agreement and continue with the installation process. The installation wizard will display the Installation Definition dialog box shown in Figure 527.4.

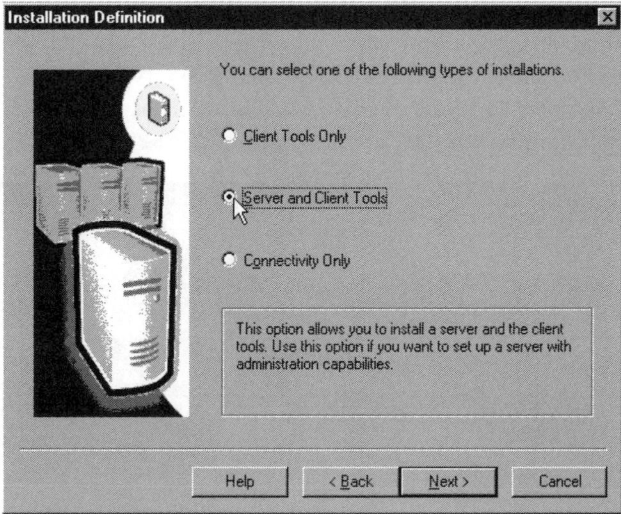

Figure 527.4 The MS-SQL Server 2000 installation wizard Installation Definition dialog box

10. Click the mouse pointer on the Server and Client Tools radio button and then on the Next button near the lower right corner of the dialog box. The installation wizard will display the Instance Name dialog box shown in Figure 527.5.

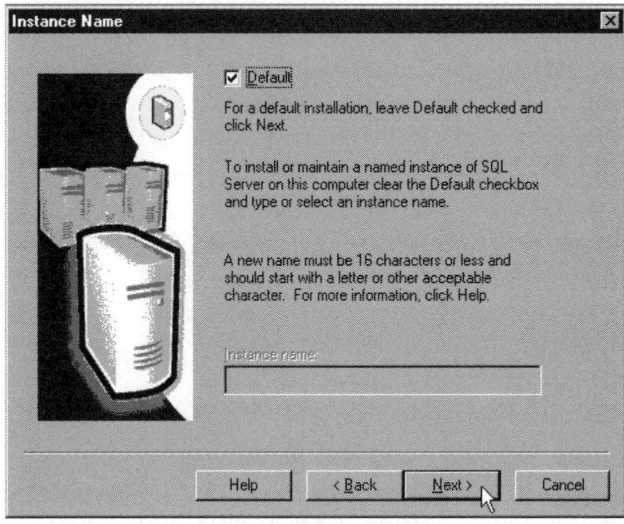

Figure 527.5 The MS-SQL Server 2000 installation wizard Instance Name dialog box

11. You can run multiple instances (copies) of the MS-SQL Server on the same computer. However, each instance of the DBMS running on the computer must have a unique name. If you are installing a single instance of the DBMS on the server, click the mouse pointer on the Default checkbox until a checkmark appears and then on the Next button near the lower right corner of the dialog box. Conversely, if you are installing an additional copy

of the DBMS, or if you plan to run more than one instance of the DBMS on the computer, clear the Default checkbox and enter an unique name for the MS-SQL Server into the Instance name field near the bottom of the dialog box. Then, click the mouse pointer on the Next button near the lower right corner of the dialog box. The install wizard will display the Setup Type dialog box shown in Figure 527.6.

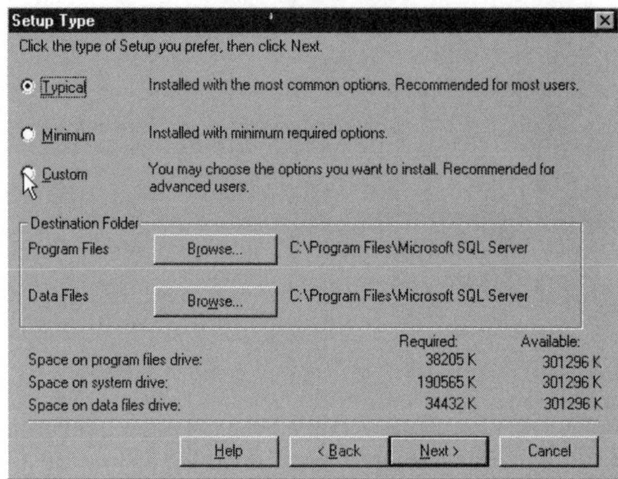

Figure 527.6 The MS-SQL Server 2000 installation wizard Setup Type dialog box

12. To install SQL programming tools and sample source code as part of the MS-SQL Server installation process, click the mouse pointer on the Custom radio button so the installation wizard will prompt you to install the sample code and SQL programming support tools on the next screen. The installation wizard will display the Select Components dialog box.

    Conversely, if you previously installed the SQL tools and code samples on this computer (and therefore do not want to install them again), click the mouse pointer on either the Typical or on the Minimum radio button—depending on the type of installation you want to perform. Then, click the mouse pointer on the Next button near the lower right corner of the dialog box. The installation wizard will display the Services Accounts screen of Step 14.

13. Scroll to the bottom of the Components scroll box on the left side of the Select Components dialog box and click the mouse pointer on the checkbox next to Code Samples until a checkmark appears. Then click the mouse pointer on the Next button near the lower right corner of the dialog box. The installation wizard will display the Services Accounts dialog box shown in Figure 527.7.

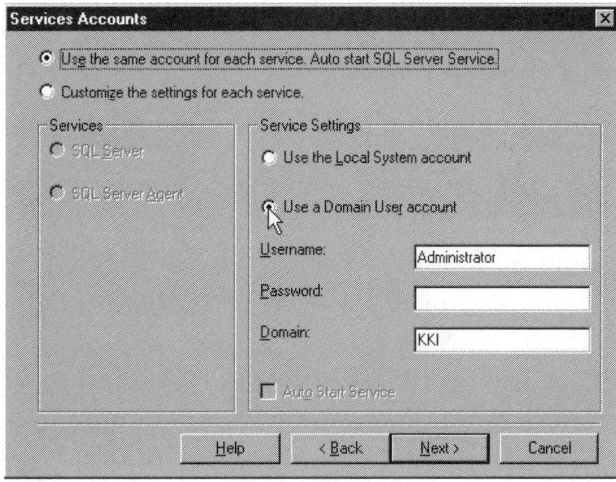

Figure 527.7 The MS-SQL Server 2000 installation wizard Services Accounts dialog box

14. To have Windows start the MS-SQL Server and the MS-SQL Server Agent automatically each time you boot the server, click the mouse pointer on the "Use the same account for each service. Auto start SQL Server Service" radio button, and on the "Use a Domain User Account" radio button. Then, into the Username and Password fields, enter the username and password you want the MS-SQL Server to use when logging into the server. Make sure that you enter the username and password of an account with system administrator access. Click your mouse pointer on the Next button near the lower right corner of the dialog box. The installation wizard will display an Authentication Mode dialog box similar to that shown in Figure 527.8.

Note: *Rather than using the system administrator's username and password, set up a separate username such as "SQLEXEC" (with a password, of course) and assign the username to the system administrators group. This will allow for administrator access to the DBMS if the system administrator changes.*

Note: *To explore the other DBMS startup options, click the mouse pointer on the Help button near the bottom center of the dialog box. The dialog box help screen gives examples of several different startup options for the MS-SQL Server. Moreover, the help screen lists the restrictions the operating system imposes on the MS-SQL Server's access rights. Keep in mind that if you choose to have the MS-SQL Server login to the local system account on startup, the MS-SQL Server will be unable to start if the system administrator later changes the password on the account.*

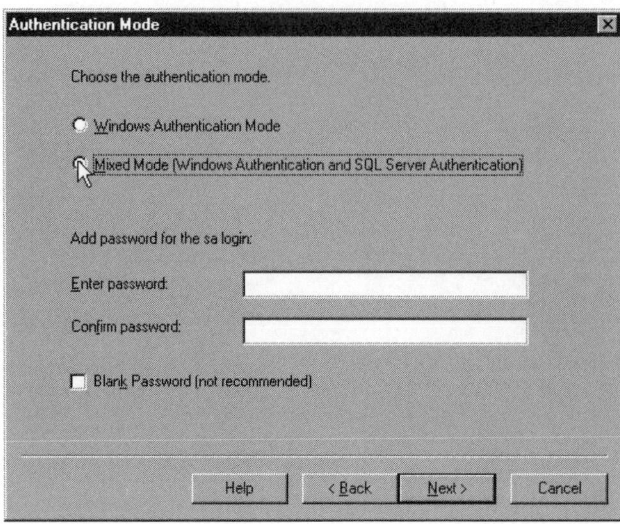

Figure 527.8 The MS-SQL Server 2000 installation wizard Authentication Mode dialog box

15. Click the mouse pointer on the Mixed Mode (Windows Authentication and SQL Server Authentication) radio button and enter a password for the MS-SQL Server sa (system administrator) account into the Enter password field and again into the Confirm password field. Click the mouse pointer on the Next button near the lower right corner of the dialog box. The installation wizard will display the Collation Settings dialog box.

Note: *The security mechanism is the same whether you select Windows Authentication Mode or Mixed Mode. However, only Mixed Mode lets you set the sa account's password. Given the importance of not leaving the sa account's password blank, now is as good of a time as any to select a password to protect the account that has all access privileges to all objects in the DBMS.*

16. Unless you need to match the collation settings of another instance of the MS-SQL Server installed on this computer, accept the default collation settings and sort order. Click the mouse pointer on the Next button near the lower right corner of the dialog box. The installation wizard will display a Network Libraries dialog box similar to that shown in Figure 527.9.

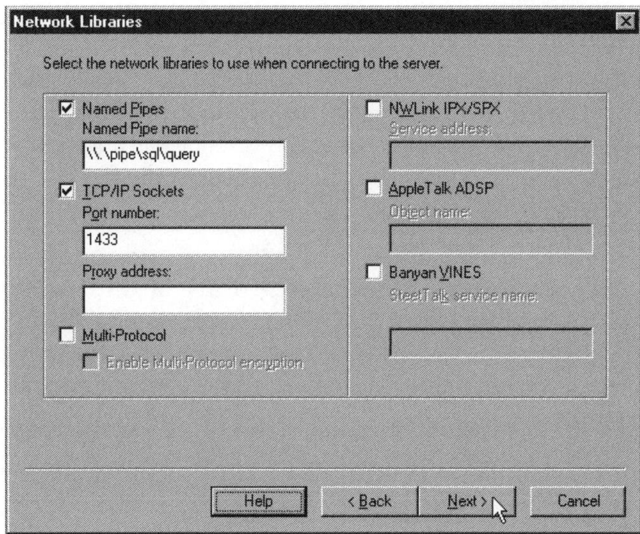

Figure 527.9 The MS-SQL Server 2000 installation wizard Network Libraries dialog box

17. The Network Libraries dialog box allows you to set up the interprocess communication (IPC) mechanism that enables MS-SQL Server client applications running on network workstations communicate with the MS-SQL Server (DBMS) running on the network server. If you are using only Windows networking, accept the dialog box defaults and click the mouse pointer on the Next button near the lower right corner of the dialog box. On the other hand, if you have a multi-protocol network, click the mouse pointer on the checkboxes next to the network libraries you want to setup and enter the information required into the field below the checkboxes you checkmark. (See your network administrator for help with service/object names and address, as necessary.) Click the mouse pointer on the Next button near the lower right corner of the dialog box. The installation wizard will display the Start Copying Files message box.

Note: *The installation program will install all of the network libraries onto the server. Therefore, if you do not see the network library you need, or if the network administrator is not available to help you with the library setup right now, you can always configure the libraries any time after you install the MS-SQL Server. See MS-SQL Server 2000's Books Online help system for additional details.*

18. Click the mouse pointer on the Next button near the lower right corner of the Start Copying Files message box.

After you complete Step 18, the MS-SQL Server 2000 installation wizard will start copying the MS-SQL Server 2000's files onto your computer and setup the MS-SQL Server DBMS software as you specified through the installation wizard's dialog boxes. Once the installation wizard starts copying files, the MS-SQL Server 2000 installation will run to completion without further intervention on your part. The installation program will display a message box and a series of status bars that tell you the name of the file it is copying and how close the program is to completing its work.

When the installation program has finished installing the MS-SQL Server 2000 on your computer, the program will display a Setup Complete dialog box. Click the mouse pointer on the Finish button at bottom of the dialog box to reboot the computer so you can start using the MS-SQL Server. Unless you specified otherwise on the Services Account screen in Step 14, the MS-SQL Server 2000 will login as a system service and startup automatically during the computer's boot process.

528 Using the MS-SQL Server SETUSER Statement to Test a User's Access to Database Objects

When you implement database security, you will give some users access privileges on certain database objects and not on others. To test a user's access rights, you can login to the user's account, or if you are the system administrator (sa) or the database owner (DBO), you can use the SETUSER statement to impersonate any database user.

The syntax of the SETUSER STATEMENT is:

```
SETUSER <username> [WITH NORESET]
```

Therefore, while logged in to the sa account you could execute the statement:

```
SETUSER MARY
```

for example, and test user MARY's access privileges on various database objects. Moreover, username MARY will own any database objects you create while the DBMS "thinks" you are MARY. As such, the SETUSER statement gives you an easy way to create new database objects and give a specific user all access privileges (as the database object owner (DBOO)) on those objects.

When you want to revert back to being the sa or DBO, execute the SETUSER statement without a username, or execute a USE statement.

If you include the WITH NORESET clause in the SETUSER statement, such as

```
SETUSER MARY NORESET
```

to impersonate another user, the DBMS will not change your identity back to the account you originally logged in on (either sa or DBO). If you include the NORESET option when you execute a SETUSER statement, the only way to get your original identity back is to logoff and then login as sa or DBO.

529 Understanding the MS-SQL Server MODEL Database

The MS-SQL Server uses the MODEL database as a template whenever you tell it to create a new database. Any new database the MS-SQL Server creates will have option settings identical to the database options of the MODEL database. Moreover, the new database will contain a copy of all objects that exist in the MODEL database when you execute the CREATE DATABASE statement. Therefore, the MODEL database provides the ideal starting place to create such things as rules, constraints, defaults, and tables that you want to exist in every database you create.

For example, if you want the rule created by

```
CREATE RULE valid_empnum
AS @employee_number BETWEEN 1000 AND 1999
```

to be available in all databases created in the future, login to the MODEL database using the system administrator (sa) account and create the VALID_EMPNUM rule. MS-SQL Server will create the VALID_EMPNUM rule in each database you create subsequent to adding the rule as an object in the MODEL database. MS-SQL Server will, of course, stop creating the VALID_EMPNUM rule in new databases if you later drop the VALID_EMPNUM object from the MODEL database.

Note: *Because the MS-SQL Server creates the TMPDB database each time the operating system starts the DBMS, make sure you never delete the MODEL database. If you remove the MODEL database from the MS-SQL Server, the DBMS will not run because it will be unable to create the TMPDB database at startup.*

530 Understanding Stored Procedures

As mentioned throughout the book, standard SQL is not a complete programming language. Rather, SQL is a non-procedural, data sublanguage with statements that let you create and delete databases and database objects; specify access privileges; enter, update, and delete data; and retrieve data for output to external applications through queries. Because SQL statements are often embedded in programs or executed as function calls using an application program interface (API), it is sometimes hard to tell where SQL ends and the procedural portion of the programming language begins.

However, standard SQL is data oriented and has no control structures for looping, keywords for conditional execution, or even a mechanism for executing multiple statements as a block. True, you can execute multiple statements as part of an open transaction. While a programming language lets you specify that a set of statements are to be executed in a specific sequence to carry out a multi-step task, an SQL transaction only identifies work to be performed by a set of autonomous statements that can be either undone or committed permanently to the database.

A stored procedure, unlike a transaction, is a sequence of Transact-SQL statements arranged in a specific order that you can assign a name, compile, and store on the MS-SQL Server. Once compiled and stored by the DBMS, you can use an application program (such as the MS-SQL Server's SQL Query Analyzer) to tell the MS-SQL Server to execute the statements in the stored procedure with a single command—similar to calling a subroutine within an application program. Moreover, also like subroutines in an application, stored procedures give you a way of executing a set of SQL statements in a specific order to carry out a multi-step task. In short, stored procedures let you use SQL statements to write "programs"—or at least multi-step subroutines you can call to perform database-related application processing within the database itself.

For example, you might use a stored procedure to transfer funds from a line of credit or savings account to a checking account if the MS-SQL Server invokes a trigger, because a check presented for processing would make the customer's checking account balance go negative. Similarly, a stored procedure might be called to accept a customer order, which requires an update of the quantities on-hand for several products in the inventory tables, followed by the insertion of records into the shipping and invoice tables, and of course, updates to the balances in the customer and salesperson tables.

Thus, stored procedures enhance standard SQL with several capabilities normally associated with programming languages (and missing from the SQL data sublanguage). These added capabilities include:

- **Conditional execution**—After placing a set of Transact-SQL statements in a stored procedure, you can use the Transact-SQL If-Then-Else structure to decide which of the stored procedure's statements to execute based on results returned on other statements in the stored procedure.
- **Looping control structures**—Transact-SQL's WHILE and FOR statements let you execute a sequence of statements repeatedly until some terminating condition is satisfied.
- **Named variables**—You can use named memory locations (i.e. variables) in a stored procedure to hold values passed to the procedure through parameters in the stored proce-

dure's heading, returned by queries within the stored procedure, or calculated by some other means.

- **Named procedures**—After placing one or more Transact-SQL statements in a stored procedure and adding the desired Transact-SQL conditional execution and loop control structures, you can give the stored procedure a name and pass data to and from it through formal input and output parameters. In short, a stored procedure has the look and feel of a subroutine in a procedural or object-oriented programming language. Moreover, once defined and compiled, you can call the stored procedure by name in a trigger, interactively through the MS-SQL Server SQL Query Analyzer, from an application program, or as one of the clauses or predicates in a standard SQL statement.
- **Statement blocking**—By calling the stored procedure as you would a subroutine in a program, you can cause the DBMS to execute a sequence of SQL statements as if they were a single statement that performs several different yet related tasks.

In addition to extending the capabilities of standard SQL to make it more of a programming language than a pure data sublanguage, stored procedures also offer the following benefits over interactive SQL statement execution:

- **Encapsulation**—In the world of object-oriented programming, stored procedures are *methods* that can be used to manipulate database objects. By using SQL security to disallow all direct access to SQL statements and database objects, you can *encapsulate* both statements and objects within stored procedures. Forcing everyone to use only stored procedures to work with the data in the database can prevent users from circumventing business rules by not applying them or skipping integrity checks in application programs that work with the database. Moreover, stored procedures make it possible for users that know nothing about database objects, structures, or even SQL statement execution, to work with the database in a safe manner. To call a stored procedure, a user only needs to know the input and output parameters in the procedure call and an understanding of the stored procedure's purpose.
- **Improved performance**—Each time you submit an SQL statement to the MS-SQL Server for execution, the DBMS must parse, validate, optimize, and generate an execution plan before it can execute the statement. By compiling stored procedures and then storing them on the SQL server, you can parse, validate, optimize, and generate an execution plan for the entire sequence of SQL statements in the stored procedure in advance. As such, when you call the stored procedure at run-time, the DBMS can execute the statements in the stored procedure more quickly because it can go directly to statement execution, bypassing the parse, validate, optimize, and execution plan generation steps, which it performed earlier.
- **Reduced network traffic**—Each time you submit an SQL statement to the DBMS for execution, your workstation must send the statement across the network to the MS-SQL Server, and the DBMS must return the statement's results set to your workstation. This back and forth traffic between workstation and SQL server can lead to network congestion if you have an SQL statement batch whose statements generate large results sets. Conversely, if you call a stored procedure that contains the same batch of statements, the

DBMS executes the statements on the server and only sends the final results set, or perhaps only a single value, back to the workstation that called the stored procedure.

- **Reusability**—After you compile a stored procedure, many users and application programs can execute the same sequence of statements without having to retype and resubmit them to the DBMS. Executing already debugged and tested SQL statement batches reduces the risk of introducing programmer error when performing work that requires many SQL statements or statements with complex logic.
- **Security**—If the database owner (DBO) or system administrator (sa) compiles and stores a stored procedure, the stored procedure will have all access privileges on the database objects it uses. Therefore, the system administrator can grant minimal access privileges on database objects to individual users. Instead of letting users work with database objects directly, the SA can control the way in which work is accomplished by granting users execute privilege on the stored procedures that they need to do their jobs. The stored procedures let the users manipulate the data in the only in a pre-approved manner—as defined in the stored procedure's *methods*.

The next two tips will show you how to create and execute stored procedures, and Tips 533–537 will show you how to pass data into and out of stored procedures through variables and server based cursors.

531 Using the CREATE PROCEDURE Statement to Create a Stored Procedure

A CREATE PROCEDURE statement lets you create, compile, and save a stored procedure on an MS-SQL Server. By default, only the database owner (DBO) has CREATE PROCEDURE access to the database. However, the DBO can execute a GRANT in the form

```
GRANT CREATE PROCEDURE <username>
```

to grant CREATE PROCEDURE access to the user ID identified by <username>.

The syntax of the CREATE PROCEDURE statement is

```
CREATE PROCEDURE <procedure name> [; <version number>]
  [{@<parameter name> <data type> [VARYING]
   [=<default value>][OUTPUT]
   [...,n]}]
  [WITH {RECOMPILE|ENCRYPTION|RECOMPILE,ENCRYPTION}]
  [FOR REPLICATION]
AS <Transact-SQL statement(s)>
```

where:

- **<procedure name>** is the name of the stored procedure and can be, at most, 128 characters in length.
- **<version number>** allows you to create multiple stored procedures with the same name. You can execute a specific version of the stored procedure by including the version number in the execute command, as in: **EXEC usp_proc;2**. If you call a stored procedure without specifying a version number, the DBMS will execute the stored procedure with the highest version number in the group of stored procedures with the same name.

  You can also drop a specific version of a stored procedure by including the version number in the DROP statement as in: **DROP PROCEDURE usp_proc;2** or you can drop all versions of the stored procedure at once by omitting the version number, as in: **DROP PROCEDURE usp_proc.**
- **<parameter name>** is the name of a parameter that can be used as a variable within the stored procedure. The value of each parameter must be supplied in the stored procedure call or set to a default value as part of the CREATE PROCEDURE statement. While parameters can be used as variable names within the stored procedure, parameters cannot be used as column names, table names, or the names of other database objects.
- **<data type>** is the parameter's data type. A parameter may be any of the valid SQL data types (including TEXT, NTEXT, and IMAGE) or a user-defined data type. If the parameter is data type CURSOR, the parameter must also be specified as VARYING and OUTPUT.
- **VARYING** is only valid with parameters of data type CURSOR. Specifies that the parameter will contain a result set whose content will vary and will be constructed dynamically by statements within the stored procedure.
- **<default value>** is the default (initial) value for a parameter. If specified, the procedure can be executed without specifying the value of the parameter.
- **OUTPUT** indicates that the value of the parameter may be changed within the stored procedure and that the modified value is to be returned to the calling procedure.
- **...,n** indicates that the CREATE PROCEDURE statement can have up to 2,100 parameters.
- **RECOMPILE** tells the MS-SQL Server to compile (i.e., generate a new execution plan) for the stored procedure each time it is called. Without the RECOMPILE option, the DBMS will compile the stored procedure when it executes the CREATE PROCEDURE statement and will use the same execution plan each time the stored procedure is called.
- **ENCRYPTION** tells the MS-SQL Server to encrypt the text of stored procedure's entry in the SYSCOMMENTS table to prevent users from viewing the statements in a compiled stored procedure. Specifying the ENCRYPTION option also prevents the stored procedure from being published as part of the MS-SQL Server replication process.

- **FOR REPLICATION** is the stored procedure that can only be executed during the replication process. You cannot specify both RECOMPILE and FOR REPLICATION in the same CREATE PROCEDURE statement.
- **<Transact-SQL statements>** is the Transact-SQL statements. The maximum size of a stored procedure is 128MB.

For example, to create a stored procedure that displays the contents of an EMPLOYEES file, you could execute a CREATE PROCEDURE statement such as:

```
CREATE PROCEDURE usp_show_all_employees
AS SELECT * FROM employees
```

Note: *You should come up with a standard naming convention for stored procedures. Unless you create and store a stored procedure with the other stored procedures in the MASTER database, avoid the temptation to prefix your stored procedures with an "sp_" like the system stored procedures. After receiving the command to execute a stored procedure that starts with "sp_", the MS-SQL Server first looks for the stored procedure in the MASTER database. The search can be quite time consuming at worst (if there are many stored procedures in the MASTER database), and is wasteful at best, since the stored procedure you want to execute is not located in the MASTER database. Use a standard prefix such as "usp_" for user-stored procedures. If you do so, the DBMS will search the current database when a user calls the stored procedure, thus avoiding the time wasted searching the MASTER database first.*

When the DBMS executes a CREATE PROCEDURE statement, the DBMS parses, validates, optimizes, and generates an execution plan for each of the statements in the stored procedure. If any of the stored procedure's statements are syntactically incorrect or refer to nonexistent database objects (other than stored procedures), the DBMS will reject the stored procedure and report the errors it found so you can correct the statements and resubmit the updated CREATE PROCEDURE statement to the DBMS for execution. If one or more statements in the stored procedure refer to other, as yet unimplemented (i.e. currently nonexistent) stored procedures, the DBMS will generate a warning message, but will still compile and install the stored procedure on the MS-SQL Server.

Note: *When validating the statements in a stored procedure, the DBMS does not take access privileges on database objects referenced in the stored procedure's statements into account. As such, a user could execute a CREATE STORED procedure statement and create a stored procedure the user cannot then execute.*

---

532 Using the EXECUTE Statement to Call a Stored Procedure

After creating a stored procedure (as you learned to do in the previous tip), you can tell the DBMS to execute the Transact-SQL statements in the stored by procedure by:

- Submitting an SQL statement execution request that calls the stored procedure from within an application program.
- Entering the stored procedure's name as the first line in a statement batch.
- Submitting an EXECUTE (or EXEC) statement that names the stored procedure during an interactive session, while in another stored procedure, or in a TRIGGER.
- Using the stored procedure's name as an argument in an SQL statement.

For example, to call a stored procedure without parameters (such as the USP_SHOW_ALL_EMPLOYEES stored procedure created near the end of the previous tip), simply type EXECUTE (or EXEC) followed by a space and the procedure name, as in

```
EXECUTE usp_show_all_employees
```

or:

```
EXEC usp_show_all_employees
```

After submitting either of the preceding two statements to the DBMS for execution, the DBMS will execute the statements in the stored procedure named USP_SHOW_ALL_EMPLOYEES.

If you do not own the stored procedure, but have been granted EXECUTE rights on it, you must include the owner's username in the EXECUTE statement, as in:

```
EXEC frank.usp_show_all_employees
```

This tells the DBMS to execute the USP_SHOW_ALL_EMPLOYEES stored procedure owned by username FRANK.

Note: *If you have EXECUTE privilege on a stored procedure owned by the database owner (DBO), you do not have to specify "DBO" in the stored procedure's name when you use the EXECUTE statement to call it. The DBMS automatically searches the list of stored procedures you own and those owned by the DBO.*

If the stored procedure has a parameter list, include parameter values after the procedure's name in the EXECUTE statement. List the parameter values in the order in which they appear in the stored procedure's CREATE statement. Separate parameters in the list with a comma, and enclose character string values in quotes.

For example, to call stored procedure created by

```
CREATE PROCEDURE usp_add_employee @first_name VARCHAR(30),
                                  @last_name  VARCHAR(30),
                                  @address    VARCHAR(30),
                                  @office     INTEGER = 1,
                                  @manager    INTEGER = 1
AS INSERT INTO employees
     (first_name, last_name, address, office, manager)
   VALUES
     (@first_name, @last_name, @address, @office, @manager)
```

submit an EXEC statement such as:

```
EXEC usp_add_employee 'Wally', 'Wallberg',
      '777 Sunset Strip', 5
```

If you prefer, you can explicitly specify the parameter names in the procedure call, which allows you to list the parameters in any order you wish. For example, the procedure call

```
EXEC usp_add_employee @office = 5,
       @address = '777 Sunset Strip',
       @first_name = 'Wally', @last_name = 'Wallberg'
```

is equivalent to the preceding procedure call that assigns parameter values by position.

533 Understanding How to Declare Variables Within a Stored Procedure

In addition to the parameters passed into a stored procedure, you may find it necessary or at least convenient, to define additional variables to hold intermediate values during the procedure's execution. The SQL DECLARE statement lets you create one or more local variables the DBMS can use while executing the statements in a stored procedure.

Although not required, declare the variables you plan to use at the beginning of the stored procedure—between the end of the stored procedure's heading and its first Transact-SQL statement.

The syntax of the DECLARE statement used to create variables for use in a stored procedure is:

```
DECLARE @<variable name> <data type>
        [..., @<last variable name> <last data type>]
```

For example, the following stored procedure declaration creates three local variables: @AUTH_COUNT, @TOT_SALES, and @AUTH_TOT_SALES.

```
CREATE PROCEDURE usp_compare_author_sales @author_ID ID
AS
/*** DECLARE local variables ***/
  DECLARE @auth_count     INTEGER,
          @tot_sales      MONEY,
          @auth_tot_sales MONEY

/*** Count the number of authors ***/
  SELECT @auth_count = COUNT(*) FROM authors

/*** Compute the total sales YTD for all authors ***/
  SELECT @tot_sales = SUM(ytd_sales) FROM titles
                      WHERE ytd_sales IS NOT NULL

/*** Compute the total sales YTD for a specific author ***/
  SELECT @auth_tot_sales = SUM(ytd_sales)
                           FROM  titles t, titleauthor ta
                           WHERE t.title_ID = ta.title_ID
                           AND   au_ID      = @author_ID
/*** Display the results ***/
  SELECT @auth_count 'authors',
         @tot_sales / @auth_count 'avg YTD sales / author',
         au_ID, @auth_tot_sales 'Total Sales',
         (au_lname + ', ' + au_fname) 'Name'
  FROM authors WHERE au_ID = @author_ID
```

Notice that the name of each variable declared in a stored procedure, like the name of each parameter passed to the stored procedure, begins with an "at" sign (@). Also like parameters, variables declared in a stored procedure can be of any SQL or user-defined data type.

SELECT statements can be used to *assign* values to variables and to *display* the values of variable's and other table data.

534 Using Stored Procedure Parameters to Return Values

Within the four preceding tips, you learned how to create and call stored procedures. As you learned in Tip 530 "Understanding Stored Procedures," you use a stored procedure to execute a sequence of statements arranged in a specific order. Once compiled and stored by the DBMS, you can execute the statements within a stored procedure by submitting it to the DBMS using the keyword EXEC (or EXECUTE) followed by the stored procedure's name.

For example, to execute the stored procedure USP_PROCESS_CHECK, you might submit the following statement to the DBMS:

```
EXEC usp_process_check 112233, 123, 258.59
```

You use parameters to pass values to statements within a stored procedure. A stored procedure's parameters, like other variables, are named memory locations in which you can store values. In this example, 112233, 123, and 258.59 are *input* parameters in that they pass values *into* the stored procedure. Thus, given the following declaration, the stored procedure call in this example passes 112233 to statements within the stored procedure as @ACCOUNT_NUMBER, 123 as @CHECK_NUMBER, and 258.59 as @CHECK_AMOUNT:

```
CREATE PROCEDURE usp_process_check @account_number INTEGER,
                                   @check_number   INTEGER,
                                   @check_amount   REAL
AS
  INSERT INTO checks (@account_number, @check_number,
                      @check_amount)
```

While input parameters let you pass values into a stored procedure, you use *output* parameters to return values to the caller. Suppose the stored procedure in this example updated the customer's checking and line of credit balances, in addition to storing check information within the CHECKS table. The stored procedure declaration might then be as follows:

```
CREATE PROCEDURE usp_process_check
                   @account_number   INTEGER,
                   @check_number     INTEGER,
                   @check_amount     REAL,
                   @checking_balance REAL OUTPUT,
                   @loc_used         REAL OUTPUT,
                   @loc_balance      REAL OUTPUT
AS
  SET @loc_used = 0

/* Retrieve current account balances */

  SELECT @checking_balance =
    (SELECT checking_balance FROM customers
     WHERE account_number = @account_number)

  SELECT @loc_balance =
    (SELECT loc_balance FROM customers
     WHERE account_number = @account_number)

/* If check amount would overdraw the checking balance,
   tap the line of credit */
```

```
  IF @checking_balance < @check_amount
    SET @loc_used = (@check_amount - @checking_balance)

/* Store the check within the CHECKS table and update the
   customer's balance(s) */

  SET @loc_balance = @loc_balance + @loc_used
  SET @checking_balance =
        @checking_balance - @check_amount + @loc_used

  INSERT INTO checks
    VALUES (@account_number, @check_number, @check_amount)

  UPDATE customers
     SET loc_balance = @loc_balance,
         checking_balance = @checking_balance
   WHERE account_number = @account_number
```

In this example, @CHECKING_BALANCE, @LOC_USED, and @LOC_BALANCE are *output* parameters, meaning the stored procedure will pass the changes it makes to the values of these parameters within the stored procedure back to the statement that invoked it. Don't be overly concerned with what the stored procedure in this example does. The important thing to understand is that Transact-SQL lets you designate input and output parameters. A parameter is an output parameter (that is, able to pass an updated value back to the stored procedure's caller) only when the keyword OUTPUT follows the parameter's data type declaration in the CREATE PROCEDURE statement.

It seems that each DMBS product has its own way to designate output parameters. Oracle, for example, has you label parameters as in, out, or in out and to place the designation prior to the parameter's data type declaration. Informix uses the keyword RETURNING to specify the parameters that are to return values. Thus, if you are using a DBMS other than MS-SQL Server, be sure to check your system documentation for the specific way in which you must specify which parameters are input and which are output within the stored procedure declaration.

Note: *You can use pass values into a stored procedure through both input and output parameters. However, if the stored procedure changes the value of input parameters, their new values will not be returned to the caller when the stored procedure completes its execution. Conversely, any changes the stored procedure makes to output parameters will be passed back. Thus, input parameters are, in effect, one-way valves that let you pass values into a stored procedure but do not let you retrieve values from it. Conversely, output parameters allow the flow in both directions—initial values into the stored procedures and updated values back out to the caller.*

To allow statements within a stored procedure to update the value of an output parameter, the procedure call must have an acceptable "target" that can receive the value to be returned.

For example, you might call USP_PROCESS_CHECK with an EXEC statement such as the following:

```
EXEC usp_process_check 112233, 123, 258.59,
       @checking_balance OUTPUT, @loc_balance OUTPUT,
       @loc_used OUTPUT
```

To pass input parameter values, you can use either literal values (such as the first three parameters passed in this example), or you can pass the names of variables that contain the values you want passed within the input parameters. For output parameters however, you must use the names of variables (that is, names of memory locations and not literal values), because the stored procedure must have access to a memory location in which to place the parameters value before returning control to the stored procedure's caller. In addition, Transact-SQL requires that when calling a stored procedure you include the keyword OUTPUT after each variable whose value the stored procedure is allowed to change. If you omit the keyword OUTPUT, the DBMS will still execute the procedure call without error. However, the output parameters will retain the value they had prior to the stored procedure's execution even after they are changed within the stored procedure.

As noted previously, though certain parameters are designated as "output" parameters for Transact-SQL, output parameter communication is not truly one-way. In fact, Transact-SQL passes the current value of an output parameter *into* the stored procedure as well as passing its updated value back out to the stored procedure's caller. Therefore, in this example, if you removed the first two SELECT statements from within the stored procedure and executed them before calling it, you could pass the balances in @CHECKING_BALANCE and @LOC_BALANCE into the stored procedure. Whether initially set within the stored procedure or external to it, the two output parameters will hold the updated balance information (for the checking account and line of credit, respectively) when the stored procedure returns control to the statement that called it.

535 Returning a Value from a Stored Function Using the Keyword RETURN

When you want to execute a sequence of statements to produce a scalar (single) value or a table, use a stored function rather than a stored procedure. Unlike a stored procedure, which can return multiple values through output parameters, a stored function can return only a single value or a table (which, may contain multiple values). Moreover, a function cannot execute INSERT, UPDATE, DELETE, or other statements that modify database objects external to the stored function. However, if it returns a table, the stored function can execute INSERT, UPDATE, or DELETE statements that change the temporary table the function returns.

Thus, if you want to change the contents or structure of permanent database objects, or return multiple values through parameters, use a stored procedure. If you want to return a single value or set of values within a single table without changing any permanent database objects, use a function.

To create a function, you use the CREATE FUNCTION statement, which has the following syntax:

```
CREATE FUNCTION [owner_name.]<function name>
  ([{@<parameter name> [AS]
     <data type>[=<default value>]}[...,n]])
RETURNS <scalar data type>
[AS]
BEGIN
  <Transact-SQL statement(s)>
  RETURN <scalar expression>
END
```

In Tip 537 "Using the CREATE FUNCTION Statement to Create a Stored Function," you will learn the syntax for each of the three forms of the CREATE FUNCTION statement. The syntax differs depending on the type of value the function returns—one syntax for returning a scalar (as shown in the following code within this tip), a second to return an inline table, and a third for a multi-statement table return.)

For now, simply note the keyword RETURNS that follows the stored function's parameter list. When a stored function is to return a single (scalar) value, you specify the returned value's data type after the keyword RETURNS. Note too, the RETURN statement immediately before the keyword END, which ends the function's declaration. For functions that return a scalar value, you specify the value that the function returns immediately after the keyword RETURN either as a literal value, as a variable that contains the value, or as an expression.

Suppose, for example, that you want to make a list of salespeople who have generated over $100,000.00 in sales during their employment. You could submit a SELECT statement with a correlated subquery (as you learned to do in Tip 339 "Understanding Correlated Subqueries Introduced with Comparison Operators"). Or, you could encapsulate the subquery as a simple SELECT statement within a function. If you named the function that returns the total sales for an employee UFN_GET_TOTAL_SALES for example, your query will be similar to that shown here:

```
SELECT first_name, last_name,
       dbo.ufn_get_total_sales(salesrep_ID)
FROM employees
WHERE dbo.ufn_get_total_sales(salesrep_ID) > 100000.0
```

Given the following definition, the stored function UFN_GET_TOTAL_SALES returns a single value (the total sales made by a particular employee), each time it is called:

```
CREATE FUNCTION ufn_get_total_sales(@salesrep_ID INTEGER)
RETURNS REAL
BEGIN
  RETURN (SELECT SUM(order_total)
          FROM cust_orders
          WHERE cust_orders.salesrep_ID = @salesrep_ID)
END
```

Thus, the WHERE clause in the original query is satisfied only when the total orders booked by a sales rep (as returned by the stored function) are greater than $100,000.00.

As mentioned previously within this tip, you can write a function that returns a table of values rather than a single (scalar) value. Suppose, for example, that you want a list of all checks and deposits made by a particular customer. You might create the following function:

```
CREATE FUNCTION ufn_cust_trans(@cust_ID INTEGER)
RETURNS @trans_list TABLE
  (trans_date   DATETIME,
   trans_ID     INTEGER,
   trans_type   CHAR(1),
   trans_amount REAL)
BEGIN
  INSERT @trans_list
    SELECT deposit_date, deposit_ID, 'D', deposit_amount
      FROM deposits
     WHERE deposits.cust_ID = @cust_ID
     ORDER BY deposit_date

  INSERT @trans_list
    SELECT check_date, check_number, 'C', check_amount
      FROM checks
     WHERE checks.cust_ID = @cust_ID
     ORDER BY check_date

  RETURN
END
```

When called, UFN_CUST_TRANS will return a table with a list of all deposits in date order followed by a list of all checks in order by check date. Note that when used to return a table, a stored function works much like a database VIEW. However, as shown by this example, whereas a database VIEW must be based on a single SELECT statement, you can use multiple SELECT statements (and perform other Transact-SQL processing) to generate the table returned by a stored function.

You can execute queries on a table returned by a function as you can on any other "normal" database table. For example, you might execute the following query to list all transaction within the table:

```
SELECT * FROM ufn_cust_trns(123456)
```

Or, you might use aggregate functions to display the total count of deposits, checks, and the grand total of each:

```
SELECT trans_type, COUNT(*), SUM(trans_amount)
FROM ufn_cust_trans(123456)
GROUP BY trans_type
```

Note: *When calling a user-defined function that returns a scalar value, you must include the owner's name—even if the stored function is one you created under your own username. Unlike stored procedures, the DBMS searches neither the list of stored functions you own nor those owned by the DBO for a matching name if you omit the owner's ID from the function call. As such, the DBMS will report an error such as*

```
'ufn_get_total_sales' is not a recognized function name'
```

if you omit the owner ID from the function call as shown here:

```
PRINT ufn_get_total_sales(1)
```

You can however, call a function you own or one owned by the DBO without providing the owner's ID if the function returns a table (versus a scalar value), as shown by the second example earlier within this tip.

536 Working with Cursors in Stored Procedures

Operations within a relational database typically act on a complete set of rows at one time. When executing a SELECT statement, for example, the DBMS returns all rows that satisfy the search condition in the query's WHERE clause at once, versus returning one row at a time. Similarly, an UPDATE statement makes the same changes to all rows that satisfy the search criteria in its WHERE clause at once. Sometimes, however, you must work with data one row (or small block of rows) at a time rather than with all rows within the results set at the same time. You can use database cursors within a stored procedure when you must work with a results set row-by-row.

Suppose, for example, that you have a stored procedure USP_CLEAR_CHECKS, which must clear checks for your customers. To reduce the number of overdrafts, you want the procedure to apply the checks in ascending order by amount. (That way, the maximum number of checks will clear if the customer's balance won't quite cover the total amount of all checks written.) In this example, you want the checks to end up in one of two tables: CLEARED_ITEMS or OVERDRAFT_ITEMS, and you want to insert a $10.00 fee for each overdraft item into the FEES table.

To create and work with a database cursor within a stored procedure (or within a stored function, for that matter) use the same DECLARE CURSOR, OPEN, FETCH, and CLOSE statements you learned about when you worked with database cursors in Tips 427–445. For example, you might declare the USP_CLEAR_CHECKS procedure as shown here:

```
CREATE PROCEDURE usp_clear_checks
                   @account_no        INTEGER,
                   @date_processed    DATETIME,
                   @checking_balance MONEY OUTPUT
AS
/* Create temporary variables into which to FETCH values
   with the columns values from a table row */

  DECLARE @check_amt  MONEY
  DECLARE @check_date DATETIME
  DECLARE @check_no   INTEGER

/* Declare the cursor in which to store the query results
   temporarily during row-by-row processing */

  DECLARE  cur_unproc_checks CURSOR FOR
    SELECT check_date, check_no, check_amount
      FROM unprocessed_checks
     WHERE account_no = @account_no
    ORDER BY check_amount

/* OPEN the cursor and then FETCH the first row within the
   results set */

  OPEN  cur_unproc_checks
  FETCH cur_unproc_checks
   INTO @check_date, @check_no, @check_amt

/* If no rows within the results set (because the customer
   has no outstanding checks) CLOSE the cursor and RETURN
   to the caller */

  IF (@@fetch_status <> 0)
    BEGIN
      CLOSE cur_unproc_checks
      DEALLOCATE cur_unproc_checks
      RETURN
    END
```

```
  SET NOCOUNT ON

/* Work through the cursor one row (check) at a time. Check
   to make sure the last FETCH was successful, then process
   the row of results. After processing, FETCH the next row
   and repeat the process until the FETCH is unsuccessful-
   meaning there are no more rows to process. */

  WHILE (@@fetch_status = 0)
  BEGIN
    IF @checking_balance - @check_amt >= 0
      BEGIN
        SET @checking_balance =
              @checking_balance - @check_amt

        INSERT INTO cleared_items
          VALUES (@date_processed, @account_no,
                  @check_date, @check_no, @check_amt)
      END
    ELSE
      BEGIN
        INSERT INTO overdraft_items
          VALUES (@date_processed, @account_no,
                  @check_date, @check_no, @check_amt)

        INSERT INTO fees
          VALUES ('OD', @date_processed, @account_no,
                  @check_date, @check_no, @check_amt,
                  10.00)
      END

/* FETCH the next row from the results set */

    FETCH cur_unproc_checks
     INTO @check_date, @check_no, @check_amt
  END

  CLOSE cur_unproc_checks
  DEALLOCATE cur_unproc_checks
RETURN
```

The preceding code represents the Transact-SQL statements you would use to process cursor results on an MS-SQL Server. If you are using a DBMS product other than MS-SQL Server, your statements will vary. In Oracle, for example, you would use a FOR loop to move through the cursor one row at a time and you will work directly with the cursor's column values without first transferring them to interim variables. Informix, on the other hand, will have you use a FOREACH loop to transfer the rows of values within a cursor, on row at a time, into temporary variables for processing. Therefore, check your DBMS system manual for the exact statements you must use to work with cursors in your DBMS. While the exact statements may differ, in general, cursor processing proceeds as follows:

1. Use the DECLARE CURSOR statement to associate a cursor with an SQL SELECT statement. (A cursor is in effect, a virtual table that lets you work with the results set returned by query one row at a time.)
2. Submit an OPEN (cursor) statement to the DBMS to execute the cursor's SELECT statement and fill (or populate) the cursor with the SELECT statement's results set.
3. Execute a series of FETCH statements to retrieve the rows within the cursor and process each row after you retrieve it.
4. Use the CLOSE (cursor) statement to "close" the cursor, and then DEALLOCATE the cursor to delete the cursor, thereby freeing up memory (and perhaps disk resources) used to hold the SELECT statement's results set temporarily.

537 Using the CREATE FUNCTION Statement to Create a Stored Function

A CREATE FUNCTION statement lets you create, compile, and save a stored procedure on an MS-SQL Server. By default, only the database owner (DBO) has CREATE FUNCTION access to the database. However, the DBO can execute a GRANT statement in the form

```
GRANT CREATE FUNCTION <username>
```

to give CREATE FUNCTION access to the user ID identified by <username>. When allowing users to create stored functions, bear in mind that when executed, the stored function has the owner's access privileges on database objects. Therefore, make sure the owner of the stored function has at least REFERENCES access to all database objects used within the stored function.

As you will learn within this Tip, the syntax of the CREATE FUNCTION statement has one of three forms depending on the data type the function is to return. Stored functions are limited to returning either a single, scalar value or a table.

To create a scalar function that returns a single (scalar) value versus a table of values, use the following syntax

```
CREATE FUNCTION [<owner name>.]<function name>
  ([{@<parameter name> [AS] <scalar data type>
   [=<default value>]}[...,n]])
RETURNS <scalar return data type>
[WITH {ENCRYPTION|SCHEMABINDING}]
[AS]
```

```
BEGIN
  <Transact-SQL statements>
  RETURN <scalar expression>
END
```

where:

- **<owner name>** is the username of the user that owns the user-defined function being created. The username you enter for <owner name> must be an existing user ID. When creating a function, bear in mind that the stored function operates on database objects with its owner's access rights.
- **<function name>** is the name of the stored function and can be at most 128 characters in length.
- **<parameter name>** is the name of a parameter which can be used as a variable within the stored function. The value of each parameter must be supplied in the stored function call or set to a default value as part of the CREATE FUNCTION statement. (When the user invokes the function, he or she must supply the keyword DEFAULT in place of each parameter omitted from the function call.) While parameters can be used as variable names within the stored function, parameters cannot be used as column names, table names, or the names of other database objects.
- **<scalar data type>** is the parameter's data type. A parameter may be any of the valid SQL scalar data types (including TEXT, NTEXT, and IMAGE). User-defined data types, even when scalar, are not permitted. The stored function's "scalar data type only" restriction means none of the function's input parameters can be a table or cursor.
- **<default value>** is the default (initial) value for a parameter. If specified, the user can call the function by specifying the keyword DEFAULT in place of the parameter.
- **...,n** indicates that the CREATE FUNCTION statement can have up to 2,100 parameters.
- **ENCRYPTION** tells the MS-SQL Server to encrypt the text of stored function's entry in the SYSCOMMENTS table to prevent users from viewing the statements in a compiled stored function.
- **SCHEMABINDING** tells the MS-SQL Server to bind the function to the database objects it references. If bound to database objects, the objects the function references cannot be altered (using the ALTER statement) or removed (using the DROP statement). To remove the function's "binding," so you can alter or drop database objects referenced within the function, you must either DROP the function or execute an ALTER function statement with the SCHEMABINDING option not specified. To create a stored function with SCHEMABINDING, the following conditions must be true: any user-defined functions and views within the function must also be schema-bound; objects referenced by the function cannot have a two-part name; the stored function and the objects it references must be within the same database; and the user executing the CREATE FUNCTION statement must have REFERENCES rights on all database objects used within the function.

- **<scalar return data type>** is the data type of the value that the stored function returns to its caller. Because all stored function parameters are "input" parameters, the function can return only a single scalar value (or a single table of values in the case of inline table or multi-statement table functions, whose syntax is discussed next). The value the function returns may be of any of the valid SQL scalar data types (including TEXT, NTEXT, and IMAGE). User-defined data types, even when scalar, are not permitted.
- **<Transact-SQL statements>** is the Transact-SQL statements. The maximum size of a stored procedure is 128MB. Unlike stored procedures, the statements within a stored function may not alter database objects defined outside the function (such as global cursors, tables, views, and so on) in any way.

For example, to create a stored function that returns the total sales for a particular employee, you could execute a CREATE FUNCTION statement such as:

```
CREATE FUNCTION ufn_employee_total_sales
         (@salesrep_ID INTEGER)
RETURNS REAL
BEGIN
  RETURN (SELECT SUM(order_total)
          FROM cust_orders
          WHERE cust_orders.salesrep_ID = @salesrep_ID)
END
```

To create an inline table-valued stored function—a function that returns a table whose columns are *not* defined within the function's RETURNS clause—use the following syntax:

```
CREATE FUNCTION [<owner name>.]<function name>
  ([{@<parameter name> [AS] <scalar data type>
   [=<default value>]}[...,n]])
RETURNS TABLE
[WITH {ENCRYPTION|SCHEMABINDING}]
[AS]
RETURN [(] <SELECT statement> [)]
```

In this form, the keyword TABLE within the CREATE FUNCTION statement's RETURNS clause indicates the function will return a table (of values) to the caller. Because there is no description of the table itself within the RETURNS clause, the table is defined by the SELECT statement within the RETURN clause at the end of the function.

For example, to create a function that returns a table of all customer information for customers assigned to a particular salesperson, you might use the following CREATE FUNCTION statement:

```
CREATE FUNCTION ufn_employee_customer_list
         (@salesrep_ID INTEGER)
RETURNS TABLE
AS
RETURN SELECT * FROM customers
       WHERE customers.salesperson = @salesrep_ID
```

The third form of the CREATE FUNCTION statement also defines a function that returns a table (versus a scalar value). However, while the definition of the inline function's table is given by a single SELECT statement (within the function's RETURN clause), the syntax for a multi-statement table function contains the table definition within the function's RETURNS clause as shown here:

```
CREATE FUNCTION [<owner name>.]<function name>
  ([{@<parameter name> [AS] <scalar data type>
   [=<default value>]}[...,n]])
RETURNS @<table name> TABLE <table definition>
[WITH {ENCRYPTION|SCHEMABINDING}]
[AS]
BEGIN
  <Transact-SQL statements>
  RETURN
END
```

For example, to create a function that returns a table with a list of all customers from three sales offices (each with its own customer list), you might use the following CREATE FUNCTION statement:

```
CREATE FUNCTION ufn_composite_customer_list ()
RETURNS @composite_customer_list TABLE
  (cust_ID      INTEGER,
   first_name   VARCHAR(30),
   last_name    VARCHAR(30),
   sales_office SMALLINT,
   salesperson  INTEGER)
AS
BEGIN
/* Build the consolidated list from office 1 customers */

  INSERT @composite_customer_list
    SELECT cust_ID, first_name, last_name, 1, salesperson
      FROM Office1_Customers

/* Add office 2 customers to the consolidated list */

  INSERT @composite_customer_list
    SELECT cust_ID, first_name, last_name, 2, salesperson
      FROM Office2_Customers

/* Add office 3 customers to the consolidated list */

  INSERT @composite_customer_list
    SELECT cust_ID, first_name, last_name, 3, salesperson
      FROM Office3_Customers

  RETURN
END
```

When it executes a CREATE FUNCTION statement, the DBMS parses, validates, optimizes, and generates an execution plan for each of the statements in the stored function. If any of the stored function's statements are syntactically incorrect or attempt to change, the structure of, or data within database objects external to the function, the DBMS will reject the stored function and report the errors it found. If the DBMS fails to create the stored function due to an error, correct the error reported and then resubmit the (updated) CREATE FUNCTION statement to the DBMS for execution. If one or more statements in the stored function refer to other, as yet unimplemented (i.e. currently nonexistent) stored functions, the DBMS will generate a warning message, but will still compile and install the stored function on the MS-SQL Server. Note that while a stored function can call other user-defined and built-in stored functions, a stored function cannot call a user-defined stored procedure.

Note: *Stored functions handle statement errors differently from stored procedures. If a Transact-SQL error causes the DBMS to stop executing a statement within a stored procedure, the DBMS continues statement execution at the next statement within the stored procedure. Conversely, if an error halts statement execution within a function, the DBMS returns immediately to the caller and stops executing the statement that invoked the stored function as well.*

---

538 Using the MS-SQL Server Enterprise Manager to View or Modify a Stored Procedure or Function

If you are using the MS-SQL Server DBMS, you can call the system-stored procedure SP_HELPTEXT with the following syntax to display the contents of a default, rule, view, or unencrypted stored function, procedure, or trigger:

```
SP_HELPTEXT <object name>
```

For example, to display the code for the stored procedure USP_PROCESS_CHECK (described in Tip 534 "Using Stored Procedure Parameters to Return Values"), you would call the SP_HELPTEXT stored procedure as:

```
SP_HELPTEXT usp_process_check
```

If you want to modify (as well as view) the contents of a stored procedure or user-defined function, use the MS-SQL Server Enterprise manager to display the procedure or function by performing the following steps:

1. Click on the Windows Start button. Windows will display the Start menu.
2. Move your mouse pointer to Programs on the Start menu, select the Microsoft SQL Server option, and click your mouse on Enterprise Manager. Windows will start the Enterprise Manager in a new application window.

3. Click on the plus (+) to the left of SQL Server Group to display the list of MS-SQL Servers available on your network.
4. Click on the plus (+) to the left of the SQL server that has the database with the stored procedure or function you want to display (and perhaps modify). Enterprise Manager will display the Databases, Data Transformation, Management, Security, and Support Services folders for the SQL Server you selected.
5. Click on the plus (+) to the left of the Databases folder to display the list of databases managed by the MS-SQL Server, and then on the plus (+) to the left of the database with the stored procedure or function you want to display. For the current project, click on the plus (+) to the left of the SQLTips folder. MS-SQL Server will display icons for the tables, views, stored procedures, and other resources managed within the database.
6. To display a list of stored procedures within the database, click the Stored Procedures icon. Or, to display a list of stored functions, click the User-Defined Functions icon. The Enterprise Manager will use its right pane to display the list of the stored procedures or functions within the database you selected in Step 5.
7. Within the Enterprise Managers right pane, right-click your mouse on the stored procedure or function you want to view or modify. The Enterprise Manager will display a pop-up menu from which you will select Properties. For the current project, right-click your mouse on USP_PROCESS_CHECK534, and then select Properties from the pop-up menu to display the stored procedure's code as shown in Figure 538.1.

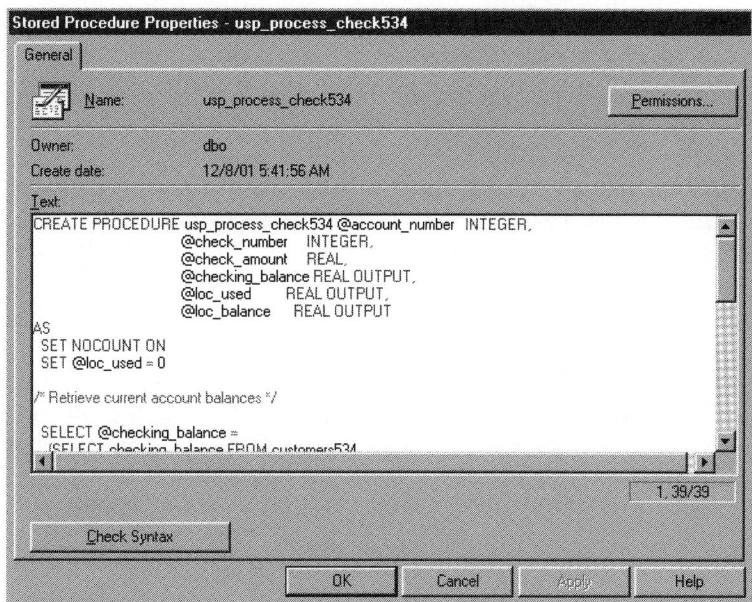

Figure 538.1 The MS-SQL Server Enterprise Manager Stored Procedure Properties dialog box

8. If you want to modify the stored procedure or function's behavior, make the desired changes, deletions, and additions in the within the Text window of the Stored Procedure (or User-Defined Function) Properties dialog box, and then click your mouse on the Check Syntax button.
9. Repeat Step 8 as necessary to correct any errors reported by the Enterprise Manager's syntax check of the procedure or function in the Text window.
10. To update the list of users allowed to execute the stored procedure or function, click the Permissions button. The Enterprise Manager will display the Object Properties dialog box with Permissions tab. Click a checkmark into the checkbox to the right of the usernames of those users allowed to execute the stored procedure. (To give all users permission to execute the stored procedure, click a checkmark into the checkbox to the right of the "public" role.) Then, click your mouse on the OK button to save your permissions updates and return to the Stored Procedure (or User-Defined Function) Properties dialog box.
11. To save your changes and make the updated stored procedure or function available to the DBMS, click your mouse pointer on the OK button.

After you complete Step 11, the Enterprise Manager will save the stored procedure (or user-defined function) text to disk and save it as a database object (by inserting the stored procedure or function text into the server's system tables). Then, the Enterprise Manager will exit the Stored Procedure (or User-Defined Function) Properties dialog box.

To create a new stored procedure or function, right-click your mouse on any unused space within the Enterprise Manager's right pane in Step 7. Then select New Stored Procedure (or New User-Defined Function) from the pop-up menu. Next, complete Steps 8–11, entering the stored procedure (or function) header and statements you want the DBMS to execute when the user calls the procedure or function in Step 8.

Note: *If you include the WITH ENCRYPTION clause within the CREATE PROCEDURE or CREATE FUNCTION statement, neither SP_HELPTEXT nor the Enterprise Manager will be able to display the stored procedure (or the User-Defined Function) source code. Moreover, you will not be able to use the Enterprise Manager to change the stored procedure or function's behavior by editing its text within the Stored Procedure (or User-Defined Function) Properties dialog box any time after saving the stored procedure or function to disk. In fact, the only way to change the behavior of an encrypted stored procedure or stored function is to drop the stored procedure or function and then recreate it. (You will learn how to delete stored procedures and functions within Tip 540 "Using the DROP Statement to Remove a Stored Procedure or User-Defined Function from the Database.")*

---

539 Using Transact-SQL Keywords DECLARE and SELECT to Define Variables in a Stored Procedure and Assign Initial Values to Them

When executing a batch of statements within a stored procedure or function, you often need variables to store data temporarily. As you learned in Tip 536 "Working with Cursors in Stored Procedures," you might use variables to store running totals as you work through a cursor, one row at a time. In addition, before you can use data stored within a cursor row, you must first transfer the data values from the cursor row's columns into temporary variables that your Transact-SQL statements can access.

To declare a variable, use the DECLARE statement with the following syntax:

```
DECLARE @<variable name> <data type>
        [...,@<last variable name> <last data type>]
```

Thus, to declare variables in which to store INTEGER, REAL, and DATETIME values, you might write the following DECLARE statement:

```
DECLARE @customer_count INTEGER, @total_sales REAL,
        @best_sales_date DATETIME
```

If you prefer, you can write multiple DECLARE statements within the same statement batch, or split a single declare statement across multiple lines so you can add comments about each variable's purpose such as:

```
DECLARE
  @customer_count INTEGER    /* number of customers serviced
                                by the salesperson */
  @total_sales REAL          /* grand total sales made */
  @best_sales_date DATETIME /* date most sales made */
```

Note that a variable's name may consist of any number of letters and numbers, but must begin with an at sign (@).

To assign values to variables, use a SET or SELECT statement. For example, to initialize variables your statement batch might include statements such as the following:

```
SET @customer_count = 0
SET @total_sales = 0.00
SET @best_sales_date = ''
```

Similarly, you can use the SELECT statement to set variable values as shown here:

```
SELECT @customer_count = 0, @total_sales = 0.00,
  @best_sales_date = ''
```

Bear in mind that the SELECT statement, used to initialize variable values here, is the standard SQL SELECT statement. As such, you can write the SELECT statement using the following syntax:

```
SELECT @variable_name = {expression | SELECT statement}
  [...{, @<last variable name> =
  {expression | SELECT statement}}
[FROM <list of tables>]
[WHERE expression]
[GROUP BY <column names>]
[HAVING expression]
[ORDER BY <column names>]
```

Thus, to print the name of the customer that placed the largest order along with the ID and the total sales for that salesperson you might use the following statement batch:

```
DECLARE
  @customer_name VARCHAR(26)
  @largest_order MONEY       /* largest order placed by a
                                single customer */
  @total_sales MONEY         /* grand total sales made */
  @salesperson_ID

SELECT @customer_name =
         RTRIM(first_name) + ' ' + RTRIM(last_name),
       @largest_order = order_total,
       @salesperson_ID = salesperson_ID
FROM customers
ORDER BY order_total

SELECT @total_sales = SUM(order_total)
FROM customers
WHERE salesperson_ID = @salesperson_ID

PRINT 'Largest order ('+CONVERT(VARCHAR(10),@largest_order)
  +') placed by'+@customer_name+' Sales Rep: '
  +CONVERT(VARCHAR(6),@salesperson_ID)
PRINT 'Total sales for rep: '
  +CONVERT(VARCHAR(6),@salesperson_ID)+' = '
  +CONVERT(VARCHAR(10),@total_sales)
```

If the SELECT statement used to assign values to variables returns multiple rows, (as is the case with the first SELECT statement in this example), the DBMS assigns the variables the values from the last row in the results set returned.

Note that variables created using DECLARE statements are "local" variables. This means that after the DBMS executes the last statement in the statement batch, procedure, or function, variables declared within the batch, procedure, or function are no longer available for use.

540 Using the DROP Statement to Remove a Stored Procedure or User-Defined Function from the Database

When you no longer need a stored procedure or stored function, you can remove it from the database with a DROP statement. Although the DBMS can manage a virtually unlimited number of stored procedures and functions, you should only keep online those currently used by system users.

During the lifetime of any DBMS, many once-important stored procedures and functions will fall into disuse as business conditions or data storage requirements change over time. By keeping obsolete procedures and functions in the database, you increase the amount of system documentation a user must review when searching for a procedure or function he or she needs. In addition, you increase server overhead by forcing the DBMS to search an ever-increasing list of stored procedures and functions each time a user invokes a stored procedure or function by name. Finally, (and perhaps most importantly), as table names are changed and tables are dropped from the database, some stored procedures may no longer function properly, because they attempt to operate on database objects that no longer exist.

To remove an existing stored procedure, use a DROP statement in the form:

```
DROP PROCEDURE <procedure name>
       [..., <last procedure name>]
```

Thus, to remove the stored procedures USP_PROCESS_CHECK, USP_ADD_ITEM, you would use a DROP PROCEDURE statement such as:

```
DROP PROCEDURE usp_process_check, usp_add_item
```

Note: *When removing a stored procedure you must drop all versions of the stored procedure at once. In Tip 531,"Using the CREATE PROCEDURE Statement to Create a Stored Procedure," you learned that you can create multiple versions of the same stored procedure within the same DBMS. Although you can modify and execute specific versions of a stored procedure by providing the version number when executing an ALTER PROCEDURE or EXEC statement, the DROP PROCEDURE statement does not allow you to enter a version number. Therefore, dropping a stored procedure means removing all its versions.*

Similarly, to delete an existing user-defined function us a DROP statement of the form:

```
DROP FUNCTION <function name>
       [..., <last function name>]
```

Therefore to remove the function UFN_REP_TOTAL_SALES, for example, you would submit the following statement to the DBMS for execution:

```
DROP FUNCTION ufn_rep_total_sales
```

DROP PROCEDURE and DROP FUNCTION rights default to the owner of the stored procedure or user-defined function, and are not transferable. However, any member of the SYSADMIN role, the DB_DDLADMIN (that is, the database data definition language administration) role, and the DBO can DROP any procedure or function by including the owner's ID in the DROP statement. For example, the DBO might remove a stored procedure owned by username "Konrad" with the following:

```
DROP PROCEDURE Konrad.usp_increase_my_pay
```

541 Understanding the MS-SQL Server Database Consistency Checker (DBCC)

The Database Consistency Checker (DBCC) is a tool you can use to get detailed information about database objects that the MS-SQL Server manages. In general terms, the DBCC is a set of statements (sometimes referred to as Database Console Commands), which you can use to make sure that all is well within the DBMS. As you will see from their descriptions within this tip and Tips 542–545, DBCC statements check the physical and logical consistency of the database. Many statements not only detect, but also fix the problems they detect.

Typically, you execute DBCC statements either to fix a reported problem within the DBMS (before resorting to a database restore, which may result in some data loss), or to determine the source of general DBMS "sluggishness" or stored procedure calls seemingly to yield wrong or inconsistent results.

DBCC statements fall into the following four categories:

- **Maintenance**—Perform maintenance tasks on a database, indexes within the database, or on the physical files that make up the logical file group in which the database is stored.
- **Miscellaneous**—Perform miscellaneous tasks such as displaying syntax information for a specified DBCC statement, changing the way the DBMS handles the storage of table data in memory, and unloading a DLL (extended-system stored procedure) from memory.
- **Status**—Check the status of such things as the amount of empty space within the transaction log, open transactions, stored procedures within the stored procedure cache and so on.

- **Validation**—Perform validation (and repair) operations on the database or its system tables, a table, index, or catalog within the database, on the files that make up the file group, or the allocation of database pages.

When you perform DBCC Maintenance tasks and Validation operations, you normally want to do so when there is as little activity as possible on the MS-SQL Server. If you attempt to run consistency checks and repairs while users are making a lot of updates and changes, you may receive false errors, because many DBCC system calls require near-exclusive use of the database. Therefore, if you must run DBCC statements on a database while it is in use, check the warning and error messages reported carefully. See if any reported errors are due to user-caused deadlocks (which you learned about in Tip 356 "Understanding Deadlocks and How the DBMS Resolves Them") or other timing issues resulting from a general high-level of DBMS activity. If in doubt, (and definitely before taking drastic repair measures), use the system stored procedure SP_DBOPTION to place the database in single-user mode before running DBCC maintenance or validation statements on it.

Suppose, for example, that you want to run some consistency checks on the SQLTips database. First, take exclusive control of the database by asking all users to logout and then place the database to single-user mode with the following statement:

```
sp_dboption SQLTips, 'single user', TRUE
```

Note: *Setting a database to single-user mode only means that one user can login to the database at a time. Therefore, if you called SP_DBOPTION while using a database other than the one you changed to single-user mode, make sure that you are the one user allowed access to the database by executing a "USE <database name>" statement immediately after you set the database to single-user mode. Thus, in the following example, you would make the preceding SP_DBOPTION call and then execute the following USE statement immediately thereafter:*

```
USE SQLTips
```

After you run the DBCC checks, you will want to perform any necessary maintenance or repair operations. Be sure to return the database state to multi-user mode so users can once again login to the database. To change the database back to multi-user mode, execute the following statement:

```
sp_dboption SQLTips, 'single user', FALSE
```

You will of course, substitute the name of your database for "SQLTips" in both the SP_DBOPTION call to set the database to single-user mode and the subsequent call to the same-system stored procedure to restore multi-user access.

Tips 542–545 will provide the syntax and discuss each of the DBCC statements available within the four DBCC statement categories.

542 Understanding DBCC Maintenance Statements

You can use the following five DBCC maintenance options to rebuild and defragment indexes, shrink database files, and update space usage tables:

- DBREINDEX—Rebuild one or more indexes for a table within a database.
- INDEXDEFRAG—Defragment clustered and secondary indexes on a specific table or view.
- SHRINKDATABASE—Reduces the file size of the physical data files that make up the database.
- SHRINKFILE—Used to reduce the file size of individual physical database files or of the transaction log file.
- UPDATEUSAGE—Reports and corrects inaccuracies in the SYSINDEXES table.

The syntax of the DBCC DBREINDEX statement is

```
DBCC DBREINDEX (['database.owner.<table name>'
      [,<index name> [,<fill factor>]]]) [WITH NO_INFOMSGS]
```

where:

- **database.owner.<table name>** is the fully qualified name of the table with the indexes you want to rebuild. You can omit the database and owner and give only the table name.
- **<index name>** is the name of the index that you want the DBMS to rebuild. If you omit the <index name> or specify it as '', the DBMS will rebuild all the table's indexes.
- **<fill factor>** is the percentage of space on each index page that the DBMS is to use for storing data. Each time an index page gets full (with data), the DBMS must split the page in two. This impacts performance as page-splits are expensive in terms of system resources. Thus, the lower fill factor (percentage), the more disk space the index consumes, but the less often the DBMS must add new pages to it. For more information on the "fill factor," see the FILLFACTOR section within Tip 162 "Understanding MS-SQL Server CREATE INDEX Statement Options." The <fill factor> you supply here becomes the new default FILLFACTOR for the index. If you supply a <fill factor> of zero (0), the DBMS uses the original FILLFACTOR defined for the index (again, as described in Tip 162).
- **<WITH NO_INFOMSGS>** tells the DBCC to suppress all informational messages—those with severity levels from 0 through 10.

You can use DBCC DBREINDEX to rebuild either an individual index for a table or all the table's indexes at once. Being able to rebuild all indexes at once is especially convenient when you perform a bulk copy of data into a table. It lets you create the PRIMARY KEY and UNIQUE indexes automatically without knowing the table's structure or constraints.

Moreover, DBCC DBREINDEX lets you recreate all indexes without having to code multiple DROP INDEX and CREATE INDEX statements. For example, to recreate all indexes on the PRODUCTS table within the NORTHWIND (sample) database with a FILLFACTOR of 50 percent, you would execute the following statement:

```
DBCC DBREINDEX('northwind.dbo.products','',50)
```

The syntax of the DBCC INDEXDEFRAG statement is

```
DBCC INDEXDEFRAG (
  {<database name>|<database ID>|0}
   ,{<table name>|<table ID>|'<view name>'|<view ID>}
   ,{<index name>|<index ID>} ) [WITH NO_INFOMSGS]
```

where:

- **<database name>|<database ID>|0** is the name of the database with the index you want the DBMS to defragment. As shown here, you can specify the database by name or by ID number. Specifying an ID of zero (0) tells the DBMS the table with the index is within the current database.
- **<table name>|<table ID>|<view name>|<view ID>** is the name or numeric ID of the table or view with the index you want to defragment.
- **<index name>|<index ID>** is the name or ID number of the index the DBMS is to defragment.
- **<WITH NO_INFOMSGS>** tells the DBMS to suppress all informational messages—those with severity levels from 0 through 10.

You can use DBCC INDEXDEFRAG to defragment both clustered and non-clustered indexes. DBCC INDEXDEFRAG performs two actions:

- It defragments the leaf level of an index so that the physical order of pages matches the left-to-right order of the leaf nodes, which improves the performance of an index scan.
- It compacts the index, moving data from one index and taking the FILLFACTOR into account. The DBMS removes any "empty" pages created as a result of shifting data from one index page to another.

Because defragmenting a large, fragmented index may take a long time, DBCC INDEXDEFRAG reports its progress every five minutes by giving an estimated percentage completed. You can terminate the defragmentation process at any time, and the DBMS will retain any work already performed by the procedure. When deciding whether to defragment an index or rebuild it entirely, keep the following in mind:

- DBCC INDEXDEFRAG (unlike DBCC DBREINDEX) does not hold locks long term and thus will not block users from executing queries and updates while it defragments an index.
- You can defragment a relatively unfragmented index in much less time than it will take to rebuild the same index. Conversely, a very fragmented index typically takes much longer to defragment than to rebuild.

- Defragmenting an index is always a fully-logged process. It inserts more entries into the database transaction log than rebuilding the the same index.

The syntax of the DBCC SHRINKDATABASE statement is

```
DBCC SHRINKDATABASE ( <database name> [,<target percent>]
      [, {NOTRUNCATE|TRUNCATEONLY}] )
```

where:

- **<database name>** is the name of the database whose files you want the DBMS to shrink (in size). The DBMS shrinks database files by removing the empty space available for additional data within each database file.
- **<target percent>** is the percentage of empty space the DBMS is to leave within the file after performing the "shrink" operation.
- **NOTRUNCATE** is the NOTRUNCATE option causes the DBMS to leave "freed" space within the database files. Omit NOTRUNCATE and specify only the <target percent> if you want DBCC SHRINKDATABASE to reduce the size of database files.
- **TRUNCATEONLY** releases the "freed" space back to the operating system for use. If you want to leave a percentage of free space within database files (as specified by <target percent>), omit the TRUNCATEONLY option. If you specify both (a <target percent> and TRUNCATEONLY), the DBMS ignores the <target percent> and truncates database files, returning any free space at the end of each file to the operating system.

If you want the DBMS to reduce the size of database files while leaving a certain percentage of each file "empty," execute the DBCC SHRINKDATABASE statement specifying the percentage of free space in each file. Suppose, for example, that you have a database named SQLTips with two data files and a transaction log file. Each of the three files is 20 megabytes in size and contains 12 megabytes of data. Executing the following statement then tells the DBMS to reduce each of the files to 15 megabytes:

```
DBCC SHRINKDATABASE (SQLTips, 20)
```

Each file will then have 12 megabytes of data plus three megabytes of free space (20 percent of 15 megabyte is three megabytes). The DBMS will move any data within the last five megabytes of each file to free space within the first 15 megabytes and reduce the total size of the 20-megabyte file to 15 megabytes.

If you specify the NOTRUNCATE option when executing the DBCC SHRINKDATABASE statement, the DBMS still moves data from allocated (8Kb) pages at the end of each file to unallocated (8Kb) pages at the front of the file. However, the file's size does not change. In this example, executing the following statement has the DBMS move all data to the first 12 megabytes within each file, leaving eight megabytes of free space at the end of each 20-megabyte file:

```
DBCC SHRINKDATABASE (SQLTips, NOTRUNCATE)
```

If you specify the TRUNCATE option when executing the DBCC SHRINKDATABASE statement, the DBMS does not move data within the data files. Instead, the DBMS simply truncates all unallocated (8Kb) pages from the end of each file. For example, if a 20-megabyte file has 12 megabytes of data spread across the first 17 megabytes within a file, the following statement will reduce the file's size to 17 megabytes, returning the last three megabytes of contiguous "free space" (or slack) to the operating system:

```
DBCC SHRINKDATABASE (SQLTips, TRUNCATEONLY)
```

Bear in mind that DBCC SHRINKDATABASE (unlike DBCC SHRINKFILE) will not reduce the physical size of any database files (neither data nor transaction log files) below the minimum size specified when the files were created (with a CREATE DATABASE statement) or the minimum file size later explicitly set within an ALTER DATABASE statement.

The syntax of the DBCC SHRINKFILE statement is

```
DBCC SHRINKFILE ( {<file name>|<file ID>
  {[,<target size>]|[,{EMPTYFILE|NOTRUNCATE|TRUNCATEONLY}]}
)
```

where:

- **<file name>|<file ID>** is the name of the file whose size you want the DBMS to reduce. You can specify the file by name or by ID number.
- **<target size>** is the integer value that specifies the "target" size for the file in megabytes. For example, if a 20 megabyte file has 12 megabytes of data and you specify a <target size> of 14, the DBMS will move the data within the last six megabytes of the file to unused (8Kb) pages within the first 14 megabytes, and truncate the file at 14 megabytes. The DBMS will not however, make a file smaller than the size required to hold all data within the file. For example, given the same 20 megabyte file with 12 megabytes of data, specifying a <target size> of 10 will reduce the file's size to 12 megabytes (not 10 megabytes).
- **EMPTYFILE** tells the DBMS to move all data within the target file to other files within the same file group, leaving an empty file which you can drop using the ALTER DATABASE statement. After you specify the EMPTYFILE option for a file, MS-SQL Server will no longer place any data into the file.
- **NOTRUNCATE** tells the DBMS to move all allocated (8Kb) pages past the <target size> to unallocated (8Kb) pages prior to <target size> within the file. If you omit <target size>, the DBMS moves all allocated (8Kb) pages to the front of the file such that all free space (or slack) remains at the end of the file. When specified, NOTRUNCATE prevents the DBMS from releasing any "free" space within the file to the operating system. As such, the file size will not change.
- **TRUNCATEONLY** tells the DBMS to shrink the file size to the last allocated extent. Thus, if the 20-megabyte file has 12 megabytes of data spread across the first 15 megabytes, specifying TRUNCATEONLY will reduce the file's size to 15 megabytes. The DBMS does not shift any data within the file.

You can use the DBCC SHRINKFILE statement to reduce the size of a file to smaller than the minimum size specified within the CREATE DATABASE statement used to create the file (or the explicit file size specified within an ALTER DATABASE statement). If you reduce the file's size below the minimum file size, the <file size> you specify within the DBCC SHRINKFILE statement becomes the new minimum file size for the file.

The syntax of the DBCC UPDATEUSAGE statement is

```
DBCC UPDATEUSAGE ( {'<database name>'|0}
  [,{'<table name>'|'<view name>'}
   [,{'<index name>'|'<index ID>'}]] )
  [WITH {[COUNT_ROWS[,NO_INFOMSGS]]|NO_INFOMSGS}]
```

where:

- **<database name>|0** is the name of the database for which to report the correct file usage statistics. Zero (0) means use the current database.
- **<table name>|<view name>** is the name of the table or indexed view for which to report the correct usage statistics.
- **<index name>|<index ID>** is the name or ID number of the index for which to report usage statistics. If you do not specify an <index name> (or an <index ID>), the DBMS will update the statistics for all indexes on the table or view.
- **COUNT_ROWS** tells the DBMS to update the ROWS column of rows within the SYSINDEXES table for the current table or view specified with the current count of the rows within the table or view. If you do not specify a table or view, the DBMS will update the ROWS column within the corresponding SYSINDEX rows for each table and view within the database. The COUNT_ROWS option only affects the ROWS column of SYSINDEX rows in which the INDID column is 0 or 1.
- **NO_INFOMSGS** tells the DBMS to suppress the display of all informational messages.

DBCC UPDATEUSAGE will correct the ROWS, USED, RESERVED, and DPAGES columns within the SYSINDEXES table for tables, views, and clustered indexes. Size information is not stored for non-clustered indexes.

Typically, you will run DBCC UPDATEUSAGE only when you suspect the system-stored procedure SP_SPACEUSED is reporting inaccurate results. In fact, SP_SPACEUSED accepts an optional parameter to run DBCC UPDATEUSAGE before returning the space usage information for the table, view, or index. If it finds no inaccuracies within the SYSINDEXES table, DBCC UPDATEUSAGE returns no data. Conversely, if DBCC UPDATEUSAGE finds inaccuracies (which it corrects), the statement returns messages that give the rows and columns it updated within SYSINDEXES—so long as you did not specify the NO_INFOMSGS option.

543 Understanding DBCC Miscellaneous Statements

You can use the following four DBCC miscellaneous options to manage the MS-SQL Server's memory usage or display the syntax of any DBCC statement:

- <DLL name> (FREE)—Unloads the DLL for an extended stored procedure from memory.
- HELP—Returns the syntax for the specified DBCC statement.
- PINTABLE—Tells the DBMS not to flush data for the specified table from memory.
- UNPINTABLE—Tells the DBMS it can flush table pages from the buffer cache as necessary.

The syntax of the DBCC <DLL name> (FREE) statement is

```
DBCC <DLL name> (FREE)
```

where:

- **<DLL name>**—Is the name of the extended stored procedure dynamic-link library (DLL) file you want the DBMS to remove from memory.

When you tell the DBMS to execute an extended stored procedure the DBMS loads a DLL program file into memory. For example, to execute XP_SENDMAIL the DBMS loads "sqlmap70.dll." Any DLLs that extended stored procedures load into memory remain in memory until you shut down the MS-SQL Server. To unload an extended stored procedure's DLL (to free up memory), you can execute the DBCC <DLL NAME> (FREE) statement. For example, to unload sqlmap70.dll from memory, submit the following statement to the DBMS:

```
DBCC xp_sendmail (FREE)
```

You can display a list of all the extended stored procedure DLL files currently available on the MS-SQL Server by executing SP_HELPEXTENDEDPROC.

The syntax of the DBCC HELP statement is

```
DBCC HELP ( '<DBCC statement>'|@<variable name>|'?' )
```

where:

- **<DBCC statement>|@<variable name>|** is a (quoted) literal string ('<DBCC statement>') or a variable (@<variable name>) with the name of the DBCC statement, that is, the keyword following "DBCC" in a DBCC statement.
- **?** tells the DBMS to return a list of all DBCC statements for which you can obtain "help" information.

For example, to display the syntax of the DBCC statement "DBCC UPDATEUSAGE," you would submit the following DBCC HELP statement to the DBMS:

```
DBCC HELP ('UPDATEUSAGE')
```

Or, you could place the statement name into a variable (such as @DBCC_STATEMENT, for example) and use the variable in place of the string literal ('UPDATEUSAGE') by executing the following statement batch:

```
DECLARE @DBCC_statement SYSNAME
SET @DBCC_statement = 'UPDATEUSAGE'
DBCC HELP (@DBCC_statement)
```

The syntax of the DBCC PINTABLE statement is

```
DBCC PINTABLE ( <database ID>,<table ID>] )
```

where:

- **<database ID>** is the ID number of the database with the table to be "pinned." To determine the database ID number, call the DB_ID function as SELECT DB_ID(['<database name>']).
- **<table ID>** is the ID number of the table to be "pinned." To determine the table ID number, call the OBJECT_ID function as SELECT OBJECT_ID('[<database name>..]<table name>').

DBCC PINTABLE does not cause the DBMS to read a table's data into memory. Whether "pinned" or not, a table's data is read into the server's memory cache as normal while executing Transact-SQL statements. However, when the MS-SQL Server needs space to read in a new page, the DBMS will not flush the cached pages from a "pinned" table from memory. Use DBCC PINTABLE to read small, frequently-used tables into memory. That way, the DBMS reads table data into memory the first time the DBMS retrieves and/or updates it, and subsequent references the DBMS makes to the same table data will be satisfied from memory versus requiring a disk read.

Note: *Be very careful when using the DBCC PINTABLE statement. If you pin too large a table or too many tables, you can severely degrade system performance. By pinning memory to a specific table (or set of tables) you can make large portions of the buffer cache unavailable for use to service data requests on other tables. In fact, if you have pinned a table that is larger than the buffer cache, it can fill the entire cache and thereby slow the DBMS to a crawl. If the buffer cache becomes filled, a member of the SYSADMIN role must shut down the MS-SQL Server, restart the DBMS, and then use DBCC UNPINTABLE to unpin the table (or tables).*

The syntax of the DBCC UNPINTABLE statement is

```
DBCC UNPINTABLE ( <database ID>,<table ID>] )
```

where:

- **<database ID>** is the ID number of the database with the table to be unpinned. To determine the database ID number, call the DB_ID function as SELECT DB_ID(['<database name>']).
- **<table ID>** is the ID number of the table to be unpinned. To determine the table ID number, call the OBJECT_ID function as SELECT OBJECT_ID('[<database name>..]<table name>').

When you execute the DBCC UNPINTABLE statement, the DBMS does not immediately flush the table data from its cache buffers. The DBCC UNPINTABLE statement simply marks the table as unpinned, which tells the DBMS that it can remove the table's data from memory if the DBMS needs space to read in a new page from disk.

544 Understanding DBCC Status Statements

You can use the first two of the following six DBCC status statements to display the most recent statement each active user connection sent to the DBMS and the results set that the DBMS returned. The remaining four statements let you check the fragmentation statistics for indexes and table data, monitor transaction log usage, and display the connection options settings for the current session:

- INPUTBUFFER—Displays the last statement the MS-SQL Server received from a particular client connected to the DBMS.
- OUTPUTBUFFER—Displays in hexadecimal and ASCII, the last set of results sent to a particular client attached to the DBMS.
- SHOWCONTIG—Displays fragmentation information for a table and its indexes.
- OPENTRAN—Displays information about the oldest active transaction, if any, being processed by the DBMS.
- SQLPERF—Displays statistics about the transaction log in all database managed by the MS-SQL Server.
- USEROPTIONS—Displays the user options set for the current connection with the DBMS.

The syntax of the DBCC INPUTBUFFER statement is

```
DBCC INPUTBUFFER ( <system process ID> )
```

where:

- **<system process ID>** is the ID number (SPID) of the user connection to the DBMS. You can call the system stored procedure SP_WHO to get the list of processes currently running on the DBMS. Each row of the results set returned by SP_WHO gives the system process ID (SPID), current status, user's login name, name of the database the process is using, and the name of the last request submitted to the DBMS for execution.

To display the full text of the last statement a specific connection submitted to the DBMS, first execute the following stored procedure call to determine the connection's SPID:

```
SP_WHO
```

Look at the LOGINAME and HOSTNAME columns to find the row with the username on the MS-SQL Server whose last transaction you want to display. Then, use the number displayed in the row's SPID column as the <system process ID> for the DBCC INPUTBUFFER statement. The DBCC process will display the last statement the DBMS received from the connection. For example, to display the last statement received from the user at connection 13 you would submit the following statement:

```
DBCC INPUTBUFFER(13)
```

The syntax of the DBCC OUTPUTBUFFER statement is

```
DBCC OUTPUTBUFFER ( <system process ID>)
```

where:

- **<system process ID>** is the ID number (SPID) of the user connection to the DBMS. You can call the system stored procedure SP_WHO to get the list of processes currently running on the DBMS. Each row within the results set returned by SP_WHO gives the system process ID (SPID), current status, login name, name of the database the process is using, and the name of the last request submitted to the DBMS for execution.

To display the most recent results set sent from the DBMS to the user at connection 20, for example, submit the following statement to the DBMS:

```
DBCC OUTPUTBUFFER (20)
```

The DBMS will display a results set with each character the DBMS last sent to the client at connection 20. Each row within the table shows the hexadecimal values for the characters sent at the left and the ASCII representation for those characters (if any) along the right side of each row.

The syntax of the DBCC SHOWCONTIG statement is:

```
DBCC SHOWCONTIG
  [( {<table name>|<table ID>|<view name>|<view ID>}
     [,<index name>|<index ID>] )]
  [WITH {ALL_INDEXES|FAST[,ALLINDEXES]|
    TABLERESULTS[,{ALL_INDEXES}][,{FAST|ALL_LEVELS}] }]
```

where:

- **<table name>|<table ID>|<view name>|<view ID>** is the name of the table or indexed view for which to report fragmentation data. (You can specify the table or indexed view by name or by ID number.) If you specify neither the table nor the view name or ID, the DBMS will check and report on the fragmentation for all tables and indexed views within the database.
- **<index name>|<index ID>** is the name or ID number of the index for which to report fragmentation statistics. If you do not specify an <index name> (or an <index ID>), the DBMS will report fragmentation stats for the base index (that is, for the PRIMARY KEY) on the specified table or view.
- **FAST** tells the DBCC process to perform a fast scan and report minimal information. When performing a fast scan, the DBMS does not read the "leaf" or data-level pages within the index.
- **TABLERESULTS** tells the DBCC process to display the fragmentation information returned in tabular form versus a summary report. In addition to changing the output format (from report to table), each row within the results table includes the table name, index name, record size, page count, and disk extent data, in addition to all the fragmentation data returned when you do not specify the TABLERESULTS option.
- **ALL_INDEXES** tells the DBCC to display fragmentation information about all indexes for a table, even when a specific index is specified with <index name> or <index ID>.
- **ALL_LEVELS** tells the DBCC to produce a row of output for each level within the index tree for each index processed. You can only specify the ALL_LEVELS option if you also specify the TABLERESULTS option and do not specify the FAST option. When you do not specify ALL_LEVELS, the DBMS only processes the table data and the highest level within the index tree, the leaf level.

Index and table files become fragmented because users execute INSERT, UPDATE, and DELETE statements that over time cause unused (8Kb) pages to appear among partially-filled pages that make up the index and table data files. As data gets spread across multiple pages, it is no longer stored compactly within the minimum possible number of (8Kb) pages. DBMS performance degrades, because fragmented data and/or index files cause DBMS to perform more and more page retrievals to retrieve the same amount of data.

You can defragment table data by executing the DBCC SHRINKDATABASE statement with the NOTRUNCATE option (as you learned in Tip 542 "Understanding DBCC Maintenance Statements"). To defragment indexes, either rebuild them using the DBCC REINDEX statement or defragment them (without rebuilding them) by executing the DBCC INDEX DEFRAG statement. (You learned about both these statements in Tip 542.)

To retrieve the information you need in order to determine the fragmentation levels of all indexes and tables within a database, execute the DBCC SHOWCONTIG statement without parameters as:

```
DBCC SHOWCONTIG WITH ALL_INDEXES
```

If you want to check only the fragmentation of a single table within the database, supply the table name. For example, to check the fragmentation level of the ORDER DETAILS table within the NORTHWIND database, you would execute the following statement batch to produce the report shown in Figure 544.1:

```
USE NORTHWIND
DBCC SHOWCONTIG('order details') WITH ALL_INDEXES
```

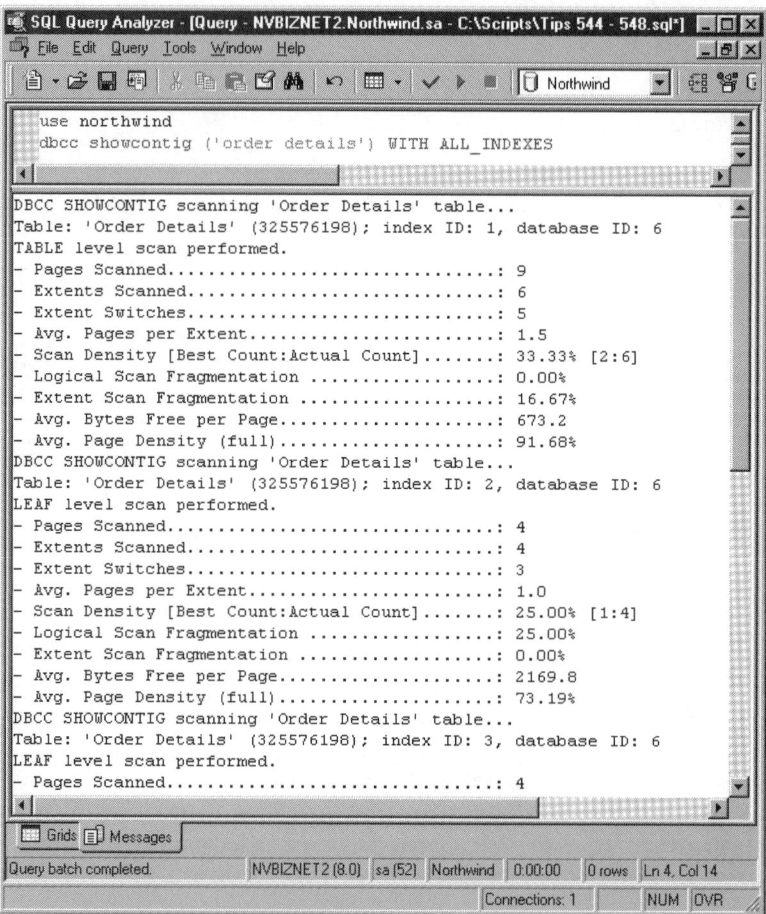

Figure 544.1 Output from an MS-SQL Server DBCC SHOWCONTIG statement

Note that you can enclose the name of the table (or view) within single quotes. In fact, you must enclose the name within quotes if the name consists of multiple words separated by spaces (such as the table named ORDER DETAILS in this example).

The fragmentation data returned by the DBCC SHOWCONTIG statement consists of the following:

- **Pages Scanned**—The number of (8Kb) pages the table or index contains. (TABLERESULTS column, PAGES.)

- **Extents Scanned**—The number of disk extents the table or index contains. The operating system adds space to a disk file one "extent" worth of bytes at a time. You set the size of an extent when you format the disk for the operating system. The optimal extent size for MS-SQL Server running under the Windows NT, NTFS file system is 64Kb. (TABLERESULTS column, EXTENTS.)
- **Extent Switches**—The number of times the DBCC process had to move from one disk extent to another while traversing the (8Kb) pages within the table or index. (TABLERESULTS column, EXTENTSWITCHES.)
- **Avg. Pages per Extent**—The average number of (8Kb) pages stored within each (64Kb) disk extent.
- **Scan Density (Best Count, Actual Count)**—Best Count is the number of extent changes the DBCC process would encounter if everything were contiguously linked (that is, if there were no fragmentation within the data file or index). Actual Count is the actual number of extent changes the DBCC process encountered when processing the table or index. Scan Density is the Best Count divided by the Actual Count, expressed as a percentage. If Scan Density is 100 percent, everything is contiguous (that is, there is no fragmentation); if Scan Density is less than 100 percent, some fragmentation exists. (TABLERESULTS columns, SCANDENSITY, BESTCOUNT, ACTUALCOUNT.)
- **Logical Scan Fragmentation**—The percentage of times when the next page indicated in an IAM (Indexed Access Method) is a different (8Kb) page than the page pointed to by the next page pointer in the index leaf page. (TABLERESULTS column, LOGICALFRAGMENTATION.)
- **Extent Scan Fragmentation**—The percentage of times the disk extent with the current (8Kb) page for an index is not physically the next extent after the extent that contains the previous (8kb) page for an index. (TABLERESULTS column, EXTENTFRAGMENTATION.)
- **Avg. Bytes Free per Page**—The average number of free (unused) bytes on the (8Kb) pages scanned. Although less unused space per page is better, the row size can affect the amount of free space in that the larger the row size, the more unused space per (8Kb) page. (TABLERESULTS column, AVERAGEFREEBYTES.)
- **Avg. Page Density (full)**—The page density expressed as a percentage that takes into account the table's row size. As such, this is a more accurate indication of how full the (8Kb) pages in the table or index are. (TABLERESULTS column, AVERAGEPAGEDENSITY.)

When deciding whether to defragment a table or index:

- Check the Avg. Page Density (full), it should be a high percentage.
- Check Logical Scan Fragmentation and Extent Scan Fragmentation, both these numbers should be as close to zero (0) as possible (0–10 percent is an acceptable range). Bear in mind Extent Scan Fragmentation will be high if the index spans multiple files.

- Compare Extent Switches and Extents Scanned—ideally, both numbers will be equal. Note this indication of fragmentation does not work for an index that spans multiple files.
- Check the Scan Density—it should be as high as possible.

If you determine a table or its indexes are fragmented, use what you learned in Tip 542 "Understanding DBCC Maintenance Statements" to either rebuild or defragment the indexes and move unused pages to the end of the table data file.

The syntax of the DBCC SQLPERF statement is:

```
DBCC SQLPERF (LOGSPACE)
```

When executed, DBCC SQLPERF (LOGSPACE) returns a table with rows that show the name of each database managed by the DBMS, the size of the transaction log file (in Megabytes), and the percentage of the transaction log file currently occupied by transaction data.

The syntax of the DBCC OPENTRAN statement is

```
DBCC OPENTRAN ( {'<database name>'|<database ID>} )
  [WITH TABLERESULTS [,NO_INFOMSGS]]
```

where:

- **<database name>|<database ID>** is the name (or numeric ID) of the database whose transaction log you want to query for a list of transactions not yet written permanently to the database.
- **<WITH TABLERESULTS>** tells the DBMS to format the results set in a tabular format you can easily load into a table. If you do not specify the TABLERESULTS option, the DBMS returns results set as a "readable" report versus in tabular form.
- **<NO_INFOMSGS>** tells the DBMS to suppress all informational messages.

If you specify neither the <database name> nor the <database ID> the DBMS will assume you want to display the uncommitted statements in the transaction log for the current database. You can use DBCC OPENTRAN to clear uncommitted transactions without having all users logoff or shutting down and then restarting the MS-SQL Server. Instead, you can use DBCC OPENTRAN to determine which user connections have uncommitted transactions. Then you can either have each user with an open transaction either submit a COMMIT statement or a ROLLBACK statement to close the transaction. Or, you can use the output from an SP_WHO stored procedure call to determine the user's SPID and terminate the connection if necessary.

The syntax of the DBCC USEROPTIONS is:

```
DBCC USEROPTIONS
```

When executed, DBCC USEROPTIONS returns a table such as that shown in Figure 544.2, which has a row for each session option set and its current value.

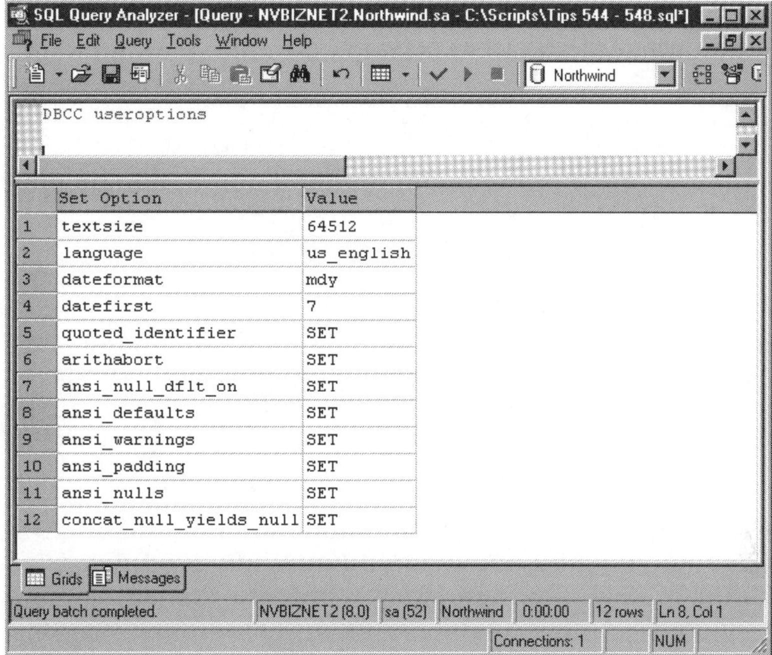

	Set Option	Value
1	textsize	64512
2	language	us_english
3	dateformat	mdy
4	datefirst	7
5	quoted_identifier	SET
6	arithabort	SET
7	ansi_null_dflt_on	SET
8	ansi_defaults	SET
9	ansi_warnings	SET
10	ansi_padding	SET
11	ansi_nulls	SET
12	concat_null_yields_null	SET

Figure 544.2 Results set from an MS-SQL Server DBCC USEROPTIONS statement

545 Understanding DBCC Validation Statements

You can use the following seven DBCC validation statements to check for and correct problems in your database files. Using DBCC validation statements, you can check the integrity of disk allocation structures, the integrity of database tables, indexes, and views, and the consistency of the data within the tables that make up the system catalog. You an also check for constraint violations, and set the value of a table's IDENTITY property. In addition to reporting problems found, most DBCC statements have "repair" options you can use to correct errors when executed in single-user mode:

- CHECKALLOC—Checks (and can repair) the disk allocation structures for a specified database.
- CHECKCATALOG—Checks for consistency in and between system tables within a database.
- CHECKCONSTRAINTS—Checks the integrity of one or all FOREIGN KEY and CHECK constraints on one or all tables in a database.

- CHECKDB—Checks (and can repair) both the disk allocation structures and the integrity of all objects within the database.
- CHECKFILEGROUP—Checks (and can repair) the disk allocation and structural integrity of all tables in within a file group.
- CHECKIDENT—Checks and lets you set the value of the IDENTITY property for tables that have an IDENTITY column.
- CHECKTABLE—Checks (and can repair) the integrity of the data within a table.

The syntax of the DBCC CHECKALLOC statement is

```
DBCC CHECKALLOC ( '<database name>'
  [,{REPAIR_ALLOW_DATA_LOSS|REPAIR_FAST|REPAIR_REBUILD}] )
  [WITH
    {[ALL_ERRORMSGS|NOINFOMSGS][,[ESTIMATEONLY]]} ]
```

where:

- **<database name>** is the name of the database for which you want the DBCC to check for allocation errors. When it is run with the REPAIR_ALLOW_DATA_LOSS option, DBCC CHECKALLOC will ensure that the index structures that tell the DBMS where to find data within the database file on disk actually point to table or index data and that the disk extent in which the data resides is allocated to the database object's storage area within the database file.
- **REPAIR_FAST** tells the DBCC process to perform minor, non-time-consuming repairs such as removing extra keys in non-clustered indexes. Repairs performed under the REPAIR_FAST option will not result in any data loss.
- **REPAIR_REBUILD** tells the DBCC process to perform the same repairs as specified by the REPAIR_FAST option plus time-consuming repairs such as rebuilding indexes. Repairs performed under the REPAIR_REBUILD option will not result in any data loss.
- **REPAIR_ALLOW_DATA_LOSS** tells the DBCC process to perform the same repairs as it would when you specify the REPAIR_REBUILD option plus repair allocation errors, structural row errors, and delete invalid text objects. Repairs performed under the REPAIR_ALLOW_DATA_LOSS option may (as its name implies) result in some data loss if the DBCC process must remove corrupted data.
- **ALL_ERRORMSGS** tells the DBCC process to display all error messages. If NO_INFOMSGS is specified and ALL_ERRORMSGS is not, DBCC CHECKALLOC will only display the first 200 error messages per object.
- **NO_INFOMSGS** tells the DBCC process to suppress all informational messages (and display only error messages).
- **ESTIMATE_ONLY** tells the DBCC process to display the estimated amount of space within TEMPDB that the DBCC CHECKALLOC statement will require when executed with the options and parameters specified.

Note: *To execute DBCC CHECKALLOC with one of the repair options (REPAIR_FAST, REPAIR_REBUILD, or REPAIR_ALLOW_DATA_LOSS), you must first set the database to be repaired to single-user mode.*

The syntax of the DBCC CHECKCATALOG statement is

```
DBCC CHECKCATALOG ( '<database name>' ) [WITH NO_INFOMSGS]
```

where:

- **<database name>** is the name of the database in which you want the DBCC to check the consistency of the data within the system tables.
- **NO_INFOMSGS** tells the DBCC process to suppress all informational messages in the report of space used by the system catalog. If you specify the NO_INFOMSGS option, DBCC CHECKCATALOG will display only the first 200 error messages the process encounters. To display all error messages, omit the NO_INFOMSGS option from the DBCC CHECKCATALOG statement.

When executed, DBCC CHECKCATALOG does such things as make sure that every data type within the SYSCOLUMNS table has a matching entry within the SYSTYPES table and that every view listed in the SYSOBJECTS table has at least one column within the SYSCOLUMNS table.

The syntax of the DBCC CHECKCONSTRAINTS statement is

```
DBCC CHECKCONSTRAINTS
  [( '<table name>'|'<constraint name>' )]
  [WITH {ALL_ERRORMSGS|ALL_CONSTRAINTS}]
```

where:

- **<table_name>** is the name of the table with the constraints you want the DBCC process to check. If you specify a table name, the DBCC checks all the table's enabled constraints.
- **<constraint name>** is the name of the constraint you want the DBCC to check.
- **ALL_CONSTRAINTS** tells DBCC to check all constraints (both enabled and disabled) on the table specified by <table name>. Or, if neither <table name> nor <constraint name> are specified, tells the DBCC process to check all constraints on all tables. (If you specify a <constraint name>, ALL_CONSTRAINTS has no effect.)
- **ALL_ERRORMSGS** tells the DBCC process to display all rows that violate the constraints checked. If you omit the ALL_ERRORMSGS option, the DBCC process will report only the first 200 constraint violations within each table it checks.

If you specify neither a <table name> nor a <constraint name> the DBCC CHECKCONSTRAINTS statement will check all enabled constraints on all tables within the current database.

For each FOREIGN KEY and CHECK constraint violation it finds, DBCC CHECKCONSTRAINTS returns the name of the table, the name of the constraint, and the data value that caused the constraint violation.

The syntax of the DBCC CHECKDB statement is

```
DBCC CHECKDB ( '<database name>'
   [,NOINDEX|{REPAIR_ALLOW_DATA_LOSS|REPAIR_FAST|
     REPAIR_REBUILD}] )
   [WITH {[ALL_ERRORMSGS][,[NO_INFOMSGS]][,[TABLOCK]]
           [,[ESTIMATEONLY]][,[PHYSICAL_ONLY]] }]
```

where:

- **<database name>** is the name of the database in which you want the DBCC to check for allocation and structural integrity errors.
- **NOINDEX** specifies that non-clustered indexes on non-system (that is, on user-defined) tables should not be checked.
- **REPAIR_FAST** tells the DBCC process to perform minor, non-time-consuming repairs such as removing extra keys in non-clustered indexes. Repairs performed under the REPAIR_FAST option will not result in any data loss.
- **REPAIR_REBUILD** tells the DBCC process to perform the same repairs as specified by the REPAIR_FAST option plus time-consuming repairs such as rebuilding indexes. Repairs performed under the REPAIR_REBUILD option will not result in any data loss.
- **REPAIR_ALLOW_DATA_LOSS** tells the DBCC process to perform the same repairs as it would when you specify the REPAIR_REBUILD option plus repair allocation errors, structural row errors, and delete invalid text objects. Repairs performed under the REPAIR_ALLOW_DATA_LOSS option may (as its name implies) result in some data loss if the DBCC process must remove corrupted data.
- **ALL_ERRORMSGS** tells the DBCC process to display all error messages. If NO_INFOMSGS is specified and ALL_ERRORMSGS is not, DBCC CHECKDB will only display the first 200 error messages per object.
- **NO_INFOMSGS** tells the DBCC process to suppress all informational messages (and display only error messages).
- **TABLOCK** tells the DBCC to obtain a shared table locks (versus row or perhaps, page locks). Specifying the TABLOCK option makes DBCC CHECKDB run faster on a DBMS that has a heavy processing load. However, issuing table locks will decrease concurrency as users are forced to wait for the DBCC process to complete its work on the entire table (versus on a single row or 8Kb page of rows).
- **ESTIMATE_ONLY** tells the DBCC process to display the estimated amount of space within TEMPDB that the DBCC CHECKDB statement will need when executed given the options and parameters specified.

- **PHYSICAL_ONLY** tells the DBCC process to check only the physical consistency of the database by checking the structure of page and record headers, the database file allocation structures, and the allocated disk extents for hardware failures that can corrupt data. PHYSICAL_ONLY implies that you want NO_INFOMSGS, and you cannot specify PHYSICAL_ONLY with any of the three repair options (REPAIR_FAST, or REPAIR_REBUILD, REPAIR_ALLOW_DATA_LOSS).

Note: *To execute DBCC CHECKDB with one of the repair options (REPAIR_FAST, REPAIR_REBUILD, or REPAIR_ALLOW_DATA_LOSS), you must first set the database to be repaired to single-user mode.*

When executed without the PHYSICAL ONLY option, DBCC CHECKDB is the most comprehensive DBCC validation statement in that it will identify and repair the widest possible range of errors. In short, DBCC CHECKDB validates the integrity of everything within the database. As such, if you run DBCC CHECKDB, you need not run DBCC CHECKALLOC or DBCC CHECKTABLE, because DBCC CHECKDB performs all the validation and repair operations those statements provide.

The syntax of the DBCC CHECKFILEGROUP statement is

```
DBCC CHECKFILEGROUP ( [{'<filegroup name>'|<filegroup ID>}]
  [,NOINDEX] )
  [WITH {[ALL_ERRORMSGS][,[NO_INFOMSGS]][,[TABLOCK]]
         [,[ESTIMATEONLY]] }]
```

where:

- **<filegroup name>** is the name of the file group for which you want to check table allocation and structural integrity. (You learned how to put database objects within file groups in Tip 496 "Adding Files and Filegroups to an Existing Database" and Tip 497 "Using the MS-SQL Server Enterprise Manager to Add Files and Filegroups to an Existing Database.")
- **<filegroup ID>** is the unique integer ID assigned to each file group within a database. To determine the filegroup ID, first find the filegroup's name within the GROUPNAME column of the SYSFILEGROUPS table. Then, look at the integer within the GROUPID column of that row for the filegroup ID.
- **NOINDEX** specifies that non-clustered indexes on non-system (that is, on user-defined) tables should not be checked. (DBCC CHECKFILEGROUP always checks all indexes on system tables when run on the PRIMARY file group.)
- **ALL_ERRORMSGS** tells the DBCC process to display all error messages. If NO_INFOMSGS is specified and ALL_ERRORMSGS is not, DBCC CHECKFILEGROUP will only display the first 200 error messages per table.
- **NO_INFOMSGS** tells the DBCC process to suppress all informational messages (and display only error messages).

- **TABLOCK** tells the DBCC process to obtain a shared table lock (versus row or perhaps, a page lock) while checking (and repairing) a table. Specifying the TABLOCK option makes DBCC CHECKFILEGROUP run faster on a DBMS with a heavy processing load. However, issuing table locks decreases concurrency as other users are forced to wait for the DBCC process to complete its work on the entire table (versus on a single row or 8Kb page of rows) before they can work with the data in the table.
- **ESTIMATE_ONLY** tells the DBCC process to display the estimated amount of space in TEMPDB the DBCC CHECKFILEGROUP statement will need when executed with the options and parameters specified.

DBCC CHECKFILEGROUP and DBCC CHECKDB are similar in that they both check the allocation and structural integrity of tables within the database. However, while DBCC CHECKDB checks the integrity for all tables, DBCC CHECKFILEGROUP checks only the integrity for tables either located within or that have indexes located within the file group specified by the <filegroup name> (or <filegroup ID>) parameter.

The syntax of the DBCC CHECKIDENT statement is

```
DBCC CHECKIDENT ( '<table name>'
  [,{NORESEED|RESEED[,<new reseed value>]}] )
```

where:

- **<table name>** is the name of the table with an IDENTITY column whose IDENTITY property you want to check or change. (You learned how to use the identity property to have the DBMS insert an incrementing non-NULL value into a table column each time you insert a row into the table in Tip 32 "Understanding the MS-SQL Server IDENTITY Property.")
- **NORESEED** specifies that the DBCC process should report but not change the value of the IDENTITY property.
- **RESEED** specifies that the DBCC process should correct the value of the IDENTITY property. If the IDENTITY property is less than the highest value within the table's IDENDITY column, DBCC CHECKIDENT will set the IDENTITY property to maximum value within the column. Conversely, if the IDENTITY property has a value greater than or equal to the maximum value within the table's IDENTITY column, DBCC CHECKIDENT will not change the IDENTITY property's value.
- **<new reseed value>** is the value to which the DBCC process will set the identity property for the table. If specified, the <new reseed value> must follow the RESEED option.

There is no intrinsic requirement that the values within an IDENTITY column must be unique. However, you typically use the IDENTITY property to have the DBMS insert a non-null, incrementing value into a PRIMARY KEY or into a column with a UNIQUE constraint. In so doing, you tell the DBMS to insert a unique value by which you can identify each row you insert within a table. Therefore, be careful when using the DBCC CHECKIDENT statement to change the IDENTITY property. If the table's IDENTITY column is a PRIMARY KEY or is subject to the UNIQUE constraint, you must set the IDENTITY property equal to or higher than the maximum value already within the column. If you do not, the DBMS will at some point, generate a duplicate IDENTITY (seed) value, which will prevent users from inserting additional rows into the table.

To report the IDENTITY property's value and the maximum value within the table's IDENTITY column—without changing the IDENTITY property's value, execute the DBCC CHECKIDENT statement as:

```
DBCC CHECKIDENT ('<table name>',NORESEED)
```

To report the IDENTITY property's value, execute the DBCC CHECKIDENT statement as:

```
DBCC CHECKIDENT ('<table name>',RESEED)
```

If the IDENTITY property's value is less than the maximum value within the table's IDENTITY column, executing DBCC CHECKIDENT using the format shown in this example tells the DBMS to set the property's value to the maximum value within the column.

To report the IDENTITY property's current value and set it to a new value (that is, to the <new reseed value>) without regard to the maximum value within the table's IDENTITY column, execute the DBCC CHECKIDENT statement as:

```
DBCC CHECKIDENT ('<table name>',RESEED,<new reseed value>)
```

If the table's IDENTITY property has a value greater than the maximum value within the table's IDENTITY column and you want to set the IDENTITY property to the maximum value within the IDENTITY column, execute the following statement batch:

```
DBCC CHECKIDENT ('<table name>',RESEED,0)
DBCC CHECKIDENT ('<table name>',RESEED)
```

(You would of course, substitute the name of the table with the IDENTITY property you want to adjust for <table name> and the actual value you want the IDENTITY property to have for <new reseed value> in the previous statements.)

The syntax of the DBCC CHECKTABLE statement is

```
DBCC CHECTABLE ( '<table name>'|'<view name>'
  [,NOINDEX|<index ID>|
    {REPAIR_ALLOW_DATA_LOSS|REPAIR_FAST|REPAIR_REBUILD}] )
  [WITH {[ALL_ERRORMSGS][,[NO_INFOMSGS]][,[TABLOCK]]
          [,[ESTIMATEONLY]][,[PHYSICAL_ONLY]] }]
```

where:

- **<table name>|<view name>** is the name of the table or indexed view that you want the DBCC process to check for structural integrity errors. (While DBCC CHECKTABLE checks the linkages and sizes of TEXT, NTEXT, and IMAGE pages, it does not check the consistency of all allocation structures in the database; you must run DBCC CHECKALLOC or DBCC CHECKDB to do that verification.)
- **NOINDEX** specifies that non-clustered indexes on non-system (that is, on user-defined) tables should not be checked.

- **<index ID>** instructs the DBCC process to check only the integrity of the table and a specific index (given by <index ID>).
- **REPAIR_FAST** tells the DBCC process to perform minor, non-time-consuming repairs such as removing extra keys in non-clustered indexes. Repairs performed under the REPAIR_FAST option will not result in any data loss.
- **REPAIR_REBUILD** tells the DBCC process to perform the same repairs as specified by the REPAIR_FAST option plus time-consuming repairs such as rebuilding indexes. Repairs performed under the REPAIR_REBUILD option will not result in any data loss.
- **REPAIR_ALLOW_DATA_LOSS** tells the DBCC process to perform the same repairs as it would when you specify the REPAIR_REBUILD option plus repair allocation errors, structural row errors, and delete invalid text objects. Repairs performed under the REPAIR_ALLOW_DATA_LOSS option may (as its name implies) result in some data loss if the DBCC process must remove corrupted data.
- **ALL_ERRORMSGS** tells the DBCC process to display all error messages. If NO_INFOMSGS is specified and ALL_ERRORMSGS is not, DBCC CHECKTABLE will only display the first 200 error messages per object.
- **NO_INFOMSGS** tells the DBCC process to suppress all informational messages (and display only error messages).
- **TABLOCK** tells the DBCC process to obtain a shared table lock (versus row or perhaps, a page lock). Specifying the TABLOCK option makes DBCC CHECKTABLE run faster on a DBMS with a heavy processing load. However, issuing table locks decreases concurrency as other users are forced to wait for the DBCC process to complete its work on the entire table (versus on a single row or [8Kb] page of rows) before they can work with the data in the table.
- **ESTIMATE_ONLY** tells the DBCC process to display the estimated amount of space within TEMPDB that the DBCC CHECKTABLE statement must have when executed with the options and parameters specified.
- **PHYSICAL_ONLY** tells the DBCC process to check only the physical consistency of the table by checking the structure of page and record headers, the table's file allocation structures, and for common hardware failures that can corrupt data. PHYSICAL_ONLY implies that you want NO_INFOMSGS and you cannot specify PHYSICAL_ONLY with any of the three repair options (REPAIR_FAST, REPAIR_REBUILD, or REPAIR_ALLOW_DATA_LOSS).

Note: *To execute DBCC CHECKTABLE with one of the repair options (REPAIR_FAST, REPAIR_REBUILD, or REPAIR_ALLOW_DATA_LOSS), you must first set the database to be repaired to single-user mode.*

If you want you to check the integrity of all tables within a database, use DBCC CHECKDB rather than DBCC CHECKTABLE.

546 Understanding the Restrictions on Subqueries Used as Predicates for a Comparison Operator

Many queries use a comparison operator within the WHERE clause to select rows in which one or more columns have a particular value or range of values. For example, to display a list of employees hired after 2/1/2002 you might use the query:

```
SELECT first_name, last_name
FROM employees
WHERE hire_date > '2/1/2002'
```

Similarly, to list the chemistry grades for all students from California you might use a query such as:

```
SELECT first_name, last_name, grade
FROM students AS s, grades AS g
WHERE s.home_state = 'CA'
  AND s.student_ID = g.student_ID
  AND g.class      = 'chemistry'
```

While the substance of the two queries differs, the WHERE clauses are similar in that they both have comparison operators nestled between a pair of scalar values. In fact, a comparison operator (=, <>, >, <, >=, or <=) can only be used to compare two scalar values—a scalar value to the left of the operator with the value to the right of the operator. However, unlike the comparisons made in the two preceding examples, you don't always know the scalar values you want to use within the comparison when you write a query. Fortunately, you can use a subquery (either correlated or uncorrelated) in place of the scalar value on either or both sides of a comparison operator.

The restriction on using a subquery in place of a scalar value is that the subquery must return one value at most. That is, the SELECT statement in the subquery must return a results set that consists of either zero or one row with only one column. SQL programmers often refer to subqueries that return a scalar value as scalar subqueries.

To make a list of students with GPAs 25 percent greater than the average GPA, you might write the following query:

```
SELECT first_name, last_name, gpa
FROM students
WHERE gpa > ((SELECT AVG(gpa) FROM students) * 1.25)
```

Without knowing the average GPA, you can still write the query that selects rows based on its value by using an uncorrelated, scalar subquery (which follows the greater than [>] comparison operator) to compute it when the DBMS executes the query. Because the subquery in this example is uncorrelated, the DBMS need only execute it once. An uncorrelated subquery would return the same results set no matter how many times it is called during the query. In this example, the optimizer reduces it to a constant value before scanning the tables listed in the FROM clause within the query—STUDENTS.

You are not limited to using only uncorrelated subqueries with comparison operators. Although the processing is a bit more complex (for the DMBS), you can use correlated subqueries as well. Suppose, for example, that you want a list of realtors that have sold homes with an average sale price of $500,000 or more. You might write the query as:

```
SELECT first_name, last_name
FROM realtors AS r
WHERE 500000.00 <= (SELECT AVG(sales_price)
                    FROM sales AS s
                    WHERE s.realtor_ID = r.realtor_ID)
```

In this example, the DBMS must execute the correlated subquery repeatedly—once for each realtor as the DBMS scans the REALTORS table. Each time the DBMS executes it, the correlated subquery returns a single (albeit, different), value. (To be a legal predicate for an unmodified comparison operator, a subquery must return a scalar value.)

547 Using a VIEW to Allow a Self-Join on the Working Table in a Subquery

Typically, multi-table queries involve a relationship between two or more tables. Suppose, for example, that you want to list all customers that purchased a red Corvette. You might write the following query that relates personal information within the CUSTOMERS table with purchase data within the SALES table:

```
SELECT first_name, last_name, date_sold, price
FROM customers AS c, sales AS s
WHERE c.cust_ID = s.sold_to
  AND make='Corvette'
  AND color='red'
```

Sometimes, however, you want to write a mutli-table query that involves a relationship with itself. Suppose, for example, that you want to list all employees that have been with the company longer than their managers. When executing the query, the DBMS must compare column values from one row within a table to column values within another row of the same table. In Tip 313, "Using a Table Alias to do a Single-Table JOIN (i.e. Self-JOIN)," you learned how to write multi-table queries that involve relationships within a single table. To write the query in this example, you might use the following SELECT statement:

```
SELECT e.emp_ID, e.first_name, e.last_name,
  e.date_hired AS 'Employee Hired',
  m.emp_ID AS 'Manager ID', m.date_hired AS 'Manager Hired'
FROM employees AS e, employees AS m
WHERE e.manager_ID = m.emp_ID
  AND e.date_hired < m.date_hired
```

By assigning correlation names ("e" and "m") to the EMPLOYEES table, you make it possible for the DBMS to perform a self-join. In a self-join, the DBMS works with the rows within a table as if it were working with rows from two separate tables—table "e" and table "m," in this example. The DBMS joins rows from the EMPLOYEES table "e" with rows from the EMPLOYEES table "m" and returns column values from those (virtual) joined rows in which the column values satisfy the search criteria in the query's WHERE clause.

Unfortunately, not all SQL statements let you use a correlation name for the target table. Suppose, for example, that you want to reduce the salary of any employee by 25 percent. The employee was hired prior to his or her manager. Although it seems to express (in SQL terms) the update you want to perform, the following UPDATE statement is syntactically incorrect—an UPDATE statement does not let you specify a correlation name in its UPDATE clause as shown here:

```
UPDATE employees AS m SET salary = salary * 0.75
WHERE employees.manager_ID = m.emp_ID
  AND e.date_hired < m.date_hired
```

To eliminate the invalid correlation name "m" in this UPDATE statement, you can create on the EMPLOYEES table a VIEW that lists all managers. Then, you can use the VIEW as a second table for the subquery within the UPDATE statement's WHERE clause.

Suppose, for example, that all non-management employees have a non-null value in the MANAGER_ID column whereas managers do not. The following VIEW will then return a list of all managers:

```
CREATE vw_managers
AS SELECT * FROM employees WHERE manager_ID IS NULL
```

Given the VW_MANAGERS VIEW, which returns the DATE_HIRED and EMP_ID for the management employees, you could write the preceding UPDATE statement as:

```
UPDATE employees SET salary = salary * 0.75
WHERE EXISTS (SELECT *
              FROM vw_managers AS m
              WHERE employees.manager_ID = m.emp_ID
                AND employees.date_hired < m.date_hired)
```

Note: *Some DBMS products (such as MS-SQL Server, for example) let you reference the UPDATE (or DELETE) statement's target table within a subquery without listing the table within the subquery's FROM clause. As such, you need not create a VIEW to* *make an outer reference to the target table within the subquery on these DBMS platforms. On MS-SQL Server for example, you can write the UPDATE statement in the preceding example without using a VIEW as:*

```
UPDATE employees SET salary = salary * 0.75
WHERE EXISTS (SELECT *
              FROM employees AS m
              WHERE employees.manager_ID = m.manager_ID
                AND employees.date_hired < m.date_hired)
```

MS-SQL Server will correctly use values from the outer reference to columns within the EMPLOYEES table in the statement's UPDATE clause when making comparisons with column values (from the same table) within the subquery's WHERE clause.

548 Using a Temporary Table to Remove Duplicate Data

If you create a table without a PRIMARY KEY or at least one column constrained as both UNIQUE and NOT NULL, users can (and according to Murphy's law, probably will) insert duplicate rows of data. Duplicate relations (that is, duplicate rows) within a table are seldom, if ever, desirable. Duplicate data not only takes up extra space and increases retrieval time and memory usage, but also prevents you from normalizing the database. To prevent database corruption due to DELETE, INSERT, and UPDATE anomalies, you must normalize the database, which, you learned to do in Tips 200–203.

The first step in the normalization process is to put all database tables into first normal form (1NF). (You learned about 1NF in Tip 201 "Understanding First Normal Form [1NF].") Because one of the requirements of 1NF is that a table has no duplicate rows, eliminating duplicate data will be one or your first tasks on the road to the desired, anomaly-free third normal form (3NF).

Unfortunately, deleting duplicate data is not as simple as executing a DELETE statement with the appropriate WHERE clause. Remember, when executed, a DELETE statement will remove all rows that satisfy the search conditions within its WHERE clause. Thus, the DELETE statement that eliminates one row of duplicate data will remove all duplicate rows—without leaving the desired *one* (now non-duplicated) row in the table.

One way to delete all but one row from each set of duplicate rows is to perform the following steps:

1. Create a temporary table with the same structure as the table that contains the duplicate data.

2. Use an INSERT statement that has a SELECT statement with a DISTINCT clause to move rows from the table with duplicate data into a new, temporary table.
3. Truncate (that is, drop all rows within) the original table.
4. Use the ALTER TABLE statement to add a UNIQUE constraint, which will prevent the insertion of duplicate rows in the future.
5. Use an INSERT statement that has a SELECT statement to copy all rows from the temporary table back into the (now) empty, original table.
6. Drop the temporary table.

Suppose, for example, that you had a table name ITEMS with the following structure:

```
ITEM_NUMBER INTEGER
DESCRIPTION VARCHAR(45)
COST        MONEY
```

To remove duplicates from the ITEMS table, you might execute the following statement batch:

```
/* Create a temporary table */
CREATE TABLE #temp_items
(item_number INTEGER,
 description VARCHAR(45),
 cost        MONEY)

/* Use the DISTINCT clause to prevent the INSERT statement
   from putting duplicate data into the temporary table */

INSERT INTO #temp_items
  SELECT DISTINCT * FROM items

/* Delete all rows from the ITEMS table */

TRUNCATE TABLE items

/* (Optional) - Apply a uniqueness constraint to the
    original table to prevent future duplicates /

ALTER TABLE items ADD UNIQUE (item_number)

/* Return data from the temporary data */

INSERT INTO items
  SELECT * FROM #temp_items

/* Drop the temporary table */

DROP #temp_items
```

Note: If the table with the duplicate data has any FOREIGN KEY constraints with an ON DELETE CASCADE rule or if the table has a DELETE or INSERT trigger, make sure you turn them all off before you start the duplicate row removal procedure. After moving the data from the temporary table back into the original table, turn the constraints and triggers back on.

549 Using a Temporary Table to Delete Rows from Multiple Tables

All commercially available DMBS products support referential integrity constraints that let the user setup parent/child relationships between pairs of tables. A referential integrity constraint requires that a FOREIGN KEY value in a child table must have a matching PRIMARY KEY value within the parent table. However, some DBMS products do not yet support DELETE triggers or the ON DELETE CASCADE referential integrity rule. Without these features, it can be difficult to delete rows from the parent table when some or all the parent table's rows are referenced by FOREIGN KEY values within rows of one or more child tables. To maintain referential integrity, you must first delete the child rows before you delete a child row's parent row.

A DELETE trigger is nothing more than a stored procedure the DBMS executes when you attempt to delete a row from the table to which you attached the trigger. What makes a trigger more handy than a stored procedure in this instance is that the DBMS executes the trigger's statements *before* deleting the row from the table to which the trigger is attached (as you learned in Tip 451 "Understanding DELETE Triggers"). Thus, by using a DELETE trigger you can have the DBMS delete child rows (in one or more tables) before deleting the parent row—even though you submit to the DBMS only the DELETE statement that removes one or more rows from the parent table.

Similarly, if your DMBS supports it, you can apply the ON DELETE CASCADE rule to FOREIGN KEY constraints and have the DBMS delete any child rows whenever you delete a parent row from the table with the PRIMARY KEY referenced by the child's FOREIGN KEY. (You learned how the ON DELETE CASCADE rule works in Tip 183 "Understanding How Applying the CASCADE Rule to Updates and Deletes Helps Maintain Referential Integrity.")

If your DBMS supports neither DELETE triggers nor the ON DELETE CASCADE rule for FOREIGN KEY constraints, you can still delete rows from multiple tables. Simply build a temporary table with the list of rows you want to delete before executing the necessary DELETE statements to remove corresponding rows from child tables and then from the parent table. You might also use the following method to DELETE "child" rows from tables in which you have not used FOREIGN KEY references to setup explicit parent/child relationships.

To delete rows from multiple tables without referential integrity (or DELETE triggers), perform the following steps:

1. Create a temporary table in which to hold the key (usually PRIMARY KEY) values you can use to identify "child" rows you want to delete in other tables.
2. Use a SELECT statement to insert the key values into the temporary table.
3. Use a DELETE statement with a subquery in its WHERE clause to delete the child rows from each of the related tables.
4. Use a DELETE statement with a subquery in its WHERE clause to delete from the parent table the rows identified by the key values within the temporary table.
5. DROP the temporary table.

Suppose, for example, that your company sends a free gift to customers along with the products they ordered. If the company later decides to discontinue the free gift products, you must remove them from the ITEM_MASTER, INVENTORY, and ORDERS tables. To do so, you might execute the following statement batch to delete rows from all three tables as a single transaction:

```
/* Create a temporary table */
CREATE TABLE #temp_discontinued
(item_number INTEGER)

/* Use the DISTINCT clause to prevent the INSERT statement
   from putting duplicate data into the temporary table */
INSERT INTO #temp_discontinued
  SELECT DISTINCT item_number
  FROM item_master WHERE type = 'gift'

/* Delete child rows from related tables */

DELETE FROM inventory
WHERE item_no IN (SELECT item_number
                  FROM #temp_discontinued)
DELETE FROM orders
WHERE item_no IN (SELECT item_number
                  FROM #temp_discontinued)

/* Delete the "parent" row from the parent table */

DELETE FROM item_master
WHERE item_number IN (SELECT item_number
                      FROM #temp_discontinued)

/* Drop the temporary table */

DROP #temp_discontinued
```

Although executing the same subquery multiple times may appear inefficient, bear in mind that the DBMS optimizer reviews all the statements in a statement batch and creates an execution plan prior to executing them. When the optimizer sees the same subquery used repeatedly, the optimizer executes the subquery only once and then uses subquery's (virtual) results table (without re-executing the subquery) each time the subquery appears within the statement batch.

Note: *Although you could execute the following DELETE statement at the end of the statement batch to remove the gift items from the ITEM_MASTER table, it is better to use the subquery, as shown in the example instead:*

```
DELETE FROM item_master WHERE type = 'gift'
```

By using the same, static subquery results table for all DELETE statements, you avoid the possibility of removing items from the ITEM_MASTER that you have not removed from its child tables. For example, if a user marks additional items as gift after the DBMS executes INSERT statement within the statement batch to build the #TEMP_DISCONTINUED table, executing the preceding DELETE statement would cause the DBMS to delete items from the ITEM_MASTER that it has not yet deleted from its child tables.

---

550 Using the UPDATE Statement to Set the Values in One Table Based on the Values in a Second Table

Unless you are performing maintenance operations or correcting inaccurate data values within a table, you typically use a data-entry program to accept new data or changes to existing data from database users. As a result, most UPDATE statements you write will be simple expressions that set the value of a column to the number or character string the user entered into a data entry field within an application program. If the user entered a number, you might set a column's value based on the results of a mathematical formula involving a column's current value and the number the user entered. As such, most UPDATE statements will be of the form:

```
UPDATE <table name>
SET <column name> = <variable name or simple expression>
WHERE <search condition>
```

However, you are not limited to this simple form for the UPDATE statement. For example, there is no rule against placing a column name on both sides of the equal sign. While the following UPDATE statement does not actually change the column's value, you can use it to trigger referential integrity actions. This can happen if the column being "updated" is a PRIMARY KEY referenced by a FOREIGN KEY with an ON UPDATE rule. You can also use it to execute a trigger if there is an UPDATE trigger on the column or on the table:

```
UPDATE customers SET cust_no = cust_no
```

In addition, you are not limited to using only a column name, variable, literal, or simple expression on the right of any equal sign (=) within an UPDATE statement's SET clause. You can also set a column to the value returned by a scalar subquery (that is, a subquery that returns a single, scalar value). Moreover, the UPDATE statement's WHERE clause can also contain a subquery, so long as the subquery is part of an expression that returns a TRUE or FALSE result.

For example, you might use a subquery within a SET clause (and within the WHERE clause) to write an UPDATE statement that collects summary data about one table and posts it to rows within another table. Suppose, for example, that you have CUSTOMERS, UNPOSTED_PAYMENTS, and PAYMENT_HISTORY tables. To update each customer's ACCOUNT_BALANCE and AVERAGE_PAYMENT data (within the CUSTOMERS table), you could execute the following statement batch:

```
/* Mark the payments to be posted and insert them into the
   payment history table */

UPDATE unposted_payments SET post = 'Y'
INSERT INTO payment_history SELECT * FROM unposted_payments
                            WHERE post = 'Y'
/* Execute the UPDATE statement that posts the unposted
   payments marked for posting */

UPDATE customers
SET account_balance = account_balance -
      (SELECT SUM(amount_paid)
       FROM unposted_payments AS up
       WHERE customers.cust_ID = up.cust_ID),

    average_payment =
      (SELECT avg(amount_paid)
       FROM payment_history as ph
       WHERE customers.cust_ID = ph.cust_ID)

WHERE EXISTS (SELECT *
              FROM unposted_payments as up
              WHERE customers.cust_ID = up.cust_ID
                AND up.post = 'Y')

/* Remove posted payments from the unposted payments
   table */

DELETE FROM unposted_payments WHERE post = 'Y'
```

As mentioned previously within this tip, each SELECT statement used in the UPDATE statement's SET clause must return a single scalar value. This example uses aggregate functions to ensure a scalar result. Although you might be tempted to write the SELECT clause in the first subquery as "SELECT amount_paid," it could be a mistake. If a customer makes more than one payment, "SELECT amount_paid" will return multiple values, and the entire UPDATE process would fail.

Note, too, that the UPDATE statement's WHERE clause uses a subquery to determine if there are any unposted payments from the customer. If not, the DBMS need not compute the average payment, since there can be no change to the average payment already within the AVERAGE_PAYMENT column of the CUSTOMERS table. More importantly, checking for the existence of payments also ensures that the AVG() aggregate will not return a NULL value. AVG() would return a NULL value if there were no payments from a customer and the subquery passed an empty table to the aggregate.

The scalar subqueries in this example are able to select payments from a particular customer, because a table referenced in the UPDATE clause is available for use throughout the remaining clauses within the UPDATE statement. Therefore, column values from the current row within the CUSTOMERS table are available for use throughout all the UPDATE statement's subqueries.

551 Optimizing the EXISTS Predicate

To check if a column (or literal) value is within a list of values, use an IN predicate. For example, if you want a list of all customers whose salesperson was either Mary, Mark, or Sue, you would use an IN predicate such as that in the following query:

```
SELECT * FROM customers
WHERE salesperson IN ('Mary','Mark','Sue')
```

Rather than list values individually, you can use a subquery to build the list of possible values you want to check. For example, to remove the phone numbers of all the current customers from the PROSPECTS list, you might write the following DELETE statement:

```
DELETE FROM prospects
WHERE phone_number IN (SELECT phone_number FROM customers)
```

When you want to perform an action when there is at least one item within a results set, use the EXISTS predicate. For example, in Tip 550, "Using the UPDATE Statement to Set the Values in One Table Based on the Values in a Second Table," you want the DBMS to update the customer account balance and average payment data if there is at least one payment from the customer within the UNPOSTED_PAYMENTS table. If you had only wanted to execute the UPDATE statement if the customer made a payment of a particular amount, you might have written the UPDATE statement's WHERE clause as:

```
WHERE customer.normal_payment IN
      (SELECT amount_paid
       FROM unposted_payments AS up
       WHERE customers.cust_ID = up.cust_ID
       AND up.post = 'Y')
```

However, since you were not checking for a specific AMOUNT_PAID and wanted the DBMS to execute the UPDATE statement if the UNPOSTED_PAYMENTS table contained a payment in any amount from the customer, you can use the EXISTS predicate in the statement's WHERE clause as:

```
WHERE EXISTS (SELECT *
              FROM unposted_payments as up
              WHERE customers.cust_ID = up.cust_ID
                AND up.post = 'Y')
```

As you will learn from the following discussion, there are three ways you can write an EXISTS predicate, and the one you choose depends on your DBMS platform. To decide which is the optimum EXISTS predicate for your DMBS platform, try executing the same query using each the three forms. Use the one that your DBMS optimizer reports as the "least costly." When you submit a query, the DBMS optimizer generates an execution plan. You learned how to review a statement's execution plan in Tip 524 "Understanding the MS-SQL Server SHOWPLAN_ALL Option for Displaying Statement Execution Plans and Statistics."

In SQL-89, the rule was that the subquery used in an EXISTS predicate had to have a SELECT clause which contained either a single column or an asterisk (*). When you used SELECT *, the DBMS (at least in theory) picked one of the columns from the tables listed in the SELECT statement's FROM clause and used it. (Remember, when you use an EXISTS predicate you are not looking for a specific value of any particular type; you are just checking to see if the subquery returns any value at all.)

SQL-92, which can handle row-valued comparison, no longer restricts you to listing only a single column or asterisk (*) in the EXISTS predicate's subquery. However, as of this writing, most DBMS products still do not support row-valued comparisons. Thus, the three most popular forms for the EXISTS predicate are:

- `EXISTS (SELECT * FROM <table name>`

  `WHERE <search criteria>)`
- `EXISTS (SELECT <column name> FROM <table name>`

  `WHERE <search criteria>)`
- `EXISTS (SELECT <constant value> FROM <table name>`

  `WHERE <search criteria>)`

In general, the first form, SELECT * FROM ... should work better than specifying either a column name or constant value. SELECT * FROM ... lets the optimizer decide which column to use. As such, if there is an INDEX on the column used in the subquery's WHERE clause, the optimizer can use the indexed column and never have to touch the table data at all. In the preceding example, if there is an index on the CUST_ID column of the UNPOSTED_PAYMENTS table, the DBMS need only check the index (on CUST_ID). Indexes are typically smaller than tables and structured for very fast searching. If the DBMS finds the value within the index, the EXISTS predicate is true; if the value is not in the index, the predicate is FALSE. In either case, the DBMS need not retrieve actual values from the UNPOSTED_PAYMENTS table.

Although SELECT * FROM ... should, in theory, be the optimal form of the EXISTS predicate, some DBMS products will actually execute the subquery and build a "virtual" table of query results. In other words, instead of just check for a value within any one of the table's columns, the DBMS builds an in-memory table that contains the values from all columns within rows that satisfy the subquery's search criteria. On such systems, limiting the results table to a single column by using the SELECT <column name> form of the EXISTS predicate is better than having the DBMS build a multi-column, multi-row interim table.

Finally, you should use the third form of the EXISTS predicate (SELECT <constant value>) on those DBMS products, like Oracle, that must be told they do not have to retrieve the actual column values when building the subquery's virtual table. If you supply a literal (constant) value, the DBMS simply repeats that value for each row that satisfies the subquery's search criteria. Although, the DBMS still has to scan the subquery's base table, it does not have to retrieve the actual data values from table columns into memory.

552 Using the ALL Predicate to Combine Two Queries into One

In Tip 546 "Understanding the Restrictions on Subqueries Used as Predicates for a Comparison Operator," you learned that you can use a subquery as one of the values in a comparison—as long as the subquery returns a single scalar value. Thus, you can use a scalar subquery (that is, a subquery that returns a scalar value) to execute queries such as the following, which lists the names and total sales for the employees with the highest TOTAL_SALES within the EMPLOYEES table:

```
SELECT first_name, last_name, total_sales
FROM employees
WHERE total_sales = (SELECT MAX(total_sales)
                     FROM employees)
```

SQL provides three quantifiers (sometimes called qualifiers) that let you use subqueries that return a set of (multiple) values in a comparison. The quantifiers are ALL, SOME, and ANY. A *quantifier* then, is a logical operator that asserts the quantity of objects for which a statement (in this case a comparison) is TRUE. Thus, you could rewrite the preceding query as:

```
SELECT first_name, last_name, total_sales
FROM employees
WHERE total_sales >= ALL (SELECT total_sales
                          FROM employees
                          WHERE total_sales IS NOT NULL)
```

The subquery in this example will return multiple values if there are two or more rows with TOTAL_SALES figures within the EMPLOYEES table. However, the second query will return the same results set as the first. The WHERE clause in the second query evaluates TRUE only when the value of TOTAL_SALES for a particular employee is greater than or equal to every TOTAL_SALES value returned by the subquery that follows the ALL quantifier.

Note: *When using the ALL quantifier, you must eliminate NULL values. The MAX() and MIN() functions do this for you automatically. When applying the ALL quantifier, the DBMS compares the scalar value on the left of the comparison operator with each value returned by the subquery that follows the quantifier. In order for the WHERE clause to evaluate TRUE, every comparison performed must evaluate TRUE. When comparing any value to NULL, the result is UNKNOWN. As a result, the WHERE clause will evaluate FALSE if the subquery results set contains any NULL values, because all comparisons performed did not evaluate TRUE.*

In this case, the first query is more intuitive and therefore easier to understand than the second. In fact, whenever you have a query that involves comparing a scalar value with the results from a subquery that you can write as a scalar subquery, you will find the query easier to understand when you write it using a comparison operator without a quantifier. When you must compare two summary values, quantifiers come in handy.

Suppose, for example, that you want to list the realtors with the highest number of houses under contract. Without a quantifier, you must write two queries (one within a VIEW) to get your answer as:

```
CREATE VIEW vw_total_listings(realtor_ID, listing_count)
SELECT realtor_ID, COUNT(*)
FROM listings
GROUP BY realtor_ID

SELECT realtor_ID, listing_count
FROM vw_total_listings
WHERE listing_count = (SELECT MAX(listing_count)
                       FROM vw_total_listing)
```

Note that the query to summarize the listings is hidden within a VIEW, so you can use the aggregate listing count for each realtor as a scalar value on the left side of the comparison operator. By using the ALL quantifier, you can write the same query as a single SELECT statement that shows the summary computation:

```
SELECT realtor_ID, COUNT(*)
FROM listings
GROUP BY realtor_ID
```

```
HAVING COUNT(*) >= ALL (SELECT DISTINCT COUNT(*)
                        FROM listings
                        GROUP BY realtor_ID)
```

The DISTINCT clause within the subquery eliminates duplicate values. Remember, when executing the query, the DBMS must compare the scalar value on the leftside of the comparison operator with each value returned by the subquery that follows the quantifier. As such, the shorter the list of values within the subquery's results set, the faster the DBMS can complete all the comparisons.

553 Using the EXISTS Predicate to Check for Duplicate Rows in a Table

The SQL-92 standard includes a UNIQUE predicate—not to be confused with the UNIQUE column constraint. Whereas the UNIQUE column constraint prevents users from inserting duplicate values into a column, the UNIQUE predicate lets you test for the absence (or presence) of duplicate rows in the results set returned by a subquery. The UNIQUE predicate returns TRUE if the subquery's results set contains no duplicate rows and FALSE if it does. Thus, to test whether a column (or set of columns) contains a unique value within each row of a table, you could write a query in the form:

```
SELECT 'All Unique'
WHERE UNIQUE (SELECT <column list> FROM <table name>)
```

When executed (with valid column and table names, of course), the SELECT statement in this example displays the words "All Unique" if the value in the column (or set of columns) given by <column list> is different within every row of the table named by <table name>.

If you use the logical connective "NOT" with the UNIQUE predicate, you can check for duplicate values in a column (or set of columns) within a table. For example, to determine if there are any duplicate values in the ITEM_NUMBER column of the ITEM_MASTER table, you can add "NOT" to the "UNIQUE" predicate and write the query as follows:

```
SELECT DISTINCT 'Contains Duplicates'
WHERE NOT UNIQUE (SELECT item_number FROM item_master)
```

Unfortunately, many DBMS products do not yet support the UNIQUE predicate. However, you can perform this same "uniqueness" test using the EXISTS predicate (available in all commercial DBMS products). For example, you could rewrite the preceding query, which checks for duplicate values within the ITEM_NUMBER column as shown here:

```
SELECT DISTINCT 'Contains Duplicates'
WHERE EXISTS (SELECT item_number, COUNT(*)
              FROM item_master
```

```
        GROUP BY item_number
        HAVING COUNT(*) > 1)
```

Note that the EXISTS predicate returns TRUE when there is at least one duplicate value, whereas the UNIQUE predicate returns FALSE if there are no duplicates. Also, while the example queries shown in this tip check for duplicates within a single column, you can use EXISTS (and UNIQUE) to check for duplicates within a set of columns as well. Simply list within the subquery's FROM and the GROUP BY clauses the set of columns you want to test for a composite duplicate value. If you want to test a table for duplicate rows, you would list all the table's columns within the two clauses.

554 Joining Table Contents and Function Results

After working with SQL data for a while, you will notice that most queries you write combine data from two or more tables. However, SQL does not limit you to joining only rows from one table with related rows from another table. You can also join a table row with the result returned by a function call.

Suppose, for example, you were in charge of storing survey results for a political party. To minimize the amount of storage required to house a large number of responses, you could separate the responses and the lists of questions into two tables. Each row in the survey responses table would consist of a string of 1's and 0's to indicate affirmative (1) and negative (0) responses to the survey questions. The SURVEY_QUESTIONS and SURVEY_RESPONSES tables might be defined as follows:

```
CREATE TABLE survey_questions
(survey_number   SMALLINT,
 question_number TINYINT,
 question_text   VARCHAR(256))

CREATE TABLE survey_responses
(survey_number   SMALLINT,
 response_string VARCHAR(50))
```

The number of characters required for the RESPONSE_STRING would depend on the number of questions within the survey. In this example, the response string can handle up to 50 responses (that is, up to 50 1's and 0's) to indicate yes and no responses for up to 50 questions.

The response to survey QUESTION_NUMBER 1 is stored in character 1 of the RESPONSE_STRING; the response to survey QUESTION_NUMBER 2 is stored in character 2 of the RESPONSE_STRING, and so on. Thus, a row in the SURVEY_RESPONSES table with a RESPONSE_STRING of 1010 would indicate the person taking the survey responded yes to questions 1 and 3 of the survey and "no" to questions 2 and 4.

Now, suppose you loaded the following four questions into the SURVEY_QUESTIONS table as SURVEY_NUMBER 1

```
1,1,"Do you support home schooling?"
1,2,"Do you want public school vouchers?"
1,3,"Do you support lower taxes over deficit reduction?"
1,4,"Do you support placing the nuclear repository in
     Nevada?"
```

and loaded the following responses into the SURVEY_RESPONSES table:

```
1,"1111"
1,"1000"
1,"1100"
1,"1110"
1,"0000"
```

To produce reports based on survey data stored within the two tables (SURVEY_QUESTIONS and SURVEY_RESPONSES), you need a third table such as the following in which to merge questions and responses from a particular survey:

```
CREATE TABLE survey_results
(question VARCHAR(256),
 response CHAR(1))
```

Then, to place the results of survey "1" into the SURVEY_RESULTS table you would use the following INSERT INTO statement:

```
INSERT INTO survey_results (question, response)
  SELECT question_text,
         SUBSTRING(response_string, question_number, 1)
  FROM survey_responses, survey_questions
  WHERE survey_responses = 1
    AND survey_questions = 1
```

The SELECT statement joins a row from SURVEY_QUESTIONS with the result returned by the SUBSTRING() function. The INSERT INTO statement then inserts the "joined" row into the SURVEY_RESULTS table. The QUESTION_NUMBER parameter shifts the SUBSTRING() function through the RESPONSE_STRING one character at a time from left to right as the query moves from QUESTION_NUMBER 1 through QUESTION_NUMBER *n*. Thus, whether there are four questions or 50, you need not change the query. Based on the number of questions, the query automatically adjusts itself to work through any length RESPONSE_STRING, one response (character) at a time.

To generate a report based on the information with the SURVEY_RESULTS table, you might execute a grouped SELECT statement such as the following, to produce the results shown in Figure 554.1 for the survey questions and responses in this example:

```
SELECT question 'Question to 5 Respondents', COUNT(*) 'Yes'
FROM survey_results
WHERE response = '1'
GROUP BY question
```

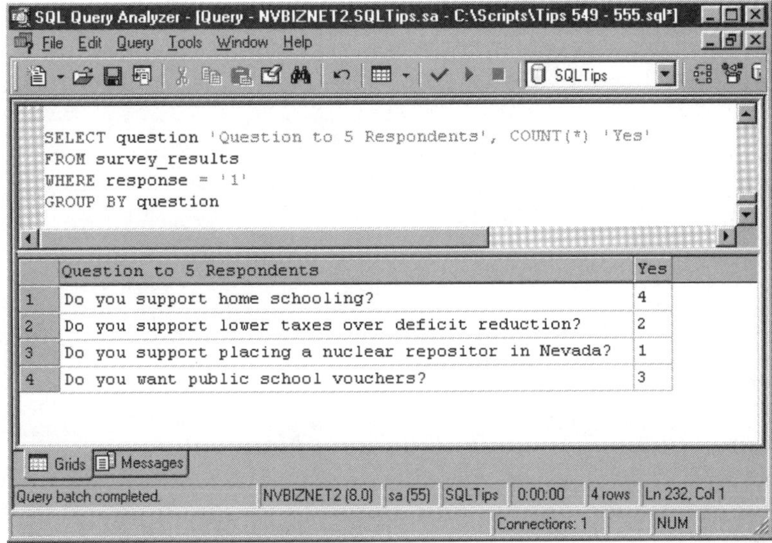

Figure 554.1 Grouped query results from the merged survey questions and responses working table

555 Using Views to Display a Hierarchy of Aggregation Levels

Most businesses are organized as hierarchies in which the span of responsibility and control increases as you move up the chain of command from worker to chief executive officer. At each level within the hierarchy, managers need summary reports to see how well their subordinates are doing. For example, in a sales organization, individual sales are grouped under the salesperson that made the sale. The department manager can then compare the effectiveness of one salesperson to another based on the total sales for each. Next, sales are grouped by department within region, so the regional vice president for sales can get a feel for how well his or her department managers are doing. Finally, regional sales are grouped together to give the company CEO the total sales information he or she must have to report on the company's overall sales growth (or lack thereof) to the board of directors and shareholders.

To build this hierarchy of summary information, you can use a sequence of SELECT statements and views to aggregate totals at each level of the hierarchy. As you work your way up the hierarchy of summary reports, each view is based on the summary of views from the previous step within the hierarchy. For example, you might create the following views to summarize company sales data by employee, department, and region:

```
CREATE VIEW vw_salesrep_sales (region, department,
                                salesprep_ID, total_sales)
AS SELECT region, department, salesrep_ID SUM(amount)
FROM sales
GROUP BY region, department, salesrep_ID

CREATE VIEW vw_department_sales (region, department,
                                 total_sales
AS SELECT region, department, SUM(total_sales)
FROM vw_salesrep_sales
GROUP BY region, department

CREATE VIEW vw_regional_sales (region, total_sales)
AS SELECT region, SUM(total_sales)
FROM vw_department_sales
GROUP BY region
```

To generate a summary reports, execute SELECT statements based on the preceding views as shown here:

```
SELECT * FROM vw_salesrep_sales
SELECT * FROM vw_department_sales
SELECT * FROM vw_region_sales

SELECT SUM (total_sales)
FROM vw_regional_sales
```

When run as a statement batch, executing these SELECT statements on views will likely run faster than executing the four queries directly on the base (SALES) table. If you query the SALES table without a VIEW, the DBMS must scan all the rows in the SALES table repeatedly (once for each query). By using views, the DBMS need only scan the SALES table once. Thereafter, the DBMS scans the virtual (either in memory or in disk cached) table created when the DBMS materialized the view at the preceding level within the hierarchy.

556 Understanding the MS-SQL Server TOP n Operator

When querying a table, you sometimes want the DBMS to return only a certain number of rows. Suppose, for example, that you have 50 salespeople working for you. You might want a list of the top three salespeople by total sales so you can single them out for praise. Or, if you must cut your staff by 10 percent, you will want a list of the five salespeople with the least total sales so you can keep the 45 best producers. The MS-SQL Server TOP operator will scan the output from a query (or subquery) and return the first *n* rows it finds.

For example, to get a list of the three highest TOTAL_SALES values in the EMPLOYEES table within an MS-SQL Server database you could write a query similar to:

```
SELECT DISTINCT TOP 3 total_sales
FROM employees
ORDER BY total_sales DESC
```

The ORDER BY clause instructs the DBMS to build a virtual (in-memory) table of TOTAL_SALES values arranged in descending order. After building the virtual table, the DBMS applies the DISTINCT clause and eliminates any duplicate rows from the interim table. Finally, the TOP operator has the DBMS return only the first *n*, in this case three rows from the virtual table as the query's results set.

If you omit the DISTINCT clause, the results set will have less than three unique values when there is a tie between two or more of the top three values within the list. Suppose, for example, that the EMPLOYEES table had the following values within the TOTAL_SALES column:

```
TOTAL_SALES
-----------
115,000.00
100,000.00
105,000.00
100,000.00
 85,000.00
 85,000.00
105,000.00
 65,000.00
 95,000.00
 95,000.00
```

The query (with the DISTINCT clause) in this example will return the three values: 115,000.00, 105,000.00, and 100,000.00. However, if you rewrote the query without the DISTINCT clause as

```
SELECT TOP 3 total_sales
FROM employees
ORDER BY total_sales DESC
```

the results set would be 115,000.00, 105,000.00, and 105,000.00. Note that you still get three rows of results. However, the results set has only two unique TOTAL_SALES values due to the tie at 105,000.00.

Transact-SQL has no BOTTOM operator you can use to tell the DBMS to return the BOTTOM *n* rows of query results. However, you can use the TOP operator to retrieve the bottom or last *n* rows of query results just as you had TOP return the top or first *n* rows. If you want to get a list of the bottom three TOTAL_SALES values (versus the top three), simply reverse the query's sort order from DESC to ASC as shown here:

```
SELECT DISTINCT TOP 3 total_sales
FROM employees
ORDER BY total_sales ASC
```

Once again the DBMS will build a virtual (in-memory) table of TOTAL_SALES values. Only this time, the ORDER BY clause instructs the DBMS to build the virtual table with the values arranged in ascending order . After building the virtual table of TOTAL_SALES values, the DBMS eliminates any duplicate rows (as instructed by the DISTINCT clause). Then, the TOP operator has the DBMS return the first three rows from the virtual table as the query's results set.

Because the ORDER BY clause has the DBMS sort the virtual table from lowest to highest value, the results set will have the three lowest TOTAL_SALES values in the first (that is, the top) three rows within the virtual table. As such, the query (with the ascending sort) in this example will return the values: 65,000.00, 85,000.00, and 95,000.00.

To list the names and TOTAL_SALES figures for your top *n* (or bottom *n*) salespeople, use a SELECT statement with the TOP operator as a subquery to build the list of top TOTAL_SALES values. For example, the following query will display the names and total sales amounts (in descending order by TOTAL_SALES value) of the employees with TOTAL_SALES equal to one of the top three values in the TOTAL_SALES column:

```
SELECT first_name, last_name, total_sales
FROM employees
WHERE total_sales IN (SELECT DISTINCT TOP 3 total_sales
                      FROM employees
                      ORDER BY total_sales DESC)
```

By the way, Transact-SQL also lets you express the number of rows you want the DBMS to return as a percentage of the total number or rows that satisfy the query's search conditions. Therefore, in this example in which the EMPLOYEES table has 10 rows, you could limit the results set from the following query to five rows by setting the TOP operator to 50 percent:

```
SELECT TOP 50 percent total_sales
FROM employees
ORDER BY total_sales DESC
```

If you apply the DISTINCT clause by writing the query as follows, the DBMS will return only three rows, because the EMPLOYEES table in this tip's example has only six unique values within the TOTAL_SALES column:

```
SELECT DISTINCT TOP 50 percent total_sales
FROM employees
ORDER BY total_sales DESC
```

(The DBMS returns three rows, because three represents 50 percent of the six unique rows the query leaves in the interim [virtual] table it generates prior to returning the final results set.)

557 Constructing a Top n or Bottom n Query Within a DBMS Without a TOP n Operator

In the preceding tip "Understanding the MS-SQL Server TOP *n* Operator," you learned how to use the Transact-SQL TOP operator to have the MS-SQL Server return the first *n* results that satisfy a query's search conditions. Unfortunately, some DBMS products do not have a TOP operator. If your DBMS is one of these, all is not lost. You can limit the number of rows within a results set by using either a grouped query or a SELECT statement with a correlated subquery.

Suppose for example that you had the following data within an EMPLOYEES table and wanted the retrieve the rows with the top three TOTAL_SALES values:

```
FIRST_NAME  LAST_NAME  TOTAL_SALES
----------  ---------  -----------
Konrad      Kernin      115,000.00
Joseph      King        100,000.00
Sally       Hardy       105,000.00
Robert      Fields      100,000.00
Walter      Berry        85,000.00
Susan       Mathau       85,000.00
Karen       Berry       105,000.00
Kregg       King         65,000.00
Kris        Smith        95,000.00
Debbie      Jones        95,000.00
```

To construct a grouped query that will return the top *n* TOTAL_SALES values, you must apply a bit of set logic. The idea is to take each value within the TOTALS_SALES column and build a set (or group) of other TOTAL_SALES values that are greater than or equal to it. The lowest TOTAL_SALES value within the sets (or groups) that have *n* or fewer unique members are the ones you want the DBMS to return. In this example, you want the DBMS to return the lowest TOTAL_SALES value from sets that have at most three unique members. (If you wanted the top five TOTAL_SALES values, you'd have the DBMS to return the SETS with at most five unique members, and so on.)

Therefore, you write the grouped query that will return the top three TOTAL_SALES values as follows:

```
SELECT MIN(e1.total_sales) 'Top Three TOTAL_SALES'
FROM employees AS e1, employees AS e2
WHERE e1.total_sales >= e2.total_sales
GROUP BY e2.total_sales
HAVING COUNT(DISTINCT e1.total_sales) <= 3
```

The query's HAVING clause tells the DBMS to keep within the interim (virtual) table only those sets of TOTAL_SALES values that have three or less unique members. Then, the MIN()

aggregate in the query's SELECT clause tells the DBMS to return the minimum TOTAL_SALES value from each of the remaining sets (with three, two, or one unique values).

To return the bottom three (that is the three lowest) TOTAL_SALES values, simply change the comparison operator within the HAVING clause from "<=" to ">" as follows:

```
SELECT MIN(e1.total_sales) 'Bottom Three TOTAL_SALES'
FROM employees AS e1, employees AS e2
WHERE e1.total_sales >= e2.total_sales
GROUP BY e2.total_sales
HAVING COUNT(DISTINCT e1.total_sales) > 3
```

If you want the query to return something other than the top (or bottom) three values, change the "3" within the HAVING clause to the number of rows you want the query to return.

Rather than write the SELECT statement as a grouped query, you can have the DBMS return the top (or bottom) *n* values using a SELECT statement that has a correlated subquery that builds and eliminates the sets of TOTAL_SALES values with more than *n* unique members. For example, to have the DBMS return the top three TOTAL_SALES values from the employees table, you can write the query as:

```
SELECT DISTINCT e1.total_sales 'Top Three TOTAL_SALES'
FROM employees AS e1
WHERE 3 < (SELECT COUNT(*) FROM employees AS e2
           WHERE e1.total_sales > e2.total_sales)
```

The DISTINCT clause eliminates duplicate TOTAL_SALES values from the results set in case of a tie among two or more of the top values within the TOTAL_SALES column in the EMPLOYEES table.

To display the list of the bottom (that is, the lowest) *n* values within a column, simply change the comparison operator within the correlated subquery's WHERE clause from less than (<) to greater than (>) as shown here:

```
SELECT DISTINCT e1.total_sales 'Bottom Three TOTAL_SALES'
FROM employees AS e1
WHERE 3 < (SELECT COUNT(*) FROM employees AS e2
           WHERE e1.total_sales < e2.total_sales)
```

If you want to list the names as well as the TOTAL_SALES figures for your top *n* (or bottom *n*) salespeople, add the columns whose values you want to display to the SELECT clause as shown in the following query:

```
SELECT first_name, last_name, total_sales
FROM employees AS e1
WHERE 3 < (SELECT COUNT(*) FROM employees AS e2
           WHERE e1.total_sales > e2.total_sales)
ORDER BY total_sales DESC
```

It probably goes without saying, however there is nothing magic about the "3" used in the preceding examples. If you wanted to list the top (or bottom) five salespeople by

TOTAL_SALES, you would simply replace the "3" within the WHERE clause of each query with "5."

558 Using a SELECT Statement with a Scalar Subquery to Display Running Totals

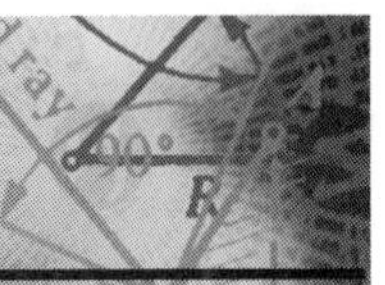

While SQL is an excellent language for data storage and retrieval, it is not much of a report writer. SQL can compute the total, average, minimum, or maximum value for a column easily. However, SQL's ability to provide totals for columns of numbers within groups of rows is limited. Whereas a report writer can make multiple passes through report data to provide descriptive statistics for groups (and groups of groups) while still providing the detail rows, SQL's totaling ability (provided by GROUP BY clause) forces you to give up detail rows if you want group totals.

For example, a report writer can provide total sales by salesperson, grand total sales for all salespeople, along with the rows of data that provide information on each sale. If you want SQL to provide total sales by salesperson, you must execute a grouped query such as the following and give up the detailed sales information:

```
SELECT salesrep_ID, SUM(amount_invoiced) 'Total Sales'
FROM sales
GROUP BY salesrep_ID
ORDER BY salesrep_ID
```

Although you could have reported both totals and detail by computing the total sales with a subquery within the main query's SELECT clause (as shown next), seeing the same total sales figure repeatedly down one column of the report can be confusing:

```
SELECT *, (SELECT SUM(amount_invoiced)
           FROM sales AS s2
           WHERE s2.salesrep_ID = s1.salesrep_ID) AS
            'Total Sales'
FROM sales AS s1
ORDER BY salesrep_ID, invoice_date
```

Whereas displaying a grand total on every detail line is less than desirable, using a scalar subquery to provide a running total can sometimes increase a report's usefulness. Suppose, for example that you have a table with check (or withdrawal) and deposit transactions. If the TRANS_AMOUNT column contains a negative value for withdrawals and positive value for deposits, you can use the following query to list the transactions, as well as the running total of deposits less withdrawals:

```
SELECT t1.trans_date, trans_type, trans_amount AS 'Amount'
       (SELECT SUM(t2.trans_amount)
```

```
        FROM transactions AS t2
        WHERE t2.trans_date <= t1.trans_date) AS
         'Net (Deposits - Checks)'
FROM transactions AS t1
ORDER BY trans_date
```

Of course, to be truly useful, you will want to execute the preceding query within a stored procedure or a statement batch in which you have the account counter within a variable such as @ACCT_NO and the account's beginning balance would be @BEGIN_BAL. You could then add the beginning balance to the net transaction amount to display a running account balance and limit the query to showing only a particular account's transactions (versus all checks and deposits within the TRANSACTIONS table):

```
SELECT t1.trans_date, trans_type, trans_amount AS 'Amount'
       (SELECT SUM(t2.trans_amount)
        FROM transactions AS t2
        WHERE t2.trans_date <= t1.trans_date
          AND t2.acct_number = @acct_no) + @begin_bal)
        AS 'Account Balance'
FROM transactions AS t1
WHERE t1.acct_number = @acct_no
ORDER BY trans_date
```

559 Using an EXCEPT Predicate to Determine the Difference Between Two Tables

The set difference operator, EXCEPT, lets you determine the rows in TABLE_A that are not also in TABLE_B. Thus, if you load the list of all students into TABLE_A and the list of students that have completed their core requirements into TABLE_B, you can use the following statement to display all students *except* those that have completed their core requirements:

```
  SELECT * FROM table_a
EXCEPT
  SELECT * FROM table_b
```

Note that the EXCEPT operator eliminates all duplicates from the first query (SELECT * FROM TABLE_A) before comparing its results set with that of the second query (SELECT * FROM TABLE_B). Thus, the results set from an EXCEPT query will never contain any duplicate rows.

Although the query in this example assumed they were, the EXCEPT statement does not require that TABLE_A and TABLE_B be union compatible. As you learned previously, two tables are *union-compatible* if both have the same number of columns and if the data type of each column in one table is the same as the data type of its corresponding column (by ordinal position) in the other table.

Because the EXCEPT operator returns all rows in the first results set that do not appear in the second, you can use EXCEPT with two dissimilar (that is, non union-compatible) tables by simply listing the columns from each table the operator is to compare. Thus, to list all customers that are not also employees, you might write the following query:

```
  SELECT first_name, last_name, phone_number FROM customers
EXCEPT
  SELECT first_name, last_name, phone_number FROM employees
```

Unfortunately, many DBMS products have not yet implemented the EXCEPT operator. As such, you may have to use a LEFT OUTER JOIN instead. Suppose, for example, that you buy a prospect list and want to eliminate your current customers before turning the list over to your sales force. You could load the prospect list data into a table named PROSPECTS and use the following LEFT OUTER JOIN to generate a list of PROSPECTS that are not also CUSTOMERS:

```
SELECT DISTINCT prospects.*
FROM (prospects LEFT OUTER JOIN customers
  ON prospects.phone_number = customers.phone_number)
WHERE customers.phone_number IS NULL
```

The preceding query assumes that PHONE_NUMBER is either a PRIMARY KEY or a column with values that uniquely identify both individual prospects and customers.

Note: *Some DBMS products implement the EXCEPT operator under a different name. Oracle for example, uses MINUS. Therefore, before substituting a less efficient LEFT OUTER JOIN for EXCEPT, check your DBMS documentation to see if EXCEPT is implemented.*

560 Using the EXISTS Predicate to Generate the Intersection Between Two Tables

When you want to know which rows two tables have in common, use the INTERSECTION operator. Whereas the EXCEPT operator (which you learned about in Tip 559 " Using an EXCEPT Predicate to Determine the Difference Between Two Tables") returns the rows within the first results set that are not within the second, the INTERSECT operator returns only those rows that appear in both results sets. Thus, if your company sells insurance and you want a list of customers that purchase both life and auto insurance from you, you might use a query similar to the following:

```
  SELECT cust_ID, first_name, last_name, phone_number
  FROM life_cust_list
INTERSECT
  SELECT cust_ID, first_name, last_name, phone_number
  FROM auto_cust_list
```

As was the case with the EXCEPT operator, the two tables you use with the INTERSECT operator need not be union-compatible. However, the component queries before and after the INTERSECT keyword must return the same number of columns and corresponding columns must be of the compatible data types. In addition to returning only rows that appear in both results sets, the INTERSECT operator also eliminates all duplicates.

Only a few DBMS products have implemented the INTERSECT operator at present. However, you can use a SELECT statement with an EXISTS predicate to generate the intersection of two tables instead. For example, if you want to generate the list of students that are both on the Dean's List and the football team, you might generate the following query:

```
SELECT DISTINCT student_id, first_name, last_name, GPA
FROM students
WHERE EXISTS (SELECT * FROM football_team
              WHERE students.student_ID =
                      football_team.student_ID)
```

You can also write the same query using an INNER JOIN as:

```
SELECT DISTINCT student_id, first_name, last_name, GPA
FROM students INNER JOIN football_team
  ON students.student_ID = football_team.student_ID
```

561 Using sp_detach_db to Remove a Database From and sp_attach_db to Add a Database to an MS-SQL Server

To remove a database from an MS-SQL Server—while leaving the database data (.mdf) and transaction log (.ldf) files intact on the hard drive—call the built-in stored procedure sp_detach_db. Although you cannot access the data within a database while it is not attached to an MS-SQL Server, you can copy or move the database .mdf file (which contains the database data and all its objects) onto another hard drive or onto another server altogether. Then, as we will discuss later within this tip, you can reattach the database data file (and optionally, its transaction log file) onto the same or a different MS-SQL Server. When that is completed, you can once again work with the data and objects within the database.

The built-in stored procedure sp_detach_db, which allows you to remove a database from the MS-SQL Server without deleting the database's files from the hard drive, has the following syntax

```
sp_detach_db [@dbname=]'<database name>'
             [,[@skipchecks=]{'TRUE'|'FALSE'}]
```

where:

- **@dbname** is the name of the database you want to remove from the MS-SQL Server.
- **@skipchecks** specifies whether the MS-SQL Server is to run the Transact-SQL UPDATE STATISTICS statement on each table and indexed view within the database before detaching the database from the DBMS. If FALSE or NULL, the DBMS runs UPDATE STATISTICS; if TRUE (which is the default if you don't specify a value for @SKIPCHECKS), the DBMS does not run UPDATE STATISTICS.

Note that the MS-SQL Server keeps statistics about the distribution of key values within an index and (sometimes) the same statistics about values stored within some of the table's non-indexed columns. The optimizer uses these statistics to determine which index or table column to use when executing a query. Whenever there is a significant change to the values stored within a table, or if someone added a large amount of data (with a bulk INSERT INTO) or removed a lot of data (with a TRUNCATE), you should set @SKIPCHECKS to FALSE so the DBMS will update table and index statistics. In addition, if you plan to move the DBMS to a read-only device, set @SKIPCHECKS to FALSE, so that permanent database has the most up-to-date indexes, which will allow queries to retrieve data as efficiently and quickly as possible. Otherwise, set @SKIPCHECKS TRUE or omit its value from the stored procedure call.

To remove the database SQLTips from an MS-SQL Server without updating statistics on INDEXES and table column values, submit the following EXEC statement to the DBMS:

```
EXEC sp_detach_db @dbname='SQLTips', @skipchecks='TRUE'
```

When you must reattach to an MS-SQL Server a database (.mdf) file that you previously detached with sp_detach_db, use the built-in stored procedure call sp_attach_db, whose syntax is shown here

```
sp_attach_db [@dbname=]'<database name>'
             ,[@filename<n>=]
                 '<pathname of an .mdf or .ldf file>'
             [...,@filename16]
```

where:

- **@dbname** is the name of the database you want to attach to an MS-SQL Server. You do not have to use the same name the database had when it was previously attached to an MS-SQL Server; any valid database name will do.

- **@filename<*n*>** is the full pathname of the database (.mdf) or transaction log (.ldf) file. Whereas an .ldf file holds the database transaction log, the .mdf file holds all database data, objects, user, and role information.

Suppose, for example, that you want to reattach the SQLTips database whose data is stored within the file C:\MSSQL\Data\SQLTips_data.mdf and whose transaction log is stored within the file in D:\MSSQL\LogFiles\SQLTips_log.ldf. To reattach SQLTips to an MS-SQL Server, you would execute the following EXEC statement:

```
EXEC sp_attach_db @dbname='MySQLTips',
     @filename1='C:\MSSQL\Data\SqlTips_data.mdf',
     @filename2='D:\MSSQL\LogFiles\SQLTips_log.ldf'
```

If you have only the database data (.mdf) file, you would call sp_attach_db as follows, instead:

```
EXEC sp_attach_db @dbname='MySQLTips',
     @filename1='C:\MSSQL\Data\SqlTips_data.mdf'
```

When you have only the database .mdf (data), the stored procedure will attach the data file to the MS-SQL Server and then create a new transaction log.

When you reattach a database to an MS-SQL Server, the database will again be accessible to DBMS users who were previously granted permission to use the database. All database objects and data, as well as user and role definitions are stored within a database .mdf file. As such, after executing the sp_attach_db procedure, the objects, data, logins, and security created within the original, previously detached database will be available within the database on the MS-SQL Server to which it was reattached.

562 Adding and Removing User-Defined Data Types with the MS-SQL Server Stored Procedures sp_addtype and sp_droptype

While creating a table, you must assign each column a data type that defines the type of data the column can hold. For example, if a column is of type INTEGER, users and applications can store only whole numbers within the column—characters and numbers with a decimal point are not allowed within the column. Similarly, when you define a column as being of type CHAR(10), the column can hold up to 10 characters, symbols, or numeric digits.

By creating a user-defined data, you can assign a descriptive name to one of the standard SQL data types. The name you assign should describe for the user the type of data and/or range of data values a user will find within a column. Suppose, for example, that you are working with the SALARY column in an EMPLOYEE table. You could define the column's data type as NUMERIC(10,2), or you could use a more descriptive user-defined data type such as EXECUTIVE_SALARY, MANAGER_SALARY, or SUPERVISOR_SALARY. Moreover, by creating a rule and binding it to the user-defined data type assigned to a column, you can ensure that numbers entered into the column (SALARY, in this example) fall within a certain range of values.

Tip 53 "Using the MS-SQL Server Enterprise Manager to Create a User-Defined Data Type," showed you how to create user-defined data types. In addition to creating data types within the Enterprise Manager, MS-SQL Server lets you create data types from the command line by calling the built-in stored procedure sp_addtype, which has the following syntax

```
sp_addtype [@typename=]'<data type name>'
           ,[@phystype=]'<valid system data type>'
           [,[@nulltype=]'{NULL|NOT NULL|NONULL}'
           [,[@owner=]'<username>']
```

where:

- **@typename** is the name that describes the type of data or range of values a table column can hold. For example, you might use names like HOURLY_PAYRATE, EXECUTIVE_SALARY, SSAN, and so on for your user-defined data types.
- **@phystype** is a valid built-in data type on your DBMS product. Most DBMS products support all the data types defined within the SQL specification and add a few of their own. Therefore, check your system documentation for a complete list of pre-defined data types you can assign to the @PHYSTYPE parameter.
- **@nulltype** specifies whether a column defined as being of the user-defined data type can hold NULL values. You can override this default nullability setting by providing a different setting when you use the user-defined type in a CREATE TABLE or ALTER TABLE statement.
- **@owner** specifies the username that owns the data type being created. If you do not pass a username to the stored procedure through the @OWNER parameter, the user executing the sp_addtype stored procedure will be the new data type's owner.

For example, to create the user-defined data type SALES_TAX, which defines a numeric value with a maximum of six digits, five of which might follow the decimal point, you would call sp_addtype as shown here:

```
EXEC sp_addtype @typename='SALES_TAX',
@phystype='NUMERIC(6,5),@owner='dbo'
```

Note that the sp_addtype stored procedure call in this example makes the DBO the user-defined data type's owner. Whenever you make the DBO a user-defined data type's owner, all users can refer to the new data type by name. If a user other than DBO owns a data type, the user must provide both the owner's username and user-defined data type's name when using the data type within a column definition.

When you no longer need a data type, you can drop it from the database using the sp_droptype stored procedure, with the following syntax

```
sp_droptype [@typename=]'<data type name>'
```

where:

- **@typename** is the name of the user-defined data type you want to delete.

Note: *You can only drop (that is, delete) user-defined types not currently in use. Thus, before you can drop a user-defined type, you must remove it from all table definitions in which it is applied to a column. In addition, you must unbind any rules or defaults (using sp_unbindrule or sp_unbindefault) you previously bound to the data type.*

Thus, to drop the user-defined data type "SSAN" from the DBMS use:

```
EXEC sp_droptype @typename='SSAN'
```

563 Using sp_help to Display Database Object Properties

The built-in stored procedure sp_help lets you display the properties of objects within a database. Just as Windows displays an object's description after you right-click the object and select Properties from the pop-up menu, sp_help returns a description of the object whose name you pass as a parameter to the stored procedure.

The syntax of the sp_help stored procedure call is

```
sp_help [[@objname=]<database object name>]
```

where:

- **@objname** is the name of the database object whose properties you want the DBMS to describe. @OBJNAME can be any database object including a user-defined data type, or the name of a table, index, constraint, view, stored procedure, and so on.

If you call sp_help without supplying the name of an object (within the @OBJNAME parameter) as shown in the following code line, the MS-SQL Server will return a results set that lists the name, owner, and data type of each object within the database:

```
EXEC sp_help
```

Therefore, calling sp_help without supplying an object's name is a convenient way to get a list of all database objects. You can then pass the names of objects, one at a time, to sp_help and get additional information on the objects you want.

The results set (that is, the specific properties information) that the DBMS returns when you call sp_help, depends on the type of object you pass to the stored procedure through its @OBJNAME parameter. For example, if you pass the name of a constraint, the DBMS will return a table listing:

- CONSTRAINT_TYPE—The constraint's type.
- CONSTRAINT_NAME—The constraint's name.
- DELETE_ACTION—Either Cascade or No Action for a FOREIGN KEY constraint. Not applicable for all other constraints. DELETE_ACTION is Cascade only when a FOREIGN KEY definition has an ON DELETE CASCADE option.
- UPDATE_ACTION—Either Cascade or No Action for a FOREIGN KEY constraint. Not applicable for all other constraints. UPDATE_ACTION is Cascade only when a FOREIGN KEY definition has an ON UPDATE CASCADE option.
- STATUS_ENABLED—Indicates whether a FOREIGN KEY or CHECK constraint is enabled. Not applicable for all other constraint types.
- STATUS_FOR_REPLICATION—Indicates whether a FOREIGN KEY or CHECK constraint is to be enforced during replication Not applicable for all other constraint types.
- CONSTRAINT_KEYS—The names of the columns that make up the constraint, or for defaults, rules, and check constraints, the text that defines the constraint.

Similarly, to display information about a stored procedure such as USP_PROCESS_CHECK, for example, you would call sp_help as follows:

```
EXEC sp_help 'USP_PROCESS_CHECK'
```

MS-SQL Server will display the name of the stored procedure, the username of its owner, and the date and time it was created. Next, the DBMS will return a results set with information about each of the stored procedure's parameters. The results set includes:

- PARAMETER_NAME—The parameter variable's name, such as @account_number, @check_number, @check_date, and so on.
- TYPE—The parameter's data type.
- LENGTH—The parameter's maximum physical storage size in bytes.
- PREC—The total number of digits (for numeric parameters) or number of characters (for non-numeric parameters).
- SCALE—For numeric parameters, the number of digits allowed to the right of the decimal point, otherwise NULL.
- PARAM_ORDER—The ordinal position of the parameter, that is 1 for the first parameter, 2 for the second, 3 for the third, and so on.

564 Using sp_helptext to Display the Text That Defines a Stored Procedure, User-Defined Function, Trigger, Default, Rule, or View

MS-SQL Server stores the batch of statements you enter to define a stored procedure, user-defined function, trigger, default, rule, or view within the TEXT column of a row within the SYSCOMMENTS table. If you did not encrypt the stored procedure, function, or trigger when you created it, you can display its statements by calling the stored procedure sp_helptext using the following syntax

```
sp_helptext [[@objname=]<database object name>]
```

where:

@objname is the name of the stored procedure, user-defined data type, function, trigger, default, rule or view.

You can only use sp_helptext to display the statement batch for objects within the current database. For example, the built-in stored procedure sp_helptext is defined within the MASTER database. As such, to display the definition of the stored procedure sp_helptext, you must first execute a "USE master" statement and then you call the stored procedure sp_helptext as shown here:

```
EXEC sp_helptext 'sp_helptext'
```

If you encrypt an object's definition by including the WITH ENCRYPTION clause with the CREATE statement that you executed to create the object, sp_helptext will not be able to display the object's text. Instead, sp_helptext will display the message "The object <encrypted object name> has been encrypted." Sp_helptext will, of course, display the object's name in place for <encrypted object name>.

565 Using sp_depends to Display the Tables and/or Views That Define a View

Before altering tables or views, especially when changing the number or order of columns in either type of object, be sure to call sp_depends. As you learned in Tip 11 "Understanding Views," a view is a virtual table that derives its columns and its rows of data either from other views or from base tables within the database. Therefore, if you drop a table, views that reference column values within the table will no longer work. When a user queries a view whose underlying table (or view) has been deleted, the DBMS returns error messages such as the following:

```
Server: Msg 208, State 1, Procedure vw_show_high_rollers,
Line2

Invalid object name 'high_rollers'.

Server: Msg 4413, Level 16, State 1, Line 1

Could not use view or function 'vw_show_high_rollers'
because of binding errors
```

While the actual text of the error messages will vary, their point is the same: Views whose base tables (or base views) have been deleted stop displaying data. Moreover, views that stop working may cause a cascade of errors throughout the DBMS as stored procedures and user-defined functions may stop working because the views that feed data to them no longer work. To prevent such data outages, you must remove dependencies before dropping tables or views upon which other views are dependant.

When database object A references a column within database object B, object A is said to be dependent on object B. A view, for example, is dependant on a table when a column within the view references a column within the table. Similarly, a view is dependant upon another view when one of the columns within the first view references a column within the second.

MS-SQL Server makes a note of all dependencies between database objects within the SYSDEPENDS table. Unfortunately, SYSDEPENDS refers to all database objects by ID number rather than by name. As a result, checking which objects are dependant by querying SYSDEPENDS can be challenging. Fortunately, you can use the built-in stored procedure sp_depends to check the dependencies between and among objects by name.

The syntax for the sp_depends stored procedure call is

```
sp_depends [[@objname=]<database object name>]
```

where:

@objname is the name of the view, table, or other database object whose dependencies you want to examine.

Sp_depends reports not only those objects that depend on the object whose name you pass to the stored procedure (through the @OBJNAME parameter), but also the database objects on which the object itself depends. Thus, before dropping or altering the view VW_HIGH_ROLLERS, for example, call sp_depends (as shown by the following code) to determine if there are any database views that reference columns within the VW_HIGH_ROLLERS view:

```
sp_depends 'vw_high_rollers'
```

If sp_depends reports there are database objects dependant on the view you want to delete, don't delete it. Or, if you delete the view anyway, either change the references within dependant objects, such that they refer to other database objects that have the same data, or delete the dependant objects views as well, because they will no longer work. Of course, before you delete any dependant objects, you should use sp_depends to see if other objects depend on them as well.

566 Using sp_helpconstraint to Display Information on Table Constraints

A constraint, as you learned in Tip 15 "Understanding Constraints," is a database object that restricts the range of values and type of data a user or application can place within a table column. There are seven types of constraints: assertions, domains, check constraints, foreign key constraints, primary key constraints, required data, and uniqueness constraints. Tip 15 explains the role that each type of constraint plays in maintaining database integrity. The bottom line is that the DBMS prevents users and applications from inserting rows with data that violates any constraints on the table's column or on the table as a whole.

If you are inserting rows manually (by executing INSERT statements through the SQL Query Analyzer, for example), the MS-SQL Server will report any constraint violations onscreen if it rejects the rows you are trying to insert. When you use an external application to insert data into a database table or when you call on a stored procedure to do so, the DBMS still rejects rows with illegal values. However, if the application or stored procedure does not handle errors properly, you might never see the system's error messages—data that you think was inserted into the database will simply go missing.

When writing batch routines that insert or update table data, it is critical that you understand the table's column constraints. Therefore, before you write stored procedures or external applications that update the database, call the built-in stored procedure sp_helpconstraint to get a list of all constraints to which column values in new rows must adhere. Then, include within your programs and stored procedures code that ensures that data to be inserted does not violate these constraints.

The syntax of an sp_helpconstraint stored procedure call is

```
sp_helpconstraint [@objname=]'<table name>'
            [,[@nomsg=]{'nomsg'}]
```

where:

- **@objname** is the name of the table for which you want the stored procedure to list constraint information.

- **@nomsg** specifies whether sp_helpconstraint is to display the name of the table whose list of constraints the stored procedure is reporting. Set @NOMSG to nomsg if you want to suppress the table name display, or omit the parameter to display the name of the table along with the table's list of constraints.

For each table constraint, sp_helpconstraint returns a results set that includes:

- CONSTRAINT_TYPE—The type of constraint (CHECK, DEFAULT, PRIMARY KEY, FOREIGN KEY, and so on) and the columns to which the constraint applies.
- CONSTRAINT_NAME—The constraint's unique user- or system-supplied name. User-supplied constraint names are often descriptive of the constraint's purpose. System-supplied names of the table name, followed by the names of the columns to which the constraint applies, and end with a randomly generated sequence of letters and numbers to guarantee the uniqueness of the constraint's name.
- DELETE_ACTION—Either Cascade or No Action for a FOREIGN KEY constraint and not applicable for all other constraints. DELETE_ACTION is Cascade only when a FOREIGN KEY definition has an ON DELETE CASCADE rule.
- UPDATE_ACTION—Either Cascade or No Action for a FOREIGN KEY constraint and not applicable for all other constraints. (UPDATE_ACTION is Cascade only when a FOREIGN KEY definition has an ON UPDATE CASCADE rule.)
- STATUS_ENABLED—Indicates whether a FOREIGN KEY or CHECK constraint is enabled and not applicable for all other constraint types.
- STATUS_FOR_REPLICATION—Indicates whether a FOREIGN KEY or CHECK constraint is to be enforced during replication and not applicable for all other types of constraints.

In addition to the preceding information about column constraints, sp_helpconstraint also lists any FOREIGN KEY constraints that reference the table—giving the name of each FOREIGN KEY and the name of the table in which the FOREIGN KEY is defined.

For example, to display the constraints on the AUTHORS table within the PUBS database you would execute the following statement batch:

```
USE PUBS
EXEC sp_helpconstraint 'authors'
```

Note: *You must call sp_helpconstraint from within the database that has the table for which you want the stored procedure to report constraints. In this example, PUBS must be the current database for the sp_helpconstraint procedure to report the constraints on the AUTHORS table as shown in Figure 566.1.*

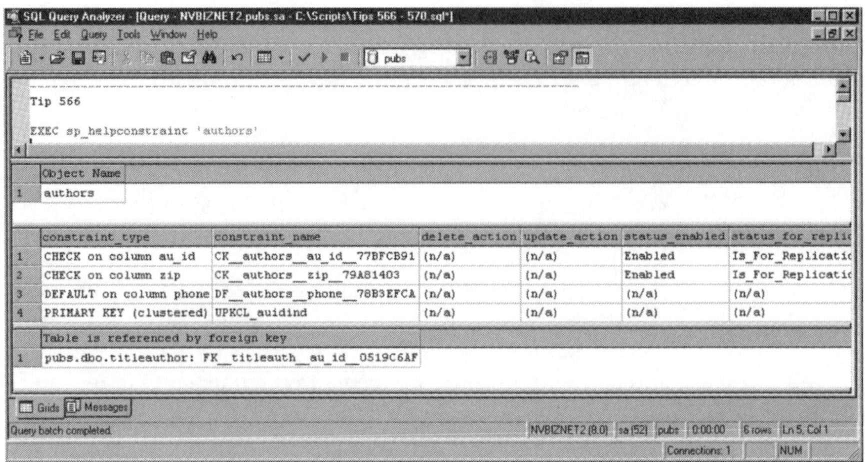

Figure 566.1 Constraint information returned by the stored procedure sp_helpconstraint about the AUTHORS table

To display the text of CHECK and DEFAULT constraints, use the built-in stored procedure sp_helptext (which you learned about in Tip 564 "Using the MS-SQL Server Stored Procedure sp_helptext to Display the Text that Defines a Stored Procedure, User-Defined Function, Trigger, Default, Rule, or View"). In this example, you would execute the following EXEC command to display the text of the CHECK constraint on the AU_ID column within the AUTHORS table:

```
EXEC sp_helptext 'CK__authors__au_id__77BFCB91'
```

When passing a system-supplied constraint name to the sp_helptext stored procedure, be sure to note the two underscores that precede the table name (AUTHORS), the column name (AU_ID), and the random string ("77BFCB91") within the constraint.

567 Using sp_pkeys to Display Information on a Table's PRIMARY KEY

You can establish a parent/child relationship between any two tables by making a FOREIGN KEY reference within the child table to the PRIMARY KEY within the parent table. A PRIMARY KEY is nothing more than one or more columns within a table to which the PRIMARY KEY constraint has been applied. Similarly, a FOREIGN KEY is a column or set of columns that have a FOREIGN KEY constraint. The importance of the PRIMARY KEY is that each PRIMARY KEY value uniquely identifies a single row within the parent table. In other words, every row in the column (or set of columns) that is the table's PRIMARY KEY must have a unique, non-NULL value. The values within the rows of a FOREIGN KEY column, on the other hand, need not be, and, in fact, are ideally not unique to any row within the child table.

Suppose, for example you want to setup a parent/child relationship between a CUSTOMERS table and an ORDERS table. In this relationship, the rows within the CUSTOMERS table are "parents" and the "child" rows are within the ORDERS table. A customer can (and hopefully does) place more than one order. However, any particular order can only belong to one customer.

To setup the parent/child relationship between CUSTOMERS and ORDERS, you would use the built-in stored procedure sp_pkeys to identify the PRIMARY KEY columns that uniquely identifies each customer (that is, each row) within the CUSTOMERS table. Then you can define within the child table (ORDERS) a FOREIGN KEY constraint that references the PRIMARY KEY within the parent table (CUSTOMERS).

The syntax of an sp_pkeys stored procedure call is

```
sp_pkeys [@table_name=]'<table name>'
          [,[@table_owner=]'<table owner's username>'
          [,[@table_qualifier=]'<database name>'
```

where:

- **@table_name** is the name of the table for which you want the stored procedure to report information about the PRIMARY KEY.
- **@table_owner** is the username of the table owner. If you omit the @TABLE_OWNER from the procedure call, the DBMS will search for the table given by <table name> among the tables you own, and then among the tables owned by the database owner (DBO).
- **@table_qualifier** the name of the database in which the table resides. If omitted, the DBMS assumes the table exists within the current database.

Thus, to display information about the PRIMARY KEY defined on the CUSTOMERS table within the NORTHWIND database, you might write the following EXEC statement:

```
EXEC sp_pkeys @table_name='customers',
              @table_qualifier='Northwind'
```

When called, sp_pkeys will return a results set with the following information about the PRIMARY KEY:

- TABLE_QUALIFIER—The name of the database in which the table resides.
- TABLE_OWNER—The username of the table's owner.
- TABLE_NAME—The table's name.
- COLUMN_NAME—The name of a column within the PRIMARY KEY.
- KEY_SEQ—The ordinal position within the PRIMARY KEY of the column named within the COLUMN_NAME column.

- PK_NAME—The name of the primary key.

After calling the sp_pkeys stored procedure, look in the COLUMN_NAME column within the results table to determine the column your FOREIGN KEY (within the ORDERS table, in this example) must reference within the parent (CUSTOMERS) table. Then, apply a FOREIGN KEY constraint to the appropriate columns within the child (ORDERS) table. You learned how to apply FOREIGN KEY constraints while creating a new table within Tip 62, "Using the CREATE TABLE Statement to Assign Foreign Key Constraints." You also learned how to change the structure of an existing table within Tip 60, "Using the ALTER TABLE Statement to Change Primary and Foreign Keys."

If the PRIMARY KEY has multiple columns, the results set returned by the sp_pkeys stored procedure will have multiple rows—one for each column within the PRIMARY KEY. When working with multi-column PRIMARY KEYs, pay particular attention to the value in both the COLUMN_NAME and KEY_SEQ columns. Make sure you list each column within the FOREIGN KEY in the same ordinal position as its corresponding column within the PRIMARY KEY. In other words, the number of columns within the FOREIGN KEY must match the number of columns in the PRIMARY KEY, and corresponding columns must be in the same ordinal position within each key. The number in the KEY_SEQ column gives you the ordinal position within the PRIMARY KEY of the column named in the COLUMN_NAME column.

568 Using sp_fkeys to Display Information on the Foreign Keys That Reference a Table's PRIMARY KEY

When creating a relational database, be sure to exploit the ability of the DBMS to maintain referential integrity. Although you can set up multi-table SELECT statements that join parent and child rows without PRIMARY KEY and FOREIGN KEY constraints, resist the temptation to do so. While it takes some prior planning to set up PRIMARY KEY and FOREIGN KEY constraints properly, doing so frees you from having to worry about users being able to insert duplicate rows into the parent table or being able to create orphan rows within the child table.

Duplicate rows in a parent table and/or orphans within a child table are undesirable because they lead to errors in reporting and can cause real-life problems. Suppose, for example, that you have a CUSTOMERS parent table and an ORDERS child table. If you have duplicate rows within the CUSTOMERS (parent) table, a child row within the ORDERS table could have two (or more) parents within the CUSTOMERS table—which means a customer will likely be billed twice for the one order that shipped. Conversely, orphan rows within the child (ORDERS) table means there are orders with no customer information. Therefore, if the

"Ship To" address is stored within the ORDERS table and the "Bill To" information is stored in the CUSTOMERS table, orders will ship without customers being billed.

After you set up PRIMARY KEY and FOREIGN KEY constraints that let the DBMS manage parent/child relationships between related tables (that is, to maintain referential integrity within the database), you will find it convenient to produce a list of FOREIGN KEY constraints that reference each parent table. This list will come in handy when you want to drop a parent table or change its structure. In addition, when executing a DELETE statement to remove parent rows or an UPDATE statement that changes values within PRIMARY KEY columns, you may have to drop or update columns in rows within the child table as well. The list of FOREIGN KEY references to the parent table's PRIMARY KEY will tell you which child tables require attention when you make changes within the parent table.

The built-in stored procedure sp_fkeys lets you get a list of FOREIGN_KEY references on any table within a database managed by an MS-SQL Server. To call sp_fkeys, use the following syntax

```
sp_fkeys
  [@pktable_name=]'<PRIMARY KEY table name>'
  [,[@pktable_owner=]'<PRIMARY KEY table owner's name>'
  [,[@fktable_name=]'<FOREIGN KEY table name>'
  [,[@fktable_owner=]'<FOREIGN KEY table owner's name>'
  [,[@fktable_qualifier=]'<FOREIGN KEY table database>'
```

where:

- **@pktable_name** is the name of the parent table (with the PRIMARY KEY) for which you want the stored procedure to list the FOREIGN KEY references.
- **@pktable_owner** is the username of the parent table's owner. If you omit the @PKTABLE_OWNER parameter from the procedure call, the DBMS will search for the table name by @PKTABLE_NAME among the tables you own and then among the tables owned by the database owner (DBO).
- **@fktable_name** is the name of the child table (with the FOREIGN KEY). If you provide both the parent table (@PKTABLE_NAME) and child table (@FKTABLE_NAME) names, the stored procedure will list only the FOREIGN KEY reference on the parent (named in @PKTABLE_NAME parameter) within the one child table (named in the @FKTABLE_NAME parameter). Conversely, if you provide only the name of the child table (in the @FKTABLE_NAME parameter) and omit the parent table's name, the stored procedure will list all the parent tables referenced by foreign keys within the child table.
- **@fktable_owner** is the username of the child table's owner. If you omit the @FKTABLE_OWNER parameter, the DBMS will search for the child table named by @FKTABLE_NAME among the tables you own and then among the tables owned by the database owner (DBO).
- **@fktable_qualifier** is the name of the database in which the child table (with the FOREIGN KEY constraint) resides. If omitted, the DBMS assumes the child (FOREIGN KEY) table exists within the current database.

Thus, if you want a list of all FOREIGN KEY constraints that reference the PRIMARY KEY within the CUSTOMERS table in the NORTHWIND database, you would execute the following statement batch:

```
USE Northwind
EXEC sp_fkeys @pktable_name='Customers'
```

The stored procedure sp_fkeys, in turn, will return a results set with at least one row per FOREIGN KEY reference and the following columns within each row:

- PKTABLE_QUALIFIER—The name of the database in which the (parent) table with the PRIMARY KEY constraint reside.
- PKTABLE_OWNER—The username of the parent table's owner.
- PKTABLE_NAME—The name of the (parent) table with the PRIMARY KEY constraint.
- PKCOLUMN_NAME—The name of the column in the PRIMARY KEY. If the PRIMARY KEY has multiple columns, sp_fkeys will return multiple rows—one for each column within the PRIMARY KEY constraint.
- FKTABLE_QUALIFIER—The name of the database in which the (child) table with the FOREIGN KEY constraint reside.
- FKTABLE_OWNER—The username of the child table's owner.
- FKTABLE_NAME—The name of the (child) table with the FORIEGN KEY constraint.
- FKCOLUMN_NAME—The name of the column within the FOREIGN KEY that corresponds to the PRIMARY KEY column named in PKCOLUMN_name (within the current row of the results set).
- KEY_SEQ—The ordinal position within the PRIMARY KEY and FOREIGN KEY of the columns described by the current row within the results table.
- UPDATE_RULE—0, 1, or 2 indicate the action the DBMS takes on the value within the FOREIGN KEY column when the value in the corresponding column within the PRIMARY KEY is updated. 0 = Cascade; 1 = No Action, and 2 = Set Null.
- DELETE_RULE—0, 1, or 2 indicate the action the DBMS takes on the value within the FOREIGN KEY column when the value in the child's corresponding row in the parent table is deleted. 0 = Cascade; 1 = No Action, and 2 = Set Null.
- FK_NAME—The user- or system-supplied name of the FOREIGN KEY constraint.
- PK_NAME—The user- or system-supplied name of the PRIMARY KEY constraint.

To display the above listed information for all parent tables referenced by FOREIGN KEYS within a child table, you would call sp_fkey and supply to it only the information about the child table (which has the FOREIGN KEY constraints). For example, to list all tables referenced by FOREIGN KEY constraints within the ORDERS table in the NORTHWIND database, you would execute the following statement batch:

```
USE Northwind
EXEC sp_fkeys @fktable_name='Orders'
```

569 Using sp_procoption to Control Which Stored Procedures the MS-SQL Server Will Run at Startup

In Tips 530–532 you learned what a stored procedure does, how to use the CREATE PROCEDURE statement to create a stored procedure, and how to call a stored procedure using the Transact-SQL EXEC command. In short, a stored procedure is a batch of SQL and/or Transact-SQL statements the DBMS executes whenever a user calls the stored procedure by name. Stored procedures are a powerful feature, because they let you write SQL Programs. That is, stored procedures let you combine SQL data management statements with procedural Transact-SQL programming statements so you can create statement batches that perform complex queries, database updates, or execute any sequence of SQL (and Transact-SQL statements) you like. Stored procedures make it possible for a database user to execute complex queries or a large batch of database management statements by submitting a single EXEC statement that calls the stored procedure, which then performs the work required.

In addition to letting users and external applications execute stored procedures, you can have the MS-SQL Server execute specific stored procedures automatically each time you start the DBMS. For example, if you have set of maintenance tasks such as creating and or clearing global temporary tables or cursors, creating executive summary tables, or some other cleanup/preparatory tasks that you want the DBMS to perform each time you start the MS-SQL Server, put the statements that perform the work into one or several stored procedures. Then, use the built-in stored procedure sp_procoption to mark the stored procedures you want to be called at startup.

To create stored procedures the DBMS will execute at startup, you must login to the MASTER database as the database owner (DBO). As DBO, and within the MASTER database, use the CREATE PROCEDURE statement to create a stored procedure you want the DBMS to execute at startup. Next, call the sp_procoption stored procedure with the the following syntax to mark the stored procedure you created for execution at startup

```
sp_procoption [@procname=]'<stored procedure name>'
              ,[@optionname=]'startup'
              ,[@optionvalue=]'{true|false}'
```

where:

- **@procname** is the name of the stored procedure you want to MS-SQL Server to run at startup. Or, if you set the @OPTIONVALUE to FALSE, @PROCNAME is the name of the stored procedure you no longer want the MS-SQL Server to run at startup.
- **@optionname** is always “startup.”

- **@optionvalue** is either TRUE or FALSE. Set @OPTIONVALUE to TRUE if you want the DBMS to execute the procedure named in @PROCNAME at startup. Set @OPTIONVALUE to FALSE if you no longer want the DBMS to execute the procedure at startup.

Suppose for example, that you create the stored procedure su_sp_CreateExecSummary as the DBO within the MASTER database. To have the DBMS call su_sp_CreateExecSummary each time you restart the MS-SQL Server, execute the following statement batch:

```
USE master
EXEC sp_procoption @procname = 'su_sp_CreateExecSummary',
                   @optionname = 'startup',
                   @optionvalue = 'true'
```

Note: *Because MS-SQL Server will not let you execute a USE statement within a stored procedure, you must refer to database objects using their fully qualified names as: <database name>.<owner ID>.<table name> within stored procedures you have the DBMS execute at startup.*

To make it easy to track stored procedures executed at startup, give each of them a descriptive name starting with "su_sp_"—for "startup stored procedure."

When you no longer want the MS-SQL Server to execute a stored procedure at startup, call the sp_procoption stored procedure as before, only this time, set @OPTIONVALUE to FALSE as shown here:

```
USE master
EXEC sp_procoption @procname = 'su_sp_CreateExecSummary',
                   @optionname = 'startup',
                   @optionvalue = 'false'
```

In this example, the DBMS will turn the execute at startup option off for the stored procedure su_sp_CreateExecSummary.

570 Using sp_helpdb to Display the Size and Physical Location of Database Files

The MS-SQL Server can manage several databases simultaneously. The DBMS places all objects that make up a database within a single disk file and stores the database transaction log within a second file. Although you can change the names of the data and transaction log files to something other than the MS-SQL Server defaults, there is no advantage to doing so.

On an MS-SQL Server 2000 installation, you will normally find the database data and transaction log files within the \SQLServer2000\MSSQL\data\ folder on the fileserver's hard drive. The name of the database file on disk is typically the same as the name of the database followed by _Data.MDF. For example, whether there are ten or 1,000 tables and other objects within the SQLTips database, you will find the entire database (that is, all its objects and security information) within a single file named SQLTips_Data.MDF in the MS-SQL Server's data folder (\SQLServer2000\MSSQL\data\). Similarly, the database transaction log file typically starts with the database name followed by _Log,LDF. Thus, the name of the file in which the DBMS keeps the SQLTips transaction log is usually SQLTips_Log.LDF.

You learned how to use the MS-SQL Server Enterprise Manager to create a new database (and therefore new database and transaction log files) in Tip 42, "Using the MS-SQL Server Enterprise Manager to Create a Database and Transaction Log." Then, in Tip 497, "Using the MS-SQL Server Enterprise Manager to Add Files and Filegroups to an Existing Database," you learned how to add additional database and transaction log files to those the DBMS created when you created the database.

To check on the current size, status, and location of the physical files in which the DBMS maintains your database objects, data, and transactions log, call the built-in stored procedure sp_helpdb using the following syntax

```
sp_helpdb [[@dbname=]'<database name>']
```

where:

- **@dbname** is the name of the database on whose files you want the stored procedure to provide information.

For example, to display file information for the SQLTips database, you would use the following EXEC statement to display the information shown in Figure 570.1:

```
EXEC sp_helpdb @dbname='SQLTips'
```

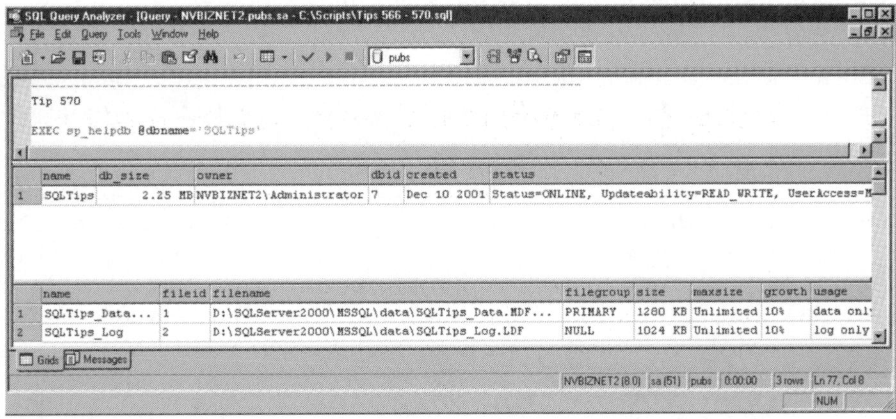

Figure 570.1 Information about the physical database files returned by the built-in stored procedure sp_helpdb

To display only the name, current size (in megabytes), owner, date created, and status information (that is, only the first results set shown below the stored procedure call in Figure 570.1), use the following EXEC statement to call the sp_helpdb stored procedure:

```
EXEC sp_helpdb
```

When you call sp_helpdb without providing the database name, as shown in this example, the stored procedure provides the information from the first results set in Figure 570.1 for all databases under management by the current MS-SQL Server.

571 Using sp_spaceused to Display the Amount of Used and Unused Space Allocated to the Database or Individual Database Objects

In Tip 542, "Understanding DBCC Maintenance Statements," you learned how to use DBCC SHRINKDATABASE and DBCC SHRINKFILE to reduce the size of database data (.mdf) and transaction log (.ldf) files. Both of these DBCC options involve removing unused space from the database data and transaction log files, and then returning the unused space to the operating system's control.

Database data (.mdf) files sometimes end up with too much empty/unused space, because the DBMS expands the size of its files as you add data to tables within the database. Unless you specify the autoshrink option, the DBMS does not reduce the size of its files on disk even when you delete large amounts of data from database tables or drop large indexes. Rather than release space previously filled with data to the operating system, the DBMS keeps the now unused space within its data files and simply marks the space available for data users might add to the database in the future.

You can set the autoshrink option for a database; however this is not recommended as it may increase overhead unnecessarily. For example, the DBMS may be forced to shrink and then re-grow the database file when unused disk space within the database files is not needed for some other purpose.

The built-in stored procedure sp_spaceused will tell you how much used and unused space there is within the database data file. In fact, you can use call the stored procedure with the following syntax to get space usage information on the entire database or for individual tables within the database

```
sp_spaceused [[@objname=]'<table name>'
              [,[@updateusage=]'updateusage']
```

where:

- **@objname** is the name of the table for which you want the stored procedure to display space usage data. If you omit the @OBJNAME parameter, the stored procedure reports space usage information for the current database (versus for an individual table within the database).
- **@updateusage** specifies whether the DBMS must scan data and index pages on disk for the actual disk usage data and make corrections to the usage figures within the SYSINDEXES table. Typically, you only want to specify the @UPDATEUSAGE option if you have recently dropped a large index from the database, because the SYSINDEXES table may not have the most up-to-date space usage information as a result.

For example, to determine the total size (in megabytes) of the SQLTips database data (.mdf) file as well as the amount of unallocated space retained within the file, submit the following EXEC statement to the DBMS:

```
EXEC sp_spaceused
```

MS-SQL Server, in turn, will display a results set with the following columns:

- DATABASE_NAME—The name of the current database.
- DATABASE_SIZE—The size (in megabytes) of the current database data (.mdf) file(s).
- UNALLOCATED_SPACE—The amount of space (in megabytes) not yet allocated to database objects.
- RESERVED—Space allocated to the 8Kb pages assigned to tables and indexes within the data base that is not yet filled with data.
- DATA—Total amount of space used to hold data in all tables.
- INDEX_SIZE—Total amount of space used to hold data by all indexes within the database.
- UNUSED—Amount of space within the database file that is not yet assigned to any database objects.

If you call the sp_spaceused stored procedure and provide the name of a table within the current database as follows, sp_spaceused reports usage stats for only that one table:

```
USE pubs
EXEC sp_spaceused @objname='authors'
```

In this example, the DBMS will report the following space usage information for the AUTHORS table within the PUBS database:

- NAME—The name of the table for which space usage information was requested.
- ROWS—The number of rows of data within in the table.
- RESERVED—Space allocated to the 8Kb pages assigned to the table and its indexes that is not yet filled with data.

- DATA—Total amount of space used to hold data within the table.
- INDEX_SIZE—Total amount of space used by index files on the table.
- UNUSED—Amount of space allocated to the table but not yet used as part of an 8Kb data page.

572 Using sp_helptrigger to Display Information About Triggers on Tables

As you learned in Tips 448–453, triggers are a special type of stored procedure that the DBMS executes in response to an INSERT, UPDATE, or DELETE operation against a specific table. For example, after you execute a CREATE TRIGGER statement to create an INSERT TRIGGER on a table, the DBMS will "fire" (that is, execute) the statements within the trigger before, after, or instead of all INSERT statements that target the table. You specify whether the DBMS is to fire the trigger before, after, or instead of an INSERT, UPDATE, or DELETE statement as one of the options when you create a trigger.

Other than the fact that the DBMS executes a trigger automatically (in response to an INSERT, UPDATE, or DELETE statement—depending on the type of trigger), a trigger looks and works exactly like a stored procedure. Unfortunately, you will not see triggers you've created on tables listed among the normal (non-trigger) stored procedures. You can get a list of non-trigger stored procedures defined within a database by clicking on the Stored Procedures icon for the database within the MS-SQL Server Enterprise Manager.

Moreover, while the built-in stored procedure sp_help displays information on FOREIGN KEY constraints (which may have an ON DELETE or an ON UPDATE rule), sp_help does not tell you anything about the triggers defined on a table. As a result, you must maintain good, up-to-date documentation on every trigger defined on tables within each database on the MS-SQL Server. If you do not, the server will appear to take random actions in response to some, but not all, INSERT, UPDATE, and DELETE statements.

You can use the built-in stored procedure sp_helptrigger, called with the following syntax, to list the triggers defined on a database table

```
sp_helptrigger [@tabname=]'<table name>'
               [,[@triggertype=']'{DELETE|INSERT|UPDATE}']
```

where:

- **@tabname** is the name of the table within the current database for which you want the stored procedure to provide information on the triggers defined.

- **@triggertype** specifies the type of trigger for which the stored procedure is to provide information. If you omit @TRIGGERTYPE, sp_helptrigger will return information about all triggers defined on the table.

For each trigger (or for each trigger of the trigger type you specify for @TRIGGERTYPE), sp_helptrigger returns a results set that includes the following columns:

- TRIGGER_NAME—The name of the trigger.
- TRIGGER_OWNER—The username of the trigger's owner.
- ISUPDATE—1, if the trigger is an UPDATE trigger; 0, if not.
- ISDELETE—1, if the trigger is a DELETE trigger; 0, if not.
- ISINSERT—1, if the trigger is an INSERT trigger; 0, if not.
- ISAFTER—1, if the DBMS is to execute the trigger *after* (versus before or instead of) executing the triggering UPDATE, DELETE, or INSERT statement on the table on which the trigger is defined. 0, if the DBMS is to execute the trigger before or instead of executing the triggering UPDATE, DELETE, or INSERT statement.
- ISINSTEADOF—1, if the DBMS is to execute the trigger *instead of* (versus before or after) executing the triggering UPDATE, DELETE, or INSERT statement on the table on which the trigger is defined. 0, if the DBMS is to execute the trigger before or after executing the triggering UPDATE, DELETE, or INSERT statement.

Thus, to display information about all the triggers defined on the EMPLOYEES table within the SQLTips database, you would execute the following statement batch:

```
USE SQLTips
EXEC sp_helptrigger 'employees'
```

Or, if SQLTips is already the current database, you would simply call the sp_helptrigger stored procedure without executing the USE statement. For example, to display only the UPDATE triggers on the EMPLOYEES table (while already in the SQLTips database) you would use the EXEC statement:

```
EXEC sp_helptrigger 'employees', 'update'
```

Note: *To save yourself a lot of grief, keep up-to-date documentation that lists and describes every trigger defined on tables within the databases managed by your MS-SQL Server. If you do not, DBMS will appear to do strange things. Remember that each database may have hundreds of tables and dozens of users submitting INSERT, UPDATE, and DELETE statements at any one time. Therefore, trying to pinpoint the specific INSERT, UPDATE, or DELETE statements that are causing seemingly errant DBMS behavior, will be a non-trivial task. As you learned within this tip, the sp_helptrigger stored procedure requires that you know at least the name of the table on which the trigger is defined.*

If you lose your documentation, you can get a list of triggers defined on tables within the current database by executing the following query on the SYSOBJECTS table:

```
SELECT * FROM sysobjects WHERE type = 'TR'
```

Look at the NAME column within the rows of the results set for the names of the triggers defined on tables within the database. Then, execute the following statement (substituting a trigger name from the results set for <name of trigger>) to review the trigger's definition—which includes the name of the table on which the trigger is defined:

```
EXEC sp_helptext <name of trigger>
```

573 Using sp_who and the KILL Command to Control Processing Running on the MS-SQL Server

Sometimes you need all users to logout from a database so you can perform scheduled maintenance tasks or unscheduled repair work. For example, to run the DBCC statements you learned about in Tip 545 "Understanding DBCC Validation Statements," you must first change the database to single-user mode if you want to run a DBCC validation task with a repair option. To change from multi-user to single-user mode, you need everyone to logout from the database. Similarly, if you want to transfer database files from one drive to another, all users must logout. Then, you can detach, move to a new disk, and then re-attach the database disk files. (You learned how to detach and re-attach database files in Tip 561 "Using sp_detach_db and sp_attach_db to Remove and Add a Database to an MS-SQL Server.")

After making a system-wide announcement for the staff to please logout, you must check a list of processes running on the MS-SQL Server to find out when everyone has indeed logged out. To get a list of users and applications logged into the MS-SQL Server, call the built-in stored procedure sp_who, using the following syntax

```
EXEC sp_who [[@loginame=]'<login name>']
```

where:

- **@loginame** is the username of the person associated with the process or login for which you want the stored procedure to supply the SPID and other process status information.

Thus, to display a list of current processes running and users logged onto the MS-SQL Server, submit the following EXEC statement to display the process list as shown in Figure 573.1:

```
EXEC sp_who
```

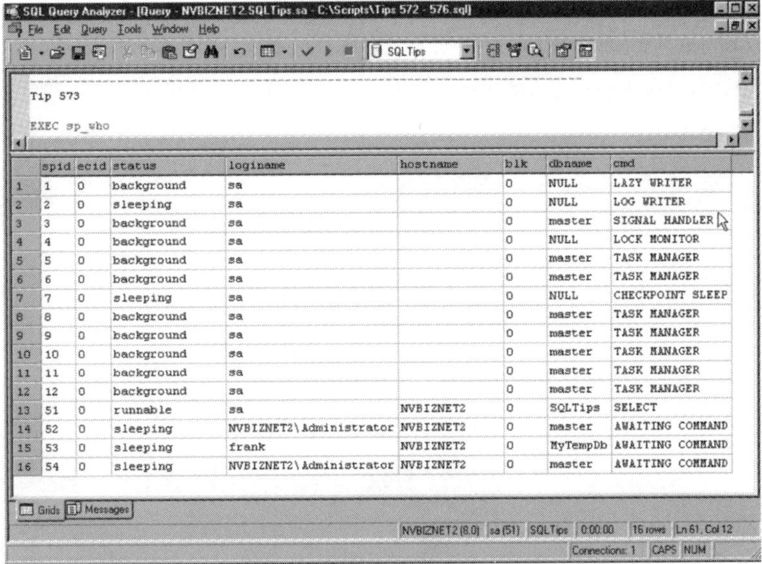

Figure 573.1 Output from a sp_who built-in stored procedure call

To determine which process to terminate, check the DBNAME column for the name of the database from which you want all users to logout. Make a note of each user's system process ID shown within the SPID column. If the user does not logout in the prescribed amount of time, you can supply the SPID to the Transact-SQL KILL command to terminate the user's session.

To terminate a user's connection, execute the Transact-SQL KILL command using the following syntax

```
EXEC KILL {spid}[WITH STATUSONLY]
```

where:

- **@spid** is the system process ID of the session you want to terminate.
- **WITH STATUSONLY** specifies that the DBMS provide a status report only to show how long it will take to finish rolling back (that is, undoing) work already performed within an uncommitted transaction.

For example, to terminate user FRANK's connection on the MS-SQL Server (shown previously in Figure 573.1 as SPID 53), you would execute the following KILL command:

```
KILL 53
```

When you use KILL to terminate a connection, the DBMS must roll back any uncommitted work performed by the connection you are terminating. While the DBMS is in the process of undoing uncommitted work performed, the process will remain on process lists displayed by the sp_who. However, the status of the connection will show as "KILLED/ROLLBACK."

To get an idea of how much longer it will take to finish a roll back in progress, execute the KILL command with the WITH STATUSONLY option as shown here:

```
KILL 53 WITH STATUSONLY
```

MS-SQL Server, in turn, will respond with a message similar to the following:

```
Spid 53: Transaction rollback in progress. Estimated
rollback completion: 75% Estimated time left: 30 seconds.
```

In addition to terminating processes so you can get everyone out of a database, you might also use KILL to terminate a process executing an errant query or whose locks are blocking other processes, as discussed within the next tip.

574 Using sp_lock to Display Information on Locks Held in a Database

In Tips 357–360, you learned about transaction isolation levels. In summary, each of the three transaction isolation levels (SERIALIZABLE, REPEATABLE READ, and READ COMMITTED) is meant to prevent certain errors in updates and reporting that occur when two or more users update and query the same table concurrently. The highest level of isolation, SERIALIZABLE, prevents all update and reporting errors by giving a user an exclusive lock on all pages with data the user reads, updates, or inserts within a table. Until the user closes a SERIALZABLE transaction, he or she maintains an exclusive lock on data read or changed within one or more tables. Other users that want to execute an INSERT or UPDATE statement on data in locked pages must wait until the user with the exclusive lock either ends the transaction (with a COMMIT or ROLLBACK), or lowers the transaction's isolation level to allow shared access.

If a user has been waiting an inordinate amount of time for an INSERT or UPDATE statement to finishing running, you can use the built-in stored procedure sp_lock to determine which other user (or process) is holding an exclusive lock on the table (or a page within the table). After you use sp_lock to determine the locking session's system process ID (SPID), you can use the KILL command to terminate the session that has the data locked, if necessary.

The syntax you use to call the sp_lock stored procedure is

```
sp_lock [[@spid1=]'<a SPID>'],[,[@spid2=]'<a second SPID>']
```

where:

- **@spid1** is the SPID of the process whose lock information you want to display.
- **@spid2** is the SPID of a second process whose lock information you want to display.

Thus, you can call sp_lock specifying either zero, one, or two parameters. If you supply zero parameters (that is, if you call sp_lock without supplying either @SPID1 or @SPID2), the stored procedure will display the lock status for all sessions within the current database. Alternatively, if you supply @SPID1, sp_lock will report lock information for one session, and if you supply both @SPID1 and @SPID2, the stored procedure will report location for two sessions.

To resolve a lock issue, first use the built-in stored procedure sp_who to determine the locked session's SPID. Suppose, for example, that Frank reports he has been waiting for hours (at least it seems that way to Frank) for his INSERT statement to run. To determine Frank's SPID, execute the following statement:

```
EXEC sp_who 'frank'
```

When sp_who returns its results set, look in the SPID column and make a note of Frank's SPID—let's say it's 54 for the current example.

Next, execute the following call of the sp_lock stored procedure to display the SPID and lock status for all connections with open locks granted by the DBMS:

```
EXEC sp_lock
```

When the stored procedure sp_lock returns a results set similar to that shown in Figure 574.1, look for Frank's SPID (54, in this example) in the results set's SPID column. Then look across to the right of all rows with Frank's SPID to see find the rows with "WAIT" in the STATUS column.

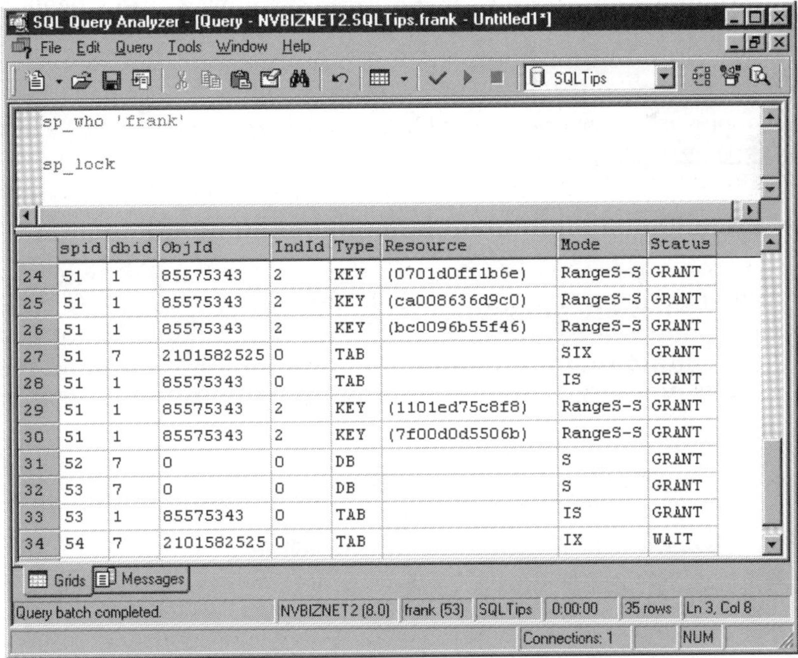

	spid	dbid	ObjId	IndId	Type	Resource	Mode	Status
24	51	1	85575343	2	KEY	(0701d0ff1b6e)	RangeS-S	GRANT
25	51	1	85575343	2	KEY	(ca0086 36d9c0)	RangeS-S	GRANT
26	51	1	85575343	2	KEY	(bc0096b55f46)	RangeS-S	GRANT
27	51	7	2101582525	0	TAB		SIX	GRANT
28	51	1	85575343	0	TAB		IS	GRANT
29	51	1	85575343	2	KEY	(1101ed75c8f8)	RangeS-S	GRANT
30	51	1	85575343	2	KEY	(7f00d0d5506b)	RangeS-S	GRANT
31	52	7	0	0	DB		S	GRANT
32	53	7	0	0	DB		S	GRANT
33	53	1	85575343	0	TAB		IS	GRANT
34	54	7	2101582525	0	TAB		IX	WAIT

Figure 574.1 Output from a sp_lock built-in stored procedure call

After you find a row with a "WAIT" in the STATUS column, look back to the left within the row and note the object ID within the DBID column. Move up or down within the DBID column until you find another process using with the same ID within the column.

In this example, SPID 51 is using DBID 7, which is the same DBID for which Frank's connection is "waiting" (as shown previously in Figure 574). Now that you have the two SPID's with the apparent conflict, call sp_lock again, supplying the two SPIDs—just to verify that the one really has locks on the resource the other wants:

```
EXEC sp_lock 51, 53
```

After you see that the one user (51, in this example) was indeed granted locks (indicated by the word GRANT within the row's STATUS column) on the table (or other resource) for which the second is waiting, you can either contact the user holding the lock, or simply terminate the SPID. To determine the name of the user holding the lock, call the sp_who stored procedure and pass to it the SPID of the session whose username you want as in:

```
EXEC sp_who 51
```

When the stored procedure returns the results set, look in the LOGINAME column for the username of the user who's session you may want to terminate. Then, give the user a courtesy call. It is always possible that the user holding the lock on a resource is in the middle of a long update or query process, or that he or she needs exclusive access to the table for some legitimate reason.

If necessary, you can terminate the locking process (to let Frank's session assert a lock on the table and execute its INSERT statement) by executing a KILL command such as the following:

```
KILL 51
```

In this example, the locking session's SPID was 51; your KILL command will likely have a different SPID altogether.

575 Using sp_password to Change Account Passwords

To access the data within a database, users must first login. While a user may use his or her name or perhaps a job title for a username, you should require that each user select a password that others cannot easily guess. As such, first names, last names, children's names, words from favorite sayings, and anything easily guessable by someone who knows the user, should not be a used as a password.

In Tip 137, "Using the MS-SQL Server Enterprise Manager to Add Logins and Users," you learned how to give users access to an MS-SQL Server. When granting database access to a username, you must select either Windows Authentication or SQL Server Authentication.

If you select Windows authentication, the MS-SQL Server will not ask you to assign the new username a password. Instead, the DBMS depends on the Windows (NT, 2000, XP) operating system to authenticate the user's login. After logging onto the Windows network, the user can login to the MS-SQL Server simply by telling the DBMS to use Windows authentication for his or her username. The MS-SQL Server retrieves the username under which the user logged onto the Windows network and checks it against its list of valid usernames. If it finds the username on the list of usernames for which Windows authentication is allowed, the MS-SQL Server logs the username onto the DBMS.

If you select SQL server authentication, the MS-SQL Server prompts you to enter a password for the new username you are creating. When you select SQL server authentication, the DBMS does not depend on the Windows (NT, 2000, XP) operating system to authenticate the user's login. Instead, whenever a user attempts to login, the DBMS challenges to the user to enter the matching password for the username under which he or she is logging in. After the user enters his or her username and password, the DBMS checks the username/password pair against those within its access list. If it finds the username/password pair on its access list, the MS-SQL Server logs the username onto the DBMS.

When you use either the MS-SQL Server Enterprise Manager or a built-in stored procedure to create an account that uses SQL server authentication, the only way to change the account's password is by calling the built-in stored procedure sp_password. Note that when you create a Windows authenticated account, the Windows (NT, 2000, XP) operating system, (not the MS-SQL Server,) maintains each account's password. Therefore, to change the password on a Windows network account, the user must use a Windows network facility or contact the network's system manager. In short, MS-SQL Server can only change passwords on accounts that the MS-SQL Server authenticates—and then only through the stored procedure sp_password.

To change an MS-SQL Server authenticated account's password, call the sp_password stored procedure using the following syntax

```
sp_password [[@old=]'<the current password>,]'
            {[@new]'<the new password>'}
            [,[@loginame=]'<username>'
```

where:

- **@old** is the current password on the account. Any user can change his or her password, but must supply the account's current password in order to do so. Members of the SYSADMIN or SECURITYADMIN role can change passwords without supplying the current password through @OLD.
- **@new** is the new password you want to assign to the account.
- **@loginame** is the username on the account whose password sp_password is to change.

Users change passwords for various reasons—another user may have learned the current password, company policy may require periodic password changes, or perhaps the user simply chose too long of a password initially, and is tired of typing it each time he or she logs onto the DBMS. By calling sp_password and supplying the account's current password (through the @OLD parameter) and a new password (through the @NEW parameter), any user can change the password on his or her own account.

If a user has forgotten his or her password, the user must see a member of the SYSADMIN or SECURITYADMIN role. A member of either group can omit the @OLD parameter and simply supply the new password (through the @NEW parameter). Suppose, for example, user Sue wanted to change her password. To do so, Sue must login to the DBMS and then call the sp_password stored procedure as follows:

```
EXEC sp_password @old='OldPass', @new='newpass'
```

Note that a non-privileged user must supply both the current (old) password and the desired (new) password for the account under which the user is logged onto the DBMS. The system administrator (or any member of the SYSADMIN or SECURTYADMIN role) can change the password on another user's account by supplying the new password (through @NEW parameter) and the username (through the @LOGINAME parameter) on the account whose password is to be changed. Suppose for example, that Konrad, a member of the SYSADMIN role, wants to change Oscar's password to MEYER. To change the password on Oscar's account, Konrad would call the sp_password stored procedure as follows:

```
EXEC sp_password @new='MEYER', @loginame='OSCAR'
```

576 Using Built-In Stored Procedures to Manage MS-SQL Server User Accounts

In Tips 137–138, you learned how to use the MS-SQL Server Enterprise Manager to add and remove user accounts. For those times when you are working on a system that does not have the MS-SQL Server Enterprise Manager installed, or when you are accessing the MS-SQL Server either remotely or locally through an application program (such as the SQL Query Analyzer), you can use built-in stored procedures to manage DBMS user accounts.

When creating (and removing) accounts, bear in mind that there are two types of accounts—MS-SQL Server accounts, which exist exclusively within the DBMS, and Windows accounts, which are Windows (NT, 2000, or XP) network accounts granted access to the DBMS. To create new MS-SQL Server accounts, use sp_addlogin. To create Windows security accounts, use sp_grantlogin. The first stored procedure (sp_addlogin) creates a new account while the second (sp_grantlogin) lets an existing Windows (NT, 2000, or XP) network account login to the database.

If you want the MS-SQL Server to authenticate a user's login to the DBMS by requiring the user to enter valid username/password pair, create an MS-SQL Server account. To create a new MS-SQL Server account, call the built-in stored procedure sp_addlogin using the following syntax

```
sp_addlogin [@loginame=]'<username>'
            [,[@password=]'<password>']
            [,[@defdb=]'<database name>']
            [,[@deflanguage='<languge>']
            [,[@SID=]'<security ID>']
            [,[@encryptopt=]
              {'NULL|skip_encryption|skip_encryption_old'}]
```

where:

- **@loginame** is the username you want to assign to the new account you are adding. The user must supply the correct username/password pair to login to an account.
- **@passwd** is the password you want to assign to the new account you are adding. Though optional, for security reasons you should require that all accounts have a password. When @PASSWORD is not NULL, the user must supply the correct username/password pair to login to an account.
- **@defdb** is the name of the accounts default database, that is, the database to which the user is connected after login.
- **@deflanguage** is the default language assigned when the user logs in. You typically omit this parameter and let the DBMS assign its default language to each user session.
- **@sid** is the security identification (SID) number you want the DBMS to assign to an account. When specified @SID must be exactly 16 bytes in length and must not already exist. You typically let the DBMS create a unique SID when it creates an account. As such, only supply the SID if you are transferring or duplicating user accounts from one server on onto another and want the logins to be identical.
- **@encryptopt** specifies whether the accounts password is to be encrypted when stored within the system tables.
    - NULL—The password is encrypted.
    - SKIP_ENCRYPTION—The password is already encrypted, so MS-SQL Server does not need to re-encrypt it.
    - SKIP_ENCRYPTION_OLD—The password was encrypted on a previous version of the MS-SQL Server and does not need to be re-encrypted prior to storage.

For example, to create an account with username WALTER and password JONES223, and whose login defaults to using the SQLTips database, execute the following statement:

```
EXEC sp_addlogin @loginame='walter', @passwd='JONES223',
                 @defdb='SQLTips'
```

After creating a new user account, you must also grant the user access to a database—including the account's default database—or the user will not be able to login to the MS-SQL Server. You will learn how to use the built-in stored procedure sp_grantdbaccess to grant users access to a database following the discussion of sp_grantlogin.

If you want the DBMS to let the Windows (NT, 2000, or XP) server take care of login authentication, use the built-in stored procedure sp_grantlogin to create a Windows security account on the MS-SQL Server. When using a Windows security account to access the DBMS, the user logs into the Windows network (versus the MS-SQL Server) by providing the network server a valid username/password pair. The Windows (NT, 2000, or XP) operating system validates the username/password pair the user entered and logs the user's account into the network. When the user then requests access to the DBMS, the MS-SQL Server reads the username on the user's network login and makes sure the username is a valid Windows security account on the DBMS. If the MS-SQL Server determines the username belongs to a valid Windows security account, the user is logged into the DBMS—without being challenged for the account's password.

To create a Windows security account, use the following syntax to call the sp_grantlogin stored procedure:

```
EXEC sp_grantlogin [@loginame=]'<domain\username>'
```

Note that you do include a password for Windows user (or group) accounts that you want to let access the DBMS. The MS-SQL Server has no need to know the password for these accounts, because the DBMS lets the Windows (NT, 2000, or XP) server handle account authentication. Thus, to let the Windows network account CLARISSA within the NVBIZNET2 domain login to the network using Windows security, you would execute the following command:

```
EXEC sp_grantlogin 'NVBizNet2\clarissa'
```

As mentioned previously within this tip, after you use sp_addlogin to create a new MS-SQL Server account or use sp_grantlogin to create a Windows security account, you must grant the user access to at least one database before the user can login to the DBMS. To grant an account access to a database, use the built-in stored procedure sp_grantdbaccess, which has the following syntax

```
sp_grantdbaccess [@loginame=]{<domain\username|username>}
                 [,[@name_in_db=]'<db username>'
```

where:

- **@loginame** is the username on the account to which you want to grant access to the current database. If the account is a Windows (NT, 2000, XP) account (which you used sp_grantlogin to give access to the MS-SQL Server), pass the <domain\username> to the stored procedure as @LOGIN. If the account is an MS-SQL Server account (which you created with sp_addlogin), only pass the <username> to sp_grantdbaccess.
- **@name_in_db** is the name you want to use when referring to the account within the database. For MS-SQL Server accounts, omit @NAME_IN_DB altogether. For Windows (NT,

2000, XP) accounts supply the <username> portion of the <domain/username> you passed to the stored procedure through the @LOGINAME parameter.

Note that sp_grantdbaccess grants the account you specify in @LOGINAME access to the current database. As such, be sure to execute a USE statement that takes you to the database to which you want to grant access before you call the sp_grantdbaccess stored procedure. For example, to grant username WALTER access to the SQLTips database, execute the following statement batch:

```
USE SQLTips
EXEC sp_grantdbaccess 'walter'
```

Because WALTER is an MS-SQL Server account (that is, an account for which the DBMS authenticates the login username and password) you omit the @NAME_IN_DB parameter. Similarly, to make it possible for the Windows security account with username CLARISSA to login to the MyTempDb database, execute the following statement batch:

```
USE MyTempDb
EXEC sp_grantdbaccess 'NVBizNet2\Clarissa', 'Clarissa'
```

As shown in this example, for Windows security accounts, you supply both the account's username (CLARISSA) and the domain in which the account exists (NVBIZNET2) on the Windows network. In addition, you should set the @NAME_IN_DB parameter to the username portion of the <domain name/username> you passed to the stored procedure through the @LOGINAME parameter. If you do not supply the database username, the stored procedure will use the value of @LOGIN for the database username, and you will not be able to use the SQL GRANT statement to grant privileges on database objects to the Windows security account user.

If you later decide you no longer want an account to have access to a particular database, call the built-in stored procedure sp_revokedbaccess. To remove database access from both MS-SQL Server and Windows security accounts, use sp_revokedbaccess which has the following syntax:

```
EXEC sp_revokedbaccess [@name_in_db=] <db username>
```

As was the case with sp_grantdbaccess, the sp_revokedbaccess stored procedure affects the rights the account has to access the current database. Therefore, be sure to execute a USE statement to make the database to which you no longer want the account to have access before you call the sp_revokedbaccess stored procedure. For example, to remove Clarissa's access to the MyTempDb database, execute the following statement batch:

```
USE MyTempDb
EXEC sp_revokedbaccess 'Clarissa'
```

If you no longer want an MS-SQL Server user account to have access to the database, first use sp_revokedbaccess to remove the accounts access from each database to which you previously granted the account access (by calling the stored procedure sp_grantdbaccess). Then, call the built-in stored procedure sp_droplogin (which uses the following syntax), to remove the user's account from the MS-SQL Server altogether:

```
EXEC sp_droplogin [@loginame=]<username>
```

Note that you can only use sp_droplogin to remove MS-SQL Server accounts (and not Windows security accounts).

If you want to remove a Windows security account's ability to access the DBMS, call the built-in stored procedure sp_revokelogin using the following syntax:

```
EXEC sp_revokelogin [@loginame=]<domain\username>
```

577 Using sp_makewebtask to Create a Task That Generates a Web Page

The MS-SQL Server built-in stored procedure sp_makewebtask makes it simple to place the results of an SQL query or set of queries within HTML tables on a Web page. To use sp_makewebtask, you must write the queries whose results sets you want displayed beforehand. As such, sp_makewebtask does not let your Web site visitors submit ad hoc queries to the MS-SQL Server. (You will learn how to let site visitors write their own queries on-the-fly within Tip 592 "Submitting an SQL Query through an HTML Form.") However, sp_makewebtask does let you create Web pages with self-updating reports on such things as sales statistics, inventory levels, personnel data, customer lists, vendor lists, and so on.

In short, if you find that you are executing the same SQL query repeatedly, you can use sp_makewebtask to create a Web task the MS-SQL Server will execute for you on demand or periodically. Rather than display query results onscreen, the tasks sp_makewebtask creates generate Web pages and insert query results within HTML tables on those pages. Moreover, the SQL data displayed on the Web pages need not be static.

Using sp_makewebtask, you can create dynamic Web content by specifying that the MS-SQL Server Agent execute the Web task's queries periodically or whenever users change data within the database that effects the information displayed on the page. Each time the MS-SQL Server Agent runs the Web task, the stored procedure the Web task executes re-generates the Web page with the most up-to-date information from the database.

To create the Web (page generation) task you want the MS-SQL Server to execute on demand, according to a preset schedule, or whenever users make changes to the report's underlying data, call the sp_makewebtask stored procedure, which has the following syntax

```
sp_makewebtask
  [@outputfile=]'<Web page document pathname>',
  [@query=]<one or more SELECT statements>
  [,[@fixedfont=]{0|1}]
```

```
[,[@bold=]{0|1}]
[,[@italic=]{0|1}]
[,[@colheaders=]{0|1}]
[,[@lastupdated=]{0|1}]
[,[@HTMLheader=]{1|2|3|4|5|6}]
[,[@username=]<username>]
[,[@dbname=]<database name>]
[,[@templatefile=]'<pathname of HTML template>']
[,[@webpagetitle=]'<Web page title text>']
[,[@resultstitle=]'<Title text above HTML table(s)>]
[,{[@URL=]'<Web page URL>',[@reftext=]'<anchor text>']}|
  {[@table_urls=]{0|1},
     [@url_query=]'<2-column table of URL queries>']}]
[,[whentype@=]{1|2|3|4|5|6|7|8|9|10}]
[,[@targetdate=]<date in YYYMMDD format>]
[,[@targettime=]<time in HHMMSS format>]
[,[@dayflags=]<day(s) of week flag>]
[,[@numunits=]<number of @UNITTYPE units in each period>]
[,[@unittype=]{1|2|3|4}]
[,[@procname=]<Web task name>]
[,[@maketask=]{0|1|2}]
[,[@rowcnt=]<maximum number of rows in results set>]
[,[@tabborder=]{0|1}]
[,[@singlerow=]{0|1}]
[,[@blobfmt=]<blob data disposition>]
[,[@nrowsperpage=]<results set rows per Web page>]
[,[@datachg=]{TABLE=<table name>[COLUMN=<column name>]
    [,...TABLE=<last table name>
      [COLUMN=<last column name>]}]
```

where:

- **@outputfile** specifies the full pathname of the HTML document that the stored procedure is to create. For example, to create the Web page INVENTORY_LIST.HTM within the folder \WEBS\SQLTIPS on the D: drive, you would use @outputfile='D:\WEBS\SQLTIPS\INVENTORY_LIST.HTM'.
- **@query** specifies the query or set of queries that the MS-SQL Server is to execute. The stored procedure sp_makewebtask displays the query results set from each query within an HTML table on the Web page specified by @OUTPUTFILE.
- **@fixedfont** is 1 if the query results are to be displayed in a fixed font or 0 if they are to be displayed in a proportional font. Default: 1.
- **@bold** is 1 if the query results are to be displayed in boldface or 0 if they are to be displayed with a regular (non-boldface) character weight. Default: 0.
- **@italic** is 1 if the query results are to be displayed in italic or 0 if they are to be displayed as non-italic. Default: 0.

- **@colheaders** is 1 if the column names from the query results set are to be used as headings within the HTML table or 0 to display the query results without the column names. Default: 1.
- **@lastupdated** is 1 if the stored procedure is to insert a "Last updated: <date and time>" one line before the first HTML table with query results, or 0 to suppress the date last generated information. Default: 1.
- **@HTMLheader** specifies which of the six HTML heading levels to use when formatting the text in @RESULTSTITLE. For example, setting @HTMLHEADER to 1, and the stored procedure will format the title above the query results tables as "<h1>Title</h1>," 2 to format it as "<h2>Title</h2>," and so on (up to 6).
- **@username** is the username under which to execute the query (or queries) assigned to @QUERY. The default is to use the current username (that is, the username of the person creating the Web task). Only the system administrator (sa) or database owner (dbo) are allowed specify a username other than the current username.
- **@dbname** specifies the name of the database in which the stored procedure's query (or queries) is to be executed. The default is to use the current database.
- **@templatefile** is the pathname of the file to be used as the template for the Web page the stored procedure generates. The HTML template contains HTML tags and text that are to appear on the Web page in addition to the HTML table with the query results. The stored procedure will replace each <%insert_data_here%> marker within the Web page template file with data returned by an SQL query.
- **@webpagetitle** is the text that the stored procedure is to place between start and end title tags (<title></title>) within the Web page header section. The default title is SQL Server Web Assistant.
- **@resultstitle** is the text that the stored procedure is to display as a title before the first (and perhaps only) HTML table of query results inserted on the Web page.
- **@URL** is the Web address (that is, the uniform resource locator or URL) to another HTML document. The stored procedure sets the hyperlink's *href* attribute to the URL passed as @URL.
- **@reftext** is the hyperlink anchor text to be displayed on the line following the last HTML table of query results on the Web page. The stored procedure creates the hyperlink to another Web page by substituting the text passed as @URL and @REFTEXT for @URL and @REFTEXT in a the following hyperlink syntax: <a href='@URL'>@REFTEXT</a>
- **@table_urls** is 1 if the hyperlinks the stored procedure is to insert on the Web page are to be generated by the query within the @URL_QUERY parameter. The default, 0 indicates there is no query to generate hyperlinks. If @TABLE_URLS is 1, @URL_QUERY must have a SELECT statement that returns a two-column results table.

- **@url_query** is a SELECT statement that returns a two-column results table of hyperlink Web addresses (URLs) and anchor text. The stored procedure displays the hyperlinks returned by executing the query (within @URL_QUERY) after the last HTML table of SQL query results that the stored procedures inserts on the Web page. The first column of each row within the URL results table contains the URL of a Web page and the second column contains the hyperlink's anchor text.
- **@whentype** specifies when the MS-SQL Server Agent is to run the Web task that creates the Web page with query results. The default of 1 instructs the MS-SQL Server is to run the task immediately and delete the task (and stored procedure that creates the Web page) immediately after execution. The possible values for the @WHENTYPE parameter are:

  1. **Create the Web page now.** The stored procedure creates a Web task that the MS-SQL Server executes and then deletes immediately after execution.
  2. **Create the Web page later.** The stored procedure creates a Web task that the MS-SQL Server Agent runs at the date and time specified by @TARGETDATE and @TARGETTIME parameters. After executing the Web task (once), the MS-SQL Server deletes the Web task. (If @TARGETTIME is omitted the Web task executes at 12:00 a.m.)
  3. **Create the Web page every *n* day(s) of the week.** The stored procedure creates a Web task that the MS-SQL Server Agent runs on the day(s) of the week specified by the @DAYFLAGS parameter. MS-SQL Server Agent starts the Web task beginning on the date specified by @TARGETDATE at @TARGETTIME and then executes the task again every *n* day(s) of the week. (If @TARGETTIME is omitted, the Web task starts at 12:00 a.m. each *n* day.)
  4. **Create the Web page every *n* minutes, hours, days, or weeks.** The stored procedure creates a Web task that the MS-SQL Server Agent executes every *n* period. The period (minutes, hours, days, or weeks) is specified by the @UNITTYPE parameter. MS-SQL Server Agent starts the Web task beginning on the date specified by @TARGETDATE at @TARGETTIME and executes the task again every *n* period. (If @TARGETTIME is omitted the Web task executes at 12:00 a.m.)
  5. **Create the Web page upon request.** The stored procedure creates a Web task that the MS-SQL Server will execute only when the user calls the stored procedure using sp_runwebtask.
  6. **Create the Web page now and later.** The stored procedure creates a Web task that the MS-SQL Server executes now and which the MS-SQL Server Agent will run one additional time when @WHENTYPE is 2.
  7. **Create the Web page now and every *n* day(s) of the week.** The stored procedure creates a Web task that the MS-SQL Server executes now. Then, the MS-SQL Server Agent will run the Web task again periodically thereafter as when @WHENTYPE is 3, except @TARGETDATE is not required.
  8. **Create the Web page now and then periodically thereafter.** The stored procedure creates a Web task that the MS-SQL Server will execute now and that the MS-SQL Server

Agent will then run periodically as when @WHENTYPE is "4," except @TARGETDATE is not required.

9. **Create the Web page now and upon request.** The stored procedure creates a Web task that the MS-SQL Server executes now and again only by user request as when @WHENTYPE is 5.

10. **Create the Web page now and when data changes.** The stored procedure creates a Web task that the MS-SQL Server executes now and again whenever a user changes a value within one of the columns listed within the @DATACHG parameter.

- **@targetdate** specifies the date that the MS-SQL Server Agent is to run the Web task. @TARGETDATE is required when @WHENTYPE is 2 (later), 3 (days of week), 4 (periodic), or 6 (now and later). The format for @TARGETDATE is YYYYMMDD.
- **@targettime** specifies the time at which the MS-SQL Server Agent is to run the Web task on the date in @TARGETDATE. The format for @TARGETTIME is HHMMSS.
- **@dayflags** specifies which days of the week the MS-SQL Server Agent is to execute the Web task. If the Web task is to be executed multiple days each week, add the date flags for the execution days together. For example, to have the MS-SQL Server Agent run a Web tasks on Monday, Wednesday, and Friday, set @DAYFLAGS to 42—2 (Monday) + 8 (Wednesday) + 32 (Friday).
  - 1 = Sunday
  - 2 = Monday
  - 4 = Tuesday
  - 8 = Wednesday
  - 16 = Thursday
  - 32 = Friday
  - 64 = Saturday

  If the Web task is to be executed multiple days each week, add the date flags for the execution days together. For example, to have the MS-SQL Server Agent run a Web tasks on Monday, Wednesday, and Friday, set @DAYFLAGS to 42—2 (Monday) + 8 (Wednesday) + 32 (Friday).
- **@numunits** specifies the number of minutes, hours, days, or weeks between successive executions of a periodic Web task—that is, for Web tasks with @WHENTYPE 4 (periodic) or 8 (now and periodically thereafter). The @UNITTYPE parameter specifies the period between successive executions.
- **@unittype** specifies the time unit between executions of the Web task when @WHENTYPE is 4 (periodic) or 8 (now and periodically thereafter)—1 = hours, 2 = days, 3 = weeks, and 4 = minutes.

- **@procname** is the name of the Web task. If omitted, the system will generate the name as WEB_<YYMMDDHHMMSS><SPID>.
- **@maketask** specifies whether to schedule a Web task along with creating the stored procedure that generates the Web page.
  - 0 = generate an unencrypted stored procedure but do not create the Web task.
  - 1 = generate an encrypted stored procedure and the Web task.
  - 2 (default) = generate an unencrypted stored procedure and the Web task that executes it.
- **@rowcnt** specifies the maximum number of rows from the results set to display within the HTML table on the Web page. The default is "0," which means to display all the rows in the results set.
- **@tabborder** is 1 (the default) if the there is to be a border around the HTML query results table, or 0 for an HTML table without borders.
- **@singlerow** specifies whether the query results are to be displayed all on one page or on multiple pages, with one row per page. The default, 0 specifies all rows from the results set will appear within a single HTML table. 1 specifies that the Web task is to create a new Web page for each row of query results. Successive HTML pages are generated with a number appended onto the filename specified by the @OUTPUTFILE parameter. For example, if @OUTPUTFILE is WEB_PAGE.HTML and there are three rows within the results set, the Web task will create the Web pages: WEB_PAGE1.HTML, WEB_PAGE2.HTML, and WEB_PAGE3.HTML.
- **@blobfmt** specifies whether a data "blob" (that is, data within a column of data type IMAGE, NTEXT, or TEXT) is to be displayed within the HTML table on the Web page or if these columns should be written to an external file and linked to the current Web page by a URL. See Tip 580 "Using the MS-SQL Server Stored Procedure sp_makewebtask to Display IMAGE and TEXT Data on Linked Web Pages," for details on handling IMAGE, NTEXT, and TEXT data.
- **@nrowsperpage** specifies the number of query results set rows to display on each Web page. Successive pages are linked with NEXT and PREVIOUS hyperlinks.
- **@datachg** is the list of table (and optionally) column names that trigger execution of the Web task after changes are made. @DATACHG is required when @WHENTYPE is 10. Specifying the @DATACHG parameter creates three triggers (UPDATE, INSERT, and DELETE) on each table specified by the @DATACHG parameter. The MS-SQL Server will execute the stored procedure (which generates the Web page) when triggered by an UPDATE, INSERT, or DELETE executed on the table named by @DATACHG. If a trigger already exists on a table, sp_createwebtask adds its sp_runwebtask call to the end of the existing trigger—provided the existing trigger was not created WITH ENCRYPTION. (If the existing trigger is encrypted, sp_makewebtask will fail.)

Suppose, for example, that you want the MS-SQL Server to create a Web page (such as that shown in Figure 577.1) daily at 12:00 a.m.

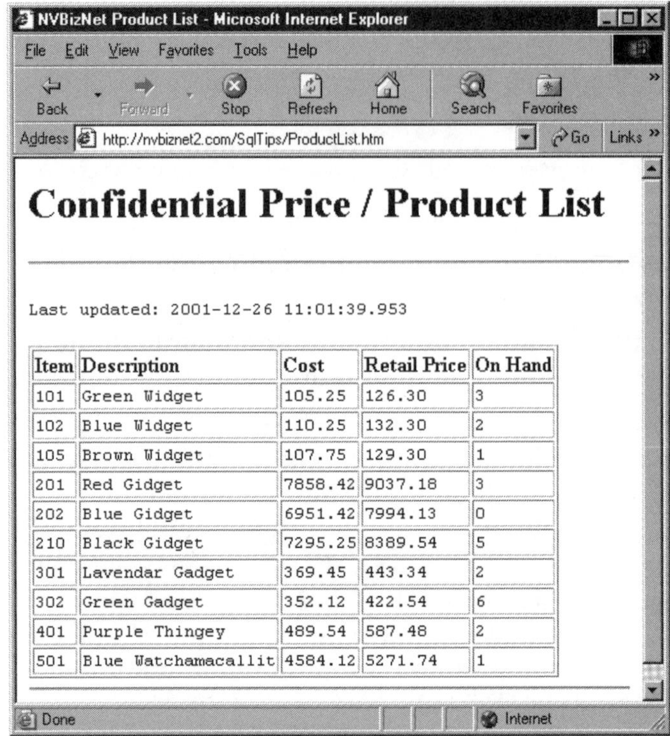

Figure 577.1 A generic Web page generated by a stored procedure created by sp_makewebtask

If the tables required for the report are within the SQLTips database, execute the following statement batch:

```
USE SQLTips

EXEC sp_makewebtask
  @outputfile='D:\InetPub\WWWRoot\SqlTips\ProductList.htm',
  @query='SELECT p.Item_Number AS ''Item'', Description,
                 Cost, Sales_Price AS ''Retail Price'',
                (SELECT COUNT(*) FROM inventory AS i
                 WHERE i.item_number = p.item_number) AS
                  ''On Hand''
          FROM products AS p
          ORDER BY p.item_number',
  @HTMLHeader=1,
  @webpagetitle='NVBizNet Product List',
  @resultstitle='Confidential Price / Product List',
  @whentype=8,
  @numunits=1,
  @unittype=2,
  @procname=web_CreateProductsPage
```

Note that calling the sp_makewebtask stored procedure creates not only a stored procedure (web_CreateProductsPage, in this example) that generates the Web page (shown previously in Figure 577), but also the Web task that executes the stored procedure according to the schedule prescribed through the @WHENTYPE parameter.

578 Creating a Web Page Template for MS-SQL Server Query Results

In the preceding tip ("Using sp_makewebtask to Create a Task That Generates a Web Page"), you learned how to create a stored procedure that displays the results set from an SQL query within an HTML table on a Web page. Figure 577 showed a Web page such a stored procedure might generate. Although the Web page displays query results within an HTML table "as advertised," you most likely want more control over the content on and layout of the Web page. Fortunately, you can create a Web page template and have the stored procedure insert the HTML table with the SQL query results among other elements as desired.

You can give the file in which you create the Web page template any name you like. You must however, store the template within a folder accessible to the MS-SQL Server when the DBMS executes the stored procedure to create the Web page based on the template. The Web page template is an ordinary HTML (or XHTML) document with an <%insert_data_here%> marker inserted wherever you want the HTML table(s) of query results to appear on the Web page.

Suppose, for example, that you want to create a Web page similar to that shown previously in Figure 577. However, instead of black text on a white background, you want a Web page with blue text on a light yellow background. In addition, you want the company logo centered above the list of products. To control elements that appear on the Web page that the MS-SQL Server generates, create a template file such as the following:

```
<html>
<head>
  <title>NVBizNet - Product List</title>
  <style type="text/css">
    h1 {color:blue; font-size:40px; font-family:verdana}
    body {color:blue; background:lightyellow;
           font-family:helvetica}
  </style>
</head>
<body>
  <center>
    <h1>Confidential Price / Product list</h1>
  </center>
```

```
  <hr>
  <center><img src='images/CompanyLogo.gif'></center>
  <hr>
  <center>
    <%insert_data_here%>
  </center>
  <hr>
</body>
</html>
```

After you save the template to a file named PRODLIST.TF within the D:\INETPUB\WWWROOT\SQLTIPS\TEMPLATES\ folder, for example, add a @TEMPLATEFILE parameter to the sp_makewebtask stored procedure call as follows:

```
EXEC sp_makewebtask
  @outputfile='D:\InetPub\WWWRoot\SqlTips\ProductList.htm',
  @query='SELECT p.Item_Number AS ''Item'', Description,
                 Cost, Sales_Price AS ''Retail Price'',
                (SELECT COUNT(*) FROM inventory AS i
                 WHERE i.item_number = p.item_number) AS
                   ''On Hand''
          FROM products p
          ORDER BY p.item_number',
  @templatefile=
   'D:\InetPub\WWWRoot\SQLTips\Templates\ProdList.TF',
  @whentype=8,
  @numunits=1,
  @unittype=2,
  @procname=web_CreateProductsPage
```

The .TF extension on the template file (PRODLIST.TF) is arbitrary, and stands for "Template File." Note that when you specify a Web page template you can omit from the sp_makewebtask stored procedure, call all Web page element parameters (such as @LASTUPDATED, @HTMLHEADER, @WEBPAGETITLE, and @RESULTSTITLE). The MS-SQL Server ignores them when you use a template to specify the format of and/or other content on the Web page.

By the way, you are not limited to displaying only a single results set per page. If you want to display the results sets from multiple queries within the Web page template, simply place one <%insert_data_here%> marker for each results set. For example, if you want to display the data within the CUSTOMERS table and the data within the EMPLOYEES table as two HTML tables on the same Web page, you might use a template such as the following:

```
<html>
<head>
  <title>NVBizNet - Customers & Employees</title>
  <style type="text/css">
    body {background:lightyellow; font-family:helvetica}
  </style>
</head>
```

```
<body>
  <center><h1>Confidential Lists</h1></center>
  <hr>
  <center><h2>Customer List</h2></center>
  <center><%insert_data_here%></center>
  <hr>
  <center><h2>Employee List</h2></center>
  <center><%insert_data_here%></center>
  <hr>
</body>
</html>
```

The specific type of information and other miscellaneous Web page elements and formatting instructions shown within this Tip are not important—you can use any legal HTML or XHTML elements and text content within your templates. Note however, that you must insert an <%insert_data_here%> marker wherever you want the MS-SQL Server to display the results table from an SQL query on the Web page. Within the next tip, "Formatting the Query Results Table on a Web Page Created by an MS-SQL Server Stored Procedure," you will learn that between <%begindetail%> and <%enddetail%> markers, you can insert an <%insert_data_here%> marker for each column within the query results table.

After you create a template with multiple <%insert_data_here%> markers and save it to a disk file with a name such as CUSTS_N_EMPS.TF, for example, you can assign multiple SELECT statements to the sp_createwebtask's @QUERY parameter. In this example, there are two <%insert_data_here%> markers, so you would change the @QUERY parameter to pass two queries as shown here:

```
EXEC sp_makewebtask
  @outputfile='D:\InetPub\WWWRoot\SqlTips\Custs_Emps.htm',
  @query='SELECT * FROM customers
          SELECT * FROM employeesp'
  @templatefile=
   'D:\InetPub\WWWRoot\SQLTips\Templates\Custs_N_Emps.TF',
  @whentype=8,
  @numunits=1,
  @unittype=2,
  @procname=web_CreateEmpsAndCustsPage
```

Although shown on two lines here for formatting purposes, the second SELECT statement could have begun on the same line on which the first ended. All that is required is that you leave at least one space between the last character of one query and the keyword SELECT that starts the next.

579 Formatting the Query Results Table on a Web Page Created by an MS-SQL Server Stored Procedure

In Tip 577, "Using sp_makewebtask to Create a Task That Generates a Web Page," you learned how to create a stored procedure that, in turn, generates a Web page with SQL Query results. Then, in Tip 578 "Creating a Web Page Template for MS-SQL Server Query Results," you learned how to insert one or several HTML tables with SQL query results onto a Web page along with other content.

In addition to inserting text and images on the page along with one or more query results tables, you learned that the Web page template lets you format text and layout the page exactly as you want. In fact, you can use any legal HTML or XHTML document as a Web page template. Simply insert <%insert_data_here%> markers wherever you want SQL query results to appear, and save the updated document to a new filename. Then, set the @TEMPLATEFILE parameter (within the sp_createwebtask stored procedure call) to the full pathname of the template file. The MS-SQL Server will then generate a new Web page with all the elements and appearance of the original page plus one or more HTML tables with the data returned from SQL queries.

Because sp_makewebtask provides very few typeface and text formatting options, you might find it necessary to write additional formatting instructions for the query results text. Fortunately, you can use <%begindetail%> and <%enddetail%> markers to tell the MS-SQL Server that it is simply to insert column data into an HTML table formatted per your instructions within the Web page template.

To format the query results on the Web page, you must write the tags that define the HTML table within the Web page template (versus letting the MS-SQL Server create the HTML tags for you). For example, to format the table with the Product/Price List you saw in Tip 578 "Creating a Web Page Template for MS-SQL Server Query Results," you might write the Web page template as follows:

```
<!DOCTYPE html PUBLIC
 "-//W3C//DTD XHTML 1.0 Transitional//EN"
 "http://www.w3.org/TR/xhtml1/DTD/xhtml1-transitional.dtd">
<html xmlns="http://www.w3.org/1999/xhtml">
<head>
  <title>NVBizNet - Product List</title>

  <style type="text/css">
     th {text-align:center; background:white}
     td {border-style:solid; border-width:1px 1px;
         border-color:black; padding-left:10px;
         padding-right:10px}
     thead {color:black; background:lightgreen;
            font-weight:bold; text-align:center}
```

```
     tfoot {color:white; background:blue; font-weight:bold;
            text-align:center}
     tbody {text-align:right; background:lightblue}

    h1 {color:blue; font-size:40px; font-family:verdana}
    body {color:blue; background:lightyellow;
          font-family:helvetica}
  </style>
</head>
<body>
  <center><h1>Confidential Price/Product List</h1></center>
  <hr />
  <center><img src='images/CompanyLogo.gif'></center>
  <hr />
  <center>
  <table cellspacing="0">
    <thead>
      <tr>
        <td colspan="5">Prices & Products</td>
      </tr>
    </thead>

    <tfoot>
      <tr>
        <td colspan="5">
           &copy; NVBizNet.com (702)-361-0141</td>
      </tr>
    </tfoot>

    <tbody>
      <tr>
        <th>Item</th><th>Description</th><th>Cost</th>
        <th>Retail Price</th><th>On Hand</th>
      </tr>

<%begindetail%>
      <tr>
        <td><%insert_data_here%></td>
        <td><%insert_data_here%></td>
        <td><%insert_data_here%></td>
        <td><%insert_data_here%></td>
        <td><%insert_data_here%></td>
      </tr>
<%enddetail%>

    </tbody>
  </table>
  </center>
</body>
</html>
```

The th and td rules within the style sheet (at the beginning of this example) style the table heading (<th>) and table data (<td>) cells within the table. In addition thead, tbody, and tfoot rules set the appearance of the three sections of an HTML table—the header (<thead>), body (<tbody>), and footer (<tfoot>). The important things to notice are:

- The Web page template includes the table definition between start and end table tags (<table></table>).
- You define text of the table heading cells between the start and end table heading tags (<th></th>) within the Web page template versus relying on the MS-SQL Server to add them to the results table.
- You place <%begindetail%> and <%enddetail%> tags around one row of table data tags within the table definition and insert one <%insert_date_here%> marker within each set of start and end table data tags (<td></td>). In this case, the each <%insert_data_here%> marker tells the MS-SQL Server to insert the data from one column within a row in the query results set.

The sp_createwebtask stored procedure call remains largely unchanged as

```
EXEC sp_makewebtask
  @outputfile='D:\InetPub\WWWRoot\SqlTips\ProductList.htm',
  @query='SELECT p.Item_Number, Description, Cost,
                 Sales_Price, (SELECT COUNT(*)
                               FROM inventory AS i
                               WHERE i.item_number =
                                     p.item_number)
          FROM products p
          ORDER BY p.item_number',
  @templatefile=
'D:\InetPub\WWWRoot\SQLTips\Templates\FmtProdList.TF',
  @whentype=8,
  @numunits=1,
  @unittype=2,
  @procname=web_CreateProductsPage
```

Since the headings for the HTML table are written into the Web page template, the SELECT clause within the stored procedure that creates the Web page no longer needs to provide user-friendly headings.

The most important thing to understand is that you must define one row within the HTML table the Web page, similar to that shown here:

```
<%begindetail%>
  <tr>
    <td><%insert_data_here%></td>
    <td><%insert_data_here%></td>
    <td><%insert_data_here%></td>
    <td><%insert_data_here%></td>
    <td><%insert_data_here%></td>
  </tr>
<%enddetail%>
```

The MS-SQL Server replaces the <%insert_data_here%> markers with the column data from the current row within the results set, and then uses the table definition again for next row, and the next, and so one. In this example, the SQL query's SELECT clause has five columns, and as a result, the table definition too must have five sets of start and end table data tags (<td></td>) to create a row with five data cells. If the SELECT clause had ten columns, the table data row defined within the HTML table in the Web page template would need ten cells (that is, ten sets of start and end table data tags [<td></td>]).

580 Using sp_makewebtask to Display IMAGE and TEXT Data on Linked Web Pages

The MS-SQL Server lets you store character strings longer than 8,000 characters within columns of data type TEXT and graphics image files within columns of data type IMAGE. (A single TEXT and IMAGE column can hold up to 2 gigabytes of data.) Although you could use what you learned in Tips 577–579 to execute a query and have the MS-SQL Server display the contents of a TEXT column within the cells of an HTML table, you typically don't want to do that. The amount of data within the column used to display the TEXT data will dwarf the remaining data items within the HTML table and thereby make the table unusable as a tabular display of related information.

When you store a graphics image within an SQL table, the DBMS stores the image as a binary string (that is, as a string of 1's and 0's). MS-SQL Server leaves it up to the program retrieving the data from an IMAGE column to interpret the string of 1's and 0's and reconstitute it into the graphics image the binary string represents. As such, you don't want to display the contents of an IMAGE column within a cell in an HTML table either. The DBMS would place the IMAGE data into the table cell as a binary string and not the graphics image you want to see.

The built-in stored procedure sp_makewebtask lets you use the @BLOBFMT parameter to specify what the DBMS is to do with the data within TEXT and IMAGE columns returned as part of a query's results set. You can either have the DBMS display TEXT and IMAGE data within the HTML table's cells (which, as discussed, is undesirable), or you can have the DBMS write the data to external files and place a hyperlink to those files within the HTML table. Placing a hyperlink into the HTML table of query results is a good solution, because it lets you review the query results in tabular form, and if you want to read a large (that is, a long) text item or see a graphics image, you need only click its hyperlink within the HTML table.

To write a TEXT or IMAGE column to an external file, use the sp_makewebtask stored procedure's @BLOBFMT parameter with the following syntax

```
@BLOBFMT='%<TEXT/IMAGE column number>%
          file=<output filename>
          [tplt=<template filename>]
          URL=<Web address of output file>

         [...%<last TEXT/IMAGE column number>%
          file=<last output filename>
          [tplt=<last template filename>]
          URL=<Web address of last output file>]'
```

Note that you can work with multiple TEXT and/or IMAGE data columns. Just repeat the "%<column #>%[<template file>]<Web address>" pattern within the @BLOBFMT parameter once for each TEXT and IMAGE column you want to write to an external file. (Each external file is accessible by a hyperlink within the HTML table of SQL query results.)

Suppose, for example, that the sp_makewebtask @QUERY parameter has the following SELECT statement, which returns TEXT data in column #1 and IMAGE data in column 6:

```
SELECT pr_info AS 'Publisher Name', pub_name, city, state,
       country, logo, 'Company Logo'
FROM  pub_info AS pub_info, publishers
where pub_info.pub_id = publishers.pub_id
```

Given the preceding query, the @BLOBFMT parameter for this example would be set as follows:

```
@blobfmt=
  '%1% file=D:\InetPub\WWWRoot\SqlTips\Temp\PR_Text.htm
       URL=http://NVBizNet2.com/SQLTips/Temp/PR_Text.htm
   %6% file=D:\InetPub\WWWRoot\SqlTips\images\publogo.gif
       URL=http://NVBizNet2.com/SQLTips/images/publogo.GIF'
```

Thus, the full text of the sp_createwebtask stored procedure call would be something like the following to produce the Web page shown in Figure 580.1:

```
USE pubs
EXEC sp_makewebtask
  @outputfile='D:\InetPub\WWWRoot\SqlTips\Publishers.htm',
  @query='SELECT pr_info AS ''Publisher Name'', pub_name,
                 city, state, country, logo,
                 ''Company Logo''
          FROM  pub_info AS pub_info, publishers
          where pub_info.pub_id = publishers.pub_id',
  @blobfmt='%1%
file=D:\InetPub\WWWRoot\SqlTips\Temp\PR_Text.htm
URL=http://NVBizNet2.com/SQLTips/Temp/PR_Text.htm
            %6%
file=D:\InetPub\WWWRoot\SqlTips\images\publogo.gif
URL=http://NVBizNet2.com/SQLTips/images/publogo.GIF',
```

```
@whentype=9,
@procname=web_CreatePublishersPage
```

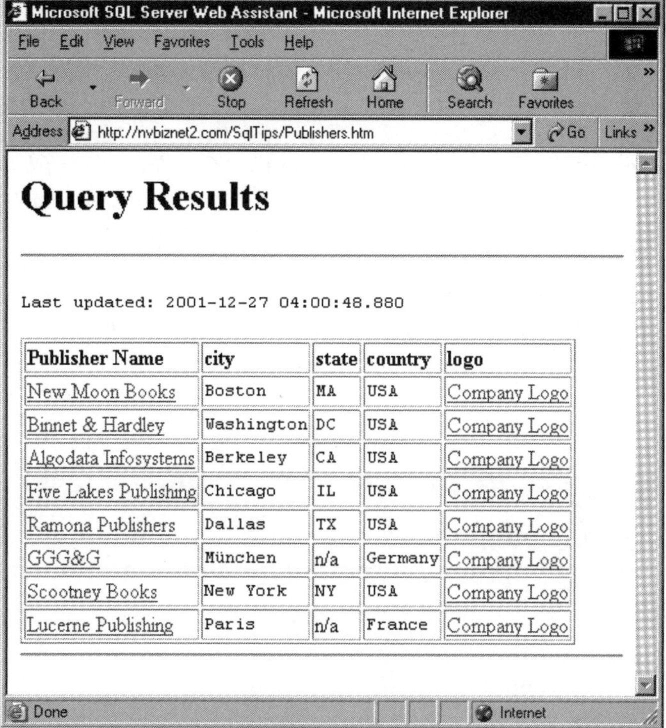

Figure 580.1 A generic Web page with hyperlinks to TEXT and IMAGE data generated by the stored procedure web_CreatePublisherPage

The stored procedure uses the contents of the column that follows an IMAGE or TEXT column within the query results as the anchor text for the hyperlinks that point to the external files into which the stored procedures writes the TEXT and IMAGE data. In this example, the values returned in column 2 (PUB_NAME) serve as the anchor text strings for the hyperlinks that point to external files that hold the TEXT data returned in column 1 (PR_INFO). Similarly, the values returned in column 7 (the string literal "Company Logo") serve as the anchor text strings for the hyperlinks that point to external files that hold the IMAGE data returned in column 6 (LOGO).

Thus, as shown previously in Figure 580.1, the stored procedure does not display TEXT and IMAGE content within the columns of the HTML table. Instead, the stored procedure writes the BLOB content to disk files and stores a hyperlink to the content within the HTML table. Notice then in this example where the query returns seven columns, only five are displayed within the HTML table, because two (the first and the sixth) columns are written to disk files.

Although this example uses no template files, you can specify an HTML template file for the main Web page (that is, the Web page with the HTML table of query results) and another for the Web pages in which the stored procedure writes the TEXT column's data. (You don't use template files for IMAGE columns because you want the stored procedure to write the binary string within the table's IMAGE column exactly as-is to the graphics file on disk.)

Note: *For TEXT data, use a filename with an extension that a Web browser will recognize as a Web page (that is, .htm, .html, .asp, .php, and so on). In order for the .php and .asp extension to work, the Web server must have the Active Server Pages for .Asp or PHP script engine for .php installed. For IMAGE data use a filename with the extension that corresponds to the format used to encode the image (typically .GIF, .JPG, .TIF, and so on). By using a Web page extension for TEXT data and a graphics file extension for IMAGE data, you instruct the Web browser to display the file of TEXT data as a Web page (with a long string of many characters) and to interpreted the binary string within the IMAGE file as a graphics image.*

---

581 Using Built-In Stored Procedures to Launch or Delete Web Tasks

The MS-SQL Server has three built-in stored procedures you can use to manage Web tasks: sp_createwebtask, sp_runwebtask, and sp_dropwebtask. While sp_createwebtask lets you create new Web tasks, sp_runwebtask lets you execute existing tasks—whether scheduled for execution or not. Finally, when you no longer want to execute a particular Web task, you can use the built-in stored procedure sp_dropwebtask to remove the web task from the DBMS.

You learned how to use sp_createwebtask in Tips 577–580. In short, sp_createwebtask lets you create a special type of stored procedure that executes one or more queries whose results set the DBMS writes to an HTML table on a Web page. One thing shown by example but not pointed out within the four previous tips is that you should always use the sp_createwebtask's @PROCNAME parameter to name each Web task you create. True, you can omit the parameter and let the system generate a name for you. However, the system-generated name of the form web_<YYMMDDHHMMSS><SPID> will not be easy to remember. In addition, a system-generated name like web_20011227042606552682 doesn't tell you anything about what the stored procedure associated with the Web task does. As such, when it comes time to start a Web task manually or to edit or drop one, you will have to search your written documentation or edit Web task's stored procedure to figure out which one you want to run, change, or delete. By using a descriptive name (such as web_CreateProductList), you can often zero-in on the Web task with which you want to work by simply reviewing the list of Web tasks defined within the database.

When you create a Web task, you specify when and how often you want the MS-SQL Server Agent to execute the task. However, you may sometimes want to start the task manually between scheduled executions. Suppose, for example, that you have a scheduled task that re-creates a Web page with the company's inventory each Sunday at 12:00 a.m. If receive a large shipment of products arrive on Wednesday, you will want to update the inventory on the Web page immediately versus waiting until the end of the week.

The built-in stored procedure sp_runwebtask that lets you start a Web task immediately (even one scheduled for execution in the future) has the following syntax:

```
sp_runwebtask [[@procname=]'<Web task process name>']
              [,[@outputfile=]'<pathname of output file>']
```

where:

- **@procname** is the name of the Web task you want to execute.
- **@outputfile** is the name of the Web page (output file) that the Web task creates.

When starting a Web task, you must be in the same database in which the particular Web task you want to run was created. To start the task, call sp_runwebtask and supply either the tasks's name or the full pathname of the Web page the task creates. Suppose, for example, that you have a Web task named web_CreatePublishersPage that creates the Web page PUBLISHERS.HTM within the D:\INETPUB\WWWROOT\SQLTIPS\ folder. You can call sp_runwebtask to run the Web task immediately by executing either of the following statements:

```
EXEC sp_runwebtask @procname='web_CreatePublishersPage'

EXEC sp_runwebtask @outputfile=
      'D:\InetPub\WWWRoot\SqlTips\Publishers.htm'
```

If you want to delete a Web task, call sp_dropwebtask to delete both the Web task and its related stored procedure from the DBMS. To call sp_dropwebtask, you use the same syntax you use to call sp_runwebtask:

```
sp_dropwebtask [[@procname=]'<Web task process name>']
               [,[@outputfile=]'<pathname of output file>']
```

As with sp_runwebtask, you can supply either the Web task's name or the full pathname of its output file when calling the built-in stored procedure sp_dropwebtask. As such, to delete a Web task named "web_CreatePublishersPage" that creates the Web page PUBLISHERS.HTM within the D:\INETPUB\WWWROOT\SQLTIPS\ folder, you first execute a USE statement to move to the DBMS in which you created the Web task and then execute either one of the following statements to delete the Web task and its stored procedure:

```
EXEC sp_dropwebtask @procname='web_CreatePublishersPage'

EXEC sp_dropwebtask @outputfile=
      'D:\InetPub\WWWRoot\SqlTips\Publishers.htm'
```

582 Using the MS-SQL Server Web Assistant Wizard to Create a Web Task That Executes a Stored Procedure

In Tip 577 "Using sp_makewebtask to Create a Task That Generates a Web Page," you learned how to use the built-in stored procedure sp_makewebtask to create a Web task that displays SQL database data on a Web page. While sp_makewebtask is easy to use, the number of parameters available for formatting output data and scheduling the task is rather daunting at first. Until you get used to all the options available, you might consider using MS-SQL Server's Web Assistant Wizard to create Web tasks.

As you will learn in this tip, the Web Assistant Wizard guides you through the process of creating a Web task. By grouping related options within various dialog boxes, the Wizard makes the list of options easier to deal with. In addition, the Web Assistant Wizard helps you to formulate queries you want the Web task to execute by letting you select the table columns (from a graphical display) whose values you want to see on the Web page. From the entries and selections you make within a dialog box (displayed after you select the SQL Table columns you want displayed), the Wizard generates the query that selects the rows of data to include in the HTML table that the Web task inserts in the Web page it creates.

The Web Assistant Wizard is located within the MS-SQL Server Enterprise Manager. To start the Wizard and create a Web task that executes a stored procedure, perform the following steps:

1. Click your mouse on the Start button. Windows will display the Start menu.
2. Move your mouse pointer to Programs on the Start menu, select the Microsoft SQL Server group, and then click your mouse on Enterprise Manager. Windows will start the SQL Server Enterprise Manager.
3. Click your mouse on the plus (+) to the left of the Microsoft SQL Servers icon to display the SQL Server Group. Then, click your mouse on the plus (+) to the left of the SQL Server Group icon to display the list of MS-SQL Servers available on your network.
4. To display the list of resources on the MS-SQL Server with the database in which you want to create a Web task, click on the plus (+) to the left of the MS-SQL Server's name. For example, if you want to work with the MS-SQL Server NVBizNet2, click on the plus (+) to the left of NVBizNet2. Enterprise Manager will display a list of folders that represent the resources available on the MS-SQL Server NVBizNet2 (for the current project).
5. Click your mouse on the Databases folder. Then, select the Tools menu, Wizards option. The Enterprise Manager will display the Select Wizard dialog box.

6. Click your mouse on the plus (+) to the left of Management to display the list of Management Wizards. Next, click your mouse on the Web Assistant Wizard within the list of Management Wizards and then on the OK button at the bottom of the dialog box. The Web Assistant Wizard will display its Welcome screen.

7. Click the Next button at the bottom of the Welcome screen. The Web Assistant Wizard will display the Select Database dialog box.

8. Click the drop-down list button to the right of the Database name field and select the database in which you want to create the Web task. For the current project, select SQLTips from the selection list, and then click the Next button. The Web Assistant Wizard will display a Start a New Web Assistant Job dialog box similar to that shown in Figure 582.1.

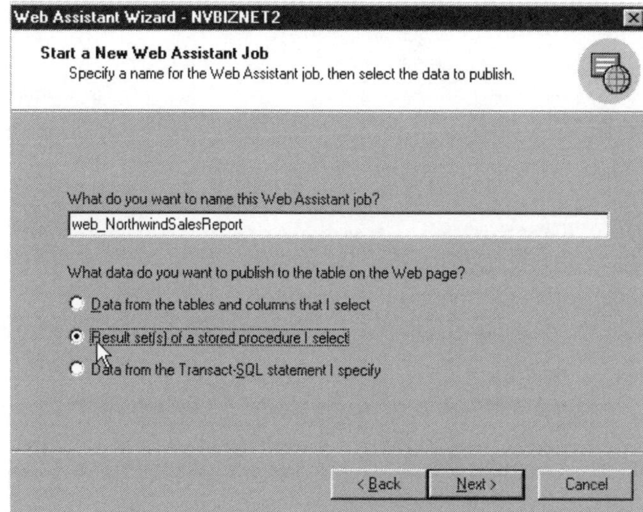

Figure 582.1 The Web Assistant Wizard Start a New Web Assistant Job dialog box

9. Into the "What do you want to name this Web Assistant job?" field, enter a name for the Web task. For the current project, enter **web_NorthwindSalesReport**.

10. Click your mouse on the radio button to the left of "Result set(s) of a stored procedure I select" within the column of radio buttons below the Web task name field. Note that you can also use the Web Assistant Wizard to create Web tasks that publish results sets from queries on tables by clicking the first radio button in the list and the results set produced generated from executing a Transact-SQL statement by clicking the third radio button. Click the Next button. The Web Assistant Wizard will display the Select Stored Procedure dialog box.

11. Within the list box with stored procedures at the center of the Select Stored Procedure Dialog box, click your mouse on the stored procedure you want the Web task to execute. For the current project, click "usp_ShowNorthwindSales" and then on the Next button at the bottom of the dialog box. The Web Assistant Wizard will Display the Schedule the Web Assistant Job dialog box shown in Figure 582.2.

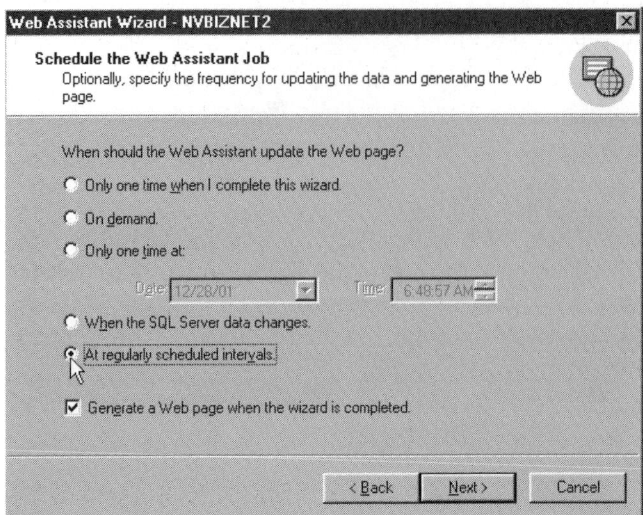

Figure 582.2 The Web Assistant Wizard Schedule the Web Assistant Job dialog box

12. Decide when you want the Web task you are creating to run and how often it is to repeat. Then, click the radio button next to your choice. For the current project, click the radio button to the left of "At regularly scheduled intervals" and then on the Next button. The Web Assistant Wizard will display the Schedule the Update Interval dialog box shown in Figure 582.3.

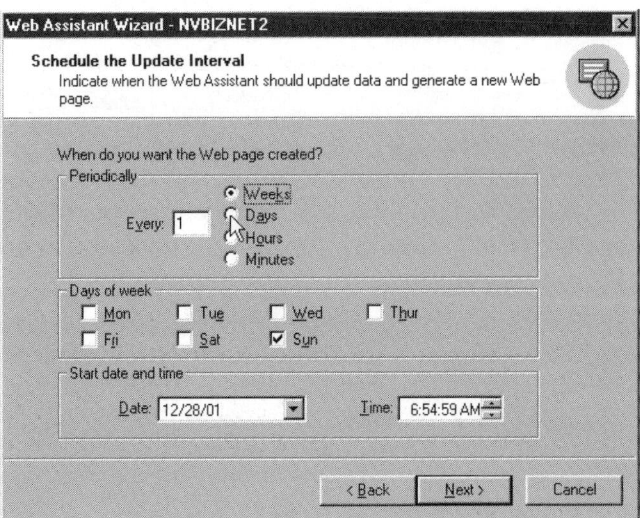

Figure 582.3 The Web Assistant Wizard Schedule the Update Interval dialog box

13. Use the check boxes and radio buttons within the dialog box to select the dates, times, and/or days of the week on which you want the Web task to run. For the current project, have the Web task update the Northwind sales report on the Web page monthly by click-

ing the Days radio button and entering **30** into the Every field within the Periodically section near the top of the dialog box. Then, click the Next button. The Web Assistant Wizard will display the Publish the Web Page dialog box.

14. Into the File name field within the Publish the Web Page dialog box, enter the pathname to which you want the MS-SQL Server to publish the Web page. If the folder is accessible to the MS-SQL Server, enter the pathname of a Web page within a folder on the Web site where you want the Web page with the SQL data displayed. Note that if you enter a pathname that points to location other than a folder within the Web site, you must copy the Web page that the Web task creates into one of the site's folders before Web site visitors can see the Web page generated. For the current project, assume the MS-SQL Server has write access to the Web site's folders. As such, enter **D:\InetPub\WWWRoot\SQLTips\NorthwindSalesReport.htm** into the File name field. Then, click the Next button at the bottom of the dialog box. The Web Assistant Wizard will display the Format the Web Page dialog box shown in Figure 582.4.

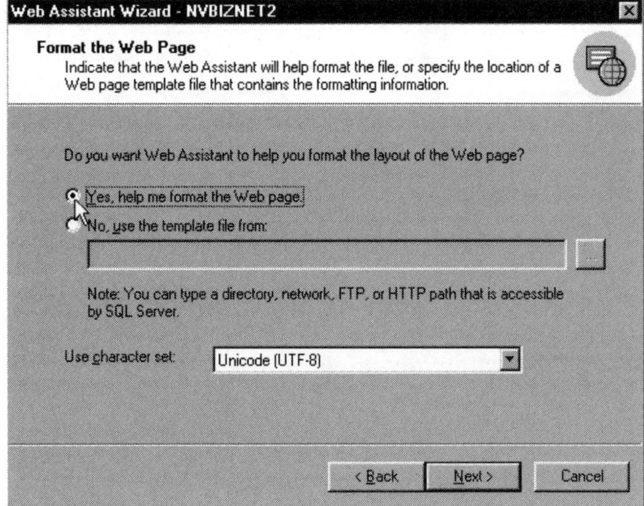

Figure 582.4 The Web Assistant Wizard Format the Web Page dialog box

15. If you want the Web task to use a Web page template, click the radio button to the left of "No, use the template file from" and enter the pathname of the Web page template you want to the Web task to use. (You learned how to create Web page templates within Tip 578, "Creating a Web Page Template for MS-SQL Server Query Results" and Tip 579, "Formatting the Query Results Table on a Web Page Created by an MS-SQL Server Stored Procedure.") For the current project, assume you have no Web page template and want the Web task to format the Web page. Therefore, click the "Yes, help me format the Web page" radio button. Then, click the Next button at the bottom of the dialog box. The Web Assistant Wizard will display the Specify Titles dialog box shown in Figure 582.5.

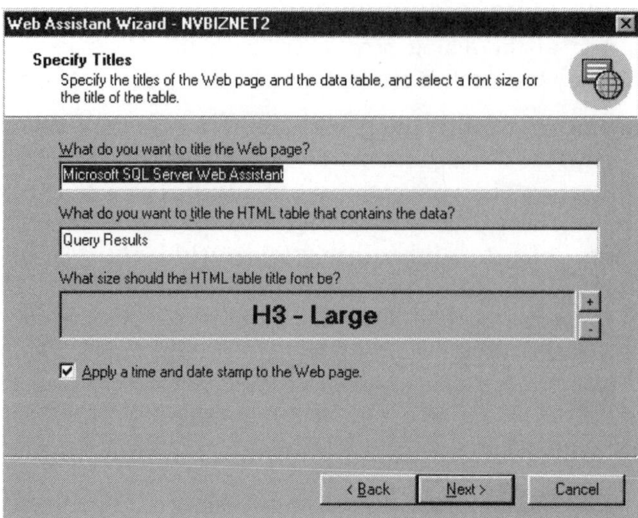

Figure 582.5 The Web Assistant Wizard Specify Titles dialog box

16. Into the "What do you want to title the Web page?" field, enter the Web page title text you want the Web task to insert between start and end title tags (<title></title>) within the Web page header section. (The Web browser displays the Web page title within the title bar across the top of the browser's application window and not on the Web page itself.) For the current project, enter **Northwind Cumulative Sales Report**.

17. Into the "What do you want to title the HTML table that contains the data?" field, enter the text you want to appear on the Web page as a title above the HTML table with the query results set. For the current project, enter **Northwind Cumulative Annual Sales Figures**.

18. Use the plus (+) and minus (-) buttons to the right of the "What size should the HTML table title font be?" field to set the size of the title text. For the current project, assume you want the title formatted using HTML level-1 heading tags, so click the minus (+) button until you see "H1–Largest."

19. Decide if you want the Web task to insert a line that writes the date and time of the last update on the Web page. If not, clear the "Apply a time and date stamp to the Web page." check box by clicking your mouse on the check box it until the checkmark disappears. For the current project, assume that you want the Web task to display the date and time of the most recent update, and leave the check box checked. Then, click on the Next button at the bottom of the dialog box. The Web Assistant Wizard will display the Format a Table dialog box shown in Figure 582.6.

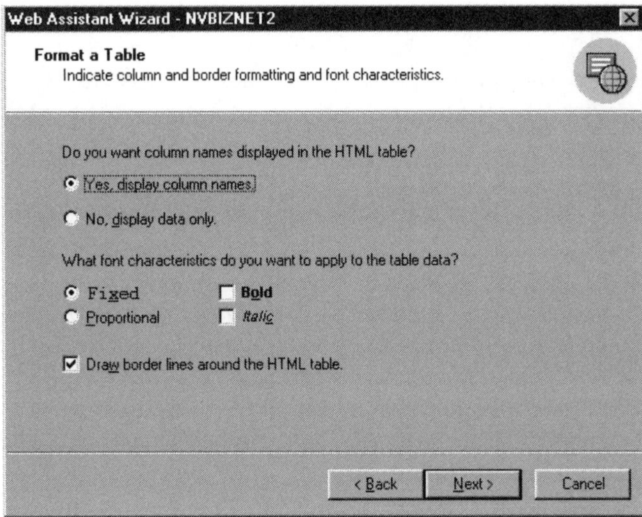

Figure 582.6 The Web Assistant Wizard Format a Table dialog box

20. Decide whether you want the Web task to use the column names from the query's SELECT clause as headings across the first row within the HTML table and how you want the non-heading data within the table to look. Then, make the appropriate radio button and check box selections. For the current project, accept the defaults to have the Web task use the SELECT clause column names as HTML table headings, write table data with fixed width spacing, in a non-bold, non-italic font, and draw a border around the HTML table and each of its cells. Then, click the Next button. The Web Assistant Wizard will display the Add Hyperlinks to Web Page dialog box shown in Figure 582.7.

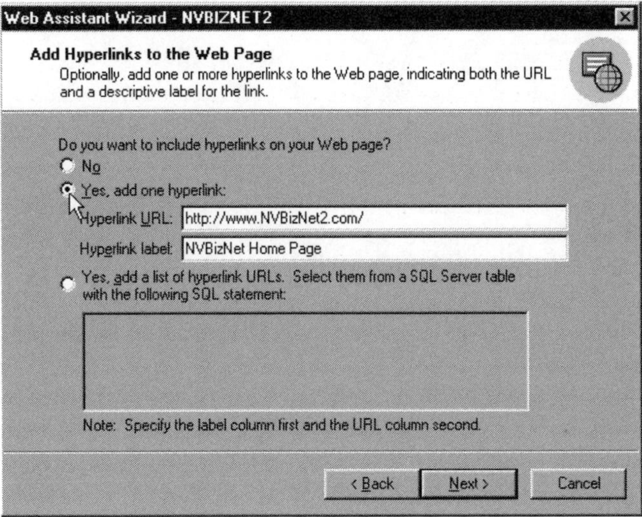

Figure 582.7 The Web Assistant Wizard Add Hyperlinks to the Web Page dialog box

21. You should always provide at least one hyperlink the visitor can use to navigate to the site's home page, to the "next" page on a hierarchical site, or to a Web page with the site map or menu. For the current project, have the Web task insert a hyperlink to the site's homepage (www.NVBizNet2.com) on the line following the HTML table with the SQL data. As such, click the "Yes, add one hyperlink" radio button, enter **HTTP://www.NVBizNet2.com/** into the "Hyperlink URL" field, and "NVBizNet Home Page" into the "Hyperlink label" field. Click your mouse on the Next button. The Web Assistant Wizard will display the Limit Rows dialog box shown in Figure 582.8.

Note: *You can have the Web task display at the bottom of the Web page a list of hyperlinks (versus a single hyperlink). To do so, you must have an SQL table with hyperlinks in one column and the associated anchor text in another. Then, in to the textbox at the bottom of the Add Hyperlinks to the Web Page dialog box, you would enter an SELECT statement that returns two columns (<Web address> and then <anchor text>) for each hyperlink within the table.*

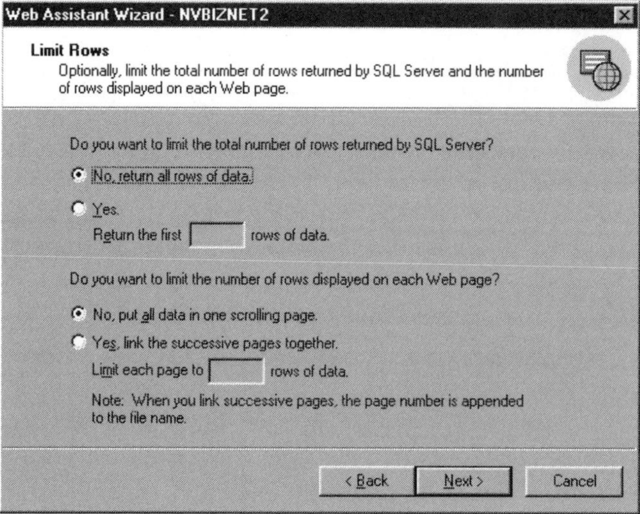

Figure 582.8 The Web Assistant Wizard Limit Rows dialog box

22. If you want to limit the number of results set rows the Web task displays and/or to display only a certain number or rows within an HTML table, click the appropriate radio buttons and enter the row counts. For the current project, accept the Web defaults to display all rows of query results within a single HTML table on a Web page. Then, click the Next button.

After you complete Step 22, the Web Assistant Wizard will display its final screen, which has a textbox that lists the options you've chosen. Review your selections and use the Back button if necessary to move back through the Wizard's dialog boxes to make any corrections. When all is OK, click the Finish button on the Wizard's last screen. The Web Assistant Wizard will generate the Web task within the database you selected and display the "Web Assistant successfully completed the task." message box.

583 Understanding Active Server Pages (ASP) and ActiveX Data Objects (ADO)

In Tips 577–582, you learned how to create and run MS-SQL Server Web tasks. As you now know, a Web task calls a stored procedure the DBMS creates for the Web task when it adds the task to the list of MS-SQL Server Agent's "to do" list. Web task-associated stored procedures execute queries or (as you learned in Tip 582 "Using the MS-SQL Server Web Assistant Wizard to Create a Web task that Executes a Stored Procedure") call other stored procedures, which in turn, execute queries. What makes a Web task different from "normal" MS-SQL Server Agent scheduled jobs (tasks), is that a Web task creates a Web page on which the task inserts (within an HTML table) the results set from the query its stored procedure executes.

The "problem" with a Web task is that it is static. That is, a Web task always executes the same query—the one you wrote when you created the task. Moreover, Web site visitors cannot use the task to submit their own queries to the DBMS. Web tasks that generate a set of pre-defined reports with up-to-date information from the database are a powerful feature. However, there will be many times when users require more or different information than that provided within the HTML tables your Web tasks create.

In addition, a Web task only provides communication in one direction—from the database to the site visitor. Therefore, while a Web task lets site visitors view data stored within database tables, it does not let visitors add, change, or delete anything. Thus, for a truly robust Web interface with the DBMS, you need more capabilities than Web tasks have to offer. That's where ActiveX Data Objects (ADO) and Web server-side script processors such as the Active Server Page (ASP) script host and the PHP script engine (discussed within the next tip) come in.

ADO consists of a set of objects that programming languages (like Visual Basic and Visual C++) and scripting languages (like VBScript, JavaScript, and JScript) can use to access data within an SQL database. The three most commonly used ADO objects are:

- **connection** objects, which let scripts establish connections with the DBMS;
- **command** objects, which scripts use to submit commands (such as SELECT, INSERT, UPDATE, and DELETE statements) to the DBMS for execution;
- **recordset** objects, which include field and row objects that scripts can use to view and manipulate query results sets.

Thus, as you will see in Tips 589–596, ADO lets you use Web server-side scripts to query an SQL DBMS for information and then integrate that data returned into Web pages as requested by Web site visitors. In addition, by combining scripts with HTML forms, you can use ADO to update the data within the database. The great thing is that the dynamic linked library (DLL) files you must have to access database data with ADO come standard with most DBMS products. As such, when you install the DBMS, you also install ADO support.

Think of the ADO Connection object as establishing a two-way pipeline between the script on the Web page and the SQL DBMS. The script, embedded within the Web page, uses the ADO Command object to send SQL statements to the DBMS through the "pipeline" established by the ADO Connection object. Note that any valid SQL statement is fair game. As long as the username under which the script connects to the DBMS has the required security privileges, the DBMS will execute the statement sent.

After executing the SQL statements it receives, the DBMS uses the ADO Recordset object to send query results and error messages (through the ADO Connection object) back to the script that submitted the SQL statements to the DBMS. The script, in turn, uses the Recordset object to display (on the Web page) and manipulate the data within the database. This two-way, ADO enabled communication between script and DBMS continues until the script connection times out or the script closes it.

To run server-side scripts embedded within a Web page and thereby exploit ADO to display and/or manipulate data within an SQL database, you need a script engine to execute the script's commands. The two most popular script engines are ASP (discussed within this tip) and PHP (discussed within the next tip).

The ASP script host lets you create dynamic Web pages by combining HTML tags and text content with instructions written in a scripting language such as VBScript, JScript, PerlScript, Python, Rexx, and more. HTML tags and text within an Active Server Page provide the static (unchanging) portion of the Web page content. Meanwhile, the embedded script generates the dynamic (that is, changing) content you want the Web server to insert. For example, rather than have a Web task generate a Web page that lists all orders placed by all customers, you can use an HTML form and VBScript embedded within an Active Server Page to let site visitors display a Web page with order details for a particular customer or set of customers. Moreover, although visitors retrieve the same Active Server Page, each of them can view data on the same or different customers—without you having to make any changes to the ASP Web page.

When a Web browser requests an Active Server Page (typically a file with an .asp extension), the Web server finds the page and passes the Web document to the ASP script host on the Web server. The ASP script host parses the Web page and sends the script statements it finds enclosed within start and end script tags (<% ... %>) to a script engine for processing.

The script engine, in turn, interprets the script's statements and returns the output (if any) as a string of HTML (tags and text) to the *asp.dll* script host. As you will see in Tips 590–596, a script can connect with an SQL DBMS, retrieve data, and return that data to the script host. Then, the script host inserts the script's output (which might be data from an SQL DBMS) in place of the script statements within the ASP document and passes the updated Active Server Page to the Web server. The Web server, in turn, sends the ASP Web page to the site visitor that requested it.

Thus, with the proper scripts, you can customize Web page content based on who is visiting the Active Server Page. Suppose for example, that your bank stores your account information within an SQL database. Using Active Server Pages on your bank's Web site you can manage your checking, savings, or credit card accounts. Scripts embedded within the ASP Web pages, let you connect with the DBMS and submit queries that generate the HTML tags and retrieve the data necessary to display your account information. When another customer logs in to your bank's Web site, that customer retrieves and works with his or her account data (and not yours) at the same Web address.

In addition to displaying dynamic and custom content, you can write ASP scripts that change data within a database. Suppose, for example, that you login to your bank's Web site and fill out an HTML form to transfer money from one account to another. After you click the form's Submit button, your Web browser sends the information you entered into the HTML form to the URL given by the *action* attribute within the form's <form> tag. If the URL names an Active Server Page, the Web server passes the Web document (specified by the URL) along with form results to the ASP script host. The script host passes the amount you specified and the account selections you made (or entered) on the HTML form to a script engine, which in turn, executes script statements that login to the DBMS and update your account balances stored within the database tables.

To create an Active Server Page, you need only a text editor, such as Notepad (which comes standard with all versions of Windows), because an Active Server Page is nothing more than an ASCII text file. To be treated as an Active Server Page, a Web document's filename must have an extension that associates the file with the asp.dll scripting engine. Typically, ASP files have an .asp extension, because site administrators associate (designate) files with an .asp extension for processing by the asp.dll application.

To make Active Server Pages available on the Internet or your company's intranet, you need a Web server that supports ASP. Both Microsoft's Internet Information Server (IIS) and its Personal Web Server (PWS) have built-in ASP support. If the ISP hosting your Web site is running Windows NT 4, he or she may have installed IIS 2 (which has ASP 1.0 support). IIS 3 is part of Windows NT 4 Service Pack 3, and IIS 4 is available free as part of the Windows NT 4 Option Pack. (You can download Option Pack 4 from the Microsoft site at http://www.microsoft.com/NTServer/downloads/recommended/NT4OptPk/default.asp.) Both IIS 3 and IIS 4 come with the asp.dll that provides ASP 2.0 support. Windows 2000 includes IIS 5, which supports ASP 3.0.

As mentioned previously within this tip, in addition to IIS, Microsoft's PWS (available within the Windows NT 4 Option Pack) also provides ASP support. (By the way, you can run the PWS on Windows NT Workstation or Windows 95 and above.) If you publish your Web site on a non-IIS (or PWS) Web server, you may still be able to use ASP. Find out if your ISP installed ASP extensions from a company like Chili!Soft or Halcyon Software. Once installed, Chili!Soft ASP, for example, lets you run Active Server Pages on Web servers from Apache, Lotus, Netscape, and Microsoft running on Microsoft, Sun, and IBM platforms.

To view Active Server Pages, you need both a Web server and a Web browser. Because the Web server (and not the Web browser) executes scripts embedded in Active Server Pages, any Web browser will do. One of the strengths in having the Web server rather than the Web browser execute scripts is that only the Web server must support the scripting languages used to write scripts embedded within Web pages. The script host running on the Web server is responsible for sending the script to the proper scripting engine and for inserting script output (including results sets returned from SQL queries) within the Web page as standard HTML tags and text the Web browser can understand and display.

584 Downloading and Installing PHP

PHP (which originally stood for Personal Home Page tools), like ASP, lets you run server-side scripts embedded within Web pages. These embedded scripts can access database data and other resources available to the Web server to build Web pages on-the-fly. Also like ASP, you can use PHP free of charge. However, unlike ASP, PHP does not come standard with a Web server. To use PHP, you must download it across the Internet, as you will learn how to do within this tip.

When a site visitor requests a PHP Web page—that is, an HTML document that has an extension, usually .php, associated to the PHP processor—the Web server sends the request to the PHP processor. The PHP processor retrieves the document and goes through it line by line, executing all PHP statements the processor finds enclosed within start PHP (<?php or <?) and end PHP (?>) script tags. The processor writes the output generated by the statements as well as all the text and HTML outside the start and end PHP script tags to a virtual Web page within the Web server's memory. When the PHP processor instructs it to do so, the Web server sends this (in-memory) Web page to the site visitor that requested the PHP document.

In short, the PHP processor creates a Web page each time a site visitor requests a document with a .php extension from the Web site. As such, you can use PHP to convert your Web site from a collection of static Web pages into a Web server-based database application that has a Web page user interface.

Whereas client-side scripting languages (such as JavaScript) run within the Web browser, PHP is a server-side scripting language, which means a program on the Web server (and not code within the Web browser) executes PHP statements embedded within the PHP Web page. In technical terms, PHP is a cross-platform, markup language embedded, server-side scripting language, which means:

- You can use the same PHP scripts on Web servers running a variety of operating systems such as Linux, Mac OS, RISC OS, Unix, and Windows.
- You embed PHP statements within your Web page file either alone or alongside the HTML, XHTML, or XML tags that describe the Web page to the Web browser.
- When the site visitor requests a Web page with a .php extension, the Web server sends the request to the PHP processor. The PHP processor locates the requested file and executes the script embedded within the Web document. The processor replaces PHP statements with their output (which might include data return within results sets from SQL queries) as it builds the virtual Web page within the Web server's memory. The Web server then

sends to the site visitor the Web page built by the PHP processor running at the Web server.

The beauty in using PHP lies in the fact that the Web browser never sees the PHP code embedded within the Web page. When you write PHP scripts, you need not worry whether the visitor's Web browser supports PHP. To create a PHP-enabled Web page, you simply embed the PHP scripts you want executed within the Web page and save the document to a file with an extension (such as .php) associated with execution by the PHP processor. When the site visitor requests a Web page with a .php extension, the Web server knows to send the request to the PHP processor and then to send the Web page that the PHP processor generates to the Web site visitor that requested it.

Before you can execute PHP scripts, you must download and install a PHP processor. If you are working with a Linux or Unix machine, you must not only retrieve the PHP processor's source code but must also compile it using an ANSI C compiler such as gcc or g++. You can retrieve the latest version of PHP for Unix/Linux from http://www.php.net. Be sure to download both the PHP source code to compile and the PHP documentation, which will guide you through the installation and help you select the necessary configuration options.

Configuring PHP on Windows NT running IIS is much simpler than compiling and configuring PHP for the Apache Web server on a Linux or Unix machine. Proceed to the PHP Web site at http://www.php.net and click the Downloads hyperlink. In the Win32 Binaries section of the downloads Web page, click the hyperlink to download the PHP archive file and then on the hyperlink to download the PHP installation program (as of this writing, you download PHP 4.0.6 Zip Package and PHP 4.0.6 Installer, respectively). When prompted, store both files within the same folder (such as C:\PHP) on the Web server. Remember, PHP is a server-side scripting language. As such, you install and run the language processor on the Web server.

Next, unzip the PHP compressed file (currently, php-4.0.6-Win32.zip) and then execute the PHP InstallShield installation program (currently, php406-installer.exe). The installation program will prompt you to enter the pathname of the folder in which you unzipped the PHP processor's files and the folder and version of IIS (or Personal Web Server) to which you want to add PHP support. After completing its work, the installation program will ask you to let it reboot your Windows (NT, 2000, or XP) server to finish the installation process. If you have any problems during the installation, or want to perform a manual installation, print and review the contents of the install.txt file within the PHP folder.

585 Understanding Open Database Connectivity (ODBC) and Data Source Names (DSNs)

Before it can submit queries and other SQL statements for processing, an ASP or PHP script must establish a connection with the DBMS. To connect with a DBMS, a server-side script must use an open database connectivity (ODBC) driver to act as a go-between. The script passes a string (with connection/login instructions or an SQL statement) to the ODBC driver. The ODBC driver puts the string into a format that the DBMS (such as MS-SQL Server) understands and then sends the connection/command string to the DBMS for processing. When the DBMS responds by sending data back to the user, the ODBC driver formats the output (such as a query results sets and data filled cursors) from the DBMS and passes the data from the DBMS to the script.

If you are working with Windows on an Intel platform and have installed Microsoft Office products, chances are excellent that you already have the ODBC drivers you need to connect with the MS-SQL Server. ODBC drivers are installed when you install MS-SQL Server client utilities and such products as Microsoft Office and Microsoft Access, which make SQL data available within Word documents, spreadsheets, and Access databases. If you are using a DBMS product other than MS-SQL Server, check your server's documentation. Most SQL products provide an ODBC driver you can use to communicate with the database from external applications written in C, C++, Visual Basic, VBScript, JavaScript, and so on.

When installing an ODBC driver, bear in mind that you must sometimes install the driver on the server and other times on the client, that is on your network workstation. The location at which the application that must communicate with the DBMS runs determines where you must install the ODBC driver. For example, to allow a Visual Basic program running at your workstation to communicate with an SQL DBMS, you must install the ODBC driver for the DBMS on your workstation. Conversely, when a script running at the Web server must communicate with a DBMS running either on the same computer or on another computer across the network (or the Internet), you must install the ODBC driver the script needs on the computer with the Web server.

After you install the requisite ODBC driver on your system, you can create data source names (DSNs) that let your applications connect with the SQL DBMS of your choice and work with its data. As is the case with ODBC drivers, you can create a DSN either at the server or on the client workstation. Again, the determining factor in deciding where to create the DSN is where the application that needs it is running. If the application is running at the workstation, perform the steps in the following procedure at the workstation. Conversely, if you are creating a DSN to support server-side scripts embedded within (PHP or ASP) Web pages, execute the following procedure at the computer with the script processor—typically the same computer running the Web server.

To create a DSN (on either a client workstation or server), you use the ODBC administrator on the Windows Control Panel by performing the following steps:

1. Click your mouse on the Start button. Windows will display the Start menu.
2. Move your mouse pointer to Settings on the Start menu and select Control Panel. Windows will open the Control Panel in a new window.
3. Double-click the Data Sources (ODBC) icon. (If you are using Windows 2000, versus Windows NT, you must open the Administrative Tools folder before you will see the Data Sources icon.) Windows will start the ODBC Data Source Administrator similar to that shown in Figure 585.1.

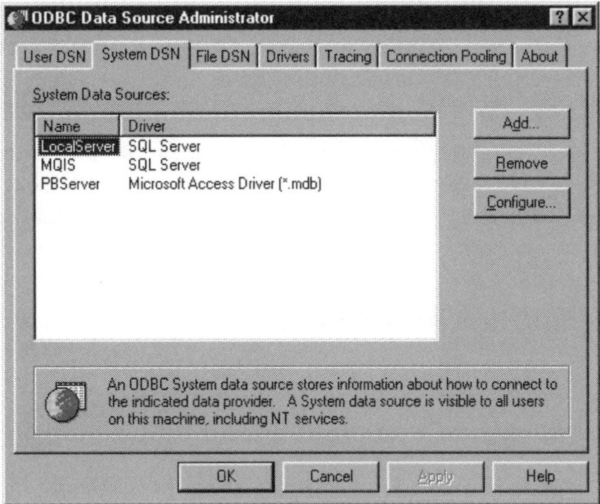

Figure 585.1 The System DSN tab within the ODBC Data Source Administrator Dialog box

---

Note: *When installing a DSN on a Windows (NT, 2000, or XP) server, make sure you are working with the System DSN (versus the User DSN) tab in Step 4. If you install the DSN on the User DSN tab, the script processor, running as a system process (and not logged in as a user) will not be able to "see" the DSN you create. When you create a DSN on the System DSN tab it is available to all users and system services (like the script processor).*

---

4. Click the Add button on the System DSN tab. The ODBC Data Source Administrator will display the Create New Data Source dialog box similar to that shown in Figure 585.2.

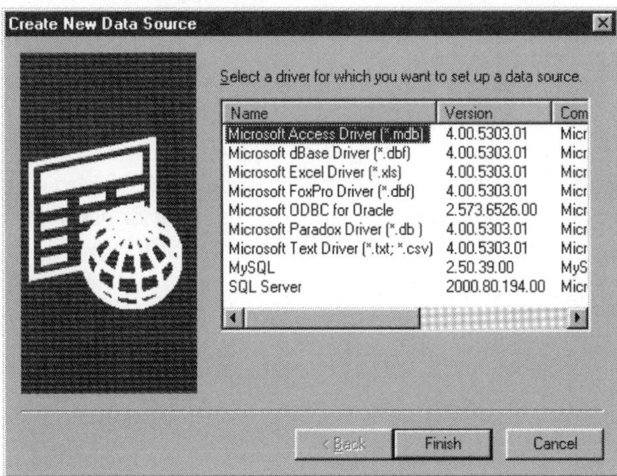

Figure 585.2 The ODBC Data Source Administrator Create New Data Source dialog box

5. Select the ODBC driver for your DBMS product. Click the Finish button. The ODBC Data Source Administrator will display the screen 1 of the Create a New Data Source to SQL Server dialog box similar to that shown in Figure 585.3.

Note: *If the ODBC driver for your DBMS product is not among those listed in the text box within the New Data Source Dialog box, check your DBMS documentation or installation instructions. One of these documents will tell you where you can obtain the ODBC driver you need and how to install it on your system. Before continuing with the next step of this procedure, you must have the ODBC driver for the DBMS product with which you want an application or script to communicate installed on your computer.*

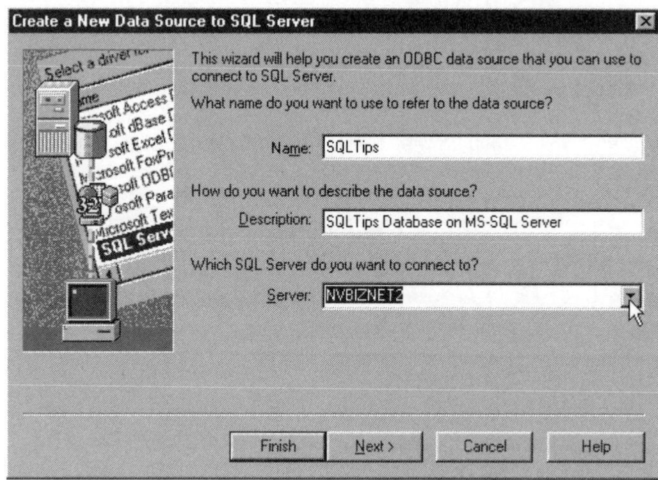

Figure 585.3 Screen 1 of the ODBC Data Source Administrator Create a New Data Source to SQL Server dialog box

6. Into the Name field enter the name you want to use when referring to the DSN within your script or application. Because a DSN points to a particular data source, such as one of several databases managed by an SQL DBMS, enter the name of the database or a one-word description of the data source. For current project, enter **SQLTips** into the Name field. Into the Description field, enter an (optional) brief description of the DSN. For the current project, enter **SQLTips Database on an MS-SQL Server** into the Description field. Use the drop-down list button to the right of the Server field to display a list of SQL servers accessible from the computer on which you are installing the DSN, pick the one to which you want the DSN to connect. For the current project select NVBizNet2. Click the Next button. The ODBC Data Source Administrator will display screen 2 of the Create a New Data Source to SQL Server dialog box similar to that shown in Figure 585.4.

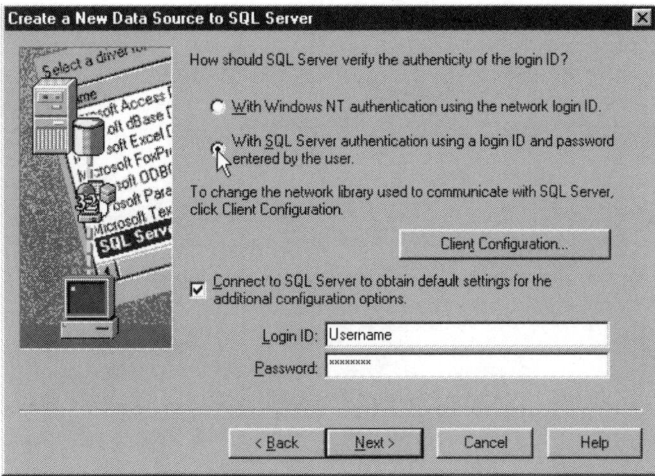

Figure 585.4 Screen 2 of the ODBC Data Source Administrator Create a New Data Source to SQL Server dialog box

7. Select the method by which you want to authenticate the login to the DBMS through the DSN. For the current project, click your mouse on the radio button to the left of "With SQL Server authentication using a login ID and password entered by the user." Click a checkmark into the "Connect to SQL Server to obtain default settings for the additional configuration options" check box. (Let the MS-SQL Server driver obtain initial settings from the MS-SQL Server you selected or entered into the Server field in Step 6.) Into the "Login ID" and "Password" fields, enter a username and password (respectively) that you want the ODBC driver to use when connecting to the MS-SQL Server while determining and testing default settings. The username/password you enter here are only used during the setup process. When connecting with the DSN from within a script or application later, the script or application will be required to supply a valid username/password pair. Click the Next button. The ODBC Data Source Administrator will attempt to use the username/password pair to connect with the MS-SQL Server (you specified in step 6). If successful, the ODBC Data Source Administrator will display screen 3 of the Create a New Data Source to SQL Server dialog box similar to that shown in Figure 585.5.

8. Click the drop-down list button to the right of the "Change the default database to" field, and select the database you want to use as the default connection for any process using this DSN. For the current project, select SQLTips from the drop-down list. (Bear in mind that this is only the default database. A script or application connecting to the DBMS through the DSN can always submit an SQL USE statement and switch to a different database.) Click the Next button. The ODBC Data Source Administrator will display screen 4 of the Create a New Data Source to SQL Server dialog box similar to that shown in Figure 585.6.

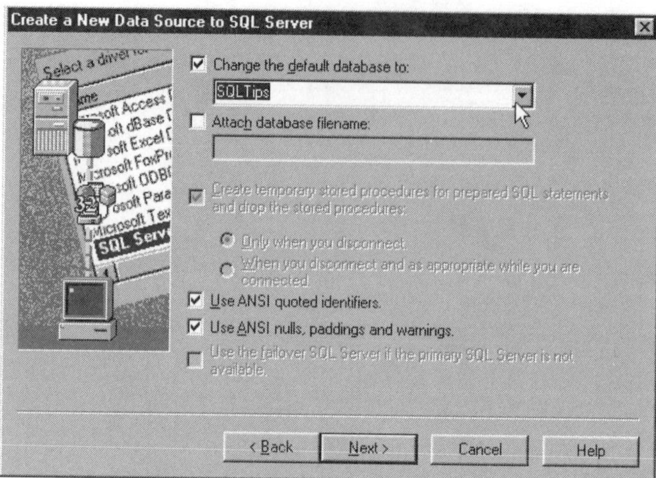

Figure 585.5 Screen 3 of the ODBC Data Source Administrator Create a New Data Source to SQL Server dialog box

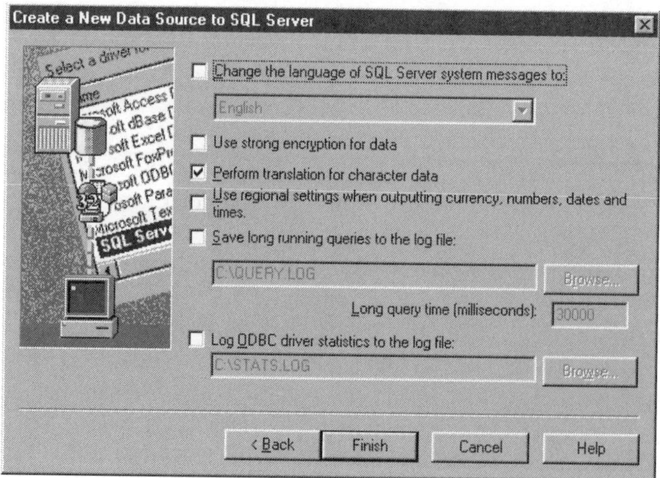

Figure 585.6 Screen 4 of the ODBC Data Source Administrator Create a New Data Source to SQL Server dialog box

9. Click the Finish button. The ODBC Data Source Administrator will display an ODBC Microsoft SQL Server Setup dialog box similar to that shown in Figure 585.7.

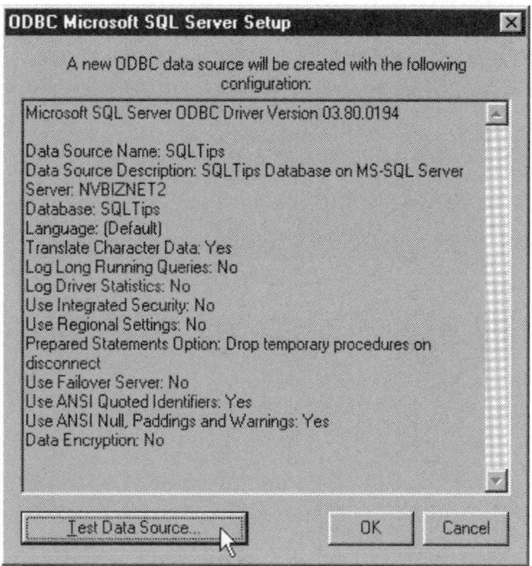

Figure 585.7 The ODBC Data Source Administrator ODBC Microsoft SQL Server Setup dialog box

10. Reviewing the settings listed within the dialog box. If any are incorrect, click the Cancel button, and move back to the appropriate screen of the Create a New Data Source dialog box to make the corrections you must make. If the new DSN's configuration options are correct, click the Test Data Source button to test whether the DSN can truly connect with the default database on the MS-SQL Server selected in Step 6. The ODBC Data Source Administrator will display its connection and options test results within the SQL Server ODBC Data Source Test dialog box shown in Figure 585.8.

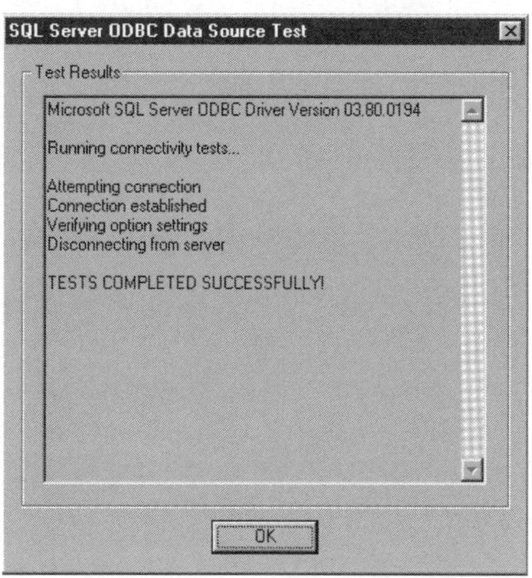

Figure 585.8 The ODBC Data Source Administrator SQL Server ODBC Data Source Test dialog box

11. Note any errors and then click the OK button to return to the ODBC Microsoft SQL Server Setup dialog box. If there were errors report within the SQL Server ODBC Data Source Test dialog box, click the Cancel button and proceed back to the appropriate dialog box to make any necessary changes to correct the problems reported. Otherwise, click the OK button to save your new DSN and return to the System DSN tab of the ODBC Data Source Administrator dialog box.

After you complete Step 11, click the OK button near the bottom center of the dialog box to exit the ODBC Data Source Administrator application.

Within the next tip you will learn how to use the DSN you created in this tip to let a script login and open a connection with a DBMS.

586 Establishing a Data Source Name (DSN) Connection with an SQL DBMS

To work with data in a database managed by an SQL DBMS, an application (such as an embedded script on an ASP or PHP Web page) must first login. After you create a DSN (as you learned to do in Tip 585 "Understanding Open Database Connectivity [ODBC] and Data Source Names [DSNs]"), the login process is simple. Because the DSN supplies the ODBC driver with all the session information, your script need only specify the DSN through which it will use to connect with the DBMS and supply a valid username/password pair. In short, logging in though a DSN is no more difficult than logging in to the MS-SQL Server DBMS through the SQL Query Analyzer's login screen.

For example, the following JavaScript when embedded within a PHP Web page (that is a Web page, with a .php extension) will use the SQLTips DSN created within the preceding tip to connect with the SQLTips database on the MS-SQL Server name NVBizNet2:

```
<!DOCTYPE HTML PUBLIC '-//W3C//DTD HTML 4.0//EN'>
<html>
<head>
  function open_DSN_connection()
  {
   $conn = odbc_connect("SQLTips","Maggy","Evans");
   return $conn;
  }
</head>
<body>

<?php
//Connect Call the function to connect with the DBMS
```

```
  $conn = open_DSN_Connection();

//Check the connection status
  if(!$conn)
   echo "Failed to connect!";
  else
  {
//Code that works with the data within the DBMS goes here
   echo "DSN Connection through SQLTips successful!";
  }
?>
</body>
</html>
```

In this example, the PHP script uses the odbc_connect() function to establish a connection with the DBMS. The three parameters passed to the function are "SQLTips" (the name of the DSN), "Maggy" (the username), and "Evans" (the password). If the connection attempt succeeds, the odbc_connect() function returns the connection handle to the $CONN variable. While this example only checks the value within the connection handle and then displays the connection status, your scripts will use the connection handle ($CONN) to send queries and other commands to the DBMS and to retrieve query results—as you will learn to do in Tips 590–592.

Whereas you use the odbc_connect() function to establish a connection between the script on a PHP Web page and an SQL DBMS, you use the ADO Connection object to do the same thing within a VBScript embedded within an ASP Web page. For example, the following script will use the same SQLTips DSN used for the preceding example to connect with an SQL DBMS. However, as shown in Figure 586.1, this script provides a little more detail about its connection than did the previous JavaScript example:

```
<!DOCTYPE HTML PUBLIC "-//W3C//DTD HTML 4.0//EN">
<html>
<body>

<%
'Function which establishes a connection with a DBMS
'through the DSN "SQLTips" when called.

 Sub open_DSN_connection (byref connObjDSN)
   CONST dsnConnection = "DSN=SQLTips;UID=Maggy;pwd=Evans;"

'Create the ADO Connection object
   Set connObjDSN = server.createobject("adodb.connection")

'Place the connection string into the ConnectionString
'property with the ADO Connection object and then try to
'establish a connection with the DBMS.

   With connObjDSN
```

```
     .ConnectionString = dsnConnection
     .open
   End With
 End Sub
DIM connObjDSN
call open_DSN_Connection (connObjDSN)

'After calling the function that opens the connection,
'display on the PHP Web page the connection details
'available from ADO Connection object properties.

   With connObjDSN
     Response.write _
       "<b>Attributes</b> = " & .Attributes & "<br>" & _
       "<b>ADO Provider</b> = " & .Provider & "<br>" & _
       "<b>Command Timeout</b> = " _
                       & .CommandTImeOut     & "<br>" & _
       "<b>Default Database</b> = " _
                       & .DefaultDatabase    & "<br>" & _
       "<b>Connection String</b> = " _
                       & .ConnectionString   & "<br>" & _
       "<b>Connection TimeOut</b> = " _
                       & .ConnectionTimeout  & "<br>" & _
       "<b>Provider</b> = " & .Provider      & "<br>" & _
       "<b>CursorLocation</b> = " _
                       & .CursorLocation     & "<br>" & _
       "<b>Isolation Level</b> = " _
                       & .IsolationLevel     & "<br>" & _
       "<b>State</b> = " & .State            & "<br>" & _
       "<b>Version</b> = " & .Version        & "<br>" & _
   End With
%>

</body>
</html>"
```

Note that an ADO object (such as the ADO Connect object [connObjDSN] used in this example) has "methods" and "properties." The *methods* are the actions or things the object can do. The ADO Connection object, for example has the following methods:

- **Cancel**—Instructs the DBMS to cancel execution of the last command asynchronous "Open" or SQL statement sent through the Connection object to the DBMS.
- **Open**—Opens a connection with the DBMS.
- **Close**—Closes the object's open connection with the DBMS.
- **BeginTrans**—Starts a new transaction on the DBMS.
- **CommitTrans**—COMMIT, that is, make permanent the work performed since the last BeginTrans method call.

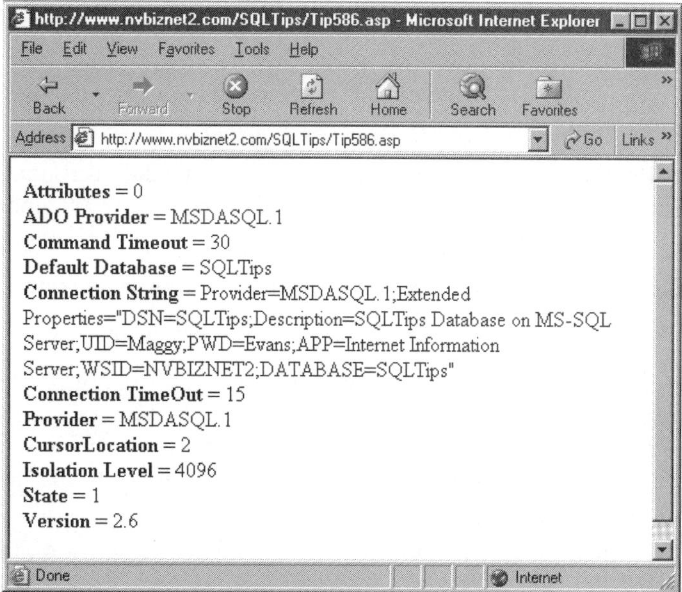

Figure 586.1 Information about an open DSN connection stored within an ADO Connection object's properties

- **RollBackTrans**—Rolls back, that is, undoes any work performed since the last BeginTrans method call.
- **Execute**—Submits a statement that is not expected to return any rows of query results to the DBMS for execution.

An object's properties, on the other hand, tell you something about the object or hold some value placed within the object either by one of the object's methods, or by the script to pass some parameter value to a method. The ADO Connection object, for example, has the following properties:

- **Attributes**—Specifies whether a new transaction is to start after a COMMIT or ROLLBACK is executed.
- **CommandTimeout**—Indicates, in seconds, how long to wait for a command to execute. The default is 30 seconds.
- **DefaultDatabase**—Lets you specify the connection's initial database when the Open method opens a connection to the DBMS.
- **ConnectionString**—Series of arguments separated by semicolons (;), which specify all the information the connection must have to connect with a datasource. When connecting through a DSN, the Open method copies the DSN's data into the ConnectionString property along with the username and password provided by the script.
- **ConnectionTimeout**—Indicates in seconds, how long to wait for the connection to open.
- **Provider**—Indicates the connection's data provider.

- **CursorLocation**—Specifies where ADO is to build the cursors to temporarily hold query results.
- **IsolationLevel**—Indicates whether on transaction can see uncommitted data within another transaction.
- **Mode**—Indicates the available permissions for accessing data through the connection. The mode might be unknown (which is the default until set) or the connection might have read-only, read/write, or write-only access.
- **State**—Indicates whether a connection is open, closed, or busy trying to connect.
- **Version**—Returns the version number of the ADO implementation.

You will learn how to use the ADO Command object's Execute method to send queries and the Connection object's Execute method to send other (non-query) statements to the DBMS within Tips 590–596. In addition, these tips will also show you how the ADO Recordset object lets you work with the multiple row results sets that SQL queries return to the ASP script within an SQL cursor.

The important thing to understand now is the odbc_connect() function and the ADO Connect object let server-side scripts use a DSN to establish a connection between the script and the DBMS. The script then sends commands to the server through the open connection and uses it to retrieve query results from the DBMS as well.

587 Downloading, Installing, and Connecting with a MySQL Database Using the MyODBC Driver

As you work with ASP and PHP, you will find that one of the most powerful (and often used) features of these server-side script processors is their ability to work with data within an SQL database. You can use scripts embedded within ASP or PHP Web pages to not only retrieve and display information retrieved from an SQL database, but also to insert, delete, and update the information stored within database tables. In fact, with the appropriate ODBC driver installed, you can send any command to the DBMS that you could execute after logging in at the server or at a workstation connected to the server's local area network (LAN).

When you go online to visit Web sites at which you access your bank, brokerage, or other account information, make purchases, or check the status of orders, chances are excellent that you are working with an SQL database. Although you typically don't type SQL SELECT, INSERT, UPDATE, or DELETE statements while online, behind the scenes, server-side scripts retrieve data from database tables to generate the Web page content you see. In addition, scripts update the data within the database when directed to do so by instructions you enter and send to the Web server through HTML forms.

Large, established companies have funds available to purchase the latest SQL DBMS product from such vendors as Microsoft, Oracle, and IBM. If you are just getting started (on your road to riches) or if you are launching a non-commercial Web site that must store information about or data submitted by a visitor within an SQL database, consider using the MySQL DBMS. MySQL is a full-featured, multi-user DBMS that can run on many of today's popular operating systems such as AIX, BSDI, DEC Unix, HP Unix, SCO UnixWare, Tru64 Unix, FreeBSD, NetBSD, OpenBSD, Linux, MacOS X Server, OS/2 Warp, Solaris, Windows (95, 98, ME, NT, 2000, XP), and more.

You can download MySQL from the Internet at www.MySQL.com and use it free of charge.

MySQL supports all the standard SQL-92 data types, statements, and transaction processing. Although MySQL does not support stored procedures, scripts embedded within PHP or ASP Web pages. You can use MySQL's ODBC interface to submit one or a batch of SQL statements to the DBMS and retrieve data from it. Therefore, you can code the statement batch usually found within a stored procedure as the statements submitted to the DBMS (through the ODBC interface) by a script function or subroutine.

Before it can submit queries and other SQL statements for processing, a Web page script must establish a connection with the DBMS. As you learned in Tip 585 "Understanding Open Database Connectivity [ODBC] and Data Source Names [DSNs]," to connect with a DBMS, a script must have an ODBC driver to act as a go-between. To login, and thereby open a connection with the DBMS, the script passes a string with connection and login details to the ODBC driver. The ODBC driver, in turn, puts the string into a format that the DBMS understands and then sends the connection string to the DBMS for processing. Next, the ODBC driver formats the output produced by the DBMS and passes the results of the login attempt back to the script.

As of this writing, the MyODBC driver that a script needs in order to communicate with the MySQL DBMS does not come bundled with the DBMS. However, like the MySQL DBMS itself, you can download the MyODBC (ODBC) driver from the Internet at the MySQL Web site at www.MySQL.com/Downloads/. Simply click on the MyODBC hyperlink within the APIs (Application Program Interface) section of the "downloads" Web page. Then follow the download instructions for your operating system.

If you installed MySQL on a Windows system, for example, retrieve the MyODBC.zip (archive) file and store it within a folder (such as C:\My Download Files) on the same computer in which you installed the MySQL DBMS. Next, extract the files within the archive (.zip) file to a folder such as C:\My Download Files\MyODBC, and then perform the steps in the following procedure to complete the installation process:

1. Find Setup.exe within the folder in which you extracted the files within the MyODBC archive file.
2. Double-click Setup.exe to start the installation program. Setup.exewill display the Microsoft ODBC Setup message box.
3. Click Continue. The installation program will display the Install Drivers dialog box.

4. Click MySQL in the Available ODBC Drivers list box and then click on the OK button. The installation program will display the Data Sources dialog box.
5. Click on the Close button. The installation program will display the "Setup Succeeded!" message box.
6. Click on the OK button at the bottom of the message box to exit the installation program.

After you install the ODBC driver for the MySQL DBMS (MyODBC), you can create a DSN through which your scripts can communicate with the MySQL DBMS. (You learned how to create DSNs in Tip 585 "Understanding Open Database Connectivity [ODBC] and Data Source Names [DSNs].")

The ODBC Data Source Administrator will display the TDX MYSQL Driver Default Configuration dialog box shown in Figure 587.1 after you select MySQL within the ODBC Data Source Administrator's Create New Data Source dialog box.

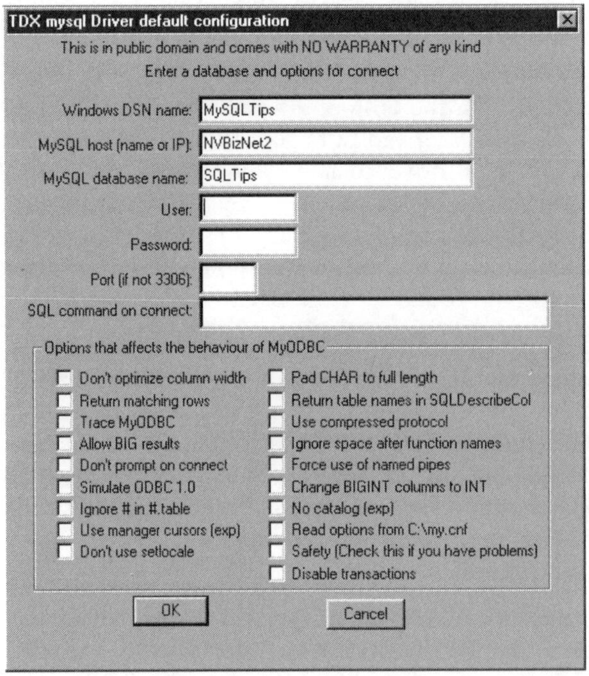

Figure 587.1 TDX MYSQL Driver Default Configuration dialog box

You need only fill in the first three fields within the TDX MYSQL dialog box whose fields include:

- **Windows DSN name**—The name you want to use when referring to the DSN within your script or application. Because a DSN points to a particular data source, such as one of several databases managed by the MySQL DBMS, enter the name of the database or a one-word description of the data source. For the current project, enter **MySQLTips** into the "Windows DSN Name" field.

- **MySQL host (name or IP)**—Enter the name or IP address of the computer on which you installed the MySQL DBMS. For example, if you installed MySQL on a Windows NT server named NVBizNet2, you would enter **NVBizNet2** into the "MySQL host (name or IP)" field.
- **MySQL database name**—The name of the initial database you want the script or application to use when it connects to the MySQL DBMS through the DSN being defined. For the current project, enter **SQLTips** into the "MySQL database name" field.
- **User**—The username under which the DSN is to login to the database. Typically, you will leave both the User and Password fields blank and let the script log in using the username (and password) desired when establishing a connection with the DBMS.
- **Password**—The password portion of the username/password pair for the DSN to use when logging in to the DBMS. Leave both the Password and User fields blank and let the script log in under the username desired when it establishes a connection with the DBMS.
- **Port (if not 3306)**—Normally you must only change the port setting if you installed MySQL on a computer behind a firewall that doesn't allow access across port 3306. In this case, you must contact your network administrator to have him or her either open port 3306 for access, or provide another open port and then change the value within the "Port" field accordingly.
- **SQL command on connect**—Lets you specify an SQL statement to be executed each time an application logs into the DBMS using the DSN being defined. Typically left blank, you might use this field to execute an INSERT statement to log access through the DSN into an audit table.

You can also use the check boxes within the bottom half of the dialog box to set up to 19 different options that affect the behavior of the MyODBC driver. Typically, the default settings—with no check boxes checked—are the ones you want. If you experience problems while using MySQL, you can return to the ODBC driver setup screen for the SQLTips DSN later and click a checkmark into the "Trace MyODBC" check box and the "Safety" check box to gather additional information that will help you resolve any issues.

After you click on the OK button at the bottom of the TDX MySQL Driver Default Configuration dialog box (shown previously in Figure 587), your scripts can use the DSN you created to open a connection with the MySQL DBMS. For example, on a PHP Web page, you can use the same odbc_connect() function you learned about in Tip 586 "Establishing a Data Source Name (DSN) Connection with an SQL DBMS" to use the MySQLTips DSN (you created within this tip) to connect with the MySQL DBMS:

```
<head>
  function open_DSN_connection()
  {
   $conn = odbc_connect("SQLTips","Konrad","King");
   return $conn;
  }
</head>
```

Similarly, if you are using an ASP Web page, you can use the ADO Connection object within a script written with VBScript as follows:

```
<%
 Sub open_DSN_connection (byref connObjDSN)
   CONST dsnConnection = "DSN=SQLTips;UID=Konrad;pwd=King;"

'Create the ADO Connection object
   Set connObjDSN = server.createobject("adodb.connection")

'Place the connection string into the ConnectionString
'property within the ADO Connection object and then try
'to establish a connection with the DBMS.

   With connObjDSN
     .ConnectionString = dsnConnection
     .open
   End With
 End Sub
%>
```

588 Establishing a DSN-Less Connection with the MS-SQL Server or MySQL DBMS

Opening a connection between a script embedded within a Web page and a SQL DBMS through a data source name (DSN) is convenient because the DSN handles the connection details. Therefore, as you saw in Tip 586 "Establishing a Data Source Name (DSN) Connection with an SQL DBMS," the script need only provide the DSN and a valid username/password pair to login to the DBMS. In fact, as you saw from the code samples at the end of Tip 587 "Downloading, Installing, and Connecting with a MySQL Database Using the MyODBC Driver," the script need not even know the specific DBMS product with which it is connecting. Although the parameters the ODBC driver must pass when connecting a script with an MS-SQL Server, for example, differ from those required to connect with a MySQL database, when using a DSN, the script still only specifies the name of the DSN and a valid username/password pair to connect with either DBMS product.

Therefore, connecting a script with an SQL database through a DSN reduces the amount of code you have to write. All connection details, such as the name and location of the DBMS, the ODBC driver selection, and session settings, are coded within the DSN and not your script. In addition, using a DSN lets you reuse the same code to connect with different DBMS products.

While convenient, using a DSN to connect with a DBMS has a couple of disadvantages. First, although a script can submit a USE statement to select any database managed by the DBMS once connected, the system administrator must create at least one DSN for each DBMS to which scripts might connect. Second, a script takes a performance hit when using a DSN versus communicating directly with the DBMS through a vendor supplied OLE DB provider. (An OLE DB provider is a software interface, which lets external applications send commands into and retrieve data from a data source such as an MS-SQL Server DBMS, an Oracle DBMS, a MySQL database, and so on.) Because a DSN sends statements to the ODBC driver which then passes the commands to the OLE DB provider for the data source. Using a DSN means you add an extra level of SQL statement and data handling (the ODBC layer) when sending commands to the DBMS and retrieving data from it.

Fortunately, the ADO Connect object lets your scripts connect and communicate directly with the OLE DB provider for a DBMS—thereby avoiding the performance impact of using the ODBC layer by eliminating it. For example, to connect with a MySQL database through a DSN-less connection, you would use code similar to the following:

```
<%
 Sub open_OLEDB_connection (byref connObj)
   connectString = _
     "PROVIDER=SQLOLEDB;DATA SOURCE=NVBizNet2;" & _
     "UID=Konrad;PWD=King;DATABASE=SQLTips"

'Create the ADO Connection object
   Set connObj = server.createobject("adodb.connection")

'Place the connection string into the ConnectionString
'property within the ADO Connection object and then call
'the .open method to establish a connection with the DBMS.

   With connObjDSN
     .ConnectionString = dsnConnection
     .open
   End With
 End Sub
%>
```

Notice that opening a DSN-less connection is similar to opening a connection through a DSN—you need only change the string you place within the connection object. For a DSN connection, you specify only the DSN, username, and password within the connection string. Conversely, when opening a DSN-less connection you use the following syntax for the connection string:

```
"PROVIDER=<name of OLE DB provider>;
 DATA SOURCE=<name of the DBMS>;
 UID=<username>;
 PWD=<password>;
 DATABASE=<initial database>"
```

Whereas MS-SQL Server uses the OLE DB provider SQLOLEDB, Oracle uses MSDAORA, and MS-Access uses Microsoft.Jet.OLEDB.4.0. Therefore, check your DBMS documentation for the name of the OLE DB driver for your DBMS.

Unfortunately, as of this writing, the MySQL DBMS does not provide a native OLE DB driver through which you can connect to the DBMS using ADO. However, you can still open an DSN-less connection with a MySQL database using the MyODBC (ODBC) driver as shown in the following connection string:

```
connectString = "DRIVER={MYSQL};SERVER=NVBizNet2;" & _
                "UID=Konrad;PWD=King;DATABASE=SQLTips"
```

You would, of course, replace "NVBizNet2" with the name of the server on which you installed your MySQL DBMS, supply a valid username/password pair for UID and PWD, and replace "SQLTips" with the name of a database managed by your MySQL server.

Whether you establish a DSN or a DSN-less connection with the DBMS, you will use the same ADO Command and Recordset object methods to work with the data within the DBMS.

589 Using an ADO Connection to Execute a SELECT Statement to Set Up Username/Password Access to a Web Site

When you must send SQL statements (such as a SELECT statement) to the DBMS, use the ADO Command object. Suppose, for example, that you want to setup username/password access to a Web site. You would use an HTML form to let the site visitor enter the username and password. Then, by specifying the address of an ASP or PHP Web page for the <form> tag's *action* attribute, you can have an embedded script connect to an SQL DBMS, send a query for the username and password entered, and then use the query results to determine whether the visitor may access the members-only area within a Web site.

A Web page with a login form might be defined as follows:

```
<!DOCTYPE HTML PUBLIC "-//W3C//DTD HTML 4.0//EN">
<html>
<head>
  <title>Login and Start a Session</title>
</head>
<body bgcolor="lightyellow">
  <center><h1>SQL Tips and Techniques</center></h1>
  <hr>
<form
```

```
  action="http://www.NVBizNet2.com/SQLTips/Login.asp"
  method="POST">
  Username: <input type="text" name="username"
            size="20"><br>
  Password: <input type="password" name="password"
            size="20"><br><br>
  <input type="submit" value="Login">
  <input type="reset" value="Reset">
</form>
</body>
</html>
```

Within the ASP Web page (LOGIN.ASP) then, you would embed a script similar to the following:

```
<%
'********************************
'*** OPEN DSN-Less Connection ***
'********************************
 Sub open_OLEDB_connection (byref connObj)
   connectString = _
     "PROVIDER=SQLOLEDB;DATA SOURCE=NVBizNet2;" & _
     "UID=sa;PWD=michele;DATABASE=SQLTips"

   With connObj
     .ConnectionString = connectString
     .open
   End With
 End Sub

'********************
'*** MAIN ROUTINE ***
'********************
 Dim connObj, objResultsSet, queryString

'open the connection to the DBMS
 Set connObj = server.createobject ("adodb.connection")
 open_OLEDB_connection (connObj)

'setup the SELECT statement to submit to the DBMS
 queryString = _
   "SELECT COUNT(*) Count FROM siteAccessList " & _
   "WHERE username = '" & Request.Form("username") & _
   "' AND password = '" & Request.Form("password") & "'"

 With connObj

'submit the SELECT statement to the DBMS

   Set objResultsSet = .Execute (queryString)
```

```
'save the session variables and then
'move the visitor member to the member area

   If objResultsSet.Fields("count") = 1 Then
     Session("username") = Request.Form("username")
     Session("password") = Request.Form("password")
     Response.Redirect "/SQLTips/StartSession.asp"
   End If
 End With
%>
```

The ASP REQUEST object's FORM collection lets you retrieve data entered into the fields (called *elements*) within an HTML form. In this example, the script retrieves the entries made into the "username" and "password" elements and uses them to form a SELECT statement as:

```
SELECT COUNT(*) FROM siteAccessList
WHERE username='<data from username field in form>'
  AND password='<data from password field in form>'
```

After assigning the query string (that is, the preceding select statement with data from the HTML form) to the QUERYSTRING variable, the script uses the ADO Command object's Execute method to send the SELECT statement (within the QUERYSTRING variable) to the DBMS for execution. The DBMS, in turn, executes the SELECT statement and returns the query results to the script within the ADO Recordset object (OBJRESULTSSET, in this example). Note that the VBScript Set statement within the preceding script both calls the Execute method and accepts the query results set into the ADO Recordset object (OBJRESULTSSET):

```
With conObj
  Set objResultsSet = .Execute (queryString)
End With
```

In this example, the Recordset object has a field named COUNT that contains the result returned by the SQL COUNT(*) aggregate function within the query's SELECT clause. The login validation script is supposed to determine if the username/password pair entered within the HTML form's input elements matches the username and password stored within a row in the SITEACCESSLIST table. If the DBMS returns a "matching" row (in which case COUNT(*) aggregate will return 1), the username/password pair entered is valid and script redirects the visitor to the STARTSESSION.ASP Web page. Conversely, if the "count" field has a value of 0 (versus 1), the username/password pair entered was not valid and the script does not move the site visitor into the members-only section of the Web site.

The following three tips will show you how to submit queries through HTML forms and how to display within an HTML table on a Web page the results sets that SQL SELECT statements return to a script.

590 Displaying Query Results Within an HTML Table on a Web Page

Typically, you will want to display the query results set returned by a SELECT statement within a HTML table on a Web page. Think of the last time you visited your bank's Web site. You most likely reviewed your account balances and item detail for deposits made and checks presented for payment within a particular period. Similarly, when you visit a credit card's Web site, you can get the listing of charges and payments made on the account during a particular billing cycle. By visiting an online store's Web site, you can get a list of the items on your last order, when the order was shipped, and if shipped via UPS or Federal Express, a tracking number. Using the tracking number, you can then get a detailed list of dates and times your shipment reached various points within the UPS or Federal Express delivery system. In all these cases, the results sets returned by your queries were most likely displayed within HTML tables on the Web pages you viewed.

Rather than write a different routine to display the results set from each query you submit, you can write a single, reusable function or subroutine to display a query results set within an HTML table. As you will see in a moment, you can write a script that displays query results without knowing the names of the columns or the number of columns returned within the query results set beforehand.

The ADO Recordset object's Fields collection has a Count property you can use to determine the number of fields (that is, columns) returned within a results set. To retrieve the number of fields (columns) returned within a results set, you would use a statement similar to:

```
columnCount = objResultsSet.Fields.Count
```

Each field, in turn, has a Value and Name property you can use to extract the field's name and value (respectively) from the Fields collection. Thus, to retrieve a field's name, you might use a statement such as:

```
columnName = objResultsSet.Fields(0).Name
```

When working with the items within the Fields collection, bear in mind that the first item has an index of 0 and not 1. Thus, the preceding example returns the name of the first column (which has an index of 0) within the Fields collection.

Meanwhile, to retrieve a field's value, you would use:

```
columnName = objResultsSet.Fields(0)
```

Note that you need not explicitly reference the Value property when you want to retrieve the value stored in an item within an ADO collection. If you omit the property name when referring to an item within a collection, the default property Value is assumed. In general, the fewer periods you use when referencing objects and collections items, the better the script's performance. Thus, of the following two statements, the second will execute more quickly than the first because it uses the collection item's default property versus referencing the property explicitly:

```
columnValue = objResultsSet.Fields(0)
columnValue = objResultsSet.Fields(0).Value
```

Putting it all together then, you could use the following VBScript subroutine to display the results set from any query as an HTML table on a Web page:

```
Sub display_In_Table (objResultsSet)
  With Response
    .Write "<center><table border='1' cellpadding='5'>"
    .Write "<tr>"
    For column = 0 To objResultsSet.Fields.Count - 1
      .Write "<th>" & objResultsSet.Fields(column).Name _
      & "</th>"
    Next
    .Write "<tr>"

    Do While Not objResultsSet.EOF
      .Write "<tr>"

      For column = 0 To objResultsSet.Fields.Count - 1
        If objResultsSet.Fields(column) <> "" Then
          .Write "<td>" & objResultsSet.Fields(column) _
          & "</td>"
        Else
          .Write "<td> </td>"
        End If
      Next
      .Write "<tr>"

      objResultsSet.MoveNext
    Loop

    .write "</table>"
  End With
End Sub
```

In addition to the Fields collection properties discussed previously, the subroutine in this example uses the Recordset object's EOF property and its MoveNext method to move through the rows within the query results set. The MoveNext method moves the row pointer to the next row within the ADO Recordset object. When the row pointer is located beyond the last row within the Recordset object, the Recordset's EOF property (OBJRESULTSSET.EOF, in this example) is set to TRUE. (If there are no rows within the Recordset object, then the SELECT statement returned no rows that satisfied the search criteria in its WHERE clause, the row pointer is positioned beyond the "last" row within the Recordset object initially, and the Recordset object's EOF property is TRUE immediately.)

591 Writing a Reusable PHP Routine to Display Query Results on a Web Page

In Tip 590, "Displaying within an HTML Table on a Web Page Query Results Returned through an ADO Recordset Object," you learned how to work with the ADO Command object to send a query to the DBMS and display its results set within an HTML table. In place of ADO objects, some server-side script engines provide functions you can use to work with the data within various DBMS products. PHP, for example, provides functions you can use to access data stored within dBase, Informix, InterBase, MS-SQL Server, mSQL, MySQL, Oracle, PostgreSQL, Sybase, and more. (In addition to functions that work only with a specific vendor's DBMS product, PHP also provides a general set of ODBC functions that you can use to work with the data within any vendor's DBMS product.)

When using PHP (or other server-side script engines) to generate Web pages, create a set of modules that do the following:

- Writes the starting and ending blocks of text and tags for a Web page—such as STARTHTML.PHP and ENDHTML.PHP in the following example.
- Connects with a DBMS—such as MSSQLCONNECT.PHP in the following example.
- Sends queries to the DBMS—such as MSSQLQUERY.PHP in the following example.
- Displays query results within an HTML table—such as SHOWTABLE.PHP in the following example.

The following code shows how you might define a PHP Web page with a script that calls on reusable modules to displays SQL query results on a Web page:

```
<?php
 include ('incFiles/StartHtml.php');
 include ('incFiles/EndHTML.php');
 include ('incFiles/MSSQLConnect.php');
 include ('incFiles/MSSQLQuery.php');
 include ('incFiles/ShowTable.php');

//** database constants **

 $db_host = "NVBizNet2";
 $db_user = "Konrad";
 $db_pass = "King";
 $db_name = "Pubs";

//** global variables **
 $link = null;  //handle/channel opened to MS-SQL Server
 $result = null;
```

```
//** WRITE THE TEXT AND TAGS THAT START A WEB PAGE **

 startHTML ("Display Query Results",
   "Authors Table Data from the Pubs Database");

//** CALL THE ROUTINE TO CONNECT WITH THE DBMS **
 if (connectToDB($db_host, $db_user, $db_pass, $db_name))
   {
//** FORMULATE THE QUERY THEN PASS IT TO THE ROUTINE **
//** THAT WILL SEND IT TO THE DBMS AND DISPLAY THE   **
//** QUERY RESULTS WITHIN AN HTML TABLE

    $query = "SELECT * FROM Authors ".
             "ORDERED BY au_fname, au_lname";
    showTable($query);
   }

//** WRITE THE TEXT AND TAGS THAT END A WEB PAGE **
 endHTML();
?>
```

Each of the PHP INCLUDE directives (used in each of the first six lines within this example), tell the PHP script engine to insert the contents from an external file. Placing script modules within external files is convenient when you want to reuse the same code on several Web pages. Moreover, by leaving the code in an external file versus cutting and pasting it into other Web pages, you can change content on several Web pages at once by changing a single file—the external file whose script (code) you INCLUDE within the other pages.

Suppose, for example, that you have the following code within the file **STARTHTML.PHP**:

```
<?PHP
 function startHTML($title, $heading = "")
{
 echo '<html><head>';
 echo "   <title>$title</title>";
 echo '</head>
        <body  bgcolor="LightYellow">
        <h1><center>SQL Tips & Techniques</center></h1>
        <hr>';
 if ($heading <> "")
   echo "<h2><center>$heading</center></h2>";
 return;
}
?>
```

Within the file, you can include content that you want the script to place at the start of each of the site's Web pages. Although in this example, the STARTHTML() function only inserts title and heading text, it could easily be written to echo an HTML image tag (<img>) to insert a company logo at the top of each Web page as well.

Similarly, to write the text content and HTML tags for elements found at the end of each Web page on the Web site, you might use the following code for the ENDHTML() subroutine stored within the external file ENDHTML.PHP:

```
<?PHP
 function endHTML()
 {
  echo '<hr>
        Created by <a href="mailto:kki@NVBizNet.com">
        Konrad King</a>.<br>
        &copy; 2002 - all rights reserved!';
  echo "</body></html>";
  return;
 }
?>
```

In this example, each Web page that calls ENDHTML() will end by displaying the Web master's name and a copyright notice. To make your Web site more user-friendly, you might also include a site map or menu with hyperlinks to all the site's pages at the bottom of each page. By echoing the text content and hyperlinks within a file such as ENDHTML.PHP, you need only type the text, hyperlinks, and HTML tags for the elements you want to appear at the bottom of all the site's pages only one time. Simply code them within the function within a file like ENDHTML.PHP, and then call the function that writes the element on the Web page within the file.

The CONNECTTODB function within the file MSSQLCONNECT.PHP file accepts the name of the MS-SQL Server ($DB_HOST) and uses it and the username ($DB_USER) and password ($DB_PASS) to log in to the DBMS. After successfully logging in, the script sets the initial database to that specified in $DB_NAME:

```
<?PHP
  function connectToDB($db_host, $db_user, $db_pass,
                       $db_name)
  {
   global $link;

   $success = true;

//If not already connected, connect to the MS-SQL Server
   if (!$link = mssql_connect($db_host, $db_user,
                              $db_pass))
    {
     $success = false;
     echo "<font color='red'><br><br><hr>".
          "<center><b>** Error ** Unable to connect ".
          "to DMBS: $db_host!</b></center>".
          "<hr><br>\n</font>";
    }
   else
    {
```

```
//Select the database with the data you want to query
     if (!mssql_select_db($db_name, $link))
      {
       $success = false;
       echo "<font color='red'><br><br><hr>".
             "<center><b>** Error ** Unable to select ".
             "the database: $db_name!</b></center>".
             "<hr><br>\n</font>";
      }
    }
  return $success;
 }
?>
```

Note that the function CONNECTTODB places the connection handle (through which the script can send statements to and receive results sets from the DBMS) within the global variable $LINK. If unable to connect with the DBMS or to select the initial database specified, the function displays an error message on the Web page and returns FALSE. The following code within the script on the main Web page (which starts with the INCLUDE statements that insert the code from the external files as discussed within this tip), calls the routine to query the DBMS and display query results only if CONNECTTODB was able to connect with the DBMS:

```
//** CALL THE ROUTINE TO CONNECT WITH THE DBMS **
 if (connectToDB($db_host, $db_user, $db_pass, $db_name))
   {
//** FORMULATE THE QUERY THEN PASS IT TO THE ROUTINE **
//** THAT WILL SEND IT TO THE DBMS AND DISPLAY THE   **
//** QUERY RESULTS WITHIN AN HTML TABLE

    $query = "SELECT * FROM Authors ".
             "ORDERED BY au_fname, au_lname";
    showTable($query);
   }

//** WRITE THE TEXT AND TAGS THAT END A WEB PAGE **
 endHTML();
?>
```

If not able to connect, the script simply writes the content and HTML tags that must appear at the bottom of each Web page. This is done without calling the SHOWTABLE() function, which submits a query to the DBMS and then displays the query's results set on the page. As a result, the page will either display an HTML table of query results (if the script successfully connects with the DBMS and selects the database that contains the data desired), or an error message (if the DBMS connection or database selection fails).

The external file SHOWQUERY.PHP contains the script statements that call the EXECUTE-QUERY function (which submits the SELECT statement within $QUERY to the DBMS) and displays the query results set within an HTML table:

```
<?
  function showTable($query)
  {
   global $link, $result;

//Submit SQL Query to the MS-SQL Server

   executeQuery($query);

//determine the number of fields within in the results set

   $fields = mssql_num_fields($result);

//display the query results set in an HTML table

   echo "<center><table border='1' cellpadding='5'>";

//display column names as table headings

   echo "<tr>";
     for ($i=0; $i < $fields; $i++)
       {
        echo "<th>" .
          mssql_field_name($result, $i) . "</th>";
        $fieldType[$i] = mssql_field_type($result, $i);
       }
   echo "</tr>";

//display query results (that is, the column) values
//within the table's rows below the headings (column names)
//that run across the top of the HTML table

   while ($array = mssql_fetch_array($result))
    {
     echo "<tr>";
     for ($i=0; $i < $fields; $i++)
       {
        if (($fieldType[$i] <> "char") and
            ($fieldType[$i] <> "blob"))
          echo '<td align="right">';
        else
          echo '<td align="left">';

        if ($array[$i] <> null)
          echo "$array[$i]</td>";
        else
          echo " </td>";
       }
     echo "</tr>";
```

```
    }

   echo "</table></center>";
   return;
  }
?>
```

Note that the script checks the data type of each field and aligns non-character data flush with the right side of each table cell. The script aligns character data flush with a cell's left side.

Of course, there will only be results set data for the script to display within the HTML table only if the EXECUTEQUERY() function successfully submits its query to the DBMS for execution. As shown by the following code from the external file MSSQLQUERY.PHP, EXECUTEQUERY() will either return the rows within the query's results set or display an error message if the DBMS was unable to execute the query for some reason:

```
<?
  function executeQuery($query)
  {
   global $link;
   global $result;

//Submit SQL Query to the MySQL DBMS
   if (!$result = mssql_query($query, $link))
    {
     echo "<font color='red'><br><br><hr>".
          "<center><b>** Error ** The DBMS reported ".
          "an error in executing query!</b></center>".
          "<hr><br>\n</font>";
    }
   return;
  }
?>
```

Note that, as is the case throughout the script's statements (both within the main Web page and within external files), the EXECUTEQUERY function communicates with the DBMS through the $LINK connection handle. ($LINK was initially set by the MSSQL_CONNECT() function call within the external file MSSQLCONNECT.PHP.)

The EXECUTEQUERY() function returns the query results set to the script that called it by placing the query results within the global variable $RESULT. Even if the results set contains no rows because no data matched the search criteria within the query's WHERE clause, $RESULT will still contain the column names. Therefore, $RESULT is NULL (and !$RESULT is TRUE) only when the DBMS experiences an error of some kind when executing a query.

You can find the script files used within this tip on the book's companion Web site at www.premierpressbooks.com/downloads.asp. If you are using a DBMS other than MS-SQL Server, simply change the "MSSQL_" references within the files to the string that starts the function calls for your DBMS product. For example, if you are using the MySQL DBMS, your function calls will start "MySQL_" versus "MSSQL_". Similarly, Oracle functions start "Ora_," Sybase functions start "Sybase_," and so on. The PHP manual available online at http://www.PHP.net/manual/en/ lists and fully describes each of the function calls to access the various DBMS products PHP supports.

592 Submitting an SQL Query Through an HTML Form

Using HTML forms to submit SQL queries requires only that you apply what you learned about SELECT statements within the tips throughout this book and about using scripts to connect to and communicate with an SQL DBMS. As you learned in Tip 589 "Using an ADO Connection to Execute a SELECT Statement to Setup Username/Password Access to a Web Site," you use an HTML form to accept input from a site visitor. After the visitor clicks the HTML form's submit button, the Web browser sends the selections and entries the visitor made within the form's elements to the Web address (that is, to the URL) given by the *action* attribute within the HTML form's <form> tag.

When a form's *action* attribute specifies the URL (or Web address) of a PHP or ASP Web page, the scripts embedded within the page can retrieve the entries that the visitor made on the HTML form by name. Suppose, for example, that you create a "query" page such as the one shown in Figure 592.1, which has the following form definition:

```
<form action="http://www.NVBizNet2.com/SQLTips/Query.php"
      method="POST">
  SELECT: <input type="text" name="selectClause"
          size="40"><br>
  FROM: <input type="text" name="fromClause" size="40"><br>
  WHERE: <input type="text" name="whereClause"
         size="40"><br>
  ORDER BY: <input type="text" name="orderBy"
            size="40"><br><br>
  <input type="submit" value="Submit Query">
</form>
```

In this example, the PHP processor copies data that the visitor entered into the form's elements into variables that scripts within the PHP Web page QUERY.PHP can access. The name of each variable with data from a form element consists of the element's name preceded by a dollar sign ($). As such, scripts within QUERY.PHP can retrieve text entered into the form's selectClause element from the variable $selectClause, text entered into the fromClause element from the variable $fromClause, text entered into the whereClause element from the variable $whereClause, and text entered into the orderBy element from the variable $orderBy.

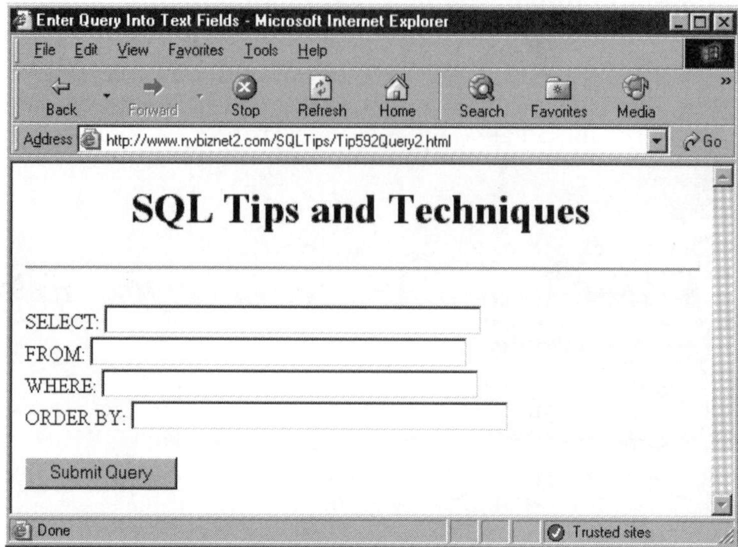

Figure 592.1 A Web page with an HTML form through which a site visitor can submit an SQL Query

To submit to the DBMS the SQL query the visitor defined with his or her entries into the four fields within the HTML form, you might define the PHP Web page QUERY.PHP as follows:

```
<?PHP
 include ('incFiles/MSSQLConnect.php');
 include ('incFiles/MSSQLQuery.php');
 include ('incFiles/StartHtml.php');
 include ('incFiles/EndHTML.php');
 include ('incFiles/ShowTable.php');

//** database connection constants **

 $db_host = "NVBizNet2";
 $db_user = "konrad";
 $db_pass = "king";
 $db_name = "pubs";

//** global variabls **

 $link = null; //handle/channel opened to the DBMS
 $result = null;

//*************************************************
//** Put the form data into an HTML table display   **
//** as a heading before the table of query results **
//*************************************************

 $headingQuery =
```

```
  "<table border='0'>" .
    "<tr><td><b>SELECT</b> " . $selectClause . "</td></tr>"
    "<tr><td><b>FROM</b> " . $fromClause . "</td></tr>";
 IF (trim($whereClause) <> "")
   $headingQuery .=
     "<tr><td><b>WHERE</b> " . $whereClause . "</td></tr>";
 If (trim($orderBy) <> "")
   $headingQuery .=
     "<tr><td><b>ORDER BY</b> " . $orderBy . "</td></tr>";

 $headingQuery = str_replace("\\", "", $headingQuery);

//********************************
//** Display the Web Page Title **
//********************************

 startHTML ("Display Query Results", $headingQuery);

//*****************************************************
//** Connect to the DBMS, and call showTable, which   **
//** submits the query and displays the query results **
//*****************************************************

 if (connectToDB($db_host, $db_user, $db_pass, $db_name))
   {
    $query = "SELECT " . $selectClause . " " .
             "FROM " . $fromClause;
    IF (trim($whereClause) <> "")
      $query .= " WHERE " . $whereClause;
    If (trim($orderBy) <> "")
      $query .= " ORDER BY " . $orderBy;

    $query = str_replace("\\", "", $query);
    showTable($query);
   }
 endHTML();
?>
```

Similarly, if the form's *action* attribute specifies the URL of an ASP Web page, such as http://www.NVBizNet2.com/SQLTips/Query.ASP for example, you might use the following VBScript to formulate and submit a query based on the visitor's entries into an HTML form:

```
<%
 Dim connObj, objResultsSet, queryString

'open the connection to the DBMS

 Set connObj = server.createobject ("adodb.connection")
 open_OLEDB_connection (connObj)
```

```
queryString = "SELECT " & Request.Form("selectClause") & _
              "FROM   " & Request.Form("fromClause")
If Trim(Request.Form("whereClause")) <> "" Then
  queryString = _
    queryString & " WHERE " & Request.Form("whereClause")
End If

If Trim(Request.Form("orderBy")) <> "" Then
  queryString = _
    queryString & " ORDER BY " & Request.Form("orderBy")
End If

'submit the SELECT statement (the query) to the DBMS

Set objResultsSet = connObj.Execute (queryString)

'call the routine that displays the query results set
'within an HTML table on the Web page
display_In_Table (objResultsSet)
%>
```

Code used but not repeated here is that within the subroutines open_OLEDB_connection() (shown previously within Tip 588 "Establishing a DSN-Less Connection with the MS-SQL Server or MySQL DBMS") and display_In_Table() (shown previously within Tip 590 "Displaying within an HTML Table on a Web Page Query Results Returned through an ADO Recordset Object").

Note that VBScript lets you retrieve entries made into HTML form elements by using the Request object's Form collection. The Form collection is an array (within the Request object) into which the ASP script host copies the selections and entries the visitor made on the HTML form and whose data the Web browser sent to the ASP Web page for processing. As shown in this example, your scripts can extract the value entered into each form element by referring to the item that has the same name within the Form collection.

The Web page shown previously in Figure 592.1 has the minimum content you want to display when letting the site visitor submit an SQL query to the DBMS. However, simply displaying a form into which a Web site visitor enters the clauses within a SELECT statement is not at all user-friendly. To make use of the query form, the visitor must know not only the names of the tables within the database, but also the names of the table columns as well. In addition, the visitor must know the correct syntax for each clause within an SQL SELECT statement.

The query forms you create for your users (typically managers accessing the DBMS through the company's intranet) to use should look more like that shown in Figure 592.2.

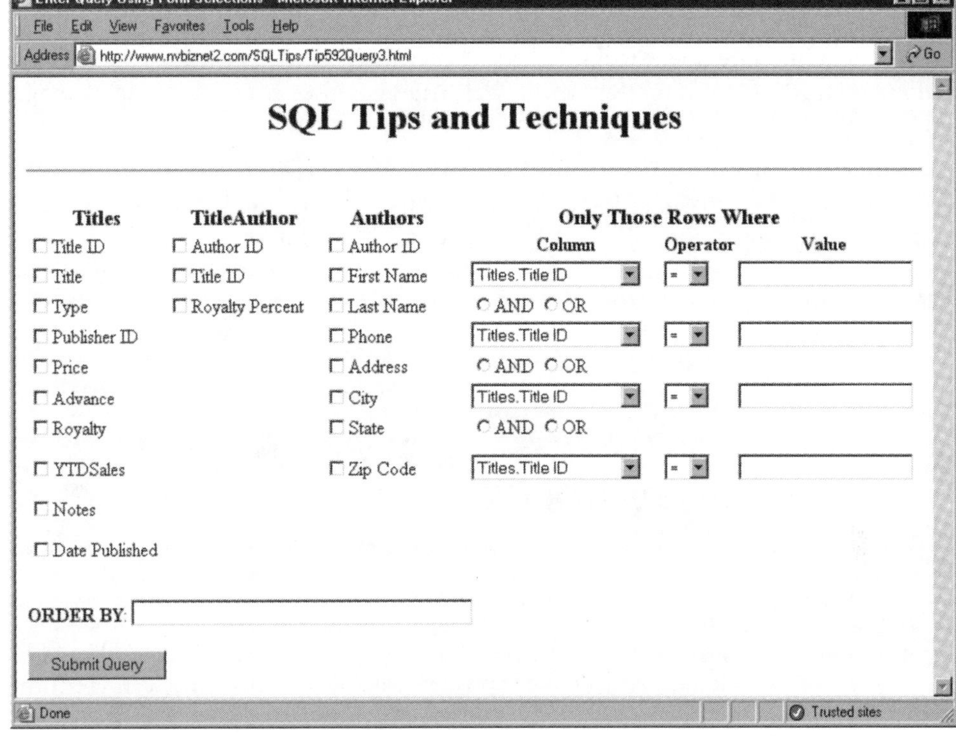

Figure 592.2 A Web page with an HTML form on which the visitor can make selections and some data entry to formulate and submit an SQL query

The Web page shown in Figure 592.2 is much more user-friendly. The visitor no longer has to know the names and structures of the tables within the database to submit a query. Instead, the visitor simply clicks a checkmark into the check boxes next to the names of the columns whose values the DBMS is to report. Based on the columns selected, the script that formulates the query—inserting into the SELECT statements FROM clause the names of the tables whose columns appear within the query's SELECT clause. Radio buttons at the bottom of the form help the visitor specify the search criteria the DBMS is to use when selecting rows it will add to the query's results set.

Creating Web pages with HTML forms that let users submit queries to the DBMS often involves making a tradeoff between creating a user-friendly Web interface for DBMS and letting the users write queries that involve as many tables, columns, and search criteria as they want. For example, the HTML form in Figure 592.1, though not user-friendly, lets the user submit a query that involves any number of tables, columns, and search conditions. Conversely, the form on the Web page in Figure 592.2 requires less knowledge about the database structure and about writing SQL SELECT statements; however, the form in this example limits the user's choices to columns within three tables and at most four search criteria to be used in the SELECT statements WHERE clause.

The HTML forms you create will, of course, depend on the knowledge and query requirements of the users on your system. Don't be surprised when you find yourself writing one set of Web page interface pages for power users that must view data within the database from various perspectives and another set of Web page based queries for use by managers who need specific, predefined reports on a daily, weekly, or monthly basis.

The important thing to understand is that you can use HTML forms to let DBMS users (or Web site visitors) specify data for which they want to search the DBMS. Using a server-side scripting language such as VBScript, PHP, JScript, and so on, you can write SELECT statements based on the user's input into HTML form, submit the queries to the DBMS, and then display the query results sets for the users within HTML tables on Web pages.

593 Using an HTML Form to Insert Data into an SQL Table

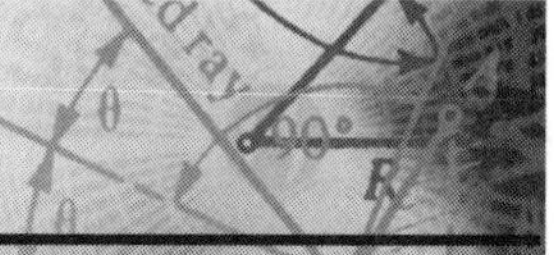

As you learned within the preceding tip, HTML forms let Web site (either Internet or intranet) visitors send data and commands to scripts embedded within ASP or PHP Web pages. In addition to letting visitors use forms to write SQL queries, you can use forms to let visitors insert, update, or remove data from a database. In fact, handling database updates through an HTML form involves the same communications process between visitor and script and between script and DBMS that you use to handle queries.

Within a PHP script, you process HTML form-based database updates by retrieving form data from variables with the same names as the form elements. Similarly, within VBScript you access form element values from the Request object's Form collection. Then, based on the information received from the HTML form, the script submits the desired INSERT, UPDATE, or DELETE statement to the DBMS for execution.

Suppose, for example, that you want salespeople to maintain information about their customers online. You might use a form similar to that shown within Figure 593.1 to add a new customer to the salesperson's list of customers.

To retrieve customer information entered into the HTML form and insert it into the CUSTOMERS table, set the *action* attribute within the HTML form's <form> tag to the URL of an ASP Web page as shown here:

```
<form
   action="http://www.NVBizNet2.com/SQLTips/AddCust.asp"
   method="POST">
```

Figure 593.1 HTML form used to insert and/or update customer data

Then, within the ASP Web page (ADDCUST.ASP, in this example), embed a VBScript such as the following:

```
<%
 Dim connObj, objResultsSet, statementString

'create a connection object and then call a subroutine
'to open a connection to the DBMS

 Set connObj = server.createobject ("adodb.connection")
 open_OLEDB_connection (connObj)

'Formulate the INSERT statement based on the visitor's
'inputs within the HTML form

 statementString = _
   "INSERT INTO customers " & _
   "(first_name, last_name, street_addr, city, state, " & _
   " zip_code, phone_number, salesrep_ID) VALUES (" & _
   "'"  & Request.Form("fName") & "'" & _
   ",'" & Request.Form("lName") & "'" & _
   ",'" & Request.Form("stAddress") & "'" & _
   ",'" & Request.Form("city") & "'" & _
```

```
    ",'" & Request.Form("state") & "'" & _
    ",'" & Request.Form("zipCode") & "'" & _
    ",'" & Request.Form("phoneNumber") & "'" & _
    "," & Request.Form("salesrepID") & ")"

'submit the INSERT statement to the DBMS for execution

 connObj.Execute statementString,,adExecuteNoRecords
%>
```

The VBScript in this example calls the open_OLEDB_connection() subroutine that you learned about in Tip 588 "Establishing a DSN-Less Connection with the MS-SQL Server or MySQL DBMS" to open a DSN-less connection with the DBMS. To build the SQL INSERT statement, the script uses the Request object's Form collection to retrieve information entered into the form (shown previously in Figure 593.1). Finally, to submit the INSERT statement to the DBMS for execution, the VBScript uses the ADO Connection object's Execute method.

Note that when using the Execute method to submit an INSERT, DELETE, or UPDATE statement, you don't expect the DBMS to return a results set. As such, you can avoid the overhead of creating a Recordset object by changing the syntax of the Execute method call to the following

```
<connection object>.EXECUTE <SQL statement>,ra,options
```

where:

- **<SQL statement>** is the SQL INSERT, DELETE or UPDATE statement the DBMS is to execute.
- **ra** is an optional parameter indicating the number of rows effected by the query.
- **options** specifies how the DBMS is to execute the SQL statement passed within the <SQL statement> parameter.

The execute method call in this example tells the DBMS to execute the SQL statement (within STATEMENTSTRING) without returning any records within a results set.

```
connObj.Execute statementString,,adExecuteNoRecords
```

Note: *For a list of enumerated values (such as adExecuteNoRecords) you can use to set options and properties within various ADO objects and methods (such as the Connect object's Execute method), visit http://www.w3schools.com/ado/ and click on one of the ADO objects listed along the left side of the Web page. After your Web browser displays the W3Schools information about the ADO object, click your mouse on the hyperlink for one of the object's properties or methods. If the method or property has enumerated values (that is, named constants) you can use to set its options or properties, you will find the enumerated values listed following the example code that shows how to use the property or method.*

For a complete list of all enumerated values for all ADO object properties and methods, visit the Microsoft Developer Network (MSDN) library at http://msdn.microsoft.com/library/. To reach the ADO enumerated type list, from the menu along the left side of the screen, make the following selections:

1. Click the plus (+) to the left of Data Access.
2. Within the Data Access menu, click the plus (+) to the left of Microsoft Data Access Components (MDAC).
3. Within the MDAC menu, click the plus (+) to the left of SDK Documentation.
4. Within the SDK Documentation menu, click the plus (+) to the left of Microsoft ActiveX Data Objects (ADO).
5. Within the ADO menu, click the plus (+) to the left of ADO Programmer's Reference.
6. Within the ADO Programmer's Reference menu, click the plus (+) to the left of ADO API Reference.
7. Within the ADO API Reference menu, click on ADO Enumerated Constants. Note: Click on the words "ADO Enumerated Constants" and not on the plus (+) to the left of the menu choice.

After you select "ADO Enumerated Constants," the MSDN site will display a page with hyperlinks to the constants you can use with ADO objects and methods along the right-hand side of the page. Because, getting to this point involves a lot of selections, be sure to add the page to your browser's list of bookmarks or favorites, so you can return to the page with a single mouse-click in the future.

594 Updating and Deleting Database Data Through an HTML Form

Before updating or deleting data within a database, you must first search for the rows with the columns whose data you want to change or the rows you want to remove. Then you execute an UPDATE or DELETE statement to change or remove data, respectively. Of course, you perform the search and update or search and delete within the same statement. The WHERE clause within an UPDATE or DELETE statement contains the search criteria the DBMS uses to identify target rows to remove or those with data to change. In an UPDATE statement, the SET clause specifies the column values to change.

A form such as the following provides the greatest flexibility for updating records within a table:

```
<form action="http://www.NVBizNet2.com/SQLTips/Update.asp"
      method="POST">
  UPDATE: <input type="text" name="tableName"
           size="40"><br>
  SET: <input type="text" name="setClause" size="40"><br>
  WHERE: <input type="text" name="whereClause"
          size="40"><br>
 <input type="submit" value="Update Record">
</form>
```

To process the update form, you would embed a VBScript such as the following within the ASP Web page (UPDATE.ASP, in this example):

```
<%
 Dim connObj, objResultsSet, statementString

'create a connection object and then call a subroutine
'to open a connection to the DBMS

 Set connObj = server.createobject ("adodb.connection")
 open_OLEDB_connection (connObj)

'Formulate the UPDATE statement based on the visitor's
'inputs within the HTML form

 statementString = _
   "UPDATE " &  Request.Form("tableName") & _
   " SET " & Request.Form("setClause") & _
   " WHERE " & Request.Form("whereClause")

'submit the UPDATE statement to the DBMS for execution

 connObj.Execute statementString,,adExecuteNoRecords
%>
```

Similarly, you can use the following form to delete rows from a table:

```
<form action="http://www.NVBizNet2.com/SQLTips/Delete.asp"
      method="POST">
  DELETE: <input type="text" name="tableName"
           size="40"><br>
  WHERE: <input type="text" name="whereClause"
          size="40"><br>
 <input type="submit" value="Delete Record">
</form>
```

To process the delete form, you would embed a VBScript such as the following within the ASP Web page (DELETE.ASP, in this example):

```
<%
 Dim connObj, objResultsSet, statementString

'create a connection object and then call a subroutine
'to open a connection to the DBMS

 Set connObj = server.createobject ("adodb.connection")
 open_OLEDB_connection (connObj)

'Formulate the DELETE statement based on the visitor's
'inputs within the HTML form

 statementString = _
   "DELETE FROM " &  Request.Form("tableName") & _
   " WHERE " & Request.Form("whereClause")

'submit the DELETE statement to the DBMS for execution

 connObj.Execute statementString,,adExecuteNoRecords
%>
```

Although the forms within the preceding examples within this tip make it easy to update or delete rows in DBMS tables, the user must know how to write SQL DELETE and UPDATE statements to use them. In addition, if the user enters the wrong criteria into the whereClause element in either form, he or she may inadvertently UPDATE or DELETE the wrong, too many, or all rows within a table. As such, you should setup delete and update access such that it occurs after the user executes a query that displays the target rows. Then, let the user select onscreen which rows to UPDATE or DELETE.

For example, to setup DELETE access on the CUSTOMERS table through an HTML form, you could use a query form such as the following to let the user display a list of customers that he or she might delete:

```
<form
  action="http://www.NVBizNet2.com/SQLTips/DelCustSel.asp
  method="POST">

  SELECT: cust_ID, <input type="text" name="selectClause"
                    size="40"><br>
  FROM: <input type="text" name="fromClause" size="40"
         value=customers593><br>
  WHERE: <input type="text" name="whereClause"
          size="40"><br>
  ORDER BY: <input type="text" name="orderBy"
             size="40"><br><br>
  <input type="submit" value="Submit Query">
</form>
```

Note that the form in this example forces the user to include the CUST_ID column within the list of columns he or she decides to display within the query's SELECT clause. For the CUSTOMERS table in this example, the CUST_ID column is the PRIMARY KEY. To delete customers marked for deletion on the form described next, the query results must include a column that the VBScript that deletes rows from the CUSTOMERS table can use to identify those rows within the CUSTOMERS table that the user marked for deletion.

When the user clicks the Submit button (labeled "Submit Query") in this example, the following subroutine embedded within the ASP Web page DELCUSTSEL.ASP, will present the list of customers matching the user's search criteria as shown in Figure 594.1:

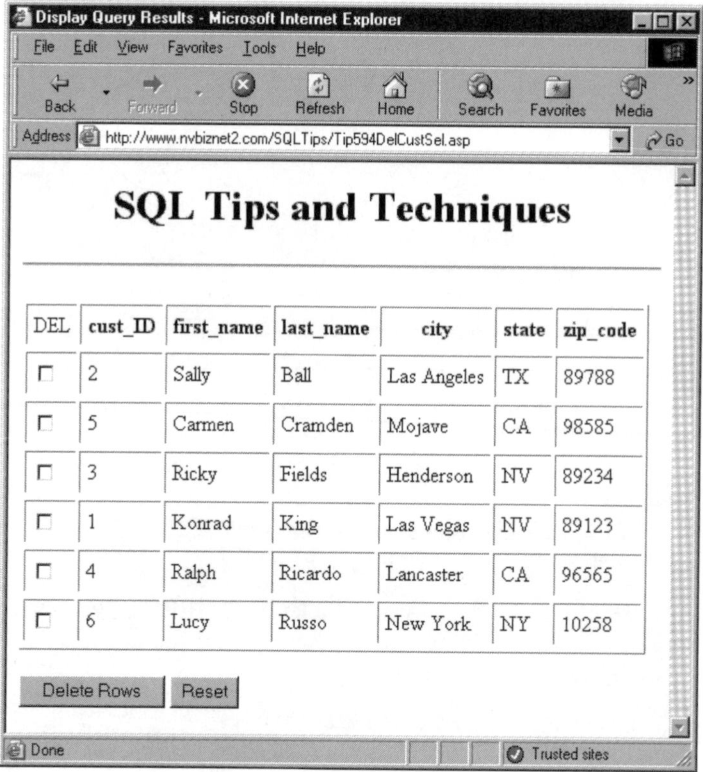

DEL	cust_ID	first_name	last_name	city	state	zip_code
☐	2	Sally	Ball	Las Angeles	TX	89788
☐	5	Carmen	Cramden	Mojave	CA	98585
☐	3	Ricky	Fields	Henderson	NV	89234
☐	1	Konrad	King	Las Vegas	NV	89123
☐	4	Ralph	Ricardo	Lancaster	CA	96565
☐	6	Lucy	Russo	New York	NY	10258

Figure 594.1 An HTML form that has a check box which displays the CUSTOMERS query results set and has a check box the user can use to mark customers for deletion

```
Sub display_In_Table (objResultsSet)
  With Response
    .Write "<form action=" & _
   "'http://www.NVBizNet2.com/SQLTips/DelCustRows.asp'" & _
          "method='POST'>"

    .Write "<table border='1' cellpadding='5'>"
    .Write "<tr>"
    .Write "<td>DEL</td>"
```

```
    For column = 0 To objResultsSet.Fields.Count - 1
      .Write "<th>" & objResultsSet.Fields(column).Name _
      & "</th>"
    Next
    .Write "<tr>"

    DIM row_number
    row_number = 0
    Do While Not objResultsSet.EOF
      .Write "<tr>"
      row_number = row_number + 1

'place a check box within the first column of each row

      .Write "<td><input type='checkbox' name='row" & _
             row_number & "' Value='" & _
             objResultsSet.Fields("cust_ID") & "'></td>"

'Display column values from the SQL table

      For column = 0 To objResultsSet.Fields.Count - 1
        If objResultsSet.Fields(column) <> "" Then
          .Write "<td>" & objResultsSet.Fields(column) _
          & "</td>"
        Else
          .Write "<td> </td>"
        End If
      Next
      .Write "<tr>"

      objResultsSet.MoveNext
    Loop

    .write "</table><br>"
    .Write "<input type='submit' value='Delete Rows'> " & _
           "<input type='reset' value='Reset'>"
    .Write "</form>"
  End With
End Sub
```

Note that the display_In_Table() subroutine shown in this example, displays the query results within an HTML table that is itself within an HTML form. The first cell of each row within the table contains a check box in which the user can click to mark a row in the CUSTOMERS table for deletion.

When the user clicks the Submit button (labeled "Delete Rows") within this form, the Web browser sends the check box selections the user made to the script on the ASP Web page DELCUSTROWS.ASP. DELCUSTROWS.ASP, then uses the following script that removes from the CUSTOMERS table the rows selected by the check boxes in the form shown previously in Figure 594.1:

```
<%
 Dim connObj, statementString, i

'open the connection to the DBMS

 Set connObj = server.createobject ("adodb.connection")
 open_OLEDB_connection (connObj)

'setup each DELETE statement to submit to the DBMS

 For i = 1 To Request.Form.Count
   statementString = "DELETE FROM CUSTOMERS593 " & _
                     " WHERE cust_ID=" & Request.Form(i)

'submit the DELETE statement to the DBMS

   connObj.Execute statementString,,adExecuteNoRecords
 Next

'return to the original CUSTOMERS search page

 Response.Redirect "DeleteCust.HTML"
%>
```

595 Calling Stored Procedures from Within a Script

Whenever possible, you should use stored procedures to execute SQL statements on behalf of the scripts embedded within your Web pages. Using stored procedures leads to enhanced DBMS performance and faster statement execution.

When executing an SQL statement submitted through an ADO Connect or Command object's Execute method, the DBMS must first generate an execution plan. Conversely, when a script calls a stored procedure, the DBMS can begin executing the stored procedure's statements immediately. Because the DBMS creates the stored procedure's execution plan when it executes the CREATE PROCEDURE statement, the DBMS avoids having to generate the same execution plan multiple times for the batch of statements within the stored procedure. Not having to generate execution plans reduces the processing load on the DBMS. Moreover, the DBMS is able to finish executing the statements faster, because it does not have to take time to create execution plans for the stored procedures statements in real-time, in addition to executing them.

In addition, using stored procedures lets you ensure all steps within an insert, update, or delete process are completed. Suppose, for example, that you have a VBScript that customers can call (through a hyperlink on a Web page) to cancel an order. In addition to deleting the order from the ORDERS table, the script must also remove the ORDERDETAILS rows for the order (so as not to leave orphans within the ORDERDTAILS table), update the COMMISSIONS table, so the salesperson does not get paid commission on the cancelled order, and must add items back into the INVENTORY table. Rather than code these statements separately into a script, it is much easier (and more reliable) to have the script call a stored procedure that executes all the required statements without inadvertently forgetting one or more or the steps. (True, a script will always execute all the statements coded within it. However, a programmer updating the Web page later may omit a line of code by accident, or there may be a communications failure of some kind between the script process and the DBMS while sending multiple statements across the network or the Internet.)

To call a stored procedure from within a script, simply pass to the ADO Connect object's Execute method the name of the stored procedure you want to call in place of an SQL statement. Suppose, for example, that a customer uses an HTML form on a Web page to cancel an order. Without a stored procedure, a script must call the Connection (or Command) object's Execute method four times to update the ORDERS, ORDERDETAILS, COMMISSIONS, and INVENTORY tables to reflect the order cancellation. By relying on a stored procedure that updates the four tables, the script need only call the Execute method once, as shown here:

```
<%
 Dim connObj, statementString

'Formulate the statement that calls the stored procedure

 statementString = "usp_cancel_order " & _
   "@order_number='" & Request.Form("order_number") & "'"

'open the connection to the DBMS and execute the stored
'procedure call

 Set connObj = server.createobject ("adodb.connection")
 open_OLEDB_connection (connObj)

 connObj.Execute statementString,,adExecuteNoRecords
%>
```

Note that a script can pass parameters values to the stored procedure as necessary. In this example, the script uses the Form collection within the Request object to retrieve the order number that the customer entered (or selected) within the HTML form on the Web page. The script then creates a statement string that passes the order number to the stored procedure through the @ORDER_NUMBER parameter.

Although the stored procedure within the preceding example returned no query results, your scripts can call stored procedures that execute queries and return results sets as well. Rather than execute the stored procedure call with the adExecuteNoRecords options setting, simply create a Recordset object in which the DBMS can place the query results the stored procedure returns, as shown here:

```
<%
 Dim connObj, objResultsSet, statementString

'Formulate the statement that calls the stored procedure

 statementString = "sales_by_year " & _
   " @beginning_date='" & Request.form("start_date") & _
   "', @ending_date='"  & Request.form("end_date")   & "'"

'open the connection to the DBMS

 Set connObj = server.createobject ("adodb.connection")
 open_OLEDB_connection (connObj)

'call the stored procedure that executes the query

 Set objResultsSet = connObj.Execute (statementString)

'display the query results returned by the stored procedure
'within an HTML table

 display_In_Table (objResultsSet)
%>
```

596 Using VBScript to Process a Recordset

In Tip 594 "Updating and Deleting Database Data Through an HTML Form," you learned how to create HTML forms that let users generate and execute SQL UPDATE and DELETE statements. You also learned that the best way to let most users remove table rows or change data within a database is to require that they first execute a query that displays potential target rows onscreen. Then, with data displayed within an HTML form, the user can select the rows to change or delete visually, which is much easier and less prone to error than writing selection criteria for the WHERE clause within an SQL UPDATE or DELETE statement.

Whereas users may, at times, want to delete several table rows at once, modifying column values within a table is typically a one-row-at-a-time operation. As such, you might replace the check box you placed at the start of each row of query results in Tip 594 with a hyperlink that retrieves the column values from a particular row in an database table. By placing the row's column values within the elements of an HTML form, you can let the user modify each value within the row as desired. When finished modifying the row's values, the user clicks the HTML form's Submit button to send the form results (that is, the update row values) to a server-side script that submits an UPDATE statement to the DBMS for execution.

Suppose, for example, that you wanted to create a Web-based application that lets users update the data within a CUSTOMERS table. First, create a Web page with a form such as the following that lets the user select the row (or rows) within the CUSTOMERS table that he or she might want to change:

```
<form
 action="http://www.NVBizNet2.com/SQLTips/CustList.asp"
 method="POST">

  SELECT: cust_ID, <input type="text" name="selectClause"
                   size="40"><br>
  FROM: <input type="text" name="fromClause" size="40"
         value=customers593><br>
  WHERE: <input type="text" name="whereClause"
          size="40"><br>
  ORDER BY: <input type="text" name="orderBy"
             size="40"><br><br>

  <input type="submit" value="Submit Query">
</form>
```

After the user clicks the form's Submit button (labeled "Submit Query," in this example), the Web browser sends the form results (that is, the information entered into the form) to an ASP (or PHP) Web page (CUSTLIST.ASP, in this example). Embedded within CUSTLIST.ASP is a script, such as the following, which creates an SQL SELECT statement based on the form results and submits the query to the DBMS:

```
<%
 Sub SubmitQuery(objConn, byref objRecordset)
   DIM queryString

   If (Trim(Request.Form("selectClause")) = "*") Then
     queryString = "SELECT * "
   else
     queryString = "SELECT cust_ID "

     If (Trim(Request.form("selectClause")) <> "") Then
       queryString = queryString & ", " &
                         Trim(Request.form("selectClause"))
     End If
   End If

   queryString = _
     queryString & " FROM    " & Request.Form("fromClause")

   If Trim(Request.Form("whereClause")) <> "" Then
     queryString = queryString & " WHERE " & _
```

```
                        Request.Form("whereClause")
   End If

   If Trim(Request.Form("orderBy")) <> "" Then
     queryString =
       queryString & " ORDER BY " & Request.Form("orderBy")
   End If

'submit the query, the SELECT statement to the DBMS

   Set objRecordset = objConn.Execute (queryString)
 End Sub
%>
```

Note that the script must include within the query's SELECT clause the PRIMARY KEY column from the target table (CUST_ID, in this example). During the update process, other scripts will use the PRIMARY KEY value to retrieve and then modify the values in a specific row within the target table (CUSTOMERS, in this example). After submitting the query, another script within the CUSTLIST.ASP Web page must process the query results returned from the DBMS. DisplayInTable() is a VBScript subroutine that processes the rows of query results returned within an ADO Recordset object to display the customer list, as shown in Figure 596.1:

```
<%
 Sub DisplayInTable(objRecordset)
   With Response
    .Write "<table border='1' cellpadding='5'>"
    .Write "<tr>"

'use Recordset field names as HTML table column headings

    .Write "<th>EDIT</th>"
    For column = 0 To objRecordset.Fields.Count - 1
      .Write "<th>" & objRecordset.Fields(column).Name _
      & "</th>"
    Next
    .Write "<tr>"

'display the value in the Recordset within the HTML table

    Do While Not objRecordset.EOF
      .Write "<tr>"

'Put an "EDIT" hyperlink in the First column of each row

      .Write "<td><a href='EditCust.asp?cust_ID=" & _
         objRecordset.Fields("cust_ID") & "'>EDIT</a></td>"

      For column = 0 To objRecordset.Fields.Count - 1
```

```
        If objRecordset.Fields(column) <> "" Then
          .Write "<td>" & objRecordset.Fields(column) _
          & "</td>"
        Else
          .Write "<td> </td>"
        End If
      Next
      .Write "<tr>"

      objRecordset.MoveNext
    Loop

    .write "</table>"
  End With
 End Sub
%>
```

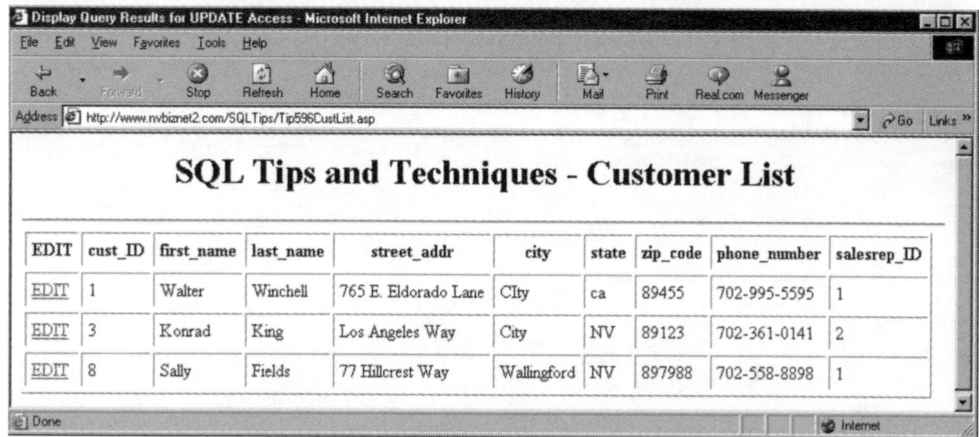

SQL Tips and Techniques - Customer List

EDIT	cust_ID	first_name	last_name	street_addr	city	state	zip_code	phone_number	salesrep_ID
EDIT	1	Walter	Winchell	765 E. Eldorado Lane	CIty	ca	89455	702-995-5595	1
EDIT	3	Konrad	King	Los Angeles Way	City	NV	89123	702-361-0141	2
EDIT	8	Sally	Fields	77 Hillcrest Way	Wallingford	NV	897988	702-558-8898	1

Figure 596.1 An HTML form that lets users click on the "Edit" hyperlink within the first column to select a row within the CUSTOMERS table to update

After the user clicks one of the "Edit" hyperlinks within the first column of the table shown in Figure 596.1, the Web browser retrieves the ASP Web page EDITCUST.ASP and passes to it a query string with the PRIMARY KEY value for the customer's row within the CUSTOMERS table. A VBScript embedded within EDITCUST.ASP uses the PRIMARY KEY value to retrieve the customer's row and calls the following DisplayInForm() subroutine to display the row's current column values within an HTML form:

```
<%
 Sub DisplayInForm(objRecordset)
  With Response
    .Write _
    "<form action=" & _
    "'http://www.NVBizNet2.com/SQLTips/UpdateCust.asp'" & _
    "method='POST'>"
```

```
    .Write "<table border='1' cellpadding='5'>"
    .Write "<tr>"

'use Recordset field names as HTML table column headings

    For column = 0 To objRecordset.Fields.Count - 1
      .Write "<th>" & objRecordset.Fields(column).Name _
      & "</th>"
    Next
    .Write "<tr>"

'display the value in the Recordset within the HTML table

    Do While Not objRecordset.EOF
      .Write "<tr>"

'Put an "EDIT" hyperlink into the first column of each row

      For column = 0 To objRecordset.Fields.Count - 1
        .Write "<td>" & _
          "<input type='text' " & _
          "name='" &
          objRecordset.Fields(column).Name & "'" & _
          "size='" &
          objRecordset.Fields(column).ActualSize & "'" & _
          "value='" & objRecordset.Fields(column) & _
          "'" & "</td>"
      Next
      .Write "<tr>"

      objRecordset.MoveNext
    Loop

    .write "</table>"
    .Write "<input name='primaryKey'
             type='hidden' value='" & _
             Request.Querystring("cust_ID") & "'>"
    .Write "<br><input type='submit' value='Save Changes'>"
    .Write " <input type='reset' value='Reset'>"
    .Write "</form>"
   End With
 End Sub
%>
```

When the user clicks the form's Submit button (labeled "Save Changes"), the Web browser sends the form results to VBScripts embedded within the ASP Web page UPDATECUST.ASP. The SubmitUpdate() subroutine embedded within UPDATECUST creates and submits to the

DBMS an UPDATE statement, which writes the new column values to the customer's row within the CUSTOMERS table:

```
<%
 Sub SubmitUpdate(objConn)
   DIM queryString, i, setCount

   setCount = 0
   queryString = "UPDATE customers593 SET "

   For i = 1 To Request.Form.count - 1
     If Request.Form.Key(i) <> "cust_ID" Then
       setCount = setCount + 1

       If setCount > 1 Then
         queryString = queryString & ","
       End If

       queryString = _
         queryString & Request.Form.key(i) & "='" & _
           Request.Form(i) & "'"
     End If
   Next

   queryString = queryString & "WHERE cust_ID =" &
                 Request.Form("cust_ID")

'submit the UPDATE statement to the DBMS

   Set objRecordset = objConn.Execute (queryString)
 End Sub
%>
```

597 Working with SQL Transaction Processing Across the Internet

SQL transaction processing lets you treat multiple SQL statements as a single unit of work. According to relational database processing rules, either the DBMS executes *all* statements within a transaction successfully or any work performed by any of the statements is undone. In other words, if a statement within a transaction fails, the DBMS will make the database data appear as if none of the statements in the transaction was executed.

If you have an open transaction and a script embedded within a Web page aborts or if the user closes his or her connection with the DBMS without executing a COMMIT statement, the DBMS is responsible for undoing any work performed and restoring database tables back to their original, unmodified condition. A user can close his or her connection with the DBMS either explicitly (by calling the ADO Connection object's Close method, for example) or implicitly (by moving on to another Web page or by disconnecting from the Internet altogether). In addition, a long period of inactivity will cause the DBMS to close an open connection—even if the user remains on the same Web page as the script used to open the connection to the DBMS.

The ADO Connection object has three methods you can use to manage SQL transactions:

- **BeginTrans** begins a new transaction. If your DBMS product allows nested transactions, you can make multiple BeginTrans method calls without first closing an open transaction by calling the CommitTrans or the RollbackTrans method. Conversely, if your DBMS does not support nested transaction, calling BeginTrans while a connection has an open transaction already will result in an error.
- **CommitTrans** makes permanent any work performed by statements since the last BeginTrans method call and ends (or closes) the current transaction. If your DBMS product supports nested transaction, each CommitTrans method call closes the innermost transaction. Thus, if the script has made three BeginTrans method calls (without any intervening RollbackTrans or CommitTrans calls), the first CommitTrans method call closes and makes permanent the work performed since the third BeginTrans method call. A second CommitTrans method call makes permanent any uncommitted work perform since the start of the second transaction (and prior to the start of the now closed third transaction). Finally, a third CommitTrans method call makes permanent any work performed since the start of the first transaction and prior to the start of the (now closed) second transaction.
- **RollbackTrans** cancels (or undoes) all changes made since the last BeginTrans method call and ends the current transaction. If your DBMS product supports nested transaction, each RollbackTrans method call closes the innermost transaction while leaving any outer transactions open and the work performed by statements within them in place.

Unless you make a BeginTrans method call to open a transaction, the DBMS automatically commits (that is, makes permanent) work performed by each statement you submit by calling a Connect or Command object's Execute method. Thus, if you have the following statement flow, no work is undone (or rolled back) by the RollbackTrans method call, because the statements were executed (and their work committed) outside an open transaction:

```
<%
  objConn.Execute "<SQL statement - MOD 1...>"
  objConn.Execute "<SQL statement - MOD 2...>"
  objConn.Execute "<SQL statement - MOD 3...>"

  objConn.RollbackTrans        'undoes nothing
%>
```

After calling the RollbackTrans method, three modifications remain in effect since their work was automatically committed by the DBMS.

Conversely, if you have the following statement flow, the DBMS does not automatically commit (make permanent) any work performed while a transaction remains open:

```
<%
  objConn.Execute "<SQL statement - MOD 1...>"

  objConn.BeginTrans
  objConn.Execute "<SQL statement - MOD 2...>"
  objConn.Execute "<SQL statement - MOD 3...>"

  objConn.RollbackTrans       'undoes MOD 2 & MOD 3
%>
```

The RollBackTrans method call undoes any work performed by MOD 2 and MOD 3 and closes the open transaction. Work performed by MOD 1 remains in place however, because the DBMS automatically committed the MOD 1 work, since it occurred outside an open transaction.

Similarly, if you have the following statement flow, the CommitTrans method call makes permanent the work performed by MOD 1, and the RollbackTrans method call will therefore only undo work performed by MOD 2 and MOD 3:

```
<%
  objConn.BeginTrans
  objConn.Execute "<SQL statement - MOD 1...>"

  objConn.CommitTrans         'makes permanent MOD 1

  objConn.BeginTrans
  objConn.Execute "<SQL statement - MOD 2...>"
  objConn.Execute "<SQL statement - MOD 3...>"

  objConn.RollbackTrans       'undoes MOD 2 & MOD 3
%>
```

Finally, when working with nested transactions, such as the following, a CommitTrans or RollbackTrans method call only effects the work performed within the current, innermost transaction:

```
<%
  objConn.BeginTrans
  objConn.Execute "<SQL statement - MOD 1...>"
  objConn.Execute "<SQL statement - MOD 2...>"

  objConn.BeginTrans
  objConn.Execute "<SQL statement - MOD 3...>"

  objConn.BeginTrans
  objConn.Execute "<SQL statement - MOD 4...>"

  objConn.RollbackTrans       'undoes MOD 4
```

```
  objConn.CommitTrans          'makes permanent MOD 3

  objConn.RollbackTrans        'undoes MOD 1 & MOD 2
%>
```

In this example, the first RollbackTrans method call undoes the work performed by MOD 4, and closes the inner-most (third-level) transaction. MOD 1, MOD 2, and MOD 3 remain in place until the first CommitTrans method call makes permanent the work performed by MOD 3 and closes the inner-most (second-level) transaction. Finally, the second RollbackTrans method call undoes the work performed by MOD 1 and MOD 2 and the closes the remaining open transaction.

598 Creating a Virtual Connection with the MS-SQL Server

If you use the MS-SQL Server DBMS, you are no doubt familiar with the SQL Query Analyzer, because the SQL Query Analyzer is the MS-SQL Server-supplied client application that lets you login to the DBMS and work with database objects. You can use the Query Analyzer to submit standard SQL statements and MS-SQL Server-specific, Transact-SQL commands and built-in system stored procedures.

Though a powerful and somewhat user-friendly interface for the MS-SQL Server DBMS, SQL Query Analyzer is still just an application program that happens to be able to communicate with an MS-SQL Server. By reading Tips within this book, you learned to write Visual Basic applications (Tips 390–425) and Visual C++ applications (Tips 372–389) that could submit SQL statements and Transact-SQL commands to the DBMS and retrieve data from it. In Tips 583–597 you learned now to use ODBC drivers, OLE DB providers, and ADO objects to let scripts embedded within ASP and PHP Web pages communicate with the MS-SQL Server DBMS as well.

Within this tip, you will learn how to create MS-SQL Server Virtual connections through the Internet Information Server (IIS). These virtual connections act as pipelines that let you communicate directly with the DBMS using hypertext transport protocol (HTTP). In other words, after you setup a Virtual Connection on the MS-SQL Server, you can type SQL statements and Transact-SQL commands into your Web browser's Address field and send those statements and commands directly to the MS-SQL Server—without going through a PHP engine or ASP script host. In addition to sending commands and statements to the DBMS, you can have the MS-SQL Server return query results sets as XML documents that your Web browser can display. In short, MS-SQL Server virtual connections let you manage and work with MS-SQL Server database objects using a Web browser (running on your PC or other Web-enabled device) or any other application able to send and receive HTTP messages.

To create virtual connections through the IIS Web server to an MS-SQL Server DBMS, perform the following steps:

1. Create a folder on the Web server computer's hard drive for each database to which you want HTTP access. Because the Web server must have read and write access to these folders, you may want to create them within the IIS server's root directory. For example, on an IIS Web server whose root folder is D:\InetPub\WWWRoot, you might create the folder for the virtual connection to the NORTHWIND database as D:\InetPub\WWWRoot\Nwind.
2. Within the folder you created in Step 1, create two subfolders: SCHEMA and TEMPLATE. For example, if you created the NWind folder as indicated in Step 1, you would create the SCHEMA and TEMPLATE folders as D:\InetPub\WWWRoot\NWind\Schema and D:\InetPub\WWWRoot\NWind\Template, respectively.
3. Start the IIS Virtual Directory Management for SQL Server program by clicking your mouse on the Windows Start button. When Windows displays the Start menu, select Programs, move your mouse pointer to the Microsoft SQL Server program group, and then click your mouse on Configure SQL XML Support in IIS. Windows will start the IIS Virtual Directory Management for SQL Server program in a window similar to that shown in Figure 598.1.

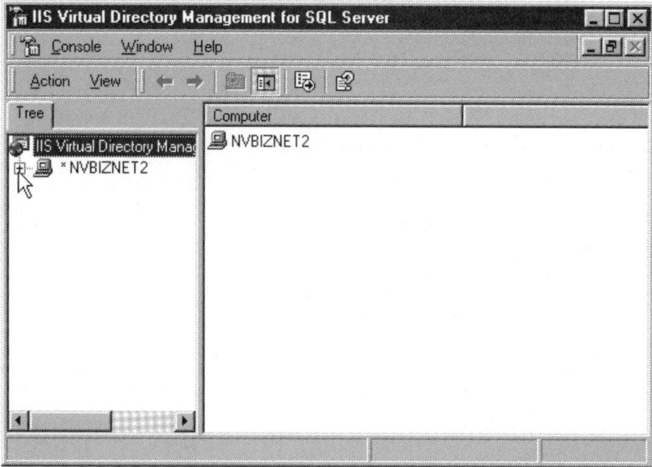

Figure 598.1 The IIS Virtual Directory Manage for SQL Server window

4. Click the plus (+) to the left of the IIS Web server with the Web site through which you want to access the MS-SQL Server. The configuration program will display the Web sites managed by the Web server.
5. Click your mouse on the Web site in which you want to create the database virtual directory. For the current project, click your mouse on "Default Web Site."
6. Select the Action menu, New option and click your mouse on "Virtual Directory." The configuration program will open the New Virtual Directory Properties dialog box shown in Figure 598.2.

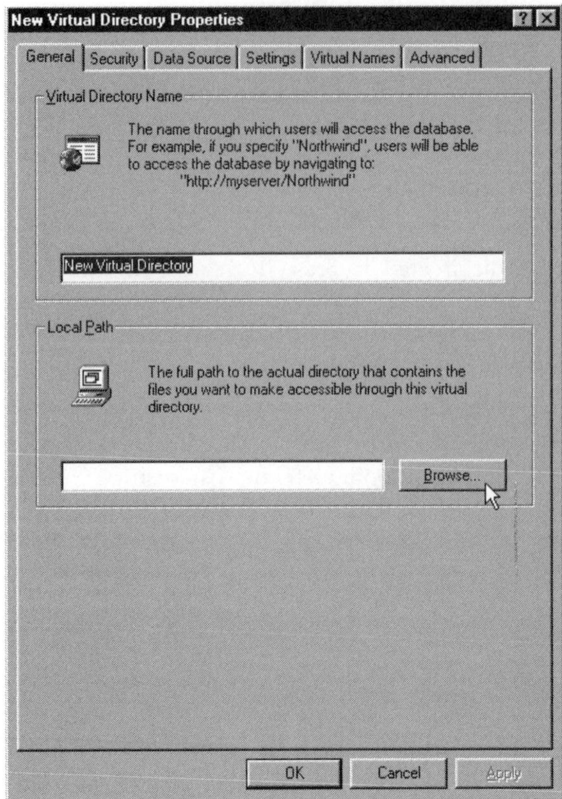

Figure 598.2 The General tab of the New Virtual Directory Properties dialog box

7. Into the "Virtual Directory Name" field within the General tab, enter the name for the virtual directory. You use the virtual directory name when specifying the database to which you are sending the SQL (or Transact-SQL) statement in the Web browser's Address field, so use something that reflects the database name. For the current project, enter **Northwind** into the "Virtual Directory Name" field.

8. Into the "Local Path" field enter the pathname to the virtual connection's "root" folder, which you created in Step 1. For the current project, enter **D:\InetPub\WWWRoot\NWind** into the "Local Path" field.

9. On the Security tab (shown in Figure 598.3), specify the authentication method you want the MS-SQL Server to use in allowing HTTP access to the database. If you enter a username and password into the Credentials area of the Security tab, make sure the username you specify has only SELECT access on tables unless you want to make it available to *everyone* on the the Internet! Bear in mind that anyone accessing the database across the

Web will have the access rights of the username you specify here. To prompt the user for a username/password, select either "Use Windows Integrated Authentication" (to allow access to users with both a valid Windows NT, 2000, or XP account and a valid MS-SQL Server account) or "Use Basic Authentication (Clear Text) to SQL Server Account" (to allow access to users with a valid MS-SQL Server account). For the current project click the "Use Basic Authentication (Clear Text) to SQL Server Account" to prompt the user for a valid MS-SQL Server username/password pair.

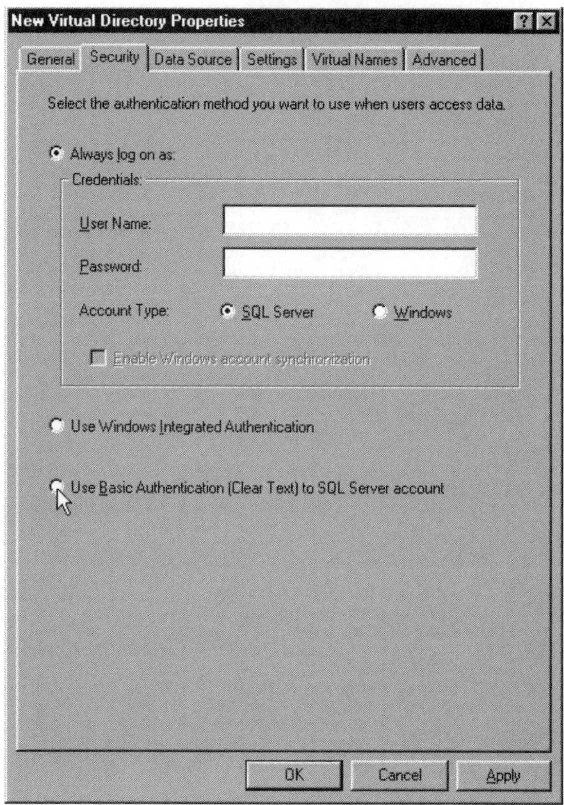

Figure 598-3 The Security tab of the New Virtual Directory Properties dialog box

10. On the Data Source tab (shown in Figure 598.4), enter the name of the MS-SQL Server with the database for which you are setting up HTTP access into the SQL Server field. Or, click your mouse on the search button to the right of the field to have the configuration program search your network and display the list of available MS-SQL Servers within a Select Server dialog box, and click your mouse on the MS-SQL Server's name and then on the OK button within the Select Server dialog box.

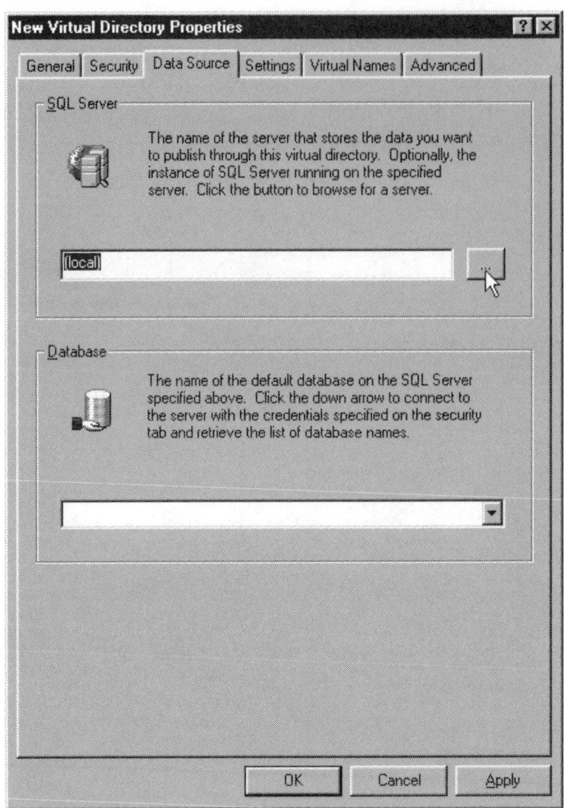

Figure 598.4 The Data Source tab of the New Virtual Directory Properties dialog box

11. Into the Database field, enter the name of the database to which you are setting up HTTP access. For the current project, enter **Northwind** into the Database field.

12. On the Settings tab (shown in Figure 598.5), click a checkmark into the "Allow URL queries," "Allow template queries," "Allow XPath," and "Allow POST" check boxes.

13. On the Virtual Names tab (shown in Figure 598.6), create the virtual names that users will use to work with templates (within the TEMPLATE subfolder), schemas (within the SCHEMA subfolder), and database objects within the database. Click your mouse on the New button. The configuration program will display the Virtual Name Configuration dialog box shown in Figure 598.7.

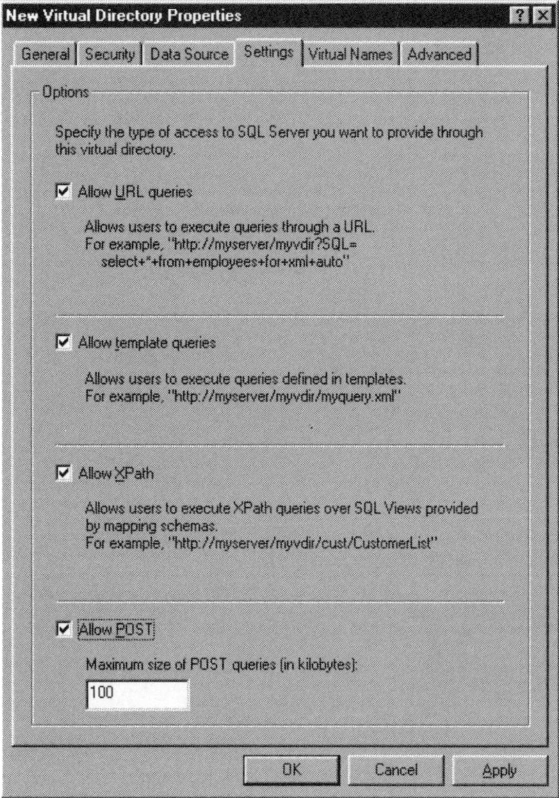

Figure 598.5 The Settings tab of the New Virtual Directory Properties dialog box

14. Into the "Virtual name" field, enter **schema**.
15. Click the drop-down list button to the right of the Type field and select "schema" from the selection list.
16. Into the Path field enter the path name to the SCHEMA subfolder you created in Step 2. For the current project, enter **D:\InetPub\WWWRoot\NWind\Schema** into the Path field. Then click on the Save button. The configuration program will return to the Virtual Names tab and add the virtual name you entered in Step 14 to the "Defined virtual names" list box within the Virtual Names tab.
17. On the Virtual Names tab click your mouse on the New button. The configuration program will again display the Virtual Name Configuration dialog box (shown previously in Figure 598.7).

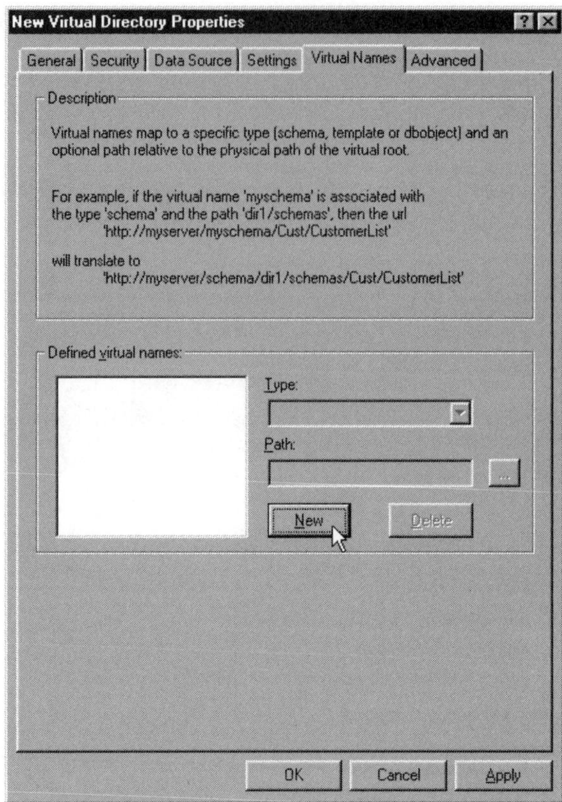

Figure 598.6 The Virtual Names tab of the New Virtual Directory Properties dialog box

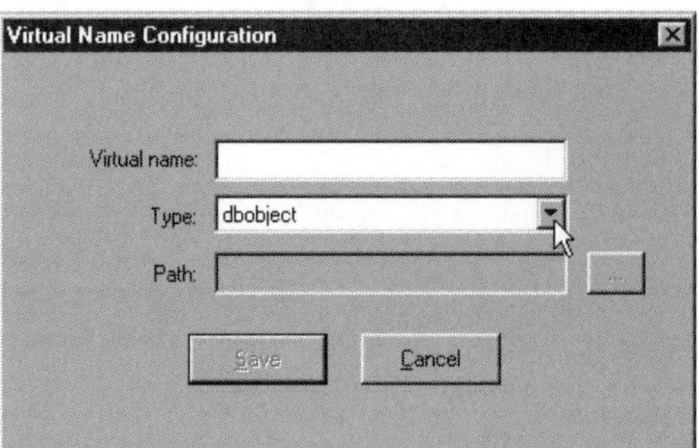

Figure 598.7 The Virtual Name Configuration dialog box

18. Into the "Virtual name" field enter **template**.
19. Click the drop-down list button to the right of the Type field and select "template" from the selection list.

20. Into the Path field enter the path name to the TEMPLATE subfolder you created in step 2. For the current project, enter **D:\InetPub\WWWRoot\NWind\Template** into the Path field. Then click on the Save button. The configuration program will return to the Virtual Names tab and add the virtual name you entered in Step 18 to the "Defined virtual names" list box within the Virtual Names tab.
21. On the Virtual Names tab click your mouse on the New button. The configuration program will again display the Virtual Name Configuration dialog box (shown previously in Figure 598.7).
22. Into the "Virtual name" field enter **dbobject**.
23. Click the drop-down list button to the right of the Type field and select "dbobject" from the selection list. Then click on the Save button. The configuration program will return to the Virtual Names tab and add the virtual name you entered in Step 21 to the "Defined virtual names" list box within the Virtual Names tab.
24. Click the OK button at the bottom of the New Virtual Directory Properties dialog box.

After you complete Step 24, the configuration program will create the Northwind virtual connection on the IIS Web server Web site you selected in Step 5 and return to the IIS Virtual Directory Management for SQL Server window.

To test the virtual connection you created, start your Web browser (and dial-up Internet connection, if necessary). Then, within the browser's Address field enter a simple query using the following syntax:

```
http://<Web Site Address>/<virtual connection>?sql=
<sql statement>+FOR+XML+AUTO&root=root
```

Although shown on two lines here, you would enter your query within the Address field as a single, albeit long, URL.

For example, if you created the Northwind virtual connection on the Web site www.NVBizNet2.com you might enter a query like

```
http://www.nvbiznet2.com/Northwind?sql=
SELECT+*+FROM+shippers+FOR+XML+AUTO&root=root
```

into the browser's Address field and then press the ENTER key. The Web browser will execute the following query against the SHIPPERS table within the NORTHWIND database:

```
SELECT * FROM shippers
```

Note that you substitute a plus (+) for each space within the command that you enter into the Web browser's Address field.

The DBMS will have Windows prompt you for a valid MS-SQL Server username/password pair and then send the query results to your Web browser as an XML document as shown in Figure 598.8.

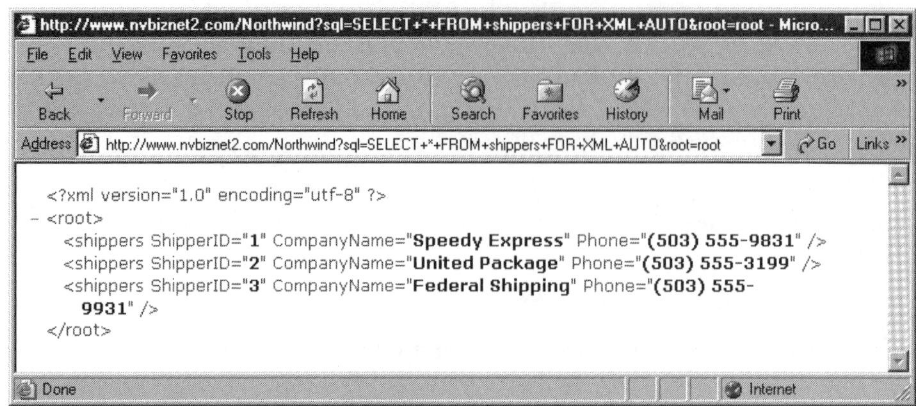

Figure 598.8 An XML document with the results set from an SQL query submitted to an MS-SQL Server using HTTP

599 Executing SQL Statements Using HTTP

After you create a virtual connection to an MS-SQL Server (by performing the steps within the procedure in Tip 598 "Creating a Virtual Connection with the MS-SQL Server"), you can use the virtual connection to send any SQL statement or other command you want to the DBMS. The virtual connection acts as a conduit that lets HTTP traffic flow into and out of the DBMS. If the message contains an SQL query, the DBMS will execute the SELECT statement and return the results set to your Web browser (or other application) as an XML document. Figure 598.8 (shown previously) shows how the Internet Explorer (IE) displays query results returned within an XML document. Within this tip you will learn how to execute SQL and Transact-SQL statements using HTTP. Then, within the next tip, you will learn how to get the DBMS to include an XSL style sheet with the XML document it returns. (The XSL style sheet instructs the Web browser what to do with the XML defined entities it finds within the XML document, so the Web browser will display query results within an HTML table instead of raw XML code.)

Being able to use virtual connections to send HTTP-based queries to an MS-SQL Server is an excellent feature, because it makes data within a database available for display within your Web browser across the Internet to anywhere in the world. However, the true power of the virtual connections lies in the fact that you can use them to send *any* command you want the DBMS to execute—including Transact-SQL statements that modify data within the database, create or change the structure of database objects, add or drop users, execute stored procedures, and more.

Because users accessing the DBMS through a virtual connection can take any action for which the account used to login to the DBMS (through the connection) has the necessary privileges, be very careful when setting up the security scheme for your virtual connection. Do not supply a username/password that logs the virtual connection in to the DBMS (within step 9 of the procedure in the preceding tip)—unless the username you are using has only SELECT access to particular database objects containing data you want to make available to anyone on the Internet. The virtual connection will pass any HTTP messages it receives to the DBMS. The DBMS, in turn, will execute any statement for which the virtual connection's username has the required access privileges.

To send a statement to the DBMS through your Web browser, you enter the statement into the browser's Address field using the following syntax:

```
http://<IIS Web Site Address>/<name of virtual connection>
?sql=<statement string>+FOR+XML+AUTO&root=root
```

Thus, to send the following select statement through the Northwind virtual connection on the NVBizNet2.com Web site:

```
SELECT CompanyName, ContactName, City, Country
FROM suppliers
WHERE Country <> 'USA'
ORDER BY City, Country
```

you would enter the following URL into your Web browser's Address field:

```
http://www.NVBizNet2.com/Northwind/?sql=SELECT+CompanyName,
+ContactName,+City,+Country+FROM+suppliers+WHERE+Country+<>
+'USA'+ORDER+BY+City,+Country+FOR+XML+AUTO&root=root
```

Note that you replace each space between words within the SQL statement or transact-SQL command with a plus (+).

To have the DBMS execute a stored procedure you would use a similar syntax, which includes the stored procedure's parameter values (if any) within the statement string the DBMS is to execute:

```
http://<IIS Web Site Address>/<name of virtual connection>
?sql={EXEC|EXECUTE}<stored procedure name>
    [+@<parameter>='<value>'
     [...,+@<last parameter>='<last value>']]&root=root
```

Note the absence of the "+FOR+XML+AUTO" (which inserts column names as XML tags within the XML document) from the URL. If the stored procedure returns a results set, you must append the "FOR XML AUTO" at the end of the query within the stored procedure, (as you will see in a moment). If the stored procedures performs some operation(s) on the database and does not return a set of row and column values, you can omit "FOR XML AUTO" altogether.

For example, to have the DBMS execute the stored procedure "TenMostExpensiveProducts," which has the following definition

```
CREATE PROCEDURE TenMostExpensiveProducts AS
SET ROWCOUNT 10
SELECT ProductName, UnitPrice
FROM products
ORDER BY UnitPrice DESC
FOR XML AUTO
```

you would enter the following URL into your browser's Address field:

```
http://www.NVBizNet2.com/Northwind/?sql=
EXECUTE+TenMostExpensiveProducts&root=root
```

(You would of course, use the Web site address and name of your virtual connection instead of www.NVBizNet2.com and Northwind used in this example.)

If you must pass parameter values to a stored procedure, specify each parameter's value by name as "@<parameter name>=<value>" within the URL that you type into the Web browser's address field. For example, you would enter the following URL in to the browser's Address field

```
http://www.nvbiznet2.com/Northwind/?sql=EXECUTE+SalesByYear
+@Beginning_Date='06/01/1996',+@Ending_Date='05/31/1997'
&root=root
```

to have the DBMS execute a stored procedure defined as follows:

```
CREATE PROCEDURE SalesByYear
   @Beginning_Date DateTime, @Ending_Date DateTime AS

SELECT Orders.ShippedDate, Orders.OrderID,
       "Order Subtotals".Subtotal,
       DATENAME(yy,ShippedDate) AS Year
FROM Orders INNER JOIN "Order Subtotals"
  ON Orders.OrderID = "Order Subtotals".OrderID
WHERE Orders.ShippedDate
      BETWEEN @Beginning_Date AND @Ending_Date
ORDER BY Year
FOR XML AUTO
```

600 Using XML Schemas to Submit Queries Using HTTP and XSL Style Sheets to Format Query Results

Within the preceding tip, you learned how to submit SQL statements and Transact-SQL commands to an MS-SQL Server using HTTP. In general, after you create a virtual connection between an Internet Information Server (IIS) Web server and a database on an MS-SQL Server (which you learned to do within Tip 598 "Creating a Virtual Connection with the MS-SQL Server"), you can use HTTP to submit any statement string you want the DBMS to execute. Simply enter into your Web browser's Address field the Web address (that is, the URL) of the virtual connection along with the statement you want executed. What makes a DBMS virtual connection so powerful is that through a virtual connection you can query, update, and manage database objects from anywhere in the world across the Internet.

Unfortunately, without an XSL style sheet, most Web browsers don't know what to do with XML entities described within the XML documents in which the DBMS returns query results sets. As a result, Web browsers simply display everything within the XML file onscreen as plain text. For example, Internet Explorer (IE) displays the XML document of query results for the following HTTP based query as shown within Figure 600.1:

```
http://www.NVBizNet2.com/Northwind/?sql=SELECT+employeeID,+
FirstName,+LastName,+Title,+Photo+FROM+employees+
FOR+XML+AUTO&root=root
```

To display the query results within an HTML table as shown within Figure 600.2, create an XSL style sheet such as the following:

```
<?xml version='1.0' encoding='UTF-8'?>
 <xsl:stylesheet xmlns:xsl='http://www.w3.org/TR/WD-xsl' >
    <xsl:template match = '*'>
        <xsl:apply-templates />
    </xsl:template>
    <xsl:template match = 'employees'>
       <TR>
         <TD><xsl:value-of select = '@employeeID' /></TD>
         <TD><xsl:value-of select = '@FirstName' /></TD>
         <TD><xsl:value-of select = '@LastName' /></TD>
         <TD><xsl:value-of select = '@Title' /></TD>
         <TD><B> <IMG><xsl:attribute name='src'>
                    <xsl:value-of select = '@Photo'/>
                    </xsl:attribute>
                 </IMG>
         </B></TD>
       </TR>
    </xsl:template>
```

```
    <xsl:template match = '/'>
      <HTML>
        <HEAD>
          <STYLE>th     {background-color : lightblue }
                 table {background-color : lightyellow}
          </STYLE>
          <BASE href='http://www.NVBizNet2.com/Northwind/'>
          </BASE>
        </HEAD>
        <BODY>
         <TABLE border='1' style='width:680;'>
           <TR><TH colspan='5'>Employee Information
               </TH></TR>
           <TR><TH  width='30'>ID</TH>
               <TH  width='100'>First Name</TH>
               <TH  width='100'>Last Name</TH>
               <TH  width='200'>Job Title</TH>
               <TH  width='250'>Photo</TH></TR>
           <xsl:apply-templates select = 'root' />
         </TABLE>
        </BODY>
      </HTML>
    </xsl:template>
</xsl:stylesheet>
```

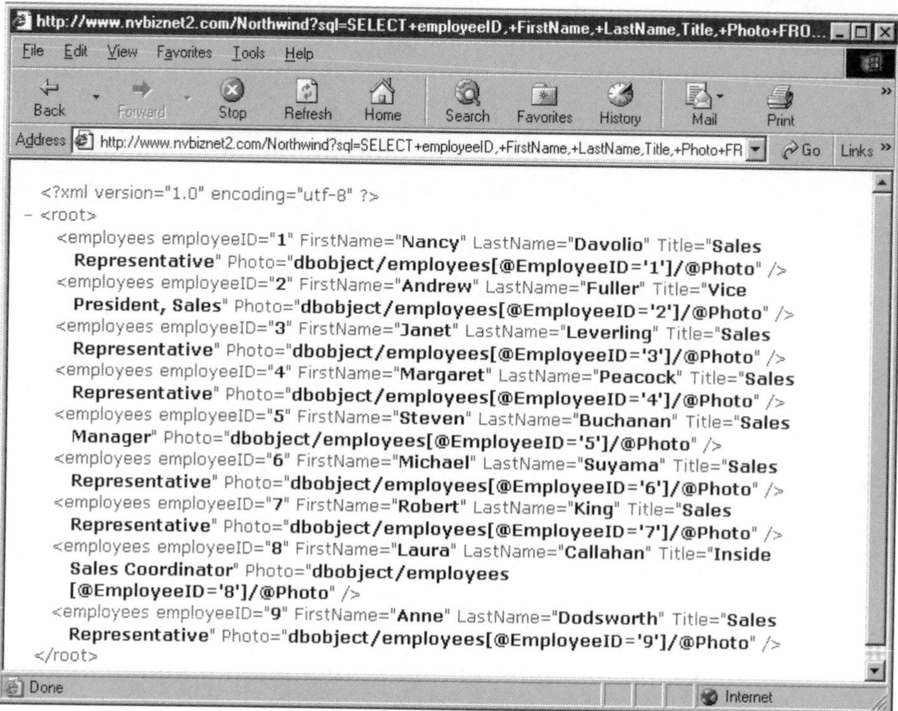

Figure 600.1 XML document displayed without an XSL style sheet as displayed by IE

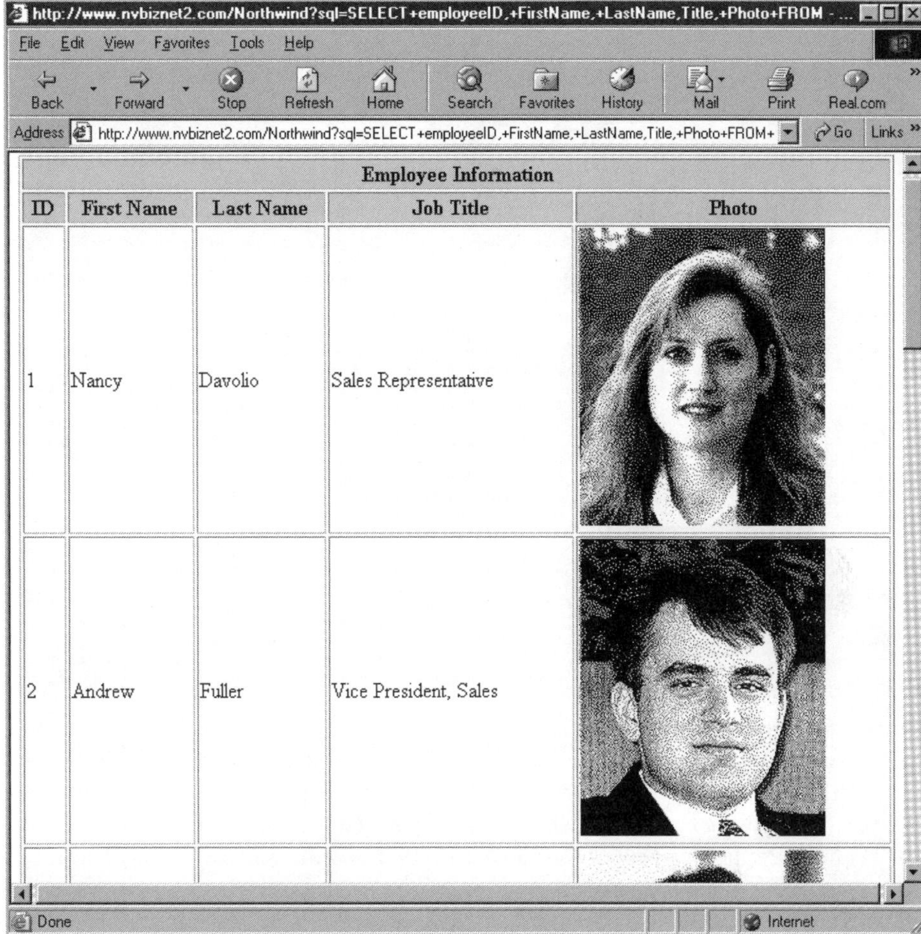

Figure 600.2 XML document formatted with an XSL style sheet and then displayed by IE

Whereas XML simply describes what makes up an entity such as a row of query results, HTML tags tell the Web browser how Web page objects like text, graphics images, video clips, animations, and sound data should appear onscreen. In other words, XML describes the individual items within the query results while HTML describes how the Web browser should display each item. An XSL style sheet tells the Web browser how to convert entities within an XML document into the HTML that defines a Web page, which displays those entities (in a more optimal format than plain text).

For example, in the XSL style sheet that precedes Figure 600.2 (shown previously), each row of query results is described by the following code within the XML document

```
<employees
  employeeID="1" FirstName="Nancy"
  LastName="Davolio" Title="Sales Representative"
  Photo="dbobject/employees[@EmployeeID='1']/@Photo" />
```

is translated into the following HTML:

```
<TR>
 <TD>1</TD><TD>Nancy</TD>
 <TD>Davolio</TD><TD>Sales Representative</TD>
 <TD><B>
   <IMG src="dbobject/employees[@EmployeeID='1']/@Photo" />
     </B></TD>
</TR>
```

To do so, the Web browser applies the following rule from the XSL style sheet used in this example:

```
<xsl:template match = 'employees'>
  <TR>
    <TD><xsl:value-of select = '@employeeID' /></TD>
    <TD><xsl:value-of select = '@FirstName' /></TD>
    <TD><xsl:value-of select = '@LastName' /></TD>
    <TD><xsl:value-of select = '@Title' /></TD>
    <TD><B> <IMG><xsl:attribute name='src'>
              <xsl:value-of select = '@Photo'/>
              </xsl:attribute>
            </IMG>
    </B></TD>
  </TR>
```

As mentioned previously within this tip, XSL templates tell the Web browser what HTML tags and text to substitute for XML entity references within the XML document. In this example, the employees template within the XSL style sheet tells the Web browser the HTML with which to replace each employees entity found within the XML document. The replacement HTML supplied by the XSL style sheet has the Web browser display the value of each of the employees entity's parts (employeeID, FirstName, LastName, Title, Photo) within a cell (between <td></td> tags) of a row (between <tr></tr> tags) within an HTML table. After it applies the XSL templates to make all the necessary conversions (from XML entity descriptions to sets of HTML tags, attributes, and text), the Web browser displays the query results returned within the XML document as Web page content such as that shown previously in Figure 600.2.

To create XSL style sheets that tell the Web browser to display results sets from HTTP-based queries you submit to the DBMS, simply change the templates shown within the XSL file in this example to match the column names in your query's SELECT clause. Be sure to change the quoted entity name ("employees") referenced within the XSL start template description line ("<xsl:template match = 'employees'>," in this example) to match the name of the XML entity to which the template applies.

For example, to handle the XML "suppliers" description returned for the query

```
SELECT CompanyName, ContactName, Phone
FROM suppliers
```

you would change the template description within the preceding example XSL style sheet to:

```
<xsl:template match = 'suppliers'>
  <TR>
    <TD><xsl:value-of select = '@CompanyName' /></TD>
    <TD><xsl:value-of select = '@ContactName' /></TD>
    <TD><xsl:value-of select = '@Phone' /></TD>
  </TR>
```

In addition, you would change the HTML table description (defined within <table></table> tags) toward the end of the XS file to:

```
<TABLE border='1' style='width:230;'>
  <TR><TH colspan='5'>Supplier Information
      </TH></TR>
  <TR><TH  width='30'>Company Name</TH>
      <TH  width='100'>Contact Name</TH>
      <TH  width='100'>Phone Number</TH>
  <xsl:apply-templates select = 'root' />
</TABLE>
```

To have the Web browser apply the templates within an XSL style sheet file to an XML document, create the XSL file within the virtual connection's root folder. Then, reference the style sheet file within the URL you use to submit the query to the DBMS. Suppose, for example, that you save within the file EmpNamePhoto.xsl the XSL style sheet you want to apply to the following HTTP-based query:

```
http://www.NVBizNet2.com/Northwind/?sql=SELECT+employeeID,+
FirstName,+LastName,+Title,+Photo+FROM+employees+
FOR+XML+AUTO&root=root
```

You can tell the Web browser to apply the XSL style sheet (EmpNamePhoto.xsl) when displaying the query results, by inserting "&xsl=<xsl filename>" reference in front of the "&root=root" within the URL as shown here:

```
http://www.NVBizNet2.com/Northwind/?sql=SELECT+employeeID,+
FirstName,+LastName,+Title,+Photo+FROM+employees+
FOR+XML+AUTO&xsl=EmpNamePhoto.xsl&root=root
```

Now that you know how to solve the display issues you encounter when submitting HTTP-based queries, the only thing left to fix is the amount of typing you have to do each time you want to submit even a simple query to the DBMS. The solution for the typing problem is to store the query as an XML template file within the TEMPLATE subfolder you created for the virtual connection. For example, you would store the query, including XSL style sheet file specification within an XML template file as follows:

```
<?xml version ='1.0' encoding='UTF-8'?>
<root xmlns:sql='urn:schemas-microsoft-com:xml-sql'
  sql:xsl='../EmpNamePhoto.xsl'>
  <sql:query >
     SELECT employeeID, FirstName, LastName, Title, Photo
     FROM employees FOR XML AUTO
  </sql:query>
</root>
```

Assuming you save the XML template within the file EmpQuery.xml within the TEMPLATE subfolder, you would then type the URL for the preceding HTTP-based query as:

```
http://www.NVBizNet2.com/Northwind/template/EmpQuery.xml
?contenttype=text/html
```

Of course, the longer the statement string, the greater the typing effort you avoid by referring to the XML template file rather than typing the query itself.

Note: *Throughout this tip, the examples used a virtual connection named "Northwind" on the www.NVBizNet2.com Web site. When writing HTTP-based SQL statements of your own, substitute for www.NVBizNet2.com the .com address on which you defined the virtual connection to the database you want to use, and the name of your virtual connection for "Northwind." Note also that the Web site and virtual connection name appear between <base></base> tags within the XSL style sheet file. In order for your database object (dboject) references to work properly, you must substitute your .com address and virtual connection name for that in the example XSL style sheet shown after Figure 600.1 within this tip.*

---

601 Displaying Image Data Stored Within an SQL Table

To display image data (that is, graphics images, animations, video clips, or other binary data) stored within a table, a Web server-side script must first write the image data to a disk file. After storing the image data within a disk file, the script embedded within the PHP or ASP Web page on which the image is to appear must set the *src* attribute within the <img> tag used to display the image to the pathname of the file in which the script saved the binary data. Before we review a VBScript that an ASP Web page might use to retrieve and display image data, let's see how easy the process is if you happen to be using all Microsoft products.

There are three applications involved in displaying an SQL table-stored image on a Web page—the SQL DBMS, the Web server, and the Web browser. If you are using the Microsoft MS-SQL Server DBMS, Internet Information Server (IIS) Web server, and the Internet Explorer (IE) Web browser, you can display image data stored within an SQL table by inserting an <img> tag such as the following within the Web page HTML:

```
<img src=
"http://www.NVBizNet2.com/Northwind/dbobject/employees
[@employeeID='1']/@photo" >
```

The <img> tag's *src* attribute instructs the IE Web browser to send an HTTP-based query to the MS-SQL Server. In this example, the Web browser requests that the DBMS send the contents of the PHOTO column from the row within EMPLOYEES table where the EMPLOY-

EEID is equal to 1. Of course, IE can only retrieve and display the image data if NVBizNet2.com has a virtual connection to the DBMS named NORTHWIND, and the virtual database object DBOBJECT is defined. (You learned how to setup virtual connections that provide HTTP access to MS-SQL Server database objects within Tip 598 "Creating a Virtual Connection with the MS-SQL Server.")

In Tip 599 "Executing SQL Statements Using HTTP," you learned how to submit SQL queries within a URL you enter into the Web browser's Address field. Using what you learned then, you can display image data stored within a database table by entering a URL such as the following into the Web browser's Address field:

```
http://www.NVBizNet2.com/Northwind/dbobject/Employees
[@EmployeeID='1']/@photo
```

Again, in order for IE to display image data stored within the EMPLOYEES table's PHOTO column, the IIS Web server for the NVBizNet2.com Web site must have a virtual connection named NORTHWIND to the MS-SQL Server database that contains the EMPLOYEES table.

Finally, in Tip 600 "Using XML Schemas to Submit Queries Using HTTP and XSL Style Sheets to Format Query Results," you learned how to write the following <img> tag definition within an XSL style sheet to display multiple images on a Web page as shown previously in Figure 600.2:

```
<TD><IMG><xsl:attribute name='src'>
       <xsl:value-of select = '@Photo'/>
       </xsl:attribute>
    </IMG>
</TD>
```

Unfortunately, each of the three preceding techniques for displaying image data on a Web page require an all-Microsoft setup as well as a virtual connection between the IIS Web server and a database on an MS-SQL Server. To make image data available within a variety of Web browsers and DBMS platforms, you can use ADO and a VBScript such as the following embedded within an ASP Web page:

```
<%@ Language=VBScript %>
<% option explicit %>
<!- #include file="adovbs.inc" ->
<%
'*********************************
'*** OPEN DSN-Less Connection ***
'*********************************
 Sub open_OLEDB_connection (byVal ServerName, DbName,
                                  Username, Password,
                            byRef objConn)
 Dim connectString

   connectString = "PROVIDER=SQLOLEDB;DATA SOURCE=" & _
     ServerName & ";UID=" & UserName & ";PWD=" & _
```

```
     Password & ";DATABASE=" & DbName

   With objConn
     .ConnectionString = connectString
     .open
   End With
 End Sub

'****************************
'*** Variable Declarations ***
'****************************
 Dim objDiskAccess
 Dim objConn
 Dim objRecordset

 Dim ADO_field_header
 Dim block_size

'connection properties & query string

 Dim Username
 Dim Password
 Dim ServerName
 Dim DBName

 Dim query_string

'image file processing variables

 Dim block_count
 Dim image_chunk
 Dim image_file_extension
 Dim image_file_size
 Dim offset
 Dim remainder
 Dim temp_image_filename
 Dim temp_image_pathname
 Dim temp_image_physical_folder
 Dim temp_image_virtual_folder

 Dim html_image_tag

'**********************
'*** Setup Constants ***
'**********************
 ADO_field_header = 78
 block_size = 256

'Determine where you want the image stored on disk
```

```
'***Change these to match where you want the image stored.
 temp_image_filename = "Image"
 temp_image_physical_folder = _
   "D:\Inetpub\wwwroot\NWind\Temp\"
 temp_image_virtual_folder = "/NWind/Temp/"
 image_file_extension = ".bmp"

'ADO connection string properties
'*** Change these to match your DB access needs.
 UserName = "username"
 Password = "password"
 ServerName = "NVBizNet2"
 DBName = "Northwind"

'***Change the query string to retrieve the image you want
'***To retrieve from the DBMS
 query_string =  _
   "select Photo from Employees where EmployeeID='1'"

'********************
'*** Main Routine ***
'********************
 on error resume next

'***You can download a copy of "FileAccessor.dll" from
'  the book's companion Web page at
'  www.PremierPressBooks.com/
 Set objDiskAccess = _
      CreateObject("FileAccessor.FileWriter")

'Formulate the pathname for the image file the script will
'  create on disk.
'Delete the previously written file of the same name (if it
'  exists).
'Then open the disk file into which the script will write
'  the contents of the image column from the table.
'***You need to change this "delete action" to match your
'  image file retention requirements.

 temp_image_pathname = _
   temp_image_physical_folder & temp_image_filename & _
     image_file_extension

 objDiskAccess.RemoveFile temp_image_pathname
 objDiskAccess.OpenFile temp_image_pathname

'Open a connection to the DBMS and call the method that
'  executes the query.
```

```
 Set objConn = Server.CreateObject("ADODB.Connection")

 Open_OLEDB_Connection _
   ServerName, DbName, Username, Password, objConn
 Set objRecordset = objConn.Execute (query_string)

'Compute the image file's size (in bytes) by subtracting
'  the bytes within the ADO field header
'Then, after discarding the header bytes stored at the
'  start of the image field's column within the ADO
'  Recordset object, Compute the number of "block size"
'  blocks there are within the image field.

 image_file_size = _
   objRecordset.fields("Photo").ActualSize - _
     ADO_field_header
 image_chunk = _
   objRecordset.fields("Photo").GetChunk(ADO_field_header)
 block_count = image_file_size \ block_size

'To make the last write ouptput a full "block size"
'  buffer, divide the block size into the image's total
'  size and then retrieve and write to the disk file any
'  "left over" bytes so that when looping the read you
'  always have exactly some number of "block size" (and no
'  extra) bytes to read and write

 remainder = image_file_size Mod block_size
 If Remainder > 0 Then
   image_chunk = _
     objRecordset.fields("photo").GetChunk(remainder)
   objDiskAccess.WriteToFile image_chunk
 End If

'Work through the image field "block size" bytes at a time
'  and append each block of bytes onto the disk file.

 offset = remainder
 Do While Offset < image_file_size
   image_chunk = _
     objRecordset.fields("photo").GetChunk(block_size)
   objDiskAccess.WriteToFile image_chunk
   offset = offset + block_size
 Loop

 html_image_tag = _
   "<img src='" & temp_image_virtual_folder & _
     temp_image_filename & image_file_extension & "'/>"
```

```
'Close the disk file, recordset and the DBMS connection.

 objDiskAccess.CloseFile
 objRecordset.Close
 objConn.Close
%>
<html>
<head>
  <title>Display Image Data from Table Column</title>
</head>
<body>
  <center>
    <h1>"Photo" Image Column Contents</h1>

    <table border='2'>
      <tr><td><%=html_image_tag%></td></tr>
    </table>
  </center>
</body>
</html>
```

Note that the script in this example retrieves the contents of the PHOTO column from one row of the EMPLOYEES table within the NORTHWIND database. However, you can customize the routine to retrieve and display the contents of any image column you like. Simply download DisplayImage.ASP from the book's companion Web page at www.premierpress-books.com/downloads.asp. Then, change the image file, connection string, and query string information define within the Constants section at the beginning of the script to suit your needs.

In addition to VBScript, which any ASP script engine will process, the script in this example uses disk access methods from an ActiveX control named FileAccesor.DLL. If you do not have an application you can use to read and write disk files, download a copy of FileAccessor.DLL from the book's companion Web page and save it within a folder on the Web server (that is on the system on which the ASP Web page DisplayImage.ASP will run). For example, you might store FileAccessor.DLL within the Web site's root folder D:\InetPub\wwwroot\. Wherever you store the ActiveX control, make sure to note the location, because you must register the control using REGSVR32.EXE before ASP scripts can use the control's methods. For example, if you stored the control within the folder D:\InetPub\wwwroot, you would use following command to register the ActiveX control on the Web server:

```
REGSVR32 D:\InetPub\WWWRoot\FileAccessor.DLL
```

If you already have a VB application that lets you create and write to disk files, feel free to use it in place of FileAccessor.DLL. The important thing to understand is that you can use ADO to retrieve image data from a database table into your VBScript. Then, you must use an external application program (such as FileAccessor.DLL) that lets you write data within an ADO Recordset object to a file on the hard drive. As mentioned at the start of this tip, you must write the image data to a physical disk file before you can display the graphics image on a Web page.

Index

Numbers refer to tip numbers not page numbers.

E

T

U

X

GAME DEVELOPMENT.

IT'S SERIOUS BUSINESS.

"Game programming is without a doubt the most intellectually challenging field of Computer Science in the world. However, we would be fooling ourselves if we said that we are 'serious' people! Writing (and reading) a game programming book should be an exciting adventure for both the author and the reader."

—André LaMothe,
Series Editor

Premier Press, Inc.
www.premierpressbooks.com

PREMIER PRESS

GAME DEVELOPMENT